Statistics for Business Decision Making

Statistics for Business Decision Making

Charles L. Olson
Governors State University

Mario J. Picconi
University of San Diego

Scott, Foresman and Company • Glenview, Illinois

Dallas, Texas   Oakland, New Jersey   Palo Alto, California
Tucker, Georgia   London, England

To Professor Harry V. Roberts, University of Chicago

Cover photograph by Hedrich-Blessing, Chicago. Photograph is of the Chicago skyline, transformed into an implied statistical bar graph.

Library of Congress Cataloging in Publication Data

Olson, Charles L., 1936–
  Statistics for business decision making.

  Includes index.
  1. Commercial statistics.   2. Industrial management—
Statistical methods.   3. Statistics.   I. Picconi,
Mario J.   1942–   II. Title.
HF1017.045   1983   519.5'024658   82-16948
ISBN 0-673-16000-9

Acknowledgments

Figure 2.4, page 44, from Dik Warren Twedt, "How Important to Marketing Strategy is the 'Heavy User'?" *Journal of Marketing*, Vol. 28, January 1964, p. 72. Copyright © 1964 by the American Marketing Association.   Graph, page 53, Chicago Tribune Graphic, copyrighted 1979. Used with permission.   Table 3.5, page 67, from Oswald D. Bowlin, "The Refunding Decision: Another Special Case of Capital Budgeting," *Journal of Finance*, March 1966, pp. 55–68. Copyright © 1966 by The American Finance Association.   Figure 4.6, page 118, reprinted from Eugene F. Fama, "The Behavior of Stock Prices," *Journal of Business*, January 1965, p. 96, by permission of The University of Chicago Press. © 1965 by the University of Chicago.   Table 14.10, page 515, from *Exploring Statistics with IDA*, © 1979 by the Scientific Press. Used with permission.   Table 15.2, page 547, reprinted by permission from *Sales and Marketing Management* magazine. Copyright 1977.   Figure 18.1, page 671, reprinted by permission, *The San Diego Union*, and *Business Week*, January 11, 1982, page 2, by special permission.   Chapter 18, quotes throughout, from "Our Flawed Inflation Indexes" by Edward Meadows, *Fortune* Magazine, April 24, 1978. Copyright © 1978 Time Inc. All rights reserved. Reprinted by permission. Page 839, "Up to knees in galoshes, he begs snow" by Jeff Lyon, *Chicago Tribune*, January 24, 1980. Copyrighted 1980, Chicago Tribune. Used with permission.   Appendix Table 2; 5, 10, 15, 20, and 25 values, from William Mendenhall, *Statistics for Management and Economics*, 3rd edition, pp. 705–8. © 1978 by Wadsworth Publishing Company, Inc. All other values from Roger Pfaffenberger and James Patterson, *Statistical Methods for Business and Economics*, © 1977 by Richard D. Irwin, Inc. Used with permission.   Appendix Table 3, from *Statistics for Modern Business Decisions*, Third Edition, by Lawrence Lapin. © 1982 by Harcourt Brace Jovanovich, Inc. Reprinted by permission of the publisher.

Preface

Statistics is a subject with much promise. Properly handled it is interesting, challenging, and a valuable tool for decision making. Badly handled it is boring and baggage soon discarded. Student evaluations seem to confirm that quite often its promise goes unfulfilled. Many reasons can be cited for this shortfall: the rigor of the subject matter, the poor quantitative preparation of students taking the course, the quality of the educational material. If the gap between promise and achievement is to be narrowed, a good textbook is required. The text can't replace the good instructor who brings personal enthusiasm to the subject but it is a key ingredient in a successful pedagogical mix. Statistical concepts must be presented clearly without a loss of integrity. At the same time practice must be shown to confirm theory. Numerous examples must show that concepts can be usefully applied to aid in decision making. We believe (supported by our reviewer's comments) that we have produced a textbook that illustrates the link between sound statistical reasoning and real business problem solving and decision making.

Statistics for Business Decision Making can be used for either undergraduate or graduate business statistics courses. It does not require calculus or other advanced mathematical knowledge. In fact, we believe our book is unique in achieving a high level of conceptual sophistication by employing a wide range of intuitive examples, rather than examples requiring advanced mathematical knowledge.

Statistics for Business Decision Making has been extensively class tested and developed over the past twelve years, in both undergraduate and graduate statistics courses taught at business schools. At the undergraduate level at the University of Notre Dame, it has been used in its full version in a two semester sequence. In selected form at the University of San Diego, it has been used in a one semester follow-up course to a previous elementary statistics course and also in a one semester course at the MBA level.

Statistics for Business Decision Making contains all of the traditional topics expected in a business statistics textbook, as well as several innovative topics. The book deals with the 4Ds of business statistics: description, drawing inference, design, and decision theory. Chapter One speaks to the student about the subject of statistics by illustrating its uses in various fields, and lays the groundwork for the remaining topics discussed in the text. Chapters Two, Three, and Four are concerned with the descriptive branch of statistics. Chapters Five through Ten develop the concepts of probability and probability distributions—the basis of inference. These chapters give consideration to the bivariate probability distribution, the binomial, Poisson, hypergeometric, and the normal distributions. Chapters Eleven and Twelve deal with inference-estimation and hypothesis testing. Chapter Thirteen shows the interplay between design and inference. Chapters Fourteen, Fifteen, and Sixteen investigate the regression model (simple and multiple) and the inferences that can be made once model accuracy is established. Importantly, these chapters point out both the promise and the hazards in using regression analysis, and represent the main emphasis of the text. Chapters Seventeen and Eighteen return us to descriptive statistics with the discussion of descriptive time series analysis and index numbers—the latter emphasizing inflation and the CPI. Chapter Nineteen brings us to inferential time series analysis in the context of business forecasting, including a workable illustration of autoregression in light of Box-Jenkins analysis. Chapters Twenty and Twenty-one illustrate inference for qualitative variables with chi-Square analysis and analysis of variance. Chapter Twenty-two offers a collection of techniques which allow us to make inferences about data for which parametric population assumptions cannot be met or are unnecessary to stipulate. Chapter Twenty-three is the concluding chapter and presents the fundamentals of decision theory, including decision tree analysis, Bayes' Theorem, and an illustration of incremental inventory analysis.

Statistics for Business Decision Making has the following features:

Chapter previews provide a short synopsis of each chapter and link each chapter to the general plan of the book.

Numerous examples, located throughout each chapter, give practical applications of concepts and extend discussions to the business world.

Managerial Issues in Practice, found in key chapters, are in-depth review exercises which present statistical concepts in the context of managerial issues such as common stock analysis and wholesaling strategy.

Chapter summaries, called "Concluding Comments," provide a brief review of the key points of the chapter.

Questions and problems, at the end of each chapter, *reinforce* concepts developed in the body of the text and, in the case of the more challenging problems, *enrich* the discussion of business statistics concepts and issues.

Answers are found at the end of the book for selected problems. Since problems sometimes build upon one another, answers to *selected* problems ensure that students will have a guide to follow through the various steps.

Statistics for Business Decision Making has a complete supplemental package. A *Student Solutions Manual* has been prepared by Joan Anderson, Chuck Teplitz, and the authors. It provides detailed worked-out solutions for selected end of chapter problems and for review exercises. These solutions contain an extended commentary on the statistical principle at issue and its practical business application. An *Instructor's Manual—Solutions Manual* contains teaching tips and solutions not found in the Student Solutions Manual. For those instructors who desire it, these other solutions are available to students in a separately bound edition. A *Study Guide*, prepared by Jules LeBon, gives a step-by-step analysis of the highlights of each chapter in the format of self-correcting exercises. It also includes a review of key words and concepts. A *Test Bank*, prepared by Don Holbert and William Stewart, gives 1400 multiple choice test questions, with alternate data sets. *Transparency Masters* are also available.

Acknowledgments

During the twelve years of development of this text we have made the acquaintance of many supportive people. We received encouragement (food and shelter) from our parents and in-laws, Mrs. Anna Olson and Mr. and Mrs. Alexander Budzinsky, who we know share the satisfaction of this accomplishment. From our respective universities we received administrative and secretarial support. A special thanks goes to Jim Burns, Dean at the University of San Diego, for providing us with the opportunity to team teach and with the secretarial support to prepare a pre-publication copy for classroom use. Before listing the many reviewers who took the time to examine at least part of the project, we would like to extend a special note of thanks and gratitude to two individuals: Ron Koot of Penn State, Department of Management Science, who, over the past four years, has spent many, many hours reading and commenting on several versions of our manuscript and supporting material; and Al Romano of San Diego State University, Department of Mathematics, who spent one semester going through the statistical concepts and notation in the first eight chapters of this book. We would also like to thank Marilyn Hart for problems she provided for early chapters of the text. Our colleagues at the University of Notre Dame, Byung T. Cho and Yu-Chi Chang, were extremely helpful to us in our discussions on how to develop a beginning statistics course based upon statistical reasoning.

We would like to thank the following reviewers for their comments and advice:

Frank Alt, University of Maryland
Joan Anderson, University of San Diego
John E. Anderson, Eastern Michigan University
Katy Azoury, University of Illinois, Chicago Circle
M. David Beveridge, Western Illinois University
Warren Boe, University of Iowa
Janet Goulet, Wittenberg University
Marilyn Hart, Governors State University
David K. Hildebrand, University of Pennsylvania
Don Holbert, Oklahoma State University
Bob Johnson, University of San Diego
Peggy Kem, Golden Gate University
Don Mann, University of San Diego
Robert Markland, University of South Carolina
W. B. Martin, University of Texas, El Paso
Leon F. Marzillier, Los Angeles Valley College
Gary M. Mullet, Berry College
Dennis Oberhelman, University of South Carolina
David Rocke, University of California at Davis
William Stewart, Oklahoma State University
Chuck Teplitz, University of San Diego
Jane Wells, Governors State University
John C. Windsor, Miami University of Ohio

We are grateful to the Literary Executor of the late Sir Ronald A. Fisher, F. R. S. to Dr. Frank Yates, F. R. S. and to Longman Group Ltd, London for permission to reprint Table III from their book *Statistical Tables for Biological, Agricultural and Medical Research* (6th Edition, 1974).

We would also like to acknowledge the important contribution made by the staff of Scott, Foresman. Jim Boyd, our acquiring editor, has been most closely involved with the project over the years. His drive and energy was a delightful luxury to have. He sought out useful reviewers which spared us from countless hours of second-guessing. His good sense of humor relieved tense situations and saved our sanity. A special note of thanks goes to Patty Boyd, who graciously accepted our frequent "urgent" phone calls. Bruce Kaplan, our developmental-copy editor "extraordinaire," steered us through the straits of the production process. His 3Ps—patience, persistence, and perspective—gave us the opportunity to make key adjustments and at the same time kept us on that all important production timetable. Jim Sitlington, the executive editor, must be commended for his positive attitude and for providing the necessary resources to get the job done. To our secretarial support: Julie Bays, Joanne Cote, Margaret Peters, Juanita Morrison, Fran Meadows, Ann Smith, Colleen Gallagher, Helen Lipke, Lois Smith, we extend our deep appreciation and admiration for a job well done. Irene Picconi typed many drafts of the text chapters over the years.

We owe our greatest debt of gratitude to our wives, Marilyn and Irene. They had to manage the household during our absences stretching from a few days to several months and did it well. Additionally they ran countless errands for us and provided some "clutch" typing at several stages of the manuscript. Their care and concern were always forthcoming and sustained us through many dark hours. More materially, their excellent desserts and coffee rewarded our daily efforts. To all involved, thanks again.

C. L. Olson, M. J. Picconi

Contents

3 Constructing Frequency Distributions, Histograms, and Smooth Curves

54

4 Summary Measures of Frequency Distributions

100

5 Basic Probability Concepts *140*

6 Probability Calculations for Composite Events *174*

7 Probability Distributions and Their Summary Measures 212

8 Random Sampling for Attributes: The Binomial Distribution 246

9 Random Sampling for Attributes: Other Discrete Distributions 292

10 Random Sampling for Measured Characteristics and the Normal Distribution *318*

11 Estimation *356*

12 Hypothesis Testing 392

13 Sampling Design and Experimental Design: The Two Sample Case 422

14 Regression and Correlation: The Basic Model 458

15 Regression and Correlation: Issues and Extensions *532*

16 Multiple Regression   *578*

19 Business Forecasting *708*

20 Contingency Tables and Chi-Square Analysis *758*

23 Decision Theory
838

Statistics for Business Decision Making

Understanding Statistics and Statistical Reasoning

Preview.   This introductory chapter raises five key topics that should prepare you for what lies ahead and that should indicate the benefits of learning statistics as an analytical tool: (1) there is a good reason why greater numbers of students are studying statistics; (2) preconceived notions about statistics blunt your understanding of statistical concepts and methods and your effectiveness in solving business problems; (3) lack of knowledge of the reasoning underlying statistical methods can cause statistical gullibility and poor statistical intuition— better educated intuition is an important objective in studying the subject; (4) the statistical sampling method known as random sampling is a keystone methodology referred to throughout the text. It defines a way of choosing sample members from a population to obtain ''representativeness'' without reliance upon human judgment; (5) a balanced view of the world of statistics embraces four branches which we shall call the four Ds of statistics: Design, Description, Drawing of Inferences, and Decision Analysis.

Early in the 1970s an obscure Federal government test of passenger car tires produced some disconcerting evidence—a failure rate of 6% among the tires tested. The tire manufacturers pooh-poohed the evidence, noting that the few thousand tested tires amounted to only a few hundredths of a percent of the 180 million tires produced annually. But U.S. Senator Gaylord Nelson didn't accept their argument. After studying the statistical report, he told the public the evidence indicates that:

> there are hundreds of thousands of inadequate or defective tires manufactured annually, leaving unsuspecting drivers traveling around the country on a time bomb.[1]

Before the decade ended, Senator Nelson's time bomb blew up for the Firestone Tire and Rubber Company. The consistently high failure rate on their popular 500 model steel-belted radial tire led to costly lawsuits and eventually forced a massive recall. The net result was millions of dollars of red ink on the firm's profit and loss statement and a tarnished reputation besides.

How could a sample representing such a small percentage of tires manufactured signal the developing failure-rate problem? Confidence in the signal is warranted because the sample was designed, taken, and analyzed using modern statistical tools—tools that very often don't require the sample to be a large percentage of the population studied.

The chapter section on random sampling will describe the actual sample design procedure for drawing random samples which the modern statistical tool of probability employs. We will now provide illustrations of the pervasiveness of the use of modern statistics in various fields as well as in everyday life.

1.1. Statistics Is Everybody's Business

The common usage of the word "statistics" has a double meaning. In one sense, "statistics" is the plural of "statistic" and refers to a collection of numerical facts. The facts might be yards gained rushing by NFL football teams, closing stock prices on the New York Stock Exchange, or housing prices in U.S. cities. But in a different sense, "statistics" (singular) refers to a *field of study* which can be exciting and informative. Information in numerical form, called data, is its raw material; the host of techniques for generating, organizing, and processing the data are its machinery. And the finished products? These are the analyses and interpretations of the data for decision-making.

This book is designed to lead the reader through the workings of statistics. The goal is to help develop a proficiency in handling and fashioning data for performing the kind of statistical analysis from which accurate conclusions can be reached.

Changing Its Image

Statistics is improving its public image as more persons learn about its use as an analytical tool. In the past, statistical manipulators have been able to perpetrate numerous frauds. As more prople learn statistical theory, more people can begin to recognize the distinguishing trademarks of sound statistical analysis from analysis which is seriously flawed.

The field of statistics is today recognized as an invaluable tool for testing concepts and for perceiving new directions in numerous disciplines. In fact, the need for statistical know-how is hard to escape. It is needed in academia; it is needed in business; it is needed in everyday affairs.

Statistics in Academia

In an expanding variety of academic disciplines, statistics is needed to achieve a better grasp of knowledge. The statistics course, long an integral part of business and economics curricula, is now well-established in several behavioral sciences—psychology, sociology, anthropology—and in such natural sciences as biology and geology. The professional fields—medicine, engineering, education, and urban planning—also demand an understanding of statistics. Even such disciplines as history, linguistics, and Greek classics, once thought unquantifiable, have joined the list of fields in which the application of statistics has produced important contributions.

Is statistics a panacea for solving difficult questions? Of course not. But the subject has proven to be useful in so many disciplines and professional fields that a background in statistics is beneficial regardless of career objectives.

Statistics in Business

In the business world, statistical issues abound. Every day, executives ask themselves questions like these:

In Marketing How sensitive is customer demand to changes in price and quality? This information is needed to market the right product at the right price.

In Manufacturing How accurately can the quality of a batch of 30,000 transistors be determined from a sample consisting of just fifty transistors? Such information is necessary to hold down the cost of producing quality products.

In Accounting What fraction of the accounts receivable balance should be regarded as uncollectible? This information may be needed in order to certify a company's financial statements.

In the Insurance Industry How does the risk of fully insuring thirty jet airplanes, each of which costs $10 million, compare with sharing the risk on 300 similar airplanes with nine other companies? Answers to this kind of question may be sought in order to know whether co-insurance is desirable.

In Banking   How long will it take before an increase in the money supply begins to have a noticeable effect on home mortgage rates? Bank economists want answers to questions like this in order to forecast the impact of Federal Reserve Board policies.

These examples merely skim the surface of business problems having statistical foundations.

Statistics—an Everyday Affair

Vital as statistics is in the academic and business worlds, its most frequent need is in everyday affairs. People are often asked to make judgments about statistical evidence on controversial issues. Here are just a few illustrations:

Do crime statistics suggest that either gun control or the death penalty are effective deterrents to crimes of violence?

Does the available evidence show that frequent marijuana usage leads to heroin addiction or to the abuse of hallucinogenic drugs?

Do laboratory experiments on dogs lead us to conclude that cigarette smoking causes cancer in human beings?

Do accident statistics indicate that the elderly are safer drivers than young marrieds (the elderly *do* have a record of fewer accidents)?

Does statistical evidence establish that the diffusion of lead into the atmosphere from the paint on automobiles contributes significantly to the pollution of the air we breathe?

Such questions cannot be answered intelligently without an understanding of statistical analysis. In fact, it is difficult to escape the need for statistical understanding. Even armchair sports enthusiasts may have to bone up on statistics to keep pace with the strategy of their favorite sport. First it was football, with former NFL quarterback Virgil Carter using statistical analysis to study field position strategy. Carter co-authored a technical paper, "Operations Research on Football," which was published in a professional journal called *Operations Research* and which helped him earn his MBA degree: "until our study, no one applied the mathematical equations of statistical analysis to assess the significance of field positions," said Carter.[2] Now it's baseball's turn. Both the American and National Leagues sponsor computerized statistical information systems to help teams determine their field strategy, evaluate players in the free-agent market—and even gauge a pitcher's speed to recognize the moment arm fatigue sets in.[3]

The Iceberg Principle

The statistical roots of many business problems are not always evident to untrained observers. Like the captain of a ship who is unaware of the iceberg's bulk, the unschooled business decision-maker oblivious to underlying statistical issues may be charting a hazardous and potentially costly course. Business leaders are often paid high salaries to make important decisions affecting not only their own reputation, but also the careers and aspirations of everyone in their organization. Responsible persons will want the statistical training which can help them evaluate the situation properly. And remember: other members of the organization won't want a leader who, like the captain of the Titanic, can't see the hidden bulk of the iceberg. The next two sections provide some perspective on how statistics is currently viewed and how it upgrades our intuition.

1.2. Attitudes Towards Statistical Training

Untrained persons hold a variety of attitudes toward statistical training. Unfortunately, many of these attitudes are related to bad feelings about arithmetic and mathematics. It's quite common, for example, to find students apprehensive about statistics courses. Intimidated by its symbols, the student is convinced at the start that statistics is a subject best left to those blessed with greater mathematical gifts. This fear prompts the rationalization, "I've never been good at math" (or figures or symbols). At the other end of the spectrum is the individual who feels that common sense and education grant authority to speak out definitively on any and all statistical issues: "special training in statistics is unnecessary—a lot of hocus pocus."

Underlying both of these all-too-common attitudes is the misguided notion that statistics is fancy arithmetic. Intimidation and arrogance tend to muddle the relationship between statistics, arithmetic, and mathematics.

Statistics Is More Than Arithmetic

Arithmetic, along with other aspects of mathematics, is certainly encountered in statistical computations. But statistics is much more than fancy arithmetic computations. Arithmetic plays the same auxiliary role in statistics as it plays in fields such as accounting, banking, retailing, or computer programming. It's only one of many spokes that keep the statistical bicycle rolling.

Statistics Is More Than a Branch of Mathematics

Statistics is sometimes considered a branch of mathematics, exactly like algebra or calculus or topology. From a novice's vantage point, one look at the mathematical symbols and equations used in statistics is usually enough to verify this notion. But statistics can be viewed as a separate and independent endeavor—and is viewed this way by most statisticians.

The relationship between mathematics and statistics is somewhat akin to that between psychology and sociology, between economics and political science, or between accounting and management. Sociology draws extensively on psychological principles but it is nevertheless considered a distinct field. Knowledge of economics is one part, but certainly not the whole, of political science. Accounting is a tool of good management, but there is obviously more to management than accounting. So it is with mathematics and statistics. Mathematics is definitely used in statistics. But statistics is much more than a branch of mathematics.

Statistics Is Thinking Clearly About Data

As a student, you cannot escape the fact that mathematics *is* used in statistics. And the higher your level of mathematical maturity, the more quickly you may grasp the meaning of some important statistical concepts. But beginning students who fear statistics because of a real or fancied deficiency in mathematics may rest assured that in statistics, mathematical maturity is a means to an end, not the end itself. The ability to manipulate symbols and equations is not what makes statistical reasoning so valuable in real-life situations. The value is rather the ability to think clearly about data, to draw valid conclusions for oneself and to recognize the erroneous conclusions drawn by others. Since one of the functions of a business school is to provide students with the analytical means of critically evaluating the quantitative impact of decision-making, it is little wonder that statistics is required in virtually every business school in the country.

1.3. Statistical Intuition

Knowingly or not, nearly everyone has been exposed to fallacious statistical reasoning at one time or another. Such fallacies are not always easy to spot, even for the well-trained. Persons lacking a statistical background are handicapped because they must rely solely on their intuition or common sense to detect erroneous statistical reasoning.

Is Your Raw Intuition Reliable?

Sometimes intuition and common sense *are* adequate. For example, when the same set of numerical facts is used by different persons to "prove" opposite conclusions, common sense tells us that the reasoning behind one or both "proofs" must be erroneous. But intuition and common sense have their limitations and at times are dangerously unreliable. In fact, uninformed intuition and preconceived notions are the culprits behind many of the statistical errors people commit.

There is a story about pioneer aviators which illustrates the danger of overreliance on intuition.

Example 1.3A. **Flying in the Days of "The Red Baron"**

During World War I, when aeronautical engineering was in its infancy, there was no sophisticated guidance equipment to lead aviators safely through inclement weather. Pilots had to rely on the use of a jar of water fastened to the instrument panel to help them maintain a level flight. Pilots could judge whether they were ascending, descending, or flying level by watching the position of the water in the jar. In clear weather these crude devices seemed quite reliable, so reliable, in fact, that pilots began to use them for flying in bad weather. Unfortunately, an inordinately large number of planes equipped with the devices crashed during bad weather.

After some investigation, an interesting fact was discovered. Pilots tended to lose their equilibrium when they could not see the horizon. In some instances their intuitive feeling contradicted the water jar reading, but most often pilots simply had no intuitive feeling at all about whether they were ascending or descending. The pilots who had developed confidence in the reliability of the water jar landed safely, while many unfortunate pilots who had not done so crashed when they could not see the horizon. At the important moment, intuition failed to help them land their planes.

Over-reliance on intuition got them into trouble they couldn't handle. With less blind faith in their own intuition and more understanding of the tools available to help them, they too could have landed safely.

Like the pilots, we often encounter situations which tend to upset our sense of statistical balance. What seems intuitively correct may turn out to be entirely wrong, and what seems intuitively wrong can often turn out to be quite correct. The unreliability of our intuition and common sense can be frustrating and sometimes embarrassing to people working with statistics without the benefit of proper statistical training.

Educated Intuition?

Despite the complexities of life, and despite the availability of powerful analytical tools for dealing with these problems, most of the countless daily decisions in our lives are still made on the basis of intuition. This is as it should be. Too much time would be used up if every decision had to be analyzed mathematically or statistically. The important thing is to know how to check intuition to avoid wrong conclusions and bad decisions with serious consequences. Here we can call upon our statistical training for help. With a proper understanding of statistical principles (theory), our intuition can be educated to ask intelligent questions on whether the data were properly collected (statistical design) and properly reported (statistical description), and whether the conclusion drawn and decision made (statistical inference and decision) are consistent with the statistical evidence at hand. Thus, in essence, statistical theory alerts us to the "traps" that exist when analyzing statistical data and, importantly, provides us with a set of procedures to avoid them.

Intuition and the Volunteer Trap

To check your own intuition, consider the statistical evidence and issues raised in the following newspaper excerpt.

Example 1.3B.   Driver Training and Highway Accidents

A traffic safety committee of the federal government reported that research showed accident rates of the professionally trained automobile driver to be about half those of untrained drivers. The research also showed fewer traffic violations for the professionally trained drivers.

Let us assume that the stated historical rates are correct. Intuitively, what do you think the findings suggest about the effectiveness of driver training? In particular, does it seem that the findings provide good evidence for concluding that future accident rates could be reduced by making driver training mandatory for all new drivers? This is what people really want to know and was probably the motivation for conducting the study.

Intuitively, most people interpret the findings as rather strong evidence for mandatory driver training. As corroborative evidence, they may point to the fact that insurance companies often offer lower rates to persons who have completed a driver training program.

Actually, this common interpretation is quite hazardous. It is based on the idea that mandatory driver education would reduce the *overall* accident rate to approximately the low level experienced by drivers who have *volunteered for driver education.* Some insights as to why this is a rash conclusion can be obtained by reading other excerpts from the same article:

> Recent research showed factors other than driver training may have produced the favorable results. For example, the committee said some of the studies failed to take in such key factors as "safety proneness" of students who wanted to take driver education courses in the first place. They also tended to ignore the questions of whether a person who takes a driver training course goes on "to significantly less or more [driving] than those who do not." Nor is there much information to indicate whether there is a "consequential relationship" between the number of violations charged against a driver and the number of accidents . . . , the report said. It also said that there was no proof that a youngster trained by a "competent, concerned, but not anxious father" would not get better instruction than one taught in high school.

The key point in interpreting the statistical reasoning of this example is that the proportion of safety-conscious drivers is almost sure to be higher among those who volunteer for driver education than among those who do not. And safety-conscious drivers, as a group, can be expected to have a lower accident rate than other drivers.

Mandatory driver education would, in effect, mix a low and high accident rate group, necessarily yielding a rate for the combined group somewhere between the high and low rates. In statistical language, we say that the accident rate for volunteer driver education programs is not representative of the rate for mandatory programs because of *self-selection bias.*

Self-selection bias distorts the true picture because the characteristic we seek to measure (the accident rate) goes hand in hand with the decision to become a voluntary member of the driver training group. Hence, it is difficult to disentangle the effect of driver education from the effect of differing attitudes towards safety. We don't know how much of the better driving record to attribute to good training, and how much to attribute to good attitudes.

Population Tagging

Yet another interesting aspect of this driver training example is the effect on insurance rates. So long as driver education is on a voluntary basis, the decision to take driver education "tags" a person as a member of a group identifiable as low risk. Therefore, it makes sense to offer premium discounts to people taking driver education. But when driver education is made mandatory, the training no longer serves to identify graduates as members of a low risk group because drivers are no longer divided according to their attitudes toward safety. As a result, insurance premium discounts for persons with driver education may have to be revoked.

Intuition and the Population Size Trap

What does your intuition suggest about the size of the sample that should be taken and investigated relative to the size of population? Do you sympathize with the manufacturer's contention in the opening chapter illustration that sampling a few thousand randomly selected tires is a shaky basis for estimating the failure rate among 180 million tires? Write down the sample size you would recommend if you were investigating the failure rate among 180 million tires. Do you suggest a sample of 10,000? 100,000? One million? Perhaps twenty million? Forty million? Changing the situation slightly, what size sample would you require if the population contained only 180 tires instead of 180 million? Now compare the percentage of tires you recommended in your sample for each of the two population sizes: 180 million and 180. Are the percentages the same? Should they be the same?

The answers to the question of how large a sample to consider taking will depend upon how much confidence we want to place in our results as an estimate of the population. The more confidence we wish, the larger the sample must be. Let's be specific. To guarantee at least ninety-five chances out of a hundred that the sample tire failure rate differs by two percentage points or less from the failure rate for the 180 million tires, a sample of only 2500 tires would be large enough—a surprisingly small amount and percentage given the size of the population. Do you want to revise your estimate for the sample size of the population of 180 tires? Don't be lead into thinking in strictly comparative terms. To guarantee the same confidence (at least ninety-five chances out of a hundred of two percentage points accuracy) requires a minimum sample size of 168 tires out of the 180, quite a turnabout in comparative terms from the first situation.

Debunking the Percentage-sample Myth

Most untrained persons guess a number much larger than 2500 in the first case and a number considerably lower than 168 in the second case. Relating the sample size to population size, a population of 180 million required only one item in the sample for each 72,000 in the population (180 million/2500), while a population of 180 items requires that nearly everyone in the population be included in the sample in order to obtain the same degree of reliability. In percentage terms a sampling percentage well below 1% is sufficient for a population of 180 million; but, a sampling percentage of 92% is required for a population of 180.

At this point you haven't yet been instructed as to how to make the correct calculation to determine the sample size required (this procedure is explained in Chapter 11), but you have learned a key idea about sampling. It is now recognized that it is misleading to believe that a sample should represent a fixed percentage of the population in order to be reliably informative. The "fixed percentage" is a myth with no basis in statistical theory. The tire manufacturers' argument is unconvincing.

The View of Someone with Statistical Training

How might someone with statistical training view the issue of the accident rate in the driver education example and failure rate in the tire testing example?

Someone with statistical training should reserve judgment about the impact of mandatory driver education on accident rates. Despite the very large amount of historical data available on accident rates, it is necessary to focus on the amount of self-selection bias for the various kinds of drivers. By contrast, in the tire testing example, someone with statistical training would feel quite comfortable in concluding that the failure rate among 180 million tires is comparable to the failure rate found in only a few thousand tires tested. The basis for the difference in attitude is the term "randomly selected", a term soon to be formally introduced. The tire article states that tested tires were randomly selected. This fact removes any worry about selection bias. A level of confidence can now be attached to the statement about the prevailing failure rate among the 180 million tires annually. With a random sample, the accumulated sample data will not be tainted by selection bias of one kind or another. For this reason, someone with statistical training, given a choice in the matter, will avoid using abundantly available data in favor of collecting a much smaller random sample.

Once the sample items are appropriately obtained, the type of reasoning that allows for generalization is known as *statistical reasoning*. The next section discusses the type of logic that allows us to generalize and shows us why this procedure cannot guarantee with absolute certainty the truth of the generalization.

1.4. Statistical Reasoning and Its Logic

There are two types of logical reasoning: deductive logic and inductive logic.

Deductive Logic

Deductive logic reasons from the general to the particular. It is extensively employed in syllogisms, which is why deductive logic is sometimes called *syllogistic* reasoning. A syllogism is a sequence of three statements in which the third statement follows directly from the first two statements. Here is an example of a simple syllogism:

> Every automobile has an air conditioner.
> All Chevrolets are automobiles.
> Therefore, all Chevrolets have air conditioners.

The first statement of a simple syllogism is called the *major premise*. It defines a group or collection of objects which have a specific characteristic in common. In the above syllogism, the major premise identifies automobiles as the collection of objects with the common feature, air conditioner.

The second statement of a simple syllogism is the *minor premise*. It defines another group and identifies them as members of the group specified in the major premise. In the above syllogism, Chevrolets are the second group identified as members of the first group, automobiles.

The third statement of the simple syllogism is the *conclusion* and is a logical result of the two premises. It concludes that the specific characteristic common to every member of the major premise group must (necessarily) be a specific characteristic of the *particular* members of the minor premise group.

In summary, a simple syllogism illustrates that a feature known to be common to the total or general class of objects (major premise) is known to be common to a subgroup of that class (minor premise).

If you reject the conclusion of a syllogism, it must be because you reject one or both of the premises. If you accept both premises of the syllogism given above, you cannot escape the conclusion that every Chevrolet has an air conditioner. This conclusion rules out the possibility that even a tiny percentage of Chevrolets lack air conditioners: what is true of every automobile must also be true for a particular Chevrolet automobile.

Venn Diagrams

Deductive reasoning can be demonstrated graphically by a *Venn Diagram*, an example of which is shown in Figure 1.1. The larger area corresponds to the major premise, and represents the group of all automobiles. The smaller area corresponds to the minor premise, and represents the group of all Chevrolets. Since the "Chevrolet area" is completely inside the large "automobile area," it follows that what is true of every automobile is also true of every Chevrolet.

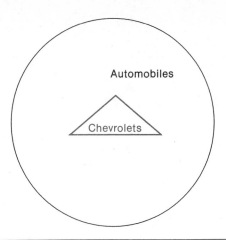

FIGURE 1.1 Venn Diagram

Inductive Logic Is Needed

Deductive logic is structured to lead us to a conclusion about the particular members of a group, given knowledge of a property common to all members of the group. But deductive logic is inadequate in generalizing from an individual member to the whole group—yet this is an important consideration in the study of statistics. The following example should help you see why.

Example 1.4A. **Not All Diesel-Engine Cars Are Alike**

In the Venn Diagram of Figure 1.2, the smaller area represents the group of diesel-engine cars with which we are familiar. Now whatever is true of all diesel-engine cars is certainly true of the ones with which we are familiar. But the reverse is not true. It does not follow that whatever is true of every diesel-engine car *with which we are famliar* is also true of all diesel-engine cars, because it may not be true of the diesel-engine cars *with which we are unfamiliar.*

The diesel-engine car example is important because it illustrates a kind of relationship and introduces the kind of logic which is extensively studied in inferential statistics. The larger area in Figure 1.2 can be thought of as the *population* of automobiles, and the smaller area as a *sample* of automobiles. The automobiles we have sampled do not constitute the entire population. It is the central task of inferential statistics to find out what conclusions can be drawn about the population on the basis of what has already been learned about a *sample* of items from the population. To draw conclusions about a population from sample evidence, one needs a different type of logic known as *induction*. A continuation of the diesel-engined car example points out the need for induction.

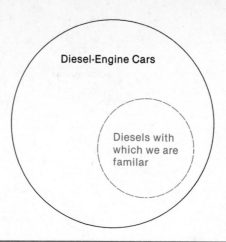

Diesel-Engine Cars

Diesels with which we are familar

FIGURE 1.2 Venn Diagram for Diesel-Engine Cars

Example 1.4B. Lemons and Diesel-Engine Cars

Suppose we are planning to buy a new diesel-engine car and every diesel-engine car can be unambiguously classified according to whether or not it is a "lemon" (defective car). Suppose that all diesel-engine cars with which we are familiar are "lemons". What can be said about diesel-engine cars we have not yet seen?

We can certainly compute a sample statistic, "percent lemons," from what we know about diesel-engine cars familiar to us. Using this sample statistic, we need inductive logic to make a statement about the corresponding percent lemons in the population of all diesel-engine cars.

We Can't Live by Deductive Reasoning Alone

Elaborating a little more on our automobile example may help clarify the main issues.

Example 1.4C. How Many Lemons Spoil the Lot?

Suppose you're at a dealer's showroom on the brink of purchasing a new automobile. Suddenly you recall that four of your friends have recently purchased the same brand and model you are considering buying with your hard-earned dollars. All four labeled their cars lemons, and said they were sorry they bought them.

Deductive reasoning does not offer any guideline about whether the car you're thinking of buying will also be a lemon. This is portrayed graphically in the Venn Diagram of Figure 1.3. There is no overlapping area between the autos known to be lemons and the autos yet to be purchased. But common sense dictates that it would be rather unusual for a prospective buyer to completely ignore such one-sided

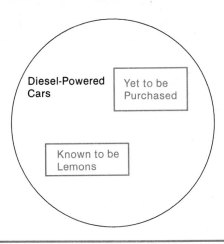

FIGURE 1.3 Venn Diagram for Lemon Diesels

bad experience as four lemons out of four cars. More likely, a rational buyer would infer that what is true of these four cars may be true of all cars of this make and model. And if all cars of this make and model are lemons, then the one you purchase will be a lemon too.

Most people will properly wonder if four lemons out of four cars is enough evidence to indicate anything of substance about the rest of a population. The automobile dealer can be counted upon to say something like, "well, a few bad apples won't spoil the whole lot," or "I'm sure you've just seen an unusual sample." But make the evidence forty lemons out of forty cars or four hundred lemons out of four hundred cars and see if the dealer can still make the sale.

The main point of the automobile lemon example is that we constantly rely on inductive inference. By applying inductive logic, we use the limited evidence at hand to form conclusions about the facts not experienced. Since we all do it frequently, we might as well learn to do it correctly. This is what sound statistical reasoning is all about.

Thus far we have seen that: (1) a sharpened statistical intuition follows directly from statistical training; (2) a person trained in statistics will employ statistical reasoning rather than other types of reasoning in order to gain reliability in making generalizations from a representative sample. Let us now discuss the mechanics of random sampling, the procedure that provides representativeness to the sample taken.

1.5. Random Sampling

Sampling is a key ingredient for statistical reasoning. Information on observed items is the basis for a conclusion about all the items. More precisely, the observed characteristic of a sample is used to imply (infer) the condition of the population characteristic. Recall that the observed six percent failure rate on the statistical sample of a few thousand automobile tires discussed in the opening illustration forms the basis for a statement about the failure rate among the population of 180 million tires produced annually.

Expert Judgment

There are essentially two ways to obtain a sample from the population. One way is to rely on the human judgment of an "expert" who can pick out key features of the population items which will make a sample of them representative of the total population. Political polls are one of the better known types of judgment sample.

Example 1.5A.   Expert Pollsters

In political elections, "experts" may believe that religion, ethnic background, income, and previous voting patterns, among other things, are decisive factors in voting behvavior. So long as the experts are correct in their judgment, they can select a sample which closely resembles the population with regard to those factors and use that sample to make a good forecast of the election outcome. Of course, the validity of their inferences reflects the accuracy of their judgment. If they believe race and religion are decisive factors in voting behavior while a candidate's physical appearance and ability to field questions are, in fact, the decisive factors, then the inferences of the "experts" are likely to err by a wide margin.

Random Samples

The second way to obtain a sample relies upon mechanical methods rather than upon human judgment to obtain the sample items. The method is *random sampling*.

Random sampling is a method of selection which gives every possible sample of the same given size a predetermined chance of being drawn from the population; very commonly, every possible sample has an *equal* chance of being selected from the population, a situation known as *simple* random sampling. The following example shows how a simple random sample might be obtained.

Example 1.5B.   Drawing a Simple Random Sample

A simple way to obtain a random sample of items from a population utilizes poker chips and a large mixing bowl. Suppose we wish to draw a random sample of size five from a population of fifty-two items. The procedure is as follows:

1. Assign the numbers 1-52 to the fifty-two items in the population.

2. Number fifty-two different poker chips to correspond to the numbers assigned the items.

3. Mix the chips thoroughly in a bowl.

4. Select five chips from the bowl.

5. Use as the sample the five population items having the same numbers as found on the selected chips.

Why use this indirect approach? Why not just put the fifty-two population items right into the bowl? The problem is the population items might not fit into a bowl for thorough mixing, as, for example, if computers were being considered.

Does the random sampling process sound vaguely similar to that of drawing a poker hand dealt from a well-shuffled deck of cards? It should, because a card hand fairly dealt from a properly shuffled deck *is* a random sampling from the deck.

Random Samples: A Necessary Ingredient

Why are random sample results so important in statistics? Only for random sample results can the extent and pattern of the variation in results be systematically investigated for insight into their usefulness and reliability. Take the tire-testing case in which the population consists of the 180 million automobile tires produced annually. Suppose we repeatedly draw random samples of 2500 tires from this population, recording the failure rate for each sample. After recording the results of many samples, what will we learn? That the failure rate varies from one sample to the next and that some failure rates occur more frequently than others. That is, we will have a table which describes how frequently the different failure rates occur. Obviously, it would be a tremendous task to continually draw and establish the shape of the failure rate distribution. Isn't there a shortcut way to obtain this distribution?

We would very much like to be able to predict analytically, in advance, what the failure rate distribution would look like—that is, how much variation there is—without having to go through a lengthy sampling procedure. Fortunately, statisticians can do this, but only if the mathematical laws of probability are applicable. These probability laws apply objectively only to random samples.[5] These laws make it possible to know the pattern of sampling variability upon which the quality of statistical reasoning depends.

The overall quality of an investigation that begins with a random sample depends on how well each phase is conducted. Let us discuss the various fields of statistics and see how they can be involved in a full investigation.

1.6. The Field of Statistics

Statistics can be divided into four rather distinct, but highly complementary, areas. The four D's of statistics are:

Designing the investigation,
Describing the data,
Drawing inferences,
Deciding on a course of action.

Statistical Design

Statistical *design* deals with procedures for efficient and economic gathering of sample data suitable for statistical analysis. There are numerous statistical designs offering schemes to gather necessary sample data. No single one of these is always the best. Instead, the circumstances of the individual problem will determine which of the design possibilities is most appropriate.

It's hard to overestimate the importance of good statistical design. Only if sample data are collected in a way compatible with the assumptions which underpin the various statistical techniques can the results be used for valid statistical conclusions.

The government test of automobile tire failures described in the opening illustration suggests that a *simple* random sampling design was used. This design avoided (among other things) the self-selection bias which posed such serious problems in the driver education sample and, more importantly, provided the basis for reliable statistical inference.

Statistical Description

Statistical *description* is concerned with techniques for communicating statistical information. These techniques involve condensing, summarizing, and reporting data in order to distinguish the important regularities and patterns of variation from the erratic or nonsystematic component of the data. The following example illustrates why we might want to report less information than is available.

Example 1.6.   **Expenditures at the Supermarket**

Suppose that we are interested in learning how much families spend in supermarkets. If we survey 10,000 households and obtain expenditures down to the last penny for the weekly grocery list, we may well end up with 3000 different figures, many of which differ by only one or two cents. Does it really serve our purpose to report all the individual amounts? Most probably it does not. Instead, we will group the figures into a few classes and report that 3612 households spend at least $40, but less than $55; 2742 households spend at least $55, but less than $70, and so forth. Summarizing the data in this way makes it easier to focus on and comprehend the main pattern of variability in household expenditures—without getting bogged down with presenting the minor differences between individual expenditures.

Statistical Inference

Statistical inference concerns making valid generalizations about a reference group's relevant characteristics. The reference group is called the *statistical population;* the relevant characteristics, the *population parameters.* In the tire example, the 180 million tires made annually constituted the statistical population; the failure rate among the 180 million tires was the population parameter.

The generalization is a reasonable conclusion arrived at by obtaining the relevant characteristic of only some of the members of the reference group. The process of selecting the members is known as sampling and the members selected are a *sample* from the population. The predominance of that characteristic in the sample (*the sample statistic*) provides the basis for drawing an inference (the prediction) about the predominance of that characteristic in the population (*the population parameter*). That is,

STATISTICAL INFERENCE

$$\text{Sample Statistic} \xrightarrow{\text{infers}} \text{Population Parameter}$$

In the tire example, the condition of the tires tested constituted the relevant characteristic of the sample. Therefore, the 6% failure rate among these tires is the sample statistic used to draw an inference about the failure rate of the 180 million tires in the population.

A statistical inference based on sampling is an alternative to gathering information on the entire population, a procedure known as a population *census*. Sampling has two obvious potential advantages over a census: reduced cost and reduced time to obtain the information. However, we shall encounter other important reasons for sampling. For example, gathering data for a population census may be either physically impossible or physically destructive. Surprisingly, perhaps, a census may also lead to more measurement errors than a sample.[6]

Although our objective is to know the values of the population parameters, limitations of data gathering mentioned above usually restrict us to using the values of the sample statistics. Since a sample is only a partial view of the population, the values of the sample statistics can only serve as an *estimate* of the corresponding values of the population parameters. These estimates, therefore, are ordinarily subject to error (known technically as *sampling error*). The basic methodology of statistical inference involves the study of the patterns of the estimation errors arising from the sampling process.

Statistical Decision Theory

Statistical *decision theory* is concerned with the selection of the single most desirable course of action from among a set of alternative actions when the consequences of the actions are not known with certainty at the time the decision must be made. For example, the question of whether an automobile manufacturer should introduce a new subcompact car would depend on the size of the market for this type of car and costs of manufacturing and marketing the car. Since neither market size nor costs can be forecast with perfect certainty, the decision problem is a candidate for statistical decision theory.

Some statistical problems encompass only one of the four areas while other problems encompass all four areas. The decision of an automobile manufacturer to market a new subcompact car would undoubtedly involve all four areas of statistics. A market research study would be designed to learn consumer attitudes toward subcompact cars. The results of the survey would have to be condensed and summarized for presentation to top management, and the results would be generalized from the surveyed group to the entire car-buying public. Finally, in considering the pros and cons of introducing the car, top management would have to weigh the likelihood of success (obtained from the research findings) against the profit prospects of favorable and unfavorable public reaction to the car.

A flow chart of the four Ds is given in Figure 1.4.

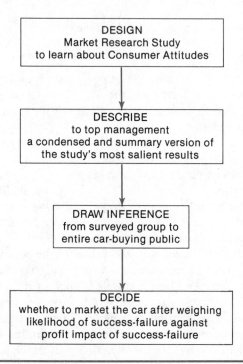

FIGURE 1.4 Flow Chart of the Four Ds for Decision to Market New Subcompact Car

1.7. Concluding Comments

Intuition is something we all have and would be lost without. When faced with a bundle of information and uncertainty as to its meaning, we use this quick internal information sorter to identify the important facts and to draw conclusions upon which we can act. However, as we try to cope with complex phenomena, we often find our intuition inadequate, in error, or lacking altogether. Faced with the need to improve our information sorter, we turn to the discipline of statistics.

By formally studying statistical principles (its theory), intelligent questions can be asked and one can recognize the statistical pitfalls prevalent in generating, presenting, and analyzing statistical data. Without an understanding and use of theory, one can hardly be expected to develop precise inferential statements. In fact, conclusions formulated without theory must remain judgmental and objectively nonverifiable.

The body of statistical theory is divided into four distinct branches: statistical design, statistical description, statistical inference, and statistical decision theory. Although each of the branches involves a distinct set of statistical principles, a statistical investigation often involves a combination or even all of the branches to answer the question being asked.

The raw material of statistics and its component branches is the variation in data. Statistical description attempts to organize the data in order to gain informational insight about the variation and its interpretation in the problem being investigated. The other three branches share the same informational concern about the variation in data, but they employ the powerful analytical tool of probability theory to deal more explicitly with the uncertainty brought about by variation in the data. In a nutshell, statistics is an information system which attempts to organize data and ferret out and deliver the messages embodied there.

In the next chapter, we begin our investigation of statistics with the most often encountered branch of statistical description.

Footnotes and References

[1] *Wall Street Journal*, June 4, 1970.
[2] *The South Bend Tribune*, February 17, 1971
[3] *Mainliner*, June issue 1980
[4] *The South Bend Tribune*, March 29, 1968
[5] For this reason, random samples are sometimes called probability samples.
[6] An interesting article illustrating this point with respect to the 1970 Census of Population is "How to Count Better: Using Statistics to Improve the Census," by Morris H. Hansen, in *Statistics: A Guide to the Unknown*, edited by Judith M. Taner, et al. (Holden-Day, 1972).

Questions and Problems

1. A newspaper clipping appeared stating: A random inspection of 4500 tires removed from cars in four American cities showed that 1125 were worn down below tread indicators, Firestone (tire company) reports. The tire company said this is a potentially dangerous practice because 90 percent of tire trouble occurs in the last 10 percent of trend life.[1]

Having read the clipping carefully, do the statistics and information presented mislead or illuminate the issue of tire safety?

2. The dust jacket of the revised edition of a well-advertised college textbook stated that the new edition was an "updated expanded edition of the best seller in the field." It also claimed there were "more than 100,000 copies of the first edition in use."

a. Explain what you think "best seller in the field" means. Are there any plausible alternative explanations?

b. Explain what you think "in use" means. Are there any plausible alternative explanations?

c. What sales figures would you suggest be compared to assess the relative popularity of the book?

d. With what other sales figure should the 100,000 copies be compared?

e. A comparison of publication dates reveals that eight years elapsed between the publication of the first and second editions of the textbook. Does this knowledge change any of your answers to the previous question?

3. *Education and Heroin Usage* Data from the National Institute on Drug Abuse reveals that Americans with college backgrounds are far less likely to use heroin than people with less education. Youngsters with at least some college education have a heroin use rate one twentieth that of high school dropouts.[2]

a. Does the comparatively high heroin usage rate among high school dropouts versus the lower usage rate among college educated people "prove" that less education causes heroin use? Explain.

b. Can the large disparity between the rates of heroin usage (the high school dropout rate twenty times as large as the rate among the better educated) result from the fact that there are more users in total among high school dropouts than among college educated users? Explain.

c. Could the usage rate differential be partly attributable to the way data on heroin usage is found and recorded? Explain.

4. Studded snow tires—curse or cure? In the late 1960s and early 1970s metal-studded snow tires were widely used during winter months in Canada and northern parts of the United States to increase traction on icy roads. The studs were blamed for tearing up road surfaces and were ultimately banned in most states. A newspaper article reported that "National Safety Council tests have demonstrated that studs improve stopping distance by as much as 50 percent and best starting traction in some instances as high as 50 percent on 'glaze ice' near the freezing point—soft ice that is easy for the studs to grip." Nevertheless, according to the article, a survey in Ontario, Canada "concluded that vehicles with studded tires are involved in a somewhat bigger percentage of accidents on icy roads than those on clear surfaces."[3]

a. Give as many plausible explanations as you can for the higher accident rates for drivers with studded snow tires on icy roads.

b. List at least one flaw each in the design of the Ontario study, in the description of the findings, in the drawing of inferences, and in the (implied) decision stage of the study.

5. The following article is from the August 16, 1972 *South Bend Tribune*:

"Airline pilots flying in and out of Love Field may not be aware of all the rules that they have to contend with.

"Among these U.S. Air Service rules, laid down in 1920 and still on the books, are:

'Don't turn sharply while taxiing. Instead, have someone lift the tail around.'

'Pilots should carry handkerchiefs to wipe off their goggles.'

'Hedge-hopping won't be tolerated.'

'Pilots will not wear spurs while flying.'

'Don't trust altitude instruments.'

'Don't leave the ground with your motor leaking.'

'And last, but not least, if an emergency occurs while flying, land as soon as you can.'"

Which of the rules do you think were based on common sense (whatever that is), which on statistical evidence, and which on unfounded intuition?

6. "There are always many thorny statistical issues connected with this type of business decision. I'm sure I'd be opening a statistical can of worms if I investigate the issues closely. I'd rather let sleeping dogs lie. The way I figure it, I'll take a good look at the situation, play my hunch, and roll the dice, so to speak. If I win, I win. If I lose, I lose. What I'm not going to do is waste time and lose sleep trying to figure out a statistical game."

Comment on the relationship between this attitude and the "iceberg principle". (Hint: How will a ship sailing iceberg-laden waters fare if the captain refuses to acknowledge and deal with the icebergs in the waters? How is the likelihood of disaster affected by the number of crossings over iceberg-laden waters?)

7. Are statistical "icebergs" usually hard to recognize? Are professional statisticians or persons with extensive statistical training the only ones that can identify them? Explain. (Hint: Draw a distinction between the task of the maritime professionals who locate and map the flow of icebergs and the ship's captain who has the responsibility to use the map to avoid hitting an iceberg.)

8. "Statistics is just fancy arithmetic. If you can't handle arithmetic, watch out for the statistics course. If you're good at arithmetic you ought to breeze through statistics." Comment.

9. Mathematical maturity, including the ability to comprehend symbols and equations, is thought to be helpful in studying statistics. Is gaining this mathematical maturity the real objective of studying business statistics?

10. Are statistical procedures a replacement for intuition and common sense? Is the reverse true? What should be done if the conclusions from a statistical analysis seem to conflict with intuition and common sense?

11. What is counter-intuitive about the correct conclusion in the driver training example (1.3B)? How can this hidden "statistical iceberg" be spotted and averted?

12. The tire safety study reported in the opening illustration of the chapter is usually considered counter-intuitive to persons who have not studied statistics. Explain. Is there a "statistical iceberg" that a person should know about to properly interpret this study as well as its modified version for a smaller population size given in Section 1.3?

13. Before using evidence from a sample to draw conclusions about a population, a statistician would likely be more concerned about:
a. how the sample is obtained *or* how large it is?
b. how large a random sample is *or* how large a percentage of the population it is?

14. Below are the major and minor premises of a syllogism. What conclusion follows from the premises?
Herbert Smith is a basketball player.
All basketball players are tall.

15. Suppose that the minor premise of the syllogism in Problem 14 is not true. Is the syllogism then invalid?

16. Would the syllogism in Problem 14 be valid if the major and minor premises were interchanged?

17. Draw a Venn Diagram illustrating the syllogism in Problem 14.

18. For each set of statements below, indicate whether the set of statements constitutes a valid syllogism, an invalid syllogism, or an inductive inference.
a. All Pintos are grey.
Herbert's car is a Pinto.
Herbert's car is grey.
b. Herbert's Pinto is grey.
Herbert's car is a Pinto.
Therefore, some Pintos are grey.
c. I have seen many Pintos.
All the Pintos I have seen are grey.
Therefore, the next Pinto I see is likely to be grey.

Footnotes for Questions and Problems

[1]*Akron Beacon Journal*, September 30, 1977, p. C5.
[2]*Parade Magazine*, August 15, 1976, p. 4.
[3]*South Bend Tribune*, September 19, 1971.

Classification and Organization of Data

Preview.   A central theme of this chapter is the importance of statistical data—a set of numbers—as a medium of communication. Contrary to a popular cliche, (statistical) facts do *not* ''speak for themselves.'' Depending upon the way data are classified and compared, more than one clear message can emerge from the same set of numbers. Consequently, there is a critical need for business people to master the art of organizing numerical information to fashion effectively the messages to be sent and received. This skill also serves as a protection against the deceptive statistical messages of another sender. A classification scheme presented in this chapter provides the structure for comprehending statistical messages. Cognizance of this structure is as necessary to understanding statistical communication as is knowledge of the baseball rules to understanding the importance of the difference between a long out that retires the side and a short home run that scores four runs. From this structure important distinctions are made according to (1) the purpose of analysis, (2) the types of statistical variables being compared (qualitative versus quantitative), and (3) the measurement scale appropriate to the data. Finally, the frequency distribution, an extremely useful tool for presenting and analyzing data, is introduced.

2

It was a business nightmare for one of America's oldest and largest corporations. After fifteen years of developmental and test marketing, Procter and Gamble launched its Rely brand of feminine tampons. Consumer approval quickly gave the brand significant market share. Rely showed every sign of becoming a market leader, joining a stable of the company's other household-word brands, such as Tide, Crest, Pampers, Folgers, and Prell. Then, in September 1980, Procter and Gamble withdrew its successful new entry from the market. This was a stunning reversal. The decision was the culmination of several days of intensive deliberations by the company's top management.

What triggered such a drastic move? A just published September study by the U.S. Government's Center for Disease Control linked Rely usage with the alarming increase in reported cases of Toxic Shock Syndrome (TSS). TSS was a newly discovered, potentially serious disease affecting mainly women under 30 who used tampons during their menstrual periods.

The initial reaction of P & G executives was to fight to save the Rely brand. But newspapers quickly began to publish articles linking Rely tampons to TSS deaths. By mid-September, Rely's troubles had become a front page story. One big headline read, "Rely Causes 25 Deaths." There was extensive radio and television coverage of the issue. Facing potentially monumental liability suits, a persistent negative press, and threat of government (FDA) action, Procter and Gamble capitulated and withdrew the product from the market. Top management ordered a halt in production and the removal of Rely from dealers' shelves. Paid ads appeared in newspapers urging women to discontinue their use of Rely because of the possible risk involved and to send back the unused product for a refund. Rely as a brand was dead.

A post-mortem analysis of the Rely fiasco reveals several interesting aspects about Procter and Gamble's decision. Financially, the product withdrawal was very costly. In the form of after-tax loss, industry analysts put a $75 million price tag on the action. No doubt a $75 million loss would financially hurt P & G, but were the real stakes in the Rely episode even higher? From the statements made by P & G executives, it appears there was a fear that the kind of negative publicity that Rely was getting could readily spill over and tarnish, perhaps permanently, the consumer images of P & G's other brands. More importantly, there was the issue of public trust. The company was afraid that consumer reaction would be doubly severe and more long lasting if the public concluded that the company had not dealt with the Rely situation in an honest and responsible manner.

What was this fear based on? Did P & G know something about Rely that it wasn't telling the public? Should it, as Ralph Nader's group claims, have pulled Rely off the market long before it did? P & G concluded that if these charges were left unanswered, suspicions about the company's trustworthiness would be fueled and cause the public to question the integrity of P & G's entire product line. Procter and Gamble therefore set out to convince the public it was a company that could be trusted. A media blitz followed. P & G published its own version of the Rely story.

Procter and Gamble's advertising campaign was successful. Initial negative publicity evaporated. Surveys of public opinion after the ad campaign on P & G's handling of the Rely withdrawal showed that the public were convinced that P & G had acted responsibly in light of the evidence.

What allowed Procter and Gamble to successfully defend its actions in the Rely case? The answer is P & G's specially prepared statistical message. P & G's well-designed ads presented statistics that delivered the message that stopped the finger of guilt from pointing at the company. The message P & G sent used statistics to show: first, that the evidence initially available to P & G did not warrant early product withdrawal; and second, that it wasn't until the September government report and its statistical evidence that P & G could consider the problem to be attributable to use of Rely. Highlighting the key role of statistics at each stage of the Rely episode, we have:

it was a statistical study that persuaded the government to single out and pursue Rely among all other brands of tampons.

it was Procter and Gamble's interpretation of the same available statistical evidence used by the government that initially led the company to fight for the Rely brand (among tens of millions of tampon users, 242 cases of TSS were reported, of which 76 involved Rely).

it was statistics that led Ralph Nader's group to charge that P & G should have pulled Rely from the market earlier.

it was public reporting and interpretation of statistics that caused a public reaction to mount against the continued marketing of Rely.

it was carefully prepared statistical evidence that gave P & G an opportunity to present its defense and successfully defuse the "public trust" issue.

In short, one can see in the Rely episode an illustration of the importance of statistics as a medium of communication. The federal government and Procter and Gamble alike used carefully organized and presented data as the medium to convey their respective messages. The government carefully gathered and submitted the data in a statistical format to show the public that Rely was an unsafe product. Similarly, Procter and Gamble, by its own compilation of data, made a well-prepared response that effectively minimized the damage. Although Procter and Gamble was forced to withdraw Rely, P & G's advertisement appeared to have averted the repercussions that would follow from public opinion, which concluded that P & G acted irresponsibly by not withdrawing Rely earlier.[1]

In this chapter we shall see how Procter and Gamble presented statistical information in defense of its move and what more can be said about the meaning of the information. The important point to realize from Procter and Gamble's response is that one needs to know how statistical data can be fashioned to deliver the message intended.

2.1. Communicating Numerical Information

No business person can afford to be statistically uninformed. The consequences could be disastrous. Had Procter and Gamble executives been simple-minded in handling the Rely statistics (knowingly or not) they might have faced an insurmountable loss of public trust in the statistics they published on their products—a blow with potential financial consequences that would have far exceeded the $75 million corporate loss they suffered on the Rely brand alone.

What lesson does this provide? It shows that it is incorrect to believe that only *one* clear message must emerge from a set of numbers. Procter and Gamble and the government each were able to fashion a message from the same set of statistics on TSS that suited their needs.

In every business firm, there is a critical need for people to master the art of organizing numerical information to know how to develop the messages that need to be sent and received. Finding the person who can make numbers talk means finding the one who knows how to organize numerical information.

The Focus of the Next Three Chapters

Why has knowing how to organize numerical information become such a key issue today? There is little doubt that the amount of numerical facts to be digested has expanded greatly without a corresponding increase in the capability of comprehending and absorbing detail. What can be done? By devising a classification scheme and appropriate statistical procedures, large amounts of numerical detail, called *data*, can be effectively squeezed, processed, and summarized for manageable consumption. This chapter and the two chapters that follow deal with describing a classification scheme and the methods for properly organizing and presenting data. The purpose is to learn how to convey meaning through numbers and how to find the message in data reported by others. These chapters are generally characterized by the term *descriptive statistics*. Descriptive statistics therefore defines the communicative and reporting branch of statistics.

Descriptive Methods

The methods of descriptive statistics generally fall into two broad categories:

1. data presentation and
2. data reduction and summarization.

Data presentation methods refer to methods of constructing tables and graphs which accurately portray the desired information. Data reduction methods suppress unnecessary detail to highlight some of the more significant features, whereas data summarization methods are used to describe the most significant features of the data in just a few numbers.

2.2. A Schematic Approach to Data Classifications

In one respect, the person learning statistics faces an obstacle similar to a person learning about baseball, soccer, or football. Some terms and concepts that are second-nature to statistically knowledgeable persons could be serious obstacles to persons trying to learn the subject. Comprehending these terms and concepts can't make you a statistical super-star any more than comprehension of the rules and language of baseball will make you a .400 hitter. But learning the rules and language of the game, statistical or otherwise, is a prerequisite to receiving fruitful instruction from one who knows the game. With this perspective we begin the study of statistics from a data classification scheme.

The Elementary Unit

In statistical terminology, the entity about which information is gathered is called an *elementary unit;* the numerical information is recorded as *data*. In business, elementary units are entities such as customers, suppliers, competitive firms, etc. Their features may be asset size, profits, days overdue on account, different lines of business, type of executive positions, plant locations.

Classifying Realizable Possibilities: The Statistical Variable

The concept of a statistical variable provides for the classification of all the realizable possibilities that should be considered. Historically, some possibilities have occurred and others have not. The concept of a variable accounts for both.

Let's demonstrate this idea with a business planning example. For planning purposes, many possible growth rates must be considered. The concept of a variable allows for growth rates which may never have been observed in the past, but which may yet appear in the future. It is a concept which is essential in understanding how the field of statistics attempts to handle the problem of prediction.

Kinds of Statistical Variables

Fundamentally, there are two different kinds of statistical variables—quantitative and qualitative. If the possible numerical values of a measurable characteristic, say next quarter's earnings on the Fortune 500, are the points of interest, a *quantitative* variable is used. A *qualitative* variable is used if the possible characteristics can only be described, say the different types of composition used in tennis rackets to be marketed next season. An *attribute* qualitative variable means that the quality has only its presence or absence as alternatives, for example, house purchasing with or without a mortgage. A *categorical* qualitative variable implies the availability of several alternatives—such attributes as suggested by the tennis racket types just mentioned.

Figure 2.1 presents an overview of the components of a classification scheme and a comparison of the concepts of a statistical variable with the observational world. Any characteristic of an elementary unit fits into the scheme shown here. The distinction between the different kinds of statistical variables is shown in the bottom half of the diagram. The distinction between reality and the related statistical variable is seen by comparing the top half with the bottom half of the diagram.

Using the scheme in Figure 2.1, an observation of a described characteristic of a person or thing is analogous, in statistical terminology, to data on an attribute of an elementary unit. Likewise, an observation on a measured characteristic of a person or thing is analogous, in statistical terminology, to data on a *variate* of an elementary unit.

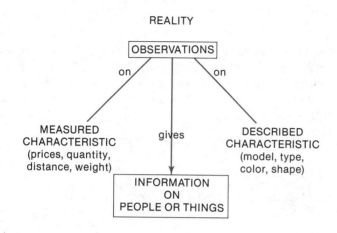

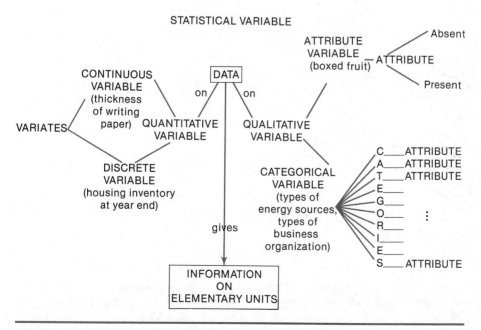

FIGURE 2.1 A Statistical Variable Used for Classifying Observations

How Many Variables Per Elementary Unit?

On many occasions, there will be more than one characteristic observed for the same elementary unit. Data, therefore, are also classified according to *how many characteristics* of each elementary unit are recorded.

If only one variable is recorded for an elementary unit, the data are *univariate*.

If two variables are recorded per elementary unit, the data are *bivariate*.

If there are more than two variables per elementary unit, the data are *multivariate*.

For example, suppose data are collected on the size of firms in the chemical industry. These data would be univariate, because only one variable (size) is recorded for each elementary unit (firm). But if size, profitability, and market share are recorded for each firm, the data are multivariate. These differences are shown graphically in Figure 2.2.

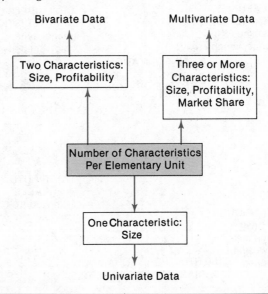

FIGURE 2.2 The Number of Statistical Variables for an Elementary Unit

2.3. What Type of Analysis? The Purpose of Using Data

An executive recruiter once said that a well-prepared job hunter is one who has in mind a model of how he will proceed in the problem-solving situations of the company. Similar advice applies in statistical reporting. Before trying your hand at data analysis, you should have in mind a statistical model which will offer guidance so that you can carry out sensible data analysis.

Data analysis can be classified into two common types. These two types can be distinguished according to whether or not there is information of interest in the *sequence* in which the data are recorded.

If there is useful informational content in the sequence of described or numerical characteristics, then the data are subject to *time series analysis*.

On the other hand, if the sequence of the observations does not exhibit a pattern of informational interest, then the study must focus on the frequency or percentage of occurrence of the characteristic. In the latter case, the data are organized for *cross-section* analysis.

Time series analysis or cross-section analysis can be conducted on the same elementary unit or different elementary units. Time series analysis, however, usually deals with the message in the *sequence* of attributes or variates on the *same elementary unit;* for example, the trend in the monthly sequence of General Motors' sales over the last 48 months. Cross-section analysis, on the other hand, refers usually to the *frequency* of occurrence. How often does a particular attribute or numerical value occur given a set of *different elementary units,* setting aside the sequence in which they were reported?

If recordings on different elementary units were reported in sequence, analysis could first be conducted to see if there is useful information in the sequence pattern. If the series shows no exploitable pattern sequence, then the sequence could be disregarded. In this case, time series analysis would be bypassed in favor of cross-section analysis.

A summary schematic diagram of the various combinations in which data on elementary units can be classified is shown in Figure 2.3.

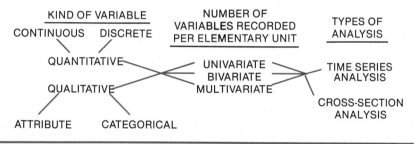

FIGURE 2.3 Schematic Diagram for Classifying Data and Types of Analysis

2.4. Qualitative Variables

Data collected on qualitative variables can be organized easily. If the qualitative variable is of the categorical variety, each elementary unit, say respondent in a sample survey, possesses an attribute and is assigned to a category. Since the attributes of the categorical variable are mutually exclusive and collectively exhaustive, the elementary unit possesses one attribute (and only one) of several possible, for example the respondent's health status. Each category represents a mutually exclusive attribute. An elementary unit can also be assigned to the absent or present column of an attribute type qualitative variable—for example, classified as either a "user" or "non-user" of a ready-to-eat breakfast cereal.

The following examples will illustrate the difference between the two types and show that the recognition of the distinction is not a trivial matter.

Example 2.4A. Advertising on "Hollywood Squares": Evaluating the Sales Impact of Network TV Advertising

The advertising budget of a leading liquid starch producer supports a network television program called the "Hollywood Squares". The program invites well-known personalities to play a game similar to tic-tac-toe. A liquid starch usage survey produced 305 viewers of the program and 1411 nonviewers. Among other things, the extent of liquid starch usage among the respondents was determined.

Each respondent was classified in either the attribute "user" column or in the "non-user" column. Non-user means the absence of a user and is the only mutually exclusive alternative to "user". Whether the respondent is a user or non-user of liquid starch products, no further implication follows about the presence or absence of the respondents' other attributes. The attribute liquid starch user speaks for itself only and is therefore an attribute variable. Table 2.1 shows the extent of usage for both viewers and nonviewers.[2]

TABLE 2.1. Usership of Liquid Starch Analyzed by Viewership of "Hollywood Squares" Program

	VIEWERS		NONVIEWERS	
	Number	Percentage	Number	Percentage
Do not use liquid starch	133	44	725	51
Do use liquid starch	172	56	686	49
Total respondents	305	100	1,411	100

There are additional questions of interest. One involves the degree of competitiveness among the existing brands; the other brand-switching between brands. Data on the brand most recently purchased by the product users provide the required information. With about a dozen other competing brands of liquid starch available in the marketplace, the liquid starch *brand* is a *categorical* variable. The presence of one brand (attribute) implies the absence of all the other brands (other attributes in the set). Designating a respondent as a user of this advertised brand says more than that he or she is a member of the "user" family as opposed to the "non-user" family of liquid starch products. It asserts that within the user family, the respondent belongs to this advertised brand branch of the family and not to any of the dozen other branches identified with competing brands.

Table 2.2 shows the assignments to liquid starch categories of brand users. Note that

> the totals for all brands combined equal the figures presented in the previous table for product usership;

> the percentages add to 100 per cent in each column, but they do not add to 100 per cent across each row.

This latter point implies that the analysis is for the variable listed down—"brand usership"—and not the variable listed across—"program viewership". The brand-switching phenomenon between brands can be investigated by surveying consumer panel usage over successive time periods, constructing a usage table like Table 2.2 for each, and comparing the changing usage percentages for the brands.

TABLE 2.2. Brand Usership of Liquid Starch Analyzed by Viewership of "Hollywood Squares" Program

| | VIEWERS | | NONVIEWERS | |
	Number	Percentage	Number	Percentage
The Advertised Brand	76	45	204	30
Competing Brand: A	4	2	24	3
B	6	3	51	8
C	1	1	16	2
D	19	11	86	13
E	4	2	7	1
F	12	7	35	5
G	3	2	8	1
H	15	9	59	9
I	2	1	17	2
J	0	0	17	2
Don't Know Brand Used	16	9	80	12
All Other Brands	14	8	82	12
Total, All Brands	172	100	686	100

The distinction between attribute and categorical variables is often misunderstood and causes needless confusion in interpreting the information presented. The following example describes a situation in which seven different attribute variables can easily be mistaken for one categorical variable.

Example 2.4B.   Consumer Profiles for Heavy Users of Shotgun Ammunition

To study the differences between consumer profiles of heavy users and non-users of shotgun ammunition, data were collected over different regions of the country. Table 2.3 indicates the geographic location of the 536 men interviewed.

TABLE 2.3. Geographic Location of 141 Heavy Users and 395 Nonusers of Shotgun Ammunition

	HEAVY USERS (Percentage)	NONUSERS (Percentage)
New England—Mid-Atlantic	21	33
N.W. Central	22	30
South Atlantic	23	12
E. South Central	10	3
W. South Central	10	5
Mountain	6	3
Pacific	9	15

TABLE 2.4. Psychographic Profiles of 141 Heavy Users and 395 Nonusers of Shotgun Ammunition

	PERCENTAGE ANSWERING "YES"	
	Heavy Users	Nonusers
I like danger.	19	8
I often do a lot of repair work on my own car.	36	12
I read the newspaper every day.	51	72
I like fishing.	68	26
I would like to be on the police force.	22	8
If given a chance, most men would cheat on their wives.	33	14
There is too much violence on television.	35	45

Notice that the percentages in each column sum to 100 (except for a slight rounding error).

This asserts the seven regions of the country are the entire set of mutually exclusive categories for one variable: location.

The percentages shown in the columns of Table 2.4, on the other hand, do *not* sum to 100.

This is not a mistake and the explanation is simple. The data refer to *seven different attribute variables* rather than to seven categories of one categorical variable. The table merely shows the number of affirmative answers assignable to each attribute variable. For example, out of 141 heavy users polled, 19 of the men responded "yes" to the question, "I like danger." The other 122 men who do not possess the attribute of responding "yes" to this question presumably are asserting the absence of this attribute from their psychographic profile.

Statistical Iceberg 2.4B: Ambiguous Categories

It is the hallmark of good data presentation to be clear about the basis of classification. How are qualitative data fitted into the proper categories? Sometimes, no effort is needed since the classification scheme is obvious. The qualitative variable sex has the two clearly defined and obvious categories "male" and "female". In other cases, misinterpretation can easily occur because the exact meaning of the categories is not so obvious. In these cases, unambiguous categories along with proper labeling is imperative. In the following example, ambiguously defined categories can easily dupe the reader who doesn't bother to clarify what responses would be classified into the stated categories.

Example 2.4C. Surveying Customer Satisfaction

In a survey of attitudes towards a particular product, it is not immediately obvious how the categories "satisfied", "mixed feelings", and "not satisfied" should be interpreted; nor is it even clear that these are the appropriate categories. Consider Table 2.5:

TABLE 2.5. Degree of Satisfaction with Product

Satisfied	30%
Mixed feelings	25
Not satisfied	20
Other (don't know, can't be classified, etc.)	25
Total (N = 2400)	100%

You can see what the table above has *not* told us by examining Table 2.6, based upon the same survey.

TABLE 2.6. Degree of Satisfaction with Product (among those who have used it)

Satisfied	40%
(Fantastic product; it couldn't be improved; exactly what I'd been looking for)	
Mixed Feelings	33
(It's not perfect, but I'd use it again; not too bad.)	
Dissatisfied	26
(Not as good as some others; I prefer a competitor's product; I hope they improve it.)	
Other	1
(Don't know, can't say)	
Total (N = 1800)	100%

In the second table, you learned something you might not have suspected about the first table—namely, that both users and non-users of the product had been grouped together. Simply taking the non-users out of the sample (N is now only 1800) improved the apparent degree of satisfaction from 30 to 40 percent. But you are also told the sorts of answers classified under the various headings. From this, you may conclude that the evaluation of the respondents' enthusiasm is excessively conservative. In any event, a product manager would surely be happier getting informational content of the second table rather than the first. Therefore, two points have been cleared up:

1. what the categories "satisfied, etc." mean; and,

2. the reference group that is being tagged with these categories.

2.5. Procter and Gamble's Rely Advertising: The Anatomy of a Statistical Message

The opening example reported that Procter and Gamble successfully used statistics to sway public opinion in its favor in the Rely tampon TSS incident. How could Procter and Gamble convince a concerned public that it had not acted in an irresponsible manner?

Let's examine P & G's newspaper ads on withdrawing Rely from the market. Prominently displayed in the ad was Table 2.7, labeled "the key data available to date."

TABLE 2.7. Definite TSS Cases Reported to CDC

	# Cases Involved	Rely Brand	Other Identified Tampon Brands	Brands Uniden- tified
		BRANDS USED		
CDC Study # 1 (completed June 20)	52	17	43	2
CDC Study # 2 (completed September 12)	50	35	22	0
Other cases reported to CDC	140	24	19	100
Total CDC cases (through September 23)	242	76	84	102

"Brands used" totals more than the number of cases reported because some women used more than one brand.

What message was communicated by these numbers? The table presents the numerical change in the number of TSS cases between the two studies cited.

> The first study shows 17 TSS cases linked to the use of Rely compared to 43 cases linked to the use of other brands.

> In the second study, the numbers show 35 cases linked to Rely and only 22 linked to other brands.

The evidence seemingly suggests that there has been a dramatic shift in incidence of TSS to Rely users between the two studies which was now a cause for alarm. The level of incidence of TSS among Rely users in the first study does not appear either substantive or conclusive enough for P & G to have acted on. The implication is that something "different" has been found in the second study which was not observable in the first study. In other words, it seemingly would have been unwarranted for P & G to conclude from the June study alone that the percentage of Rely users contracting TSS was any higher than the percentage linked to other brands. As surveys showed, this is the message the public found in the data.

Procter and Gamble's way of presenting the data was well designed. It gave readers the opportunity to see the comparison intended, interpret it, and reach their own conclusions.

Although some liability action suits have been filed subsequently contending negligence on the part of P & G for marketing Rely, no public outcry has arisen because of P & G's behavior in the incident. This suggests that P & G did successfully use statistical information to convey its intended message that it had acted responsibly in light of the evidence at hand.

Could other statistical comparisons, however, have been made which would not have reflected as favorably on P & G? Omitted from the table of statistical information which P & G furnished in its ad was the fact that Rely had been launched nationally only a few months before the first study was completed. This study included reported cases over the previous year and a half. Thus, Rely wasn't even on the market during part of the time data were collected for the first study. By the second study, however, Rely's market share had quickly climbed to a hefty 24 percent.

The sharp rise in the company's market share in the tampon market is critical for analysis. Why? Because it defines the base on which TSS incidence must be evaluated for a fair comparison. The base of Rely users was much smaller for the 17 cases in Study One than for the 35 cases in Study Two. Therefore, on a relative basis, the 17 cases of TSS associated with the use of Rely is significant in itself, given Rely's small share of the market in Study One. It seems that Procter and Gamble might have known that. Whether it actually did is a matter of conjecture.

2.6. Quantitative Variables

Quantitative variables refer to the numerically measured characteristics of elementary units. Yearly sales of color TVs, weekly family expenditures on food, daily stock prices on the New York Stock Exchange are but a few of the many possible examples.

Every quantitative variable ranges from a low value to a high value. However, there are two measurement yardsticks on which a quantitative variable can be measured. One is a *continuous* yardstick and the other is a *discrete* yardstick.

The size of a land parcel, the diameter of a ball bearing, the time to maturity of a bond are examples of measurements on continuous quantitative variables. They are continuous measurements because the recorded measurements can always be made more precise merely by making the measuring instruments more accurate. For example, in surveying a real estate parcel between the size 141.67 and 141.68 acres, there are still an infinite number of measurements possible (but surely not practical) to measure.

A quantitative variable measured by a *discrete* yardstick is called a *discrete quantitative variable*. The number of cars produced daily, or the yearly sales of color TVs are examples of discrete quantitative variables because the variables (production, sales) change only by whole unit jumps—one car at a time, or one TV set at a time.

2.7. Measurement Scales

The assignment of numbers to characteristics of objects, persons, states, or events according to a prescribed set of rules is called a *measurement*. The goal is to assign numbers so that the properties of the numbers are paralleled by the properties of the objects or events that we are measuring. This implies that we have different kinds of numbers. It is common to distinguish four different types of numbers or *scales of measurement* according to the kinds of comparisons that can be made.

Nominal.   Nominally scaled numbers simply *identify* an object or person as a member of a particular category, such as male-female, sole proprietorship-partnership-corporation, professional-technical-clerical, etc. The objects in each category are viewed as equivalent with respect to the characteristics. No category is considered more meritorious than another. The categories are viewed as merely descriptive. The only arithmetic operation that can be performed on nominal data is counting. For instance, consider the prevalence of business organizations in Table 2.8:

TABLE 2.8. United States Business
Organizations, 1975

TYPE	NUMBER (Thousands)
Proprietorship	10,882
Partnership	1073
Corporation	2022

Source: Internal Revenue Service, Statistics of Income
1975, Business Income Tax Returns

So comparison of nominal data can involve a comparison of counts or incidence of the categories.

Ordinal.   Ordinally scaled numbers indicate *relative order* or *rank* in addition to identity. They indicate whether an object has more or less of a characteristic than another object, but not how much more or less. Consider brand preference data, market position, attitude measure, social class, commodity grades for meat as typical examples. For instance "prime" meat is a higher grade than "choice" meat which in turn is higher than "standard" meat. Therefore "prime" would receive a rank of 1, choice a rank of 2, and standard a rank of 3. Note that the ranking does not reveal whether the same difference exists between the ranks. The arithmetic operations that are consistent with this level of comparison are counting and ranking.

Interval.   Intervally scaled numbers tell us the distance between measured characteristics. This means the *differences* between them can be compared in addition to identity and rank. Numerically equal distances on the scale represent equal distances in the property being measured. The unit of measurement and the zero or base level to start measuring are arbitrary. Index numbers, awareness of product and advertising attitudes, and temperature are examples. For instance, the Consumer Price Index has arbitrarily set its base year at 1967, so 1967 = 100. The freezing point of water is set at zero on the centigrade temperature scale, but zero does not mean the absence of heat. Addition and subtraction are permissible arithmetic operations for interval scale comparisons, but multiplication and division are not. It would not be correct to say that 50°C is twice as hot as 25°C.

Ratio. Ratio scaled numbers possess a natural or absolute zero, one for which there is universal agreement as to its location. Height and weight are obvious examples. Sales, units produced, costs, age, number of customers are other examples. Since ratio scale numbers have a natural zero point, multiplication and division are permissible arithmetic operations along with addition and subtraction. It is fair to compare 10 million in sales to 20 million in sales and say sales have doubled.

Table 2.9 summarizes the four scales of measurement, their appropriate types of arithmetic operations, and the comparisons that can be made.

TABLE 2.9. Overview of the Type of Measurement Scales and Their Implications

SCALE	ARITHMETIC OPERATION	IMPLICATION
1. Nominal	Counting	Categorizes
2. Ordinal	Counting	Categorizes
	Ranking	Ranks
3. Interval	Counting	Categorizes
	Ranking	Ranks
	Addition	Has equal measurement units
	Subtraction	Arbitrary zero or base point
4. Ratio	Counting	Categorizes
	Ranking	Ranks
	Addition	Has equal measurement units
	Subtraction	Has absolute or natural zero
	Multiplication	
	Division	

Many statistical pitfalls await the person who does not carefully consider the measurement scale of the data being investigated.

Quantifying a Qualitative Variable: A Potential Pitfall

It may seem feasible and advantageous at times to convert information on a qualitative variable to quantitative form. Expressed qualitatively, there is no way to determine how much one categorical value of the variable exceeds another categorical value. With the values expressed quantitatively, it is easy to make these comparisons. It is tempting then to try and "pull the rabbit out of the hat" by assigning quantitative values to the qualitative categories. But herein lies the problem. The comparisons depend on the coding scheme used and this is completely arbitrary. Just as the rabbit in the hat was not there until the magician put it there, so the comparisons which result from quantification of a categorical variable are a product of the particular coding scheme chosen.

The information embodied in the qualitative variable can become badly distorted by quantitative coding even if the categories of the qualitative variable are ranked.

A particularly prevalent distortion occurs when the relationship among ranked categories is assumed to be identical to the relationship among the magnitudes of the numbers assigned to the ranks.

For example, the U.S. Department of Agriculture ranks prime grade beef first, choice grade beef second, and good grade beef third. This does not mean that prime grade beef is two times better (or worse) than choice grade beef, and three times better (or worse) than good grade beef. In fact, it would be a gross oversimplification to say that prime grade beef "exceeds" choice grade beef by the same amount that choice grade beef "exceeds" good grade beef.

A business example which shows the communicative distortion that can crop up if numerical weights are assigned to a categorical variable is reported in Buzzell, Cox, Brown.[3]

Example 2.7. Measuring Corporate Images

A marketing research study, shown in Table 2.10, reports the frequency of responses to questions about the fairness of price and value of five companies. The companies produce crush and grind equipment for the chemical process industry:

TABLE 2.10. Fairness of Price and Value

	EXCELLENT	GOOD	FAIR	POOR	DON'T KNOW
Collins, Inc.	18	74	18	2	132
Diamond Co.	27	95	23	7	92
Ferguson, Inc.	32	103	37	4	68
Hammond Machine Co.	19	65	26	6	128
Maxwell Mfg.	26	83	48	7	80

Although the table is quite informative as it stands, the frequencies were condensed to an "average value" by assigning each response a value according to the following weights:

Excellent = 2
Good = 1
Fair = 0
Poor = −1

This leads to the following "average attitude scores":

Collins   .96
Diamond   .93
Ferguson   .93
Hammond   .84
Maxwell   .78

with Collins leading the way.

The crux of the problem lies in the arbitrariness of the weights assigned to the categories. Had one wanted Diamond to top the list the following equally arbitrary (and justifiable) weighting scheme below could have been used:

Excellent = 60
Good = 35
Fair = 25
Poor = 20

Now Diamond tops the list of "average attitude scores":

Diamond   37.2
Collins   37.1
Ferguson   37.1
Hammond   36.1
Maxwell   35.4

Interpreting an ordinally scaled qualitative variable as if the measurement scale were interval is only one of the ways measurement scales are abused. The message in a data set can also be badly distorted when the categories of a nominally-scaled categorical variable are interpreted as if the measurement scale were ordinal, that is, when the data ought not to be ranked at all. For example, in distinguishing types of U.S. business organizations, it would not be meaningful to rank "sole proprietorship" over "partnership" or "partnership" over "corporation". These are categories of a nominally-scaled variable. Each exists for different reasons. Likewise, from Table 2.3, it does not make sense to think of the South Atlantic region as greater or less than the Pacific region or the mountain region; the region variable is nominally scaled, not ordinally scaled. However, it is legitimate to view a newly issued ATT bond rated by Moody's Investment Service on an ordinal scale, *Aaa* a rank higher than a rating of *Aa* or of simply *A*.

2.8. Frequency Distributions

A frequency distribution is a statistical device that effectively assembles individual data items so that a comprehensive message about the pattern of variation in the data can be gained. For example, an unorganized listing of the earnings of the approximately 80 million U.S. workers would be overwhelming and certainly would not be very informative. A frequency distribution is used to suppress unnecessary detail and to effectively organize the data. This organization facilitates comprehension of the pattern of wage and salary variation for U.S. workers.

A frequency distribution divides attributes or variates into groups called classes. Once completed, it describes the range and concentration of the observations among the classes.

Frequency distributions of either a qualitative or a quantitative variable can be presented in either tabular form or graphically. The qualitative frequency distribution shown as a table describes the frequency of the attribute appearance. A table of the quantitative frequency distribution describes how frequent the different variates occur. The remainder of this chapter is devoted to the exposition of frequency distributions, their extensions and their role in data analysis.

2.9. Qualitative Frequency Distributions

Making business decisions often requires information about the *proportion* or percentage that a category holds of the entire distribution. An example which few business people dare ignore is their firm's market share.

Example 2.9A.   **Market Share Strategy**

A well known management consulting firm, The Boston Consulting Group, advises clients to pursue a high market share strategy. The basis of its advice is a series of "Profit Impact of Market Share" (PIMS) studies that associate long run profitability with high market share relative to competitors. Thus a firm's decision to enter or not to enter a particular market should depend on its anticipated ability to gain market share. A critical factor in making this assessment is how the market is presently divided. What market configuration represents a profitable opportunity to new firms willing to pursue aggressively a market share policy? A highly fragmented market showing a broad competitive scatter among many existing firms is desirable. On the other hand, a market controlled by a few dominant firms would represent a formidable obstacle for a new entrant. A firm formulating a strategy for entry requires two pieces of relevant information:

> data on the competitors' market positions in particular markets

> data on the importance of various products in the overall market

Table 2.11 illustrates the kind of information about market position that is needed. It lists the names of firms as the relevant nominal categories of the qualitative variable, hand calculator firms, along with each firm's market share.

TABLE 2.11. Market Share of the Hand Calculator Market

CATEGORY	MARKET SHARE, 1982 (Percentage)
Texas Instruments	30
Casio	20
Sharp	15
Hewlett-Packard	12
Commodore	8
All Others	15
	100%

Source: Hypothetical

The second concern of a potential entrant is the importance of major segments within the overall market. This can be measured by the proportion of total market sales accounted for by particular products or lines of products. This can be seen in Table 2.12.

TABLE 2.12. Market Share for Products Using Integrated Circuitry

CATEGORY	MARKET SHARE, 1982 (Percentage)
Hand-Held Calculators	60
Digital Watches	25
Random Access Memory	15
	100

Source: Hypothetical

Such tabular frequency distributions of the market share across firms and product lines are standard items used by management in thinking about the competitive environment and the resources it will take to overcome its competitors to achieve significant market share status.

The qualitative frequency distribution in graphic form presents pictorially the percentage distribution of the various categories of the qualitative variable. In marketing, for example, a particular kind of bar chart has become popular in assessing the degree of market segmentation.

Example 2.9B.   Heavy User Segmentation

Usage differs from product to product. It is important in setting marketing strategy to know consumer usage habits. If there is a heavy usage group consuming as a group a very large percentage of the total product used, then a marketing plan should be set in motion to segment, pursue, and cultivate this group. In terms of productivity per dollar of advertising, it seems that money should be channeled to reach the heavy users. Consider the chart in Figure 2.4. It represents a study of how important heavy user segmentation can be to producers of particular products.

Each bar in Figure 2.4 designates a different product. The first bar examines household purchases of lemon-lime softdrinks. The household percentages *above* the bar show that 42% are non-users—therefore their volume of purchase of lemon-lime is zero. This zero percentage volume is always shown in the first segment of the bar, which we see is lengthwise proportional to the percentage of non-users. This means that 58% of the bar represents households that are users. Forming two *equal size* user groups with the heaviest users of lemon-lime in one group and the lighter users in the other group, places half of 58%, or 29%, in each group. The 29% group which represents the heaviest purchasers of lemon-lime we will call the "heavy half," the other 29% group which comprises the lighter purchasers the "light half". How much of the total volume of the product does the "heavy half" purchase? How much does the "light half" purchase? The figures in the bar beneath the "heavy half" and the "light half" labels show us the volume percentages. In the case of lemon-lime, the "heavy half" purchases a whopping 91% of the *total* volume purchases. The "light half" user group purchases only 9% of the total volume. In the case of lemon-lime soft drink, it shows that purchases are very concentrated in the

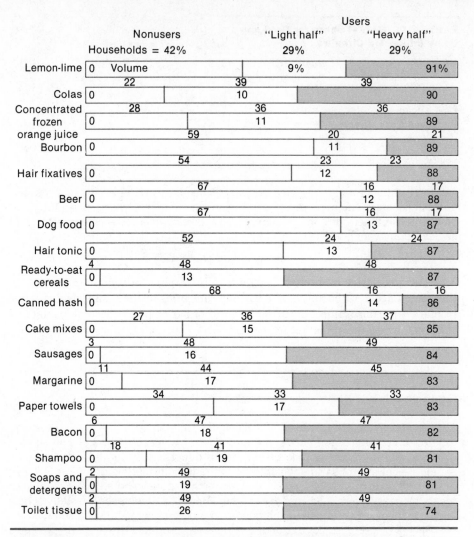

	Nonusers Households = 42%	Users "Light half" 29%	"Heavy half" 29%
Lemon-lime (households 22 / 39 / 39)	0 Volume	9%	91%
Colas (28 / 36 / 36)	0	10	90
Concentrated frozen orange juice (59 / 20 / 21)	0	11	89
Bourbon (54 / 23 / 23)	0	11	89
Hair fixatives (67 / 16 / 17)	0	12	88
Beer (67 / 16 / 17)	0	12	88
Dog food (52 / 24 / 24)	0	13	87
Hair tonic (4 / 48 / 48)	0	13	87
Ready-to-eat cereals (68 / 16 / 16)	0	13	87
Canned hash (27 / 36 / 37)	0	14	86
Cake mixes (3 / 48 / 49)	0	15	85
Sausages (11 / 44 / 45)	0	16	84
Margarine (34 / 33 / 33)	0	17	83
Paper towels (6 / 47 / 47)	0	17	83
Bacon (18 / 41 / 41)	0	18	82
Shampoo (2 / 49 / 49)	0	19	81
Soaps and detergents (2 / 49 / 49)	0	19	81
Toilet tissue	0	26	74

FIGURE 2.4   Percentage of Purchase Volume Accounted for by Different Usage Groups

Source: Dik Warren Twedt. "How Important to Marketing Strategy is the 'Heavy User'?" *Journal of Marketing,* Vol 28 (January 1964), p. 72. Published by the American Marketing Association.

"heavy half" user group. In fact they are so heavy that perhaps a lemon-lime producer should direct all advertising to convince this group that his brand of lemon-lime, for example 7-Up, ought to be their brand.

Each bar has the same designations for *households:* non-users and its percentage and users with its percentage dividing equally between the "light half" and "heavy half". The respective volume percentage that is assigned to each household designation is shown within that segment of the bar. Notice in all of these cases that the "heavy half" of users dominates the purchasing volume. One can now recognize why such charts are key guideposts for producers in determining where their marketing efforts should be directed. In the following section we will show how such bars can be obtained from compiled data on usage.

Another graphic illustration that is often used to depict changes in the size of the market over time and changes in the market share of competing factors in the market is the pie chart. Figure 2.5 is an example of this type of organization of data.

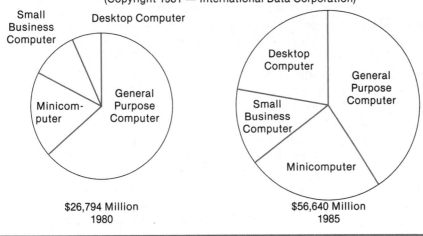

VALUE OF WORLDWIDE SHIPMENTS OF
U.S. MANUFACTURERS 1980–1985
(Copyright 1981 — International Data Corporation)

$26,794 Million
1980

$56,640 Million
1985

FIGURE 2.5   Actual 1980 and Projected 1985 Total Value of Worldwide Shipments by U.S.
Manufacturers and Market Share of Computer Categories

Source: *San Diego Union,* Tuesday, November 3, 1981.

The pie chart shows that the pie is expanding, with the value of worldwide shipments of computers more than doubling in five years. At the same time, by 1985 the general purpose computer will have a smaller share—a smaller piece of the expanded pie. Desk top computers, small business computers, and minicomputers will all increase their market share of the expanded pie.

2.10. Quantitative Frequency Distributions

A quantitative frequency distribution reports the frequencies corresponding to the variates or variate classes of a quantitative variable. Table 2.13 presents a frequency distribution for the usage of a golf course by 234 club members during a one week period, compiled by the management.

**TABLE 2.13. Golf Course Usage by Members
Over a One Week Period**

NUMBER OF OCCASIONS MEMBER USED GOLF COURSE	FREQUENCY
0	27
1	43
2	60
3	29
4	25
5	17
6	11
7	18
8	4

The table shows that the overwhelming majority of members used the golf course during the particular week, although there was considerable variation in the amount of usage. The most common usage pattern was two times over the week, but 27 members were nonusers and 4 members played golf on average more than once a day.

Usage Concentration

What aspect of golf course usage would management likely be interested in? For example, can management tell from the concentration of usage among members whether there is a "hard core" group of members who used the course intensively throughout the week or whether the weekend type predominates? On the other hand, management may want to know what percentage of total golf course membership usage is accounted for by members who used the course on more than two occasions during the week. Usage concentration can be determined from the frequency distribution by following the procedure shown in Table 2.14.

TABLE 2.14. Determination of Usage Concentration

USAGE	FREQUENCY	USAGE SUBTOTALS (Usage Times Frequency)	USAGE CONCENTRATION Usage Subtotals as Percent of Total Usage
0 (non-user)	27	0	0
1	43	43	$\frac{43}{659} \times 100 = $ 6.5%
2	60	120	$\frac{120}{659} \times 100 = 18.2$
3	29	87	$\frac{87}{659} \times 100 = 13.2$
4	25	100	$\frac{100}{659} \times 100 = 15.2$
5	17	85	$\frac{85}{659} \times 100 = 12.9$
6	11	66	$\frac{66}{659} \times 100 = 10.0$
7	18	126	$\frac{126}{659} \times 100 = 19.1$
8	4	32	$\frac{32}{659} \times 100 = $ 4.9
Total Usage		659	

The usage concentration for each variate is the product of the variate and its frequency, expressed as a percentage of total usage. Note that the number of non-users has no impact when the intensity among users is the question at hand. For instance, to find the concentration of golf course usage among members who used the course on more than two occasions during the week, one sums the percentages on the last column from the fourth to the last row. This comes to 75.3 percent. Thus, the 104 members who used the golf course on more than two occasions during the week account for less than half of the membership (44.4 percent), but more than three-quarters (75.3 percent) of the golf course usage.

Usage concentration can be further summarized by partitioning the population into usage groups, such as non-users, light users, and heavy users. Bar graphs, such as that shown in Figure 2.6, are another convenient way of summarizing the data. How is the bar graph constructed? The frequency distribution on golf course usage by members in Table 2.8 is first partitioned into non-users (27) and users (207). The 207 users are then evenly split (nearly) into two variate subgroups so that one can designate the "heavy half" (104) and "light half" (103). The "heavy half" group uses the golf course more than twice a week and represents about 75.3 percent of total usage. The "light half" represent the remaining 24.7 percent of total usage. The figures on usage are summarized in Table 2.15.

TABLE 2.15. Usage Concentration by Groups

SEGMENT	PERCENT OF MEMBERS	PERCENT OF USAGE
Heavy Half	44.4	75.3
Light Half	44.0	24.7
Nonusers	11.6	0

The corresponding bar graph for the segments shows the same breakdown:

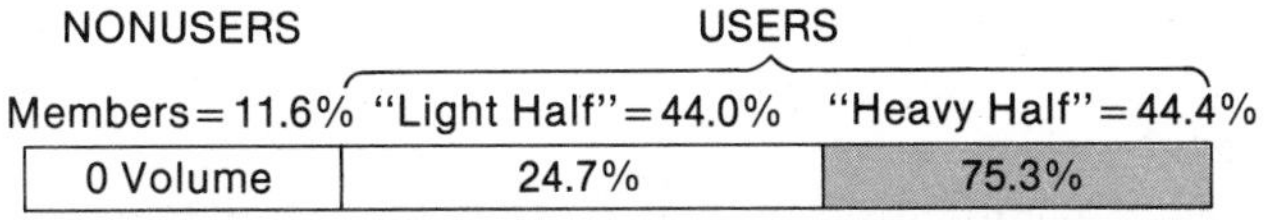

FIGURE 2.6   Bar Graph of Golf Course Usage Concentration

2.11. Concluding Comments

A structural framework for classifying and comparing data is essential to understanding the basis for effective statistical communication. The framework uses the concept of a *statistical variable* for classifying observations. The entity about which information is gathered is called an *elementary unit;* the numerical information is recorded as *data.* The data will either provide information on a *measured* characteristic of the elementary unit or on a *described* characteristic. In the former situation a *quantitative* variable is involved, in the latter case a *qualitative* variable. Quantitative variables are either *discrete,* meaning that the possible values only occur in discrete steps or jumps, or else the variable is *continuous.* Qualitative variables are either of the *attribute* or of the *categorical* variety, depending upon whether the observational choices are merely the presence or absence of one particular attribute, or a choice among two or more different attributes.

Comparisons among different values of the same variable are made on one of four different kinds of measurement scale: *nominal, ordinal, interval,* and *ratio.* A nominal (name only) scale distinguishes different categories, but not a hierarchy among the categories. A qualitative variable of the attribute type can only be measured on this scale. An ordinal scale distinguishes rank, or order of values. All quantitative and some, but not all, categorical variables can be measured on this scale. An interval scale measures how much greater one quantitative value is than another. A ratio scale measures how many times greater one quantitative value is than another. Ordinarily, all quantitative variables can be measured on an interval scale. The exception is a qualitative variable that has been converted by coding into a quantitative variable.

Moving beyond a simple comparison of two values of the variable to the pattern of variation found among many values actually recorded on a variable calls for a *frequency* distribution. A frequency distribution organizes the data into classes of attributes or variates from which the range and concentration of values can be readily discerned. In the case of quantitative data, a variant of the frequency distribution formed by finding the product of the values and their frequencies is sometimes very useful. For example, when the variable represents intensity of usage of a product, the distribution of products of values and frequencies shows the concentration of usage among the variate classes. This latter type of distribution is particularly useful in analyzing sales and marketing data to determine the source of business attributable to the different customer classes.

A distinction is made between two different types of data analysis, *cross-sectional* and *time-series*. In cross-sectional analysis, the values compared are for different elementary units. In time-series analysis, the comparison of values is for patterns of variation in a specific sequence of recordings. In most of the chapters that follow, it is assumed that the sequential pattern of variation has no special significance. However, Chapters 17 and 19 are devoted to problems in time-series analysis.

When data are recorded on only one variable for a given elementary unit, the analysis is said to be *univariate*. When data are recorded on more than one variable for the same elementary unit, the analysis is *bivariate* or *multivariate* depending whether two, three, or more variables are involved. This kind of analysis entails consideration of the relationships (if any) that exist among the variables as well as the pattern of variation among values of each variable. Bivariate, trivariate, and multivariate analysis is discussed in Chapters 14, 15, 16, 20, 21, and 22.

Finally, it is worth stressing that clearly understanding the scheme by which the data are classified can be an important deterrent to erroneous comparisons and interpretations. Thus, saying that 76 persons or 44 percent of *viewers* in the Hollywood Squares survey use the advertised brand implies that the classification of categories is according to product or brand usage, and *not* according to program viewership. Likewise, knowing that the percentage of TSS cases involving tampons took a sharp jump is definitely *not* the same thing as knowing that a sudden increase occurred in the percentage of TSS cases among users of Rely. The classification schemes for categories are entirely different. The change of user base from tampon user to Rely user tells us that the classification scheme is no longer the same.

Footnotes and References

[1] The description of the Rely episode is the authors' interpretation based upon a front page *Wall Street Journal* article of November 3, 1980, Procter and Gamble advertisements during and subsequent to the product withdrawal, and various other news media headlines and reports at the time of the incident.

[2] The data in this example is adapted from data given in the "Staten Manufacturing Company" case, Boyd, Westfall and Stasch, *Marketing Research: Text and Cases*, Richard D. Irwin, Fourth Edition, 1977.

[3] Robert D. Buzzell, Donald F. Cox, Rex V. Brown, *Marketing Research and Information Systems: Text and Cases*, McGraw-Hill, 1971, p. 253.

Questions and Problems

1. What are the two broad categories into which the methods of descriptive statistics can be classified? In what way do they differ?

2. Why is it necessary to have a scheme for classifying, organizing, and presenting data?

3. Give an example of a measured characteristic. Can it also be described or can it only be measured?

4. In what way does an elementary unit differ from a measured or described characteristic?

5. What is the purpose of a statistical variable?

6. What are the two fundamentally different kinds of statistical variables?

7. Both attribute variables and categorical variables are concerned with attributes. What distinguishes an attribute variable from a categorical variable?

8. Can the values of a discrete quantitative variable be nonintegers? Explain.

9. What is the distinction between an attribute and a variate?

10. Must every observed characteristic refer to a different elementary unit or can more than one characteristic be observed for the same elementary unit?

11. What distinguishes multivariate data from bivariate data?

12. Why is it important to know whether there is information of interest in the sequence in which data are recorded? If there is interest in the sequence, what type of analysis is appropriate? If there is no interest in the sequence, what is the appropriate type of analysis?

13. What is a variable and why is it a useful concept?

14. Why do we distinguish between time-series and cross-sectional data?

15. What is the major goal in assigning numbers to characteristics of objects?

16. What are the four different scales of measurement?

17. If two numbers are ordinally scaled, can nominal comparisons be made? Explain.

18. Can interval scaled numbers be used to make comparisons? Explain.

19. Under what circumstances can a qualitative variable legitimately be quantified? What pitfall must be avoided in quantifying a qualitative variable?

20. What is a frequency distribution and what is its purpose?

21. Do all frequency distributions describe the frequency of variates?

22. Ratio-scaled numbers such as a firm's profits, inventories, and sales are commonly expressed as financial ratios (for example, a firm's profit margin equals the firm's profits divided by a firm's sales). Why do financial ratios facilitate a financial comparison across firms with differing amounts of sales?

23. An interpretation problem arises in determining a firm's financial position, if there is a change by an equal amount in the numerator and denominator of the firm's financial ratio: for example, the effect on the firm's liquidity if the current assets in the numerator and current liabilities in the denominator change by the same magnitude. Explain.

24. Classify each of the following as time-series data or as cross-sectional data:
a. population of Cook County, Illinois, 1956–1981
b. population of Cook County, Illinois, by census tract, 1980
c. the number of customers of Allstate Insurance in San Diego County for 1981
d. sales of Fotomat, monthly, 1976–1981
e. number of employees, by department, of Goodyear Tire and Rubber Co., 1980
f. number of homicides, Pittsburgh, Pennsylvania, 1962–1981
g. number of homicides, Pittsburgh, Pennsylvania, by census tract, 1981

25. For each of the measurements described, indicate whether a *nominal, ordinal, interval,* or *ratio* scale was used. Explain why you think your answer is correct.
a. a measurement of brand preference between *Peak* and *Shell* antifreeze
b. a compilation of total *Peak* antifreeze sales in Ohio, 1980
c. a determination of the temperature at which the mixture of two gallons of *Peak* and two gallons of water will freeze.

26. What kind of measurement scale is implied by the following statement? "A sample of 600 adults was asked to rank aspirin, *Anacin, Bufferin, Excedrin, Emperin,* and *Tylenol* in order of preference for relief of headaches. The most preferred was given a ranking of one and least preferred a ranking of 6. The average for Tylenol was 2.76."

27. Two stores, profiled below by their customers, are attempting to sell to the same target customers, using basically the same approach (merchandise, advertising, and price). What are the managerial implications of this profile for Store A? Store B?

(28.–38.) Assessing the User Image of Fresh Pineapples

In an attempt to determine what direction to take in promoting fresh pineapples, a pineapple growers' trade association commissions a study of pineapple users which leads to Table 2.16. Problems 28 through 38 refer to this table.

28. Are the variables in this table qualitative or are they quantitative in nature? Give the names of three variables.

29. Are the 6 attributes under the heading "qualities" mutually exclusive categories? Explain.

30. Heavy, moderate, and light are mutually exclusive user designations. Why do the percentages across the "rich in vitamin C" row (or any other row) not add to 100 percent?

31. Why isn't the sum of the percentages across the heavy, moderate, and light user columns for each row equal to the percentage figure given in the "total" column for that row?

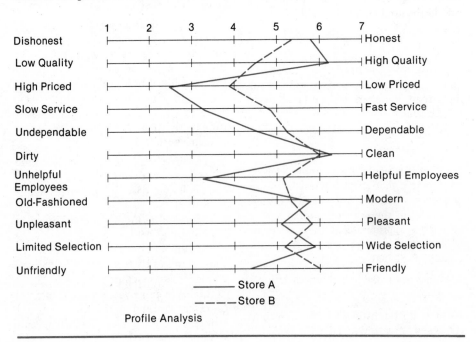

Profile Analysis

PROBLEM 2.27

TABLE 2.16. Extent of General Agreement* About Certain Characteristics of Fresh Pineapples

Qualities:	Total (in %)	FRESH PINEAPPLE		
		Heavy Users (in %)	Moderate Users (in %)	Light Users (in %)
Low calorie fruit	62	65	61	59
Extra special/gourmet fruit	56	53	57	60
Rich in Vitamin C	49	50	52	45
Most delicious flavor of any fruit	48	53	49	42
Spoil more quickly than other fruits	74	69	76	77
Expensive compared with most fresh fruit	43	40	43	48
Season:				
Best ones come in the spring	73	72	75	72
Except in springtime, almost never in the stores	57	52	55	63
Uses-versatility:				
More ways to use than most other fruit	67	71	68	61
Very few recipes for using them	13	11	13	16
Hawaiian quality:				
Best pineapples come from Hawaii	20	23	16	21
Flavor-appearance Relationship:				
Very difficult to judge their taste by how they look	65	66	64	65
(No. of respondents)	(2,344)	(852)	(734)	(758)

*Difference between percentages shown and the 100 percent is accounted for by "disagree" or "don't know" answers.

32. Since the total number of respondents (2344) is the sum of the number of respondents in each of the user categories, why isn't each of the percentages in the total column a 100% figure?

33. What does add to 100 percent? (Hint: note the footnote on the bottom of the table.)

34. If asked to express an overall judgment about the image of fresh pineapples based upon the data given in this table, how would you go about *forming* your opinion?

35. Which descriptive adjective best characterizes the image of fresh pineapples: positive, neutral, negative?

36. What are the relative strengths and weaknesses of the fresh pineapple image?

37. In tailoring your advertising campaign to heavy users, what features would you promote?

38. To a large extent, the image assessment is dependent upon the importance (weight) attached to the different features.

For another individual to arrive at the same image assessment you have, what assumptions must be made about the importance of the various features?

39. A survey of purchases of six-packs of beer reported by households for the preceding week is given in Table 2.17.

TABLE 2.17. Purchases of Beer

NUMBER OF SIX PACKS PURCHASED LAST WEEK	NUMBER OF HOUSE-HOLDS REPORTING SIX PACK PURCHASE QUANTITY
0	643
1	92
2	79
3	64
4	53
5	45
6	33
7	31
8	22
9	17
10	11
11	7
12	3

a. How many households participated in the survey?
b. How many households were purchasers of beer? Non-purchasers?
c. Eliminating the non-purchaser group, split the number of households purchasing beer into two equal size groups. One group (one half of the purchasing households) constitutes those who purchase relatively fewer six packs and consequently are called the "light half". The other group (the other half of the purchasing households) represents those households which purchase relatively a greater number of six packs and therefore are called the "heavy half" category. How many households are in the "heavy half" category? How many are in the "light half" category?
d. How many households purchased four six-packs during the week? Are they in the light half or the heavy half?

40. For the beer purchase data given in Problem 39 determine:
a. How many six-packs were purchased in total by households purchasing four six-packs?
b. What was the highest purchase quantity for a household included in the light user group? What was the lowest purchase quantity for a household included in the heavy purchaser group?
c. How many six-packs were purchased in total by households purchasing at least three six-packs?
d. How many six-packs were purchased by the "heavy purchasing" households?
e. How many six-packs were purchased by the entire group surveyed?
f. What percentage of total purchases were made by heavy purchasing households?
g. From the data in your table, what is your assessment of the importance of heavy purchasing households to the beer marketers?

41. The data provided in Table 2.18 shows beer purchasing information for two age groups. What additional conclusions can you draw from this table about usage concentration?

TABLE 2.18. Beer Purchases by Age Group

NO. OF SIX-PACKS PURCHASED LAST WEEK	NO. OF HOUSEHOLDS REPORTING THIS PURCHASE QUANTITY (by Age of Oldest Person in Household)	
	Under 30	Over 30
0	311	332
1	47	45
2	41	38
3	32	32
4	29	24
5	25	20
6	16	17
7	15	16
8	12	10
9	11	6
10	7	4
11	5	2
12	2	1

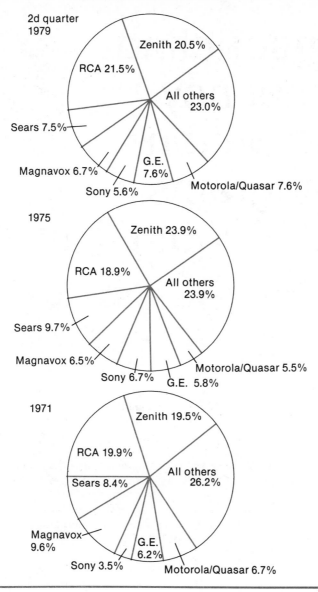

Market Shares of Color TV Sales

PROBLEM 2.42

Source: *Chicago Tribune*, August 15, 1979.

42. Analyze the pie chart.

a. Which company has had the most significant gain in market share?

b. Has the gain in market share been at the expense of any particular company?

c. Does the pie change over time suggest what has happened to the total size of the color TV market?

Constructing Frequency Distributions, Histograms, and Smooth Curves

Preview. The quantitative frequency distribution is an important tool of statistical analysis. It facilitates analysis of the pattern of variation among the observed data values. An experienced analyst can quickly discern from a frequency distribution the range of values, clustering tendencies, and other salient characteristics of the data. Abrupt changes in the frequency of adjacent or nearby values sometimes signal an important message about the people or objects on which the data recordings were made. However, abrupt frequency changes can also result from random sources of variation. To construct a frequency distribution which attenuates variation attributable to extraneous sources, a number of potential problems must be surmounted. Many of these problems stem from having too few observations compared to the number of possible values that might be recorded. Most of the possible values will then have a frequency of zero and the other values will have very low frequencies. The emerging pattern of variation will be unlike that which would be seen had the observations been more plentiful. In this chapter most of the procedures considered deal with the sparse data problem and show how to bring out the data's key statistical message that otherwise would have been obscured. Grouping the data into classes, smoothing the data to the shape of a smooth curve, and associating values with relative position in the data set are three procedures which may be useful for accomplishing this task.

3.1. Introduction

Mixing conversation with martinis at a popular Chicago watering hole, two senior advertising executives lamented a failing they found too prevalent among the advertising industry's new crop of young recruits. It wasn't the recruits' energy, intelligence, or ambition that they found fault with; rather it was their surprising lack of form and style. This shortcoming, they agreed, spawned superfluous ideas, confusing illustrations, and excessive detail. Predictably the fallout came in terms of garbled messages with little appeal. What the industry must do, the ad execs decided, was to make a concerted effort to cultivate and develop top-notch presenters—people who could deliver the intended message smoothly.

Just as polished delivery is the hallmark of the competent ad recruit, so also is it the identifying mark of the able user of statistics. This chapter demonstrates that making statistical messages effective and appealing requires the use of structure and technique. One of the basic tools of statistical analysis, which smooths out the rough edges in presenting statistical messages, is the quantitative frequency distribution. It provides:

1. a structure to efficiently organize a massive amount of detail, at the same time avoiding statistical ambiguity,

2. a format for delivering the results concisely and attractively.

3.2. Constructing Quantitative Frequency Distributions

When the measurements to be considered are discrete and cover a limited range of values, quantitative frequency distributions are simple to construct yet very informative. Suppose a hospital administrator wants to organize and interpret hospital records on the number of days nurses call in sick during the year. What key features of the data could a quantitative frequency distribution bring out? The following example will show not only that there are regular patterns which may be of great interest, but also that peculiar deviations from them may also be of great interest.

Example 3.2.   A Personnel Manager's Problem: How Many "Sick" Nurses Are Really Sick?

Employee abuse of sick leave is a very common problem in both profit and nonprofit organizations. Personnel policy ordinarily specifies the maximum number of days each employee may stay home because of illness without losing pay. However, some employees are inclined to treat unused sick leave as extra vacation days; they call in sick when, in fact, they just don't feel like going to work. A quantitative frequency distribution is a convenient device for checking the seriousness of sick leave abuse.

Table 3.1 shows the annual sick leave of 120 nurses at a hospital permitting eleven sick days annually. What things might we like to know about the data?

1. What is the spread or "range" of the annual sick leave taken by the nurses?

2. Do the different values of sick leave occur with about equal frequency, or is there a clustering of data near certain values?

3. If there is a clustering, does the frequency of observations fall off sharply or gradually for sick leave values higher or lower than the values near the center of the cluster?

4. Are there any peculiarities in the frequencies which stand out?

The first question is easily answered by looking for the highest and lowest values in Table 3.1. Fourteen is the most sick days that were taken and zero is the least. The other three questions require some organization of the raw data. The first step is to organize the data into a frequency distribution.

TABLE 3.1. Raw Data on Annual Sick Leave Days Taken by 120 Hospital Nurses

3	1	10	0	4	4	5	5	2	11	14	11
9	2	13	7	4	11	4	11	11	9	6	12
13	10	9	4	3	5	7	5	1	4	10	6
10	2	11	4	3	1	10	5	6	11	8	3
11	6	1	6	1	14	7	1	11	4	6	5
7	11	7	10	13	2	4	11	3	11	3	7
3	5	14	1	5	9	0	11	11	4	7	11
1	13	4	2	5	10	14	0	5	3	13	4
6	6	3	0	6	11	8	3	8	3	2	5
12	7	2	7	5	11	4	11.	3	0	1	1

The Array: Keeping Score

In constructing a quantitative frequency distribution, the first step is to arrange the observations in rank order—from low to high, or vice versa. An array for the raw data on nurses' annual sick leave shown in Table 3.1 is presented in the second column of Table 3.2. The tallying procedure requires that a tally mark be placed to the right of a value each time that value occurs. When the values of all the elementary units in the array have been tallied and counted, the counts are recorded as the frequencies (column three). Raw data reduced to an array format provides ready access to some significant features of the data— the highest, the lowest, and the most frequent numerical values (14, 0, and 11, respectively).

TABLE 3.2. Array and Frequency Distribution for Annual Sick Leave Days Taken by 120 Hospital Nurses

Number of Sick Leave Days	Tally	Frequency
0	‖‖‖		6
1	‖‖‖ ‖‖‖	10
2	‖‖‖ ||	7
3	‖‖‖ ‖‖‖ ||	12
4	‖‖‖ ‖‖‖ |||	13
5	‖‖‖ ‖‖‖ ||	12
6	‖‖‖ ||||	9
7	‖‖‖ ||||	9
8					3
9					3
10	‖‖‖ ||	7
11	‖‖‖ ‖‖‖ ‖‖‖ |||	18
12				2
13	‖‖‖	5
14						4
		120

Frequency Tables and Line Charts

The variation in sick leave frequencies is illustrated graphically by drawing a vertical line directly above the value to which the frequency refers. The height of each line represents frequency and the diagram is called a *line chart*. The line chart for the Nursing Department is shown in Figure 3.1.[1]

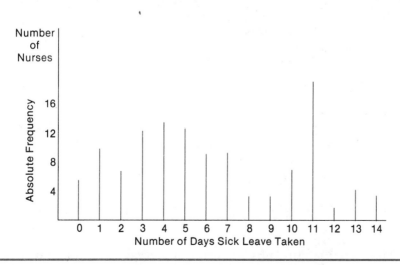

FIGURE 3.1 Number of Days Called in Sick by a Nursing Department

Data Spikes May Pinpoint a Problem

Notice that the predominant number of sick days taken by nurses is eleven days. This is quite apparent from the shape of the line chart. It peaks at eleven days. What could have caused the spike? Could it be coincidentally related to the company's sick leave policy? Could it be that healthy nurses view unused sick leave as an opportunity to take extra vacation? If so, a data spike at eleven days is exactly what we would expect.

Don't Jump to Conclusions

As tempting as it may be to conclude that the spike proves the existence of sick leave abuse, this conclusion may be incorrect. Why? The data spike is also consistent with an alternative explanation. It may be that some nurses who are really sick *more* than eleven days report to work while sick to avoid losing a day's pay. Does this new consideration diminish the usefulness of the line chart? Not at all. It is extremely important that hospital management recognizes that sick leave policy strongly influences the number of sick days taken, whatever the cause. The line chart did identify this message. The *why* behind the spike at 11 days—"vacationitis" or the reluctance to lose pay—is a matter that calls for further investigation.

Some Statistical Detective Work May Be Required

How could one proceed to delve deeper into the sick leave problem? A good way to start is by looking for additional data that would discriminate between the two explanations. To repeat, the two explanations are: use of sick leave as extra vacation days, or reporting to work while sick to avoid losing pay. Data should substantiate one explanation over the other.

If nurses plan to use sick leave as extra vacation days, one would expect that they might wait until later in the year to feign illness. This would reduce the chances of succumbing to a real illness after having used up their sick leave. Consequently, one would expect an increase in sick leave usage towards the end of the sick leave year.

On the other hand, if nurses are reporting for work while sick to avoid losing pay, one would expect their records to show the sick leave maximum to have been reached substantially before the end of their sick leave year. Consequently, as the end of the sick leave year approaches, a decrease in sick leave usage ought to materialize.

The key statistical information needed to discriminate between the alternative explanations for the "spike" at eleven days is sick leave usage throughout the year. Assuming that sick leave is not cumulative from year to year, a year end rise would suggest "vacationitis". A year end decline, on the other hand, does not support a charge of "vacationitis".

3.3. Relative Frequency Distributions

When a comparison between the pattern of variation in two different distributions is important, it is usually a good idea to present the data in terms of *relative* rather than absolute frequencies. For instance, how would you check the impact of an eleven day sick leave policy on the pattern of sick leave usage between two hospitals, one employing 120 nurses, the other 1080? An adjustment for the size of the hospitals is needed. Finding that the smaller hospital had 18 nurses taking the maximum sick leave while the larger had 162 reveals relatively little about the similarity of the sick leave usage patterns. Reporting *relative* frequencies—that both hospitals had 15 per cent of the nurses taking maximum sick leave—establishes that the policy impact on sick leave usage is virtually the same for both institutions.

A relative frequency distribution therefore is a simple and straightforward technique to facilitate a complete comparison between distributions. It is obtained by dividing each absolute frequency by the total number of elementary units in the entire distribution. The resulting pure numbers are called *relative frequencies.*

Since the relative frequency is the absolute frequency changed by a constant scale factor, both can be easily graphed on the same line chart. Figure 3.2 shows the data on nurses' absenteeism on these bases. Relative frequency is read on the left-hand scale; absolute frequency is read on the right-hand scale.

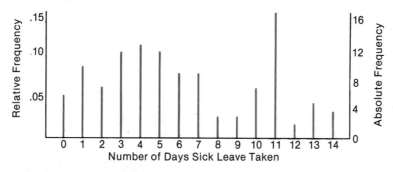

FIGURE 3.2   Relative and Absolute Frequency Distributions for Sick Leave Data for 120 Nurses

3.4. Many-Valued Distributions

Line charts were shown to be excellent devices for conveying information about the pattern of variation in the data, especially when there is a small number of different variates, say a dozen, needed to construct the frequency distribution for the set of data. More often, the number of different values needed to construct the frequency distribution is very large, forcing the frequencies of most variates to be small. In fact, a good example of this is sales forecasting.

Example 3.4. A Sales Manager's Problem: How Good Are Your Sales Forecasts?

Businesses like to have accurate sales forecasts because so many other decisions depend upon the level of sales. But even the best sales forecasting systems do not hit the target all the time, so it is important to know just how much accuracy you are getting from your forecasts. Table 3.3 is a set of data revealing the track record of a firm's marketing department in forecasting district sales to the nearest tenth of a percent.

TABLE 3.3. Per Cent Difference Between Actual and Forecasted Sales Volume (nearest tenth of a percent)

− 6.3	+13.9	−10.2	+ 4.3	+ 9.1	− 3.8	+13.5	+ 0.7
+ 2.4	+ 9.4	− 8.2	− 8.1	+ 3.2	+ 3.5	+ 3.7	+ 7.2
−18.7	− 1.5	−28.5	− 8.8	− 5.9	+ 5.8	− 2.4	+ 9.6
+ 3.6	− 5.6	+16.4	+ 0.8	+ 0.7	+ 3.2	− 6.1	−17.9
− 7.3	−24.1	−18.4	− 4.8	− 7.6	− 1.1	− 8.6	−22.1
−26.3	+ 8.1	−22.3	− 8.1	−10.3	−16.3	−17.6	−16.3
− 0.2	+16.3	+ 1.8	− 3.1	− 4.4	− 2.7	− 5.5	−15.0
−12.5	− 2.0	− 6.0	− 6.9	− 8.2	−32.5	+ 1.4	− 9.9
+ 5.4	− 0.8	−10.4	−23.4	−13.3	−19.8	+ 3.0	− 0.2
+ 7.0	− 1.1	+ 4.4	−12.7	−21.5	−13.7	+ 3.6	+ 4.2
−12.8	− 9.1	−15.3	−17.4	−24.8	− 6.9	− 6.0	− 3.4
+19.1	+ 3.1	−31.5	− 8.8	+14.8	− 2.4	−14.9	− 7.0
−13.9	−14.3	+ 2.4	+ 4.8	− 1.5	− 7.0	+ 9.8	−18.8
+ 9.9	− 1.0	−20.8	− 6.6	− 8.4	−18.5	− 3.0	− 0.7
+11.5	+ 6.6	−22.4	−24.2	− 7.8	−13.3	−16.4	− 7.1
− 6.2	−14.5	−19.7	+ 5.3	−15.1	− 7.5	−12.9	−21.0
− 1.2	+ 1.0	− 5.5	− 3.0	−25.6	− 1.5	−20.9	− 9.5
−23.2	+18.0	+ 0.1	0.0	+11.8	+ 0.3	− 9.4	− 1.6
− 4.7	− 6.9	−14.1	+ 1.5	− 1.1	+ 1.8	−12.1	−10.3
−11.5	−10.6	−29.9	− 4.7	− 8.1	− 1.2	−21.9	−11.0
− 7.9	+ 5.9	−14.3	−15.2	+ 9.9	− 8.6	− 5.4	+ 3.2
+ 3.6	− 9.9	−22.3	− 2.3	− 9.5	−11.0	− 1.9	+ 0.7
+ 5.6	−17.0	+ 1.4	−22.5	− 1.4	−20.2	− 1.5	−11.4
− 1.3	−18.6	+10.6	− 4.3	− 5.8	−19.5	− 5.3	−12.2
− 7.5	+ 6.7	−13.6	−18.1	− 6.9	−17.7	+ 1.0	− 2.4

In assessing the accuracy of forecasts, two key questions invariably arise:

1. How frequent are large errors?
2. Is there a tendency for the forecasts to be either too optimistic or too pessimistic?

Organizing the data into a frequency distribution and its graphical counterpart is a good way to learn about the answers to these questions. We shall carry out this analysis before drawing conclusions about how good the sales forecasts are.

A first step to consider in the analysis is a line chart of the percentage differences between the actual and forecasted values.

It is rather difficult to interpret the pattern of variation in forecast errors in Figure 3.3. There are two reasons for this difficulty. First, there is not much amplitude in the frequencies of the error percentages. In fact, most of the observed error rates have a frequency of one. Second, there is a considerable variation in the length of the "gaps" or spaces between the error sizes for which the data are recorded. It almost seems that more can be learned from the distribution by studying the gaps than by focusing on the height of the frequency lines. The frequency lines are so small that they are hardly noticeable. However, studying the gaps is not the answer either. With so many gaps, it is likewise difficult to discern much of a pattern to the errors.

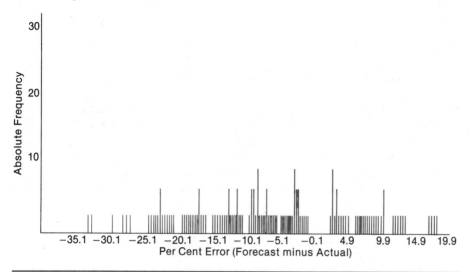

FIGURE 3.3   Distribution of Forecasting Errors: A Picture But No Message

The trouble with line charts like Figure 3.3 is that the underlying pattern of the variation is obscured by too much detail. The variable's many different values render the number of observations too sparse for a useful pattern to emerge. Data reduction and organization is the solution to this problem.

Two Ways to Treat Many-Valued Variables

There are essentially two different organizational approaches that can be used to simplify the treatment of data which take on a large number of different variates. These two approaches work in opposite directions.

> Reduce the number of alternative variates to be examined by "grouping" the data; that is, by considering only ranges of variates rather than individual variates.

> Take precisely the opposite approach; smooth the data over an infinite number of variates.

Which of the two data simplification procedures is more useful depends on the situation. Both procedures are used to *filter out erratic variation*. In other words, both techniques attempt to shed some light on the shape of what might be thought of as the frequency distribution which would be obtained if the data series were infinite.

3.5. Grouped Data

How can one simultaneously bring out the broad pattern of variation in the population, yet screen out the minor fluctuations attributable to the incompleteness of the sample data? One way is to organize the data into several variate classes, in effect grouping the data.

The Assignment Method of Grouping Data

How do you go about grouping data? One way is to construct a small number of variate classes and then assign each observation to one of the variate classes. The data on sales forecasting errors in Table 3.3 can be used to illustrate the assignment method of grouping data. First, variate classes are chosen by inspection of the data. Then, one by one, every observation is assigned to a class. What emerges is the absolute and relative frequency distribution showing *class frequencies* (Table 3.4).

TABLE 3.4. Per Cent Difference Between Actual and Forecasted Sales Volume (nearest tenth of a percent)

CLASS	CLASS INTERVAL, X	CLASS FREQUENCY, f	CLASS RELATIVE FREQUENCY, r.f.
1	−35.0 to −30.1	2	.01
2	−30.0 to −25.1	4	.02
3	−25.0 to −20.1	16	.08
4	−20.0 to −15.1	20	.10
5	−15.0 to −10.1	26	.13
6	−10.0 to − 5.1	42	.21
7	− 5.0 to − 0.1	34	.17
8	0.0 to + 4.9	30	.15
9	+ 5.0 to + 9.9	16	.08
10	+10.0 to +14.9	6	.03
11	+15.0 to +19.9	4	.02
		200	1.00

Frequency Histograms

Line charts are not generally used to portray class frequencies. The danger is that an unsuspecting reader might not realize that the vertical frequency lines refer to classes of values rather than individual values on which the vertical line is placed. Instead of using vertical lines, vertical bars are generally used to represent class frequencies, the width of the bar indicating the range of values included in the class. A diagram of this kind is called a frequency histogram (Figure 3.4). Although the frequencies portrayed on the vertical axis may be either absolute frequencies or relative frequencies, our convention shall be to construct the frequency histogram using relative frequencies unless stated otherwise.

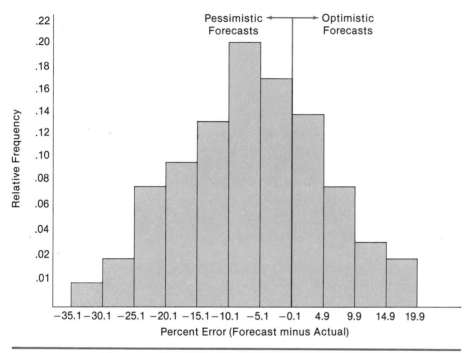

FIGURE 3.4 Distribution of Forecasting Errors

How Large Are the Errors?

The grouped data-based frequency distribution presented in Table 3.4 and Figure 3.4 reveals much more about the pattern of sales forecast errors than the line chart based on the ungrouped data. For instance, notice the range of errors:

Overestimates—in the two most extreme instances, actual sales were from 30.1 to 35 percent below the forecast.

Underestimates—in the four most extreme instances, actual sales exceeded the forecast level by between 15 and 19.9 percent.

Since those six instances represent the extremes and amount to only three percent of the 200 forecasts, it seems that neither unexpectedly high nor unexpectedly low sales pose a major problem. Although we observe that few if any of the forecasts were right on target, by adding up the relative frequencies within an error range of plus or minus 10% we find most (61% to be exact) fell within that error range. Assuming that this past error pattern prevails in the future, management will want to make sure that the inventory it carries reflects the uncertainties involved in forecasting sales.

Look for Pessimism and Optimism

An important point brought out by the relative frequency histogram is that 72 percent of the forecasts were too pessimistic. About eight times as many forecasts were ten percent too low as were ten percent too high. If management is unaware of this situation, it may be losing both sales and good will by incurring stockouts too frequently. However, once the situation is recognized, a correction can easily be made by adjusting each forecast upward by about five percent.

Surprising as it may seem, it is generally not a wise policy to stock enough inventory to satisfy every customer who might, but seldom does, come in. This is because carrying inventory costs money. No business likes to lose a customer, but at some point the likelihood of a forecasting error this large becomes too remote to justify the costs of carrying the additional inventory. Although the details are deferred until Chapter 23, it should be evident that the forecasting error frequency distribution plays an important role in deciding how much inventory is the right amount to keep on hand.

Class Limits and Class Interval

After the observations have been recorded (including rounding if necessary), the assignment of a recorded value to a particular class is determined by the *stated class limits*. The *lower* and *upper* stated class limits refer to the smallest and largest recording that can go into a particular class. For example, the lowest recorded error percentage which would fall into the third class is -25.0 while the highest recorded error percentage which would fall in the third class is -20.1. The lower class limit of the kth class is designated by the symbol L_k, and the upper class limit of the class is designated by the symbol U_k. A *class interval* of the kth class, C_k, is the difference between the lower limit of the kth class and the lower limit of the $(k$th $+ 1)$ class; or, alternatively, between the upper limit of the kth class and the upper limit of the next lower class, the $(k$th $- 1)$ class. All of the class intervals for the sales forecasting error data are 5.0 percentage points. Symbolically, the class interval of the kth class can be written either as: $C_k = L_{k+1} - L_k$ or as $C_k = U_k - U_{k-1}$. For instance, the class interval for the 3rd class in Table 3.4 is computed as $C_3 = L_4 - L_3 = (-20.0) - (-25.0) = 5.0$ or alternatively as $C_3 = U_3 - U_2 = (-20.1) - (-25.1) = 5.0$. As we can see both approaches agree.

Data Gaps May Spell Trouble

In the nurses sick leave example, a data spike of eleven days sick leave, the maximum permitted by the hospital, alerted management to a problem created by its sick leave policy. In the sales forecasting example, the predominance of mildly pessimistic forecasts suggested to management that a possible improvement in their forecasting system could be achieved. Gaps in the data are another type of message pattern that deserves investigation. Frequency distributions and their graphs are amazingly simple yet effective tools for this purpose, as the following example illustrates.

Example 3.5A. A Production Manager's Problem: Are Your Inspectors Doing Their Jobs?[2]

Inspection is a very important function in manufacturing and considerable effort is often expended in weeding out faulty parts and assemblies. However, sometimes it is the inspectors themselves who need to be inspected!

Consider the relative frequency histogram shown in Figure 3.5. It shows the distribution of diameters in centimeters of 500 steel rods. The lower tolerance limit (LTL) on these rods was set at 1.000 centimeters, because rods smaller than this would be too loose when fitted to a hole in a later operation.

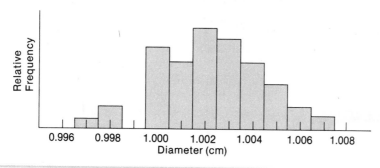

FIGURE 3.5   Distribution of Measurements on the Inside Diameter of 500 Steel Rods

Notice the gap at .999 and the peak at 1.000 centimeters, the lowest acceptable diameter. Although we can not be sure of the reason for this gap, its location just to the left of the lower tolerance limit arouses suspicion. It appears as if the inspectors might have been fudging the data a bit, passing parts that were just below the tolerance limit. A follow-up investigation revealed that this indeed is exactly what happened.

The inspectors knew that rejecting a rod meant losing not only the material but also the labor that had been expended up to that point. Consequently, they were reluctant to scrap a part so close to being acceptable. They were unaware of how much trouble was caused later on by fudging the data, and quickly changed their practice once the problem was called to their attention.

The Rounding Method of Grouping Data: Implicit Interval Estimates

The assignment method requires a deliberate selection of variate classes. The lazy way omits this deliberation. The procedure is simply to *round* the measurement. In effect, this establishes variate classes. The following example describes this situation.

Example 3.5B. Reporting Automobile Sales

Suppose the value of the variable "number of automobiles sold" is found to be 5.2 million and suppose you decide to round all figures to the nearest million units. The observed number 5.2 million will be rounded to 5 million. This means that, after rounding, the frequency found for 5 million represents the frequency for the implicit variate class "4.5 million but less than 5.5 million"—a class one million in size. That is, all the observations with values of "4.5 million but less than 5.5 million" will form the "5 million class" and its associated frequency.

Both the assignment method and the rounding method are legitimate ways of grouping data. The assignment method is more flexible in choosing classes, but the rounding method is simpler and may be more convenient.

Bars, Not Lines, For Rounded Data

Since recordings of rounded data (5 million) actually refer to a class or range of values—"4.5 million but less than 5.5 million"—it is appropriate to think of the recorded value as just the midpoint of a class of values. With this in mind, the appropriate graphic presentation of the frequency distribution on rounded data (even ungrouped data) should always be a bar rather than a line. This is why Figure 3.5 uses bars rather than lines in the relative frqeuency histogram even though the data on diameters were not grouped.

Real Versus Stated Class Limits

Whenever our measurements are rounded the stated class limits for the recorded data values do not exactly coincide with the limits of the actual values of the variable corresponding to the recorded measurements, which are referred to as *real class limits*. This point is illustrated by rounded data on rates of return earned by firms on bond refundings.

Example 3.5C. A Finance Manager's Problem: How Profitable Are Bond Refunding Decisions?

When interest rates decline substantially from previous levels and they are not antici-pated to go much lower, it is often financially advantageous for a firm to incur the cost of paying current bondholders a premium for recalling the outstanding bonds and to float (at an additional cost) a new issue of bonds at the lower interest rate to replace the current outstanding bond issue. The interest savings between the two

TABLE 3.5. Rates of Return on Forty Bond Refundings by Public Utilities in 1962 and 1963 (Raw Data and Array)

RAW DATA

14.7	5.5	16.1	8.7	8.0	10.4
11.5	15.3	6.8	11.3	10.4	7.3
9.1	12.3	9.9	14.6	13.1	7.1
3.6	9.6	12.3	26.7	23.8	10.1
14.8	6.5	16.1	13.8	19.7	12.8
11.9	9.7	5.7	11.2	13.0	19.7
9.5	12.3	43.4	8.2		

VARIATE, X	TALLY	f	VARIATE, X	TALLY	f
3.6	I	1	11.3	I	1
5.5	I	1	11.5	I	1
5.7	I	1	11.9	I	1
6.5	I	1	12.3	I I	2
6.8	I	1	12.8	I I	2
7.1	I	1	13.0	I	1
7.3	I	1	13.1	I	1
8.0	I	1	13.8	I	1
8.2	I	1	14.6	I	1
8.7	I	1	14.7	I	1
9.1	I	1	14.8	I	1
9.5	I	1	15.3	I	1
9.6	I	1	16.1	I I	2
9.7	I	1	17.2	I	1
9.9	I	1	19.7	I	1
10.1	I	1	23.8	I	1
10.4	I I	2	26.7	I	1
11.2	I	1	43.4	I	1

Source: Oswald D. Bowlin, "The Refunding Decision: Another Special Case of Capital Budgeting," *Journal of Finance* (March, 1966) pp. 55–68.

issues versus the new float cost and call cost will determine the rate of return earned. Data presented in Table 3.5 were collected to show the profitability of these refunding decisions.

The data have been rounded to the nearest tenth of a percentage point. Consequently, the range of actual values corresponding to a class is slightly larger than the stated class limits. For example, in Table 3.6, the stated class limits for the third class are 13.5 and 18.4 percent. However, all actual rates of return between 13.45 and 18.45 will fall into the class. The values 13.45 and 18.45 will fall into the class. The values 13.45 and 18.45 are the real class limits for the third class. Notice in Figure 3.6 that it is the real class limits, not the stated class limits, which are plotted on the frequency histogram for the rounded data. So the values 13.45 and 18.45 are the plotted bounds of the third class.

In Table 3.6 and Figure 3.6, the data have been grouped into eight equal classes. (Ignore the dotted line in Figure 3.6.) Notice the single observation in the highest-valued class, preceded by two empty classes and one other class with a single observation. This is important information, because it shows the rapid fall-off of frequency for returns above 20 percent.

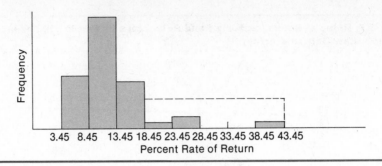

FIGURE 3.6   Rates of Return on Forty Bond Refundings

TABLE 3.6. Frequency Distribution Based on Equal Class Intervals

INTERVAL	FREQUENCY
3.5– 8.4	9
8.5–13.4	19
13.5–18.4	8
18.5–23.4	1
23.5–28.4	2
28.5–33.4	0
33.5–38.4	0
38.5–43.4	1

3.6. What's Wrong with Unequal Class Intervals?

In using a frequency histogram to compare class frequencies our eye focuses on the height and area of the rectangular bars. When class intervals are equal, as in the frequency histogram for sales forecasting errors, both the heights and areas are proportional to the relative frequencies of the observations in the intervals. Consequently, we get a correct visual presentation of the differences among relative frequencies of the classes. But sometimes equal class intervals cannot be used because the data available are already grouped in unequal class intervals, or because two or more classes have been combined to eliminate some intervals with zero or near-zero frequencies. In these cases the areas of a frequency histogram for unequal class intervals will not be proportional to the class frequencies. Thus, if our eyes focus on area for informational content on the relative frequencies, a distorted message will be conveyed. Comparing the height of the bars to one another does not eliminate the distortion since our eyes now have to contend with a changing dimension—interval width.

The problem created by unequal class intervals is similar to the problem of comparing prices at different stores when bottle sizes are unequal. When prices at some stores are on a per-gallon basis and prices at other stores are expressed on a fraction of a gallon or on a quart basis, direct price comparisons are not very meaningful. The price at all the stores must first be mentally converted to a common dimensional unit, such as a quart, to accomplish direct price comparison. Likewise, the relative frequency bars in a frequency histogram must mentally be expressed on a common dimensional base: relative frequency *per unit* of whatever is measured on the horizontal axis. Otherwise, a visual distortion occurs. This phenomenon is illustrated by rearranging the data from Table 3.6 (which has equal class intervals) into a relative frequency distribution of unequal class intervals, Table 3.7.

TABLE 3.7. Frequency Distribution Based on Unequal Class Intervals

INTERVAL	FREQUENCY
3.5– 8.4	9
8.5–13.4	19
13.5–18.4	8
18.5–43.4	4

The last five classes in Table 3.6 (including two empty classes) have been combined into one class having four observations. This eliminates the need for a larger table to accommodate all those empty classes. The revised frequency histogram (indicated by the dotted line in Figure 3.6) shows the visual distortion caused by the use of unequal class intervals.

Deceptive Frequency Histograms: The Visual Illusion

The two versions of frequency histograms shown in Figure 3.6 try to impart the same information about the intensity of observations among the classes, but the visual impression is distinctly different. The frequency histogram for unequal class intervals (the dotted line) gives the clear impression that the relative frequency in the combined six classes has greatly increased. This erroneous impression is obtained because our eyes do not naturally make an adjustment for the expanded interval width. The area under the newly formed rectangle is much larger than the combined area included in the original rectangles for the five classes, and the height of the new rectangular bar is greater than that of any of the original bars.

3.7. Density Histograms

The distorted visual impression caused by using unequal classes in a frequency histogram can be easily corrected, simply by making one important conceptual change. Represent relative frequency by the *area* rather than the height of the rectangles.

Use Area Rather Than Height to Represent Frequency

If relative frequency is to be represented by the area of a rectangle rather than its height, what does height represent? Since the area of every rectangle is the product of its base and its height, and the base of each bar is the number of units in the class, the height has to represent relative frequency *per unit* within the class (of whatever is measured along the horizontal axis). This is usually called relative frequency *density.*[3] Frequency density, like frequency, can be diagramed, as we will see in Figure 3.7.

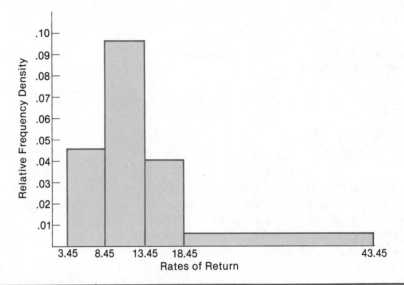

FIGURE 3.7   Density Histogram on Bond Refunding Rates of Return
(area under rectangles represents density of observations in the intervals)

Relative Frequency Density

Relative frequency *density* of the kth class equals the relative frequency of the kth class divided by the class interval of the kth class:

$$\text{r.f.d.}(X_k) = \frac{\text{r.f.}(X_k)}{C_k}$$

In Table 3.8, relative frequency density has been added to the data on rates of return given in Table 3.7. For example, the second class has an interval width of 5 percentage points and a relative frequency of .475. Therefore, the relative frequency density is $^{.475}\!/_{5.0} = .095$; the rectangular bar has area (base times height) of 5 × .095 = .475, the same numerical value as the relative frequency. For the fourth class, the computation for relative frequency density is $^{.125}\!/_{25} = .005$. Notice that the intervals vary in width from five to twenty-five. This means that relative frequency density (shown in the last column) will *not* be directly proportional to relative frequency (next to last column).

TABLE 3.8. Frequency Distribution of Rates of Return With Unequal Classes

INTERVAL	RELATIVE FREQUENCY	RELATIVE FREQUENCY DENSITY
3.5– 8.4	.225	.045
8.5–13.4	.475	.095
13.5–18.4	.200	.040
18.5–43.4	.125	.005
	1.000	

Density Histograms Permit the Right Comparisons

Graphs of frequency distributions which portray relative frequency as an area rather than height are called *density histograms*. Density histograms not only solve the practical problem of unequal class intervals, they are conceptually better as well. They do what the graph is really expected to do—convey information on the variation in intensity of observations per unit interval among the different classes; that is, the change in frequency density from class to class. Figure 3.7 is a density histogram of the data in Table 3.8. Area now represents the intensity of bond refundings in the interval, and thus a correct visual impression of the actual circumstance is given.

3.8. The Less-Looks-Like-More Trap

The frequency histogram has been shown to be a useful tool in the proper hands. Improperly used, frequency histograms can make less look like more, or more look like less. The secret is in selecting the number of classes into which the data will be grouped.

Squashing a Frequency Histogram

The problem with frequency histograms stems from the fact that as the number of classes increases, a frequency histogram tends to flatten out. That is, the larger the number of classes, the smaller the relative frequency of each class. If the number of classes doubles, the frequency histogram squashes to about one-half of its original height and half its original area.

Figure 3.8 shows how the size of a frequency histogram is related to the number of classes used to construct it. The frequency histograms in that figure are both based upon the tabular frequency distributions of Table 3.9. In other words, the two histograms refer to the same set of data. But they don't look the same. The colored histogram is only about half the size of the solid line histogram.

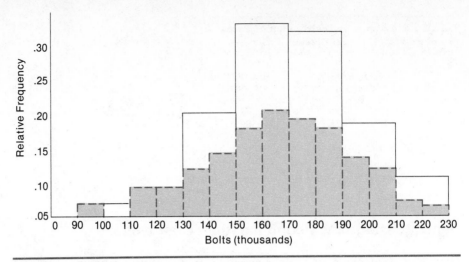

FIGURE 3.8 Comparison of Frequency Histograms Before and After Doubling the Number of Classes

TABLE 3.9. Comparison of the Frequency Distributions of the Number of Bolts in 200 Standard Crates with 7 and 14 Classes (doubling the classes)

SEVEN CLASSES

Class, x (Thousands)	Frequency, f(x)	Relative Frequency, r.f.(x)	Relative Frequency Density, r.f.d.(x)
90 up to 110	1	.005	.00015
110 up to 130	5	.025	.00125
130 up to 150	33	.165	.00825
150 up to 170	63	.315	.01650
170 up to 190	61	.305	.01550
190 up to 210	31	.155	.00775
210 up to 230	6	.030	.00150
	200	1.000	

SEVEN CLASSES DOUBLED (*Fourteen Classes*)

Class, x (Thousands)	Frequency, f(x)	Relative Frequency, r.f.(x)	Relative Frequency Density, r.f.d.(x)
90 up to 100	1	.005	.0005
100 up to 110	0	.000	.0000
110 up to 120	3	.015	.0015
120 up to 130	2	.010	.0010
130 up to 140	13	.065	.0065
140 up to 150	20	.100	.0100
150 up to 160	28	.140	.0140
160 up to 170	35	.175	.0175
170 up to 180	31	.155	.0155
180 up to 190	30	.150	.0150
190 up to 200	18	.090	.0090
200 up to 210	13	.065	.0065
210 up to 220	4	.020	.0020
220 up to 230	2	.010	.0010
	200	1.000	

You Can't Squash a Density Histogram

Unlike a frequency histogram, density histograms are not compressed towards the horizontal axis when the number of classes is increased. This is an important advantage of density histograms. Doubling the number of density histogram classes merely halves the *area* per class, leaving the *height* per class (relative frequency density) essentially unchanged. The total area under the entire density histogram remains unchanged.

Although the *area* under a density histogram does not change as the number of classes increases, the *outline* of the density histogram does change. The outline can become either smoother or more jagged as the number of classes is increased, primarily depending upon whether the total number of observations is large or small.

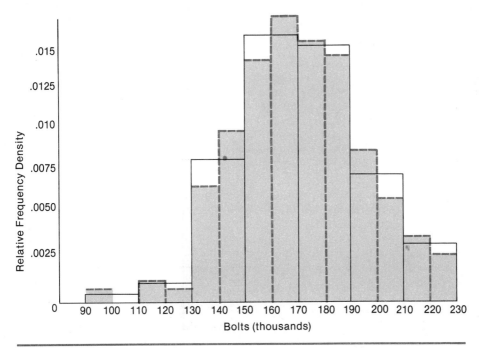

FIGURE 3.9 Comparison of Density Histograms Before and After Doubling the
Number of Classes

Figure 3.9 shows what happens to the density histogram for bolts-per-crate when the number of classes is doubled. The solid outline represents the original density histogram with class intervals of twenty thousand bolts. The colored outline represents the revised density histogram obtained by cutting the class intervals in half (to ten thousand bolts), thereby doubling the number of classes from seven to fourteen. A key point to notice is that doubling the classes did *not* cause the density histogram to be squashed down towards the horizontal axis, as it did to the frequency histogram.

In comparing two distributions which do not have the same size class intervals, the use of density histograms rather than frequency histograms can be crucially important for proper interpretation. An example from the supermarket industry illustrates a frequency histogram trap and how that trap can be corrected by the use of density histograms.

Example 3.8. Supermarket Drawing Power

In the supermarket industry, expanding a store's trade area can be a route to higher sales and profits. Since department stores and large discount stores draw customers from a large trade area, building a supermarket in close proximity to these stores is one way supermarket executives may attempt to expand a supermarket's trade area. However, increased traffic congestion and closer proximity to competing supermarkets can significantly reduce the advantage or even bring about a reduced volume of sales. Thus, a feasibility study with a careful analysis of the trade area of a proposed store is a must before a site is selected. One of the popular measures of a store's trade area is the relative frequency distribution of the store's current customers by distance from the store. This measure is commonly called store *drawing power*.

The drawing power of two comparable supermarkets obtained from customer spotting surveys is graphed in Figure 3.10. Store *A* is a free-standing store, while Store *B* is a supermarket associated with a large self-service department store. The data from Store *A* are reported in intervals of one mile, while the data from Store *B* are reported in intervals of one-half mile.

A comparison of the two frequency histograms in Figure 3.10 indicates that the height of the drawing power of Store *B* is below that of Store *A* at every trade area distance, and the total area under the Store *B* drawing power distribution is much less than the area under the Store *A* distribution. From this, some people may jump to the (erroneous) conclusion that the free-standing store has more customers in every trading area zone.

Misinterpreting Figure 3.10 this way stems from the fact that the two relative frequency histograms are based on different size class intervals. Since Store *B*'s intervals are only half the width of the intervals for Store *A*, the heights of the bars for Store *B* are on average only half the height of the bars for Store *A*, because the

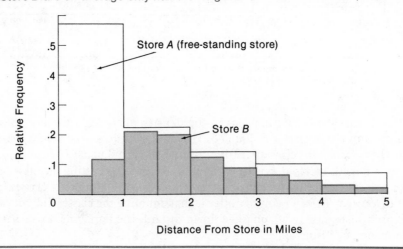

FIGURE 3.10   Frequency Histograms for Supermarket Drawing Power

concentration of observations has been divided between two classes. The wider the interval, the more intact the concentration remains. Thus, the area under the frequency histogram of Store *B* bars is half Store *A*'s. This visual distortion cannot be avoided so long as drawing power is shown as height.

Density histograms avoid all the problems of unequal intervals. In a density histogram (Figure 3.11), the amount of drawing power is by design made proportional to the area under a bar rather than to the bar's height. A comparison of the two density histograms in Figure 3.11 reveals a new perspective. Supermarket *B*, associated with the self-service department store, has a greater drawing power than Store *A* in the more distant zones. This shows that the actual situation is in exact conformity with what is expected if the self-service department store helps the supermarket attract new customers from more distant zones.

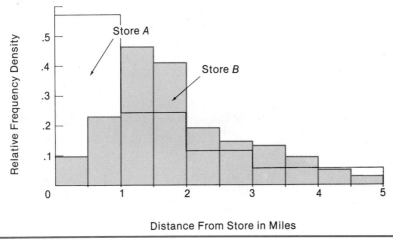

FIGURE 3.11   Density Histograms for Supermarket Drawing Power

3.9. The Right Class Size Depends on the Number of Observations

Sometimes the information on the pattern of variation is best discerned by grouping the data into a small number of classes of rather wide intervals. But in other instances, a much larger number of classes of narrower interval is more informative. How do we know whether to group data into a small number of wide intervals or a larger number of narrower intervals to deliver the message?

How Wide Should Class Intervals Be Made?

Are there relatively few observations? If so, grouping the data into a small number of classes will highlight the informational pattern of variation by smoothing out some of the jaggedness. Conversely, increasing the number of classes leads to a more jagged outline. How much more jagged? Quite a bit, as can be clearly seen by comparing density histograms for the following example on hospital patient waiting time.

Example 3.9. Patient Waiting Time at a Hospital Emergency Room

The Joint Committee for Accreditation of Hospitals requires that reasonable standards be set for various hospital services. Administrators at a group of large city hospitals believe an "ideal" hospital should be able to treat a certain class of emergency cases within thirty minutes of arrival. However, they know that this ideal standard would be impossible for most hospitals to implement within reasonable budgeting limitations. To encourage hospitals to move towards this ideal, the administrators want to set a standard that can realistically be met by hospitals putting forth a sincere effort, and that if met will result in a significant reduction in patient waiting time. To help determine the standard, hospitals have been asked to supply data on the waiting times presently experienced by their patients.

The data in Table 3.10 give the excess time (beyond the thirty minute ideal) it took for two hundred patients to receive treatments. No negative values appear since no waiting was less than thirty minutes. How should these data be presented in order to facilitate an assessment of a feasible and acceptable standard?

TABLE 3.10. Raw Data: 200 Recordings on Excess Patient Waiting Time at a Hospital Emergency Room (nearest minute)

39	41	53	54	85	69	81	36
40	79	50	39	59	46	52	51
100	45	49	60	76	49	66	48
72	40	60	44	56	46	92	36
47	88	63	14	30	51	26	25
32	51	41	49	23	53	46	48
0	33	33	38	51	34	40	57
73	15	6	31	44	48	29	41
74	25	78	52	37	24	35	54
53	46	49	53	63	64	43	48
27	45	15	61	74	32	87	60
47	56	79	41	62	60	42	32
68	62	46	70	69	49	63	76
26	52	33	73	71	50	62	87
64	1	29	22	85	77	68	58
26	59	53	23	50	41	58	36
51	31	89	30	55	60	9	61
97	79	52	69	54	49	67	59
34	43	40	31	27	65	51	78
56	29	29	64	49	71	41	37
32	33	51	44	31	58	74	50
12	0	80	25	41	78	61	66
55	48	23	81	25	59	89	51
36	73	50	45	36	52	69	31
44	54	64	36	66	62	42	36

Three density histograms, based on the same 200 patient waiting time, are presented in Figure 3.12. The data have been grouped into classes having an interval of twenty minutes in one case, ten minutes in another, and only one minute in the third.

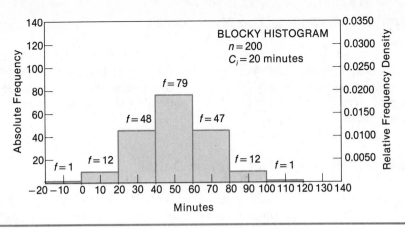

FIGURE 3.12a Density Histogram of Excess Patient Waiting Time

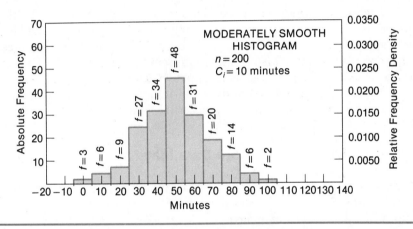

FIGURE 3.12b Density Histogram of Excess Patient Waiting Time

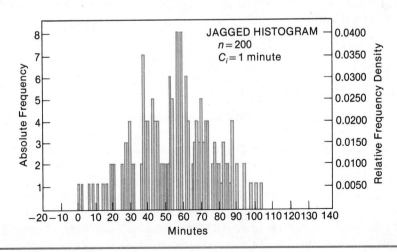

FIGURE 3.12c Density Histogram of Excess Patient Waiting Time

Jaggedness Indicates Too Much Detail

The density histogram with the narrowest classes (Figure 3.12c) is the most jagged. It is riddled with many empty classes and gives an unclear picture of how relative frequency density varies among the waiting time classes. The two density histograms with wider class intervals are noticeably less jagged and are much more informative.

Blockiness Indicates Not Enough Detail

The density histogram with the widest classes (Figure 3.12a) is the least jagged but it is not the most informative of the three. There is a "blockiness" to that histogram which obscures the pattern of the change in relative frequency density from class to class.

The density histogram which seems to best capture the pattern of the change in the relative frequency density is the middle histogram (Figure 3.12b), the one with a class interval of ten minutes. This moderately smooth histogram presents neither excessive detail to distract attention from the basic pattern of variation, nor excessive aggregation to obscure informative detail.

By trying out several different interval widths as we did in this example, it will usually become apparent which interval size is appropriate.

With Large Class Sizes, More Data May Not Help

The conclusion as to which size class interval is best may change when data are more plentiful. Figure 3.13 shows how the density histograms of Figure 3.12 change when the number of observations is increased from 200 to 6000, a thirty-fold increase. Since data sets containing more than 6000 observations are rarely encountered, Figure 3.13 can be considered representative of a large sample.

The two density histograms in Figure 3.13a and b look almost like carbon copies of the two histograms in Figure 3.12a and b. Therefore, it can be concluded that adding the extra observations didn't provide much useful new information when class intervals were ten minutes or larger.

Use Smaller Class Sizes When Data Are Plentiful

The really striking difference between Figures 3.12 and 3.13 is found in the two histograms where the class interval is only one minute. In Figure 3.12c, where there were only 200 observations, the underlying pattern of variation in waiting time tends to be obscured by extreme jaggedness, a condition not present when intervals of ten minutes or twenty minutes were used. However, in Figure 3.13c, which is based upon a sample size of 6000 observations, jaggedness no longer poses a serious problem and the one minute interval width reveals additional information about the main pattern of variation not obtainable from the histogram based on wider intervals. *The moral is this: take advantage of more plentiful*

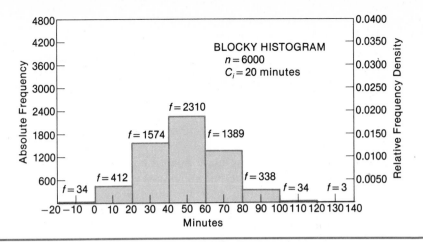

FIGURE 3.13a   Density Histogram of Excess Patient Waiting Time

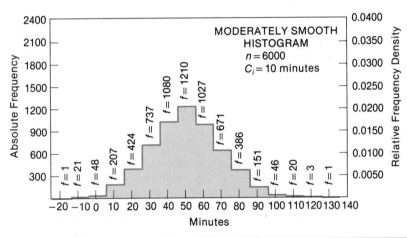

FIGURE 3.13b   Density Histogram of Excess Patient Waiting Time

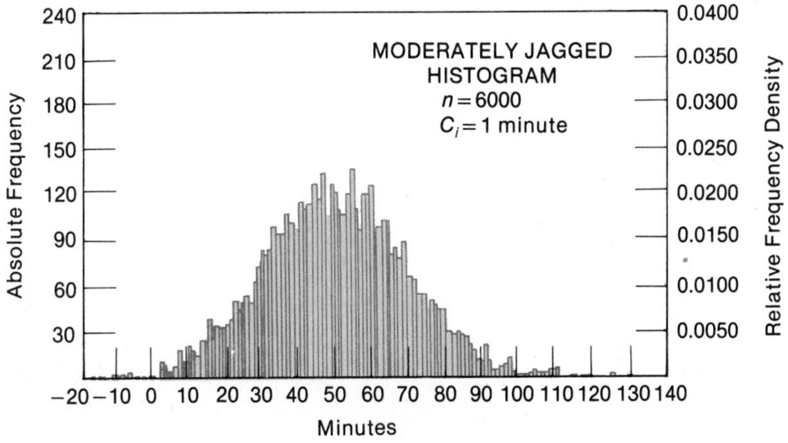

FIGURE 3.13c   Density Histogram of Excess Patient Waiting Time

data by making the interval class size smaller; but don't reduce the interval size to the point where jaggedness obscures the main pattern of variation.

Sparse Data and Fuzzy Messages

Why is the jaggedness of the waiting time data so pronounced when the data are sparse? And why does it iron out when the number of observations becomes very large? The reason is simple.

For a particular observation, the main opposing forces influencing patient waiting time by various amounts are not all simultaneously present to balance each other out. The net result is that merely by chance, one or another of these forces may exert the dominant influence on patient waiting time. Over a small number of observations this influence may not be offset (hence the jaggedness of Figure 3.12c). But over a larger number of observations, the forces of chance do have an opportunity to offset each other and cancel out (as in Figure 3.13c).

Filling the Slots: Make Classes Wide Enough to Include Several Observations

The dramatic difference in appearance of the two histograms (Figures 3.12c and 3.13c) brings out the two important points about the smoothness of the outline of density histograms.

The first point pertains to the *number of observations per class:*

> In order to smooth out the jaggedness due to sources of variation of secondary interest and focus attention on the source of variation of primary interest, several observations are required in most of the classes.

The more observations in a class, the stronger is the tendency for the secondary sources of variation to cancel each other out. The villain which makes the histogram in Figure 3.12c more jagged than Figure 3.13c is the small number of observations in each class, not the large number of classes.

The second point pertains to the *number of classes:*

> Increasing the number of classes leads to a smoother outline (less blockiness) if, but only if, the secondary sources of variation do not exert a strong influence within classes.

Neither Blocky Nor Jagged?

Most classes in Figure 3.13c have several observations, enough so that the secondary sources of variation do not affect the outline of the histogram to any great extent. Reducing the class interval to one minute, histogram 3.13c leads to a smoother outline even though the same technique does not work well in histogram 3.12c.

Although histogram 3.13c adds useful detail not observable in the top two histograms, some jaggedness is still apparent. Might it be possible to keep much of the detail while eliminating a portion of the jaggedness by using a class interval somewhere between one and ten minutes?

The answer is apparent from Figure 3.14 which is a density histogram of class interval of five minutes. This appears to be the most informative of all the histograms. It is neither blocky nor jagged and has detail not contained in the histograms based on wider intervals.

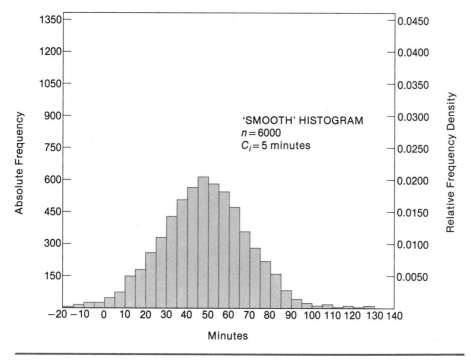

FIGURE 3.14   Density Histogram of Excess Patient Waiting Time

3.10. Deciding on the Number of Classes

The overriding goal in grouping data is to emphasize the primary or major patterns of variation and de-emphasize erratic or secondary patterns of minor interest. To bring out the major pattern of variation, we want to avoid both blockiness and jaggedness. Jaggedness, which results from secondary variation, can be reduced by increasing the number of observations in each class. This is accomplished by using wider intervals, thereby reducing the number of classes. On the other hand, reducing the number of classes introduces blockiness, which tends to obscure the major patterns of variation. So there is usually a trade-off between blockiness and jaggedness.

Since increasing the number of classes reduces blockiness and leads to a more accurate picture of the variation's pattern, the general principle to be used in selecting the number of classes is rather simple: continue to increase the number of classes as long as jaggedness doesn't set in. But because the amount of variation due to secondary sources differs considerably from one situation to the next, the number of classes which would effectively filter out secondary variation differs from one situation to the next.

No Mechanical Rule Is Entirely Satisfactory

However, the smoothness of the outline of a histogram is closely related to the number of classes. Therefore, it is important to be able to find the "right" number of classes. But how does one establish the "best" number of classes? Must it be by trial and error as in the previous section, constructing and examining various histograms? Or is there some mechanical rule for grouping data into classes?

It turns out that there's no universally applicable definitive rule for the optimal grouping of data into classes. But there are three rules of thumb which are rather widely used to decide upon the number of classes for grouping the data.

1. The Six-Fifteen Rule

One rule suggests a *minimum of six classes for small samples and a maximum of fifteen classes for large samples.* The motivation for this rule stems from the fact that the reduction in class size without jaggedness made possible by a larger sample size is less than proportional to the increase in the number of observations. Consider the patient waiting time graphed in Figures 3.12 and 3.13. With 200 observations, there was no jaggedness using eleven classes (Figure 3.12b). But, with a fifteenfold increase in the number of classes, some jaggedness appeared even though the number of observations increased thirtyfold (Figure 3.13c).

2. Sturges' Rule

Another convenient and popular rule known as *Sturges' Rule* gives explicit guidelines for the number of classes to use. This number is found according to the following formula:

$$k = 1 + 3.3(\log_{10}n),$$

where the integer value of k is the number of classes and n is the number of observations. For example, if there are 100 observations, Sturges' Rule suggests 7 classes;

$$k = 1 + 3.3(\log 100)$$
$$= 1 + 3.3(2)$$
$$= 7.6$$

By dropping the numbers to the right of the decimal, we find the integer value of $7.6 = 7$. If there are 1000 observations, Sturges' Rule suggests 10 classes:

$$k = 1 + 3.3(\log 1000)$$
$$= 1 + 3.3(3)$$
$$= 10.9$$

and the integer value of $10.9 = 10$.

3. Split-Sample Comparison

A third approach, known as the *split-sample comparison*, requires the following steps:

1. Select a number of classes which you feel might be appropriate.

2. Divide the data into two groups by assigning alternate data items to the two groups.

3. Construct a histogram from each of the two groups, but use only one-half the selected number of classes.

4. If these two histograms are quite similar in appearance, the selected number of classes is probably about right.

5. If the two histograms obtained in Step 3 are quite dissimilar, go back to Step 1 and repeat the procedure, using a smaller number of classes.

3.11. Frequency Polygons

An interesting variant of the density histogram is the *frequency polygon*. Like density histograms, frequency polygons measure frequency or relative frequency as area under the curve. But frequency polygons use trapezoidal rather than rectangular areas to represent frequency.

A frequency polygon is simple to construct from a histogram. There are three steps:

1. At each end of the histogram, presume there is an extra class having zero frequency.

2. Locate the midpoints of all classes.

3. Connect the midpoints with straight lines.

Frequency polygons for the 6000 patient waiting time observations have been constructed in Figure 3.15. The polygons are based on class intervals of twenty minutes, ten minutes, and five minutes and are superimposed over the corresponding density histograms. It can be seen from Figure 3.15 that frequency polygons enhance the smoothing effect of small class intervals combined with large numbers of observations.

A density histogram and a frequency polygon enclose an identical area so long as all the class intervals are of equal width. This is because the triangular area chopped off one rectangle of a density histogram by a superimposed frequency polygon always equals the triangular area in the polygon above the adjacent rectangle in the histogram. Note, however, the shift of triangular areas means that the total areas of individual classes of a frequency polygon are no longer exactly equal to the actual frequency or relative frequencies of the class.

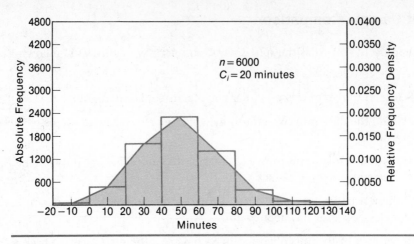

FIGURE 3.15a   Frequency Polygon of Excess Patient Waiting Time

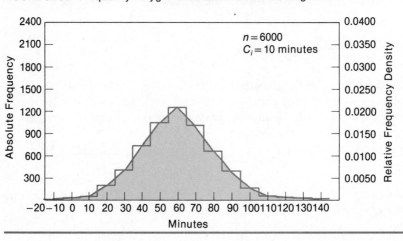

FIGURE 3.15b   Frequency Polygon of Excess Patient Waiting Time

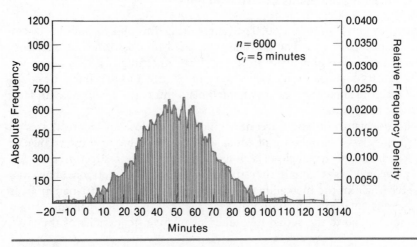

FIGURE 3.15c   Frequency Polygon of Excess Patient Waiting Time

3.12. Density Functions and Smooth Curves

We have now completed consideration of the first of two approaches toward simplifying the treatment of variables which take on a large number of different values: grouping the data so as to reduce the number of alternatives to be considered. The second approach simplifies the treatment not by reducing, but rather by increasing, the number of possible values unendingly. The effect of this procedure is easily seen using the concept of a frequency polygon.

Smooth Curves: Another Way to Simplify Data

Compare once again the three frequency polygons shown in Figure 3.15a, b, and c. As the number of classes (and the number of observations) is increased, the polygon becomes smoother. Our interest lies in the extreme case:

> in the limit, as both the number of classes and the number of observations approach infinity, the frequency polygon tends to become a smoothly continuous curve.

This is illustrated in Figure 3.16, where the bottom frequency polygon of Figure 3.15 has been smoothed to show what would happen in the extreme case.

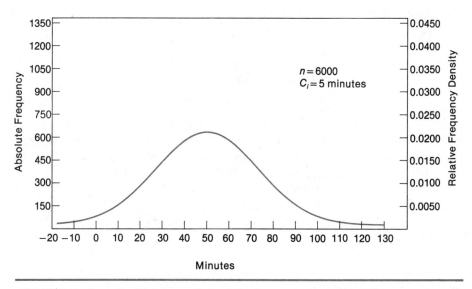

FIGURE 3.16   Smoothed Frequency Polygon for Excess Patient Waiting Time

What's So Special About Smooth Curves?

Smooth curves are of special interest because they can often be expressed in the form of a mathematical equation, the ultimate in data reduction. The height of the curve, representing relative frequency density, is expressed as some function of the variable measured on the horizontal axis. Functions of this type are known as *density functions*.

Density functions measure the rate of change of density for minute changes in the interval size. Density functions, therefore, are the mathematical equations which define the long-run (theoretical) relative frequency distributions towards which the historical (empirical) relative frequency distributions approach as the number of observations becomes infinitely large and the intervals infinitely small. It can therefore be said that the long-run, theoretical distribution is the abstract model underlying an empirical frequency distribution based on historical data. In Chapter 7, this approach is used to assess probability from a smoothed empirical frequency distribution of the historical data available.

Density Functions Offer Three Advantages

There are three reasons why density functions are especially convenient devices for describing data.

Density functions are a compact way of summarizing information contained in a set of data.

All the pertinent information can be communicated in the short space it takes to write the equation for the density function. Persons familiar with the function can immediately recognize the shape of the function as well as other important features even without graphing it.

Density functions often facilitate computations.

For example, it is often easier to compute the area under a density function than a histogram over any specified interval.

Density functions simplify the treatment of data and facilitate comparisons.

Instead of studying the pattern of variation within each data set as if the pattern were unique, it is often helpful to relate the data to one of about a dozen density functions for which the pattern of variation is already known. In this way, the study of variation can be largely limited to a few frequently recurring types so that these can be given the special attention they properly deserve.

We shall mention one frequently encountered type of density function here—the normal density function. We will consider other types of density functions in a subsequent chapter.

Normal Density Functions

All density functions of the so-called "normal" family resemble the bell-shaped curve shown in Figure 3.17. Areas under normal curves are ordinarily obtained from a table which has been prepared for this purpose rather than by evaluating a mathematical function.[4] In Chapter 10, we shall have the opportunity to study the normal family of density functions in considerably more detail.

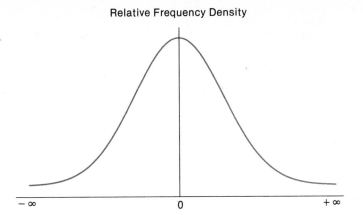

Relative Frequency Density

$-\infty$ 0 $+\infty$

FIGURE 3.17 Standardized Normal Density Function

3.13. Cumulative Distributions and Ogives

A frequency distribution is not the best device for finding the frequency between any two values. A variant known as a *cumulative* distribution is usually more convenient for this purpose. As the name suggests, cumulative distributions differ from frequency distributions in that the listed frequencies are cumulative.

For ungrouped data, cumulative frequencies indicate the number of observations which have a value *less than or equal to* the specified values of the variable; for example, seven executives at Megabyte were less than 35 years old and twenty were less than 40 years old. Therefore, the frequency between any two values of a variable is simply the difference between the cumulative frequencies for those values; for example, thirteen executives at Megabyte were between 35 and 40 years old.

For data grouped into classes, cumulative frequencies indicate the number of observations which have a value less than the lower limit of the designated class. Table 3.11 gives the relative frequency distribution for the data on excess patient waiting time using ten minute class intervals. The corresponding cumulative relative frequency (c.r.f.) distribution is shown in Table 3.12. Notice that the first class has a c.r.f. of zero, because no observations were recorded for values less than the lower limit of this class. For the other classes, the cumulative relative frequency is the sum of all the relative frequencies for lesser-valued classes. For example, the fifth class has a c.r.f. of .225, the sum of .015, .030, .045, and .135.

Ogives

An *ogive* is a chart of a cumulative distribution. Figure 3.18 is an ogive constructed from the data in Table 3.12. A point and the ogive are plotted by:

TABLE 3.11. Frequency Distribution of 200 Recordings on Excess Patient Waiting Time at a Hospital Emergency Room (nearest minute)

Class Interval (x)	CLASS INTERVAL SIZE 10 f(x)	r.f.(x)
−4 to 5	3	.015
6 to 15	6	.030
16 to 25	9	.045
26 to 35	27	.135
36 to 45	34	.175
46 to 55	48	.240
56 to 65	31	.155
66 to 75	20	.100
76 to 85	14	.070
86 to 95	6	.030
96 to 105	2	.010

Source: Table 3.10

TABLE 3.12. Cumulative Frequency Distribution of 200 Recordings on Excess Patient Waiting Time at a Hospital Emergency Room (nearest minute)

Class	Lower Limit of Class Interval (x)	Cumulative Relative Frequency c.r.f.(x)
1	less than −4	.000
2	less than 6	.015
3	less than 16	.045
4	less than 26	.090
5	less than 36	.225
6	less than 46	.395
7	less than 56	.635
8	less than 66	.790
9	less than 76	.890
10	less than 86	.960
11	less than 96	.990
12	less than 106	1.000

1. moving to the right from the origin until the value equal to the lower class limit of the designated class is reached (for example, 36 for the fifth class);

2. then, moving vertically upward until a value equal to the cumulative relative frequency value is reached (for example, .225 for the fifth class). This is where the point is plotted.

3. Connecting the points by line segments produced the ogive.

Since the waiting time data are on a continuous variable (time), points on the ogive could be connected by a smooth curve (under the assumption that values of the continuous variable change in infinitesimally small increments rather than in discrete steps or jumps).

Ogives obtained from density functions will always be smooth since the

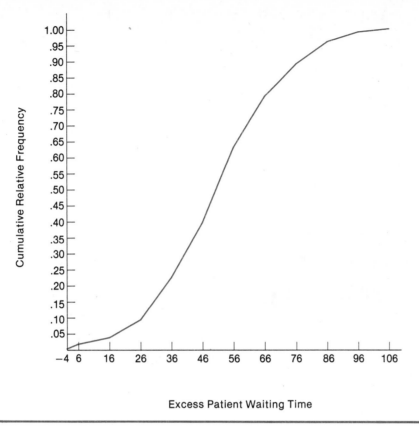

FIGURE 3.18 Ogive (Cumulative Relative Frequency Diagram) for Excess Patient Waiting Time

underlying variable is continuous. Figure 3.19 shows the ogive for the commonly encountered normal density function portrayed in Figure 3.17. Smooth ogives are often called *cumulative distribution functions.*

If the cumulative distribution is based upon a discrete variable, then the ogive will always increase in discrete jumps or steps as in Figure 3.20. Ogives of this kind are sometimes called *step functions.*

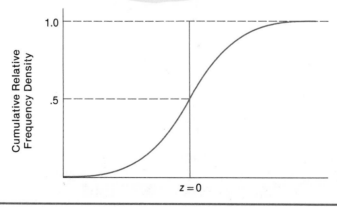

FIGURE 3.19 Ogive for the Standard Normal Density Function

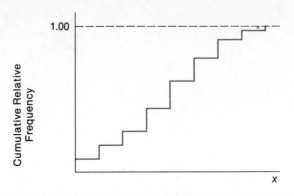

FIGURE 3.20   Step Function for Discrete Variable *x*

Ogives, which are properly charts, are sometimes referred to as *cumulative frequency distributions* or just cumulative distributions, terms which more properly refer to equations or tables rather than to charts.

One advantage of ogives over histograms and frequency polygons is that the actual data can be plotted without any need for grouping the data. This not only eliminates the need for deciding the "right" size interval, but also eliminates the loss of information which results from grouping data; that is, you no longer need to know the value of the individual observations.

3.14. Measures of Relative Position Say a Lot: Fractiles

Fractiles are the standard measure of relative position within a frequency distribution.

> A fractile of a distribution is a cumulative relative frequency. It denotes the proportion of the observations which have a numerical value less than or equal to the fractile value.

In other words, a .4 fractile having a fractile value of 57 denotes that forty percent of the total observations have values less than or equal to 57.

Consider the following ungrouped scores recorded on ten elementary units;

17, 25, 13, 37, 31, 26, 22, 20, 31, 25.

Rearranging them in order of magnitude, we find that four of the ten elementary units have values *less than* or *equal to* 22. This means that the .4 fractile has a fractile value equal to 22 and that four-tenths, four out of ten in this case, of the elementary units have a score of 22 or less.

Percentiles

Percentiles are simply fractiles multiplied by one hundred. They are expressible in percentage terms. For example, a .37 fractile is also a 37th percentile; both indicate that 63 percent of the observations have values which exceed the value associated with the .37 fractile (37th percentile). Percentiles are more commonly used than fractiles in reporting data to the general public. For example, college board scores are often reported in terms of percentiles. If someone tells you that she scored in the 78th percentile on her college boards, she should mean that 78 percent of the other examinees received a score lower than or equal to her own. It should also mean that 22 percent of the people taking the examinations scored higher than she did.

Deciles, Quintiles, and Quartiles

Certain fractiles and percentiles are used often enough to have their own names. For example, *deciles* partition a frequency distribution into ten approximately equal groups—the first decile is the .10 fractile; the second decile is the .20 fractile, etc. *Quintiles* partition a frequency distribution into five approximately equal groups—the first quintile is the .20 fractile; the second quintile is the .40 fractile, etc. The .25, .50 and .75 fractiles divide a distribution into quarters and are called the first, second, and third *quartiles*, respectively. The .50 fractile partitions a distribution into two approximately equal parts and is called the *median* of the distribution. It is also the second quartile and fifth decile of the distribution.

A Few Fractiles May Tell the Story

Fractiles and percentiles are so useful as descriptive measures because just a few fractiles can convey a great deal of information about a frequency distribution. Better than words ever could, a simple example will show just how well the important features of the original frequency distribution can be summarized by a few fractiles. Constructing individual freehand ogives from a few fractiles gives a visual impression of the dissimilarity (or similarity) that exists between two frequency distributions.

 With only the four quintile values of a distribution reported: 200, 300, 350, and 400, an approximation of the entire ogive of the original distribution can be made merely by connecting the four quintiles with a smooth freehand curve as shown in Figure 3.21a. It is evident from the ogive that the original distribution has an inflection point (change in the *rate* of increase) in the vicinity of 325.

 Now suppose the reported quintile values of another distribution are 100, 250, 500, and 800. The freehand ogive for this distribution is shown in Figure 3.21b. Note the visual difference.

 The contrast between the two freehand ogives reflects important differences between the two underlying frequency distributions from which the quintile values were obtained. More accuracy would undoubtedly be added to the sketch by using a greater number of fractile values, but this is not the point. The crucial point to be understood is that only a few measures of relative location (in our case, four) is sufficient to highlight the basic difference between two frequency distributions.

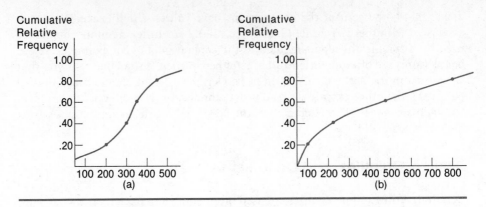

FIGURE 3.21 Freehand Ogives Constructed from Two Different Distributions

Another Plus for Fractiles

In organizing and reporting statistical information, fractiles can be advantageous for an entirely different reason. The use and effectiveness of fractiles in communicating information does not depend on the number of observations in the frequency distribution. In other words, the quintiles of a distribution based upon forty elementary units imparts the same information about the spread and concentration of the elementary units as do the quintiles of a distribution of forty thousand elementary units. Thus, in the following example on the tax burden, the number of observations is not even stated, yet the important statistical message is effectively communicated.

Example 3.14.   The Tax Burden: Who Bears More and More of It?

The House Ways and Means Committee of Congress is faced with the task of screening tax bills for tax reform policy for the nation. A key consideration in granting tax relief to income groups is to ascertain which group is currently bearing the tax burden and whether that burden is becoming more oppressive. An excellent statistical device to detect how the burden is being shared and whether that burden is shifting is the *ogive*. From Figure 3.22, can one surmise that the poor are bearing more than their share of the tax burden and that this burden is becoming greater and greater?

Using the IRS Statistics on Income, an ogive for 1975 shows that the top 10 per cent paid about 50 per cent of the total personal income taxes collected in 1975. The top 50 per cent income earner—those with adjusted gross income of $8431 or more in 1975—paid 92.9 per cent of the total tax bill. Also, the tax burden is shifting away from lower income people. For the bottom 50 percent of income

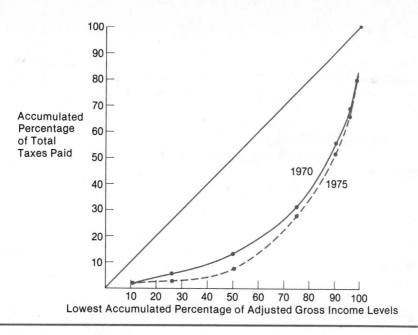

FIGURE 3.22 Ogives of the Percentage of Total Taxes Paid by High and Low Income Taxpayers, 1970 and 1975

TABLE 3.13. Percentage of Total Taxes Paid by High and Low Income Taxpayer, 1970 and 1975

ADJUSTED GROSS INCOME CLASS	ADJUSTED GROSS INCOME LEVEL		PERCENTAGE OF TAX PAID	
	1970	1975	1970	1975
Lowest 10%	$ 1258 or less	1526 or less	.1	.1
Lowest 25%	3156 or less	4043 or less	.9	.4
Lowest 50%	6918 or less	8930 or less	10.3	7.1
Lowest 75%	11,466 or less	15,897 or less	31.7	28.0
Lowest 90%	16,964 or less	23,419 or less	55.0	51.3
Lowest 95%	20,866 or less	29,271 or less	65.9	63.4
Lowest 99%	43,248 or less	59,337 or less	82.4	81.3

earners, the tax burden share declined from 10.3 to 7.1 from 1970 to 1975. The 45° straight line represents equal percentages of total taxes to equal percentages of adjusted gross income and depicts a situation of "equal" tax burden. The further away from the 45° straight line the more disproportionate is the tax burden relative to income. Shifts further away indicate the disproportionate burden is becoming greater (as is the case from 1970 to 1975).

3.15. Concluding Comments

Frequency distributions can be represented graphically by a *line chart* or by a *histogram*. If the frequency distribution shows the frequency of individual values, a line chart is used. When the frequencies of the distribution correspond to a range of variate values or classes, a histogram is the preferred method. Frequency in this later case is shown by the height of, or the area under, a vertical bar. *Frequency histograms* show the frequency (absolute or relative) proportional to the bar height. *Density histograms* show frequency proportional to bar area.

The use of density histograms instead of frequency histograms solves two problems: one, the distorted visual impression the frequency histogram gives when unequal class sizes are used; second, the squashing effect problem on the frequency histogram with increasing number of classes.

In constructing histograms, a decision must be made as to the number of classes into which the data will be grouped. The fewer the classes, the "blockier" will the outline of the histogram be. Increasing the number of classes for a given number of observations, however, eventually leads to a "jagged" outline. The right number of classes, avoiding blockiness and jaggedness, cannot be determined by a definite rule. However, three rules of thumb are helpful in this regard. The simplest of the three advises no less than six and no more than fifteen classes. The second rule, *Sturges' rule*, is more precise; it sets the number of classes equal to one plus (3.3 times the log of the number of observations). The last rule, the split-sample rule, advises changing the number of classes until the outline of two histograms, each based on half the data, becomes similar.

Frequency polygons, a variant of density histograms, are obtained by connecting the midpoints of adjacent bars of a density histogram. If there are both a large number of classes and a large number of observations, the frequency polygon may resemble a smooth curve. Smooth curves are of special interest because they can often be expressed in the form of a mathematical equation, the ultimate in data reduction. These equations are called *density functions*. Certain families of density functions are of special importance in statistics; one of these is the normal family of density functions.

A *cumulative distribution* aggregates frequencies. For ungrouped data, it reports the number of observations which have a value less than or equal to a particular single value. For grouped data, it reports the number of observations which have less than the value of a particular class limit. A graph of the cumulative frequencies is called an *ogive*. Interestingly, its construction does not require that the data be grouped into classes first. This eliminates the chore of determining the "right" number of classes and avoids any loss of information resulting from the grouping process.

Much of the information contained in a data set can be tersely presented by a few *fractiles* and their corresponding fractile values. A fractile merely indicates the proportion of observations, whereas the fractile value specifies the particular numerical magnitude not exceeded by that proportion of the observations. Multiplying fractiles by 100 converts them to *percentiles*. *Deciles, quin-*

tiles, and *quartiles* are fractiles or percentiles that partition the frequency distribution into approximately equal groups of ten in the case of deciles, of five in the case of quintiles, and of four in the case of quartiles. It is easy to compare important features of different distributions from fractile values particularly when fractile values are used to construct freehand ogives.

Frequency distributions as well as cumulative distributions, whether in tabular or graphical form, provide us with information about patterns in the data. What features or patterns should one be searching for? Some suggestions to look for are:

the range of values over which the data are dispersed;

the degree of uniformity in the dispersion of the observations over the range of values;

clustering near certain values, particularly those locations for which one has expectations that clusters will appear (for example, the clustering of sales forecast errors at positive values in Example 3.4, if sales forecasts are generally too pessimistic);

the lopsidedness versus the symmetry of the distribution of values around the middle of the range;

the peculiar "spikes" or "gaps" in the data.

Finding one or more of the above features or patterns will typically provide some implication worth noting for the business decision maker.

Footnotes and References

[1]The data in this example are hypothetical but the problem is quite real. The problem is based on newspaper accounts of a nurses' strike at the Oak Forest Hospital, Oak Forest, Illinois in the fall of 1976. Included in the final settlement was a controversial stipulation that nurses would not be paid for the first two days of each sick leave absence, a provision inserted by management to discourage nurses from treating unused sick leave as vacation days.

[2]W. Edwards Deming, "Making Things Right" in Judith Tanur et al. (editors), *STATISTICS: A Guide to the Unknown.* (San Francisco: Holden Day, 1971) pp. 229–236.

[3]base $\times$ height = area

height = area/base

but area = relative frequency

then height = $\dfrac{\text{relative frequency}}{\text{units in base}}$

and height = relative frequency per unit

= relative frequency density

[4]Actually, the table is for the standard normal variable, Z, which has a density function of the form $D(z) = \dfrac{e^{-\frac{1}{2}z^2}}{\sqrt{2\pi}}$

Questions and Problems

1. What is the first step in constructing a quantitative frequency distribution?

2. In constructing an array, is it better to arrange the data in ascending order from low to high than in descending order from high to low?

3. What is the purpose of a tally mark?

4. Name six features of the data set that a frequency distribution can be helpful in describing.

5. What distinguishes relative frequencies from frequencies?

6. How is a line chart constructed? Does it have as many lines as there are data?

7. Are comparisons between two sets of data better facilitated by frequency distributions or relative frequency distributions? Why?

8. What is the major disadvantage of a line chart in situations where the number of variates is large and the number of observations is small?

9. What are the two alternative approaches that can be used to simplify the treatment of data which take on a large number of variates? Do these approaches differ in objective?

10. What are the two different methods of grouping data and how do they differ? Is the choice between these methods a matter of personal preference? Do the two methods always lead to the same data classes?

11. Why are line charts not generally used to portray class frequencies?

12. What is the purpose of lower and upper class limits? Should the upper limit of one class be equal in value to the lower limit of the next class?

13. What is the difference between the stated class limits and the real class limits? Which are plotted on a histogram? Which are reported in describing the class? Which are used to determine the class interval? Are there ever any circumstances where the stated and real class limits coincide?

14. Must all the classes have equal intervals?

15. What is the advantage of a density histogram over a frequency histogram? Is it ever proper to use a frequency histogram?

16. Explain how the use of unequal class intervals can distort the comparison between two frequency histograms.

17. Explain how the choice of number of classes can distort the comparison between two frequency histograms.

18. A graphical distortion can be alleviated by widening the class interval and hence decreasing the number of classes. Explain.

19. A graphical distortion can be alleviated by narrowing the class interval (and thereby increasing the number of classes). Explain.

20. What is the overriding goal in grouping data? What indicates achievement in reaching the goal?

21. Name and explain three rules for deciding on the number of classes in grouping data.

22. Using Sturges' rule, how many classes should there be if there are 84 observations? 400 observations?

23. Why is the area of a class under a frequency polygon not exactly equal to the frequency (or relative frequency) of that class? Is the actual class frequency always overstated, always understated, or sometimes overstated, sometimes understated?

24. What distinguishes a density function from a smoothed frequency polygon?

25. Give three advantages of density functions as a means of describing data.

26. In what way does a cumulative frequency distribution differ from a frequency distribution? What advantage does a cumulative distribution offer?

27. What is the graph of a cumulative frequency distribution called? What advantage does it offer compared to a histogram?

28. Why are fractiles and percentiles so useful as descriptive measures of data? What are their advantages over histograms, ogives, etc.? Disadvantages?

29. Given the following quintile values, construct a freehand ogive.

First Quintile	80
Second Quintile	120
Third Quintile	135
Fourth Quintile	175

30. Explain how a frequency distribution is used to indicate the clustering of values. In comparing two frequency distributions, how would you determine which one exhibits the greater clustering?

31. In comparing two frequency distributions, how would you determine which one has a greater dispersion of values?

32. Suppose you have been asked to find out whether pediatricians tend to earn more than family practitioners in their practice of medicine. How would you use a frequency distribution of pediatricians' earnings and a frequency distribution of family practitioners' earnings to answer this question?

33. Suppose you have been asked to determine whether the rate of return on investment tends to be higher among transportation companies than among utility companies. How would you use frequency distributions of the rates of return on investment for the two types of companies to answer this question?

34. Suppose you have been asked to determine whether the consumption of diet soft drinks tends to be higher among white collar workers than among blue collar workers. How would you use frequency distributions of diet soft drink consumption for the two worker classes to answer this question?

35. Why do statistical analysts pay special attention to data gaps and spikes in an otherwise smooth frequency polygon or histogram?

36. A survey of 45 randomly selected households led to the following data on the number of days ready-to-eat breakfast cereal had been served to at least one member of the household during the previous week.

5	4	1	1	5	6	4	3	6	4
1	3	7	5	5	0	2	2	0	6
0	1	1	0	5	2	6	3	0	7
3	4	1	3	1	0	6	2	3	7
1	4	4	5	3					

Construct an absolute and relative frequency distribution on the cereal usage of households.

37. Use the data in Problem 36 for the following:
a. Construct a cumulative frequency and cumulative relative frequency distribution for the data.
b. Construct an ogive for the data.
c. Construct an ogive with the accumulated percentage of households on the horizontal axis and the accumulated percentage of cereal-usage-days on the vertical axis. (Hint: see Figure 3.22 and Table 2.14.)
d. Write a brief paragraph describing your findings on usage of breakfast cereal and draw some conclusion about marketing ready-to-eat breakfast cereal.

38. A manufacturer of recreational vehicles has compiled the following data about absenteeism among workers at its Tennessee plant during the previous month:

2	1	2	4	1	3	6	1
9	1	0	5	1	0	1	6
0	1	7	1	0	0	0	2
5	3	2	3	2	1	3	3
0	1	1	2	4	1	11	0

a. Construct frequency and relative frequency distributions for the data.
b. Construct a line chart for the data.
c. Write a brief description of your findings about absenteeism at the Tennessee plant.

39. Use the data in Problem 38 for the following:
a. Construct a cumulative frequency and cumulative relative frequency distribution for the data.
b. Construct an ogive for the data.
c. Construct an ogive with accumulated percentage of workers on the horizontal

axis and accumulated percentage of absences on the vertical axis. (Hint: Your ogive should have an appearance similar to that of Figure 3.22. See Table 2.14 for the computation of the data.)

d. Does the constructed ogive serve a particular purpose not achieved by the figure drawn in Part b above?

40. Data on the sales price (in thousands of dollars) of single family houses in a suburban real estate market are given below:

60.0	121.5	99.0	127.5	102.0
36.5	77.7	129.6	136.5	108.2
75.6	92.7	71.4	100.5	39.0
93.0	114.3	76.2	85.2	60.6
117.0	100.5	91.5	142.5	91.5
106.0	115.5	154.8	82.5	134.4

a. Construct frequency and relative frequency distributions for these data. Use Sturges' rule to determine the number of classes.

b. Construct frequency and density histograms for these data.

c. Construct a frequency polygon for these data.

41. Use the data in Problem 40 for the following:

a. Construct cumulative frequency and cumulative relative frequency distributions for these data.

b. Construct an ogive for these data.

c. Determine the quintiles of the distribution from the constructed ogive.

42. Use the data in Problem 40 for the following:

a. Construct an ogive in which the horizontal axis represents the accumulated percentage of houses sold and the vertical axis represents the accumulated percentage of housing value. (See Problem 39c.)

b. Assume that real estate sales commissions amount to 7% of sales value on every home sold. What percentage of total real estate commissions are earned on homes sold at a value of $100,000 or more? What percentage of the homes sold is this?

c. Write a brief paragraph explaining in your own words the findings on real estate transactions of single family homes and on sales commissions earned.

43. Data on the number of gallons of diesel fuel purchased by truckers at a large truck stop are given below.

191	147	123	146	148
132	136	159	174	158
119	181	148	170	178
180	172	137	115	163
182	205	174	140	174
161	203	121	150	182
177	197	98	94	120
206	146	114	128	

a. Construct frequency and relative frequency distributions for these data.

b. Construct frequency and density histograms for these data.

c. Construct a frequency polygon for these data.

44. Use the data in Problem 43 for the following:

a. Construct cumulative frequency and cumulative relative frequency distributions for these data.

b. Construct an ogive for these data.

c. Find the quartiles of the distribution.

d. Construct an ogive in which the horizontal axis represents the cumulative percentage of customers and the vertical axis represents the accumulated percentage of diesel fuel sold. (See Problem 39c.)

45. Use the data in Problem 43 for the following:

a. Double the number of classes used to construct the histograms in Problem 45 and reconstruct the histograms using the larger number of classes. What differences do you note in the outline of the histograms?

b. Halve the number of classes used to construct the histograms in Problem 45. Reconstruct the histograms using the smaller number of classes. What differences do you note between the original histograms and the new ones?

c. Does one histogram have an advantage over the other? Explain.

46. Data on the scores attained on a civil service promotion test given by the Sanitary District of a large urban area follow.

72	91	75	73	63
69	75	90	78	75
95	72	62	75	86
70	74	75	74	81
82	70	92	85	86

a. Construct a frequency distribution for these data.

b. Construct a histogram for these data using Sturges' rule to determine the number of classes.

c. Do you notice any peculiar data gaps or data spikes? If so, what do you think might have caused them?

47. A real estate broker is keeping track of the percentage that actual recorded selling price represents of the listed price on units of residential real estate handled over the month. Because of the high mortgage rates, there is currently a slow real estate market in which a broker encourages sellers to lend to buyers at below the unaffordably high mortgage rates. The data below on 30 transactions are listed in the broker's percentage figures (ratio of selling price to listed price in percentage terms).

95%	99%	100%	85%	94%
85%	100%	86%	86%	100%
90%	98%	99%	89%	90%
87%	93%	100%	89%	92%
100%	97%	99%	98%	99%
88%	98%	90%	98%	100%

a. Construct a relative frequency distribution for these data.

b. Construct a density histogram for these data.

c. Do you notice any peculiar data spikes or data gaps? If so, what do you think might have caused it?

d. What complicating factor is presented here and should be accounted for in a full discussion?

48. Data on the amount of the dinner check paid by individual customers at an Italian restaurant in Chicago are given below in dollars.

37.60	42.93	42.69	74.75	34.10
50.06	31.10	75.00	38.44	59.97
45.83	35.82	68.78	31.33	40.22
55.98	24.35	70.40	45.61	54.37

a. Round the data to the nearest dollar and construct a frequency distribution based on the rounded data.

b. Construct a density histogram based upon the rounded data.

c. What are the quartiles of the distribution?

d. Write a brief paragraph explaining in your own words the findings on the amount of the dinner checks at this restaurant and any conclusions that management should draw.

Summary Measures of Frequency Distributions

Preview. In the previous chapter, a frequency histogram for sales forecast errors had a majority of its area lying to the left of the zero point. This implied a tendency for overly pessimistic forecasts. Had the location of the histogram been shifted to the right of the zero point, overly optimistic forecasts would have resulted. Thus changes in the *location* of the histogram are important. So are changes in other characteristics of the data; for example, how widely and how uniformly dispersed the data values are. In describing a set of data, we do not always have the opportunity to use a histogram for the purpose of description. We may have to capture the important information by reporting just a few characteristics of the data. These are called *summary measures.* In this chapter we study the common summary measures of important data characteristics, particularly *location* or *central tendency, dispersion,* and *skewness.* Although the main purpose of reporting these characteristics is to provide useful information about the distribution, we must also consider situations in which important parts of the message are suppressed by summary measures.

Deluged with much more numerical detail than can be readily comprehended, one's instinctive reaction is to "number crunch". That means finding some way of reducing the entire data set to a few numbers that speak for the whole set. Number crunching relieves the excess detail problem and, if properly done, can bring order out of chaos. Too much number crunching can destroy vital information. Perhaps the greatest danger in using crunched numbers is reading into them something that isn't there. For instance, "averages" are often accused of causing misunderstandings about actual situations. Merton Miller, a distinguished University of Chicago Business School professor, when asked by a finance student why individual rates of return in an industry seldom equal or even come close to the industry average, reportedly quipped, "Harry Roberts (another well-known professor at the school) and I average eight miles of running per day. Harry runs sixteen."

Much of the message of this chapter is wrapped up in that one quip. Sixteen is a lot of miles to run; however, split between two persons, the resulting average of eight miles per day is more plausible. But this average fails to tell us whether one professor is doing more running and, if so, by how much. Persons unaware of how statistics are computed often jump to the erroneous conclusion that both professors are avid runners, or worse yet that the two professors run approximately the same distance. As the example clearly shows, nothing ought to be inferred from the "average" about the mileage breakdown for the two professors. We only know that the total mileage run is sixteen.

4.1. Introduction

Frequency distributions, histograms, and smooth curves are all important statistical devices designed to reduce data, to highlight significant features, and to convey the intended message. But often the communication of the important informational features of a set of data requires the reporting of only a few *summary measures* or *summary statistics*. Each measure describes an important characteristic of the set of data.

Does the elimination of details cause a practical problem? It can. But generally the benefits of data reduction outweigh the costs of losing detail. Here is an example:

Example 4.1A. How Much Do You Need to Know About Battery Life?

Automobile battery manufacturers yearly sell millions of batteries with a several-year replacement guarantee. For planning purposes, the length of life of each and every battery produced is unimportant. The information that management needs to know can be condensed by a few summary statistics. For example, one useful statistic would be the percentage of batteries which become inoperative before the warranty expires. Another would be the average length of battery life. With these two measures, management's most important questions could be answered. Some other questions management would need helpful answers to are: what frequency of replacement should be expected and what frequency of customer's complaints is likely?

Lost Detail Is Not Recoverable

Once a set of data has been reduced to a few summary statistics, one loses not only the ability to reproduce the original numbers in the data set, but also the possibility of recovering the class frequencies if the original data were grouped. Usually, this is of little consequence. But there are exceptions to the rule. For example, the sharp spike in nurses' absenteeism (Example 3.2) and the absence of parts with diameters just below the acceptable level (Example 3.5A) might have gone unnoticed had the entire frequency distribution not been presented. And, as the following example shows, summary statistics can also hide vital information.

Example 4.1B. Campaign Financing and the Watergate Incident

In 1973 and 1974, the Watergate scandal focused public attention on several issues surrounding political campaigns. One hotly debated issue was the financing of President Nixon's 1972 election campaign. Who contributed and how much each contributed were important facts in determining whether any contributions were of a size large enough to raise suspicions about the motivation of the contribution. These questions could be readily answered had the entire list of contributors been made public. However, only summary statistics such as the total number of contributors and the average size of contribution were published. Without statistics indicating how prevalent large contributions were in financing the campaign, any investigation attempting to identify the donors of large contributions would be stymied. In this particular instance, summary statistics concealed rather than revealed the important information.

4.2. Characteristics of Frequency Distributions

Four characteristics of frequency distributions are commonly described by summary statistics. One is the central *location* of the entire distribution considered as a whole: do values of the variable tend to be in the vicinity of 50, or in the vicinity of 50,000? The *dispersion* or variability of the values around the central location is a second commonly described characteristic. A third characteristic is the distribution's symmetry or lack of it, called *skewness*. The fourth is the peakedness of the distribution, called *kurtosis*.

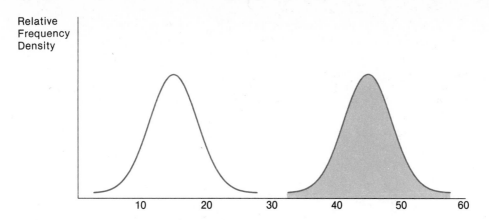

FIGURE 4.1 Location Comparison: Two Identically Shaped Distributions Differing in Location

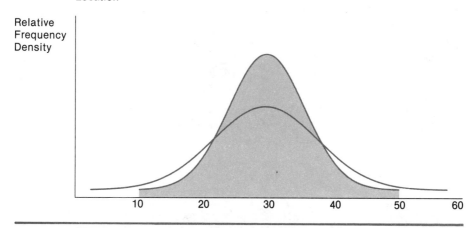

FIGURE 4.2 Dispersion Comparison: Two Distributions of Same Central Location but Differing in Dispersion

The location characteristic is illustrated in Figure 4.1. Two identically shaped distributions differ in central location, the shaded distribution having values concentrated at a higher level than the other.

The dispersion characteristic describes the spread of the distribution around its central location. Figure 4.2 indicates that the shaded distribution has the lesser dispersion of the two.

The skewness characteristic is illustrated in Figure 4.3. The shaded distribution is highly skewed (one long-tail); the unshaded distribution is not skewed at all (even-tailed).

The peakedness characteristic is illustrated in Figure 4.4. The shaded distribution has the higher degree of kurtosis.

The summary measures considered so far have all been calculated by performing arithmetic operations on all the data. Alternatively, summary measures can be based upon the relative position of a value within the distribution. A simple example will illustrate the difference between the two categories of summary statistics.

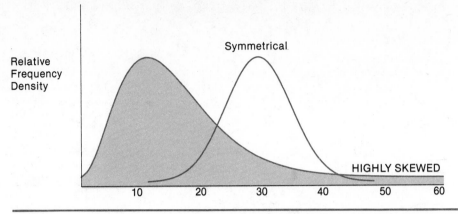

FIGURE 4.3 Skewness Comparison: A Highly Skewed Distribution Contrasted with a Symmetrical Distribution

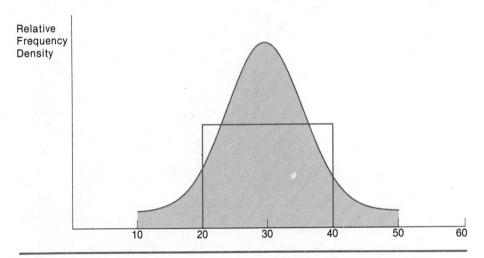

FIGURE 4.4 Kurtosis Comparison: Two Distributions of Same Central Location but Differing in Kurtosis

Example 4.2. Statistical Fountain of Youth?

Suppose three men are 20, 30 and 70 years old. Summing the ages and dividing by three would give an average age of 40 years. This is an example of a descriptive measure calculated by arithmetic operations. Alternatively, a relative position descriptive statistic for the same data is the "middle" age position—30 years.

In the next four sections, we will consider location. Then we will go on to discuss dispersion, skewness, and kurtosis.

4.3. Measures of the Location Characteristic: Mode, Median, and Mean

Locational measures, also called measures of *central tendency*, refer to the location of "clustering" or "bunching" tendencies of the data.

The Mode: The Value You See the Most

One measure of central tendency is the positional value of the distribution which occurs more frequently than any other. This value is called the *mode* of the distribution. For example, suppose the number of days spaghetti was served during the past week by households participating in a consumer panel is given by the frequency distribution in Table 4.1.

TABLE 4.1. Consumption of Spaghetti

NUMBER OF DAYS HOUSEHOLDS SERVED SPAGHETTI	NUMBER OF HOUSE-HOLDS (Frequency)
0	36
1	42
2	12
3	3
4	1
5	0
6	0
7	0

The mode of this distribution is one time per week since this value is more prevalent among the households (42 households) than any other value.

If there is a single value which occurs most often, the distribution is said to be *unimodal* (one peak). If two different values, say 43 and 44, tie for the highest frequency, there are then two modes and the distribution is said to be *bimodal*. A distribution is also called bimodal if the histogram shows a dip or valley between two peaks. For example, 43 and 44 could be 2 modes, no valley, or 43 and 55, two modes and one valley between them.

Median: The "Middle of the Road"

The *median* is another positional measure of central tendency. The median position partitions, as best as possible, a frequency distribution into two equal parts when the observations have been ranked by magnitude. The value associated with the median position is called the median value, or "middle value" of a distribution.

The median will always have a unique value so long as the data set contains an odd number of elementary units. In Example 4.2, the median age is the unique value 30, because this value splits the two remaining observations equally, one value above thirty, the other value below thirty. The median could not be 29.5 or 30.5 or any value other than 30, because this would lead to a partition with an uneven division of items. But when there are an even number of elementary units, the median may or may not be a unique value because there may be two or more "middle-most" values. For example, consider the following exam scores of ten children:

75, 86, 92, 77, 79, 80, 91, 83, 77, 86.

Rearranging by magnitude, we get: 75, 77, 77, 79, 80, 83, 86, 86, 91, 92. The values 80 and 83 are the two middle-most observed. However, if 80 is used as the median, there would be more higher-valued than lower-valued observations compared to 80. The reverse is true if 83 is chosen. For any value *between* 80 and 83, there are exactly as many higher-valued observations as lower-valued observations. Therefore, in this case, the median is not a unique value, but the entire range of values which are more than eighty but less than eighty-three.

Although there is no logical necessity for a single-valued median, it is awkward to compare a single value from one distribution with a range of values from another. As a result, it has become widespread practice to "split the difference" between the values of the two middle-most observations in an even-numbered data set and call this new value "the" median. After splitting the difference between the two middle-most observed values of the ten exam scores, the value of 81.5 becomes the median value. This leads to a simple rule for determining the median position:

$$\frac{n + 1}{2} = \text{median position}$$

where the symbol n stands for the number of sample observations. The value at the median position is the median value. For the ten exam scores, the median position is

$$\frac{10 + 1}{2} = 5.5$$

so the median value is halfway between the fifth and sixth ranked values; that is, halfway between 83 and 80.

Arithmetic Mean: Weighing Things Out

The most widely used of all summary measures is probably the *arithmetic mean*, or simply, the *mean* of a distribution. The arithmetic mean is the sum of the values of all the observations divided by the number of observations n. The symbol which is almost universally used to designate the mean of a sample data set is $\overline{X}$ (read X-bar); the Greek symbol μ represents the mean of all the observations in the population. The formulas for the arithmetic mean are given below. In these formulas, the symbol Σ is the Greek capital letter sigma. It is the mathematical notation used to indicate summation. In the first formula the summation is over all the X values in the sample. In the second formula the summation is over all the X values in the population.

1. For the mean of n sample observations: $\overline{X} = \dfrac{\Sigma X}{n}$

2. For the mean of N population values: $\mu = \dfrac{\Sigma X}{N}$

For example, if a sample of five observations gives 30, 42, 14, 17, and 25 as values for X, the mean of the five values is:

$$\overline{X} = \frac{\Sigma X}{n} = \frac{30 + 42 + 14 + 17 + 25}{5} = 25.6$$

When there are many observed values, say 1000, an alternative computational procedure may be more practical. The arithmetic mean is the weighted average of all of the different values of the observations in a frequency distribution, where the weight assigned to each value is its relative frequency. Thus, for ungrouped data it is simply the products of each X value multiplied by its relative frequency and summed over the observations. The computation of the arithmetic mean for the ten exam scores is illustrated in Table 4.2. The computational formulas are given below:

1. for the mean of n sample observations

$\overline{X} = \Sigma [X][\text{r.f.}(X)]$

where the summation is over all values of X in the sample

2. for the mean of the population of N observations

$\mu = \Sigma [X][\text{r.f.}(X)]$

where the summation is over all values of X in the population

TABLE 4.2. Computation of the Arithmetic Mean for the Exam Scores Data

X	r.f.(X)	$[X]$ $[\text{r.f.}(X)]$
75	.1	7.5
77	.2	15.4
79	.1	7.9
80	.1	8.0
83	.1	8.3
86	.2	17.2
91	.1	9.1
92	.1	9.2
	1.0	82.6 $= \Sigma[X][\text{r.f.}(X)]$

Therefore, $\overline{X} = 82.6$.

The mean is the result of mathematical operations on values which have been observed. Except by coincidence, it is not itself a value which has actually been observed. This is probably why the mean, which is one form of average, has become the butt of cynics' jokes.

Example 4.3.   The Arithmetic Mean: Often Computed But Seldom Seen

The average man has $\frac{4}{5}$ of a wife and 2.7 children who help drive their 1.4 automobiles to their 1.3 homes, where they have $\frac{3}{5}$ of a washer and one and one-half TV sets and 3.2 radios.

4.4. Is There a "Best" Measure of Central Location?

Which measure is the "best" measure of central location—the mode, the median, or the arithmetic mean? Often asked, this question misleads one to believe that there is one measure which *is* universally best. In fact, each measure describes a different feature of the data. For some purposes, knowing the middle-most value may be most important; for other purposes, the "most common" value or a weighted average will contain more valuable information than the middle-most value. That is why there are three different measures of central location. The original question, properly rephrased, should be: "When is one measure of central tendency better than another?" Very shortly, we shall discuss an example which brings out the circumstances favoring one measure of central tendency over the others.

In some cases, there may not be a choice as to which measure of central location to report because they cannot all be computed. If only one measure can be computed, it is by definition the "best" one to report. For example, frequency distributions are sometimes encountered in which either the upper or lower class will be open ended. The upper class might consist of, say, all incomes above $30,000. This is illustrated in Table 4.3.

TABLE 4.3. Income Distribution

RANGE OF INCOMES	FREQUENCY
Below 1000	3 million
:	:
:	:
Above 30,000	1 million

The last class would include $2,000,001 as well as $30,001. Without additional information about the incomes within the uppermost class, it would be impossible to compute the arithmetic mean for the distribution. The median, on the other hand, does not require knowledge of these incomes. Therefore, the median is reported because it can be computed and the mean cannot.

Generosity Is the Best Policy

When all three measures of central location can be computed, it may be better to report them all than to single one out to report. Although all three are loosely referred to as "averages" they describe different characteristics of the data. By reporting all three, readers can decide for themselves whether the most common value, the middle-most value, or a weighted average of all the values would best suit their purposes. If you decide to report only one of the measures, you should make it very clear which measure you have computed.

4.5. The Mean Is Popular for a Very Good Reason

Of the three common measures of central location, the arithmetic mean is undoubtedly the most popular. At least part of the popularity is attributable to the fact that the mean has mathematical properties which are very desirable. One of these is the algebraic relationship which makes it possible to go from a mean to a total. This is an especially desirable property when sample surveys are used in lieu of a population census.

Example 4.5. **Estimating the Number of Cameras in Michigan**

A camera manufacturer wanting to estimate the total number of cameras in existence among Michigan households surveys a sample of Michigan households and calculates the mean number of cameras per household in the sample. Using the sample mean of the survey as an estimate of the mean for the entire state of Michigan, and knowing that the mean $\overline{X}$ is the sum of all data items divided by the number of data items n, one need only multiply the survey mean by the number of households in Michigan to get an estimate of the total number of cameras in Michigan. For example, if the mean number of cameras per household was 1.2 and the number of Michigan households was 2 million, the estimated number of cameras in Michigan would be (1.2)(2 million) = 2.4 million.

Since both the median and the mode are positional measures, there is no simple algebraic relationship between the median and the total or between the mode and the total. In survey work, especially in business and economics, the real interest often centers on the total for some population and this unquestionably contributes to the popularity of the mean as a summary measure.

4.6. Summary Measures of Central Location for Grouped Data

If the data have been grouped into classes, then the true values of the mean, mode, and median of the original data cannot be found. The practical significance of this theoretical problem is seldom critical. It is always possible to report the *median class* or *modal class*, and this often is sufficient for the purpose at hand.

When more than a median or modal class is required, it has become a widespread practice to *estimate* the mean, median, or mode of the original data. This is accomplished by making a convenient assumption about the nature of variation within a class.

Estimating the Mode

Since the mode of the original data is a positional average, its estimated value can be easily located by smoothing the histogram. The highest point of the smoothed curve locates the estimated mode. This procedure is illustrated in Figure 4.5.

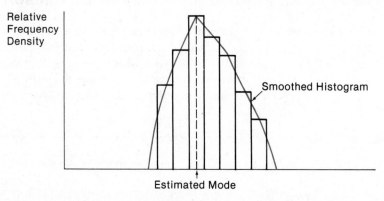

FIGURE 4.5   Estimating the Mode Using Grouped Data

Estimating the Median

The median of the original data, another positional average, is also easily estimated if it is assumed that the observations are equally distributed within the median class. On the basis of this assumption, let us use the rates of return on bond refunding found in Table 4.4, which contains eight classes and a record of the frequencies for each class.

TABLE 4.4. Frequency Distributions of the Rates of Return of a Sample of 40 Bond Refundings

RATE OF RETURN		FREQUENCY
3.5– 8.4		9
8.5–13.4	Median Class →	19
13.5–18.4		8
18.5–23.4		1
23.5–28.4		2
28.5–33.4		0
33.5–38.4		0
38.5–43.4		1
		40

The first step to take to compute the median rate of return of these bond refundings is to determine which of the eight class intervals *contains* the median. To do this, we must add the frequencies in the frequency column until we reach the $\frac{(n + 1)}{2}$ positioned item. Since there are 40 accounts, the positioned item $\frac{(n + 1)}{2}$ is 20.5 (the average of the 20th and 21st items).

Next, we find the class interval containing the 20th and 21st items. The frequency for the first class is 9. Moving to the second class, 19 elements are added to 9 for a total of 28. Therefore, the 20th and 21st observations must be located in this class (the interval from 8.5 percent to 13.4 percent). Therefore, the *median class* for this data contains 19 items. If we assume that these 19 items begin at the class boundary of 8.45 percent and *are evenly spaced over the entire class interval* from 8.45 percent to 13.45 percent, then we can interpolate and find values for the 20th and 21st items. First, notice that the 20th and 21st items are the 11th and 12th elements in the median class:

20 minus 9 [items in the first class] = 11
21 minus 9 [items in the first class] = 12

Calculating the *width* of the 19 equal steps from 8.45 percent to 13.45 percent:

Lower Boundary of Next Class   Lower Boundary of Median Class

$$\frac{13.45\% - 8.45\%}{19} = 0.26316\% \text{ in width}$$

Knowing that there are 19 steps of 0.26316 percent each and that 11 steps will take us to the end of the 11th item, the value at that point is:

$(0.26316 \times 11) + 8.45\% = 11.34474\%$

This point is also the beginning of the 12th item, so it is the point halfway between the midpoint of the 11th interval and the midpoint of the 12th interval. Thus, it is the value of the median.

In summary, the steps to follow to estimate the median of grouped data are:

1. Determine by the formula $\frac{(n + 1)}{2}$ which sample observation in the distribution is at the centermost (median) position (in this case, the average of the 20th and 21st items).

2. Add the frequencies in each class to find the class that contains that centermost observation (the second class, or 8.45% − 13.45%).

3. Find the number of observations in the median class (19) and the location of the median item (item 20 was the 11th element; item 21, the 12th element).

4. Determine the width of each step in the median class by dividing the size of the class interval by the number of observations in the class (width = 0.26316%).

5. Determine the number of steps from the lower bound of the median class to the appropriate position for the median (11 steps to the end of the 11th item in the median class. Note: if the total number of observations had been 41, an odd number, we would have to take an extra half-step).

Estimating the Mean

The mean of the original data is estimated from grouped data by assuming that the typical value of each individual class lies at the class midpoint, m_k. The more evenly the original data is distributed within a class, and the more symmetrical the entire distribution about the true mean, the closer will the value of the mean estimated in this way be to the true mean of the original data.

The computational procedure for estimating the mean from grouped data requires five steps:

1. Determine the midpoint of each class, m_k.

2. Assume that the class midpoint, m_k, is representative of each observation within the class.

3. Determine the relative frequency of each class.

4. For each class, determine the product of the class midpoint and the relative frequency of the class.

5. Sum the products obtained in Step 4. This sum is the estimated value of the mean.

In summary, the estimated mean is a weighted average of the class midpoints where the weights are the class relative frequencies.

The above procedure for computing the mean of sample data that have been grouped can be expressed algebraically as:

$$\overline{X} = \sum_{k=1}^{K} [m_k][r.f.\ (X_k)]$$

where K represents the number of classes, m_k represents the midpoint of the kth class, and r.f.(X_k) represents the relative frequency of the X values within the kth class.

To illustrate, consider again the grouped data on a sample of bond refunding rates of return originally presented in Table 3.6. The data are repeated in Table 4.5 where the calculations leading to an estimated mean rate of return of 12.575 percent are shown.

TABLE 4.5. Computation of the Mean for Rates of Return of a Sample of Bond Refundings

Class k	Class Interval X_k	f.(X_k)	m_k	r.f.(X_k)	$[m_k][r.f.(X_k)]$
1	−3.5 − 8.4	9	5.95	.225	1.33875
2	8.5 − 13.4	19	10.95	.475	5.20125
3	13.5 − 18.4	8	15.95	.200	3.19000
4	18.5 − 23.4	1	20.95	.025	0.52375
5	23.5 − 28.4	2	25.95	.050	1.29750
6	28.5 − 33.4	0	30.95	.000	.00000
7	33.5 − 38.4	0	35.95	.000	.00000
8	38.5 − 43.4	1	40.95	.025	1.02375
		40		1.000	12.57500

$$\overline{X} = \sum_{k=1}^{8} [m_k][\text{r.f.}(X_k)]$$

For $k = 1$, $m_k = 5.95$, $\text{r.f.}(X_1) = .225$ and

$$[m_1][\text{r.f.}(X_1)] = (5.95)(.225) = 1.33875.$$

Following this procedure for $k = 2$, $k = 3$, . . . $k = 8$ and summing gives:

$$\overline{X} = 12.575.$$

4.7. Summary Measures of Dispersion: Variance, Standard Deviation, and Mean Absolute Deviation

Attempts to summarize the present data can go too far. Knowing that a particular characteristic of a distribution can be captured by a single summary statistic does not imply that it is unnecessary to report the other important characteristics of a distribution—an error which is all too common. The danger in trying to summarize an entire frequency distribution by a single summary number was demonstrated in the chapter's opening example on "average miles run per day." In most cases when a single statistic is reported, the statistic refers to the central location or central tendency of the distribution. This is understandable because central location is usually the most important characteristic of a distribution. But it should also be remembered that information about the central location must often be complemented by information on the other important characteristics of the distribution—dispersion, skewness, kurtosis.

Dispersion Matters

Failing to consider dispersion can lead to many seemingly paradoxical situations, such as a person drowning in a river with an average depth of only one foot of water, or a person freezing to death where the mean daily temperature never varied more than a few degrees from 75° Fahrenheit (the Mojave Desert). Here is another example which shows that disregarding dispersion can be disastrous.

Example 4.7A.   Pot Luck With Hand Grenades

Two boxes of hand grenades are identical in appearance with both having identical five-second mean time to explosion from the moment the pins are pulled and the safety released. However, in one box all the grenades explode at exactly five seconds, while in the other box they explode anywhere from zero to ten seconds. If you were a combat soldier, would there be any doubt as to the box from which you would prefer to select your grenades?

Positional Measures of Dispersion: A Partial View of Dispersion

Computationally simple and perhaps the most easily understood of all summary measures of dispersion is the *range.*. The range is merely the difference between the maximum and minimum values in the data set. For example, if the high temperature for the day is 82°F. and the low is 51°F., the temperature range for the day is 31°F. The range's most serious deficiency is that it gives no indication of the degree of variation of the observations *within* the range, only the relative location of the dispersion.

A popular variant of the range is the *interquartile range*, which is the distance between the first and third quartiles (where the first and third quartile represent the lowest 25 percent and lowest 75 percent of all the data). This figure indicates the span of the middle 50 percent of the data. A close relative of the interquartile range is the *semi-interquartile range*, also called the *quartile deviation*. It is equal to one-half of the value of the interquartile range.

All of the positional measures of dispersion have the same key drawback as the range; individually, they don't provide information on the *density* of observations and so give little idea as to the concentration of the observations around some central point. This drawback can partially be alleviated by reporting two or more positional measures; for example, both the range and the quartile deviation.

Measures of Dispersion Based Upon Arithmetic Calculations: The Spread Around a Central Point

The drawback in measuring dispersion by positional summary measures is that they are calculated from only two data points in the distribution and thus do not reflect all the observations. This inadequacy can be circumvented by employing a summary measure of dispersion based on arithmetic calculations rather than one based on relative location. Three such measures are considered. All three summarize the spread of *all* the observations around a central location. Moreover, the information is reported in a single number. The calculations required to obtain these measures involve finding the deviations of the individual values from the arithmetic mean $(X - \overline{X})$. A problem arises, however, because the sum of these deviations would always be zero, regardless of the data. By definition, the mean is the value which balances off the negative and positive deviations around it. Symbolically,

$$\Sigma(X - \overline{X}) = 0.$$

There are two simple ways to combine deviations from the mean while avoiding a zero sum. One is to sum the *squares* of the deviations. The other is to sum the *absolute values* of the deviations. Either procedure leads to a positive sum. The first procedure leads to a measure called the variance and its corollary, the standard deviation; the latter procedure leads to a measure called the mean absolute deviation. Of the two procedures (squaring and absolute value) the squaring procedure is more common because the resulting value has a more useful mathematical interpretation.

The Variance

The most commonly used summary measure of dispersion based upon the squaring operation is the *variance*.

The magnitude of the variance is determined by the scatter of the observations from the mean. The more scattered the individual observations from the mean, the greater the sum of the squared deviations and the greater the variance. This is exactly what is expected of a summary measure of dispersion. Nevertheless, a modification is necessary because the sum is influenced by the number of observations. That is, if we double the number of observations, the sum of squared deviations will increase. This would make it difficult to interpret the variances (as measures of comparative dispersion) between two distributions that are not based on the same number of observations.

A Base for Comparison

To facilitate comparisons among distributions having different numbers of observations, dispersion is described on a "per-observation" basis. In other words, the *average* squared deviation is computed. To find the average squared deviation, the sum of squared deviations is divided by N, the number of observations in the population (which is also the number of deviations). The result is the summary measure known as the *population variance* designated by the symbol σ^2 (sigma squared) and expressed by the formula:

$$\sigma^2 = \frac{\Sigma (X - \mu)^2}{N}$$

Suppose the sum of squared deviations is 3000 for one distribution and 2000 for a second distribution. If the number of observations for the first distribution is 200, and 100 for the second, the first distribution has a smaller variance. The variance for the first distribution is $^{3000}\!/_{200} = 15$ compared to $^{2000}\!/_{100} = 20$ for the second distribution.

Sample Variance

If the variance from a *sample* set of data is to be used to obtain an estimate of the variance of the population, a required change is needed in the sample variance formula. The denominator must be $n - 1$ (known as the degrees of freedom adjustment) instead of the anticipated value n. The purpose of this change is to make the average of the sample variances obtainable from repeated sampling equal to the variance in the population from which the samples were drawn. This is a property which becomes important in statistical inference (Chapter 11). Therefore, when the data series is a sample from the population, the formula for the sample variance is sometimes defined as:

$$\hat{\sigma}^2 = S^2 = \frac{\Sigma (X - \bar{X})^2}{n - 1}$$

In this book we will use both the symbol $\hat{\sigma}^2$ and the symbol S^2 for the sample variance.

The Standard Deviation

An unfortunate disadvantage of the variance is that it is not measured in the same units as other summary measures (such as the mean) of the original data. For example, in describing the distribution of the rates of return on common stock, the mean (or median) would be measured in percentages, but the variance in *percentages squared.* Because the measurement units are different, one cannot readily put together the mean and the variance—two summary measures needed to adequately describe the features of a distribution, for example, the rates of return distribution. How can this situation be corrected?

Simply by taking the positive square root of the variance, one gets a derivative measure of dispersion called the population *standard deviation.* It is designated by the symbol σ and has the formula:

$$\sigma = +\sqrt{\frac{\Sigma (X - \mu)^2}{N}}$$

The measurement units for σ are expressed in the original measurement units, not squared units, and thus in units compatible with the mean and median.

When the data set is a sample drawn from a population, the sample standard deviation formula which gives an unbiased estimate of the standard deviation of the population is:

$$S = +\sqrt{\frac{\Sigma (X - \overline{X})^2}{n - 1}}$$

For grouped sample data, S can be computed by using the formula:

$$S = +\sqrt{\Sigma \left[(m_k - \overline{X})^2\right]\left[\text{r.f.}(X_k)\right]} \cdot \sqrt{\frac{n}{n - 1}}$$

The computations according to the grouped data formula are shown in Table 4.6.

TABLE 4.6. Computation of Estimated Standard Deviation for Rates of Return on Bond Refundings (recorded to nearest tenth of a percent)

Class k	Class Interval X_k	f.(X_k)	m_k	r.f.(X_k)	$[m_k][\text{r.f.}(X_k)]$	$(m_k - \overline{X})$	$(m_k - \overline{X})^2$	$[(m_k - \overline{X})^2] \cdot [\text{r.f.}(X_k)]$
1	3.5– 8.4	9	5.95	.225	1.338	−6.625	43.89	9.875
2	8.5–13.4	19	10.95	.475	5.201	−1.625	2.64	1.254
3	13.5–18.4	8	15.95	.200	3.190	3.375	11.39	2.278
4	18.5–23.4	1	20.95	.025	0.523	8.375	70.14	1.754
5	23.5–28.4	2	25.95	.050	1.297	13.375	178.89	8.945
6	28.5–33.4	0	30.95	.000	.000	18.375	337.64	0.000
7	33.5–38.4	0	35.95	.000	.000	23.375	546.39	0.000
8	38.5–43.4	1	40.95	.0250	1.023	28.375	805.14	20.129
		40			12.575 = $\overline{X}$			44.234

$$\overline{X} = \sum [m_k][\text{r.f.}(X_k)]$$

$$\overline{X} = 12.575$$

The sum of the values in the last column is the left hand term in the formula below.

$$S = +\sqrt{\sum[(m_k - \overline{X})^2][\text{r.f.}(X_k)]} \cdot \sqrt{\frac{n}{n-1}}$$
$$S = \sqrt{44.235 \cdot {}^{40}\!/_{39}}$$
$$S = (6.65094)(1.01274)$$
$$= 6.736$$

The value of $\overline{X}$ was previously computed to be 12.575. The calculations which lead to this value are given in the first six columns of Table 4.6. Column 7 of the table shows the deviation from the mean value of each of the midpoints of the classes. In column 8, the deviations given in column 7 are squared. A value in column 8 is multiplied by the class relative frequency given in column 5 to get the value shown in column 9.

The Mean Absolute Deviation

The *mean absolute deviation* (M.A.D.) is calculated by summing the absolute deviations around the mean and dividing by the number of observations. For n sample observations, the *average* deviation (typical deviation per observation) is defined by the formula:

$$\text{M.A.D.} = \frac{\sum|X - \overline{X}|}{n}$$

For all N observations in the population, the value μ substitutes for $\overline{X}$ and N substitutes for n. The M.A.D. is encountered in business statistical practice primarily in the fields of quality control, statistical forecasting, and financial analysis.

Example 4.7B. **Describing the Risk of Listed New York Stock Exchange Securities**

The two key factors financial analysts use to describe the attractiveness of corporate securities are the risk and the expected rate of return. Generally the higher the risk, the higher the expected rate of return. To quantify this direct relationship between risk and return and to reliably compare the risk of different securities, what is required of a measure of risk? Financial analysts need a measure of risk that is consistent, one that doesn't fluctuate erratically as the historical evidence on a security's return accumulates. Usually, for the types of data encountered in business, the standard deviation is an adequate measure of risk. However, in a pioneering study of stock securities price behavior, Professor Eugene Fama showed that the M.A.D. provides a more stable measure of securities risk than the standard deviation.

Professor Fama showed that the distribution of investment returns on stock market securities is characterized by extreme variation. There is a greater concentration of observations at the tails of the distribution than in other business risk situations that had been studied.[1] (His study is discussed in more detail in Appendix Example 4B). Squaring the values of the extreme observations—outliers—causes more problems than not squaring them in this stock securities case. The sample standard deviation is subject to more erratic fluctuations than is the M.A.D. Hence M.A.D. is a better measure of stock securities risk.

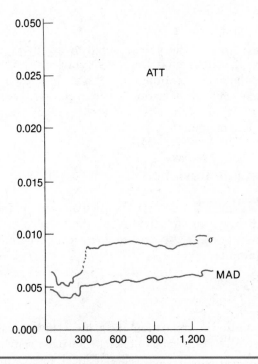

FIGURE 4.6 Sequential Values of the Standard Deviation and Mean Absolute Deviation from Population with Infinite Variance

The tendency of the standard deviation to be a more erratic measure of stock securities risk than M.A.D. is illustrated in Figure 4.6 for AT&T stock returns. It can be seen that the value of the standard deviation exceeds that of M.A.D. for all sample sizes. This is not important in comparing the risk of AT&T against different securities, for one would always use the same measure (either the standard deviation or M.A.D.). The important difference is in the stability of the two measures. Notice the large upward shift in the value of the standard deviation as the sample size approaches 300. Another upward shift is located near the sample size of 1100. These erratic fluctuations are not evident in the M.A.D. series.

4.8. Chebyshev's Inequality: An Application of the Standard Deviation

The popularity of the variance and standard deviation as measures of dispersion is attributable to the usefulness of the mathematical properties which they possess. An especially important conclusion is given by a theorem known as *Chebyshev's Inequality*. According to this theorem, it is always true for *any* set of data that:

> the total relative frequency of all the values which are *more than* k *standard deviations from the mean* (in either direction) *cannot be greater than* $1/k^2$.

It is also true that for any distribution, the fraction which lies within k standard deviations of the mean is at least $1 - (1/k^2)$. According to Chebyshev's Inequality, the maximum relative frequency which can lie more than two standard deviations from the mean is $\frac{1}{4}$. The minimum relative frequency which must lie within two standard deviations is $\frac{3}{4}$. Because of this rule, the standard deviation can be used as a valuable measuring stick for comparing the dispersion of two distributions.

Example 4.8.   Preventive Maintenance: Time Is Money

Replacing light bulbs in large office buildings can be an expensive proposition if it is done on an individual basis each time a bulb burns out. To save on labor costs, many firms replace all the lights in a given section of the building (including the ones that are still working) at regularly scheduled intervals. This policy makes the most sense when there is not much variability in the length of lamp life, because then they can all be replaced shortly before they start burning out.

Suppose the service characteristics of two types of lamps are as shown in Table 4.7.

TABLE 4.7. Lamp Life

	Type A	Type B
Mean Life	1000 hours	1100 hours
Standard Deviation	50 hours	200 hours

	Range for Mean $\pm$ k Standard Deviations		
K	$1 - (1/k^2)$	Type A	Type B
1	0	950–1050	900–1300
2	$\frac{3}{4}$	900–1100	700–1500
3	$\frac{8}{9}$	850–1150	500–1700

Chebyshev's Inequality guarantees that at least $\frac{8}{9}$ of the Type A bulbs last 850 hours, but for the Type B bulbs the guarantee is only that at least $\frac{8}{9}$ of them last 500 hours. Thus, assuming the bulbs sell at the same price, a firm replacing bulbs at regular intervals would probably be better off using Type *A* bulbs even though they have a shorter mean life. A firm replacing bulbs one at a time, however, would be better off with Type *B* because of its higher average. That is, on average, the time between replacement of individual bulbs would be longer for Type *B* bulbs. A comparison of the two distributions is given in Figure 4.7.

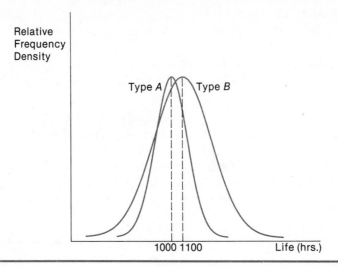

FIGURE 4.7 A Comparison of the Frequency Distribution of Two Types of Light Bulbs

4.9. Relative Dispersion

The numerical value of the standard deviation and variance represent absolute measures of dispersion, that is, their values do not change with a shift of the location of the distribution. This property is helpful when one is simply comparing the dispersion of distributions expressed in different units, such as wheat and egg production. But often when the units of measurement of the two distributions are the same, the required perspective is achieved by comparing the dispersion of two distributions *relative to the magnitude of the respective means.* The amount of dispersion on a comparable per-unit basis distinguishes the *relative* dispersion. For this purpose, there is the *coefficient of variation.* Its formula for sample observations is:

$$V = \frac{(\text{std.dev.})}{\text{mean}} = \frac{S}{\overline{X}}$$

For the entire set of observations in the population, the value of V is determined by substituting σ for S and μ for $\overline{X}$.

Suppose the distributions of lawyers' income has a mean of $60,000 per year and a standard deviation of $24,000 per year. Suppose accountants have a mean of \$50,000 per year and a standard deviation of \$10,000. Then

$$V_{\text{lawyers}} = \frac{(24,000)}{60,000} = .40 \text{ and } V_{\text{accountants}} = \frac{(10,000)}{50,000} = .20.$$

Thus lawyers' income is relatively more dispersed than accountants'. The following example illustrates the importance of relative dispersion in the financial world.

Example 4.9. Financial Leveraging and the Risk-Return Relationship

A key financial decision that must be made by a corporate financial officer is how to finance corporate expansion. Should the capital funds come from selling bonds or from selling common stock? With bonds, the firm has a contractual obligation to pay interest to bondholders every six months. A default on the interest payment could cause the entire debt to be due immediately and might force the firm to declare bankruptcy. No such threat of bankruptcy exists with the issuance of common stock.

What advantage does bond financing rather than 100 percent stock financing provide? With debt financing comes financial *leverage*. For instance, a million dollar expansion financed by \$800 thousand of bondholder money is an expansion which is *80 percent leveraged*. The importance of leverage lies in the fact that the return to stockholders can be positively magnified and the more leverage, the greater the positive magnification. In other words, the earnings on the assets financed by other people's money (the bondholders') go first to cover the bondholders' interest payment; the rest goes to the owners. But leverage isn't always a positive influence. Since bondholders demand interest payments regardless of the level of earnings the firm makes on its operations, any shortfall must be made up by stockholders. This is a risk they bear by leveraging. It follows that the greater the leveraging, the more burdensome is the interest payment obligation on stockholders. This renders their return (earnings per share) more variable (positive and negative) and thus more risky with additional leverage. Thus financial leverage can be correctly viewed as a double-edged sword—promising higher earnings per share (EPS) to stockholders in good years, but depressing their EPS (perhaps to the negative range) in bad years.

How can the financial manager make a choice about the use of leverage? It requires quantifying the impact on EPS. The conservative choice of no leverage with complete reliance on stock financing offers a stockholders' earnings per share distribution shown in Figure 4.8. The EPS distribution for choosing debt and so financial leverage is shown by distribution *B*. It is clear from the diagram that stockholders face a higher *mean* earnings per share in distribution *B* (the leverage route) than in distribution *S* (the non leverage route). But in turn stockholders must live with a greater EPS *dispersion* with distribution *B*.

Can the *relative* impact on EPS of bond versus stock financing be correctly summarized? Granted bond financing entails a higher absolute risk as measured by the standard deviation, but doesn't it also achieve a higher mean EPS? What then is the relative risk? That is, how much absolute risk is there per dollar of mean (expected) EPS gained? This type of adjustment calls for a ratio of the standard devi-

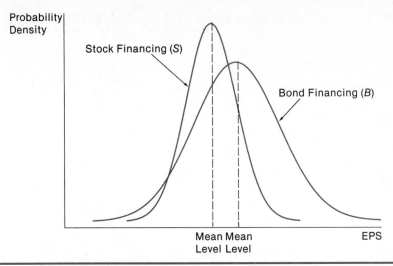

FIGURE 4.8 Probability Curves for Stock and Bond Financing

ation of the different distributions and their respective mean earnings per share. This ratio, called the *coefficient of variation,* is:

$$V = \frac{\text{std. deviation of earnings per share (EPS)}}{\text{mean level of earnings per share (EPS)}}$$

The coefficient shows the variability of EPS per dollar of mean EPS. It is interpreted as the amount of risk *per unit of return.* The higher the value of V, the more risk associated with each dollar of mean earnings per share.

How does the financial manager use these results to avoid making an ill-advised decision? One aid that helps the financial manager better understand the situation is a schedule (Table 4.8) comparing mean earnings per share and V for different levels of leverage. Ideally the financial officer would like to have high earnings per share combined with low V. But this would be like having your cake and eating it too—high return with low risk. What the table shows instead is a positive *risk-return tradeoff.*

TABLE 4.8. Risk-Return Tradeoff for Various Degrees of Leverage

LEVERAGE PERCENTAGE	MEAN (Expected) EPS	STANDARD DEVIATION	COEFFICIENT OF VARIATION
0%*	1.80	.99	.55
10	1.95	1.11	.57
20	2.00	1.18	.59
30	2.10	1.30	.62
40	2.20	1.43	.65
50	2.30	1.54	.67

*(stock financing)

Examining the figures closely, one can see that higher leverage (column 1) produces higher mean earnings (column 2) at the price of increased variability in the distribution of earnings per share (column 3). On a relative risk basis higher leverage goes hand in hand with higher values of the coefficient of variation (column 4). Thus, there is no free lunch. It brings a higher mean earnings per share, but each dollar of mean earnings per share now carries greater risk. At what point does the additional risk become *too* burdensome? There lies the heart of the crucial choice for the financial officer. The schedule described in Table 4.8 shows the options available and their consequences. With such facts at hand, the financial officer can resolve in a more informed way the financial leverage decision.

The leveraging example points out an important consideration in comparing distributions. Although both distributions may be measured in the same units, the fact that they have different means tells one not to rely on absolute measures of dispersion such as the standard deviation to make relevant comparisons. Instead a measure of *relative* dispersion such as V ought to be employed.

4.10. The Effect of Skewness on Measures of Central Tendency

Using statistics to deceive someone is a well developed and much practiced art. Using an unspecified average in conjunction with a highly skewed distribution is part of the statistical con artist's stock in trade. To illustrate, consider the desire to find a business opportunity that will make one a millionaire overnight. Without a clear understanding of the different kinds of averages and the way these averages are affected by skewness, the chances are that the would-be member of the millionaire's club may instead become a living example of how easy it is to be conned.

Example 4.10. **Getting Plucked in the Chicken Business: Nothing But the Truth Need Not Be the Whole Truth**

Imagine that you're looking into fried chicken franchises for your big opportunity and that we are your potential franchisors. Having sized you up as an over-eager investor, we show you financial statements on our existing chicken franchises. We guarantee that on the average, $40,000 pure profit is returned to first-year holders of our franchises on a $40,000 initial investment. Furthermore, we guarantee that the average profit the following year is also in the same bracket. The promised rate of return certainly beats the prospects that your local savings and loan association offer you.

Let's suppose you decide to buy our franchise. Because you are good at business and lucky too, perhaps you make your $40,000 profit the first year. But then some disconcerting information reaches your ear. You hear that lawsuits have been filed against the parent company, with swindle being claimed by a host of unsuccessful franchise buyers. Details of the case bring out the fact that although some franchises are very successful ventures, 75% of newly-bought franchises go broke within a year. Luckily, you weren't one of the many casualties but that is not the point—the point is that had you known the facts, you might not have taken the risk.

The pitfall in the chicken deal was that the mean had been carefully selected for reporting purposes precisely *because* it helped hide the high failure rate. The great thing about lying with averages (carefully choosing the "right" one) is that you can't be convicted for it. After all, the parent company never said what *kind* of average that $40,000 return was. There's no law against presenting the average which will give the most favorable impression of the profit outlook. You were given the arithmetic mean because it was the highest average of the three. The relatively few highly successful investors pulled the mean up far beyond that of the majority of investors, many of whom lost their entire investment. Had you asked about the median and modal profits for first year franchises, you would undoubtedly have realized that chicken franchises are extremely risky ventures where most people lose their investments, but the few who do make money make lots of it. It's the old story that "nothing but the truth" does not necessarily imply the "whole truth."

Skewness Makes the Difference

There may or may not be a big difference between the three different measures of central tendency. It all depends on the shape or skewness of the distribution. If a frequency distribution is symmetrical about the mean, then all three measures will have the same value. See Figure 4.9A. Instead of being symmetrical, the distribution for our chicken franchises would be highly skewed. See Figure 4.9B. To quote a classic description by Darrel Huff, "its shape would be a little like that of a child's slide, the ladder rising sharply to a peak, the working part sloping gradually down."[2]

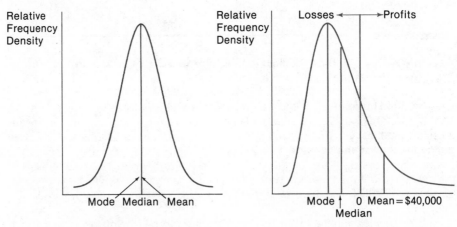

FIGURE 4.9a. FIGURE 4.9b.

Although a skewed distribution will have mean, mode, and median values which differ, comparing these values is not the best way to determine how skewed the distribution is. If it is important to measure skewness by a summary statistic, one of the formulas given in Appendix 4A should be used.

By now you should be thoroughly convinced that the "best" measure of central location is the one which suits your purpose. To avoid possible deception, all three measures should be reported. Also, use the words mean, mode, and median for the ones you do report rather than the ambiguous term "average".

4.11. Summary Measures in Decision Making: The Median

The usefulness of a summary measure is not limited to merely describing an existing set of data. The properties of a summary measure may make that measure useful for decision making purposes too. The median is a case in point.

One unique property of the median is that the sum of the absolute deviations around it is minimum. Regardless of what other value one uses—including the mean and the mode—the sum of the absolute deviations around any other value will not be less than the sum of the absolute deviations around the median. Symbolically, $\sum |X - \text{Median}|$ is minimum.

For physical distribution and logistics specialists, this is a good property to remember, because it may help them when it comes time to pick the site for a warehouse or supply depot.

Example 4.11. **A Warehouse Location Problem**

In the food franchising business, the location of a supply warehouse as the distribution point for trucking food to each franchise can be a key decision. If all the franchises are located along a fairly straight highway and one truck is sent from each franchise to the warehouse, then one can picture the highway beginning at point zero and continuing for 200 miles with franchises A to I along the route (Figure 4.10).

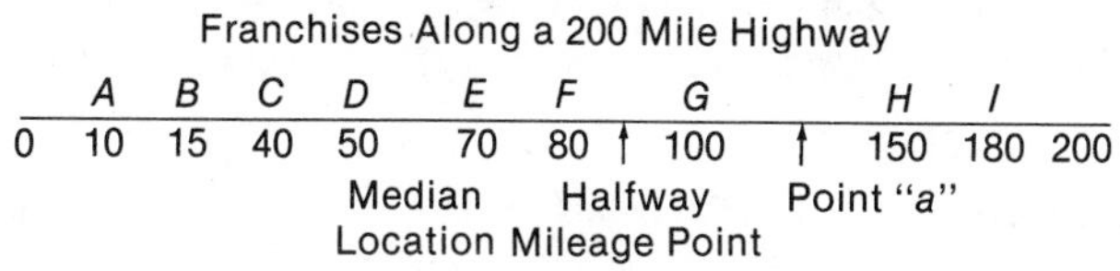

Franchises Along a 200 Mile Highway

	A	B	C	D	E	F	G		H	I	
0	10	15	40	50	70	80 †	100	†	150	180	200

Median   Halfway   Point "a"
Location   Mileage Point

FIGURE 4.10   Using the Median to Locate a Warehouse

The first guess of an unschooled manager might be to locate the warehouse at the 95-mile marker, the halfway point between the two extreme franchises A (10 miles) and I (180 miles), that is, 10 + (180 − 10)/2 = 95 miles. Alternatively, the warehouse might be put at Franchise G, the franchise nearest the halfway point of mileage between A and I. Both guesses would be a mistake if traveling distance is to be minimized. The best place to put the warehouse to minimize traveling is at E, the median position—the halfway point counting *franchises* rather than miles.

Both intuitively and mathematically, point E has an advantage over any other point. Intuitively, the advantage of E can be seen by picking any arbitrary point on the map for the warehouse location and moving the point along the horizontal axis either left or right. For example, pick point "a" and move to the right. As the point is shifted to the right, there is an increase in travel from each of the six franchise locations, A to G, by an amount exactly equal to the distance of the shift. There is also a reduction in travel by the amount of the shift, but to only two franchises, H and I. Therefore, the total distance traveled to make the deliveries increases. If point a is moved to the left instead, there is a travel reduction to each four franchises and a travel increase to each of the two franchises by the shift amount. Therefore, such a move reduces total travel. In fact, as long as there are more franchises to the left of the warehouse than the right, a leftward movement will reduce total travel costs. With this in mind, the movement will lead us past franchises G and F (the first guesses) until we get to E—the "middle-most" position of the franchises. Mathematically, the advantage of location E over location G can be seen from Table 4.9, where the sum of the deviations around points G and E are compared. The deviations represent the travel distance to each franchise. As the numbers show, the total distance traveled is lower from point E.

TABLE 4.9. Comparison of Locations _G_ and _E_

FRANCHISE	DISTANCE FROM G	DISTANCE FROM E
A	90	60
B	75	45
C	60	30
D	50	20
E	30	0
F	20	10
G	0	30
H	50	80
I	60	110
	455	385

4.12. Concluding Comments

Summary measures provide valuable, but by no means complete, information on the values in a data set. _Central tendency_, _dispersion_, and _skewness_ are the characteristics which ordinarily need to be described.

The _arithmetic mean_, _median_, and _mode_ are all measures of central tendency. The mean can be used to determine a population total (as in estimating the number of cameras in Michigan); the median is used when a "middle-most" measure is desired, one which is influenced only by how many and not by how far values are above and below it. Because of this property, the median can be computed for open-ended distributions; the mean cannot.

Measures of dispersion describe the variation in the data values. Measures based upon the position of values within the distribution—the _range_, _interquartile range_, _quartile deviation_—are easy to compute but do not indicate the variation in intensity of observations around some central point. Measures based upon arithmetic calculations—the *mean, absolute deviation,* the *variance,* the *standard deviation*—do not have this drawback.

Skewness refers to the asymmetry of a distribution, the fact that there may be many more observations a given distance away from the mean in one direction than the other. This information will often be important and is signalled by differences among the values of the mean, mode, and median.

When it is important to know an upper limit on the percentage of observations lying beyond a given distance (in either direction) from the mean, Chebyshev's Inequality can be employed if the mean and standard deviation are known.

Finally, it is worth stressing that summary measures can be used to hide as well as provide information. For example, if only the mean is given (as in the chicken business example), an erroneous conclusion might result. If only the mean and standard deviation are given, no information can be gleaned about skewness.

Appendix

Appendix 4A. Measures of Skewness

Skewness refers to lopsidedness or the lack of symmetry in the shape of a frequency distribution. Of the several measures of skewness, one measure, called the third moment about the mean, bears a close resemblance to the formula for the variance (which is referred to as the second moment about the mean). The formula for the third moment is:

$$M_3 = \sum_{\text{all} X} [\text{r.f.}(X)][(X - \overline{X})^3]$$

If the distribution is symmetrical, this measure has a value of zero. The more lopsided the distribution, the larger the value of the third moment. As can be surmised, the name third moment comes from the fact that deviations from the mean are raised to the third power.

The example of the fried chicken franchise used earlier in the chapter demonstrates the importance of knowing whether the distribution is highly skewed. Skewness to the left or the right depends on whether the long tail of the distribution trails off to the left or the right. The distribution of fried chicken franchise profits was highly skewed to the right (see Appendix Figure 4A).

In a highly skewed distribution, the mean is pulled out in the direction of the extreme values and the mode stays on the lopsided part on the highest point of the curve. The median falls somewhere in between the mean and mode because it is affected by the number (not the value) of the extreme observations. If the skewness is moderate, the median tends to fall about one-third of the way

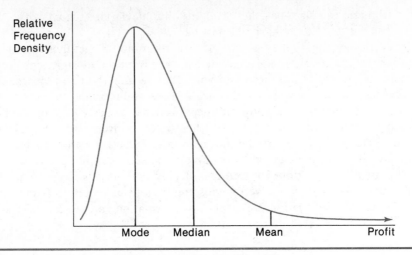

APPENDIX FIGURE 4.A. Profits of Fried Chicken Franchise

from the mean to the mode. A simple measure of skewness known as the *coefficient of skewness* is based upon this relationship:

$$Sk = \frac{3(\overline{X} - \text{median})}{S}$$

The value of the coefficient of skewness can range between plus and minus three. Positive values indicate skewness to the right, negative values indicate skewness to the left, and a value of zero indicates a symmetrical distribution.

Appendix 4B. Kurtosis

Kurtosis—the relative peakedness of a distribution—is ordinarily measured by the ratio of the fourth moment about the mean to the square of the second moment (the second moment is the variance). The formula is:

$$\text{kurtosis ratio} = \frac{\sum_{\text{all}X} [\text{r.f.}(X)][(X - \overline{X})^4]}{\left[\sum_{\text{all}X} [\text{r.f.}(X)][(X - \overline{X})^2]\right]^2}$$

This ratio measures the degree of peakedness relative to the level of dispersion. Of two distributions having the same dispersion, the one having the larger value of the kurtosis ratio will have more observations concentrated near the mean and also at the tails of the distribution (at the expense of intermediate area). The degree of peakedness is described as *leptokurtic, mesokurtic,* or *platykurtic* according to the value of the ratio.

The bell-shaped normal curve encountered in Chapter Three is characterized by the mesokurtic shape with a value of 3 for the kurtosis ratio. Distributions with values of the kurtosis ratio greater than 3 are leptokurtic. Relative to the standard mesokurtic (normal curve) shape, these distributions will be more peaked and more fat-tailed. Distributions with values of the kurtosis ratio less than three are platykurtic, flatter in shape than the standard normal distribution. Each of these types of distributions is illustrated in Appendix Figure 4-B1.

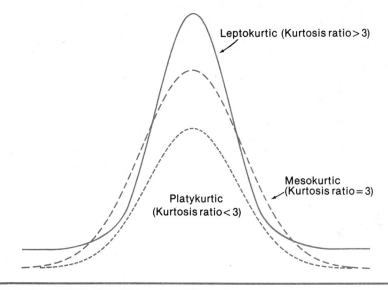

APPENDIX FIGURE 4.B1. Illustration of Kurtosis

The following example discusses the importance of kurtosis in analyzing stock market returns.

Appendix Example 4B.   Stock Price Changes: A Random Walk or Not?

Perhaps no other subject in the investment community has generated so much attention and controversy as the pattern of behavior of stock market prices. One side of the debate espouses the theory that changes of stock prices move in a random fashion, unpredictable from past movements. If this is so, no amount of investigation of past stock price data will be any good in predicting future stock prices. This claim rests on the belief that the organized stock markets are *efficient* markets. That is, organized exchanges are characterized by sophisticated investors and speculators who are constantly searching for relevant information on the earnings of listed stocks. With many analysts involved, this dynamic condition does not enable any one analyst to have a monopoly on information, but does enable the market to reflect quickly in the current price any relevant information on a particular company's earnings. Current market price therefore always reflects the general market's assessment of the *latest* information affecting a firm's future earnings. Any *changes* in price can only come from unanticipated new information on a company's earnings. Such relevant new information cannot come in a predictable way, otherwise it would have been already anticipated and impounded in the current price. Since changes in stock prices are linked with unpredictable relevant events, there is no way for the average analyst to systematically "beat" the market nor take advantage of some magic formula for analyzing past market trends in the hope of predicting future market trends. Simply stated, the Random Walk Theory of Efficient Markets asserts that although it is clear that trends and fluctuations exist in the market, *when* they occur and *how long they persist* cannot be predicted (the famous timing problem). For the *average* analyst in the market, therefore, profits and losses will fluctuate randomly as if playing roulette at a Las Vegas casino. Thus, the strategy of the random walk advocates is *not* to try and "beat" the market by trying to predict its up and down movements (timing) but to count on the fact that in the long run the market rises. With this in mind, the plan for the random walk believer is to *buy and hold* a diversified portfolio of stocks, thereby eliminating the timing problem of when to buy and when to sell and the brokerage fees of moving in and out of different stocks.

Confirmation of the random walk theory has received much attention in academic literature as well as on Wall Street. The tests have involved comparing the empirical frequency distributions of the rates of return (usually on a monthly basis) to the standard normal distribution. The implication of this comparison is that if the random walk theory is correct, the empirical distribution should be in close conformity to a normal distribution. Close conformity implies that the key characteristics (dispersion, symmetry, kurtosis) of the empirical distribution match the summary measures for a normal distribution.

The evidence shows that rather close conformity does exist, but it is not perfect. As the superimposed distributions in Figure 4-B2 indicate, the empirical distribution is more peaked at middle values and more fat-tailed at more extreme rates of return than the normal distribution would predict. This implies that small deviations and large deviations from the average rate of return are more prevalent in the market than the theory (normal curve) would have us believe. Attempts to explain this discrepancy have spurred continuing research in stock price behavior.

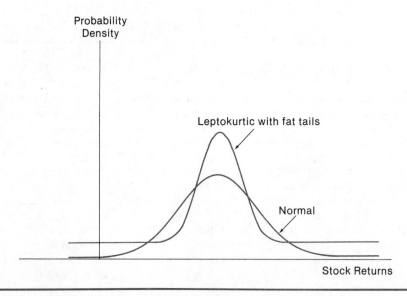

APPENDIX FIGURE 4.B2. Normal Distribution Compared with Leptokurtic Distribution with Fat Tails

Appendix 4C. The Geometric and Harmonic Means

There are two situations where a mean is desired but where the arithmetic mean is misleading. One involves averaging growth rates, or rates of return (often expressed in percentage terms); this requires the computation of the *geometric mean* instead of the arithmetic mean. The other situation arises where the units are expressed inversely to what is desired in the mean, as in kilowatts (energy usage) per barrel of oil instead of barrels of oil per kilowatt; this latter situation necessitates the use of the *harmonic mean* instead of the arithmetic mean to get a result in desired units.

Geometric Mean

The geometric mean is the nth root of the product of a sequence of positive numbers. This kind of a mean is needed when the numbers represent rates of change from some base number which shifts from period to period.

Appendix Example 4C.1. **How to Make Zero Profits Look Profitable**

Let's say you have $1000 to invest and decide to put your money in gold stock. With the current speculation on gold, suppose your gold stock doubles in one year so that by year-end your holdings are now worth $2000. But, like many speculative bubbles, the price of gold declines and by the end of the next year the gold stock has gone back to $1000, your original purchase price. The arithmetic average of return is the average of the 100 percent rate of return earned the first year and the -50 percent rate of return earned the second year:

$$\frac{100\% + (-50\%)}{2} = 25\% \text{ per year}$$

But your original holdings were worth $1000 and at the end of the two-year period the stocks were again valued at $1000, so really you earned no profit at all and certainly not the 25% return you calculated! It is clear that the arithmetic average of successive period rates of returns is not equal to the true rate of return.

The true rate of return over n periods is the geometric mean return which is calculated by *subtracting one from the antilog of the arithmetic mean of the logarithms of the return relative* (the rate of return plus one, $r + 1$). The geometric mean formula is:

$$gr = \left(\text{antilog}\left[\frac{1}{n}\sum_{t=1}^{n}\log(1 + r_t)\right]\right) - 1$$

where r is the rate of return defined as:

$$r = \frac{\text{value at end of period} - \text{value at start of period}}{\text{value at start of period}}$$

The computation would be:

End of Period	$t = 0$	$t = 1$	$t = 2$
Market Value, V	$V_0 = 1000$	$V_1 = 2000$	$V_2 = 1000$
Return, r		$r_1 = \dfrac{2000 - 1000}{1000} = 1$	$r_2 = \dfrac{1000 - 2000}{2000} = -.5$
Natural log, Log_e of $(1 + r)^*$		$\text{Log}_e(1+1) = .693$	$\text{Log}_e(1-.5) = -.693$

$$gr = \text{antilog} \frac{1}{2}(.693 + [-.693]) - 1$$
$$= \text{antilog}\,(0) - 1$$
$$gr = 1 - 1$$
$$gr = 0$$

This makes sense. Your true rate of return over the two periods was zero.

*Logarithms are used for simplification, to aid in numerical calculations. Calculating the logarithm identifies the exponent to which a number called the *base* must be raised to obtain the original number. For example, consider the original number 1000 which can be written as

$$1000 = 10^3$$

In this expression 3 is the logarithm of 1000 to the base 10 because it is the exponent to which 10 is raised to obtain 1000. The notation commonly used is $\log_{10}(1000) = 3$. Since 10 is a very common base number, it is usually understood to be the base if no base number is given. For example, in $\log (1000) = 3$ no base is given, so it is assumed to be 10. Finding the antilog of a number reverses the process in order to find the original number for which the log has been calculated. For example, if 10 is the base, the antilog of 3 is $10^3 = 1000$, so 1000 is the original number.

Harmonic Mean

The purpose of the harmonic mean is best understood by considering an example.

Appendix Example 4C.2.   Trucking Logistics

A business economist for Roadway, a Midwest trucking firm, is attempting to get an estimate of fuel usage and subsequent cost figures for a new route the company is thinking of acquiring in the Far West. The haul for the specific route will be averaging

1680 miles and traveling at different speeds and in different traffic situations. One part of the haul involves city traffic where the truck is expected to get two miles per gallon driving at 25 miles per hour; another part of the trip is on an interstate highway where the truck expects to drive 55 miles per hour, with gasoline mileage rising to seven miles per gallon; another stretch of the haul is on the country roads where five miles per gallon is expected of the truck. The total trip is expected to be accomplished in three days with each part of the trip expected to take 14 hours of driving time.

A first thought in problems of this kind might be to find the arithmetic mean of the three mileage figures, because each part of the trip will take one day and the truck will get 2, 5 and 7 miles per gallon for each part. One might think the mean of these numbers, 4.67, would be your mean miles per gallon (mpg) for the entire trip. Based on this assumption, the truck will consume 360 gallons of diesel fuel to complete the 1680-mile haul. However, the answer is wrong; it understates your actual fuel consumption. You might also suppose that the three mpg should be weighted by the 350 (14 × 25) miles driven at this speed; 7 mpg should be weighted by the 770 (14 × 55) miles driven at this speed; and the 5 mpg should be weighted by the 560 (14 × 40) miles driven at this speed. Using these weights, you get a weighted arithmetic mean of 5.29 mpg, which implies 317.58 gallons should bring you to your destination. This answer is also wrong; it too understates your gasoline consumption. The correct mean mileage would be 4.23 miles per gallon calculated by using the harmonic mean formula, with 397 gallons of diesel fuel consumption.

All means, whether arithmetic, geometric, or harmonic, are expressed in some base measurement unit. The base units for gasoline mileage are gallons. The two erroneous figures for the mean mpg resulted because fuel usage measured in gallons was being weighted by either driving time (in hours) or distance (in miles). But gallons do not make sense as a base, whereas distance in miles does. In order to find the correct average miles per gallon, the data must first be converted into fuel consumption for a unit distance (gallons per mile), then averaged to obtain the mean gallons per mile, and finally the mean gallons per mile must be converted to miles per gallon. The harmonic mean makes that conversion. The harmonic mean is the overall reciprocal of the mileage weighted arithmetic mean of the reciprocals of the original mpg data. For this example, the formula is:

$$ H = \frac{1}{w_1 \left(\dfrac{1}{mpg_1} \right) + w_2 \left(\dfrac{1}{mpg_2} \right) + w_3 \left(\dfrac{1}{mpg_3} \right)} $$

where w is weight. Computationally, for this data:

$$ H = \frac{1}{\dfrac{350}{1680} \left(\dfrac{1}{2\ mpg} \right) + \dfrac{560}{1680} \left(\dfrac{1}{5\ mpg} \right) + \dfrac{770}{1680} \left(\dfrac{1}{7\ mpg} \right)} = 4.232\ mpg. $$

Once you know what a harmonic mean is supposed to do, you may wish to abandon it. Its real value is in demonstrating the necessity of expressing a problem in consistent units. If you keep the units straight and think the problem through step by step, it is not necessary to use the harmonic mean to get the correct answer. In the trucking example, gasoline consumption for the three legs of the trip is:

350 miles @ 2 miles/gallon = 175 gallons
770 miles @ 7 miles/gallon = 110 gallons
560 miles @ 5 miles/gallon = 112 gallons
1680 miles   divided by   397 gallons = 4.232 mpg.

Consider a motorist who wishes to average 60 miles per hour on a 100-mile trip. If she can average only 30 miles per hour over the first 50 miles due to traffic congestion, can she average 60 miles per hour over the entire distance by averaging 90 miles per hour over the last 50 miles? Of course not; in order to average 60 miles per hour over the entire distance, the trip must take 100 minutes; at 30 miles per hour, the first 50 miles takes 100 minutes of driving time; no matter how fast she averages on the last half, she can't average 60 miles per hour for the entire trip. How fast would she average over the entire distance if she averaged 90 miles per hour over the last half? The easiest conceptual route to the answer is to find the total elapsed time and divide this into the distance. The elapsed time on the first half is 100 minutes; the elapsed time on the second half is 50 minutes; total elapsed time for the entire trip is 150 minutes or two and one-half hours. Dividing this into 100 miles gives 40 miles per hour for the entire trip.

Footnotes and References

[1]Fama's study, "The Behavior of Stock Prices," described stock market returns as fitting a Paretian distribution. This type of distribution is characterized by infinite variance (in the population). The study was published in the January 1965 issue of the *Journal of Business of the University of Chicago.*

[2]Huff, Darrel. *How To Lie With Statistics*, W.W. Norton and Co., 1954, p. 30.

Questions and Problems

1. Is the value of every item in the data set taken into account in the computation of this summary measure of central tendency? (Mean? Mode? Median?)

2. Can this summary measure be determined from a frequency distribution which has an open-ended class interval? (Mean? Mode? Median?)

3. Can this summary measure be determined from a frequency distribution with unequal class intervals? (Mean? Mode? Median?)

4. Do the values of extreme items in a frequency distribution influence the value of this summary measure? (Mean? Mode? Median?)

5. Is it true that the values of the mean, median and mode become identical when the whole population, and not just a sample, is examined? Explain.

6. Can the value of this summary measure be used to find the summation of all the values in the data set? (Mean? Mode? Median?)

7. Many alumni of a certain university base their annual gift to the university on the reported "average" donation of alumni as a whole. The distribution of contributions is highly skewed; most of the funds come from a few extremely generous donors. Which of the three averages (mean,

mode, median) would you compute to report:

a. the largest "average" donation?

b. the donation most frequently received?

c. the donation which is exceeded in size by about as many donations as it exceeds?

8. Which of the three common averages of weights of persons in an elevator would you want to know to determine whether the elevator's maximum safe passenger weight was being exceeded? Explain.

9. Which type of average would you use to report the average percentage change in price of haircuts among barbershops from one year to the next?

10. What type of average would you use to report the average rate of change in price of a house over five years of ownership?

11. A truck replacement part is sold at $4296 per thousand on the West Coast, $3775 per thousand on the East Coast, and $4520 per thousand in the Midwest. Use the harmonic mean to calculate the average posted price among the three regions.

12. Four optical scanners will scan typewritten pages at the rates of 80 pages per hour, 60 pages per hour, 100 pages per hour, and 40 pages per hour.

a. What is the average scanning rate of the four machines?

b. What average was used to make the computation?

13. What is meant by the term "relative dispersion"? How would this term be used?

14. Is it true that the arithmetic mean computed from an array of items will always be the same as the one determined from a frequency distribution of the same data set? Explain.

15. Is it true that the sum of the absolute deviations of the items in a data set will always be less if deviations are taken from the mean than if taken from any other value? Explain.

16. Is it true that the variance cannot be computed for an open-ended frequency distribution? Explain.

17. A marketer of breakfast cereals asked its advertising agency to survey households to learn about consumer behavior with respect to ready-to-eat breakfast cereals. A total of 45 randomly selected households were surveyed. Respondents reported the number of days ready-to-eat breakfast cereal had been served to at least one member of the household during the previous week. The frequency distribution in Table 4.10 resulted.

TABLE 4.10. Cereal Usage

USAGE RATE: NO. OF DAYS READY-TO-EAT CEREAL SERVED	NO. OF HOUSE-HOLDS REPORTING THIS USAGE RATE
0	5
1	9
2	4
3	7
4	6
5	6
6	5
7	3

a. Construct a line chart for this frequency distribution.

b. What is the mean cereal usage rate by the households in the survey for the week?

c. What is the median cereal usage rate for the surveyed households?

18. What is the standard deviation of cereal usage among the surveyed households in Problem 17?

19. Use the data in Problem 17 to answer the following questions.

a. How many days in total was cereal used by the households?

b. Is it necessary to have the frequency distribution to determine your answer to Part a? Explain.

c. How many days in total was cereal used by the households which used cereal everyday?

d. What percentage of total usage days is accounted for by households in which cereal was served everyday?

20. In Problem 17:
a. What is the mean percentage of days on which cereal is served by the surveyed households?
b. What percentage of households in the survey did not use cereal during the week studied?

21. In Problem 17:
a. At what usage rate is the greatest single concentration of customers found?
b. Which summary statistic reports this value?
c. What percentage of surveyed households have this usage rate?

22. In Problem 17:
a. Which of the summary statistics you computed might be used to estimate the size of the ready-to-eat cereal market? (Assume that the households in the market are the ones from which the surveyed households have been randomly selected.)
b. If the market contains 12 million households, what would be the estimated cereal market size?

23. In Problem 17, is a large percentage of the usage accounted for by a small percentage of households? If this is true, then the market strategy of the cereal marketer might be to identify, pursue, and cultivate these high intensity users. This strategy of aiming promotional efforts directly at a particular group of households is sometimes called the "rifle approach". If usage is not concentrated among a small percentage of the households, then a broad-coverage or "shotgun" promotional approach would likely be more appropriate.
a. If there is little or no dispersion of usage rate among households, cereal consumption would not be highly concentrated among a small percentage of the households. What summary statistic indicates the amount of dispersion in usage of ready-to-eat cereal among households?
b. Use Chebyshev's theorem in conjunction with this summary statistic to make a statement about the variation in cereal usage among the surveyed households.
c. Explain why concentration of cereal usage is so closely linked to dispersion of usage among households.

d. In accounting for cereal usage by households, explain why the percentage of cereal usage accounted for by heavy users exceeds the percentage of all households that represent this usage category.

24. In Problem 17 how do the differences in values between the mean, median, and mode suggest the skewness of the distribution and in turn the potentially large concentration of non-users?

25. In Problem 17:
a. The user group of households surveyed was split into two groups, the "heavy half" and the "light half". What percentage of all the households surveyed fall into the heavy user category?
b. A major objective of the survey was to learn how important heavy users are to the cereal marketer's strategy. An indication of this importance is given by the percentage of days of cereal usage accounted for by heavy users. What is this percentage for the survey data?
c. Construct a horizontal bar display showing the percentage breakdown of households among heavy users, light users, and non-users.
d. Indicate on the bar display the percentage breakdown of cereal usage among heavy users and light users.
e. What implications do your findings have for cereal marketing strategy?

26. In Problem 17, the cereal marketer's advertising agency wants to know who the heavy users are in terms of certain demographics, personal characteristics, and media habits, particularly those they have in common. Summary statistics for the survey report a mean household income of $24 thousand and a standard deviation of $7 thousand for the heavy users. Based on these summary measures, what income range does Chebyshev's theorem say includes at least 75 percent of the heavy users in the survey?

27. In Problem 17, suppose you know that the total volume of cereal sold has increased over the last two years. However, you want to know how pervasive the usage increase has been. Has the usage increase

occurred because a small percentage of households have greatly increased their purchase rate, or has it occurred because most households have been increasing their usage of cereal? Could you answer this question by comparing the values over the last two years for

a. the mean usage per household? Explain.

b. the modal usage? Explain.

c. the median usage? Explain.

28. Midwest Airlines commissioned a survey of 250 randomly selected households. The purpose was to learn about consumer behavior with respect to air travel for other-than-business purposes. Respondents reported the number of non-business trips taken by members of the household during the previous year. The following summary statistics resulted:

Mean = 1.46 trips/household
Median = 0 trips/household
Mode = 0 trips/household
Standard Deviation = 2.54 trips/household

a. How many flights in total were taken by households in the survey?

b. Can you determine what percentage of households in the survey did not use air travel for non-business purposes? If so, what is it?

c. At what usage rate is the single greatest concentration of customers found?

d. Which summary statistic reports this value?

e. Which of the summary statistics you computed might be used to estimate the size of the total air travel market for other-than-business purposes?

f. If the market contains 2 million households, what would be the estimated size of the nonbusiness air travel market?

29. In Problem 28:

a. What summary statistic indicates the amount of dispersion in air travel usage among the households?

b. Use Chebyshev's Inequality to make a statement about the maximum percentage of households surveyed that could have flown more than six times during the study period.

30. In Problem 28, do the values of the mean, mode, and median suggest a distribution which is symmetrical or one which is skewed? If skewed, in which direction?

31. In Problem 28, the airline learns that 78 percent of all flights are taken by only 18 percent of the households, the "heavy users". The airline wants to know who the heavy users are in terms of certain demographics, personal characteristics, and media habits, particularly those they have in common. Summary statistics for the survey report a mean household income of $36 thousand and a standard deviation of $7 thousand for the heavy users. Based on these summary measures, what income range does Chebyshev's theorem say includes at least 75 percent of the heavy users in the survey? Have you found a way to segment your market for purposes of promotion?

32. The Midlothian Paramedic Service took a sample of 201 paramedic emergency runs. The data in Table 4.11 are for the time required to reach the scene of the emergency.

TABLE 4.11. Time of Emergency Runs

TIME REQUIRED IN MINUTES	NUMBER OF RUNS
0.0—0.9	11
1.0—1.9	55
2.0—2.9	74
3.0—3.9	36
4.0—4.9	17
5.0—5.9	5
6.0—6.9	2
7.0—7.9	1
8.0 or more	0

a. What is the mean time to the scene of the emergency?

b. Median Time?

c. Modal Time?

d. What is the standard deviation of time?

e. Range?

f. Mean Absolute Deviation?

g. Coefficient of Variation?

33. The paramedic service in another city reported the following summary statistics for the time to the scene of the emergency:

Mean = 3.1 minutes
Median = 1.9 minutes
Standard Deviation = 2.2 minutes
Mean Absolute Deviation = 1.5 minutes

Compare the performance of the paramedic response time in the two cities.

34. A manufacturer of recreational vehicles recorded (in Table 4.12) data on absenteeism at its Michigan plant over a one month period.

TABLE 4.12. Absenteeism

NO. OF DAYS ABSENT	NO. OF EMPLOYEES
0	192
1	76
2	79
3	64
4	47
5	30
6	28
7	21
8	13
9	5
10	4
11	1
12 or more	0

---

a. What is the mean number of absences per employee?
b. Median?
c. Mode?
d. Range?
e. Mean Absolute Deviation?
f. Standard Deviation?
g. Coefficient of Variation?

35. In Problem 34
a. What percentage of employees were absent within two standard deviations of the mean number of absences per employee?
b. How does your answer to Part a compare with the minimum percentage which follows from Chebyshev's Inequality?

c. What percentage of employees were absent at least twice as frequently as the median rate?
d. What percentage of all absences were due to employees who were absent at least twice as frequently as the median rate?
e. Compare your answers to c and d and make a brief statement about absenteeism at the Michigan plant.

36. In Problem 34 assume that the total number of absences has doubled from the year-ago level, while the number of employees has remained the same. You want to know whether the increased absenteeism is a pervasive problem among the employees or whether it is attributable to a few employees who become chronically absent. Which statistic, the mean, mode, or median, best provides the information you seek? Explain.

37. The recreational vehicle manufacturer described in Problem 34 has another plant in Tennessee. There the mean number of absences per employee was 1.9, the median was 1, and the standard deviation was 1.3.
a. In which plant was the problem of the chronically absent employee more severe? Explain how you made this determination.
b. Write a brief paragraph comparing the absenteeism problem at the Michigan and Tennessee plants?

38. A major credit card company has encountered a situation in which the unpaid balances on its accounts has increased substantially, even though account holders are making fewer new purchases with their cards. A sample of accounts revealed the frequency distribution in Table 4.13.
a. What is the mean percentage of account balance unpaid?
b. Median class?
c. Mode?
d. Variance?
e. Standard Deviation?
f. Coefficient of Variation?

39. In Problem 38 the mean and median are both near fifty percent. Does this imply that:
a. the distribution is nearly symmetrical?
b. the distribution is bell shaped?

TABLE 4.13. Unpaid Account Balances

PERCENTAGE OF JANUARY ENDING BALANCE NOT PAID BY THE END OF FEBRUARY	NUMBER OF ACCOUNTS
0 (entire amt. paid)	349
More than 0 but not more than 10	86
More than 10 but not more than 25	53
More than 25 but not more than 40	168
More than 40 but not more than 60	230
More than 60 but not more than 85	414
More than 85 but less than 100	271
100 (entire amt. unpaid)	115

c. the most commonly found values are close to fifty percent?

d. the credit card holders have very similar account payment patterns?

40. The credit card company in Problem 38 knew that the economic situation had worsened considerably for many of its cardholders over the past six months. Some cardholders reduce payments on their accounts when this happens. The company wanted to know whether payment slowdown was quite pervasive among its customers or whether the larger unpaid accounts balance was caused by a small percentage of households which were using its cards extensively without paying much on its balances. Six months ago the percentage distribution of account balances unpaid one month later had a mean of 35 percent and a median of 38 percent.

a. Write a brief paragraph reporting on the source of the increase in percentage of account balances unpaid.

b. If every sampled account had a January balance of $1000, what percentage of the total amount outstanding in this group at the end of February would be attributable to the slowest paying quintile of the cardholders?

41. The prices in Table 4.14 were observed for the shares of a steel corporation and a computer manufacturer over a three year period.

TABLE 4.14. Comparison of Share Prices

TIME	STEEL CORPORATION	COMPUTER MANUFACTURER
Present	$50	$135
One Year Ago	$63	$115
Two Years Ago	$90	$110
Three Years Ago	$100	$100

a. Calculate the arithmetic and geometric mean rates of return for an investment made three years ago in one share of the computer manufacturer's stock.

b. Do the same for the steel corporation stock.

c. Compare your computed arithmetic and geometric values for each of the two stocks. Does there appear to be a systematic difference? If so, which mean gives the bigger value? Why?

d. Which of the two means you computed for each stock would be more useful in measuring the average annual rate of return? Why?

42. A sales manager expects her representatives to make calls on customer accounts as shown in Table 4.15.

TABLE 4.15. Expected Sales Calls Per Day

TYPE OF ACCOUNT	CALLS/DAY
Class A	2
Class B	4
Class C	7

If a sales rep is assigned 20 class A accounts, 40 class B accounts, and 70 class C accounts,

a. what should be the mean number of calls per day?

b. what type of mean was used to make the computation? Why?

Basic Probability Concepts

Preview. In this chapter we begin the formal study of uncertainty by introducing basic concepts of probability theory. First, a framework is established: the *random experiment.* In this context interpretations of probability as a measure of uncertainty are discussed. Then, drawing on concepts of set theory, rules are developed which govern probability assignments for different results of a random experiment. The advantage of rules over uneducated intuition in making probability assessments is demonstrated. Then the procedure for using the probabilities assigned to simple "building block" events to find the probability of other events formed from them is illustrated. Situations with unequal as well as equal probabilities are considered. Finally, an example is given showing how the building block probabilities are arrived at by Morgan Bank financial experts.

The sting of uncertainty isn't pleasant. You know it's touched the people on the street when they mumble, "There's no such thing as a sure thing." Football coaches know the feeling, too, when their premier place kicker misses the point after a touchdown. The emotion reaches Wall Street brokers when "Black Tuesday" type days hit and the market takes a nosedive. As unpleasant as it may be, uncertainty is here to stay and needs to be considered when we make our decisions.

There are some people who deal with uncertainty on a professional basis. The old riverboat gambler, stereotyped by green eye shades and fancy shirt, is the classic example. Today the big time risk takers aren't found in the smoke filled rooms of a riverboat. They may reside instead in the executive office of a commercial bank. The green eye shade has been replaced by a pin-striped suit. But don't let the conservative suit fool you, bank lending officers probably take risks for bigger stakes than the riverboat gambler ever dreamed of. To top it off, the banker takes the risks with someone else's money.

The bank lending officer takes money deposited by customers and, at an interest rate, lends to commercial enterprises needing and willing to borrow. The difference between the interest rate charged to the commercial borrower and the interest rate the bank pays to the depositor represents a contribution to the bank's profits.

There is an element of risk in banking. Why? First, the bank is obligated to come up with cash upon the depositor's demand, cash which the bank may not have on hand. The bank is always uncertain of the *exact* time and size of depositor withdrawals. Second, the bank faces the uncertain possibility of a loan default.

Loans and cash reserves generally fall within certain calculable risk ranges. Generally these calculations work quite well. Banks generally take a conservative approach to loans. However, sometimes foolish loans are made or unforeseen changes in the market lead to default. An overextended bank might fail, as happened to a large bank in Philadelphia in the Seventies. Thus, there is an element of risk in banking and a definite need for probability assessment. This and the next chapter will give the basic concepts in understanding and applying probability.

5.1. Introduction

Commercial bank loan officers are not the only members of the business community who deal with uncertainty. Business decisions made under uncertainty are the rule rather than the exception. With every business decision, a variety of outcomes is possible. While hoping for the most favorable outcome, the decision-maker unavoidably knows there is a chance—call it risk—of less favorable outcomes.

An automobile dealer, purchasing an inventory of new cars, reckons with the uncertainty of demand from the buying public. Lost sales from an inventory shortage and a glut of unsold cars from overstocking are possible unfavorable outcomes once an inventory decision has been made.

An advertising executive, having chosen a media mix for a product, is subject to the uncertainty about the effectiveness of the mix in reaching and convincing the target audience.

A stockbroker, before recommending whether to buy a company's stock, has to consider how uncertain future economic conditions will affect the expected future earnings of the company.

Knowing that uncertainty is present in their business decisions, business executives make efforts to measure and compare the uncertainty of their gambles. Their position is similar to that of the poker player who wants to know the odds before playing his hand. Those who can calculate the proper odds gain a distinct advantage over potential competitors who have incorrectly assessed the risks involved.

Uncertainty and Probability

Probability theory is the branch of mathematics that deals with uncertainty. It is useful in two different ways. First, it helps us remove inconsistencies in our thinking about uncertainty. For example, suppose heads and tails represent two equally likely outcomes for any fair coin toss. Probability theory shows that for *two* independently tossed fair coins, it would be inconsistent to believe anything else than that the outcome "one head" is twice as likely as the outcome "zero heads". Second, probability theory provides the cornerstone for statistical inference.

In Chapters Five through Ten, we will elaborate on the use of probability to remove inconsistencies in thought. Also, we will see how repeated sampling from a population allows us to determine the probability of any one sample result. Armed with this probability for a single sample result, we can then make statistical inferences about the general population. For example, knowing the rules of probability and the percentage of defective tires in a single sample, we can then go on to make statements about the percentage of defective tires in the population. Once the groundwork in probability is set in the next chapters, procedures for applying probability for statistical inferences will be presented in Chapter Eleven.

5.2. Random Sampling Experiments and Probability

The term "random sampling" was first introduced in Chapter One. It refers to the type of *selection mechanism which insures that the laws of probability apply to the variation* in results that come from repeated sampling from a population. The set of conditions under which the selection is performed and which assures the consistency of the selection process is called the "random sampling experiment".

Two distinguishing features common to all random sampling experiments are:

1. repetitions of the random sampling experiment do not always lead to the same result; and,

2. in any repetition, there is always uncertainty as to which of the possible outcomes will occur.

Example 5.2A. **Dice Rolling Experiment**

Rolling an ordinary six-sided die (singular of dice) is one example of a random sampling experiment.
1. Repetitions of the die roll lead to varying results: sometimes a one appears on the face of the die, sometimes a six, etc.

2. Before any roll, there is uncertainty as to which face will show after the roll.

In essence, all random sampling experiments exhibit both variation of outcomes and uncertainty about which possible outcome will be realized. The second condition is particularly important when considering sequences of random sampling experiments (see Example 5.2B).

Mutually Exclusive and Exhaustive Outcomes

Before it is conducted, every random sampling experiment must have two or more possible outcomes which are both *mutually exclusive* and *exhaustive*. Mutually exclusive simply means that the realization of any one of the possibilities precludes the realization of any others. Exhaustive means that one of the possible outcomes must be realized. Together, the two requirements of mutually exclusive and exhaustive outcomes guarantee that one and only one of the possible outcomes will be realized.

Example 5.2B. **Coin Tossing Experiment**

In a random sampling experiment of tossing an ordinary quarter, the two possible outcomes are "heads" and "tails". Since heads and tails cannot occur simultaneously on the same toss, these outcomes are mutually exclusive. That is, the appearance of one outcome on a toss excludes the appearance of the other. Also, since at each coin toss either heads or tails must result, heads and tails are collectively exhaustive outcomes.

What is Meant by the Probability of an Outcome?

Each possible outcome of a random sampling experiment can be assigned a probability—a number which indicates its likelihood of occurring. Probabilities are always assigned on a scale from zero to one, where zero stands for no chance at all and one stands for complete certainty.

Example 5.2C.   **Probability as a Measure of the Likelihood of an Outcome**

From an urn containing twenty red balls and eighty white balls, ten balls are randomly drawn. The drawn ball is always replaced before the next draw. Thus for this experiment, the ten draws constitute one repetition of the experiment. The number of red balls could range anywhere from zero to ten—eleven possibilities in all. Each of these eleven possibilities will be assigned a corresponding probability value. What are the implications of the probability values assessed? For example, what are the implications of saying that the "probability" of obtaining two red balls in ten draws is .3020 and the "probability" of obtaining five red balls in ten draws is .0264? (In Chapter Eight we show a simple way to calculate these probabilities.) Two implications are:

  1. we cannot be certain as to exactly how many of the selected balls will be red until the experiment is completed;

  2. recognizing that there are degrees of uncertainty, it is appropriate to say that the outcome "two red balls" is more likely to occur than the outcome "five red balls," because .3020 is greater than .0264. Moreover, with probability values measured on a ratio scale, it is also correct to say that the occurrence of five red balls is only 264/3020 as likely as two red balls (the ratio of the two probabilities).

5.3. Applying Knowledge of Probability Concepts to Business Problems

The desire to know the relative predictability of outcomes for casino games led gamblers to use convenient artifices, such as drawing balls from an urn. By studying the results, they learned the usable underlying outcome patterns and how to rely on them. Business executives today have a similar concern. They want to know the predictability of outcomes of real business situations. So the business executive may also find it useful to do as the gamblers did. The merits of using the balls and urn device can be seen in the following example.

Example 5.3.   **Life Insurance**

In the life insurance business, historical actuarial tables indicate what proportion of people of a given age class and in normal health will die in a year's time. The age category can be viewed as the urn, the proportion of people in the category who die can be likened to the proportion of red balls in the urn, and the company's policy-holders can be considered as a random sample from the given age class. Then just as one can use probability theory to figure out the probability of drawing a given number of red balls with the urn sample, the company can figure out the probability that it will have to pay out death benefits on a given number of the policies held by its insurees.

By investigating the pattern that uncertainty produces in random sampling experiments (for example, balls and urn), we are in effect gaining insight into and coming to grips with the nature of business decision-making in reality—a reality which includes uncertainty arising from the incompleteness of information about future events and the inability of decision-makers to predict future events perfectly. What does this process of learning about predictability start with? The process of learning about predictability under uncertainty requires: (1) knowledge about the yardstick that gauges predictability under uncertainty—probability; and (2) a method of specifying outcomes to which probabilities can be assigned. The way of making these appropriate specifications follows directly from understanding the principles of set theory.

5.4. Sets, Elements, and Sample Spaces

A set is a well-defined collection of distinct objects of any sort. The collection could be the corporate officers of Eastman Kodak, stock prices on the New York Stock Exchange at the end of the year, or any other group of people or numbers of interest. If the frame of reference is a random sampling experiment, a well-defined collection is the possible outcomes (or simply "outcomes") of the random sampling experiment.

What does it mean to say that the collection of objects is well-defined? A set is well-defined if an unequivocal "yes" or "no" answer can be given to the question: does the distinct object under consideration belong to the set?

The phrase "distinct object" means the objects in the collection have unique features that cannot overlap with other features listed. For example, a "head" is a distinguishable feature from a "tail" on a coin. But the feature "student" is not distinctly different from the feature "football player," since some persons might be both a football player and a student.

The individual objects that collectively make up a set are called its *elements.* Each element is said to belong to, be a member of, or be contained in the set. It is common in set notation to use a lower case letter "*e*" for an element and a capital letter "*A*" for a set. The expression $e \in A$ is the symbolic abbreviation for "*e* is an element of the set *A*."

How Is a Set Specified?

A set is specified in either of two ways:

 1. by listing its elements in brackets, or

2. by enclosing a defining property of the elements in brackets.

As an example of the first approach, a set *A* consisting of the two brands Budweiser and Coors could be specified by:

A = [Budweiser, Coors].

For the second approach, a set *B* consisting of all million dollar corporate customers could be specified by:

B = [x | x = million dollar corporate customers].

The quantity in brackets is read "x such that x is million dollar corporate customers."

Equality of Sets

Two sets are said to be equal if and only if both contain exactly the same elements. For example, let us define sets *A* and *B* as

A = [Big Mac, Whopper, Super Chef].
B = [Super Chef, Whopper, Big Mac].

These two sets contain exactly the same elements and are therefore equal, even though the elements are listed in different order.

Sets and Random Sampling Experiments

Sets can be defined from the possible outcomes of a random sampling experiment. For example, consider defining a set from the experiment of rolling a die once. The elements of the set could be defined as the numbers appearing on the top face, one through six. The two-stage experiment of rolling the die twice expands the possible outcomes that can be used as elements of a set. The set of elements which describes the complete list of possible outcomes of a random sampling experiment is referred to as the *sample space* of the experiment. The sample space in such a case is properly defined when:

1. each of the elements of the sample space denotes a possible outcome of the experiment, and

2. the observed outcome of the performance of the experiment is one and only one element of the sample space.

Since the outcomes of a random sampling experiment are mutually exclusive and collectively exhaustive, the elements of the sample space for the random sampling experiment must likewise be mutually exclusive and collectively exhaustive. We shall use *S* as the mathematical symbol for sample space.[1]

Different Sample Spaces for the Same Experiment

It should not be assumed that only one sample space of elements can be defined for a given random sampling experiment. Consider a one trial random sampling experiment in which a single account is drawn from the accounts receivable ledger of a firm. There are numerous ways to define the elements so that they would collectively be a sample space. One sample space could be stated as:

S = [Account current, Account overdue].

An alternative sample space for the experiment could be

S = [Account current, Account 30 days overdue, Account 40 days overdue, Account 50 days overdue, Account 60 days overdue].

With both satisfying the definition of a sample space, what guidelines determine which one to use? The needs of the actual business decision suggest the amount of detail wanted. Generally, however, it can be said that the more useful information provided by the sample space the greater flexibility one has for the investigation at hand. This guideline should be followed in the absence of compelling reasons to the contrary. Accordingly, the second sample space is the preferred one to use.

5.5. Subsets and Events

Probability discussions often focus on features of particular interest. Consider a common business problem.

Example 5.5A. Uncollectible Accounts Receivable

Consider a CPA's role in auditing a firm to assess its financial position. The CPA's interest in the accounts receivable of the firm generally lie with the long overdue accounts since a portion of them become uncollectible. After a stratification of the accounts receivable by age ("aging the accounts"), a random sampling experiment is conducted on the overdue accounts to detect the subset of uncollectibles.

Subsets

A collection of some of the elements in the sample space is called a subset of the sample space. Each of the elements of the subset must be an element of the sample space. Thus, if the sample space for the number of dots on the upper face for one roll of a six-sided die is defined as

S = [1, 2, 3, 4, 5, 6]

then the set

A = [1, 2, 3]

is a legitimate subset of this sample space. Since every element of A is also an element of the sample space S, one can write

A ⊂ S

that is, the set A is contained in S.

Events

The subsets used in conjunction with probability theory are given the special term, *events*. Different collections of the different possible outcomes of a random sampling experiment to which probability can be assigned qualify as events. The subset *A* defined in the previous paragraph is also event *A* because all of its elements are possible outcomes of a random sampling experiment.

Once an event is defined and one of its elements turns out to be the actual outcome of the random sampling experiment, the event is said to occur. For example, if the roll of the die in the experiment yields a three, then the event *A* defined as

$$A = [1, 2, 3]$$

is said to have occurred. Is event *A* the only event to have occurred? Not necessarily. If there are other events having three as one of their elements, they have also occurred. For example, the event "value greater than one" has also occurred. Notice, though, that the occurrence of one of the possible outcomes of an event mutually excludes the occurrence of the other possible outcomes.

Events Can Occur—Subsets Cannot

Since every event is also a subset, is the concept of an event necessary? Why not just stick with subset? The answer is that an event can "occur" but, literally speaking, a subset cannot be said either to "occur" or to "not occur". It is just a collection of elements. It need not define a collection of elements to which a probability can be assigned.

Grouping Outcomes into Events

The outcomes of random sampling experiments should be grouped into events so that their occurrence or nonoccurrence will provide significant information for management decision-making. In fact, the first step in formulating a decision is to decide which of the different possible outcomes dictate different plans of action. The following example illustrates how this might be done.

Example 5.5B. Diesel Engine Lemons

Consider a random sampling experiment of drawing a sample of four diesels from the population of all diesels. In this experiment, the characteristic of interest is the number of "lemons" in the sample. Assume that our decision-making scheme is as follows: if two or more of the diesels in the sample turn out to be lemons, then we definitely would not buy a diesel; if one lemon appears we would investigate further; if no lemons are found, a diesel will be purchased.

5.6. Elementary Events, Composite Events, and the Sample Space

An *elementary event* is an event which contains only one of the possible outcomes. Thus, there is one elementary event corresponding to each of the different possible outcomes of the random sampling experiment and there are as many elementary events as there are possible outcomes. We shall use a subscripted E to designate an elementary event.

Example 5.6A.   Possible Outcomes and Elementary Events for a Dice Experiment

Rolling a die twice is a random sampling experiment with two identical representative trials. On each of these trials, any one of the six faces of the die can be the actual result. So the experiment leads to an ordered pair of faces, of which there are thirty-six possibilities. Each of these is a possible outcome. Thus, there are thirty-six possible outcomes, which are:[2]

(1,1)	(2,1)	(3,1)	(4,1)	(5,1)	(6,1)
(1,2)	(2,2)	(3,2)	(4,2)	(5,2)	(6,2)
(1,3)	(2,3)	(3,3)	(4,3)	(5,3)	(6,3)
(1,4)	(2,4)	(3,4)	(4,4)	(5,4)	(6,4)
(1,5)	(2,5)	(3,5)	(4,5)	(5,5)	(6,5)
(1,6)	(2,6)	(3,6)	(4,6)	(5,6)	(6,6)

Each possible outcome constitutes one element of the sample space. Corresponding to each outcome is an elementary event having that outcome as its only element. By letting capital E and an identifying subscript represent the elementary events, we can list the thirty-six events E_1 to E_{36} corresponding to the thirty-six outcomes.

$$E_1 = [(1,1)]$$
$$E_2 = [(1,2)]$$
$$E_3 = [(1,3)]$$
$$\vdots$$
$$E_{35} = [(6,5)]$$
$$E_{36} = [(6,6)]$$

A *composite event* is one which contains more than one possible outcome. For example, $[(1,1),(1,2)]$ is a composite event in the dice rolling experiment. We shall use a subscripted A to designate a composite event.

The sample space of the random sampling experiment, S, is referred to as a *certain* event because it includes all the possible outcomes and therefore each elementary event. When the random sampling experiment is performed, one of the elementary events it includes *must occur.*

Example 5.6B. Certain Event and Elementary Events for the Experiment of Rolling One Die

In a one trial die rolling experiment the sample space would be:

$S = [1, 2, 3, 4, 5, 6]$ where $E_1 = [1]$, $E_2 = [2]$ etc.

The sample space S is a certain event since one of its elementary events (outcomes) must occur when a die is rolled.

Example 5.6C. Certain Event and Elementary Events for the Experiment of Tossing Coins Twice

Consider a coin tossing experiment of two trials. One can define four events E_1 to E_4 that would represent the four elementary events. Each elementary event has only one of the four possible outcomes of the experiment.

$E_1 = [(h\ h)]$: heads on both tosses
$E_2 = [(h\ t)]$: heads on the first toss of the coin, tails on the second toss of the coin
$E_3 = [(t\ h)]$: tails on the first toss of the coin, heads on the second toss of the coin
$E_4 = [(t\ t)]$: tails on both tosses

Again, the certain event is the sample space with all four of the outcomes representing all four elementary events.

$S = [(h\ h), (h\ t), (t\ h), (t\ t)]$ where $E_1 = [(h\ h)]$, $E_2 = [(h\ t)]$, etc.

Null Event

The event containing no elementary events at all is called the *null* event. It is designated by the symbol $\emptyset$.

Example 5.6D. Null Event for the Die Rolling Experiment

The null event for the die rolling experiment is:

$\emptyset = [\qquad\qquad]$.

Since *one* of the outcomes of an experiment *must* occur, and since the null event occurs only if *none* of the outcomes do occur, the null event cannot actually occur. For this reason, it is sometimes referred to as the *impossible* event.

5.7. Probability Rules

Probability rules are devised to insure consistency in our thinking about uncertainty. They provide uniformity in assigning probabilities to events and facilitate the use of the known probabilities of some events to calculate the initially unknown probabilities of related events.

The probability assigned to any event A, denoted by $P(A)$, must satisfy three basic rules:

Rule 1: Every event must be assigned a non-negative number less than or equal to one.

Rule 2: The sample space (the certain event, designated by S) must be assigned a probability of exactly one.

Rule 3: If $E_1, E_2, \ldots E_k$ are the elementary events which represent the individual outcomes included in event A, then $P(A) = P(E_1) + P(E_2) \ldots + P(E_k)$.

Rule 3 is very important because it implies that knowledge of the probabilities assigned to all the elementary events is sufficient to determine the probability of any formulated event. For example, if we know the probabilities of the six elementary events for a die toss, we can compute the probability of evens.

The rules for making probability assignments fall into two categories. Some of the rules place restrictions on the choice of probability values which can be assigned to an event. Rules 1 and 2 are of this kind. Other rules indicate how the unknown probability of one event can be ascertained from the known probabilities of related events. Rule 3 is in this category.

The Role of Rules

The role of rules is frequently misunderstood. Probability rules are similar to traffic rules. Traffic rules limit a motorist's freedom to select the route, speed, and lanes which are permissible in traveling to a destination, but they do not choose the destination for the motorist. Probability rules set out the ground rules for assigning and calculating probabilities. Except in the case of the null event and the certain event, though, the rules do not dictate exactly which acceptable number should be assigned to an event. Thus, assigning the probability value is still up to us. Legitimately, therefore, different sets of probabilities can be assigned.

Tossing a coin once is a familiar random sampling experiment in which four events can be defined from the two possible outcomes: heads and tails. The events can be described as "either heads or tails," "heads but not tails," "tails but not heads," and "neither heads nor tails." The latter event is the null event, $\emptyset$. The certain event (heads *or* tails) is the sample space S; Rule 2 tells us its probability must be the value one. The assigned probabilities to the other events must be non-negative (Rule 1); also, since $P(S) = 1$ (by Rule 2) and since there are only two elementary events in the sample space, S, then the sum of their probabilities must equal one (Rule 3). That is,

$$P(h) + P(t) = P(S) = 1.$$

There are many equally valid probability assignments for the possible events of this experiment, as Table 5.1 shows.

TABLE 5.1. Probability Assignments for Coin Experiment

Event A	Comment	ONE SET OF LEGITIMATE PROBABILITY ASSIGNMENTS $P(A)$	EQUALLY LEGITIMATE SET OF PROBABILITY ASSIGNMENTS $P(A)$
(Either heads or tails)	sample space S	1.0	1.0
(Heads but not tails)	one of two elementary events	0.5	0.85
(Tails but not heads)	the other elementary event	0.5	0.15
(Neither heads nor tails)	the null event, $\emptyset$	0	0

Note that neither of these probability assignments violate any of the probability rules. Hence, they are both legitimate assignments.

Given that different probability assignments can legitimately be made for the same group of possible events, is there a procedure which *should* be used to tackle probabilities? Unfortunately, there is not one assignment procedure, but three.

5.8. How Are Probabilities Assigned to Events?

People who have found probability theory useful employ three procedures for assigning probabilities to events:

1. *Equiprobable Elementary Events Procedure: Assign to each elementary event a probability equal to one divided by the number of elementary events.* This procedure treats all elementary events as equally likely. For example, if there are eight elementary events, each would be assigned a probability of one divided by eight, or .125.

2. *Relative Frequency Procedure: Use relative frequencies from numerous past repetitions* of the same or similar random sampling experiments as probabilities for the present experiment. For example, if 52 percent of the babies born in the past decade have been boys, use .52 as the probability of a boy on the next birth.

3. *Subjective Probability Procedure: Quantify personal judgment about the relative likelihood of different events.* This is accomplished by estab-

lishing personal "betting odds" for each event based upon both objective and subjective information pertaining to the event. For example, if all things considered your personal betting odds on a forthcoming heavyweight championship fight are three to one in favor of the current champion retaining his title, assign a probability of .75 to this event.

The three assignment procedures are not equally appropriate under all circumstances. For instance, the first two procedures cannot be used in new and unique situations in which unequal probability assessments are desired. An example is assessing the probability of heads on a bent coin which has never been tossed. Experience does indicate that one of the three procedures proves particularly useful in certain cases.

Assigning equal probability to each elementary event is an appropriate common practice when the sampling procedure employs a method of random selection. This gives each and every member of a population an "equal chance" of being included in the sample from that population. Consider the calculation of the probability of obtaining three Democrats in a *sample of five voters* randomly drawn from a list of twenty voters. It would be appropriate in this case to assign equal probability to each of the 15,504 possible sample results. We will discuss how to calculate this figure in Section 5.12.

Subjective judgment, on the other hand, tends to be called on for probability assignment when the stakes are large and relevant historical evidence is too sparse or too hard to come by. For instance, in deciding whether to market an innovative product, a young firm might not be able to devote a substantial portion of its organizational resources to obtain market evidence on whether the new product will be well received. Instead, the firm might make a decision on the basis of subjective probability judgment developed from interpreting rather limited marketing and sales evidence.

A problem sometimes encountered in assessing probabilities is that it may not be immediately apparent what the elementary events are. The tree diagram approach discussed in the next section can be very helpful in dealing with this problem.

5.9. Tree Diagrams for Elementary Events

Elementary events can be successfully used as building blocks in making probability calculations. Knowing their probabilities, one can derive the probability of any event defined in terms of the elementary events. How many elementary events are there in a particular sample space? What are they? This will depend on how many characteristics (variables) are observed, and how many possible variations there are (attributes or variates) for each characteristic. The more characteristics to be observed and the more variations that are possible for each characteristic, the more elementary events there will be.

A device known as a *tree diagram* is very helpful in determining how many elementary events there are and what collections of characteristics they represent. A tree diagram is a pictorial way of tracing a multi-stage selection of the characteristics which define the possible outcomes. Figure 5.1 shows a three-stage tree diagram, one stage for each characteristic to be observed in the outcomes of the experiment. After explaining this diagram, we shall consider an example of how tree diagrams can be used to determine the number and the precise composition of the elementary events.

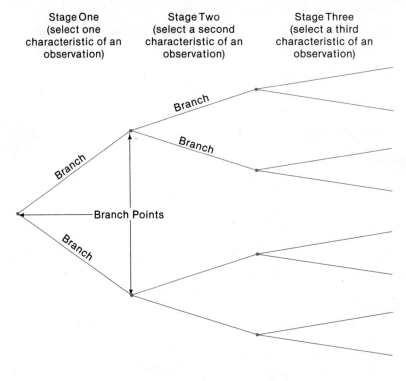

Stage One
(select one
characteristic of an
observation)

Stage Two
(select a second
characteristic of an
observation)

Stage Three
(select a third
characteristic of an
observation)

Branch

Branch

Branch

Branch Points

Branch

FIGURE 5.1 Three Stage Tree Diagram for Selecting Characteristics of a
Trivariate Observation

By reading from left to right, the tree diagram portrays the anatomy of the successive stages of the selection process. At each stage there is one or more branch points. Exiting from each branch point towards the right are the branches. The branches show the possible choices at that stage of the selection process. Tracing a single path through the branches from left to right indicates the particular choices taken over the various stages of the selection process. Each complete branch path results in a possible outcome; the complete paths in total define all the possible outcomes. Only one path is taken and only one outcome will actually materialize in the actual performance of the experiment. The following example illustrates how a tree diagram might be used in determining the possible outcomes and elementary events for a sample space.

Example 5.9. Elementary Events for Survey Sampling

A department store wants to find out whether a customer service problem exists at the lingerie department. Two "professional" customers are hired to purchase

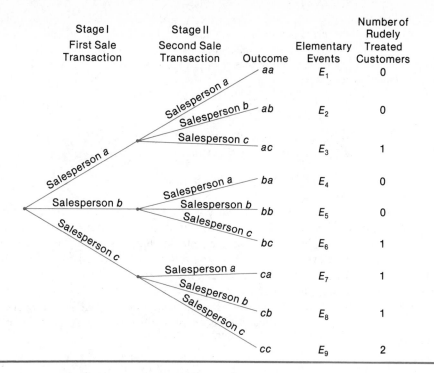

Stage I First Sale Transaction	Stage II Second Sale Transaction	Outcome	Elementary Events	Number of Rudely Treated Customers
	Salesperson a	aa	E_1	0
	Salesperson b	ab	E_2	0
	Salesperson c	ac	E_3	1
Salesperson a	Salesperson a	ba	E_4	0
Salesperson b	Salesperson b	bb	E_5	0
Salesperson c	Salesperson c	bc	E_6	1
	Salesperson a	ca	E_7	1
	Salesperson b	cb	E_8	1
	Salesperson c	cc	E_9	2

FIGURE 5.2 Tree Diagram Showing Elementary Events for Customer Service Sample
Space

lingerie and secretly note the salesperson's service. Any problems encountered are
reported to management. Independently, the two professional customers each
randomly choose one of the three salespersons. This process can be viewed as a
sample survey based upon a simple random sample of size two drawn with replacement from a population of three salespersons.

For the salespersons who served the two professional customers, what are the
possible outcomes (ordered salesperson pairs) of the sample? The two stage tree
diagram given in Figure 5.2 provides the answer. The characteristic (salesperson)
identified with the first sales transaction represents one stage of the tree diagram.
The characteristic (salesperson) identified with the second transaction represents
the other stage of the tree diagram. The salesperson alternatives are the exiting
branches from each branch point.

How many elementary event paths are there for this two-stage selection process? The tree diagram shows that regardless of which salesperson serves the customer at the first stage transaction, there are three salesperson possibilities at the
second stage transaction. This is indicated by three branches exiting each of the
three branching points at the second stage. The end result of this assumption is
nine complete two stage paths. What do the paths show?

Each path yields as an end product a different ordered salesperson pair. For
example, one unique ordered pair would be:

salesperson a servicing customer transaction one, and
salesperson c servicing customer transaction two.

Each ordered pair shows the anatomy of a possible outcome. Collectively the outcomes represent the sample space and the elements of the certain event. By count-

ing these outcomes one can find out how many elementary events there are. With the assumption that the elementary events are equiprobable, one can calculate the probability of events defined in terms of the elementary events. The procedure described in the following section shows how to take advantage of the tree diagrams in probability calculations.

5.10. Probability Calculations in Simple Random Sampling: An Application of the Equiprobable Elementary Events Procedure

In this and some of the following sections the three procedures for assigning probabilities to elementary events are illustrated in the context of typical situations where they might apply. The example in this section applies the equiprobable elementary events approach. In the following section historical relative frequencies are used. In Section 5.15 an example is given of the use of subjective probabilities by a large New York bank.

The type of probability question that comes from random sampling some population of interest can be illustrated by carrying the customer service example a bit further.

Example 5.10. **Monitoring Sales Service: Some Calculations**

Suppose Mrs. c in the previous example (a salesperson employed in the lingerie department) is always rude to customers. On the other hand, Mr. a and Mrs. b are always courteous to customers. Assume salesperson's compensation is straight salary. It is plausible to believe that each of the nine salesperson pairs can occur with equal chance. What then is the probability of the event: "neither of the ("professional") customers is rudely treated?" With each elementary event (salesperson pair) equally probable, the answer can be obtained by an appropriate reading of the tree diagram shown in Figure 5.2. Before proceeding, let's record your intuitive feeling as to the answer.

_____ (Your intuitive answer)

Step I:
The first step of the probability calculation procedure is to determine the number of elementary events associated with this sample space. This is easily accomplished by counting the number of complete branch paths that result in outcomes in the tree diagram. The result is nine.

Step II:
Next, the probability of each equiprobable elementary event is found by dividing into one the number of elementary events. The result in this case is one-ninth and represents the probability of each particular ordered pair of salespersons serving the two customers.

Step III:

The third step requires determining how many possible outcomes at the end of the branches possess the attribute under consideration. The outcomes possessing the attribute "no customer is rudely treated" are (*aa*), (*ab*), (*ba*), and (*bb*). The corresponding elementary events are E_1, E_2, E_4, and E_5.

Step IV:

The last step, finding the probability of the event in question, combines the results of the first three steps. The one-ninth probability of each elementary event from step two is multiplied by four, the number of elementary events found in step three in which no customer is rudely treated. The four-ninths result is the correct probability of the event "no customer is rudely treated." Did your intuition lead you to the correct answer?

The probabilities for the different possible numbers of rudely treated customers are in Table 5.2.

TABLE 5.2. Probabilities for Rudely Treated Customers

EVENT, NUMBER OF RUDELY TREATED CUSTOMERS	OUTCOMES INCLUDED	ELEMENTARY EVENTS	PROBABILITY
0	(aa),(ab),(ba),(bb)	E_1,E_2,E_4,E_5	4/9
1	(ac),(bc),(ca),(cb)	E_3,E_6,E_7,E_8	4/9
2	(cc)	E_9	1/9

In summary, the four steps are:

1. Determine the number of elementary events, bearing in mind that each elementary event represents a different sample outcome.

2. Assign to each elementary event a probability equal to one divided by the total number of elementary events.

3. Determine how many of the outcomes possess the attribute or characteristic in question. This determines the number of elementary events which represent outcomes contained in the event for which the probability is sought.

4. Find the product of the second and third step. This is the probability of the event in question.

Under what conditions do these four steps lead to the correct probability calculations? Under simple random sampling, the possible sample outcomes will all be equiprobable elementary events and in conformity with the assumption that is made in carrying out step two. What guarantees equiprobable elementary events? The equiprobable feature follows when at each draw all the population members available have an equal chance of actually being drawn. There are two versions of simple random sampling:

1. *Sampling With Replacement:* After each draw, the selected item is replaced before the next sample item is drawn. Each draw can then be viewed as coming from the complete original population.

2. *Sampling Without Replacement:* Once drawn, the item is not replaced in the population and cannot, therefore, be drawn more than once. The draws can be viewed as coming from a changing population but on each draw all of the items in the available population have an equal chance of being drawn.

Probability questions for either type of simple random sample can be answered by following this four-step procedure.

Educated Intuition

An important lesson is often shown by this simple example. The lesson concerns the reliability of your intuition. Is the intuitive approach to probability assessment as reliable as the calculated approach to probability assessment? Your intuition usually falters when asked for such answers. In fact, many people have no intuition at all as to the correct answer. Others are wrongly led by their intuition and answer $\frac{1}{9}$, $\frac{1}{3}$, or $\frac{2}{3}$. Surely they need the help of an analytical approach to problem solving. But even if your intuition did lead you to the correct answer, $\frac{4}{9}$, this particular problem is relatively simple. In more complex and more realistic situations involving stock market movements, quality control, new product decisions, and insurance risk analysis, one cannot be expected to rely on intuition. The point is this: in modern business, where important assessments are made every day, business people should not rely solely on raw intuition; appropriate statistical procedures which check and aid intuition should be employed.

5.11. Probability Calculations When Elementary Events Have Unequal Probabilities

In the previous section, the purpose of the tree diagram was simply to find out how many equiprobable elementary events there were (Figure 5.2). What if probability is assigned on a subjective or a relative frequency basis, in which case equally likely events should not be expected? Determining event probabilities is then no longer simply a matter of following the four-step procedure described in Section 5.10. Nevertheless, it still holds true that the sum of the probabilities of the elementary events which represent outcomes included in an event defines the probability of the event. However, sometimes it is not obvious what the elementary events are. In this case, just as with equiprobable elementary events, a tree diagram can be used to portray graphically the outcomes and elementary events. The tree diagram may also reveal more clearly which of the possible outcomes are included in the composite event for which a probability value is sought. In the following example a tree diagram shows the possible outcomes; probabilities for the elementary events corresponding to these outcomes are assigned on the basis of historical relative frequencies. These probabilities are then used to determine the probabilities for the composite events of interest.

Example 5.11. Event Probabilities When Elementary Events Are Not Equiprobable: Automobile Insurance

An automobile insurance company classifies applicants for automobile insurance according to criteria on which accident risk is thought to depend. It is typical for a company to keep track of the incidence of accidents and of various types of claims for the different risk categories. The risk categories are defined in terms of policy-holder characteristics such as age, marital status, geographic location, etc. For example, one risk category might be married women over age 35 living in rural areas. Suppose records are kept on the status of each policyholder in this risk category for three characteristics:

1. whether or not the person was involved in an accident during the last year;
2. whether or not the person filed a liability claim during the last year;
3. whether or not the person filed a collision claim during the last year.

For this specific risk category, consider the number and type of cross-classifications: accident status, collision-claim status, and liability-claim status. What are the historical relative frequencies for policyholders in the specific risk category with respect to different cross-classifications? If policyholders in this risk category are considered indistinguishable with regard to accident and claim proneness, the historical relative frequency questions become the key factor in the insurance company's deliberation on how much to charge such customers. In other words, these cross-classifications permit the insurance company to define the possible outcomes of next year's insurance history for the individuals in this group. Insurance premiums are determined with the relative frequencies of the outcomes as estimates of the probabilities of the elementary events corresponding to these outcomes. Thus the "risk profile" applicable to a married woman over age 35 from a rural area who applies for insurance would describe the set of elementary events and their probabilities assessed from the relative frequencies.

The three stage tree diagram shown in Figure 5.3 illustrates the possible outcomes and their corresponding elementary events, E_1 through E_8. Each path through the diagram sketches the individual attribute composition of a particular outcome. Collectively the set of outcomes define the sample space and show the different attribute combination paths possible. At the end of each year, the individual married woman policyholder over age 35 who lives in a rural area will have proceeded through a path and possess the combination of attribute characteristics for a particular outcome. That is, readings of accident status, liability claim status, and collision claim status together determine the outcome. The elementary event corresponding to that outcome will then have "occurred".

The three stage tree diagram assembles the possible outcomes and their individual attribute composition as shown in Figure 5.3. Each outcome is represented by one of the elementary events E_1 through E_8.

Suppose that company records of married women over age 35 living in rural areas show the following relative frequencies for the elementary events for a one year period:

E_1: involved in accident leading to both liability and collision claims   .025
E_2: involved in accident leading to a collision claim only   .015
E_3: involved in accident leading to a liability claim only   .005

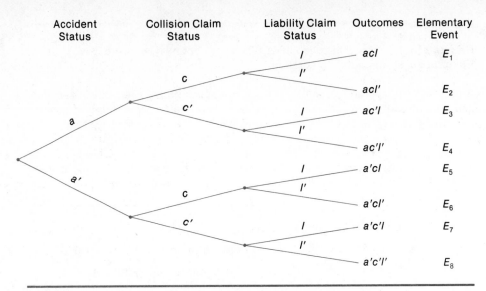

Accident Status	Collision Claim Status	Liability Claim Status	Outcomes	Elementary Event
		l	acl	E_1
	c	l'		
			acl'	E_2
	c'	l	$ac'l$	E_3
a		l'		
			$ac'l'$	E_4
		l	$a'cl$	E_5
	c	l'		
a'			$a'cl'$	E_6
	c'	l	$a'c'l$	E_7
		l'		
			$a'c'l'$	E_8

FIGURE 5.3 Tree Diagram of Automobile Company Risk Profiles

E_4: involved in accident but no claims against the company	.035
E_5, E_6, E_7: claim(s) without an accident	.000
E_8: not involved in any accident	.920

Note that only five of the eight elementary events are relevant: E_1, E_2, E_3, E_4, E_8. Elementary events E_5, E_6, E_7 cannot be on the company's record since they cannot occur. Therefore they have a zero relative frequency.

Let us assume that these historical relative frequencies are the appropriate elementary event probabilities for the next married female applicant over the age of 35 living in a rural area. Using probability rule three (the probability of any event is the sum of the elementary event probabilities for the elements it contains), is it possible to calculate any other claim or accident probability of interest for the coming year? For example, what is the probability that during the next year the applicant will be involved in:

  a. a liability claim accident?
  b. a collision claim accident?
  c. an accident with a claim against the insurer?
  d. an accident?

From the outcomes represented by the five elementary events which have non-zero probability, composite events of the elementary events can be formed. Included among these are the four events specified. Their probabilities are computed as follows:

Solution to a:

$$P(\text{a liability claim accident}) = P[(acl),(ac'l)]$$
$$= P(E_1) + P(E_3)$$
$$= .025 + .005 = .030.$$

Solution to b:

$$P(\text{a collision claim accident}) = P[(acl),(acl')]$$
$$= P(E_1) + P(E_2)$$
$$= .025 + .015 = .040.$$

Solution to c:

$$P(\text{accident with claim against the company}) = P[(acl),(acl'),(ac'l)]$$
$$= P(E_1) + P(E_2) + P(E_3)$$
$$= .025 + .015 + .005 = .045.$$

Solution to d:

$$P(\text{an accident}) = P[(acl),(acl'),(ac'l),(ac'l')]$$
$$= P(E_1) + P(E_2) + P(E_3) + P(E_4)$$
$$= .025 + .015 + .005 + .035 = .080.$$

In the probability calculations shown, it should not be overlooked that a defined event must include all the outcomes where the event occurs. No concern should arise about other events also occurring with the appearance of these outcomes. For instance, the outcome represented by elementary event E_1 is included in the event "liability claim accident" even though this outcome's appearance also means the occurrence of a collision claim.

Outcome Grid

When the experiment involves recordings on two or three characteristics (that is, bivariate or trivariate observations), a graphic device which we shall call an *outcome grid* can be constructed to better visualize the relationship between characteristics and possible outcomes. The outcome grid is a Venn diagram in which the attributes or categories of each characteristic (variable) are shown on a different dimension of the diagram. Each square or block (depending on whether there are two or three dimensions) represents one of the possible outcomes. The composition of the possible outcomes describes the attributes present and absent and occupies a particular position in the grid. Figure 5.4 shows an outcome grid for the insurance example.

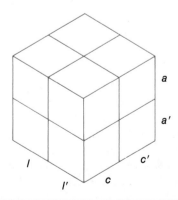

FIGURE 5.4 Outcome Grid of the Risk Profile of a Holder of Automobile Insurance

This section and the last have used tree diagrams to decompose possible outcomes into combinations of attributes. Some of the outcomes have the attribute we seek. The probabilities of the corresponding elementary events provide "building blocks" and are summed to determine the probability of obtaining the specified attribute. Although this basic approach is similar in both sections, there is a difference in the calculation of the elementary event probabilities. In this section we took advantage of historical relative frequencies of claim and accident reports among policyholders in the particular risk category studied. On the other hand, in the previous section we saw that the process of finding the probability of various events in simple random sampling requires equiprobable possible outcomes or elementary events.

In the next section our attention returns to equiprobable events. We shall describe a shortcut rule for counting the number of possible outcomes, a prerequisite to learning how much probability should be assigned to each outcome.

5.12. The Fundamental Principles of Counting

Tree diagrams have provided a basic procedure for counting the possible sample outcomes in random sampling. For very small samples, tree diagrams are an ideal way to show the possible sample outcomes; but, for moderate and large size samples, the procedure becomes too unwieldy. The necessity of time-saving counting rules for determining the number of tree diagram branches for a modest size random sample becomes clear when it is realized that a sample involving only six draws (with replacement) from a population of ten items would require a tree diagram with a million branches! In Chapter Six we shall describe a procedure that can often be used that doesn't involve so many branches. Presently, however, we need a rule for counting the branches.

The Number of Branches of a Tree Diagram

The grandfather of all counting shortcuts is the fundamental principle of counting:

> In order to count the number of branches that span an n-stage tree diagram, simply multiply together the number of choices (V_i) available at each and every stage; that is, $V_{\text{total}} = (V_1)(V_2)(V_3) \ldots (V_n)$.

A simple example will show how it works.

Consider a three-stage tree diagram (Figure 5.5). Stage one has three branches at its only branching point, stage two has four branches at each of its three branching points, and stage three has two branches exiting from each of its branching points. The number of branches leaving the branching points indicate the number of alternative choices available at that point.

Counting the branches at the last stage gives the total number of alternative n-stage branches. In this case there were 24 branches. The key point of the fundamental principle is that the correct count of branches that span the n-stages

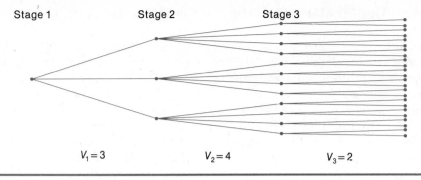

$V_1 = 3$ $V_2 = 4$ $V_3 = 2$

FIGURE 5.5 Three Stage Tree Diagram with 24 Branches

can be obtained without counting the branches one by one and without even drawing the tree diagram.

Applying the fundamental principle,

$$V = (V_{i=1})(V_{i=2})(V_{i=3})$$

$$= \begin{pmatrix} \text{Number of} \\ \text{branches at first} \\ \text{stage, for each} \\ \text{branching point} \end{pmatrix} \begin{pmatrix} \text{Number of} \\ \text{branches at sec-} \\ \text{ond stage, for} \\ \text{each branching} \\ \text{point} \end{pmatrix} \begin{pmatrix} \text{Number of} \\ \text{branches at third} \\ \text{stage, for each} \\ \text{branching point} \end{pmatrix}$$

$$= (3)(4)(2)$$
$$= 24 \ branches$$

The Number of Elementary Events in Sampling With Replacement

The fundamental principle of counting greatly simplifies the task of determining the number of elementary events in random sampling. Let each stage in the tree diagram represent a draw from a population of N items: the first stage represents the first draw, the second stage represents the second draw, etc. Sampling with replacement provides that there are N items in the population at all times for each draw and therefore N choices to pick from at every stage (draw). Thus, for a sample of size n,

$$V = (V_1)(V_2) \ . \ . \ . \ (V_n)$$
$$= (N)(N) \ . \ . \ . \ (N)$$
$$V = N^n$$

Applying this simple rule to the customer service monitoring survey in Example 5.10 but extending the sample survey from a sample of two to a sample of ten means ten stages with the same a, b, c salesperson choices at each stage.

$$V = 3^{10}$$
$$= 59{,}049$$

equiprobable elementary events, each of sample size ten with each having one chance in 59,049 of turning up when the survey is conducted.

Caveat: The Fundamental Principle Isn't Always Applicable

It should be noted that the fundamental principle of counting does not apply to a process for which the number of branches coming from each branching point at a given stage is not equal. For example, suppose the first stage of a selection process is to determine the outcome of a coin toss, heads or tails. If the outcome is heads, a second coin is tossed. If the outcome is tails, a die is rolled at the second stage. The fundamental principle doesn't apply because of the different number of branches at the two second stage branching points. There are two branches exiting from the second stage branching point representing the coin toss; there are six branches exiting from the branching point representing the die toss. Fortunately, in simple random sampling the number of choices available at a given draw are the same regardless of which choices are made on previous draws. Hence, the fundamental principle is always applicable to simple random sampling.

5.13. Event Spaces

Is there a way to determine how many different events can be defined from the elements of a given sample space? Knowing that different combinations of outcomes, hence corresponding elementary events, represent different events means that there are exactly as many events as there are combinations. But how many different combinations are there?

The set which contains all the different events (all the combinations of outcomes or elementary events) as elements defines a sample space known as the *event space*. One way to find out how many elements the event space contains is to simply list and count all the possible subsets of outcomes. For example, consider the following sample space for the "Big Three" Automakers:

$S = [\text{GM, Ford, Chrysler}]$.

The elementary events for this sample space are the three different outcomes. Eight different events can be formed from the three outcomes. These are:

[   ] (this is the "null" event)
[GM]
[Ford]
[Chrysler]
[GM, Ford]
[GM, Chrysler]
[Ford, Chrysler]
[GM, Ford, Chrysler] (this is the "certain" event)

The number of possible events is always larger than the number of outcomes or elementary events. As an aid in avoiding omissions when compiling the list of possible events, it is often helpful to utilize the event space tree diagram.

Example 5.13.   Using a Tree Diagram to Show Event Possibilities

As an example of how tree diagrams can be used to show the elements of an event space, we shall again use the sample space of the "Big Three" Automakers,

S = [GM, Ford, Chrysler].

To determine the event possibilities which can be formed from the three elementary events, we set up a three-stage selection process—one stage for each elementary event. At each stage, the choice is whether to include (IN) or exclude (OUT) the elementary event considered at that stage in the event being formed. Figure 5.6 traces the eight different paths leading to the construction of the eight events that would define the event space.

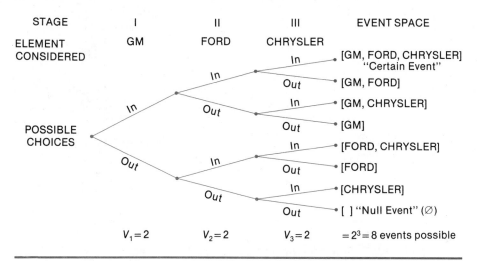

FIGURE 5.6 Tree Diagram Showing Event Space for Three-Element Sample

5.14. How Many Events?

If there are more than a handful of elementary events, the list of possible events gets very long and the counting task becomes onerous. For example, suppose that instead of three elementary events there are twenty. How many elements make up the event space? More than a million elements! Consequently, there is a very strong incentive to learn how to determine the total number of possible events without having to list and count them one by one.

Fortunately, it is not necessary to construct a tree diagram every time we want to determine how many different events can be formed from a given number of elementary events in the sample space. The calculations follow the fundamental principle:

If the number of different elementary events (outcomes of the random experiment) is k, then the number of different events possible (combinations of elementary events) is 2^k.

Figure 5.7 shows this to be a k-stage experiment with each stage's branching point having two branches. This means that each elementary event at that stage has two options—either to be "in" the event being constructed or to be "out" of the event being constructed. For the "Big Three" Automakers example with its three elementary events, there are $2^3 = 8$ events possible as is shown in Figure 5.6. Each branching point, no matter which stage, has two branches suggesting that the number of choices V open for the elementary event is always two.

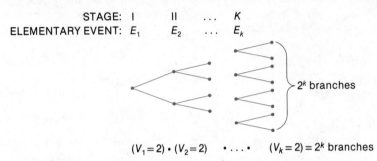

FIGURE 5.7 Applying the Fundamental Principle to Determine the Number of Events in the Event Space

5.15. Subjective Assessment of Probabilities

In the probability examples illustrated to this point, we did not consider the role of personal judgment in assessing probability values. Personal judgment should not be a factor when the equally likely elementary events approach or the relative frequency approach is used. In business, however, personal judgment is often a necessity. An example of probability assessment follows in which the subjective expectations of knowledgeable people carry the day.

Example 5.15. **Subjective Probabilities at the Morgan Bank**

The Morgan Guaranty Trust Company is a large New York City bank. The Sources and Uses Committee of the Morgan was comprised of top ranking executives. The committee met about twice a month to receive information and recommendations concerning basic asset and liability policy decisions. Typical topics considered were the buying and selling of bonds and notes for the firm's investment portfolio, and the quantity and maturity period of CDs (certificates of deposit) to be issued.

At each meeting the committee received information and recommendations on money market developments anticipated by a group of seven financial market specialists who closely monitored changes in market conditions. Considerable discussion among this group of specialists normally preceded their presentation.

Opinions typically differed among the specialists about the likely value of interest rate changes. Yet the discussion always concluded with a single-valued estimate of the future interest rate. Thus, the specialist group might report they expected a 7% prime rate in three months, or a 6% certificate of deposit rate in one month, and so forth, even though the group members all had their individual expectations about the rate. There was no formal procedure for quantifying the collective interest rate expectations of the participants. Nor was there any procedure for describing the uncertainty surrounding the single value reported as the group's expectation.

In the early 1970s, the bank's top management set about introducing an element of quantification for the uncertainty that existed. The procedure employed subjective probabilities. For example, on November 13, 1972, the group of financial market specialists met to express a view as to what the ninety-day CD rate would be on February 7, 1973. Instead of a single-valued interest rate expectation, the meeting led to the subjective probability assignment for the interest rate in Table 5.3.

TABLE 5.3. Subjective Probability Assignment

INTEREST RATE RANGE		PROBABILITY
At least	But less than	
$4\frac{7}{8}$	$5\frac{1}{8}$%	.15
$5\frac{1}{8}$	$5\frac{3}{8}$%	.30
$5\frac{3}{8}$	$5\frac{5}{8}$%	.30
$5\frac{5}{8}$	$5\frac{7}{8}$%	.20
$5\frac{7}{8}$	$6\frac{1}{8}$%	.05

As quoted in an article in the *Harvard Business Review,* here is the interpretation which the group gave to this assignment:[3]

> the [probabilities] group feels that on February 7, 1973 the 90-day CD rate will most likely have a value between $5\frac{1}{8}$% and $5\frac{5}{8}$% with equal likelihood for any rate within that range; that if the rate falls outside that range, it will have a value either between $4\frac{7}{8}$% and $5\frac{1}{8}$% (not below that range) or between $5\frac{5}{8}$% and $5\frac{7}{8}$% (with only a very small chance it might exceed that range and go as high as $6\frac{1}{8}$%); and that it is unlikely the rate will be lower than its present value but quite likely (about 2 to 1 odds) that it will be higher.

5.16. Concluding Comments

The framework for studying uncertainty is the *random experiment.* Mutually exclusive *outcomes* of the experiment are the elements of the experiment's *sample space.* Subsets of these outcomes are the possible *events* for the experiment. Subsets containing only one outcome are called *elementary events,* or *simple events.* The probabilities of these elementary events are "building block" probabilities in that they are used to determine the probabilities of *composite events* containing more than one outcome. The composite event probability is the sum of the "building block" probabilities of the elementary events corresponding to the outcomes contained in the composite event.

The building block probabilities for the elementary events can be assigned according to one of three procedures. (1) All elementary events may be treated as equally likely, in which case 1/(number of elementary events) gives the probability of each. (2) Historical relative frequencies may be used to divide the total probability (of 1) among the elementary events. (3) Subjective personal judgment may be the basis of the assignment.

For probability assignments based on equally likely elementary events, the major stumbling block may be in knowing how many elementary events there are. When the outcomes of the experiment are characterized by multiple attributes, a *tree diagram* with one branch for each outcome can be employed to describe and count the number of outcomes and corresponding elementary events. From the *fundamental principle of counting*, the number of outcomes can be determined without having to draw the tree diagram.

Finally, the *event space* consisting of all the different events which can be formed from n possible outcomes contains 2^n members.

Footnotes and References

[1] S has been previously used to denote the sample standard deviation. Since the sample space commonly is also denoted by S, we will also use this latter convention. The meaning of S will be obvious from the context of the discussion.

[2] Note each element or outcome is enclosed in parentheses and the comma separates the number to avoid misreading the element (for example, without the comma one might misread the first element as the number eleven). No commas are required when qualitative features are within the parentheses. Commas are required, however, to separate the different elements included in an event.

[3] Material for this example, as well as the quote itself, came from Irwin Kabus, "You can bank on uncertainty," *Harvard Business Review*, May/June, 1976, pp. 95–105.

Questions and Problems

For Problems 1–7, identify the type of probability interpretation you think is employed, and any assumption necessary to make that interpretation plausible.

1. During the Vietnam War, a draft lottery was conducted to assign callup priorities for each of the 365 birthdates within a year (not a leap year). A draft registrant born on June 29 said he had a probability of $\frac{100}{365}$ of having his birthdate on the list of the first 100 birthdates selected for the draft.

2. A Post Office study of the "undeliverable letter" problem resulted in the finding that 1742 of 10,000 first class letters monitored were eventually classified as "undeliverable". A post office worker comments that the probability is .1742 that the next first class letter handled will be undeliverable.

3. A Las Vegas oddsmaker quotes odds of 9 to 5 that the reigning heavyweight boxing champion will retain his title in a forthcoming title fight against an opponent he has never fought.

4. A marketing manager says the probability is .7 that a new product her company is introducing will be successful at the marketplace.

5. A production manager at a disposable baby diaper plant says that the probability of a randomly selected diaper being defective upon inspection is .2, according to recent records.

6. A telephone book survey is conducted by interviewing every fiftieth household listed in the telephone book. The probability of the Herbert Jones household being included in the sample is .02.

7. The marketing manager referred to in Problem 4 is in a meeting to discuss plans for introducing the new product. In response to her assessment of .7 as the probability of the new product's success, other persons attending comment as follows:

a. one person says that historically, only 2% of new product ideas ever become market successes, so .02 would be better than .7 as an assessment of the probability of the new product's successful introduction;

b. a second person says that the success rate of new products actually introduced to the marketplace is 40%, so .4 is the appropriate probability assessment;

c. a third person says that historically, this particular company has had a new product success rate that exceeds that experienced by most other companies. Thus, the probability of the new product's success should be assessed at .5 to correspond to the 50% success rate actually experienced;

d. a fourth person agrees with the third person's assessment of .5, but for a different reason. According to this person, there are two things that can happen to any new product. It can succeed or it can fail in the marketplace. Given that these are the only two possibilities, the outcome should be treated like a roll of the dice, because any new product is a gamble. Thus, each outcome has a fifty-fifty chance;

e. the marketing manager responds to the above comments by saying that the new product she is introducing is unique and cannot be lumped together with all kinds of other products which may have had prospects quite different from the present one. Her assessment of .7 is based on marketing research reports of consumer acceptance of the product and on her confidence in the organization's ability to do what has to be done to pave the way for a new product's success.

Formulate your own response to each of the above comments.

Information For Problems 8–24

Marketing managers often try to identify particular market segments which have substantial sales potential and then develop products to meet specific needs of the most promising segments. User surveys are widely employed to learn about the needs and sales potential of the different segments. The various market segments can be portrayed in a diagram like Figure 5.8, commonly known as a *market grid*. In this diagram, each dimension represents a basis of segmentation. In this example, there are three bases: extent of product usage, annual income, and residential location. The colored block in the upper front

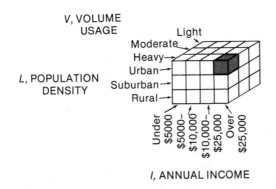

FIGURE 5.8 Market Grid

corner represents the segment "urban, heavy user, with income under $5000".

The market grid also serves as the sample space of a Venn Diagram for a user survey. The possible outcomes of the random experiment correspond to the different market segments. Each random draw from the population (trial of the random sampling experiment) results in a joint recording on a user. Each recording classifies the user into a market segment according to the joint attributes: product usage, annual income, and residential location.

In the problems, let

v_1, v_2, v_3 represent light user, moderate user, and heavy user, respectively;

l_1, l_2, l_3 represent urban location, suburban location, and rural location, respectively;

i_1, i_2, i_3, i_4 represent the income classes "under $5000", "$5000 to $9999", "$10,000 to $25,000", and "over $25,000", respectively.

Use as elementary event probabilities the relative frequencies given in Table 5.4.

8. How many outcomes (market segments) are included in the sample space?

9. Is the event "heavy user" an elementary event? Is the event "heavy urban user" an elementary event? Is the event "heavy urban user with annual income over $25,000" an elementary event? Explain clearly the reason for each answer.

10. a. In the event "heavy user" which outcomes are included?
b. In the event "heavy urban user" which outcomes are included?
c. In the event "annual income over $25,000" which outcomes are included? How would the probability of this event be found? Why is this procedure possible? What is the probability of this event?

11. Which outcomes are included in the event "heavy user with annual income over $25,000"? What is the probability of this event?

12. Does the event "user with annual income over $25,000" contain outcomes across all user categories?

13. Do the events "heavy user" and "user with annual income over $25,000" have any outcomes in common? If so, what?

TABLE 5.4. Relative Frequencies for Use, Location, and Income

CLASSI-FICATION	RELATIVE FREQUENCY AMONG RESPON-DENTS	CLASSI-FICATION	RELATIVE FREQUENCY AMONG RESPON-DENTS	CLASSI-FICATION	RELATIVE FREQUENCY AMONG RESPON-DENTS
$v_1 l_1 i_1$	.010	$v_2 l_1 i_1$	.020	$v_3 l_1 i_1$	.020
$v_1 l_1 i_2$	.015	$v_2 l_1 i_2$	.030	$v_3 l_1 i_2$	.030
$v_1 l_1 i_3$	.020	$v_2 l_1 i_3$	.040	$v_3 l_1 i_3$	.040
$v_1 l_1 i_4$	.025	$v_2 l_1 i_4$	.050	$v_3 l_1 i_4$	.050
$v_1 l_2 i_1$	.020	$v_2 l_2 i_1$	.040	$v_3 l_2 i_1$	.040
$v_1 l_2 i_2$	.010	$v_2 l_2 i_2$	.020	$v_3 l_2 i_2$	.020
$v_1 l_2 i_3$	.015	$v_2 l_2 i_3$	.025	$v_3 l_2 i_3$	.010
$v_1 l_2 i_4$	.022	$v_2 l_2 i_4$	.038	$v_3 l_2 i_4$	.015
$v_1 l_3 i_1$	.030	$v_2 l_3 i_1$	.050	$v_3 l_3 i_1$	.020
$v_1 l_3 i_2$	.038	$v_2 l_3 i_2$	.062	$v_3 l_3 i_2$	.025
$v_1 l_3 i_3$	.030	$v_2 l_3 i_3$	.050	$v_3 l_3 i_3$	.020
$v_1 l_3 i_4$	.015	$v_2 l_3 i_4$	.025	$v_3 l_3 i_4$	.010

14. Does the composite event "suburban user" contain outcomes across all user categories? Location categories?

15. Do the events "heavy user" and "suburban user" have any outcomes in common? If so, what are they?

16. Do the events "heavy user" and "light user" have any outcomes in common? If so, what are they?

17. What outcomes are included in the event "urban user with annual income over $25,000"? What is the probability of this event?

18. Which outcomes are included in the event "light user with income over $25,000"? What is the probability of this event?

19. Are the events "urban user" and "user with income over $25,000" mutually exclusive?

20. Which outcomes are included in the composite event "urban user or a user with income over $25,000"? What is the probability of this event? Hint: don't count twice an outcome in common.

21. Which outcomes are included in the composite event "heavy user or urban user"? What is the probability of this event? Do the events "heavy user" and "urban user" have outcomes in common? If so, what are they?

22. Which outcomes are included in the composite event "heavy suburban user or a moderate user with income over $25,000"? What is the probability of this event? Do the events "heavy suburban user" and "user with income over $25,000" have outcomes in common? If so, what are they?

23. How many outcomes are included in the composite event "not a light or rural user"? What is the probability of this event? Do the events "not a light user" and "rural user" have outcomes in common? If so, what are they?

24. a. How many outcomes are included in the null event?

b. How many outcomes are included in the sample space?

c. How many different events can be defined on the sample space?

25. Why is probability theory important in statistics?

26. Why is the sample space assigned the probability one?

27. Why is it significant that the probability of a composite event is found by merely adding the sum of the "building block" probabilities of the elementary events corresponding to the outcomes contained in the composite event?

28. Assume that an honest die is rolled once. What is the probability of:
a. an even number?
b. an even number greater than 3?
c. a number that is greater than 5 or less than 3?

29. An urn contains 3 green balls, 2 red balls, and 4 yellow balls. If a ball is chosen at random, find
a. P (green)
b. P (red)
c. P (yellow)
d. P (red or green)
e. P (yellow and red)
f. P (red or not yellow)
g. P (blue)
h. P (not red and not green)
i. P (not red or not green)
j. P (red or not green)

30. Two dice are rolled. Give the probability that the sum is:
a. 8
b. 7 or 11
c. less than 7
d. less than 9
e. even
f. at least 6 but less than 11
g. 14

31. Employees at the McDunn Corporation were categorized according to their length of service with the company. The results are shown in Table 5.5, which is given on the following page.

TABLE 5.5. Length of Service

CATEGORY	NUMBER OF EMPLOYEES
Less than 1 year	35
1–5 years,	123
6–10 years	82
11–15 years	79
More than 15 years	11

What is the probability that an employee selected at random has been with the company
a. less than 1 year?
b. 6–10 years?
c. more than 10 years?
d. less than 6 years?

32. From past experience a small company found that the probability that one employee will be absent on a Monday morning is .15, two employees is .07, three employees is .04, more than three is .01. What is the probability that everyone will show up next Monday morning?

33. An owner of a small business claims that the probability that he will break even this year is .3, that he will lose money is .25, but that he will enjoy a profit is .6. What can you say about his claim?

34. Suppose out of ten new AMC wagons sitting in a dealer's lot, 5 have air-conditioning, 6 have an AM-FM radio, 3 have both. What is the probability that a car selected at random off the lot:
a. will have either air-conditioning or an AM-FM radio?
b. will have neither?
c. will have air-conditioning but not an AM-FM radio?
d. will have air-conditioning or not have an AM-FM radio?

35. Suppose at Aftex Corporation, the employee make-up is as follows:

production	60
sales	25
management	15
TOTAL	100

Suppose three people are randomly selected with replacement for the three prizes in the office pool. How many different possible sample results are there? Was it necessary to break down employees by department to answer this?

36. Two dice are rolled. What is the probability that both are 4s? What is the probability that both are 6s? What is the probability that both are the same number?

37. Three cards are drawn from a poker deck. What is the probability that all three are aces?

38. By mistake 3 defective light bulbs were mixed with 4 good ones. Randomly one is chosen and tried in a socket. If it is defective it is discarded and another bulb is tried. Once a good bulb is found, the search ends. What is the probability that only one trial has to be made to get a good bulb?

39. A manufacturer must sub-contract for two parts. There are three companies in Indiana and five in Illinois (all equiprobable) that she can choose from.
a. If she has no objections to giving both contracts to the same company, what is the probability that both will be from Indiana? One from Indiana and one from Illinois? Both from Illinois?
b. Given that the manufacturer will not give both contracts to the same company, what is the probability that both will be from Indiana? One from Indiana and one from Illinois? Both from Illinois?

40. No corporate purchasing director wants performance to depend on unreliable suppliers. To avoid this risk, corporate purchasing directors cultivate a group of "in-list" suppliers. Firms that qualify for this list are those that can be depended upon to deliver quality products and services on time at favorable prices and in accordance with the conditions agreed upon when the order was placed. Not all suppliers meet these criteria. Screening among the firms which appear to have the potential for being a reliable supplier is a key aspect of the purchasing director's job. Of the many firms eager to do business with the company, those having obvious deficiencies

must be weeded out, leaving a pool of seemingly good suppliers. The director is constantly updating the list, particularly when an "in-list" supplier cannot provide what is needed. With no prior information to go on, choosing a supplier can be treated as a random selection. If that supplier shows a record of reliable service for the probationary period, the supplier joins the "in-list" and becomes eligible for routine reorders on a regular basis. Unreliable suppliers join the "out" supplier group and are only used in emergency situations.

Among the pool of untried suppliers of an important electronics component part, suppose three actually have serious deficiencies and five are reliable suppliers.

a. What is the probability that only one supplier has to be tried to find a reliable one that can be added to the in-list for these electronics component parts?

b. What is the probability that exactly two suppliers have to be tried? (Hint: Use the fundamental principle of counting for both Steps 1 and 3; for counting purposes complete the second stage even if the process would actually terminate at the end of the first stage.)

Probability Calculations for Composite Events

Preview. In the previous chapter, the concept of "building block" probabilities was extensively employed to determine the probabilities of composite events. Probabilities were assigned by one of three procedures to the elementary events corresponding to the outcomes of a random experiment. For the situations considered, it was implicitly assumed both that (1) information would be sufficient to assess all the elementary event probabilities and that (2) knowledge of these probabilities would be the most efficient way to determine the desired composite event probabilities. In actuality, situations arise in which one or the other of these assumptions is not valid. For example, suppose defective parts occur randomly with probability of .2 among the parts produced by an assembly line operation. Consider the question: "what is the probability that of two parts examined, at least one will be defective?" This question cannot be answered using the building block approach because the elementary event probabilities are not known. However, the correct probability, .36, can be calculated by applying a rule explained in this chapter.

This chapter will deal with the following. If probabilities for some of the composite events can be directly assessed quite easily, it may be possible and even desirable to use these known composite event probabilities to determine the probabilities of the other composite events. Moreover, it may be possible to reverse the procedure of the previous chapter and take advantage of the known composite event probabilities in determining the probabilities to be assigned to the elementary events.

Two very important probability laws known as the *addition rule* and the *multiplication rule* greatly expand our ability to use known probabilities of some events to determine the unknown probabilities of other events. The application of the multiplication rule necessitates a distinction between *conditional* and *unconditional* (or *marginal*) probability. This distinction between probabilities in turn leads to a distinction between two kinds of event relationships: *statistically dependent events* versus *statistically independent events*.

Grammar school arithmetic rules are simple enough. Two plus two always equal four; one-sixth and one-sixth always equal two-sixths or one-third. Do these simple grammar school adding rules apply to probabilities? An editorial presented in the *Wall Street Journal* implied this. The editorial quoted Herman Kahn, the physicist who runs the Hudson Institute. Kahn described the prospects of an economic depression as follows:

> it is now no longer beyond the realm of possibility that the United States might have to endure a severe economic depression.

The editorial reported Kahn as believing the chances of a depression the next year to be one in six. Kahn was also cited as believing the chances to be one in six that, if the depression doesn't occur the next year, it will occur sometime during the remainder of the decade. Then, putting its own words in Kahn's mouth, the editorial concluded:

> in other words, he sees one chance in three that in this decade we will experience depression.[1]

From these calculations, the editor apparently thought that Kahn was giving similar kinds of probability—the unqualified probability of a depression in the coming year and the unqualified probability of a depression for the remainder of the decade. For that reason, their sum seemingly is the probability of a depression for the decade.

Unfortunately, that calculation is misguided on two counts. First, the two probabilities Kahn gave were not of the same type. Kahn's initial probability is the unqualified probability of a depression in the coming year, but the subsequent probability he gave *isn't* the unqualified probability of a depression for the remainder of the decade. It is applicable only if there isn't a depression this year. Second, even if the subsequent probability was the appropriate unqualified probability, it couldn't legitimately be added to the first probability value except in very special circumstances. In order to add the probabilities, one would have to assume that there could only be *one* depression in the decade. These addition rules are explained in Section 6.2.

What kind of probability was Kahn giving as the probability of a depression later in the decade? If you read carefully what he said, Kahn gave $\frac{1}{6}$ as the probability of a depression later in the decade *if* there was no depression now. He did not say what the probability of a depression later in the decade would be if there was a depression the coming year; nor did he make an unqualified assessment of the probability of a depression later in the decade. Interestingly, all of these figures can be calculated from what Kahn did give, but *not* just by addition alone. Multiplication is required first and then addition. The procedure isn't difficult and the approach that is needed is discussed fully in this chapter.

Using Herman Kahn's figures, the correct procedure gives a value of $\frac{11}{36}$ for the probability of a depression in the decade. The one-third ($\frac{12}{36}$) obtained by the editor's misguided approach came within $\frac{1}{36}$ of the correct value of $\frac{11}{36}$. Is this discrepancy trivial? For most, like newspaper editors, probability questions do not arise daily and when they arise have little importance. But what on the surface seems to be a case of editorial license with little ill-consequence is in fact indicative of a potentially hazardous lack of knowledge of the rules that govern probability calculation.

In business, where probabilities are a fact of life and important decisions rest on their calculation, one can not afford to be caught adding when in fact preliminary subtracting and multiplying steps are warranted. Keeping correct score on probabilities by following the correct rules is a sign of professional business competence—the same kind of professionalism one expects an accountant to have in keeping accurate financial records in accordance with generally accepted accounting principles. In both cases, prolonged disregard of the guiding rules produces muddled decision-making within the firm, a diminished financial performance, and, at worst, even the firm's financial failure.

6.1. Unions, Intersections, and Marginal Events

In the previous chapter we saw that the probability of an event is the sum of the probabilities assigned to the elementary events which represent the possible outcomes. This rule is true without exception and it frequently can be advantageously used to calculate the probability of the event of interest. But the values of the elementary event probabilities are not always known. Sometimes all or most of the known probabilities are for composite events rather than for elementary events. What then? Is there a set of rules that informs us how to determine probabilities of events of interest to us from composite event probabilities?

Consider a random sampling experiment from a bivariate population. For example, suppose each member being sampled either possesses or does not possess one or both of two attributes a and b. A random draw will produce one of four possible outcomes with each outcome showing a joint recording on the presence or absence of attribute a and of attribute b. The four possible outcomes are the elements of the sample space of the two-attribute experiment. For simplicity of notation we shall denote the elements by e_1, e_2, e_3, and e_4, and their corresponding elementary events E_1, E_2, E_3 and E_4 respectively. Note that in Table 6.1 the elementary events need not be equiprobable.

TABLE 6.1. Possible Outcomes of a Random Sampling Experiment

ATTRIBUTE a	ATTRIBUTE b	POSSIBLE OUTCOME	CORRESPONDING ELEMENTARY EVENT
Present, a	Present, b	$(ab) = e_1$	E_1
	Absent, b'	$(ab') = e_2$	E_2
Absent, a'	Present, b	$(a'b) = e_3$	E_3
	Absent, b'	$(a'b') = e_4$	E_4

Each of the four possible outcomes in the sample space can be included or excluded in forming various events. In Chapter Five we learned that a total of

2^n events can be formed from n possible outcomes. Thus in this particular case, a total of $2^4 = 16$ events can be formed from the four possible outcomes. The entire collection of derived events comprises the event space for the experiment. These are shown in Figure 6.1.

FIGURE 6.1 Event Space for Random Sampling Experiment with Four Elementary Events

(ELEMENTARY) EVENTS CONTAINING *ONE* ELEMENT	(COMPOSITE) EVENTS CONTAINING *TWO* ELEMENTS	(COMPOSITE) EVENTS CONTAINING *THREE* ELEMENTS	SAMPLE SPACE CONTAINING *ALL* ELEMENTS	NULL EVENT CONTAINING *NO* ELEMENTS
$E_1 = [e_1]$ $E_2 = [e_2]$ $E_3 = [e_3]$ $E_4 = [e_4]$	$C_1 = [e_1, e_2]$ $C_2 = [e_1, e_3]$ $C_3 = [e_1, e_4]$ $C_4 = [e_2, e_3]$ $C_5 = [e_2, e_4]$ $C_6 = [e_3, e_4]$	$C_7 = [e_1, e_2, e_3]$ $C_8 = [e_1, e_2, e_4]$ $C_9 = [e_1, e_3, e_4]$ $C_{10} = [e_2, e_3, e_4]$	$S = [e_1, e_2, e_3, e_4]$	$\emptyset = [\quad]$

Several noteworthy relationships among these events and their probabilities are of key interest to us. We begin by defining the following three types of events.

union of two events
intersection of two events
marginal event

Union

For some purposes it is desirable to treat a pair of attributes as a single entity. For example, suppose Fiona MacTavish and Fergus MacTavish are a married couple who rent an apartment from their landlord, Angus MacDonald. When Mac-Donald looks over the rent receipts to see who has paid and who has not paid him rent, he looks at the two MacTavishes as a single entity: "the MacTavishes have paid their rent" or "the MacTavishes are delinquent in their rent." He does not care whether it was Fiona MacTavish or Fergus MacTavish who signed the check, because payment by either one constitutes payment for the pair considered as a single entity.

Closely related to the idea of treating a pair of attributes as a single entity is the concept of the *union* of two events. Consider any pair of events A and B defined on the sample space for the experiment. There will be a third event defined on the same sample space which occurs if (and only if):

A occurs, or
B occurs, or
both A and B occur.

For example, suppose A is the event accident "liability claim" and B is the event accident "collision claim". The event accident "claim" occurs if either of the other two events occur or if both occur. This event is called the *union* of events A and B. The union includes as elements:

all the possible outcomes which are included in either A or B or both, *but* no other possible outcomes.

The union of two events is designated mathematically by the symbol $\cup$, so the union of A and B is written $A \cup B$. This is read as "A union B."

For example, of the events described in the event space given in Figure 6.1, event C_7 is the union of the events C_1 and C_2, because C_7 includes sample space elements e_1, e_2, and e_3. These are the elements which are either in event C_1 (e_1 and e_2) or in event C_2 (e_1 and e_3). Thus,

$$C_1 \cup C_2 = [e_1, e_2, e_3] = C_7.$$

Note that the event which is the union of two other events necessarily occurs whenever either one of the two events occurs. Thus, C_7 occurs whenever C_1 occurs or C_2 occurs. For this reason the rule for forming unions is sometimes referred to informally as the "either-or" rule.

Intersection

Again consider any pair of events A and B, defined on the sample space. There will be another event defined on the sample space which includes as elements:

all the sample space elements (possible outcomes) *common* to both of the events, *but* no other elements.

For example, suppose A is the event "even number" and B is the event "number less than nine." The event which includes all the elements common to both A and B is $[2, 4, 6, 8]$.

This event is called the *intersection* of A and B. The intersection of two events is designated mathematically by the symbol $\cap$, and is written $A \cap B$. This is read "A intersect B."

The rule for forming intersections is informally referred to as the "both-and" rule. The name follows from the fact that the event which is the intersection of two other events necessarily requires both of these events to overlap: A and B both must occur. For the event space described in Figure 6.1, event E_1 with possible outcome e_1 as its only element is the intersection (overlap) of the events C_1 (with elements e_1 and e_2) and event C_2 (with elements e_1 and e_2). That is,

$$C_1 \cap C_2 = [e_1] = E_1.$$

The intersection $A \cap B$ is sometimes called a *joint* event. Its occurrence indicates a situation in which the two events A and B occur simultaneously or jointly.

Marginal Events

For reasons which will become clear shortly, we want to focus on what is called the *marginal event*. Its definition requires some elaboration. Suppose we want to focus on attribute a, even though the experiment concerns both attributes a and b. Attribute a appears in elements e_1 and e_2. It does not appear in elements e_3 or e_4. We want to look at that one composite event which has as elements all those outcomes that have attribute a present (e_1 and e_2), but which does *not* contain any other outcome where a is absent (e_3 and e_4). For example, composite event C_7 has as elements e_1 and e_2, in which attribute a appears, but also includes e_3 in which a does not appear, so C_7 is not the composite event we are interested in. Composite event C_5 contains e_2, in which a appears, but it also contains e_4, which does not have a, so this composite event is not the one either. E_1 has e_1, in which a appears, but it excludes e_2, in which a also appears, so it is not the composite event. We want that composite event which only contains all the elements in which a appears. In this case, only C_1 has both e_1 and e_2, and does *not* contain e_3 or e_4. Event C_1 is called the marginal event for attribute a. To summarize:

> a *marginal event for attribute a* is that event which includes as elements all the possible outcomes in which attribute a appears and none of the possible outcomes in which the attribute a is absent.

What is the marginal event for attribute b? It is the composite event which occurs if and only if attribute b appears in the experiment's outcome. This is event C_2 which includes as elements the two possible outcomes e_1 and e_3. We shall designate this event as B. Thus,

$$B = \text{Marginal event for attribute } b = [e_1, e_3] = C_2.$$

A New Look at the Event Space

Figure 6.2 delineates the composition of the possible outcomes in the sample space for this experiment and the entire collection of events in the event space. In the columns on the right hand side, event $C_1 = [e_1, e_2]$ has been labeled A and event $C_2 = [e_1, e_3]$ has been labeled B. These are the marginal events corresponding to the appearance of attributes a and b, respectively, in the experiment's outcome. Note that all the events in the event space (including the elementary events) can be derived from the four marginal events A, A', B, B', where

$$A' = C_6 = [e_3, e_4]$$
$$B' = C_5 = [e_2, e_4]$$

Also, note that the four elementary events are the four possible intersections of the marginal events. For example, $E_1 = A \cap B$ as shown below:

$$A = [e_1, e_2] \qquad B = [e_1, e_3]$$
$$A \cap B = [e_1] = E_1$$

There are other points worth noting: The *joint* events (intersections) are *elementary* events; that is, they each contain only one element ($A \cap B = [e_1]$, $A \cap B' = [e_2]$, etc.) The marginal events are all *composite* events; all of them contain more than one element (for example, A contains two elements, e_1 and e_2). The *marginal* events are *unions of joint* events ($A = E_1 \cup E_2 = (A \cap B) \cup (A \cap B')$, etc.)

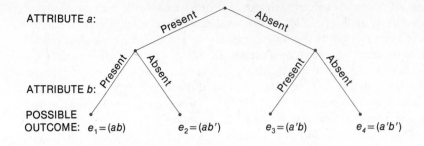

ATTRIBUTE a: Present Absent

ATTRIBUTE b: Present Absent Present Absent

POSSIBLE OUTCOME: $e_1 = (ab)$ $e_2 = (ab')$ $e_3 = (a'b)$ $e_4 = (a'b')$

Description in Terms of Possible Outcome Status, by Event

EVENT	COMPOSITE EVENTS EXPRESSED AS THE UNION OF ELEMENTARY EVENTS	e_1	e_2	e_3	e_4	EVENT EXPRESSED IN TERMS OF MARGINAL EVENTS	THIS EVENT IS ALSO DE-SCRIBED AS:
E_1		In	Out	Out	Out	$A \cap B$	Joint Event—
E_2		Out	In	Out	Out	$A \cap B'$	Intersec-
E_3		Out	Out	In	Out	$A' \cap B$	tion of A
E_4		Out	Out	Out	In	$A' \cap B'$	and B
	$C_1 = E_1 \cup E_2$	In	In	Out	Out	A	Marginal event A
	$C_2 = E_1 \cup E_3$	In	Out	In	Out	B	Marginal event B
	$C_3 = E_1 \cup E_4$	In	Out	Out	In	$(A \cap B) \cup (A' \cap B')$	
	$C_4 = E_2 \cup E_3$	Out	In	In	Out	$(A \cap B') \cup (A' \cap B)$	
	$C_5 = E_2 \cup E_4$	Out	In	Out	In	B'	Marginal event B'
	$C_6 = E_3 \cup E_4$	Out	Out	In	In	A'	Marginal event A'
	$C_7 = E_1 \cup E_2 \cup E_3$	In	In	In	Out	$A \cup B$	Either A or B or both
	$C_8 = E_1 \cup E_2 \cup E_4$	In	In	Out	In	$(A' \cap B)'$	
	$C_9 = E_1 \cup E_3 \cup E_4$	In	Out	In	In	$(A \cap B')'$	
	$C_{10} = E_2 \cup E_3 \cup E_4$	Out	In	In	In	$(A \cap B)'$	
	S	In	In	In	In		Sample space
	$\emptyset$	Out	Out	Out	Out		Null event

FIGURE 6.2 Event Space Formed from Intersection of Marginal Events

The three new concepts introduced in this section:

1. events which are unions of other events,

2. events which are intersections of other events, and

3. marginal events,

give us a new framework for describing and using all the events in the event space. Used in conjunction with probability rules presented in the remainder of this chapter, this framework will provide a valuable supplement and in some cases an alternative to the "building blocks" approach of calculating event probabilities. There are two advantages to this new structure.

> Rather than describe outcomes in terms of all the detail that can be distinguished as in the building blocks approach, we need describe only those attributes we *want* to distinguish; the latter approach may reduce the number of elementary events and permit simplified calculations of probabilities for the events to be considered. For example, suppose we are to draw a sample of two poker chips from an urn (with replacement of the chip after each draw), distinguishing the order (red or white) of the chip. If the urn contains 10 chips there would be $10^2 = 100$ possible outcomes. Using our new approach we would distinguish only 4 possible outcomes, one for each possible color arrangement (RR, RW, WR, WW).

The new framework facilitates calculation of unknown elementary event probabilities from known composite event probabilities; since the elementary event probabilities are required in the building block approach, the new framework facilitates implementation of the building block procedure. This will be shown later in this chapter (Sections 6.6 and 6.7).

6.2. The Addition Rule

The first rule we shall study for calculating probabilities using the new framework is the addition rule.

Let $P(A)$ represent the probability of event A and $P(B)$ the probability of event B. What is the relationship between these two event probabilities and the probability of the union, $P(A \cup B)$? The relationship is known as the *addition rule*.

> **The Addition Rule (General Case): For any two events A and B, the probability of their union is obtained from**
> $$P(A \cup B) = P(A) + P(B) - P(A \cap B).$$

Thus the probability of a union requires that the probability of the intersection be subtracted from the simple sum of the probabilities of the events comprising the union. Why?

Figure 6.3 illustrates the situation in a Venn diagram. In the sample space S, the shaded area shows the possible outcomes common to both A and B. Adding the probabilities of the elementary events corresponding to the outcomes in A to the probabilities of the elementary events corresponding to the outcomes in B does *not* give the correct answer. This value *double counts* the elementary event probabilities in the shaded area. A correction is made by subtracting the probability associated with the overlapping elementary events from the sum. This procedure adjusts the sum so that what remains is the probability of the union

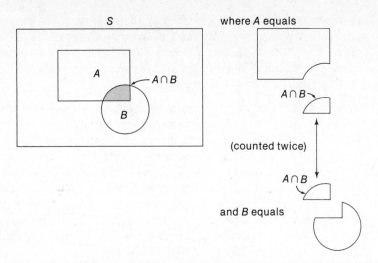

S

where A equals

A

A∩B

A∩B

(counted twice)

A∩B

and B equals

FIGURE 6.3   Venn Diagram Showing Intersection of Two Events

of events A and B. This shaded area, the intersection $(A \cap B)$, shows graphically why $P(A \cap B)$ has to be subtracted from $P(A) + P(B)$ in the equation $P(A \cup B) = P(A) + P(B) - P(A \cap B)$. This equation shows that "the probability of the union of any two events is the sum of the probabilities of the individual events minus the probability of both events occurring jointly."

Example 6.2A.   Illustration of the Addition Rule with the Building Blocks Approach

From ten cars in a parking lot one car is to be selected at random. The probability of being selected is .1 for each car. Six of the cars are Fords and the rest are Chevrolets. Four Fords and one Chevrolet are equipped with air conditioning. The symbols f, c, and a represent the attributes Ford, Chevrolet, and air conditioning, respectively.

Suppose we define the sample space so that each car represents one element (possible outcome). Columns 1 and 2 in Figure 6.4 list the elements and their status

Element of Sample Space (car drawn)	Attributes	Event A	Event F	Event A∪F	Event A∩F
e_1	fa	●	●	●	●
e_2	fa	●	●	●	●
e_3	fa	●	●	●	●
e_4	fa	●	●	●	●
e_5	fa'		●	●	
e_6	fa'		●	●	
e_7	ca	●		●	
e_8	ca'				
e_9	ca'				
e_{10}	ca'				

FIGURE 6.4   Events Based Upon Sample Space of Ten Cars

with respect to car make and air conditioning equipment. Let A represent the marginal event "air conditioning" and let F represent the marginal event "Ford". In column 3, the five dots indicate the five elements in marginal event A. Likewise, the six dots in column 4 indicate the six elements included in marginal event F. The seven dots in column 5 indicate the seven elements in the union, $A \cup F$. The four dots in column 6 indicate the four elements included in the intersection $A \cap F$.

Using the building blocks approach and adding elementary event probabilities to find composite event probabilities leads to the following:

$$P(A) = P[e_1, e_2, e_3, e_4, e_7] = P(E_1) + \ldots + P(E_4) + P(E_7) = .5$$
$$P(F) = P[e_1, e_2, e_3, e_4, e_5, e_6] = P(E_1) + \ldots + P(E_6) = .6$$
$$P(A \cup F) = P[e_1, e_2, e_3, e_4, e_5, e_6, e_7] = P(E_1) + \ldots + P(E_7) = .7$$
$$P(A \cap F) = P[e_1, e_2, e_3, e_4] = P(E_1) + \ldots + P(E_4) = .4$$

The probability of the union of A and F ($P(A \cup F)$) was obtained by adding the elementary event probabilities. However, note that by using the addition rule, we *could* have obtained the same answer for the union probability from knowledge of marginal and intersection event probabilities *without* knowing the elementary event probabilities:

$$P(A \cup F) = P(A) + P(F) - P(A \cap F)$$
$$= .5 + .6 - .4 = .7$$

The addition rule shows we could have obtained the correct answer without using the building block approach, provided we knew the marginal event probabilities and the probability of their intersection. In this particular case it was not *necessary* to use the addition rule because the building block approach led to the answer. However, in the next example, the building block approach will not work and we *must* use the addition rule.

Example 6.2B.   Illustration of the Addition Rule When the Building Block Approach Doesn't Provide Answers

Let us reconsider the problem developed in Example 6.2A, except that this time we are *not told how many cars there are.* We are told only that sixty percent of the cars are Fords, fifty percent are air conditioned, and forty percent are air-conditioned Fords. Again, we are asked to find the probability of drawing in a random sample either a Ford or an air-conditioned car (or both).

In trying to solve this problem the building block approach leads to a dead end. We do not know how many cars there are (possible outcomes). However, this problem can be solved by applying the addition rule. A different sample space must be used, one based upon the attributes to be considered: make of car and air-conditioning status. Viewed this way, there are four possible outcomes in the sample space and they lead to marginal and union events as shown in Figure 6.5.

The probability of the event (F union A) is the sum of the probabilities of the elementary events corresponding to the elements the union includes (Rule 3 in Chapter 5):

$$P(F \cup A) = P(E_1) + P(E_2) + P(E_3). \text{ But these probabilities are unknown.}$$

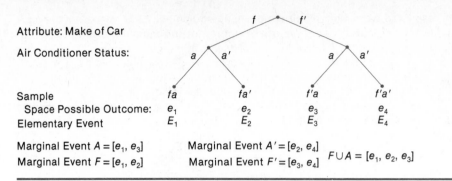

Attribute: Make of Car

Air Conditioner Status:

	fa	fa'	$f'a$	$f'a'$
Sample Space Possible Outcome:	e_1	e_2	e_3	e_4
Elementary Event	E_1	E_2	E_3	E_4

Marginal Event $A = [e_1, e_3]$ Marginal Event $A' = [e_2, e_4]$

Marginal Event $F = [e_1, e_2]$ Marginal Event $F' = [e_3, e_4]$ $F \cup A = [e_1, e_2, e_3]$

FIGURE 6.5 Marginal Events Based Upon Sample Space of Four Outcomes

According to the addition rule:

$$P(A \cup F) = P(A) + P(F) - P(A \cap F)$$
$$P(A \cup F) = .5 + .6 - .4$$
$$P(A \cup F) = .7$$

In other words, we sum the probabilities of the two marginal events forming the union and subtract their *joint* probability (subtract the probability of their intersection). *Why did we subtract the joint probability,* $P(A \cap F)$? This was necessary to avoid double counting the four air-conditioned Fords which are included in both A and F. Remember, double counting joint probabilities is a frequent mistake.

The addition rule approach not only solved the problem, but is much quicker. Had we *started* with the addition rule, we could have easily and quickly solved the problem by using F, A, and $A \cap F$.

In the process of illustrating the usefulness of the addition rule, we also demonstrated a different approach to sample space construction. This new approach is based upon considering the attributes that are of interest in the possible outcomes, rather than focusing on the units that were actually sampled (cars). This new approach was not sufficient by itself to give us the required probability. We needed the help of the addition rule. However, with the help of some other probability rules soon to be introduced, we may be able to find elementary event probabilities from the given information. Thus, the building block approach could once again prove useful in finding still other unknown probabilities of interest.

6.3. Assigning Probabilities for the Null Event, for Mutually Exclusive Events, and for Complementary Events

The event containing no possible outcomes was defined in the previous chapter as the "null event," $\emptyset$. With no possible outcomes there is nothing to occur, which is why the null event is also called the "impossible" event. What permissible probability value should be given to an event that cannot occur? The lowest? From the previous rule it can be shown that:

the null event must be assigned a value of zero.[2] $P(\emptyset) = 0$.

Probability of Mutually Exclusive Events

Any two events defined on the same sample space which have no possible outcomes in common are said to be *mutually exclusive*. The intersection of two events which are mutually exclusive is the null or impossible event, $\emptyset$. In other words, if two events are mutually exclusive, the occurrence of one eliminates the possible occurrence of the other. It follows from the probability rule for the null event that

> if A and B are two mutually exclusive events, the probability assigned to their intersection must be zero: $P(A \cap B) = 0$ if $(A \cap B) = \emptyset$.

Example 6.3A. **Mutually Exclusive Events for a Die Experiment**

The two events "even number of spots" and "odd number of spots" on a roll of a die contain no common elements and are therefore mutually exclusive in the sense that they cannot occur simultaneously. That is,

> if event A = [evens] = [2, 4, 6]
> and event B = [odds] = [1, 3, 5]
> $A \cap B = \emptyset$.
> Thus $P(\text{evens} \cap \text{odds}) = P(A \cap B) = P(\emptyset) = 0$

Probability of Complementary Events

Every event has a complementary event. For any event A, the complementary event A' is defined to be the event containing all the possible outcomes not included in A.

Example 6.3B. **Complementary Event for the Die Experiment**

If in the experiment of rolling a pair of dice the event A contains the possible outcomes:

> [3, 5, 7, 9, 11],

then the complementary event A' contains

> [2, 4, 6, 8, 10, 12].

In other words, if event A is "odds," then the complementary event A' is "evens".

Situations arise in which the probability of the event wanted is not known, and the probability of its complementary event is either known, or can easily be determined. In this situation, it is important to know

> A', the complement of event A, has probability equal to one minus the probability assigned to event A. $P(A') = 1 - P(A)$

Example 6.3C. Calculating the Probability of a Complementary Event: Mortgage Default Rates

Because of high administration costs, an important concern of a Saving and Loan Association is the mortgage default rate. The U.S. Saving and Loan League which monitors home mortgage defaults reports a .02 default rate. Considering this relative frequency as the probability of a home mortgage default, what is the probability that the next mortgage loan made will *not* be a default account?

Let *A* represent the event that the mortgage loan goes into default. The complementary event *A'* represents the probability that we want to find. Its probability is

$$P(A') = 1 - P(A)$$
$$= 1 - .02 = .98$$

There is a .98 chance that the next mortgage loan made will not default.

In the above example the desired probability was not known and could not be computed directly. Thus the probability rule for the complementary event was essential in obtaining the desired probability from the probability that *was* known. However, even when enough information is available to compute the desired probability directly, the alternative approach of first calculating the probability of the complementary event may prove advantageous. For example, in Review Exercise VI at the end of this chapter, an otherwise difficult problem is easily solved by employing the probability rule for the complementary event. Instead of calculating and summing 15 individual probabilities, one probability calculation is made for the complementary event and this is used to obtain the probability of the event in question.

6.4. Managerial Issues in Practice—
Review Exercise I:
Consolidating the Corporate Profit Picture

A large corporation has an aerospace division and a consumer products division. After extensive study and consultation, it is reported by the corporate staff that the probability of a favorable profit picture in the aerospace division next year is .65 compared to .45 for the consumer products division. The probability of not ending up with favorable profits at either division is assessed at .20.

1. What are the elementary events in the sample space showing the possible joint recordings on the profitability status of the two firm divisions?

The recordings for this experiment are the profitability status of the aerospace division and the profitability status of the consumer division. There are two possible recordings with respect to the aerospace division:

a: Profit picture at the aerospace division is favorable.
a': Profit picture at the aerospace division is not favorable.

There are also two possible recordings with respect to the consumer division:

c: Profit picture at the consumer division is favorable.
c': Profit picture at the consumer division is not favorable.

Thus, a tree diagram (Figure 6.6) shows four possible profitability status recordings. These are the elementary events of the sample space formed from the intersection of one marginal event with respect to aerospace division profitability (a or a') and one marginal event with respect to consumer division profitability (c or c'). The sample space is shown graphically by the Venn Diagram in Figure 6.7 which identifies the four marginal events and their appropriate elementary events.

2. How many events can be formed from the four possible outcomes which comprise the sample space for this experiment and what are they?

The general rule given in Chapter 5 is that there are 2^n possible events for n elements. Thus, there are $2^4 = 16$ possible events which can be formed from different arrangements of the four elements. These are shown in Table 6.2.

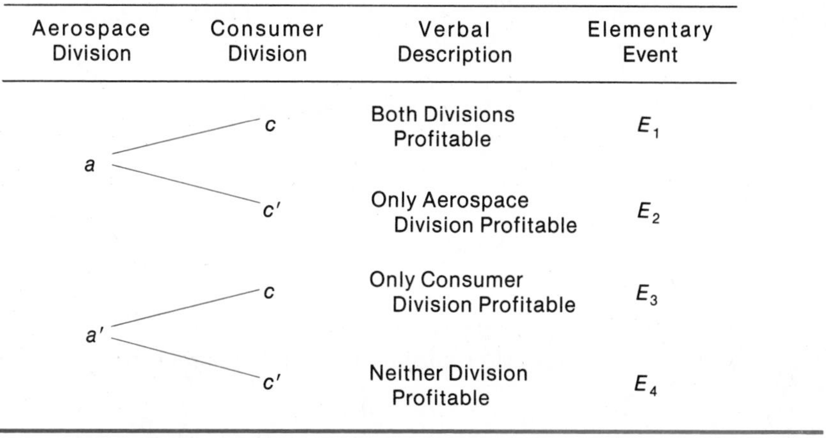

Aerospace Division	Consumer Division	Verbal Description	Elementary Event
a	c	Both Divisions Profitable	E_1
	c'	Only Aerospace Division Profitable	E_2
a'	c	Only Consumer Division Profitable	E_3
	c'	Neither Division Profitable	E_4

FIGURE 6.6   Tree Diagram for Elementary Events

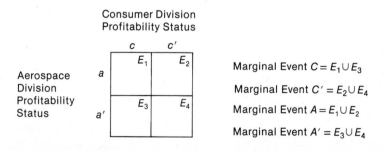

Consumer Division Profitability Status

Marginal Event $C = E_1 \cup E_3$

Marginal Event $C' = E_2 \cup E_4$

Marginal Event $A = E_1 \cup E_2$

Marginal Event $A' = E_3 \cup E_4$

FIGURE 6.7   Venn Diagram for Sample Space of Experiment on Division Profitability Status

TABLE 6.2. Possible Events from Four Elements

EVENT	VERBAL DESCRIPTION	KEY MARGINAL AND JOINT EVENTS
$\emptyset$	Null Event	
E_1	Both Divisions Profitable	$A \cap C$
E_2	Only Aerospace Profitable	$A \cap C'$
E_3	Only Consumer Profitable	$A' \cap C$
E_4	Neither Division Profitable	$A' \cap C'$
$E_1 \cup E_2$	Aerospace Division Profitable	A
$E_1 \cup E_3$	Consumer Division Profitable	C
$E_1 \cup E_4$	Same Result at Both Divisions	
$E_2 \cup E_3$	Only One of the Divisions Profitable	
$E_2 \cup E_4$	Consumer Division Not Profitable	C'
$E_3 \cup E_4$	Aerospace Division Not Profitable	A'
$E_1 \cup E_2 \cup E_3$	At Least One Profitable Division	
$E_1 \cup E_2 \cup E_4$	Consumer Division Profitable only if Aerospace Profitable	
$E_1 \cup E_3 \cup E_4$	Aerospace Division Profitable only if Consumer Profitable	
$E_2 \cup E_3 \cup E_4$	At Least One Unprofitable Division	
$S = E_1 \cup E_2 \cup E_3 \cup E_4$	Sample Space	

3. Must the elementary events be equiprobable?

No. In fact, they cannot be equiprobable in this problem because E_4 is assigned a probability of only .20.

4. What is the probability that the consumer products division does not end up with a favorable profit picture?

This is event C'. Using elementary events as the building blocks,

$$P(C') = P(E_2) + P(E_4) = P(E_2) + .20.$$

Thus, the probability of the desired event cannot be found (at this point) using the building block approach since $P(E_2)$ is not known. Another approach must be tried. Since C' has as its complement C, one can employ the rule for the probability of a complement.

$$P(C') = 1 - P(C) = 1 - .45 = .55.$$

5. What is the probability that at least one of the two divisions ends up with a favorable profit picture?

This is the event which is the union of the elementary events E_1, E_2, and E_3. Since the probabilities of these elementary events are not known at this point, the building block approach cannot be used. However, this event has as its complement E_4. Since the probability of E_4 is known, we can use the probability rule for the complementary event to compute:

$$P(E_1 \cup E_2 \cup E_3) = 1 - P(E_4) = 1 - .20 = .80.$$

6. What is the probability that at least one of the two divisions end up with an unfavorable profit picture?

This is the union of the elementary events E_2, E_3, and E_4. Of these, only the probability of E_4 is known so the building block approach cannot be used. However, the union of A' and C' is the event in question. The probability of C' was previously computed to be .55. A' has as its complement A so its probability is

$$P(A') = 1 - P(A) = 1 - .65 = .35.$$

From the addition rule,

$$P(E_2 \cup E_3 \cup E_4) = P(A' \cup C') = P(A') + P(C') - P(A' \cap C').$$

The intersection of A' and C' is the elementary event E_4, which has probability .20. Then

$$P(E_2 \cup E_3 \cup E_4) = .35 + .55 - .20 = .70.$$

7. What is the probability that the aerospace division's profit picture is favorable, but the consumer division's is not favorable?

This is event E_2. The probability of event C' is .55 and C' is the union of elementary events E_2 and E_4.

$$P(C') = P(E_2 \cup E_4) = P(E_2) + P(E_4)$$
$$.55 = P(E_2) + .20$$
$$P(E_2) = .55 - .20 = .35$$

8. What is the probability that both of the divisions end up with a favorable profit picture?

This is elementary event E_1, the probability of which is not known at this point. However, E_1 is the complement of $E_2 \cup E_3 \cup E_4$ and that probability has already been determined as .7. Thus,

$$P(E_1) = 1 - P(E_2 \cup E_3 \cup E_4) = 1 - .70 = .30$$

6.5. Conditional Probability

Probability calculations so far have been concerned with the probability of an event with respect to the entire sample space. However, information that a particular event has occurred can be relevant information and affect the probability of other events. The concept of conditional probability uses the certainty of one event to better assess the probability of the event of interest. In other words, information that a particular event has occurred (or that it didn't occur) is relevant if this knowledge enables us to focus in on a narrower range of possible outcomes, thereby enhancing our probability assessment of the event in question.

Example 6.5.   Sixty Minutes and the Reported A.C. Nielsen Television Ratings

From a list of 1000 names and phone numbers, outgoing randomly selected phone calls are made subsequent to the *Sixty Minutes* television program. Respondents are asked whether they were watching television and if so, which program. For a single randomly selective phone call, what is the probability that *Sixty Minutes* was being watched?

There are really two different *Sixty Minutes* probabilities of potential interest which can be inferred from the sampling done and relative frequency reported by the A.C. Nielsen TV rating service. One can compare *Sixty Minutes* with other programs slated at the same time (audience share, in the advertising vernacular), in which case we want the conditional probability that if our respondent was classified as a TV viewer, he or she is a *Sixty Minutes* viewer. By way of contrast, the unconditional probability (or simply the marginal probability) refers to the probability that the respondent is a *Sixty Minutes* viewer (regardless of TV viewing status).

Both conditional and unconditional probabilities can be important and useful, but for different reasons. Evaluating how the *Sixty Minutes* show compares with its immediate competition (the conditional probability) is one concern. Evaluating *Sixty Minutes's* overall drawing power, that is, how well *Sixty Minutes* draws viewers away from other (non-television) activities (the unconditional probability), is a different, but also important, concern.

If we seek the probability for event A where B is the event for which information is available, we use the notation $P(A|B)$. It reads "the *conditional* probability of A, given or conditional upon the information about the occurrence of event B." If A is the event, *Sixty Minutes watcher*, and B is the event *television viewer*, than $P(A|B)$ is the probability of a *Sixty Minutes watcher* if the respondent is a TV viewer.

The use of the word probability without any additional specification ordinarily refers to marginal (unconditional) probability defined over the entire sample space, not a reduced sample space. However, to avoid any confusion which might lead to calculating an inappropriate probability, the phrase *unconditional* probability should be used. This makes clear that the reference is to the probability of an event with respect to the entire sample space (in this case, all phone call respondents) and not a smaller group (TV viewers). Perhaps the Venn Diagram in Figure 6.8 will help clarify the reduced sample space concept.

Getting Things in Proper Perspective

What is the relationship between conditional probabilities and unconditional probabilities? Intuitively, the relationship is quite easy to see. We know that $P(S) = 1$; in other words, the probabilities assigned to all the elementary events defined on the sample space must sum to 1. This value of 1 indicates of course that one of the elementary events *must* occur. Analogously, the summation of the probabilities defined over the reduced sample space (a subset of S) also sums to one. For example, $P(A|B) + P(A'|B) = 1$. That is, given the reduced sample space B, one of the conditional outcomes $A|B$ or $A'|B$ must occur. What this

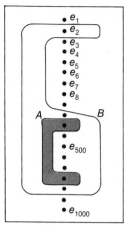

(1). Knowing that B has occurred makes the original sample space, S, irrelevant.

(2). B, the reduced sample space, is now the relevant sample space.

(3). $A \cap B$ (shaded area) represents those possible outcomes in reduced sample space B which are included in A.

FIGURE 6.8   Venn Diagram Showing a Reduced Sample Space

amounts to is that the probability of each elementary event defined on the reduced sample space (B in our case) must be evaluated relative to the *reduced space reference probability* $P(B)$ rather than $P(S)$. This will make the sum of the *conditional probabilities*, given that B has occurred, equal one.

What particular event of the original sample space contains the same possible outcomes as the conditional event ($A|B$) defined on the reduced sample space, B? It is the intersection ($B \cap A$)—the joint event that the respondent must be **both** a TV viewer **and** a *Sixty Minutes* watcher. But the probability of the joint event ($B \cap A$) must be judged relative to the probability of the reduced space B in order to arrive at $P(A|B)$. This ratio of the probability of ($B \cap A$) to the probability of (B) is by definition the **conditional probability of ($A|B$).** Symbolically,

$$P(A|B) = \frac{P(B \cap A)}{P(B)}$$

Suppose the probability that a randomly selected respondent is a television viewer is .30, [$P(B)$]. Suppose the probability that a respondent who is jointly a television viewer and a *Sixty Minutes* viewer is .18 [$P(B \cap A)$]. The probability of drawing a *Sixty Minutes* watcher, if we know that the respondent is a television viewer, is $^{.18}/_{.30}$ or .60, $P(A|B)$. The information that the respondent is a television viewer has changed (conditioned) the chances (the probability) of finding a *Sixty Minutes* watcher. What this example illustrates is an idea you've known all along; that is, relevant information is the kind of information which changes the chance of finding something else.

6.6. The Probability of Two Events Occurring Jointly: The Multiplication Law

A simple transposition of the definition of conditional probability gives an expression for the probability of obtaining the joint occurrences of two events, A

and B. Starting with the conditional probability definition:

$$P(A|B) = \frac{P(A \cap B)}{P(B)}$$

$$P(B)P(A \cap B) = P(A \cap B)$$

$$\mathbf{P(A \cap B) = P(B)P(A|B)}$$

This last equation is called the *multiplication law of probability*. The multiplication law shows that the probability of B and A occurring together is the product of the *unconditional* probability that B occurs, times the *conditional* probability that A occurs if B does (that is, given the information B). The following example illustrates how these statistical concepts relate to business concepts.

Example 6.6.   Brand Usage

Thirty percent of the households in a certain area are users of automatic dishwashers, and of those that are dishwasher users, forty percent use the brand produced by your company. What is the probability that a randomly selected household in the area will turn out to be a user of an automatic dishwasher and your brand?
    Define the following events:

    A = user of your brand
    B = user of an automatic dishwasher
    $P(B \cap A) = P(B)P(A|B)$

In words, P(dishwasher user and user of your brand) = P(dishwasher user) times P(user of your brand, given a dishwasher user)

    $= (.30)(.40)$

    $= .12$

In marketing terminology, .12 is *brand penetration*; .30 is *product penetration*; .40 is *market share*.

It should be noted that since the events $(A \cap B)$ and $(B \cap A)$ mean the same thing (the events occur jointly), then the two event probabilities are also equal. That is:

$$P(A \cap B) = P(B \cap A).$$

6.7. Probability Trees

The tree diagram or the fundamental principle of counting was employed in Chapter 5 to find out how many elementary events there are, and from this the probability of each one. Important problems in statistics are by no means all like this. Certainly when probability is assigned on a subjective or a relative frequency basis, equally likely elementary events should not be expected. Moreover, the subjective or relative frequency probabilities assigned typically do not refer to elementary events. Is there a way of using the probabilities that have been assigned subjectively or on the basis of relative frequency to determine the elementary event probabilities? Fortunately, for these types of problems, the *probability tree diagram* can be an exceptionally valuable aid.

Tracking by Trees

A probability tree is a diagramatic method of explaining the relationship among probabilities in which unconditional and conditional probabilities are expressed on the branches of a tree; the product of the probabilities along a path through the branches is a joint probability—the probability of the elementary event represented by that path. In the following example, a probability tree is used to compute elementary event probabilities which are initially unknown and cannot be assumed equally likely.

Example 6.7. Calculating Joint Probabilities by Probability Trees: Life Insurance

A population of 1000 persons is invited to participate in a group life insurance program designed specifically for that population. Four hundred persons from this population are exposed to favorable promotion about the program prior to their invitation and eighty of these exposed persons accept the invitation. Of six hundred persons not exposed to the promotion prior to their invitation, ninety accept the invitation.

Randomly selecting a person from the population and classifying the selection with respect to the attribute "promotion" and the attribute "status of the invitation" offers four possible joint recordings. Each possible joint recording recognizes that every randomly selected person will have simultaneously promotion status and invitation status.

One can define the unconditional (marginal) events:

E: the person exposed to the promotion
E': the person not exposed to the promotion
A: the person accepting the invitation
A': the person refusing the invitation

One can express the joint events as:

1. exposed to the promotion and accepted the invitation, $E \cap A$

2. exposed to the promotion but did not accept the invitation, $E \cap A'$

3. was not exposed to the promotion but accepted the invitation anyway, $E' \cap A$

4. was not exposed to the promotion and did not accept the invitation, $E' \cap A'$

These four possible joint events are shown on a tree diagram by constructing four branches, one for each joint event (Figure 6.9). The branches cover two stages. The first stage classifies the selected person according to possible promotion status; the second stage, according to the invitation status. The tree diagram can now be converted to a probability tree by filling in the appropriate unconditional probabilities at the first stage and the appropriate conditional probabilities at the second stage (given the first stage has occurred). Importantly, the probability tree now offers a scheme for computing the probability for each of the four joint events—the elementary events of the random sampling experiments.

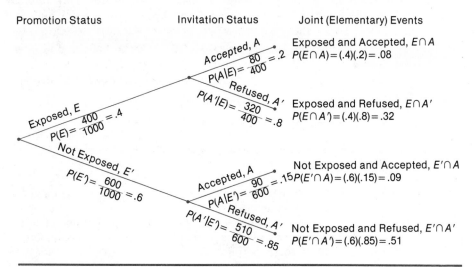

FIGURE 6.9 Probability Tree for Obtaining Joint Probabilities

Using the Tree in Calculating Joint Probabilities

The multiplication rule can be applied to determine the probabilities of the four joint events:

$$P(E \cap A) = P(E)P(A|E)$$
$$P(E \cap A') = P(E)P(A'|E)$$
$$P(E' \cap A) = P(E')P(A|E')$$
$$P(E' \cap A') = P(E')P(A'|E')$$

The connection between the multiplication rule and the tree diagram in Figure 6.9 is both important and simple. It is:

1. The first term on the path (left-hand side) is the probability of selecting the indicated branch at the first stage of the tree diagram. This will always be an unconditional probability.

2. The second term on the path is the conditional probability of exiting from the second stage branching point along the branch indicated by the expression in parenthesis. For example, $P(A|E)$ is the probability of taking branch A from the branching point E; whereas $P(A|E')$ is the probability of taking branch A from the branching point E'.

3. The product of the unconditional and conditional probabilities along each path is the joint probability. It is the probability of finding on a random draw a person with both the promotional status and invitational status stated along the path.

All of the probabilities are easily obtained from the information given. Since forty percent of the persons were exposed to promotion, $P(E) = .4$, it follows that the probability of the complementary event E' is $P(E') = .6$. Since eighty of four hundred persons exposed accepted the invitation, $P(A|E) = {}^{80}\!/_{400} = .2$. It follows that $P(A'|E) = {}^{320}\!/_{400} = .8$ from the fact that the probability of $A|E$ and the probability of the complement event $A'|E$ must sum to one. Since ninety of six hundred persons not exposed accepted the invitation, $P(A|E') = {}^{90}\!/_{600} = .15$, and it follows that $P(A'|E') = {}^{540}\!/_{600} = .85$. The probability of.the joint event at the end of a path is the product of all the probabilities on the sequence of branches leading through the event path. Thus, $P(A \cap E) = P(E)P(A|E) = (.4)(.2) = .08$. The set of joint probabilities at the path ends are again the elementary event probabilities. From them, the probability of any other event in the event space can be calculated. It is important to note that these elementary event probabilities were not known in advance and the equiprobable assumption for elementary events was not tenable. But using the probability tree concept, it was easy to compute the elementary event probabilities from the information given.

Two Things to Note

Two concluding observations about probability trees are important to note and remember:

> the branches at the initial stage always represent unconditional probabilities, while branches at succeeding stages always represent conditional probabilities;

> the sum of the conditional probabilities on the branches exiting from each branching point must be one. This follows from the fact that the entire collection of conditional probabilities over the same given event exhausts the reduced sample space.

6.8. Managerial Issues in Practice— Review Exercise II: Multiplication Rule Checkpoint: Knowing Your Quality Control

Consider a manufacturing situation in which experience indicates that only sixty percent of parts produced by a certain machine will be acceptable. The part can be inspected and they will definitely pass inspection if they are not defective. But twenty percent of the defective parts will also pass inspection. What is the probability that a randomly selected part will be defective and will slip through inspection?

Viewing the status of the part and the outcome of the inspection as the two attributes recorded for each random draw, we are led to a sample space with four possible outcomes to each of which there is a corresponding elementary (joint) event. Each of the elementary events is represented by one of the paths in the probability tree of Figure 6.10. The four elementary (joint) events all have different probabilities. These probabilities are the product of the probabilities of the branches in the path. The joint probability that a randomly selected path is both defective (event D) and okay at inspection (event O) is

$$P(D \cap O) = P(D)P(O|D) = (.4)(.2) = .08.$$

Interpreting this probability as a long-run relative frequency, we can thus say that eight percent of the parts are defective and slip through inspection.

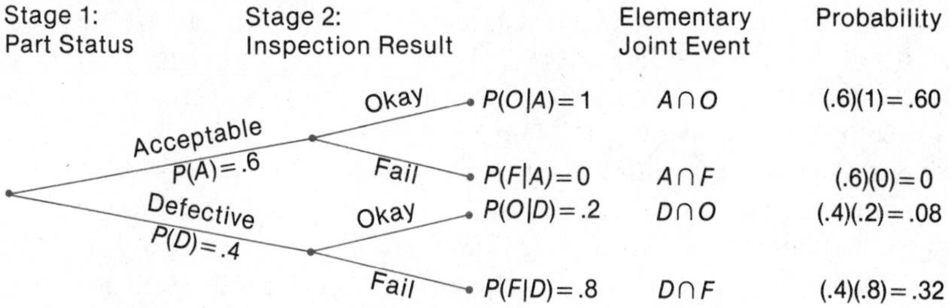

Stage 1: Part Status	Stage 2: Inspection Result		Elementary Joint Event	Probability
Acceptable $P(A)=.6$	Okay	$P(O|A)=1$	$A \cap O$	$(.6)(1)=.60$
	Fail	$P(F|A)=0$	$A \cap F$	$(.6)(0)=0$
Defective $P(D)=.4$	Okay	$P(O|D)=.2$	$D \cap O$	$(.4)(.2)=.08$
	Fail	$P(F|D)=.8$	$D \cap F$	$(.4)(.8)=.32$

FIGURE 6.10   Probability Tree for Quality Control Problem

6.9. Managerial Issues in Practice—
Review Exercise III: Multiplication Rule
Checkpoint: Advertising Effectiveness

Probability trees can be very helpful in studying the effectiveness of advertising. Two conditions are usually regarded as imperative in order for advertising to be effective. First, the advertising message must reach the intended receiver and, second, the message must be influential in converting the recipient into a buyer. The *effectiveness of the medium* can be judged by the probability that a potential buyer is reached. The *effectiveness of the message* can be judged by the conditional probability of purchase for a buyer who is reached as compared to the purchase probability for a buyer who is not reached. The *effectiveness of the advertising program* should be judged by comparing the probability that a potential buyer is both reached and becomes a purchaser with the probability that a potential buyer is not reached but nevertheless becomes a purchaser.

Construct a probability tree showing how the reach and purchase probabilities are used to determine the probabilities used in assessing advertising program effectiveness.

Figure 6.11 depicts the situation as a probability tree. Increasing either $P(R)$ or $P(B|R)$ will improve the level of advertising effectiveness. But it is the product of the two, $P(B \cap R)$, which should be compared with $P(B|R')$ to determine how well the overall effectiveness of the advertising program has fared. For example, suppose $P(B \cap R) = .3$ and $P(B|R') = .1$. Then the probability of being reached and then buying exceeds by 0.2 the probability of buying if not reached by the advertising. Expressed in terms of an expected long run percentage, the impli-

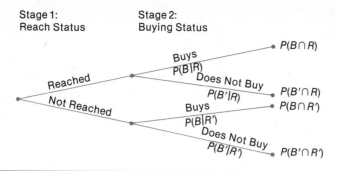

Stage 1:
Reach Status

Stage 2:
Buying Status

FIGURE 6.11   Advertising Effectiveness Probability Tree

cation is that advertising leads to an additional 20 percent of the target population becoming buyers.

6.10. Statistical Independence

Probability trees show conditional probabilities on the branches of the second stage after a branch was selected at the first stage. This situation informs us that the second stage probabilities are statistically dependent upon the event at the first stage. "Statistically independent" means that the probabilities at a particular stage are not affected (conditioned) by the path of branches taken, whether in preceding or subsequent stages. The statistical independence of two events indicates that the chance of the occurrence of one event is undisturbed by the occurrence of the other event. Alternatively stated, if knowledge of B does not alter or change the chances that A will occur, then A and B are independent events. For example, if A is "heads on the first toss" of a coin, and B is "heads on the second toss" of a coin, A and B are independent only if the probability of heads is the same on both tosses.

The formal definition of statistical independence relies on the comparison of conditional and unconditional probabilities. The unconditional probability of an event A is always defined on the original sample space of all the possible outcomes. It is expressed simply as $P(A)$. The conditional probability of A given B recognizes that the relevant sample space is B—a subset of the original sample space. Now the relevant sample space consists of only the possible outcomes included in event B.

> Two events, A and B, are said to be statistically independent if (and only if) $P(A|B) = P(A)$. (Definition of statistical independence)

> Two events are said to be statistically dependent if $P(A|B) \neq P(A)$. (Definition of statistical dependence)

If A and B are statistically independent events, then the occurrence of B can neither increase nor decrease the chances for the occurrence of A.

In recent years the concept of statistical independence has been employed in judging whether or not employers have discriminated against women and minorities in hiring and promotion.

Example 6.10A. Employment Discrimination

Under equal opportunity laws, individuals are supposed to be given an equal chance at hiring and promotion regardless of sex, race, or religion. In statistical language, this means that the conditional probability of promotion given sex, race, or religion should be the same as the unconditional probability of promotion. Promotion and sex, race, or religion should be independent events.

In a lawsuit emanating from employment discrimination claims on the basis of sex, the concept of independence may arise in the following way. First, the ratio of the relative frequency of promoted women to women qualified for promotion would be computed. Then, the ratio of relative frequency of promoted men to men qualified for promotion would be computed and compared to the first ratio. If the difference between the two ratios is too large to ascribe to chance alone (that is, promotion is not independent of sex), the charge of discrimination may be pursued.

Multiplication Rule for Statistically Independent Events

In the special case of independent events, the multiplication rule simplifies as follows:

$P(A \cap B) = P(A)P(A|B) = P(A)P(B)$. (Multiplication rule for independent events)

In other words, the probability that events A and B occur jointly is simply the product of their individual probabilities. Information that B occurs does not change the chances of A occurring.

Example 6.10B. Sampling with Replacement Versus Sampling without Replacement

The distinction between independent and dependent events is important in sampling.

> In sampling with replacement, the results of the draws are statistically independent; that is, the (conditional) probability of observing a particular result on a draw is identical for all draws, regardless of the result of previous draws.

> In sampling without replacement, the results of draws are statistically dependent; that is, the (conditional) probability of observing a particular result on a draw changes with each draw.

Knowing that sample results are statistically independent simplifies the procedure for calculating the probability of a specified sequence of sample results. Suppose a simple random sample of four students is drawn with replacement from a population having 30 percent freshmen, 25 percent sophomores, 25 percent juniors, and 20 percent seniors. Without having to use a tree diagram, the (joint) probability of drawing a particular outcome, say freshman, sophomore, junior, and senior can be easily obtained. It is the product of the four unconditional (marginal) probabilities:

the sampling with replacement assures the applicability of the multiplication rule for independent events.

$$\left.\begin{array}{l}\text{Joint Probability of the sequence:}\\ \text{Freshman, } F; \text{Sophomore, } S_1; \text{Junior, } J; \text{Senior, } S_2\end{array}\right] = P(F \cap S_1 \cap J \cap S_2)$$
$$= (.30)(.25)(.25)(.20)$$
$$= .00375$$

6.11. Managerial Issues in Practice—
Review Exercise IV: Competitive Bidding

A contractor submits separate contract bids for the plumbing and heating of a building. The contractor estimates subjectively that the odds are 60–40 in favor or being awarded the plumbing contract. Further, she estimates that there is a $\frac{2}{3}$ chance of receiving the heating contract if the plumbing contract is received. Should the contractor not receive the plumbing contract, she nevertheless feels that she has a $\frac{1}{4}$ chance of receiving the heating contract.

a. What is the probability that the heating contract will be received and the plumbing contract will not?

b. What is the probability of receiving the heating contract?

c. Are the two events *state of the heating contract* and *state of the plumbing contract* dependent?

Solution Step 1: Identify the elementary events. In this experiment, two characteristics are observed: plumbing contract status and heating contract status. A two stage tree diagram identifies the elementary events corresponding to the four possible outcomes in the sample space. The following symbols are used for the four marginal events:

P: plumbing contract awarded
P': plumbing contract not awarded
H: heating contract awarded
H': heating contract not awarded

Step 2: Construct a probability tree showing how the product of marginal and conditional event probabilities lead to the elementary event probabilities.

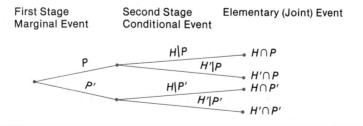

First Stage Marginal Event	Second Stage Conditional Event	Elementary (Joint) Event

STEP 1

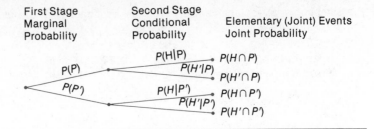

First Stage Marginal Probability	Second Stage Conditional Probability	Elementary (Joint) Events Joint Probability

STEP 2

Let $P(P)$ represent the probability of being awarded the plumbing contract, and let $P(P')$ represent its complement, the probability of not being awarded the plumbing contract. Let $P(H|P)$ and $P(H'|P)$ represent the conditional probabilities of the heating contract being awarded and not awarded, respectively, given that the plumbing contract is awarded. Let $P(H|P')$ and $P(H'|P')$ represent the conditional probabilities of the heating contract being awarded and not awarded, respectively, given that the plumbing contract *is not* awarded.

Step 3: Insert in the probability tree the probabilities given in the problem. Odds of 60–40 in favor of being awarded the contract means that $P(P) = .60$. $P(H|P)$ is given as $\frac{2}{3}$ or .67. $P(H|P')$ is given as $\frac{1}{4}$ or .25.

Step 4: Fill in the remainder of the probabilities on the branches by finding the complementary event probabilities.

$$P(P') = 1 - P(P) = 1 - .6 = .4$$

$$P(H'|P) = 1 - P(H|P) = 1 - .67 = .33$$

$$P(H'|P') = 1 - P(H|P') = 1 - .25 = .75$$

Step 5: The event that the heating contract will be received and the plumbing contract will not is the joint event $H \cap P'$. The probability of this joint event is obtained by applying the multiplication rule to the probabilities shown on the third branch of the probability tree. This is the answer to the first equation.

$$P(H \cap P') = P(H|P')P(P') = (.25)(.40) = .10$$

Step 6: Answering the second question requires knowing two elementary event probabilities. The unconditional (marginal) probability $P(H)$ is the sum of the joint (elementary events) probabilities in which H occurs. Thus, $P(H) = P(H \cap P) + P(H \cap P')$. The latter two probabilities are given by the first and third probability tree branches. $P(H \cap P')$ was found in the previous step to be .10. The probability of the joint event $H \cap P$ is obtained by applying the multiplication rule to the probabilities shown on the first branch of the probability tree:

$$P(H \cap P) = P(H|P)P(P) = (.67)(.60) = .40$$

Step 7: The probability of obtaining the heating contract can now be obtained by summing the probabilities of the two elementary events included in event H:

$$P(H) = P(H \cap P) + P(H \cap P') = .40 + .10 = .50.$$

Step 8: To determine whether the two event states of the heating contract and the two event states of the plumbing contract are dependent or independent, one approach would be to compare $P(H|P)$ or $P(H|P')$ with $P(H)$. These two conditional probability values, $\frac{2}{3}$ and $\frac{1}{4}$ respectively, are not the same as the unconditional probability value $\frac{1}{2}$. It implies that the occurrence of one state of the plumbing contract is information that changes the probability of occurrence of the heating contract; in other words, they are not events which occur independently.

In the next example, the steps to the solution are again provided but with a somewhat reduced explanation.

6.12. Managerial Issues in Practice— Review Exercise V: Stock Price Changes

Stock G is a glamour stock and stock B is a blue chip. The probability that Gs price increases in a given day is .4; the probability that it remains unchanged in price is also .4. The probability that Bs price increases is .3, and the probability that it remains unchanged is .5. If Bs price does increase, the probability that G also increases is .6, but the probability that G remains unchanged is .2. If Bs price remains unchanged, the probability is .4 that G increases, but the probability is .5 that G remains unchanged in price.

What is the probability that on a given day

a. both G and B increase in price?
b. at least one of the two stocks increases in price?
c. either G or B but not both increases in price?
d. exactly one of the two stocks increases in price?
e. neither of the two stocks go up in price?
f. both stocks remain unchanged in price?
g. both stocks decrease in price?
h. neither stock decreases in price?
i. one stock increases while the other decreases in price?
j. if B decreases in price, G increases?
k. if G decreases in price, B increases?

Before answering the individual parts of the problem, let us compute the various elements that will be needed.

Step 1: Identify the nine elementary events corresponding to the possible outcomes in the sample space. The following symbols are used:

$B+$	B increases in price
$B°$	B remains unchanged in price
$B-$	B decreases in price
$G+$	G increases in price
$G°$	G remains unchanged in price
$G-$	G decreases in price

The tree diagram on the left is drawn with B leading to G. The tree diagram on the right is drawn with G leading to B. Either way will give the same set of joint events at the end of the branches. For example, $G-\cap B+$ is one of the joint events on the left diagram. It is also one of the events on the right diagram. It does not matter whether the event is written $G-\cap B+$ or $B+\cap G-$. Note, though, that $G-|B+$ is *not* the same event as $B+|G-$.

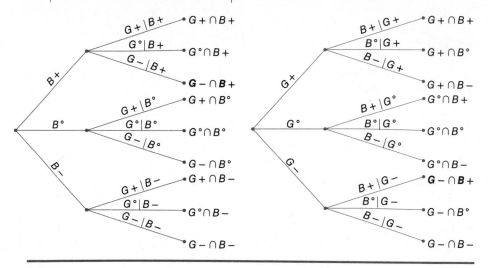

STEP 1

Step 2:

$$P(B-) = 1 - P(B+) - P(B°)$$
$$= 1 - .3 - .5 = .2$$

The sum of the probabilities exiting from any branching point must equal one.

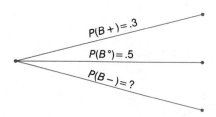

STEP 2

Step 3:

$$P(G-|B+) = 1 - .6 - .2 = .2$$

Same reasoning as in Step 2.

Step 4:

$$P(G-|B°) = 1 - .4 - .5 = .1$$

Same reasoning as in Step 2.

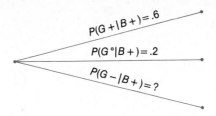

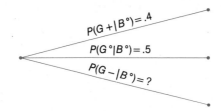

Step 5:
Computation of probabilities of the joint events described by the different possible paths through the probability tree are determined by application of the multiplication rule.

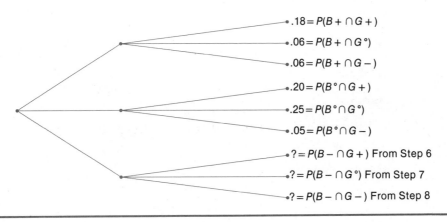

Step 6:

$$P(G+) = P(B+ \cap G+) + P(B° \cap G+) + P(B- \cap G+) = .4$$
$$= \quad .18 \quad + \quad .20 \quad + P(B- \cap G+) = .4$$

Therefore, $P(B- \cap G+) = .4 - .18 - .20 = .02$

The unconditional (marginal) probability of an event is the sum of the joint probabilities for each of the paths through the probability tree in which the event occurs. For example, $P(B+ \cap G+) = P(B+)P(G+|B+) = .18$. This is a critical step for all subsequent probability calculations. Both trees will be needed.

Step 7:

$$P(G°) = P(B+ \cap G°) + P(B° \cap G°) + P(B- \cap G°) = .4$$
$$= \quad .06 \quad + \quad .25 \quad + P(B-\cap G°) = .4$$

Therefore, $P(B- \cap G°) = .4 - .06 - .25 = .09$

Same reasoning as in Step 6.

Step 8:

$$P(G-) = P(B+ \cap G-) + P(B° \cap G-) + P(B- \cap G-) = .2$$
$$= \quad .06 \quad + \quad .05 \quad + P(B-\cap G-) = .2$$

Therefore, $P(B- \cap G-) = .2 - .06 - .05 = .09$

Same reasoning as in Step 6.

We can now proceed to answer the individual parts of the problem.

a. Probability that both B and G increase in price? $P(B+ \cap G+) = .18$

b. Probability that at least one of the two stocks increase?

$$P(B+ \cup G+) = P(B+) + P(G+) - P(B+ \cap G+)$$
$$= \quad .3 \quad + \quad .4 \quad - \quad .18 \quad = .52$$

The general form of the addition rule.

c. Probability that G or B but not both increase?

$$P(B+ \cap G+') \cup (B+' \cap G+) = P(B+ \cap G+') + P(B+' \cap G+)$$
$$= P(B+ \cap G°) + P(B+ \cap G-) + P(B° \cap G+) + P(B- \cap G+)$$
$$= \quad .06 \quad + \quad .06 \quad + \quad .20 \quad + \quad .02 \quad = .34$$

Special case of the addition rule for mutually exclusive events. Note that the intersection of the two events forming the union has zero probability; $P[(B+ \cap G+') \cap (B+' \cap G+)] = 0.$

d. Probability that exactly one of the two stocks increase? Since "exactly one" is the same event as "G or B, but not both," the answer is .34, as for Part C.

e. Probability that neither of the two stocks increase?

$$P(B+' \cap G+') = P(B° \cap G°) +$$
$$P(B° \cap G-) + P(B- \cap G°) + P(B- \cap G-)$$
$$= .25 + .05 + .09 + .09 = .48$$

Sum of mutually exclusive events.

f. Probability that both stocks remain unchanged?

$$P(B° \cap G°) = .25$$

One of the numerated joint events in Step 5.

g. Probability that both stocks decrease in price?

$$P(B- \cap G-) = .09$$

Calculated in Step 8.

h. Probability that neither stock decreases in price?

$$P(B-' \cap G-') = 1 - P(B- \cup G-)$$
$$= 1 - [P(B-) + P(G-) - P(B- \cap G-)]$$
$$= 1 - [.2 + .2 - .09] = .69$$

Use of complementary event axiom and general addition rule.

i. Probability that one stock decreases while the other increases?

$$P(B+ \cap G-) + P(B- \cap G+) = .06 + .02 = .08$$

Sum of mutually exclusive events.

j. Probability that if B decreases, G increases?

$$P(G+|B-) = \frac{P(G+ \cap B-)}{P(B-)} = \frac{.02}{.20} = .10$$

Conditional probability from rearranging the multiplication rule.

k. Probability that if G decreases, B increases?

$$P(B+|G-) = \frac{P(B+ \cap G-)}{P(G-)} = \frac{.06}{.20} = .3$$

Same reasoning as calculation in Part j.

6.13. Managerial Issues in Practice—
Review Exercise VI: Sampling Accounts
Receivable

An audit-update was taken by a local CPA firm having 65 client accounts, six known from last period's check to be behind in their payments of their billings. If four accounts are selected at random without replacement from the 65, what is the probability that at least one of the accounts selected falls in the late-payment category? (*Hint:* the probability that at least one account selected is a late payer is one minus the probability that all accounts are current in their payments. The calculations leading to this latter probability are much simpler than the calculations required to calculate directly the former probability.)

In this problem there will be four recordings, one for each of the accounts selected. Since there are two possibilities (in default, not in default) for the recordings on each account, there are $2^4 = 16$ elementary events. Each of these can be depicted by a branch on a tree diagram. A probability tree is constructed by assigning probabilities to the branches. Application of the multiplication rule to the probabilities on a branch gives the elementary event probability at the end of the branch. We have not shown the tree diagram or probability tree because we will be working with only one branch.

Of the 16 branches on the probability tree only one corresponds to the event that all accounts are current. Let A_i represent the ith account drawn being current. Thus A_1 indicates that the first account drawn is current, $A_2|A_1$ means that the second account drawn is current given that the first one is current, etc.

The probability that the first account is current, $P(A_1)$, is $^{59}\!/_{65}$. Having drawn a current account, the probability that the second account is current is the conditional probability, $P(A_2|A_1)$, which is $^{58}\!/_{64}$ (sampling without replacement leaves only 64 accounts remaining, of which 58 are current). So the joint probability of two current accounts is

$$P(A_1 \cap A_2) = P(A_1)P(A_2|A_1) = {}^{59}\!/_{65} \cdot {}^{58}\!/_{64}$$

by way of the multiplication rule. To calculate the subsequent joint probabilities of the first three accounts drawn being current, $P(A_1 \cap A_2 \cap A_3)$, one needs the conditional probability that the third account is current given the first two accounts being current; that is, $P(A_3|A_1 \cap A_2) = {}^{57}\!/_{63}$. Then

$$P(A_1 \cap A_2 \cap A_3) = P(A_1)P(A_2|A_1)P(A_3|A_1 \cap A_2) = {}^{59}\!/_{65} \cdot {}^{58}\!/_{64} \cdot {}^{57}\!/_{63}.$$

Continuing the pattern, the probability that all four accounts are current is given by the following:

$$P(A_1 \cap A_2 \cap A_3 \cap A_4)$$
$$= P(A_1)P(A_2|A_1)P(A_3|A_1 \cap A_2)P(A_4|A_1 \cap A_2 \cap A_3)$$
$$= {}^{59}\!/_{65} \cdot {}^{58}\!/_{64} \cdot {}^{57}\!/_{63} \cdot {}^{56}\!/_{62} = .67$$

Using the complementary event rule, we can say that

$$P(\text{at least one late paying account}) = 1 - P(\text{none late paying})$$
$$= 1 - P(\text{all current})$$
$$= 1 - .67$$
$$= .33$$

6.14. Concluding Comments

In this chapter we have considered rules concerning the probabilities of events. It was necessary to distinguish between *unconditional* probability and *conditional* probability, the latter being based upon only a subset of elements in the original sample space. From the concept of the *intersection* of two events, $A \cap B$, we developed the *multiplication rule* for the probability that the two events jointly occur:

$$P(A \cap B) = P(A)P(B|A)$$
$$= P(B)P(A|B).$$

From the concept of the *union* of two events, $A \cup B$, we developed the *addition rule* for the probability that at least one of the two events occur:

$$P(A \cup B) = P(A) + P(B) - P(A \cap B).$$

A distinction was drawn between two events that are *statistically dependent*, a situation in which

$$P(B) \neq P(B|A),$$

and two events that are *statistically independent*, a situation in which

$$P(B) = P(B|A).$$

Another helpful rule relating event probabilities is the rule for the *complement* of an event:

$$P(A') = 1 - P(A).$$

The concept of statistically independent events is all too frequently confused with the concept of *mutually exclusive* events. Two events are statistically independent if the occurrence of one does not affect the probability of the other's occurrence. Two events are mutually exclusive if their intersection is the *null* or impossible event, which has zero probability. Since the occurrence of one of the mutually exclusive events depends upon the nonoccurrence of the other, the two cannot be statistically independent; quite the opposite, they are perfectly dependent.

The distinction between statistical independence and mutual exclusivity can be illustrated in coin tossing. If we let H_2 represent heads on the second toss and H_1 represent heads on the first toss, statistical independence means that $P(H_2) = P(H_2|H_1)$. That is, the probability of heads on the second toss is not affected by the outcome of the first toss. If we represent tails on the second toss by T_2, we can say that H_2 and T_2 are mutually exclusive. If they were also independent, this would require $P(H_2) = P(H_2|T_2)$. The latter probability is zero, because we cannot get both heads and tails on the same toss.

When elementary event probabilities are not readily assigned directly, they may sometimes be found indirectly from the multiplication rule. This is accomplished by describing the elementary events as the intersection of two composite events having known unconditional and conditional probabilities. A graphical counterpart of the multiplication rule known as a *probability tree* can often be exploited to show the relationship between unconditional, conditional, and elementary events and their respective probabilities.

In Chapter Five and in this chapter, we have looked exclusively at probability questions for attributes or categories. In the next chapter our attention turns to quantitative variables. There we shall find probability counterparts to the frequency distributions studied in Chapter Three, and to the summary measures studied in Chapter Four.

Footnotes and References

[1] *Wall Street Journal*, October 4, 1974
[2] Since:

$$S \cup \emptyset = S$$
$$P(S \cup \emptyset) = P(S)$$

so $P(S) + P(\emptyset) = 1$

or $P(\emptyset) = 1 - P(S) = 0$

Questions and Problems

1. The intersection of two mutually exclusive events is the null event, which is assigned a probability of zero. Explain the logic of this assignment.

2. In determining the probability of the union of two events, is it important to know if the two events are mutually exclusive? Explain.

3. The terms $P(A \cap B)$ and $P(B \cap A)$ are identical in meaning, but the terms $P(A|B)$ and $P(B|A)$ are not. Discuss.

4. In conducting a marketing survey, is it important to know that the probable response of A given B is merely the probable response of A? What are the implications?

5. Can two events which are mutually exclusive also be statistically independent? Explain.

6. If the probability that a newborn baby will be a boy is .51, what is the probability of a girl?

7. The probability that a parcel of real estate will increase in price is .40 and the probability that it will remain unchanged in price is .15. What is the probability of a price decrease?

8. The probability that a bet on the Detroit Tigers baseball team will win is .4; the probability that a bet on the Detroit Lions football team will win is .7; the probability that both bets will win is .25. What is the probability that
a. at least one bet will win;
b. both bets lose?

9. Compute the answers to Problem 5-29 taking advantage of the probability rules given in this chapter. Were you able to find shortcuts to the answers you previously found?

10. An investor in a certain stock figured her probability of making money is .75, of breaking even is .10. What does she figure is her probability of losing money?

11. If the probability that a person selected at random is a female *Time* magazine reader is .3, and the probability that the person is a male *Time* magazine reader is .4, what is the probability that a person selected at random is a *Time* reader?

12. It is estimated that the probability that a fuse coming off a certain assembly line is defective and passed is .02, but that it is defective and rejected is .07. What is the probability that a fuse coming off this assembly line is defective?

13. If 72% of the purchasers of hair blowers are women, 60% of all purchasers are over 25 years old, and 90% of all purchasers are either women or over 25, what percentage of the purchasers are women over 25?

14. Compute the answer to Problem 5-34a using the probability rules given in this chapter.

15. Determine $P(A)$ if $P(A \text{ or } B) = .6$, $P(B) = .4$ and
a. $P(A') = .43$
b. $P(A \text{ and } B) = .3$
c. $P(A|B) = .5$
d. A and B are independent
e. A and B are mutually exclusive

16. Given: C_0 Family does not have a car
C_1 Family has one car
C_2 Family has 2 or more cars
I_1 Family income is under \$12,000
I_2 Family income is \$12,000 or more
and that from the area under study it was found that:

$$P(C_0) = .10 \qquad P(I_1) = .70$$
$$P(C_1) = .65 \qquad P(C_2|I_2) = .4$$

a. Find $P(C_2 \cap I_2)$
b. Find $P(C_2 \cup I_2)$
c. Find $P(I_2|C_2)$

17. Marketers generally assume a hierarchy of stages before a product is actually purchased. A potential buyer has to become aware of and knowledgeable about the product, then become convinced that the product should be purchased, and then get around to making the purchase. After trying the product the buyer may adopt the product and become a repeat purchaser.

Much of marketing research is directed to finding out the appropriate probability associated with the potential buyer at each buying stage. Suppose a member of the target market for a particular new product has a probability of .6 of becoming aware of and knowledgeable about it: if that happens, a .3 probability of becoming convinced to purchase it; and if that happens, a .8 probability of actually making the purchase; and if that happens, a .7 probability of becoming a repeat purchaser. Use the multiplication rule to find the probability that the target market member becomes a repeat purchaser.

18. Given S_1 Person is male
S_2 Person is female
F_1 Person owns a Ford
F_2 Person does not own a Ford
The employees at a Ford Plant were surveyed to see if they owned a Ford. It was found:

$$P(S_1) = .6$$
$$P(F_1) = .45$$
$$P(F_2|S_2) = .75$$

a. Find $P(F_2 \text{ and } S_2)$
b. Find $P(F_2 \text{ or } S_2)$
c. Find $P(S_2|F_2)$

19. The probability that an automobile insurance policyholder will be involved in an accident leading to liability claims is .030; the probability of collision damage claims is .040; the probability of both liability and collision claims is .025. What is the probability of
a. either liability or collision claims;
b. neither liability nor collision claims?

20. Suppose the probability that a randomly selected young adult male is a *Sports Illustrated* reader is .4, the probability of drawing a *Time* reader is .5, and the probability of drawing a reader of both *Sports Illustrated* and *Time* is .15. What is the probability of drawing
a. a *Time* reader, given that the person reads *Sports Illustrated*?
b. a *Sports Illustrated* reader, given that the person reads *Time*?

21. A manufacturer is making bids for 3

contracts. She is sure to get at least one, and after subjectively analyzing the situation she feels that the probability that she will get two is .3, and that she will get all three is .2. From past experience she has found that if she gets one contract, the probability that she makes a profit that year is .4, whereas the probability of profit is .8 if she gets all three. The probability of a loss is .3 if she gets only one contract, .2 if she gets two contracts. The probability of breaking even with two contracts is .3, but is .15 with three contracts.

Make the appropriate diagram and compute the probability that:
a. given two contracts, she makes a profit.
b. she gets two contracts and makes a profit.
c. she gets three contracts and suffers a loss.
d. doesn't suffer a loss.
e. either suffers a loss or breaks even.
f. either gets three contracts or makes a profit.

22. Recompute the answers to Parts a–k of Review Exercise V (Section 6.12) using the following information: the probability that in a given day Gs price decreases is .3 and remains the same is .3, the probability that Bs price increases is .2 and decreases is .3, and the conditional probabilities given in the review exercise remain unchanged. (Hint: construct both forward and reverse tree diagrams, filling in all known probabilities. Compute as many elementary event probabilities as you can from the forward tree. Transfer these to the reverse tree and solve for the remaining probabilities.)

23. In order to check the effectiveness of a store's advertising in a local paper, the store manager asked each person as they checked out if they had seen the ad. He also noted if they had purchased the sale item. The results are summarized in Table 6.3, given on the following page.

Using relative frequencies as probabilities, find:

a. $P(A)$
b. $P(A')$
c. $P(P)$
d. $P(P')$
e. $P(A|P)$
f. $P(A|P')$
g. $P(P|A)$
h. $P(P|A')$
i. $P(A'|P)$
j. $P(A'|P')$
k. $P(P'|A)$
l. $P(P'|A')$
m. $P(A \cap P)$
n. $P(A' \cap P)$
o. $P(A \cap P')$
p. $P(A' \cap P')$

TABLE 6.3. Advertising Effectiveness

	SAW AD (A)	DIDN'T SEE AD (A')	TOTALS
Purchased sale item (P)	20	15	35
Didn't purchase sale item (P')	35	30	65
TOTALS	55	45	100

24. Tell if the following are independent events.

a. On a role of two dice
E_1: a 5 on one die
E_2: a 3 on the other die

b. With 3 red and 6 green chips in a box, drawing without replacement
E_1: first chip drawn is red
E_2: second chip drawn is red

c. With 3 red and 6 green chips in a box, drawing with replacement
E_1: first chip drawn is red
E_2: second chip drawn is red

d. Two fair dice are rolled once
E_1: the sum of the two dice is 7
E_2: the two dice have the same number

25. A firm has two mini-computers. Due to the demand of use and the chance of breakdown, the probability that a specific computer will be available when needed is .85. Assuming the availability of each is independent of the other, what is the probability:

a. at least one will be available when needed?

b. neither will be available?

26. A company has two loading docks and is concerned about the availability of one when needed. The probability that a specific dock is unused at a given time is .6. Assuming the availability of each is independent of the other, what is the probability:

a. both will be available if 2 trucks come in at the same time?

b. only one will be available?

c. neither will be available?

27. A point-of-purchase survey reveals that 90 percent of men's razor blade purchasers selected *Blue Blades*, and 10 percent selected *Sword Blades*. A follow-up survey reveals that ninety percent of the original *Blue Blade* purchasers remained loyal to the brand on their next purchase (with the other ten percent switching to *Sword Blades*). The follow-up survey also reveals that ninety percent of the original *Sword Blade* users remained loyal to the brand on their next purchase (with the other ten percent switching to *Blue Blades*). Assume that one of the surveyed purchasers is selected at random. What is the probability that the selected person:

a. originally purchased *Blue Blades?*

b. purchased *Blue Blades* the second time, if the original purchase was *Blue Blades?*

c. purchased *Blue Blades* the second time, if the original purchase was *Sword Blades?*

d. purchased *Blue Blades* both times?

e. purchased *Blue Blades* the second time?

28. Is the purchase of razor blades in Problem 27 statistically dependent upon or independent of the previous brand purchased? Did the survey market share of *Blue Blades* increase, decrease, or remain the same between the original survey and the follow-up survey?

29. For the situation described in Problem 38 in Chapter 5:

a. What is the probability that two bulbs have to be tried?

b. Three?

c. Four?

d. Five?

e. Six?

30. On a certain assembly line, an article gets inspected twice. The probability a defective gets passed by the first inspector is .05, and of those, .12 is the probability of getting passed by the second. What is the probability that a defective gets passed by both inspectors?

31. For the situation described in Problem 40 in Chapter 5, use a probability tree to find the probability that it will take three suppliers to find a reliable one that can be added to the in-list.

32. Effective managers are hard to come by, but essential for the success of a corporation. Many firms recognize this and set up management development programs to identify managerial talent. Suppose a firm hires at the nonmanagerial level a pool of candidates from which it intends to pick future managers. All persons hired have been assessed as having managerial potential. Among those hopefuls some will make good managers. Personnel records suggest that historically, half of the persons initially screened for the management opening prove to be effective, while the other half are ineffective.

With an entry position currently open, the corporate personnel director screens candidates who appear qualified for the opportunity to earn his or her "management spurs" and chooses one for a series of management assignments. Effective performance on these assignments leads to a promotion to managerial ranks, whereas ineffective performance leads to firing, a dead end job, or some other not-so-subtle hint to find employment elsewhere. If the first hopeful selected does not achieve management status, the personnel director goes back to the candidate pool and chooses another candidate. The search continues until one of the candidates proves to be effective and is promoted to management ranks.

a. What is the probability that only one candidate has to be given the opportunity to fill the management opening?

b. What is the probability that it will take exactly two candidates?

33. The corporate staff described in Review Exercise I is now planning a two year investment program. The funds for financing the program depend upon the ability of the firm to generate retained earnings (earnings that are not distributed to stockholders) from the profits on current projects of its Aerospace and Consumer Divisions. The corporate staff believes that the profit picture will be identical in the second year to the one described in Review Exercise I. Because current projects are designed with a one year payback criterion (the initial investment is recoverable in one year), assume that one year's profit picture is independent of the other year's profit picture.

a. What is the probability that over the two years at least one division will be profitable each year?

b. Both divisions will be profitable in both years?

c. Neither division will be profitable in any year?

d. Do the events defined in a, b, c, exhaust the sample space? Explain briefly.

e. Are they mutually exclusive? Explain briefly.

34. The corporate-staff report referred to in Review Exercise I was developed in three stages. First, the firm's economic, political, technological, and ecological environments were studied. On the basis of emerging trends that were observed the staff developed two alternative environmental outcomes they thought possible. Alternative A was subjectively assigned probability of $\frac{2}{3}$; Alternative B was assigned probability $\frac{1}{3}$. Next, the financial group at the aerospace division was contacted. The financial group of the division was asked to assess the probability of a favorable profit outlook for each alternative. They assessed the probability of a favorable profit outlook at .6 for Alternative A and .75 for Alternative B. Then the consumer products financial group at the division was contacted and asked the same thing. They assessed the probability of a favorable profit outlook at .36 for Alternative A and .63 for Alternative B. Finally, the corporate staff used the information to develop a probability tree. Assume that for a given state of the environment, A or B, the status of profitability at one division is unrelated to the profitability of the other.

a. What is the (joint) probability of Alternative B and a favorable profit outlook at both divisions?

b. Complete the probability tree and use it to find the probability for each of the profit possibilities for the entire corporation (both divisions).

Probability Distributions and Their Summary Measures

Preview. In Chapters 3 and 4 we looked at the frequency distribution of a single variable and its summary measures such as the mean and standard deviation; for example, the frequency distribution and summary measures of bond refundings. In Chapters 5 and 6 we developed rules of probability for measuring uncertainty. Now we want to put these chapters together and apply the idea of probability to the distribution of a variable and its summary measures. The purpose of this probability framework is to establish a useful way of dealing with uncertainty. This is necessary because business decisions are made under uncertainty.

The first part of this chapter presents a general way of defining the numerical value for a single variable of interest and of assigning probabilities to the values. The complete description of the distribution of numerical values and their probabilities is called the probability distribution. The probability distribution serves as a basis for defining events and calculating their probabilities. The summary measures of the distribution are often sufficient to answer questions about the nature of the probability distribution. Similar to the summary measures of empirical frequency distributions, the summary measures describe the central tendency and the amount of spread (as opposed to the amount of concentration) shown by the values of the distribution. With the aid of the summary measures and Chebyshev's Inequality, general probability statements about finding a range of numerical values can be made.

The second part of the chapter focuses on two numerically defined variables of interest, the probabilities of the variables jointly occurring and the nature of the relationship between their joint movement or variation. Summary measures describing the joint distribution are also discussed. The chapter ends with a discussion about a linear combination of variables and what can be said about the summary measures that describe the center and variability of the distribution that represents their sum and their average.

7.1. Random Variables

In Chapter Six we saw how tree diagrams simplify the task of determining probabilities, especially when the number of possible outcomes is very large. Since each branch of the tree represents one of the possible outcomes, the tree is a complete description of the random experiment. However, we also saw that the number of branches of the tree can be astronomical even for seemingly simple random experiments. For example, in drawing a random sample of fifty persons from a population defined according to users and non-users of a product, the number of possible outcomes is 2^{50}—an astronomically large number. Is it necessary to work with all the possible outcomes? How could we manage information on the possible outcomes and events? The amount of detailed information is almost certainly more than we can easily comprehend. What is needed is an effective way of organizing and condensing information on the possible outcomes, the corresponding elementary events, and their probabilities.

In many, if not most, random experiments we neither need nor want all of the detailed information about possible outcomes of the sample space. Let's illustrate this point.

Example 7.1.   Eliminate the Information You Don't Need to Know: Inspecting Defective Products

Suppose a manufacturer's incoming inspection department receives a vendor's shipment of three parts produced by a process which frequently yields defective output. Let us say that each part has probability .5 of being defective. Classifying each part as either good or defective, we have eight possible outcomes as shown in Figure 7.1. However, for purposes of describing the overall quality level of the shipment, we would have little interest in knowing whether a defective part happened to be the first one sampled, or the second, or the third. Our interest would center on *how many* of the parts turn out to be defective. For this purpose, the key piece of information about the possible outcome is whether number zero, one, two, or three correctly describes the number of defective parts it contains. In other words, although there are eight descriptive possible outcomes, the information of interest can be captured numerically by one of only four numbers.

A quick glance at Figure 7.2 shows that the transformation from the original sample space to the new sample space is accomplished by the introduction of the concept of a *random variable*. Defined over the numerical valued sample space, the random variable provides a numerical rule of correspondence which links the descriptive outcomes and the numerical values. The random variable is commonly expressed as a capital letter, say X, Y, Z.[1] The random variable specifies our point of interest. From the listed outcomes showing the good-defective categorical features our attention has focused on the number of defectives. For our example, the random variable X can refer to the number of defectives. Hypo-

1st Part Inspected	2nd Part Inspected	3rd Part Inspected	Possible Outcomes	Number of Defective Parts

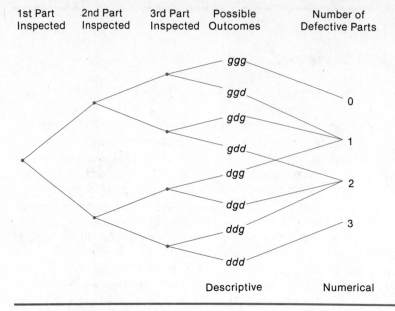

FIGURE 7.1 Tree Diagram Showing Descriptive Outcomes Summarized Numerically

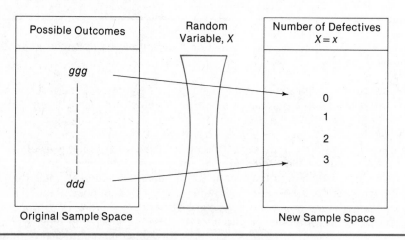

FIGURE 7.2 Random Variable X: The Number of Defectives

thetically, interest could have focused on the random variable Y, which could stand for the number of good parts.

Let specific assignments to the value of the random variable be denoted by

$$X = x.$$

The small letter x therefore represents any specific values for the random variable. In the case of defectives, $x = 0, 1, 2, 3$. Figure 7.2 shows the scheme of the random variable transformation in the case where the random variable is X, the number of defectives.

Limiting our attention to the number of defectives, we need notation for the different events that can be specified, say the event *two defective*. Commonly this event is symbolized as:

$$X = 2$$

and is read "where the value of the random variable assumes the value two."

The notation for the probabilities of such events as $(X = 0)$, $(X = 1)$, . . . $(X = x)$ is denoted by: $P(X = 1)$, $P(X = 2)$, . . . $P(X = x)$. At times this notation becomes cumbersome to write and $P(1)$, $P(2)$, . . . $P(x)$ is substituted.

7.2. Probability Distributions

The array of the specific values of the random variable together with the associated probabilities is customarily referred to as a *probability distribution*. Once the probability distribution is known, all the questions pertaining to our interest about X can be easily answered. For example, to find the probability of "no more than one defective" the expression would be $P(X \leq 1)$, where the math symbol $\leq$ means less than or equal to. The relevant probabilities in the probability distribution for this event are the probability of zero defectives $P(X = 0)$ and the probability of one defective part $P(X = 1)$. But, how do we obtain the probability distribution in the first place?

To find the probability distribution for a random variable, one can start with the elementary events derived from the outcomes of the original sample space. The probability of any value of a random variable is simply the sum of the probabilities of the elementary events. The probability of each elementary event (see Figure 7.1) is ⅛. Thus, the event "two defectives" ($X = 2$) is the union of 3 of the 8 equally probable elementary events derived from the outcomes *ddg, dgd, gdd*. Each of the three elementary events has the same probability ⅛, and their summed probability is ⅜. The probability of each of the other values of the random variable can be similarly computed. The results are shown in Figure 7.3.

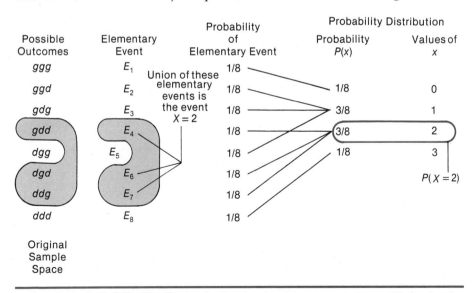

FIGURE 7.3 Probability Distribution for Random Variable X = "Number of Defectives"

A graphic version of the defective parts probability distribution is shown in Figure 7.4.

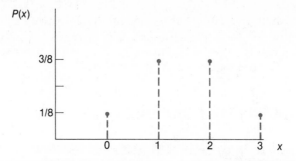

FIGURE 7.4 Graph of Probability Distribution for Defective Parts Example

7.3. Probability Distributions Versus Relative Frequency Distributions: Theory Versus Reality

Probability distributions are the theoretical counterpart to the empirical relative frequency distributions discussed in Chapters Two through Four. Probability distributions describe the range of uncertainty about the forthcoming values of the random experiment. Empirical relative frequency distributions describe the variation that *has* occurred for the variable. That is, relative frequency distributions show the distribution of values that result from actual successive repetitions of the random experiment. Successive repetitions of the random experiment provide actual outcomes from the probability distribution. Figure 7.5 shows two empirical (relative frequency) distributions obtained by drawing random samples with event probabilities specified by the theoretical (probability) distribution shown in Figure 7.4. The empirical distribution on the left is based

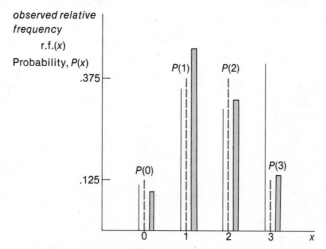

FIGURE 7.5 Comparison of Theoretical and Empirical Distributions

on several samples of size ten. The one on the right is based on samples of size one-hundred. It is apparent from the figure that relative frequencies come closer to the theoretical probabilities the larger the sample. With an extremely large sample size, the sampling empirical relative frequencies should "settle down" very near the underlying theoretical probability values. This is consistent with the view that the probabilities assigned to the values of a random variable are identical to the *long run* relative frequencies.

7.4. Probability Distribution Assessment by Smoothing Historical Data

Knowing that probabilities represent long run relative frequencies is of key importance. It confirms the eventual similarity of probability distributions and *long run* relative frequency distributions. In addition, it provides the basis for using observed relative frequency to make assessments about the features of the underlying probability distribution. This connection is valuable when (1) one is willing to assume that future occurrences will be determined by the same underlying mechanisms as the past (historical data); (2) one wants to use the probability distributions as a sensible way of thinking about the underlying model as the basis of an observed relative frequency distribution.

Usually, however, only a limited number of observations are available to calculate the relative frequencies. From limited historical data, only *estimates of long-run* relative frequencies can be obtained. More precisely, to overcome the fact that a limited historical series cannot exactly reveal the long-run relative frequencies, an adjustment (smoothing) procedure applied to the observed relative frequency distribution is often required to get reasonable estimates of the long-run frequencies. Let us illustrate that process.

Example 7.4.   Predicting Airline No-Shows

A common occurrence in the airline industry is the "no show"—people making airline reservations but failing either to take the flight or cancel the reservation. After accounting for the known factors affecting the no-show rate—season of the year, time of day, flight origin and destination, etc.—the exact no-show rate still remains uncertain. Collecting historical data, as in Table 7.1, offers the opportunity to plot a step function from the data (the staircase outline in Figure 7.6). But as it stands, the step function is inadequate for estimating cumulative *long-run* frequencies and, in turn, probabilities.

Usually, the historical relative frequency of any one particular event, such as "13 no-shows," is a reasonable estimate of the long-run relative frequency of that event. But not always. In the latter case, a simple composite of the individual estimate may not provide a good picture of the long-run relative frequency distribution or a good assessment of the underlying probability distribution. For instance, consider the events surrounding the event "12 no-shows." The historical 16 day record shows a relative frequency of .125 for "13 no-shows" and .063 for "11 no-shows," and zero for "12 no-shows." It would be poor judgment for an airline to think that zero is a reasonable estimate of "12 no-shows." A very long series of days, if available, would

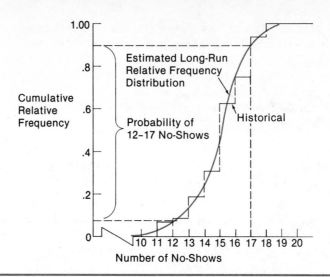

FIGURE 7.6   Cumulative Historical Relative Frequencies and Estimated
Cumulative Long-Run Relative Frequencies

TABLE 7.1. Historical Record of Airline No-shows

NUMBER OF NO-SHOWS	FREQUENCY	RELATIVE FREQUENCY	CUMULATIVE RELATIVE FREQUENCY
10 or less	0	0	0
11	1	.063	.063
12	0	.000	.063
13	2	.125	.188
14	3	.187	.375
15	4	.250	.625
16	2	.125	.750
17	3	.187	.937
18	1	.063	1.000
19 or more	0	0	1.000
	16	1.000	

reflect the true relative frequency value for "12 no-shows" consistent with the values
for "11 no-shows" and "13 no-shows." A short series, as in this case, is less likely
to do so. Unless some compelling reason can be given why "12 no-shows" is an
impossible event, the assumption should be that the underlying no-show probability
distribution has no perceptible break at "12 no-shows."

A useful way of approaching the assessment problem given a shorter series
is to assume that the long-run relative frequencies change smoothly. A reasonable
impression of the shape of the underlying probability distribution can be attained
by drawing a smooth curve through the horizontal segments of the step function
as was done for the historical data in Figure 7.6. The drawn smooth curve is an
ogive from which estimated cumulative long-run relative frequencies can be read.
The difference between the long-run cumulative relative frequencies for two "no-
show" values is the probability assessment for the interval between them. The prob-

ability of "12 to 16 no-shows" would be the cumulative *long-run* relative frequency of "17 no-shows" minus the cumulative long-run relative frequency of "12 no-shows." For instance, if

cumulative (long run) relative frequency, c.r.f. $(X \leq 12) = .136$

cumulative (long run) relative frequency, c.r.f. $(X \leq 17) = .875$, then

$$P(12 \leq X \leq 16) \approx \text{c.r.f. } (X \leq 17) - \text{c.r.f. } (X \leq 12)$$
$$\approx .875 - .136$$
$$\approx .739$$

A word of caution is in order at this point. It may not be sensible at times to assume that a theoretical probability distribution underlies the observed frequency distribution. The observed frequency distribution may *not* be a summary of successive repetitions of an unchanging random experiment but simply a descriptive way of presenting a collection of features. Geographical size distribution of the states of the U.S. or their respective income tax rates distribution are purely descriptive in nature. No underlying theoretical probability distribution is involved or should be assumed.

7.5. Summary Measures of Location

As with their empirical counterparts, important features of an entire probability distribution can often be condensed to a few summary measures. Foremost on the list of summary measures is the measure of central location of the distribution.

Once again, the three commonly encountered summary measures of location highlight: (1) the one value of the distribution which is more probable than any other, the *mode* of the distribution; (2) the value of the random variable which divides the total probability into two parts as equally as possible, the *median* of a probability distribution; (3) lastly, the value most frequently used of all locational summary measures, the *mean* of a probability distribution. The mean is a weighted average. Each possible value of the distribution is assigned its probability as a weight. The mean of the probability distribution of X is denoted by μ_X and its formula is

$$\mu_X = \sum_i (X = x_i)P(X = x_i) = \sum_i x_i P(x_i)$$

Let's now illustrate its calculation.

Example 7.5.   **Weighting the Possible Values**

Let X be the random variable "number of heads" in a coin tossing experiment consisting of two tosses (repetitions). Let the coin be biased in such a way that the probability of heads on any one toss is .3 and of tails is .7. The calculation of the mean is shown in Table 7.2.

**TABLE 7.2. Mean Calculation for
Probability Distribution of** X

NUMBER OF HEADS x	PROBABILITY $P(x)$	$xP(x)$
0	.490	.0
1	.420	.420
2	.090	.180

$$\sum xP(x) = .600 = \mu_x$$

The three possible values of X are 0, 1, and 2 because heads can appear 0, 1, or 2 times in two coin tosses. Their probabilities are .490, .420, .090 respectively. The value 0 has the highest probability and so is the mode of the distribution. At the numerical value 1, the total probability divides into the lower and upper half; so, one is the median of the distribution.

The Mean By Any Other Name Is Still a Mean

The term *expected value* is a legitimate name often used for the mean of a distribution. For instance, μ_X can be written as $E(X)$. The meaning of the term has often been misunderstood. Example 7.5 demonstrates that the "expected" value is not one of the three possible values (0, 1, 2). So the expected value may not actually be a value one should expect to occur if the experiment is performed. If the expected value does happen to be one of the possible values of the random variable, often the other possible random values represent a more probable occurrence (sum of all the individual probabilities) than the expected value alone. So frequently the other values collectively are more "expected" to appear than the expected value itself. For instance, the number 7 on tossing two dice is the expected value and has a one-sixth chance of occurring. The other possible values (2 . . . 6, 8 . . . 12) have a five-sixth chance and therefore are expected to appear five times out of six.

7.6. Measures of Variability (Dispersion)

However helpful the median, mean, or mode may be in describing the central tendency of a probability distribution, none of these measures describe the variability or *dispersion* of a distribution.

One very simple measure of dispersion is the *range* of the distribution. The range is the difference between the maximum and minimum values of the random variable. For example, if the random variable is the number of spots showing on the roll of an ordinary die, then the range would be 5, the difference between the maximum number of spots, 6, and the minimum number, 1.

Variance

Although the range is somewhat informative in that all variability of a random variable is restricted to values within its range, it is not a completely satisfactory measure of dispersion because no information is conveyed as to the pattern of variation among values within the range.

Example 7.6.   Stock Price Spread

Barron's Review publishes weekly the range of prices that a stock trades for on the market. This information is not completely satisfactory for some investors following closely the activity of a stock. Before taking any action themselves, they want to know more information than just the trading range. For instance, if a stock trades in a price range of 7 from 17–24 over the week, at what price was most of the trading taking place? 23 or 24? or 17? 18?

To describe dispersion within the range, a different measure is needed. Largely for mathematical reasons, the *variance* of a probability distribution has come to be widely accepted as a measure of dispersion.

In words, the variance of a probability distribution is the expected value of the *squared deviations* from the mean of the distribution. The notation for the variance is σ^2, read "sigma squared":

$$\sigma^2 = \sum_i (x_i - \mu)^2 \, P(x_i)$$

An informal interpretation of variance would be that the probability of distributions with large variances is more dispersed than for distributions with smaller variance. For example, consider the distributions shown in Figures 7.7a and 7.7b.

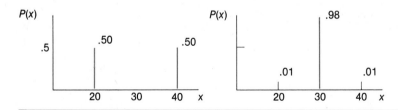

FIGURE 7.7a   Distribution A   FIGURE 7.7b   Distribution B

Both distributions have a mean of 30 and a range of 20, but the variance of the distribution in Figure 7.7a is 100, whereas the variance of the distribution in Figure 7.7b is only 2, as Table 7.3 shows.

TABLE 7.3. Computation of Variance for Distribution A and B

	DISTRIBUTION A				DISTRIBUTION B		
x	$P(x)$	$(x - \mu_x)^2$	$P(x)(x - \mu_x)^2$	x	$P(x)$	$(x - \mu_x)^2$	$P(x)(x - \mu_x)^2$
20	.5	$(20 - 30)^2$	.5(100)	20	.01	$(20 - 30)^2$	.01(100)
30	0	$(30 - 30)^2$	0(0)	30	.98	$(30 - 30)^2$	.98(0)
40	.5	$(40 - 30)^2$	.5(100)	40	.01	$(40 - 30)^2$	.01(100)
			$\sum P(x)(x - \mu_x)^2$ $= 100$				$\sum P(x)(x - \mu_x)^2$ $= 2$

The smaller variance of 2 suggests that the chances of getting a value near the mean value 30 is greater with distribution B than with distribution A with its variance of 100. A visual comparison of Figure 7.7a and 7.7b confirms that this is correct.

Standard Deviation

One inconvenient feature of the variance is that it is not measured in the same units as the random variable. For example, if the random variable X is measured in units of dollars, then σ^2 is measured in units of dollars squared. It is helpful to have a measure of dispersion which uses the same units as the original random variable. A convenient measure of this kind is the *standard deviation*, which is merely the square root of the variance. It has the symbol σ. As an example, consider again the distribution of Figure 7.7a. If the random variable is measured in dollars, then the variance of this distribution is 100 dollars *squared* and the standard deviation is 10 dollars. For the distribution in Figure 7.7b, the variance is 2 dollars *squared* and the standard deviation is 1.41 dollars.

The standard deviation of X is expressed algebraically as

$$\sigma = +\sqrt{\sum_i (x_i - \mu)^2 \, P(x_i)}$$

Note that the conclusion reached above about the comparison between distributions A and B will be unaltered if the standard deviation is used as the measure of dispersion. This correctly suggests the variance and standard deviation provide the dispersion information that is consistent with each other.

7.7. Other Summary Measures

Measures of location and dispersion are the most commonly used measures in describing a probability distribution, but they are not the only ones. Of two probability distributions with identical means and variances, one may be more symmetrically distributed about the mean or mode than the other, or one may be more peaked than the other.

If a probability distribution is unimodal and symmetrical about the mode, then the mean, median, and mode all have the same numerical value. If the distribution is unimodal but not symmetrical about the mode, then the distribution is said to be "skewed" in the direction in which the long tail of the distribution stretches. A measure of skewness is the following:

$$\sum_i (x_i - \mu)^3 \, P(x_i)$$

If this quantity is positive, the distribution is skewed to the right. If it is negative, the distribution is skewed to the left. If it is zero, the distribution is symmetrical.

7.8. Chebyshev's Inequality

First discussed in Chapter Four for empirical distributions, the important theorem known as *Chebyshev's Inequality* can once again be called upon in the case of theoretical distributions to suggest just how close one can expect the value of a random variable to be to the mean of its distribution.

> If X is a discrete random variable having a distribution with mean μ and standard deviation σ, then for any positive constant k, the probability that X assumes a specific value more than k standard deviations away from the mean is less than $1/k^2$.

In other words, we now see that important *probability statements* about a probability distribution can also be made without knowing its exact shape. We only need to know the mean and standard deviation of the distribution.

Example 7.8.   Incoming Telephone Calls

Suppose the probability distribution for incoming telephone calls at a busy switchboard has a mean of 64 calls per minute and a standard deviation of 8 calls per minute. Then, according to Chebyshev's inequality, the probability of receiving either less than 48 or more than 80 calls in a minute is less than .25. The probability of receiving less than 24 or more than 104 calls is less than .04. Having a switchboard that can handle about 104 calls per minute reduces the chance of a system overload to less than 4%.

7.9. Using One Probability Distribution to Approximate Another

Summary measures such as the mean and variance are often relied on to make comparisons between two distributions. Although it is possible that two probability distributions having identical means and identical standard deviations will not have identical probability assigned to each value of the random variable, it generally is decided that, at least as a first approximation, the two distributions can be used interchangeably.

Why Accept a Substitute?

A strong motivation for wanting to use one distribution in place of another is that it may be much easier to calculate probabilities for the substitute distribution than for the original. The incentive to use a substitute distribution is especially great if the substitute can be expressed as a mathematical equation or if its values can be read from a published table.

As it turns out, a small number of types or families of probability distributions provide yeoman service in statistics. The most important of these are discussed in the next three chapters. Very frequently, the actual probability distribution which describes a situation either is a member of one of these families or can be well-approximated by one of them. Consequently, they will be worthy of our attention.

7.10. Continuous Probability Distributions

All of the random variable sample spaces considered to this point have been of the kind where the possible values of the random variable move in discrete steps or jumps. These are called *discrete* sample spaces; likewise, the random variable is called a *discrete random variable.*

Not all random variables are discrete. Suppose that between any two possible values of the variable, no matter how close they may be, it is possible to list an intermediate value. This variable is called a *continuous random variable.*

The concept of a continuous random variable is a useful abstraction of reality. In reality, we never observe continuous data. The impreciseness of the measuring instruments limits the accuracy of the value that can be recorded. Even if the underlying variable is continuous (say temperature), the data recorded will be a discrete value (degrees). Nevertheless, a continuous probability distribution is often the theoretical model underlying the empirical data. As the size of sample increases and the width of class intervals narrows, the empirical frequency distribution comes closer and closer to the theoretical probability distribution.

Probability Represented by Area Rather Than by Height

When the random variable is continuous, probability is not *represented by the height of the graph at any given point as is true for discrete distributions.* In the continuous case, height represents probability *density;* probability is measured by the *area* under the curve between two points. As with relative frequency histograms and polygons, area under the entire curve sums to one.

In Figure 7.8, the probability of a value between 20 and 30 is given by the shaded area of the triangle with height of .10 value and base of 10, the length between 30 and 20. Thus, since the area of a triangle equals one-half of the base times the height ($A = \frac{1}{2}bh$), the probability is

$$P(20 < X < 30) = \frac{1}{2}(30 - 20)(.10) = .50$$

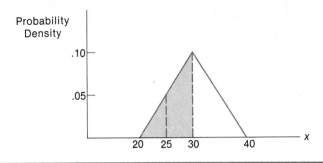

FIGURE 7.8 Continuous Probability Distribution

Likewise, the probability of a value between 20 and 25 is

$$P(20 < X < 25) = \tfrac{1}{2}(25 - 20)(.05) = .125$$

Zero Probability Is Associated with Every Value

It must be pointed out that probability is associated only with an interval and not a point. Probability is measured by area above an interval; since points have no width or thickness, they have no area, and hence no probability can lie above it. Thus, the probability attached to an individual point must be zero. Consequently, the probability for the following two intervals is identical:

$$P(20 < X < 30) = .50$$
$$P(20 \leq X \leq 30) = .50$$

It is important to recognize that in the continuous case, *zero probability for a given value of the random variable does not imply logical impossibility of the value.* Quite the contrary. Since every value is assigned zero probability and since one of the values must occur, one of the values assigned zero probability must occur. This seeming paradox is explained by the fact that the zero probability is really a limiting value obtained as the interval width is made infinitely short. However, the whole matter is largely academic and of little practical concern because our ultimately inaccurate measuring instruments force us to deal only with the probabilities of intervals and not of isolated points.

7.11. Cumulative Probability

An alternative approach sometimes used in specifying the probability distribution of a random variable is the *cumulative probability distribution*. In a cumulative distribution, the probability associated at a given value x_k represents the (accumulated) probability of obtaining values of X *less than or equal to the* given value. For a *discrete distribution*, this means:

$$P(X \leq x_k) = \sum_{i=1}^{k} P(X = x_i).$$

For instance, using Table 7.2 we can write

$$P(X \leq 1) = P(X = 0) + P(X = 1)$$
$$= .490 + .420$$
$$= .910$$

Read the first term, $P(X \leq 1)$, as "the probability of no more than one head."

If the cumulative distribution is based upon a discrete random variable, then the graph of cumulative probability will always increase in discrete steps or jumps (staircase fashion) as shown in Figure 7.9.

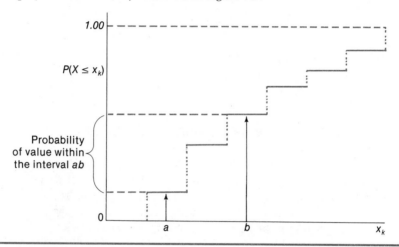

FIGURE 7.9   Cumulative Probability Graph for Discrete Distribution

In a cumulative probability graph, each point on the horizontal segment of a step has a cumulative probability read from the vertical axis. The cumulative probability is a summation of the probabilities that associate with all the values on the horizontal axis up to and including that point. The dotted vertical lines define the boundary of each step and specify the range of values of the random variable included in that step.

To find the probability of a value within the interval *a-b*, the following procedure is used:

1. From points *a* and *b*, construct vertical lines up to the horizontal segment of the staircase.

2. Draw horizontal lines over to the vertical axis from the two steps indicated in (1).

3. Subtract the lower of the two probability values obtained in (2) from the higher. The result is the probability of a value within the interval *ab*.

In the case of a *continuous random variable*, the cumulative probability graph is a smooth curve, as shown in Figure 7.10. The same procedure just defined for the cumulative discrete distribution can be followed to obtain the probability for the interval ab.

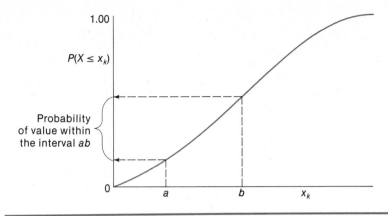

FIGURE 7.10 Cumulative Probability Graph for Continuous Distribution

7.12. Bivariate Probability Distributions and Correlation

A bivariate (joint) probability distribution shows the different ordered combinations of values of two random variables and their joint probabilities. For example, let X and Y be two random variables. For any ordered pair of specific values (x_i, y_j), there is $P(x_i, y_j)$, the value of the *joint probability* distribution at (x_i, y_j). To illustrate, consider the experiment of tossing a coin and a three sided die. Define the following:

$X = $ number of heads
$Y = $ number on upper face of die

The joint distribution showing the joint probabilities $P(x, y)$ in the cell is shown in Figure 7.11. From the joint distribution, one can describe the degree of association between the values of the two variables. In the following example a joint distribution is used to bring out a very important point for persons in the financial world.

y x	1	2	3
0	$P(0,1)$	$P(0,2)$	$P(0,3)$
1	$P(1,1)$	$P(1,2)$	$P(1,3)$

FIGURE 7.11 Joint Probability of a Coin Toss and a Three-Sided Die

Example 7.12 Investment Diversification—Does Putting Your Eggs in Different Baskets Really Reduce Risk?

An old investment maxim says "don't put all your eggs in one basket." In the real estate business, this maxim applies even to relatively conservative income property such as apartment buildings. In recent years, Real Estate Investment Trusts (REITs) have become a popular means for investors to diversify by pooling assets. The trusts have thus been used to reduce risk.

Suppose you and I separately have apartment projects that will return $1.2 million if successful and $0.8 million if unsuccessful. For each project, the probability of a successful investment is .75; the probability of unsuccessful investment, its complement, is .25.

Can we reduce the risk of the lower return by pooling our projects—you take half of mine and I take half of yours? The answer depends on the co-movements of the investment values of the two variables indicated by the joint probability distribution. If the joint probabilities are as shown within the cells in Figure 7.12, the answer is no.

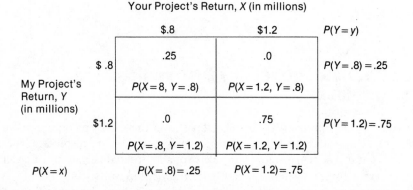

FIGURE 7.12 Joint Distribution of Apartment Projects' Returns

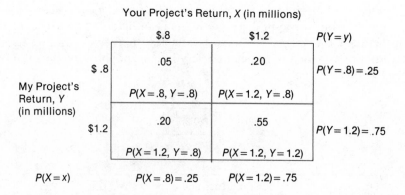

FIGURE 7.13 Joint Distribution of Apartment Projects' Returns

In Figure 7.12, pooling would not help reduce risk. The values of X and Y move together in lock step. The return on your project is the same as the return on my project. This might be expected if the projects shared a common risk, say the risk of a population loss in the town in which they both are located. In situations of this kind, you have in effect put your eggs in the "same" basket.

In Figure 7.13, pooling definitely would help reduce risk. Instead of a 25 percent chance of the minimum return, $0.8 million, the risk drops to 5 percent. Of course, the chance of the maximum return, $1.2 million, also declines. Some of the probability, .40 in fact, falls on the intermediate possibility of $1.0 million (half of $0.8 million and half of $1.2 million).

The reason pooling works in Figure 7.13 is that the return on the two projects tends to move in *opposite* directions. This tendency might be expected if the two projects are in competition for the same business. For example, your project is successful if our town's population growth occurs on your side of town instead of mine. In projects of this kind, pooling the two projects definitely does help reduce the risk of the worst return.

Covariance

The co-movement of two random variables can be summarized by a measure known as their *covariance*. In words, the covariance of two random variables is the mean value of the product of the individual paired deviations from their respective means weighted by their joint probabilities. In symbols:

$$\text{Cov}(X, Y) = \sum_{x_i y_j} [(x_i - \mu_X)(y_j - \mu_Y)] \, P(x_i, y_j)$$

The covariance can be either positive or negative or zero. Regardless of the size of the covariance term, a positive covariance indicates the two variables tend to move together; a negative value indicates that the variables tend to move in opposite directions, and a zero value indicates the movements in the two variables are unrelated. For the joint probability distribution shown in Figure 7.12, the covariance calculation is as follows:

Since $\mu_X = \sum x P(X = x)$

$$\begin{aligned}
\mu_X &= .8 \, P(X = .8) + 1.2 \, P(X = 1.2) \\
&= .8(.25) + 1.2(.75) \\
&= 1.1
\end{aligned}$$

Similarly $\mu_Y = \sum y P(Y = y)$

$$\begin{aligned}
\mu_Y &= .8 \, P(Y = .8) + 1.2 \, P(Y = 1.2) \\
&= .8(.25) + 1.2(.75) \\
&= 1.1
\end{aligned}$$

$$\begin{aligned}
\text{Cov}(X, Y) &= (.8 - 1.1)(.8 - 1.1)(.25) + (.8 - 1.1)(1.2 - 1.1)(0) \\
&\quad + (1.2 - 1.1)(.8 - 1.1)(0) + (1.2 - 1.1)(1.2 - 1.1)(.75) \\
&= (-.3)(-.3)(.25) + 0 + 0 + (.1)(.1)(.75) \\
&= .25(-.3)(-.3) + .75(.1)(.1) \\
&= .03
\end{aligned}$$

Thus the positive association between the return on the two projects is confirmed by the positive covariance value.

The covariance calculation for the joint distribution shown in Figure 7.13 is as follows:

$$\mu_X = .8\,P(X = .8) + 1.2\,P(X = 1.2)$$
$$= .8(.25) + 1.2(.75)$$
$$= 1.1$$

$$\mu_Y = .8\,P(Y = .8) + 1.2\,P(Y = 1.2)$$
$$= .8(.25) + 1.2(.75)$$
$$= 1.1$$

$$\text{Cov}(X, Y) = (.8 - 1.1)(.8 - 1.1)(.05) + (.8 - 1.1)(1.2 - 1.1)(.20)$$
$$+ (1.2 - 1.1)(.8 - 1.1)(.20) + (1.2 - 1.1)(1.2 - 1.1)(.55)$$
$$= .0045 - .006 - .006 + .0055$$
$$= -.002$$

Here, the negative covariance value confirms the negative association between the returns on the two apartment projects.

Correlation Coefficient

The sign of the covariance indicates whether the co-movement in the values of X and Y tends to be in the same or in opposite directions. However, the *degree* of co-movement *cannot* be inferred from the magnitude of the covariance since the covariance term is influenced by the unit of measurement used. The degree of co-movement reported should be independent of the units of measurement of the two variables. A popular measure known as the *correlation coefficient*, denoted by ρ, is a pure number and achieves this objective:

$$\rho_{XY} = \frac{\text{Cov}(X, Y)}{\sigma_X\,\sigma_Y}$$

The values of ρ can range from -1 to $+1$ inclusive. The extreme case of $\rho = +1$ is called *perfect positive correlation* and is obtained only when all the possible values of the variables fall on a straight line with a positive incline. The extreme case of $\rho = -1$ is called *perfect negative correlation* and is obtained only when all the possible values of the variables fall on a straight line with a negative incline. If $\rho = 0$, the two variables are said to be uncorrelated.

To compute the correlation coefficients for the two distributions shown in Figures 7.12 and 7.13, we must first find the standard deviations of X and of Y:

$$\sigma_X = \sqrt{\sum_{x_i} P(x_i)[x_i - \mu_X]^2} = \sqrt{.25(.8 - 1.1)^2 + .75(1.2 - 1.1)^2}$$
$$= \sqrt{.03} \text{ or } .173$$

$$\sigma_Y = \sqrt{\sum_{y_j} P(y_j)[y_j - \mu_Y]^2} = \sqrt{.25(.8 - 1.1)^2 + .75(1.2 - 1.1)^2}$$
$$= \sqrt{.03} \text{ or } .173$$

Then, to find the correlation coefficient for the distribution in Figure 7.12, we compute:

$$\rho_{XY} = \frac{\text{Cov}(X, Y)}{\sigma_X \sigma_Y} = \frac{.03}{\sqrt{.03}\sqrt{.03}} = 1$$

Thus, the returns from the two apartment projects are perfectly correlated in the positive direction. The correlation coefficient for the distribution in Figure 7.13 is:

$$\sigma_X = \sqrt{.25(.8 - 1.1)^2 + .75(1.2 - 1.1)^2}$$
$$= \sqrt{.0225 + .0075}$$
$$= .173$$

$$\sigma_Y = \sqrt{.25(.8 - 1.1)^2 + .75(1.2 - 1.1)^2}$$
$$= \sqrt{.0225 + .0075}$$
$$= .173$$

$$\rho_{XY} = \frac{\text{Cov}(X, Y)}{\sigma_X \sigma_Y} = \frac{-.002}{(.173)(.173)} = -.067$$

This confirms the negative relationship between the variables and indicates that correlation is not perfect.

A Caveat in Interpreting ρ

The value of ρ can be misleading; ρ is an ordinal number, not a ratio number. In other words, a ρ value of 0.6 indicates a stronger association than does a ρ value of 0.2. but *not* three times as strong.

We have seen in this section that investment "pooling" effectively reduces risk to the owner when the returns on two projects are negatively correlated. We have also seen that pooling does not reduce risk when the returns on the projects are perfectly and positively correlated. In the next section, we shall see that risk can also be reduced when the two variables are independent of each other, implying a covariance of zero.

7.13. Linear Combinations of Random Variables

The pooled apartment projects example was concerned with a *combination* of random variables. Suppose that X_1 is the random variable representing the return on your apartment project and X_2 is the random variable representing the return on my apartment project. Then, a new random variable which we shall call W can be obtained by combining the two original variables. The value of W will depend on how much weight is given to X_1 as compared to X_2. Let us designate these weights as a_1 and a_2, respectively. The weighted sum

$$W = a_1X_1 + a_2X_2$$

is called a *linear combination* of the two original random variables. Linear combinations are encountered extensively in statistics, so we shall review some important aspects of their probability distributions.

In the pooled apartments projects example, the pooling was accomplished by assuming equal share investments and so assigning a weight of one-half to each of the two variables X_1 and X_2. That is, $a_1 = a_2 = \frac{1}{2}$:

$$W = \frac{1}{2}X_1 + \frac{1}{2}X_2 = \frac{X_1 + X_2}{2}$$

The combination leads to a simple average. An average will result any time each variable is given the same weight. The weights given will equal one divided by the number of variables. Learning about what happens when we average random variables is one of the important reasons we study linear combinations.

Another important special case of linear combinations sets all the a coefficients equal to one. In this case, the linear combination is simply the total or sum of individual values. Designating the total by T, we have

$$T = a_1 X_1 + a_2 X_2 = (1)X_1 + (1)X_2 = X_1 + X_2$$

Too Many Combinations?

The probability distribution for the linearly combined variable W is determined by the joint distribution of X_1 and X_2. There is one value of W for each combination of X_1 and X_2 values. Thus, if X_1 and X_2 each have a dozen values, W will have 144 values.

If X_1 and X_2 have only a few possible values, determining their joint probability distribution (and therefore Ws distribution) may not be difficult. But if X_1 and X_2 each have 100 values, their joint distribution will have 10,000 possible values and its computation from X_1 and X_2 will not be so simple. If there are six variables to be combined (X_1 through X_6) instead of just two, the number of computations required to obtain the joint distribution quickly reaches astronomical levels. A simplified approach is clearly in order.

Start by Focusing on the Summary Measures

Most of the questions about W do not pertain to individual values but rather to more general measures such as:

The location or average value of W.

The probability that a value of W will be above a certain value, below a certain value.

The probability that W will lie within a specified interval.

Is there a simplified approach for answering most questions about the probability distribution of W? The use of summary measures to describe the distribution is one common approach. The two most important characteristics to describe are location and dispersion. Location of the combined distribution is generally described by the mean, and dispersion by the variance or standard deviation of the distribution.

Save Work by Relating Summary Measures of the Combined Distribution to Summary Measures of the Original Distribution

The trick in using summary measures as a way to simplify the process of combining X_1 and X_2 to get W is in relating the summary measures of the combined distribution to the summary measures for the original distribution. If W can be adequately described by its mean and variance, and if these can be expressed in terms of the means and variance of X_1 and X_2, an astronomical number of computations can be reduced to just a handful. Fortunately, it *is* possible to do exactly that.

7.14. The Mean of a Linear Combination

We shall assume in the remainder of this section that all of the random variables have finite means and variances. Given this assumption, the relationship between the mean of the combined variable $W = a_1 X_1 + a_2 X_2$ is simply:

$$\mu_W = a_1 \mu_{X_1} + a_2 \mu_{X_2}$$

In other words, the mean of the combined variable is just the weighted average of the means of the original variables. The weights applied to the means (a_1 and a_2) are the same as the weights used in forming the linear combination. For instance, from the data in Figure 7.13 and assuming my investment is twice yours, the mean return is

$$\mu_W = a_1 \mu_X + a_2 \mu_Y \text{ where } a_1 = .33 \text{ and } a_2 = .67$$

since $\mu_X = 1.1$ million and $\mu_Y = 1.1$ million

$$\mu_W = .33(1.1) + .67(1.1)$$
$$= .363 + .737$$
$$= 1.1$$

The "Average Total"

One of the more common kinds of linear combination results from summing the values of two or more random variables to obtain a total. Since both a_1 and a_2 equal one in this special case, the mean or "average total" of two random variables X_1 and X_2 is simply the sum of their individual means. That is,

$$\mu_T = \mu_{X_1} + \mu_{X_2}$$

Example 7.14. Merger Profitability

Suppose two firms agree to merge and the profitability of each firm is a random variable. If the mean of the probability distribution for the first firm's profits is 30 million dollars, and the mean for the second firm is 40 million dollars, then the mean of the probability distribution for the merged firm's profitability is

$$\mu_T = \mu_{X_1} + \mu_{X_2}$$
$$= 30 + 40 = 70 \text{ million dollars.}$$

The "Average Average"

The pooled apartment project shown in Figure 7.12 illustrates how the expression for the mean of a linear combination of random variables can save computational effort. The pooled investment return is a straight average of the returns from the two projects, assuming equal weights. Each investment has a mean return of $1.1 million. The mean return on the pooled investment (the "average average") can be obtained by weighting or pooling the individual mean returns:

$$\mu_W = \tfrac{1}{2}\mu_{X_1} + \tfrac{1}{2}\mu_{X_2}$$
$$= \tfrac{1}{2}(1.1) + \tfrac{1}{2}(1.1) = 1.1 \text{ million dollars.}$$

7.15. The Variance of a Linear Combination

The variance of a linear combination of random variables can also be determined directly from summary measures of the original variables. However, the expression is a little more complicated than that for the mean because a covariance term is included:

$$\sigma_W^2 = a_1^2\sigma_{X_1}^2 + a_2^2\sigma_{X_2}^2 + 2a_1a_2\,\text{Cov}(X_1, X_2)$$

Alternatively, we could express the variance using ρ_{12}. That is

$$\sigma_W^2 = a_1^2\sigma_{X_1}^2 + a_2^2\sigma_{X_2}^2 + 2a_1a_2\rho_{12}\sigma_{X_1}\sigma_{X_2}$$

For the pooled apartment projects having negative covariance, the result is:

$$\sigma_W^2 = (\tfrac{1}{2})^2.030 + (\tfrac{1}{2})^2.030 + 2(\tfrac{1}{2})(\tfrac{1}{2})(-.002)$$
$$= .014$$

The standard deviation of W, σ_W is:

$$\sigma_W = \sqrt{.014} = .118$$

Notice that the negative covariance term enters to reduce the variance and standard deviation reflecting an overall reduction of dispersion. The result would be the same had we used the negative correlation coefficient, $\rho_{12} = -.067$ in the alternative formula for σ_W^2.

Does Pooling Reduce Risk?—a Simple Check

One of the objectives of pooling the two investments was to reduce risk, that is, to obtain an investment return which has the same mean value as the single investment but less dispersion about the mean.

Less dispersion determines less risk. With less dispersion comes the increased assurance that outlying returns, both positive and negative, will not be very likely to appear. Avoiding the large downside or negative return is important to a business, especially small businesses which cannot absorb large losses and continue to operate.

How do we know whether risk is actually reduced without comparing the entire distributions? Simply by comparing the summary measures of dispersion—either the variance or the standard deviation.

The two apartment projects with negative covariance have individual standard deviations of .173 and .173. The standard deviation figure for the pooled project is .118, less than either standard deviation of the projects alone. Thus, the pooled investment definitely has less dispersion and, therefore, less risk.

The Variance of Independent Random Variables

If the variables forming the linear combination are independent, the expression for the variance of the combination is somewhat simplified:

$$\sigma_W^2 = a_1^2 \sigma_{X_1}^2 + a_2^2 \sigma_{X_2}^2 \text{ (only if } X_1 \text{ and } X_2 \text{ are independent)}.$$

This simplification occurs because the covariance of two independent random variables is zero; the term $2a_1 a_2 \text{Cov}(X_1, X_2)$ drops out of the equation. Thus, in this special case, the variance of the combination can be determined from the variances of the individual components and their weight in the combination.

Although the expression above has been stated for just two variables, it also applies to any number of variables. If there are n independent variables:

$$\sigma_W^2 = a_1^2 \sigma_{X_1}^2 + a_2^2 \sigma_{X_2}^2 + a_3^2 \sigma_{X_3}^2 + \ldots a_n^2 \sigma_{X_n}^2$$

(only if all variables are independent)

To obtain an average of n random variables, we simply weight each variable by the constant $1/n$. That is,

$$W = (1/n)X_1 + (1/n)X_2 + (1/n)X_3 + \ldots (1/n)X_n$$

Consequently, the variance of W is:

$$\sigma_W^2 = (1/n)^2 \sigma_{X_1}^2 + (1/n)^2 \sigma_{X_2}^2 + (1/n)^2 \sigma_{X_3}^2 + \ldots (1/n)^2 \sigma_{X_n}^2$$

Factoring out the common term $(1/n)^2$,

$$\sigma_W^2 = (1/n)^2 [\sigma_{X_1}^2 + \sigma_{X_2}^2 + \sigma_{X_3}^2 + \ldots \sigma_{X_n}^2]$$

(only if all variables are independent)

A further simplification is possible if all n variables have the same probability distribution. This situation occurs in simple random sampling (with replacement). Here, the probability distribution for any one draw is the same as for all the others. Let us designate the common variance by σ^2. Thus, the variance of the sample *average* (mean), denoted by $\sigma_{\bar{X}}^2$ is:

$$\sigma_{\bar{X}}^2 = (1/n)^2[\sigma^2 + \sigma^2 + \sigma^2 \ldots \sigma^2 \ (n \text{ terms})]$$
$$= (1/n)^2[n\sigma^2]$$
$$\sigma_{\bar{X}}^2 = \sigma^2/n$$

The standard deviation is the square root of the variance. Hence, the standard deviation of the probability distribution for a sample mean is:

$$\sigma_{\bar{X}} = \sigma/\sqrt{n}$$

This is a very important result in statistics. It not only says that the variation of sample means is less than that of the population from which the sample is drawn, it says by how much. Let us illustrate a business situation where this knowledge becomes important.

Example 7.15A.   Potential Gain from Diversification

Suppose an investor could purchase a large tract of land for $100,000 or could instead invest in five smaller lots at $20,000 apiece in different areas of town. The percentage return on the large lot and on each of the small lots has a variance σ^2 of 25 and standard deviation σ of 5%.

The investor believes that lot prices will fluctuate almost independently of each other in the near future. Therefore, the returns experienced by holding the five small lots will show a variance $\sigma_{\bar{X}}^2$ of only $\sigma^2/n = 25/5$ or 5% and so standard deviation of only $5\%/\sqrt{5}$ or 2.24%. This is one fifth the variability (overall risk variance) in returns associated with an investment in the single large lot with σ^2 of 25.

In chapter ten these results will be very useful in our consideration of randomly drawn samples from a population.

More Uncertainty About a Total Than About Its Components

The expression for the variance of independent chance variables has some important implications. One of these pertains to the sum of independent random variables. Intuitively, many people feel that there should be less variation in the total than in the values of the individual variables. Actually, the opposite is true. Since a equals one for summing operations, the expression for the variance of the total is:

$$\sigma_T^2 = \sigma_{X_1}^2 + \sigma_{X_2}^2 + \sigma_{X_3}^2 + \ldots \sigma_{X_n}^2$$
(only if all variables are independent)

In other words, the variance of the total is the *sum* of the variances of the individual variables and is therefore greater than any one of them.

Example 7.15B.   Conglomerate Versus Subsidiary Profits

Suppose a large conglomerate is comprised of five subsidiaries, each of which has a probability distribution for profits with a mean of ten million dollars and a standard deviation of one million dollars. Is the standard deviation of profits for the entire firm less than that for one of its subsidiaries? Definitely not.

Assuming that the profit variables for the subsidiaries are all independent of each other, the following relationship holds:

$$\sigma_T^2 = 1^2 + 1^2 + 1^2 + 1^2 + 1^2 = 5$$

The square root of 5 gives 2.236 million dollars as the standard deviation of the profit distribution for the entire firm. This is more than double the value for any single subsidiary. The increased dollar amount of profit must be viewed relative to the mean profit for the conglomerate which is now 100 million. Percentage wise, given their mean and standard deviation, this is a smaller fluctuation than what any subsidiary experiences. This result points up the advantage of the conglomerate in stabilizing its relative profit picture.

It's Averaging—Not Summing—That Reduces Variation

One of the most important implications of the expression for the variance of independent random variables concerns averages. How does the variance of the average of several random variables compare with the variance of the individual variables? If the variables are independent, the variance of the average is *less* than that of any single variable included in the average, as was first pointed out in Example 7.15A. Let us now consider another perspective on the same issue.

Example 7.15C.   Finding the Standard Deviation of Sample Proportions

Suppose simple random samples are to be drawn with replacement from a population which contains a proportion p of instant coffee users. How much variation can we expect in the proportion of coffee users among samples of 10,000 persons?

The number of instant coffee users on each draw must be either zero or one. The value one has probability p and zero has probability $1 - p$. Both p and $1 - p$ must be values between 0 and 1. Therefore, the mean μ on a single draw is:

$$\mu = 0(1 - p) + 1(p) = p$$

and the variance is:

$$
\begin{aligned}
\sigma^2 &= (0 - p)^2(1 - p) + (1 - p)^2 p \\
&= p^2 - p^3 + p - 2p^2 + p^3 \\
&= p - p^2 \\
&= p(1 - p)
\end{aligned}
$$

Hence, the variance in the sample proportion among samples of size 10,000 would be:

$$\sigma_{\bar{X}}^2 = \sigma^2/n = p(1 - p)/n = p(1 - p)/10{,}000$$

The standard deviation would be:

$$\sigma_{\bar{x}} = \sqrt{p(1-p)}/100$$

If the value of p is set at .5, the expression $p(1-p)$ is as large as possible and equal to .25. Thus, the largest possible value of $\sigma_{\bar{x}}$ would be

$$\sigma_{\bar{x}} = \sqrt{(.5)(.5)}/100 = .005$$

Multiplying by 100 to obtain a percentage, the result says that the maximum value of the standard deviation of sample proportions is just half a percentage point.

From Chebyshev's Inequality, we know that the probability of a random variable's value falling within k standard deviations of the mean is at least $1 - 1/k^2$. Let us choose $k = 4$, which is equivalent to two percentage points. This means that there is *at least* a

$$1 - 1/k^2 = 1 - 1/4^2 = 15/16$$

probability that the proportion of instant coffee users in the sample will be within plus or minus two percentage points of the percentage in the population.

Would you have guessed such a high probability of being so accurate?

7.16. Concluding Comments

To avoid trial and error, business people must incorporate uncertainty in their decision-making process. A positive first step is to make explicit the uncertainty that cloaks the outcomes of their decisions. By means of a random variable the type of information wanted can be specified. A probability distribution listing the numerical values and their associated probabilities can then follow. Whatever the interpretation of probability, the probability numbers should always add up to one (1.0). If the decision maker has properly described the possible numerical outcomes, one of them must always occur; 100% of the time, the actual result should be one of the outcome values. For the same reason, the probability of any one outcome can never be greater than one or less than zero. Besides probabilities of the outcomes, businesses can use summary measures—expected value, variance, standard deviation—of the probability distribution as indicators of the likely value and surrounding uncertainty that can result from an action.

But involvement with uncertainty and the method of dealing with it are not only restricted to one variable at a time. Risk or uncertainty surface in business with concern for the relationship between two variables of interest. Informed businesses will distinguish themselves by their ability to know how to control this risk, and control is tied by an umbilical cord to measurement. By calculating the statistical measures, the variance and its ally measure, the correlation coefficient, businesses will have key information about the risk taken.

With such information, a decision can be made whether the level of risk is too burdensome or if it is desirable. Risk declines as more independent variables are pooled. The overall risk (variance) declines to $\frac{1}{n}^{th}$ the initial size provided the n variables averaged are independent and identically distributed. For example, the diversification gains for 10 similar size but independent investments is a 90% reduction in variance over no diversification at all.

Footnotes and References

[1]Strictly speaking, we ought to have different symbols noting the distinction between the random variable and actual data values. But we have used X for both. The ambiguity this causes has been allowed for the sake of minimizing symbols and because it conforms to the treatment offered by widely used business statistics texts.

Questions and Problems

1. Define a random experiment. Why must there be more than one possible outcome? Can a possible outcome have a probability of zero?

2. Define a random variable. Why is it used to describe the results of a random experiment?

3. Identify whether the experiment is a random experiment or not and define a random variable of interest if it is
a. rolling a blank die
b. conducting an opinion poll of President Reagan's performance
c. fixed monthly contribution to a common stock mutual fund
d. weekly value of 100 shares of Pan Am stock
e. length of waiting time in a supermarket
f. gas use to and from work over a specific route
g. playing "Russian Roulette" with a completely loaded gun
h. number of mortgage defaults weekly
i. volume of beer produced daily
j. number of newspapers delivered to subscription customers on a given route

4. Identify in Problem 3 whether the random variable is discrete or continuous.

5. Using relative frequency of transformer usage daily as a probability measure of daily usage, what is the expected number of transformers in usage for the PUCO electric and gas company in Orange County, California on a given day? Historical records give the data in Table 7.4.

TABLE 7.4. Relative Frequency of Transformer Usage

NUMBER OF TRANSFORMERS IN USAGE DAILY	RELATIVE FREQUENCY
1	.07
2	.19
3	.23
4	.46
5	.05
	1.00

If it is not possible to have a part of a transformer in use on a given day, what is the usefulness of having the expected value calculation in estimating total usage over a planning period.

6. What implications can be drawn about PUCOs costs and its revenues in Problem 5, if PUCO discovered that over two successive 5 year periods, the mean number of transformers used has not changed, but that the standard deviation has increased?

7. The owner of a custom order fabricating shop is trying to decide whether to accept or reject a million dollar order. The cost of making the item is not known with cer-

tainty, but he estimates that it will cost either $900,000 or $1,100,000, depending on how long it takes to complete. The owner regards the two production schedules as equally likely. Should he decide to reject the offer, he anticipates no adverse reaction from the customer and the net change in profits to be zero. Will the owner accept the order if positive expected profit is a requirement?

8. Suppose the owner in Problem 7 can postpone the decision and analyze a set of similar types of orders already in progress instead and thereby gain information that will aid him in his decision. The cost of setting up the necessary internal accounting record-keeping to analyze the data is $10,000. This will change the net results to a net loss of $10,000 if he rejects the order. A net gain of $90,000 or a net loss of $110,000 will result if he accepts the order.

a. The owner finds that the accounting reports indicate *low* recent production cost. He now regards the $90,000 gain as probable at the .9 level and the $110,000 loss probable at only the .1 level. On the basis of the expected value, what should be the owner's decision?

b. The accounting report is not able to identify the level of production cost. The net gain of $90,000 and loss of $110,000 will be equally likely and thus have the 50-50 probability status originally used in Problem 7. Which decision (accept or reject) should be made on the basis of expected value?

c. The accounting report indicated *high* recent production cost so that the probability of a $90,000 gain is now .10 and the loss of $110,000 is now .90. Which decision, on the basis of expected value, should be made?

d. From the above results indicate the link between the decision taken and the usefulness of the accounting system in determining that choice.

9. How does an increase in the cost of the accounting system in Problem 8 affect the outcome, if no additional relevant information is gained as the cost increases?

10. A toy manufacturer wants to determine

the best sales price for a new electronic game. The marketing manager from survey information has estimated possibilities of reaching annual sales levels for various selling prices as shown in Table 7.5.

TABLE 7.5. Sales Level and Prices

SALES LEVEL (UNIT)	SELLING PRICE			
	$40	$50	$60	$70
40,000	—	—	.3	.7
60,000	—	.2	.4	.3
80,000	.5	.5	.2	—
100,000	.5	.3	.1	—

a. Does the sum of the probabilities down a column for given price come to the value 1.00? Explain.

b. Does the sum of the probabilities across the row for a given level of sales come to one? Explain.

c. Calculate the expected dollar sales for a given price.

d. Which sales price produces the largest value for expected revenue?

11. Consider the random experiment in which four accounts are drawn from a department store's credit card files and called about their preference in using multi-purpose credit cards such as Mastercard, Visa, and American Express instead of the department store's card in making purchases at the store. The responses can be classified as either no preference, N, or preference, P.

a. Using the number of preferences as the random variable, trace a tree diagram specifying the elementary events and link the elementary events with each value of the random variable.

b. What additional information about the responses P and N would we need in order to obtain the probability associated with each value of the random variable?

12. A regional used-book dealer stocks two accounting texts, A & B. From past experience, the dealer assesses the chances for college accounting text adoptions at institutions to be divided equally among text A, text B, and all others. A randomly selected

calling of three college bookstores is conducted in the spring to find out the intention of the bookstore about book orders for the fall term. (Assume each bookstore orders only one type of text.)

a. What are the elementary events?

b. What are the values of the random variable "adoptions of A or B?"

c. What are the associated probabilities for these values if the regional dealer is correct?

d. What benefit could the information gained in the calling serve?

13. Pick out the situation which portrays the empirical distribution of a random experiment from those which are purely descriptive in nature with no underlying random experiment implied.

a. the distribution of lot sizes in a housing tract development.

b. the distribution of avocado yields from several standardized area plantings treated similarly by owners recorded for 1983.

c. the total dollar sales of North County shopping malls recorded weekly.

14. Historical records over two years at the Rancho Bernardo supermarket indicate the distribution of the number of check-out counters on Saturday mornings (between 9:00 AM and 1:00 PM) is as shown in Table 7.6.

TABLE 7.6. Relative Frequency of Check-out Counter Use

NUMBER OF CHECK-OUT COUNTERS IN USE	RELATIVE FREQUENCY
6	.11
7	.21
8	.32
9	.24
10	.12
	100

Using the relative frequency as a probability measure, what is

a. the modal value of the distribution?

b. the median value of the distribution?

c. the mean of the distribution?

15. Using the random experiment of one toss of two dice:

a. Enumerate by tree diagram the elementary events.

b. Derive the values of the random variable "sum of face dots."

c. Give probabilities for the values of the random variable.

d. Calculate the mean (expected) value of the random variable. Is it a value of the random variable?

e. Explain why other values other than the expected value are usually the values one expects to turn up on a single toss of the dice.

f. Would the expected value be a value of the random variable, if the random experiment involved only one die? Is something wrong? Explain.

16. Using Problem 15, calculate the standard deviation of the random experiment involving two dice.

17. Apply Chebyshev's inequality for $k = 2$ to the mean and standard deviation calculated in the dice tossing random experiment described in Problems 15 and 16. Did this application of the inequality serve some benefit?

18. An investments study by Ibbotson-Sinquefield compiled information on the annual returns investors holding a broadly diversified portfolio of high-grade common stocks experienced during the period 1926–1976. This information in probability distribution form is condensed in Table 7.7.

A further summarizing of the data shows that common stocks earn on average 11.6% a year with the standard deviation of return of 22.4%.

a. Using Chebyshev's Inequality, construct the interval around the mean for $k = 1, 2, 3, 4$, and make an appropriate statement for each.

b. Compare the statements made in (a) with the actual distribution of returns to verify Chebyshev's theorem. How useful in a practical sense was Chebyshev's theorem in describing the actual distribution? Was any valuable information lost?

TABLE 7.7. Annual Returns of High-grade Common Stock

GAIN OR LOSS, X (PERCENTAGE TERMS)	PROBABILITY OF GAIN	PROBABILITY OF LOSS
0 to 10	.171	.133
10 to 25	.254	.117
25 to 50	.230	.049
50 to 75	.042	.002
75 or more	.002	very small
	Sum .699	Sum .301

19. Survey findings on investment decision making of 1000 randomly selected customer accounts at a brokerage house produced some surprising results. When asked the question, "Approximately how many hours do you spend monthly on your securities portfolio?" investors answered as shown in Table 7.8.

TABLE 7.8. Hours Spent on Securities Portfolio

FRACTION OF THE SAMPLE	X, NUMBER OF HOURS EACH MONTH
.600	1
.240	2
.096	3
.035	4
.015	5
.006	6
.002	7
.001	8
.005	8*

*individual values greater than 8 had a total fraction of .005.

The sample mean value is 2 and the sample standard deviation is 1.05. Using this rela-

tive frequency distribution as an adequate approximation of the probability distribution of X:

a. Find the probability that X will be more than two standard deviations from its mean.

b. Find the probability that X will be more than three standard deviations from its mean.

c. Is Chebyshev's theorem applicable even though the distribution is highly skewed to the right?

20. Bartoldi Construction Company, which specializes in shopping mall construction, recognizes that its profitability depends on how accurately it bids on jobs that it takes. Bartoldi's management wants to assess the dependability of its cost accounting department. How close are the estimated costs to the actual cost? Estimates must effectively deal with the uncertainties, such as the price of lumber, brick, and other materials, labor costs, union strike action, and the weather, that cause sizable differences between actual realized costs and the cost estimates made beforehand.

Bartoldi recently has been involved in the construction of several Southland shopping centers and is now involved in submitting a bid for the proposed Mount Carmel shopping complex. Before bidding, Bartoldi decided to examine closely the actual costs incurred with the beforehand cost estimates on the previous shopping malls it constructed. Table 7.9 shows this comparison of these two cost figures for 10 shopping malls constructed over the last five years.

The ratios are above one in five cases, indicating the estimates exceeded the cost. There are three cases in which the costs exceeded the estimates. Consider the historical data an appropriate basis for the probability distribution of the ratio.

a. Construct a probability distribution for the ratio.

b. Construct a cumulative probability distribution for the ratio.

TABLE 7.9. Comparative Costs: Actual vs. Estimate (nearest thousand dollars)

PROJECT	ESTIMATED COST, E	ACTUAL COST, A	RATIO: $R = E/A$
1. Westwood	66	60	1.1
2. Rancho Santa Fe	56	70	.8
3. Fashion Valley	73	81	.9
4. Broadmoor	101	112	.9
5. Eastview	107	107	1.0
6. Mission Valley	85	85	1.0
7. Eastgate	96	80	1.2
8. Westfield	106	95	1.1
9. Northridge	55	50	1.1
10. Rancho Mirage	93	84	1.1

c. Graph the cumulative probability distribution.

d. For the cost estimating department to be reliable, its estimates must be consistent in how *much* they miss the actual cost. Do you judge the estimates reliable?

e. Calculate the expected ratio-value, $E(R)$, and interpret whether on average Bartoldi underestimates or over estimates actual cost.

f. Biased ratio estimates from a cost accounting system show a tendency to be on one side of one such that $E(R)$ no longer equals one. No bias is found when $E(R)$ = 1.0. What is your assessment of the reliability in this case? Can management deal with bias easily when found?

g. Calculate the standard deviation σ_R of the ratios. What implication does a small value of σ_R have about reliability?

h. Does reliability imply no biases? Does no bias imply reliability?

21. The joint distribution of returns between gold coin futures and U.S. Treasury bill futures over the next year is assessed to be the following:

a. Calculate the mean of the X distribution and Y distribution.

b. Calculate the covariance of X and Y. Interpret the value obtained and the type of relationship suggested.

c. Calculate the values of the standard deviation of X and standard deviation of Y.

d. Calculate the correlation coefficient between X and Y. Interpret the coefficient.

e. What advantage is gained by using the correlation coefficient rather than the covariance in discussing the degree of association between two variables?

22. The following joint distribution (Table 7.11) describes the potential returns for the stock of UAL and the less risky convertible bond of UAL.

a. Calculate the mean of the X distribution and Y distribution.

b. Calculate the covariance of X and Y. Interpret the value obtained and the type of relationship suggested.

c. Calculate the values of the standard deviation of X and standard deviation of Y.

d. Calculate the correlation coefficient between X and Y. Interpret the coefficient.

TABLE 7.10. Gold and Treasury Bill Futures

		PERCENTAGE RETURN FOR GOLD COIN FUTURES, Y		
		Zero	Ten	Twenty
PERCENTAGE RETURN FOR U.S.	Zero	0	0	.2
TREASURY BILL FUTURES, X	Ten	0	.2	.2
	Twenty	.4	0	0

TABLE 7.11. Potential Returns of UAL Stock and Bonds

| | | PERCENTAGE RETURN ON UNITED AIRLINE STOCK, Y | | |
		5%	15%	25%
PERCENTAGE RETURN	10%	.40	.20	.20
ON UAL BOND, X	15%	.10	.05	.05

e. What advantage is gained by using the correlation coefficient rather than the covariance in discussing the degree of association between these two variables?

23. What is the expected return on the portfolio of investments shown in Table 7.12?

TABLE 7.12. Investment Expected Return

TYPE OF INVESTMENT	VALUE	EXPECTED RETURN, %
Stocks	$30,000	14
Corporate Bonds	$50,000	12
Municipal Bonds	$20,000	8

24. The expected return of a portfolio equals the weighted average of the returns on each investment. Why is the variance of a portfolio usually not equal to the weighted average of the variance of each investment?

25. Assume a financial world in which (1) all stocks move independently of each other and (2) the standard deviation of annual returns equals 10% for every stock. Calculate the variance of a randomly diversified portfolio of n independent equally weighted investments for
a. $n = 1$ (population).
b. $n = 8$.

c. $n = 128$.
d. Draw a conclusion about what happens to the variation of portfolio returns as the sample of investments increases.

26. Does diversification reduce the expected return of a portfolio? What characteristic of the returns does it reduce?

27. The securities of two large portfolios, one for bonds and one for stocks, have distributions of returns with the features in Table 7.13.
Complete the entries in the table. Assume that
a. The investor invested equally in each portfolio and wishes to calculate a simple average return of two securities, one from each portfolio. That is, $\bar{X} = (X_1 + X_2)/2$
b. The investor invested twice as much in the stock portfolio than in the bond portfolio. The weighted average, W, is $W = \frac{1}{3} X_1 + \frac{2}{3} X_2$

28. Using Problem 27, adjust for the following and solve.
a. If the covariance $X_1, X_2 = -120$, what interpretation might you give the negative covariance? What has it done to the variance of the simple and weighted average?
b. If the covariance $X_1, X_2 = 0$, what happens to the simple and weighted average?
c. Summarize the changing effect that a positive, negative, and zero covariance has on the variance of the average. Which is most beneficial and why?

TABLE 7.13. Distribution of Bond and Stock Returns

	MEAN RETURN	STANDARD DEVIATION	VARIANCE
Bond Portfolio, X_1	15%	12%	____
Stock Portfolio, X_2	18%	12%	____
a. Average, $\bar{X}$	____	____	____
b. Weighted Average, W	____	____	____
Covariance, Cov(X_1, X_2), = 15			

TABLE 7.14. Correlation Matrix for Individual Securities

	AT&T Common	AT&T Bond	Mobil	Lockheed	TWA
AT&T Common	1.00				
AT&T Bond	.34	1.00			
Mobil	.55	.66	1.00		
Lockheed	.40	.26	.37	1.00	
TWA	−.01	.35	.27	.42	1.00

29. The correlation matrix allows the investor to obtain an indication of the potential risk reducing ability of each security under consideration. Table 7.14 shows the correlation matrix for individual securities.

a. Which two securities provide the best risk reduction potential in a portfolio? Why?

b. Which two securities offer the least risk reduction potential in a portfolio? Why?

Random Sampling for Attributes: The Binomial Distribution

Preview. The meaning and importance of random sampling was first discovered in Chapter One, while Chapters Five and Six covered probability measurements. Probability measurements are useful analytical tools in evaluating random samples. These tools will now be used to verify the applicability and reliability of results of random sampling. If sampling produces results that are helter-skelter and probability measures don't apply, there is no way to ascertain reliability: the results will generally be off target.

In this chapter we will examine random sampling for attributes. In this type of random sampling, the prospective user of the sampling information wants to know the prevalence in percentage terms of an attribute in the population under consideration. The nature of the sampling results can be approached both empirically and theoretically. This chapter considers both approaches to confirm that the answers provided by theoretical (probability) distributions are perfectly consistent with the answers arrived at by a long term empirical project. This allows us to be confident about our future use of the theoretical probability distribution. Additionally, the role of sample size will be observed as the accuracy and reliability of the sample results change with increased sample size.

8.1. The Random Sample and the Population

Are all randomly drawn samples miniature replicas of the population from which they are drawn? If they are, then for every random sample, no matter what size, the value of the characteristic of interest in the sample will be the same as the value found in the population. For example, if a population of college students is comprised of sixty percent men and forty percent women, all you would want to know about the population could be obtained directly from the sample. There would be no need for inferential statistics.

How do we know whether or not random samples are miniature replicas of the population? The answer lies with *sequence* of successive outcomes of random draws from the population. If there were a regular and predictable pattern to the successive outcomes, then the incidence of a characteristic in the population would be duplicated in every random sample. In this sense, they would all be miniature replicas of the population.

But if there is no regular, predictable pattern to the sequence of random draws, even for random samples of the same size, then there must be variability between the sample results. Hence, the samples would *not* be small replicas of the population. And for any sample drawn, there would be uncertainty about the relationship between the composition of the sample and of the population.

The results of the example below should shed some light on the issue.

Example 8.1.   Drawing Poker Chips from an Urn

An urn containing ninety white poker chips and ten red chips was thoroughly stirred and a blindfolded experimenter withdrew a chip from the urn. The color of the chip was recorded and then the chip was replaced in the urn. After thoroughly stirring the urn again, a second chip was withdrawn and its color recorded. This procedure was repeated until forty chips had been withdrawn. The outcome of each draw is shown in Figure 8.1. Viewed collectively, the forty outcomes can be called a *random sample of size forty* (poker chips) from the urn.

```
              Mapping of One Poker Chip Experiment
                  (each X represents one draw)

 Color of
 Poker Chip

   Red            X          X              X    X

   White     XXXX   XXXXXXXXX  XXXXXXXXXXXXXXXX  XXX   XXXX
             1                  Draw                    40
```

FIGURE 8.1   Sequence Plot of the Results for a Random Sample of Size 40

Four of the forty draws resulted in a red chip. In other words, the proportion of red chips in this particular sample is the same as that in the population—a welcome result if we want to use the sample proportion as an estimate of the population proportion. However, in the next section we shall find that this is a fortuitous result. Exact equality between population and sample proportions occur much less frequently than might be supposed. Chance variation is the reason for the differences. Statistics deals with chance, with uncertainty, and hence, with the study of these differences.

Now let's study the *sequence* of the red chips. Notice that the four red chips are not equally spaced among the white chips. It took:

> four white chips to get the first red chip
> nine whites to get the second red chip
> sixteen whites to get the third red chip
> three whites to get the fourth red chip

In other words, there does *not* appear to be a regular predictable pattern to the red outcomes.

Perfect Replicas Are Hard to Get

The fact that there is no regular and predictable sequence to the outcomes of drawing chips from an urn helps us answer the second of our initial questions. Are random samples small replicas of the population from which they are drawn? *The answer is no.* The fact that chance causes the sequence of outcomes to be irregular and unpredictable implies that there will be variation (sometimes considerable) in the color composition of random samples of the same size. Since sample composition will vary somewhat, it follows that samples cannot all be exact replicas of the population.

8.2. The Nature of Sampling Variation and Sampling Error

Variability of sample results is an inherent part of the random sampling process. Because random sample results are used as estimates of the population parameter (the characteristic of the population which is of interest to us), variability among sample results causes variability among the estimates. The extent of variability will determine the reliability of random sample results as population estimators.

Variability Causes Estimation Error

What is the link between sampling variability and estimation error? The answer is straightforward. The amount by which a sample statistic (result) differs from the population parameter is exactly the same as the amount by which the population estimate we use differs from the actual population value. Suppose thirty percent of law school students are women. A sample of law school students has twenty percent women. The sample statistic is ten percentage points less than the population parameter. If the sample percentage of women is used to estimate the population percentage, the estimate errs by ten percentage points, the same amount as the difference between population parameter and sample statistic.

> The difference between the estimate and the true value of the parameter is called the (*random*) *sampling error*.

How large can we expect the sampling error to be? Since the error arises from the variability of sample results, to learn about sampling error we must first study the sampling variability prevalent in every sampling process. Sampling variation is objectively studied by means of the random sampling design.

This section seeks to give perspective on sampling variability and sampling errors by investigating the sampling errors which actually occurred in a set of poker chip experiments involving the use of simple random samples. In these experiments, the parameter (ten percent in the first set of experiments) being estimated is known; therefore, the sampling error associated with any given estimate or sample statistic follows directly. More specifically, because there is a one-to-one correspondence between the sample result (the estimate of the population parameter) and the sampling error, the nature of the sampling error can be established by discovering the key features of the distribution of the sample statistic. Attention centers on two key questions.

> 1. Among same-size samples drawn at random from the same population, how close do the sample values tend to be to the actual value of the corresponding population characteristic?

> 2. How close do the population estimates tend to be to the actual values of the population characteristic?

These two questions have the same answer, because the sample values are used as population estimates.

Statistical Inference

The sample statistic, computed and studied in the experiments, is the proportion, $\hat{p}$ (called "p-hat"), of poker chips in the sample which are red. This sample statistic is an estimate of the proportion of chips which are red in the population. Thus, $\hat{p}$ is an *inference or prediction* about the population value, p. Based upon this particular piece of evidence (the sample statistic), we make generalizations about the entire population. Since this inference is made by determining the characteristics of the *sampling distribution of the sample statistic*, we term the process *statistical inference*.

The Sampling Distribution

What is the sampling distribution of a sample statistic? It is defined as:

> the distribution of values of the sample statistic for all the possible samples of the same size from the same population.

The key characteristics of the sampling distribution can be ascertained in two alternative ways:

1. *empirically*, by constructing a frequency distribution of the results from repeated random sampling from the same population, or,

2. *analytically*, by applying the laws of probability.

This and the following two chapters consider both empirical and analytical methods. The goal of the first approach is to develop a sensible perspective about sampling variation by empirically establishing the broad features of the sampling distribution of the sample statistic for one particular situation. Having acquired an initial perspective, the goal of the second approach is to show how the analytical tool of probability can be used to make precise statements with a high degree of confidence about the true value of the population parameter. Let's begin with the empirical demonstration.

8.3. The Empirical Experiment

To establish empirically the broad features of the sampling distribution of the sample statistic, one must take the following steps:

Start with an experimental sampling situation in which the population parameter is known.

As each sample is drawn, tabulate the empirical sample results and compute the sample statistic of interest.

Construct a frequency distribution of the sample statistic. Use the horizontal axis to record the magnitude of the values of the statistic and the vertical axis to record the corresponding frequency of occurrence of each observed value.

As the empirical distribution takes "shape," we can get a good reading (but not a perfect reading) as to how closely sample values are distributed around the population value. Additionally, perspective is gained on the range within which a sample value would most likely fall relative to the population value.

Repetitions of the sampling experiments are performed using the poker chip experiment previously described. That is, forty chips are randomly drawn with replacement from an urn containing ninety white and ten red chips. The nature and the achievement of sampling variation is learned by comparing the color composition of the resulting samples with that of the urn's (population) composition.

One might be unpleasantly surprised if the results of any series of poker chip draws did not reflect the color composition in the urn from which the chips were drawn. If there are mostly white chips in the urn, then a series of random draws will yield mostly white chips. But what of the incidence of the particular color in the urn compared to the sample? How often will they not be identical? *How much will they differ?* This question requires the results of sampling experiments.

Commonly Used Symbols

The relationship between the color composition of the urn and the color composition of the chips drawn from the urn is the relationship between a population value and the corresponding sample statistic. We shall indicate these values by the following symbols:

p: the proportion of red chips in the population (called a *parameter* of the population);

$\hat{p}$: the proportion of red chips in a sample drawn from the urn (called a *statistic* of the sample).

The relationship between a population parameter and the corresponding statistic for a sample drawn from that population is of utmost importance in the field of statistics. Were it not for random variation, the relationship would be extremely simple. The statistic of the sample would always have a value identical to that of the population parameter. But random variation is unavoidable. Hence, the actual value of the sample statistic will depend upon how far the sample statistic deviates from the population parameter.

8.4. Variation: Some Empirical Results

Does a sample very often yield the same color composition as the population from which it was drawn? That's what happened the first time the sampling was tried. The fact that four out of forty draws resulted in a red chip means that the proportion of red chips for this particular sample happened to have exactly the same value as that in the population, .10. In other words, the sample statistic, $\hat{p}_{red}$, turned out to be identical to the population parameter, p_{red}. Both had the value of .10. But this result suggests a host of questions.

Are samples where $\hat{p}_{red} = p_{red}$ sampling flukes or rather common results?

How frequently *does* a sample statistic have the same value as the population from which it was drawn?

And, when differences do occur, how large do they tend to be?

Concise answers to the above questions cannot be obtained without resorting to probability theory. Nevertheless, the cumulative evidence of successive poker chip experiments can provide strong hints as to the correct answers.

Example 8.4. Poker Chip Experiments: Series I

The random experiment of randomly drawing forty poker chips (with replacement) was repeated fifty times. After each set of 40 draws, the number of red chips obtained in that sample was recorded. The process was repeated fifty times. The results ranged from a low of zero red chips to a high of nine red chips. Each of these extremes happened only once in the fifty repetitions. The most common outcome, four red chips,

Number of
Red Chips
Per Sample
(Experiment)

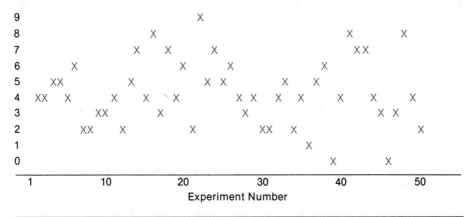

FIGURE 8.2   *Poker Chip Experiments: Series I*
Sequence Chart Mapping Number of Red Poker Chips per Sample for Fifty
Experiments (Each X Represents a Sample of Size Forty)

Overall
Frequency

```
13                        X
12                        X
11                        X
10                        X
 9                        X
 8            X           X
 7            X           X     X
 6            X     X     X     X
 5            X     X     X     X           X
 4            X     X     X     X     X     X
 3            X     X     X     X     X     X     X
 2  X        X     X     X     X     X     X     X
 1  X     X  X     X     X     X     X     X     X     X

    0     1  2     3     4     5     6     7     8     9
         Number of Red Chips Drawn Per Sample
```

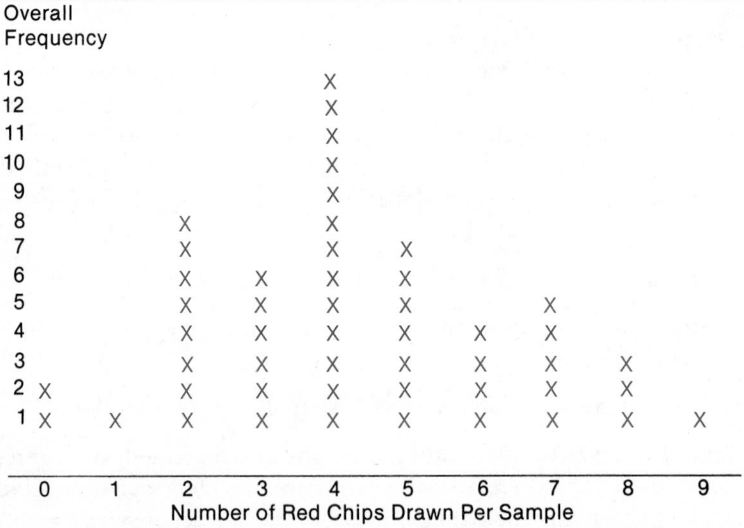

FIGURE 8.3   *Poker Chip Experiments: Series I*
Frequency Chart of Occurrence of Various Outcomes, Based
on Fifty Experiments (Each X Represents a Sample of Size Forty)

occurred thirteen times (26 percent of the outcomes). A sequence chart of the number of red chips obtained in each of the fifty repetitions is shown in Figure 8.2. The number of times each result, zero through nine, occurred is summarized in the *frequency distribution* shown in Figure 8.3.

Figures 8.2 and 8.3 clearly show that when it comes to drawing poker chips, variation is the rule, not the exception. Yet, while the variation does have a wide range, zero through nine chips, half (26) of the outcomes do not deviate by more than one chip from the most common value: four chips. Moreover, nearly three quarters (37) of the outcomes do not deviate from four chips by more than two chips.

A Pattern Exists

The poker chip experiments demonstrate *a pattern*. We will want to capitalize on it. The pattern which is encountered over and over again in studying random variation is: *small deviations from a central value occur frequently; large deviations also occur, but not nearly as often.*

Is $\hat{p}_{red}$ Reliable as an Estimator?

It was found that:

$\hat{p}_{red}$ was different from $p_{red} = .10$ much more often than not.

How often? Had $\hat{p}_{red}$ been used to estimate p_{red}, thirty-seven of the fifty estimates would have been off-target.

The error rate amounts to a whopping 74 percent!

On the surface, these results are rather discouraging, especially if we intend to use the sample result to estimate the population parameter. They seem to indicate that $\hat{p}_{red}$ is not a good estimator of p_{red}.

The Size of the Errors

But, wait a minute! A closer look at the magnitude of the errors qualifies the 74 percent error rate: most of the errors were rather small.

From Figure 8.4, it can be observed that forty-four of the fifty estimates would have been within ±.08 of the p_{red} value. Sixteen are between .125 and .175, thirteen are at .100 and fifteen are between .025 and .075. The largest error amounted to only .125 (12.5 percentage points). Maybe the sample results make good estimates of the population parameter after all.

The results of Figure 8.4 bring out a point which hardly can be overemphasized and which is a central theme of inferential statistics:

Estimation errors will be the rule rather than the exception, but this is hardly a matter of great concern. The real question pertains to the *size* of the errors; that is, what are the chances that the results will be within a *tolerable* range of the target?

Suppose that any error of eight percentage points or less is tolerable. In this case, Figure 8.4 shows that *88 percent of the estimates (44 out of 50) would have been tolerably accurate.* This is quite a different picture from that painted by the simple error rate computed without regard to the size of the error.

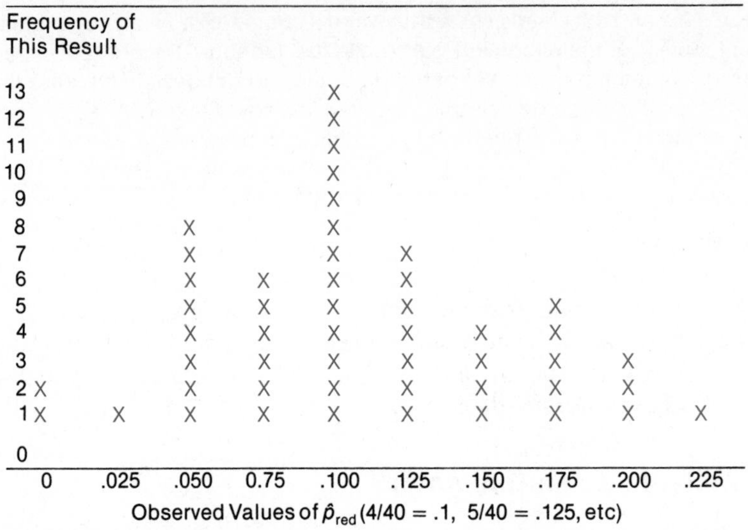

Frequency of
This Result

```
13                          X
12                          X
11                          X
10                          X
 9                          X
 8            X             X
 7            X             X       X
 6            X     X       X       X
 5            X     X       X       X               X
 4            X     X       X       X       X       X
 3            X     X       X       X       X       X       X
 2 X          X     X       X       X       X       X       X
 1 X    X     X     X       X       X       X       X       X       X

 0
   0   .025  .050  0.75   .100   .125   .150   .175   .200   .225
        Observed Values of p̂_red (4/40 = .1,  5/40 = .125, etc)
```

FIGURE 8.4   *Poker Chip Experiments: Series I*
Frequency Chart of Occurrence of Various Sample
Proportions, $\hat{p}_{red}$, for Fifty Experiments when $p_{red} = .1$
(Each X Represents a Sample of Size Forty)

We have learned so far about sampling from the poker chip experiments:

First: The drawn red chips were observed to be spaced irregularly among the outcomes. This suggests that it is *not* possible to *predict* the sequence or pattern of the next draw from preceding draws.

Second: The sample proportion, $\hat{p}_{red}$, the proportion of red chips in each sample, varied over a wide range of values but tended to bunch or concentrate around the population parameter, p_{red}.

This suggests two points:

The sample statistic is usually not exactly on target but usually high or low.

More importantly, the chance that the estimation error is small is quite high.

8.5. Changing the Value of the Population Proportion

What happens if the color composition of the urn, the underlying population parameter, is changed? What would you expect to change about the two main findings? Surely the unpredictability of sequence from one draw to the next would still be maintained. But what of the second finding about the proportion of red chips? To answer these questions, a second series of experiments was conducted.

Example 8.5.   **Poker Chip Experiments: Series II**

The experiment of drawing a random sample of forty chips was again repeated fifty times, just as in Example 8.4. However, in the new series of experiments, the color composition of the poker chips in the urn was changed. In the original experiments, white chips predominated, ninety of the one hundred chips being white. In the new series of experiments, the colors were equally balanced—fifty red and fifty white chips. In other words, the value of p_{red} increased from .10 to .50.

The experiments were conducted as before. A chip was randomly drawn, its color recorded and then replaced in the urn. After forty chips were drawn in this manner, the number of red chips obtained in the forty draws was ascertained and recorded as the sample result. The entire process was repeated fifty times and the fifty sample results are shown in Figure 8.5.

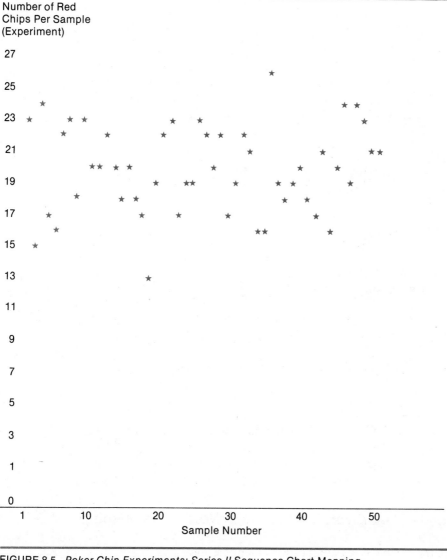

FIGURE 8.5 *Poker Chip Experiments: Series II* Sequence Chart Mapping of Number of Red Poker Chips per Sample for Fifty Experiments (Each * Represents a Sample Size Forty)

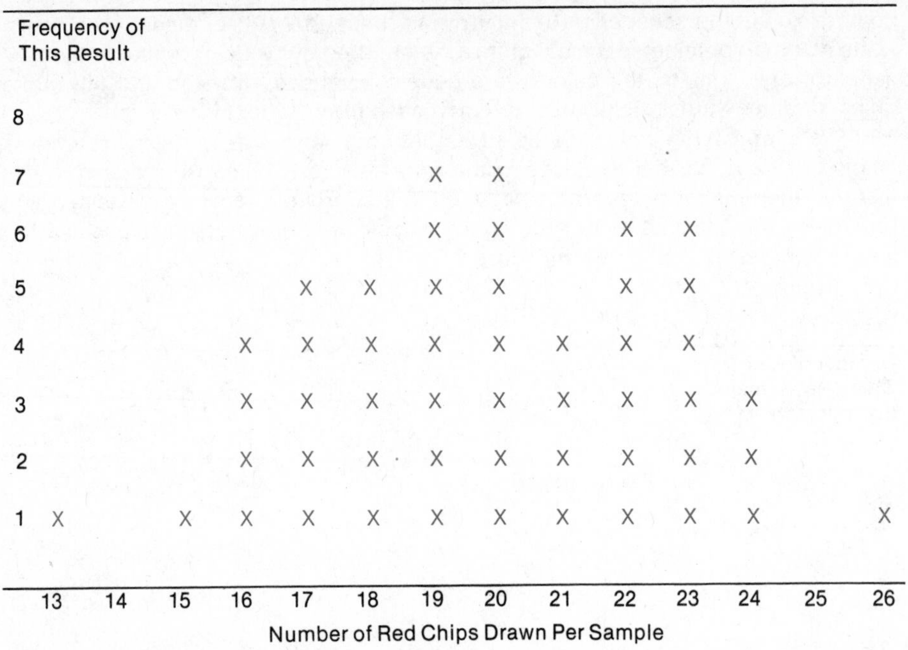

This Result	13	14	15	16	17	18	19	20	21	22	23	24	25	26
8														
7							X	X						
6							X	X		X	X			
5					X	X	X	X		X	X			
4				X	X	X	X	X	X	X	X			
3				X	X	X	X	X	X	X	X	X		
2				X	X	X	X	X	X	X	X	X		
1	X		X	X	X	X	X	X	X	X	X	X		X

Number of Red Chips Drawn Per Sample

FIGURE 8.6 *Poker Chip Experiments: Series II*
Frequency Chart of Occurrence of Various Outcomes

A frequency distribution showing the number of times each of the different sample results occurred is charted in Figure 8.6. Since $p_{red} = .5$ and the sample size is 40, $\hat{p}_{red}$ would equal p_{red} if the sample has twenty red chips. The number of red chips ranged from a low of thirteen to a high of twenty-six. The most common outcome was nineteen and twenty red chips. These values occurred seven times each among the fifty samples.

Sample Variability Is a General Phenomenon

Has increasing the percentage of red chips in the urn eliminated variability in the sample results? Definitely not. Figure 8.6 clearly illustrates that samples of the same size drawn from the same population will exhibit considerable variation in the number of times an attribute (in this case, red chips) is observed. In other words, it appears that *variability of sample outcomes is a general phenomenon which should be expected regardless of the value of the population parameter.*

Estimation Error: A Household Word in Sampling

Is the sample color composition identical to that in the population? Again, the answer is a resounding "no!" Figure 8.6 shows that of the fifty samples, only six had 20 red chips and thus a sample proportion $\hat{p}_{red}$ identical to p_{red}.

Had $\hat{p}_{red}$ been used to estimate p_{red}, the error rate would have been 88 percent. This figure compares with a 74 percent error rate when the urn contained mostly white chips. Both figures are high and suggest that *errors will occur regardless of the value of population parameter.*

Is the Size of Estimation Errors Tolerable?

How large are the differences between $\hat{p}_{red}$ and p_{red}? Are they so large that you can't live with the errors obtained by using $\hat{p}_{red}$ to estimate p_{red}? To answer this question, Figure 8.7 was constructed. Figure 8.7 differs from Figure 8.6 only in that the horizontal scale has been changed to indicate the *proportion* of red chips instead of the number of red chips obtained for each of the samples.

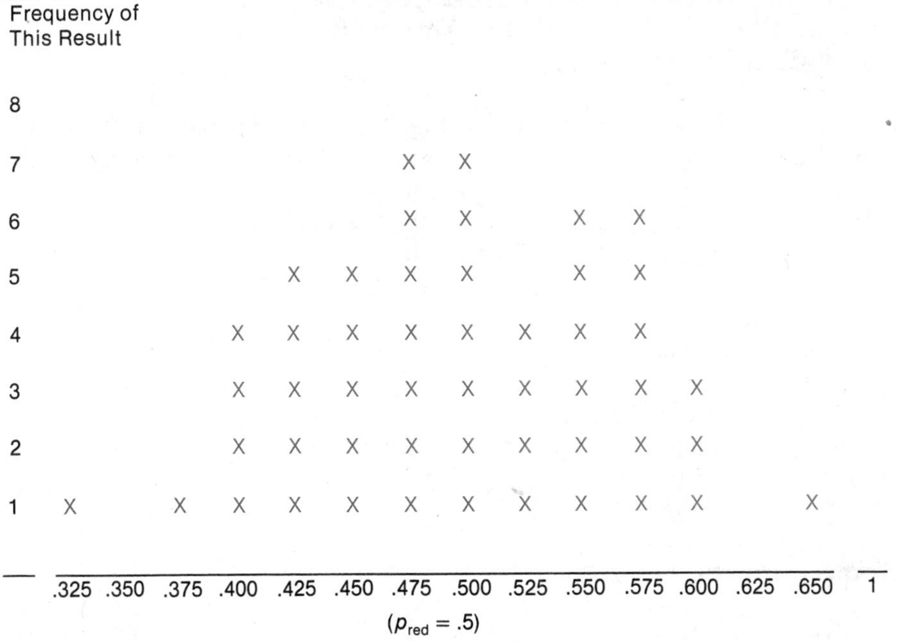

```
Frequency of
This Result

8

7                              X   X

6                              X   X           X   X

5                      X   X   X   X           X   X

4                  X   X   X   X   X   X   X   X

3                  X   X   X   X   X   X   X   X   X

2                  X   X   X   X   X   X   X   X   X

1      X       X   X   X   X   X   X   X   X   X           X
─────────────────────────────────────────────────────────────
    .325 .350 .375 .400 .425 .450 .475 .500 .525 .550 .575 .600 .625 .650   1
                              (p_red = .5)
```

FIGURE 8.7 *Poker Chip Experiments: Series II*
Frequency Chart of Occurrence of Various Samples

Although the error rate in Figure 8.7 is very high (88 percent), the size of the errors for the most part is not very large. For example, it can be observed from Figure 8.7 that forty of the fifty estimates would have a value within .075 of the p_{red} value of .500. In other words, *if eight percentage points is defined as the maximum tolerable error, then 80 percent of the errors would be tolerable.* The conclusion with the new population parameter (color composition) is that the overwhelming majority of the errors are tolerable. This conclusion is the same as when the urn contained only ten red chips. This suggests that the conclusion is quite general and probably not restricted to just one random sampling situation from a population.

There are three major similarities in the conclusions for the two different color composition experiments, each of which can be generalized. They are

It is impossible to predict the *sequence* of future results from past results.

Estimates of p_{red} based on $\hat{p}_{red}$ are quite likely to be in error.

The chances are that the *size* of the estimation error will be tolerably small (provided that errors of plus or minus eight percentage points are considered tolerable).

An important point to keep in mind is that these conclusions hold for two *widely different* population parameters. Thus, it is plausible to suppose that they will be true regardless of the value of the population parameter.

The Question of Inference: How Effectively Does the Sample Statistic Discriminate Among Alternative Population Parameters?

An intriguing question about the sampling experiments remains unanswered. Can sample outcomes be used to identify precisely the underlying population characteristics? Suppose it is known that the urn contains either ten red chips or fifty red chips. But, suppose it is *not* known which value is correct. Is it possible to identify the correct value by comparing the observed value of $\hat{p}_{red}$ to the two possibilities?

As a simple decision rule, suppose it is decided to guess that p_{red} is .50 any time the value of $\hat{p}_{red}$ for the sample is closer to .50 than to .10. How frequently would we guess the right answer?

To help answer the identification questions, Figure 8.8 was constructed. In that figure, the results of both series of experiments are recorded so that they can be compared.

Some Important Clues

It is apparent from the chart that both sets of experiments are plagued by random variation—wide variation of sample results. However, there are two distinguishing features of the different series which give telltale clues to the underlying population parameter generating the sample outcomes:

Clue One: The most obvious difference is that the *values of the sample results have a cluster at quite different levels.* None of the Series I experiments resulted in more than ten red chips; none of the Series II experiments resulted in less than thirteen red chips.

Clue Two: A less obvious difference between the two sets of results is that the *range* of variation is different. Only nine red chips separated the high from the low result for the Series I experiments, compared to thirteen red chips for the Series II experiments.

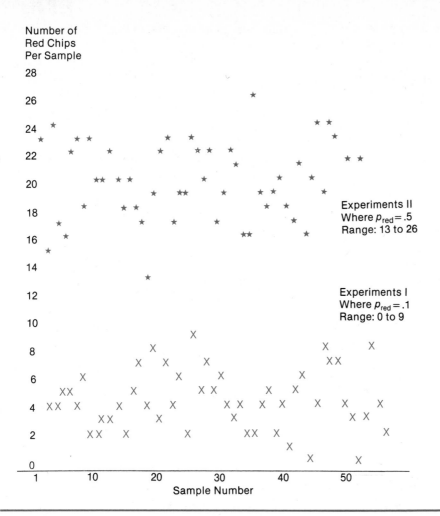

FIGURE 8.8 *Poker Chip Experiments: Series I and II*
Sequence Chart of the Number of Red Poker Chips per Sample for Two
Populations (Each X or * Represents a Sample Size of Forty)

We have learned something of great interest and importance. It was previously established that samples don't *have* to have identical characteristics to
those of the population from which they were drawn. Nevertheless, considerable
similarity between the sample proportion and the population parameter *was
actually found* in the poker chip experiments. In fact, *the similarity was strong
enough so that the sample outcome could be used to identify the population
parameter which produced the results.*

Suppose we had been told after each sample (of size 40) how many red chips
it contained, but not which urn the sample was drawn from. A guess is made
about the urn. If one accepts the simple decision rule to guess Urn I if the sample
contained twelve or less red chips and Urn II if the sample contained thirteen
or more red chips, what percentage of the guesses would have been correct? All

of the guesses would have yielded the correct answer. In other words, for underlying population parameters as different as $p_{red} = .10$ and $p_{red} = .50$, it appears that the results of samples of size forty bunch closely enough around the target to identify the population parameter.

It would be wrong to suppose that sample results can *always* discriminate between population parameters as successfully as was the case this time. To understand why, take a closer look at Figure 8.8. Imagine what the sample results would look like if the two population parameter values had been closer, say $p_{red} = .50$ and $p_{red} = .40$. Many of the sample results for the two series would have overlapped. It would have been very difficult to discern which population had generated a particular sample result.

Larger Samples Improve the Situation

How can the population parameter be identified by a sample outcome when the two possible values are close together? The only way to reduce the amount of chance variation is by increasing the size of the sample, thereby causing tighter bunching of the sample results around the target population parameter. The important relationship between sample size and sample variability is discussed later in this chapter.

8.6. Emerging Truths

Two conclusions tentatively emerge from our limited experimentation:

> *First:* The sample results of chance experiments are plagued with variation.

> *Second:* The configuration of the sample results does suggest the value of the underlying population parameter.

As one could guess, it is true that large samples yield better information about the underlying population parameter. However, complete knowledge of the configuration of sample results for pinpointing the underlying population parameter should not be expected unless we sample ad infinitum—an impossible task.

Some Mileage Out of What We Learned

Our interest in sampling poker chips from an urn is merely a means to another end. We shall conclude our discussion of empirical sampling with an example of how knowledge of sampling gained from the poker chip experiments can be put to good administrative use.

Example 8.6. **Work Sampling**

Industrial engineers use a sampling procedure known as *work sampling* to determine the extent to which a machine or an operator is being utilized. For example, suppose consideration is being given to enlarging the job of a certain punch press operator in the stamping department to include parts inspection. It is important to know what proportion of the time on the job the punch press operator spends actually operating the press as opposed to waiting for parts, setting up the machine, etc. Instead of stationing a time-study engineer at the punch press for several days, an engineer will merely check the press operator at forty randomly selected intervals over the study period, recording each time whether or not the press is being operated. The proportion of observations in which the press was being operated is used as the estimate of the total time spent in actual operation of the punch press.

Work Sampling is analogous to the poker chip experiment in these respects:

1. the proportion of on-the-job time actually spent operating the punch press corresponds to p_{red}, the proportion of red chips in the urn;

2. drawing a random sample of forty times to observe the punch press operator corresponds to drawing a random sample of forty chips from the urn;

3. finding that the operator was actually operating the press corresponds to drawing a red chip;

4. the proportion of sample observations in which the press was being operated corresponds to $\hat{p}_{red}$.

Applying what we learned from the poker chip experiments to work sampling, we can conclude that with a sample as small as forty, it would be possible to distinguish a situation in which the machine was being operated 50 percent of the time from one in which the machine was being operated only 10 percent of the time.

8.7. Tree Diagram for Sampling Experiments: Counting the Number of Elementary Events

The poker chip experiments provided many important insights into sampling variability. Yet the insights do not provide answers to specific probability questions we might have. Correct answers to these probability questions can be obtained by an extension of the four-step procedure described and used in Chapter Five (Example 5.10) to calculate the probabilities for simple random sampling. In that procedure we determined the number of elementary events, the probability of each, the number of elementary events in which the characteristic of interest is present, and the product of the last two steps. As before, the objective of the first step is obtained by using a tree diagram. The number of branches on the tree determines how many elementary events the experiment has. Assigning equal probability to each elementary event requires each of these probabilities to be "one divided by the number of tree diagram branches." Let us illustrate the probability calculations for a specific problem.

Figure 8.9 shows the structure of the tree diagram branches for a sample of $n = 4$ chips drawn from the population of $N = 100$ poker chips. The four stages of the tree diagram, one for each chip drawn, start with 100 chips in the urn at the first stage. This means that for the specific chip to be drawn there are 100 different possibilities that can appear. The second, third, and fourth chips to be drawn also have 100 possibilities since the sampling is done with replacement.

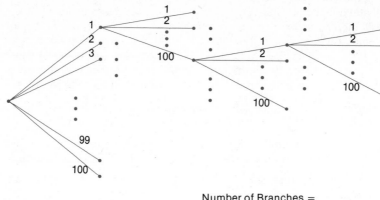

Number of Branches =
100 × 100 × 100 × 100 = 100 million

FIGURE 8.9 Four-Stage Tree Diagram for $n = 4$, $N = 100$

Applying the fundamental principle of counting (section 5.12), the total number of complete four-stage branches and elementary events is:

Stage I   Stage II   Stage III   Stage IV
 100 ·   100   ·   100   ·   100 $= N^n = 100^4$
                                          $= 100$ million

The probability of each equiprobable elementary event must be $1/N^n =$ one/(100 million). To determine the probability of any specific number of red chips in the sample requires one to obtain the number of elementary events that correspond to the possible sample results possessing the specified number of red chips.

8.8. Probability Calculations for Sampling Experiments

Assuming a population of $R = 30$ red chips and $N - R = 70$ white chips, what is the probability that a simple random sample of $n = 4$ will result in exactly x (say, one) red chips? The probability calculation involves the product of:

1. the number of elementary events out of the 100 million total that corresponds to the outcomes possessing the described characteristic of exactly one red chip.

2. the probability of each equiprobable elementary event, $1/N^n$, which in this case equals 1/(100 million).

Having determined the latter, let's now determine the former.
     Each elementary event of interest corresponds to an outcome which contains

exactly one red chip. This one red chip (x) must be drawn from the $R = 30$ red chips in the urn. To fill out the sample, $n - x = 3$ white chips must be drawn (with replacement) from the $N - R = 70$ white chips in the urn. Once it is known which red chip and which three white chips will be in the sample, the next task is to determine the sequential position the red chip occupies along the branch. There are four possible positions, one for each of the tree diagram's four stages. With selection and sequencing tasks accomplished, the complete set of outcomes with one red chip has been singled out. Let's now illustrate this procedure in detail.

Every outcome with one red chip (x) and three white chips $(n - x)$ can be viewed as the end product of three tasks. Each task involves one aspect needed to identify a tree diagram branch. The three tasks are presented in Figure 8.10.

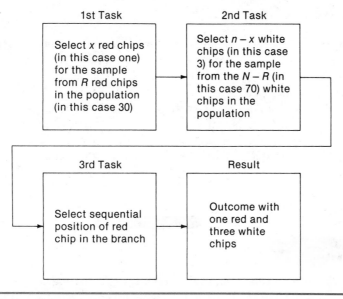

FIGURE 8.10   Identifying an Outcome with One Red Chip

From the fundamental principle of counting the number of ways of accomplishing all three tasks is the product of the number of ways of accomplishing each one individually.

There are $R^x = 30^1$ ways of selecting one red chip in the sample from the thirty red chips in the population.

There are $(N - R)^{(n - x)} = 70^3$ ways of selecting the three white chips in the sample from the seventy white chips in the population.

There are 4 possible sequential positions for the red chip to occupy in the sample.

Thus, *the number of elementary events including exactly one red chip* is:

$$R^x(N - R)^{(n - x)}(4) = (30)^1(70)^3(4) = 41.16 \text{ million.}$$

The probability of exactly one red chip is now easily computed: It is the product of two terms:

$$\begin{pmatrix} \text{Probability of} \\ \text{exactly one red chip} \\ \text{in sample of } n = 4 \end{pmatrix} = \begin{pmatrix} \text{Probability of} \\ \text{each elemen-} \\ \text{tary event} \end{pmatrix} \text{ times } \begin{pmatrix} \text{Number of elementary} \\ \text{events that correspond} \\ \text{to outcomes including} \\ \text{exactly one red chip} \end{pmatrix}$$

$= 1/(100 \text{ million}) \text{ times } 41.16 \text{ million} = .4116.$

Thus, in a random sample of four poker chips drawn with replacement from an urn containing 30 red and 70 white chips, the probability of one red chip is .4116.

8.9. Counting Combinations

Does the procedure used in the preceding section to compute the probability of one red chip in a sample of size four illustrate a general approach to these kinds of problems? Yes, however, it is not always so easy to see possible sequential positions if more than one red chip is involved. For example, to compute the probability of two red chips in a sample of $n = 4$, how many different sequential arrangements of the red chips are possible? In making this determination we have no concern for which one of the two red chips occupies the position (assume the red chips are indistinguishable). The answer is six, as shown below:

```
rrww     rwwr     wrwr
rwrw     wrrw     wwrr
```

A simple counting formula called the *combination rule* gives the correct number.

$$C_x^n = \frac{n!}{x!(n - x)!}$$

The symbol ! is a mathematical symbol for the *factorial* operation which refers to the product of a series of integers, where the first term is n and each successive term declines by one. The last term 0! is defined to equal the value one. Thus,

$$n! = (n)(n - 1)(n - 2) \ldots \ldots \ldots (3)(2)(1)(0!)$$

For example, $5! = (5)(4)(3)(2)(1)(0!) = 120$. Note, the series can be split at any position, such as $n! = (n)(n - 1)(n - 2)!$ In Section 9.3 we explain the derivation of the combination formula. For the present, let's see how the combination formula applies.

Example 8.9A.   **Counting Sample Sequences**

The number of different sequential arrangements of two red chips in a sample of size $n = 4$ was found to be six by listing the arrangements. This answer can be obtained without resorting to a listing by taking advantage of the combination rule. Each possible sample sequence can be viewed as a *n*-size poker chip sample composed of two groups, one group of exactly *x* (two) red chips and the other group of exactly

$n - x$ (two) white chips. There are C_x^n different sequential arrangements that have this same sample composition. Thus,

$$C_2^4 = \frac{4!}{2!(4-2)!}$$

$$= \frac{4 \cdot 3 \cdot 2 \cdot 1}{2 \cdot 1 \cdot 2 \cdot 1} \text{ or } \frac{4 \cdot 3(2!)}{2!(2!)} = \frac{4 \cdot 3}{2!} = \frac{12}{2}$$

$$= 6$$

Using the combination rule spared us the time required to list and enumerate all the different sequences. This advantage becomes greater the more sequences there are. Left to uneducated intuition, most people tend to vastly underestimate the number of combinations which are possible in commonly encountered situations. What number would you guess for a sample size $n = 20$, where the number of red chips is $x = 10$? For C_{10}^{20} there are 184,756 arrangements with the same composition of red and white chips. The following example illustrates a business situation in which there are far more combinations than most people realize.

Example 8.9B.   **Selecting a Common Stock Portfolio**

Suppose common stock is to be purchased of five different companies from the fourteen hundred companies listed on the New York Stock Exchange. How many different portfolios of five companies are there? According to the combination rule, there are

$$C_5^{1400} = \frac{1400!}{5!(1400 - 5)!} = 44{,}499{,}332{,}850{,}000.$$

This staggering number amounts to more than 10,000 different portfolios for every person living on the earth.

8.10. Formula for the Binomial Distribution

The terms given in Section 8.8 for the probability of exactly x occurrences of a specified attribute (one red chip) in a random sample of size n can be expressed simply with the inclusion of the counting rule for combinations. That is,

$$P(x) = \frac{1}{N^n} C_x^n R^x (N - R)^{n-x}$$

In this formula, N is the number of items in the population; R is the number of items in the population in which the specified attribute is present; $N - R$ is the number of population items in which the specified attribute is absent; $n - x$ is the number of sample items in which the specified attribute is absent.

The resulting expression is a certified way to find the probability of a sample result for any given sample size. However, even more can be gained by slightly restructuring the right hand side of the expression.

First, rewrite the denominator N^n as $N^x \cdot N^{n-x}$

These are equivalent expressions. This gives the expression:

$$P(x) = \frac{C_x^n R^x (N-R)^{n-x}}{N^x \cdot N^{n-x}}$$

Next, note that the terms R^x in the numerator and N^x in the denominator are raised to the same exponent, x. A simplification of the expression is possible.
Write the ratio R^x/N^x as $(R/N)^x$

These are equivalent expressions. The terms $(N-R)^{n-x}$ in the numerator and N^{n-x} in the denominator simplify to $[(N-R)/(N)]^{n-x}$ since they have the same exponent, $n-x$. Thus,

$$P(x) = C_x^n (R/N)^x [(N-R)/N]^{n-x}$$

A key point to recognize is that the ratio R/N is a constant. Its value does not change in sampling the population of size N. Likewise the ratio $(N-R)/N$ is a constant throughout the sampling. For instance, in the urn example replacement of the ball after each draw restores the original number of R items and $N-R$ items so that N items are again in the population.

Now let's further simplify and let p equal the value R/N which represents the constant proportion of items in the population having the characteristic specified. Let $1-p$ equal the constant for the unchanged $(N-R)/N$ proportion of the population not having the specified characteristic. This leads to a very terse and usable probability formula called the *Binomial Sampling Formula*:

$$\mathbf{P(x) = C_x^n (p)^x (1-p)^{n-x}}$$

where n is the sample size, x is the number of items in the sample having the desired characteristic, p is the proportion of items in the population having the desired characteristic, $1-p$ is the proportion of items in the population which do not have the desired characteristic, and $P(x)$ is the probability of obtaining exactly x items having the desired characteristic in a sample of size n.

Let's use the binomial sampling formula to find the probability of three Democrats voting in a random sample with replacement of ten voters where 40 percent of the registered voters in the population are Democrats. We have:

$$
\begin{aligned}
n &= 10, \\
x &= 3, \\
p &= .4 \\
1-p &= .6
\end{aligned}
$$

$$P(3) = \left[\frac{10 \cdot 9 \cdot 8 \cdot 7 \cdot 6 \cdot 5 \cdot 4 \cdot 3 \cdot 2 \cdot 1}{(3 \cdot 2 \cdot 1)(7 \cdot 6 \cdot 5 \cdot 4 \cdot 3 \cdot 2 \cdot 1)} \right] [.4^3][.6^7]$$

$$= \left[\frac{10 \cdot 9 \cdot 8}{3 \cdot 2 \cdot 1} \right] [.064][.0280]$$

$$= [120][.064][.0280]$$

$$= .2150$$

This means that if the population parameter of Democrats is .4, then out of ten registered voters randomly selected, the chances of finding three Democrats is a little more than one in five. The formula uses the product of the number of ways of obtaining the desired outcome and the probability of each desired outcome to shortcut the lengthy and cumbersome (yet valid) process of working with the elementary events of tree diagrams to find the probability of the event in question.

8.11. A Simplified Probability Tree

Whenever sampling is done with replacement from a population of attribute characteristics, the binomial formula is applicable. The binomial formula was obtained by a fairly straightforward application of the four-step procedure developed in Chapter Five. After asserting that the probability of any event is the sum of the probabilities of the elementary events which it includes, the procedure prescribes:

Defining the elementary events from outcomes that are equally likely

Finding the total count for the elementary events

Defining the probability of any elementary event as one divided by the count

Finding the count for those elementary events that correspond to outcomes which include the specified attribute

Multiplying together the last two calculations

The binomial formula can also be obtained by another procedure first developed in Chapter Six. It is instructive to pursue this alternative approach. It utilizes the probability tree concept (Section 6.7). The tree does not require that elementary events be equally likely and it accomplishes a drastic reduction in the number of elementary events. Figure 8.11 shows a probability tree for the four-stage poker chip experiment described in Section 8.8, where there are 30

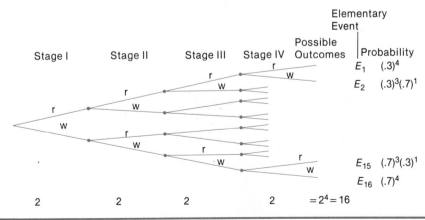

FIGURE 8.11 Probability Tree for the Elementary Events and Their Probabilities in the Poker Chip Experiment ($R = 30$, $N - R = 70$)

red chips and 70 white chips. The tree requires only 16 branches, not the 100 million previously required. By viewing the outcome of each draw in terms of which *color* (red or white) is drawn rather than in terms of which *chip* (of the 100 in the urn) is drawn, each stage can be shown with two choices, red or white. The product 2^4 indicates there are sixteen branches showing the possible sequential arrangements and defining the sixteen possible outcomes and corresponding elementary events at the terminal position of each branch.

The probability of each elementary event is obtainable from the multiplication rule described in Section 6.6 and is the product of the probabilities on the different segments of the branch. Since the sample is drawn with replacement, the probability of red is the same .3 value at every stage and the same .7 value for white at every stage. Thus the probability of the elementary event representing the sequence *rwrw* is:

$$(.3)(.7)(.3)(.7) = .0441$$

Collecting like terms, this can be written

$$(.3)^2(.7)^2 = .0441,$$

which in p and $1 - p$ terms is,

$$p^2(1 - p)^2$$

This can be viewed in general terms as,

$$p^x(1 - p)^{n-x}$$

The combination rule tells us that there are C_x^n combinations of distinguishable arrangements of x red chips among the n draws. Each distinguishable arrangement represents a different outcome and corresponding elementary event. Thus with C_x^n giving the count and $p^x(1 - p)^{n-x}$ giving the individual probability, the sum of their individual probabilities must be:

$$P(x) = C_x^n p^x(1 - p)^{n-x}$$

This different approach derives the same expression of the binomial formula first shown in Section 8.10. It is read:

> the probability of x occurrences of the specified attribute in a sample of size n drawn with replacement.

An additional and common sampling interpretation is to view the *population as infinite* and interpret the probability given by the binomial formula as:

> x occurrences on n distinct, repetitive, independent trials of an experiment having only two possible outcomes; one of these is designated a success and the other is designated a failure. The probability of a success is denoted by p and it must be constant from trial to trial.

As the following example suggests, the binomial distribution can be of great value in situations requiring the assessment of decision risk.

Example 8.11. The Aborted Attempt to Rescue American Hostages in Iran

In the spring of 1980 a difficult and dangerous helicopter rescue mission was launched to release the Americans held hostage by Iranians at the American embassy in Tehran. Eight helicopters had to fly more than 800 miles at low altitude during the night over sandy desert to reach their rendezvous point. The mission was aborted. Three of the eight helicopters failed to reach their rendezvous point in workable condition. The mission commander required six helicopters at that point in order to proceed with the mission. A controversy soon developed over whether more helicopters should have been sent in view of the known hazards (both mechanical and navigational) of such a long nighttime desert flying mission.

Let us assume, for the moment, that past experience from practice missions and previous low altitude trips over sand at night made the military planners quite aware of the risk that a helicopter would not be successful in its attempt. Based upon the number sent (eight) and the number required (six), let us further assume that each helicopter was thought to have a .75 chance of getting to the rendezvous point in satisfactory condition. What would be the probability that a sufficient number (at least six) helicopters make the trip successfully?

Plugging into the binomial formula the appropriate values of the parameters, one can determine the probability of exactly six successes. It is:

$$P(6) = C_6^8(.75)^6(.25)^2$$
$$= 28(.177979)(.0625)$$
$$= .3115$$

The probability of exactly seven successes is:

$$P(7) = C_7^8(.75)^7(.25)^1 = .2670$$

The probability of eight successes is:

$$P(8) = C_8^8(.75)^8(.25)^0 = .1001$$

The probability of a sufficient number of helicopters reaching the rendezvous point is the sum of these probabilities or .6786.

With the assumption of $p = .75$, it appears that there was nearly one chance in three that the mission would fail because of too few helicopters reaching the rendezvous point. How would this risk be decreased by a few extra helicopters? Further calculations indicate that the risk of failure could have been cut from .3214 to .0343, or less than one chance in twenty, with *just three* additional helicopters.

At first one might want to assume the obvious, that the probability of success for a particular helicopter must have been higher than our assumed .75 figure, say .95. This would make it more plausible that only eight helicopters were sent. But claiming such a high probability of success creates an inconsistency. The statements issued to the press by the mission's military planners strongly suggested that the mission was highly risky to begin with—a logical assessment, if the probability of a helicopter being trouble-free was a moderate value, say .75, rather than .95. If this is true, then certainly eight helicopters were not enough to be highly confident that the mission would succeed.

It is easy to say from hindsight that the mission might have gone better if more helicopters had been sent. Our point is directed more to the statistical thinking behind the strategy. Many people are unaware of what is meant by a probability of success of $^6/_8$, or as some people would say, "6 chances out of 8." They erroneously think it means that out of *every* 8 there will be 6 successes. One can daily witness such thinking at the Las Vegas slot machines. People will watch for machines which have been paying off "below average" because they think this indicates the machines are now "due to catch up" with the long run averages. At Las Vegas, the consequences of this are confined primarily to the individual gambler. What if this statistical mentality dominates the planning of military strategists? The consequences of their decisions could be very costly or even disastrous nationally and internationally.

8.12. Binomial Tables

The binomial sampling formula is so frequently used in statistics that special tables have been constructed from which many binomial probabilities can be read directly rather than having to be calculated. These tables are constructed for various sample sizes and values of p, the probability of obtaining an item with the desired characteristic. Table 1 in the appendix of this book shows the probability for each individual value of x for samples of size n from 1 through 50 and for selected values of p from .01 through .50. To illustrate its use, refer to Table 1 where for $n = 10, p = .4$ and $x = 3$, the value .2150 is read from the body of the table. This agrees with the value previously calculated.

If the value of p exceeds .5, the problem must be restated in order to use the binomial tables. For an urn containing only red and white chips, where $p_{red} = .7$, what is the probability of five red chips in a sample of size eight? Since p only goes to .5 in the tables, the problem is restated by phrasing the question in terms of white chips instead of red. Since $p_{red} = .7$, p_{white} must equal .3. If there are to be five red chips in a sample of eight chips, then three chips must be white. So, we can ask for the probability of three white chips in eight, given $p_{white} = .3$. From Table 1, the answer is .2541.

Determining Probability for a Range

In addition to listing the probabilities of individual sample results, the binomial tables can also be used to find the probability that the number of items having a desired characteristic in a sample lies within a specified *range* of values. For example, suppose we want to know how probable it is that the number of red chips in a sample of size twenty-five will lie within the range fifteen to nineteen if 50 percent of the chips in the population are red. We can use Table 1 in the appendix to find the individual probabilities; summing the individual probabilities gives the probability for the range:

$$P(15) = .0974$$
$$P(16) = .0609$$
$$P(17) = .0322$$
$$P(18) = .0143$$
$$P(19) = .0053$$
$$P(15 \leq X \leq 19) = .2101$$

Cumulative Probability

Table 2 in the appendix is a table of *cumulative* binomial probabilities. It provides a shortcut method of determining the probability for a range. The values in the table represent the probabilities of all values *less than* or *equal to* the indicated number. For example, the probability of nineteen or less red chips, given $n = 25$ and $p = .5$, is listed in the table as:

$$P(X \leq 19) = .998$$

The probability that the number of red chips lies within the range fifteen to nineteen inclusive can be obtained by finding the difference between the probability of nineteen or less red chips and fourteen or less red chips:

$$\begin{aligned} P(15 \leq X \leq 19) &= P(X \leq 19) - P(X \leq 14) \\ &= .998 - .788 \\ &= .210 \end{aligned}$$

This is nearly the same value obtained earlier by the more tedious procedure of summing the probabilities of individual values within the range.

8.13. Summary Measures for the Binomial Distribution

A useful, important feature of the binomial distribution is that the general procedure for calculating the mean, variance, and standard deviation described in the previous chapter can be condensed to a short expression. For the mean, the expression is:

$$\mu_{\text{binomial}} = np.$$

That is, the mean of a binomial distribution is the product of the size of the sample and the constant probability of finding a success on each draw from the population. The expression for the variance is:

$$\sigma^2_{\text{binomial}} = np(1 - p)$$

For example, in the second series of poker chip experiments, $n = 40$ and $p = .5$.

$$\mu_{\text{binomial}} = np = (40)(.5) = 20$$
$$\sigma^2_{\text{binomial}} = np(1 - p) = (40)(.5)(.5) = 10.$$

This implies that the variance of any binomial is the product of the sample size, the probability of success, and the probability of failure. The shortcut expression for the standard deviation is:

$$\sigma_{\text{binomial}} = \sqrt{np(1 - p)}$$

For the series II poker chip experiments,

$$\sigma_{\text{binomial}} = \sqrt{np(1 - p)} = \sqrt{40(.5)(.5)} = 3.162$$

The standard deviation is merely the positive square root of the variance. The application of Chebyshev's Inequality (Section 7.8) can provide insight into the extent of sampling variability. These expressions facilitate the quick computations needed to implement the Inequality. In a probability context, Chebyshev's Inequality states that

$$P\left[\frac{|X - \mu|}{\sigma} \geq k\right] \leq \frac{1}{k^2}$$

This inequality states that the probability of a value more than k standard deviations from the mean is less than $1/k^2$. For example, choosing 2 as the value for k, we say that the probability of a value more than two standard deviations from the mean is less than $\frac{1}{4}$, or less than .25.

Example 8.13. Using the Shortcut Formulas for the Mean and Standard Deviation of a Binomial Distribution

Suppose a large sample of 10,000 chips is randomly drawn with replacement from a population in which 50 percent of the chips are red. Taking advantage of the shortcut formulas, we find that

$$\mu_{binomial} = np = 10{,}000(.50) = 5000$$

$$\sigma^2_{binomial} = np(1 - p) = 10{,}000(.50)(.50) = 2500$$

$$\sigma_{binomial} = \sqrt{np(1 - p)} = \sqrt{10{,}000(.50)(.50)} = 50.$$

Knowing that the mean number of red chips in samples of size 10,000 is 5000, with a standard deviation of 50, we can apply Chebyshev's Inequality to learn about sampling variation. Let's pick the range 4800–5200 red chips and find the maximum probability of a sample result outside this range:

$$\frac{x - \mu}{\sigma} = \frac{5200 - 5000}{50} = 4; \qquad \frac{x - \mu}{\sigma} = \frac{4800 - 5000}{50} = -4$$

Both the value 5200 and the value 4800 are four standard deviations from the mean, 5000. Therefore, in setting up the inequality we have:

$$P\left[\frac{|X - \mu|}{\sigma} > 4\right] \leq \frac{1}{4^2} \text{ or } \frac{1}{16}.$$

In other words, the chance of finding more than 5200 or less than 4800 red chips in a sample of 10,000 is less than one in sixteen.

8.14. The Sampling Distribution for the Sample Proportion, $\hat{p}$

It should be recognized that there is a direct correspondence between the *number* and the *proportion* of items in a sample having a desired characteristic. The proportion is simply the number of such items divided by the sample size:

$$\hat{p} = \frac{x}{n}$$

Therefore, a table of binomial sampling probabilities also gives the probabilities for all the different possible sample proportions, $\hat{p}$.

Suppose there is a population in which 30 percent of the items are classified as defective. A random sample of size eight is drawn with replacement. What are the probabilities for the possible values of the proportion defective *in the sample?* Following is a list of the sample proportion defective corresponding to each possible *number* of defective items in the sample:

Number of Defectives, x:	0	1	2	3	4	5	6	7	8
Proportion of Defectives, $\hat{p}$:	.000	.125	.250	.375	.500	.625	.750	.875	1.000

Examining the table of binomial probabilities for $n = 8$ and $p = .30$, the probabilities for the different possible number of defectives, x, and for the proportion defective in the sample are:

Number of Defectives; x:	0	1	2	3	4
Sample Proportion Defective; $\hat{p}$:	0	.125	.250	.375	.500
Probability:	.0576	.1977	.2965	.2541	.1361

Number of Defectives; x:	5	6	7	8
Sample Proportion Defective; $\hat{p}$:	.625	.750	.875	1.000
Probability:	.0467	.0100	.0012	.0001

The most probable sample outcome is two defectives among the eight items in the sample, or a proportion defective of $\frac{2}{8}$ or .25. Comparing the sample proportion $\hat{p}$ to the population proportion $p = .30$, we find that the probability of $\hat{p}$ differing from p by more than .10 is .4494:

$$.0576 + .1977 + .1361 + .0467 + .0100 + .0012 + .0001 = .4494$$

The probability that $\hat{p}$ will differ from p by more than .20 is .1156. Check this for yourself.

In one of the poker chip experiments, samples of size forty were drawn with replacement from a population in which fifty percent of the chips were red. The probabilities for the different possible values of the proportion red in a sample are listed in the table of binomial probabilities for $n = 40$ and $p = .5$. Rounded to four digits, the probabilities for the sample proportion values are given in Table 8.1 and graphed in Figure 8.12.

With this table in hand, the probability of obtaining a sample proportion with any specified range can be easily computed. There is only .3642 probability (.1194 + .1254 + .1194) of obtaining a sample proportion within the range .475 to .525; that is, within plus or minus two and one half percentage points of the percent in the population. Similarly, there is a very substantial .9194 probability of obtaining a sample proportion within the range .375 to .625; that is, within plus or minus twelve and one half points of the percent in the population.

TABLE 8.1. Probabilities for the Proportion of Red Chips in a Sample; $n = 40$, $p_{red} = .5$

SAMPLE PROPORTION, $\hat{p}$	PROBABILITY
.175*	.0000
.200	.0001
.225	.0002
.250	.0008
.275	.0021
.300	.0051
.325	.0109
.350	.0211
.375	.0366
.400	.0572
.425	.0807
.450	.1031
.475	.1194
.500	.1254
.525	.1194
.550	.1031
.575	.0807
.600	.0572
.625	.0366
.650	.0211
.675	.0109
.700	.0051
.725	.0021
.750	.0008
.775	.0002
.800**	.0001

*and all smaller proportions
**and all larger proportions

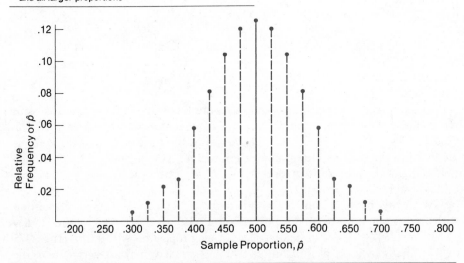

FIGURE 8.12 Sampling Distribution for Sample Proportion Red in Sample of Size 40 from Population with $p_{red} = .50$

Error Tolerance and Reliability Level

In Section 8.5 the sampling experiments were used to investigate the reliability of $\hat{p}$, the sample proportion, as an estimate of p, the population proportion. It was learned that some amount of error $(p - \hat{p})$ usually occurred. In that particular case, 88 percent of the experiments had errors, but only twenty percent of the experiments had errors exceeding eight percentage points. Having studied the binomial distribution, we can now be more precise in our statements about reliability and estimation error. First let us define two terms:

the error tolerance is the maximum acceptable difference (error) between the sample proportion and the population proportion.

the reliability level of the sampling process is the probability that a sample proportion will actually fall within the range of tolerable error.

Consider the error tolerance of $\pm .08$ which for p of .5 captures the range of sample proportion between $\hat{p} = .425$ and $\hat{p} = .575$. From Table 8.1 it is seen that the sum of the probabilities of the sample proportions between $\hat{p} = .425$ and $\hat{p} = .575$ is .7318. The value .7318 is the reliability level of the sampling process given the specified error tolerance and the sample size used. Thus, the sampling experiments conducted early in this chapter correctly foretold an important conclusion about sampling variability that we have now established formally by calculating probabilities: the majority of sample proportions lie within $\pm .08$ error tolerance of the population proportion. A graph showing the exact sampling probability distribution for the sample proportion $\hat{p}$ is shown in Figure 8.12.

The relationship between error tolerance and the reliability level of the sampling process is important. Table 8.2 presents the levels for the two factors from a population with $p = .5$. The table's figures show that increased reliability is bought at the price of increased error tolerance. How are the reliability levels calculated? As before, the reliability levels are obtained by summing the appropriate probabilities in Table 8.1 for the range of $\hat{p}$ implied from error tolerance.

TABLE 8.2. Reliability Levels Corresponding to Different Error Tolerances For Samples of Size $n = 40$ with $p = .5$

ERROR TOLERANCE	RELIABILITY LEVEL
$\pm .025$	.3642
$\pm .050$	.5704
$\pm .075$	.7318
$\pm .100$	.8462
$\pm .125$	.9194
$\pm .150$	.9616
$\pm .175$	.9834
$\pm .200$	.9936

It is not necessary to construct special tables for the sampling distribution of $\hat{p}$ in order to determine the reliability level of the sample process. The calculations can be made directly from the binomial distribution tables for individual values. The following example illustrates how this is done.

Example 8.14. Using Binomial Tables to Determine the Reliability Level of the Sampling Process

Suppose for a population with equal numbers of red and white chips, we want to know how probable it is that the percentage of red chips in a sample of size forty will lie within ten percentage points of the population percentage. This is equivalent to asking for the reliability level of the sampling process associated with an error tolerance of $\pm.10$. Thus, the reliability level we seek to know is the probability that $\hat{p}$ will fall within the range .4 to .6. The number of red chips corresponding to $\hat{p} = .4$ is:

$$\hat{p} = \frac{x}{n}$$

$$x = n\hat{p}$$

$$= (40)(.4) = 16$$

and the number of red chips corresponding to $\hat{p} = .6$ is:

$$x = n\hat{p} = (40)(.6) = 24$$

Therefore, the probability that $\hat{p}_{red}$ lies between .4 and .6 inclusive is equivalent to $P(16 \leq X \leq 24)$. We need then only calculate:

$$P(16 \leq X \leq 24) = P(X \leq 24) - P(X \leq 15)$$
$$= .9231 - .0769$$
$$= .8462.$$

This is the reliability level for the sampling process where $p_{red} = .5$, $n = 40$, and an error tolerance of $\pm.10$ is imposed.

8.15. The Effect of Sample Size on the Sampling Distribution of $\hat{p}$

The tradeoff between reliability level and error tolerance shown in Table 8.2 for a sample of size $n = 40$ is not an isolated case. It is a generalizable phenomenon:

> *for any given size sample,* there is no way to increase the reliability level of a particular sampling process without accepting a greater error tolerance.

Increasing the reliability level without simultaneously changing the error tolerance requires reducing the variability of the sample statistic. This reduction can be accomplished by increasing the sample size. How much can be accomplished? The relationship between the size of a sample and its level of reliability will be investigated shortly by finding the mean and standard deviation of the sampling probability distribution of $\hat{p}$ and applying Chebyshev's Inequality.

The Standard Deviation of the Sampling (Probability) Distribution of Sample Proportions

Knowing that for a binomial variable X the mean of the probability distribution of the x values equals np and that $\hat{p} = x/n$, then the mean of the probability distribution for the $\hat{p}$ values must be np/n or simply p, the population proportion. Similarly knowing that the variance of the x values equals $np(1 - p)$, we can find the variance of the $\hat{p}$ values. From the rule that the variance of random variable X with a constant, here $\frac{1}{n}$, is the constant squared, $(\frac{1}{n})^2$, times the variance of X, we obtain $(\frac{1}{n})^2[np(1 - p)]$, which simplifies to $p(1 - p)/n$. We can then write the mean and standard deviation of the sampling probability distribution of $\hat{p}$ as:

$$\mu_{\hat{p}} = p \qquad \sigma_{\hat{p}} = \sqrt{\frac{p(1 - p)}{n}}$$

Note that $\sigma_{\hat{p}}$ is inversely related to n, the sample size. If the sample size quadrupled, the standard deviation of $\hat{p}$ would be cut in half. In the poker chip experiments, the mean, p_{red}, = .5, and the standard deviation is

$$\sigma_{\hat{p}} = \sqrt{\frac{(.5)(.5)}{n}} = \frac{.5}{\sqrt{n}}$$

Thus for the sample of size 100, the standard deviation is $.5/\sqrt{100} = .05$; quadrupling the sample size to 400 cuts the standard deviation to $.5/\sqrt{400} = .025$; quadrupling the sample size again to 1600 halves again the standard deviation to $.5/\sqrt{1600} = .0125$. For a sample of 10,000 the standard deviation is $.5/\sqrt{10,000} = .005$.

Greater Reliability from Larger Samples

Chebyshev's Inequality provides a minimum reliability level for the sampling process. Chebyshev's Inequality states that the maximum probability of finding a value more than k standard deviations from the mean is $1/k^2$. This implies that the minimum reliability level is $1 - 1/k^2$. With the population $p = .5$ and the error tolerance at $\pm.05$, the minimum reliability level calculation that follows for a sample of size 10,000 is:

$$\sigma_{\hat{p}} = \sqrt{\frac{p(1 - p)}{n}} = \sqrt{\frac{(.5)(.5)}{10,000}} = .005$$

$$k = \frac{\text{Error Tolerance}}{\sigma_{\hat{p}}} = \pm\frac{.05}{.005} = 10$$

Minimum reliability level = $1 - 1/k^2 = 1 - 1/100 = .99$

This means that 99 times out of a hundred the sampling process will produce a $\hat{p}$ within $\pm.05$ of the true mean value, p. The calculations for other size samples are shown in Table 8.3. The table highlights the fact that reliability level improves dramatically as the sample size increases from 100 to 400; and a substantial improvement occurs when the sample size is increased to 1600. Gains continue to come beyond 1600, but at a much slower pace.

TABLE 8.3. Relationship Between Sample Size and Minimum Reliability Level for Population With $p = .5$ and Error Tolerance of $\pm.05$

SAMPLE SIZE, n	$\sigma_{\hat{p}}$	k	MINIMUM RELIABILITY LEVEL
100	.05	1	0
400	.025	2	.75
1600	.0125	4	.9375
10,000	.0050	10	.99

Precision and Reliability Level

The gains in error tolerance achieved as sample size increases given a required 95 percent reliability level is indicated by the narrowing gap between the two converging lines graphed in Figure 8.13. The reductions in error tolerance are viewed as increases in *precision*. Precision improves remarkably with modest increases in sample size. Additions to sample size to achieve the same improvement in sample precision become very burdensome as the sample size expands. At what point should the improvement in precision stop? How large a size sample is worthwhile? The worth of the extra sampling is determined by the need for accuracy.

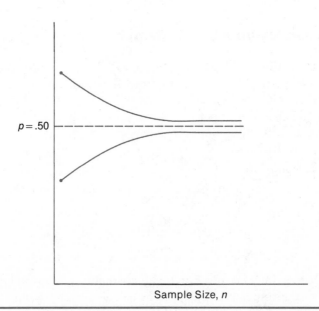

FIGURE 8.13   Upper and Lower Boundaries of the Sample Proportion Values for a Given .95 Reliability Level

The Law Of Averages: Larger Samples Reduce Sampling Variability

There are many important aspects of random variation which are explainable by the so-called *law of large numbers*, popularly known as the *law of averages*. Loosely stated, this law says that the numerical value of a *sample statistic (such as $\hat{p}_{red}$) tends to approximate more closely the value of the corresponding population parameter, (such as p_{red}), the larger the sample from that population*. The following example illustrates the law of large numbers in a familiar context.

Example 8.15.   Sampling Batting Averages

Consider a major league baseball player who has a batting average of .310 for a 160-game season. For each of the 160 games, record the batting percentage for each game on an individual slip of paper and put all 160 slips into a hat. The law of large numbers predicts that the batting average computed from randomly selected samples of twenty slips will tend to vary less from the season average of .310 than will the batting average computed from randomly selected samples of ten slips. That is, $\hat{p}$ for $n = 20$ will vary less from p than will $\hat{p}$ for $n = 10$.

   What is the practical significance of the law of averages? In baseball, it is simply this: a .310 hitter (based on the entire season) is likely to average closer to .310 in a randomly picked month (sample size of 30) than in a randomly picked week (sample size of 7).

8.16. Sampling Experiments Confirm the Law of Averages

Many persons are startled by the relationship between sample size and reliability level exhibited in Table 8.3. The results seem particularly surprising when one realizes that since the sampling is done with replacement, population size is not involved in the calculations. The results are just as attainable from a population of 100 million as from a population of 100 poker chips!

   The surprisingly large reduction in sampling variability associated with only moderately larger samples is a key point demonstrated by the poker chip sampling experiments. The details are given in the following example.

Example 8.16.   Use Larger Samples to Obtain Less Sampling Variability

The Series II poker chip experiments described in Example 8.5 consisted of fifty samples of forty chips each, or collectively two thousand draws. By regrouping the two thousand draws into ten larger samples of two hundred chips each, sample size can be related to sampling variability.

The first 200-size sample was formed by pooling the first five original samples of forty chips each. Similarly, the second five forty-chip samples were pooled to make a second 200-chip sample, etc.

The values of $\hat{p}_{red}$ for the fifty original samples of forty chips described in Figure 8.7 are mapped in Figure 8.14. Data for the ten pooled samples of two hundred chips are given in Table 8.4 and are mapped in Figure 8.15.

A comparison of Figures 8.14 and 8.15 is revealing on two counts. First, it is evident from the figures that pooling the chips to form 200-chip samples has not entirely eliminated variability among sample results. Second, pooling the two thousand draws into ten samples considerably reduced the magnitude of the variation of the original fifty sampling experiments. That is, the sampling variability of sampling results is reduced by calculating the sampling result from the larger scale.

TABLE 8.4. Results of Pooled Series II Poker Chip Experiments

FIRST POOLED SAMPLE		SECOND POOLED SAMPLE		THIRD POOLED SAMPLE		FOURTH POOLED SAMPLE	
Orig. Exp. No.	No. Red Chips	Orig. Exp. No.	No. Red Chips	Orig. Exp. No.	No. Red Chips	Orig. Exp. No.	No. Red Chips
1	23	6	22	11	20	16	18
2	15	7	23	12	22	17	17
3	24	8	18	13	20	18	13
4	17	9	23	14	18	19	19
5	16	10	20	15	20	20	22
Total	95	Total	106	Total	100	Total	89
Proportion Red:	.475	Proportion Red:	.530	Proportion Red:	.500	Proportion Red:	.445

FIFTH POOLED SAMPLE		SIXTH POOLED SAMPLE		SEVENTH POOLED SAMPLE		EIGHTH POOLED SAMPLE	
Orig. Exp. No.	No. Red Chips	Orig. Exp. No.	No. Red Chips	Orig. Exp. No.	No. Red Chips	Orig. Exp. No.	No. Red Chips
21	23	26	22	31	22	36	19
22	17	27	20	32	21	37	18
23	19	28	22	33	16	38	19
24	19	29	17	34	16	39	20
25	23	30	19	35	26	40	18
Total	101	Total	100	Total	101	Total	94
Proportion Red:	.505	Proportion Red:	.500	Proportion Red:	.505	Proportion Red:	.470

NINTH POOLED SAMPLE		TENTH POOLED SAMPLE	
Orig. Exp. No.	No. Red Chips	Orig. Exp. No.	No. Red Chips
41	17	46	19
42	21	47	24
43	16	48	23
44	20	49	21
45	24	50	21
Total	98	Total	108
Proportion Red:	.490	Proportion Red:	.540

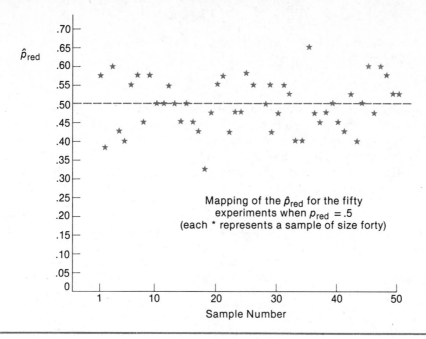

FIGURE 8.14   Series II Poker Chip Experiments (Ungrouped)

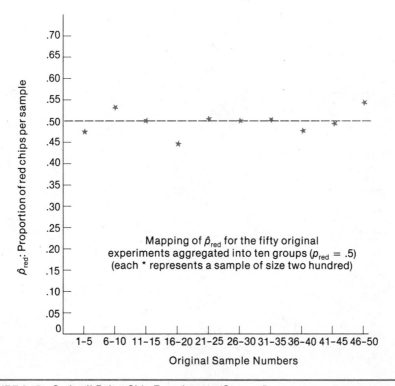

FIGURE 8.15   Series II Poker Chip Experiments (Grouped)

8.17. Sampling Has Diminishing Returns—The More You Already Know, The Less You Can Learn by Additional Sampling

Because larger samples require additional expenditures of time and money, it is important to know how rapidly the divergence between population and sample proportions tends to diminish as sample size increases. A formal consideration of the economics of sample size involves statistical decision theory. Informally, some indication of diminishing returns follows from further consideration of the poker chip experiments.

Example 8.17. The Value of $\hat{p}$ "Settles Down" Quickly as Sample Size Increases

The Series II poker chip data was reorganized to show what happened to $\hat{p}_{red}$ as the sample size increased. To find the relationship, the *cumulative* value of $\hat{p}_{red}$ was calculated at forty-chip intervals. The results are in Table 8.5 and are presented graphically in Figure 8.16.

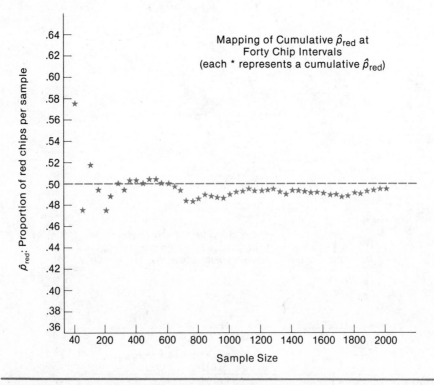

FIGURE 8.16   Series II Poker Chip Experiments (Cumulative)

TABLE 8.5. Cumulative Results of 2000 Poker Chips Drawn, Recorded at 40 Chip Intervals

SIZE OF SAMPLE (CUMULATIVE NUMBER OF CHIPS DRAWN)	CUMULATIVE NUMBER OF RED CHIPS	CUMULATIVE PROPORTION OF RED CHIPS	SIZE OF SAMPLE (CUMULATIVE NUMBER OF CHIPS DRAWN)	CUMULATIVE NUMBER OF RED CHIPS	CUMULATIVE PROPORTION OF RED CHIPS
40	23	.575	1040	512	.492
80	38	.475	1080	532	.493
120	62	.517	1120	554	.495
160	79	.494	1160	571	.492
200	95	.475	1200	590	.492
240	117	.488	1240	612	.494
280	140	.500	1280	633	.495
320	158	.494	1320	649	.492
360	181	.503	1360	665	.489
400	201	.503	1400	691	.494
440	220	.500	1440	710	.493
480	242	.504	1480	728	.492
520	262	.504	1520	747	.491
560	280	.500	1560	767	.492
600	300	.500	1600	785	.491
640	318	.497	1640	802	.489
680	335	.493	1680	823	.490
720	348	.483	1720	839	.488
760	367	.483	1760	859	.488
800	389	.486	1800	883	.491
840	412	.490	1840	902	.490
880	429	.488	1880	926	.493
920	448	.487	1920	949	.494
960	467	.486	1960	970	.495
1000	490	.490	2000	991	.496

In the first forty draws, twenty-three red chips were obtained, giving a $\hat{p}_{red}$ value of .575. This is indicated in Figure 8.16 by the first asterisk.

The first eighty draws yielded a total of thirty-eight red chips (twenty-three in the first forty and fifteen in the second forty). Therefore, the value of $\hat{p}_{red}$ dropped to .475 after eighty draws as indicated by the second asterisk in Figure 8.16.

Sixty-two red chips were obtained in the first 120 draws, leading to a value of .517 for $\hat{p}_{red}$ after 120 draws, as indicated by the third asterisk.

Near the left-hand side of Figure 8.16 where sample sizes are small, there is considerable variation in the value of $\hat{p}_{red}$. Near the right hand side, however, where sample sizes are much larger, the value of $\hat{p}_{red}$ has "settled down" near .50, the population proportion of red (p_{red}).

Figure 8.16 illustrates that there are diminishing returns to larger sample sizes. The more you know before the sample is taken, the less information is gained from the sample. That is, a sample of size 100 provides more information if no previous sample had been taken than if a sample of size 10,000 has already been taken. In Figure 8.16 the first few cumulative $\hat{p}_{red}$ fluctuate within the range .46

to .58. Limited as this information may be, it seems to suggest that it is unlikely that p_{red} is a value far above, say, .62 or far below .42. In other words, the results for a few modest size samples (of size forty each) isolate the range of the population parameter to only one-fifth of the total range. By how much more can additional sampling reduce this range? The best that can be accomplished with additional sampling is to further narrow the range (.42 to .62) in the same manner that had eliminated four-fifths (0 to .42 and .62 to 1.00) of the range with a sample size of 200 chips. Why? There are diminishing returns to additional sampling.

How quickly do the returns to additional sampling diminish? Starting at the left hand side of Figure 8.16, each asterisk shows how a new sample of size forty changes the cumulative value of $\hat{p}_{red}$. Although there are still some mild waves beyond 400 draws in the cumulative value of $\hat{p}_{red}$, it is evident that all the cumulative $\hat{p}_{red}$ values lie well within the range .48 to .52, a much narrower range than achieved by looking at the samples individually (Figure 8.14). The first few samples combined (200 chips) narrowed the original 0–1.00 range down by about 80 percent; later samples of 1800 additional chips further narrowed the original range for the population parameter by only 16 percent. Here are these calculations in tabular form:

TABLE 8.6. Reduction of Probability Range Because of Sample Size

NUMBER OF CHIPS SAMPLED PRIOR TO THIS EXAMPLE	INCREMENT TO SAMPLE	RANGE OF LIKELY VALUES FOR $\hat{p}_{red}$		REDUCTION IN RANGE	REDUCTION AS % OF ORIGINAL RANGE
		PRIOR TO THIS INCREMENT OF SAMPLE	AFTER THIS INCREMENT OF SAMPLE		
Zero	200	0–1.00	.42–.62	.80	80
200	1800	.42–.62	.48–.52	.16	16

The key point demonstrated is: the *extra eighteen hundred* observations were less informative about the range of the true population parameter than the *first two hundred* observations. If an extra eighteen hundred observations could not reduce the range of uncertainty by as much as the first two hundred, it is clear that an extra two hundred (instead of eighteen hundred) wouldn't have either. An important conclusion is clear: each additional successive same-size sample reduces the range of uncertainty about the true population value, but by a lesser amount than the previous one. That is, each additional sample *yields less new information about the true population value the larger the cumulative size* of the sample we already have. When will the value of the information contained in a larger sample fail to exceed the cost of obtaining the larger sample? It is evident from Figure 8.16 that the variation in the sample proportion has settled down to within a few hundredths of the true population value of .50 after two thousand observations.

This pattern of declining variability with increasing sample size is not a fluke. Fifty successive samples of forty chips were aggregated to a size of 2000 chips. Repeated four times, the results are presented graphically in Figure 8.17. All of

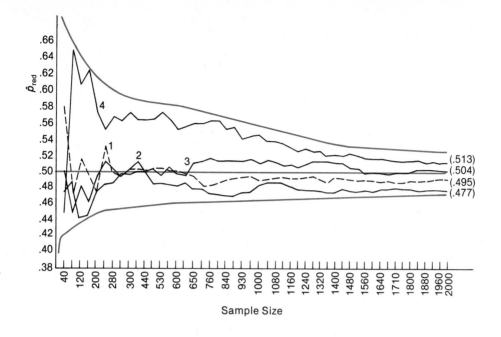

FIGURE 8.17 Relationship Between $\hat{p}_{red}$ and Sample Size

the series exhibit considerable fluctuation in $\hat{p}_{red}$ with smaller sample sizes (towards the left); as sample size increases, the fluctuations rapidly diminish; as the sample size approaches 2000 chips, they gradually settle down near .50.

The empirical sampling results (summarized in Figure 8.17) strongly suggest that sample sizes exceeding a few thousand items would be worthwhile only if estimation accuracy more refined than within a few hundredths of the true population value is required. This is empirical confirmation of the theoretical conclusion reached in Section 8.15 and portrayed graphically in Figure 8.13.

8.18. Managerial Issues in Practice—
Review Exercise: The Logistics of Marketing
Replacement Parts

Ellen Carlyle is a newly employed staff analyst in the corporate controller's office at Rohrton Controls, an industrial temperature control manufacturer. Ellen is recommending that replacement regulators for Rohrton equipment be supplied from the central parts warehouse in Detroit, rather than from one of the fifty regional sales and distribution centers.

The marketing manager in charge of replacement parts disagreed. "Look, inventory is inventory. The regulators have to be stored somewhere and that costs money. Why should storage cost be less in Detroit? Besides, regulators are needed at the regional centers. Customers calling for a replacement regulator usually expect next day delivery. To do this Detroit must ship by air at the extra cost of $8 per regulator. Shipping, say 1300 regulators by air will incur an additional transportation cost of more than $10,000. So I don't see how distributing out of Detroit could result in saving money."

Ellen stuck to her guns. She knew that each regulator cost $1000 to make and at the current 20% annual cost of capital the holding cost in inventory comes to about $200 per year. Ellen recognized that air transportation would have to be used, but felt sure that the extra $10,000 transportation cost could be absorbed and still save nearly $35,000 per year from the drastic cutback in inventory required. "That might just pay your salary next year," she told the replacement parts manager. She told him to bone up on the binomial distribution that night so that tomorrow she could show him how the saving would be achieved.

Assume the daily demand at each of the fifty regional sales and distribution centers for a replacement regulator has a probability distribution with .10 probability for one regulator and .90 probability for zero regulators. Thus, there is zero probability of more than one regulator being demanded on a given day. Delivery time of a part from Detroit is ten working days. When a part is used, it is immediately reordered. Inventory stocking at the regional center anticipates meeting ten days' demand. The company requires that each regional center keep to less than .01 the probability of running out of parts.

a. What is the binomial probability that no regulators are demanded at a particular regional center during a ten day period? More than two regulators demanded during a ten day period?

b. How many regulators must be stocked in inventory to assure each regional center meets the company's requirement that the probability of being out of stock when a customer needs a regulator be less than .01?

c. What total inventory of regulators need to be stocked at all fifty regional centers?

d. At $200 holding cost per year per regulator, what would be the annual holding cost of the inventory?

e. If all replacement demand were to be supplied from a central warehouse in Detroit by air, what would be the required inventory level to meet the .01 stockout probability stipulation?

f. What is your estimate of the amount that Ellen's plan would save or lose, based upon 1300 regulators ordered annually?

Solution

a. $P_{\text{binomial}} (X = 0|n = 10, p = .1) = .3487$
$P_{\text{binomial}} (X > 2|n = 10, p = .1) = 1 - P(X \leq 2|n = 10, p = .1)$
$$= 1 - .930 = .07$$

b. $P_{binomial}\ (X > x|n = 10, p = .1) \le .01$; looking at the cumulative binomial table at $n = 10$, we find: for $X = 3$, $P(X \le 3) = .987$; for $X = 4$, $P(X \le 4) = .998$

$1 - .998$ is less than .01

Therefore, 4 parts must be stocked at each warehouse while a part is on order. Before selling the part there must have been *five* in inventory.

c. $50 \times 5 = 250$

d. $\$200 \times 250 = \$50,000$ holding cost

e. $P_{binomial}\ (X > x|n = 50, p = .1) \le .01$ (for fifty regional centers)
for $X = 9$, $P(X \le 9) = .975$; for $X = 10$, $P(X \le 10) = .991$
$1 - .991$ is less than .01: $P(X > 10) \le .01$

Therefore, the chance that more than 10 parts will be requested by the 50 regional centers is less than 1%. With 10 parts held in stock at all times at the central warehouse, one meets the 1% reliability level and reduces by 240 units the total stock that using the regionals requires.

f. holding cost $= \$200 \times 10 = \$2000$ (assuming no units stocked now at central headquarters)
extra transportation cost $= \$8 \times 1300 = \$10,400$
total cost $= \$2000 + \$10,400 = \$12,400$
Difference: $\$50,000 - \$12,400 = \$37,600$ savings
Therefore, this still saves a replacement parts manager's salary of $\$37,600$.

8.19. Concluding Comments

Using the method of random sampling, one is not guaranteed the certainty that each and every result will reflect perfectly the population being sampled. But the method does provide confidence in the results. The empirical demonstrations consistently show that, although sampling results are not picture perfect, they are very reputable reflections. This is very encouraging because it means we have a feasible scheme that we can depend on and one for which the results can be derived analytically through the use of probability. The probability framework called the binomial distribution provides the technique to find the probability of the possible sample results once we can specify the sample size and assume constant the chance of finding the presence of the attribute in the population as the sampling process continues. These two key pieces of information, symbolized by n for the sample size and p for the unchanging probability of the attribute's presence in the population, are called the parameters of the binomial distribution. They distinguish one binomial distribution from another and are all that is needed to use printed binomial tables that show the probability of finding a particular number or percentage of the attribute in an n size sample. Given that there is variability in the values $\hat{p}$ coming from the same binomial distribution, it is difficult to infer the exact value of the underlying p just by seeing sample results on $\hat{p}$. In other words, sample results from the same binomial distribution (population) can at times be suggestive of a variety of similar p values, but not suggestive of vastly different p values. The uncertainty that surrounds the underlying p value can be whittled away by using larger samples, since the sample percentages ($\hat{p}$) will settle down closer to p for large sample sizes. We have in effect gone full circle. By learning how to calculate and discuss the probability of obtaining various $\hat{p}$ values from random sampling given the binomial parameters n and p, we have shown how much confidence one should have in using a $\hat{p}$ value observed from a random sample of size n to infer what the underlying value p can be.

Questions and Problems

1. Is it correct to say that a random sample is a miniature replica of the population from which it is drawn? Why or why not?

2. Why must we study sampling variability to learn about the size of errors that might be expected in estimating a population characteristic (parameter)?

3. What is meant by the *sampling distribution of the sample statistic* and how does it pertain to the process of statistical inference?

4. Are there any advantages in determining the key characteristics of the sampling distribution analytically rather than empirically? If so, what are they?

5. In the first series of poker chip experiments, the first sample drawn had a value of $\hat{p}_{red}$ exactly equal to the value of p_{red} for the population sampled. (Both had a value of 0.10.) Is it common for the sample statistic to have the same value as the population parameter? Explain, using (a) the results of both series of poker chip experiments, and (b) using the binomial probability tables.

6. Do large estimation errors tend to occur more frequently, less frequently, or with about the same frequency as smaller estimation errors? Explain.

7. In the poker chip experiments, why was it important to learn that the *sequence* of future red and white chip outcomes could not be predicted from the sequence of past outcomes?

8. Every value of $\hat{p}_{red}$ in the second series of poker chip experiments exceeded (with $p_{red} = .5$) the value of the highest $\hat{p}_{red}$ in the first series (with $p_{red} = .1$). Does this imply or suggest that the sample statistic from a population with a higher-valued population parameter will always exceed the value of a sample statistic drawn from a population having a lower-valued parameter? Explain.

9. Construct a graph which compares the empirical sampling distribution obtained for the Series II poker chip experiments ($p_{red} = .5$) with the analytical (probability) distribution for this same set of experiments. The empirical distribution can be obtained by converting the frequencies given in Figure 8.7 into relative frequencies. The analytical distribution is given in Figure 8.12.

10. A sample of $n = 3$ chips is to be drawn from a population of $N = 50$ poker chips. If a tree diagram is constructed to represent the equiprobable elementary events, how many branches will there be at each stage? How many complete three-stage branches (elementary events) will there be?

11. Of the fifty poker chips in Problem 10, forty are red and ten are white. How many ways are there to draw (a) two red chips? (b) one white chip? (c) a sample sequence which includes two red and one white chip? (d) two red chips and one white chip in any sequence?

12. From the population described in Problems 10 and 11, what is the probability of two red chips in a sample of three chips? (Express your answer as the ratio of your answer to Part d of Problem 11 to your answer to the last question in Problem 10.)

13. According to the combination rule there are ten different sample sequences which include three red and two white

chips. List the sequences and then show how the correct number of sequences can be obtained without listing by employing the combination rule.

14. A portfolio of four stocks is to be selected from the 500 stocks included in the "Fortune 500" list. How many different portfolios are possible? How many of these include both General Motors stock and Standard Oil of New Jersey stock (both of which are included in the Fortune 500 list)?

15. A sample of eight stores is to be selected from the 200 stores in a retail chain. Use the combination rule to determine how many different samples are possible.

16. A random sample of five persons is to be selected from a group of 12 persons, four of whom are Republicans. If the sample is drawn with replacement, what is the probability that exactly three persons in the sample are Republicans? Use the binomial formula for the probability calculations.

17. A sample of seven women is to be randomly selected with replacement from twenty mothers of children in a nursery school. Fourteen of the mothers are employed full-time. Use the binomial distribution formula to determine the probability that five of the mothers in the sample are employed full-time. Verify your calculations against the value given in the binomial tables.

18. For the experiment described in Problem 17, find the probability that at least five of the seven women in the sample are employed full-time. Verify your calculations against the values given in the binomial tables.

19. A sample of three chips is to be drawn with replacement from a population containing sixty poker chips—35 red chips and 25 white chips. Construct a simplified tree diagram for the elementary events of this experiment. In constructing this diagram, distinguish only the color of a chip (red or white) and not which of the sixty chips it is. How many branches (elementary events) does the tree have? Are they equiprobable? Why are there fewer branches than for the tree constructed in Problem 10?

20. A sample of six observations on the work pattern of an electrician is taken at a construction site. One of two possible recordings is made for each observation. The recording W indicates that the electrician is working on an assigned task. The recording A indicates that the electrician is in attendance on the job, but is not actually working on an assigned task. Construct a simplified tree diagram for the outcomes of the sample. How many branches does the tree diagram have? Are the elementary events which the branches represent equiprobable? Could you construct an alternative tree diagram for this experiment? Why or why not?

21. For the situation described in Problem 20 assume that the electrician works on an assigned task 60 percent of the time. What is the probability that four or more of the recordings will be W? What is the probability of the sequence WWAWWA?

22. What is wrong with thinking that the Las Vegas or Atlantic City slot machines which have been paying off below average are now due to "catch up" with the long run averages?

23. Why is it unnecessary for binomial tables to include probabilities for values of p exceeding .50?

24. According to the binomial tables, the probability of $X = 3$ successes in $n = 5$ trials with $p = .45$ probability of success on each trial is .3369. What would the probability be of three successes in the following sequence: SFSFS? (Hint: Use the combination rule to find out how many different sequences of three successes in five trials are possible. Then divide this number into the binomial probability.)

25. It can be determined from the binomial probability tables that $P(X \leq 8|n = 20, p = .40)$ has a value of .5956. This can be interpreted as the probability of "eight or less success in twenty trials". However, the result can be described in other ways also. Complete the alternative descriptions:
a. "at most ____ successes"
b. "not more than ____ successes"
c. "less than ____ successes"

d. "_____ or more failures"

e. "at least _____ failures"

f. "not less than _____ failures"

g. "more than _____ failures"

26. Use the binomial tables to find $P(9 \leq X \leq 13 | n = 17, p = .35)$.

27. Use the binomial tables to find the probability that in twenty trials with $p = .55$, the number of successes is:

a. greater than or equal to nine and less than or equal to thirteen?

b. at least nine and at most thirteen?

c. more than eleven, but less than fifteen?

28. From the binomial tables the probability of zero successes in eighteen trials, with $p = .10$ on each trial, is .1501. What is the probability that it takes more than eighteen trials to obtain a success?

29. Given that $p = .10$, what is the probability of at most two successes in twelve independent trials? What is the probability that it takes at least thirteen trials to obtain the third success?

30. A random sample is drawn with replacement from a population of poker chips, thirty percent of which are red. Given that the sample size is $n = 1000$ chips, what is:

a. the mean of the probability distribution of the number of red chips in the sample?

b. the variance of the probability distribution of red chips?

c. the standard deviation of the number of red chips in the sample?

d. the maximum probability of a sample result outside the range 250–300 red chips?

31. Show that the mean of the binomial distribution with probability p of success on each of n trials is np. (Hint: use the rule given in Chapter Seven for the expected value of the sum of independent random variables. Code the result of each trial as 0 if the outcome is not a success and 1 if the outcome is a success).

32. Use the rule given in Chapter Seven for the variance of a sum of independent random variables to show that the variance of a binomial distribution is $np(1 - p)$.

33. Use the rule given in Chapter Seven for the expected value of the sum of independent random variables to show that the mean of the distribution of sample proportions is p.

34. Use the rule given in Chapter Seven for the variance of a sum of independent random variables to show that the variance of the sampling distribution of proportions in sampling with replacement is $p(1 - p)/n$.

35. A sample of size $n = 20$ chips is drawn from a population of poker chips (with replacement), thirty percent of which are red. Use the binomial tables to determine the probability of a sample proportion $\hat{p} = .35$ and $\hat{p} = .375$.

36. Twenty-five percent of the chips in a poker chip population are red. A sample of n chips is drawn with replacement and the proportion, $\hat{p}$, of red chips is computed. What is the probability that $\hat{p}$ will lie within the range .20 to .30 if the sample size is:

a. $n = 3$?

b. $n = 15$?

c. $n = 30$?

d. $n = 300$? (Use Chebyshev's theorem to approximate this probability)

37. What is the distinction between the terms *reliability level* and *error tolerance*?

38. Use Chebyshev's inequality to determine the minimum reliability level of a sample drawn with replacement being within error tolerance limits of $\pm .02$ for the following sample sizes, assuming that $p = .5$.

a. $n = 100$

b. $n = 400$

c. $n = 1000$

d. $n = 2500$

39. A sample drawn with replacement from a population with $p = .5$ is required to have a minimum reliability level of .95. What error tolerance can be assured for this sample if the sample size is:

a. $n = 100$?

b. $n = 400$?

c. $n = 1000$?

d. $n = 2500$?

40. For a sample of given size from a population with $p = .5$, is it possible to increase

the minimum reliability level without relaxing the acceptable error tolerance?

41. Suppose the proportion of insured automobile drivers that will be involved in an accident this year is denoted by p. According to the law of averages, the proportion $\hat{p}$ of insured drivers involved in an accident will tend to be closer to p among samples of large size than among samples of smaller size. Is it also true that the *number* of insured drivers involved in an accident will tend to exhibit less variability among samples of a larger size than among samples of a smaller size? Explain.

42. Explain the implications of your answer to Problem 41 for an automobile insurance company having 50,000 insurees randomly drawn from the pool of "high-risk" drivers as compared to an insurance company having only 10,000 drivers randomly drawn from the high-risk pool. In practice, will the company having more insurance tend to exhibit less year-to-year fluctuation than the other company in (a) the *proportion* and (b) the *number* of its insured drivers involved in an accident?

43. Each of ten natural gas wells drilled has a probability of .10 of becoming productive. Assuming independent outcomes, what is the probability that none of the wells become productive? No more than two wells become productive?

44. A restaurant employs 11 waiters on the evening shift. The probability that any given waiter will not report to work is .05. Assume each waiter's decision on whether to report or not is not influenced by the behavior of the other waiters. Calculate the probability that:
a. no waiter will be absent?
b. only one waiter will be absent?
c. at least one waiter will be absent?
d. more than one waiter will be absent?

45. For the restaurant situation described in Problem 44, assume that a serious customer service problem would develop, if fewer than ten of the waiters report for work on the evening shift.
a. What is the probability that fewer than

ten waiters report for work?
b. If the probability of fewer than ten waiters reporting to work must be less than .01, how many waiters will have to be scheduled to report for work?
c. If each day can be regarded as independent of other days, what is the probability that a customer service problem will develop during the course of 25 working days due to excessive absenteeism?

46. A small hospital in California needs at least three medical-surgical registered nurses on duty on the night shift each day. There is also a twenty percent chance each day that a fourth nurse will be needed due to a higher than usual bed-count of patients. The hospital cannot be without the nursing help when needed or it will eventually lose its accreditation. However, the nursing administrator is reluctant to lock the hospital into a full time contract to pay $100 per day for an extra nurse knowing that there are days when the fourth nurse is not needed. A local nursing registry (employment service) will provide a qualified nurse on the night shift on an as-needed basis for $200 per night. Given the probability distribution for the number of days the fourth nurse is needed over a ten day stretch, what would be the expected savings (if any) from hiring the registry nurse as needed over a ten day stretch rather than employ a full-time nurse?

47. The California nursing registry referred to in Problem 46 employs two full time nurses and co-operates with eight small hospitals. Each hospital, independently of the other hospitals, on any given night has a .20 probability of asking the registry to supply one nurse.
a. Give the probability distribution for the total number of nurses that the registry could be called on to supply to the client hospitals on a given night.
b. If two nurses hired by the registry on a full time basis are each paid an average $120 per day, does it appear that the registry can cover its costs? Explain.
c. What is the probability that the demand for the registry's nurses exceeds two?

Random Sampling for Attributes: Other Discrete Distributions

Preview. In the previous chapter, we looked at attribute sampling distributions and developed the binomial sampling formula for samples made with replacement. In this chapter we want to look at two variations: sampling without replacement and sampling done over time or space.

The first variation, sampling done without replacement, requires adjustments in the sampling formula. These adjustments lead to the hypergeometric sampling formula. For small populations, substantial errors occur in calculating probabilities if adjustments are not made. For small samples from large populations, however, we will see that the binomial sampling formula gives probabilities which are good approximations of the correct values and have the advantage of being much simpler to obtain.

The second variation considered is that of sampling over a continuum such as time or space rather than from a population which consists of a collection of distinct items or individuals. This variation leads to a sampling distribution known as the Poisson distribution. In certain situations involving sample sizes larger than those the binomial tables cover, the binomial probabilities can be well-approximated by easily computed Poisson probabilities.

9.1. Sampling Without Replacement

In Chapter 8 the binomial sampling formula was used to compute the probabilities for simple random samples drawn with replacement. Simple random samples can be and sometimes are drawn *without* replacement. Generally the expense, the inconvenience, and in some cases sheer impossibility preclude the restoration of the sampled element to the population after every draw. Here are some factors that make sampling without replacement required or recommended.

1. Not restoring the drawn item to the population eliminates the possibility that the same item will be drawn twice with no new information gained. In surveying human populations, for example, samples are almost always drawn without replacement to avoid interviewing the same person twice.

2. Situations commonly arise in which the sampling process is destructive; the sampled items cannot be restored to the population because they are physically consumed or are no longer usable. In quality control, for example, testing of light bulbs and hand grenades destroys the product; in taste testing of food items like wine and hamburgers, the sampled products could not be reused.

In sampling without replacement, a key assumption of the binomial distribution is not met. The probability of obtaining a specified characteristic, such as a red poker chip, changes from draw to draw depending on what was drawn the last time. For example, if there are sixty red chips in an urn of 100 chips, the probability of red on the first draw is $^{60}/_{100}$; on the second draw, however, there are only 99 chips in the urn and the probability of red is either $^{59}/_{99}$ or $^{60}/_{99}$, depending on whether or not a red chip was drawn the first time. Since the probability of a characteristic is not constant, but changing with each draw, the binomial distribution is not applicable in computing probabilities. Instead the *hypergeometric* distribution must be used. However, before learning about this distribution, some additional counting principles must be learned to aid our discussion and computations.

9.2. Permutations

Consider a poker chip sampling problem in which there are $N = 100$ chips from which a random sample of $n = 4$ chips is to be drawn. This can be pictured as a four stage tree diagram with each sample draw representing one stage. The number of branches on the tree diagram is the number of elementary events of the experiment. Sampling *with* replacement, the product of the number of choices at each stage is:

STAGE 1   STAGE 2   STAGE 3   STAGE 4
$100 \times$ $100 \times$ $100 \times$ $100 = 100$ million branches

This means there are 100 million distinguishable arrangements of chips possible among the four stages. For sampling *without* replacement, there will be fewer branches and fewer elementary events. The number of chips from which to choose will be 100 on the first draw, 99 on the second draw (because the first drawn chip is not replaced). There will be only 98 chips on the third draw (because the first two chips drawn have not been replaced). On the fourth draw there will be 97 chips from which to choose because the first three chips drawn are no longer available.

> In general, the number of chips from which to choose is equal to the number you started with minus the number already drawn.

Thus, in sampling without replacement the number of branches in the tree diagram (distinguishable arrangements of chips among the stages) and, hence, the number of elementary events is:

$$100 \times 99 \times 98 \times 97 = 94{,}109{,}400$$

branches and elementary events.

Approximately six percent fewer elementary events are defined for this sampling experiment when the sampling is done without replacement as compared to sampling with replacement.

This particular problem of selecting a sample of four chips from a population of 100 chips is an example of the more general problem:

> How many ways can a smaller group of distinguishable objects be selected from a larger group? Each possible smaller group is called a *permutation* of the larger group.

A tree diagram shows the possible permutations. Each branch represents one permutation. Each segment of the branch represents one of the objects in the group.

The number of permutations is designated by P_n^N, which is read "the number of permutations of N things taken n at a time." The superscript and subscript of P indicate the number of items in the larger and smaller groups, respectively. The symbols N and n are arbitrary.

There is a simple rule for counting the number of branches (permutations) in a tree diagram of permutations. It is:

> *Counting Rule for Permutations:* If there are n different stages to a tree diagram and N distinct choices at the first stage, where $(n \le N)$, and one less choice in each subsequent stage, then there are (N) choices at the first stage, $(N - 1)$ choices at the second stage, $(N - 2)$ choices at the third stage, etc. There are $(N - n + 1)$ choices at the last, or n^{th} stage. Altogether, there are $P_n^N = (N)(N - 1)(N - 2) \ldots (N - n + 1)$ branches. Notice that there must be n terms in the product, one term for each of the stages.

What is the importance of this counting rule? If uneducated intuition rather than the permutation rule is used to arrive at the number of permutations, there is a very great danger of a large underestimation error. The following example illustrates how large the underestimation error can be.

Example 9.2A.   Professional Sports Drafts

Suppose four basketball teams are each to draft one player from a draft list of 100 eligible basketball players.

Would you have guessed that there are more than *ninety million* different possible outcomes to the draft (94,109,400) to be exact)? Most untrained persons would not. Their intuition would lead them to a much smaller number; many guess as low as 400. But if the permutation rule is applied, the correct answer of 94 million plus is easily obtainable. In the predraft more than four teams choose so the number of possible outcomes is astronomical.

Suppose a betting pool is established on the basketball draft described in this example. One "ticket" is issued for each different possible draft outcome. Bettors pay \$1 for the right to receive a ticket which is randomly drawn from the 94 million possibilities. The winning ticket is the one with the correct draft choices; the holder of this ticket claims the "prize" of \$1 million. Bettors are *not* told how many tickets are issued. Given that there are only 100 basketball players in the draft, and only 4 players to be drafted, how many ticket buyers do you think will be duped into thinking that the million dollar prize is really a "good bet"? How many will realize that the sponsor of the betting pool is actually keeping \$93 million out of the \$94 million collected? The moral of the example is simple. If you can't intuitively tell a situation in which a \$1 ticket on a \$1 million prize really is a good bet from the one described in which the prize must exceed \$94 million to be a good bet, then you need to become familiar with the permutation rule before committing yourself to the bet.

How Many Ways Are There To Order a Group?

An important special case of the permutation counting rule uses all the members of the original set. In this case $n = N$, so the number of different possible permutations of N things taken N at a time is designated by the symbol P_N^N. Importantly, P_N^N is the number of different ways a group of N items can be arranged or ordered. Applying the previously given permutation rule to the present situation where $n = N$, one gets

$$P_n^N = P_N^N = N(N - 1)(N - 2) \ . \ . \ . \ (N - N + 1).$$

However, the last term, $(N - N + 1)$, is simply 1. Therefore,

$$P_N^N = (N)(N - 1)(N - 2) \ . \ . \ . \ (1)$$

is the number of different ways of ordering a group of N items. The expression $(N)(N - 1)(N - 2) \ . \ . \ . \ (1)$ is rather cumbersome. Recall from the previous chapter the definition of $N!$ (factorial).

$$N! = N(N - 1)(N - 2) \ . \ . \ . \ (1)(0!)$$

where 0! is defined to have a value of 1. Thus, the right hand side of the equations for P_N^N and for $N!$ are equivalent. It follows, therefore, that

$$P_N^N = N!$$

In the following example, the permutation rule for ordered arrangements is used to show why a sales manager would like to avoid having to evaluate all the different possible arrangements of sales representatives to territories.

Example 9.2B. **Assigning Sales Representatives to Territories**

Each of a group of seven sales reps is completing a training program and will soon be assigned to a different one of the country's seven different sales territories. How many different ways are there to assign the reps to the territories?

Solution: The problem involves assigning all seven (N) reps to seven (n) territories to obtain a particular unique arrangement (a permutation). Assigning one rep to a territory depletes by one the number available for the next territory, and the permutation rule is applicable. Since $n = N$, this situation qualifies for the special case of the permutation rule. We find that there are

$$P_7^7 = 7! = (7)(6)(5)(4)(3)(2)(1) = 5040$$

different ways to assign the seven reps to the seven territories. If it took only six minutes each to evaluate an assignment permutation, more than twelve forty-hour work weeks would be required to complete the task.

Persons who rely on uneducated intuition rather than the permutation rule tend to greatly underestimate the number of possible permutations. With only 7 sales representatives and seven territories, the tendency is to think that there are only 49 or perhaps only 7 different possible sets of assignments. This is a trap in that it can lead to thinking that it might be worthwhile to spend time evaluating the merits of each individual assignment arrangement. Eventually, perhaps after a period of time of calculations that merely scratch the surface of the possibilities, the sales manager will realize there are too many permutations to individually evaluate. Time will have been wasted. The advantage of knowing and using the permutation rule is that a quick calculation reveals there are 5040 permutations of the reps among the territories; the manager should be alert to the evaluation sinkhole. The manager will know better than to evaluate them all individually. Attention can immediately turn to more feasible methods of making the assignments. There is no need to experience the futility of wasting time before learning this lesson.

9.3. The Relationship Between the Number of Permutations and the Number of Combinations

In calculating probabilities for sampling with replacement (Chapter 8), the number of *combinations* of n things taken x at a time, C_x^n, was required. The number of combinations, C_x^n, differs from the number of permutations, P_x^n. The difference is that the objects of a combination are not regarded as an *ordered* arrangement. For example, the number of combinations of $n = 3$ poker chips taken $x = 2$ at a time is

$$C_2^3 = \frac{3!}{2!} = 3, \text{ while}$$

$$P_2^3 = (3)(2) = 6.$$

The *composition* of a combination is its only identifying characteristic. Nevertheless, there is a general relationship between the number of combinations (unordered arrangements) and the number of permutations (ordered arrangements). It is:

$$\begin{bmatrix} \text{Number of} \\ \text{Combinations} \end{bmatrix} \quad \text{times} \quad \begin{bmatrix} \text{Number of ways} \\ \text{to order each} \\ \text{combination} \end{bmatrix} = \begin{bmatrix} \text{Number of} \\ \text{Permutations} \end{bmatrix}$$

which can be expressed notationally as:

$$C_x^n \begin{bmatrix} \text{Number of ways} \\ \text{to order each} \\ \text{combination} \end{bmatrix} = P_x^n$$

By rearranging terms in the above relationship, a shortcut formula for the number of *combinations* is derived:

$$C_x^n = \frac{P_x^n}{\text{Number of ways to order each combination}}$$

Recalling from the previous section that the number of ways of ordering the entire group of n items is $n!$, the number of ways of ordering x items is $x!$ The number of combinations of n things x at a time can then be written as:

$$C_x^n = \frac{P_x^n}{x!}$$

For example,

$$C_2^3 = \frac{P_2^3}{2!} = \frac{6}{(2)(1)} = 3.$$

9.4. Sampling Without Replacement: The Hypergeometric Distribution

Suppose we are given a population of N items, R of which have a specific attribute of interest. It was shown in the previous chapter that the probability of obtaining exactly x occurrences of the specific attribute in a simple random sample of size n drawn *with replacement* from the population is a binomial probability expressed by the formula:

$$\begin{bmatrix} \text{Probability of exactly } x \text{ occurrences of the} \\ \text{specified attribute in a simple random sample} \\ \text{of size } n \text{ drawn with replacement} \end{bmatrix} = C_x^n p^x (1-p)^{n-x}$$

In this formula, p is the probability of an occurrence of the specified attribute on each draw. The value of p is equal to the proportion of items in the population in which the specified attribute is present. That is, $p = R/N$. How would the probability of exactly x occurrences change if the sample is drawn *without* replacement? To find out, we first revert to a version of the binomial formula presented in Section 8.8.

$$P(X = x) = \frac{1}{N^n}[C_x^n R^x (N - R)^{n-x}].$$

In this formula, the term in brackets on the right hand side gives the number of elementary events corresponding to x occurrences of the desired attribute. Sampling without replacement, the number of choices available declines as each sample member is drawn. The binomial formula must be adjusted to show the decline. The adjustment for the declining number of choices available at each stage of the tree diagram reflects two important facts about sampling without replacement:

1. There are fewer elementary events—P_n^N instead of N^n
2. Fewer of the elementary events have exactly x occurrences of the specified characteristics—$C_x^n P_x^R P_{n-x}^{N-R}$ rather than $C_x^n R^x (N - R)^{n-x}$.

The latter expression is the one given by the terms in brackets on the right hand side of the formula given above. Thus, the formula becomes:

$$\frac{1}{P_n^N} C_x^n P_x^R P_{n-x}^{N-R}$$

This is called the *hypergeometric* probability. The formula can be further simplified somewhat by replacing the combination term C_x^n by its equivalence in permutation terms, $P_x^n/x!$ This gives

$$\frac{1}{P_n^N}\left(\frac{P_x^n}{x!}\right) P_x^R P_{n-x}^{N-R}, \text{ or, since } \frac{P_x^n}{x!} = \frac{n!}{x!(n-x)!}$$

$$\frac{1}{P_n^N}\left[\frac{n!}{x!(n-x)!} P_x^R P_{n-x}^{N-R}\right]$$

This can be rearranged to give

$$\frac{n!}{P_n^N}\left[\frac{P_x^R}{x!}\right]\left[\frac{P_{n-x}^{N-R}}{(n-x)!}\right], \text{ or}$$

$$\frac{\left[\frac{P_x^R}{x!}\right]\left[\frac{P_{n-x}^{N-R}}{(n-x)!}\right]}{\frac{P_n^N}{n!}}$$

Written this way each of the three terms can be expressed by its equivalent combination term. Thus the hypergeometric formula is commonly expressed as:

$$\left[\begin{array}{c} \text{Probability of exactly x items having the} \\ \text{specified attribute in a simple random sample} \\ \text{of size } n \text{ drawn } without \text{ replacement} \end{array}\right] = \frac{C_x^R C_{n-x}^{N-R}}{C_n^N}$$

The example below applies the formula.

Example 9.4. Discounting Accounts Receivable

A firm which is attempting to borrow using its accounts receivable as collateral (known as discounting its accounts receivables) finds that of its 50 largest accounts, five are more than 120 days overdue. Its commercial bank (before lending the funds) makes an assessment of the collateral value of the accounts, checking on the credit worthiness of the firm's customers. For ten accounts sampled, is it likely that the bank will find at least one account more than 120 days overdue?

$$P\text{(at least one account found 120 days overdue)} = 1 - P\text{(no account found 120 days overdue)}$$

$$P\binom{\text{no account found}}{\text{120 days overdue}} = \frac{C_0^5 C_{10}^{45}}{C_{10}^{50}}$$

$$= \frac{\dfrac{R!}{x!(R-x)!} \dfrac{(N-R)!}{(n-x)!((N-R)-(n-x))!}}{\dfrac{N!}{n!(N-n)!}}$$

$$= \frac{\dfrac{5!}{0!(5-0)!} \dfrac{(50-5)!}{(10-0)!((50-5)-(10-0))!}}{\dfrac{50!}{10!(50-10)!}}$$

$$= \frac{\dfrac{45!}{10!(45-10)!}}{\dfrac{50!}{10!40!}} = \frac{(45)(44)\cdots(36)}{(50)(49)\cdots(41)}$$

$$= \frac{(40)(39)(38)(37)(36)}{(50)(49)(48)(47)(46)} = .31$$

It can be concluded that out of 10 large accounts sampled, there is a slightly over three in ten chance (.31) that all five of the accounts more than 120 days overdue will be completely missed even though the bank creditors followed a 20% sampling rate (10 accounts sampled out of 50). Therefore, one minus this probability, or $1 - .31 = .69$, is the probability that the commercial bank will find at least one overdue by more than 120 days.

9.5. Sampling Distribution for the Sample Proportion in Sampling Without Replacement

In simple random samples, the focus is often on the *proportion* $\hat{p}$ of items in the sample which have a particular characteristic. Probabilities for the sampling distribution of the sample proportion $\hat{p}$ depend upon whether sampling is done with or without replacement. In sampling with replacement the probabilities are given by a modified version of the binomial distribution (Section 8.14). In sampling *without* replacement, these probabilities are given by a modified version of the hypergeometric distribution. That is, in a sample of size n the probability of x occurrences of the specified characteristic given by the hypergeometric distribution is also the probability for the sample proportion $\hat{p} = x/n$. Thus, for a sample of size $n = 8$, the probability of $\hat{p} = .25$ would be the same as the probability of $x = 2$, which is given by the hypergeometric distribution. The following example illustrates how to use a hypergeometric distribution to find the probability of values for $\hat{p}$.

Example 9.5. Narcotics Smuggling

Suppose the Federal government recently compiled a list of 100 persons on the West coast suspected of smuggling cocaine into the United States. The Narcotics Bureau will commit the substantial resources necessary to place all one hundred persons under close surveillance if they can obtain some reliable evidence showing that a high percentage of the suspects actually are smugglers. The need, therefore, is for a reliable preliminary estimate of the percentage of smugglers among persons on the list. To obtain this estimate a simple random sample of ten names is selected for a pilot surveillance project.

If, unknown to the Narcotics Bureau, sixty persons on the list are in fact smugglers (and the other forty are not), how probable is it that the sample evidence will reveal a sixty percent figure or a figure close to sixty percent? The answer, of course, depends on how much of the probability is associated with sample values clustered near the sixty percent figure.

We might start by considering the probability for the fortuitous case in which the sample figure is right on the sixty percent target. This would mean six smugglers in our sample of size ten. This probability calculation is:

$$P(\hat{p} = .6) = \frac{[C_6^{60}][C_4^{40}]}{C_{10}^{100}}$$

$$= \frac{\dfrac{(60)(59)\cdots(55)}{6!}\dfrac{(40)(39)(38)(37)}{4!}}{\dfrac{(100)(99)\cdots(91)}{10!}}$$

$$= .264$$

In other words, the odds are nearly three to one (.736:.264) against finding the same percentage of smugglers in the sample as in the population. On the other hand, it is somewhat reassuring that it is even more unlikely that the sample contains no smugglers at all:

$$P(\hat{p} = 0) = \frac{[C_0^{60}][C_{10}^{40}]}{C_{10}^{100}}$$

$$= .00005$$

Shortly the calculation for a clustering of sample values will be demonstrated, but first it is advantageous to learn the shortcut formula for the mean and standard deviation of the hypergeometric distribution.

9.6. Summary Measures of the Hypergeometric Distribution

The mean of the hypergeometric distribution is given by the expression:

$$\mu_{\text{hypergeometric}} = np$$

This is the same expression as the mean of the binomial distribution, that is, the product of the sample size, n, and the probability of the specific characteristic of interest, p.

The variance and standard deviation of the hypergeometric distribution are:

$$\sigma^2_{\text{hypergeometric}} = np(1 - p)\left[\frac{N - n}{N - 1}\right]$$

$$\sigma_{\text{hypergeometric}} = \sqrt{np(1 - p)\left[\frac{N - n}{N - 1}\right]}$$

The term in brackets is called the *finite population adjustment*. If the population is large relative to the sample size, this adjustment term is approximately equal to:

1 minus the fraction of the population sampled.

With the help of Chebyshev's Inequality, the mean and standard deviation are used to assess how probable it is that a sample proportion will deviate from the population proportion by specified amounts.

Example 9.6.   Using the Mean and Standard Deviation to Assess the Clustering of Sampling Results

To obtain the exact total probability for a cluster of sample results in the narcotic smuggling example would involve the use of hypergeometric tables. These tables are seldom readily available and, even if they were available, would involve time con-suming calculations for several individual probabilities. Fortunately Chebyshev's Inequality in conjunction with the mean and standard deviation of the distribution offers a plausible alternative approach to solving the probability calculation. Solving for the mean and standard deviation, we obtain:

$$\mu = np = 10(.60) = 6$$

$$\sigma = \sqrt{np(1 - p)\left[\frac{N - n}{N - 1}\right]} = \sqrt{10(.60)(.40)\frac{100 - 10}{100 - 1}}$$

$$= \sqrt{(2.4)(.909)}$$

$$= (1.55)(.953) = 1.477$$

According to Chebyshev's Inequality, the chance of finding a value beyond the $k\sigma$ range is at most $1/k^2$ (for values of 2, 3, and 4 this probability is $\frac{1}{4}$, $\frac{1}{9}$, and $\frac{1}{16}$, respec-tively). Since the hypergeometric distribution is discrete, the probability of obtaining a sample value within the range of, say 5 to 7, is the same as the total probability of *not* obtaining sample values "4 or less" combined with not obtaining values "8 or more." Table 9.1 illustrates how to handle this situation to estimate hypergeometric probabilities:

TABLE 9.1. Application Of Chebyshev's Inequality to Hypergeometric Distribution with $N = 100$, $X = 60$, and $n = 10$.

1 CLUSTER OF SAMPLE VALUES OF INTEREST	2 CORRESPONDING PERCENTAGE POINT ERROR FROM TARGET VALUE OF 60 PERCENT	3 k	4 MAXIMUM PROB. OF VALUE OUTSIDE RANGE OF INTEREST	5 MINIMUM PROB. OF VALUE WITHIN RANGE OF INTEREST
6	0	—	—	.264 (exact value-
5–7	10	1.354	.545	.455 from Ex. 9.5)
4–8	20	2.031	.242	.758
3–9	30	2.708	.136	.864

Because of the discreteness problem mentioned above, the values in the third column were used for k so that the range $\mu \pm k\sigma$ would not include the next lower and higher integer numbers (the k for the range $5 = \mu - k\sigma$ to $7 = \mu + k\sigma$ is computed on the basis of 4.0001 to 7.9999 to exclude the next integers, 4 and 8).

The important point Table 9.1 reveals is that the range of sample values needed to attain .864 of the total probability is rather wide. More precisely, the needed range can be off from the 60 percent target by as much as 30 percentage points. This points out the glaring inadequacy of using a small sample in the hope that one can rely on the sampling process to produce sample results that achieve both closeness to the target value (precision) and are associated with a substantial portion of the total probability (reliability). In summary, one shouldn't be surprised that for small samples the probability of sampling results doesn't cluster within a narrow range of its target parameter.

9.7. Binomial Approximation of the Hypergeometric Probabilities

We have learned that the choice between the binomial and hypergeometric probability distributions depends on the sampling method employed. If sampling is performed without replacement the appropriate distribution to use is the hypergeometric. Actually, these two distributions are close relatives. Their kinship can be established by comparing the formulas for their summary measures. If two distributions have virtually identical means and variances, their shape and location are likely to be nearly the same. Comparing the means of these two distributions,

$$\mu_{\text{binomial}} = np \text{ and } \mu_{\text{hypergeometric}} = np,$$

we find that the shortcut formulas are identical. There is, however, a disparity in variance due to the finite population adjustment factor, $(N - n)/(N - 1)$:

$$\sigma^2_{\text{binomial}} = np(1 - p) \text{ and } \sigma^2_{\text{hypergeometric}} = np(1 - p)\left(\frac{N - n}{N - 1}\right).$$

Because of the adjustment factor, the hypergeometric distribution has a smaller variance than the binomial. The magnitude of this disparity is greater the larger the fraction of the population sampled. Example 9.7 compares two situations—one in which the fraction sampled is a substantial portion of the population and the other in which the fraction sampled is a less significant portion of the population.

Example 9.7. **A Comparison of the Binomial and Hypergeometric Probabilities for Different Fractions Sampled**

Suppose a shipment of electronic finished goods has fifty units, three of which are defective. That is,

$N = 50$,
$R = 3$,

thus: $p = \dfrac{R}{N} = \dfrac{3}{50} = .06$

If a sample of five units is drawn randomly and tested by the customer, the possible number of defective units and their respective probabilities are as shown in Table 9.2.

TABLE 9.2. The Hypergeometric (Exact) Probabilities Versus the Binomial (Approximate) Probabilities for a Sample, n, of Five Units Drawn from a Population, N, of Fifty Units. Three of the Units are Malfunctioning ($R = 3$).

NUMBER OF DEFECTIVES	HYPERGEOMETRIC PROBABILITY	BINOMIAL PROBABILITY
0	$\dfrac{C_5^{47} C_0^3}{C_5^{50}} = .7239$	$C_0^5(.06)^0(.94)^5 = .7339$
1	$\dfrac{C_4^{47} C_1^3}{C_5^{50}} = .2526$	$C_1^5(.06)^1(.94)^4 = .2342$
2	$\dfrac{C_3^{47} C_2^3}{C_5^{50}} = .0230$	$C_2^5(.06)^2(.94)^3 = .0299$
3	$\dfrac{C_2^{47} C_3^3}{C_5^{50}} = .0005$	$C_3^5(.06)^3(.94)^2 = .0019$

A comparison of the hypergeometric and binomial probabilities is informative. It shows that:

the binomial probabilities are close approximations to the corresponding hypergeometric (exact) probabilities when the sample is not a large fraction of the population, $n/N = 5/50 = 10\%$.

This evidence supports the use of the more readily available binomial tables to approximate the hypergeometric probability.

Let us now look at the situation where the sample represents a large fraction of a small population. If the population size, N, is 10 and the sample size, n, is 5, the sample represents $n/N = 5/10 = 50$ percent of the population. If three of the units are malfunctioning, then $p = R/N = 3/10 = .3$. The hypergeometric probability distribution for the possible sample outcomes is given in Table 9.3 along with the corresponding binomial probabilities.

TABLE 9.3. The Hypergeometric (Exact) Probabilities Versus the Binomial (Approximate) Probabilities for a Sample, n, of Five Units Drawn from a Population, N, of Ten Units. Three of the Units are Malfunctioning ($R = 3$).

NUMBER OF DEFECTIVES	HYPERGEOMETRIC PROBABILITY	BINOMIAL PROBABILITY
0	$\dfrac{C_5^7 C_0^3}{C_5^{10}} = .0833$	$C_0^5 (.3)^0 (.7)^5 = .1681$
1	$\dfrac{C_4^7 C_1^3}{C_5^{10}} = .4166$	$C_1^5 (.3)^1 (.7)^4 = .3602$
2	$\dfrac{C_3^7 C_2^3}{C_5^{10}} = .4166$	$C_2^5 (.3)^2 (.7)^3 = .3087$
3	$\dfrac{C_2^7 C_3^3}{C_5^{10}} = .0833$	$C_3^5 (.3)^3 (.7)^2 = .1323$

Table 9.3 reveals a broad dissimilarity between the binomial and hypergeometric probabilities. Thus:

the disparity between the hypergeometric and binomial probabilities becomes substantial as the sample represents a larger portion of the population.

This disparity is also reflected by a larger difference in variances between the two distributions as the sample fraction of the population increases. In this case, using binomial tables would produce results which are far from the exact probabilities. Thus the larger the population from which the sample is drawn, the more assurance one has that the binomial tables will offer close approximations of the exact hypergeometric probabilities.

Why does the binomial look like the hypergeometric for small samples? As n gets larger for a given population size N, the comparable expressions will tend to diverge. For example, consider a population of $N = 100$ with $R = 40$. The binomial expression of three successes for $n = 3$ written as

$$\frac{40}{100} \times \frac{40}{100} \times \frac{40}{100}$$

is closer to the hypergeometric expression of three successes for $n = 3$,

$$\frac{40}{100} \times \frac{40 - 1}{100 - 1} \times \frac{40 - 2}{100 - 2}$$

than, say, the binomial expression of ten successes for $n = 10$, the product of $^{40}/_{100}$ ten times, is to its corresponding hypergeometric expression

$$\frac{40}{100} \times \frac{40 - 1}{100 - 1} \cdot \cdot \cdot \frac{40 - 10}{100 - 10}.$$

9.8. Sampling Over Time or Space: The Poisson Distribution

The sampling process which leads to the binomial and hypergeometric distributions has two important characteristics.

1. There are a series of "distinct trials" (such as draws from an urn).

2. There are only two outcomes possible on each trial. One outcome possibility is the occurrence of a specific attribute (red chip); the other is the attribute's nonoccurrence.

This situation of "distinct trials with exactly two possible outcomes" is not always applicable. Often sampling is done on a continuum, such as time or space, rather than "distinct trials."

Some examples of sampling on a continuum of time or space are:

1. the number of incoming calls at a telephone switchboard in a five minute interval.

2. The number of paint bubble defects on the surface paint of refrigerators coming off an assembly line.

3. The particulate pollutants of smoke spewing forth from an industrial chimney in an eight hour shift.

What is an appropriate model for these situations? In all three cases, the appropriate model seemingly is the *Poisson* distribution, named after the French mathematician Simeon Poisson. However, there are four important assumptions which must be satisfied before the Poisson model can be deemed appropriate.

1. A defined continuous interval of time or space (five minutes in the telephone example above).

2. Identical probability of an occurrence for each and every infinitely short interval (instant) of time. (This probability need not be known—it is only a logical necessity.)

3. A negligible possibility of more than one occurrence in the interval defined as short.

4. Independence of occurrences: the occurrence observed in any one instant must not in any way affect the chances of an occurrence during any other interval.

At first sight, the Poisson assumptions seem similar to the preconditions necessary to compute the binomial probabilities for occurrences in a sequence of *distinct* trials.

Pursuing this more closely, let's calculate the binomial probability of incoming calls for a telephone switchboard.

Example 9.8. Incoming Telephone Calls

Assume that an incoming call is just as likely at any one moment of time as any other (assumption two) and suppose there is interest in knowing the probability that exactly three incoming calls are received during an interval of five minutes.

As it stands there are no distinct trials in this problem. The binomial distribution is not applicable. But now partition the five minute interval into convenient units of, say, one minute each. Each minute interval is then similar to a distinct binomial trial with two possible outcomes (success if an incoming call is received, failure otherwise). We will also assume that the probability of success, p, although unknown remains constant from trial to trial.

Given these assumptions, one could approach the probability for the number of successes in five minutes as a binomial distribution calculation with parameters $n = 5$ and p the probability of *three successes* in five minutes. Going one step further, the probability of *three incoming calls* in five minutes is $C_3^5 p^3 q^2$. Unfortunately, this seemingly plausible statement would be incorrect. Let us explain.

9.9. Understanding the Poisson Distribution

Because it is entirely possible to receive two, three, four, or even more calls during any interval, the probability distribution for the number of "incoming calls" during a minute cannot be confined to *exactly* one (as the Binomial model requires) but must be defined as *at least* one incoming call during a minute. This lumping together of incoming calls as one "success" forecloses the use of the binomial as the appropriate model, since the binomial requires that each success be associated with only one incoming call. Allowing too much "time" to be a "trial" blocks the use of the Binomial. Does this suggest a solution?

> Make the time interval so short that only one incoming call could possibly be received during the interval.

With one problem solved another arises. What's wrong with shortening the time interval to define one "trial" in which at most one incoming call can be received? It produces a prodigious number of trials in a five-minute interval. In fact, since a call can occur at *any* instant, we must make our unit time interval *infinitely* short. This means that

> there will be an infinite number of trials in a five-minute interval.

The computation of the expression of binomial probability of three incoming calls during the five-minute interval for n equal to infinity is

$$C_3^n p^3 (1 - p)^{n-3} = C_3^\infty p^3 (1 - p)^{\infty-3} \quad (\infty = \text{infinity})$$

Is this computation an insurmountable problem? Fortunately, the problem is resolved with some subtle algebraic manipulations of the binomial formula not presented here. However, the underlying logic and the results are important enough to deserve our attention.

1. Divide the continuum of time or space into equal intervals, letting each interval represent an individual trial.

2. The outcome of each trial is assumed to be independent of all the others.

3. The probability of success on each and every independent trial is defined to be the constant value, p.

Now we are ready for an important idea that will facilitate our computation.

Let μ represent the *average* number of occurrences of the event we are recording over the continuum.

In our illustration, μ would be the average number of incoming telephone calls received at a switchboard during a five-minute interval. This value may be zero, 1, 3, 30 or perhaps 3000 during some busy periods. But the average of all these is some specific number, a constant which we call μ.

Since the time period of an individual trial has to be so short as to permit the occurrence of at most one success during this period, μ must also be the average number of successes in the n *trials* (comprising the overall interval of five minutes), so that for the n trials, μ/n is the average proportion of trials which result in a success. For example, if the mean number of occurrences μ in 5 minutes is 20, then for intervals of one minute each, $\mu/n = 20/5 = 4$ occurrences per interval. For intervals of $1/100$ of a minute, $\mu/n = 20/500 = .04$. This would be the average *proportion* of $1/100$ minute intervals during which a success occurs.

Reviving the relative frequency interpretation of probability, one can state a very useful conclusion. As n approaches infinity, the ratio μ/n becomes extremely small, approaching by increasingly smaller decrements a value we shall define as p, which we call the *limiting* value of the ratio. Thus,

$$\text{limit}_{n \to \infty} \left[\frac{\mu}{n} \right] = p$$

We interpret p as the probability of an incoming call during one of the infinitely short intervals, as the limit of the proportion (relative frequency) of times this event occurs out of the n opportunities as the number of opportunities n approaches infinity. Under this working premise, p, the probability of receiving a telephone call in an infinitely short period of time, can be replaced by μ/n.

Why the interest of replacing p with μ/n? The value μ can be estimated from observation, whereas p cannot be measured because the interval to which p applies is infinitely small. The formula expressed in terms of p is conceptually insightful, but since p cannot be measured, it has no practical value. With p replaced by μ/n, and μ estimatable, the theory can be empirically implemented.

9.10. Calculating Poisson Probabilities

Letting x represent the number of occurrences of the event of interest (incoming telephone calls at a switchboard), and after carrying out some additional algebraic steps we do not show, the expression for the probability of x given the parameter is:

$$P(x|\mu) = \frac{\mu^x e^{-\mu}}{x!}$$

This expression defines the Poisson probability distribution. The elimination of n and p simplifies the final equation and makes the computation attainable. The value of e is a constant, equal to 2.718281828459. Many inexpensive pocket calculators give the value of e raised to a power.

Remarkably, the calculation of any desired probability with the Poisson distribution requires the specification of only one parameter, μ, the *average* number of occurrences. In actual practice, a good estimate of μ for the continuum used is obtained by finding the average for a large number of observations.

Example 9.10A.   **Calculating Poisson Probabilities**

Suppose the records on incoming telephone calls show that 960 incoming telephone calls were received in total during 120 randomly selected five minute intervals. The mean number of telephone calls per five minute interval can then be estimated as

$$\mu \approx \frac{960 \text{ calls}}{120 \text{ five minute intervals}} = 8$$

Inserting this estimate into the Poisson formula gives

$$P(X = 3 | \mu = 8) = \frac{\mu^x e^{-\mu}}{x!}$$

$$= \frac{8^3 e^{-8}}{3!}$$

$$= \frac{(512)\left(\dfrac{1}{2980.958}\right)}{6}$$

$$= .028626$$

In the above calculation, a pocket calculator was used to find the value of e^{-8}. According to this result, three calls in a five minute interval is not highly probable when the mean number is 8 calls per five minute interval.

Now, suppose that instead of desiring the probability of exactly three calls during a five-minute interval (as in Example 9.8), we ask for the probability of exactly 18 calls during a ten-minute interval. There are 60 ten-minute intervals in ten hours. Therefore, μ for the ten-minute interval must be estimated as 960/60 = 16 calls per ten-minute interval, on the average. In other words, doubling the time interval doubles the average number of occurrences during the interval. What this means is that if the Poisson assumptions are met, one need only know μ for *one* interval in order to find the probability of any event whatsoever. For example, knowing only that $\mu = 8$ for a five-minute interval, we can calculate the probability of three incoming calls in a 37.5-second interval. Since there are 300 seconds in a five minute interval, we would use $(37.5/300)8$ as our estimate of μ. Thus,

$$P(X = 3 \mid \mu = (37.5/300)8) = \mu^x e^{-\mu}/x!$$

$$= \frac{\left[\left(\frac{37.5}{300}\right)8\right]^3 e^{-\left[\frac{37.5 \times 8}{300}\right]}}{3!}$$

$$= \frac{(1)e^{-1}}{6} = .0613$$

Although doubling the magnitude of the time interval considered does double the *average* number of occurrences one expects, the probability of a particular number of occurrences is *not* thereby doubled. Should the latter be the case, then doubling all the probabilities would imply that the sum of all the doubled probabilities would be two rather than one, which, of course, is not possible. An example illustrates the point.

Example 9.10B.   A Pitfall to Avoid in Poisson Calculations

Suppose $\mu = 1$ for a five-minute interval. Then $\mu = 2$ for a ten-minute interval. The probability of exactly one telephone call in ten minutes is:

$$P(X = 1 \mid \mu = 2) = \frac{\mu^x e^{-\mu}}{x!} = \frac{2^1 e^{-2}}{1} = 2e^{-2}$$

$$= .2707.$$

In the above calculation the value of e^{-2} is .135335, obtained with the help of a pocket calculator. The probability of one telephone call in five minutes is:

$$P(X = 1 \mid \mu = 1) = \frac{\mu^x e^{-\mu}}{x!} = \frac{1^1 e^{-1}}{1} = e^{-1} = .3679$$

Thus, the probability of one telephone call in ten minutes is *not* twice the probability of one call in five minutes. In practice, Poisson probabilities can usually be found by using published tables like the one given in the Appendix. At this point the student should try to use Table 3 to find the probabilities calculated above.

9.11. Using the Poisson to Approximate the Binomial

What is the main motivation for wanting to use one distribution in place of another? It may be much easier to calculate probabilities for one of the distributions than the other. What is the criterion for deciding whether an approximation is appropriate? If summary measures of the two distributions (central tendency and dispersion) are the same, one may decide to assume that one distribution is a good approximation of the other. That is, binomial probabilities, say, could be calculated using the Poisson formula. In what situations does the Poisson serve as an appropriate substitute for the binomial? Appropriateness arises when the binomial is characterized by *large n* and *small p*, (the probability of success, *p*, is "small" and the number of trials, *n*, is "large"). In these situations there will be a Poisson distribution having mean and standard deviations very similar to that of the binomial distribution it approaches.

Example 9.11.   The Poisson Substitutes for the Binomial

Suppose a machine turns out defective parts with probability $p = .001$. What is the probability that a group of 10,000 parts contains exactly eight defectives? The theoretically correct calculation would be the Binomial probability using the formula

$$P(X = 8 | n = 10,000; p = .001) = C_8^{10,000}(.001)^8(.999)^{9992}$$

Obviously, it would be extremely burdensome to solve the equation arithmetically. Furthermore, the Binomial tables available do not include answers for *n* of this size. There is a good approximation to the correct binomial probability—the Poisson probability. What is often done in such cases is to calculate the mean and variance of the binomial distribution and then apply the values to the needed conditions for the substitute Poisson distribution.

The mean of the binomial distribution is:

$$np = (10,000)(.001) = 10.$$

The variance is:

$$np(1 - p) = (10,000)(.001)(.999) = 9.99.$$

As can be seen, the values of the mean and variance are almost identical: this suggests that a Poisson distribution with $\mu = 10$ might be a good approximation to the binomial. From the cumulative Poisson probability values given in Table 3 for various values of μ and *x* (the occurrences), the probability of eight occurrences when $\mu = 10$ can be computed to be .1126. In general, it can be asserted that the Poisson serves as a better approximating model for the binomial the larger the *n* and the smaller the *p*. The reason for this closer correspondence is that with larger *n* and smaller *p* the binomial variance $np(1 - p)$ approaches the binomial mean, np—the underlying assumption in using the Poisson.

Using the Poisson Formula to Calculate Waiting Time Probabilities

The Poisson probability formula is very useful in answering questions about waiting time probabilities. For example, suppose one wishes to know the probability that it will take at least *t* minutes in order to get the third occurrence of an attribute, say a telephone call. This would necessitate there being no more than two occurrences during the first *t* minutes. The latter probability can be computed as $P(X \leq 2)$ using a Poisson distribution with μ estimated for *t* minutes. For example, if .371 is the probability of two or less occurrences in six minutes, then .371 is also the probability that it takes more than six minutes to get the third occurrence.

9.12. Managerial Issues in Practice—Review Exercise: Operations Research During World War II

The field of operations research was born in World War II when military planners called upon mathematicians and statisticians to help them solve important problems. The Poisson distribution has an important role in operations research. To see how a military planner might apply what we have learned about the Poisson and other probability distributions, imagine that you are Commander of Allied Forces during World War II. Your objective is to land 85,000 combat troops on a remote beach in Northern Europe. The troops will land from ships carrying 5000 troops each. The problem is that the sea entry to the beach has been mined by the enemy. Intelligence reports indicate that 100 mines have been randomly placed in the beach approach, which is 10 miles wide and extends four miles from shore. Assume that all ships are $\frac{1}{50}$ of a mile wide and approach the beach in different lanes. The location of the mines cannot be determined, but a mine will detonate if any part of a ship passes directly over it.

a. Use the Poisson distribution to find the probability that a particular ship reaches the beach landing area without detonating a mine.
b. If seventeen ships are sent, what is the probability that none detonate a mine?
c. If seventeen ships are sent, what is the expected number to reach the beach with out detonating a mine?
d. What is the minimum number of ships which must be sent to assure at least a .95 probability that at least seventeen ships successfully reach the beach without detonating a mine?

Solutions

a. The mean number of mines per square mile in the beach approach area is:

$$\mu = \frac{100}{4 \times 10} = 2.5 \text{ per square mile.}$$

To reach the beach without detonating a mine a ship must travel over a water lane with an area of 4 miles long $\times \frac{1}{50} = .08$ square miles. The mean number of mines in strips of .08 square miles is:

$$\mu = (2.5)(.08) = .2 \text{ mines per .08 square mile strip.}$$

The fact that mines are randomly distributed over the 40 square miles implies a Poisson distribution. To safely reach the beach, zero mines must be encountered by a ship in its approach strip. Thus,

$$P(X = 0 | \mu = .2) = \frac{\mu^x e^{-\mu}}{x!} = \frac{.2^0 e^{-.2}}{0!} = .8187$$

Thus, any one ship has a high probability of not encountering any mines.

b. Each ship has a binomial probability $= .8187$ of success, or $.1813$ probability of failure. Assuming (approximate) independence of outcomes,

$$P(X = 0 | n = 17, p = .1813) = C_0^{17} (.1813)^0 (.8187)^{17} = .0334$$

c. $\mu_{\text{binomial}} = np = (17)(.8187) = 13.9179$

d. Try successively higher values of n until the required probability is reached. Using $p = .18$ as the probability of a particular ship encountering a mine, the probability of 17 or more ships safely reaching the beach area (or no more than $n - 17$ failing to do so) is given for the following values of n in the cumulative binomial table (not available in this text) as

n	Probability
23	.896
24	.947
25	.975

Thus, $n = 25$ is the fewest number of ships that would assure at least .95 probability of getting 85,000 troops or more to the beach approach area.

9.13. Concluding Comments

In simple random sampling for the presence or absence of an attribute, the probability calculations depend upon whether the sample is drawn with or without replacement. If the sample is drawn with replacement, the binomial sampling formula discussed in the previous chapter is appropriate. If the sample is drawn without replacement, the correct probability is given by the Hypergeometric sampling formula. According to this formula, the probability of exactly x occurrences of the attribute in a sample of size n will depend upon the population size, N, and the number of population members which possess the attribute, R:

$$P(X = x) = \frac{1}{C_n^N} C_x^R C_{n-x}^{N-R}$$

For very small populations, say a few dozen or less, the calculations required by this formula are quite manageable and their results can be startlingly different from those obtained by the binomial sampling formula; hence, the hypergeometric probabilities should be used.

For moderate sized samples from large populations, the calculations required by the hypergeometric sampling formula can be very onerous. However, it may not be necessary to calculate the exact hypergeometric probabilities. If the sample size is only a small fraction of the population size, say no more than .1, then the probability obtained from the binomial tables for that sample size will approximate the exact hypergeometric probability closely enough for most purposes.

When the sample is not a small fraction of the population, an alternative to direct calculation of hypergeometric probabilities is to apply Chebyshev's Inequality. The Inequality can be used to determine the minimum probability of obtaining a value beyond a specified range above and below the mean value. The distribution's mean and standard deviation are needed for this; they can be calculated from:

$$\mu = np$$

$$\sigma = \sqrt{np(1-p)} \sqrt{\frac{N-n}{N-1}}$$

In the next chapter, another alternative, the normal distribution approximation, will be presented.

Many attribute sampling situations involve counting the number of occurrences of an attribute over some continuum of time or space. Sampling incoming telephone calls or the number of truck accidents per million miles of over-the-road driving are two typical examples. In these problems there is not a finite population to be sampled. Indeed, the very concept of a population is nebulous, because there is no rigid or tangible division of the time or space corresponding to an independent item or person; breaking up time into brief instants, seconds, minutes, hours, or days is quite arbitrary. Also, there typically can be more than one occurrence of an attribute, say a telephone call, in a period of time. Nevertheless, if the occurrence can be considered an event which occurs independently with constant probability per each infinitesimally small unit of time or space, then the Poisson distribution provides probabilities for the number of occurrences:

$$P(x \mid \mu) = \frac{\mu^x e^{-\mu}}{x!}$$

In the formula, μ is the mean number of occurrences for the interval of time or space considered. The value of μ is ordinarily estimated from the past history of occurrences for the process.

The Poisson distribution shows the expected variation in the actual number of occurrences of an attribute for a given mean value of occurrences.

The Poisson probability formula can also be used to approximate binomial probabilities when the product of $np(1 - p)$ is close to np. This will happen when the value of n is large and p is small, say .1 or less. The Poisson approximation to the binomial probability is advantageous when the sample size is too large to be found in Binomial Tables.

Questions and Problems

1. Does the investigator always have a choice as to whether a sample is drawn with or without replacement? Explain.

2. How does the number of elementary events in sampling without replacement compare with the number of elementary events in sampling with replacement? Give an expression relating the two.

3. The number of permutations of n things taken x at a time is always equal to the number of ordered combinations of n things taken x at a time. Does this mean that permutations always involve ordering? Explain.

4. Given that the number of permutations of n things taken three at a time is 210, what is:

a. the number of combinations?
b. the value of n?

5. Suppose the number of permutations of the n sample members taken x at a time is 5040. Also suppose that the number of combinations of the n sample members taken x at a time is 210.

a. How many ways are there to order the sample?
b. What is the value of x?
c. What is the value of n?

6. A population consists of N poker chips, of which R are red and $N - R$ are white. A sample of size n is to be drawn. For both sampling with replacement and sampling without replacement give the expression for the following quantities:

a. the number of different sequences of x red chips (and hence $n - x$ white chips) in the sample of size n.

b. the number of different ways to select x red chips from the R red chips in the population.

c. the number of different ways to select $n - x$ white chips from the $N - R$ white chips in the population.

d. the number of different sample results (elementary events) which include x red chips in the sample of size n. (Hint: this should be the product of your answers to a, b, and c.)

e. the number of different elementary events.

f. the probability of x red chips in the sample of size n (Hint: this should be the ratio of your answers to d and e.)

7. Given that $N = 100, R = 70, x = 3$, and $n = 5$, calculate the values for the expressions in parts a through f of Problem 6.

8. Is there a difference between "sampling without replacement" and "finite population sampling"? Explain.

9. An auditor samples $n = 8$ acounts from a population of $N = 200$ accounts to verify their balance. If $R = 6$ account balances have been falsified by an embezzler, what is the probability that the auditor will draw:

a. none of the falsified accounts?

b. at least one falsified account?

c. all of the falsified accounts?

10. What are the sample proportions of the falsified accounts corresponding to your probability calculations in Problem 9? Does the sample proportion of falsified accounts refer to the same thing as the proportion of falsified accounts included in the sample?

11. For the population and sample size given in Problem 9, what is:

a. the mean of the binomial sampling distribution? Use sampling with replacement.

b. the standard deviation of the binomial sampling distribution? Assume as above.

c. the mean of the hypergeometric sampling distribution?

d. the standard deviation of the hypergeometric sampling distribution?

e. the finite population correction factor?

12. The finite population correction factor is needed to calculate the standard deviation of the sampling distribution when sampling is done without replacement from a finite population. Is the correction factor also used in calculating the mean? Explain.

13. Will the standard deviation of the sampling distribution be smaller if sampling is done with replacement or without replacement? Explain.

14. What does your answer to Problem 13 suggest about the variability of sample proportions in sampling without replacement as compared to sampling with replacement?

15. When should the binomial probabilities for sampling with replacement be used as good approximations to the hypergeometric probabilities for sampling without replacement? When shouldn't they be used?

16. In what types of sampling situations would a Poisson distribution be more appropriate than a binomial or a hypergeometric distribution?

17. Assume that telephone calls occur independently of one another. Why would it be inappropriate to use the binomial distribution for $n = 5$ and $x = 3$ to find the probability of three telephone calls in five minutes?

18. Why would the use of the binomial distribution for the probability of three telephone calls in five minutes have to assume infinity for the value of n and not 5 as one might think?

19. How many parameters does a Poisson distribution have?

20. How is the Poisson parameter, μ, determined or estimated?

21. Suppose a Poisson parameter is stated in an interval of time or space not identical to the interval for which information on the mean number of occurrences is available. What adjustment procedure should be followed?

22. Using a Poisson distribution, calculate the probability of five telephone calls in ten minutes for the following available information:

a. the mean number of telephone calls in ten-minute intervals is ten.

b. the telephone calls average one per minute.

c. the telephone calls average two per five minutes.

d. the telephone calls average one call every two minutes.

23. For the information provided in Problem 22d, what is the probability of three telephone calls in the ten minutes? Six telephone calls?

24. For the information provided in Problem 22a, what is the probability of three telephone calls in the ten minutes? Is your answer twice the value of your answer to Problem 23? Why or why not?

25. For the situation described in Problem 22a, what is the probability of six telephone calls in the ten minute interval? Is this probability the same as that computed in Problem 23 for three telephone calls with a parameter value only half that of the 22a parameter value? Why or why not?

26. A machine turns out defective parts with probability .002, from which a group of 4000 parts has been assembled. The production supervisor wants to know the probability that the group contains six defective parts.

a. Find the theoretically correct binomial expression for the probability.

b. Why would the probability for Part a be difficult to obtain using the binomial expression?

c. What is the mean of the binomial distribution for the number of defective parts in the group of 4000 parts?

d. What is the variance of the binomial distribution?

e. What is the mean of the Poisson distribution that can be used to approximate the theoretically correct binomial probability?

f. What is the Poisson probability value that can be used to approximate the theoretically correct binomial probability?

27. In what situations will a Poisson distribution give a good approximation to binomial probabilities? Does the situation in Problem 26 fall into this category?

28. Are there any circumstances in which it would make sense to approximate theoretically correct Poisson probabilities by binomial probabilities? Explain.

29. Compare the binomial probabilities for $n = 50$ and $p = .01$ with the Poisson probabilities used to approximate them. How accurate are the approximations?

30. A box contains twenty hand grenades, three of which are duds. Five grenades are randomly chosen from the box and thrown at a target. What is the probability that:

a. the first grenade tossed is a dud?

b. at least one of the grenades is a dud?

c. three of the grenades are duds?

d. more than three grenades are duds?

31. A company has received a group of twenty guidance system components for its line of industrial robots. These components are critical to the operation of the robot. It is extremely expensive to test the individual components to find out if they are operationally acceptable, so the company will employ a sampling plan to decide whether the group should be accepted. Quality control inspectors will choose four components randomly and subject them to thorough testing. If any one of the four fails the test, the entire group of twenty components is sent back to the manufacturer. If no defective components are found, then the entire group is accepted without further testing. If there are actually four defective components in the lot, what is the probability that at least one of them will be among the four tested?

32. A company has eight products in the final development stage, all of which appear to the company officials to be equally promising candidates for market introduction. Actually, however, only three will be market successes if introduced; the other five will be market failures. If the company decides to introduce three products and chooses on the basis of criteria which are unrelated to the actual outcome (effectively chooses randomly), what is the probability that:

a. all three products introduced will be market successes?

b. none of the three products chosen will be market successes?

c. at least one of the products will be a market success?

33. Twelve missiles are directed at a target. Three of these are armed and nine are decoys. A defense system sends up nine ZAP antimissile missiles, each targeted at one of the incoming missiles. Assuming that decoys cannot be distinguished from the armed missiles, so that the choice of which missiles to go after is essentially random, what is the probability that:

a. all three of the armed missiles are targeted by the ZAP defense system?

b. all the missiles targeted by the ZAP defense system turn out to be the decoys?

34. Suppose that each of the ZAP missiles in the defense system described in Problem 33 has a fifty-fifty chance of finding and destroying its target missile before it could cause damage.

a. How many ZAP missiles would have to be aimed at each incoming missile to assure a .99 chance that it does not get through to cause damage?

b. How many ZAP missiles would have to be fired in order to assure that the chances of any of the twelve incoming missiles getting through to the target would be less than .01?

35. A large corporation puts a few newly hired MBA graduates into an elite training program each year. The program exposes the trainees to many important aspects of the business that less privileged management trainees do not ordinarily get until they have accumulated many years of managerial experience. Sixteen men and nine women have completed the training program to date. Seven men and two women were appointed to "fast track" line executive positions upon completion of the program; the others were appointed to less desirable staff positions. An employment discrimination suit against the company points to the training program as evidence that women are given only "token" advancement opportunities. The company argues that the lower rate of "fast track" positions for women is coincidental.

a. Assume that sexual status is unrelated to job advancement, so that the appointment outcomes can essentially be regarded as a random sample from the population of trainees. What is the probability that merely by chance two or fewer women would end up in the fast-track group?

b. Suppose your answer to Part a seems too small to be due to sampling fluctuation. Is there an explanation that would not involve discrimination on the part of the company? If so, what is it?

36. At a suburban paramedic service, the probability of an emergency call for aid is identical at every instant of time, with the calls averaging four per eight hour shift. Use the Poisson distribution to find the probability of:

a. no calls during an eight hour shift.

b. one call during an eight hour shift.

c. three calls during an eight hour shift.

d. more than three calls during an eight hour shift.

e. at least three calls during an eight hour shift.

f. at most three calls during an eight hour shift.

37. For the paramedic described in Problem 36, find the following probabilities:

a. no calls during a one hour time interval.

b. one call during a one hour time interval.

c. more than one call during a one hour time interval.

d. more than one hour to get the third call.

e. less than one hour to get two calls.

f. the first call comes during the second hour.

38. For the paramedic service described in Problem 36, assume that the service's only unit has just been called to an emergency that will take two hours to handle. No other paramedic service is available in the suburb until this call is completed and the paramedic crew checks back with the base. What is the probability that:

a. no new calls come in while the paramedic unit is responding to the two hour call?

b. at least one call is received while the paramedic unit is still responding to the first emergency?

c. only one call is received while the paramedic unit is responding to the first emergency?

d. three calls have stacked up at the base during the two hours the paramedics have been responding to the first emergency?

39. A travel agent operates the travel concession at a small bank. Customer arrivals average 1.5 per hour during her six hour day. The probability of a customer arrival is identical for every instant of time. Use the Poisson distribution to find the probability of:

a. no customers during a day.

b. only one customer during the day.

c. at least three customers during the day.

d. more than twelve customers during the day.

e. no more than ten customers during the day.

40. For the travel agent described in Problem 39, what is the probability of:

a. no calls during the first hour?

b. six calls in two hours?

c. more than three hours before the first customer arrives?

d. less than two hours to get three customer arrivals?

e. five customers in the same hour?

f. at most two hours before the first customer arrives?

41. For the travel agent described in Problem 39, assume that it takes twenty minutes to complete a transaction with a customer. What is the probability that:

a. no new customer comes in while the travel agent is working on a customer transaction?

b. only one customer comes in while the travel agent is working on a transaction with a customer?

c. at least two new customers come in while the travel agent is working on a customer's transaction?

42. The Arden Cartage Company operates a fleet of over-the-road trucks. Company drivers have achieved an excellent safety record. They have averaged only three accidents per million miles. Assume that accidents occur with identical probability on every part of the route system. What is the probability that:

a. at least three accidents will occur during a period for which 100,000 miles are scheduled to be driven?

b. drivers will accumulate three million miles before the sixth accident occurs?

43. A man-made floor covering is produced in strips twelve feet wide. Defects in the product serious enough to cause rejection by quality control inspectors occur randomly, but at a mean rate of 0.8 per thousand square feet. When a defect occurs the material is cut at that point across the entire twelve foot width. The manufacturer would like to be able to cut material at lengths of 100 feet for shipment to dealers, but there cannot be any defects in the material shipped. Hint: use square feet.

a. What is the probability that a 100-foot strip contains no defects?

b. What is the longest strip which would have less than a .01 probability of having a defect?

44. For the man-made floor covering described in Problem 43, assume that the production process requires that the material be cut into standardized lengths before inspection for defects takes place. If the material is cut into strips of 80-foot lengths:

a. What is the probability that of five randomly selected strips, four contain no defects?

b. What percentage of the strips would be expected to contain serious defects?

45. At a soft drink bottling factory, production line stoppages occasionally occur due to bottle breakage or other malfunction of the bottling process. Assume that the probability of a malfunction is identical for every bottle going through the process. The mean rate of malfunction has been 0.7 per 10,000 bottles produced.

a. Is the distribution of malfunctions more appropriately thought of as a binomial distribution or as a Poisson distribution?

b. If weekly production is scheduled at 50,000 bottles, what is the probability that there will be no stoppages due to malfunctions during the week? More than 20 malfunctions?

Random Sampling for Measured Characteristics and the Normal Distribution

Preview. Problems can arise with the binomial distribution when the sample size is too large for the binomial tables. This generally doesn't pose a problem because the mean can be approximated by "normal" distributions. This chapter will be concerned with the normal family of distributions.

Normal distributions are the most important and best known of all sampling distributions. Normal distributions are versatile. They are all related in a way that makes it possible to use a table of probabilities for one "standardized" normal distribution to find probabilities for any other distribution in the normal family. Importantly, the mean of a large sample drawn from nearly any population will have a probability distribution which can be well approximated by a member of the normal family. Normal distributions model rather closely many actual empirical distributions encountered in the physical, social, and management sciences.

10.1. Large Sample Binomial Distributions Have a Limiting Form: The Bell-Shaped Normal Curve

In Chapter 8 we used the binomial sampling formula to compute the probabilities of sample results and then learned how to avoid the computations by using the published binomial distribution tables. However, for samples larger than 50 or 100, we can't rely on published tables since for samples larger than 50 tables are rarely available.

One reason for this unavailability is that the number of pages required to express all the different probabilities becomes unwieldy. A more compelling reason is that binomial tables become largely unnecessary. Very close approximations to binomial probabilities can be obtained by employing probabilities of the *standardized normal density function* for which there are easy to use published tables. How is this accomplished? The key lies with sample size.

It has been found that as the sample size is increased the shape of the binomial probability distribution for the sample results gradually loses its step-like appearance and becomes a nearly smooth bell-shaped curve. For samples as small as 25, the shape of symmetrical binomial distributions (for example, those with $p = .5$), begins to closely resemble that of the bell-shaped family of normal density functions or *normal curves* first introduced in Chapter 3. This can be illustrated by the series of binomial distributions shown in Figure 10.1.

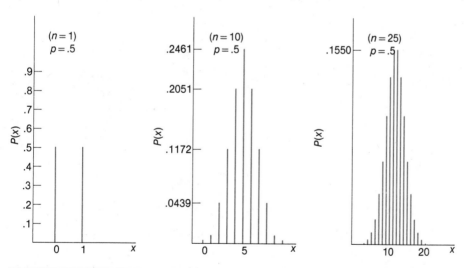

FIGURE 10.1 Binomial Distributions, $p = .5$

The Normal Approximation Works for Skewed Binomial Distributions Too!

When the parent population has a binomial parameter different from .5, the distribution for the population (one draw) and for small sample sizes is skewed to

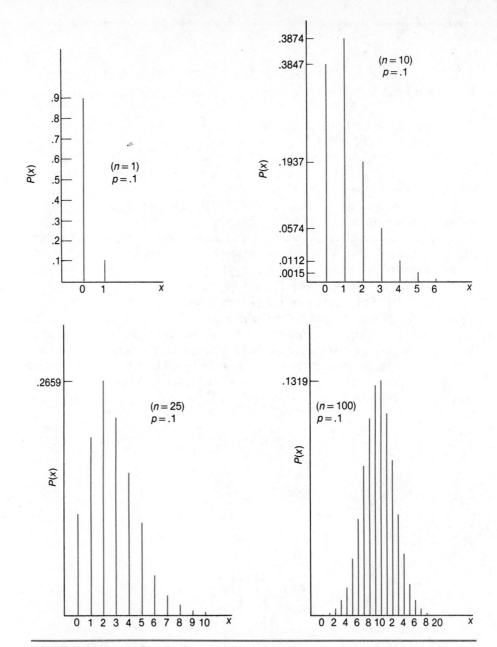

FIGURE 10.2 Binomial Distributions, $p = .1$

the left or right. The direction of skewness depends upon whether p is less than .5 (skewed right) or greater than .5 (skewed left). However, this skewed shape largely disappears if one looks at the average results of larger samples. One can see from examining Figure 10.2 that for large samples, the shape of the distribution of sample means approaches that of the normal curve. The series of distributions shown in Figure 10.2 demonstrates that for population parameters far removed from .5 ($p = .1$ in this case),

1. the binomial distribution tends toward symmetry as n increases and

2. begins to resemble a normal curve when the sample size reaches 100.

10.2. The Standard Normal Density Function

The equation describing the normal family of density functions (as the limiting form of the binomial distribution as n becomes very large) was first derived by a French mathematician, Abraham DeMoivre, in 1733. Interestingly and fortunately, all normal density functions can be related to one particular normal curve, the *standard normal density function*. The height of the curve is defined by the values of the random variable of the standard normal density function designated by the letter Z. The height (density) of this function is given by the equation

$$\text{height (probability density)} \atop \text{of the standard normal density} \atop \text{function over the range of } Z = \frac{1}{\sqrt{2\pi}} e^{-[z^2/2]}$$

This density function, graphed in Figure 10.3, has a mean of zero ($\mu_Z = 0$) and a standard deviation of one ($\sigma_Z = 1$). It is bell-shaped and symmetrical about the mean, so that the mean, median, and mode all coincide. Both tails of the normal curve extend indefinitely, moving toward but never quite reaching the horizontal axis.

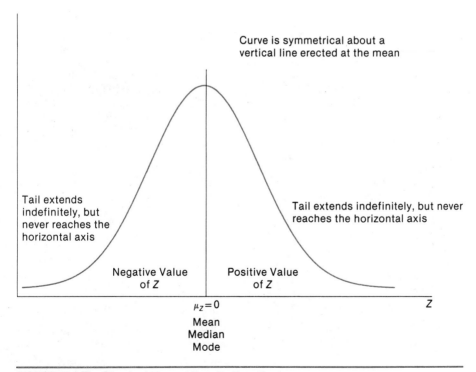

Curve is symmetrical about a
vertical line erected at the mean

Tail extends
indefinitely, but
never reaches the
horizontal axis

Tail extends indefinitely, but never
reaches the horizontal axis

Negative Value
of Z

Positive Value
of Z

$\mu_Z = 0$

Mean
Median
Mode

Z

FIGURE 10.3 The Standard Normal Density Function

It should be noted that since the standard deviation of this density function is one, the value of Z also represents the *number of standard deviations from the mean.* For example, a value of $Z = 2$ indicates a value two standard deviations above the mean, while $Z = -1$ indicates a value one standard deviation below the mean. Negative values of Z merely indicate that the Z value is on the left hand side of (below) the mean, which has a zero value. Positive values of Z are always on the right hand side of (above) the mean.

Probability for a Normal Curve Is Measured By Area, Not By Height

A random variable following a normal density function is a *continuous* random variable. Probability is measured by the *area beneath the curve between two points,* rather than by the height of the curve; height measures probability *density.* The term density is used here in the same sense as in population density—a high population density tells you that people are crowded together, but does not tell you how many people there are in the population. The probability values for the standard normal density function can be read from Table 4 in the appendix. The procedure is quite simple.

Table 10.1 has been cut from Appendix Table 4 for illustrative purposes.

TABLE 10.1. Areas Under the Normal Curve

Z	.00	.01	.02	.03	.04	.05	.06	.07	.08	.09
0.0	.0000	.0040	.0080	.0120	.0160	.0199	.0239	.0279	.0319	.0359
0.1	.0398	.0438	.0478	.0517	.0557	.0596	.0636	.0675	.0714	.0753
0.2	.0793	.0832	.0871	.0910	.0948	.0987	.1026	.1064	.1103	.1141
0.3	.1179	.1217	.1255	.1293	.1331	.1368	.1406	.1443	.1480	.1517
0.4	.1554	.1591	.1628	.1664	.1700	.1736	.1772	.1808	.1844	.1879
0.5	.1915	.1950	.1985	.2019	.2054	.2088	.2123	.2157	.2190	.2224
0.6	.2257	.2291	.2324	.2357	.2389	.2422	.2454	.2486	.2518	.2549
0.7	.2580	.2612	.2642	.2673	.2704	.2734	.2764	.2794	.2823	.2852
0.8	.2881	.2910	.2939	.2967	.2995	.3023	.3051	.3078	.3106	.3133
0.9	.3159	.3186	.3212	.3238	.3264	.3289	.3315	.3340	.3365	.3389
1.0	.3413	.3438	.3461	.3485	.3508	.3531	.3554	.3577	.3599	.3621
1.1	.3643	.3665	.3686	.3708	.3729	.3749	.3770	.3790	.3810	.3830
1.2	.3849	.3869	.3888	.3907	.3925	.3944	.3962	.3980	.3997	.4015
1.3	.4032	.4049	.4066	.4082	.4099	.4115	.4131	.4147	.4162	.4177
1.4	.4192	.4207	.4222	.4236	.4251	.4265	.4279	.4292	.4306	.4319

The arrows placed in the table show that Z is read down initially in the first column for the integer digit and the first decimal digit and then across the top row for the columns of the second decimal digit. For example, the value of Z at 1.24 has an integer and first decimal digit of 1.2 and second decimal digit of .04. Reading down the Z column to 1.2, then across the Z row until .04, the number in color represents the area proportion linked to 1.24. It is .3925 and represents the area under the standard normal curve from the center, $Z = 0$, to a value of $Z = 1.24$. Try reading the area proportion associated with $Z = .87$. You should have found the area to be .3078.

Let us now illustrate the calculations involved in obtaining the area under the curve between any two Z values (say $Z = 2.12$ and $Z = .53$). One must:

1. Start with the higher of the two Z values and look up the entry in the main body of Table 4 corresponding to this Z value. This will be the area under the normal density function between the mean, which has a value $Z = 0$, and the Z value you have chosen. (The entry corresponding to 2.12 is .4830, shown in Figure 10.4a.)

2. Next take the lower of the two Z values and look up the corresponding entry in the main body of the table. This will be the area under the curve between the mean and the lower of the two Z values. (The entry corresponding to $Z = 0.53$ is .2019—shown in Figure 10.4b.)

3a. If the two Z values are of *like* sign, find the *difference* between the two areas determined in steps one and two. This is the area under the density function between the two values, and represents probability that on a random draw from this distribution one would obtain a value within the range defined by the two values. (.4830 − .2019 = .2811, which is the probability of a Z value within the range $Z = 0.53$ to $Z = 2.12$—shown in Figure 10.4c.)

3b. If the two Z values are of *opposite* signs, find the *sum* of the two areas determined in steps one and two. This is the probability that on a random draw from the distribution one finds a value within the range defined by the two values. This is illustrated in the following example.

Example 10.2. **Finding Areas Under Segments of the Standard Normal Density Function**

Find the area under the standardized normal density function between $Z = -1.75$ and $Z = 1.50$, shown in Figure 10.5.

1. In Table 4 the entry corresponding to $Z = 1.50$ is .4332.
2. The entry corresponding to -1.75 is .4599.
3. Add because the Z signs are different. The sum of the two entries determined in steps one and two is $.4332 + .4599 = .8931$.

Thus, .8931 is the probability of randomly drawing a value between $Z = -1.75$ and $Z = 1.50$.

The probability calculation between two Z values on opposite sides of the mean requires addition. Had both Z values been on the same side of the mean, step 3 would have required that the *difference* rather than the sum be computed for the two areas obtained in steps 1 and 2.

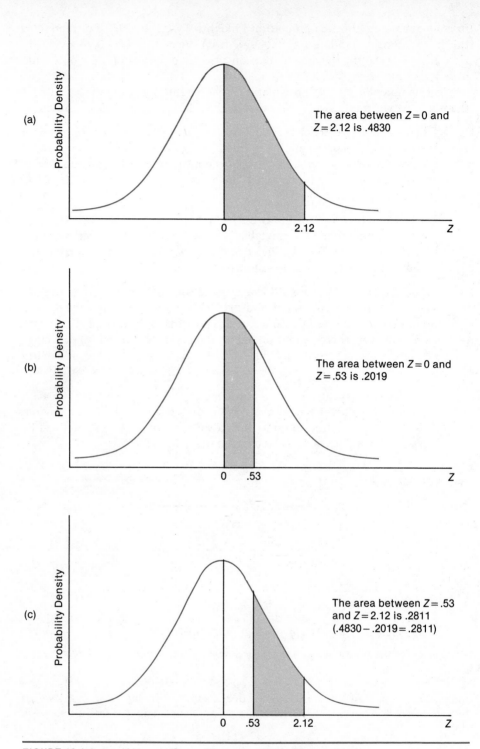

(a)

The area between $Z = 0$ and $Z = 2.12$ is .4830

(b)

The area between $Z = 0$ and $Z = .53$ is .2019

(c)

The area between $Z = .53$ and $Z = 2.12$ is .2811 $(.4830 - .2019 = .2811)$

FIGURE 10.4 Areas of Normal Curve Corresponding to Various Z-Values

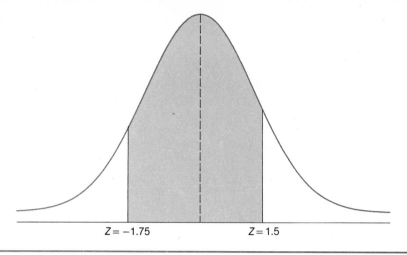

$Z = -1.75$ $Z = 1.5$

FIGURE 10.5 Finding the Probability Under a Z Curve

How Rapidly Does Probability Decline with Distance from the Mean?

With any normal curve, the most probable values lie close to the mean and the least probable values are those most distant from the mean. To appreciate how rapidly probability density declines with distance from the mean, it is instructive· to compare the area under the curve for increasing distances from the mean (measured in terms of units which indicate the number of standard deviations from the mean). Table 10.2 gives this information for distances of 1, 2, and 3 standard deviations.

TABLE 10.2. Probability Corresponding to Various Z Values

NO. OF STANDARD DEVIATIONS ABOVE AND BELOW THE MEAN	CORRESPONDING RANGE OF THE Z-VALUES	AREA INCLUDED WITHIN THIS RANGE	PROBABILITY OF VALUE BEYOND THIS RANGE
1	-1 to $+1$	.6826	.3174
2	-2 to $+2$	.9544	.0456
3	-3 to $+3$	.9974	.0026

Thus, about two thirds of the area lies within one standard deviation of the mean, about 95 percent lies within two standard deviations, and nearly all the area lies within three standard deviations. This is shown graphically in Figure 10.6. For example, if AT&T's monthly stock market returns can be viewed as

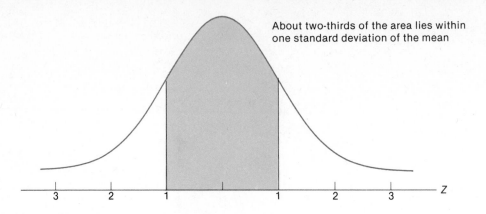

About two-thirds of the area lies within one standard deviation of the mean

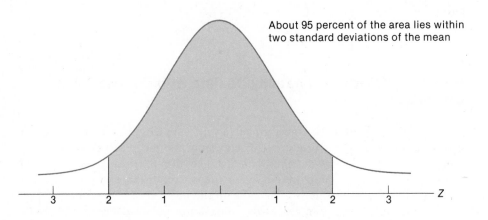

About 95 percent of the area lies within two standard deviations of the mean

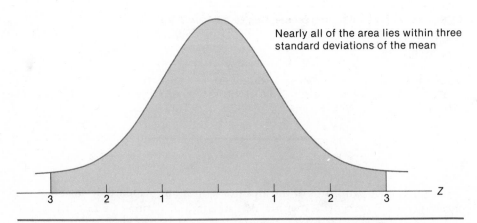

Nearly all of the area lies within three standard deviations of the mean

FIGURE 10.6 Area Under the Normal Curve Within One, Two, and Three Standard Deviations of the Mean

following a normal distribution with mean of 12 percent and standard deviation of 3 percent, then about 68 percent of the time we find that monthly returns fall in the range $12 \pm 1(3)$ or between 9 and 15 percent and virtually all of the time in the range $12 \pm 3(3)$ or between 3 and 21 percent.

10.3. Using the Probability Table for the Standard Normal Curve to Find Probabilities for Other Normal Curves

Normal curves share an important common characteristic: an identical proportion of each curve's area lies between (a) the mean, and (b) a point a given number of standard deviations from the mean. Thus, by finding out that one normal curve has .4332 of its area between the mean and a point 1.5 standard deviations above the mean, we know that *all* normal curves possess this same property. Knowing this property, one can readily use the table of area under the *standardized* normal curve to find the area between two points under *any* normal curve. All normal curve probability assessments require that the distances from the mean be stated in terms of standard deviations; that is, in terms of the Z units of the standard normal curve. In other words, the deviation of any value of X from its mean μ_X in a normal distribution can be standardized by dividing by the distribution's standard deviation σ_X. The operation results in a value of Z. Generalizing,

$$\frac{X - \mu_X}{\sigma_X} = Z$$

As can be noticed from the expression, a value of X at the mean μ_X has a value of $Z = 0$ (the value of X is zero standard deviations away from its mean μ_X). So the value of Z always represents the number of standard deviations which the value of X is away from its mean μ_X. A positive value of Z indicates that X lies *above* its mean μ_X whereas a negative value of Z lies *below* its mean. Once the calculated value of Z is obtained, the next step is to look up the value in Table 4 and find the area proportion associated with the particular value of Z.

Suppose a normal curve has a mean μ_X of 100 and a standard deviation σ_X of 20, and suppose we want to know how much area lies under the curve between the mean and a value of $X = 130$. Expressed in terms of the *number of standard deviations* above the mean, this becomes

$$Z = \frac{X - \mu_X}{\sigma_X} = \frac{130 - 100}{20} = \frac{30}{20} = 1.5$$

The calculated Z value is 1.5 and indicates that X lies 1.5 standard deviations above its mean. Since we found in Example 10.2 that the area between the mean and a value 1.5 standard deviations above the mean included .4332 of the total area under the standardized normal density function, we know that this same proportion, .4332, applies also to the present problem. Thus, the probability that a random draw will result in a value between 100 and 130 is .4332.

The procedure for using the standardized normal density function to find the area under any normal curve between any two points is as follows:

1. Start with the higher of the two values of X and find the corresponding value of Z on the standardized normal density function according to

$$Z = \frac{X - \mu_X}{\sigma_X}$$

2. Next take the lower of the two values of X and find the corresponding value of Z on the standardized normal density function.

3. Use the table of areas for the standardized normal density function to find the area between the two values of Z. This is also the area between the two values of X under the original (unstandardized) normal density function.

Example 10.3.   Using the Table of Areas for the Standardized Normal Density Function to Find Areas Under Other Normal Density Functions

To find the area between $X = 560$ and $X = 680$ for a normal density function having mean $\mu_X = 600$ and standard deviation $\sigma_X = 50$:
First, convert 680 to a Z value.

$$Z = \frac{X - \mu_X}{\sigma_X} = \frac{680 - 600}{50} = 1.6$$

Second, convert 560 to a Z value.

$$Z = \frac{X - \mu_X}{\sigma_X} = \frac{560 - 600}{50} = -.8$$

Third, determine the area under the standardized normal density function between $Z = 1.6$ and $Z = -.8$.

a. The area between $Z = 0$ and $Z = 1.6$ is .4452.
b. The area between $Z = 0$ and $Z = -.8$ is .2881.
c. Therefore, the area between $Z = -.8$ and $Z = 1.6$ is .4452 + .2881 = .7333. (The areas obtained in a and b are added because the two Z values have opposite signs.)

Thus, the area between $X = 560$ and $X = 680$ is .7333. This is shown graphically in Figure 10.7.

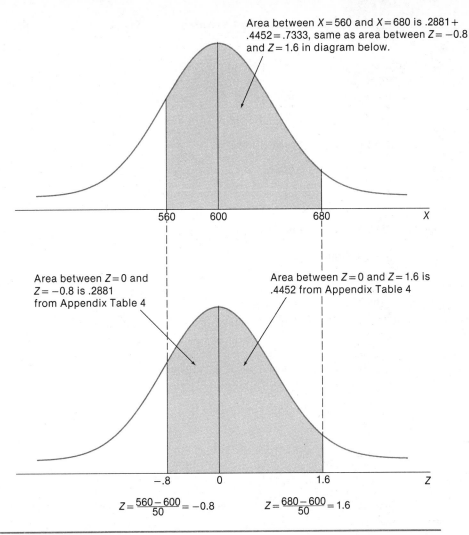

Area between $X = 560$ and $X = 680$ is $.2881 + .4452 = .7333$, same as area between $Z = -0.8$ and $Z = 1.6$ in diagram below.

Area between $Z = 0$ and $Z = -0.8$ is $.2881$ from Appendix Table 4

Area between $Z = 0$ and $Z = 1.6$ is $.4452$ from Appendix Table 4

$$Z = \frac{560 - 600}{50} = -0.8 \qquad Z = \frac{680 - 600}{50} = 1.6$$

FIGURE 10.7 Using the Table of Probabilities for the Standard Normal Curve to Find Probability for Another Normal Curve

10.4. Using the Normal Density Function to Approximate a Binomial Distribution

The table of areas for the standardized normal density function will now be used to facilitate the computation of binomial probabilities for sample sizes beyond the range generally found in binomial tables. This takes advantage of the fact that the binomial distribution approaches the normal density function as n increases. The assumption is that *if two distributions have the same summary measures (mean, dispersion, degree of skewness and kurtosis), it is appropriate* to use computed probabilities of one to approximate the corresponding probabilities of the other.

Approximating binomial probabilities from normal probability tables involves using a normal density function with the same mean and standard deviation as the binomial.

Thus, to approximate the normal distribution mean, we use

$\mu_X = np$ (the mean of the binomial)

and to approximate the standard deviation, we use

$\sigma_X = \sqrt{np(1 - p)}$ (the standard deviation of the binomial)

Continuity Correction

With area rather than height representing probability for a normal curve, the probability calculation requires that the total area under the normal curve be divided into segments indicating the corresponding binomial distribution. Each segment will feature one of $n + 1$ integer values of the particular binomial distribution. To illustrate this notion, consider the daily up and down movements of the Dow stock market index during a particular week ($n = 5$ days). The Dow index can experience 0, 1, 2, 3, 4, or 5 down days; that is, $n + 1$ or 6 possible values. In other words, dividing the normal curve produces intervals representing the possible integer values of the binomial. The interval

a. extends to the left from the integer to a point halfway down to the next lower integer and

b. extends to the right from the integer to a point halfway up to the next higher integer.

Thus, if we want to use the normal approximation to find the binomial probability of a value falling between the binomial values 80 and 82 inclusively, we would find the area under the normal curve between 79.5 and 82.5 (see Figure 10.8). The use of 79.5, the lower boundary of the segment representing 80, and 82.5, the upper boundary of the segment representing 82, is called a *continuity correction*.

Limitations of the Normal Approximation

The normal approximation to the binomial distribution is better the larger the value of n and the closer p is to .5. But how *small* a sample, and for how *far* from $p = .5$, is the normal approximation acceptably accurate? *As a rule of thumb, statisticians want both np and n(1 − p) to equal or exceed 5; so for p = .1, n should be at least 50 before using the normal approximation.* The following example illustrates a business situation in which the underlying distribution is binomial, but a normal distribution is advantageously used to approximate these probabilities.

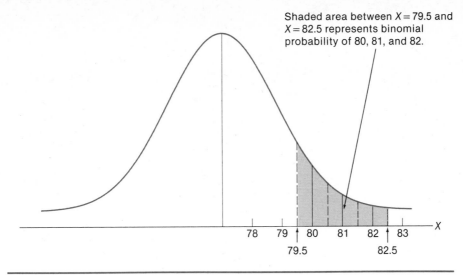

Shaded area between $X = 79.5$ and $X = 82.5$ represents binomial probability of 80, 81, and 82.

FIGURE 10.8 Continuity Correction Is Required When a (Continuous) Normal Curve Is Used to Approximate a (Discrete) Binomial Distribution

Example 10.4A.   Airline Passengers Meal Choices

A passenger airline offers all 160 passengers on a Chicago–San Diego flight a luncheon choice of boneless breast of chicken or sirloin tip of beef in burgundy sauce. Because the passengers do not select their meal until the flight is in progress, there is no way to be sure in advance how many will choose chicken and how many will choose beef. Yet to avoid excess food waste and cost, the airline cannot afford to carry many excess meals on the flight. A careful study of historical records reveals that

1. 60% of the passengers have chosen beef when offered the chicken-beef choice

2. passenger choices appear to be independent, so that a binomial distribution is appropriate.

What is the probability that on this particular flight, the number of passengers choosing beef will be more than 110?

In this problem the sample size is too large to find the probabilities from binomial tables. To use the normal approximation:

a. the mean and standard deviation of the binomial distribution of meal choice must first be found, where the beef choice is the feature of interest.

$$\mu_x = np = 160 \times .6 = 96$$

$$\sigma_x = \sqrt{np(1 - p)} = \sqrt{160 \times .6 \times .4} = \sqrt{38.4} = 6.197$$

b. Next we compute $P(X > 110)$, which corresponds to $P(Z > ?)$

$$Z = \frac{X - \mu_X}{\sigma_X} = \frac{110.5 - 96}{6.197} = \frac{14.5}{6.197} = 2.34$$

c. Turning to Table 4, the table of areas under the standardized normal density function, we find the area between the mean and a value 2.34 standard deviations above the mean is .4904.

d. Since the normal curve is symmetrical, half the area, or .5000, lies to the right of the mean. To find the probability of a value in excess of 110 meals, we therefore identify the area under the normal curve *to the right of* $Z = 2.34$ as the area which must be determined. This is shown by the shaded area in Figure 10.9.

e. Since we know that .4904 of the area lies between $Z = 0$ and $Z = 2.34$ and that .5000 is the total area to the right of $Z = 0$, the difference between .5000 − .4904 or .0096 (approximately 1 chance in a hundred) is the probability that the number of passengers choosing beef in burgundy sauce will exceed 110.

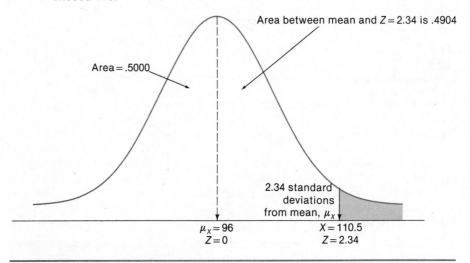

FIGURE 10.9 Normal Distribution Approximation of Beef Meals X for Airline Flight Obtained from Past Records

Practically all business people must make business decisions in the face of the risk of adverse consequences. They must make sure that the risks they take are "calculated" risks. Sometimes this may be a purely subjective judgment, but there are many situations in which risk can be assessed statistically. In the following example we show how risk can be calculated.

Example 10.4B.   Executing a Calculated Risk

Suppose in the airline meal service problem (Example 10.4A) that the airline decided it wants to take a .10 chance (risk) of not being able to serve its passengers the meal of their choice (chicken or beef). How do we calculate the number of beef meals to put on board the plane if there are 160 passengers on the flight?

a. The first step is to find the value of Z on the standardized normal density function which has .10 of the area to its right: in the upper tail, the shaded area in Figure 10.10.

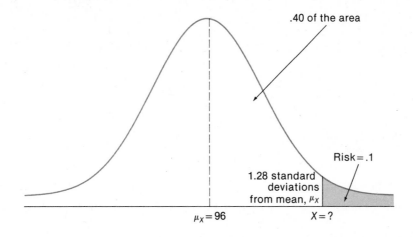

FIGURE 10.10 Using the Normal Approximation to Obtain the Number of Meals to Assume .1 Risk

b. Since .10 of the area lies to its right, .90 of the area must lie to its left. Since .50 of the area lies to the left of the mean, $.90 - .50 = .40$ must lie between the mean and the value of Z we seek.

c. Search the main body of the normal tables for the area value nearest to .40; the closest value is .3997.

d. The Z value to which .3997 (almost .40) refers is 1.28, and represents the *number* of standard deviations above the mean we must go to exclude only .10 of the total probability.

e. The next step is to multiply the Z value of 1.28 by the standard deviation of 6.197 meals computed in Example 10.4A. This gives the number of meals we must bring aboard above the mean value of the binomial distribution. (You can think of this as a "safety reserve".) This is

$$1.28 \times 6.197 = 7.932 \text{ meals.}$$

f. Add 7.932 meals to the mean value of 96 meals computed in Example 10.4A. This gives

$$96 + 7.932 = 103.932 \text{ meals.}$$

g. Rounding this up to the nearest integer, we obtain 104 beef meals as the total number we must bring aboard in order to assure only a .10 probability of not being able to serve all the passengers who request beef meals.

10.5. Probability Calculations for the Sampling Distribution of $\hat{p}$

For large samples (for example, $n = 30$ or larger), the sampling distribution for any sample proportion can be approximated by a normal distribution having the same mean and standard deviation. The mean and standard deviation of this sampling distribution were given in Section 8.14:

$$\mu_{\hat{p}} = p$$

$$\sigma_{\hat{p}} = \sqrt{\frac{p(1 - p)}{n}}$$

Let us now illustrate the calculations by answering the question:

> What is the probability that a sample of size $n = 100$ from a population with $p = .5$ will yield a sample proportion in the range .47 to .53?

A five step procedure using the continuity correction factor $\hat{p} \pm .5/n$ follows.

1. Find the mean and standard deviation of the sampling distribution:

$$\mu_{\hat{p}} = p = .5$$

$$\sigma_{\hat{p}} = \sqrt{\frac{p(1 - p)}{n}} = \sqrt{\frac{(.5)(.5)}{100}} = .05$$

2. Determine the number of standard deviations, Z, between the population mean and the lowest value in the range adjusted by subtracting $.5/n$, so that $Z = (\hat{p} - .5/n - p)/\sigma_{\hat{p}} = (.47 - .005 - .50)/.05 = (.465 - .50)/.05 = -0.7$.

3. For the number of standard deviations obtained in step 2, find the corresponding probability from the table of the standardized normal distribution. For .7 standard deviations, the corresponding probability is .2580.

4. Repeat steps 2 and 3 for the highest value in the range, adding $.5/n$ to $\hat{p}$.

5. Sum the two probabilities obtained in steps 2 and 3:

$.2580 + .2580 = .5160$

This is the probability that $(.47 \leq \hat{p} \leq .53)$. It can also be interpreted as the reliability level corresponding to an error tolerance of $\pm .03$.

Following the same five steps, we find the probability is .9930 that a sample of size 100 will give a sample proportion within the range .37 to .63.

Expressing Chapter Eight's results for the poker chip experiment in percentage terms, we can say that for a sample of size 100, the probability is .5160 that a sample proportion will lie within three percentage points of the population percentage, and .9930 that it will lie within thirteen percentage points of the population mean.

To underscore the value of larger sample size, one need only compare the probability that different size samples will produce a sample proportion within a given percentage point range of the population percentage. Table 10.3 shows that for a specified range around the population percentage, the larger the sample the higher the probability that the sample will produce a sample proportion within the given three percentage point range. This probability increases from .4108 to .9836 with an increase in sample size from 40 to 1600.

TABLE 10.3. Probabilities that a Sample Proportion Will Lie Within Specified Ranges of the Population Percentage (Population Percentage = Fifty; $p = .5$)

SAMPLE SIZE	PROBABILITY OF SAMPLE PROPORTION LYING WITHIN RANGE OF	
	Three Percentage Points	Eight Percentage Points
40	.4108	.7580
100	.3160	.9108
400*	.7698	.99862
1600	.9836	.99999

*For very large samples, the correction factor is very small and can be ignored.

Graphically, this can be illustrated by showing that for the larger sample size the greatest portion of the probability distribution is concentrated within the specified three percentage point range. See Figure 10.11.

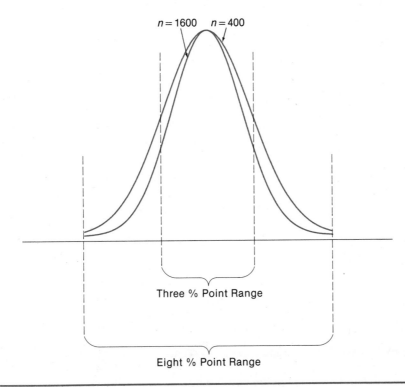

FIGURE 10.11 The Effect of Sample Size on the Concentration for Given Tolerance Ranges

Obviously, expanding the tolerance range to eight percentage points around the population proportion encompasses a larger area of the distribution of possible sample results. From the third column of Table 10.3 one sees that the chances of obtaining a sample result of $\hat{p}_{red}$ within eight percentage points of the target p_{red} jumps to .7580 for samples of size forty, to .9108 for samples of size one hundred, and to virtual assurity (.9999) for samples of size sixteen hundred. Increasing the tolerance range from three percentage points to eight assures one that the sample percentage will be within the specified range. However, the greater the tolerance range, the less certain one can be about the nearness of the sample percentage to its target.

Instead of asking for the probability that a sample proportion will lie within a specified range of the population proportion, we can reverse the question. What is the range within which a sample will fall with specified probability, say .95? To answer this question we (ignoring the continuity correction):

1. divide the total .95 probability into .475 probability of a value above the population proportion and .475 probability of a value below the population proportion.

2. From the probability table for the standardized normal distribution, we find the number of standard deviations, 1.96, corresponding to an area of .475 under the curve between the population proportion and the sample proportion.

3. We multiply the *number* of standard deviations by the value of the standard deviation of sample proportions for the sample size we have chosen.

For example, for a sample of 100 in the poker chip experiment where the percentage of red chips in the population p_{red} is 50 percent, the calculation for the percentage point deviation is

$$1.96\ \sigma_{\hat{p}} = 1.96\ \sqrt{\frac{p(1-p)}{n}} = 1.96\ \sqrt{\frac{(.5)(.5)}{100}} = .098$$

or 9.8 in percentage terms.

With the percentage point deviation at 9.8, the sample proportion $\hat{p}_{red}$ will fall with .95 probability in the range $50 \pm 1.96(9.8)$, that is, the range of 40.2 percent to 59.8 percent. For a sample of size 400, the percentage point deviation is cut in half (that is, $1.96\ \sqrt{(.5)(.5)/400} = .049$) and the range of $\hat{p}_{red}$ reduced to a range of 45.1 percent to 54.9 percent. Quadrupling the same size once more to 1600 reduces in half again the percentage point deviation (that is, $1.96\ \sqrt{(.5)(.5)/1600} = .0245$) and narrows the range of $\hat{p}_{red}$ with .95 probability to between 47.55 percent and 52.45 percent.

Example 10.5.   Copying Machine Down Time

An office manager notes that the copying machine in the office seems to be down (not operating properly) a substantial portion of the time. To check this out, the machine will be observed at 400 randomly selected instants of time during regular working hours over the next few months. The proportion of observations will be calculated for when the machine was inoperative. Suppose the true proportion of downtime is $p = .2$. What is the standard deviation of the sampling distribution of $\hat{p}$?

Answer: $\sigma_{\hat{p}} = \sqrt{\dfrac{p(1 - p)}{n}} = \sqrt{\dfrac{(.2)(.8)}{400}} = .02$

What is the probability that the computed value of $\hat{p}$ will exceed .25?

Answer: $P(\hat{p} > .25) = P\left(Z > \dfrac{\hat{p} - p}{\sigma_{\hat{p}}}\right) = P\left(Z > \dfrac{.25 - .20}{.04}\right)$

$$= P(Z > 2.5) = .5000 - .4938 = .0062$$

What is the reliability level corresponding to an error tolerance $(\hat{p} - p)$ of $\pm.05$?

Answer: Reliability level $= P((\hat{p} - p) < \pm.05)$

$$= P\left(\left(\dfrac{\hat{p} - p}{\sigma_{\hat{p}}}\right) < \pm\dfrac{.05}{\sigma_{\hat{p}}}\right)$$

Since $\sigma_{\hat{p}} = .02$ and $\dfrac{\hat{p} - p}{\sigma_{\hat{p}}} = Z$, we have

$$P(Z < \pm 2.5);$$

Recognizing the symmetry we can write $2P(Z < 2.5)$
$$= 2(.4938) = .9876$$

10.6. An Empirical Demonstration

We have already seen that the normal distribution makes a good approximation to the binomial sampling distribution. Interestingly, the normal distribution is also the limiting form of the sampling distribution when sampling from other populations. One example is the uniform distribution. We can gain an impression of the uniform sampling distribution's shape by constructing an empirical distribution based upon repeated sampling. For instance, the probability distribution (parent population) of spots on the roll of a die (values 1 through 6) is a uniform distribution, shown in Figure 10.12.

For this uniform parent population, what is the shape of the sampling distribution for means of 200 samples of size five drawn randomly from it? By recording the results of each sample and finding the average number of spots, we obtain Table 10.4.

The empirical (frequency) distribution of sample means constructed from the results shown in Table 10.4 is presented in Figure 10.13. As can be seen from this figure, the distribution is not in perfect conformity with the specifications of the normal distribution (that would take many more than our 200 repetitions). Importantly though, it is clear that even for our very small sample size ($n = 5$), the outline sketched of the empirical distribution of sample means bears a strong resemblance to a normal distribution.

TABLE 10.4. Sampling Results for Die Throws (Sample Size, $n = 5$)

SAMPLE NUMBER	SAMPLE MEASUREMENTS	$\sum X_i$	$\overline{X}$	SAMPLE NUMBER	SAMPLE MEASUREMENTS	$\sum X_i$	$\overline{X}$
1	13112	8	1.6	53	34564	22	4.4
2	36552	21	4.2	54	44656	25	5.0
3	56223	18	3.6	55	46235	20	4.0
4	11224	10	2.0	56	41565	21	4.2
5	25146	18	3.6	57	22161	12	2.4
6	34421	14	2.8	58	44351	17	3.4
7	16644	21	4.2	59	16626	21	4.2
8	52521	15	3.0	60	36115	16	3.2
9	15533	17	3.4	61	24226	16	3.2
10	66622	22	4.4	62	42316	16	3.2
11	11546	17	3.4	63	36236	20	4.0
12	64423	19	3.8	64	15525	18	3.6
13	65121	15	3.0	65	26313	15	3.0
14	16543	19	3.8	66	12426	15	3.0
15	53643	21	4.2	67	33664	22	4.4
16	33355	19	3.8	68	65646	27	5.4
17	53445	21	4.2	69	16653	21	4.2
18	53421	15	3.0	70	15251	14	2.8
19	32133	12	2.4	71	46222	16	3.2
20	53325	18	3.6	72	46244	20	4.0
21	61124	14	2.8	73	56233	19	3.8
22	55456	25	5.0	74	62214	15	3.0
23	64654	25	5.0	75	52232	14	2.8
24	23542	16	3.2	76	25366	22	4.4
25	33412	13	2.6	77	53466	24	4.8
26	11265	15	3.0	78	21344	14	2.8
27	66362	23	4.6	79	51635	20	4.0
28	22544	17	3.4	80	45343	19	3.8
29	26542	19	3.8	81	22112	8	1.6
30	11542	13	2.6	82	26631	18	3.6
31	44426	20	4.0	83	44242	16	3.2
32	43545	21	4.2	84	43632	18	3.6
33	12313	10	2.0	85	16563	21	4.2
34	54124	16	3.2	86	51261	15	3.0
35	54521	17	3.4	87	31524	15	3.0
36	52633	19	3.8	88	43624	19	3.8
37	55452	21	4.2	89	56542	22	4.4
38	55366	25	5.0	90	14131	10	2.0
39	66514	22	4.4	91	63365	23	4.6
40	53421	15	3.0	92	23435	17	3.4
41	61542	18	3.6	93	56462	23	4.6
42	61156	19	3.8	94	53121	12	2.4
43	56633	23	4.6	95	21231	9	1.8
44	44644	22	4.4	96	13445	17	3.4
45	11154	12	2.4	97	26544	21	4.2
46	54551	20	4.0	98	21422	11	2.2
47	62235	18	3.6	99	66642	24	4.8
48	56423	20	4.0	100	23623	16	3.2
49	41611	13	2.6	101	33353	17	3.4
50	46423	19	3.8	102	62363	20	4.0
51	12522	12	2.4	103	15153	15	3.0
52	15366	21	4.2	104	31431	12	2.4

SAMPLE NUMBER	SAMPLE MEASUREMENTS	$\sum X$	$\bar{X}$	SAMPLE NUMBER	SAMPLE MEASUREMENTS	$\sum X_i$	$\bar{X}$
105	23451	15	3.0	153	42416	17	3.4
106	53153	17	3.4	154	55442	20	4.0
107	52146	18	3.6	155	13154	14	2.8
108	21345	15	3.0	156	55441	19	3.8
109	16162	16	3.2	157	15525	18	3.6
110	26134	16	3.2	158	63454	22	4.4
111	11522	11	2.2	159	23312	11	2.2
112	54465	24	4.8	160	12312	9	1.8
113	22263	15	3.0	161	65621	20	4.0
114	66251	20	4.0	162	64542	21	4.2
115	42244	16	3.2	163	33264	18	3.6
116	56142	18	3.6	164	51532	16	3.2
117	64462	22	4.4	165	54213	15	3.0
118	31243	13	2.6	166	52663	22	4.4
119	35562	21	4.2	167	21135	12	2.4
120	34164	18	3.6	168	26113	13	2.6
121	16533	18	3.6	169	25166	20	4.0
122	11526	15	3.0	170	65326	22	4.4
123	42113	11	2.2	171	42622	16	3.2
124	12351	12	2.4	172	63251	17	3.4
125	42232	13	2.6	173	62166	21	4.2
126	55232	17	3.4	174	24332	14	2.8
127	43626	21	4.2	175	53511	15	3.0
128	21215	11	2.2	176	34112	11	2.2
129	26462	20	4.0	177	31433	14	2.8
130	53235	18	3.6	178	62116	16	3.2
131	25526	20	4.0	179	22441	13	2.6
132	33262	16	3.2	180	12662	17	3.4
133	26141	14	2.8	181	44625	21	4.2
134	31326	15	3.0	182	24266	20	4.0
135	44353	19	3.8	183	14453	17	3.4
136	66533	23	4.6	184	56343	21	4.2
137	41443	16	3.2	185	25122	12	2.4
138	54524	20	4.0	186	32565	21	4.2
139	23256	18	3.6	187	16613	17	3.4
140	32124	12	2.4	188	56324	20	4.0
141	61631	17	3.4	189	22336	16	3.2
142	31334	14	2.8	190	56356	25	5.0
143	31122	9	1.8	191	13451	14	2.8
144	44534	20	4.0	192	54166	22	4.4
145	45453	21	4.2	193	24165	18	3.6
146	61563	21	4.2	194	16625	20	4.0
147	61254	18	3.6	195	54646	25	5.0
148	23123	11	2.2	196	26413	16	3.2
149	11613	12	2.4	197	54211	13	2.6
150	35336	20	4.0	198	66534	24	4.8
151	46125	18	3.6	199	61315	16	3.2
152	62333	17	3.4	200	15126	15	3.0

The mean and standard deviation of the empirical distribution of sample results will, of course, be related to the mean and standard deviation of the parent population from which the sample came. In this particular example, the mean of the 200 sample means is 3.472, whereas the mean of the parent population is 3.5.

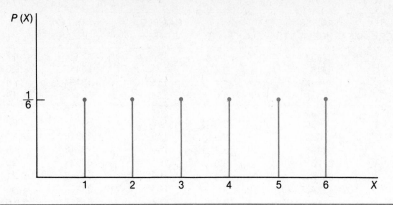

FIGURE 10.12 Parent Population for the Number of Spots on the Face of One Rolled Die

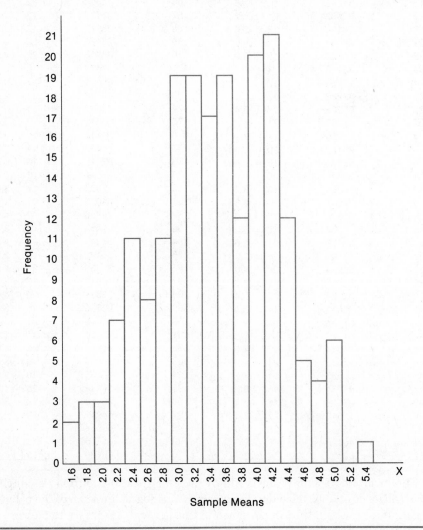

FIGURE 10.13 Frequency Distribution of Sample Results (Means) of Sampling from the Die Population (Sample Size)

10.7. The Ever-Present Normal Curve in Sampling: The Central Limit Theorem

The normal density function is usually regarded as the most important of the sampling distributions. Its stature among the other distributions lies not just in the fact that the normal curve represents the limiting form for the binomial sampling distribution, but from the fact that the binomial case is illustrative of a general phenomenon. The statement of this general phenomenon is provided by the *Central Limit Theorem*. The theorem assures that:

> For random sampling with replacement from any population (with finite variance), the shape of the distribution for the sample sum and for the sample mean tends toward a normal curve as n becomes large.

An example of a sampling distribution for the *sample sum* (of whatever characteristic we are counting) is the binomial. Similarly, an example of a distribution of *sample means* is the sampling distribution of sample means drawn from a uniform distribution. And as we have shown graphically in previous sections of this chapter, both distributions take on the shape of the normal curve as n becomes large.

The remarkable fact about the central limit theorem is that it is not restrictive about the shape of the parent population from which we sample. No matter what the shape of the parent population, the sampling distribution for the mean of a large sample drawn from that population will end up looking like a normal curve—*even if the population distribution bears no resemblance to the shape of a normal curve!*

Knowing that for large samples, the sampling distribution of sample means always ends up looking like a normal curve is of great importance when a sample mean is used to estimate the population mean. It implies that the magnitude of potential estimation errors obtained by using sample means as estimates can be described by a normal curve, *regardless* of the population from which the sample is drawn.

As a practical matter, it is crucial to know how large a sample must be in order for its sampling distribution to be in close conformity with the shape of a normal curve. Is a sample of $n = 5$ large enough? Or if not, would n have to exceed 100, 1000 or even 10,000? Certainly if the latter size is needed, the Central Limit Theorem would not be very useful in application. Fortunately, statisticians have learned that the normal density function is a good approximation to the sampling distribution for sample means (and sample sums) whenever n is at least 30. Since samples of size 30 or more are commonplace, the central limit theorem becomes of very great practical importance.

Some perspective on the tendency toward normality in the sampling distribution of the sample mean ($\overline{X}$) as n increases can be gained by examining the populations and their respective sampling distributions shown in Figure 10.14.

One set of sampling distributions shown in Figure 10.14 is for the means of samples of size 2, 4, and 25 from a uniformly distributed population. Another is for the means of samples of size 2, 4, and 25 from an exponentially distributed population. Neither parent population distribution resembles a normal curve. For samples of size 4, the sampling distribution exhibits some similarity to a

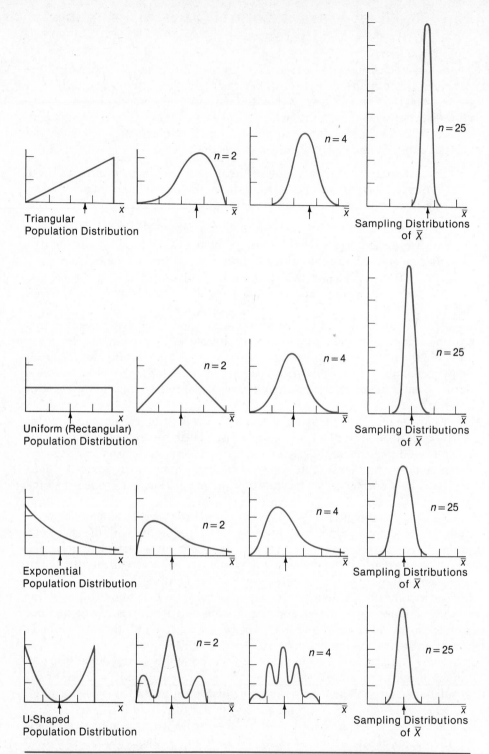

FIGURE 10.14 The Central Limit Theorem: The Tendency of the Sampling Distribution of $\overline{X}$ toward Normality as n Increases for Different Populations

normal curve for these two populations, but not for the other two populations shown. And for samples of size 25, all four sampling distributions bear an unmistakable resemblance to a normal curve.

10.8. The Sampling Distribution of the Sample Mean

In the previous sections empirical sampling and the Central Limit Theorem illustrated that

the empirical distribution of $\overline{X}$ tends to center itself on the mean of the population

the empirical distribution of $\overline{X}$ will become a normal distribution as successive large sampling repetitions are performed.

Through probability theory the theoretical analogue of the empirical sampling distribution can be found. The sampling (probability) distribution of $\overline{X}$ provides valuable information about the role of the sample means as estimators of the population. It shows that

its mean is identical to that of the population mean

$$\mu_{\overline{X}} = \mu_X$$

The variability of the distribution of sample means diminishes with increasing sample size. Its standard deviation depends both upon the sample size and the variation within the present population:

$$\sigma_{\overline{X}} = \frac{\sigma_X}{\sqrt{n}}$$

$\sigma_{\overline{X}}$ is often called the *standard error of the mean*. Presumably, the word "error" is used in place of "deviation" here to emphasize that variation among sample means is due to sampling error.

As the formula indicates, the standard error of the mean varies directly with the standard deviation of the population, σ_X, and inversely with the square root of sample size. By increasing the sample size, the standard error can be reduced to any level desired. However, the reduction is not proportional to the increase in sample size. To cut the standard error in half, the sample size must be quadrupled.

Example 10.8. "Hero" Sandwiches

A deli in a large supermarket advertises that its family "hero" sandwich contains a full pound of whichever cold cut the customer prefers. The perennial favorites are the expensive cuts: roast beef, ham, and turkey. About 1000 sandwiches are made each week. Because customers ask for different thicknesses of meat and also want to see the meat sliced fresh for the sandwich, the owner cannot pre-cut and pre-weigh each pound portion. The owner of the deli believes that the butcher is consistently a bit generous in making up the sandwiches and has a tendency to add a few slices over the pound mark rather than to underweigh the meat. The butcher, a member of the United Meat Cutters union, insists that the overweight sandwiches balance out with the underweight sandwiches. The deli owner comes to you, the store manager, since with your formal quantitative business training you might be able to suggest how to make a proper evaluation from a sample of 100 weighings. Assuming the historical $\sigma_x = .03$ lb. (slightly under half-ounce), find the probability that the mean sample weight would be:

  a. as large as one pound (1 lb.)
  b. as large as one pound and a half ounce (1.031 lb.)

if the butcher is holding to a true mean weight of 1.00 lb.
Solutions: The standard error is

$$\sigma_{\bar{x}} = \frac{\sigma_x}{\sqrt{n}} = \frac{.03}{\sqrt{100}} = .003$$

The sampling distribution of $\bar{X}$ has $\mu_{\bar{x}} = 1.000$ and $\sigma_{\bar{x}} = .003$. From the table of standardized normal distribution, we determine the areas under the curve between $Z = 0$ and

  a. $Z = \dfrac{\bar{X} - \mu_{\bar{x}}}{\sigma_{\bar{x}}} = \dfrac{1.000 - 1.000}{.003} = 0$

  b. $Z = \dfrac{1.031 - 1.00}{.003} = \dfrac{.031}{.003} = 10.33$

These areas are 0 and approximately .5, respectively. To each of these areas we must add .5000, the area to the left of the population mean. Thus, the probabilities that the mean sample weight exceeds the stated values are

  a. .5000
  b. approximately zero

Thus, because of sampling variation, a sample mean above the prescribed mean of 1.000 lbs. would not be unusual, but in a sample of 100, a value above 1.031 lbs. would be extremely unusual.

10.9. The Normal Model

Besides its use in simplifying the computations for the binomial and its use in the Central Limit Theorem, the Normal Distribution can serve as a useful model on its own. It has been said that if one is allowed to learn about only one distribution, it should be the normal distribution. One might ask why, since according to the statistician John Tukey, "There never was and never will be a normal distribution." Taken literally, this suggests that even under the best of circumstances raw data does not conform exactly to the specification prescribed by the normal distribution. What good then is the normal distribution model?

One would be led astray by reading too much into John Tukey's words. Recall that a model *per se* is a sensible sketch of reality. When one gathers data from the real world, one should expect some non-conformity between the empirical values and the theoretical values given by the normal distribution used as a model. The important point is this—model usability or adequacy can be achieved even without perfect conformity between the empirical data and the prescribed values of the chosen model. Model adequacy means only that the model is a good approximation to the underlying process generating the actual data. This approximate conformity is usable in the sense that the model characteristics can be relied on to generate tolerably accurate inferences (predictions) about the parameters of the process producing the data.

What underlying situations are needed for the normal model to be appropriate? Suppose we consider observations as the end product of two types of factors; some factors can be identified and assigned to the phenomenon as determinants, but others are too numerous and their impact too diverse to specify. Cumulatively, these diverse factors have a significant total effect, but individually they are not measurable. These diverse elements are usually identified as "independent, random" factors. They are random in the sense that for each observation we regard the individual impact of a factor as unpredictable. Independence implies that the chance of any one random element occurring is unaffected by the occurrence of another random factor. The cumulative effect of these independent random elements is considered as the additive summation of the factors—some factors augmenting others and some negating others. No one random factor systematically predominates over the group. If one factor did, it ought to be classified as a determinant, not a random factor. Empirical evidence frequently has shown that when there exists a random process of these type of factors at work, the distribution which is most appropriate is the normal.

Some situations characterized by these random factors (so that the normal model usefully describes the process generating the data) are:

1. In controlled production processes the variation in yields, weights, or lengths from a prescribed standard has been noted to follow a normal distribution; for example, overfill and underfill measurements from a set standard in vending machines dispensing liquids, and oversize and undersize parts in mass production industrial processes.

2. The variation around an average for anatomical and intelligence measurements for particular groups; for example, heart pulses for given stress condition, IQs for first graders.

3. In measuring economic activity there is an "unexplainable" portion of the economic activity which can be viewed as the product of a numerous variety of individual random happenings (shocks) after having accounted for certain assignable factors. For example, the sales of automobiles in a given year are a function of people's income level, but also their individual taste for style, safety features, prestige, etc.—all of which are contributory in explaining the sales level, but are individually non-measurable.

Basically, so much importance is attached to the normal model that it often serves as a *benchmark* model for studying a process. Non-conformity to the normal model can spur further investigation of the reason for the non-conformity. For instance, the non-conformity of stock price changes to the normal model has had a significant effect on the theory of investments. Non-conformity also can lead the researcher to seek a more appropriate model or some effective way to transform the data to achieve a normal model conformity.[1]

Although there are no laws of nature that dictate that the normal distribution ought to be the end goal of analysis, data manipulation to reach such a stage has considerable merit. If achieved, the nature of the true process can be better understood and used in subsequent analyses for prediction purposes. A word of caution is in order here. It should be understood at the outset that the lack of pattern in the sequence of the observations (called randomness) does not imply normality. However, the histogram of the non-random observations can follow a normal pattern. Normality and randomness are key concerns when the data analysis deals with finding the pattern in data collected sequentially over time.

Example 10.9. Controlling Cash Balances: An Application of the Normal Model

A prime concern of the comptroller of a firm is to prevent technical insolvency (a shortage of cash) since it likely impairs the firm's credit position among its creditors and ultimately the firm's profitability. Avoiding technical insolvency requires the firm to have the cash on hand when debt obligations are due. Holding too much cash in reserve, however, is also a condition which is to be avoided, since idle cash could be earning interest in marketable securities. It is important, therefore, to balance off the cost and benefits and hold the optimal amount of cash on hand. Miller and Orr have developed a decision rule on the amount of cash to hold, given that the cash drawn to meet maturing obligations follows a normal distribution—a working assumption against which the actual situation is compared.[2] See Figure 10.15.

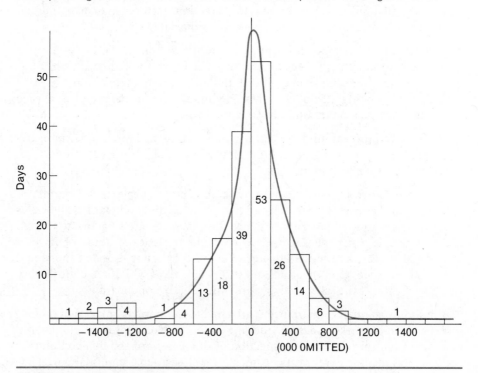

FIGURE 10.15 Daily Cash Changes

Interestingly, the decision rule of when to buy and sell marketable securities developed from the normal model assumption proved to be more effective in monitoring and managing the cash reserves of the firm than the firm's comptroller, who made decisions on a purely subjective basis.

10.10. Managerial Issues in Practice— Review Exercise: Wholesaling Strategy—An Application of the Law of Averages

Frank Cazmier's restaurant concession at a Northeastern Ohio truckstop displays, near the cash register, giant stuffed toy animals which some truckers purchase for their children. The animals cost Frank $50 each. Once a month a salesman for the toy company which makes the animals calls on Frank, takes Frank's order, promises delivery within four weeks, and checks to see that the previous month's order has arrived. He also collects the amount Frank owes on the animals he purchased two months ago and which were delivered prior to the salesman's last visit.

Like many other small retailers, Frank orders conservatively. He invariably orders four of the stuffed toy animals, fewer than he could sell. "Turnover," he says. "I could sell on average, about nine of these stuffed toy animals a month. But demand is sporadic and some months I wouldn't sell any at all. The restaurant business is pretty much a cash and carry type of operation. If I have a bad month with the stuffed animals and none of them sell, I still have to open up the cash register and come up with $450 when the toy salesman stops in. That really hurts. It means I may have to cut back on my food buying or send a waitress or waiter home. I can't afford to do that, because food service, not toys, is my bread and butter. So I only order what I'm ninety-five percent sure can be sold to my own customers before the toy salesman's next call. At that time I pay him an amount usually covering the price of four toy animals. I make a nice profit on them and don't have to worry about tying up my own cash in the inventory."

Moose Crowley, a tobacco and candy wholesaler, has talked with Frank about the toy animals. One day Moose told Frank he had decided to add stuffed toy animals to his line of merchandise. "I wouldn't be able to save you any money, Frank, because the manufacturer won't give me a price break. I have to pay $50 just like you do and so I'll have to charge you $60. But the way I figure it, you'll come out ahead. With a $90 selling price, you'll clear on average $270 per month, a definite improvement over the previous $160. You'll have the big advantage of animals in stock since I can deliver to you on my regular twice weekly calls. When the animals don't sell quickly, I'll give you the same thirty day terms as the manufacturer. When they do sell quickly, you can pay me when I deliver the replacement stock and avoid tying up your own cash in inventory. With a fresh supply of stuffed animals in your hands quickly, you'll never run low, but instead be in position to capture about five extra sales a month and surprisingly without putting up your own money for inventory. It's like having your cake and eating it too."

Frank did some quick figuring and said, "It looks good, Moose. The only thing I don't understand is why you want to do it for ten bucks profit per animal.

You know how sporadic the sales are and you don't like having your cash tied up in inventory any more than I do."

"It's the Law of Averages," Moose said. "You're only one of thirty-six customers I'll have. Your monthly sales vary a lot. Mine won't, thanks to the Law of Averages. If you want to be a good wholesaler, you gotta know about the Law of Averages."

Assume that each of Moose's customers is like Frank and has a probability distribution for stuffed toy animal sales which has a mean, μ, of nine per month and a standard deviation of $\sigma = 3$ per month. Additionally, measure relative risk by the ratio of the standard deviation to the mean sales per month. This shows how much variation in monthly sales there is for the average size of monthly sales and standardizes risk per unit sale.

a. What is the ratio of the standard deviation σ to the mean μ_X of Frank's sales probability distribution? *Answer:* For Frank, $\mu = 9$ and $\sigma = 3$ so Frank's relative risk is

$$\frac{\sigma}{\mu} = \frac{3}{9} = \frac{1}{3}$$

b. What are the mean $\mu_{\overline{X}}$, and standard deviation $\sigma_{\overline{X}}$, of the sampling distribution of the mean sales per month faced by Moose using 36 retailers? *Answer:* $\mu_{\overline{X}} = 9$; the average monthly sales figure over his 36 retailers with

$$\sigma_{\overline{X}} = \frac{\sigma_X}{\sqrt{n}} = \frac{3}{\sqrt{36}} = .5$$

c. What is the ratio of the standard deviation $\sigma_{\overline{X}}$ to the mean $\mu_{\overline{X}}$ of Moose's sales probability distribution? *Answer:* For Moose, relative risk per unit sale is

$$\frac{\sigma_{\overline{X}}}{\mu_{\overline{X}}} = \frac{.5}{9} = \frac{1}{18}$$

We now see that Frank, as one retailer, has a monthly average of 9 and Moose has a monthly average of *9 per retailer over 36 retailers.* Yet Moose encounters considerably less variation of monthly mean sales than Frank. In fact, on a relative basis it is six times greater for Frank since $\frac{1}{3}$ is six times greater than $\frac{1}{18}$. This shows that Moose faces much less downside sales risk on a unit sales basis than Frank, even though both stock to meet their average demand.

d. What are the upper and lower values of the central range within which there is a 95 percent chance that the 36 customer mean, $\overline{X}$, will fall? *Answer:* For the central 95% range, the value of Z at the boundaries will be $+1.96$ and -1.96. Thus, the upper boundary is

$$\mu + Z\sigma_{\overline{X}} = 9 + 1.96(.5) = 9.98$$

The lower boundary is

$$\mu - Z\sigma_{\overline{X}} = 9 - 1.96(.5) = 8.02$$

e. Explain how the law of averages relates to Moose's wholesaling strategy.

Answer: Moose's wholesaling strategy appeals to customers like Frank because it helps them capture sales they presently lose without increasing their risk of cash shortage. Moose carries and makes available to his customers the inventory they want on short notice but are not willing to risk holding.

It is a common notion that middlemen like Moose sell and profit without benefiting anyone else. This simply is not true. Manufacturers, retailers (like Frank), and customers (such as Frank's customers) all benefit from Moose's wholesaling operation. There is an increased profit for the manufacturer and the retailer (Frank) from the larger volume of sales. Additionally, customers find a greater availability of the product to better suit their purchase time preference. It is of particular interest to note that Moose's strategy does not depend at all on volume price discounts from the manufacturer as is generally believed. If discounts are available because of volume production and shipping, it is an additional benefit of the wholesaling system.

The key to Moose's wholesaling strategy is that the individual retailer's holding risk is diversified and reduced by Moose's inventory holding operation. Individual retailers' demand fluctuations are generally not perfectly linked so that if one retailer's demand slumps they all do not slump. If they did, there would be no net gain from Moose's wholesaling strategy. So long as individual retailers' demand exhibits independent movement, one retail customer's demand slump will likely be offset by another's rise. This averaging out process lowers the per unit risk of Moose to a level that is *lower than any one of Moose's retail customers*. The law of averages is a foundation of this risk reduction advantage. Moose and other wholesalers recognize why it is critical to understand how the law of averages works for them.

10.11. Concluding Comments

The normal family of distributions is perhaps the most versatile of the distributions we study. First, normal distributions serve as good models for many phenomena encountered in the physical, social, and management sciences—from variations in mass production to variations in IQ. Second, normal distributions are often used to simplify probability calculations even when another distribution better models the phenomenon studied, as was seen in Example 10.4A concerning airline meal choice. Third, the normal distribution can be used to provide approximate probability calculations for summary statistics such as $\overline{X}$ and $\hat{p}$ from large sampling distributions.

Since the normal distribution is measured over a continuum of values, the height of the normal curve at any point measures probability *density*. The probability that an observation will lie between any two particular values is given by the *area* under the curve between these two values. If the probability calculation is to approximate the probability for a discrete distribution, then a continuity correction is required. The normal curve must be divided into segments which correspond to the discrete values. The area under the normal curve which approximates the discrete probability will be the area in the segments corresponding to the discrete values, not just the area between the two values. Thus, to approximate the probability between 45 and 55 inclusive for an integer-valued distribution, one would find the area between 44.5 and 55.5 under the matching normal curve. It is appropriate to use a normal curve for binomial distribution approximation if the binomial meets the conditions that both np and $n(1 - p)$ exceed the value of five.

An important concept in the study of sampling distributions is the Central Limit Theorem. The theorem states that the sampling distribution of a sample summary statistic, say the sample mean $\overline{X}$ or sample proportion $\hat{p}$, approaches the form of a normal distribution for large sample sizes. Interestingly, the theorem holds regardless of the underlying shape of the original population's distribution from which the samples are drawn. For the sampling distribution of $\overline{X}$, the mean of the distribution $\mu_{\overline{X}}$ will equal the population mean $\mu_X(\mu_{\overline{X}} = \mu_X)$. The dispersion of the sampling distribution $\sigma_{\overline{X}}$ will vary inversely with the size of n, as can be seen from the formula:

$$\sigma_{\overline{X}} = \frac{\sigma_X}{\sqrt{n}}$$

This means that a quadrupling of n cuts $\sigma_{\overline{X}}$ in half.

Another important case of interest is the sampling distribution of the sample proportion $\hat{p}$. Its mean $\mu_{\hat{p}}$ equals p, the population proportion, and its dispersion is:

$$\sigma_{\hat{p}} = \sqrt{\frac{p(1 - p)}{n}}$$

Again as the formula shows, a fourfold increase in the sample size n lowers the dispersion of $\hat{p}$ by fifty percent.

These features of the sampling distribution will be used in the next two chapters to construct inference statements about the underlying population parameter from a one sample value of $\overline{X}$ or $\hat{p}$.

Footnotes and References

[1] For a good discussion of this approach to data analysis, see *Conversational Statistics* by Harry Roberts, Hewlett Packard Co., 1975.
[2] Merton Miller and Daniel Orr, "Mathematical Models for Financial Management" *Selected Paper No. 23* (Chicago, University of Chicago Graduate School of Business, 1966).

Questions and Problems

1. Distinguish whether the random sampling is from a binomial distribution or from a normal distribution.

a. sampling numerical grades from a large number of grades

b. sampling business schools with respect

to AACSB accreditation
c. sampling firms with respect to net income over net worth
d. sampling accounts receivable with respect to uncollectible status
e. sampling from a large number of job applicants with respect to their years of experience
f. sampling from the large number of New York Stock Exchange returns over the past year

2. The following statements are true or false. If false, explain and offer a reasonable way of correcting them.
a. The binomial distribution takes on a symmetrical shape only when $p = .5$ regardless of the sample size.
b. The binomial distribution should always be normalized for computational accuracy.
c. The smaller the size of the sample, the more confident one should be in using a standardized normal distribution to approximate the binomial.
d. The use of the standardized normal table will always give more accurate probability calculations than the use of the binomial table.
e. The normal curve shouldn't be used to approximate the binomial when the binomial random variable takes on values smaller than zero.
f. Samples of size 1 give a sampling distribution equivalent to the original distribution.

3. Calculate the area under the normal curve between the following two values.
a. $Z = 0$ and $Z = .40$
b. $Z = 0$ and $Z = -.40$
c. $Z = .65$ and $Z = 2.65$
d. $Z = -.65$ and $Z = -2.65$
e. $Z = -.80$ and $Z = -1.20$
f. $Z = -1.20$ and $Z = 1.20$
g. $Z = -2.0$ and $Z = 1.45$
h. $Z = +1.58$ and $Z = -1.58$

4. Calculate the area under the standard normal probability curve:
a. to the right of $Z = .58$
b. to the left of $Z = -1.25$
c. to the right of $Z = -.66$
d. to the left of $Z = -1.30$
e. between $Z = 1.48$ and $Z = 1.33$

5. Find the appropriate Z value, Z_c, that partitions the area under the Z distribution such that
a. the probability to the right of $Z_c = .01$, or $P(Z > Z_c) = .01$
b. the probability to the left of $Z_c = .05$, or $P(Z < Z_c) = .05$
c. the probability within $\pm Z_c = .68$, or $P(-Z_c < Z < Z_c) = .68$
d. $P(Z > Z_c) = .10$
e. $P(Z < Z_c) = .1314$
f. $P(-Z_c < Z < Z_c) = .90$
g. $P(-Z_c < Z < Z_c) = .99$

6. Suppose X is a normally distributed random variable with mean 125 and standard deviation of 25. Convert the probability expression for X in terms of Z and then determine the probability
a. $P(50 < X < 125)$
b. $P(X < 100)$
c. $P(125 < X < 155)$
d. $P(100 < X < 150)$
e. $P(X > 125)$
f. $P(X > 45)$

7. Observed price earnings ratios (market price per share divided by earnings per share) can provide useful information to financial analysts. Suppose the distribution of P/E ratios across the stocks are approximately normally distributed with a mean value of 9.2 and a standard deviation of 5.2. For the purpose of screening the lower 10% of the P/E ratio stocks "for more intensive analysis in the hope they are currently undervalued in terms of price for the level of earnings," what should be set as the critical screening P/E value?

8. As vice president of operations for a state wide bank with 16 branches, you wish to formulate bank policy for the installation of an ATM (Automatic Teller Machine) system. The pilot program installed an ATM at a single branch location considered typical by past records. After several months of operations, the figures of monthly usage were shown to follow a normal distribution pattern with a monthly average of 1140 transactions and a standard deviation of 96 transactions. Historically these figures can be assumed to be the population monthly usage pattern.

a. If 1000 transactions represent a break-even point for ordering an ATM, what is the pilot program's chance of failing to reach this figure in a given month?

b. As a bank officer you are more concerned with the break-even point of the proposed ATM system to be installed in all the 16 branches. Assuming all branches follow the same normal distribution as the pilot branch, what is the chance that the break-even average of 1000 transactions per branch will not be achieved in a given month by the entire system? Compare this result with that in (a).

9. Suppose a business student in a class presentation on small businesses cites the census data on the dollar sales volume as follows:

> Average = 1.5 million
> Standard Deviation = 1.1 Million
> Distribution is said to be normal

What would your reaction be?

10. One of the key components required in performing an analysis of a firm's financial ratios is its degree of financial leverage. The degree of financial leverage reflects the use of debt to fund the firm's assets and is measured by the ratio of total debt to total assets. The higher the ratio, the greater the use of debt and degree of financial leverage, and the higher the financial risk to the firm since debt *requires* interest payments be made generally every six months regardless of earnings level. Assume in 1979 all the chemical firms had a mean debt ratio, in percentage terms, of 43.3% with a standard deviation of 11.2%. The chemical firm you were given to analyze has a debt ratio of 36.5%. How unusual is the degree of financial leverage the firm uses relative to the industry at this time? Assume a normal distribution.

11. Candy manufacturers believe that there is a "right" price to charge for slot machine candy. Wanting to hold the "right" price of the candy bar at 25¢ in spite of the dramatic rise in chocolate prices, the manufacturer has no alternative but to reduce the size of the bar. The chocolate dis-pensing apparatus needs to be reset. If the amount of chocolate coating on a bar is normally distributed with a standard deviation of .05 ounces, what average setting will cause 95% of the production run to have candy bars with no more than .5 ounces of chocolate coating?

12. Spier Industries, a high technology firm, requires constant infusions of new capital for research and development and growth. As the parent company of a wholly owned subsidiary, PPD Drilling, Spier views PPD Drilling as a "cash cow"—a chief source of cash from operations. PPD Drilling pays back fifty percent of after-tax profit as cash dividend and is designed to serve Spier's cash flow needs. The annual after-tax profit probability distribution for PPD Drilling is assessed to have a mean of 16 million and a standard deviation of 3.4 million. If after-tax profit falls below 10 million, given its burdensome dividend policy, PPD will have to go to the market and borrow to maintain its plant and equipment. What is the probability that additional debt financing would be required?

13. E-Z Chicken Enterprises operates 140 fast food franchises in Southern California. Each franchise uses three infra-red heating lamps on a full time basis to prevent the fried food from getting cold and unappetizing. At the beginning of the fiscal year and the new operating budget, new lamps were installed. Assume that the life of the new lamps can be treated as a normally distributed random variable with a mean life of about 90 days with a standard deviation of 18 days. How many would be expected to fail by the end of first quarter?

14. Given the circumstances in Problem 13, how many lamps should E-Z Chicken Enterprises stockpile quarterly to be 99% sure (only 1% risk) that E-Z's supply of lamps will not be exhausted before next quarter's shipment?

15. The replacement of parts at specified time intervals instead of when they fail is called preventive maintenance. It lowers the shutdown cost of lost production time as well as the cost that occurs with the

disruption of service. Additionally, maintenance is scheduled to coincide with off peak time periods. Consider once again the use of heating lamps in Problem 13. To hold down the failure rate during operating hours, all the lamps are replaced after a specific period of operation. How often must the lamps be replaced in order to have 90% assurance that no more than 2% fail between the replacement times.

16. On your breakfast flight from Chicago to Hilo, Hawaii, your UAL steward hands you a colorful menu which ends with the "friendly skies" saying, "If by chance your choice is not available due to previous passenger selection, please accept our apology." The entree selection offers a choice of Farmer's Omelette or French Toast. Historical records suggest a slight preference for French Toast, .55, to .45 for the omelette. If there are 425 passengers on the Jumbo 747 what is the probability that more than half will order the omelette?

17. Suppose in the airline meal service Problem 16, the airline decided to take a 5% chance (risk) of having to apologize to a passenger for not having his first choice of breakfast entree for the 425 passengers on the jet. How many orders of French Toast should UAL carry on the flight?

18. No-shows—reservations made in which the customer does not arrive—are a nagging, common (sometimes costly and embarrassing) problem to both the airline and motel-hotel industries. It is standard policy for reservation agents to "overbook" reservations in excess of capacity, counting on the fact that historically some percentage of the confirmed reservations are no-shows. A large metropolitan hotel has found that 4% of its reservations during early Spring months of the year will be no-shows. If because of a convention schedule, the hotel has accepted ten excess reservations for its 140 room hotel, what is the probability that all the customers with a valid reservation will be able to have rooms?

19. Suppose in Problem 18, the hotel wants to accept reservations so that there is no more than a 10% chance that a valid reser-

vation cannot be honored. How many reservations should be accepted? What if the room capacity was 180 rooms?

20. Assume (as recent investments research suggests) that the commodity markets can be played naively as a fair game (chance of winning equal to chance of losing) on a daily basis. But daily trading (buying and selling on the same day) incurs brokerage commission costs *causing* the chance of losing to be slightly greater than the chance of winning, so the probability of losing $= .53$ while the probability of winning $= .47$. What is the approximate chance of ending up a loser (losing more times than winning) if you play the market

a. one week (5 trading days); hint: $P(3$ or more losses)?

b. two weeks (10 trading days)?

c. one month (25 trading days)?

d. one year (250 trading days plus two weeks needed vacation)?

e. What conclusion do you come to about your chances of being declared a loser when trading naively (moving in and out of the market on the basis of information already known and discounted by the market)?

f. Do you think the assumption of naive trading is questionable? In what way?

21. Considering the situation in Problem 20, how many days of trading are needed to be .99 sure that the trader would be a loser?

22. *Cost-Volume-Profit (C-V-P) Analysis, I* Probabilistic C-V-P analysis allows a financial manager to compare the risk involved for each alternative product under consideration by the firm, as well as to compare the relative break-even point and expected profit. Suppose the manager assumed that sales quantity is a random variable with a mean or expected value, $E(Q)$, of 60,000 units and with an equal chance that sales will be greater or less than the 60,000 units. Further marketing information suggests there is about a $\frac{2}{3}$ chance that actual sales will be within 5000 units of the mean: $\sigma_Q = 5000$. Overall therefore the sales can be viewed as a normally distributed ran-

dom variable around the 60,000 units mean value. Assuming that the selling price is certain at $2 per unit above variable cost per unit and that fixed cost is certain at $100,000, the break-even volume, Q_B, that follows is,

$$Q_B = \frac{\text{Fixed Cost}}{\begin{array}{c}\text{excess of price}\\\text{over variable cost}\end{array}}$$

$$= \frac{\$100,000}{\$2} = 50,000 \text{ units}$$

The expected profit, $E(Z)$, at mean level sales is therefore

$$E(Z) = \$2E(Q) - F$$
$$= \$2(60,000) - \$100,000$$
$$= \$20,000$$

and standard deviation of profit, $\sigma(Z)$ is

$$\sigma_Z = \$2\sigma_Q$$
$$= \$2(5,000) = \$10,000.$$

Since the probability distribution of sales quantity is normal, the probability distribution of profits will also be normal with $\mu_Z = \$20,000$ and $\sigma_Z = \$10,000$ as just shown.

a. Compute the probability of at least breaking even (profits equal zero).

b. Compute the probability of profits being greater than $35,000.

c. Compute the probability of incurring losses.

d. Compute the probability of the loss being greater than $25,000.

23. *C-V-P Analysis II* You as financial manager receive a sales forecast for next year of 25,000 units from the marketing research department. It has also indicated that the probability is .75 that actual sales would be between 20,000 and 30,000 units. Assume that sales are normally distributed.

a. Find the value of the standard deviation of sales, in units.

b. Calculate the probability that sales will be greater than 32,000.

c. If fixed expenses are $50,000 and excess of price over variable cost is $5 per unit, compute the probability that the firm will break even on this product in the coming year.

24. Fill in the normal probability values for Table 10.5, page 355. (Parts a–d)

e. If the firm's top management is unwilling to accept a loss because the financial distress caused would seriously impair the ability of the firm to stay in business, which product should be chosen?

f. If the firm's top management feels that any product with a probability of loss greater than .3 ought not be accepted, which product(s) would be acceptable?

g. The firm's top management believe high profit products are attractive so long as the probability of losses are low and easily controlled. Specifically, the firm is willing to accept a product proposal if the probability of profits greater than $275,000 is at least .35, provided that probability of a loss greater than $200,000 does not exceed .10. Which project meets this qualification and is most attractive?

25. Suppose a decision on two mutually exclusive Interferon projects face a genetic engineering firm, Gensystems. Each project costs $4.5 million and both projects have an expected cash flow of $5.0 million; the respective standard deviation of cash flow is .63 million for Project A and 1.26 million for Project B. The cash flow can be assumed to follow a normal distribution.

a. Fill in the values in Table 10.6.

b. Plot the cumulative normal probability for the cash flows for Project A and Project B on one graph and draw a separate curve for each project connecting the points plotted.

c. Designate on the graph how to determine the probability of achieving the break-even cash flow for each project. What is the estimated probability for each project?

d. Determine and compare the chance that Project A will yield more than $6.0 million to the chance that Project B will yield $7.0 million or more.

e. Besides the risk profile of the two projects what else would be useful in choosing between the projects?

26. Melanie's Novelty Shop has a cash management problem. She faces, on average, a positive net cash inflow in the first twenty days of the month but negative net cash

TABLE 10.5. Probability of Profits and Losses by Product

| | PRODUCTS OF THE FIRM | | |
	(1)	(2)	(3)
Expected Profit	$200,000	$200,000	$200,000
Standard Deviation of Profit	225,000	275,000	450,000
The Probability of:			
a. At least breaking even	_____	_____	_____
b. Profit at least $150,000	_____	_____	_____
c. Profit at least $275,000	_____	_____	_____
d. Loss greater than $200,000	_____	_____	_____

TABLE 10.6. Probability of Cash Flow for Two Projects

PROJECT A		
Cash Flow (Millions)	Z Value	Cumulative Normal Probability
3.0		
4.0		
5.0		
5.75		
6.00		
7.00		

PROJECT B		
Cash Flow (Millions)	Z Value	Cumulative Normal Probability
2.0		
3.0		
4.0		
5.0		
5.75		
6.00		
7.00		
8.00		

outflow during the last ten days of the month. She wants to know how much cash to have on hand at the end of day 20, if her previous experience shows that the cumulative net cash outflow during the last ten days are normally distributed with an average value of $750 and a standard deviation of $150. Assume that Melanie is willing to take a 5 percent chance of running out of cash.

27. Look again at Melanie's cash situation in Problem 26. Now consider the impact of a very tight credit market, especially for a small business which, if it could borrow, would face borrowing rates in excess of 25%. To avoid the dire consequences of running out of cash, Melanie has now taken on a very risk-averse attitude and wishes no more than a .5 percent chance of running out of cash. How much cash should she now have on hand on day 20?

28. *Commercial Bankers and the Law of Averages* Commercial bankers lend out their depositors' money to someone else everyday. Why don't the bankers lose sleep over the fact that the bank has lent out money which will have to be paid out when the depositors write checks against their deposits? A basic reason is the law of averages. Assume that a bank has 2500 depositors, each of whom maintains an average balance of $500. Net changes in the account balance occur because of deposits and withdrawals. Assume that the standard deviation of the net changes in an account's balance is $500 over a specified period of time (like a day or a week). Assume that changes in different depositors' account balances occur independently of changes in other account balances.

a. What is the standard deviation of the change in the *mean* account balance over the specified period of time?

b. What is the probability that the *mean* account balance will fall below $450 during the specified period of time?

c. Explain in your own words how the law of averages enables a banker to lend out a depositor's money and yet not be worried that there won't be enough cash to meet depositor withdrawals.

d. Why is the assumption of independent balance changes so important? How realistic do you believe the independence assumption is?

Estimation

Preview. This chapter begins the study of statistical inference. This subject builds upon our previous study of probability and sampling distributions.

In the three preceding chapters we studied the characteristics of probability distributions of sample statistics for randomly drawn samples in which the parameters of the population were known to the investigator. By learning about the features of the probability distribution of the sample statistic, one is able to make probability statements about finding a sample statistic in sampling from a population.

In this chapter we consider cases where the population parameter is unknown. We have only a single sample, and will have to estimate the underlying population parameters from it. By applying our knowledge of the sampling distributions, we can come up with good population estimates from samples.

11.1. Point Versus Interval Estimation

In estimating a population parameter, a *point* estimate is distinguished from an *interval* estimate. A point estimate is a single value guess about the parameter and hence makes no allowance for the uncertainty about its accuracy as an estimate of the parameter. To estimate by an interval recognizes the uncertainty about the accuracy of the point estimate and compensates for it by specifying a range of values around the point estimate within which the population parameter may actually lie. That is,

interval estimate = point estimate + allowance for uncertainty.

Let's consider point estimates first, beginning with the desirable properties of a good estimator and then move on to the interval estimate as an approach to estimation.

11.2. Criteria for a Good Estimator

There is a distinction between the terms point *estimate* and point *estimator*. The former is the actual numerical value used as the estimate of the population parameter. The latter is a rule or method which tells us how to calculate this value. Considering the sample statistics which we have already encountered, we can say that,

$\overline{X}$ is an estimator of μ, the population mean;
$\hat{p}$ is an estimator of p, the population proportion.

Three criteria are usually used to evaluate the desirability of a point estimator. The criteria are *consistency*, *unbiasedness*, and *efficiency*.

Consistency

A consistent estimator distinguishes itself by its ability to come closer and closer to the population parameter as the sample size becomes larger and larger. In other words, the reliability of a consistent estimator becomes greater with larger sample sizes.

The sample mean, $\overline{X}$, is a consistent estimator of the population mean, μ. The sample proportion, $\hat{p}$, is a consistent estimator of the population proportion, p.

Unbiasedness

For an estimator to be unbiased, the mean of the probability distribution of the sample statistic used as the estimator must meet an important condition. It must have a value equal to the value of the unknown population parameter being estimated. For instance, if the unknown population parameter $\theta = 10$ then the mean of the sample statistic $\hat{\theta}$ must equal 10 ($\mu_{\hat{\theta}} = 10$). Note, do not confuse the concept of bias used here with *the way in which the sample items are drawn*. If the mean of the estimator's probability distribution is not the population parameter, the estimator is biased.

> The mean of the sampling distribution of $\overline{X}$, $\mu_{\overline{X}}$, is equal to the mean of the population from which the sample was taken, μ. Hence, the sample statistic $\overline{X}$ is an unbiased estimator of the population mean μ.

> The sample proportion, $\hat{p}$, is an unbiased estimator of the population proportion.

> The sample variance, S^2, is an unbiased estimator of the population variance, σ^2.

Efficiency

If two unbiased estimators are available, the one having the tightest (least dispersed) distribution of estimation error about the target population parameter is said to be the more efficient of the two. For unbiased estimators, the error in estimating the population parameter of interest has an important property. It is identical to the sampling error of the sample statistic since the mean of the probability (sampling) distribution equals the target population parameter. Hence, the standard deviation of the sampling distribution will be identical to the standard deviation of the estimation error. This is shown in Figure 11.1, in which the mean of the sampling distribution for the unbiased estimator is located at the same point as the parameter value you are trying to estimate.

For a biased estimator, the inherent sampling error that comes with sampling will not be identical to the estimation error. Regrettably, the estimation error will

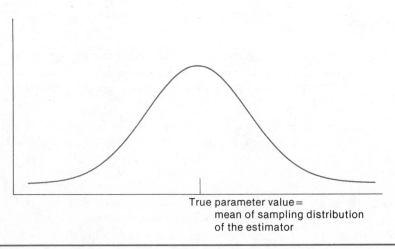

True parameter value=
mean of sampling distribution
of the estimator

FIGURE 11.1 Comparison of Parameter Value and Mean of Sampling Distribution for Unbiased Estimator

on average exceed the sampling error. By how much? That will depend upon the amount of bias. This is shown in Figure 11.2, in which the center and the bulk of the sampling distribution for the biased estimator are located far away from the parameter value you are trying to estimate.

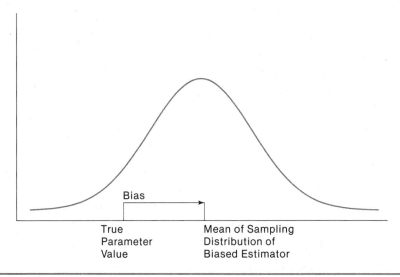

FIGURE 11.2 Comparison of True Parameter Value and Mean of Sampling Distribution of Biased Estimator

This means that an estimator can have the lowest standard deviation of *sampling* error but may not be the one having the lowest standard deviation of *estimation* error. The relationship between estimation error, sampling error, and bias is given below:

$$\frac{\text{variance of estimation}}{\text{error distribution}} = \frac{\text{variance of sampling}}{\text{error distribution}} + \text{bias}^2$$

The concept of efficiency combines the two attractive features, small sampling variance and small bias. It perhaps is the most important desirable criterion for judging the attractiveness of an estimator.

Inefficiency of Using Sample Median to Estimate the Population Mean

How does the sample mean stand with respect to the criterion of efficiency? To measure the efficiency of the mean as an estimator, you need an available alternative estimator to compare the mean. Although you may not ordinarily regard the median as your choice as estimator of the population mean, it is an unbiased estimator of the mean if the distribution is symmetrical. Moreover, there are situations in which the sample mean is not known or cannot be computed and the median can be found. The median will then be the only choice as an estimator of the population mean. But, when both are available and unbiased estimators, how does the mean compare in efficiency with the median? As expected, the mean is more efficient provided the underlying population distribution is normal. The probability distribution of the sample median has a variance equal to 1.57 times the variance of the distribution of the sample mean. This makes the sample median 57% less efficient as an estimator of the population mean. Importantly in considering sampling cost, it means that, if the median is used as the estimator, a sample would have to be 57% larger to have the same variance of estimation error that the sample mean achieves.

11.3. Interval Estimate of the Population Mean— Large Sample with σ Known

A point estimate alone provides no way to assess the uncertainty of the estimate. Why not then express the estimate as a *range* of values within which the population parameter is thought to lie? This is the idea underlying an *interval estimate*. Expressing the estimate in the form of an interval openly acknowledges the fact that sample statistics from a sampling process are not usually exactly on the target unknown population parameter being estimated. With the actual value of the population parameter unknown, constructing an interval in this way still does not guarantee the investigator that the interval estimate is correct. This is formally recognized by attaching to the interval estimate a number called the degree of *confidence* or the *confidence level*. The purpose of the confidence level is to report on the reliability of the sampling process. That is, how often would accurate interval statements about the population parameter result if the procedure were repeated many times? The interval estimate constructed is called a *confidence interval*. Its lowest value is called the *lower confidence limit*, abbreviated as LCL. The highest value is called the *upper confidence limit*, abbreviated as UCL.

It is convenient to think of the construction of a confidence interval estimate in two stages: first, establish a range of values centered on the sample statistic computed from the sample data, say around the computed $\overline{X}$; second, adjust the constructed interval for any bias known to cause the mean of the probability distribution of $\overline{X}$ to differ from the value of the population parameter being estimated. If no bias exists, the second stage is eliminated and the interval estimate obtained in the first stage is left unchanged. This is the case for all the interval estimates we shall study.

Procedure for Constructing a Confidence Interval for the Population Mean—σ Known

To construct a confidence interval for the population mean when the population standard deviation is known and the population is normally distributed, we suggest the following procedure:

1. Choose the level or degree of confidence desired, designated by $1 - \alpha$. The notation $1 - \alpha$ indicates that our confidence about our procedure is less than the certainty of 1 by the probability level α. The symbol α then reflects the probability and amount of risk accepted that the confidence interval procedure will err in making an inference statement about the unknown

parameter. When inference is made by hypothesis testing (discussed in the next chapter), it again represents the chance of error and the risk accepted by using the hypothesis testing procedure to reject a specified value as the unknown parameter value. The use of α in this same sense in both inferential procedures reflects the fact that there is a complementary relationship between the two inferential procedures. The particular value set for $1 - \alpha$ rests on the judgment of the investigator. The values popularly chosen for $1 - \alpha$ are .90, .95, and .99.

2. From the table of areas of the standard normal curve, locate the *confidence coefficient* corresponding to the degree of confidence chosen in step 1. With the sampling distribution of, say, $\overline{X}$, normally distributed, set the $1 - \alpha$ level of confidence equal to the probability area under the normal curve. See Figure 11.3a. This provides for the probability under the curve to be divided between both sides of the distribution. If the $1 - \alpha$ level of confidence is .95, then .475 of the probability is on each side of the mean of the distribution and $\alpha/2$ indicates .025 in each tail. How many standard deviations cover .475 of the probability area to leave .025 in each tail? The answer is the confidence coefficient, $Z_{\alpha/2}$. For example, if the confidence level $1 - \alpha$ is .90, then the confidence coefficient $Z_{\alpha/2}$ must leave .05 of the area in each tail. The $Z_{\alpha/2}$ value to do this equals 1.64. See Figure 11.3b.

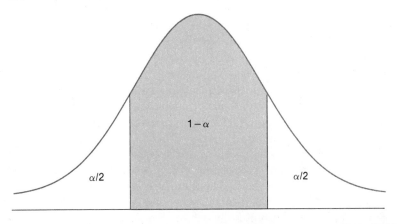

FIGURE 11.3a The Level of Confidence and Risk in Using Confidence Interval Estimation

3. Compute the standard deviation of the sampling distribution. Since σ is assumed to be known, the value of $\sigma_{\overline{X}}$ is equal to $\sigma/\sqrt{n}$.

4. Find the upper confidence limit from the expression $\text{UCL} = \overline{X} + Z_{\alpha/2}\sigma_{\overline{X}}$

5. Compute the lower confidence limit from the expression $\text{LCL} = \overline{X} - Z_{\alpha/2}\sigma_{\overline{X}}$

Thus, the confidence interval encompasses the range $\overline{X} \pm Z_{\alpha/2}\sigma_{\overline{X}}$.

With each sample drawn, only one confidence interval can be constructed for a given confidence level. Repeated sampling, known as a *sampling process*, will

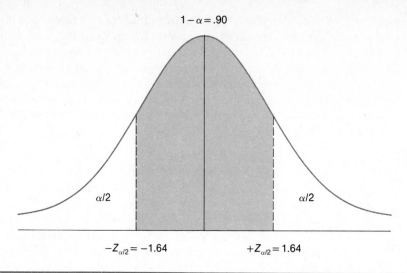

FIGURE 11.3b The Correspondence between Z Values and Level of Confidence

lead to different intervals. Each will have the *same* width but their locations will differ depending on the value of $\overline{X}$ obtained for the particular sample. Figure 11.4 illustrates the different locations of the confidence intervals constructed from the $\overline{X}$s of ten hypothetical samples from the population.

Must the computed confidence interval actually include the value of $\mu_{\overline{X}}$? Of course not, because the range covered by the confidence interval depends upon the value of $\overline{X}$ which, because of sampling error, is likely to be different from the value of $\mu_{\overline{X}}$. Figure 11.4 clearly shows that most of the intervals do include $\mu_{\overline{X}}$, but not all of them. *Which* confidence intervals will include $\mu_{\overline{X}}$ and therefore be accurate interval estimates of $\mu_{\overline{X}}$? It is *the intervals constructed from samples for which the value* of $\overline{X}$ falls within $\pm Z_{\alpha/2}\sigma_{\overline{X}}$ of $\mu_{\overline{X}}$ (shaded area in Figure 11.4). And in repetitive sampling, what proportion of the constructed confidence intervals meet this requirement? The proportion will be equal to the probability (area) under the curve, set off by the level of confidence chosen. For example, with a confidence level of 95%, 95% of the intervals will contain the parameter. After all, the level of confidence was purposefully set so that the confidence intervals constructed have a high chance of containing $\mu_{\overline{X}}$. In short, the confidence level is equal in value to the probability of obtaining a random sample with a sample mean $\overline{X}$ within $Z_{\alpha/2}\sigma_{\overline{X}}$ of the sampling distribution's center, $\mu_{\overline{X}}$. And with this recognition, the confidence level represents an assuredness that the intervals formed will embrace $\mu_{\overline{X}}$.

An important connection must now be made linking this procedure for constructing confidence intervals and the original purpose of the investigation.

So far, the confidence interval $\overline{X} \pm Z_{\alpha/2}\sigma_{\overline{X}}$ has been described only as an estimate of $\mu_{\overline{X}}$, the mean of the sampling distribution. However, our original intent was to make an inference about the parameter μ_X, the mean of the population. Fortunately this does not pose a problem, because $\mu_{\overline{X}} = \mu_X$; that is, there is no bias between the target μ_X and the mean of this sampling distribution, $\mu_{\overline{X}}$. The confidence interval for $\mu_{\overline{X}}$ is also the confidence interval for μ_X.

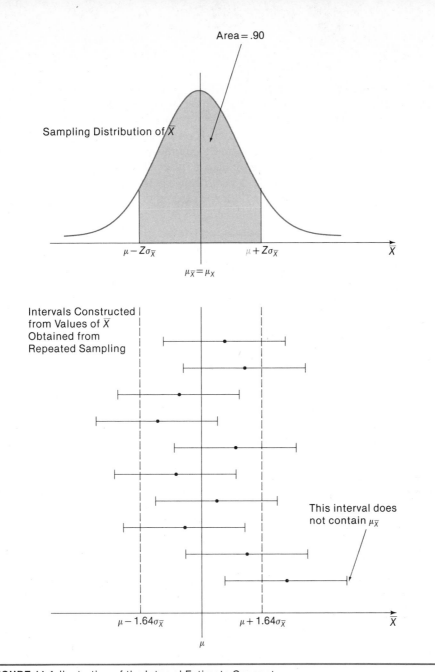

FIGURE 11.4 Ilustration of the Interval Estimate Concept

Interpreting a Confidence Interval

The concepts of a confidence interval and the level of confidence are closely allied to the concepts of error tolerance and reliability, respectively, discussed in previous chapters. Error tolerance and reliability refer to the *sampling process before-*

hand; confidence interval and confidence level are terms applied to the actual interval estimate of the parameter made *after* a particular sample result has been realized. A given sample leads to the construction of only one confidence interval and that interval is *the* estimate of the population parameter. When constructed the interval either does or does not include the population mean; at that point the interval is a correct estimation interval or an incorrect estimation interval. It cannot be (say) 95 percent correct. Thus, when we state that we are 95 percent confident that the confidence interval estimate includes the population mean, we are referring to the process used to generate the intervals. Ninety-five percent of the time it generates correct intervals. A given constructed interval, though, is either all correct or not correct at all. The following example illustrates the construction and interpretation of a confidence interval.

Example 11.3. Food Portion Control

Restaurants generally try to maintain control over food costs. One way is to control the portions of expensive food served to customers. Meat is one of these items. If not closely monitored, food costs can skyrocket. Suppose a deli-restaurant manager wants to monitor the portions of meat put into the sandwiches: turkey, corned beef, roast beef, ham, pastrami, etc. Even when food preparers are instructed to put a specific number of ounces of meat in a sandwich, there will be variation in the actual weight due to the nuisance and difficulty of adhering to the rigid standards. Let's assume that the variation of weight around the standard can be viewed as normally distributed with standard deviation of $\frac{1}{2}$ ounce. The standard deviation does not depend on the weight of meat set as the standard. A sample of $n = 64$ sandwiches is randomly selected and the meat portion weighed precisely. The sample mean is $\bar{X} = 5.20$ ounces. What is the 95 percent confidence interval estimate of the true or population mean weight of the sandwiches?

Solution: The confidence interval encompasses the range $\bar{X} \pm Z_{\alpha/2}\sigma_{\bar{X}}$. The upper and lower limits of the range are found according to the following five steps:

1. The confidence level $1 - \alpha$ is given in the problem as .95.

2. Find the confidence coefficient corresponding to a .95 confidence level. From the table of area under the normal curve, the confidence coefficient is found to be $Z_{\alpha/2} = 1.96$, since it associates with leaving .025 area in each tail of the distribution.

3. Find the standard deviation of the sampling distribution, $\sigma_{\bar{X}}$. Since $\sigma = \frac{1}{2}$ ounce and $n = 64$ sandwiches,
$\sigma_{\bar{X}} = \sigma/\sqrt{n} = (\frac{1}{2})/\sqrt{64} = .0625$.

4. The upper confidence limit is given by $\bar{X} + Z_{\alpha/2}\sigma_{\bar{X}} = 5.20 + 1.96(.0625) = 5.32$ ounces.

5. The lower confidence limit is found from the relationship
$LCL = \bar{X} - Z_{\alpha/2}\sigma_{\bar{X}} = 5.20 - 1.96(.0625) = 5.08$.

The confidence interval then is 5.08 to 5.32. Although we don't know that this interval embraces the unknown mean, we are sure that on average 95 out of 100 intervals formed this way will embrace the unknown mean.

For the situation in the above example the population standard deviation was known and the population was known to be normally distributed. The presence of both of these conditions allows us to assert that the sampling distribution of $\overline{X}$ must also be a normal distribution regardless of the size of the sample. What if the population standard deviation is known as before, but the population distribution is assumed not to be a normal distribution? In this situation the sampling distribution for $\overline{X}$ is only approximately normal and then only if the sample is large. In both situations, however, the same procedure is followed to find the upper and lower confidence limits.

11.4. Interval Estimation of the Population Mean— Large Sample with σ Unknown

The preceding example on the issue of food portion control assumed foreknowledge of the population standard deviation σ from previous investigation of this issue. Practically speaking, foreknowledge of σ is not commonly the case. Usually there are no previous studies from which σ is known, or if there have been studies the value of σ is not applicable to the new study. This latter situation will occur, for example, if the value of σ is related to the value of μ (which in fact it often is). In other words, if there is reason to believe that μ changed from what it was, there is often also reason to believe that σ has also changed. So what is the investigator to do if it cannot be assumed that σ is known?

With the sample mean $\overline{X}$ and the sample standard deviation S available from the sample, it is always possible to use the sample standard deviation as an *estimate* of the population standard deviation σ. However, since S is not generally equal to σ, there is additional inaccuracy presented by using S instead of σ. For large samples this additional inaccuracy is minimal. The main result of introducing inaccuracy about σ is that a more widely dispersed distribution called the *Student t distribution* has to be used. This distribution was named by the statistician W. S. Gosset who published under the assumed name "Student".

Instead of the previously used Z statistic and its standardized normal distribution, the *t-statistic* and its Student t distribution is used. The formula is:

$$t_{n-1} = \frac{\overline{X} - \mu_{\overline{X}}}{S_{\overline{X}}}$$

where the subscript $n - 1$ denotes a number one less than the sample size, called the *degrees of freedom*, abbreviated d.f. The degrees of freedom parameter determines the character of the Student's t distribution. This character—shape and properties—changes as the level of degrees of freedom changes. Figure 11.5 shows the standardized normal distribution and two Student t distributions, one based on 5 degrees of freedom, the other based on 25 degrees of freedom.

As can be seen, the t distribution with 25 d.f. is quite close to the normal curve. This explains why the normal distribution can be used to approximate the actual sampling distribution when the sample is large and σ is unknown. It also explains why samples above thirty or forty are usually regarded as large samples. When the degrees of freedom exceed thirty or thirty-five, the t distribution is virtually indistinguishable from a normal distribution because the value of S is very close to that of σ.

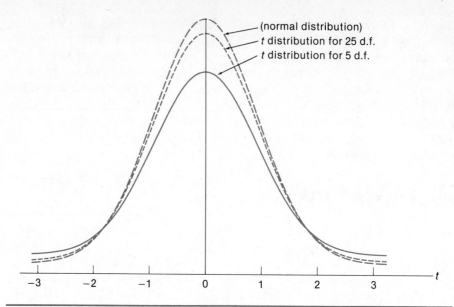

FIGURE 11.5 Comparison of Normal Distribution and Student t Distributions

Thus as a practical matter, the table for the normal distribution can be substituted to find the confidence coefficient. When the value of S replaces the value of σ, the value of $\sigma_{\bar{X}}$ is replaced by the value of $S_{\bar{X}}$ which is computed from:

$$S_{\bar{X}} = S/\sqrt{n}$$

The range of the confidence interval now becomes:

$$\bar{X} \pm Z_{\alpha/2} S_{\bar{X}}$$

Thus, the computational procedure for the confidence interval for large samples with σ unknown is as follows:

Step 1: Choose the confidence level $1 - \alpha$.
Step 2: Find the confidence coefficient $Z_{\alpha/2}$ from the normal curve table.
Step 3: Compute $S_{\bar{X}} = S/\sqrt{n}$.
Step 4: Compute the upper confidence limit: $\text{UCL} = \bar{X} + Z_{\alpha/2} S_{\bar{X}}$
Step 5: Compute the lower confidence limit: $\text{LCL} = \bar{X} - Z_{\alpha/2} S_{\bar{X}}$

The following example illustrates the confidence interval procedure when σ is unknown.

Example 11.4.   Estimating Supermarket Checkout Times

The manager of a large supermarket wants to achieve more effective scheduling of checkout personnel. She feels it will be helpful to know, on average, how long it takes an efficient clerk to handle a customer at the checkout counter. One hundred randomly chosen transactions handled by the efficient clerks are selected. The mean time per transaction, $\bar{X}$, is found to be 3.25 minutes, with a standard deviation, S, of 1.50 minutes. What is the 99 percent confidence interval for the mean time per customer transaction?

Step 1: The confidence level $1 - \alpha$ is given in the problem as .99.

Step 2: Find the confidence coefficient Z from the table of the normal curve. For $1 - \alpha = .99$, the $Z_{\alpha/2}$ value of 2.58 leaves .005 area in each tail of the distribution.

Step 3: Compute $S_{\bar{x}} = S/\sqrt{n} = 1.50/\sqrt{100} = .15$ minutes.

Step 4: The upper confidence limit is determined from:

$$\text{UCL} = \bar{X} + Z_{.005}S_{\bar{x}} = 3.25 + (2.58)(0.15) = 3.64 \text{ minutes.}$$

Step 5: The lower confidence limit is determined from:

$$\text{LCL} = \bar{X} - Z_{.005}S_{\bar{x}} = 3.25 - (2.58)(0.15) = 2.86 \text{ minutes.}$$

Thus, the 99 percent confidence interval for the mean checkout time is 2.86 to 3.64 minutes.

11.5. Confidence Interval Estimate for the Population Proportion—Large Samples

Are the analytical principles underlying the construction of a confidence interval for the population proportion the same as for the population mean? For large samples from a population of attributes, where the conditions are sample size n greater than 30 and np and $n(1 - p)$ both larger than 5, the central limit theorem assures that the sampling distribution of the sample proportion $\hat{p}$ will be approximately normally distributed. However, both σ_p and $\sigma_{\hat{p}}$ will typically be unknown since the population proportion p is both the parameter of interest in our investigation and a required value in calculating these standard deviation values. That is,

$$\sigma_{\hat{p}} = \sqrt{\frac{p(1 - p)}{n}}$$

What should be done about the unknown value of p in the expression for the standard deviation of the sampling distribution? An obvious possibility is to substitute $\hat{p}$ for p and $1 - \hat{p}$ for $1 - p$ and use the result, which we shall call $S_{\hat{p}}$, as the estimated standard deviation of the sampling distribution:

$$S_{\hat{p}} = \sqrt{\frac{\hat{p}(1 - \hat{p})}{n}}$$

This is in fact what is almost universally done, regardless of the fact that $S_{\hat{p}}$ is a biased estimate of $\sigma_{\hat{p}}$ and, to be unbiased, the denominator would have to be $n - 1$ rather than n. Once the sample is large, the difference is trivial. Expectedly the substitution of $S_{\hat{p}}$ in place of $\sigma_{\hat{p}}$ introduces another source of error, but again it does not pose a problem for large samples. The procedure for constructing the confidence interval for p is as follows:

Step 1: Choose the confidence level $1 - \alpha$.

Step 2: Find the confidence coefficient $Z_{\alpha/2}$ from the normal table.

Step 3: Compute the value of $S_{\hat{p}} = \sqrt{\hat{p}(1 - \hat{p})/n}$.

Step 4: Find the value of the upper confidence limit from:

$$UCL = \hat{p} + Z_{\alpha/2}S_{\hat{p}}$$

Step 5: Find the value of the lower confidence limit from:

$$LCL = \hat{p} - Z_{\alpha/2}S_{\hat{p}}$$

The following example illustrates the confidence interval procedure for estimating a population proportion.

Example 11.5.   A Work Sampling Application

In Example 8.6 the important management tool of *work sampling* was first introduced. We shall now illustrate that technique. Let us suppose an office administrator wants to know what proportion of the time a copying machine operator actually spends making copies compared to being in attendance on other assigned duties. A total of 400 observations were taken at random times during the study period. On 112 of these occasions the operator was making a copy. Thus,

$$\hat{p} = 112/400 = .28.$$

What is the .95 confidence interval estimate of the proportion of time the operator spends making copies?

Step 1: The confidence level is given in the problem as $1 - \alpha = .95$.

Step 2: The normal curve table shows a confidence coefficient $Z_{\alpha/2}$ of value 1.96 associated with a tail area of .025.

Step 3: The value of the standard deviation of the sampling distribution is found from:

$$S_{\hat{p}} = \sqrt{\frac{\hat{p}(1 - \hat{p})}{n}} = \sqrt{\frac{(.28)(.72)}{400}} = .0224$$

Step 4: The upper confidence limit is computed from:

$$UCL = \hat{p} + Z_{.025}(S_{\hat{p}}) = .28 + 1.96(.0224) = .28 + .044 = .324$$

Step 5: The lower confidence limit is computed from:

$$LCL = \hat{p} - Z_{.025}(S_{\hat{p}}) = .28 - 1.96(.0224) = .28 - .044 = .236$$

Thus, the .95 confidence interval is .236 to .324.

11.6. Small Samples

Is the confidence interval estimation procedure affected by a small sample, say one of size less than 30? In the case of the population mean we distinguish three situations.

The population is normal and the standard deviation is known. In this case the sampling distribution of the Z statistic is standard normal with standard deviation $\sigma_{\bar{X}} = \sigma/\sqrt{n}$. In other words, there is no change from the large sample case, so the procedure of Section 11.3 applies without alteration.

The population is normal but the standard deviation is not known. In this case the sampling distribution of the t statistic is a t distribution with $n - 1$ degrees of freedom. The procedure for constructing a confidence interval is:

Step 1: Choose the confidence level $1 - \alpha$.

Step 2: Find the confidence coefficient, $t_{\alpha/2,\,n-1}$ corresponding to the confidence level chosen in step 1. This is found from the Appendix table for the Student t distribution using $n - 1$ degrees of freedom.

Step 3: Compute the standard deviation of the sampling distribution: $S_{\bar{X}} = S/\sqrt{n}$.

Step 4: Compute the upper confidence limit from: $\text{UCL} = \bar{X} + t_{\alpha/2,\,n-1}(S_{\bar{X}})$.

Step 5: Compute the lower confidence limit: $\text{LCL} = \bar{X} - t_{\alpha/2,\,n-1}(S_{\bar{X}})$.

The population is not normal and the standard deviation σ is not known. If the deviation from normality is not severe, the procedure described in step 2 above will give the approximately correct confidence for the interval constructed; the alternative approach is nonparametric methods discussed in Chapter 22. Let us illustrate the calculation described in the second situation, that of a normally distributed population with σ unknown.

Example 11.6. Estimating Construction Cost Errors

A construction company executive is involved with the problem of estimating construction costs on large bridge projects the company bids on. The executive believes the cost estimation errors are normally distributed, but does not know either the mean size of the error to be expected or the standard deviation of the error distribution. The company has recently completed seven bridge projects. The executive believes the errors on estimating the cost of these projects can be regarded as a random sample from the estimation process. The mean estimation error, expressed as a percentage of true completed cost, is -14.3 percent. The standard deviation is 9.1 percent. What is the estimated 90 percent confidence interval for the construction cost error percentage?

Step 1: The confidence level is stated in the problem as $1 - \alpha = .90$.

Step 2: The confidence coefficient is found from a Student t distribution with $n - 1 = 6$ degrees of freedom: $t_{.05,\,6} = 1.943$.

Step 3: The value of $S_{\bar{X}}$ is computed as follows:

$$S_{\bar{X}} = S/\sqrt{n} = 9.1/\sqrt{7} = 3.44 \text{ percent.}$$

Step 4: The upper confidence limit is computed from:

$$\text{UCL} = \bar{X} + t_{.05,\,6}(S_{\bar{X}}) = -14.3 + 1.943(3.44) = -7.62 \text{ percent.}$$

Step 5: The lower confidence is computed from:

$$\text{LCL} = \bar{X} - t_{.05,\,6}(S_{\bar{X}}) = -14.3 - 1.943(3.44) = -20.98 \text{ percent.}$$

Thus, the interval estimate of the estimation error is -7.62 percent to -20.98 percent. Although we don't know whether this interval embraces the unknown parameter, we know 9 out of 10 intervals formed this way will, *on average,* embrace the unknown parameter.

Before leaving the subject of small samples, it must be noted that the t distribution is *not* used in constructing interval estimates for a population proportion. If the sample size is small ($n < 30$) the binomial distribution is used.

Finally, it must also be noted that the treatment given in this chapter on the subject of confidence interval estimation assumes that the sample data are the only source, or at least the most important source, for information on the population parameter. This implicit assumption may not be valid, particularly in the case of small samples. In this case prior information available on the parameter can swamp the scarce amount of sample information. One approach to *a priori* information is discussed in the next chapter on hypothesis testing. Another approach is *Bayesian inference,* discussed in Chapter 23.

11.7. Interval Estimation for Sampling Without Replacement

The procedures for constructing confidence intervals presented so far have not considered the effect of population size. The samples were assumed to be drawn by a sampling process generating an infinite population (like work sampling) or a finite population in which the population was replenished after every draw (sampling with replacement). But what if sampling is done *without* replacement from a finite population?

When the population is very large compared to the size of the sample, the sampling distribution will be *nearly the same* no matter whether sampling is done with or without replacement. The procedures for constructing an interval estimate described already can be used without modification. Is there a rule of thumb to determine whether the population is very large relative to the sample size? A ratio guideline suggested is 20:1. That is, a population twenty times larger than the sample size allows us to disregard the effect of diminishing population size when sampling without replacement.

Adjustment to Account for Sampling Without Replacement

What modification in procedure is required if the population is small and the sample is taken without replacement? The sampling distribution of the sample statistic, say $\overline{X}$, will have a smaller variance. This will result in a smaller range for the interval estimate. Another slight adjustment will be made depending upon whether σ is known or unknown. If σ is known, the expression for $\sigma_{\overline{X}}$ is multiplied by the finite population correction factor $\sqrt{(N - n)/(N - 1)}$. If σ is unknown, the correction factor that assures that $S_{\overline{X}}$ is an unbiased estimate of $\sigma_{\overline{X}}$ is $\sqrt{(N - n)/N}$. As a practical matter, using N rather than $N - 1$ changes the denominator little, so usually the latter version of the correction factor is used whether or not the value of σ is known.

The following example illustrates the confidence interval procedure for a sample drawn without replacement from a population too small to ignore the population size adjustment.

Example 11.7. Auditing Accounts Receivable

A retiring physician is anxious to sell his practice to another physician who would assume the collection of the patient accounts still outstanding. To settle on the asset value of these accounts, the auditor for the purchaser randomly sampled 242 of the 1476 patient accounts recorded on the selling physician's books as having an outstanding balance. The mean account balance was found to be $197.53 with a standard deviation of $87.35. What is the 95 percent confidence interval estimate for the mean account balance?

> *Step 1:* The confidence level is given in the problem as 95 percent.
> *Step 2:* From the normal curve table the confidence coefficient is found to be 1.96.
> *Step 3:* The standard deviation of the sampling distribution is found from:

$$S_{\bar{x}} = \frac{S}{\sqrt{n}}\sqrt{\frac{N-n}{N}} = \frac{87.35}{\sqrt{242}}\sqrt{\frac{1476-242}{1476}}$$

$$= \frac{87.35}{15.56}\sqrt{.836} = 5.61(.914) = 5.13$$

> *Step 4:* The upper confidence limit is computed from:

$$\text{UCL} = \bar{X} + Z_{\alpha/2}(S_{\bar{x}}) = \$197.53 + 1.96(\$5.13) = \$207.58$$

> *Step 5:* The lower confidence limit is computed from:

$$\text{LCL} = \bar{X} - Z_{\alpha/2}(S_{\bar{x}}) = \$197.53 - 1.96(\$5.13) = \$187.48$$

Thus, the interval estimate at the .95 confidence level is $187.48 to $207.58.

11.8. Confidence Interval for the Population Total

A sample may be taken for the express purpose of making an inference about the population total. The computation of the sample mean and the interval estimate of the population mean are transition steps for determining a confidence interval for the population total. Thus, in Example 11.7 the auditor's purpose is eventually to make an estimate of the total accounts receivable balances outstanding. The estimate of the *mean* balance is a critical step in making that estimate of the total.

   It is a simple matter to make an inference about the population total once an inference has been made about the population mean. Knowing the size of the population, the population total is simply the product of the population mean and the number of items in the population. That is,

   Population Total $= \mu N$

An estimate of the population total uses $\bar{X}$ as the estimate of the population mean. Thus, a point estimate of the population total is:

   Point Estimate of Population Total $= \bar{X}N$

In the auditing example given in the previous section, this leads to an estimate of:

$$\text{Point Estimate of Population Total} = \bar{X}N = (\$197.53)(1476) = \$291,554$$

A .95 confidence interval for the population total can be obtained by multiplying the upper and lower confidence limits for μ by the population size. Thus, in the auditing example, the upper confidence limit is found from:

$$\text{UCL} = N\,(\text{UCL for } \mu) = N(\bar{X} + t_{\alpha/2,\,n-1}S_{\bar{X}}) = 1476(207.58) = \$306,388$$

while the lower confidence limit is:

$$\text{LCL} = N\,(\text{LCL for } \mu) = N(\bar{X} - t_{\alpha/2,\,n-1}S_{\bar{X}}) = 1476(187.48) = \$276,720$$

The .95 confidence interval for estimating the population total is $276,720 to $306,388. It represents an interval from an estimating procedure which is reliable on average 95 times out of 100.

11.9. Determining the Required Sample Size: Sampling With Replacement

How large must the sample be to assure a sample result with a desired reliability level and error tolerance? The answer to the question is determined by satisfying the basic relationship,

$$Z_r \left[\begin{array}{l} \text{Standard Deviation of} \\ \text{Sampling Distribution} \end{array} \right] = \text{Error Tolerance}$$

where Z_r is the Z value needed for the desired reliability level. For instance, making an inference about μ, the population mean, with the aid of the sample mean, $\bar{X}$, requires $\sigma_{\bar{X}}$, the standard deviation of the sampling (probability) distribution of $\bar{X}$. The value of $\sigma_{\bar{X}}$ is given by:

$$\sigma_{\bar{X}} = \frac{\sigma}{\sqrt{n}}$$

Thus, substituting for $\sigma_{\bar{X}}$ and letting E represent the error tolerance, we have the basic relationship:

$$\frac{Z_r \sigma}{\sqrt{n}} = E$$

and by isolating n, it becomes:

$$\sqrt{n} = \left[\frac{Z_r \sigma}{E} \right]$$

$$n = \left[\frac{Z_r \sigma}{E} \right]^2$$

To determine n, the population value of σ must either be known or appropriately estimated, once the values of E and Z_r have been set.

In the case of an attribute variable, making an inference about p, the population proportion, through the aid of the sample result, $\hat{p}$, requires $\sigma_{\hat{p}}$. Since the value of $\sigma_{\hat{p}}$ is:

$$\sigma_{\hat{p}} = \sqrt{\frac{p(1-p)}{n}}$$

the basic relationship is now,

$$Z_r\sqrt{\frac{p(1-p)}{n}} = E$$

Isolating n we have,

$$\sqrt{n} = \frac{Z_r\sqrt{p(1-p)}}{E}$$

$$n = \left[\frac{Z_r\sqrt{p(1-p)}}{E}\right]^2$$

The population proportion, p, is the object of our inference. Obviously it is unknown and must be appropriately estimated for use in the equation. The most conservative estimate is the value .5. Why? Because it makes the product $p(1-p)$ the maximum value of .25. (Try your hand at exceeding .25 for any value of p you might choose. You'll find it can't be done.) With this product at a maximum, the required sample size that follows is the largest it can be, once Z_r and E are set. Thus the required sample size determined for $p = .5$ will always suffice no matter what the unknown p value is. The formula using $p = .5$ becomes:

$$n = \left[\frac{.5Z_r}{E}\right]^2$$

For example, to guarantee the sample proportion $\hat{p}$ has a .95 reliability level with a $\pm.02$ error tolerance around the unknown p value, the required sample size would have to be:

$$n = \left[\frac{.5(1.96)}{.02}\right]^2 = 49^2$$
$$= 2401$$

where 1.96 is the Z value for the .95 reliability level.

When is the above procedure applicable? It applies to three situations:

Situation One: when the sampling is from an infinite population
Situation Two: when sampling from a finite population with replacement
Situation Three: when sampling from a finite population without replacement where the sample size is small compared to the population size

Do Larger Populations Necessitate Larger Samples?

Is there a role for population size in determining the required sample size? A common thought is that when sampling from a larger population, one should take a proportionally larger sample. Yet curiously, the expression given for sample size does not include N, the population size, assuming sampling is done with replacement. Why? The chance of obtaining a particular $\hat{p}$ sample result is unchanged by the size of the population. For example, in the poker chip experiments described in Chapter 8, it is immaterial whether we draw and replace from an urn which contains five red and five white chips, fifty red and fifty white, or fifty million red and fifty million white. In each case the proportion of red chips is the same; therefore, the chances of obtaining any particular sample proportion $\hat{p}$ from a sequence of results still remains the same, no matter which urn you draw the sample from. To summarize:

> when a sample is drawn *with* replacement, the size of the population has absolutely no impact on the sample size required for the desired level of precision and confidence.

In short, the size of the population is irrelevant for the calculations.

How can the knowledge that the expression for sample size does not include a term for population size be put to good use in the business world? The following example provides a clue in that the cost to sample three different sized target audiences turns out to be identical.

Example 11.9A.   Estimating the Tonight Show Audience Size

The network television business pays constant attention to the percentage of television viewers in specific geographical areas who are watching their broadcast. Advertising revenue and the fortunes of the network depend on the network's ratings. A rating is based on the percentage of the TV-watching audience viewing the program. The rating of NBC's Tonight Show is based on an assessment of the percentage of the late night viewing audience tuned to the Tonight Show. What sample size is required for specific geographic areas to guarantee with a .95 reliability level that the obtained sample percentage is within a $\pm .02$ error tolerance of the true population percentage? Does it change with the area? According to what we have just learned, Situation Three applies. Under these stipulations of accuracy, estimation of the true percentage of viewers for specific geographic areas requires a random sample of only 2401 viewers from *each area*. That is, since Situation Three applies, the sample size required is the same regardless of whether the target audience is Cedar Rapids, Iowa, the State of New York, or the entire United States.

Economies of Scale in Information Gathering

What appeal results from this development? Finding out that the same sample size of 2401 households is needed for the State of New York, the whole United States, or for Cedar Rapids, Iowa provides a strong incentive for using mass populations in the gathering of information. In other words, there seems to be important economies of scale in gathering information. The following example shows how a national brewer like Budweiser or Millers gains a marketing cost advantage over a regional brewer like Stroh's.

Suppose both a regional brewer and a national brewer want to market survey the consumers of their beer. The regional brewer sells to a target market of 100,000 households, whereas the national brewer sells to a target market of 20 million. What is the cost per household in the two markets corresponding to a .95 reliability level with a ±10% error tolerance? Let's suppose a personal interview survey costs $10 per household surveyed and therefore $24,010 for the 2401 households surveyed. With the cost of administering the project added in, the total cost comes to $35,000. Spreading this cost over the entire target market gives the regional brewer a cost of $350 per thousand households in the regional market. This figure compares to the $1.75 per thousand households for the national brewer. The calculations show it is a lot cheaper per household to estimate the national brewer's market than it is to estimate the regional brewer's market.

The $10.00 out-of-pocket cost figure cited in the above example for personal interviews would be even lower for telephone interviews and mail surveys, perhaps $2.50 for telephone and half that for mail surveys. It should be noted that conducting a personal interview survey on a national basis generally entails higher costs than on a local basis for identical sample sizes. Ordinarily, a national survey involves more travel time and travel cost. What about the relative advantages of adding these costs? Typically, the costs are small compared to the per customer savings that come from adding customers to the population. With large research organizations usually having field personnel located in several cities, national sampling may not turn out to involve much extra cost at all. So there will still be important cost economies in sampling a large target market as compared to a small one.

11.10. Sample Size Versus Sample Precision

How do changes in the desired level of precision affect the required sample size? Is the price tag of improved precision too high? To answer these questions specifically, we shall fix the reliability level at .95 while changing (relaxing) the error tolerance from say ±.02 to ±.10.

Example 11.10A. Why Good Ballpark Estimates Can Be Inexpensive

What happens to the sample size requirement as we drop the error tolerance? Relaxing the error tolerance from ±.02 to ±.10 expectedly lowers the sample size requirement. But, does it drop dramatically? For an error tolerance of ±.02, we found n equaling 2401 to be the required sample size. The new error tolerance of ±.10 substantially reduces the required sample size all the way down to 96. The calculations are as follows:

$$n = \left[\frac{.5(1.96)}{.10} \right]^2 = 9.8^2 = 96$$

An estimate with a precision of ±10 percentage points is what many persons regard as a ballpark estimate. For many purposes this level of precision is quite satisfactory. The remarkable thing is how extremely inexpensive ballpark estimates can be. Let's use the $10 per respondent figure cited before, and turn to the problem of estimating the proportion of houses having central air conditioning. Fantastic as it may seem, a random sample of close to 100 houses can obtain for us a ballpark estimate (±10 percentage points) for the entire United States. At $10 per respondent, the cost comes to $960. What about ballpark estimates from telephone and mail surveys? This answer is cheaper yet. A ballpark telephone survey should cost a few hundred dollars and the cost for a ballpark mail survey would ordinarily be under $200.

Ballpark estimates come cheap, but very precise estimates do not. In order to halve the error tolerance, the sample size must be quadrupled.

Example 11.10B. **Why the Price of Highly Precise Estimates Is Usually Prohibitive**

To cut the error tolerance from ±.10 to ±.05 requires an increase in the sample size from 96 to 385. To cut the error tolerance from ±.02 to ±.01 requires an increase in the sample size from 2401 to 9604. And to cut the error tolerance to .005 (half percent), the sample size would have to be increased to 38416.

11.11. Sample Size Determination: Sampling Without Replacement from Small Populations

For samples drawn without replacement, the finite population diminishes at each draw. When the population is small, the loss makes a difference. No longer can that element be drawn from the population. To account for this reduction in population and reduction in the variability of outcome, a downward adjustment must be made. The adjustment reduces $\sigma_{\bar{X}}$ by a finite population correction factor. The value of $\sigma_{\bar{X}}$ becomes:

$$\sigma_{\bar{X}} = \frac{\sigma}{\sqrt{n_f}} \sqrt{\frac{N - n_f}{N - 1}}$$

where n_f is the sample size drawn from a finite population.

What does the adjustment factor tell us?

It recognizes that the sample size cannot exceed the population size. When every member of the population is sampled, the value of n_f equals N and the numerator of the second term becomes zero as does the value of $\sigma_{\bar{X}}$.

It shows that with the assumption of a large population, the dropping of the −1 in the correction factor comes with negligible consequences.

Can one link the required sample size n_f for sampling without replacement to the required sample size n for sampling with replacement? Yes, and the formula is:

$$n_f = n \left[\frac{N}{N + n} \right]$$

This expression permits us to gain some insight into the relative sizes of n_f compared to N. For instance, the sample size of 2401 required for sampling with replacement would be reduced to:

$$n_f = 2401 \left[\frac{N}{N + 2401} \right]$$

if the sample is taken without replacement. For a population of 100,000 items, the sample size would be reduced to

$$n_f = 2401 \left[\frac{100,000}{100,000 + 2401} \right] = 2345$$

This is less than a three percent reduction, barely enough to notice. But, for a population of 1000 items, the sample size would be:

$$n_f = 2401 \left[\frac{1000}{1000 + 2401} \right] = 706$$

This is a 71 percent reduction and illustrates the savings potential in the cost of sampling.

Take Larger Samples from Small Populations

People who rely on uneducated intuition are likely to go astray when it comes to the sample size requirement. They tend to vastly *understate* the sample size needed for small populations and vastly *overstate* the sample size needed for large populations. To check your intuition let's calculate the sample size needed for the Tonight Show survey, if there are only 100 homes in the target population.

$$n_f = 2401 \left[\frac{100}{100 + 2401} \right] = 96$$

Most people are startled to learn that 96 out of 100 homes have to be in the sample. The moral is this: it is hardly worthwhile sampling a small population. You may as well take a complete census and get the true value rather than an estimate.

Take Small Samples from Large Populations

Now let's try the other extreme—a very large population. For a population of 100 million homes, the calculations are as follows:

$$n_f = 2401 \left[\frac{100,000,000}{100,000,000 + 2401} \right] = 2400.9$$

Most people are very surprised to learn that the same reliability and precision that a 96 percent sample yields for a population of 100 homes can be attained with a 0.0024 percent sample when the population consists of 100 *million* homes. The moral here is, even when we sample without replacement, the percentage of the population surveyed is a very poor index of reliability and precision. Some consequences of failing to understand this point are brought out in the following example.

Example 11.11.   The Problem with 10 Percent Samples

There is a widespread belief that the sample selected should be some constant percentage of the population (often 10 percent). This percentage guideline about the "best" size sample to take is simply a foolhardy approach that can be costly and deceptive. Let's say that the relevant population contains 90,000 homes and that the desired levels of precision and reliability are as used before. Using the 10 percent "rule of thumb" and $10 per respondent, the total cost for conducting the survey would come to $90,000. The correct sample size of 2,339 would cost $23,390, permitting a $66,610 saving. Putting this another way, $66,610 was sent down the drain for information that wasn't needed.

With small populations, the danger in "rule of thumb" methods is that the desired level of precision and reliability will not be attained. Take a population of 1000 individuals. Using the 10 percent rule of thumb method would lead to a sample of only 100 persons, not nearly enough to yield the desired precision and reliability levels. Not having good information is bad enough, but using information you believe is much more accurate than it really is could have devastating consequences.

11.12. Managerial Issues in Practice—
Review Exercise: Estimating Population Size
by the "Tagging" Technique

As a market analyst for a truck rental company competing against U-Haul, you want to estimate the number of U-Haul 18 foot vans in their fleet. You could sample the trucks at randomly selected dealers, but there are always trucks on the road that would be missed. So you proceed as follows:

1. From the trucks parked at randomly selected dealer lots, you "tag" the 18 foot vans by recording their license plate numbers or other identifying marks so that if you see them again, you will know they come from this tagged group. Let the number of tagged 18 foot vans be designated by R.

2. Let enough time elapse to make it plausible to assume that the tagged trucks have been randomly dispersed among the U-Haul population of dealers.

3. Draw a second sample by again randomly selecting U-Haul dealers and then recording the license plate or other identifying features on their 18-foot U-Haul trucks. Designate the number of 18 foot vans in this sample by n.

4. Compare the vehicles in the second sample with the list of tagged vans from the first sample. Let the number of 18 foot vans that turned up in both samples be designated by x.

5. Compute the ratio x/n (the proportion of tagged vehicles found in the second sample).

a. Show how the ratio x/n can be used to estimate the number of 18 foot vans in the U-Haul fleet (a point estimate).

b. Show how to compute a 95 percent confidence interval for the number of 18 foot vans in the U-Haul fleet based on the ratio x/n. Assume that the sample is from a large enough population that the finite population adjustment can safely be ignored. (Note: This is not a crucial assumption. See Problem 42 at the end of this chapter for further consideration of the finite population adjustment.)

c. Suppose there are $R = 500$ (18 foot) U-Haul vans in the first sample and $n = 400$ vans in the second sample. In the second sample $x = 16$ vans are identified as having also been in the first sample. What is your point estimate and the .95 confidence interval estimate of the number of 18 foot vans in the U-Haul truck rental population?

Solutions:

a. The 18 foot vans in the U-Haul truck rental fleet are the population members. The total number of trucks in this population is denoted by N. The number of trucks spotted and tagged in the first sample is denoted by R. The ratio R/N is the *proportion p* tagged in the population. That is, $p = R/N$. By rearranging terms the expression for population size is obtained:

$$N = \frac{R}{p}$$

The numerator (R) of this expression is known; the denominator (p) is not known. However, p can be estimated by $\hat{p}$, the proportion of vans in the *second* U-Haul sample that were found to be tagged, indicating that they were also members of the first sample. The value of $\hat{p}$ is the ratio x/n. Thus a point estimate of the population size (denoted by $\hat{N}$) is given by:

$$\hat{N} = \frac{R}{\hat{p}} = \frac{R}{x/n} = R\left(\frac{n}{x}\right)$$

The point estimate of the population size is the product of the number of tagged vans in the population, R, and the ratio of the total number of vans in the second sample, n, to the number in that sample that were also in the first sample, x.

b. A 95 percent confidence interval for the number of 18 foot vans in the U-Haul fleet is found by replacing $\hat{p}$ in the expression for $\hat{N}$ given in Part a by the upper and lower limits of the confidence interval for p. Assuming a large sample size, the upper limit for p is $\hat{p} + 1.96\sqrt{\hat{p}(1 - \hat{p})/n}$; the lower limit is $\hat{p} - 1.96\sqrt{\hat{p}(1 - \hat{p})/n}$. Thus, substituting for $\hat{p}$ in the expression gives the upper and lower limits for N:

upper limit: $\dfrac{R}{\hat{p} - 1.96\sqrt{\hat{p}(1 - \hat{p})/n}}$ lower limit: $\dfrac{R}{\hat{p} + 1.96\sqrt{\hat{p}(1 - \hat{p})/n}}$

c. $R = 500 \quad n = 400 \quad x = 16$

Therefore, $\hat{p} = \dfrac{x}{n} = \dfrac{16}{400} = .04.$

The point estimate of the number of 18 foot vans in the U-Haul fleet is:

$$\hat{N} = \frac{R}{\hat{p}} = \frac{500}{.04} = 12,500.$$

The upper confidence limit is:

$$\frac{R}{\hat{p} - 1.96\sqrt{\hat{p}(1-\hat{p})/n}} = \frac{500}{.04 - 1.96\sqrt{(.04)(.96)/400}} = 24,043$$

The lower confidence limit is:

$$\frac{R}{\hat{p} + 1.96\sqrt{\hat{p}(1-\hat{p})/n}} = \frac{500}{.04 + 1.96\sqrt{(.04)(.96)/400}} = 8,445.$$

Thus the width of the .95 confidence interval indicates that considerable uncertainty remains about the population size when this sample of 400 trucks is the basis for inference.

Many persons are greatly surprised to learn that a sample of 400 trucks is not enough to draw reasonably precise and reliable inferences about the population size. To attain greater accuracy, both the number of tagged trucks and the number of trucks in the second sample should be increased. Suppose the number of tagged trucks is increased to 1250 and the number of trucks in the second sample is quadrupled to 1600 trucks, of which $x = 160$ are found to be tagged. The point estimate of population size is 12,500 as before, but now the 95% confidence interval is reduced drastically in width. The lower limit becomes 10,898 and the upper limit becomes 14,653.

It should be noted that one cannot feasibly determine the population size in this problem by counting the individual trucks. They are not all accessible to the investigator. The tagging technique is a resourceful solution to these problems.

11.13. Concluding Comments

Among estimators of the population mean μ, the sample mean $\overline{X}$ scores well using the traditional criteria for evaluating an estimator. Thus, $\overline{X}$ is *consistent, unbiased,* and more *efficient* than the sample median. Although the value of $\overline{X}$ computed from a sample is a valid *point* estimate of μ, it is desirable to construct an *interval* estimate of μ which indicates how much confidence can be placed in the estimate. The width of the interval depends upon the level of confidence and the sampling distribution of $\overline{X}$. For large samples, the sampling distribution is normally distributed with mean μ and standard deviation $\sigma_{\overline{X}} = \sigma/\sqrt{n}$. If the value of σ is unknown, it can be estimated by the standard deviation S computed from the sample. For small samples, nonparametric methods (discussed in Chapter

22) must be used unless the *population* is normally distributed. In the latter case, the sampling distribution will also be normally distributed if σ is known. If σ is *not* known, one must rely on the Student t distribution with $n - 1$ degrees of freedom to make interval estimates of $\overline{X}$.

A large sample confidence interval for the population proportion p is centered on the sample proportion $\hat{p}$. The width of the interval depends upon the desired level of confidence and the value of $S_{\hat{p}} = \sqrt{\hat{p}(1 - \hat{p})/n}$. A small sample confidence interval for p must be based on the binomial distribution.

A confidence interval based upon sampling without replacement will be narrower than one based upon sampling with replacement if the sample size is a large percentage of the population size. However, a small sample drawn without replacement from a large population will give virtually the same interval width as for a sample drawn with replacement, assuming equal sample sizes.

In sampling with replacement, the sample size required to assure a given level of precision does not depend upon population size. Moreover, there are diminishing returns in precision to increased sample size. In sampling without replacement, population size does influence the required sample size. However, the percentage of the population sampled is a poor indicator of sample reliability. Small populations require a large percentage of the population in the sample; large populations do not.

Questions and Problems

1. Write a brief explanation of the distinction between the concepts *point estimate* vs. *point estimator.*

2. Explain the difference between the three properties of a point estimator: consistency, unbiasedness, and efficiency.

3. Pinpoint the distinction between the concepts *statistical bias* vs. *sampling error.*

4. Describe the difference in meaning between statistical bias and selection bias.

5. Look at the probability (sampling) distributions of two estimators, A and B, shown on page 382.
a. Is the criterion of unbiasedness possessed by A, B, or both? Explain.
b. Your goal is to pick the estimator which conveys the greater stability in successive samplings. Which one, A or B, possesses this property? Why?
c. Your goal is to use an estimator which exhibits sampling errors that balance out in repeated sampling.
d. How does the criterion of efficiency combine both the stability and balancing

of sampling errors concepts? Which would you consider the more efficient, A or B? Explain.

6. Draw a rough sketch, highlighting the difference between the sampling distribution of the mean and median when the underlying population is normal.

7. From a large number of nighttime viewers in San Diego, a simple random sample of 1000 people is taken to estimate the percentage of viewers in San Diego who watch ABC Nightline News. It turns out that 357 of the viewers interviewed are Nightline watchers. With the sample percentage ($357/1000 \times 100$) at 35.7% and the standard deviation of the sample percentage ($100\sqrt{(.357)(.643)/1000}$) at 1.5%, is it valid to say that the chances are .95 that the true percentage lies within the range 35.7% $\pm$ 2 (1.5%)? Explain.

8. At a large Southern California university, 25% of the students are in the business school. A simple random sample of 1000 students surveyed on the need for a foreign language course requirement. Is the chance

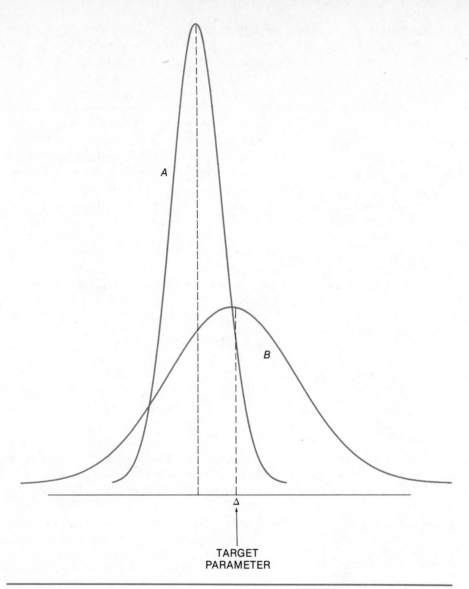

A

B

Δ

TARGET
PARAMETER

_____

PROBLEM 11.5

about two in three (one standard deviation) that the percentage of business students in the survey will lie in the range
25% ± 1.4% ($S_{\hat{p}} = 100\sqrt{(.25)(.75)/1000} =$
1.4%)? Explain.

9. Given a population with parameters
mean $\mu = 79$ and standard deviation σ
$= 12$ (assume a normal distribution):

a. Calculate the probability that, for sample
of size one, the sample mean will fall
within the interval 76 to 82.

b. Calculate the probability for a sample of
size 9 that the sample mean will fall within
the interval 76 to 82.

c. Calculate the probability for a sample
of size 81 that the sample mean will fall
within the interval 76 to 82.

d. Compare a, b, c and summarize the findings as samples increase ninefold.

e. How large a sample is needed to assume
with 99% confidence that the sample mean
will fall in the 76 to 82 interval?

10. Given a random sample with mean $\overline{X} = 79$ and population standard deviation $\sigma = 12$ drawn from a normal population, calculate for a sample of size 9 the degree of confidence that the population mean lies within the interval 76–82.

11. Do the same for a sample of size 81.

12. How much did the increase in sample size affect the degree of confidence?

13. "A random sample of the preference of 50 T.V. viewers in L.A.'s two million viewer market will provide as reliable an estimate of viewer preference as a random sample of the preference of 50 T.V. viewers in San Diego's 700,000 viewers market." Assuming that the preferences are the same, is this a questionable statement? Explain.

14. Citibank of Rancho Bernardo is in the process of organizing. You are hired by the charter investors to draw up a prospectus for a public offering of common stock of 500,000 shares at $6.25 a share. In creating the description for the stock offering, you have decided to state target deposit levels of $1 million by the end of the first month. Studies you have examined suggest that by the end of the first month the amount of deposits have stabilized with no trend up or down and can be represented as a normal distribution with a monthly average of $1.25 million and a standard deviation of $.3 million per month.
a. Compute the chance you are taking of the bank failing to reach this first month figure assuming the normal distribution given above is applicable.
b. Assuming that deposits will follow over the next year the normal distribution found in the studies, what cumulative total deposits figure range would you want to quote to have a 99% chance of being right, given the studies you examined?

15. Probability is connected with the sampling procedure beforehand, not with the parameter afterwards. The confidence level identifies the way the interval estimates are formed. On page 384 is a MINITAB simulation of 60 different intervals formed from the sample mean of the different samples, each of size 9, using the commands NRAN (for random sampling from a normal distribution) and ZINT (for Z confidence coefficient intervals). The population mean is 10 and standard deviation is 15. As one can see an interval either covers or doesn't cover the population mean, indicated by the heavy vertical line.
a. What is your best guess as to the level of confidence used to construct the intervals? On average, would changes about your best guess more likely occur with more or fewer intervals generated? Explain.
b. Could you place a mark showing the value of the mean found in the seventh sample? Why are all the intervals of the same size but have different sample means?
c. Would your best guess on the level of confidence change if you found out that the sample size used is 2500? What would you change about the intervals with respect to its length and centerpoint?
d. Why aren't interval estimates constructed at the 100% confidence level to guarantee that the population parameter is covered?
e. If the ZINT command used both the sample mean $\overline{X}$ and the sample standard deviation S from the NRAN command instead of using $\sigma = 15$ to construct the interval, what would change with respect to the interval's length and centerpoint?

16. A survey is taken to update census data on water usage in Riverside county. From the population of manufacturing firms employing over 25 employees, 58 firms from a simple random sample of 625 drawn use water in the manufacturing process. Estimate at the .95 confidence level the percentage of all manufacturing firms employing over 25 employees which use water in the manufacturing process. Ignore the finite population effect.

17. Suppose a simple random sample of 625 is taken from the population of employees obtained from the state withholding tax rolls for the manufacturing firms in Problem 16. The sample results show that 330 employees were working in firms utilizing water as a direct input on the

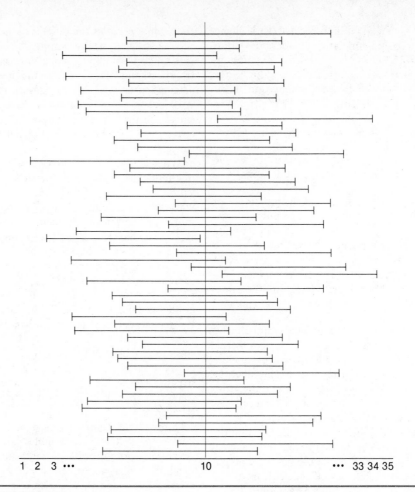

1 2 3 ···   10   ··· 33 34 35

PROBLEM 11.15

manufacturing process. Estimate, at the .95 confidence level, the percentage of people employed that are working in firms that use water in the manufacturing process for the population of firms employing over 25 persons. Ignore the finite population effect.

18. Compare the results in Problem 16 to the results in Problem 17. Do you think the difference in the percentages observed is caused by sampling error? If not, what interpretation would you offer?

19. A week-long sampling study of the productivity of the secretarial pool was conducted at a commercial publishing house. It revealed that for observations made at random times, one or more secretaries were idle 15 of the 100 recordings. Construct a 90% confidence interval for the percentage of the time that one or more secretaries are idle. Explain the meaning of the calculated interval.

20. As financial manager of IVAC, a corporation producing plastic sterile intravenous fluid-infusion sets and other medical plastics, you are responding to the highest level of short term credit in the last five years. By changing IVAC's credit terms to encourage early cash payments, you hope to reduce the money tied up in accounts receivable. The current terms offer a 1% discount on the purchase price if payment is made in 10 days; otherwise total payment with

no discount is due in 30 days (that is, 1/10/net 30). The new terms increase the discount to 3% (that is, 3/10/net 30). To set up the company's short term financing plan, an estimate of the average account receivable balance under the new credit terms needs to be assessed. You are relatively confident that the company's experience over the next billing cycle with the collection of accounts receivable will be representative of those for the coming months. A random sample of 60 accounts receivable collected from the accounts receivable ledger since the new credit terms were imposed is given in Table 11.1.

TABLE 11.1. Age of Account Receivables at Time of Collection (Numbers from 1—60)

01–10	11–20	21–30	31–40	41–50	51–60
27	28	11	8	10	31
28	29	29	10	24	28
29	29	9	30	7	29
10	9	10	10	27	25
30	8	11	28	6	10
6	11	30	28	7	5
8	28	31	29	10	7
10	32	10	9	8	20
29	10	11	27	24	27
11	27	12	9	27	11

a. Starting at any point on a random number chart, pick five successive two-digit numbers, discarding duplicates and numbers over 60. Select the account receivable corresponding with the five numbers. List the elements that represent a random sample of five accounts receivable with respect to their age.

b. What is the mean collection age in the sample? Is this an unbiased point estimate of the mean collection time for *all* accounts receivable? What is your estimate of the standard deviation of the sample mean? Interpret.

c. On inspection you notice that the majority of accounts either pay off early to obtain the cash discount or pay off near the 30th day to avoid delinquency. Should this affect the size of the sample you take to get

a good (closer) estimate of the mean collection for *all* the accounts?

d. Recognizing that you probably will get a closer estimate of the underlying mean by sampling more accounts, you continue to sample as before increasing the sample size to 10. What is your point estimate of the mean collection time now? Is it an unbiased estimate? What is your estimate of the standard deviation of the sample mean?

e. On average, do you expect the standard deviation (the uncertainty surrounding your estimate) of the sample mean to be cut in half by taking samples of 10 rather than 5? Explain.

21. In an investment seminar entitled "Gems: the Investment Vehicle to Financial Security" you became engrossed in the following conversation with the speaker. "According to my strategy," he says, "the average investment in my large gem portfolio will return about 12% per quarter." "Oh?" you say, "Is my return on gems normally distributed?"

"Just about perfectly," he answers, "with a standard deviation of about 1%."

"But," you reply, "according to the *Gem Quarterly* to which I subscribe, I see that diversified gem portfolios had a population quarterly return of only 6%."

"Well, I guess I'm doing better than most," he quickly replied.

Assuming both the 1% standard deviation and 6% mean figures are the true parameters, is the speaker's description of his return distribution believable? If not, why not? Assuming the speaker's quote about the standard deviation and about $\overline{X} = 12\%$ per quarter, what is the highest value you would expect the average return on gems to be and the lowest value, using a 90% confidence interval?

22. Your Mira Mesa Law Clinic has a word-processing system on a lease with option-to-buy condition and currently is evaluating the performance of the accompanying $10,000 picture-ready printer unit. Printers commonly come with a service contract, but the printers that can minimize shutdown cost will be the most attractive. Shutdown cost includes the opportunity cost

of lost time and out-of-pocket expenses of salaried employees left idle. The down time lapse between the point of break down and the start-up point showed an average of $4\frac{1}{2}$ hours with a standard deviation of 2 hours for sixteen observations. Assume a normal distribution for lapse time is plausible. Construct a 98% confidence interval estimate for the printer's mean "down" time per breakdown. Using the upper confidence limit as the underlying true mean down time, how probable is it that a printer remains down an entire 8 hour day?

23. As a consultant in personal financial planning serving professionals in the R.B. area, you are recommending to four of your clients a $60,000 second trust deed ($15,000 each) as a high yield, medium risk investment vehicle. Typically, a second trust deed is a borrower's promise to pay the loan plus interest backed up by the borrower's equity in the borrower's home. To assess the market value of the home securing the loan, the selling price of a sample of comparable tract homes sold in the last six months were found. The selling prices, in thousands, of the houses sold were: 113, 104, 119, 107, 110, 108, 112, 107.
a. Calculate the value of s, the standard deviation of selling prices, for $n = 8$.
b. Determine some bounds (say with 95 percent confidence) for the range of values that estimates the true mean selling price of all comparable homes.
c. Give the assumptions made and their plausibility, in coming up with the interval.

24. "It is the absolute size of the sample that counts, not the size of the population, even when sampling without replacement. For example, a sample of size 36 drawn without replacement from a population of 36,000 will provide almost as accurate an estimate of the population mean as a sample of size 36 drawn without replacement from a population of 360,000, given that the standard deviation σ in both populations are equal." From the value of the finite population correction factor, $(N - n)/N$, in calculating $\sigma_{\bar{X}}$, show that this is a reasonable statement to make.

25. A prospective corporate buyout of Learning System Press (LSP), a commercial publishing house, by Scott Freman (SF), an international commercial publishing house, is being reviewed. A preliminary audit of LSP's books reveals that 10 out of a random sample of 36 titles have been selling on average 11,000 copies or more over the past 5 years. Calculate a .95 confidence interval estimate for the proportion of titles selling on average 11,000 copies or more over the past five years for all LSP's 300 titles.

26. A human resource consulting team reporting on executive stress found that the exercise time for a random sample of 50 of the company's 325 executives averaged 17 minutes per week with a sample standard deviation of 10 minutes per week. Calculate a .98 confidence interval as an estimate of the population mean exercise time of all executives and interpret this interval.

27. As part of its job enrichment program for its middle management, a firm has agreed to pay for all the MBA tuition cost up to two courses per semester. Four hundred signed letters of intent to enroll were received from managers taking advantage of the enrichment program. To gain some attitudinal information about the program as well as an estimate of tuition expense for next year's budget, the personnel department picked and interviewed a random sample of 50 from the 400. A survey indicated that next year's average cost per manager will be $2500 with a standard deviation of $625. Calculate the interval estimate of the total cost at a .95 confidence level for all 400 managers.

28. A marketing survey at Apple Computer Corporation reveals that eight percent of a sample of 2000 households plan to consider buying a home computer during the Christmas holidays. Assuming that the sample can be viewed as an unbiased random sample of the 25 million household target market population, calculate a .98 confidence interval estimate of the total unit demand for home computers among the household population.

29. a. For a sample size of 25, what is the standard deviation of the sample percentage $\hat{p}$ if the population percentage is $p = .2$? If $p = .4$? If $p = .5$? If $p = .6$? If $p = .9$? What conclusion does the calculation suggest about symmetry? the value of p producing the greatest value for the standard deviation? the value of p producing the lowest value for the standard deviation?

b. Assuming that $p = .5$, calculate the standard deviation of the sample percentage if n is quadrupled from 25 to 100 and in turn $n = 100$ is quadrupled to 400? Just how does the successive quadrupling affect the size of the standard deviation?

30. The normal distribution can be relied on as a good approximation of the under-lying binomial distribution under certain conditions. Can we use the normal distribution for making inferences about the population proportion (percentage) if $p = .0075$ and $n = 400$? If $p = .1725$ and $n = 400$? Explain with respect to the figures below.

31. a. Calculate the standard error of the sample percentage if (1) $p = .5$, (2) the sample size is $n = 100$, (3) the population size N is 400 and (4) sampling is done without replacement.

b. Compare the result with the calculation made in Problem 29b in which $n = 100$. Explain.

32. To meet cash needs and to invest excess cash, firms transfer funds in and out of

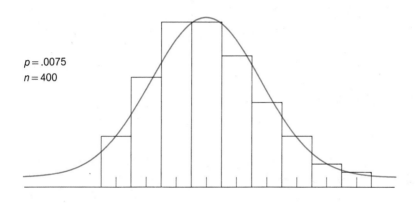

$p = .0075$
$n = 400$

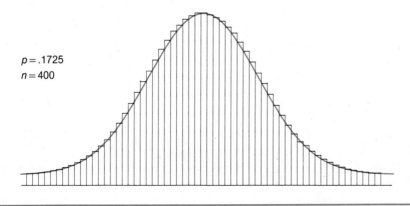

$p = .1725$
$n = 400$

PROBLEM 11.30

their interest earning marketable securities portfolio. Too many small transfers incur excessive out-of-pocket transfer costs, while too large a transfer results in lost interest. A firm wants to evaluate the performance of its treasurer. How large a sample of transfer actions is required to obtain an estimate of the average size of transfer that is within $1500 of the amount the treasurer is actually making? A .95 reliability level is wanted and the previous year's standard deviation of $5000 is believed to be a reasonable value to use.

33. Local financial institutions are engaged in an advertising war to convince the public that differences exist between their services. You, a marketing manager, at the Poway Bank of Trust and Commerce have decided to blitz the media with the slogan, "Doing More for You." To measure the extent of slogan recognition that has been achieved, county area households are surveyed by telephone a week after the media exposure. You wish the error between the estimated sample percentage and the true population percentage to be no more than $1\frac{1}{2}$ percentage points, with a confidence coefficient of 95 percent.
a. How large a sample is required if the p used is the maximum value of .5?
b. If the telephone survey cost $2.00 per call plus a $400 set-up cost, how much should the entire telephone survey cost?

34. Consider the work sampling information in Problem 19.
a. A new productivity study was requested with the qualification that the true percentage of idle time for one or more secretaries be within three percentage points of the point estimate given. How many observations will guarantee this for sure? Guarantee it at the .99 confidence level?
b. If the percentage of observations showing one or more secretaries idle increased to 20%, would the calculated sample size required in (a) be larger or smaller? Explain.

35. Your employer, a large Los Angeles amusement park, is planning its children's T.V. programming budget. With the high price T.V. spots on Saturday morning, you

as marketing manager want to document your decision if prime Saturday time is the airtime you decide to buy. It is desired to estimate (1) the percentage of viewing children who watch Saturday morning T.V. within three percentage points at the 95 percent confidence level; (2) the mean viewing time of Saturday morning T.V. within 15 minutes at the 95 percent confidence level. Previous studies suggest a mean of three hours with an hour standard deviation for Saturday morning viewing.
a. What sample size of children needs to be interviewed to achieve both objectives?
b. If the setup overhead costs of a well designed survey is $25,000, plus $15 per interviewee, what total cost should be allocated for the survey?

36. Consider the information in Problem 35. What would be the additional cost if the confidence level were raised to 99 percent? What kind of market information would serve as a key input in determining whether to incur the additional cost?

37. Again consider the promotion problem faced by the Los Angeles amusement park owner in Problem 35. You, as marketing manager, are aware that Los Angeles has about four times as many youngsters as San Diego. You think it reasonable that the size of the simple random sample of children taken in each city to estimate the percentage that watch Saturday morning T.V. ought to reflect that 4 to 1 ratio. Wanting the same level of confidence and error tolerance in both cases, a sample size of 2000 is considered for L.A. and a sample of 500 for San Diego. Just how reasonable an approach is this? How did the sample size affect the accuracy of the estimation?

38. Tandy's sales and marketing department recognizes that the recent introduction of Apple II and Apple III represents a serious threat to their market share of the small home and office computer market. In response it has allocated $120,000 to survey the sales potential of its new competitive model in the TR line. The product is to be introduced regionally at its Radio Shack outlets and sales are to be closely moni-

tored for several months and include a follow-up interview of purchasers. This monitoring will provide an assessment of the market segment it is attracting along with average sales per store per month. Tandy can then estimate the total sales potential of the new model. Fixed costs for design and central administration are estimated at $30,000 and $2000 per store over the survey period. Past records of similar marketing surveys suggest a standard deviation of sales per store of 15 per month.

a. How large a sample can the budget accommodate? Using past records as a guide, what sampling error is expected for the estimate of the average sales per store per month?

b. Because of the administrative difficulties in a few stores, only 36 stores were used and the sales estimates for the period were 40 per month per store with a standard deviation of 12. Using this latter figure as a basis, project total annual sales for the 300 store chain. Calculate a .98 confidence interval about the estimate and interpret.

c. What chance is there that the estimated total annual sales will be off by 10,000 or more either way? Off by 20,000 or more either way?

39. How large a sample would be needed to estimate the mean life of a production run of new 5 year car batteries within 30 days, at the 99% reliability level? The standard deviation of previous testing was recorded at 200 days.

40. a. Using Problem 39, what would be the required sample size if the production run was for 20,000 batteries? For 10,000 batteries? What conclusion follows when these results are compared to the result in Problem 39?

b. Is the percentage sampled changing? If so, in what way?

41. *Mercury Pedal Vehicle Company* Mercury Pedal Vehicle Company is a large toy manufacturer specializing in children's tricycles. Mercury's New Products Division is currently considering the possibility of marketing a three-wheel fiberglass pedal vehicle as an alternative to the traditional children's tricycle. The latest version of this new fiberglass model has been dubbed "The Dynawheel".

In order to assess consumer reaction to the Dynawheel, the marketing research group plans to put some of the new vehicles in the hands of a random sample of children in the appropriate age group. The objective is to learn how children in the target market like the Dynawheel as compared to their own tricycles.

Among the many questions which it is expected that the consumer test will help answer are the following:
Is the Dynawheel

preferred over traditional tricycles?
liked by boys?
liked by girls?
durable? safe?
acceptable to parents?
used in place of or in addition to regular tricycles?

Children will use the Dynawheel for a three-month test period. At the end of the test period, the responses of the children and their parents will be recorded, collected, tabulated, and summarized for evaluation by the new product group.

Assume that the research staff has decided on a .95 reliability level for its marketing information. That is, once a tolerable level of error in estimating the incidence of some characteristic among the target population from a random sample has been specified, it is expected that the sampling procedure will guarantee a 95 percent chance of yielding a sample based estimate which does not exceed the tolerance level. Suppose the target population consists of 10 million potential customers (children).

a. The marketing staff estimates that the cost of the consumer test will run about $2000 plus $15 per respondent. The fixed portion covers the cost of preparing the questionnaire. The variable portion covers the cost of interviewing, data processing, and supplying participants with Dynawheels, which they will keep after the test is completed.

Complete Table 11.2 on survey costs. Hint: Compute the required sample size for sampling with replacement, then adjust for a finite population.

TABLE 11.2. Survey Costs

	ERROR TOLERANCE			
	±.10	±.05	±.02	±.01
Total survey cost				
Average cost per respondent				
Reduction in error tolerance (expressed in percentage points) from next higher category	—	5	3	1
Average cost per one-percentage-point reduction in error tolerance	—			

Compare your answers. Does tightening the error tolerance by tenfold (from ±.10 to ±.01) increase the sample size (check one):

_____ not at all?
_____ by substantially less than tenfold?
_____ by tenfold?
_____ by substantially more than tenfold?

b. Although marketing management is convinced that a favorable consumer reaction is essential for the ultimate success of the Dynawheel, they are also keenly aware of the importance of store buyer attitudes. A favorable reaction among department and discount store toy buyers is a virtual necessity in order to obtain the distribution required to make the Dynawheel a market success.

Suppose that marketing management wants to survey the reaction of store buyers to the Dynawheel. Assume that there are 200 key buyers and that a .95 reliability level is desired.

Compute the required sample sizes and population percentages in Table 11.3 in the event that the error tolerance is reduced from ±.10 to ±.05, ±.02, and ±.01.

TABLE 11.3. Sample Size and Population Percentages

	ERROR TOLERANCE			
	±.10	±.05	±.02	±.01
Sample Size				
Percent of Population				

Compare your answers for ±.01 and ±.10. Does tightening the error tolerance by tenfold (from ±.10 to ±.01) increase the sample size (check one):

_____ not at all?
_____ by substantially less than tenfold?
_____ by tenfold?
_____ by substantially more than tenfold?

c. Complete Table 11.4.

TABLE 11.4. Error Tolerance, Sample Size, and Population Size

ERROR TOLERANCE	PERCENTAGE OF POPULATION IN THE SAMPLE Population Size	
	10,000,000	200
±.10		
±.05		
±.02		
±.01		

In Table 11.4, compare the percentage of population required to attain a given error tolerance level for a population of 200 items with that for a population of 10 million items. Is the percentage for the *smaller* population (check one):

_____ about the same as the percentage for the larger population in every case?
_____ sometimes larger, sometimes smaller than the percentage for the larger population?

_____ always larger than the percentage for the larger population?

_____ always smaller than the percentage for the larger population?

42. In the review exercise at the end of this chapter, the objective was to estimate the number of 18 foot vans in the U-Haul fleet of rental trucks. It was assumed that the population would be large enough that the finite population adjustment ($\sqrt{1 - n/N}$) could safely be ignored. This approach was convenient because the adjustment requires knowing the value of the population size, N, when the object of the study is to make an inference about the value of N. An alternative to ignoring the finite population adjustment is to replace N by its point estimator, $\hat{N} = R/\hat{p}$. Rework Parts b and c of the review exercise using this alternative procedure.

Hypothesis Testing

Preview. In this chapter a different approach is taken on inference. The previous chapter on estimation provided an interval to estimate the population parameter from a sample. Sampling results were used with no conscious hypothesis about the population value. For instance, we might want to find out what proportion of TV viewers watch the Tonight Show and we have no idea what the answer will be. But there are times when we want to use sample information to verify or reject a plausible hypothesis about the parameter. In business, it is often the case that an innovative product must be tested for market receptivity. There are definite opinions on what constitutes a good entry, and test marketing produces sample results that can be evaluated for a decision. The hypothesis testing procedure described in this chapter can serve as an important element in a complete decision process.

12.1. Basic Concepts in Testing Hypotheses

12

In Chapter 11, we saw that the *sine qua non* for confidence interval estimation is the random sample. To make an inference about the relevant population presumes that the sample used to construct the confidence interval estimate is typical or representative of the samples that could have been drawn. This stipulation of representativeness requires that the sample be drawn randomly.

This chapter presents another approach to the use of a random sample to make an inference. The approach is different in purpose from inference through confidence interval estimation. The heart of the difference between the two approaches is the role of *a priori* information—information that allows one to form a plausible hypothesis about the value of the population parameter. Attention now focuses on whether the sample drawn is atypical if the stated hypothesis about the parameter is true. Rejection or acceptance of the stated hypothesis is a consequence of the degree of atypicalness of the sample.

Contrasting the Two Approaches

Confidence intervals are designed to infer a range of values within which the population parameter lies. Importantly, by the confidence interval procedure the information necessary to infer the range is furnished directly by the sample. Examining the confidence interval estimation procedure, say for the population mean, one finds that:

> the interval is centered at the value of the sample mean;

> the width of the interval around the sample mean depends on the value of the standard deviation of the sample mean, which is determined by the sample size and the standard deviation of the sample.

No *a priori* information is taken into account in making the inference.

A second inferential approach is hypothesis testing. Unlike the methodology of using sample information directly to construct the interval in confidence interval estimation, the methodology of hypothesis testing uses the sample evidence *indirectly* to draw an inference about the parameter. The focus in hypothesis testing is directed to a simple question.

> Does the sample evidence render implausible a particular parameter value hypothesized *a priori* as plausible?

The rejection of the plausibility of this particular hypothetical value establishes indirectly the plausibility of an alternative hypothesized value or range of values. This is the way that an inference is made about the value of the population parameter. The following example describes how the hypothesis testing approach can be used to evaluate schemes for getting rich quickly in the stock market.

Example 12.1A.   Challenging the Random Walk Hypothesis: Can Stock Market Pros Outperform Blindfolded Monkeys?

Schemes claiming to identify exploitable buying and selling opportunities in the stock market have attracted high interest over the years. One could accept the validity of these schemes at face value. Otherwise, testing is required. To establish whether a particular scheme is valid requires the application of a performance test to a sample from the population of stock market returns surrounding the event of interest.

Do the sampling results when tested conflict with the hypothesis that all schemes designed to "beat the market" are doomed to failure? More precisely, does an examination of the sampling evidence of stock market returns for stocks about to split or for stocks about to be listed on the Big Board offer convincing evidence that allows one to reject the "doomed to failure" philosophy?

Is there a statistical way of pitting sample evidence for beating the market against the "doomed to failure" hypothesis?

Burton Malkiel, author of *A Random Walk Down Wall Street,* states the argument and offers a way of testing it:

> In essence, the random walk theory espouses the belief that future stock market prices cannot be predicted. It says that a *blindfolded monkey* throwing darts at the newspaper's financial page *could select a portfolio that would do just as well* as one carefully selected by the experts. Therefore, investment advisory services, earnings predictions, and complicated chart patterns are useless.[1]

What is Malkiel suggesting? Make a performance comparison with the random walk strategy. Only if the sample results investigated are convincing enough to disprove the premise of the random walk hypothesis of stock price movements can the investor claim his scheme (stock splits, listing news, etc.) is a legitimate way of beating the market. What evidence would be convincing? So far the sample evidence suggests that the rate of return earned by different schemes represent no statistically relevant gain over and above what a blindfolded monkey would have earned naively by throwing darts.

Learning how to judge statistical relevance is one of the key concepts examined in this chapter.

Hypothesis Testing and Jury Trials

The logic used in hypothesis testing is similar to that used in jury trials in our legal system. The *a priori* hypothesis in hypothesis testing is like the starting trial premise: namely, the defendant is innocent. Now, the fact that a trial is conducted means that the prosecutor already has in mind an alternative hypothesis (guilty). But the jury presumes innocence because there is a high regard for the individual. The prosecutor's task is to *discredit the innocence hypothesis.* To persuade the jury, the prosecutor must present relevant evidence that shows beyond a reasonable doubt that the *a priori* hypothesis of innocence is no longer tenable. Does beyond a reasonable doubt mean that the defendant's innocence must be *impossible* to maintain? No. But it does mean the prosecutor's evidence must be very strong because of the jury's intent to minimize the risk of wrongly rejecting the defendant's innocence. The evidence must convince the 12 independent jurors that the defendant's innocence is no longer a plausible position to maintain. Failure to present convincing evidence brings a "not guilty" verdict.

> Only after having discredited the *a priori* hypothesis of innocence can the prosecutor get the jury to turn to the alternative hypothesis of guilt.

In summary, to "prove" the alternative hypothesis of guilt—the hypothesis the prosecutor is wishing to establish—the prosecutor must do it *indirectly* by convincingly *disproving* the *a priori* hypothesis of innocence. This reasoning approach is called "proof by contradiction".

Equivalent to the evidence in a jury "trial" is the observed random sample in a statistical hypothesis test. Just as the evidence presented by a prosecuting attorney must be strong enough to disprove the "innocence" hypothesis, the sample evidence must have the strength to disprove the plausibility of the *a priori* hypothesis.

Unusual Evidence

Statistical hypothesis testing relies on the criterion of "unusualness". Can the observed sample evidence be regarded as "extremely unusual" assuming a particular hypothesized parameter value?

What is an unusual or highly unlikely sample result? Simply stated, it is one not expected to appear by chance assuming the hypothesized parameter value is correct. In other words, there is only a remote possibility of obtaining purely by chance a sample result differing that much from the hypothesized value.

When such an unusual sample *is* observed, what impact does it have on our *a priori* belief in the hypothesized value? Is our *a priori* belief shaken? Finding such an unusual sample should indeed place in question the assumption that the hypothesized parameter value is the correct parameter value. It constitutes evidence for rejecting what *a priori* was a plausible hypothesized value for the parameter.

How can one view this process in terms of probability and a stated hypothesis? Suppose there is an *a priori* hypothesis about the value of a population mean. How is the sample evidence brought to bear on the hypothesis?

It takes the form of a probability statement. "What is the *probability* that a *population* with a mean as stated in the hypothesis would produce a *sample* mean this unusual or more so as the one observed?" If the probability is very *low*, it suggests that the sample evidence is strongly *against* the *a priori* hypothesis. In other words, it would not be plausible to hold that the observed difference between the sample value and the hypothesized mean was solely due to chance. The hypothesis would therefore be rejected.

The motivation and the formal procedure for testing a hypothesis can best be explained in terms of a particular example.

Example 12.1B. A Proposal for Curbing Sick Leave Abuses

Absenteeism is a major concern of many companies. Excessive absenteeism causes a loss of valuable hours of production, over-budgeted sick-leave cost, and, if uncontrolled, a disruptive influence on worker morale. Of the many plans proposed to remedy the problem one of the more controversial involves eliminating compensation for the first few days of "sick leave," and extending substantially the benefits for sick leaves of longer duration. Supporters of the plan claim that withholding compensation, say for the first two days of sick leave, allows more benefits to be available for workers who suffer prolonged illness or disablement. Importantly, the key effect anticipated is employee reluctance to lose a day's pay. Ostensibly this should result in a general decrease in absenteeism, particularly among workers who feign sickness when they just don't feel like going to work.

Will the plan really decrease absenteeism? Certainly its backers think so. But critics argue differently. They argue that employees sick enough to stay home two days *without* pay might just decide to stay home an extra few days after sick leave compensation begins—even if they have fully recovered.

Null and Alternative Hypotheses

The language of hypothesis testing refers to the unchallenged hypothesis on which the sample evidence is brought to bear as the *null hypothesis,* with the symbol H_0.

The alternative statement to the null hypothesis is called the *alternative hypothesis* and is given the symbol H_A (some books use the symbol H_1). The alternative hypothesis is in essence the hypothesis that the investigator wishes to establish. Its acceptability depends on rejecting the null hypothesis.

12.2. Identifying Type I and II Errors

A hypothesis test concludes with a decision about whether or not to reject the null hypothesis. From this decision any one of four different situations can result depending on whether the hypothesis is true or not. The four situations are:

1. the null hypothesis is true and the decision is not to reject the hypothesis.

2. the null hypothesis is false and the decision is to reject it.

3. the null hypothesis is true and the decision is to reject it.

4. the null hypothesis is false and the decision is not to reject it.

In the first two situations, the decision made is correct with respect to the hypothesis. In the latter two situations, the decision made is erroneous with respect to the hypothesis. However, the errors are not of the same type in the last two situations. Situation 3, an erroneous decision to reject the hypothesis when (unknown to the investigator) it is actually true, is called a *Type I* error. Situation 4, an erroneous decision *not* to reject the hypothesis when (again, unknown to the investigator) it is actually false is called a *Type II* error. Table 12.1 shows the relationship between the conclusions about the null hypothesis H_0 and the actual status of H_0 for the sick leave problem. It also shows when the different types of error arise, and the probability designation for the chance of that happening.

TABLE 12.1. Relation Between the Conclusion About a Hypothesis and Its Status where the Null Hypothesis (H_0) = Mean Sick Leave Unchanged

True State: Status of H_0	Mean Sick Leave Unchanged H_0 is true	Mean Sick Leave Changed H_0 is false
Decision: Accept H_0	No Error—Correct Decision Probability $= 1 - \alpha$ $\quad$ = confidence level	Type II Error Probability $= \beta$
Reject H_0	Type I Error Probability $= \alpha$ $\quad$ = level of testing	No Error—Correct Decision Probability $= 1 - \beta$

Let us examine these designations more closely.

There is a Type I error if the null hypothesis is in fact true and the decision is to reject H_0. The probability or risk of a Type I error is designated by the Greek letter α (alpha). The investigator sets the level of α in the hypothesis testing procedure. This value has traditionally been called the *significance level* of the test.

A Type II error can only be committed if the null hypothesis is false and the decision is to accept it. The probability or risk of a Type II error is designated by the Greek letter β (beta).

Since the null hypothesis cannot simultaneously be true and false, the occurrence of one of the two types of error precludes the occurrence of the other. Type I and Type II errors cannot occur simultaneously. However, the investigator will not know which type is precluded. Therefore, it usually is worthwhile to consider the consequences of both types of error. Moreover, as we shall shortly see, lowering the risk of one type of error raises the risk of incurring the other given an unchanged size of sample. Thus, a choice must be made as to which type of error it is more important to reduce.

Our emphasis in this chapter is on the consideration of the most serious type of errors, Type I errors. This is consistent with widespread hypothesis testing practice in the social sciences and with the advice and practice of the late Sir Ronald Fisher, a famous statistician whose book, *The Design of Experiments*, became the "bible" for statistical investigations of many kinds.

12.3. Procedure for Testing the Hypothesis

The hypothesis testing procedure can be carried out in four steps:

1. State in simple terms:

a. The *null hypothesis* H_0 concerning the statistical population that the investigation seeks to discredit. This should be a formal statement about parameters (characteristics) of the population investigated.

b. The *alternative hypothesis* H_A, a conjecture made by the researcher that the investigation seeks to establish.

Usually, H_0 will refer to the summary measures (parameters) of the statistical population and not to the characteristics of the individual member. The way the alternative is stated determines what portion of the probability distribution will be used in the test.

2. Decide on the *level of significance*, α. The lower the level of α, say 5%, the less the probability of committing a Type I error. By lowering α one then raises the required level of unusualness of the sample evidence needed for rejecting the null hypothesis. The setting of α by the investigator before testing is begun reflects the investigator's high concern that a null hypothesis that in fact is true is not wrongly rejected. Highly unusual sample evidence, given the stated null, places the null hypothesis in jeopardy of being declared untenable.

Steps 1 and 2 are carried out before the statistical evidence is examined.

3. Calculate the actual *degree* of unusualness of the observed sample. Assume the null hypothesis is correct, and then find the probability of obtaining a sample result *at least* as unusual as was actually observed. This is called the computed *prob-value* (some books call this a *p*-value). See Figure 12.1.

4. Compare the computed prob-value to the significance level α.

a. If the computed prob-value is lower than α *reject* the null. Why? The sample value is more unusual than the decided upon level of unusualness that the investigator is willing to tolerate. This makes *a priori* belief about the parameter value, stated in the null, untenable; hence, the null hypothesis must be rejected. For example, if $\alpha = .05$ and the computed prob-value $= .03$, then we have the situation in Figure 12.2.

b. If the computed prob-value is *higher* than the significance level, claim the null hypothesized value *acceptable* in light of the sample evidence. That is, the level of significance defines the limiting degree of unusualness consistent with the value hypothesized *a priori* in the null as the parameter value. So a prob-value higher than the significance level indicates a sample result which is not unusual enough to reject the hypothesis. For example, if $\alpha = .05$ and the computed prob-value $= .14$, we have the situation in Figure 12.3.

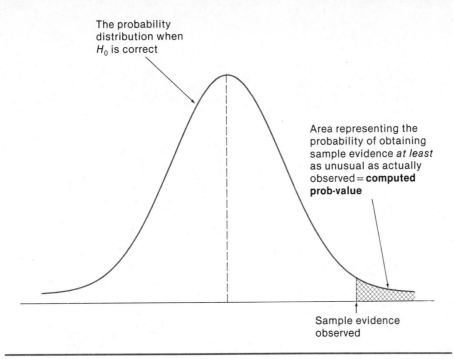

The probability
distribution when
H_0 is correct

Area representing the
probability of obtaining
sample evidence *at least*
as unusual as actually
observed = **computed
prob-value**

Sample evidence
observed

FIGURE 12.1 Computing the Prob-value

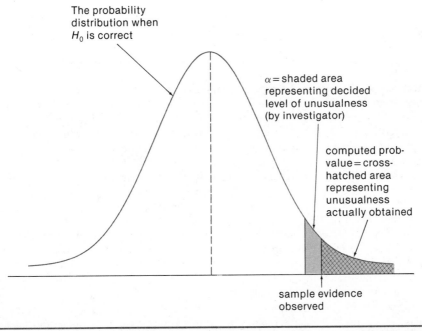

The probability
distribution when
H_0 is correct

α = shaded area
representing decided
level of unusualness
(by investigator)

computed prob-
value = cross-
hatched area
representing
unusualness
actually obtained

sample evidence
observed

FIGURE 12.2 Rejecting the Null When the Sample Is More Unusual than the Significance
Level α

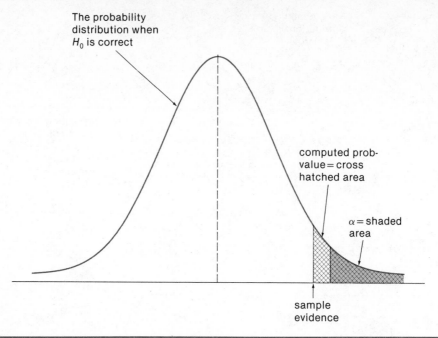

The probability distribution when H_0 is correct

computed prob-value = cross hatched area

α = shaded area

sample evidence

FIGURE 12.3 Accepting the Null When the Sample Is Less Unusual than the Significance Level α

Let's illustrate these steps in detail in the next four sections with the following specific delayed compensation sick leave plan.

Example 12.3. Record Keeping on the Effectiveness of a Delayed Sick Leave Plan

The hospital administration of a publicly-owned hospital chain which hires thousands of new employees annually has decided to introduce the delayed compensation sick leave plan of no compensation for the first few sick days and extended benefits for longer sick leaves. It will apply (for the time being at least) only to *newly hired* employees. The administration decided, because of a limited budget and costly record keeping, to monitor closely the absenteeism behavior of a random sample of 100 nurses hired under the new sick leave plan. Many different records were kept—the number of consecutive sick days taken, the notification time given for reporting in sick, the month of the year and the day of the week sick days were taken, etc. By the end of the year, the records showed that this group had averaged 7.2 sick days—1.6 days below the overall 8.8 day first-year absenteeism average found in the personnel records of all newly-hired nurses for the *past few years*.

Absenteeism can be expected to vary for different sample groups of employees. But let's assume that the 100 newly hired nurses can be regarded as a random sample from the population of all potential newly hired nurses. Does the 7.2 sick day average substantiate the claim that absenteeism (among the *population* of newly-hired nurses) changed with the introduction of the delayed sick leave plan? Or does it simply reflect the variation that expectedly comes with samples of this size? In other words, is it just the consequence of the luck-of-the-draw of putting too many healthy or conscientious nurses (who take few sick days) in the 100 being monitored under the new plan?

In short, the issue boils down to whether the absenteeism reduction could be a "fluke" attributable to sampling error. It makes sense that the smaller the study group (the sample), the more likely will be a large observed difference in results between the study group and the reference group (the population). Of course, it must also be remembered that the observed sample absenteeism also depends on the standard deviation of absenteeism in the work force. Let's say in this case that the standard deviation in the work force is 4 days.

12.4. Step One: Specify the Hypothesis

Our concern in the sick leave study is the *source* of the observed difference between the sample average and the old population value. In hypothesis testing, two claims about the source are specified. One claim is stated in the *null* hypothesis. The other claim is stated in the alternative hypothesis.

The general position taken by finding the null acceptable is that the observed difference between the sample value and the hypothesized value under the null is due merely to sampling variation. Finding the null acceptable for the sick-leave hypothesis test means that the difference the investigator is seeing is merely the luck of the draw natural with sampling. Therefore, the difference *does not represent a real change from the sick leave taken* with the old mean parameter value.

More precisely, in determining whether the sick-leave parameter 8.8 was changed by the new sick-leave compensation plan (either upward or downward), the question would be stated and answered by testing the null hypothesis:

H_0: $\mu = 8.8$ (No real changes in sick-leave days)

And, in general, the null hypothesis would be stated as:

H_0: $\mu = \mu_0$ (Premise investigator wants to reject at minimal risk of being wrong)

where μ_0 is the numerical value assigned to the null.

The *alternate* hypothesis, on the other hand, claims that the sources of the observed differences are *real*, not just due to sampling variability. *This is the position that the investigator is wishing to prove about the plan by disproving the null.* The specification of the alternative hypothesis determines two things:

the goal of the investigation and the interest of the investigator;

importantly, whether the significance level and prob-value will refer to *one or two tails* of the sampling distribution.

Let's now take up that issue.

One-sided Versus Two-sided Alternative Hypothesis

If the investigator is interested in testing whether there has been a change in the population parameter *regardless* of the direction of change, then a *two-sided* alternative hypothesis would be appropriate. A one-sided alternative would suggest the investigator has a belief in a particular directional change. For the sick-leave situation we have:

$H_A : \mu \neq 8.8$ (there is a real change in sick-leave days with the introduction of the delayed sick-leave plan)

and in general

$H_A : \mu \neq \mu_0$ (the premise the investigator wishes to prove)

where μ_0 is the particular hypothesized value of the null. Figure 12.4 shows what's at stake in these claims.

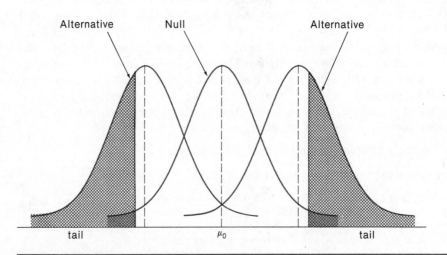

shaded area represents "tail" probability, if null is true

cross hatched area represents "tail" probabilities under two different alternative hypotheses

Alternative   Null   Alternative

tail μ_0 tail

FIGURE 12.4 Sampling Distribution for Two-Tail Test for $\mu_0 = 8.8$

The figure suggests that values in the "tail" region occur with a greater probability if the alternative hypothesis holds. By testing the null hypothesis against a *two-sided* alternative hypothesis we check on the unusualness of the observed sample value *at either extreme* of the null distribution. We use the result to possibly discredit the plausibility of the null. As can be surmised from looking at Figure 12.4,

the null hypothesis becomes a less plausible candidate for the true underlying distribution when "tail" sample results are observed.

12.5. Step Two: Choose a Significance Level

Even though the possibility of Type I error of wrongly rejecting the postulated null cannot be eliminated, within broad limits the investigator can choose the maximum risk of incurring it. At what level should this risk be set? Recalling that the null hypothesis is stated to reflect what the investigator seeks to disprove, it is customary to place the burden of proof on the investigator rather than on the null hypothesis. This is accomplished by requiring a low prob-value before concluding the sample result is "too unusual" to have been drawn from a population having the characteristics stated by the null hypothesis. The lower the prob-value chosen as the level of significance, the less the investigator's risk of Type I error.

In practice, it has become common to choose one or the other of two significance levels: 5% or 1%. So rejecting the null by finding

a computed prob-value between 5% and 1% is called a *statistically significant* finding.

a computed prob-value of less than 1% is called a *highly statistically significant* finding.

12.6. Step Three: Compute the Prob-Value

In the delayed sick leave compensation problem, there is a 1.6 day difference between the old population mean of 8.8 sick days and the sample mean of 7.2 sick days recorded for the sample group under the plan. Since the value of the standard deviation of sick leave of individual employees is four days, does this suggest that the observed difference is likely due to the chance variation that naturally results when sampling?

No. The attention is not being focused on the correct standard deviation. Four sick leave days is the standard deviation of *individual* employees and is not the appropriate standard deviation to employ in testing the hypothesis. The testing procedure uses the *mean* of the 100 employees as a summary statistic of the sample, so the testing requires the *standard error of the mean* which is:

$$\sigma_{\overline{X}} = \frac{\sigma_X}{\sqrt{n}} = \frac{4}{\sqrt{100}} = 0.4 \text{ days}$$

We can now properly test whether the null hypothesis of the 8.8 sick days is "close" to the 7.2 mean of the sample. Remember that "closeness" is measured in terms of number of standard errors. The smaller this number, the "closer" is the sample mean to the hypothesized population mean. The value to be computed is usually called the Z value. It is referred to as the *test statistic* and is calculated using the following formula:

$$Z = \frac{\overline{X} - \mu_0}{\sigma_{\overline{X}}}$$

where μ_0 is the population mean stated in the null hypothesis. The calculation for this sample is:

$$Z = \text{number of standard errors} = \frac{7.2 - 8.8}{0.4} = -4.0$$

The Z value of -4.0 indicates that the value 7.2 is four standard errors below 8.8.

What is the computed prob-value of $Z = -4.0$? That is, what is the probability that a test statistic as extreme as the Z value of -4.0 would appear, assuming the null is true? The probability calculation depends on the probability distribution of Z.

It is appropriate to assume (from the central limit theorem) that for samples of size 100 the Z-test statistic follows the standardized normal distribution and that it can be used to calculate probabilities.

> When computing the prob-value we are interested in the probability associated with the area under the standardized normal curve on both sides of the μ_0 mean beyond, in this case, four standard deviations.

Appendix Table 4 indicates that by doubling the area that lies beyond a Z of 4.0 one obtains a value of .0000634, which represents the total area that lies in the *two tails;* that is, under those portions of the curve beyond plus or minus four standard deviations. (Note: some hand-held calculators also give area under the normal curve.)

Is the computed probability associated with this area the prob-value? Yes. The prob-value is .0000634, a very, very low value. From this calculation one can conclude either:

> that the true amount of absenteeism has shifted to a new lower level, or

> if it didn't go below its current 8.8 mark, then the observed sample result is an extremely rare event since *a priori* it had less than one chance in ten thousand of appearing.

12.7. Step Four: Compare the Prob-Value and Significance Level α to Reach a Conclusion

Let's assume that the investigator decides to use the level of unusualness at 1%. With the 1% significance level (α at .01), we will distribute half of 1%, or .5%, to each of two tails as shown in Figure 12.5.

The sample result is clearly "highly unusual," but for the null hypothesis being assumed, what formal conclusion follows?

> In hypothesis testing terminology, the absenteeism reduction is *highly statistically significant* since the computed prob-value of .0000634 calculated at both tails is much less than the left and right tail areas sum, α, of .01. Thus, the null hypothesis is rejected in favor of the alternative hypothesis at the 1% level of significance.

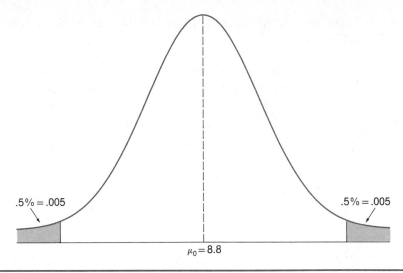

.5% = .005   .5% = .005

$\mu_0 = 8.8$

FIGURE 12.5 Two Tail Testing at the 1% Significance Level

What does the rejection conclusion mean? The observed disparity between the sample statistic and the hypothesized parameter is "too unusual" to be attributed simply to sampling variation. Hence, it is no longer plausible under the circumstances to maintain that the hypothesized value of the null is the true value of the parameter.

Does this rejection of the null hypothesis *prove* that the delayed-compensation sick leave plan caused a change in absenteeism? Not in the pure sense of the word. What the evidence has reasonably proved is that the *mean number of sick days employees use has changed*, favoring the conclusion that absenteeism has substantially decreased.

Does the verdict on the null hypothesis depend on what value was chosen for the level of significance? Only if the level of significance chosen had been smaller than .00006 would the null hypothesis not be rejected. But this would be saying that a result which occurs only six times in a hundred thousand is not rare—a bit far fetched, maybe even reckless, especially if some action hinges on the conclusion.

> The smaller the prob-value, the more far fetched it would be to consider the null hypothesis acceptable.

What the Prob-Value Is Not

Tempting as it may be to interpret the prob-value as the probability of the null hypothesis being correct, it simply isn't. The prob-value instead is the *conditional* probability of obtaining a result more unusual than the observed sample result *assuming the null hypothesis is true.* This should *not* be confused with the conditional probability of the null hypothesis *being true, given the sample result.*

Looking Back and Ahead—Estimation After Rejection of the Null Hypothesis

The null hypothesis postulated *a priori* no change in the mean number of days taken for sick leave with the introduction of the new sick leave plan. This formulation is simplistic, yet purposeful. It affords the sample evidence the opportunity to convincingly disprove this postulate before turning to the alternative hypothesis that is of particular interest to us to "prove." With the rejection of the null, the plausibility of the alternative hypothesis (that some real change in parameter has occurred) can be affirmed.

Now that the null has been rejected and the alternative affirmed, can something more be done? Yes. Confident that a change in the average number of sick days used has taken place, we can be more specific about the change.

> One approach is to make a *confidence interval* statement about the magnitude of the real reduction in sick days taken off from work.

Ruling out any further *a priori* considerations, we can proceed to construct a confidence interval from the statistics obtained from the sample. The confidence interval will specify a range of values about the new sick-day population mean. Thus, in no way does hypothesis testing preclude the subsequent construction of a confidence interval in the event that the null hypothesis is rejected. The interval $7.2 \pm (2.57)(0.4)$ or 6.17 to 8.23 days provides a 99% confidence interval estimate of the new sick day population mean.

Notice that the 99% confidence interval does not include the hypothesized value of 8.8 days. This is not a coincidence. Although the purposes of confidence interval estimation and hypothesis testing are different, the conclusions are consistent. A confidence interval represents the set of acceptable hypotheses about the parameter calculated for a level of confidence equal to one minus the significance level, $1 - \alpha$. Rejecting the null hypothesis at the α significance level is equivalent to saying that the null hypothesis value is not part of the acceptable hypotheses included in the confidence interval. Also, since the confidence interval represents the set of acceptable hypotheses, it includes all values that the null hypothesis could postulate and *not* be rejected. In this sense, the concepts of the confidence interval and a hypothesis test are equivalent.

12.8. One-Tailed Tests

If used to determine whether a population parameter has changed *regardless of the direction* of change, a hypothesis test is referred to as a *two-tailed test*. The test of the null hypothesis in the delayed sick-leave compensation plan was an example of a two-tailed test.

> With a two-tailed test the null hypothesis can be rejected if the computed Z-test statistic falls at *either* extreme of the two tails of its sampling distribution.

More specifically, the null hypothesis is rejected if the prob-value (the probability associated with the positive *and* negative values of the computed Z-statistic) does not exceed the desired level of significance.

Hypothesis testing can also be conducted on a *one-tail* basis. If the investigator is only interested in the possible alternatives to the null that lie in a particular direction, then the testing will be *one-tailed*. With a one-tailed test, the alternative hypothesis will no longer be a statement of "some change of any kind" in the population parameter value as it was for the two-tail test. Instead it will specify whether the alternative values to the null represent "an increase" or "a decrease" from the assigned value of the null.

> Suppose the test is to determine whether the old mean processing time for orders has been materially improved with the introduction of a new handling process. Then the null and alternative hypotheses would be denoted by:
>
> $H_0: \mu = \mu_0$ (no real change in the mean processing time)
> $H_A: \mu < \mu_0$ (improved (lower) mean processing time)

μ_0 is the numerical value of the population mean under the null. Likewise, the null and alternative hypotheses of "an increase" in mean processing time (for the population mean) is denoted generally by:

> $H_0: \mu = \mu_0$
> $H_A: \mu > \mu_0$

where μ_0 is again the numerical value assigned to the population mean under the null.

Computing the Prob-Value

Does the value of the computed Z-test statistic of the observed sample result depend on whether the hypothesis test is two-tailed or one-tailed? No. Recall that the Z-test transforms the observed sample value into standard units on the basis of the assigned value of the null.

> The distinguishing feature of a one-tail test is that the level of significance used and the prob-value are applied to only one tail; the other tail plays *no* part in testing the hypothesis.

Had the only concern in the delayed sick-leave compensation example been with the effectiveness of the plan in reducing sick-leave days taken, the null and alternative hypotheses would be:

> $H_0: \mu = 8.8$ (no real change in the sick-leave mean parameter)
> $H_A: \mu < 8.8$ (a real reduction in the sick-leave parameter)

Since the null hypothesis is identical to that of the previous two-tail test, the Z-test statistic is again -4.0. As shown in Figure 12.6, finding a Z-test statistic as remote or more so than -4.0 refers to the area under the standardized normal curve to the left side of $Z = -4.0$. This has a value of .00003 (rounded).

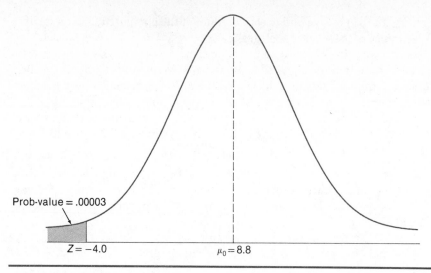

Prob-value = .00003

$Z = -4.0$

$\mu_0 = 8.8$

FIGURE 12.6 One Tail Testing of Effectiveness of Delayed Sick-Leave Plan

So .00003 is the computed *one*-tailed prob-value. On the basis of the null, the chance of finding a Z-test statistic as unusual as or more so than the one observed is no more than .00003. Thus, comparing the one-tail and two-tail versions of the test, we find:

1. the Z-statistic to be the *same*, but
2. the one-tail prob-value is only *half* that of the two-tailed prob-value.

Assume that the investigator's only consideration in evaluating the plan is the plan's ability to reduce μ, the mean number of days of absenteeism. The investigator wants to avoid the mistake of recommending a plan that actually effects an increase in absenteeism. The appropriate null hypothesis to disprove states that the mean is unchanged at 8.8 ($\mu = 8.8$) and not that the mean had increased ($\mu > 8.8$). If the plan actually increased μ beyond 8.8 days, how would testing $\mu = 8.8$ instead of $\mu > 8.8$ affect the risk of reaching the erroneous conclusion that there was a drop in mean absenteeism?

The observed sample result, 7.2 days, falls *far below* the null hypothesis value 8.8. On the grounds that the observed sample result is highly unusual, such that the prob-value is smaller than the significance level α chosen, the null is rejected. Had the null hypothesis been stated as $\mu > 8.8$, the observed sample value would be even farther away from the null hypothesis. This means that the wrong conclusion—that mean absenteeism dropped—will be even less likely. The important point to realize is that if the conclusion is reached that mean days absenteeism had been reduced ($\mu < 8.8$) while testing the null $\mu = 8.8$, the same conclusion would be reached had we tested the null at $\mu > 8.8$. Nothing was lost.

The following example illustrates a business situation which calls for a one-tailed test and employs such a tactic.

Example 12.8. Honest Hamburgers?

Millions of "Big Burgers" advertised as containing a quarter pound of ground beef are sold each year by a chain of fast food restaurants in a large city. The meat is purchased in patties from a local meat dealer, who guarantees that the patties weigh an average of .250 pounds. The variation in density of beef and other factors simply do not make it feasible to require every patty to be exactly .250 pounds; overall, the standard deviation for *all* the ground beef patties is .020 lbs.

The relatively low wholesale mark-up on meat (say 10%), combined with the fact that it is impractical for the restaurant to weigh each and every patty purchased, encourages unscrupulous meat dealers to fraudulently increase their profit margin by "shaving" just a little meat from each patty. If some of the patties are weighed upon receipt by the restaurant and found to be underweight, the unscupulous dealer simply claims it was due to a "bad (unusual) sample" which happened by chance. Often, fast food chains are reluctant to change dealers merely on the *suspicion* that a particular dealer is cheating on the weight because good meat dealers are hard to find. The retailer does not want to stop doing business with a dealer unless there is strong evidence that the dealer is dishonest. That is, the retailer wants to keep low the risk of Type I error, wrongly accusing a dealer who in fact is not shaving.

Admittedly there will be normal variation in hamburger patty weight, but how could the fast food chain detect *abnormal* variation in the weight of the burgers? One approach is to: (1) weigh random samples of the patties and (2) use the sample mean weight to test the null hypothesis about the true mean weight.

The first step was taken and a mean of .249 was reported for a random sample of 100 meat patties. Knowing the interest of the investigator, do you suggest a one or two tail test?

The intent of the investigator is to take possible action only if he reaches the conclusion that the meat dealer's hamburger patties are falling short of the .250 lb. standard. The test, therefore, is to establish a change in parameter in a *particular direction.* It follows that a *one*-tailed test should be used.

Crediting the dealer with no shaving in the null, because of the dire consequences of wrongly rejecting a true null, places μ_0 at .250 lbs. This means the burden of proof is on the sample evidence to disprove the null hypothesis. The null and the one-sided alternative which would be of interest to "prove" are:

$$H_0: \mu = .250 \text{ (no shaving)}; H_A: \mu < .250 \text{ (a decrease in the mean patty weight)}$$

Solution: On the basis of the null, a computed Z-test statistic was calculated converting the observed .249 into standard error unit terms.

$$Z = \frac{\bar{X} - \mu_0}{\sigma_{\bar{X}}} = \frac{\bar{X} - \mu_0}{\sigma_x/\sqrt{n}} = \frac{.249 - .250}{.020/\sqrt{100}} = \frac{-.001}{.002} = -.5$$

The prob-value of .3085 is the area under the left tail beyond $Z = -.5$. For any significance level chosen above .3085, the null hypothesis would be rejected. But with respect to the commonly used levels of .05 and .01, the null has to be considered not rejectable. This suggests that the observed difference between the sample value .249 and the .250 mean under the null was likely the work of chance variation. The difference did not represent a "real change" in the mean; the mean weight for *all* meat patties has not gone down.

12.9. Calculating a β Risk

In the hamburger procurement example, assume that the investigator will be testing the null of "no shaving" ($\mu_0 = .250$) at the significance level α of 5% to assure low risk of the severe consequences of a Type I error—that is, of rejecting a true null. But now the investigator also wants assurance that beta, the probability or risk of a Type II error which comes from wrongly accepting the null, does not exceed 10%. In other words, there must be at least a 90% chance of rejecting the null, if the meat supplier is actually shaving the quarterpound hamburger patties by 2% or more—.005 lbs. per patty. What is the probability of a Type II error? Does it exceed the 10% maximum for β risk?

Solution: It follows as before, from Example 12.8, that a left one-tail test is needed to establish a change in the parameter in the particular direction dictated by the alternative hypothesis. Given the level of α at .05 and the left one-tail testing, we need to obtain from Appendix Table 4 the value of Z that cuts off 5% in one tail. The table shows Z to be 1.65, and adding the negative sign for the left tail, we obtain $Z = -1.65$. This means that for the prob-value of the computed Z value to be less than .05, the computed Z must be a negative value at least as large as -1.65. That is,

$$Z = \frac{\overline{X}_c - \mu_0}{\sigma_{\overline{X}}} = -1.65$$

with $\overline{X}_c$ representing the critical $\overline{X}$ value needed to meet this condition of the investigator. So the negative value of -1.65 indicates that to reject the null at the 5% significance level the sample result $\overline{X}$ must fall below H_0 by 1.65 standard errors. Rearranging the terms to isolate $\overline{X}_c$, we get

$$\overline{X}_c = \mu_0 - 1.65\sigma_{\overline{X}}$$

Since the sample result must fall below $\overline{X}_c$, we can write

$$\overline{X} < \mu_0 - 1.65\sigma_{\overline{X}}$$

Substituting the given values, we have

$$\overline{X} < .250 - 1.65(.002)$$
$$\overline{X} < .2467$$

This means the sample result $\overline{X}$ must fall below $\overline{X}_c = .2467$.

Since the claim of the alternative hypothesis is that shaving is 2% or more (.005 lbs. or more), the $H_A: \mu \leq .245$ specifies this condition. Setting μ at .245 (the first point where the H_A condition is met) allows us to portray graphically the area designated by our conditions on α and β. The beta risk or probability of wrongly accepting the null of no shaving when in fact $\mu = .245$ (a shaving of 2% is present) is shown in Figure 12.7 by the shaded tail area to the right of $\overline{X}_c = .2467$. The Z statistic corresponding to the point $\overline{X}_c = .2467$ is 0.85, obtained as follows. Assuming the alternative hypothesis $\mu = .245$ is the true condition of shaving, then $\overline{X}_c$ in Z terms is

$$Z = \frac{\overline{X}_c - \mu_A}{\sigma_{\overline{X}}} = \frac{.2467 - .245}{.002} = \frac{.0017}{.002} = 0.85$$

From the normal probability table, we find that the area beyond $Z = .85$ is

$$P(Z > 0.85) = .1977$$

Therefore, on the basis that H_A is correct at $\mu = .245$, the β risk defines the probability of erroneously accepting H_0 when in fact H_A is true. In this case we found it to be .1977, and this exceeds the investigator's requirement that $\beta \le .10$. To bring the β risk lower, the investigator, given the definition of shaving as 2%, must tolerate a high α risk. This tradeoff will be discussed in the next section.

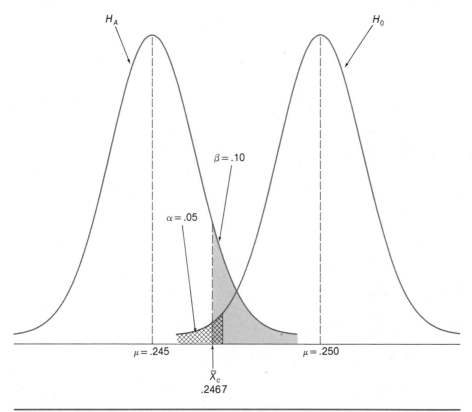

FIGURE 12.7 Determining β Risk When H_A Is True

12.10. Operating Characteristic Curves

Given the sample size and the chosen α risk, the value of β will depend on how far the actual parameter value is located from the critical value of the test statistic. The greater this distance, the less the β risk. A graph called an *operating characteristic curve* can be constructed to show how rapidly the risk of Type II error decreases as the distance of the actual parameter from the critical test statistic value increases. Figure 12.8a shows the operating characteristic curve for the hamburger procurement problem.

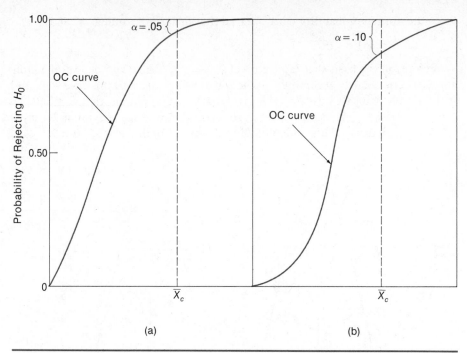

FIGURE 12.8 Operating Characteristic Curves

For a sample of given size, the α and β risks cannot be simultaneously reduced. However, it is possible to reduce one at the expense of increasing the other. Thus, if a more sharply falling β risk curve is desired, this can be accomplished by increasing the chosen level of significance—the α risk. Figure 12.8b shows the operating characteristic curve for the hamburger procurement problem using a 10% level of significance. By comparing parts a and b of Figure 12.8 the tradeoff between α and β can be observed. Notice that a sharp reduction in β risk is gained for parameter values near $\overline{X}_c$ by accepting the greater α risk.

12.11. Determining the Sample Size

The only way to simultaneously decrease the α and β risk is to take a larger sample. To find the minimum sample size which will satisfy requirements for both the critical value of $\overline{X}_c$, the two equations involving $\overline{X}_c$ are solved simultaneously. The solution is found by subtracting one equation from the other:

$$\overline{X}_c - \mu_0 = -1.65\sigma_X/\sqrt{n}$$
$$\overline{X}_c - \mu_A = 1.28\sigma_X/\sqrt{n}$$

The subtraction of equations can be expressed by

$$(\overline{X}_c - \mu_0) - (\overline{X}_c - \mu_A) = \mu_A - \mu_0$$

This can also be expressed by

$$\left(\frac{-1.65\sigma_X}{\sqrt{n}}\right) - \left(\frac{1.28\sigma_X}{\sqrt{n}}\right) = \frac{-2.93\sigma_X}{\sqrt{n}}$$

Combining the two we get

$$\mu_A - \mu_0 = \frac{-2.93\sigma_X}{\sqrt{n}}$$

Substituting the value of $\sigma_X = .02$ and solving for n gives

$$\sqrt{n} = \frac{(-2.93)\sigma_X}{\mu_A - \mu_0} = \frac{(-2.93)(.02)}{.245 - .250} = 11.72$$

$$n = (11.72)^2 = 138 \text{ (rounded to next highest integer)}$$

If we took a sample of size 138 we could feel assured that using a 5% significance level would give a reliability of 90% of rejecting the null when μ of .245 lb. is the mean weight of *all* meat patties.

12.12. Choosing the Type of Test: One-Tailed vs. Two-Tailed

Consider once again the reasoning process behind the hypotheses in the hamburger procurement example. Presumably the key concern of the fast food chain is in getting what it pays for and not being shortchanged in the weight of the patties. This one-direction concern would call for a one-tailed test. But there is another consideration. Wouldn't reliable information that the meat dealer consistently shipped *overweight* patties also be of interest? Perhaps the fast food chain could advantageously use this information. One possibility is for the retailer to renegotiate with the meat contractor for smaller patties at a lower price. This possibility of taking advantage of knowledge that $\mu > .250$ would prompt the investigator to be interested in whether there has been *any* change of weight (overweight or underweight) from the hypothesized .250 lb. A two-tailed test is then the appropriate one to use.

Consider also the example of the delayed sick leave compensation. The expectation is that the plan will *lower* absenteeism. But what if an *increase* in absenteeism is the result instead? This might have important theoretical implications for the study of work behavior. It might suggest that there are factors in the environment which cause workers to want to report sick and avoid coming to work. The chance that absenteeism can change in *either* direction calls for a *two*-sided test if the perspective is scientific research. Management's interest lies only in substantiating that the new sick leave plan is linked to lower absenteeism. Adoption of the plan depends on establishing only the positive effect of the plan. Therefore, a *one*-sided test would be appropriate.

Statistically Significant Flukes?

The key point of this discussion is that the objective of the test ought to be specified *before choosing* whether a one-tailed or a two-tailed test is needed. Those investigators who attempt to justify the value of the investigation by deciding which hypothesis to test *after* having seen the results skate on very thin ice. They run the risk of being steered into concocting a theory to explain "statistically significant" flukes. To guard against making such flukes, an independent set of data should be tested.

12.13. One Sample Tests for a Population Proportion

The step procedures for testing a hypothesis about a population proportion are similar to those just described for testing a hypothesis about a population mean. In the case of a proportion, the Z statistic is given by:

$$Z = \frac{\text{sample proportion} - \text{null hypothesized population proportion}}{\text{standard error of the sample proportion}}$$

Designating the sample proportion by $\hat{p}$, the hypothesized population proportion of the null by p_0, and the standard error of the sample proportion by $\sigma_{\hat{p}}$, the relationship is:

$$Z = \frac{\hat{p} - p_0}{\sigma_{\hat{p}}}$$

This expression for Z, like the expression for the population mean, converts into standard units the numerical discrepancy between the sample result and the value assigned to p_0, the null value. But in this case the standard deviation values cannot be calculated directly from information obtainable from the sample. The term $\sigma_{\hat{p}}$, defined as $\sqrt{p(1-p)/n}$, requires the use of the population parameter p, which of course is not known. On the basis of the null hypothesis we assume as a working premise that $p = p_0$. Thus, the Z statistic is:

$$Z = \frac{\hat{p} - p_0}{\sqrt{\dfrac{p_0(1 - p_0)}{n}}}$$

Example 12.13.   The Relationship Between Product Price and Perceived Consumer Risk

Is lowering your price relative to the competition a sure-fire way to achieve increased sales volume? *Ceteris paribus* (other things unchanged) economic theory says it should be. But *mutatis mutandis* (all things taken into account), a lower price tag needn't bring about a higher sales volume. What's the reason? A change in buyer's risk perception may be one explanation. Consumers who rely on the adage "You get what you pay for" can conclude that the lower price means an inferior product—a risk they are not willing to bear—rather than a better value for an equivalent product. The prevalence of this viewpoint for particular products can seriously undermine the effectiveness of a lower price-same quality pricing strategy.

Take the case of Bristol-Myers, a company recognized for its expertise in successfully marketing consumer products. It introduced and promoted *Behold,* a brand of spray furniture wax, as a lower price-same quality product vis-a-vis the market leader, *Lemon Pledge* and was very successful. On the other hand, its promotion of *Datril,* a brand of aspirin substitute, against the market leader *Tylenol* failed miserably. Tylenol users did not switch to Datril and Datril could not establish its own customer following. It was eventually withdrawn from the market. Why the different reaction? Perhaps to the new user of Behold there was little risk other than the price of the wax. If Behold did not deliver the quality of shine that came with Lemon Pledge, the Behold buyer's furniture would not suffer irreparable damage and the return to Lemon Pledge would be easy. An unhappy experience with a personal health product is another matter. Envisioning possible discomforting health effects, the buyer is willing to pay the price to lower the risk of an inferior product.

What if the product manager of a non-prescription digestive agent wants to reposition her brand from its present same quality-same price position relative to the market leader to a same quality-lower price position? Concern with such a strategy would be greatly simplified if she could dismiss the fear that a substantial increase in perceived consumer risk would accompany a lowering of the price. She knows from previous marketing research that 30 percent of the users of this digestive agent regard her brand as inferior to the market leader. If upon implementation of the lower price plan this figure rises to 50 percent or greater, the lower price-same quality strategy will prove to be a disaster in terms of expected lost sales to other brands and of the resources that were spent to reposition the product. Considering this information, she wants to set up a null hypothesis test with the null hypothesis stating that the proportion p of users regarding her brand as inferior

has become .5 or greater with the new lower price strategy.

That is,

$H_0: p \geq .50$ (A lowering of the price increases perceived consumer risk sufficiently to make the proposed strategy a disaster.)

$H_A: p < .50$ (A lowering of the price does *not* increase perceived consumer risk sufficiently to make the proposed strategy a disaster.)

To test the null hypothesis an 1100 member consumer panel is screened to identify users of the drug who are willing to cooperate in an attitude study. Of the forty members used, twenty nine regard her brand as inferior, so $\hat{p} = {}^{29}\!/_{40} = .725$. Treating this group as a random sample of product users, what is the prob-value of the result? What is the credibility of the hypothesis at the 5% level of significance?

For this one tail test, the standard error of the test procedure is calculated using the .5 of the null.

The standard error of $\hat{p}$ is: $\sigma_{\hat{p}} = \sqrt{\dfrac{(.50)(.50)}{40}} = .0791$

Therefore, the Z-statistic is: $Z = \dfrac{\hat{p} - p_0}{\sigma_{\hat{p}}} = \dfrac{.725 - .500}{.0791} = 2.84$

Comment: The prob-value for a Z-statistic of 2.84 is .9977. This means that if, in fact, p equals the null hypothesis value of .5, there would be a 99% chance of observing $\hat{p}$ as small as .725. The prob-value summarizes in a terse fashion the conformity between the sample data and the null hypothesis. Because of the extremely high prob-value, it appears that the null hypothesis is very plausible. Thus from this sample evidence, the product manager should conclude that using the marketing strategy of lower price-same quality would be an unprofitable route to take.

12.14. Small Sample Tests

The hypothesis testing procedures discussed in the preceding sections are appropriate for large samples. For small samples, the underlying theory is the same as that given in Section 11.6, where confidence interval estimation was discussed. In hypothesis testing as in confidence interval estimation, the distinction between large and small sample tests becomes important when the population standard deviation σ_X is *unknown*. It must then be estimated from the sample data, using S_X. No longer will the Z statistic, $(\overline{X} - \mu)/(\sigma_X/\sqrt{n})$, be useful since it depends on the unknown parameter, σ_X. However, if the population is closely approximated by a normal distribution, the sampling distribution of the t statistic, $(\overline{X} - \mu)/(S_X/\sqrt{n})$, follows a Student t distribution with $n - 1$ degrees of freedom regardless of the sample size. The test procedure is the same as that given in Sections 12.3 through 12.7, substituting the t statistic and its distribution for the Z statistic and its distribution. Appendix Table 7 provides prob-values for different t distributions.

To illustrate, suppose X is a normally distributed variable which is hypothesized to have a mean, $\mu_0 = 100$. The risk of Type I error is set at $\alpha = .05$. A random sample is taken with the following results:

$$n = 16$$
$$S = 5$$
$$\overline{X} = 106$$

The solution requires that $S_{\overline{X}}$ and t be calculated:

$$S_{\overline{X}} = S/\sqrt{n} = 5/\sqrt{16} = 1.25$$

$$t = \frac{\overline{X} - \mu_0}{S_{\overline{X}}} = \frac{106 - 100}{1.25} = 4.80$$

Since $n = 16$, the number of degrees of freedom is d.f. $= n - 1 = 15$. Looking along the row for d.f. $= 15$ in Table 7 of the Appendix, we find that the highest t-value shown is $t = 4.073$ given in the last column. This has a prob-value of .001, given at the top of the column. Thus, the computed t statistic of 4.8 must have a prob-value less than .001, which is "too unusual" to sustain credibility in a null hypothesis using .05 as the level of significance. The hypothesis is therefore rejected.

In this example, the population was assumed to be normally distributed. If this were not the case, nonparametric methods discussed in Chapter 22 should be considered. Also, it must be noted that since small samples can provide only a very limited amount of additional information, prior beliefs about the issue in question may take on greater importance. Large sample evidence can often "swamp" even firmly held prior beliefs whereas one-sided evidence from small samples may not be able to overwhelm these beliefs. This general issue of prior beliefs is considered in Chapter 23 on Bayesian statistics.

12.15. Concluding Comments

Hypothesis tests provide a useful opportunity to sort out truly meritorious business theories from those that lack validity. Following the lead of the late Ronald Fisher, the specified hypothesis is the one the investigator seeks to disprove, much as a prosecuting attorney seeks to disprove the defendant's innocence in order to get a conviction. Then the level of significance, the risk to be accepted of wrongly rejecting this hypothesis (Type I error), is decided upon. After the statistical evidence is collected, the prob-value for this evidence is computed. This value is compared with the chosen significance level: if the prob-value is smaller the hypothesis is rejected; otherwise, it is not rejected.

Particularly in applications encountered in production and operations management, as opposed to scientific research, it may be important to take explicit account of the risk of failing to reject an erroneous hypothesis (Type II error). This risk will differ depending upon how far the actual population parameter is from the hypothesized value. The operating characteristic curve describes the risks of error of the two types for different parameter values. For a given sample size, it is possible to lower either the Type I risk or the Type II risk, but not both. If it is necessary to control both types of risk, the sample size should be increased. There will be a minimum sample size which is consistent with the levels of Type I and Type II error regarded as acceptable.

Footnotes and References

[1]Burton Malkiel, *A Random Walk Down Wall Street*, W. W. Norton and Co., 1975.

Questions and Problems

1. Do confidence interval estimation and hypothesis testing share a common inferential purpose? If so, what is it? If not, in what way do the purposes differ?

2. What is the role of sample evidence in hypothesis testing?

3. Suppose an investor wants to test the validity of a stock market scheme espoused by a broker. Why is the tested hypothesis the "random walk" hypothesis and not the hypothesis proposed by the broker?

4. In what way is a statistical hypothesis test analogous to a jury trial?

5. What is meant by the phrase "proof by contradiction?"

6. When a hypothesis is tested, why is sample evidence used to disprove the credibility of a hypothesis rather than to prove the credibility of the hypothesis?

7. What is a *null* hypothesis? What distinguishes it from the *alternative* hypothesis?

8. What is a Type I Error? What distinguishes it from a Type II Error?

9. Do Type I and Type II Errors occur independently? Explain.

10. What is the risk of Type I Error if the null hypothesis is false?

11. What is the value of β (Beta) when the null hypothesis is true?

12. Do statistical investigators typically regard Type I and Type II Errors equally seriously? If not, which one is taken more seriously? Why?

13. What is the basis for determining whether a statistical hypothesis test should be one-tailed or two-tailed?

14. What is meant by the phrase "level of unusualness?"

15. What is meant by the term "prob-value?"

16. Between what computed prob-values is a finding called *statistically significant*? *Highly statistically significant*?

17. What is a "test statistic" and how is it calculated?

18. In the employee sick leave problem, the investigator wanted to know whether absenteeism is reduced by the new sick leave plan. The null hypothesis tested was that the new plan would *not* reduce absenteeism. When the null hypothesis was subsequently rejected, why had we not proved that absenteeism is reduced by the proposed sick leave plan?

19. Is the prob-value the probability of the null hypothesis being correct? Explain.

20. Are confidence intervals and hypothesis tests mutually exclusive? Explain.

21. Will a one-tailed and two-tailed test performed on the same data:
a. give the same prob-value? Explain.
b. lead to the same conclusion (reject or accept the null hypothesis)?

22. What is the rationale for expressing the null hypothesis for a one-tailed test as $\mu = \mu_0$ (rather than as $\mu \geq \mu_0$ or $\mu \leq \mu_0$)?

23. If the one-tailed null hypothesis is not rejected, does this mean that the value of μ is equal to the hypothesized value μ_0? Explain.

24. Is it wrong to express the null hypothesis for a one-tail test as $\mu < \mu_0$ (or $\mu > \mu_0$) rather than $\mu = \mu_0$? Explain.

25. Should the value of β risk be added to the value of the α risk to determine minimum acceptable risk? Explain.

26. For a given sample size and level of α risk, is there more than one beta risk value? Explain.

27. What is an "operating characteristic curve?"

28. Just how can both α and β risks simultaneously decrease?

29. When should the choice between a one or two-tailed test be made? Before or after the data is seen? Explain.

30. When the null hypothesis is about a population proportion p, rather than the mean μ, of quantitative data, the computation of the standard deviation of the sampling distribution for $\hat{p}$ relies on the hypothesized value of p rather than the observed statistic $\hat{p}$. Why? Is there an analogous procedure in the computation of S_X in hypothesis testing for the hypothesized value of μ with quantitative data? Explain.

31. Hypothesis tests involving small samples sometimes erroneously use the Student t distribution. For the t distribution to be applicable, what conditions must be met?

32. Sample size is not a condition required for the applicability of the t distribution; yet, the t distribution is almost universally associated with small samples. Why?

33. For each hypothesis testing situations listed in Table 12.2 for the mean μ_0 of a quantitative population, indicate the theoretically correct sampling distribution applicable for testing in each situation, if there is one (if none, so state). Is this theoretically correct sampling distribution likely to be used in testing the hypothesis?

If not, indicate what alternative distribution is likely to be used and why.

TABLE 12.2. Hypothesis Testing Situations

SAMPLE SIZE	POPULATION STD DEVIATION	POPULATION DISTRIBUTION
a. 225	known	normal
b. 15	known	normal
c. 225	known	unknown
d. 15	known	unknown
e. 225	unknown	normal
f. 15	unknown	normal
g. 225	unknown	unknown
h. 15	unknown	unknown

34. In hypothesis testing for a population proportion, what sampling distribution should be assumed if the sample size is:
a. 18?
b. 1800?

35. Reconsider the employee absenteeism problem (Example 12.3) using the following revised information:

$$\alpha = .01$$
$$\overline{X} = 8.5 \text{ days}$$
$$\sigma = 3 \text{ days}$$
$$n = 900 \text{ nurses}$$

a. What is the prob-value of the sample statistic, $\overline{X} = 8.5$?
b. Would the null hypothesis ($\mu_0 = 8.8$) be rejected? Explain.
c. Comparing these results with those given in Example 12.3, which have the greater degree of statistical significance?
d. As the hospital administrator, which set of results indicate the greater effectiveness of the delayed sick leave plan?
e. What is the risk of Type II error if $\mu = 8.5$ days? 8.7 days?

36. Reconsider the honest hamburger problem (Example 12.8) using a two-tailed test and the following revised information:

$$\alpha = .01$$
$$\overline{X} = .251$$
$$\sigma = .025$$

a. What is the prob-value of the sample statistic $\overline{X} = .251$?

b. Would the null hypothesis ($\mu_0 = .250$) be rejected? Explain.
c. What is the β risk if $\mu = .248$ lbs.?
d. Construct an operating characteristic curve.
e. What size sample would be required to give an alpha risk no higher than .05 and a β risk no higher than .10 when $\mu = .248$?

37. Reconsider the pricing strategy problem (Example 12.13) using the following information:

$$p_0 \geq .40$$
$$\alpha = .05$$
$$\beta = .10 \text{ at } p = .30$$
$$\hat{p} = .36$$

a. What sample size is implied by the above revisions?
b. What is the prob-value of the given sample result, $\hat{p} = .36$?
c. Should the null hypothesis be rejected or not? Why?

38. A sample of size $n = 9$ is drawn from a normal population with unknown standard deviation. The hypothesized mean of this population is $\mu_0 = 130$. The sample mean and sample standard deviation are found to be 160 and 15, respectively. The hypothesis is tested at the .05 significance level using a two-sided test.
a. What is the computed prob-value?
b. Should the hypothesis be rejected or not? Explain.

39. A hardware company claims its bolts have an average diameter of 10 mm with a standard deviation of .4 mm. A random sample of 36 bolts on Monday had an average diameter of 10.15 mm.
a. Establish the decision mode for accepting or rejecting this claim where $\alpha = 5\%$.
b. Based on Monday's sample, do you accept or reject this claim?

40. A new outdoor barbecue called the Happy Cooker advertises that on average it cooks steaks in 8 minutes. A sample of 45 steaks cooked on the Happy Cooker took an average of 9 minutes with a sample standard deviation of 3 minutes. Do you agree with the Happy Cooker's claim that it cooks steaks faster, at a 5% significance level?

41. The Santee School district is being investigated for achievement testing irregularities. The average test score in mathematics for last spring was 92. To test the validity of these results the State Attorney General's office ordered a comparable test to be given to a random sample of 64 of these students. The mean score of this sample was 80 with a standard deviation of 12 points. From this, do you accept that 92 was a valid score at the .05 level of significance? (Include an explanation of why you chose a one tail or two tailed test.)

42. According to the Wall Street Journal (3/4/82), the postal service claims that 97.5% of first class letters go coast to coast within three days. Thomas and Sons, Inc. doubt this claim and have decided to test it by mailing eight letters from California to New York and eight from New York to California at randomly chosen times. The average time for arrival of this sample ($n = 64$) is 2.5 days with a sample standard deviation of .3 days. Assume a normal distribution for delivery time.

a. Using $s = .3$ as an estimate of the standard deviation, if the Post Office's claim of 97.5 % arriving within three days is correct, what is the claimed mean arrival time? (Note: In this problem you are not using the sampling distribution of the means.)

b. Using the claimed mean arrival time as the hypothesized mean (as calculated in (a)), is the sample mean of 2.5 consistent with the Post Office's claim at the 10% level of significance? (In other words, do you accept the null hypothesis for $\alpha = .10$?)

43. City planners want to test the effectiveness of solar water heaters. To be adequate a water heater needs to be able to maintain a water temperature of at least 120° F. The population distribution of water temperatures is assumed to be normal. A test of 16 water heaters is made and the sample standard deviation S is calculated to be 8, and the sample mean $\overline{X}$ is 117°F.

a. At a .05 level of significance do you accept the null hypothesis that the water temperature is at least 120°F?

b. The sample size is increased to 64, $S = 8$, yielding a critical value or lower limit of 118.35. If the true mean were 119, what would be the value of β? $(1 - \beta)$? The latter value is called the power of the test.

c. With $n = 64$ and $\overline{X} = 118.35$, if the true mean was 117, what would be the value of β?

44. Suppose the daily records of the large volume of trading at the Chicago Mercantile Exchange shows that an average 8 out of 10 commodity futures trades lose money or break even. A national brokerage house, Pearson and Stone, wanted to test the hypothesis that their own organization's record was no better and no worse than the 20 percent rate of profitable trades reported by the Mercantile Exchange. They selected a random sample of 1600 commodity trades handled by their organization's most active brokers with respect to commodity contract trading. If the null hypothesis is true, can one say that the chances are about two in three that the percentage of profitable trades for their brokers' customers would be in the range 20% ± 1% for the 1600 sample members? Why or why not?

45. A large oil company has noticed a decline in business at one of its company owned service stations. The station operator claims that the decline is due to reduced traffic volume past the station. The oil company management doubts this, but wants to check the possibility before proceeding to investigate other causes, such as whether the station operator is falling down on the job. For 20 randomly selected hours during the prime business hours, the mean number of cars passing the location is $\overline{X} = 208.5$ with a standard deviation of 30. Previous studies established that the mean number of cars passing the location during the prime business hours has been 225 cars; assume a normally distributed population.

a. at the 5% level of significance, test the hypothesis that the traffic volume past the location during prime business hours has not fallen below the mean level of 225 cars per hour.

b. What is the prob-value of the test statistic?

46. In Problem 45, assume that the mean traffic volume per hour has actually fallen to 200 cars per hour. What would be the risk of a Type II error for a sample of size 20 if we will be testing at the 1% level of significance?

47. You are appointed as the manager at a newly opened 30,000 square feet supermarket in a high income area. You need to attract enough customer traffic and volume of business to make store utilization (average sales per square foot) profitable at competitive prices to shoppers. One strategy you decide to take is to accept not only authorized personal checks but also credit cards issued by local banks. The paperwork will be done at the checkout except when the purchase exceeds $50, which would require a phone credit check at the manager's booth. You realize that with this new policy, checkout time at the counter will increase and you are concerned about the spillover effect this will have on customer waiting time. Waiting times over 10 minutes are generally recognized to cause high levels of customer dissatisfaction. Recognizing that somewhat longer waiting periods will be encountered with the credit card plan, you decide to try the plan only if the mean waiting time is presently less than 8 minutes. The mean waiting time will be clocked for a random sample of customers at peak time on Saturday. Assuming that waiting time is normally distributed:
a. For a standard deviation of two, with $n = 20$, what is the risk of a Type II error if $\mu = 7$ minutes? Use $\alpha = .05$.
b. What is the minimum sample size that would assure a maximum risk of Type II error of $\beta = .10$ when $\mu = 7$? Again assume a standard deviation of two. Use $\alpha = .05$.
c. A sample of twenty customers was taken. Using $\overline{X} = 7.25$ minutes and the sample

standard deviation $= 1.75$ minutes, test the hypothesis $H_0 : \mu \geq 8$ against the alternative $H_A : \mu < 8$ at the 10% level of significance.

48. A Rochester, New York film plant produces ready-to-use film cartridges for instant developing pictures. The thickness of the coating material on the film is a cause for concern, because too much or not enough coating destroys the quality of the picture. When functioning properly, the manufacturing process places on average a coating of .040mm maximum thickness of film on the photographic paper used in the cartridge. The standard deviation of coating thickness is .002mm. For every batch produced, several cartridges are tested to assess the thickness of the coating applied. It is important that for the sample of ten cartridges tested, the mean thickness of coating must be no more than .043mm and no less than .037mm. A value over or under these limits is taken as serious enough to stop the process and investigate the production line.
a. Calculate the probability that the process will be stopped, even though the process is properly functioning (that is, with maximum coating thickness at .040mm average).
b. Calculate the probability that the process will be stopped if it is depositing an average .042 of film coating.

49. Referring to Problem 48, assume that the process on average is depositing .043mm film coating, an amount equal to the upper tolerance limit. What is the chance that the process is allowed to continue without investigation after the sample of 10 cartridges is tested? Do the same calculation, assuming the process on average deposits .037mm of coating, an amount equal to the lower tolerance limit.

Sampling Design and Experimental Design: The Two Sample Case

Preview. In previous chapters we have considered two of the four D's of statistics: statistical *description* and the *drawing of statistical inferences.* In this chapter we turn to a third D: statistical *design.* In an actual statistical study, the study design would or at least should be considered before the data are collected. Indeed, problems of poor design may be uncorrectible once the data have been collected. We have deferred our consideration of statistical design to this point only to gain the analytical tools helpful in distinguishing good designs from bad ones.

The design considerations studied in this chapter can be classified into two broad categories. Sections 13.1 through 13.4 focus on the plan for efficiently and economically sampling the target population to obtain sample results that can be generalized to the population with an acceptable degree of reliability. The remaining sections of the chapter explore design procedures for ascertaining the sources of the difference between two sets of sample measurements. After studying this chapter the reader should be better able to evaluate conclusions based upon statistical studies, including ones popularized by television commercials such as the "Pepsi Challenge" and the Crest fluoride toothpaste experiments.

13.1. Sampling and Sample Design

At all levels of government and industry, samples are a major source of published numerical information. Feasibility, data gathering cost, and the limitations of time are all key factors which motivate the use of sample information. Therefore, efficient gathering and proper treatment of sample information is a major concern of statisticians. Only by carefully selecting a sampling procedure (known as the *sampling plan* or *sample design*) *before* collecting any data can one achieve the efficiency of design which leads to the most reliable results.

The many available sampling plans are categorized broadly as either *random sampling plans* or *non-random sampling plans.* Random sampling plans require that each element of the population has a known probability of being selected, a key property absent from a non-random sampling plan. But what does knowledge about the probability of selection do for us? It permits us to make reliable statements about sampling error—the discrepancy between the sample value we obtain and the unknown target population value of interest to us. Probability statements about the size of the sampling error for a given sample size can be made if a random sample procedure was used. With non-random samples, there also can be factors causing discrepancies. In that case the nature and size of the errors cannot be evaluated by probability theory or by any other scientific basis. This type of disrupting influence persists even as the sample size increases.

Before moving on to the distinctions among the different sampling plans and the types of errors that occur, it would be helpful to define some terms used in sampling.

13.2. Sampling Terminology

Terms with precise meaning in statistical design are: elementary unit, population, sampling unit, frame, and sample.

Elementary Unit

Elementary Unit: The person, place, or thing on which an observation is made.

The elementary unit could range from inanimate objects such as vehicles coming off an assembly line to people at home or beef cattle on the hoof. A prevalent concern in data gathering is that the recorded observations are attributable to the elementary units one intended to sample. The following example indicates the importance of this concern.

Example 13.2A. Surveying Attitudes on the Equal Rights Amendment

In the late 1970s, an amendment was proposed to the Constitution of the United States known popularly as the Equal Rights Amendment (ERA). The proposed amendment obtained mixed voter support. Legislators, barraged by their more vocal constituents, were uncertain how public opinion split on the amendment, especially the opinion of women voters. Of the many surveys conducted, some provided useful information, others did not.

Women's opinions about the amendment were solicited by a questionnaire mailed to women of voting age. Caution was necessary to avoid including responses from persons not intended to be in the survey. Such a faulty survey design can happen in several ways:

1. *Ambiguous Addressee:* A survey questionnaire, addressed to the "occupant," "the Smith's," "Mr. and Mrs. Smith," etc, instead of a particular woman in the household, may create ambiguity. It allows the questionnaire to be completed and returned by anyone in the household.

2. *Burdensome:* The intended recipient of the questionnaire finds it burdensome to complete and asks her husband or someone else to complete the form. If the purpose of the survey is unclear to the recipient, as is frequently the case, this potential pitfall becomes more likely to occur.

3. *Composite Opinion:* Thinking the survey is supposed to represent the household's opinion, not just her own, the recipient consults with other household members and reflects their opinion in answering the question.

4. *Apathy:* The recipient, upon reflection on the purpose of the survey, has no strong views on the subject and gives the questionnaire to someone who does.

Unless these pitfalls are explicitly considered and avoided in the design chosen, the results of the survey are likely seriously to distort the prevailing opinion of women about the ERA.

Population

Population: A designated collection of elementary units about which a generalization is to be made.

The population may consist of fish in a catfish pond or people who own Chevrolet automobiles. But it is essential that the population be *clearly defined* so that it becomes possible to unambiguously identify population members. This is sometimes more difficult than might be expected. The following example illustrates a situation in which it would be important to report the population definition.

Example 13.2B. **Defining the Population of Unemployed Workers**

The federal government publishes periodic statements about the number of unemployed people and the length of time that persons remain unemployed between jobs. But which people are to be designated as unemployed? Clearly, the population of unemployed can be designated in various ways. For instance, should only those still currently collecting unemployment benefits be considered unemployed, or alternatively, should the base also include those persons actively looking for a job, but whose benefits have run out? Should the population include or exclude persons who are on strike? A choice among these population definitions must be made, although the best choice is far from obvious. Therefore, explicit information should be provided by the researcher on how the population is defined.

Sampling Unit

Sampling Unit: A non-overlapping block of elementary units.

Strange as it may seem to the uninitiated, what is sampled is not necessarily an elementary unit. The concept of a sampling unit permits us to distinguish the units being sampled from the units on which observations are recorded. The example below illustrates why that distinction is important.

Example 13.2C. **College Student Consumer Expenditure Study**

Knowledge about the items college students buy most frequently and how much money they spend weekly is essential information for corporations marketing to college students. To obtain this information, one might propose a survey (a random sample) of all college students, the population of elementary units. Even if a complete up-to-date student list could be obtained, an interview survey would not be feasible because of the expense in locating and polling students from widely dispersed geographical areas. A less costly and more convenient alternative approach is to use colleges rather than students as sampling units. From a complete list of colleges (which is easier to obtain than a complete list of students), a random sample of several colleges would be drawn. From each college included in the survey, observations on several college students (elementary units) would be obtained. The sampling unit (college) and elementary unit (college student) are not identical in this case, but in some cases they may be.

The Frame

Frame: A list enumerating the sampling units from which the sample is drawn.

The list of all colleges in our college student marketing example defines the sampling frame. Frequently, the list of elementary units in the sampling frame is not identical to the list of elementary units in the actual target population. This discrepancy occurs because published listings are usually out of date. For instance, published college student directories are frequently used as a current list for sampling purposes. These directories are generally published only annually and are completed from the list of students registered at the beginning of the academic year. Thus, they will still include the names of students who have dropped out, and will exclude students who have enrolled subsequent to the beginning of the academic year. The greater the turnover of students during the academic year, the less representative will be the published list of the current target population. Frequent up-dates of lists of elementary units give better correspondence of the elementary units in the frame to the target population of elementary units.

The Sample

Sample: A selected number of sampling units drawn from the frame.

Observations are made on every elementary unit contained in the selected sampling units. From these observations, a statistical inference is made about the totality of elementary units in the frame. Only if the frame and the target population are identical will the inference apply directly to the target population.

13.3. Types of Bias

There are numerous types of sampling bias. We will look at several of them here and explain how they can be guarded against.

Selection Bias

Selection bias is the tendency to favor the selection of certain population members with distinct traits different from the other members of the population. At times selection bias is intentional and appropriate. In choosing a panel for a roundtable discussion on the economy, panelists with particular areas of economic expertise would be preferred over a randomly selected group of citizens. On the other hand, unintended selection bias can alter the validity of a conclusion. For example, interviewers, left on their own, tend to shy away from homes in both extremely wealthy and poor neighborhoods (and probably from homes with barking Dobermans as well.) The following example illustrates a business situation in which selection bias can easily occur.

Example 13.3A. **Measuring the Sales Effectiveness of Promotional Expenditures**

Marketing studies designed to measure the sales effectiveness of various promotional expenditures often give misleading results when the beneficiaries of the expenditures are left to the discretion of sales representatives. Given a choice, sales reps often choose either their badly neglected accounts, or accounts with whom they have already developed a particularly good relationship. Over-estimates of average sales effectiveness of the promotional monies would likely result from servicing the badly neglected accounts. Catering to accounts which have nearly reached their full sales potential would likely underestimate the effectiveness of promotional monies on average sales. In either case, the conclusion drawn would be misleading.

Measurement Bias

Measurement bias is a source of error attributable to the manner in which the observation is made. A *misrecording* of a physical dimension such as weight or height is a simple kind of measurement bias. To mention a few that are common yet more subtle:

1. The *wording of a question* can influence a respondent's answer.
2. Some *persons may lie* about their age, their income, or their sexual behavior.
3. Other persons may be influenced in their responses by the *interviewer's appearance or mannerisms.*

In experiments designed to determine the effect of chance in a causal variable, such as change in product price, measurement bias may exist if the observation is recorded before full impact of the change has taken place.

Nonresponse Bias

One of the most prevalent and devastating types of unintended bias is *nonresponse bias.* It is a form of selection bias in human populations; it surfaces when certain groups selected for the sample are more predisposed to respond than others. In surveys conducted by telephone or by personal interviewing, the not-at-home intended respondent is likely an important source of nonresponse bias.

Example 13.3B.   **Marketing Microwave Ovens**

A manufacturer researching consumer opinion towards microwave ovens conducts a telephone survey of two thousand households during the morning and afternoon hours. However, the greatest demand for convenience appliances such as microwave ovens is likely to be found in households where time available for meal preparation is most scarce. Employed adults are particularly likely to fall into this category, but are also least likely to be at home during the daytime to answer the telephone. Consequently, their opinion will be underrepresented in a survey restricted to daytime hours. Replacing a not-at-home intended respondent by an at-home daytime neighbor doesn't help; in fact it actually increases the bias by giving increased weight to the opinions of those who are at-home during the daytime. Requiring interviewers to call back evenings and weekends will virtually eliminate most of the not-at-home selection bias.

Volunteer Bias

Mail surveys have a variety of selection biases as insidious as the not-at-home variety found in the telephone and personal interviews surveys. It is called *volunteer bias.* Volunteer bias is characterized by two factors: first, the sampling units decide for themselves whether to respond; second, the likelihood of response is linked to the issue being surveyed.[1] A notorious example of volunteer bias occurred in the famous 1936 election fiasco involving the now-defunct *Literary Digest Magazine.*

Example 13.3C. The 1936 *Literary Digest* Presidential Poll

In 1936 Franklin Delano Roosevelt, the incumbent Democrat, was running against Republican Alfred M. Landon. A poll was taken by the *Literary Digest* to determine voter preferences for these two candidates and several million responses were obtained. The poll predicted Landon would be a landslide winner, but Roosevelt achieved one of the most lopsided victories in the history of American presidential elections.

The poll's erroneous conclusion has been mainly attributed to volunteer bias. The *Digest* had used its own subscription lists and names from telephone directories for sampling units to obtain a mailing of 10 million sampling units. The majority of the 2.3 million who responded were strongly anti-Roosevelt, so much so that they took the time to answer the questionnaire. The great majority of the non-respondents apparently liked Roosevelt, but not intensely enough to respond to the questionnaire. Despite the enormous sample size, the poll was not representative of the voters who went to the polls. The *Literary Digest* ceased publication shortly after the poll fiasco.[2]

Non-Random Samples

Measurement bias can occur in any type of sample unless great care is taken in constructing the questionnaire, training interviewers, etc. But selection bias occurs only in non-random samples, of which there are two main types—convenience and judgment. For non-random sampling, a "convenient chunk" rather than a process of randomization is one basis for obtaining observations on the population. A judgment sample is chosen neither by a randomization procedure nor on the basis of convenience, but by a highly regarded "expert" whose judgment determines who is to be represented in the sample. Canvassing industry reactions to proposed energy legislation, a U.S. senator might ask a business consultant familiar with the energy needs of industry to get an informed overview of industry's position by selectively surveying executive officers of various corporations.

Quota Samples

Quota samples are a hybrid of the convenience and judgment type of sample. An "expert" decides that a certain proportion of various sub-groups of population members should be included in the sample. The required number in each sub-group is selected conveniently rather than judgmentally or randomly. In evaluating state conservation policy, the state commissioner may mandate that a certain proportion of executives of each industry (gas, electricity, oil) be surveyed as well as consumer environmental groups.

The main motivation for the use of judgment samples, quota samples, and convenience samples over random samples is the lower cost-per-respondent. But the amount of bias remains open to speculation. The need for reliability may dictate a random sample. Actually, as the following section illustrates, random samples can prove to be both lower in total cost and less biased than non-random samples.

The Larger-Is-Better Trap

A small random sample relatively free from bias is usually much better than a larger non-random sample with unknown bias. To the uninitiated, survey results from a questionnaire sent to the entire 20,000 name mailing list may sound much more impressive and accurate than the results from a truly random sample of only 400 names from the list. However, sheer figures on the number of questionnaires mailed are meaningless unless one also knows both the number and the representativeness of the returns. In non-random sampling, 1000 responses out of 20,000 questionnaires mailed speak only for the 1000 persons who made them and not for the 19,000 persons who failed to reply. One can always speculate about what the 19,000 non-respondents would have said had they responded, but the speculation remains just that. Without tracking down the 19,000 non-respondents, a far more costly and difficult task than the original mailing, there is no way to predict the accuracy of the speculation. The money saved by mailing out 400 rather than 20,000 questionnaires can be used to track down the non-respondents in the smaller randomly selected sample. Since the sample is random, the results can be generalized with a known degree of accuracy to the entire list of 20,000 persons.

13.4. Random Sampling Plans

Having distinguished the features of random samples from non-random samples, we can now consider the different types of random sampling plans.

Simple Random Samples

A sample is a simple random sample if it is obtained in such a way that on every draw, each sampling unit remaining in the frame has an equal chance of being included in the sample. Selection could be accomplished by physical means by assigning a tag to each sampling unit and then drawing the tags out of a thoroughly stirred bowl containing all the tags. Usually, selections are made from a *table of random numbers*.

Random numbers are digits generated by a process which allows any possible number an equal probability to appear next. For example, in a list of five-digit random numbers, each value between 00000 and 99999 has the same chance of appearing at each location in the table. Table 13.1 is a segment from the table of *105,000 Random Decimal Digits* constructed for the Bureau of Transport Economics and Statistics of the Interstate Commerce Commission. This particular source has passed many statistical tests and has been widely accepted by the scientific community.

TABLE 13.1. Table of Random Numbers

	(1)	(2)	(3)	(4)	(5)	(6)	(7)	(8)	(9)	(10)
1	54941	72711	39406	94620	27963	96478	21559	19246	88097	44026
2	02349	71389	45608	60947	60775	73181	43264	56895	04232	59604
3	98210	44546	27174	27499	53523	63110	57106	20865	91683	80688
4	11826	91326	29664	01603	23156	89223	43429	95353	44662	59433
5	96810	17100	35066	00815	01552	06392	31437	70385	45863	75971
6	81060	33449	68055	83844	90942	74857	52419	68723	47830	63010
7	56135	80647	51404	06626	10042	93629	37609	57215	08409	81906
8	57361	65304	93258	56760	63348	24949	11839	29793	37457	59377
9	24548	56415	61927	64416	29934	00755	09418	14230	62887	92683
10	66504	02036	02922	63569	17906	38076	32135	19096	96970	75917
11	45068	05520	56321	22693	35089	07694	04252	23791	60249	83010
12	99717	01542	72990	43413	59744	44595	71326	91382	45114	20245
13	05394	61840	83089	09224	78530	33996	49965	04851	18280	14039
14	38155	42661	02363	67625	34683	95372	74733	63558	09665	22610
15	74319	04318	99387	86874	12549	38369	54952	91579	26023	81076
16	18134	90062	10761	54548	49505	52685	63903	13193	33905	66936
17	92012	42710	34650	73236	66167	21788	03581	40699	10396	81827
18	78101	44392	53767	15220	66319	72953	14071	59148	95154	72852
19	23469	42846	94810	16151	08029	50554	03891	38313	34016	18671
20	35342	56119	97190	43635	84249	61254	80993	55431	90793	62603
21	55846	18076	12415	30193	42777	85611	57635	51362	79907	77364
22	22184	33998	87436	37430	45246	11400	20986	43996	73112	88474
23	83668	66236	79665	88312	93047	12088	86937	70794	01041	74867
24	50083	70696	13558	98995	58159	04700	90443	13168	31553	67891
25	97765	27552	49617	51734	20849	70198	67906	00880	82899	66065
26	40988	13176	94219	88698	41755	56216	66832	17748	04963	54859
27	78257	86249	46134	51865	09836	73966	65711	41699	11732	17173
28	30946	22210	79302	40300	08852	27528	84648	79589	95295	72895
29	19468	76358	69203	02760	28625	70476	76410	32988	10194	94917
30	30806	80857	84383	78450	26245	91763	73117	33047	03577	62599
31	42163	69332	98851	50252	56911	62693	73817	98693	18728	94741
32	39249	51463	95963	07929	66728	47761	81472	44806	15592	71357
33	88717	29289	77360	09030	39605	87507	85446	51257	89555	75520
34	16767	57345	42285	56670	88445	85799	76200	21795	38894	58070
35	77516	98648	51868	48140	13583	94911	13318	64741	64336	95103
36	87192	66483	55649	36764	86132	12463	28385	94242	32063	45233
37	74078	64120	04643	14351	71381	28133	68269	65145	28152	39087
38	94119	20108	78101	81276	00835	63835	87174	42446	08882	27067
39	62180	27453	18567	55524	86088	00069	59254	24654	77371	26409
40	56199	05993	71201	78852	65889	32719	13758	23937	90740	16866
41	04994	09879	70337	11861	69032	51915	23510	32050	52052	24004
42	21725	43827	78862	67699	01009	07050	73324	06732	27510	33761
43	24305	37661	18956	50064	39500	17450	18030	63124	48061	59412
44	14762	69734	89150	93126	17700	94400	76075	08317	27324	72723
45	28387	99781	52977	01657	92602	41043	05686	15650	29970	95877

Source: Extracted from "Table of 105,000 Random Decimal Digits," Statement No. 4914, File No. 261-A (Washington, D.C.: Interstate Commerce Commission, 1949).

Example 13.4A.   Using a Table of Random Numbers to Draw a Random Sample

As part of a brand preference marketing survey for frozen orange juice concentrate, we wish to select a random sample of eight households from a housing subdivision of eighty-four households. The following steps would lead to a random sample:

1. List all households by address and number them from 01 to 84.

2. Choose an arbitrary starting point on the page of random numbers—say the 14th row and 8th column in Table 13.1. Pick out any two-digit number—usually adjacent digits are selected for convenience. Using the first two digits, this number is 63. Then household number 63 is included in your random sample.

3. The next two digit number can be chosen by moving in any direction from the starting point, up, across, or whatever. Keep selecting two-digit numbers until you have eight numbers between 01 and 84 with no repetitions.

For instance, moving down the table, the next number after 63 is 91, but it is ineligible since no household corresponds with 91. Again, moving down the table, one encounters digits 13, 40, 59, 38, 55, 51, 43: at this point the eight households are eligible to be surveyed. Numbers 63, 13, 40, 59, 38, 55, 51, and 43 are to be surveyed.

If there are exactly 100 items in the frame, read "00" as 100. If there are more than 100 items, use as many additional adjacent digits as necessary to form numbers large enough to encompass the number of sampling units in the frame. Thus, if one begins in the first line of the second column, the adjacent digits 727 could be used to start off the three-digit numbers or 7271 to start off the four-digit numbers.

Systematic Random Samples

A systematic random sample is obtained by selecting the first sampling unit to be included in the sample on a random basis and then choosing the additional sampling units at evenly spaced intervals until the desired sample size is reached. To obtain a sample of 100 names from a frame of 700 names requires dividing the frame by the sample size to obtain the size of the interval—in this case seven. From a table of random numbers, a starting number (from one to seven) is randomly selected. If the number is three, then the third name on the list is the first person in the sample, and every seventh name thereafter (10, 17, 24, . . . 696) is included in the sample.

If the elementary units in the population appear in random order, a systematic random sample is equivalent to a simple random sample of the same size. The advantage lies in the greater ease of drawing the sample—only one item has to be selected randomly instead of every item. If nearby elementary units of a population tend to resemble each other more than those at greater distances, systematic random sampling has an advantage over simple random sampling. Adjacent houses, for instance, tend to be more similar in value than houses in different neighborhoods. Systematic interval selection of city blocks avoids adjacent or nearby houses and tends to include in the sample proportionate amounts of each housing value group. A simple random sample, on the other hand, could include adjacent similar valued housing.

Biased systematic random sampling is possible if periodic variation in the population coincides with the sampling interval. Sampling a supermarket's sales one day of the week at random and then every seventh day thereafter to estimate average daily sales would be biased by the strong daily sales pattern within each week. If Wednesday sales are below the daily average this week, they will likely be below the daily average other weeks as well. Choosing every Wednesday as the sampling interval would lead to an underestimate of the actual average daily sales.

Stratified Sampling

A *stratified sample* is selected by dividing the frame into strata and drawing part of the total sample from each stratum by random selection.

Suppose a population can be divided into strata (subgroups) within which variability of the measurements on each of the subgroups is considerably less than in the population taken as a whole. Substantial reduction in sampling variability may be achieved compared to a simple random sample of the same size. The idea is to do extensive sampling in strata of high variability and less extensive sampling in strata of low variability compared to an equal sampling effort on each stratum. In short, stratification achieves advantages if:

1. The variable used as the basis for stratification can easily be identified and is linked with the variable being investigated.

2. The elementary units grouped into a stratum are more homogeneous (alike), both with respect to the variable being investigated and with respect to the variable used for stratification, than generally are the elementary units of the population.

To meet both criteria, human populations are frequently stratified by age, occupation, sex, etc. The belief is that the stratifying feature links the members of a stratum to the variable being studied. An estimate of the average income of self-employed professionals in a city can be achieved by linking occupation to income and stratifying the professionals according to occupation (doctors, lawyers, dentists, etc.) A simple random sample from each stratum provides income values which are pooled to obtain the overall estimate of income for the frame. The greater the difference among the strata, the more likely it is that this estimate will be more accurate than an estimate obtained from a simple random sample of the same total sample size taken from the frame without the benefit of stratification.

For instance, consider the problem of estimating the average salary of a university faculty with three ranks of faculty members (assistant, associate, and full professor), each with *one* salary rate. A simple random sample would have some sampling error. However, stratifying by rank and then sampling only one professor from each rank would give an estimate with no sampling error at all! We would know exactly the average salary for the entire faculty!

Realizing then that the objective of stratification is to minimize overall sample variability for a given total sample size n, how can one determine how many items to sample from each stratum? The number of items to be sampled from a specific stratum is determined by the following formula:

$$m_i = n\left[\frac{M_i\sigma_i}{\sum(M_i\sigma_i)}\right]$$

where m_i = the number of items to be sampled in the ith stratum, M_i = the total number of items in the ith stratum, σ_i = the standard deviation of the ith stratum, n = total sample size: the sum of the items sampled across the strata, $\sum m_i$.

For example, suppose a population $N = 9000$ items is grouped into three strata with $M_1 = 2000$ items in the first stratum, $M_2 = 3000$ items in the second stratum, and $M_3 = 4000$ items in the third stratum. If the strata standard deviations are $\sigma_1 = 50$, $\sigma_2 = 20$, $\sigma_3 = 80$, a total sample of $n = 200$ items should include

$$m_2 = n\left[\frac{M_2\sigma_2}{\sum M_i\sigma_i}\right] = 200\left[\frac{(3000)(20)}{(2000)(50) + (3000)(20) + (4000)(80)}\right] = 25$$

items in the sample from the second stratum.

The means of the individual strata are pooled to obtain an estimate of the population mean:

$$\overline{X}_{\text{stratified}} = \sum\left(\frac{M_i}{N}\right)\overline{X}_i$$

where N is the population size and $\overline{X}_i$ is the sample mean of the ith stratum. Thus, in estimating the overall mean of the stratified population, an individual stratum mean is weighted according to the proportion of the population items in that stratum. The larger this proportion, the more influential is the mean of this stratum in determining the overall population mean estimate.

The standard error of the population mean is also obtained by pooling:

$$\sigma_{\overline{X}_{\text{stratified}}} = \sqrt{\sum\left(\frac{M_i}{N}\right)^2\sigma_{\overline{X}_i}^2}$$

where $\sigma_{\overline{X}_i}^2$ is the variance of the sampling distribution for sample means in the ith stratum. Thus, the larger the proportion of the total population included in a particular stratum, the more heavily weighted is that stratum's standard error in computing the standard error of the overall population mean. Let us illustrate these computations.

Example 13.4B. **Calculating the Mean and Standard Error of a Stratified Sample**

A manufacturer of truck engines wants to estimate efficiently the mean annual mileage per vehicle in which his engines are installed. It is known, however, that the 20,000 trucks used in local cartage average substantially less mileage annually than the 10,000 trucks used in intercity transportation. Because of the bimodal nature of the mileage distribution, a stratified sampling plan is suggested to reduce the sampling variability of the estimated mean. The standard deviation of mileage of the vehicles is reliably estimated as 5000 miles for the local stratum and 10,000 miles for the intercity stratum.

Table 13.2 summarizes the information needed to compute the sample size for each stratum.

TABLE 13.2. Strata Items and Standard Deviations

STRATUM	STRATUM NUMBER (i)	NUMBER OF ITEMS IN STRATUM (M_i)	STD. DEVIATION OF ITEMS IN STRATUM (σ_i)	PRODUCT ($M_i\sigma_i$)
Intercity	1	10,000	10,000	100,000,000
Local	2	20,000	5000	100,000,000
		Total = 30,000 = N	Total	200,000,000

Using a total sample size of $n = 600$ items, we can then determine the sample size for each stratum:

$$m_1 = (600)\frac{100,000,000}{200,000,000} = 300 \text{ trucks}$$

in the local stratum and

$$m_2 = (600)\frac{100,000,000}{200,000,000} = 300 \text{ trucks}$$

in the intercity stratum.

If the sample of 600 items is taken and results in a mean of $\overline{X}_1 = 94,000$ and $\overline{X}_2 = 26,000$, the estimate for the entire population is

$$\overline{X}_{\text{stratified}} = \sum\left(\frac{M_i}{N}\right)\overline{X}_i = \left(\frac{1}{3}\right)94,000 + \left(\frac{2}{3}\right)26,000$$

$$= 48,667$$

The standard error of $\overline{X}$ stratified requires that the standard errors of the individual strata first be calculated, taking into account the finite population adjustment.

$$\sigma_{\overline{X}_1} = \frac{\sigma_1}{\sqrt{m_1}}\sqrt{1 - \frac{m_1}{M_1}} = \frac{10,000}{\sqrt{300}}\sqrt{1 - \frac{300}{10,000}} = 568.6$$

$$\sigma_{\overline{X}_2} = \frac{\sigma_2}{\sqrt{m_2}}\sqrt{1 - \frac{m_2}{M_2}} = \frac{5000}{\sqrt{300}}\sqrt{1 - \frac{300}{20,000}} = 286.5$$

These standard errors are then inserted into the formula for the population standard error.

$$\sigma_{\overline{X}_{\text{stratified}}} = \sqrt{\sum\left[\left(\frac{M_i}{N}\right)^2\sigma_{\overline{X}_i}^2\right]} = \sqrt{\left(\frac{10,000}{30,000}\right)^2(568.6)^2 + \left(\frac{20,000}{30,000}\right)^2 286.5^2}$$

$$= 269.1$$

Cluster Samples

The advantages of stratification over alternative methods of sampling diminishes the greater the similarity among the individual strata. Sampling from each and every group is unnecessary if groups are similar in composition. Moreover, there is no disadvantage in leaving some groups out of the sample. More is gained for a given sample size by concentrating sample efforts within one group rather than among the various groups if the groups are similar. With no increase in sampling error, the cost of obtaining the sample would be less. Groupings with similar composition are termed clusters and sampling from clusters, *cluster sampling*.

Cluster sampling from a population requires dividing the population to achieve relative homogeneity among the clusters, although there may be considerable heterogeneity *within* a cluster. The important point is that the composition of each cluster should be similar to the others. The procedure is to select from the collection of similar (not identical) clusters, a simple random sample of clusters. The next step is to draw a simple random sample (possibly a complete census) from each and every selected cluster.

Example 13.4C.   Using Cluster Sampling to Obtain Reliable Information Inexpensively

In order to survey a sample of 1000 midwest farm families on their attitudes about a new tractor model, cluster sampling could be used to reduce both the time and expense required to collect the thousand responses. With cluster sampling, the farms in a few selected counties could be completely canvassed. Had simple random sampling of the farms been performed initially, the survey would likely involve traveling across dozens of states to collect responses from the diverse sampling units selected randomly. The traveling cost and the time spent would be far more expensive for the simple random sample.

Cluster sampling has an additional advantage over simple random sampling. Sampling by clusters does not require a listing of the elementary units in the frame being sampled. For instance, a sampling of the employees of Chicago retail stores would require far less effort if a list of the retail stores within the city was the starting point rather than a list of all their employees. With a random sample of clusters (stores) selected, one needs only a list of the employees of the stores included in the cluster sample for the interviewing.

Normally, cluster sampling does not yield a sampling error as low as a simple random sample of the same size. Why? Since there will likely be some heterogeneity among clusters, those clusters selected in the sample will vary in composition from those left out. Cluster sampling in this sense is more inefficient in gathering information and results in higher sampling error than the same size simple random sample. Has all been lost? Hardly. Despite this drawback, the reduced cost of cluster sampling may easily allow a larger cluster sample to surpass in reliability the simple random sample of 1000 respondents. At an average cost of $15 each for the simple random sample, or a total of $15,000, a better result might be obtained for $9600 with a cluster sample of 1600 respondents costing only $6 each.

It should be evident by now that systematic, stratified, and cluster sampling plans are clearly better alternatives at times than using a simple random sampling plan exclusively, although all of these plans employ a simple random sample at some stage of the sampling plan. Moreover, regardless of the sampling plan, random or non-random, simple random sampling is the standard of comparison against which all other sampling plans are measured. Understanding simple random sampling is extremely important, and in the next section we shall learn its role in experimental design.

13.5. Experimental Design

Several statistical design principles and procedures have been considered up to this point. They have all been directed towards efficiently and reliably drawing unbiased generalizations about a target population based upon a sample of elementary units from the sampling frame. Another important class of statistical design problems are considered in the remaining sections of this chapter. These are concerned with establishing the amount of difference and the reason for differences between two sets of measurements. In particular, we shall usually want to know whether the differences can plausibly be attributed to sources extraneous to our interest, or alternatively, to a source that is the object or purpose of our investigation. For example, in the Crest fluoride toothpaste experiments, a lower cavity rate was found among children using the fluoride toothpaste than among children using a toothpaste without fluoride. Is the lower cavity rate for the fluoride toothpaste attributable to the fluoride? Or, alternatively, is it attributable to other sources such as fewer children with good teeth among the non-fluoride group, or bias in the test administration? This determination should be feasible if the purpose of the investigation is properly reflected in the statistical design.

All too often a statistical study purporting to test one thing actually tests another or, worse yet, is so improperly designed that it cannot serve any useful purpose at all. The latter situation is illustrated in the following example in which a study failed to determine whether a new type of automobile battery offered improved performance compared to a conventional battery type.

Example 13.5. **Evaluating New Product Performance**

Suppose an automobile battery manufacturer, having to make a decision about which of two batteries to market to a target group of users, needs an evaluation of the service life of a new, permanently sealed battery and its alternative, a conventional battery. Six conventional batteries and six of the new type are installed in a dozen cars. With the headlights on, each car was started every three minutes until it would no longer start. Recording the number of successful starts on each car might yield the following results:

Conventional Battery:	606, 630, 586, 570, 641, 559	Mean: 598.7
New Type Battery:	513, 536, 561, 603, 595, 529	Mean: 556.2

At first glance, the conventional battery, averaging more starts than the new type, seems to offer better performance. But on careful reflection, the numbers may warrant a different conclusion. First, there is a considerable variation in the number of starts among the batteries, even of the same type. This raises the possibility that the higher conventional battery average may be attributable only to sampling error.

Leaving sampling error aside for the moment, there is still the important unanswered question as to whether the research design assures that the difference in mean number of starts truly reflects a performance difference between the battery types rather than the effect of extraneous factors. For example, the conditions under which the batteries were tested have not been specified and may have been substantially different. Cars assigned to the newer type battery may have had a larger engine, been harder to start, been tested in colder weather, the battery terminals may have been loosely connected, or the persons counting the starts for the newer type battery may have been less diligent in recording results. Thus, what at first may have seemed an obvious conclusion about the merits of the two batteries turns out to be an unwarranted conclusion. Although it may still be true that superior performance of the conventional battery is due to quality differences, previously cited factors or others could have singly or in combination accounted for the difference. The lack of information about the design should lead one to be cautious in making a judgment as to *why* the difference in service life occurred.

To assert that one particular factor (among many possible ones) is the *cause* of an observed variation, one needs the assurance that none of the other factors present could be held responsible. *Experimental design* is a branch of statistics which provides techniques to account for, and to reduce, the side effects of extraneous factors. Although experimental design is a course in itself, there are some important experimental design principles that are easily illustrated. In the battery sample, control of the effects of several factors can be achieved by holding these factors at a constant level in both treatments. One could resort to using the same car (carefully inspected for change of condition after each use), conduct the test at the same temperature, with the same operator, and with strict controls on the recording of results. Holding "constant" these conditions allows one to conclude that one battery type is superior to the other *under those rigidly controlled conditions.* However, the limitations of the conclusion (generalization of the results) must be recognized also. Would tests still favor the conventional battery if the tests were conducted with a different type of car, in colder or warmer weather, with different drivers, with a longer time between starts, or with less careful attention to cleaning the battery terminals and (in the case of the conventional battery) periodic checking of the cells to see if water should be added?

Equalizing Versus Controlling

To systematically isolate one factor at a time requires an enormous number of separate experiments. Testing the effect of eight different factors at three different levels (hot, moderate, and cold weather) would require over *six thousand* repetitions! Design procedures permitting simultaneous measurement of the effect of several variables circumvent these complications. But for the battery manufacturer there is little practical importance to knowing the effects of weather, degree of maintenance, etc. on a battery's life since the battery manufacturer has virtually no control over the weather or a car owner's maintenance standards. His concern is the service life of the two battery types under *actual usage conditions.* How do we simulate actual usage conditions? The procedure is surprisingly simple. Draw a *random sample* of registered vehicles and offer the owners free batteries in return for their cooperation in reporting battery life. By "sampling the environment," one "equalizes" (rather than controls) the test conditions for the two batteries. Performance difference too large to expect from sampling error affirms a significant difference in battery type. The message is clear: To assess data from a random sample for business decision making, one must know beforehand the nature and magnitude of sampling error to expect.

13.6. Two-Sample Designs—Independent Samples

The problem of evaluating a new battery's performance is an important inferential question not previously encountered. Our interest in the new type of battery's performance is obviously not isolated from the performance of the battery type currently being marketed and sold. A comparative performance of the two battery types would likely be the focus of a statistical investigation. But our study of inference so far has been restricted to a single population. What is the inferential procedure when two populations are compared?

For this important class of comparative problems, sample statistics are obtained from *two independent samples*. The relevant comparison is made in terms of the *difference* between two underlying population parameters (means or proportions). For example, take the difference between the means of two populations. To make a statistical inference about this difference, we look both at the difference actually observed between the means of samples drawn from the two populations, and at the standard deviations of these populations. Thus, if a sample of new style batteries has a mean life of $\overline{X}_1 = 34$ months while the sample of current style batteries has a mean life of $\overline{X}_2 = 31$ months, we look at the difference, $\overline{X}_1 - \overline{X}_2 = 3$ months. However, we cannot ignore the variation among battery lives. Moreover, the amount of this variation might differ for the two types. We need to know how this variation might affect the values of $\overline{X}_1$ and $\overline{X}_2$ that we find, and particularly their difference. The sampling distribution for this difference describes the variation we want to know about. Its standard deviation is needed to make an inference about the difference between means of the two populations of batteries.

> The standard deviation of the sampling distribution of the difference between means of two independent samples is the *square root of the sum of the two individual standard deviations squared*. This value is known as the *standard error of the difference*.

Defining $\overline{D}$ as the difference between the individual sample means calculated from two independent samples, and $\sigma_{\overline{D}}$ as its standard error, we have

$$\overline{D} = \overline{X}_2 - \overline{X}_1;$$

$$\sigma_{\overline{D}} = \sqrt{\frac{\sigma_1^2}{n_1} + \frac{\sigma_2^2}{n_2}}$$

where $\overline{X}_1$ and σ_1^2 are the sample mean and the population variance of the first population, and $\overline{X}_2$ and σ_2^2 are the comparable values for the second population.

For the battery type example above, suppose $\sigma_1 = 5$ months for the new type batteries and $\sigma_2 = 6$ months for the current type, with $n_1 = 100$ and $n_2 = 200$. Then the standard error of the difference between $\overline{X}_1$ and $\overline{X}_2$ is

$$\sigma_{\overline{D}} = \sqrt{\frac{\sigma_1^2}{n_1} + \frac{\sigma_2^2}{n_2}} = \sqrt{\frac{25}{100} + \frac{36}{200}} = \sqrt{.43} = .656$$

Population Standard Deviations Unknown

When the population standard deviations, σ_1 and σ_2, are not available, the sampling distribution used to make inferences about the true D follows a Student t distribution. For large samples ($n > 30$) however, the t distribution is well approximated by a normal distribution with the values of σ_1 and σ_2 estimated, with slight imprecision, by S_1 and S_2, the respective sample standard deviations computed from the two independent samples drawn. The substitution permits the calculation of $S_{\overline{D}}$ as an estimate of $\sigma_{\overline{D}}$:

$$S_{\overline{D}} = \sqrt{\frac{S_1^2}{n_1} + \frac{S_2^2}{n_2}}$$

An example follows where σ_1 and σ_2 are known.

Example 13.6.   **Quality Control For Part Clearances: Bolts that Don't Fit Their Bushings**

Critical clearance, an important quality control feature in general manufacturing, is used extensively in automotive part production. Consider the situation between a bolt and its bushing. Suppose a machine, when operating correctly, produces bolts with diameter dimensions X_1 that:

1. have a mean diameter μ_{X_1} of .250 inches with
2. standard deviation σ_{X_1} of .004 and
3. are normally distributed.

Properly functioning, the machine producing bushings turns out items with diameter measurements X_2 that:

1. have a mean diameter μ_{X_2} of .265 and
2. standard deviation σ_{X_2} of .003 and
3. are normally distributed.

The *clearance* between a bushing and bolt is the difference in diameters; that is,

$$D = X_2 - X_1$$

If there is not enough clearance between the bolt and bushing for quick and easy assembly, the parts are unusable for the production line. If both machines are in proper adjustment, the *probability distribution for the clearance* between a randomly drawn bolt and randomly drawn bushing has:

1. mean $\mu_D = \mu_{X_2} - \mu_{X_1}$
   $$= .265 - .250 = .015$$

2. standard deviation $\sigma_D = \sqrt{\sigma_{X_1}^2 + \sigma_{X_2}^2}$
$$= \sqrt{.004^2 + .003^2}$$
$$= .005$$

3. a normal distribution

Suppose the minimum satisfactory clearance value is $D = .005$, which is two stan-dard deviations below μ_D ($D - \mu_D = .005 - .015 = -.010 = -2\sigma_D$). Thus, from the normal curve tables it can be shown that the probability of D less than .005 pro-ducing an unsatisfactory fit is only .0228. Notice that this is a one-tailed value reading. However, if the machine slips out of adjustment, this probability increases to 0.1587 if the actual mean clearance between the bolt and the bushings produced falls to .010. Let's illustrate this.

The first step in the solution is to determine what range of values of the stan-dardized variable Z correspond to $D < .005$. Since

$$Z = \frac{D - \mu_D}{\sigma_D}$$

the range of Z values corresponding to $(D < .005 \,|\, \mu_D = .010, \sigma_D = .005)$ is

$$Z < \frac{.005 - .010}{.005} \quad \text{or}$$

$$Z < -1$$

From Appendix Table 4 (normal curve),

$$P(Z < -1) = .1587$$

In other words, if such a machine is allowed to continue to produce, sixteen per-cent of the parts would have unsatisfactory clearance.

To check the production system, random samples of $n_1 = 400$ bolts and $n_2 = 400$ bushings are taken; sample means $\overline{X}_1 = .2552$ and $\overline{X}_2 = .2668$ are found. Given these sample statistics, what are upper and lower limits of the .99 confidence inter-val for the mean clearance μ_D?

1. The sampling distribution of $\overline{D}$ has standard error

$$\sigma_{\overline{D}} = \sqrt{\frac{\sigma_1^2}{n_1} + \frac{\sigma_2^2}{n_2}} = \sqrt{\frac{(.004)^2}{400} + \frac{(.003)^2}{400}} = .00025$$

where $\overline{D} = \overline{X}_1 - \overline{X}_2$.

2. The Z statistic required for a two-sided .99 confidence interval is 2.58.

3. The upper confidence limit for μ_D is

$$\overline{D} + Z_{.005}\sigma_{\overline{D}} = (.2668 - .2552) + (2.58)(.00025)$$
$$= .0116 + .000645$$
$$= .0122$$

4. The lower confidence limit for μ_D is
$$\overline{D} - Z_{.005}\sigma_{\overline{D}} = .0116 - .000645$$
$$= .0110$$

If the actual mean clearance has the value of the lower confidence limit ($\mu_D = .0110$), what fraction of clearances between a randomly chosen bolt and bushing pair will be unsatisfactory (less than .005)?

1. The sampling distribution of $\bar{D}$ for a sample of one (pair) has a standard error the same as the population clearance probability distribution:

$$\sigma_{\bar{D}} = \sqrt{\frac{\sigma_1^2}{n_1} + \frac{\sigma_2^2}{n_2}} = \sqrt{\frac{.004^2}{1} + \frac{.003^2}{1}} = .005 = \sigma_D$$

2. Measured in standard deviations, the difference between the mean clearance, .0110 and .005, is

$$Z = \frac{D - \mu_D}{\sigma_D} = \frac{.005 - .0110}{.005} = -1.2$$

3. From the normal distribution table, the probability of a Z value below -1.2 is .1151. This is the fraction of clearances expected to be less than .005. Thus, as long as the actual mean clearance is within the computed confidence interval, the probability that a bolt will be too large for its bushing will not exceed .1151.

13.7. Inferences Concerning the Differences Between Two Proportions

The procedure for making an inference about the difference between two population proportions, $p_1 - p_2$, is similar to the steps taken to compare the difference between two population means. Similar that is, except for one common complication. The problem arises in calculating the standard error of the differences.

The formula for the standard error is:

$$\sigma_{\bar{D}} = \sqrt{\frac{p_1(1 - p_1)}{n_1} + \frac{p_2(1 - p_2)}{n_2}}$$

where $\bar{D} = \hat{p}_2 - \hat{p}_1$.

How is the value of the standard error, which depends upon the population values p_1 and p_2, to be estimated?

> One approach frequently used exploits the null hypothesis claiming *no difference* between the two population proportions. It assumes the hypothesized relationship $p_1 = p_2$ is true.

From this claim, it is plausible to *average together* the two sample proportions to form an estimate of the common value of p_1 and p_2. The average value of the two sample proportions, weighted by the sizes of the two samples, defines p_A. The computation of standard error of the difference follows:

$$\hat{p}_A = \frac{n_1 \hat{p}_1 + n_2 \hat{p}_2}{n_1 + n_2}$$

$$S_{\bar{D}} = \sqrt{\frac{\hat{p}_A(1 - \hat{p}_A)}{n_1} + \frac{\hat{p}_A(1 - \hat{p}_A)}{n_2}}$$

This inferential procedure is illustrated in the following example.

Example 13.7. Are Users of Nescafe Instant Coffee Lazy?

One of the classic studies in the marketing research literature is the famous "shopping list" study conducted by Professor Mason Haire of Harvard University.[3] A sample of one hundred Boston women were personally interviewed. Each woman was given one of two types of grocery shopping lists and told to project herself into the situation until she could "more or less characterize the woman who brought home the groceries. Then write a brief description of her personality and character."

The interviewed women were not aware of the existence of two lists and, more importantly, that the two shopping lists were identical except for the type of coffee. The coffee on one list was "Nescafe Instant Coffee"; on the other list was "1 lb. can of Maxwell House Coffee (Drip Grind)". The purpose of this shopping list approach was to isolate the attitude difference between the two coffees. It was thought that there might be a possible stigma attached to the use of instant coffee. This notion of the "shopping list" arose because at that time, when directly questioned as to why they did not purchase instant coffee, people used the acceptable answer, "I don't like the flavor," and avoided the answer, "People will think I am lazy and not a good wife."

All responses were reported literally so that no interviewer bias would be "read into" them. Twenty-four (48%) of the women in the group given the "Nescafe Instant" shopping list characterized the shopper by the word "lazy." Only two (4%) of the women with the "Maxwell House (Drip Grind)" list described the shopper using the word "lazy."

Could two random samples of 50 each produce such dramatically different rates of occurrence of the description "lazy" if in fact there were no differences in the populations from which the samples were drawn? In other words, can the seemingly wide difference between 48% and 4% plausibly be explained by the "smallness" of the sample? A hypothesis test provides an answer to this question. Since the thrust of marketing research is to find exploitable differences between brands, it seems the appropriate null the investigator wishes to disprove and the alternative are:

$$H_0: \mu_D = p_2 - p_1 = 0$$

$$H_A: \mu_D \neq 0.$$

The estimate of the common population proportion is:

$$\hat{p}_A = \frac{n_1 \hat{p}_1 + n_2 \hat{p}_2}{n_1 + n_2} = \frac{50(.48) + 50(.04)}{50 + 50} = .26$$

The standard error is:

$$S_{\bar{D}} = \sqrt{\frac{\hat{p}_A(1 - \hat{p}_A)}{n_1} + \frac{\hat{p}_A(1 - \hat{p}_A)}{n_2}}$$

$$= \sqrt{\frac{(.26)(.74)}{50} + \frac{(.26)(.74)}{50}}$$

$$= .0877$$

Therefore, the Z-statistic is

$$Z = \frac{\bar{D} - \mu_D}{S_{\bar{D}}} = \frac{p_2 - p_1}{S_{\bar{D}}} = \frac{.48 - .04}{.0877} = 5.02$$

where $\mu_D = 0$.

The prob-value of finding a Z-statistic 5.02 standard deviations away from the assumed mean of $D = 0$ is so low that it cannot be found on the normal curve table. The sample evidence is too unusual for the claim of no difference between the population proportions to remain tenable. So, the null hypothesis would be rejected even at the 1% level of significance. Thus the data suggest a real difference in the two population proportions. Is this due to a stigma against instant coffee? Or to a faulty design of the study? Whatever the cause, the observed difference is not due to "smallness of the sample."

13.8. Two-Sample Designs: Matched Pairs

So far the two-sample designs in this chapter have analyzed differences between the means or proportions of the observations of two *independent* samples. But there is another approach called *matched pair* sampling in which the differences are between two measurements on the same individuals or items. For example, when the same person is asked to compare the taste of Coke and of Pepsi, this is a matched pair design. Conceptually these paired measurement differences can be treated as a single sample of differences and statistically analyzed as such.

In matched pair sampling, the observed differences d_i are matched bivariate observations—matched measurements on two variables for the same i^{th} individual or item. Thus, if an individual rates Pepsi as 9 and Coke 7 on a 10 point scale, the "Pepsi difference" for that individual is $9 - 7 = 2$. Notationally,

$$d_i = X_{2i} - X_{1i}$$

where d_i = the *matched pair difference* for the ith unit; X_{1i} = the value of the first variable for the ith unit; X_{2i} = the value of the second variable for the ith unit. Note that d_i represents an *individual's* measurement difference and is *not* the same as the unsubscripted D used to represent the difference between the measurements on items of two independent samples. Each matched pair difference d_i can be treated like an individual observation. Consequently,

$$\bar{d} = \frac{\Sigma d_i}{n}$$

has the same properties as $\bar{X}$ and all the procedures for one-sample inferences are applicable.

Why is matched pair sampling usually a much more efficient method of testing the difference between two means than is the method of comparing the independent samples? This question can perhaps best be addressed by considering an example.

Example 13.8. Physical Conditioning at Marine Corps Boot Camp

One typical result of conditioning new recruits at Marine Corps boot camp is a change in weight. Some recruits lose, others gain, and some maintain their existing weight. To test whether *overall* there has been a mean weight change one can use either two independent samples or matched pairs sampling.

Two independent samples: Although the Marine Corps typically follows closely the progress of each recruit, assume that two independent random samples *were* taken, one upon entering and one upon finishing boot camp. The difference between the means of the two samples, $\bar{D}$, can then be used to infer whether there has been an overall average weight change for *all* recruits.

Matched pairs: One random sample of recruits is used. But *two* observations on weight are recorded for *each recruit,* one upon entering boot camp and the other upon finishing boot camp. The weight *change* would be recorded for each recruit and the average of these changes, $\bar{d}$, would then be used to infer whether a mean weight change occurred for *all* recruits.

In the first method, it is likely that *different* recruits are involved in each sample. The observed difference between the sample means (entering versus finishing) will mainly reflect the different composition of the two groups. There will be considerable weight variation among the different individual recruits within each group. This "within" group weight variation would likely make it difficult to isolate a weight change due solely to boot camp training, unless there is both a very large weight change and the two samples used are very large. Is the matched pair method, working with the weight difference on the same recruits as a single sample, subject to the same problem? No. The extraneous source of weight variation present in the independent samples method is eliminated. This focuses the observed average difference to the factor of interest: *change* in weights due to training.

13.9. Two-Sample Designs—Small Samples

For large samples, the sampling distribution of

$$Z = \frac{\bar{X} - \mu_{\bar{X}}}{\sigma_{\bar{X}}}$$

is approximately normally distributed regardless of whether the underlying population is normally distributed, and regardless of whether the population standard deviation σ_X is known or is estimated by the sample standard deviations S_X.

For small size samples, the two-sample designs employing the normal or Student t distributions necessitate some restrictive assumptions. The assumptions may not be met in practice, particularly if independent samples are taken.

A normal sampling distribution is appropriate to use only if the two populations are known to have a normal distribution with known standard deviations.

A Student t distribution is strictly appropriate to use only if the two populations are known to have normal distributions with unknown but *equal* variances.

When these conditions are not met even approximately, the investigator should turn to *nonparametric* methods discussed in Chapter 22. However, it should be noted that the t distribution is quite robust in the sense that small to moderate deviations from the assumptions often do not greatly affect test results. Deviations from the normality condition are less hazardous than deviations from the equal variances assumption. Moreover, in many formally designed experiments it is proper to assume equality of population variances. Why? It is plausible that the source of variation is the environment which is the same or common to both populations.

Matched Pair Sampling

Matched pair sampling used with small rather than large samples necessitates one procedural change. The t-statistic based on $n - 1$ degrees of freedom is used instead of a Z statistic. The following example illustrates the procedure for matched pair sampling using small samples.

Example 13.9. How Creditworthy Are a Firm's Accounts Receivable?

The commercial lending department of a large bank often buys at a discount the accounts receivable of many of its client companies, a process known as "factoring" the receivables. Before purchasing the receivables, a bank loan officer evaluates closely the ability to pay or credit-worthiness of the client company's customers who owe the receivables. Ultimately, this determines whether to purchase and how much to purchase of the outstanding receivables. The loan officer's opinion of the "quality" of the receivables is expressed as a value between 0 and 10. An excellent rating is given a ten and a zero indicates that the receivables constitute a very poor credit risk.

   The management of the bank wanted to be sure that the same standards were being applied by the two loan officers in charge of developing the ratings. Accordingly, twenty factoring applications were selected at random and two loan officers were asked to make independent evaluations of the receivables' quality. The results are given in Table 13.3.

   Is the difference significant at $\alpha = 5\%$ level?

   We first set the null and alternative hypotheses:

   H_0: $\mu_d = 0$ (no real difference between loan officer evaluations)
   H_A: $\mu_d \neq 0$ (real difference between loan officer evaluations)

Next, we need to find the t statistic.

$$t = \frac{\bar{d} - 0}{S_{\bar{d}}} = \frac{.55 - 0}{1.3945/\sqrt{20}} = \frac{.55}{.3118} = 1.764$$

TABLE 13.3. Loan Officer Ratings of Accounts Receivable Quality

APPLICATION NUMBER	LOAN OFFICER A	LOAN OFFICER B	DIFFERENCE
1	5	6	−1
2	7	4	3
3	8	6	2
4	5	5	0
5	4	2	2
6	1	2	−1
7	9	9	0
8	6	7	−1
9	5	3	2
10	8	7	1
11	4	3	1
12	8	5	3
13	8	9	−1
14	4	3	1
15	3	5	−2
16	4	3	1
17	5	5	0
18	4	4	0
19	5	4	1
20	6	6	0

$$\sum d_i = 11$$
$$\bar{d} = .55$$

$$S_d = \sqrt{\frac{\sum(d_i - \bar{d})^2}{n - 1}} = \sqrt{\frac{\sum(d_i - .55)^2}{19}} = \sqrt{\frac{36.95}{19}} = 1.3945$$

In the above calculation,

$$S_{\bar{d}} = \frac{S_d}{\sqrt{n}} = \frac{1.3945}{\sqrt{20}}$$

Next, the computed value of 1.764 must be compared with the critical value of t shown in Appendix Table 7 for $n - 1 = 19$ degrees of freedom and the .05 level of significance.

Using the t-distribution table for a two-tail test, we find 2.093 to be the critical value of t corresponding to the 5% significance level (2.5% in each tail) with 19 degrees of freedom. Since the computed t-ratio of 1.764 is less than the critical value, then its prob-value is greater than 5%. That is, there is greater than a 5% chance of finding such sample evidence assuming that the null is true. It appears that the sample evidence is *not unusual enough* to reject the null hypothesis of no real difference between the two loan officers' ratings, given the level of unusualness ($\alpha = .05$) that is required.

Independent Samples

Sample designs based on small independent samples and using the Student t distribution require an estimate of the standard deviation assumed to be common to the two populations. This estimate is obtained by *pooling the two sample standard deviations* from the two samples according to the following expression:

$$S_{D_{pooled}} = \sqrt{\frac{(n_1 - 1)S_1^2 + (n_2 - 1)S_2^2}{n_1 + n_2 - 2}}$$

Suppose two samples, one of size $n_1 = 18$ and the other of size $n_2 = 20$ are independently taken from a population. The first sample has standard deviation $S_1 = 40$ and the second has $S_2 = 50$. The pooled estimate of the population standard deviation is

$$
\begin{aligned}
S_{D_{pooled}} &= \sqrt{\frac{(n_1 - 1)S_1^2 + (n_2 - 1)S_2^2}{n_1 + n_2 - 2}} \\
&= \sqrt{\frac{(18 - 1)40^2 + (20 - 1)50^2}{18 + 20 - 2}} \\
&= \sqrt{\frac{27{,}200 + 47{,}500}{36}} \\
&= 45.5522
\end{aligned}
$$

The value of $S_{\bar{D}}$, the standard error of the sampling distribution of the difference in sample means, is given by

$$S_{\bar{D}} = S_{D_{pooled}} \sqrt{\frac{1}{n_1} + \frac{1}{n_2}}$$

For the values above,

$$S_{\bar{D}} = S_{D_{pooled}} \sqrt{\frac{1}{n_1} + \frac{1}{n_2}} = 45.5522 \sqrt{\frac{1}{18} + \frac{1}{20}} = 14.7996$$

A further application of this procedure is given in the review exercise in the next section.

13.10. Managerial Issues in Practice—Review Exercise: Selecting a New Computer

The funding for a comprehensive new computer system is usually a major capital item in a firm's budget. Whether the system is obtained by direct purchase or by long term leasing, the capital expenditure will have a key impact on the firm's cash flow situation and possibly on the firm's long run profit picture. There are many computer firms (IBM, Burroughs, SCM, National Cash Register) which offer systems for data processing as well as for analysis of business problems.

Choosing among them is a question of getting in a given price range the *right system* for the particular variety of jobs one needs done—not simply the system with the lowest price or the largest storage capacity or the fastest processing speed.

Two firms, IBM and NCR, were selected as the final choice for supplying a new computer system. Which system would give the lowest cost for the particular job needs of the firm? What game plan for evaluation should be used?

The Game Plan

Two considerations dominate the choice process.

> The first consideration is to determine the types of jobs which the new computer system will be doing.

If future demands are like past demands, then a *random sample of past jobs* will be representative of the expected demands on the new computing system.

> Comparing the cost of these jobs in the two new systems is the second consideration.

How are operating costs determined? Can they be ascertained merely by asking the computer manufacturers for their estimates? Perhaps, but only if the company doesn't mind taking the risk that the manufacturers will give an unrealistically low estimate.

To obtain *independent* cost comparisons, it is proposed that the sample of different jobs be split into two groups. The jobs in one group would be sent to a computer service bureau employing IBM equipment of the kind being considered; the other jobs would be sent to a computer service bureau employing NCR equipment of the kind to be purchased. By obtaining individual costs for each job, the mean cost per job can be computed for each of the two computer brands. To measure their cost competitiveness the mean costs per job are then compared.

Does the observed difference in mean cost per job represent a *real* difference or simply the work of sampling variation? A *t* test offers a way of determining the answer. Concluding that there is no real cost difference forces the computer system choice to be made on the basis of other dimensions than operating cost. A real cost difference, on the other hand, would have to be weighed in with other factors in arriving at the final decision.

Is splitting the sample the best way to design such a cost comparison study? On the surface it might seem so. Certainly a difference in mean cost per job will be detected using this independent sample technique if the sample is large enough. But perhaps there is a better way:

> send the *same* jobs to *both* service bureau companies.

This translates into taking *two* observations on cost, one for IBM and one for NCR on only *one* sample of jobs. The cost *difference* for each job is computed and then the *average of these differences* is used to infer whether there is a real difference in the mean cost between IBM and NCR for *all* jobs.

What recommends the matched pair design over the independent sample design? Isn't it simply wasteful to pay twice for the same job? After all, with independent samples, each job was sent only to *one* service bureau (IBM equipped or NCR equipped), not to both.

An advantage of the matched pairs design is that it drastically *reduces the required sample size.* The cost of paying twice for each job is offset by the fewer jobs which are required.

With independent samples, the two service bureaus work on *different* jobs. The observed difference between the means of the two independent samples will largely be due to the variation in cost among different types of jobs. This could possibly obscure all but a very large cost difference between the IBM system and the NCR system, unless the two samples are very large. In the matched pairs design, we eliminate this extraneous source of cost variation (different costs due to different jobs) present in the first method, focusing instead on the factor of interest: cost *difference* between the IBM system and the NCR system.

Suppose the costs on 25 different jobs using the IBM and NCR equipment are as shown in Table 13.4. A *t* test of the null hypothesis of no significant mean cost difference can be made using the method of independent samples. The required assumption of equal population variances is plausible since the two samples are drawn from the same population of computer jobs.

TABLE 13.4. Costs of 25 Computer Runs on Two Different Systems

Job	SYSTEM IBM	NCR	Difference	Job	SYSTEM IBM	NCR	Difference
1	$65	$70	−5	14	$36	$44	−8
2	32	39	−7	15	70	68	+2
3	55	57	−2	16	22	21	+1
4	6	9	−3	17	46	47	−1
5	8	11	−3	18	20	20	0
6	29	30	−1	19	15	17	−2
7	52	60	−8	20	20	23	−3
8	8	6	+2	21	4	6	−2
9	61	66	−5	22	54	53	+1
10	32	36	−4	23	60	59	+1
11	15	21	−6	24	70	75	−5
12	38	37	+1	25	43	46	−3
13	12	9	+3				
							$\Sigma d_i = -\$57$

The calculations that follow show the greater reliability (lesser sampling variability) gained by the matched pairs method.

Matched Pairs. The null hypothesis is

$$H_0: \mu_d = 0.$$

The alternative hypothesis is

$$H_A: \mu_d \neq 0.$$

To test this two-tailed hypothesis at the 5% level of significance, first find

$\bar{d} = \dfrac{\Sigma d_i}{n}$ where d_i = cost difference on the *same* job.

$$\dfrac{-\$57}{25} = -\$2.28 \text{ mean cost difference per job in favor of IBM system}$$

Then, find $S_{\bar{d}} = \dfrac{S_d}{\sqrt{n}}$

$$S_d = \sqrt{\dfrac{\Sigma(d_i - \bar{d})^2}{n-1}} = \sqrt{\dfrac{\Sigma d_i^2 - (\Sigma d_i)^2/n}{n-1}}$$

$$= \sqrt{\dfrac{(-5)^2 + (-7)^2 + \ldots - (-57)^2/25}{25 - 1}} = \$3.195$$

The numerator in the above expression is the computational way of finding the sum of the squared differences between IBM and NCR costs on the 25 jobs.

$$S_{\bar{d}} = \dfrac{S_d}{\sqrt{n}} = \dfrac{3.195}{\sqrt{25}} = \$.639.$$

Next, find the prob-value of $\bar{d} = -\$2.28$.

$$t = \dfrac{\bar{d} - \mu_{do}}{S_{\bar{d}}} = \dfrac{-2.28 - 0}{.639} = -3.568$$

From the t distribution table for $n - 1 = 24$ degrees of freedom, the (two-tailed) prob-value of $t = -3.568$ is found to be less than .01. If the significance level is set at the 1% level or any other significance level greater than 1%, the null stating no real difference between the costs of the two systems cannot be maintained. Consequently we conclude that there is a real cost difference between the two systems. Using $\bar{d}$ as a point estimate, we find the IBM system lower in cost by an average of $2.28 per job run. At this point the NCR sales representative would be at an obvious disadvantage because she cannot argue that the lower cost on the IBM system was due to differences on the jobs assigned. She can and should point out, however, that the cost advantage of the IBM system could be attributable to differences in the efficiency or profit margin of the two service bureaus. The likelihood of that possibility will have to be judged before a final evaluation of the two systems can be achieved.

Independent Samples. The null hypothesis is:

$$H_0: \mu_D = 0.$$

The alternative hypothesis is

$$H_A: \mu_D \neq 0.$$

To test this hypothesis, first find $\bar{D} = \bar{X}_2 - \bar{X}_1$ where X_2 = IBM, X_1 = NCR.

$$\bar{D} = \$34.92 - \$37.20$$
$$= -\$2.28$$

Having found that $S_1 = \$22.22$ and $S_2 = \$21.56$, we can find $S_{D_{pooled}}$ by

$$S_{D_{pooled}} = \sqrt{\frac{(n_1 - 1)S_1^2 + (n_2 - 1)S_2^2}{n_1 + n_2 - 2}}$$

$$= \sqrt{\frac{(25 - 1)(22.22)^2 + (25 - 1)(21.56)^2}{25 + 25 - 2}}$$

$$= \sqrt{479.281} = \$21.89$$

and subsequently find $S_{\bar{D}}$ by

$$S_{\bar{D}} = S_{D_{pooled}} \sqrt{\frac{1}{n_1} + \frac{1}{n_2}}$$

$$= 21.89 \sqrt{\frac{1}{25} + \frac{1}{25}} = \$6.19$$

Note that $S_{\bar{D}} = \$6.19$ is not the same as $S_{\bar{d}} = \$.639$ obtained when the samples were considered as matched pairs. The standard error of the mean difference between IBM and NCR cost per job is nearly ten times as high with the independent sampling method as compared to the matched pair method.

Find the prob-value of $\bar{D} = -\$2.28$.

$$t = \frac{\bar{D} - \mu_D}{S_{\bar{D}}} = \frac{-\$2.28 - 0}{\$6.19} = -0.368$$

The two-tailed prob-value of $t = -0.368$ with $n_1 + n_2 - 2 = 48$ degrees of freedom is found from the normal probability table (because of large sample size) to be .7114. Thus, using the 5% significance level, the results are *not* significant; although there is an observed difference of $\$-2.28$ per job, the test suggests that there is *no real difference* in the mean cost per job using IBM and NCR systems. The observed difference is merely due to sampling variability, a conclusion inconsistent with the conclusion found for the matched sample procedure.

Comparing Matched and Independent Samples

Using the matched pairs method, the difference in mean job cost between the two computer systems was highly significant; using the method of independent samples, the difference was not even close to being significant. But the two tests are *not* equally valid. The standard error of the difference using the independent samples design was nearly *ten times as large* as when the matched pairs method was employed. Thus, using the *same sample information*, the matched pairs design was much more *efficient*. This is to be expected whenever a substantial amount of variation between the means of two samples is attributable to a common source (differences among the jobs in this case) that can be blocked out by using the matched pairs design. In this situation the matched pairs design is superior and appropriate to use.

Measuring the Inefficiency of Independent Sampling

How much more efficient is the matched pairs design? We can assess this by calculating how large a sample would be required using independent samples to give the same standard error of the difference as with matched pairs—.639. Assuming $n_1 = n_2 = n$ and using the computed values for S_1 and S_2;

$$S_{\bar{D}} = \sqrt{\frac{(n-1)S_1^2 + (n-1)S_2^2}{n + n - 2}} \sqrt{\frac{1}{n} + \frac{1}{n}} = \sqrt{\frac{S_1^2}{n} + \frac{S_2^2}{n}}$$

$$S_{\bar{D}} = \sqrt{\frac{(22.22)^2}{n} + \frac{(21.56)^2}{n}} = \sqrt{\frac{958.56}{n}} = .639$$

$$n = \frac{958.56}{(.639)^2}$$

$$n = 2348$$

In other words, it would take a random sample of 2348 jobs with two independent samples to give the same results as 25 jobs with a matched pairs sample. Quite a difference!

It should be noted that for illustrative purposes only, the data set in this example was analyzed both as independent samples and as matched pairs samples. In practice, a given data set is *not* analyzed both ways. The data must be analyzed consistent with the methodology used to collect it in order to give valid conclusions.

Caveat: When to Use Independent Sampling?

Despite the advantage of matched pairs sampling when it can block out a common source of variation, it would be *disadvantageous* to use the matched pairs design if there is no common source of variation to be blocked out. Why? Because degrees of freedom are lost using the matched pairs design, which is tantamount to a smaller effective sample size. With two independent samples each of size n, the degrees of freedom are $2n - 2$. With a matched pairs, the degrees of freedom are only $n - 1$, exactly half that with independent sampling. Situations also arise in which it is not feasible or not cost effective to collect data on matched pairs. For example, if a product is being tested and the test process physically destroys the product, or affects the user in a way that interferes with subsequent testing, matched pair sampling is not feasible. In comparing two brands of beer, the taste of the second may be "contaminated" by the lingering taste of the first. In these situations, independent sampling is advantageous.

13.11. Concluding Comments

The sampling plan is an important consideration in the design of any statistical investigation. The objective is to choose a plan which assures economical, reliable, and unbiased generalizations about a target population based upon a sample of elementary units from the sampling frame. A critical choice is whether the sample will be a probability sample or a nonprobability sample. Probability samples have the advantage of a calculable degree of reliability, but may be more difficult and more costly to secure. The cost of obtaining a given degree of reliability with a probability sample can often be reduced by employing a stratified or cluster sampling plan rather than a simple random sampling plan. A stratified plan is more likely to be advantageous when the population can be segmented into groups *among* which there is a considerable heterogeneity, and *within* which there is considerable homogeneity. A cluster sampling plan is most advantageous in the opposite situation: homogeneous clusters of heterogeneous elementary units.

A good sampling plan will attempt to minimize measurement, selection, and nonresponse bias. In telephone and personal interview surveys, not-at-homes are the most important source of nonresponse bias. In mail surveys, volunteer bias can be quite serious.

Many statistical investigations require a comparison between two (or more) sets of measurements obtained by sampling. Interest centers on the amount, if any, and source of the difference between the two populations from which the samples were taken. The distribution of sample means and the distribution of sample proportions are used to test whether the observed differences between means or between proportions can be attributed plausibly to sources of variation extraneous to the purpose of the investigation. If not, confidence interval estimates for the population differences can be computed. If there is a common source of variation affecting both sets of measurements, a matched pairs design will usually be much more efficient than an independent samples design.

The experimental designs considered in this chapter were restricted to comparisons of two sets of measurements. Techniques to be used when there are more than two sets of measurements are considered in subsequent chapters, particularly Chapter 21 (Analysis of Variance) and Chapter 22 (Nonparametric Statistics).

Footnotes and References

[1] Volunteer bias is not restricted to nonresponse in mail surveys. See the discussion of the driver training example in Chapter One.

[2] In published accounts of the disastrous poll, selection bias has often been reported as the main reason for the discrepancy between the *Literary Digest* prediction about the 1936 election outcome and the actual outcome. It has been claimed that Landon voters were over-represented on the telephone and automobile registration lists from which the mailing list was drawn. However, a recent examination of the evidence about the fiasco in the *American Statistician*, Vol. 30, No. 4, November, 1976, shows that the reported selection bias story "was not only incapable of explaining the error but not even correct to begin with."

[3] Mason Haire, "Projective Techniques in Marketing Research," *Journal of Marketing*, Volume 14, pp. 649–656.

Questions and Problems

1. A proponent of random sampling plans claims that for a sample of given size, a random sample will always give you less error than any non-random sample. A critic scoffs at this, claiming that one reason non-random samples are sometimes used is that they offer smaller errors for the same sample size. Is the random sampling proponent correct? If not, then what is the advantage of random over non-random samples?

2. What is the distinction between an elementary unit and a sampling unit? Give an example of a situation in which this distinction would be important.

3. In Example 13.2A (Surveying Attitudes on the Equal Rights Amendment), it was noted that an ambiguous addressee, apathetic recipient, burdensome questionnaire, or a composite response are issues that prevent us from using a recorded observation on the intended elementary unit. Would it be correct to say that the recorded observations are attributable to the sampling unit rather than the elementary unit? Explain.

4. The terms *population* and *sampling unit* both refer to a collection of elementary units. What distinguishes a population from a sampling unit?

5. Is the distinction between members and non-members of a population generally as obvious as it may seem? Explain.

6. Is *target population* synonymous with the *frame*? Should it be, if possible? Explain.

7. A sample is commonly understood to represent a selected number of elementary units drawn from the target population. In statistical design terminology, however, a sample is a selected number of sampling units drawn from the frame. Are these interpretations interchangeable? In what circumstances?

8. State the distinction between measurement bias and selection bias. Can both occur simultaneously? Does the estimation error due to either of these sources differ from the estimation error due to random sampling variation? Explain.

9. Discuss the types of selection bias likely introduced by letting an interviewer select which homes to be included in a "random sample." How about a sales representative who selects the customers to be included in a "random sample?"

10. List at least three sources of measurement bias.

11. a. Distinguish between volunteer bias and not-at-home bias.
b. Give an example of non-response bias which does not involve volunteer or not-at-home bias.
c. Give an example of selection bias which does not involve non-response bias.

12. From a list of names defining the target population, a random sample is chosen and sent mail questionnaires. The responses are tabulated and summarized and described as a "random sample of responses from this population." Actually, the respondents are not likely to be a random sample from the target population. Why not? From what population could they be considered a random sample?

13. Compare and contrast a judgment sample and a convenience sample. Either one may be chosen over a random sample. Explain.

14. Shoppers surveyed at large malls and shopping centers are a popular source of marketing research information in recent years. Would these surveys likely be a random or non-random sample of the target population? Do you expect the information obtained from these surveys can be valuable to marketing executives? Explain.

15. In what circumstances is a systematic random sample
a. equivalent to a simple random sample?
b. at a disadvantage compared to a simple random sample?
c. at an advantage compared to a simple random sample?

16. Under what circumstances, using what criteria, would a stratified sample be:
a. superior to a simple random sample?
b. superior to a cluster sample?
c. equivalent to a systematic random sample?

17. What circumstances, and what criteria, cause a cluster sample to be:
a. superior to a simple random sample?
b. superior to a stratified sample?
c. equivalent to a systematic random sample?

18. Reconsider the manufacturer of truck engines who wants to estimate efficiently the mean annual mileage per vehicle in which his engines are installed (Example 13.4B). Assume that 30,000 of the trucks produced annually are used in local cartage and 20,000 are used in intercity transportation. The standard deviations are 6000 miles for the local stratum and 18,000 miles for the intercity stratum. A total of 900 trucks are to be included in the sample.
a. How many trucks in the sample should be from the local stratum? Intercity stratum?
b. What is the standard error of the local stratum mileage?
c. What is the standard error of the intercity stratum mileage?
d. What is the standard error of the total sample (local and intercity strata combined)?
e. If the mean mileage in the sample from the local stratum is 32,000 miles and the mean mileage in the sample from the intercity stratum is 86,000 miles, what is your point estimate of the mean mileage for the entire population of trucks produced annually?

19. Using the information in Problem 18:
a. determine the 95 percent confidence interval for the mean mileage per truck.
b. compare your answer from Part a to the 95 percent confidence interval that would be obtained if the sample were treated as a simple random sample rather than a stratified sample.

20. Hallcraft is a company that produces specialized communications equipment for business and industrial use. The company is presently developing a computerized tracking system. It is intended for organizations which deploy large numbers of motor vehicles and have to reroute vehicles frequently during the course of a day. The company wants to estimate the potential market for the new equipment. The bulk of the potential is expected to lie in applications within four types of organizations: electric utilities, telephone companies, taxicab companies, and police departments. A sample of these potential customers will be taken to estimate the number of purchases during the next year. Lists of the companies and departments have been compiled. Also, preliminary estimates have been made of the market penetration rate within each of the four categories. These are shown in Table 13.5. The preliminary estimates are needed to estimate the standard deviation within a category. A sample of 200 companies will be drawn and these companies will be studied to estimate the proportion of companies and departments in the target market which are likely to buy the new product each year.
a. What should be the allocation of sample items among the strata?

TABLE 13.5. Potential Customers and Estimate of Market Penetration

	NO. OF POTENTIAL CUSTOMERS	PRELIMINARY ESTIMATE OF PROPORTION WHICH WILL BUY WITHIN THE NEXT YEAR
Electrical Utilities	1425	.15
Telephone Companies	75	.10
Police Departments	5125	.05
Taxicab Companies	3135	.05

b. Suppose the survey is taken and the proportions classified as likely to buy are .20, .20, .07, .08 respectively, for the four categories given above. What would be the 95 percent confidence interval for the overall *proportion* likely to buy among all the four categories? The *total* number of organizations classifiable as likely to buy?

21. Both stratified and cluster samples involve dividing the population into subgroups. Distinguish between the two types in drawing the sample once the subgroups have been formed.

22. With cluster sampling, a probability sample can be taken from a population without even knowing how many members the population includes, let alone who they are. Explain.

23. A given size cluster sample likely has a larger sampling error than a stratified or a simple random sample of the same size. Despite this, cluster sampling is often able to produce lower sampling error for a given budget. Explain.

24. What is meant by "equalizing" test conditions? How is equalizing different from "controlling" the test conditions? In what situations would controlling be preferred?

25. Two brands of dripless dinner candles are tested for burning time to determine whether one brand has a longer burning time than the other, and if so, by how much. One hundred candles of Brand No. 1 and 121 candles of Brand No. 2 are burned under similar test conditions and the length of burning time is recorded. The sample statistics in Table 13.6 result.
a. Why must the comparison between these two brands be based upon independent random samples rather than matched pair samples?
b. Estimate the difference between the mean burning time between the two brands and determine a 99 percent confidence interval for the difference.

26. Reconsider the quality control problem for the fit between bolts and bushings

TABLE 13.6. Comparison of Candle Burning Time

CANDLE BRAND NO. 1	CANDLE BRAND NO. 2
$n_1 = 100$	$n_2 = 121$
$\bar{X}_1 = 29.63$ minutes	$\bar{X}_2 = 28.90$ minutes
$S_1 = 1.40$ minutes	$S_2 = 1.10$ minutes

(Example 13.6). Assuming that when the machines are operating correctly,

the mean diameter of bolts produced is .375 inches and the standard deviation of bolt diameters is .006 inches

the mean diameter of bushings produced is .388 inches and the standard deviation of bushing diameters is .008 inches

the minimum satisfactory clearance is .008 inches

$n_1 = 40$ and $n_2 = 50$

$\bar{X}_1 = .379$ inches and $\bar{X}_2 = .385$ inches

a. What are the mean and standard deviation of the probability distribution for the clearance between a randomly drawn bolt and a randomly drawn bushing, assuming that the machines producing bolts and bushings are properly adjusted?
b. Assuming a normal distribution for both bolt and bushing diameters, what is the probability that the clearance between a randomly drawn bolt and a randomly drawn bushing will meet the minimum clearance requirement if Part a applies?
c. Relying only on the sample information (ignoring the information that the machines are in correct adjustment) calculate the upper and lower limits of the .95 confidence interval for the mean clearance, μ_D.

27. To make an inference about the difference between two population proportions, p_1 and p_2, it is necessary to know the standard error of the sampling distribution of the difference between them. However, the expression for this standard error involves p_1 and p_2 which, presum-

ably, are not known (because if it were known, then the difference could simply be calculated—it wouldn't have to be inferred). How, then, is the required standard error estimated?

28. Reconsider the Nescafe instant coffee example (13.7) using the following values:

$$n_1 = 80 \qquad \hat{p}_1 = .52$$
$$n_2 = 70 \qquad \hat{p}_2 = .30$$

a. Test the null hypothesis at the .05 level of significance.
b. Why must this investigation use the independent samples design rather than the matched pairs design?

29. How does the design of the experiment (matched pairs versus independent samples) affect the calculation of the standard error of the sampling distribution used in estimating the difference between the population means?

30. You, as sales manager, felt your sales representatives were not effectively cultivating the customer accounts in their sales area, possibly because of inefficient usage of their contact time with the customer. Having sent your five sales reps to a time management workshop you collect the data in Table 13.7 on sales before and after the workshop. You hope to evaluate the impact of the workshop on performance. You are pleased that, without exception, the mean number of sales transactions per week was higher after the workshop than before. However, you are concerned about the considerable variation in the mean number of sales per week for sales reps both before and after the workshop. Can the apparent performance improvement simply be due to chance factors associated

TABLE 13.7. Sales Before and After Time Management Workshop

| | MEAN SALES PER WEEK Three Month Period Immediately | |
Sales Rep	Before Workshop	After Workshop
1	19	29
2	23	32
3	25	29
4	12	18
5	21	34

with the small sample size?
a. Indicate what assumptions are necessary to test the null hypothesis using the procedures in this chapter.
b. Based upon your assumptions in Part a, test the null hypothesis using $\alpha = .10$.
c. What conclusion do you draw about the source of the higher performance after the workshop?

31. How would the requirements in Problem 30 change if the matched pairs design was used rather than the independent samples design?

32. In what circumstances might it be plausible to assume that two populations have equal variance without knowing what the population variances are?

33. Reconsider the accounts receivable factoring example (13.9) using only the first twelve observations.
a. Test the null hypothesis at the 1 percent level of significance.
b. Why would it not be appropriate to test the hypothesis using the formula for independent samples (even though the calculation could be made)?

Regression and Correlation: The Basic Model

Preview. In this chapter, we begin the study of correlation and regression— powerful statistical tools used to examine the association and the relationship between variables. For example, correlation analysis can provide an indication of the association between success in college and student SAT scores. If SAT scores are linked closely to college success, it will be beneficial to use them as a screening device for admissions. In business, an investigation of economic issues frequently links two variables for analysis and policy formation. The relationship between interest rates and housing demand is a particular concern to the home-building industry. The impact on housing demand of a unit change in interest rates is of particular importance. Like other statistical tools of high potential, the power of correlation and regression can be mishandled. It is the purpose of this chapter to explain the basic concepts that underlie correlation and the basic simple linear regression model. Chapter Fifteen examines in detail potential hazards in using simple regression. Chapter Sixteen deals with multiple regression, an extension of regression to more than two variables. For example, while simple regression would deal with the prediction of college success based on SAT scores, multiple regression would take into account other variables such as grade point average, as well as SAT scores.

14.1. Analysis of Bivariate Quantitative Data

Business questions quite commonly involve statistical analysis of quantitative data on two variables (bivariate data). Consider these questions:

If the sales of Eastman Kodak drop off, what happens to the company's operating cost?

If the Dow Jones Industrial Average index rises, what generally is the movement in the price of Philip Morris stock?

How is transit time related to the distance traveled?

Answers to these and similar questions require measures which describe the *strength, direction,* and *form* of the statistical relationship between the two variables being examined.

Strength: the strength of the association refers to the amount of coordination between changes in the values of the two variables. The degree of coordination can be strong, weak, or nonexistent.

Direction: if values of the variables move in the same direction, the association is positive; whereas the association is termed *negative* if values of the variables move in the opposite direction.

Form: if the relationship between the two variables can be summarized best by a straight line, then the form of the equation linking the two variables will be *linear.* If, however, a curve better expresses the relationship, then X and Y are related *non-linearly.* Examples of these two forms are shown in Figures 14.1a and b for the variables X and Y.

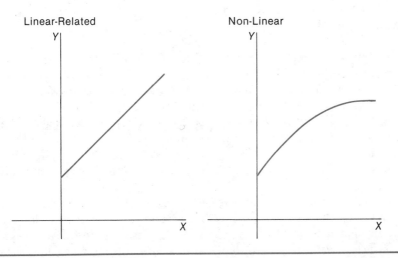

FIGURE 14.1a Linear Relationship   **FIGURE 14.1b** Non-Linear Relationship

Two important statistical analyses which provide numerical measures of this relationship's form, direction, and strength are *regression analysis* and *correlation analysis*. Correlation analysis provides a basic description of the degree of co-ordination between the values of two quantitative variables. Regression analysis is used in management for two more specific purposes: (1) *prediction*, and (2) *planning and control*. A schematic overview for classifying the association between two variables is provided in Figure 14.2. The basic ideas underlying regression analysis and correlation analysis and their two purposes are explained in the latter part of this section.

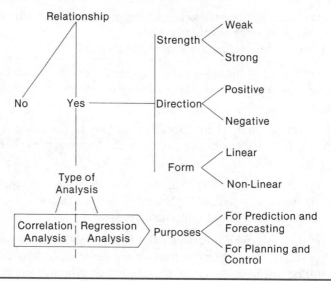

FIGURE 14.2 Schematic Overview of Regression and Correlation Analysis

Scatter Diagram

The strength, direction, and form of the association between two variables should first be assessed by a graph called a *scatter diagram*. A scatter diagram is a two dimensional plot of the paired observations, say on the variables X and Y; it provides a visual assessment of the three elements of association.

Table 14.1 reports data on two quantitative variables, research-and-development and sales, for nine firms in the drug industry. A scatter diagram of the joint observations for this sample data set is plotted in Figure 14.3. The horizontal axis measures units of research and development and the vertical axis measures units of sales.

The scatter diagram provides a visual assessment of the *association* between sales and research and development. The direction *positive* appears since higher values of sales tend to follow higher values of research and development. Although only a scant number of observations are available, a straight line seems to better represent the flow of the points than does a curve.

TABLE 14.1. Cross-section of Sales and Research and Development Expenditures of Firms in the Drug Industry (Millions of Dollars)

FIRM	SALES	RES-DEV
1. Abbott	1708.00	85.400
2. Baxter Travenol	1175.00	47.000
3. Bristol-Meyers	2575.00	103.000
4. Johnson & Johnson	3854.00	192.700
5. Eli Lilly	2186.25	174.900
6. Merck	2351.25	188.100
7. Pfizer	2754.00	137.700
8. Richardson-Merrell	1130.00	45.200
9. Schering-Plough	1496.00	74.800

Source: Information obtained from Standard & Poor's Corporation Records, 1981

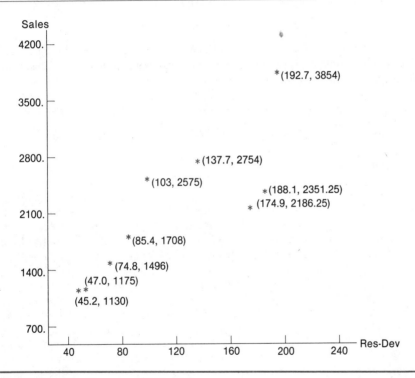

FIGURE 14.3 Scatter Diagram of Table 14.1

A. Regression for Prediction

In prediction and forecasting, the focus is on using the value of X to predict the value of Y, say using SAT scores to predict college performance. The variable Y is called the *dependent* variable or the *criterion* variable. The variable X is called the *independent* variable or the *predictor* variable. A useful predictive equation can be developed provided that:

>1. information on the value of X can be obtained more readily or more economically than the value of Y, and

>2. there exists a strong and stable relationship between the two variables.

The equation expressing the predictive relationship for Y is called the *regression* equation.

The Regression Equation

The mathematical expression that equates Y with X is called an equation. In statistics it is called the regression equation. Its structure shows the value of Y on the left side and the expression for X on the right side. That is,

$$\text{Predicted Value of } Y = \text{Predicting Expression of } X$$

The total right hand side expression as a unit determines the predicted value of Y. The goal of regression for prediction and forecasting is to obtain high accuracy in the prediction of Y. Consider the following example.

Example 14.1A.   Work Scheduling in Mail Order Houses

Daily work scheduling at mail-order houses depends on the number of incoming orders arriving each day for processing. But work scheduling plans must be made before the incoming orders are counted; in fact, even before the incoming mail is sorted, opened, and classified. To solve this problem, incoming mail is weighed early in the day. Using a regression equation expressing the historical relationship between the number of orders and the weight of the mail bags, the weight of today's mailbags is used to estimate the number of new orders received. It has been found that the relationship changes depending on the day of the week. For example, Monday has fewer orders per pound of mail than does Tuesday. Consequently, using the historical data for the same day of the week, a separate regression equation is computed for each week day. The individual regression equation predicts orders for the particular weekday.

In Example 14.1A it should be noted that a heavier mailbag weight does not *cause* an increase in the number of orders (if anything, the reverse is true). So causality is not a necessary ingredient in order to take advantage of the relationship between two variables—in this case the number of orders and mailbag weight. *Low cost accessibility of information* that will improve the prediction of the dependent variable is the compelling reason for using mailbag weight to *predict* the more difficult to obtain value of the number of orders contained in the mailbags.

B. Regression for Planning and Control

In planning and control, the purpose of regression analysis is to obtain parameter estimates of the quantitative impact of changes in the value of X on the value of

Y. That is, once *X* is identified as a component force determining *Y*, the next step is to specify the *contribution* of changes in *X* to changes in the mean level of *Y*. The parameter estimated tells specifically *how much change in the mean value of Y* to expect for a one-unit change in the *value of X*. It is termed the *slope* of the relationship. The greater the proportional impact on *Y* of a given change in *X*, the greater the slope of the relationship. The following example illustrates the way regression analysis can be used for purposes of control.

Example 14.1B. **Real Estate Appraisals**

What do real estate appraisers do when called upon to estimate the market value of land on which a building is currently standing? They rely upon recent sales of comparable nearby properties as their primary source of market value information. Frequently, however, in neighborhoods already fully developed, the obtainable sales figures are for the entire piece of property consisting of both land and buildings and not for the land alone. Is there a way to isolate the land's component value? By regressing market value (*Y*) of the total property (land and buildings together) on *building size* (*X*) for same-sized lots, the appraiser can estimate the mean change in property value for a given change in building size. From this knowledge, the appraiser can segregate and estimate the *component* of total value attributable to the land.[1]

Examples 14.1A and 14.1B highlight the distinction between the two purposes of regression analysis and show its great versatility. In Example 14.1A, the usefulness of the regression analysis depends solely on the accuracy with which incoming orders, *Y, can be predicted* from knowledge of mailbag weight. We have no interest at all in actually changing the mailbag weight. And if we did foolishly put a lead brick inside it, nothing would happen to the value of the orders. In Example 14.1B the issue is *control*. By controlling for building value, the contribution of lot size as a *component* of total (land and building) value can be isolated. The *total* value of the property in question is known, so there is no concern for prediction of *Y*. Our interest is in estimating what change in *Y* could be expected if we hypothetically change the value of *X* (to zero) in this case. Thus, regression analysis is employed to separate total property value into its land and building components.

C. Correlation Analysis

Correlation means the extent to which the values of two variables simultaneously change. A correlation statistic provides an index of the direction and magnitude of the *co-movement* of the two variables.

In conjunction with regression analysis, correlation analysis serves as a screening device, identifying those situations worthy of further study by regression. But lest we forget, the following example shows that correlation analysis can be the focus of the investigation.

Example 14.1C. Project Analysis and Earnings Correlation

Correlation is a useful tool in deciding where a firm should make new investments. One of the important considerations in making new investments is the impact of earnings that come from the new investment on the overall variability of the firm's earnings. If the earnings from the new investment reduce the variability of the firm's earnings, the new investment is said to have diversification benefits. The reduction of earnings fluctuations with diversification is important since it reduces the chance of earnings falling to a level insufficient to cover the firm's financial obligations when due. Insufficient earnings cause the firm financial distress and in the extreme case financial insolvency and bankruptcy. Companies with less fluctuating earnings get financing at lower interest costs and manage more easily their financial obligations. In other words, predictable earnings permit better financial management and sounder financial planning. Diversification benefits were certainly an important reason that Exxon, a major oil company, decided to invest in the business typewriter market (its Qwyx product line) rather than in more exploratory drilling. Diversification analysis for investment purposes rests on the statistical theory of correlation. Let us consider two different situations that highlight the linkage between diversification and correlation and why the firm of Aloha Airlines, given two diversification possibilities, would choose one over the other.

Situation A: Aloha Airlines and Wiki Wiki Wheels Car Rental Service are both transportation companies operating only in Hawaii. Suppose Aloha is considering a merger with Wiki Wiki Wheels to link its air service with ground transportation. Both companies are heavily dependent on the price and availability of gas and the Hawaiian tourist trade, and anticipate their expected earnings to fluctuate in a similar manner. Assume this is true and both firms have the same expected earnings and variability of earnings. The association between the earnings is as shown in Table 14.2. Each prospect for oil will be assumed to have exactly the same probability of occurrence.

TABLE 14.2. Positive Correlation Between Wiki Wiki Wheels Earnings and the Earnings of Aloha Airlines—Situation A

OIL PROSPECTIVE	EARNINGS OF WIKI WIKI (Thousands of Dollars)	EARNINGS OF ALOHA (Thousands of Dollars)	COMBINED EARNINGS (Thousands of Dollars)
Oversupply	75	75	150
Normal	50	50	100
Shortage	25	25	50

The last column of situation A shown in Table 14.2 verifies the fact that the variability in Aloha Airline's earnings is widened by the addition of Wiki Wiki Wheels. Since the earnings of Wiki Wiki Wheels behave exactly the same as the earnings of Aloha Airlines, Wiki Wiki Wheels provides no diversification benefits to Aloha Airlines.

Situation B: Alternatively, Aloha Airlines can invest in Islander Bicycle and Canoe Company. Again the earnings of the company are linked closely to oil prospects, but now in a different way. When gasoline is expensive, airline fares will rise to reflect the higher cost, but passenger demand and traffic will decline. Bicycle and canoe sales, on the other hand, can be stimulated. To avoid using gasoline run cars, people resort to non-gas means of travel and recreation. Assuming Aloha and Islander have identical expected earnings and earnings variability, the expected total earnings of their merger would be as shown in the last column of Table 14.3. Each oil prospect is again assumed to be equally probable.

TABLE 14.3. Negative Correlation Between Islander Bicycle and Canoe Company's Earnings and the Earnings of Aloha Airlines—Situation B

OIL PROSPECTIVE	EARNINGS OF ALOHA (Thousands of Dollars)	EARNINGS OF ISLANDER (Thousands of Dollars)	COMBINED EARNINGS (Thousands of Dollars)
Oversupply	75	25	100
Normal	50	50	100
Shortage	25	75	100

Situation B reveals ultimate diversification. The variability of Aloha's earnings has been completely eliminated by the merger. No longer is there any uncertainty about the level of the mergered earnings. The combination or portfolio which includes Islander Company and Aloha Airlines will have $100,000 of earnings regardless of the oil situation.

In combination Tables 14.2 and 14.3 make an important point—the degree of correlation determines the degree of diversification. The ability of a project to diversify away the variability of earnings in a portfolio of projects depends on the correlation between the expected earnings between the project and the earnings of the other projects in the portfolio. No variability is eliminated if the earnings have a perfect positive correlation. All the variability can be diversified away if the earnings have a perfect negative correlation. In the real world such extreme situations are rare. But extreme situations specify how the degree of correlation determines the range of diversification. The general nature of the relationship is illustrated in Table 14.4.

TABLE 14.4. Correlation and Diversification Benefits

DEGREE OF CORRELATION BETWEEN EXPECTED EARNINGS	DIVERSIFICATION BENEFITS	VARIABILITY OF EARNINGS
Perfect Positive Correlation	None	Highest
Moderate Positive Correlation		
Uncorrelated	↓	↓
Moderate Negative Correlation		
Perfect Negative Correlation	Maximum	Lowest

Let us now discuss how to define and compute an index measuring the degree of correlation.

14.2. The Coefficients of Correlation and Determination

The scatter diagram between total research and development cost and sales in Figure 14.3 gave us a sense of the direction and form of the association between X and Y, but no actual measurement of the strength of the association. Table 14.4. also seems to suggest that a numerical summary measure of the degree of correlation would be helpful in quantifying the reduction in the variability of earnings achieved for the different degrees of correlation possible.

Pearson's r

Specific numerical indices are available to gauge the strength of the association between quantitative or categorical variables regardless of whether the relationship is linear or non-linear. With our concern at present focused on quantitative variables which are linearly related, we will examine in detail the most widely used index of the strength of the association or degree of correlation between two quantitative variables—the Pearson linear *correlation coefficient*, ρ (Greek letter "rho"). The symbol ρ is assigned to the population parameter. The computed estimate of ρ for a sample is noted by the symbol r and is called the Pearson r. The value of r therefore refers to sample data and defines the degree of correlation for the quantitative bivariate observations of the sample.

Since statistical variables do not generally follow each other in a perfect linear fashion, there are different degrees of linear correlation other than perfect. The range of values for r, from $+1.00$ to -1.00, indicates the different degrees of *linearity* between variables. A visual impression of what an r value implies about the scatter of observations is given by the various scatter diagrams in Figure 14.4 with their associated Pearson r values. As we can see, perfect correlation (positive or negative) means that all the observations lie on a straight line. As we move away from perfect positive correlation, the relationship passes from strongly positive and cigar shaped to oval shaped, where there is no relationship and zero correlation. The process is the same starting from perfect negative correlation.

The *sign of* r can be positive or negative and always conveys the direction of the relationship. The earnings of Aloha Airlines and Wiki Wiki Wheels moved in the *same* direction, therefore their r value would be positive, whereas the earnings of Aloha Airlines and Islander Bicycle moved in the opposite direction with respect to each other and therefore had a negative value for r. The magnitude of r indicates the *strength* of the linear association. Perfect positive correlation is given an r value of plus one ($r = +1.00$) whereas perfect negative correlation is given an r value of minus one ($r = -1.00$). A zero value for r is given when there is no correlation ($r = 0.00$). That is, the range of r shows:

$$-1 \leq r \leq +1$$

From Figure 14.4 we can surmise that *positive values of* r imply that there is a tendency for *high* (low) values on X to be associated with *high* (low) values on Y. For negative values of r, the implication is that *low* (high) values of X are associated with *high* (low) values of Y.

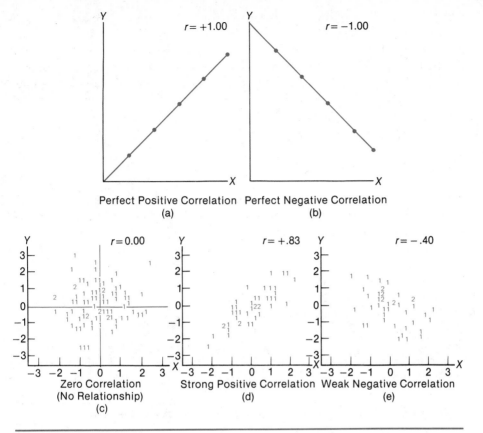

FIGURE 14.4 Scatter Diagrams Showing Various Degrees of Linear Correlation for the Observed Data

Standardizing

The term "high" means "high with respect to other observed values of that variable." Better detail of relative position is given by calculating the standardized score, Z. The Z scores for the particular sample values of X are computed by:

$$Z_X = \frac{X - \bar{X}}{S_X}$$

For example, if X is a sample value of 10 and its mean $\bar{X}$ has a value of 5 and the standard deviation of all sample observations of X, S_X, has a value of 2.5, then the Z score of X is

$$\frac{10 - 5}{2.5} = +2$$

Likewise, for the sample values of Y, the Z scores are computed by:

$$Z_Y = \frac{Y - \bar{Y}}{S_Y}$$

The particular Z score then is the relative position of a value in the standardized range of values. More precisely, the Z score measures how many standard deviations a particular sample value is above or below its sample mean. For the calculation of Z_X above, we can say that $X = 10$ is two standard deviations above its mean. If paired sample values of X and Y have the same Z score, this would mean that the particular sample X value and the particular sample Y value are the same number of standard deviations away from the respective sample means *of their respective X and Y distributions.*

Computing Pearson's *r*

The strength of linear correlation between the joint observations of X and Y is summarized by "averaging" the cross product of the Z scores. The Pearson r *correlation coefficient* is defined as,

$$r = \frac{\Sigma(Z_X Z_Y)}{n - 1}$$

where n is the sample size (number of paired observations in the sample data set) and the summation is taken over all n paired observations. Its maximum positive value of positive one ($+1$) occurs when $Z_X = Z_Y$ for each and every pair. Such perfect matching of the sign and magnitude is called *perfect positive correlation.* The paired bivariate observed on Y and X in Table 14.5 illustrates this situation and the calculated r.

TABLE 14.5. Bivariate Observations with Perfect Positive Correlation

X	Y	Z_X	Z_Y	$Z_X Z_Y$
4	7	−0.63246	−0.63246	0.4
3	6	−1.26491	−1.26491	1.6
5	8	0.00000	0.00000	0.0
7	10	1.26491	1.26491	1.6
6	9	0.63246	0.63246	0.4

$$\Sigma Z_X Z_Y = 4.0$$

$n = 5 \quad \bar{X} = 5 \quad \bar{Y} = 8 \quad S_X = S_Y = 1.5811$

$$r = \frac{\Sigma Z_X Z_Y}{n - 1}$$

$$= \frac{+4.0}{4} = +1.00$$

As can be seen from the calculations, each Z_X has a corresponding Z_Y equal in value and sign. This indicates that each pair of X, Y values deviate from their respective means in terms of standard deviations by the same amount and direction. Thus, when X is 7 (2 above its mean) and Y is 10 (2 above its mean), they are the same number of standard deviations above their respective means in the same direction.

The mirror situation yields *perfect negative correlation.* The paired bivariate observations on Y and X in Table 14.6 show this type of comovement and what it implies for the calculated r.

TABLE 14.6. Perfect Negative Correlation

X	Y	Z_X	Z_Y	$Z_X Z_Y$
4	11	−1.26491	1.26491	−1.6
7	8	0.63246	−0.63246	−0.4
6	9	0.00000	0.00000	0.0
8	7	1.26491	−1.26491	−1.6
5	10	−0.63246	0.63246	−0.4
				$\Sigma Z_X Z_Y = -4.0$

$n = 5 \quad \bar{X} = 6 \quad \bar{Y} = 9 \quad S_X = S_Y = 1.5811 \quad r = \Sigma Z_X Z_Y$

$$= \frac{-4.0}{4} = -1.00$$

The calculations show that each paired Z_X, Z_Y have the same value, but with opposite signs: $Z_X = -Z_Y$. Thus, the original value of X and Y deviate identically from their respective means in terms of standard deviations but in opposite directions. That means an X above its mean by two standard deviations matches perfectly with a Y below its mean by two standard deviations. The Pearson r value shows its minimum value of minus one when $Z_X = -Z_Y$ for every pair.

The situation which balances positive matching and negative matching defines no correlation at all ($r = 0$). A r value of zero reflects a condition in which the scatter of points show no discernible pattern. Partitioning the scatter diagram of observations shown in Figure 14.4c into four quadrants, by horizontal and vertical lines, shows an approximately equal balance of points scattered in all four quadrants. The mathematical outcome of such balancing is that the positive cross-products (points in the upper right and lower left quadrants) directly offset the negative cross products (points in the upper left and lower right quadrants) with a net result of zero.

Coefficient of Determination

Observed paired standardized values of X and Y are rarely found to be exactly on a straight line pattern or to show no discernible pattern at all. This lack of perfect correlation or non-correlation means that the value of r is generally a value other than zero, less than the value one, and greater than the value minus one. If the value of r is squared, it is given the name *coefficient of determination*. That is,

Coefficient of determination = r^2

The coefficient of determination indicates the proportion of the total variation in Y linearly associated with the variation in X. This is a very useful figure to know since it allows us to *express as a percentage* how much of the variation of Y has been explained by X. Say r was found to be $+.8$, then $r^2 = (+.8)^2 = .64$. This means that 64% of variation in Y is associated with the variation in X. Alternatively, one can assert that 36% ($1 - .64 = .36$) of the variation of Y is not linearly associated with X. The following example on portfolio formation presents a situation where r^2 is a key figure for the financial decision at hand.

Example 14.2. Common Stock Portfolio Formation: Calculating the Correlation Between Individual Stocks and the Market

One might expect that the financial returns earned from investing in different individual stocks are linked with the returns earned by the general market. Similarly, the risk (variability) of stock returns may be linked to the risk (variability) of returns experienced by the general market. Importantly, though, not all stock returns fluctuate in the same degree with respect to general market fluctuations. For example, for a given general market movement one would expect on average that a small maverick telecommunications firm like MCI to exhibit more sensitivity than the well established industry giant ATT.

To determine the actual extent of linkage, the variability of an individual stock's returns is matched to the return variability of the general market. Portfolio managers recognize that these differences exist in stock return variability and may be useful in selecting a portfolio of stock. For instance, if it is believed that there is a good chance of a downward market movement, then individual stocks that show returns fluctuations not very sensitive to the general market returns fluctuations will understandably be sought after as a defensive strategy by professional investment managers. Low sensitivity is indicated by low correlation between the stock returns and the market returns. Table 14.7 shows the annual returns for the general market and the individual annual returns for ATT and Pan Am over nine consecutive years. Figure 14.5a and b show the scatter diagrams of the original return observations.

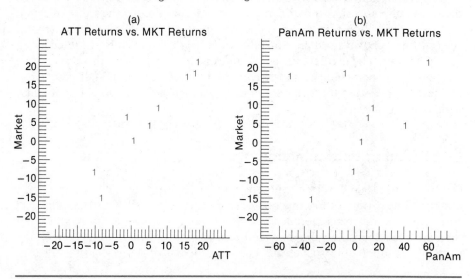

FIGURE 14.5 Scatter Diagrams of the Annual Market Returns and the Annual Returns for AT&T and PanAm

The figure indicates that for this period the returns of ATT move in harmony and in the same direction as the returns to the general market, whereas the movement of the returns of Pan Am are not closely allied to the movement of returns in the general market. But Pan Am returns generally seem to move in the same direction as the market returns. The Pearson *r* statistic for each set of sample data is calculated in Table 14.8.

TABLE 14.7. Annual Returns for the General Market, ATT, and Pan Am

	R_{MKT} (% terms)	R_{ATT} (% terms)	$R_{Pan\ Am}$ (% terms)
1	4.5	5.0	40.0
2	7.0	−1.2	10.0
3	−15.0	−8.7	−35.0
4	17.8	15.0	−52.7
5	9.2	7.5	14.0
6	0.5	0.5	5.0
7	−8.0	−10.1	−2.1
8	21.5	18.4	−8.7
9	18.7	17.2	58.7

TABLE 14.8. Calculated Pearson r for Market vs. ATT and Market vs. Pan Am

	(A) MARKET VS. ATT (Z terms)			(B) MARKET VS. PAN AM (Z terms)		
	Z_{MKT}	Z_{ATT}	$Z_{MKT}Z_{ATT}$	Z_{MKT}	$Z_{Pan\ Am}$	$Z_{MKT}Z_{Pan\ Am}$
1	−0.14120	0.01459	−0.00206	−0.14120	1.07488	−0.15177
2	0.06116	−0.56710	−0.03468	0.06116	0.19756	0.01208
3	−1.71963	−1.27077	2.18525	−1.71963	−1.11842	1.92327
4	0.93537	0.95282	0.89124	0.93537	−1.63605	−1.53031
5	0.23924	0.24915	0.05961	0.23924	0.31454	0.07525
6	−0.46498	−0.40761	0.18953	−0.46498	0.05134	−0.02387
7	−1.15302	−1.40212	1.61667	−1.15302	−0.15629	0.18021
8	1.23486	1.27181	1.57051	1.23486	−0.34930	−0.43134
9	1.00822	1.15923	1.16876	1.00822	1.62175	1.63508

$$r = \frac{\Sigma Z_{MKT}Z_{ATT}}{n-1} = \frac{7.64483}{8} = .956$$

$$r = \frac{\Sigma Z_{MKT}Z_{Pan\ Am}}{n-1} = \frac{1.68860}{8} = .211$$

The calculated values of r are .956 and .211 (the association between the returns to the market and the return to ATT and Pan Am respectively). These figures confirm our assessment of the scatter plots. That is,

a strong positive linear relationship exists between the market and AT&T and,

a weak positive association links the market and Pan Am.

Although the returns in both cases are assumed linearly related, the points do not lie on a straight line pattern. To make this degree of linear association more "usable," one needs the coefficient of determination. The calculations are:

$$\text{Coefficient of Determination} = r^2 \begin{cases} r^2_{MKT,\ ATT} = (.956)^2 = .91 \\ r^2_{MKT,\ Pan\ Am} = (.211)^2 = .04 \end{cases}$$

What interpretation does the coefficient of determination have in this case? It represents the proportion of the total variation in the return to the stock (ATT or Pan Am) linearly associated with the variation in the market return. The value of .91 indicates that a substantial proportion of the variation in the return to ATT stock was linearly associated with the variation which accompanied the annual market return for this period. On the other hand, only a small fraction of the variation in the returns to Pan Am, .04, can be linked to the variation in the market return; .96 or 96% of the variation in return experienced by Pan Am stock is *not* linearly associated with the fluctuation in return shown by the general market. This suggests that Pan Am is a superior stock for portfolio diversification compared to ATT.

14.3. Inference About the Correlation Coefficient ρ

In order to make a direct inference about the underlying parameter ρ from the sample statistic r, the estimated standard error of the correlation coefficient, s_r, must be used. The formula for s_r is:

$$s_r = \sqrt{\frac{(1 - r)^2}{n - 1}}$$

Unfortunately, the formula is limited to large samples and even then the

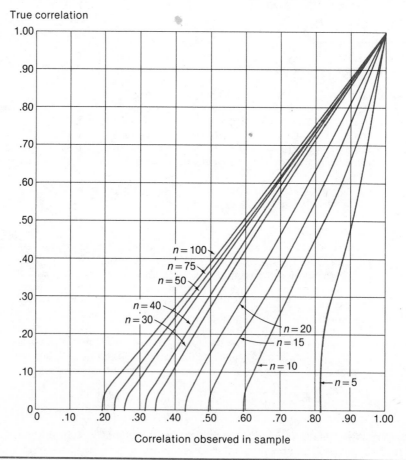

FIGURE 14.6 Minimum Correlation in Population for Varying Observed Correlation (r) and Size of Sample (n)

sampling distribution of the sample r's is highly skewed over a wide range of ρ.

Some perspective on the amount of sampling variability associated with various values of r for different sample sizes can be obtained from Figure 14.6. The figure allows us to determine the minimum value of the true correlation coefficient ρ for any observed sample value of r at the .95 confidence level. Let's now illustrate the use of the figure in the context of an example.

Example 14.3.   **95 Percent Confidence Level for Minimum Level of** ρ

Suppose a scatter diagram between Gamma and Zeta stocks for fifty monthly returns is as shown in Figure 14.7.

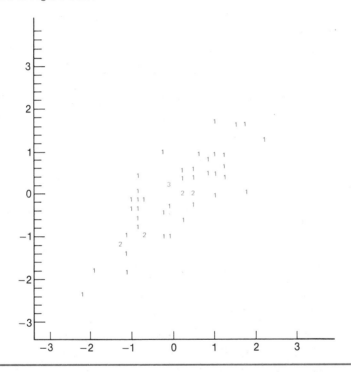

FIGURE 14.7 Scatter Diagram of 50 Standardized Returns on Gamma and Zeta Stocks

The calculated r statistic between the returns is .83. Using Figure 14.6 draw a vertical line from the value .83 on the X axis, to the $n = 50$ curve in the diagram. One finds, following the boldface line across to the Y axis, the value .74. From this reading, one can say with .95 confidence that the true correlation between the returns to Gamma and Zeta stocks is at least .74. Since the data was simulated, the true value of ρ is known to be .8.

Notice, however, the situation if one observes a moderate .6 value for r and the sample is small, say $n = 10$. One reads the graph to say that at the .95 confidence level, the true value ρ is at least zero. This means that 5 percent of all samples of size 10 would have a calculated r statistic of $\pm .60$, even if no correlation exists between the variables. Upon close examination of the graph in Figure 14.6 one sees that a high degree of imprecision exists about the value ρ when the observed r and sample size are small. This need not be of concern since regression analysis incorporates the observed r in its statistic which will be used for inference. In this way inference on ρ is made indirectly.

14.4. The Simple Linear Model

Sometimes correlation analysis alone provides sufficient information for the problem. Example 14.1C on Project Analysis and Earnings Correlation demonstrated that correlation analysis was the key tool in diversification analysis. But some issues require additional investigation beyond correlation. Business decisions that involve important organizational and financial changes often require the investigator to obtain a numerical value that specifies the impact that a policy change is thought to produce.

For instance, a more complete picture may require a statistic that measures changes in the value of Y, the dependent variable, that on average are associated with changes in the value of X, the independent variable.

A popular device that captures the essence of similar problems and is useful for analysis is the *mathematical model*. In investigating bivariate relationships a common model used universally and accepted as the standard of comparison is the *simple linear model*. It has the following form:

$$Y = \alpha + \beta X + \epsilon$$

where α and β are the intercept and slope parameters of a line which determine the average relationship between Y and X; ϵ is a random variable with expected value of zero and standard deviation σ_ϵ. Let us now explain the purposes of the model and the meaning of the terms.

Formulating the simple linear model serves two important purposes:

1. it forces us to decide and identify which variable is to be designated as the independent (or predictor) variable, X, and which variable is to be designated as the dependent (or criterion) variable, Y; it is the values of the latter variable which we wish to predict.

2. the linear parameter values, α and β, together with the random variable term, ϵ, present a sensible way of answering the following question: what portion of the value of Y, the dependent variable, can be regarded as *unrelated* to X, the independent variable, and what portion of Y results from the relationship with the independent variable?

The values of the linear parameters α and β answer these questions.

β (beta) represents the average change in the value of Y attributable to one unit change in the value of X. For instance, if $Y = 7 + 4X + \epsilon$, then 4 is the average change in Y attributable to a one unit change in X.

The sum $(\alpha + \epsilon)$ is the component part of Y *unrelated* to the values of X; this component can be broken into two parts with α representing the average or *mean* value of this component and ϵ representing the random deviations in this component of Y about its mean α. Using the illustrated equation above, we see that the value of $\alpha = 7$ units.

In other words, the simple linear model helps us understand that a change in the value of Y can arise from two sources:

> *First Source:* a change in the value of X: the corresponding change in Y equals β (the change in X).

> *Second Source:* a change in the value of the random variable ϵ.

Note that because α reflects the *mean* value of $(\alpha + \epsilon)$, it is not a variable. These two sources can and will often occur simultaneously; but, as the next example illustrates, changes in Y resulting from changes in X are of particular interest.

Example 14.4.   Rate Scheduling at Overland Express

Overland Express sees a market opportunity in linking a land delivery service and commuter and regional airlines serving market segments abandoned by the large commercial trunk carriers. Overland plans a dependable delivery truck service for small packages arriving on these new commuter airlines. The rate charges for the service, according to the firm's cost accountant, require an estimate for each of two cost factors: labor cost and truck operating cost. Since operating costs rise the farther away the delivery address, charges are distance-based. The accountant therefore needs cost changes for each extra delivery mile.

> *Truck Operating Costs:* Truck operating cost per-mile figures that come from truck dealerships and government statistics indicate a 55 cent per mile cost for the truck type considered. The accountant will use this figure as a reliable truck operating cost. Therefore regression analysis is not needed.

> *Labor Cost:* The company will use its experience to estimate the labor costs for delivery distance by regression analysis. Labor costs vary with labor time usage given that the wage per hour is assumed to be fixed. Overland must estimate the extra labor time, on average, it takes to deliver an extra delivery mile. This is the central problem Overland shall shortly address.

Several features characterize the relationship between labor time usage and delivery distance. They are:

> 1. *Direction—A priori,* one expects labor time usage increases with delivery distance. That is, the variables move in the same direction.

> 2. *Level of Non-Distance-Related Labor Time Usage—*Some labor time usage occurs regardless of the distance the package is delivered. This includes unloading time, customer contact time, driver record keeping, traffic patterns, time of day, weather conditions, etc.

> 3. *Sensitivity of Distance-Related Labor Time Usage—*This amount of labor time usage is the direct result of delivery distance. Added to the nondistance related labor time usage component, one obtains the total labor time usage. The larger the distance related component as a percentage of the total labor time usage, the more reliable must be the rate charged for this component of labor time usage.

Because the non-distance related component has many factors with varying intensity, there will be considerable variation in labor time usage due to this component. Deliveries for the same distance then are not all going to show the same amount of total labor time. That is, a given X delivery distance will be associated with various Y values of total labor time usage. This means a plot of the XY paired values generated by a simple linear model will not fall on a straight line, but instead will show up as a scatter diagram like the one pictured in Figure 14.3.

To reflect this condition the equation for labor time usage can be expressed in terms of distance-related and non distance-related components. This means

$$Y = \alpha + \beta X + \epsilon$$

can be rewritten as

$$Y = (\alpha + \epsilon) + \beta X$$

Distance-related component
Non-distance related component
Total Labor Time Usage

The expression highlights the point that holding fixed the delivery distance does not hold fixed the total labor time usage. Fluctuation of Y will occur because ϵ, in the non distance-related component, is a random variable. But why are the changes in the non distance-related component represented by a random variable?

To approach this question properly, we must analyze the nature of non-distance-related time usage. As mentioned before, the non-distance related component of time usage is a composite of many elements not related to delivery distance: traffic congestion, weather, clerical and handling time, etc. This conglomeration of factors which affects time usage is unpredictable in number and intensity from Y value to Y value. The *net impact* of these elements can be expected to take on the behavioral nature of a random variable, fluctuating from observation to observation. With the value of the random variable ϵ fluctuating from observation to observation, a statistical relationship rather than an *exact* relationship is needed to define total labor time usage (Y). What assumption can be plausibly made about the distribution of ϵ, the random part of the distribution of labor time usage not distance related?

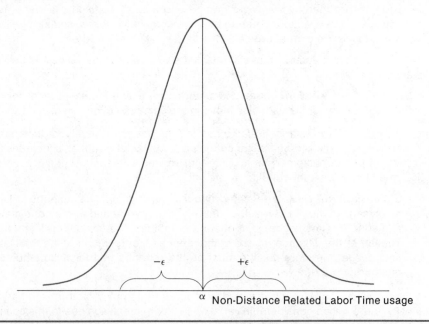

FIGURE 14.8 Distribution of Non-Distance Related Labor Time Usage

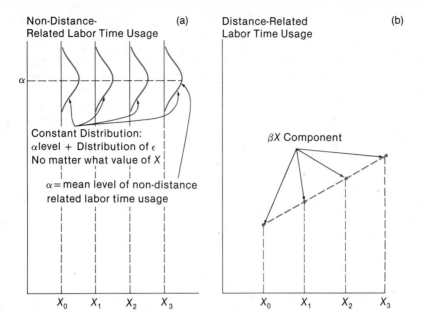

(a) Non-Distance-Related Labor Time Usage

α

Constant Distribution:
αlevel + Distribution of ϵ
No matter what value of X

α = mean level of non-distance related labor time usage

X_0 X_1 X_2 X_3

(b) Distance-Related Labor Time Usage

βX Component

X_0 X_1 X_2 X_3

Distribution of Y, Total Labor Time Usage = αlevel + βXlevel + distribution of ϵ

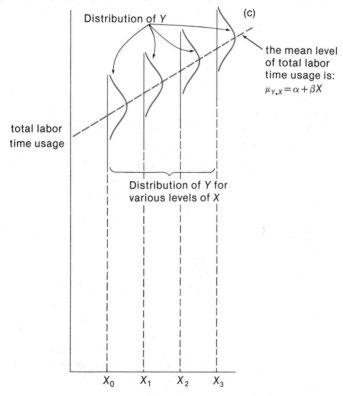

(c)

Distribution of Y

the mean level of total labor time usage is:
$\mu_{Y \cdot X} = \alpha + \beta X$

total labor time usage

Distribution of Y for various levels of X

X_0 X_1 X_2 X_3

FIGURE 14.9 Non-Distance-Related Time Usage, Distance-Related Time Usage, and Total Time Usage

The usual and plausible assumption made about the randomly occurring factors embodied in ϵ are that they are: numerous, relatively small, and independent. The underlying distribution of ($\alpha + \epsilon$) can then be assumed to be a normal distribution, with the center of the distribution at α. As can be noticed from Figure 14.8, the actual non-distance-related labor time usage of the components $\alpha + \epsilon$ is determined by how far above or below α the value of the term ϵ falls.

It is important to note that linear models commonly assume the probability distribution of ϵ unchanging across the levels of X. In this case it implies that the factors embodied in ϵ that affect time usage are unaffected by the size of the time usage associated with delivery distance, X.

Figure 14.9 graphically portrays that the *distribution* of non-distance-related labor time usage across the different levels of delivery distance, X, is unchanging and with the mean level fixed at α. The corresponding distance-related labor time usage component for these same delivery distances in Figure 14.9b follows an *exact path* that rises with distance. The total time usage shown in Figure 14.9c is a combination of (a) and (b).

14.5. The Simple Linear Regression Line

Figure 14.9 uses a broken line to indicate the path of centers of the Y distribution at different levels of X; each point on the line represents the *mean* value of Y at that level of X. This is written symbolically as $\mu_{Y.X}$. The line is called the *regression line of Y on X* and is frequently further identified as the *true* regression line. The true regression line, which might be thought of as representing the *average* relationship between Y and X, is given by:

$$\mu_{Y.X} = \alpha + \beta X.$$

In the Overland Express example, $\mu_{Y.X}$ represents the mean level of total labor time usage at delivery distance X. The linear relationship between these two variables can be graphed as shown in Figure 14.10.

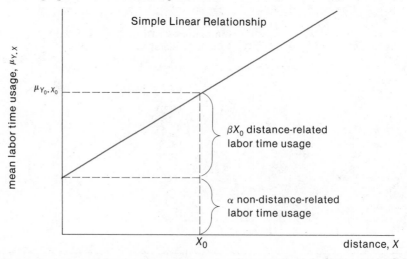

FIGURE 14.10 Simple Linear Regression Line

For a specific X_0 distance on the horizontal axis, a vertical line drawn to the relationship line pinpoints $\mu_{Y_0 \cdot X_0}$, the height of the line above point X_0. The height is divided into two segments representing the non-distance and distance related components of mean labor time usage. The lower segment, having length α, represents the non-distance related component of mean level of labor time usage. The upper segment, the distance related labor time usage component at the delivery distance X_0, is the product of two terms:

1. the slope, β, the average change in labor time usage for a one-unit change in delivery distance and

2. X_0 units of delivery distance.

In summary, the equation of the level of mean labor time usage is given by the following general relationship:

Mean Level of Labor Time Usage	=	non distance-related component of mean labor time usage	+	distance-related component of mean labor time usage
$\mu_{Y \cdot X}$	=	α	+	βX

At the specific distance X_0, the value of $\mu_{Y_0 \cdot X_0}$ (the mean labor time usage associated at distance X_0) is given by:

$$\mu_{Y_0 \cdot X_0} = \alpha + \beta X_0.$$

The simple linear regression line can be a key statistical tool in investigating a bivariate relationship. In the Overland Express situation, as in many other business situations, the primary interest will be in learning how $\mu_{Y \cdot X}$ varies with X. Why would Overland Express want to know the relationship between *mean* labor time usage and delivery distance? Because if the rates charged customers are to be based on distance, Overland must know its *mean* cost at a given distance to determine the rate it must charge to earn a profit. There will be expected differences in the labor time usage (and therefore costs) of deliveries at a given distance. Yet the customers will all be charged the same rate for that distance. What counts for profitability is whether the *mean* of these costs is below the rate charged.

Finding the value of the parameters α and β is critical in investigating the nature of the business relationship that X and Y represent. With the exact values of α and β typically not known, they must be estimated from the data available. The quantity and quality of the available data are key determinants of how well the estimation turns out. The statistical techniques used and the conditions they assume about the data for making the estimates are also important to understand. In the next section the procedure for making the estimates is discussed.

14.6. The Least Squares Method of Fitting a Regression Line

From a scatter diagram of *available sample* observations on X and Y such as Figure 14.11, we *can't locate the line* $\mu_{Y \cdot X} = \alpha + \beta X$ (miracles aside) and get the exact α and β values for our time usage analysis. But we can obtain an *estimate* of these values from a line fitted to the sample data. *But aren't there many lines which could be fitted to one set of data?* Yes, and Figure 14.11b shows a few. The question is which one to choose: which one gives the best fit?

For each individual point, it is customary to define "fit" as the *vertical* distance from the point to the fitted or estimated line. The closer the point to the line, the better the fit. That is, labeling the height of the line $\hat{Y}_0$ at the horizontal coordinate X_0, the fit is better the smaller the value of $(Y_0 - \hat{Y}_0)$; if the point is below the line, the discrepancy between the point and the line is negative. For this reason, the discrepancy will be squared, $(Y - \hat{Y}_0)^2$. See Figure 14.12. If the discrepancies above and below the line were simply added together, the positive and negative values would cancel each other out. To remove this possibility of canceling out, squaring turns these distances into ones with common signs.

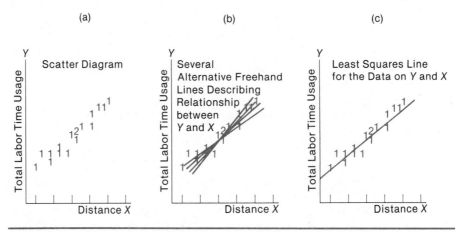

FIGURE 14.11 Scatter Diagrams with Freehand Lines and Least Squares Line

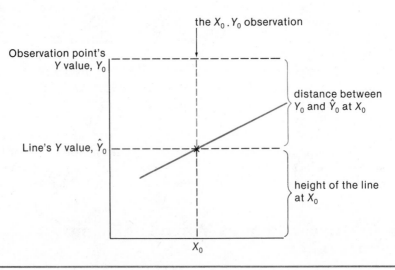

FIGURE 14.12 The Deviation between the Least Squares Line and an Observation

Quite often a scatter diagram has many dispersed points, not just one or two points. It is virtually impossible to have one (straight) line passing through all the observations. Moving the line to better fit one point generally pulls the line away from some other point(s) and worsens their fit. (Try this yourself on a scatter diagram.) Where does this leave us if we wish to take the fit for *all* points into account in deciding on the "best" line? It means that a "best" line selection with respect to a criterion ought to take account of the entire set of observations.

The most universally accepted criterion is to choose the one line which minimizes the *total squared discrepancy*, $\sum(Y - \hat{Y})^2$. This criterion is called the *"least squares" criterion* and the line which satisfies it is called the *least squares line.* Roughly speaking, this criterion corresponds to a belief that several small errors may be better than a few large ones. In business, a firm may be able to sustain small financial losses, but it may not be able to survive a financial "bath".

Since the least squares line is obtained from the available sample data, the line's Y intercept is labeled "*a*" (an *estimate* of α) and its slope is labeled "*b*" (an estimate of β). The equation for the line estimate is:

$$\hat{Y} = a + bX,$$

where $\hat{Y}$ is the height of the line measured from the horizontal axis X. The least squares line for the scatter of points in Figure 14.11a is indicated by the heavy line shown in Figure 14.11c.

14.7. Finding the Least Squares Line

In computing the least squares line, $\sum(Y - \hat{Y})^2$ is minimized. Substituting the equation for $\hat{Y}$, this becomes

$$\sum(Y - a - bX)^2,$$

an expression in which there are two unknowns, a and b.[2] How can the value of this expression be minimized? By assigning different values to a and b, the value of the expression changes. The goal is to find the right combination of a and b values which, together with the available data on X and Y, gives the lowest possible value of the expression. Mathematically, it may be shown that the combination of a and b values which simultaneously satisfies the following two equations is the combination which meets the minimization requirement.[3]

$$\sum Y = na + b \sum X$$
$$\sum XY = a \sum X + b \sum X^2$$

The values of Y, X, XY, X^2 and n are all obtained from computations on the sample data. This leaves only the values of a and b as unknowns to be obtained by solving the two equations.

Solving the two equations algebraically obtains the following solution for b:

$$b = \frac{n\Sigma XY - \Sigma X\Sigma Y}{n\Sigma X^2 - (\Sigma X)^2}$$

Note that the term in the denominator is often referred to as SS_X (the Sum Squared of X), since it is equivalent to $\Sigma(X - \bar{X})^2$. $SS_X = \Sigma(X - \bar{X})^2 = n\Sigma X^2 - (\Sigma X)^2$. The procedure for computing the value of 'a' may then be obtained in two steps:

1. substituting the value of 'b' into the first of the two simultaneous equations and

2. isolating 'a': $a = \dfrac{1}{n}(\Sigma Y - b\Sigma X)$.

Using the relationship that the sum is the number of observations n multiplied by the typical value, the mean, we can write $\Sigma X = n\bar{X}$ and $\Sigma Y = n\bar{Y}$. The expressions for a and b can be simplified to:

$$b = \frac{\Sigma XY - n\bar{X}\bar{Y}}{\Sigma X^2 - n\bar{X}^2} \quad \text{slope coefficient}$$

$$a = \bar{Y} - b\bar{X} \quad \text{intercept coefficient}$$

Using the correlation coefficient r, an expression that links b with r is,

$$b = r\frac{S_Y}{S_X}$$

where $S_Y = \dfrac{\Sigma(Y - \bar{Y})^2}{(n-1)}$ and $S_X = \dfrac{\Sigma(X - \bar{X})^2}{(n-1)}$. Notice that the value of b must be computed before 'a' can be computed.

Let us now illustrate the least squares solution for the regression coefficients 'a' and 'b' for the data on Overland Express.

Example 14.7. Illustration of the Method for Computing the Regression Coefficients

We now present the data on distance, X, and time usage, Y, and the subsequent calculations, shown in Table 14.9. The least squares regression coefficients for Overland Express (Example 14.4) can be computed with the use of this data.

$$b = \frac{n(\Sigma XY) - (\Sigma X)(\Sigma Y)}{n(\Sigma X^2) - (\Sigma X)^2} = \frac{17(8229) - (243)(503)}{17(3999) - (243)(243)} = \frac{139,893 - 122,229}{67,983 - 59,049}$$

$$= \frac{17,664}{8934} = 1.97716 = 1.98$$

$$a = \bar{Y} - b\bar{X}$$

where $\bar{X} = \Sigma X/n = 243/17 = 14.294$; $\bar{Y} = \Sigma Y/n = 503/17 = 29.588$

$a = 29.588 - 1.97716(14.294) = 1.3264 = 1.33$

TABLE 14.9. Calculating Regression Statistics for Overland Express

PACKAGE NUMBER	DISTANCE, X (MILES)	TIME USAGE, Y (MINUTES)	X^2	XY	Y^2
1	3	9	9	27	81
2	6	20	36	120	400
3	8	20	64	160	400
4	9	16	81	144	256
5	11	23	121	253	529
6	11	19	121	209	361
7	13	20	169	260	400
8	14	30	196	420	900
9	15	33	225	495	1089
10	16	27	256	432	729
11	16	32	256	512	1024
12	17	34	289	578	1156
13	19	41	361	779	1681
14	19	34	361	646	1156
15	21	47	441	987	2209
16	22	47	484	1034	2209
17	23	51	529	1173	2601
	$\sum X = 243$	$\sum Y = 503$	$\sum X^2 = 3999$	$\sum XY = 8229$	$\sum Y^2 = 17{,}181$

Inserting the computed values of a and b leads to the computed regression equation:

$$\hat{Y} = 1.33 + 1.98X.$$

This computed regression equation can now provide Overland Express an estimate of how much labor time it takes on average to deliver a package a given distance. For example, using $\hat{Y}$ to estimate $\mu_{Y.X}$, the predicted mean labor time usage that it will take to deliver a package fourteen miles is estimated to be:

$$\hat{Y} = 1.33 + 1.98(14)$$
$$= 1.33 + 27.72$$
$$= 29.05 \text{ minutes}$$

How much of the estimated mean delivery time is distance related? Interestingly, the proportion of distance related mean labor time usage, bX, to total mean time usage indicates that nearly all $[(27.72)/(29.05) = 95\%]$ of mean labor time usage is distance related at the near average delivery distance $\overline{X} \simeq 14$ miles. This means that distance alone will be a reliable index for Overland of the mean labor time expended in making a delivery.

Observed Variation in Values of Labor Time Usage for Individual Deliveries

A computational formula for r^2 that follows directly from the computation of the simple regression coefficients and the format of the computation in Table 14.9 is,

$$r^2 = \frac{a(\sum Y) + b(\sum XY) - [(\sum Y)^2/n]}{\sum Y^2 - [(\sum Y)^2/n]}$$

$$= \frac{(1.3264)(503) + (1.97716)(8229) - (503)^2/17}{17,181 - (503)^2/17}$$

$$= \frac{2054.3465}{2298.1176} = .89$$

Note: For accuracy, full decimal values are used for the values of regression coefficients "*a*" and "*b*".

The r^2 value of .89 means that 89% of the observed variation in the values of the labor time usage variable can be explained by the variation in the values of the delivery distance variable. What about the other eleven percent of the observed variation in labor time usage? It is attributable to factors other than distance which are not formally specified in the model; that is, to the random variation in ϵ, the term of the non-distance-related component.

There is an alternative way of computing r and r^2. From the already computed value of b, we can find r from the relationship

$$b = r\frac{S_Y}{S_X}$$

Isolating r and using the computed value of b, S_X, and S_Y, we have

$$r = b\frac{S_X}{S_Y} = 1.97716\left[\frac{5.7311}{11.9847}\right] = .9454$$

$$\text{where } S_X = \sqrt{\frac{\sum(X - \bar{X})^2}{n-1}} = 5.7311 \text{ and } S_Y = \sqrt{\frac{\sum(Y - \bar{Y})^2}{n-1}} = 11.9847.$$

So $r^2 = (.9454)^2 = .894$, the same value found using the computations of Table 14.9. If you have access to a computer, you may at this point want to plug in the numbers to verify the results and become familiar with the format of computer programs in presenting the results.

14.8. Standard Deviation of Residuals—A Measure of the Predictive Error in Regression

The computed regression line should help reduce prediction errors. By how much is a question which requires a two part inquiry. First, upon what prediction technique does the computed regression line improve? That is, in the absence of the computed regression line for predicting Y, what other sample statistic can we use? Second, what overall sample statistic best summarizes the prediction error? The needed summary statistic must offer a way of judging the relative prediction error of the different prediction methods.

Predicting without knowledge of an X series, by necessity, means relying completely on the Y series itself to predict the next value of Y. In this case, the best guess to give is the sample mean of the available data, $\bar{Y}$.[4] After all, the sample mean does represent the net result (average) considering all the available Y values; it best typifies an individual value of the Y series available. The predictive error encountered by using $\overline{Y}$ to predict Y is measured by S_Y, the standard deviation of Y where $S_Y = \sqrt{\dfrac{\Sigma(Y - \overline{Y})^2}{n - 1}}$. The term S_Y is a summary statistic reflecting the average difference or error between the observed values of Y and the prediction $\overline{Y}$ (see Figure 14.13a).

But what if there exists information on a linear relationship between Y and a variable X, and that information is available? By fitting a least squares line to the joint observations, we get a computed regression line which now serves to predict the value of Y. The best point prediction of Y at a particular value of X would no longer be $\overline{Y}$, but $\hat{Y}$—the predictive value of Y read off the regression line. The difference between the actual Y value and the predicted value $\hat{Y}$ is called a residual $(Y - \hat{Y} = \text{residual})$. The dispersion of residuals about the regression line is measured by the *standard deviation of residuals* and is denoted by $S_{Y.X}$. It is expressed by the formula:[5]

$$S_{Y.X} = \sqrt{\frac{\Sigma(Y - \hat{Y})^2}{n - 2}}$$

As a summary statistic, $S_{Y.X}$ reflects the square root of the *average squared deviation* between the actual Y values and the $\hat{Y}$ values—the *predicted* Ys using the regression line. Since $Y - \hat{Y}$ is the size of the predictive error, the standard deviation of residuals is also a summary measure of the *average* predicted error one expects to encounter by using regression analysis. Sometimes the variance of Y about the line of least squares fit is called the variance of e where $e = Y - \hat{Y}$. That is, it's common to see $S_{Y.X}$ written as S_e. Alternatively, the standard deviation of residuals may be called the standard error of estimate.

Can the predictive advantage gained by using the regression line be visualized? Compare Figure 14.13a with b. The indication from the graph is that the scatter around the computed regression line is less than the scatter around $\overline{Y}$. That is, $S_{Y.X}$ is less than S_Y.

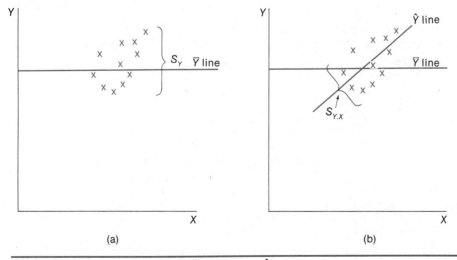

FIGURE 14.13 Predictive Error Using $\overline{Y}$ Line Versus $\hat{Y}$ Line

Except in the case of zero correlation (where nothing is gained by using information on X), the value of $S_{Y.X}$ is always smaller than S_Y. The reduction in prediction error gained by the use of regression could be expressed in terms of the difference between S_Y and $S_{Y.X}$. Instead, however, it is usually expressed in terms of the difference between the *variance* of the errors:

$$
\begin{array}{ll}
& \text{Variance of prediction errors without regression } (S_Y^2) \\
\textit{minus} & \underline{\text{variance of prediction errors using regression } (S_{Y.X}^2)} \\
\textit{equals} & \text{reduction in variance of prediction errors.}
\end{array}
$$

The *proportional* reduction in the variance of prediction errors is therefore the ratio:

$$\frac{S_Y^2 - S_{Y.X}^2}{S_Y^2} = \text{Proportional Reduction.}$$

This latter expression is r^2, the coefficient of determination.[6] Naturally, therefore, r^2 can also be interpreted as the proportional reduction in prediction error obtained by using $\hat{Y}$ rather than $\overline{Y}$ to predict Y. Thus, an r^2 of .80 indicates that using $\hat{Y}$ rather than $\overline{Y}$ to predict Y reduces the size of the average prediction error by 80 percent.

The standard deviation of residuals formula can be reworked by substituting the computed regression line $a + bX$ for $\hat{Y}$ since $\hat{Y} = a + bX$. The standard deviation rewritten is

$$S_{Y.X} = \sqrt{\frac{\sum(Y - a - bX)^2}{n - 2}}$$

By additional rearrangement, this formula will yield a more computationally usable equation which will conform to the computation made in Table 14.9. This formula rewritten becomes

$$S_{Y.X} = \sqrt{\frac{(\sum Y^2) - (a)(\sum Y) - (b)(\sum XY)}{n - 2}}$$

Note that the top portion of the computational formula is often termed the sum of squared errors (SSE) because it is equivalent to $\sum(Y - \hat{Y})^2$. It is a common computation found on regression computer printouts.

Computing the standard deviation of residuals for the Overland Express problem, we have

$$S_{Y.X} = \sqrt{\frac{(\sum Y^2) - (a)(\sum Y) - (b)(\sum XY)}{n - 2}} = \sqrt{\frac{SSE}{n - 2}}$$

$$= \sqrt{\frac{17{,}181 - (1.3264)(503) - (1.97716)(8229)}{17 - 2}}$$

$$= \sqrt{\frac{243.77116}{15}} = 4.03130$$

14.9. Inferences About the True Slope Coefficient

Once the slope b of the computed least squares regression line has been obtained, the next step is to consider β, the value of the true regression line's slope coefficient.

If the assumptions of the linear regression model are met, what will the sampling distribution of b look like? If random samples of size n are repeatedly drawn from the bivariate X,Y population, the computed regression slopes (the bs) would form a probability distribution normally distributed with mean β (the true slope), and standard deviation σ_b. That is

b is distributed as $N(\beta, \sigma_b)$

$$\text{where } \sigma_b = \sqrt{\frac{\sigma_{Y.x}^2}{\Sigma(X - \overline{X})^2}}$$

This is represented in Figure 14.14.

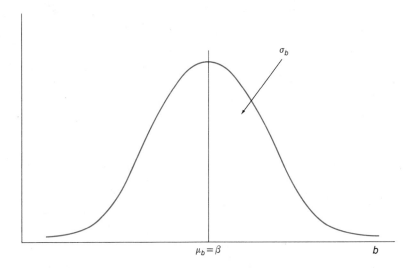

FIGURE 14.14 Sample Distribution of the Slope Coefficient, b

A good replacement for the population value σ_b is available by replacing the population error variance $\sigma_{Y.X}^2$ with its sample estimate $S_{Y.X}^2$, the calculated variance of the observed errors (residuals) surrounding the regression line. The replacement S_b is

$$S_b = \sqrt{\frac{S_{Y.X}^2}{\Sigma(X - \overline{X})^2}}$$

However, this substitution gives additional uncertainty to the sampling inference about β. The sampling distribution now employed refers to the statistic

$(b - \beta)/S_b$ which is t distributed with $n - 2$ degree of freedom. Importantly, probability statements about the statistic can be manipulated (pivoted) into confidence interval statements for β.

By rewriting the terms in the denominator a more useful form for computing S_b results. It is,

$$S_b = \sqrt{\frac{n(S^2_{Y.X})}{n(\sum X^2) - (\sum X)^2}}$$

Let us now employ S_b and estimate a confidence interval for β.

Confidence Interval for β

A confidence interval for β is built around the computed value of b, and its width is determined by the desired degree of confidence $1 - \alpha$ and the value of S_b. The interval is:

$$b \pm t_{[\alpha/2,\, n-2]} S_b$$

Example 14.9A. Computation of the Confidence Interval for the Slope Coefficient

In Example 14.7 the least squares regression of time usage on distance for Overland Express led to a computed slope coefficient of 1.98 minutes per mile. Although this figure is useful as a point estimate of the value β, we know from our study of sampling distribution that it is not very likely for b to equal the parameter β. Fortunately we can still make a statement reflecting our assuredness about where β lies given our information about b and the appropriate t distribution. An interval estimate serves to convey this message. The interval's range conveys the precision we have achieved and the degree of confidence defines the trustworthiness of that precision. The first step is to calculate S_b:

$$S_b = \sqrt{\frac{S^2_{Y.X}}{\sum(X - \overline{X})^2}} = \sqrt{\frac{nS^2_{Y.X}}{n(\sum X^2) - (\sum X)^2}} = \sqrt{\frac{17(4.03130)(4.03130)}{17(3999) - (243)(243)}} = .1758$$

Next the t value for $n - 2 = 15$ degrees of freedom is determined from the tables of the t distribution given in the appendix. For a two-sided 95% confidence interval, this would be 2.131. Thus, the .95 confidence interval is:

$$b \pm t_{.025} S_b = 1.98 \pm (2.131)(.1758) = 1.98 \pm .3746$$

The upper limit would be $1.98 + .3746 = 2.35$

The lower limit would be $1.98 - .3746 = 1.61$

This means that we strongly expect the increase in labor time usage for a one unit (one mile) increase in delivery distance to fall in the interval from 1.61 minutes to 2.35 minutes.

Testing Hypotheses About β

In some cases we have in mind a particular value of β, reflecting the way in which X and Y are related. To statistically check our hypothesis about β, a hypothesis test is performed. The test evaluates how plausible the value we have in mind is in light of the observed difference between the sample slope coefficient b and the hypothesized value of β. By dividing the observed difference by the standard deviation of the sampling distribution for b, we obtain a ratio referred to as the calculated value of t for the test statistic $(b - \beta)/S_b$. That is,

$$\text{Calculated } t = \frac{b - \text{hypothesized } \beta}{S_b}$$

This calculated t-ratio is compared with the critical value of t at the desired significance level at the prescribed $n - 2$ degrees of freedom.

Often, the hypothesized value of β is set at zero. We are, in that case, interested in testing the hypothesis that no linear relationship exists. In other words, having information on the independent variable X may not be useful in predicting the dependent variable Y in the way the linear model suggests. At the .05 significance level, the null hypothesis would be rejected if the calculated $t = (b - 0)/S_b$ exceeds the critical t-value at .05 level for $n - 2$ degrees of freedom.

Example 14.9B. **Illustration of Computations in Hypothesis Tests About the Slope Coefficient**

How strong is the sample evidence against the hypothesis that for Overland's operation time usage is linearly unrelated to distance? To answer this question, let's consider the following steps.

Steps to Consider in Testing a Hypothesis on the Slope

Step 1: Null Hypothesis, H_0: $\beta = 0$ (no linear relationship exists)

Step 2: Alternative Hypothesis, H_A: $\beta > 0$ (a positive linear relationship exists)

Step 3: Calculated t: $t = \dfrac{b - 0}{S_b}$

Step 4: Rejection Area: Choosing $\alpha = .01$, find the critical value of t_{01} for $n - 2 = 15$ degrees of freedom which designates the area of rejection of the null hypothesis (area to the right of the critical value).

Step 5: Compare Calculated t to Critical t: reject the null hypothesis if the calculated t exceeds the critical t; otherwise accept the alternative hypothesis.

Solution: $\quad$ calculated $t = \dfrac{b - \text{hypothesized } \beta}{S_b}$

$$= \frac{1.98 - 0}{.1758} = 11.26$$

Since the alternative hypothesis is directional, a one-sided hypothesis would be rejected at the 1 percent significance level since the critical t value $= 2.602$. This indicates that the sample evidence is strong enough to make the null hypothesis untenable. Overland's operation time usage has a positive linear relation to distance.

14.10. Sampling Variation of the Computed Regression Line

There is only one true regression line for each bivariate population. It is expressed by the equation $\mu_{Y.X} = \alpha + \beta X$. This equation represents the path followed by the means of the Y distributions for the particular values of X considered.

The "uniqueness" of the true regression line does not carry over to the least squares line used to estimate the "true" regression line. Each available set of data represents a particular random sample from the population. For each different random sample drawn from the population, a different *least squares regression line* (often called the *sample regression line* or *regression line of the observed data*) can be calculated. The computed regression line is expressed by the equation $\hat{Y} = a + bX$.

Each computed least squares line provides a different estimate of the true regression line. Inferences about the accuracy of these estimates require a description of the amount of sampling variation that accompanies the least squares lines. That is, the inferences must recognize the fact that the actual least squares line calculated from the particular set of available sample data is only one of a host of possible lines from the different random samples which could have been drawn.

Least Squares Line: Empirical Sampling Demonstrations

How well do the sample regression lines approximate the true regression line? One way to find out is to conduct some empirical experiments from a bivariate population with a known true regression line. The procedure we followed was to:

1. draw twenty-five random samples, each of size 50;

2. compute the least squares line for each different sample;

3. compare their position with that of the true regression line.

Figure 14.15 shows the results on a graph. The heavy line in the diagram is the true regression line; it has the equation $\mu_{Y.X} = 100 + 2X$. The other lines in the figure are the computed least squares lines for 25 bivariate random samples each of size 50. From the figure, we can conclude that:

1. these computed least squares lines form a fan-shaped band (dotted line) around the true regression line

2. the narrowest part of the band is found above the population mean of X, μ_X reflecting less uncertainty about the position of the height of the true regression line at that point

3. the band continues to widen as the distance away from the mean value increases

Is there a statistic which summarizes these conclusions on how much error is likely when using a computed sample regression line to estimate the corresponding true regression line? Fortunately there is. It is given by a statistic called the standard deviation of the computed regression line.

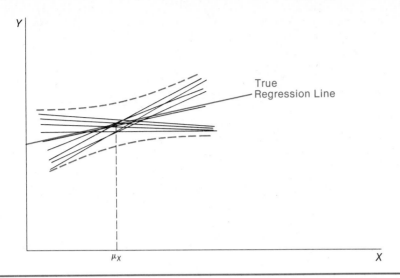

FIGURE 14.15 Least Squares Lines for Bivariate Samples of Size 50

Specifically, what role does the standard deviation of the calculated regression line play in inference? It is a key element in constructing a confidence interval for $\mu_{Y.X}$ at a *particular* value of X.

Standard Deviation of the Regression Line

The *standard deviation of the computed regression line* is the expression:

$$S_{\hat{Y}.X} = S_{Y.X}\sqrt{\frac{1}{n} + \frac{(X - \overline{X})^2}{\sum(X - \overline{X})^2}}$$

$$= S_{Y.X}\sqrt{\frac{1}{n} + \frac{(X - \overline{X})^2}{SS_X}}$$

Looking at the first term under the radical, we see that the standard deviation and likely error decreases with increasing sample size. The second term shows that the likely error depends on how close X is to $\overline{X}$. The closer $\overline{X}$ is to the particular value of X at which Y is predicted, the smaller will be the likely error. For computational purposes, the second term's denominator can be written as SS_X ($\sum(X - \overline{X})^2 = SS_X$). This simplifies the notation and conforms to standardized computer output.

Example 14.10.   Using Regression Analysis to Cut Physical Distribution Costs

A Chicago produce distributor wants to cut physical distribution costs, a major component of total costs. With a good estimate of transit time, storage and holding costs can be cut. The sooner the order is met, the lower will be the physical costs of storing and holding. Transit time tends to increase with increasing distance between origin and destination, but is also subject to random variation. Suppose a random sample of 100 orders is taken to provide data on transit times. Then a regression equation is computed with the following results:

$$\hat{Y} = 3.197 + .00309X$$

where X = straight line distance (in miles) between Chicago and the point of origin

$\hat{Y}$ = estimated average transit time (in days) for distance X

Other statistics are:

$r = .84$ $\bar{X} = 1329.410$ miles

$S_{Y.X} = 1.55$ days $SS_X = 6,303,022.7$ miles squared

For shipments coming a distance of 2000 miles, points and interval estimates of the mean transit time are computed as follows.

Point Estimate:

The point estimate represents the best single guess about the value of $\mu_{Y.X}$ at the X value considered. The calculation of its value will rely on the computed regression which represents the average relationship between X and Y. Plugging $X = 2000$ into the regression equation gives

$$\hat{Y} = 3.197 + .00309X$$
$$\hat{Y} = 3.197 + .00309(2000)$$
$$= 3.197 + 6.18$$
$$= 9.377 \text{ days}$$

Interval Estimate:

Now that we have obtained a point estimate (best single value guess), we can formally make an allowance for the uncertainty about the accuracy of the estimate. An interval compensates for the inaccuracy by specifying a range of values around the point estimate. We have

interval estimate = point estimate + allowance for uncertainty

The allowance for uncertainty is expressed by the standard error of the regression line, $S_{\hat{Y}.X}$. We can then write the general form of the confidence interval as:

confidence interval estimate = point estimate $\pm t_{\alpha/2} S_{\hat{Y}.X}$

The standard error of the regression line computation then is:

$$S_{\hat{Y}.X} = S_{Y.X} \sqrt{\frac{1}{n} + \frac{(X - \bar{X})^2}{SS_X}}$$

$$= 1.55 \sqrt{\frac{1}{100} + \frac{(2000 - 1329.410)^2}{6,303,022.7}}$$

$$= 1.55 \sqrt{.010 + 0.0713453}$$

$$= 1.55(0.285211)$$

$$= 0.442 \text{ days}$$

Thus a .95 confidence interval estimate for $\mu_{Y.X}$ when $X = 2000$ miles is:

$$\hat{Y} + t_{.025}S_{\hat{Y}.X} = 9.377 + (1.96)(0.442)$$
$$= 10.243 \text{ days}$$

$$\hat{Y} - t_{.025}S_{\hat{Y}.X} = 9.377 - (1.96)(0.442)$$
$$= 8.511 \text{ days}$$

We could conclude that the transit time for points of origin 2000 miles distant from Chicago is, on the *average*, at least 8.511 days and not more than 10.243 days. Our confidence in the correctness of this statement rests upon the procedure used, which provides intervals containing the true mean about 95 percent of the time.

14.11. Forecasting a New Observation

Having computed the least squares line, one can use it to forecast an individual value of Y for a particular value of X. The forecast is the point $\hat{Y}$, which is the height of the least squares line at the particular value of X. However, seldom is the forecast $\hat{Y}$ exactly equal to Y—the *actual* value of Y at point X. Usually there will be a forecast *error* $(Y - \hat{Y})$, defined as the discrepancy between the actual Y value and the predicted value $\hat{Y}$. In view of the prevalence of these errors, how accurate is $\hat{Y}$ as a forecast of Y?

The accuracy of $\hat{Y}$ as a forecast of the actual Y value depends on the amount of *systematic* error, if any, and on the amount of *random* error encountered in the process of sampling. Since $\hat{Y}$ is an *unbiased* estimator of the actual Y value, there is *no systematic* source of error to be concerned about. Hence, our attention turns to the random sampling error. How much variability is there at a given level of X among the e's obtained for different random samples from the same population? That is, how *reliable* is $\hat{Y}$ as a forecaster of Y?

A Measure of Forecast Reliability

The reliability of Y value forecasts is assessed by the *standard deviation of forecast error*, given by the formula:

$$S_{F.X} = S_{Y.X}\sqrt{\frac{1}{n} + \frac{(X - \overline{X})^2}{\Sigma(X - \overline{X})^2} + 1}$$

Standard Deviation of Forecast Error

alternatively written

$$S_{F.X} = S_{Y.X}\sqrt{\frac{1}{n} + \frac{(X - \overline{X})^2}{SS_X} + 1}$$

The larger the value of $S_{F.X}$, the less reliable is the forecast. Note again that computationally $\Sigma(X - \overline{X})^2$ is expressed as SS_X.

Prediction Interval for a New *Y* Value

Within what range of values can we be reasonably sure that the new *Y* value will lie, taking forecast error into consideration? The answer to this question is given by the *prediction interval of a new Y value* at a given *X* value. The prediction interval is constructed around the point forecast, $\hat{Y}$, adding a range above and below to account for forecast error. The amount added depends on:

1. the size of the standard deviation of forecast error
2. the level of confidence we wish to have for the prediction interval

In total, the amount added is a *t*-multiple (using $n - 2$ degrees of freedom) of the size of the standard deviation of forecast:

$$Upper\ Limit \text{ of Interval Prediction} = Y + t_{[\alpha/2, n-2]}S_{F.X}$$

$$Lower\ Limit \text{ of Interval Prediction} = \hat{Y} - t_{[\alpha/2, n-2]}S_{F.X}$$

where $1 - \alpha =$ the desired level of confidence in the prediction.

Example 14.11. Using Regression Analysis to Determine Delivery Dependability

In Example 14.10, an estimate of *mean* transit time for shipments coming 2000 miles enables the Chicago produce distributor to plan how much lead time to allow in placing orders. Shorter average transit time guarantees fresher produce on arrival. But there still remains concern about the *variability* of the transit times around the estimated mean for 2000 mile trips. The greater the variation in transit times, the more uncertain is the arrival time for *any particular* shipment. An actual transit time substantially different from the average will cause disastrous operating problems. For instance, lettuce from California arriving too early may wilt on the loading dock while waiting to be processed. Late arriving lettuce is likely to disrupt scheduled service to restaurants and supermarkets which depend on receiving delivery daily. Confronted with possible spoilage costs and unserviced customers, the Chicago produce distributor may forego using one mode of transit with a lower average transit time for another offering greater dependability, even if the latter on the average delivers produce which is somewhat less fresh.

For example, say the first mode of transit has transit time of 9 days on average but transit time varies from 7 to 15 days. Say the other mode has an average of 10 days but transit time varies between 8 and 12 days. The latter mode has a more dependable service since there is less of a deviation from the mean than that shown by the first mode.

The size of the forecast errors made will be (slightly) larger the further the transit distance is from $\overline{X}$ (1329.41 miles). The *standard deviation of forecast error* can be used to measure the variability of transit times at a specific distance (2000 miles). The value of $S_{F.X}$ is also needed to compute a Prediction Interval for shipment transit time. In the calculation below, a 95% confidence level is used in determining the *t*-multiple for the prediction interval.

Computation of Standard Deviation of Forecast Error for 2000 Mile Distance

$$S_{F.X} = S_{Y.X} \sqrt{\frac{1}{n} + \frac{(X - \bar{X})^2}{SS_X} + 1}$$

$$= 1.55 \sqrt{\frac{1}{100} + \frac{(2000 - 1329.41)^2}{6303022.7} + 1}$$

$$= 1.55(1.0399)$$

$$= 1.612$$

Prediction Interval of Y for 2000 Mile Distance at a 95% Confidence Level

Upper Limit: $\hat{Y}_{2000} + t_{.025} S_{F.X} = 9.377 + (1.96)(1.612) = 12.54$ days

Lower Limit: $\hat{Y}_{2000} - t_{.025} S_{F.X} = 9.377 - (1.96)(1.612) = 6.22$ days

The interpretation of the prediction interval is that over the long run, 95% of the transit times for shipments arriving from a source 2000 miles distant should take at least 6.22 days and not more than 12.54 days. Based upon this interval prediction, the produce distributor would have to allow for considerable leeway in the arrival time of produce shipments. This leeway may make this mode of transit unacceptable.

14.12. Managerial Issues in Practice—Review Exercise: Beta Stock Analysis and the Market Model

Which stocks move up the fastest when the market turns bullish? Which stocks resist downward pressure when a bearish mood grips the market? Which stocks perform like the market—are neither risky high fliers nor slow moving income stocks lacking price appreciation potential? To answer these questions you need what Wall Street calls *"Beta Analysis"*; more specifically, you need to estimate β (Beta) from regression analysis of the "market model".

The market model is a simple linear regression model linking a stock's return (the dependent variable) to the return on a stock market index (the independent variable). Typically, the broad stock market indices used are the *New York Stock Index* or the *Standard and Poor's 500 Stock Index*. Regression analysis requires collecting a historical series of bivariate return observations (usually in consecutive monthly intervals) on the stock and the market index over several years. The slope coefficient of the regression line gives an estimate of the stock's *Beta*.

Beta Measures a Stock's Sensitivity to Market Changes

Beta reflects on the average the relative sensitivity of the *individual stock's* return to the *market index return* over the period of available data. The value of beta measures the average change in the stock's return (expressed in percentage points) for a *one percentage point change* in the market return. Thus, a beta value of one for a stock indicates that the return on the investment in that stock, *on average,* changes by the same amount as the market return changes, whether the market goes up or down.

Aggressive and Defensive Stocks

Stocks with beta greater than one are called *aggressive* stocks, since investment returns in these stocks move relatively faster; so gains tend to be greater than the market when the market is bullish and rises, and losses tend to be greater than the market when the market is bearish and falls. These are stocks to buy when you are betting on a market rise, and to avoid if you expect the market to fall.

Beta values less than one belong to *defensive* stocks. Investment returns in these stocks are relatively less sensitive to market return changes. They fare better than the market in bearish times, but do not do as well when the market is bullish. These are the stocks to hold when you are concerned about a downturn, but to divest yourself of in a bull market.

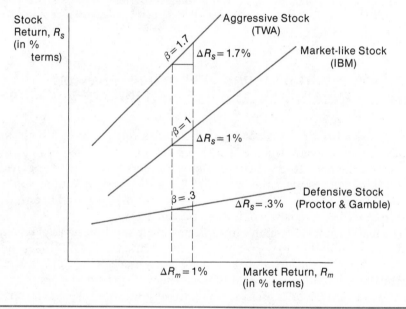

FIGURE 14.16 Market Model Line (Characteristic Line) For Three Types of Stocks

Figure 14.16 illustrates the different responses to market movement of individual stocks having different values.

Note that all three β values cited in Figure 14.16 are positive; that is, economy wide forces that affect the market in general tend to affect these individual stocks in the same direction. Much more rare is the stock that has a zero or even negative β value. One example is Homestake Mining, the gold mining stock. This means that when the market has a great fall, the value of the stock goes counter to the market since the value of gold rises. Gold stocks such as Homestake have a negative β value.

The Components of a Stock's Return

The underlying simple linear regression model expressing the component elements making up a specific stock's return for each period is written as follows:

$$Y = \alpha + \beta X + \epsilon$$

Y is the actual return to the firm's stock during each of the given time intervals being investigated. X is the actual return to the stock market index during this same time interval. β is the expected percentage point change of the stock's return for a one percentage point change in the market index return. α is the long run component of the stock's actual return which is not related to the level of the market. Rather, this component is due to other factors *specific* to the firm. These factors affect the stock's return but are not accounted for by the market index: for example, management's decision to promote an aggressive marketing campaign. ϵ is the effect on the stock's actual return due to an *unexpected* factor (such as a managerial shakeup or confiscation of assets by a foreign government) during a specific time period. These components are illustrated in Figure 14.17.

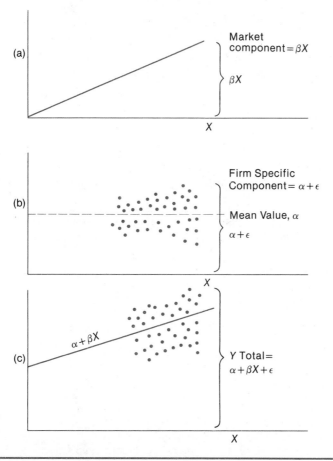

FIGURE 14.17 The Market Model: The Components of a Stock's Return

Example 14.12.   Beta Analysis of IBM Common Stock

A computer drawn scatter diagram is shown in Figure 14.18. The diagram compares monthly rates of return on IBM stock with the return on an index of the New York Stock Exchange stocks over a seven year period when IBM and the computer industry were going through rapid growth.

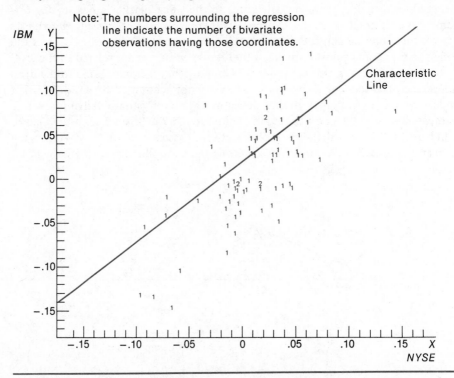

FIGURE 14.18 Scatter Plot of IBMs Monthly Stock Returns Versus Monthly Returns on New York Stock Exchange Index

Source: Computer Tapes, University of Chicago Center for Research in Security Prices

The 1s and 2s in the diagram indicate there are one and two values, respectively, at each of these points. The regression line (*characteristic* line in Wall Street terminology) computed for this data has the following equation:

$$\hat{Y} = .2596 + .998X$$

Other statistics are:

S_b $= .10837$ S_a $= .48166$
$S_{Y \cdot X} = 4.20997$ $\overline{X}$ $= 1.33731$
r^2 $= .508$ $\overline{Y}$ $= 1.59429$
S_Y $= 5.96851$ $SS_X = 1509.27$
                        S_X $= 4.26426$

Here are some important questions the computations help answer.
1. *How does the return on IBM stock compare to the market return?* The mean rate of return on IBM stock is given by $\overline{Y}$, which is approximately 1.59% per month (annualized rate of 19.30%). The mean market rate of return is given by $\overline{X}$, which is

approximately 1.34% per month (annualized rate of 15.60%). So over this seven year period, the value of IBM stock appreciated faster than the market as a whole.

2. *How sensitive is IBM stock to economy-wide forces incorporated in the market index?* This is indicated by the value of the regression slope coefficient *b*, which is the estimated value of beta. The value of .998 is very close to one, indicating that changes in the market rate of return were felt almost identically by IBM stockholders.

3. *Could IBMs greater than average price appreciation (return) than the market in general be attributed to a greater sensitivity to economy-wide forces than that which affects the market level?* No. This would imply a beta value substantially greater than one; as we have already noted, the estimated beta value is .998. Since this value is less than one, the higher rate of return on IBM stock is *not* due to its greater than average sensitivity to the economy-wide forces that affect and are reflected in the level of the market index.

4. *What is the average market-related component of IBMs monthly return over the seven years?* This is given by the product $b\overline{X} = (.998)(1.34) = 1.337\%$.

5. *If IBMs greater than average rate of return is not attributable to economy wide forces which affect the market as a whole, then what is the explanation?* Firm-specific growth factors unrelated to the movement of the market as a whole produce the mean value of this component given by the difference between the mean rate of return $\overline{Y}$ (1.594%) and the market-related component $b\overline{X}$ (1.337%). The value of this difference is the intercept term *a*(.2596% per month). $a = \overline{Y} - b\overline{X}$.
Having delineated the contributions of the specific components of IBM's *average* rate of return, an additional concern is the *variability* of the rate of return.

6. *How do the fluctuations in IBMs rate of return compare with general market movements?* Over the seven year period, IBMs actual monthly rate of return fluctuated considerably, as measured by $S_Y = 5.969\%$ per month. The general market movement was smaller, as measured by $S_X = 4.264\%$ per month.

7. *What portion of the ups and down in IBMs rate of return was merely a reflection of the general market movements?* This is given by r^2, which has a value of $[b(S_X/S_Y)]^2 = [.998(4.26426/5.96851)]^2 = (.713)^2 = .508$. Thus, changes in the market rate of return explain only half of the fluctuations in IBMs rate of return.

8. *And the remainder of the variation was due to firm-specific factors?* That's right. These factors accounted for $1 - r^2 = .492$ or 49.2% of the variation in IBMs rate of return.

9. *How can the market-related movements and the firm-specific movements in IBMs rate of return be traced on a scatter diagram?* The movement in IBMs rate of return associated with a market index movement from one *X* level to another *X* level would be given by the vertical *change in height* of the computed regression line across the *X* level change (movement *along* the regression line). The firm-specific component of IBMs rate of return at any *X* level is given by the *deviation* (vertical height) of the observation from the regression line.

10. *What statistic reports or summarizes the amount of fluctuation in IBMs rate of return attributable to variation in firm-specific factors?* The standard deviation of residuals $S_{Y.X}$ reports this variation. The population of firm-specific IBM returns is expected to be distributed as a normal curve, with approximately two-thirds falling within ± one standard deviation $S_{Y.X}$ of the regression line. The 4.2% value found for $S_{Y.X}$ then indicates that from the data it is estimated that approximately two thirds of the monthly rates of return on IBM stock fall within 4.2 percentage points of the $\hat{Y}$ values read along the regression line.

11. *How reliable is b, the estimated value of beta, β?* The uncertainty about beta (β) is measured by S_b, the standard error of the regression coefficient b. It has a value of .10837. If the Beta value is zero, how likely is it to find a sample value as far from zero as the observed b value of .998? Computing a t-ratio gives us a way to evaluate the plausibility of the hypothesis that $\beta = 0$. We find,

$$t = \frac{b - \beta}{S_b} = \frac{.998 - 0}{.10837} = 9.21$$

The regression slope coefficient is more than nine standard deviations from the value of $\beta = 0$. This leaves little doubt that the hypothesis $\beta = 0$ ought to be rejected. It is plausible then to assume that there is a linear systematic link between IBMs stock return and movements in the stock market.

12. *What is the 95% confidence interval for beta?* A 95% confidence interval for beta has a lower limit of .7856 and an upper limit of 1.2104. These are computed as follows:

Lower Limit: $b - t_{.025}S_b = .9980 - 1.96(.10837) = .7856$
Upper Limit: $b + t_{.025}S_b = .9980 + 1.96(.10837) = 1.2104$

With the aid of the computed regression line of best fit, we were able to decompose an actual IBM rate of return into two components: one linked to market related factors and the other linked to firm-specific factors. The computed regression line represents the $\hat{Y}$ values. These are best-guess estimates of the mean IBM return given information on specific levels of the market return X. But the use of the $\hat{Y}$s as point predictors did not formally acknowledge that there is uncertainty with the use of a computed regression line. This uncertainty stems from the fact that *the computed regression line is not a perfectly reliable estimator of the true regression line.* Don't we need to recognize the uncertainty about the location of the true regression line when using the computed regression line to estimate the mean IBM return at the various levels of the market return? Obviously we do. But how do we account for uncertainty about the location of the true regression line? It is measured by the *standard error of the regression line,* $S_{\hat{Y}.x}$. The value of $S_{\hat{Y}.x}$ is not constant across the value of market return, X. It is lowest at $X - \overline{X}$ and fans out the farther X is from $\overline{X}$. Let's focus on two situations for comparative purposes.

13. *How do we find the value of the standard error of the regression line at a specific value of the market rate of return? For example, at the mean market rate of return where $X = \overline{X}$?* We use the general formula for $S_{\hat{Y}.x}$:

$$S_{\hat{Y}.x} = S_{Y.x} \sqrt{\frac{1}{n} + \frac{(X - \overline{X})^2}{SS_x}}$$

$$= 4.20997 \sqrt{\frac{1}{84} + \frac{(X - 1.33731)^2}{1509.27}}$$

At the value $X = \overline{X}$, the last term drops out (because the numerator becomes zero) leaving

$$S_{\hat{Y}.x} = 4.20997 \sqrt{\frac{1}{84}} = 0.45935$$

This value depicts the typical error size that one expects to have approximately two thirds of the time when using the computed regression line to estimate the mean IBM returns from the mean market rate of return.

14. *How much does this uncertainty about the location of the regression line affect our estimate of α, the component of IBMs stock return attributable to firm-specific factors, on average?* This means considering the point $X = 0$ where $\hat{Y} = a$ and there is no market influence. To find the standard error of the regression line where $\hat{Y} = a$, the estimate of α, substitute $X = 0$ in the expression for $S_{\hat{Y} \cdot X}$. This gives:

$$S_{\hat{Y} \cdot X} = 4.20997 \sqrt{\frac{1}{84} + \frac{(0 - 1.33731)^2}{1509.27}} = 4.20997 \sqrt{.0119048 + .0011849}$$

$$= 4.20997 \sqrt{.0130897} = 4.20997(.11441) = .48166$$

This value is often reported as S_a or as the "standard error of the intercept term" on computer output. A 95% confidence interval inferring the value of α would use the estimate 'a' and its standard error S_a which we see is $S_{\hat{Y} \cdot X}$ evaluated at $X = 0$. In this case we obtain

$$a \pm t_{.025} S_a = .2596 \pm 1.96(.48166)$$
$$= .2596 \pm .9441$$
$$= -.6845 \text{ to } 1.2037$$

The interval extends all the way from $-.6845$ to 1.2037, thus clearly embracing the possibility that α equals zero. In other words, even though our point estimate 'a' suggests that the firm-specific factors contribute .2596% per month or a modest 3.12% per year, on average, to IBMs rate of return, there is considerable uncertainty about the true magnitude of this component. Enough uncertainty, in fact, that we cannot be confident the component is even positive.

14.13. Analyzing the Residuals

Is the simple linear regression model a sensible way of describing the data? One key step in verifying whether it is, is to examine the behavior of the observed *residuals*. An observed residual is the discrepancy between the observed Y value and the predicted Y value $\hat{Y}$ obtained from reading the regression line. Thus, a residual is defined as $Y - \hat{Y}$.

Let's suppose you compute the least squares line and, say, find both a high r^2 and high (statistically significant) t-ratios for the coefficients of a and b. Can you legitimately claim that the simple linear regression model is appropriate? No, not yet. You haven't plotted the observed residuals, the estimates of the regression model error terms. The claim of the simple linear regression model is that the error terms behave randomly. A test of conformity, termed diagnostic checking, between the observed residuals and the assumption made about error term conditions is needed to justify the use of the linear regression model for the data at hand. What are the assumptions about the random behavior of the error term? Basically, the key assumptions for inference are:

1. no tendency for the residuals to move in a trend or cyclical pattern (Figure 14.19a),

2. no tendency for the residuals to show a strong non-constant cloud pattern (Figure 14.19c),

3. normal distribution of the residuals.

Residual Dependency

The plotted residuals in Figure 14.19a clearly follow a non random pattern. Consecutive residuals show a strong tendency to move up and down in a cyclical way. This situation is prevalent for data recorded in consecutive time periods. Why does this happen? Probably because important unknown or unspecified variables remain in the residuals and are associated through time. Therefore, consecutive time period residuals tend to be in close proximity to each other. This tendency of residuals to trend or cycle is called *serial correlation.*

The problem with the strong residual dependency which gives rise to serial correlation is that the *computed* value of the standard deviation of residuals is *lower than it should be.* (You'll have to take our word on this.) Since the computed standard error of forecast is directly related to the standard deviation of residuals, *our predictive ability is less than the computed standard error of forecast would have us believe.*

For planning and control, the value and reliability of the regression coefficients are in jeopardy when linked residuals are present. *Residual dependency causes the computed standard error of the regression coefficients to be consistently underestimated.* Importantly, the conventional *t*-tests, which use the computed value for the standard error of the coefficients, can no longer provide an answer about the statistical reliability of the coefficients.

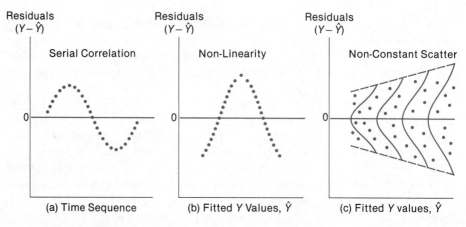

Note: The zero line in the figures is the regression line tilted to a horizontal position for ease of observation and interpretation.

FIGURE 14.19 Diagnostic Checking of Residuals: Three Types of Non-Random Residual Patterns

Non Linearity

Figure 14.19b shows another non random situation that can appear when the observed residuals are plotted against the predicted or fitted Y values, $\hat{Y}$s. A semicircle residual pattern strongly suggests that the simple linear regression model was a mistake—some non-linear model is more sensible.

Heteroskedasticity

Figure 14.19c illustrates a non-constant scatter cloud of the residuals. A widening or narrowing of the scatter cloud (variance) of the residuals violates the regression condition that the variance stay constant (homoskedastic). If there is a systematic factor operating in the residuals, a non-constant scatter (termed heteroskedasticity) is the result. Figure 14.19c shows that the systematic factor is intensifying as the fitted Y values (and underlying X values) increase.

The spread of the cloud reflects the likely error one faces in using the regression line to predict Y. Relying on the computed standard deviation of residuals as a constant value along the regression line would be a mistake. The non constant scatter causes the computed standard deviation of residuals to be a composite value of the different size scatter clouds.

A remedial adjustment often used to attain a constant scatter cloud requires the Y data to be transformed to log of Y data and X data transformed to log of X data. The basis for these transformations is that the underlying regression model should reflect percentage changes in Y to percentage changes in X and log transformations accomplish this. The log of Y, as the dependent variable, is regressed on the independent variable log of X to obtain a regression line.

Residual conformity to the regression error term assumptions is important. Without it, inferences about the linear regression model's parameters will not be reliable and prediction risk cannot be accurately estimated. In these cases, the data have to be manipulated, if they can be, to fit the model. These manipulation techniques will be given in Chapters 15 and 19.

Example 14.13.   Analyzing Market Model Residuals

The market model regression regressed IBMs monthly returns against the market index monthly returns over the same seven year period. To properly evaluate the reliability of the model's estimated regression coefficients, one needs diagnostic checking of the calculated residuals for violations of the assumptions made about ϵ, the underlying disturbance term. A scatter diagram of the residuals (Figure 14.20) on the vertical axis and the fitted Y values (the $\hat{Y}$s) provides a visual check. In Figure 14.20, the 84 residuals and fitted Ys from the market model are graphed. Checking is done by examining the residuals around the regression line horizontally drawn across from the zero point on the Y axis. The residuals are shown to be well balanced above and below the line over the entire range of values of Y with no distinctive expansion or contraction pattern. This indicates no heteroskedasticity problem. It also

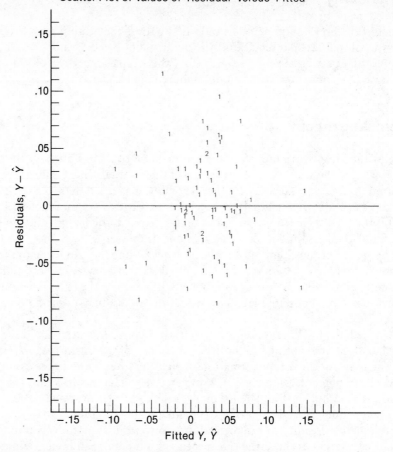

Scatter Plot of Values of 'Residual' Versus 'Fitted'

FIGURE 14.20 Scatter Plot of Market Model Residuals

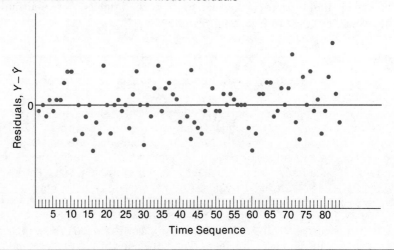

FIGURE 14.21 Sequence Plot of Market Model Residuals

shows that the line or model is an adequate representation of the flow of the data points.

The sequence plot of the residuals shown in Figure 14.21 shows the residuals exhibiting no *strong* distinctive wavelike pattern from time period to time period. This lack of dependence indicates that serial correlation bias will not plague our regression results.

14.14. Correlation and Regression: Don't Confuse It With Causation

Now that we have shown ways of statistically measuring the relationship between two variables X and Y, the issue of cause and effect briefly mentioned in the discussion of Example 14.1A deserves additional attention. Causality can not be assumed from the mere fact that two variables have a high r in correlation analysis or a high r^2 in regression analysis. In other words, a high r or r^2 does not imply that changes in the value of X *cause* changes in the value of Y. Nor does it imply that changes in the value of Y cause changes in the value of X. Correlated changes in X and Y can be induced by a third variable which affects both X and Y simultaneously. The identity of this third variable may or may not be known. In the two examples which follow, we probe the relationship between correlation and causation.

Example 14.14A.   The Stork Did It

Studies of the stork populations among towns in Belgium reportedly indicate a high (positive) correlation between the number of storks and the number of childbirths. This correlation cannot be explained away by sampling variation. Before you tell your friends that this correlation proves that storks really do bring babies, you might consider the following alternative explanation.

It is said that storks like to nest on chimneys of buildings. The larger the population of a town, the more chimneys there are likely to be to attract a large number of storks. According to this explanation, the observed (valid) correlation between storks and babies would be entirely attributable to a third variable: population.

Can causality ever be legitimately claimed? Not easily. The assurance of causality would require that the movement of the independent variable X be isolated as a determinant (at least in part) of the movement in the dependent variable Y. In most observational studies (business included) in which variables are not controlled, this cannot be accomplished. The correlation value calculated in observational studies measures the strength of the association between two variables, *not* whether there is cause and effect. Changes in a third factor not specifically accounted for may be the causal agent.

Example 14.14B.   The Federal Reserve Board Did It

Suppose there is a strong positive association between annual changes in the number of new housing starts and annual changes in the level of the Dow-Jones Industrial Average. Does this mean that bullish stock market activity causes building contractor optimism and leads to the construction of new homes? Or vice versa? It is generally the case that both variables are responding simultaneously to changes in a third variable, for instance, the interest rate on money which FED policy can influence by changing its ''Free Reserves'' policy. (See Figure 14.22.)

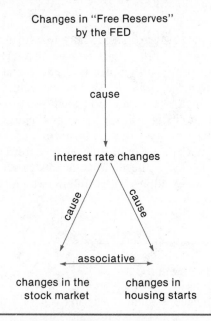

FIGURE 14.22 Causative and Associative Relationships

The distinction between mere association and causation is often at the center of controversies over the interpretation of statistical evidence. Consider the research linking cigarette smoking to lung cancer. Clearly, there is evidence of an associative relationship between the incidence of lung cancer and cigarette smoking; however, the real question is whether there is also causality. Is it the smoking which causes the cancer? Or is it (for example) emotional stress combined with genetic and personality traits which drives one both to smoke and to set in motion the type of tension which induces cancer? This kind of evidence is hard to obtain in studying cancer. Hence, debate over causality continues.

> . . . The fact that the exact mechanism of such selective association is not readily visualized is not an adequate reason for considering the suggestion of its possible existence to be—as it has been characterized—'Far fetched'. . . . Nor is it conclusive that the considerable number of statistical studies that have been published all agree in showing an association between smoking and cancer of the lung. On the contrary, . . . if correlation is produced by

some elements of the statistical procedure itself, it is almost inevitable that the correlation will appear whenever the statistical procedure is used.[7]

What methodology need be employed to pinpoint causality and the strength of the causality? To establish the existence and magnitude of a causal relationship between Y and X requires the design of a statistical experiment in which X is administered with control over a predetermined range. By randomly selecting and applying the values of X, the response of Y can be attributed to the changing values of X. The randomization procedure insures that the value of the slope coefficient will truly reflect (in addition to sampling variation) only the isolated and systematic effect of X on Y. It screens out the effect of variables other than X which may (perhaps unknowingly) also be influencing Y.

Spurious or Irrelevant Correlation

The term *spurious* or irrelevant correlation means that the correlation coefficient of the sample is found to be different from zero even though the two underlying populations being investigated are known to be uncorrelated. For instance, for a short stretch of time one may find a positive value for the correlation coefficient between the numbers of sightings of UFOs in the United States and the number of ounces of gold mined in South Africa. The sample correlation is irrelevant, however, since the two *populations* are almost certainly uncorrelated. As more observations are included in the sample, the apparent relationship will disappear and the sample correlation coefficient will reduce to zero.

Invalid Interpretation of Valid Correlation

Care should be taken not to call the correlation between storks and babies "spurious correlation." The correlation is quite valid and therefore not spurious. What *would* be invalid is the interpretation that one of the variables is a cause of the other.

14.15. Comparing Prediction Intervals and Confidence Intervals

The least squares regression line is used in two ways which should be distinguished and not confused. The computed line serves to:

1. estimate $\mu_{Y.X}$, the *average* or mean value of Y at a particular value of X having standard deviation $S_{\hat{Y}.X}$

2. forecast an *individual* value of Y at a particular value of X having standard deviation $S_{F.X}$

The procedure used to make a point estimate of the average or *mean* value of Y is identical to the procedure used to make a point forecast of an *individual* value of Y. Hence, both computations will provide the same point estimate. In both cases, the $\hat{Y}$ value read off the regression line for the X level considered is the best value to use. But the *trustworthiness* of the point estimate is different for the two situations.

There is always more likely error in predicting an *individual* Y value at a particular X value than there is in estimating $\mu_{Y.X}$, the *average* value of Y for the same level of X. This difference in likely error makes the value of $S_{F.X}$ larger than the value of $S_{\hat{Y}.X}$. The relationship between these two standard deviations is given by:

$$S_{F.X} = \sqrt{S_{Y.X}^2 + S_{\hat{Y}.X}^2}$$

The expression shows that the difference between $S_{F.X}$ and $S_{\hat{Y}.X}$ depends on the size of the standard deviation of residuals $S_{Y.X}$. The existence and size of this difference in standard deviations does not imply that one prediction ought to be employed over the other. The choice of whether to obtain an individual Y forecast or mean Y estimate rests not on the reliability feature, but rather on the purpose the result is intended to serve.

Example 14.15. **Know Your Purpose: It Determines the Computation**

The nature of the decision at hand determines whether an estimate of the mean of Y or a forecast of an individual Y is appropriate. In the Chicago produce distributor example, an estimate of the *average* transit time for a 2000 mile trip was the figure needed if better scheduling of California orders was the prime concern. In the second situation, *dependability* of the lead time estimates for individual shipments was the key factor. The value of 9.377 days served as the point estimate of the transit time in both cases. The prediction *interval* for the individual transit-time forecast (6.22 to 12.54 days) is larger than the confidence interval for the mean transit-time. And this is as it should be. There is a greater inherent uncertainty in forecasting individual shipment transit-time as compared to estimating the mean for all shipments over the same distance. This is properly reflected by the wider range of the individual Y interval.

The Role of Sample Size in Forecasting

Increasing the sample size will tend to *reduce* uncertainty about predicting an individual Y value. For an infinitely large sample the sampling variability of the *least squares line* would disappear. The *sample* regression line would coincide with the *true* regression line—the path of Y means. Although estimation of the *mean* of Y from the regression line would be perfectly reliable, there would still be prediction error in forecasting an individual Y value. Regardless of the particular level of X, forecasting an individual value of Y means predicting a single value of Y from the distribution of potential Y values. These distributions are clustered around the regression line. By using the points on the regression line as the best prediction of any individual Y value, one faces a likely predictive error. The extent of the likely error is determined by the *amount of spread* of the Y distribution around the regression line. For an infinitely large sample the summary measure reporting the magnitude of the spread is the *standard deviation of residuals*, the standard deviation of the Y distributions around the true regression line presumed to be constant over all levels of X. We can summarize the role of sample size in forecasting an individual Y value as follows: the likely predictive error measured by $S_{F.X}$ reduces to the standard deviation of residuals $S_{Y.X}$ as the sample size increases.

Confidence Bands and Prediction Bands

The preceding discussion has pointed out that readings from the least squares regression line can serve two purposes which are quite different. It was concluded that the accuracy of an estimate of a *mean* value of Y at any X value considered, is greater than that of a forecast for an *individual* observation considered at the same value of X. But *does estimation accuracy for the mean value of Y and forecast accuracy for the individual value of Y change with the level of X?* If so, then how does estimation and forecast accuracy depend on the level of X?

Consider the formulas for $S_{\hat{Y}.X}$ and $S_{F.X}$. Both standard deviations increase (accuracy decreases) as the distance between X and $\overline{X}$ increases. The value of $S_{Y.X}$ for the different X levels considered produces a changing width for any confidence or reliability level.

In Figure 14.23, this loss of accuracy is shown by the widening out of the confidence and prediction intervals the further from $\overline{X}$ we go. The outer band represents the 95% *prediction band* for forecasting individual Y values by the least squares regression line. The inner band is the 95% *confidence band* estimating the

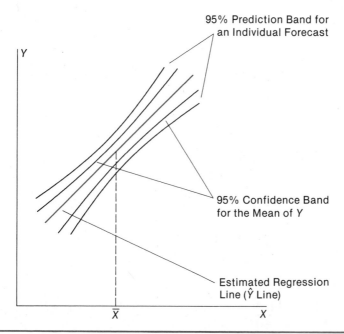

FIGURE 14.23 Confidence Band for the Mean of Y and Prediction Band for an Individual Forecast at Many Values of X

mean of Y by the regression line. The tighter fit of the inner band indicates the lower uncertainty in estimating the *mean* of Y compared to the uncertainty connected with an *individual Y* forecast.

Let us now turn to improving predictive accuracy.

14.16. Improving Predictive Accuracy

How does the reduction of sample size affect the sampling variability of the least squares lines? The least squares lines in Figure 14.24 are for samples of 25 observations, only *half* the number of observations used before for Figure 14.15. Comparing the graphs for the two sample sizes shows that both have fan-shaped bands, but the fan in Figure 14.24 is noticeably fatter. Since the width of the fan indicates how much uncertainty there is about estimating the mean Y by a computed regression line, one must conclude that *regression lines computed from larger samples offer greater reliability than those computed from smaller samples.* This notion is quantified by the measure of predictive uncertainty, $S_{\hat{Y} \cdot X}$. The formula for $S_{\hat{Y} \cdot X}$ shows n in the denominator under the square root radical. This indicates that sample size reduces $S_{\hat{Y} \cdot X}$ proportionally to the *square root* of the sample size; thus, quadrupling the sample size would halve the size of the likely error of estimation.

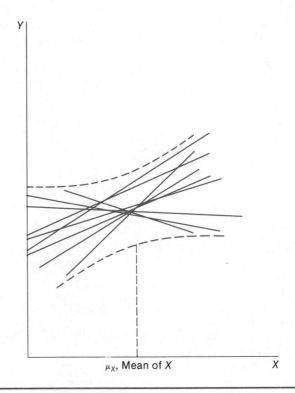

FIGURE 14.24 Least Squares Lines for Bivariate Samples of Size 25

Demonstrating the Effect of Variation in *X*

Does the amount of dispersion in *X* affect the likely error in estimating the true regression line by a computed least squares line? It very definitely does. To see how much, Figures 14.25a and 14.25b were constructed; these figures show 50 regression lines based on the same 50 random samples of data already drawn. However, each regression line in (a) was estimated from only the 25 *"middle-most"* observations for each of the 50 sample sets of data. Figure 14.25b, on the other hand, shows the 50 regression lines computed by using the 25 "outlying" or "extreme" observations falling at the end ranges of *X*. The dispersion in *X* values is much greater for (b) than for (a) and will make a difference in the variability of the computed regression lines. The fan-shaped band in (b) will be noticeably narrower. The dispersion in *X* controls the variability of the computed regression lines. The wider spread of *X*s in (b) forced the lines into a tighter pattern. This reduction in variability of the lines lowers the likely errors one makes by using the computed regression line to make predictions of *Y* for particular values of *X*. Advantage can and should be taken of this knowledge in designing the sample. A marketer assessing advertising effectiveness on purchase behavior *Y* needs to expose consumers to a wide range of advertising dosages to obtain a reliable estimate of *b*.

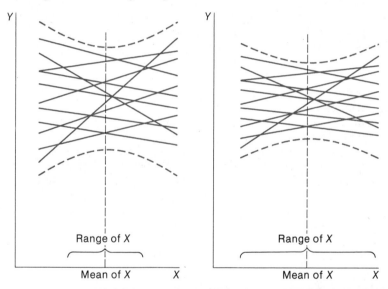

FIGURE 14.25a Computed Regression Lines for Bunched *X* Values

FIGURE 14.25b Computed Regression Lines for Spread Out *X* Values

Improving Predictions Through Better Design

When developing a sample design to achieve forecasting accuracy with a computed regression line, one can deliberately reduce the uncertainty associated with the line. The trick is in making sure that the values of *X* used in computing the line vary over a wide range. Ample dispersion of *X* values assures an improved precision of estimating the level of *Y* without sacrificing the level of confidence.

Example 14.16. **Freddie Laker Teaches the Airline Industry a Lesson**

The typical pricing strategy of firms in oligopolistic industries is very simple and conservative: avoid drastic price changes. Raising the price may cause the firm to lose practically all its customers, particularly if the rivals produce a similar product or service; lowering the price may set off a price war. But when infrequent and small changes in price are the norm, there is little information on which to base a reliable estimate of the sales response to a major price change. What would a significant price change mean for profits? As the following example illustrates, a "stand pat" approach to pricing can cause some very red faces in the executive suite when a daring entrepreneur decides to teach the industry a lesson.

The airline industry has historically been a regulated oligopoly. Because of high fixed cost operations and heavy use of debt financing, small changes in traffic volume and sales revenue can spell the difference between large profits or large losses. During the early 1970s, when both traffic and profits were in the doldrums, fare reductions were one possible response. But the airlines did not petition them through their regulating agency, the CAB, because their estimates of the traffic increase from fare reduction did not paint a promising profit picture.

Why did they have such a pessimistic market pricing strategy? Basically they had been too conservative with their price experimentation, and so had not obtained precise and reliable information about the impact of price on sales. Industry executives, fearful of competitor reaction, chose not to tinker with fares. Without significant fare experimentation, no conclusion about the real impact of fare changes on traffic demand could be isolated from the other causes (unrelated to fare changes) which substantially affect route traffic. Then along came the maverick Freddie Laker and Laker Airlines with an innovative marketing plan.

Laker's bargain basement fares and no frills service surprised the industry. It did not take long for the established airlines to recognize that their estimates were faulty and that route traffic was highly sensitive to price concessions. Since that time discount fares have been a common marketing device used by airlines to entice the non-business traveler and the key competitive weapon for capturing the business traveler on heavily traveled routes (for example, the NY-LA coast to coast route). Those airlines that survive the 80s will have learned how to effectively use as much price variation as possible in the independent variable to get reliable regression estimates of passenger demand sensitivity.

Two Ways to Improve Predictive Accuracy

In summary, the standard deviation of the computed regression line indicates that the predictive accuracy of the line at a specific value of X as a substitute for the true regression line can be enhanced in two ways:

1. by increasing the *sample size* of observed data used in computing the predicted least squares line.

2. by increasing the *dispersion* of X values of the observed data; this forces the direction and position of the computed least squares line to better conform to the unknown true regression line.

14.17. Managerial Issues in Practice—
Review Exercise: Job Evaluation at
M & M Industries*

M & M Industries is a fictitious name for an actual midwest industrial company. A number of concerns about the company's salary structure have come to the attention of the Personnel Manager at M & M Industries. One concern is *external*.

> Are the different levels of M & M salaries for similar type management positions out of line compared to the salary levels offered by other firms in the same industry, or in the same locality?

This concerns stems from a fear that the competition will pirate underpaid but talented M & M executives; other executives may be overpaid compared to the competition, causing an unnecessary drain on profits. A second concern is *internal*.

> Does the salary structure within M & M Industries compensate fairly for the job content of the different management positions?

Objective information for external and internal salary comparisons is provided by an audit of all the management ("exempt personnel") jobs. The audit is conducted by a management consulting firm which evaluates each job position according to three job content components:

1. "Know-How" (KNOWHO)
2. "Problem Solving" Ability (PROBSO)
3. "Accountability" (ACCTBL)

A numerical score is assigned to each component following a detailed set of procedures.** The procedures are designed to assure that the points assigned to one job content component, say KNOWHOW, are equivalent (and therefore additive) to the points assigned to another component, say ACCOUNTABILITY.

---

* We are indebted to Professor Harry V. Roberts of the University of Chicago Graduate School of Business for permission to use the data from his problem, *M & M Industries*, from which this case was adapted.

** For example, "Know-How" is divided into three component dimensions:

> a. Required *managerial* know-how, varying from limited performance in a narrow area to comprehensive integration and coordination.
> b. Required *technical* know-how, varying from simple practical procedures to exceptional competence and unique mastery in a scientific or other learned discipline.
> c. Required *human relations* know-how varying from ordinary courtesy in dealing with others to skill in selecting, developing, and motivating other people.

> The consulting firm rates the "know-how" component of a job on each of these three component dimensions and then, referring to a triple-entry table developed by the firm from past experience, gets a single numerical rating for "Know-How." Similar procedures are followed for the assignment of numerical ratings to "Problem-Solving" and "Accountability."

Thus the point total of the three job content components becomes a valid basis for summarizing a job's evaluation. The point total for a job is derived independently of the salary actually given for the job. Thus *external* salary comparisons can be made by comparing the salary of an M & M Industries job position to the salary of jobs having the same point total at other firms in the same industry or in the same locality. The relationship between salary and job evaluation (point total) is also the basis for *internal* analysis:

1. In general, how closely do salaries reflect job evaluations?

2. How much variation in salary is there among jobs of equivalent content (having the same point total)?

3. In principle, fairness requires that the salary compensation awarded for an additional point of job content be the same regardless of the job position. Is there any evidence of salary favoritism? For example, is there any indication that high salaried executive jobs get paid more for each addition to their content point total than do middle management jobs?

A statistical analyst is brought to M & M Industries and asked to conduct an exploratory analysis of the relationship of salaries to the corresponding management consultant's job evaluations. The data are given in Table 14.10.

One versatile and informative tool for analysis is a simple *scatterplot*. The data's scatterplot produced by the computer is presented in Figure 14.26.*** It plots the joint observations on company salary (SALARY) and total content points (TOTAL) with SALARY measured along the vertical axis and TOTAL along the horizontal axis.

Comparing the company's scatterplot to plots of similar firms in the industry reveals to the analyst the existence of any contrasts in the pattern of salary compensation which may be cause for concern.

Additional and more formal diagnostic analysis can be achieved by using *regression analysis*. The following series of questions pertain to the way regression analysis is used to obtain evidence on the pertinent issues.

1. *Managerial Issue:* How closely does the hierarchy of salaries correspond to the hierarchy of job content as evaluated by the consultant? That is, do the high salaries at M & M go to the management positions evaluated as high in job content, and do the lower salaries go to the management positions evaluated as low in job content?

Statistical Measure: Value of r^2

Comment: A high value of r^2 would indicate a close correspondence between the position on the salary scale and the position in terms of the consultant's evaluation of job content. A low value of r^2 would indicate a lack of this correspondence. At M & M there does appear to be quite a close correspondence between the two. The data are given in Table 14.10 and a scatterplot of the data appears in Figure 14.26.

***The computer package used to produce the output for this review exercise is the well-known MINITAB program designed at Penn State University.

TABLE 14.10. Data File on M & M Industries

COLUMN COUNT ROW	TOTAL	SALARY	COLUMN COUNT ROW	TOTAL	SALARY
1	1292.00	77220.0	33	332.00	37440.0
2	1184.00	77220.0	34	319.00	37440.0
3	1136.00	87516.0	35	319.00	34320.0
4	1124.00	60000.0	36	319.00	36192.0
5	954.00	54000.0	37	319.00	33540.0
6	950.00	69420.0	38	319.00	27300.0
7	805.00	48048.0	39	319.00	28860.0
8	800.00	48048.0	40	317.00	29640.0
9	775.00	65520.0	41	317.00	30600.0
10	594.00	64740.0	42	308.00	30420.0
11	539.00	47580.0	43	308.00	35100.0
12	539.00	49296.0	44	307.00	30000.0
13	462.00	42120.0	45	289.00	32760.0
14	462.00	37830.0	46	278.00	27300.0
15	449.00	45006.0	47	278.00	35100.0
16	421.00	42003.0	48	278.00	29640.0
17	421.00	50700.0	49	278.00	35100.0
18	417.00	39000.0	50	268.00	28080.0
19	417.00	41340.0	51	261.00	31980.0
20	387.00	36000.0	52	261.00	29952.0
21	376.00	35880.0	53	261.00	31980.0
22	376.00	36036.0	54	261.00	32760.0
23	363.00	36900.0	55	261.00	32760.0
24	363.00	35880.0	56	261.00	32760.0
25	353.00	35100.0	57	261.00	31980.0
26	341.00	34320.0	58	261.00	31980.0
27	332.00	36660.0	59	261.00	24960.0
28	332.00	39780.0	60	261.00	28080.0
29	332.00	29640.0	61	261.00	32760.0
30	332.00	37440.0	62	261.00	32760.0
31	332.00	39000.0	63	261.00	31980.0
32	332.00	39780.0	64	252.00	29640.0

The regression of SALARY on TOTAL has an r^2 value of .84, so 84 percent of the variation among salaries is accounted for by the difference in the job evaluation variable, TOTAL. Thus there is substantial agreement between M & M's evaluation of a job (as implied by its salary) and the management consulting firm's evaluation. The remaining 16 percent represents the salary variation not explained by TOTAL. Since TOTAL represents the management consultant's overall evaluation of a job, then 16 percent of the actual salary variation is not linked with what the consultant thought would be appropriate.

2. *Managerial Issue:* How can one estimate M & M salary for a new job by using the consultant's evaluation of Job Content?

Statistical Issue: Computed Regression Equation
What is the average linear relationship between the total content points for a new job position and the corresponding M & M job salary for the position?

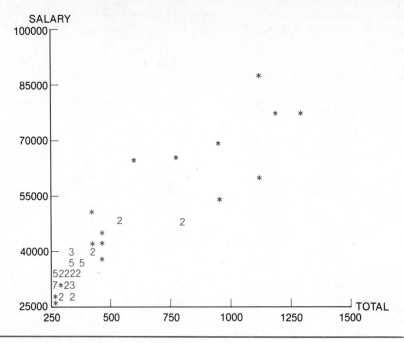

FIGURE 14.26 Scatterplot of SALARY versus TOTAL

THE REGRESSION EQUATION IS
Y = 19219. + 47.6 X1

	COLUMN	COEFFICIENT	ST. DEV. OF COEF.	T-RATIO = COEF/S.D.
	--	19218	1284	14.96
X1	TOTAL	47.581	2.583	18.41

THE ST. DEV. OF Y ABOUT REGRESSION LINE IS
S = 5212
WITH (64- 2) =   62 DEGREES OF FREEDOM

R-SQUARED = 84.5 PERCENT
R-SQUARED = 84.3 PERCENT, ADJUSTED FOR D.F.

ROW	X1 TOTAL	Y SALARY	PRED. Y VALUE	ST.DEV. PRED. Y	RESIDUAL	ST.RES.
1	1292	77220	80694	2324	-3474	-0.74 X
2	1184	77220	75555	2058	1664	0.34 X
3	1136	87516	73272	1941	14243	2.94RX
4	1124	60000	72701	1911	-12701	-2.61RX
5	954	54000	64612	1506	-10612	-2.12RX
6	950	69420	64421	1497	4998	1.00 X
10	594	64740	47482	779	17257	3.34R
17	421	50700	39250	651	11449	2.21R

R DENOTES AN OBS. WITH A LARGE ST. RES.
X DENOTES AN OBS. WHOSE X VALUE GIVES IT LARGE INFLUENCE.

FIGURE 14.27 Computer Output for Regression of SALARY on TOTAL

Comment: The best fitting linear equation using the least squares criterion is:

$$\hat{Y} = 19{,}218 + 47.581 \text{ TOTAL}$$

If, for example, a job is evaluated at 800 total points, the estimated salary average would be

$$\hat{Y} = 19{,}218 + 47.581(800) = 19{,}218 + 38{,}064.8 = \$57{,}283$$

From Figure 14.27 it can be seen that the cofficient of the computed regression coefficient (47.581) is several times the value of its standard error (2.583). The value of its *t*-ratio is 18.41. The intercept term (19,218) is also several times the value of its standard error (1284). The value of its *t*-ratio is 14.96.

Since both sample coefficients are several times larger than their standard errors (both have high *t* values), the true coefficient values are very probably not zero. ·

3. *Managerial Issue:* How much additional salary is given at M & M for each additional point of job content?

Statistical Measure: b
The regression coefficient, $47.58, means that for each additional total content point gained by a job, there is additional salary of, on average, $47.58.

4. *Managerial Issue:* How much salary, on average, is M & M paying for factors other than what the consultant records as the content of the job?

Statistical Measure: Interpretation of *a*
Assuming the linear equation validly extends to the vertical axis, the *Y* intercept value of $19,218 can be considered as the average salary amount attributable to factors other than the total content points. These factors might represent experience, favoritism, or any other reason management knowingly or unknowingly used in assigning salaries.

5. *Managerial Issue:* Does the fact that higher salaries are assigned to jobs evaluated by the consultant as having higher content mean that salaries on average are proportional to job content? That is, on average, do jobs evaluated as having twice the content of another job also have twice the salary?

Statistical Issue: Pitfall in Interpreting r^2
High values of r^2 only mean that the deviations from the mean salary are associated with deviations from the mean job content. That does *not* imply that salary is proportional to job content. To see this, imagine that the jobs evaluated as lowest in content are also the lowest paid, while the jobs evaluated as highest in content, say the presidency, receive the highest salary. This would give a high r^2. But if janitors earn $60,000 per year and the president $65,000, then salaries are undoubtedly not proportional to job content.

Statistical Procedure: Compare $\hat{Y}_2/\hat{Y}_1$ with X_2/X_1
In terms of job content, the consultant's ratings imply that salaries ought to be proportional to job content points. If one job is assigned 400 points and the other 800, the second job is worth twice as much as the first. The M & M estimated salary

for the two jobs would be estimated from the computed regression equation at $X = 400$ and $X = 800$ respectively.

$$\hat{Y} = \$19,218 + \$47.58(400) = \$38,250$$
$$\hat{Y} = \$19,218 + \$47.58(800) = \$57,282$$

Thus, M & M would assign an estimated salary to the 800 point job of only $57,282/38,250 = 1.5$ times that of the 400 point job. In other words, differences in salaries are not proportional to differences in the content points of the job.

6. *Managerial Issue:* What percentage of salary, on average, is accounted for by factors not related to the job's content?

Statistical Measures: $a/\overline{Y}$, $b\overline{X}/\overline{Y}$

The ratio $a/\overline{Y}$ measures the proportion of average salary accounted for by factors unrelated to job content. This is $\$19,218/\$39,596.67 = .485$ or 48.5 percent. The ratio $1 - (a/\overline{Y}) = b\overline{X}/\overline{Y}$ is the proportion of average salary accounted for by job content. This is $1 - .485 = .515$ or 51.5 percent.

7. *Managerial Issue:* Is there any evidence that the amount of additional salary awarded to an additional point of job content depends on the content level of the job? That is, do higher level positions receive more for an additional content point than lower level positions?

Statistical Issue: Should the functional form of the regression equation be linear or non-linear?

Suggested Procedure: Examining the scatterplot of salary levels and total content points (TOTAL) it appears that there is a positive relationship between the two variables. Does the flow of data suggest:

> a linear pattern (constant amount of salary compensation per unit increase in total points)

> a curvilinear trend (changing amount of salary compensation per unit increase in total points)

> a distinct shift, perhaps, at a particular point score. This would indicate a discontinuity and the need for two linear regressions instead of one.

The three situations mentioned are illustrated in Figure 14.28a, b, and c.

Comment: Figure 14.26 does not show an obvious curvilinear pattern nor a sudden shift in the level of the observation. Except for the unusually wide dispersion at the upper range, a *linear regression* equation may be an appropriate form. Let's fit a linear equation to the data.

8. *Managerial Issue:* How can the regression line be used in making external salary comparisons, that is, in comparing M & Ms salary structure with that of other firms or industry groupings?

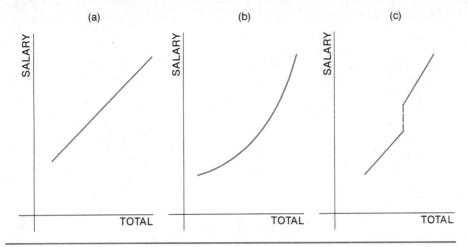

FIGURE 14.28 Three Possible Relationships between SALARY and TOTAL

Statistical Issue: Regression Equation Comparison

For a particular job point total one important comparison is the difference between what:

1. the M & M regression equation predicts for salary and
2. the known salary for the equivalent job in other firms or industry groupings.

Also, there would be interest in comparing the M & M Industries regression equation with the equation developed by another company (if available). If the regression coefficients in both equations have similar numerical values, then one can conclude that both firms view the worth of an additional total content point in much the same way. Widely different regression coefficients point to a different management compensation structure for the two companies—a situation that might demand a remedy.

9. *Managerial Issue:* Is a particular job position overcompensated or undercompensated for its job evaluation total when *compared to other M & M management jobs?* See Figure 14.29.

Statistical Issue: Interpretation of Residuals

Compute the regression *residual* for the job. Positive residuals indicate *over-compensation,* negative residuals indicate undercompensation. For example, the actual salary of the job evaluated at 800 total points is $48,048. This indicates *undercompensation* of $9,235.

$$Y - \hat{Y} = \$48,048 - \$57,283$$
$$= -\$9,235$$

10. *Managerial Issue:* Discuss the statistical significance of the regression coefficient and Y intercept values. See Figure 14.27.

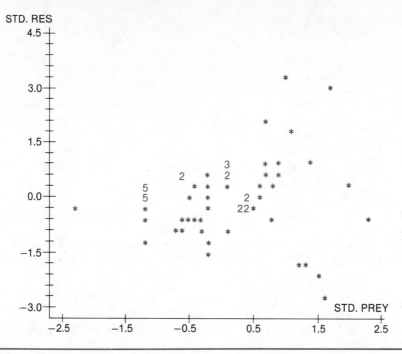

FIGURE 14.29 Standardized Residuals Scatterplot of SALARY versus PREDICTED SALARY

Statistical Issue: Heteroskedasticity

Comment: Scatterplots in Figure 14.26 and Figure 14.29 change from a tight configuration at lower total point levels to a more dispersed pattern at higher total point levels. This heteroskedasticity suggests that some transformation (for example, logarithmic) should be tried to create a more evenly-balanced dispersion. If, in this case, an adjustment is not made to correct the heteroskedasticity, the reliability of the regression coefficients and the standard deviation of residuals would be overstated. Ignoring heteroskedasticity and using at face value the regression parameter estimates would misrepresent the merits of the equation for its planning application and prediction. An adjustment procedure for dealing with the heteroskedasticity will be shown in the following chapter.

14.18. Concluding Comments

In this chapter we restricted our interest to two variables X and Y and to a discussion of the mechanics and interpretation of two powerful statistical tools—correlation analysis and simple regression analysis. Simple correlation analysis resulted in a single summary measure called the correlation coefficient, which describes the extent of the linear relationship between the two variables. Its value ranges from $+1$ to -1. The magnitude of the coefficient reveals how well the joint observations follow a linear pattern. The sign reflects whether the linear relationship is negative or positive. Values near one reflect a strong linear (cigarlike) pattern, whereas values near zero show virtually no linear pattern. One important business application of correlation is diversification analysis.

Regression analysis, on the other hand, describes the relationship between two variables in terms of the mathematical equation for a line. Regression analysis can be used for prediction or planning and control. In the first case, the equation shows the predictor variable as the independent variable and the variable being predicted as the dependent variable. If its purpose is planning and control, the contribution that the independent variable makes to the value of the dependent variable is the issue of concern. Recognizing that the relationship between X and Y is a statistical one, the estimated regression line is an expression of the average relationship between the variables. Since the observed X and Y data are sample data, there is the possibility that an observed sample relationship is spurious and would disappear if all the population data were available. An hypothesis test on the regression coefficient using the t statistic attempts to disprove the premise that no true relationship exists between X and Y. Rejecting this hypothesis still does not guarantee that X will be very useful in predicting Y. The r^2 statistic, along with the standard deviation of residuals, confirms how well the regression line fits the observations. For this reason, both values are called goodness of fit measures. The r^2 value indicates how much variation of Y has been explained by X; the standard deviation of residuals reflects the variation of Y values around the regression line. The latter value is an indicator of the uncertainty of predicting Y by using the points on the regression line and is the key element in constructing a confidence interval for the mean value of Y and in constructing a prediction interval for individual Y values. Increased sample size and a wide dispersion of X were both shown to enhance the chance of obtaining a computed regression line that is a good estimate of the true regression line.

It is important to note that a high r^2 and a significant t statistic do not guarantee the reliability of the numbers obtained as regression line estimates. That rests with the behavior of the residuals. Adequate conformity of the residuals to the underlying random model assumption prevents the regression parameter estimates from being labeled just "window dressing". A thorough statistical business study ought to give an indication of the behavior of the residuals along with the reporting of the parameter estimates and r^2. Canned interactive computer programs such as IDA and MINITAB contain routines that make the examination of the residuals very accessible.

Linking directly the existence of causality between the two variables and the finding of a regression relationship or correlation between two variables is a temptation that generally should be avoided.

Footnotes and References

[1] Alternatively, the appraiser can regress market value of the total property on *lot-size* for equivalent buildings.

[2] Usually in mathematics we think of X and Y as unknowns, but that is not true here. X and Y represent the available data values and these have to be known in order to compute the least squares line.

[3] These expressions are known as the *normal equations*, a term having nothing to do with the normal curve.

[4] A qualification is in order. The assumption here is that there exists no sequential correlation between the Y values that can be successfully employed for prediction purposes.

[5]Instead of the term n (sample size) in the denominator, the term $n - 2$, called the degree of freedom, is used to adjust $S_{Y.X}$. Defined in this way $S_{Y.X}$ becomes a reliable estimate of its population counterpart $\sigma_{Y.X}$—the true standard deviation of Y values around the true regression line.

[6]The value of r^2 calculated in this fashion is called the adjusted r^2 because it directly uses S_Y^2 and $S_{Y.X}^2$ which are adjusted terms for the degrees of freedom. This adjustment causes the value of adjusted r^2 to be never larger than the r^2 value computed in this chapter. Because the adjusted r^2 is a more useful statistic for analysis of multiple regression models, it will be the computation preferred when r^2 is read from computer output. The adjusted value is also the preferred one to use when inference about ρ is made in Section 14.3.

[7]Joseph Berkson, "The Statistical Study of Association Between Smoking and Lung Cancer," *Proceedings of the Staff Meetings of the Mayo Clinic*, vol. 30 (1955), p. 319.

Questions and Problems

1. Identify and explain the three dimensions of a statistical relationship between two variables.

2. What is the purpose of a scatter diagram and how is it constructed?

3. Two different purposes for regression analysis are distinguished, both of which are viewed as distinct from correlation analysis. Match the three different objectives given below with the three types of analysis.

Objective

a. From the known value of the independent variable X, determine the unknown value of the dependent variable Y.

b. Measure the degree of comovement in the two variables X and Y.

c. Estimate the change in the value of the dependent variable (Y) that would occur if the value of the independent variable (X) increases by one unit.

Type of Analysis	Objective
1. Regression Analysis for Planning and Control	_____
2. Regression Analysis for Prediction and Forecasting	_____
3. Correlation Analysis	_____

4. Match the different situations described below with the three different types of analysis.

Type of Analysis

a. Correlation

b. Regression for Prediction and Forecasting

c. Regression for Planning and Control

Type of Analysis	Situation
1. _____	A trucking company is determining rates to charge for local deliveries and wants to estimate how much extra driver time will be incurred, on average, for each additional mile of delivery distance.
2. _____	A trucking company is scheduling local deliveries for its drivers and wants to predict how long a delivery to a destination ten miles distant will take.
3. _____	A stock market analyst wants to determine the extent to which fluctuations in the price of U.S. Steel coincide with fluctuations in the Dow-Jones Index of Industrial Stock.
4. _____	A stock market analyst wants to estimate the sensitivity of Eastman Kodak stock to changes in the Dow-Jones Index of Industrial Stocks.
5. _____	A mail-order house wants to use the weight of Monday morning mailbags to predict the number of orders to be processed that day.

6. _____ A manufacturer of roofing shingles believes its future sales to dealers depends upon the number of new homes presently under construction. However, this information is published too late to help the roofing manufacturer. The dealer wants to use the current mortgage rate to predict the number of homes presently under construction.

7. _____ A real estate appraiser wants to assess the value of the office building at a certain address based upon the size in square feet of the building.

5. One stock market analyst wants to know the extent to which fluctuations in the price of PPG Industries stock coincide with fluctuations in the New York Stock Index. A second analyst wants to know how sensitive the price of PPG Industries stock is to changes in the New York Stock Index. Do both analysts want the same information? Explain.

6. For the annual returns data given in Table 14.7,
a. compute the coefficient of linear correlation between AT&T and Pan Am.
b. compute the coefficient of determination between AT&T and Pan Am.
c. what important information about the relationship between Pan Am and AT&T returns is given by the coefficient of linear correlation, but not by the coefficient of determination?
d. what interpretative advantage does the coefficient of determination have over the coefficient of linear correlation?

7. For the AT&T and Pan Am annual returns data given in Table 14.7,
a. compute the estimated standard error of the correlation coefficient, S_r.
b. would it be appropriate to use the value computed in part a to determine a confidence interval for the true value of ρ? Explain.

c. use Figure 14.6 to find the 95 percent confidence level for the minimum value of ρ.

8. In Example 14.1B, the real estate appraiser would purportedly regress the total property value (land and buildings together) on building size (for same sized lots).
a. Express this regression in the form of a simple linear model.
b. What portion of the total property value would be unrelated to building size? Is this the land value? Explain.
c. What interpretation is given to α?
d. What is the interpretation of β?
e. What interpretation would be given to the product βX?

9. Of the many possible lines which might be fitted to the scatter of joint observations on Y and X, the line most often chosen by statistical analysts is the "least squares" line. What is the rationale of this choice?

10. Following the procedure described in Section 14.6 for finding the least squares line, which coefficient, a or b, is computed first? Why?

11. Suppose the coefficient of linear correlation between Y and X is .6, and the standard deviation of Y is three times that of the standard deviation of X. What is the value of the slope coefficient in the least squares regression of Y on X?

12. Reconsider the Overland Express problem (Example 14.4) using only the first ten observations given in Table 14.9.
a. What is the value of the slope coefficient b?
b. What is the value of the intercept term a?
c. What is the value of the coefficient of linear correlation r?
d. What fraction of the variation in labor time usage is explained by variation in delivery distance?
e. What is the computed regression equation?
f. What is the predicted labor time incurred to make a delivery six miles distant?

13. For the revised version given in Problem 12 of the Overland Express problem,

a. what is the value of the standard deviation of residuals $S_{Y.X}$?

b. What is the value of the standard error of the regression coefficient S_b?

14. Can the value of $S_{Y.X}$, the standard deviation of residuals, ever exceed the value of S_Y? Explain.

15. Which of the computed regression statistics $(a, b, r, r^2, S_Y, S_b, S_a, S_{Y.X}, S_X, \overline{Y}, \overline{X})$ is a measure of the average predictive error one expects to encounter in using a known value of X to arrive at a prediction of the unknown value of Y? If there are several different choices of variables to use as the independent variable X, does the variable giving the lowest standard deviation of residuals also minimize the average predictive error?

16. What is the relationship between:

a. SSE and the standard deviation of residuals?

b. SS_X and the standard deviation of the independent variable?

17. Must the hypothesized value of β be zero? Explain.

18. Which of the computed regression statistics $(a, b, r, r^2, S_Y, S_X, S_{Y.X}, S_b, S_a, \overline{Y}, \overline{X})$ is a measure of the reliability of the computed regression (slope) coefficient? Does the expected value of this statistic diminish as sample size increases?

19. If the sample size is quadrupled, what would you expect to happen to the value of the standard deviation of residuals? The value of the coefficient of determination?

20. In Example 14.10, what proportion of the mean transit time for shipments originating 2000 miles from Chicago is distance-related? Is this value equal to the proportion of the variation in transit time explained by the variation in distance (r^2)? Explain.

21. Compute the following statistics for the revised Overland Express exercise given in Problem 12.

a. S_b

b. $S_{\hat{Y}.X}$ for $X = 2$ miles

c. $S_{F.X}$ for $X = 2$ miles

d. S_a

e. 95 percent confidence interval for β.

f. 90 percent confidence interval for the mean labor time usage for a delivery distance of 2 miles.

g. 99 percent prediction interval for the labor time usage on a specific delivery at a distance of 2 miles.

22. In Example 14.10, what interpretation should be given to the intercept term $a = 3.197$ days?

23. Through what point does every computed least squares line pass?

24. For rate-setting in the Overland Express Example (14.4), what is the advantage in using the computed regression line as the basis for rate differentials rather than simply the mean labor time usage per mile?

25. Both $S_{Y.X}$ (the standard deviation of residuals) and $1 - r^2$ (the "unexplained variation") measure the scatter of points about the regression. $S_{Y.X}$ is an absolute measure and $1 - r^2$ a relative measure.

a. Do $S_{Y.X}$ and $1 - r^2$ serve different purposes or the same purpose?

b. If there are several different choices of variables to use, does the variable which is most highly correlated with the dependent variable also give the lowest standard deviation of residuals? Explain.

26. In forecasting the dependent variable using regression analysis, which of the following are we most desirous of obtaining?

a. a low standard deviation of residuals

b. a high r^2

c. a small standard error of the regression (slope) coefficient

d. an unbiased regression coefficient with a high t-ratio

27. Suppose that r^2 has a very high value, say 0.98. Indicate in a few sentences why you agree or disagree that the statements below follow from this information.

a. The slope coefficient b must have a high t-value.

b. The intercept term a must have a high t-value.

c. The estimated relationship $\hat{Y} = a + bX$ is a very close approximation to the true relationship between Y and X.

d. The observed Y's do not vary much from the predicted Y's, $\hat{Y}$.

e. The variation in X accounts for a substantial proportion of the variation in Y.

f. The observed residuals ($e = Y - \hat{Y}$) show no systematic pattern.

28. The advertising manager for the Green Giant brand of frozen mixed fruit sponsors a consumer panel study to determine the productivity of advertising for the brand. A regression equation known as an advertising response function is computed regressing a family's dollar purchases for the brand (Y) on the amount of exposure opportunities to the Green Giant brand advertising (X). The computed regression equation is: $\hat{Y} = 3.15 + 0.16X$.

a. What is the average change in a family's dollar expenditure on the Green Giant brand associated with one additional exposure opportunity to Green Giant advertising?

b. For a family having 10 exposure opportunities to the Green Giant advertising, what is the estimated expenditure on the Green Giant brand?

c. Suppose a family is not exposed to the Green Giant brand advertising. What is the family's expected expenditures on the Green Giant brand?

29. In Problem 28, which of the following statistics: r^2, $S_{Y.X}$, S_b, S_a

a. would measure the proportion of variation in Green Giant sales explained by exposure to Green Giant advertising?

b. would be the best measure of the regression equation's ability to predict Green Giant sales?

c. is the best measure of reliability of the computed regression coefficient?

d. has a value approaching zero as the sample size becomes very large?

30. In Problem 28, the correlation between family expenditures on Green Giant products and advertising by Green Giant is quite low, only .13. Does this mean the regression is not very effective for measuring advertising impact on expenditures? Explain.

31. In using Beta analysis of stock price movements, indicate which of the following statements is the correct interpretation of Beta.

a. Beta represents the proportion of variation in the individual stock's return explained by corresponding changes in the level of the stock market return.

b. Beta represents the component of a stock's return which is attributable to the level of the stock market return.

c. Beta represents the average percentage point change in a stock's price for a one percentage point change in the market price.

d. Beta represents the average dollar change in a stock's return for a one dollar change in the stock market index.

e. Beta represents the average percentage point change in a stock's price for a one percentage point change in the market return.

32. For each of the statements below, indicate whether you agree or disagree, and if you disagree, why.

a. Stocks with a Beta value exceeding one will increase in value faster than stocks with a Beta value less than one.

b. The returns in stocks with a low Beta value should exhibit less variation than returns on stocks with high Beta values.

c. The returns on stocks with high Beta values should on average be higher than on stocks with low Beta values.

d. If Beta has a value of one, the intercept term should have a value of zero.

e. If two stocks have the same Beta value, the fluctuations in their rates of return should be about the same.

f. A stock with a Beta value exceeding one should earn more than the market rate of return.

g. The ratio $100b\bar{X}/\bar{Y}$ represents the average market-related component of a stock's return expressed as a percentage of the total.

h. A stock with a Beta value of one should not have a rate of return higher than that of the market as a whole.

33. a. Why is it important to examine the residuals for randomness?

b. What graphical tool is useful in checking on model adequacy?

c. What is the distinction between nonlinearity and heteroskedasticity?

d. Does serial correlation lead to a biased regression coefficient? Any other bias?

e. What remedy is suggested for treating heteroskedasticity?

34. Why is the observed correlation between smoking and the incidence of various health problems such as lung cancer not necessarily indicative that the health problem is caused by smoking?

35. Why is the observed correlation between inflation and interest rates not necessarily indicative that a reduction in interest rates will bring about a reduction in the rate of inflation?

36. What statistical approach is useful in identifying and measuring the cause and effect relationship between two variables?

37. Why is the correlation between the number of storks and the number of new babies found in some parts of the world not a "spurious" correlation?

38. The Y values read off a regression line are used to make two different kinds of point estimates. What is the distinction between them? Are they equally trustworthy?

39. What is the difference between a confidence band and a prediction band?

40. Is the amount of likely error in estimating the true regression line by a computed least squares line affected by:

a. the sample size? Explain.

b. the amount of variation in X? Explain, using the statistical lesson of Freddie Laker and the airlines industry.

41. A manufacturer of camping equipment is designing a new line of products aimed at the moderately affluent camper. The marketing manager wants to know the average annual expenditure on camping equipment presently made by households in the target market. A survey has been budgeted because "there aren't any figures available for our particular target market," she says. "We can't use the available data because it refers to households having different income levels than our target. I don't like spending the money on a survey, but we're sure the camping expenditures per capita for the income bracket our equipment is for won't be the same as for lower or higher brackets." A colleague suggested that regression analysis on the available data for other income brackets might be a good substitute for the survey.

a. Explain how regression analysis on data for different income categories than the target market might solve the problem.

b. What are the advantages and disadvantages of using regression analysis to estimate the mean value of Y at a given value of X, compared to collecting data on Y values for the specific X value considered?

42. *Predicting the Need for Temporary Help* Lehman's, a diversified department store located in the Water Tower complex in downtown Chicago, uses many part-time clerical and sales employees to supplement the regular staff during busy selling periods. The supplementary work force is hired by the personnel manager as needed on a weekly basis. The reason for this is two-fold: first, competent people are hard to get on a daily basis, especially on short notice; second, the consumer reaction to purchase may be immediate or may take several days and specials are commonly extended for the week. To better implement this plan Harry Speer, a marketing consultant with Market Planning Associates, is brought in to identify a way of predicting weekly sales. "Accurate forecasts of weekly sales will hold down the cost of hiring unnecessary help, yet it will let us take advantage of sales opportunities," explained the personnel manager. Speer thought a while and came up with the suggestion that weekly expenditures on advertising should provide a useful predictor of the fluctuation in weekly sales. Listed in Table 14.11 are the weekly records on sales and advertising.

a. Speer suggested that regression analysis can effectively be used to predict sales from the knowledge of next week's media advertising. Find the least square line.

b. As a personnel manager, check on the appropriateness of Speer's suggestion. Plot

TABLE 14.11. Weekly Sales and Advertising

WEEK	Y WEEKLY SALES (1000s of dollars)	X WEEKLY MEDIA ADVERTISING (1000s of dollars)
1	80	2
2	110	5
3	90	3
4	150	8
5	75	2
6	135	6
7	70	1
8	125	4

the observations and graph the least squares lines through the points plotted. Evaluate.

c. What is the size of the typical error in predicting sales if the computed regression equation is the true underlying regression equation? Calculate the appropriate standard deviation.

d. What gain has regression made over the use of the mean sales of past weekly sales as the best guess of the coming weekly sales? Calculate S_Y and compare it to $S_{Y.X}$. Evaluate.

e. Does the statistical evidence indicate that the regression equation can be relied on? Calculate S_b as a measure of the uncertainty surrounding the coefficient b.

f. Does S_b equal b? If it did what is the chance that the true value $\beta = 0$?

g. Form a .95 confidence interval around the value of b. Does the interval cover the value zero? Interpret.

h. Test the hypothesis that the underlying value of the parameter $\beta = 0$, using the significance level of 5 percent ($\alpha = .05$).

i. Compare and contrast the inferential approach on β in (g) to the one in (h). Which is more restrictive?

j. Should the computed value of "a" (the Y intercept) be given an economic interpretation? (for example, the value of sales when media expenditure is zero)

k. How much of variation in weekly sales were explained by the variation in weekly media advertising? Calculate r^2.

l. Should the personnel manager use the regression equation as a practical method of hiring the temporary work force? What statistics confirm this?

m. Suggest alternative factors which Speer overlooked that might be used to predict weekly sales. (Hint: seasonality)

43. Using the data in Problem 42, what is the 95% prediction interval for the weekly sales of the department store with the following weekly advertising expenditure (in thousands of dollars)?

a. 3
b. 7
c. 8
d. 1
e. Which of these four prediction intervals is least precise? Most precise? Explain
f. Does prediction beyond observational data represent speculation? Explain.

44. "We gotta hold on to our older workers" demanded the foreman of Plant 2 to Joe Purvis, the personnel manager. "They know the job and besides, they come to work everyday. Just look at the records; you'll see what I mean." After venting a few more complaints, the foreman left. Joe sipped his morning coffee a few more times, turned to his files, and pulled at random a few records on workers in Plant 2. Compiling the information, he came up with the data in Table 14.12.

TABLE 14.12. Yearly Absence Compared to Length of Service

EMPLOYEE	DAYS ABSENT OVER PAST YEAR	NUMBER OF YEARS EMPLOYED WITH THE COMPANY
Akins	10	3
Bays	0	6
Cote	1	7
Dines	4	7
Meadows	3	5
Peters	7	2
Hodges	5	1

a. Calculate the least squares line for the data.

b. Plot the points and check for the linearity assumption.

c. Calculate $S_{Y.X}$ and interpret.

d. Does the statistical evidence indicate that the regression equation can be relied upon? Calculate S_b and interpret.

e. Form a .99 confidence interval around the value of b. Does the interval cover the value zero? Interpret.

f. Test the hypothesis that the underlying value of $\beta = 0$ using the significance level of 1 percent, $\alpha = .01$.

g. Inferences on β made in (e) and (f) are similar. In fact, a confidence interval can be viewed as a set of acceptable hypotheses. Does it then follow that a (correct) rejection of the hypothesis $\beta = 0$ at the $\alpha = .10$ level means that the true value of β must not be within the .90 confidence interval estimate? Explain.

h. Is it meaningful to test for the statistical reliability of "a" in this equation if the purpose of the regression analysis is determined to be prediction? Planning and control?

i. Determine the point estimate for the mean number of workdays absent during the past year per employee for employees who have worked for the company the past five years and construct a 90% confidence interval estimate for the mean. Interpret.

j. For purposes of the investigation at hand, which interval should be of greater interest for the personnel department? Is it the prediction interval for an individual Y value at a given X or the confidence interval for the mean workday absenteeism at the same given X? Explain.

k. How much variation in daily absenteeism was explained by the variation in years employed on the job?

l. Choose true or false. If false, indicate why it is false. For the purpose of these questions you may ignore the affect of random sampling error.

  a. The employment manager noted the positive value of the intercept coefficient and said, "this equation is useless because according to it, people who haven't started to work yet have (on average) already accumulated a poor absenteeism record."

  b. The production manager said, "the negative regression (slope) coefficient tells us that the longer a person works at our company, the more likely that person is to improve his or her absenteeism record."

  c. What the production manager said is not true, because predictions made based on the regression equation are valid only for groups and not for individuals. What *would* be valid, however, is to say that on *average*, persons who have worked here seven or eight years have improved their absenteeism record since their early years with us.

  d. What we found from the regression equation is that longer work experience contributed to fewer work absences. Assuming that the regression results we obtained would be found by other companies too, so it is not just our company, that means hiring more experienced workers would lead to fewer absences.

  e. What the positive intercept tells us is the absenteeism rate our prospective employees have (on average) at *other* companies *before* coming to us. What the negative slope coefficient tells us is how quickly they tend to *improve* once they join our company.

  f. The regression equation tells us how much better the absenteeism record is, on average, for people who have worked here, say, an extra two years. What it *doesn't* tell us is how much of an improvement to expect among workers who gain two years extra work experience with us.

45. *Supermarket Marketing Research* A supermarket chain conducted an experiment to determine the relationship between the amount of display space allotted to a brand of "natural food" breakfast cereal and its weekly sales. The amount of space allotted to the brand was varied by changing the number of packages facing the shopper among 2, 4, and 6 "facings" in a random pattern over twelve weeks.

TABLE 14.13. Display Space and Sales

NUMBER OF FACINGS	NUMBER OF PACKAGES SOLD
6	469
4	371
2	145
6	397
4	324
2	229
4	385
2	211
6	436
2	248
6	368
4	230

The space allotted to competing brands was kept at two facings each. The data are given in Table 14.13.

a. Determine the least squares equation for these data.

b. Plot the points and draw in the least squares line for a visual check of the appropriateness on your calculations.

c. Calculate $S_{Y.X}$.

d. Determine the 95 percent confidence interval for the mean weekly sales corresponding to 4 facings.

e. Determine the 95 percent prediction interval for weekly sales in a week when 4 facings are allotted to the brand. Is this interval similar to the one determined in Part d? Explain.

46. *Estimating Daily Order Receipts* You are operations manager at a plant of one of the large mail order houses such as Sears, Wards, or J.C. Penney's. Your plant, depending on the season, handles between 1000 and 4000 orders in a ten, fifteen, or twenty minute cycle. This means that during each cycle anywhere from one to four thousand orders are being processed, assembled, and shipped through the same operational channels and by the same personnel. Any "bottlenecking" of machines and people represents poor planning and can cause an overlapping of the cycle and complete chaos. Early knowledge of the number of orders that are to be processed that day will be of tremendous help in organizing a work plan for that day. You feel that there is association between the weight of the mail received and the volume of orders to be filled. Daily you sort out customer mail from the junk mail. Over several days you randomly select ten sacks of sorted mail from the different weight classes ranging from two hundred to six hundred pounds of mail—two from each hundred pound class. Table 14.14 shows what you have found over several days of sampling.

a. Estimate the least squares line for the data.

b. Check the linearity assumption by plotting the data.

c. Is there a reliable relationship between the number of orders and the weight? Explain.

d. What gain does the relationship show over the alternative procedure of estimating the number of orders on a given day from the mean number of orders received over the past several days?

e. Can you suggest an improvement on the selection procedure of picking the sacks over several successive days of receipts?

f. Do you think that by applying the same procedure you can estimate how many complaints from customers you will receive daily, and perhaps more importantly, how many payments on account you will receive daily?

47. *Flexible Budgeting* Management's expectations for control over manufacturing overhead costs is commonly conveyed to each of the firm's cost centers by the use

TABLE 14.14. Association between Weight of Mail & Volume of Orders

Number of Orders, Y (in thousands)	7.2	7.5	10.3	9.7	12.9	14.0	15.4	16.2	19.1	20.0
Weight of Mail, X (in hundreds of pounds)	2	2	3	3	4	4	5	5	6	6

TABLE 14.15. Overhead Costs and Direct Machine Hours

Direct Machine Hours ($1000) X:	2.5	4	5	7.5	8
Overhead Costs ($10,000) Y:	25	35	50	65	70

of a flexible budget. A flexible budget shows cost expectations for various output levels at the cost center. Up to now MCI Electronics has been run by engineers with little background in financial control. Their procedure for estimating the budget for manufacturing overhead was simply to estimate the level of each cost at the anticipated volume for the period (so-called static budget). Although for the most part accurate, preparation was time consuming and therefore expensive and diverted their attention away from their area of expertise. You are hired and asked to develop a flexible budget system capable of estimating the variable cost component for their computer disc production. Assume that, in general, the overhead varies with direct machine hours. You gather historical data on overhead costs and direct machine hours over a certain range of production, as shown in Table 14.15.

a. Calculate the least squares lines for the data to estimate the variable overhead cost. Which variable is the independent variable and which is the dependent variable?

b. As a check on linearity, plot the points with cost on the vertical axis and machine hours on the horizontal axis and assess.

c. Since variable cost represents the cost that changes per unit change in machine hours, it is measured by the slope b of the computed regression line. Interpret the calculated value.

d. How reliable is b? Compare S_b to the value b and infer the underlying parameter using the hypothesis test $\beta = 0$ at the $\alpha = .01$ level. What do you conclude?

e. Construct a 99% confidence interval around b. Does it cover the value zero? Interpret.

48. The data in Table 14.16 are the returns to IBM common stock (column 1) and the returns to the New York Stock Exchange

Arithmetic Index (column 2) used in the beta analysis regression in Example 14.12. If you have the availability of a computer, perform the same regression analysis as was done in the chapter. Run your own simple regression on the data and verify the key regression statistics that were presented. This will give you a "hands on" demonstration of the computer output you will be working with. Notice how you obtain and where you find the key statistical details on your computer output. The returns have been slightly abbreviated for more manageable data entry and this will cause a slight discrepancy between your results and our analysis. (Note: For computer applications, such data are preferably entered in decimal form. To verbalize the results in percentage terms, as given in the text, multiply the results by 100. To get computer results in percentage terms, one could multiply each column by 100 before running the regression.)

49. As computer industry analyst for Dean Witter, you are asked to make a recommendation on whether the firm's blue chip customers should invest in IBM for the near term. Although you are sold on IBM as a long term prospect, you think over the past eighteen months IBM has been viewed as a more risky prospect because of government antitrust action coupled with competitive pressure from "plug-compatible" computer makers. To follow up on your hunch, you decide to run a beta analysis on IBMs monthly returns over the last eighteen months. Using the data given in Problem 48 run a regression of IBM returns on the market returns, calculating all statistics for a full analysis.

a. What is the proportion of variation in IBMs return attributable to variation in the level of stock market return?

b. What is the component of IBMs mean

TABLE 14.16. Returns to IBM Common Stock and Returns to New York Stock Exchange Arithmetic Index

ROW	IBM	NYSE	ROW	IBM	NYSE	ROW	IBM	NYSE
1	0.073	0.082	29	0.031	0.032	57	0.027	0.031
2	0.063	0.059	30	−0.086	−0.016	58	0.040	0.047
3	0.030	0.050	31	−0.004	−0.010	59	−0.012	0.030
4	0.027	0.008	32	0.026	0.051	60	−0.050	0.033
5	0.028	0.042	33	0.016	−0.018	61	−0.006	0.044
6	−0.027	−0.042	34	0.093	0.016	62	0.041	0.011
7	0.024	0.011	35	−0.015	−0.007	63	0.002	−0.022
8	0.068	0.021	36	0.045	0.008	64	0.080	0.034
9	0.036	−0.030	37	0.069	0.020	65	−0.022	−0.072
10	0.092	0.021	38	0.052	0.027	66	−0.030	−0.005
11	−0.012	0.046	39	0.044	0.031	67	−0.028	−0.013
12	−0.002	−0.004	40	−0.040	−0.003	68	−0.056	−0.093
13	−0.064	−0.008	41	0.055	0.012	69	−0.009	−0.014
14	−0.008	0.016	42	−0.006	0.015	70	0.046	0.013
15	−0.008	−0.006	43	−0.031	0.028	71	0.136	0.038
16	−0.148	−0.068	44	−0.044	−0.009	72	−0.012	0.016
17	−0.134	−0.098	45	−0.009	0.037	73	0.075	0.143
18	−0.136	−0.085	46	−0.038	0.017	74	0.079	0.021
19	0.141	0.064	47	−0.015	0.001	75	0.049	0.052
20	0.026	0.028	48	−0.007	−0.007	76	0.101	0.036
21	−0.108	−0.061	49	0.095	0.059	77	−0.035	−0.018
22	−0.021	−0.022	50	0.020	0.028	78	0.067	0.052
23	0.154	0.137	51	−0.003	0.005	79	0.021	0.071
24	−0.021	−0.009	52	0.068	0.036	80	−0.014	0.003
25	0.087	0.078	53	−0.011	−0.008	81	0.097	0.038
26	−0.054	−0.015	54	−0.042	−0.074	82	0.083	−0.036
27	0.053	0.021	55	0.046	0.029	83	0.033	0.007
28	0.102	0.039	56	0.045	0.045	84	0.025	0.055

return attributable to the (mean) level of the stock market return?

c. What is the average percentage point change in IBMs return attributable to a one percentage point change in the market return?

d. Does it appear that IBMs return appreciated faster than the stock market's return? Explain.

e. Does IBMs return exhibit more or less variation than the market return? Explain.

f. What statistic would you look at to assess IBMs price appreciation from factors un-

related to the stock market return?

g. What statistic measures the variation in the return from factors unrelated to the stock market return?

h. From the analysis you have done, what would you expect an investor in IBM common stock to earn if, on average, the NYSE return earning is 0.05 monthly? (Assume your estimated relationship is applicable to the next year.)

i. Does the analysis give you a practical tool for forecasting the returns on IBM common stock? Explain.

Regression and Correlation: Issues and Extensions

Preview. In a variety of circumstances the basic regression and correlation models have proven to be valuable aids in solving business problems. Yet their analytical value can be undermined if the models are inappropriately used or interpreted. Fortunately, these pitfalls can be avoided by better understanding the issues involved and by checking that the underlying specifications of the model are met. In addition, some important extensions of the basic models make regression and correlation even more versatile and valuable tools for business decision-making purposes. The issues and extensions explained in this chapter are intended to help solve such questions as (1) In economics, the Phillips curve postulates a curvilinear tradeoff between the rate of unemployment and the rate of inflation. Can regression analysis estimate a curvilinear model? Can it be used to test the validity of the controversial Phillips curve? (2) Federal Express is thinking of expanding its air cargo operations to international markets. Can the shipping cost-distance equation for domestic routes be useful in predicting the shipping costs on more distant international routes?

    The topics in this chapter fall into six broad categories. Sections 15.1 and 15.2 focus on the *form* of the true regression relationship. Techniques are presented for extending the linear regression model to the curvilinear case. Sections 15.3 to 15.5 are concerned with the implications of using a linear computed regression line when the true relationship between the variables is or may be curvilinear. Section 15.6 deals with the variables themselves as we consider problems of measurement and the substitution of surrogate variables for ones we cannot measure directly. Section 15.7 raises the subject of "nuisance" variables and attempts to alert the reader to what must *not* be done about them. In Section 15.8 we consider a particularly insidious form of selection bias for the observations and the "truncated distribution trap" to which this bias all too often leads. In Sections 15.9 and 15.10 we consider the bivariate data "regression phenomenon" and associated fallacious interpretations of the regression coefficient. Three extensive review exercises at the end of this chapter provide additional familiarity with the techniques of applied regression analysis and the possible pitfalls associated with applications of this powerful statistical tool. Considered as a group, the modifications and caveats presented in this chapter should greatly facilitate enlightened and successful application of what has come to be one of the most widely utilized statistical methods.

15.1. Curvilinear Relationships: Polynomial Regression

15

The simple linear regression model presented in Chapter Fourteen proved to be a powerful tool for analyzing bivariate quantitative linear relationships. However, the requirement that the underlying relationship be linear is a serious limitation on the versatility of regression analysis. Many bivariate relationships are curvilinear. A curvilinear relationship should provide a better fit to the data than a straight line if the following two conditions are met:

1. A plausible reason exists for believing that the underlying relationship between the variables follows a non-linear pattern.

2. A visual check of the scatter diagram suggests a curvilinear rather than a straight line pattern.

There are two popular but different techniques in handling curvilinear data:

1. *Directly fit a non-linear equation to the data* (for example, a polynomial or other higher degree equation).

2a. *Transform the original variables* so that the relationship between the transformed variables is approximately linear (for example, by taking logarithms of the original data).

2b. *Estimate the parameters* of the relationship between the transformed variables using *linear* regression (regress the logarithms of Y on the logarithms of X).

How do you determine the merits of directly fitting a curve rather than a straight line to the data? This is done by comparing the variation still unexplained for the two cases. This residual variation is measured by the *standard deviation of residuals*, which serves as the barometer of how good the equation fits the data. The lower the value of this statistic, the better the fit, provided the residuals are randomly distributed. So,

> if the standard deviation of residuals is lower for the straight line, it provides a better fit to the observed data; otherwise, a curvilinear form fits better.

We discuss the first of the two alternative curvilinear approaches, polynomial regression, in this section. The second approach is considered in the next section.

Polynomial Regression

The parabolic curve heads the list of mathematical forms used for curve fitting. The general form of an estimated parabola is

$$Y = a + b_1X + b_2X^2$$

From the observed sample data on Y and X a third variable X^2 is generated to achieve curvature. The least squares method applied to the data on the three variables gives the estimates, a, b_1, b_2. A sketch of observed data following a parabolic pattern and its fitted parabolic curve is shown in Figure 15.1.

At times the parabolic equation reduces to a special case in which the curve is U-shaped or inverted U-shaped. The expression for such estimated parabolic curve is

$$Y = a + bX^2$$

To obtain estimates a and b, the least squares method is applied to the variables Y and X^2.

In either the general or the special case, computer programs are readily available to carry out the necessary calculations for the curve fitting. But having the technique available does not eliminate the need for foresight in knowing when to employ it, as the following example shows.

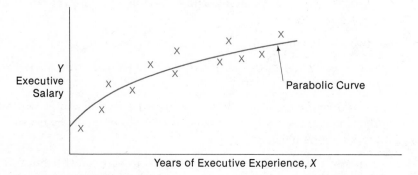

FIGURE 15.1 Fitting a Parabolic Curve

Example 15.1. Blame It on the Humidity

A multiplant company has one particular plant with a history of unusually high employee grievances of all kinds. The plant manager, suspected of being a poor administrator, invariably blames "the weather" for the high rate of grievances at the plant. Essentially, he argues that large deviations from "ideal" humidity cause employees to become disgruntled and dream up a wide variety of imaginary grievances. The only way to stop the grievances, he says, is to air condition the plant, which he happens to know is virtually impossible.

The Vice President of Industrial Relations thinks the solution to the problem may be to find a new plant manager. To check out the situation, he has data collected on Employee Grievances and on Deviation of Humidity from Ideal. Then he computes the least squares regression line. The computed r^2 is very low ($r^2 = .005$ for the equation $Y = 26 + 0.35X$) and the standard deviation of the slope coefficient is several times the value of the coefficient. On receiving that news the Vice President draws up the plant manager's pink slip.

The plant manager appeals and asks for the data (Table 15.1). To verify the suitability of a linear regression, he proceeds to draw a scatter diagram, shown in Figure 15.2a.

TABLE 15.1. Bivariate Data on the Relationship Between Grievances and Humidity

DAY	DEVIATION OF HUMIDITY INDEX FROM "IDEAL"	NUMBER OF EMPLOYEE GRIEVANCES
1	−2	6
2	+3	11
3	+7	51
4	+2	6
5	0	2
6	−9	83
7	+6	38
8	−5	27
9	+4	18
10	−5	27
11	−1	3
12	−3	11
13	+7	51

The scatter indicates non-random residuals about the computed linear regression line. Values between −4 and +4 for deviations from "ideal" humidity all lie below the computed linear regression line. Values below −4 and above 4 all lie above the computed linear regression line. This pattern of non-random residuals suggests that the relationship follows a pronounced curvilinear pattern. That grievances are definitely related to deviations from ideal humidity can be seen by

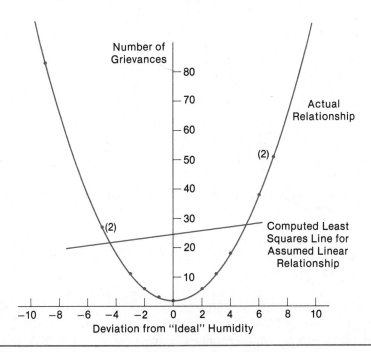

FIGURE 15.2a Relationship Between Grievances and Humidity

connecting the points on the scatter diagram. The data perfectly fit a parabolic curve with equation $Y = 2 + X^2$. According to this equation and the scatter diagram, small deviations from ideal humidity have little effect on the grievances. However, large deviations from the ideal lead to large increases in grievances. Having established this relationship, the plant manager, of course, saves his job.

It is possible in this case to transform the data in a way that permits a linear regression to bring out the curvilinear relationship. Instead of running a regression of Y on X, the values of X are first squared and then a new variable $Z = X^2$ is defined. A linear regression of Y on Z is run. The resulting computed regression equation is

$$Y = 2 + Z$$

The r^2 for this equation is one, indicating perfect positive correlation between Y and Z. Substituting X^2 for Z gives the parabolic equation

$$Y = 2 + X^2$$

In Figure 15.2b the transformed data are plotted on a graph in which the horizontal axis represents values of X^2 rather than values of X. Notice that all the points fall on a straight line, indicating a perfect positive relationship between Y and X^2. Your job should not be on the firing line every time a regression is run; but remembering to check the data for curvilinearity and to follow up on the diagnostics for good relative fit could save you considerable grief some day.

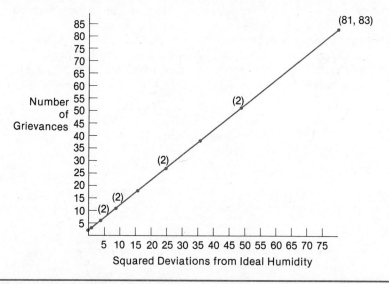

Figure 15.2b Relationship Between Grievances and Squared Deviations from Ideal Humidity

15.2. Curvilinear Relationships: The Double Log Transformation

The parabolic regression model presented in the previous section has two drawbacks. First, a parabola does not fit all curvilinear data well. Second, its two coefficients b_1 and b_2, which specify the impact of a change in X and Y, have no direct economic or business interpretation useful in planning and control.

Fortunately, not all instances of curvilinearity need be expressed by a parabolic curve. At times a convenient linear transformation of the curvilinear pattern of X and Y produces a slope coefficient with a direct interpretation.

An important example of this is in the measurement of *demand elasticity.* This term refers to the sensitivity of the quantity that can be sold to changes in the selling price. As in stretching a rubber band, greater elasticity means greater response or change for a given amount of pressure. The more elastic the demand, the greater the increase in quantity that can be sold in response to the pressure of a given degree of price reduction.

In the following example disagreement about the degree of demand elasticity emphasizes the need for its measurement.

Example 15.2.   The *Wall Street Journal* on Gasoline Price Elasticity

One of the sillier arguments federal interventionists have used against gasoline price decontrol has been that gasoline demand, unlike demand for almost everything else, is "inelastic", meaning it doesn't drop when the price rises. Hence, it would not curb demand and eliminate shortages if price controls were removed. A Utah State University group has just completed a survey of vacation plans showing that if gasoline prices rose to $1.50 a gallon, half the respondents would cancel planned motor vacations and only 19% would travel more than 500 miles. There must be some elasticity there somewhere.[1]

To quantify the concept of demand elasticity, a common definition is required. Economists define it as the ratio of the percentage change in quantity to the percentage change in price. For example, if initially quantity is 100 at a price of $10 and changes to 120 in response to a reduction in price to $9,

$$b = \text{demand elasticity} = \frac{\left(\dfrac{120 - 100}{100}\right)}{\left(\dfrac{9 - 10}{10}\right)} = \frac{20\%}{-10\%} = -2$$

The concept of demand elasticity is important to business executives because it indicates how sales volume and sales revenue will be affected by a price change. For example, if the absolute value of demand elasticity is less than one, it means that a price reduction will result in a *loss* of sales revenue. The revenue increase from new customers will not be sufficient to offset the revenue loss from lower prices to present customers.

Based upon his or her experience in a particular industry, a business executive may believe that demand in this industry is such that a 10 percent price cut will on average lead to, say, a twenty percent increase in the volume that could be sold, regardless of the initial sales level. The executive may compare this industry to others in which a 10 percent price cut is thought to lead to a 30 or 40 percent increase in the quantity that could be sold. In concluding that demand is "less elastic in my industry" the executive is implicitly or explicitly assuming a constant demand elasticity.

If the executive is correct in assuming that the value of b is a constant, it turns out that the relationship between quantity and price will be curvilinear, as shown in Figure 15.3a. Thus, the simple linear regression model of Chapter 14 would not be the appropriate one to use in estimating the demand elasticity. However, a modification of the model is appropriate in the case of constant demand elasticity. The modification is based upon the fact that, if b is a constant, then the relationship between quantity and price must be of the form

$$\text{quantity} = A(\text{price})^b$$

where A and b are constants and b is the demand elasticity. Designating quantity by Y and price by X,

$$Y = A(X)^b$$

This is a logarithmic relationship in that if $A = 1$, then b is the logarithm of Y to the base X. (A brief discussion of logarithms is given in Chapter 4.) The point is that a logarithmic transformation of the variables leads to a *linear* relationship, one that can be estimated by the simple linear regression model presented in Chapter 14.

Taking the logarithm of both sides gives:

$$\text{Log } Y = \text{Log } A + b(\text{Log } X)$$

Letting Log A be designated by a, the equation takes on the form of a linear relationship with constants a and b. This is the form of the computed regression equation of Log Y on Log X. The value of the regression coefficient b is the estimated price elasticity. This value can be estimated by following three steps.

1. Take logarithms of price and quantity.
2. Regress the Log Y values on the corresponding Log X values.
3. Use the computed value of b in the regression equation as the estimated price elasticity.

To see that the value of b actually does represent the percentage change in Y corresponding to a one percentage point change in the value of X, consider the following numerical illustration based on an elasticity of -5.

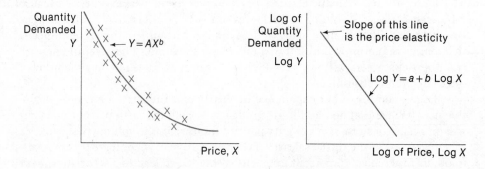

FIGURE 15.3a Constant Elasticity Demand Curve

FIGURE 15.3b Logarithmic Transformation of the Demand Curve Shown in Figure 15-3a

Price-Quantity Relationship: Log(quantity) = 13 − 5Log(Price)

At a price of $100, quantity is computed as follows:

$$
\begin{aligned}
\text{Log(quantity)} &= 13 - 5\text{Log(Price)} \\
&= 13 - 5\text{Log}(100) \\
&= 13 - 5(2) \\
&= 3.
\end{aligned}
$$

Therefore,

$$
\begin{aligned}
\text{quantity} &= \text{antilog}(3) \\
&= 1000.
\end{aligned}
$$

Increasing the price by one percentage point to 101 gives the quantity calculated from:

$$
\begin{aligned}
\text{Log(quantity)} &= 13 - 5\text{Log}(101) \\
&= 13 - 5(2.0043) \\
&= 2.9785
\end{aligned}
$$

Therefore,

$$
\begin{aligned}
\text{quantity} &= \text{antilog}(2.9785) \\
&= 952
\end{aligned}
$$

The actual quantity change is −48. The *relative* quantity change is:

$$
\frac{952 - 1000}{1000} = -4.8\%.
$$

Thus the calculated percentage change in quantity does approximately agree with the b coefficient value of −5. The reason for the difference is that, strictly speaking, the constant percentage relationship between quantity and price holds only for a point and not for a line segment. The smaller the change in price considered, the more closely will b approximate the ratio of the percentage changes in quantity and price, respectively.

The above calculations were made using logarithms to the base 10. This is the base most people used when first learning logarithms. However, any other base could also be used. A base that is very widely used in statistics is $e = 2.718$. The resulting logarithms are called *natural* logarithms. Unless the base is specifically stated, we shall assume that the base e is used and that natural logarithms are implied. For the initial quantity and price given above, the corresponding natural logarithms are:

Variable	Y (quantity)	X (price)
Value	1000	100
Transformed Variable	Log Y	Log X
Value	6.90776	4.60517

In Figure 15.3a, a constant elasticity demand curve is shown before logarithmic transformation. In Figure 15.3b, this same demand curve is shown after a logarithmic transformation. Note that the value for b in such demand studies ought to have a negative sign. The double log transformation can be used in any situation where there is a *constant percentage change* between values of the dependent and independent variables. Review Exercise I at the end of this chapter illustrates the transformation procedure for the M & M Industries job evaluation problem introduced in Chapter 14.

15.3. Linear Approximation of a Curvilinear Relationship

Suppose data have been collected on X and Y. From the diagnostics made, you have concluded that a least squares line provides a close fit to the data and that the residuals conform to the assumptions of a simple linear regression model. Given this knowledge about the fit it seems perfectly legitimate for you to use the computed regression equation to predict Y for various levels of X *within* the range of observed data. But some disturbing information comes to your attention about the true regression line for X values far removed from the range of your data. At these X values, it seems the *true* regression line passes through Y values different than the Y values for the extended computed regression. See Figure 15.4.

This information points out the potential misuse of mechanically extending the least squares line for the prediction of Y values *outside the range of observed data.* But does this raise enough suspicion about the quality of the computed regression equation to warrant not using it as a predictive model? No, the observed discrepancy does *not* undermine the equation's predictive worth *within* the range of the observed data.

Two guiding principles in judging model predictive value should be kept in mind. They are:

1. The data *must have been collected* over the range of X values used in *predicting* Y, and

2. The model should represent the observed data well.

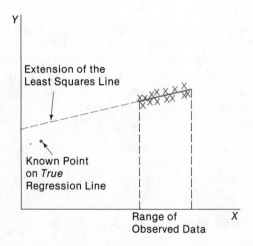

FIGURE 15.4 Extension of Computed Regression Line Fails to Pass Through Known Point on True Regression Line

Remember that the predictive power of the computed equation is definable within the range of the data at hand. Developing predictive accuracy within this range is the purpose for computing the regression line. The following example presents a classic situation in which a computed linear regression equation may give very good estimates of the dependent variable within the range of observed values of the independent variable even though an extension of the regression line does not pass through a known point on the true line.

Example 15.3.　**How Heavy are Persons of Zero Height?**

Consider Figure 15.5, where weight is shown on the Y axis and height is shown on the horizontal axis. *In the range of the actual data* (indicated by the shaded rectangle), a least squares line (*aa'*) provides a good fit. But we know that the *true* regression line must pass through the origin—that is, persons of zero height should have zero weight. Does this mean the *computed* regression line should be forced to pass through the origin also? A line (*OA*) forced through the origin would provide a terrible fit *where it really counts*—in the range of the actually observed data—and provide a poor basis for estimating weight from height.

　　Presumably the true regression line (*OC*) is curvilinear. Is this important? Not necessarily. Over the range of the observed data, the range where the predictions will be made, the curvature is small and well approximated by the straight line *aa'*.

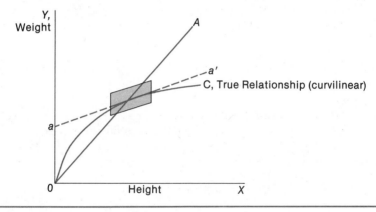

FIGURE 15.5 Regression of Weight on Height

　　The above example illustrates why one can predict with a good fitting linear regression line within the range of interpolation even though the true relationship between the variables may be curvilinear. It does *not* follow that this same line can safely be used for extrapolation (prediction beyond the range of the data observed), as we will see in the next section.

15.4. Hazards of Linear Extrapolation

Can the relationship between Y and X for a range containing no observations be estimated? Extending the regression line computed for the range where there *are* observations is one approach. The *extended regression line* is called the *extrapolated* regression line, and the predictions of Y for values of X *outside the range* of the observed data are referred to as *extrapolations*. Such predictions are highly speculative and are subject to large prediction errors.

Recall the Freddie Laker example in Chapter Fourteen. Reliance on an extrapolated regression line caused air line executives to underestimate greatly the sensitivity of passenger traffic to big discounts in air fares. Innovative pricing by Freddie Laker showed the established airlines the cost of unwarranted protracted extrapolation.

So extrapolation has led to some serious prediction errors. Perhaps the fault lies with a poor fit of the regression line to the actual data. What if the fit was good? Is extrapolation no longer a risky business? No matter how close the fit (high R^2) in the observed range, extrapolation is a gamble. It is like rolling the dice about the form of the relationship *outside* the observed range. There simply is no guarantee that the form found useful for fitting the *observed* data automatically will be a good approximation of the true relationship in the range of *extrapolation*.

The least squares regression of weight on height in the height-weight example gave a close linear fit *within* the range of the observed data. But what help does it give about the form *outside* the range of the observed data? Curvature is likely for the height-weight relationship. Linear extrapolation risks large non-random errors the farther from the observed data one extrapolates.

Without data in the extrapolated range to assess the probable departure of the model from linearity, the size of the expected non-random errors would be pure guesswork.

In the business world, true cost functions are usually non-linear. This can create a potential problem, as the following example illustrates.

Example 15.4.   Linear Extrapolation of Nonlinear Costs

Cost analysts are known to make a simplifying assumption. The relationship between total costs and sales volume over the relevant range of activity is generally considered linear. But there are sound structural cost reasons for expecting a *curvilinear* relationship over an extended volume range.

A plausible curvilinear cost structure is shown in Figure 15.6 by the curve *NA*. If prediction of costs is restricted to the range of actual volume X_0 to X_1, the straight line *aa'* represents the cost changes well. Large non-random errors should not appear. *Beyond* the range X_0 to X_1, the use of *aa'* to extrapolate cost Y would lead to serious non-random errors of unknown size. Extrapolation is warranted only if tied to a specific knowledge of operations on the outside regions.

Although extrapolation beyond the range of existing data is hazardous and should be avoided whenever possible, situations do arise in which extrapolation may be required. Problems 23 to 25 at the end of this chapter consider one possible

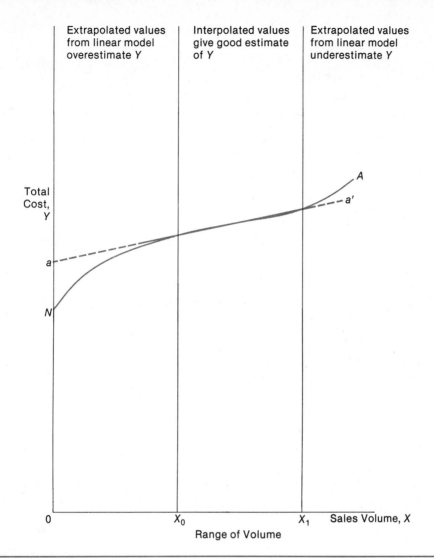

| Extrapolated values from linear model overestimate Y | Interpolated values give good estimate of Y | Extrapolated values from linear model underestimate Y |

FIGURE 15.6 Non-linear Cost Function

situation, the introduction of a new consumer product. When a new product is introduced the ultimate levels of market penetration and market share are generally thought to be related to the sales performance during the first few weeks or months after the introduction. Of necessity, the projections of future sales and market penetration must be extrapolations. In Chapter 19 (Business Fore-casting), we shall consider the contribution of modern time series analysis in reducing errors of extrapolation.

15.5. Interpreting the Y Intercept

It is particularly important to understand the hazards of extrapolation when interpreting a, the value of the Y intercept of the computed regression line. It would be best to think of 'a' as merely the mechanical extension of the regression line to the Y-axis; in other words, it should be given no economic interpretation (even though the Y-intercept for the true regression line *does* have one). The following example shows the danger in not heeding this advice.

Example 15.5A. **Properly Interpreting the Value of the Y Intercept**

If the dots in Figure 15.7 are the observed data, the fitted regression line would be *aa'*. The 'a' value of the regression line is simply the mechanical extension of the regression line to the Y-axis. No relevant economic interpretation should be given to the value of 'a'. However, if the observed data include both the dots and the cross-hatched points, the Y intercept value of the regression curve (at point N) would legitimately be an estimate of the average rate of growth of inflation not related to the rate of growth of the money supply. Had the value of 'a' been erroneously accepted as an estimate of inflation which is not money supply related, the result would have grossly overestimated the true figure N. Unfortunately, economic analysts too often blindly use the intercept term as representing a meaningful figure even though it is an extrapolation well beyond the range of the data.

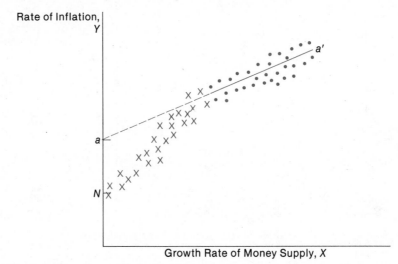

FIGURE 15.7 Rate of Inflation Versus Money Supply Growth Rate

Extrapolation of the regression to the Y axis can lead to a *negative value* of the regression line's Y intercept. In situations where it is known that the dependent variable cannot possibly have a negative value, this would indeed be puzzling if the extrapolated intercept value were taken seriously. The following example describes a situation in which a negative intercept would be impossible for the true relationship, but the negative intercept found for the computed relationship was harmless.

Example 15.5B. Negative Spending At the Supermarket?

A marketing research study on competing supermarkets was undertaken to determine the feasibility of estimating store sales by using the count of grocery bags of each customer. The field observers placed at each store recorded data on customer actual expenditure and a count of the grocery bags of customers exiting at each store at selected periods during the week. A linear regression of customer expenditures on the number of grocery bags gave a very close fit to the actual data, indicating that grocery bag count, indeed, would be a good predictor of actual expenditures. However, the intercept term was a significant *negative* value not explainable by sampling error alone. Figure 15.8 shows this situation.

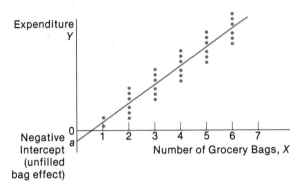

FIGURE 15.8 Observed Relationship between Expenditure at
Checkout Counter and Number of Grocery Bags

The puzzled analysts were worried. What is the implication of the negative value? Shouldn't zero bags indicate a customer who made no purchases? And shouldn't the intercept term, as the average expenditure for persons exiting with zero bags, be zero? And if the true intercept value is zero, obtaining a computed value different from zero should be explainable by sampling error. What went wrong?

Of the explanations suggested, all pointed to a possible *positive* intercept, none to a negative intercept. It was jokingly said that the supermarket managers were making payoffs to certain people to keep them away from the store, hence the negative expenditures for zero grocery bags.

Fortunately, some additional probing and insight led to quite a different conclusion. First, it was noticed that the actual data did not include any observations of customers exiting with zero bags. So the Y-intercept was an *extrapolation* of the computed regression line. Next, believing the *true* intercept value equaled zero, the analysts substituted zero in the regression equation; expenditure predictions Y were computed for different numbers of grocery bags X (one, two, three, etc.). Regardless of the number of grocery bags, the expenditure predictions tended to be *too high* compared with the actual expenditures for the number of bags. Somehow the *negative "a" term was needed to compensate* for this overestimation. But why? What was it compensating for?

After further thought about the survey's raw data, it was realized that the last grocery bag for each customer was usually not completely full. On average, the expenditure on a partially filled bag came to less than on one which was full. Typically each customer exited the store with one *partially filled*, and *less expensive*, bag of groceries relative to the other bags.

The "*b*" term in the regression equation is a constant indicating the average incremental expenditure for each additional bag of groceries bought. It is a constant applied to *X*, the number of full or partially full bags.

The problem is that the *b* term reflects the average expenditure on a *full* bag. Why? Assume, on average, one partially filled bag per customer. In comparing one bag to two-bag purchases, we in effect compare expenditures for *one partially filled bag versus one partially filled and one full bag*. Thus, the observed additional grocery expenditure reflects only the incremental effect of a *full* bag of groceries. Similarly, in comparing two-bag and three-bag purchases, the observed additional grocery expense is for an incremental full bag. Each time we consider the expenditures for an additional bag of groceries, it is always a *full* bag to which we refer.

With the *b* term showing the incremental expenditure for full bags and the *X* variable the total count of bags (including the *partially* filled bag), the aggregate product *bX* in the regression equation will *overestimate* the actual expenditure. The overestimate will reflect the difference between the average expenditure on a full bag and a partially filled bag. In what way can this overestimate (the product *bX*) be adjusted for elsewhere in the equation?

The overestimated expenditures resulting from using the *bX* term alone forces the *intercept* term to a negative value to adjust for the unfilled bag effect. Thus, the mysterious negative intercept turns out to have a logical explanation after all.

The supermarket example makes several important points.

1. It shows that economic interpretations of the intercept term should be avoided unless the underlying model and its relation to the actual data are very well understood.

2. In most instances, particularly those involving extrapolation, the intercept term should be treated simply as a mechanical extension of the computed regression line and nothing more.

3. Finding a negative intercept term in a regression equation does *not* destroy the predictive ability of the model over the range of observed data.

In this and preceding sections of the chapter we have considered the *form* of the true relationship and the implications of using a linear computed regression line when the true relationship between the variables is or may be nonlinear. In the next section we turn our attention to the variables themselves, particularly the independent variable.

15.6. Surrogate Variables

Collecting data directly on the variables we want to investigate is desirable so long as the collection of primary data:

1. does not take too long,

2. is not too costly, and

3. is easily accessible.

Otherwise, one must resort to a substitute variable which has these features and is closely allied to the variable of investigative interest. The substitute variable is referred to as a *surrogate* variable or *proxy* variable.

Properly used, surrogate variables are invaluable and perfectly legitimate devices. For instance, market research studies of consumer behavior often rely on surrogate variables to identify consumer attitudes towards a product. This is necessary because attitude is a state of mind and as such is not directly measurable, even when consumers respond to questions about their attitudes. Marketing researchers often go to great lengths to find surrogate variables which can be used as independent variables in their statistical investigations. The following example illustrates the use of a popular surrogate variable in retail marketing research.

Example 15.6. Buying Power Index

Oversized and undersized stores are costly mistakes for a retailer. The potential volume of customer traffic a prospective store's trade area can generate determines the optimal size of store which should be built. To decide whether to build a new store and, if built, what its size should be, retail executives obtain and evaluate the trade area's optimal sales potential. As useful as the concept of sales potential is, it is difficult to measure. What do planners use? Often they rely on the *Buying Power Index,* a surrogate or proxy for sales potential, published annually for several hundred market areas by *Sales and Marketing Management* magazine (see Table 15.2).

TABLE 15.2. Survey of Buying Power (Colorado)

METRO AREAS COUNTIES CITIES	BUYING POWER INDEX	METRO AREAS COUNTIES CITIES	BUYING POWER INDEX
COLORADO SPRINGS	.1326	DENVER-BOULDER	.7335
El Paso	.1304	Adams	.0965
Colorado Springs	.0967	Arapahoe	.1228
Teller	.0022	Aurora	.0573
SUBURBAN TOTAL	.0359	Boulder	.0858
FORT COLLINS	.0567	Boulder	.0484
Larimer	.0567	Denver	.2575
Fort Collins	.0320	Denver	.2575
SUBURBAN TOTAL	.0247	Douglas	.0053
GREELEY	.0455	Gilpin	.0008
Weld	.0455	Jefferson	.1648
Greeley	.0238	Arvada	.0299
SUBURBAN TOTAL	.0217	Lakewood	.0761
PUEBLO	.0581	SUBURBAN TOTAL	.4276
Pueblo	.0581		
Pueblo	.0512		
SUBURBAN TOTAL	.0069		

Source: *1977 Survey of Buying Power,* published by Sales and Marketing Management, July 25, 1977, p. C-34. Reprinted by permission. All rights reserved.

The index accounts for a region's percentage of U.S. population, percentage of total U.S. retail sales, and percentage of U.S. disposable income. Higher values of the index indicate greater buying power. The use of the BPI as a surrogate for sales potential is widespread in regression analysis, which relates 'ideal' store size to sales potential. Regressing the size of a retailer's successful stores on the BPI of their trade area makes the BPI a surrogate for the independent variable, sales potential. More precisely stated, optimal store size is a function of sales potential. Substituting the variable BPI for sales potential, the linear estimating equation is:

Optimal Store Size $= a + b$ (BPI)

Inserting a new area's BPI value into the regression equation allows the retailer to predict the size of the ideal store for that area. The final adjustment of the store size will depend on other factors that store planners feel need to be considered.

15.7. Nuisance Variables and the Induced Correlation Trap

The "nuisance" effect of a third variable can obscure the true relationship between the two variables of interest. How should it be handled?

The proper way to deal with a "nuisance" variable is to employ *multiple regression*, a technique in which the nuisance variable can be included separately as a second independent variable in the regression equation. This technique is discussed and illustrated in Chapter 16.

Does a nuisance variable really necessitate abandoning simple regression analysis? Can't some accommodation for the effect of a nuisance variable be made? After all, we are really not interested in measuring the effect of the nuisance variable, only in eliminating its interference. Perhaps one approach is simply to form *ratios* of the two variables of interest (say Y and X) to the nuisance variable (Z). We would then have only two variables, (Y/Z) and (X/Z). The former ratio would then be regressed on the latter using simple regression. Since both Y and X have been divided by the same value (Z), wouldn't the regression of the ratios be free of the nuisance variable Z?

Actually, it isn't that simple. Adjusting for the effect of the nuisance variable Z in this way can lead to a trap, the *induced correlation* trap. Dividing both sides of the equation relating Y to X by Z can artificially *induce* correlation between (Y/Z) and (X/Z).

Suppose one set of observations on X, Y, and Z is 60, 40, and 10, respectively. The value of X/Z is $60/10 = 6$ and the value of Y/Z is $40/10 = 4$. A second set of observations is 40, 60, and $\frac{1}{10}$ for X, Y, and Z. The value of X/Z becomes $40/(\frac{1}{10}) = 400$ and the value of Y/Z becomes $60/(\frac{1}{10}) = 600$. These are summarized below:

	X	Y	Z	X/Z	Y/Z
1st set of observations	60	40	10	6	4
2nd set of observations	40	60	$\frac{1}{10}$	400	600

Note that the ratio variable Y/Z has a low value when X/Z is low and a high value when X/Z has a high value. This occurs even though the values of the original variable Y and X moved in opposite directions. The point is that even when there is no correlation among the variables in the first three columns, the variables in the last two columns will be correlated.

Changes of Z over a wide range of values for the observations considered sets the stage for the trap. The wider the range of Z, the more acute will be the problem.[2] Even if X and Y are *uncorrelated*, the resulting ratios X/Z and Y/Z *will be correlated* since both contain the common and changing element, $1/Z$. In a nutshell, the apparent correlation between X and Y has been artificially induced by $1/Z$ being correlated with itself. In the following example, the danger in handling a nuisance variable by forming ratios of other variables to it is illustrated for stock market analysis.

Example 15.7.   Showing Correlation Where There is None

Does the stock market attach a "premium" to the shares of firms whose earnings are backed up by book value—net tangible assets like factories, equipment, and plain old cash? Some market "pros" think so. Or at least they think this would make a lot of sense. "Asset rich" firms, they argue, are in a better position to pay their bills and to sustain a severe business recession than are firms whose assets are less tangible—like many wholesalers or discount retailers.

Suppose one firm has plant, equipment, and other tangible assets of $100 million, liabilities of $20 million, and one million stock shares outstanding. Its net tangible assets per share would be ($100,000,000 − $20,000,000)/1,000,000 = $80. A second firm has tangible assets per share of $60. The first firm is "asset rich" compared to the second firm. Proponents of this theory would regard the first firm as worth a premium compared to the second firm.

Suppose a mutual fund manager looking for good buys for the fund's portfolio wants to investigate the relationship between a firm's stock price per-share and the book value per share. Merely regressing the first variable on the second would be unsatisfactory. It would not take into account the amount of *earnings* each share of stock is generating, an item of keen interest to investors and a factor believed by many to be the key determinant of the stock price. This creates a problem because there are three variables to be considered and for ease of interpretation we want our regression analysis to deal only with two.

One possible approach to the problem (a poor one as we'll see) is to simply crunch the three variables into two. By dividing both the firm's book value and stock value by the firm's earnings (all in per-share form), we seemingly get an adjustment for the earnings effect. That is, the resulting regression equation relates the firm's stock price *per dollar of earnings* to the firm's book value *per dollar of earnings*.

$$\frac{\text{Firm's Stock Price } (Y)}{\text{Firm's Earnings } (Z)} = a + b\left[\frac{\text{Firm's Book Value } (X)}{\text{Firm's Earnings } (Z)}\right]$$

$$\frac{\text{Stock Value per Dollar}}{\text{of Earnings}} = a + b\left[\frac{\text{Book Value per Dollar}}{\text{of Earnings}}\right]$$

In the financial world, the ratio on the left-hand side of the equation (Y/Z) is called the firm's *price-earnings ratio*, while the ratio on the right-hand side (X/Z) is called the firm's *book value to earnings ratio*. Thus,

$$\text{Price-Earnings Ratio} = a + b(\text{Book Value to Earnings Ratio})$$

$$(Y/Z) = a + b(X/Z)$$

Unfortunately, this regression of ratios likely distorts the relationship between Y and X. The equation in this form has forced Y/Z to be related to X/Z by injecting the common element $1/Z$ and then correlating this reciprocal of Z with itself. Division of the price per share and book value per share by a very *large* earnings value—say $100—will produce *low* values for both ratios. On the scatter diagram the observation will be located on the lower left hand side (Figure 15.9b). But if the same price and book value levels are divided by *low* earnings, say $2, both ratios will be inflated—fifty times as high as before. The observation this time will be in the upper right-hand side of the scatter diagram. The net effect of this earnings adjustment is obvious from Panel B. The observational plot of the points tends to stretch out upward from left to right. *We have seemingly induced a positive relation between X and Y when actually none exists.* Actually, the substitution of the ratio X/Z for X and the ratio Y/Z for Y has led us into a statistical trap, one in which it is difficult to measure how much correlation the procedure has induced, and how much it changes the regression equation.

Induced correlation between the ratios (X/Z and Y/Z) obscures the issue of real interest—the actual relationship between stock price and the book value behind each share. Can we avoid this pitfall? Yes, a better approach to the problem is discussed in Chapter 16. It involves *multiple* regression analysis. The regression has three variables, stock price (the dependent variable), and the two variables, earnings and book value, as separate independent variables. More precisely, Y(market price) $= a + b_1 X_1$ (Book Value) $+ b_2 X_2$ (Earnings). With these results in hand, the issue of association between assets and stock price can be evaluated. Although multiple regression is not a panacea for all nuisance variable problems, it generally is the right way to start the analysis.

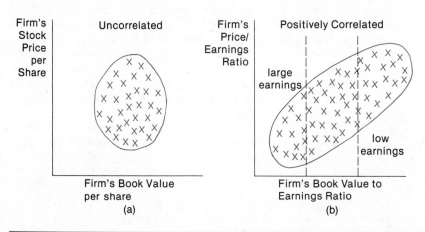

FIGURE 15.9 Firm's Book Value Earning Ratio Forecasting the Price-Earnings Ratio

Up to this point in the chapter we have discussed the form of the regression relationship and measurements on the variables. In the next section we turn to the method for choosing observations.

15.8. Truncated Distributions

In performing regression analysis on bivariate data, it is important to know whether the available data have been preselected in any systematic way. If certain portions of the complete distribution have been excluded by a screening method, our analysis is restricted to the remaining portion which we call a *truncated distribution*. What happens when the screening device used is a value of one of the bivariate variables being examined? For example, what happens if the performance of military students in military electronics school is regressed on their score on the Armed Forces Qualification Test that was used in selecting them for the school?

1. A random sample from the truncated distribution will not likely be representative of the entire bivariate distribution.

2. The regression line for the truncated distribution will also not likely be the same as the regression line for the entire distribution.

By itself, this is neither surprising nor disturbing. The potential problem is *incorrectly interpreting* the regression line for the truncated distribution as if it does provide valid inferences about the bivariate relationship in the entire population. The trap for the investigator is:

1. in believing that the relationship in the entire population is the same as that found in the truncated portion, and

2. using the estimated equation of the *truncated* distribution to form inferences about the *population* bivariate relationship.

How the investigator falls into the trap and the consequences that follow is illustrated in the following example.

Example 15.8A. **Entrance Examinations and Academic Performance**

A blizzard of admission applications from prospective students arrives every year at the admissions offices of colleges and universities. To read and evaluate subjectively every application is administratively difficult, if not an impossible task. Annually admission officers resort to the College Entrance Board scores (or similar exams) to serve as preliminary screening devices in accepting applicants for admission. The rationale for their use is that scores on these tests and academic performance are believed to be highly correlated; therefore, the scores should be good predictors of future academic performance. But does the data on grade point averages and college board scores substantiate this belief and justify the use of this screening procedure?

University officials reviewing student board scores on entering school and their subsequent academic performance are frequently startled to learn that the records show virtually no (or little) correlation. This may prompt the admissions officer to drop the board scores as a screening device for admission. If so, the director has unwittingly succumbed to the truncated distribution trap. What has happened?

Suppose the admissions director assumes (this assumption may be questionable) a strong population relationship between student's aptitude measured by the college board scores and the student's performance during college. This population characteristic ought to be reflected in the sample of students that the university accepts, *provided the university gets a random sample from the entire population.* The question then is whether a random sample of the entire population is precluded by the university's screening policy, by the type of prospective students that apply, or by some combination of both.

Screening applicants by preadmission test scores means that only students above some set minimum score will be admitted. All members of the distribution with scores below this cut off figure will not be admitted and will not appear on the academic student rolls of the university. As illustrated in Figure 15.10, this truncates the distribution at the line C_L. Those students below C_L are denied admission—the crosshatched area. Also missing on the academic rolls of most universities are students who receive the highest scores. They usually seek and gain admission to the most prestigious universities, which as a matter of policy make it attractive for them to attend. The cut off line on the higher end of the distribution represents a cut off imposed on the less prestigious universities by the high test score students. What then does this leave for the majority of universities?

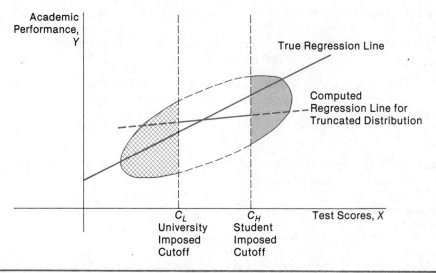

FIGURE 15.10 Truncated Distribution of Academic Performance and Test Scores

With a modestly strong population correlation between academic performance and test scores (as Figure 15.10 implies), the student rolls of most universities are restricted to students who score in the middle range (blank area). As Figure 15.10 illustrates, the regression line fitted to this middle range (truncated distribution) will be quite different from the true relationship expressed by the regression line of the total distribution.

For most universities the relationship between preadmission test scores and subsequent academic performance is weak to non-existent. Yet the practice of screening applicants by test scores continues at most universities. A knowledgeable admissions director should know that test scores are a valid indicator of future performance, but not the only valid indicator. Final admission should be a careful weighing of *all* the factors believed to influence student academic performance, including admission test scores. In some instances, the negative effect of the low test scores should be compensated by the positive effect of the other factors. In these cases the student possibly should be admitted.

Consequences of the Trap

The prevalence of the truncated distribution trap makes its study important. Camouflaging a true relationship may lead to a poor course of action. In business, the truncated distribution trap is especially likely to be encountered in evaluating job applicants based upon performance characteristics of present employees.

Example 15.8B.   Do Sour Faces Win Sales?

The manager of sales personnel wants to improve the job performance of the sales force, so she consults with the industrial relations director to screen applicants at the hiring stage by characteristics predictive of job (sales) performance.

"From my experience," the manager argues, "a pleasant personality is the most important trait of a successful sales person."

"If this association exists," the industrial relations director reasons, "a comparison between the personality ratings and performance ratings for the company's present sales force should show a strong positive correlation."

The industrial relations director's statement is correct if in fact the company's present sales force is a representative random sample from the entire sales force distribution. But here lies a possible catch. What if a pleasant personality was one of the traits considered in the *initial selection* of sales persons? Then the present sales force could *not* be considered a random sample of applicants. This would set the stage for the truncated distribution trap.

Suppose the true relationship between personality and sales success is positive and modestly strong. This is indicated by the scatter diagram in Figure 15.11. The absolute minimum personality score required before the company will consider hiring is the point 'a' on the horizontal axis. However, in order to be hired, the applicant with a personality score this low must possess other outstanding traits which are believed to be positively related to the sales performance. The higher the personality score above the 'a' level, the less compensatory need be the other traits. Conversely, the less outstanding these other traits the higher must be the applicant's personality score to achieve a satisfactory level of expected sales effectiveness. This trade off between personality score and the presence of other desirable traits creates the downward sloping hiring line AA' in Figure 15.11. Applicants to the left of this line are rejected by the company; applicants to the right are accepted.

The hiring process is usually a two way process. Companies with high growth potential and manager development programs attract talented applicants. Suppose point 'b' on the horizontal axis indicates the highest personality score that could be lured to a particular company. Because of attractive opportunities elsewhere, this company gets only persons of 'b' level personality scores who are deficient in the other important characteristics that go with good job performance, such as motivation, education, experience, intelligence, etc. Persons with *less than 'b' level* personality scores are less desirable as a group to other firms than the 'b' level type. With less attractive alternatives, the less than 'b' level group finds this firm's employment

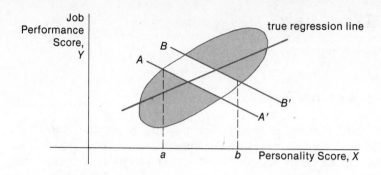

FIGURE 15.11 Inverting the Relationship by Double Truncation

opportunities relatively more attractive than would the '*b*' level group. Thus, as a group, a greater percentage of the less than '*b*' level group will choose this company. So as the personality score of the group declines, the percentage of the group of prospective sales persons attracted to (choosing) this company will increase. In essence, the lower personality score applicants are less choosy and more willing to work for this company. This "choosing out" process by the applicant is indicated by the downward sloping line, *BB'*. Generally, applicants to the right of this line refuse to work for the company because of their better opportunities elsewhere; applicants to the left of *BB'* are willing to work for this company because of less attractive benefits elsewhere.

The unshaded band between line *AA'* and *BB'* represents the pool of persons who are both acceptable to the company and willing to work for the company. From this truncated portion of the distribution come the persons currently enrolled and surveyed in the industrial relations director's study. From the figure one can see that a regression line fitted to this truncated distribution will have a negative slope, indicating negative correlation between personality score and sales success. Negative correlation leads one to erroneously conclude (trapped into thinking) that a grumpier personality makes a better sales person.

Ideally, the truncated distribution trap is avoided by sampling from the entire distribution of interest rather than a truncated segment of it. All too often this is not feasible. A personnel manager, for example, can only speculate about what the performance might have been from job applicants who were rejected because of low test scores. Faced with this dilemma, methods of multiple regression analysis considering simultaneously several of the important factors (discussed in the next chapter) frequently can be helpful.

In previous sections of this chapter, we have considered limitations of the simple linear regression model presented in Chapter 14 attributable to the form of the relationship and to problems in measuring the variables. In this section our attention turned to the method for choosing observations. We saw that if data are restricted to a truncated segment of a bivariate distribution, the resulting computed regression equation does not generalize to the entire distribution. In the next section we turn to an important issue in the interpretation of regression results. We shall see that even when the issues considered up to this point pose no problems, great care is required to avoid a pervasive misinterpretation called "the regression fallacy."

15.9. The Regression Phenomenon and the Regression Fallacy

Regression analysis, properly understood, is one of the most valuable statistical tools available to managers. Improperly understood, it can easily become the source of fallacious reasoning. Of the many improper interpretations, a particularly notorious example is often referred to as the "regression fallacy." The regression fallacy stems from a misunderstanding of the regression phenomenon first reported by Charles Galton more than a century ago.

Galton, investigating the heights of fathers and their sons, concluded that:

1. Tall fathers on the average tend to have (adult) sons who are also tall, but less so than their fathers, and

2. Short fathers tend on average to have sons who are also short, but less so than their fathers.

Galton's conclusion from the evidence was that fathers at either extreme tend to have sons whose heights are nearer to the mean of the distribution. This phenomenon is described as "regression toward the mean," or simply as the "regression phenomenon."

The regression *phenomenon* is real. If Galton's study was to be repeated today, the phenomenon would be observed. Instead of a line with a slope of one (which would indicate that sons average the same height as their fathers), a line fitted to the scatter diagram of fathers' heights (X) and sons' heights (Y) would have a slope value less than one. The latter situation indicates regression toward the mean. See Figure 15.12. The regression *fallacy* stems from interpreting this phenomenon as evidence that the heights of men are becoming less dispersed (with men tending toward a similar size) or that the number of men greater than, say, six and a half feet tall is declining. This would be fallacious because the regression phenomenon occurs whether or not dispersion is changing, or the number of tall men declining.

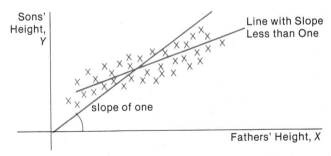

FIGURE 15.12 The "Regression Phenomenon"

Galton never knew it, but a surprising variety of modern day business problems are subject to the same regression phenomenon he encountered. Unfortunately, unless the regression phenomenon is clearly understood by business decision makers, the type of fallacious interpretations prevalent in his day likely will be repeated in interpreting current business and economic data. The following example shows how failure to comprehend the regression phenomenon can lead to marketing mistakes.

Example 15.9A.   A Consumer Panel Caveat: Don't Focus All Your Attention on the Product's Heavy Users

Marketing researchers, in an attempt to monitor trends in buying patterns, often employ consumer panels comprised of persons agreeing to maintain a diary of their product purchases. Suppose an analysis of the buying patterns of a consumer panel's members indicates that a large percentage of a frozen food brand's sales are made to only 20 or 30% of its customers. A follow-up study of the panel's heavy users shows a decline in usage rate too large to be explained by sampling variation. The marketing manager concludes that the brand is in serious trouble with its most loyal customers and orders a change in marketing strategy to head off further erosion of support.

Has the marketing manager jumped the gun—an unwitting victim of the regression fallacy? Doing a *reverse* panel study will show the trap that has been laid. Isolating *current* heavy users and tracing their level of purchases in the *previous* period reveals a startling result. Has consumption by the heavy user declined? Surprisingly, their current purchases will likely show an increase over the previous period's purchases.

How can the same source of data give us two conflicting signals on usage? More precisely, how can the same data tell us that the aggregate amount purchased by our most important customers, the heavy users, has simultaneously increased and decreased?

Drawing a direct analogy to Galton's data on fathers and sons, one can say:

> Heavy users in the first period tend to have above average consumption in the second period also, but not by as much as in the first period.

For specific brands one would find that the usage of the brand by extreme users is regressing to the mean, just as Galton's data on fathers' and sons' heights did. Additionally it would be unwise to interpret this movement as evidence of a strong downward trend in general usage, or that the ranks of the heavy users are thinning out. Why does such data give disconcerting signals that can lead one to misinterpret the survey results?

The crux of the problem lies in the failure to recognize that the changing composition patterns of this crucially important group over time cannot be traced by simply following the consumption pattern of the individuals that constitute the heavy user group currently in the survey panel. Not all current heavy users are the regular heavy users.

Current heavy users are a composite of the regular heavy users and those only temporarily in the heavy user category. The latter group will shortly return to its regular lower consumption category. Tracking from period to period the usage pattern of the individuals currently classified as heavy users means monitoring the regular heavy users and the heavy transitory users, whereas our interest is only in the consumption habit of the regular heavy users. Any conclusion about the latter group using data which include the transitory element of consumption would be an inaccurate and downward biased view of the regular heavy user consumption.

The regression *phenomenon* of the heavy user category draws attention to the regression toward the mean of the extreme usage group with its regular and transitory members. The regression *fallacy* arises by interpreting this phenomenon as evidence that the number of regular heavy users is declining, or that the average size of their purchases is declining.

Example 15.9B.   Baseball Batting Averages and the Regression Phenomenon

Interestingly, the examination of baseball batting averages in successive years shows the same regression phenomenon. The activity variable of the extreme groups regresses toward the mean from a previous period to a more recent period. For instance, if a regression is run of 1983 batting averages (*Y* variable) on 1982 batting averages (*X* variable), one would get a regression slope with a value *less than one*. The implication is that on the whole the good hitters (say .300 hitters) of 1982 did not do so well in 1983 (although, of course, some in the group did). And this drop on average will be reversed at the other extreme. The poor hitters, say below .225 in 1982, on average improved in 1983. Is this a generalizable process, and if so, what underlying mechanism is at work? Consider the *.300 hitters of 1982*. Plausibly they consist of three types of hitters in regard to luck:

1. normal .270 hitters, who having had more good luck than bad, hit thirty points above normal this year

2. normal .300 hitters, who have had an average amount of luck, with the good balancing out the bad

3. normal .330 hitters who have been unlucky enough to have more bad luck than good to end the year thirty points below their normal average.

What luck can one rightfully expect for next year? On balance one can expect an *average* amount since an average means what typically occurs. But since there are more .270 hitters than .330 hitters, what value will the group batting average regress towards in 1984? *Toward the .270 figure.* The *wrong* interpretation of these results is that the good hitters are becoming mediocre hitters—regressing towards mediocrity (the game just isn't what it was). What it *does* mean is that for a given year, good luck isn't shared by all groups to the same degree.

The lesson to be learned from the baseball example is simple:

tracking current extreme groups for the expressed purpose of generalizing to the entire population is bad practice.

There is intermingled in extreme groups (.300 hitters or .225 hitters) a segment enjoying (or suffering) extremely fortuitous (or calamitous) circumstances which will expectedly in the *next period* return to their normal situation. That is, some .300 hitters will return to their lower normal average whereas some .225 hitters will return to their higher normal average. But note that this is not a regression to mediocrity for *all* baseball players. In the next period there will be some current .270 hitters who will enjoy calamitous circumstance and move down to .225 hitters. Not understanding the regularity of this shifting composition from period to period can lead to seriously misguided conclusions, particularly if one extrapolates the experience of the extreme group to be the experience of the entire population.

> The only way to know if there has been a generalized shift for all players is to examine the entire distribution of batting averages in both periods, not just the extreme groups.

Thinking back to the heavy user consumer panel example, would all user groups experience the same changes in the pattern of consumption found for the extreme heavy user group had the study been conducted over all user levels?

15.10. The Regression Phenomenon With Cross-Sectional Data

Thus far the impression may be that the regression phenomenon is time-dependent—appearing only when there is a comparison across time periods. Actually, it is not that restrictive. It can appear in data examined cross-sectionally, such as cross-sectional consumer expenditure-family income data collected to estimate the pattern of spending across different income groups. Cross-sectional analysis of expenditures (Y) regressed on income levels (X) across different families describes the consumption expenditures of different families at their income levels at a particular time period—a snapshot of the expenditure-income situation at that time for different families.

The empirical studies for family income-expenditure data invariably find that the computed regression line has a slope less than one. The 45° line in Figure 15.13 has a slope of one. What do these findings mean?

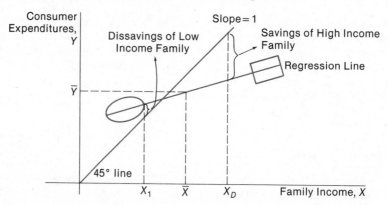

FIGURE 15.13 Cross-Sectional Regression of Family Consumption Expenditures and Family Income

A regression slope of less than one implies that families with income at the upper end of the scale (incomes at the rectangular area) tend to consume above the overall average (above $\overline{Y}$) but not as much above average as their incomes would suggest.

Graphically, this tendency places the rectangle below the 45° line. Let us now explain in savings terminology how the same regression phenomenon portrays a more dramatic conclusion.

Example 15.10.   Do the Rich Truly Get Richer While the Poor Get Poorer?

The average amount of savings or dissavings of families for a particular income level is merely the difference between the height of the regression line and the height of the 45° line (see Figure 15.13). The regression line suggests that families of above average income tend to have savings which are proportionately more above average than their incomes. Families of below average income (incomes at the circle area) tend to have savings which are proportionately more below average than their incomes. The seemingly logical conclusion from such family budget data is that "the rich are getting richer and the poor are getting poorer."

Another interesting conclusion based upon this evidence is that the percentage spent of a given incremental income (say, a tax rebate of $1000) would be different for different income groups.

Can these conclusions be wrong? Yes, because the expenditure-income picture shows the cross-sectional spending patterns of *different* income groups at *one point in time* rather than the permanent spending pattern of the *same* income groups *over* time.

Why do cross-sectional estimates at a particular point in time generally misrepresent the actual spending patterns of families who are consistently members of these groups over time? The reason is that *both* extreme groups contain some families that are transitory members. The transient element in their income (positive or negative) has temporarily moved them into a higher or lower income level than is their norm. Their spending, however, continues as if they are still making their normal level of income. For instance, a family which views the current income setback as temporary does not reduce its consumption pattern dramatically but likely spends consistent with its "permanent level" of income. This behavior gives an inflated view of the spending pattern of the families permanently in the lower income group.

This picture reverses for the higher income group. At any point in time there are families who are currently in the higher income group because they are presently enjoying positive transitory income. These families, however, continue to spend in tune with their lower permanent income. This behavior causes an understatement of the spending pattern of families *permanently* in the higher income group.

Each situation depicts the regression phenomenon at work. One can conclude that even if the true slope coefficient of the income-consumption relationship equals one, the regression *phenomenon* will cause the computed slope from a cross sectional study to be less than one. Nobel prize winning economist Milton Friedman has pointed this out, in a famous study of the consumption-income relationship. He showed that the computed regression line will appear as in Figure 15.13 *even if the marginal propensity to save incremental income is identical* for the different income groups.[3]

The regression phenomenon is very real. It is not fallacious to speak of regression towards the mean spending level. The regression *fallacy* arises if one erroneously interprets the observed spending pattern of families *currently* in the extreme group as the true spending pattern of families consistently in that group.[4]

It is important to emphasize that cross-sectional regression deals with different observational units at one point in time, not across time. The regression coefficient b obtained denotes the way Y values on average differ per unit difference in X values *across* the observational units, for example the difference on average between family expenditures per $1000 difference in family incomes. This value b does not represent how much on average an individual family expenditure will change for a $1000 change in family income. Only a time series regression b can yield that kind of information. Misguided decision making will result if an available cross-sectional regression b is employed when the unavailable time series regression b is needed.

15.11. Managerial Issues in Practice—Review Exercise I: M & M Industries (continued)

In Chapter 14 we used a simple linear regression model to study the relationship between the salary structure at M & M Industries and job point totals assessed by a consultant. A positive relationship was found, indicating that, on average, jobs with greater content (knowledge requirements, responsibility, and problem-solving ability) are more highly compensated. An estimate of the additional mean salary increment associated with an additional job point was obtained. However, analysis of residuals of the regression indicated substantial heteroskedasticity. At the higher salary levels, there appeared to be more overcompensation and undercompensation than at lower salaries. Part of what appeared to be undercompensation and overcompensation could be due to a misspecification of the form of the regression relationship. In this review exercise, we shall consider this possibility by fitting an alternative form to the data and noticing how the results change.

1. *Managerial Issue:* Could the *percentage* salary change be related to the *percentage* total point change? If so, a logarithmic transformation might improve the results.

Statistical Issue: Logarithmic Transformation for Reducing Heteroskedasticity

Suggested Procedure: Transform the original variables SALARY and TOTAL into log form and regress the *logarithm* of salary (LOGSAL) on the *logarithm* of total points (LOGTOT). We shall use natural logarithms, computed to the base $e = 2.718$. Compare the scatterplot of the original variables (Figure 14.26) to the scatterplot of the transformed variables in Figure 15.14; compare the regression results.

Comment: The scatterplot of LOGSAL vs. LOGTOT shows a more uniform scatter of observations from the lower range of the data to the upper range—a marked improvement in uniformity compared to the scatter plot exhibited by the original variables. The t value on the regression coefficients and the r^2 value show no loss in strength of significance nor explanatory power compared to the similar values of the original regression of salary and point total. Overall, therefore, the transformation has been a net improvement. See Figure 15.15.

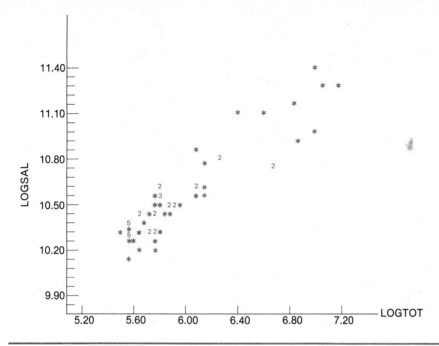

FIGURE 15.14 Scatterplot of LOGSAL vs. LOGTOT

```
THE REGRESSION EQUATION IS
Y =     7.11 + 0.578 X1


                                  ST. DEV.   T-RATIO =
          COLUMN     COEFFICIENT  OF COEF.   COEF/S.D.
          --           7.1067      0.1871     37.97
X1        LOGTOT       0.57832     0.03139    18.41


THE ST. DEV. OF Y ABOUT REGRESSION LINE IS
S = 0.1096
WITH (  64- 2) =  62 DEGREES OF FREEDOM


R-SQUARED = 84.5 PERCENT
R-SQUARED = 84.3 PERCENT, ADJUSTED FOR D.F.
```

FIGURE 15.15 Computer Output for Regression of LOGSAL on LOGTOT

2. *Managerial Issue:* Is the problem of non-constant residuals still in evidence?

Statistical Issue: Residual Adequacy

Suggested Procedure: Construct a scatter plot of the standardized residuals on the Y axis and the standardized predicted Y values on the X axis. See Figure 15.16.

Comment: The plot indicates the non-constant scatter problem of residuals (heteroskedasticity) has been lessened as compared to the situation shown in Figure 14.29 for the original variables but not completely eliminated. A few outlying residuals can still be found at the upper ranges of the data.

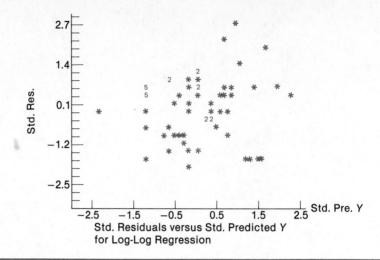

Std. Residuals versus Std. Predicted Y
for Log-Log Regression

FIGURE 15.16 Scatterplot of the Standardized Residuals

3. *Managerial Issue:* How is the regression equation to be used? Explain the meaning of the regression coefficient of LOGTOT. Discuss its statistical reliability. See Figure 15.15.

Statistical Issue: Interpretation of the Regression Equation and the Computed Coefficient of the Independent Variable

Comment: The regression coefficient of LOGTOT is over eighteen times larger than its standard error. This high value of t strongly suggests that the true value of the regression coefficient is highly unlikely to be zero. The regression coefficient value of .57 means that for each additional percentage point increase in total points, there is on average over a half percentage point increase in salary. The computed regression equation permits a prediction of salary given a value of LOGTOT. If, for example, a job is assigned a value of 950 total points, the point estimate of $\log \hat{Y}$ is

$$\widehat{\text{Log } Y} = \text{Log } A + b \text{ Log } X$$

Substituting we get

$$\widehat{\text{Log } Y} = 7.1067 + .5783 \text{ Log } (950)$$
$$= 7.1067 + .5783 (6.856)$$
$$= 7.1067 + 3.9651$$
$$\widehat{\text{Log } Y} = 11.0718$$
$$\hat{Y} = \$64{,}331$$

The actual salary (Y) for a job rated 950 points by the consultant is $69,420. This means an overcompensation of

$$Y - \hat{Y} = \$69{,}420 - \$64{,}331 = \$5089$$

given its job evaluation total and compared to other M & M management jobs.

The double log transformation has improved our fit of the regression relationship to the data as compared to the linear regression run on the original variables. This suggests that the additional salary associated with a one point addition to total job points is not constant. It is higher at higher levels of job point total. Moreover, the logarithmic regression indicates that the ratio of the mean *percentage* change in salary to mean *percentage* change in job point total is constant. Importantly, the logarithmic regression suggests that the overcompensation and undercompensation found at high salary levels in the original regression has diminished. This suggests that the original overcompensation and undercompensation estimates at these levels were too high, being partly attributable to the misspecified form of the regression relationship.

15.12. Managerial Issues in Practice— Review Exercise II: The Regression Phenomenon on Wall Street— Winners and Losers in the Corporate Profit Derby

Get-Rich-Quick schemes are commonplace on Wall Street. Most of them don't work. A clear understanding of the regression phenomenon helps avoid reading a lot into something when actually nothing is going on.

Many stock market investors, like racehorse handicappers, like to play the odds. Studying price movements and the earnings picture of numerous firms, these stock market devotees are on the lookout for corporations that are a good bet to yield consistently a high rate of return on their stockholders' equity—corporate thoroughbreds.

Is this year's track record on the rate of return on equity a good indicator that the earnings will also be superior several years in the future? In other words, is it good stock market savvy to bet that most of the corporate winners in a given year are the corporate thoroughbreds?

On the surface it might seem that these questions could be easily resolved by examining the rate of return picture of a comprehensive list of corporations between two time periods. However, this approach will encounter the pervasive regression phenomenon and, in particular, the fallacious interpretation it entices. To see how this can come about, let's organize the data in two different ways.

Table 15.3 describes the 1972 and 1978 earnings record of 492 corporations listed in the *Fortune 500* in both years. From Table 15.3, Table 15.4 has been prepared. The firms are grouped according to 1972 profits into six groups, with a column also showing the average profits that these groups earned in 1978.

Table 15.4 shows that the corporate winners of 1972, those corporations which made substantially above average earnings that year, on average lost ground in 1978 with respect to the 1978 average earnings rate for all firms. This tendency for earnings to regress toward the overall mean rate between 1972 and 1978 is seen in four of the six categories. Moreover, the spread between the mean earnings rate of the firms in the highest and lowest categories narrowed considerably (from $32.98 - 2.765 = 29.215\%$ in 1972 to $26.38 - 0.961 = 25.419\%$ in 1978). Taken together, do these findings imply a leveling-out process at work, eliminating the extremes and pushing corporations toward a middling earnings performance? This is what some people would firmly believe, interpreting Table 15.4 at face value.

TABLE 15.3. 1972 and 1978 Earnings of 492 *Fortune 500* Corporations

NET INCOME AS % OF STOCK-HOLDER EQUITY FOR 1978	less than 5	5 < 10	10 < 15	15 < 20	20 < 25	25 and more	NUMBER OF FIRMS	1972	1978
			NET INCOME AS % OF STOCKHOLDER EQUITY FOR 1972					MEAN NET INCOME AS % OF STOCK-HOLDERS EQUITY	
less than 5	23	11	0	0	0	0	34	7.597	−4.427
5 < 10	0	64	0	0	0	0	64	9.309	7.877
10 < 15	0	6	173	0	0	0	179	12.356	12.824
15 < 20	0	0	44	111	0	0	155	15.266	16.974
20 < 25	0	0	0	11	34	2	47	20.423	22.060
25 and over	0	0	0	0	0	13	13	28.254	32.069
NUMBER	23	81	217	122	34	15	492		
Mean net income as % of stockholders equity in 1972	2.765	7.906	12.761	16.86	21.609	32.980		13.738	
Mean net income as % of stockholders equity in 1978	0.961	8.122	13.23	17.238	20.118	26.380			13.686

TABLE 15.4. 492 of the *Fortune 500* Corporations Grouped According to 1972 Earnings

NUMBER OF CORPORATIONS	GROUP	1972 Average	Deviation from Overall 1972 Average	1978 Average	Deviation from Overall 1978 Average
		NET INCOME (AS PERCENT OF STOCKHOLDER EQUITY)			
23	1	2.765	−10.973	.961	−12.725
81	2	7.906	−5.832	8.122	−5.564
217	3	12.761	−0.977	13.230	−0.456
122	4	16.860	3.122	17.238	3.552
34	5	21.609	7.871	20.118	6.432
15	6	32.980	19.242	26.380	12.694
492	Overall Average 13.738			13.686	

Surprisingly, quite a different picture emerges from the figures in Table 15.5. This table again assigns the same corporations into six groups, but now according to their 1978 earnings.

TABLE 15.5. 492 of the *Fortune 500* Corporations Grouped According to 1978 Earnings

NUMBER OF CORPORATIONS	GROUP	NET INCOME (AS PERCENT OF STOCKHOLDER EQUITY)			
		1978 Average	Deviation from Overall 1978 Average	1972 Average	Deviation from Overall 1972 Average
34	1	−4.427	−18.113	7.597	−6.141
64	2	7.877	−5.859	9.309	−4.429
179	3	12.824	−0.862	12.356	−1.382
155	4	16.974	3.288	15.266	1.528
47	5	22.060	8.374	20.923	7.185
13	6	32.069	18.383	28.254	14.516
492	Overall Average	13.686		13.738	

Table 15.5 allows us to look back from 1978 to see where the high and low performers have come from in 1972. This table shows that in five of the six categories, the 1978 mean earnings performance of corporations was farther (but in the same direction) from the overall mean earnings rate than in 1972. The above-average performers in 1978 have, on average, *improved* their performance compared to their 1972 performance. The below-average performers in 1978 appear to have fared *even worse* in 1978 than they did in 1972. This widening disparity of performance between the best performers and the poorest performers could suggest to some analysts, first, an eventual shake-out of the Fortune 500 firms with the less profitable firms falling out and, second, perhaps a good stock market strategy may be to consistently buy the stocks which are currently star performers.

The unsettling question is: Why does the 1978 earnings performance

1. seem to converge toward a middle, mediocre performance compared to the 1972 dispersion if the data are grouped one way and
2. diverge further in performance in 1978 as compared to their 1972 standing when the data are grouped another way?

The answer, of course, lies with the regression phenomenon. On closer inspection, the numbers show most of the corporations in both years have earnings which are near the average level. Taking a count, we find that 234 of the 492 corporations in both years fall either into the group which includes the average performers, or the next nearest group. But who are the firms at the extremes? They consist of two types. First, firms which generally tend to have earnings performance near the average will, in any one year, have an unusually good or bad year and be off at one of the extremes. Then, of the few corporations which *consistently* tend to be at an extreme, most will be at an extreme in any one year. Thus, when we look at the extreme corporations in a given year, we expect to find a mixture of

1. those which are *generally* in the extreme group and can be expected to stay there, and

2. those which are *not* generally at the extreme and can be expected to return towards the center of the earnings performance distribution

The to and fro movement of these latter firms—some back to their norm from the extremes, others away from their norm towards the extreme—causes the membership of the extreme groups to be constantly shifting from year to year. But since each of the tables just discussed monitors the performance of the *same* group of firms over two periods, the tables *cannot* be monitoring the entire membership of the extreme groups. Why? Because the extreme groups do not contain the same firms from period to period; their membership changes. Assertions that the *extreme groups* are, *as a whole*, disappearing into the middle, as one table suggests, or *as a whole* becoming more separated groups, as the other table suggests, are *regression fallacies* which completely overlook the fact that the year-to-year membership of the extreme groups is not constant.

15.13. Managerial Issues in Practice—Review Exercise III: Checkpoint Problem on the Regression Phenomenon

The Richard Keller Brewing Company regularly monitors consumer reaction to its Big Sky brand of beer by means of a consumer panel of beer drinkers. Recently the Keller Company asked the research firm sponsoring the panel to study consumption trends across the range of Big Sky drinkers from light users to heavy users. The research firm was told to compare the latest period beer consumption with the beer consumption one year ago for each Big Sky drinker in the period. The findings of the panel study reveal some interesting trends.

Upward Trend in Heavy User Consumption Cited by Marketing Manager

Individuals in the panel consuming 30 gallons per year or more of Big Sky beer were described as *heavy users* of the Big Sky Brand. The marketing manager was particularly interested in consumption trends which might develop among the *regular heavy users* of Big Sky beer. Because of their frequent purchases, he felt the impact of any significant attitude changes affecting consumption would likely show up first among the heavy users. Thus, the marketing manager was elated to learn that the panel members currently identified as heavy users of Big Sky showed a dramatic increase in consumption from the previous year. He felt this signaled a favorable attitude change that would eventually lead moderate Big Sky users and even non-users to shift more of their purchases to the Big Sky brand.

The elation of the marketing manager over the results in the panel's heavy user category was only slightly dampened by the fact that current light users (10 gallons per year or less) of the Big Sky brand had decreased consumption from the previous year. "Naturally, we'd like to be popular with everyone," he said, "but it's our position in the heavy-user segment that really counts."

Downward Trend in Heavy User Consumption Cited by Ad Agency

Keller's Marketing Vice President was quite pleased with the report given her by the marketing manager until she attended a meeting with representatives of a reputable ad agency soliciting the Keller account. At this meeting the agency representatives argued that the Big Sky brand was facing *declining* customer loyalty and that a switch to their ad agency should be given serious consideration. As evidence of the loyalty problem, the ad agency cited the same consumer panel used by Keller. Identifying last year's heavy-users of Big Sky and observing their consumption this year, the ad agency pointed out that a dramatic decline in consumption had taken place. A consumption increase had occurred in last year's light-user group, but the ad agency, like the Marketing Manager, believed changes in the heavy-user group were much more important.

The Marketing Vice President was thoroughly perplexed by the conflicting reports. How could her Marketing Manager and the ad agency seemingly reach contradictory conclusions from the same consumer panel evidence about trends among heavy Big Sky users? She thought that either the Marketing Manager or the ad agency or both erred in citing the findings of the consumer panel study. But the research firm which did the study confirmed that both findings cited were correct.

Having eliminated that possibility, the Marketing Vice President pursued another course. She asked the research firm for three additional research items:

a scatter diagram showing both 1981 and 1982 consumption for each panel member. From the scatter diagram the marketing manager could obtain a visual impression of the strength and direction of the relationship between the panel member's consumption in the two years.

the least squares regression equation used by the marketing manager in drawing his conclusion of an upward trend in heavy user consumption. The regression equation shows the previous year's consumption as the dependent variable and the current year consumption level as the independent variable: $\hat{P} = 15 + 0.25C$, where C is an individual panel member's current year consumption (in gallons) of Big Sky beer, and $\hat{P}$ is the regression line (see Figure 15.17) estimate of an individual panel member's previous year's consumption (in gallons) associated with the value C for the member's current year consumption. The $\hat{P}$ value is also the equation's prediction of the average consumption of the previous year for panel members consuming C gallons this year. For example, panel members consuming 24 gallons this year are estimated to have averaged only 21 gallons the previous year, an increase of three gallons this year over last year.

the regression (shown in Figure 15.17) used by the ad agency in drawing its conclusion of a downward trend in heavy user consumption. This line had the following equation: $\hat{C} = 15 + .25P$, where P is an individual's previous year's consumption (in gallons), and $\hat{C}$ is the regression line estimate of current year consumption for the same individual. The $\hat{C}$ value is also the equation's prediction of the average consumption of the current year for panel members consuming P gallons last year.

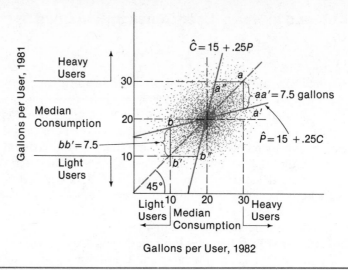

FIGURE 15.17 Comparison of 1981 and 1982 Consumption of Big Sky Brand Beer for all Panel Members

Let us first assume that the long run consumption pattern of Big Sky users is stable in the sense that the average consumption level of individual users shows no upward or downward trend. Any changes observed in a panel member's consumption between the two years reflects only random variation. Let us refer to the stable value of an individual's long run average Big Sky consumption level as that person's "regular" consumption level. If unchanged and observable, it would show up in Figure 15.17 for an individual as a point on a 45° line from the origin. Since the regular (long run average) consumption value is not observable for an individual (the data are only yearly), the 45° line connecting the regular consumption levels of the different panel members is shown as a dashed line.

Can this unobservable dashed line be derived using least squares regression analysis? If a least squares regression was run using data on long run average consumption levels, the computed regression line would closely approximate the dashed 45° line shown in Figure 15.17. However, these data are not available. So, can least squares regression lines constructed from data on yearly actual consumption reflect the line relating "regular" (long run average) consumption for the two years?

The marketing manager thought so. He regressed current year consumption on previous year consumption, thinking the resulting regression line would be the appropriate one to use. The marketing manager was wrong. As can be seen in Figure 15.17, this gives biased estimates of the relationship between regular (long run average) consumption of panel members for the two years. The computed slope coefficient is biased downward and the computed intercept term is biased upwards.

The ad agency also thought its regression equation would be appropriate but it was wrong, too. It reversed the two variables, regressing current year consumption on previous year consumption. This reversal changed the direction of the bias but did not eliminate it.

Since long run consumption patterns are stable, the line relating "regular" (long run average) consumption for an individual for two different years is a 45° line. Both regression lines computed from short term annual data are tilted. The tilt is in different directions, so their bias is opposite in direction, but they are both biased. Why do the two computed regression equations fail to give a 45° line from the origin as is necessary in this case if they are to be used as valid estimates of trends in regular (long run average) consumption patterns? The answer is the regression phenomenon, which leads to a biased line, predictable in direction depending upon which way the regression is run.

Conclusion: What should be done to obtain a correct view of the heavy user consumption pattern? The correct approach to isolate consumption changes for the heavy users is to compare the mean consumption of all heavy users in the panel in 1981 with the mean of all heavy users in the panel in 1982. If similar mean values are found, no change has taken place in the heavy user consumption profile on the whole, whereas individual members of the heavy user group will show different short term year to year consumption amounts. The crucial statistic is the average of these individuals collectively. Tracing by regression the consumption of the individuals from year to year will only trace the short term movement and produce the regression phenomenon with its interpretive pitfalls.

15.14. Concluding Comments

The simple linear regression model discussed in Chapter 14 is a valuable tool in the analysis of bivariate data. However, the tool must be used with great care and an understanding of its limitations. Modifications may be required in the case of a curvilinear relationship. However, if the curvature is not great over the range of observed data, a linear approximation of the true relationship may perform well. Yet, we must be careful not to extrapolate the computed regression line to areas where the true regression line is highly curvilinear.

If a dependent variable is causally related to the independent variable, yet values of the latter variable are unattainable, prediction of the dependent variable values may still be feasible. A surrogate variable for which data are available may be substituted as the independent variable.

If a "nuisance" variable threatens to obscure the values of the regression coefficient in simple regression, multiple regression is required (Chapter 16).

If data are restricted to a truncated segment of a bivariate distribution, a computed regression equation will not generalize to the entire distribution.

Misunderstanding of the regression phenomenon is pervasive, leading to contradictory and fallacious statements about the same set of data. The phenomenon is quite real and is encountered in both time series and cross-sectional data. The regression "fallacies" refer to incorrect statements pertaining to the regression coefficient. The source of the fallacy usually lies in a limited understanding of the impact of the shifting composition of groups, particularly groups located at the extremes of the distribution.

Footnotes and References

[1] *Wall Street Journal*, Wednesday, July 11, 1979.
[2] Of course, if the value of Z is a constant and not a random variable, then division
    by Z does not induce correlation artificially.

[3]Milton Friedman, *A Theory of the Consumption Function*, National Bureau of Economic Research, 1957.
[4]If the true slope is less than one, the regression phenomenon will still exist; it will exaggerate the under and over spending patterns of the two extreme groups.

Questions and Problems

1. Suppose the true regression relationship has a positive-valued Y intercept. Does finding that the estimated regression equation also has a positive intercept guarantee that the estimated regression will be useful in predicting the dependent variable value? Comment.

2. Let's suppose you want to develop an equation predicting how much a household will spend on fast food purchases. You think the expenditures will depend on how much the household actually earns. Can you rely on using what people *say* they earn as the independent variable, recognizing that what they earn is not necessarily what they say they earn? Explain. (Hint: Refer to the discussion in Section 15.4.)

3. Without a scatter diagram there would be no way to check on the curvilinearity of the relationship. Comment.

4. The equation for a straight line can be viewed as a special case of a parabola in which the coefficient of the X^2 is zero. Does this imply that nearly all regressions are curvilinear? Explain.

5. A scatter diagram of the regression residuals plotted against the independent variable provides a visual way to check for curvilinearity. What would you look for in such a scatter diagram?

6. The truncated distribution trap is associated with a violation of the basic regression model assumptions. Explain.

7. The computed regression line in Example No. 15.8B (Sour-Faced Salespersons) gives a misleading impression of the relationship between sales and personality for the kind of salespersons the company actually hires. Comment.

8. Assume that the true regression line in Example No. 15.8B (Sour-Faced Salespersons) is positively sloped as shown. The computed regression line has a negative slope. What does this suggest about the company's hiring and retention policies?

9. Is it ever appropriate to force a regression line through the origin? Explain.

10. If two variables are both divided by a third variable, is correlation always induced between the two ratios which result? Explain.

11. It is discovered that the correlation found between two variables is artificially induced by dividing both variables by the same third variable. How can this be corrected? What is the most probable reason this was not handled in this way previously?

12. In Example 15.3 (How Heavy Are Persons of Zero Height?) it was noted that *a priori* knowledge that the true relationship between height and weight must go through the origin was not relevant in deciding whether to use the computed regression which had a positive valued Y intercept term. Does this imply that *a priori* information about values for the true relationship can always be safely disregarded if the values lie outside the range of the observed data? Explain.

13. In Section 15.4 the hazards of extrapolating a linear regression line beyond the range of observed data were pointed out. Can you think of any situation in which you might want to extrapolate a regression relationship beyond the range of observed data even though you know it is potentially hazardous? Explain.

14. In Example 15.5B (Negative Spending at the Supermarket), the negative intercept obtained for the computed regression equation proved not to be of concern even though it was known that the intercept for the true relationship could not be negative.

Does this suggest or imply that a value for the intercept term in the computed regression equation which is the opposite in sign from that which is expected is not generally a cause for concern? Explain.

15. *The Experience Curve* A key strategic planning tool is the "experience curve". The name refers to a graph that shows average unit cost on the vertical axis and cumulative production on the horizontal axis. The curve indicates that manufacturing costs fall as experience is gained producing the product. A sharply falling curve has a special significance for planning purposes. The steep slope suggests that it is critical to be the first firm to enter a market. The advantage gained over later entrants is lower cost by virtue of greater accumulated experience. Potentially, this gives the first entrant the ability to profitably price its products below the cost of would-be rivals, thereby ensuring itself a dominant market position. The data in Table 15.6 present cost figures and accumulated experience for polyethylene.

TABLE 15.6. Changes in Unit Cost Due to Accumulated Experience

UNIT COST ($/lb.)	CUMULATIVE PRODUCTION (Millions of lbs.)
$.58	260
.50	400
.46	600
.43	1000
.39	1700
.33	2200
.31	3300
.30	4500
.29	5800
.25	7200
.23	9300
.18	20,000
.15	25,000

a. Estimate the equation for the experience curve using a double-log regression.
b. On average, what would be the impact on unit cost if cumulative production is doubled?

16. *Salesperson Burn-Out* Salespersons assigned to the same territory for a long period of time are sometimes thought to experience "burn-out," a decline in their productivity. A company has compiled the data in Table 15.7 for its sales force.

TABLE 15.7. Comparison of Sales and Time Spent in the Same Territory

SALESPERSON	SALES	YEARS IN SAME TERRITORY
1	$195 thous.	1.1
2	402	4.4
3	473	3.6
4	102	.8
5	298	4.5
6	237	1.5
7	265	1.4
8	263	5.5
9	345	2.2
10	533	3.0

a. Fit a parabolic regression equation to the data with sales as Y and years as X.
b. Assuming the territories have equal potential, what does the equation suggest about the burn-out hypothesis?
c. What recommendations might you suggest for management consideration in view of your findings?

17. *Measuring Price Elasticity for Rayon* A large manufacturer of rayon fiber wanted to know how rayon fiber consumption was influenced by changes in the price of rayon relative to its chief alternative, cotton fiber. A double-log regression was run in which Y, the annual consumption per capita of rayon fiber (in pounds) is regressed on P, the ratio of rayon fiber price to cotton fiber price. The resulting equation was:

$$\widehat{\text{Log } Y} = 2.315 - 1.150 \text{ Log } P$$

a. What would be the estimated impact on rayon fiber consumption of a 2 percent increase in rayon fiber price with cotton fiber price remaining unchanged?
b. What would be the estimated impact on rayon fiber consumption if rayon fiber price were to decrease by 19 percent while cotton fiber price declined only 5 percent?
c. What is the estimated price elasticity of

rayon fiber consumption with respect to the ratio of rayon fiber price to cotton fiber price?

d. Would the fact that this equation was estimated from the time series data rather than cross-sectional data have any bearing on the usefulness in estimating consumption response to price changes? Explain.

18. *Price Elasticity of X-Ray Film* A study of the sales response of X-Ray film Y to price changes P measured across 26 sales territories led to the following equation:

$$\widehat{\text{Log } Y} = 17.527 - 2.645 \text{ Log } P$$

a. What is the price elasticity estimate from the equation?

b. What bearing, if any, would the cross-sectional nature of the data have on your interpretation of the usefulness of the estimate? (Hint: see comment following Example 15.10.)

19. *Measuring Price Elasticity by Experimentation* The price elasticity of sour cherry preserves was estimated at -5 from a double-log regression equation. The data were collected by a formal experimental design that rotated different prices for the product among cooperating stores in a number of different trading areas. What do you see as likely advantages and disadvantages of estimating the price elasticity from controlled pricing experiments as compared to estimates obtained from:

a. an observational study based on cross-sectional data? Hint: range of X (prices)

b. an observational study based on time-series data? Hint: serial correlation

20. *The Phillips Curve* In the late 1950s A.W. Phillips published a paper linking the inflation rate and the unemployment rate. The paper suggested that there is a trade-off between inflation and unemployment which is defined by a simple curvilinear relationship. In other words, low employment would be "bought" at the price of high inflation. Using the annual data in Table 15.8 on the various unemployment rates U, and the rate of inflation P (the

TABLE 15.8. Unemployment and Inflation Rates

YEAR	OVERALL UNEMPLOYMENT RATE (Percentage)	UNEMPLOYMENT RATE (Percentage) White	Black	P, INFLATION RATE (Percentage)
1956	4.1			1.5
1957	4.3			3.6
1958	6.8	6.1	12.6	2.7
1959	5.5	4.8	10.7	.8
1960	5.5	4.9	10.2	1.6
1961	6.7	6.0	12.4	1.0
1962	5.5	4.9	10.9	1.1
1963	5.7	5.0	10.8	1.2
1964	5.2	4.6	9.6	1.3
1965	4.5	4.1	8.1	2.7
1966	3.8	3.4	7.3	2.9
1967	3.8	3.4	7.4	2.9
1968	3.6	3.2	6.7	4.2
1969	3.5	3.1	6.4	5.4
1970	4.9	4.5	8.2	5.9
1971	5.9	5.4	9.9	4.3
1972	5.6	5.0	10.0	3.3
1973	4.9	4.3	8.9	6.2
1974	5.6	5.0	9.9	11.0
1975	8.5			9.1

Source: U.S. Government Printing Office. *Economic Report of the President,* 1975 and 1976

annual percentage change in the consumer price index from December to December), fit a Phillips curve of the form:

$$\widehat{\text{Log } P_t} = a + b \text{ Log } U_t$$

Consider only the data for the overall employment rate and the inflation rate.

a. How good a fit (R^2) does the double log regression equation give?

b. Interpret the regression coefficient b.

c. How would you test the claim that the curve shifted down with President Nixon's mandatory price and wage controls in 1971?

d. Do any of the following alternative specifications provide a better R^2 fit?

1. $\hat{P}_t = a + b\,(1/U_t)$
2. $\hat{P}_t = a + b\,(1/U_t^2)$
3. $\hat{P}_t = a + b\,(1/U_t) + c(1/U_t^2)$

e. Draw in a free hand curve to "best" fit the data. What conclusion can be plausibly drawn from this sketch?

21. Consider the data for the unemployment rate (white, black) and the inflation rate in Problem 20.

a. Find the goodness of fit R^2 for the double log regression equation for a "white" Phillips curve and a "black" Phillips curve.

b. What comparative conclusions can be drawn from the fit of the two curves and the interpretation of b in the two regression equations?

22. *Worker Fatigue and Job Safety* Many companies sponsor job-related safety programs in order to reduce accidents on the job. Suppose it is hypothesized that serious accidents become more likely near the end of the workday when workers are fatigued rather than near the beginning of the day. A curvilinear model is proposed to investigate the fatigue hypothesis. Accident reports over the past year are sampled, and the number of hours the employee had worked before the accident occurred (X) and the number of days lost from work (Y) are recorded. A total of eighty accident reports are examined. The fitted regression equation is:

$$\hat{Y} = 12.5 + .23X - .0035X^2.$$
$$R^2 = .044$$

a. Use the regression equation to predict the number of days lost from work for an employee who has an accident after seven hours of work.

b. Does the low value of R^2 necessarily mean that no fatigue factor exists? Explain.

23. *Forecasting New Product Adoptions* Consumer panels are often used in developing early forecasts from test markets of long-run market penetration and sales for a new product. After establishing the panel in the test markets, the new product is introduced to those markets. The percentage of panel members buying the product for the first time is recorded at periodic intervals. The relationship is then established between the percentage of the market having bought the product and the length of time since the product was launched. This relationship is extrapolated into the future to estimate the eventual level of market penetration. Hypothetical data for a new breakfast cereal are given in Table 15.9.

TABLE 15.9. Hypothetical Data for a New Breakfast Cereal

Y	X
CUMULATIVE PERCENTAGE OF CEREAL BUYERS BUYING THE NEW PRODUCT FOR THE FIRST TIME	NUMBER OF WEEKS SINCE PRODUCT WAS LAUNCHED
7.0	2
14.1	4
18.2	6
21.2	8
23.5	10
25.4	12
27.0	14
27.8	16

a. Draw a scatter diagram of the data.

b. Does the relationship appear to be linear or curvilinear?

c. Estimate the regression equation using the form which gives the best fit to the data.

d. Assume that market penetration will eventually level off; estimate this ultimate level by extrapolating the regression line you computed in Part c.

e. How hazardous do you think the extrapolation in Part d is? Explain.

24. *Forecasting New Product Repeat Purchases* When a new consumer food product is introduced, getting customers to try the product is the most immediate hurdle a marketing manager faces. In the long run, however, gaining repeat sales from customers who do try the product is equally important. By monitoring the repeat purchase rate of consumer panel members in test market cities, early indications are gained of the product's likelihood of success. Suppose recent purchases for a new breakfast cereal are as given in Table 15.10.

TABLE 15.10. Hypothetical Data for Cereal Repeat Purchases

Y REPEAT PURCHASES OF NEW CEREAL AS PERCENTAGE OF ALL PURCHASES OF CEREAL AFTER FIRST TRIAL	X NUMBER OF WEEKS SINCE FIRST PURCHASE OF NEW CEREAL
18.2	2
16.7	4
15.6	6
14.8	8
14.1	10
13.6	12
13.1	14
12.7	16

---

a. Draw a scatter diagram of the data.
b. Does the relationship appear to be linear or non-linear?
c. Estimate the regression equation using the form which gives the best fit to the data.
d. Assume the repeat purchase rate will eventually stabilize; estimate this ultimate repeat purchase rate by extrapolating the regression line you computed in Part c.
e. How hazardous do you think the extrapolation in Part d is? Explain.

25. *Forecasting New Product Market Share* The basic model for forecasting new product market share from early consumer panel data relies on extrapolations of market penetration and the repeat purchase rate:

$$\text{Market Share} = (\text{Market Penetration}) \text{ times } (\text{Repeat Purchase Rate})$$

a. Using extrapolation find the ultimate market penetration from Problem 23 and the ultimate purchase rate from Problem 24. Forecast the ultimate market share of the new cereal discussed in those problems.
b. What would you expect to be the major source of errors encountered in using this model to forecast new product sales?

26. *Engine-less Gas Guzzlers?* A simple linear regression of average gasoline consumption on vehicle horsepower yields an intercept of 35 gallons per thousand miles and a slope coefficient of .225 gallons (per thousand miles) per horsepower. Autos tested ranged in horsepower from a low of 90 to a high of 250. The value of r^2 was found to be .80. However, a critic argues that the intercept of 35 gallons per thousand miles "doesn't make any sense because autos with zero horsepower don't consume any gasoline. If the regression could be made to go through the origin, the resulting equation would be useful." Comment.

27. *Artificially Induced Correlation?* In Problem 26 the effect of an automobile's weight on gasoline consumption has been ignored. It seems almost certain that the weight of an automobile would affect gasoline consumption. To account for this, a new regression is run expressing consumption as "gallons per thousand miles per pound of automobile" and horsepower is expressed as "horsepower per pound". Does this technique artificially inflate the correlation, or is it a legitimate, in fact, a rather clever way to deal with the weight factor? Explain.

28. *Poorer Performance from Smarter Diemakers?* A study of a corporation's tool and die workers reveals a highly significant negative correlation between the score on an intelligence test and the performance on the job. The industrial relations director

examines the results and concludes that "more intelligent persons are apparently bored with tool and die work, so we would be wise to encourage persons of lesser intelligence to apply for tool and die jobs." Three statements about the conclusion are given below:

a. the conclusion is apparently correct.

b. because the sample data is based upon a truncated segment of the population distribution, inferences concerning the population are unwarranted.

c. the advice is correct, but we cannot conclude that the lower performance of persons of higher intelligence is caused by boredom.

Which of the three statements is most appropriate? Explain.

29. *Smart Students Are Lazy—Or Are They?* A study of Air Force enlisted men reveals a significant negative correlation between the score on Armed Forces Qualification (AFQT) Tests and the rank in class in electronics schools. The study concludes: "to get better students in our electronic schools, we should take persons with lower AFQT scores." Comment on this statement using your understanding of the truncated distribution trap.

30. *Estimating the Vulnerability of a New Product to an Economic Recession* The Purity Diaper Division of Eagle Products Company had introduced a disposable diaper which sold well among higher income households. However, disposable diapers are a luxury good and the marketing staff was concerned about possible sales dropoff during a recession which had been predicted. Since the product was new, historical data on sensitivity to income fluctuations were not available; consequently, a cross-sectional survey was conducted. Although the survey did show that expenditure on disposable diapers was related to income, it appeared that only a large income decline would bring about any sizeable cutback in expenditure. Much to the dismay of management, when the rather

mild recession did take place, the bottom fell out of the disposable diaper market.

Explain the effect of the regression phenomenon on the measurement of the sensitivity of disposable diaper expenditures to income changes.

31. *Mutual Fund Performance "For a Winning Mutual Fund, Check the Past?"* (*Chicago Tribune*, June 11, 1979)—One of the most popular ways for individual investors, large and small, to obtain a diversified portfolio of stocks with the guidance of professional investment management is to buy shares of a mutual fund. But which of the hundreds of such funds open to the public will consistently yield a superior rate of return over a long period? A *Chicago Tribune* financial writer examined the problem with the help of data supplied by Lipper Analytical Distributors. a New York firm which monitors the returns performance of over 480 mutual funds. The writer drew this conclusion from the performances in Table 15.11: "One way not to pick a winning fund is to select one which has been among the top 10 in performance for several years."

A detailed look at the annual performance of mutual funds between successive years is shown in Table 15.12.

a. In what way does this table confirm or refute the conclusion made by the financial writer from the performance table (Table 15.10) previously excerpted from Lipper?

b. Can any additional insight be added to this statement from the 1977–1978 table (Table 15.12) presented below?

c. What additional analysis could be performed on the original data to get an interpretation quite different from those made in Part b?

32. *The Polaroid Corporation: Early Estimates of Retail Sales* (This problem is adapted from a Harvard Business School Case Study.) The Polaroid Corporation had been experiencing difficulties in obtaining accurate and timely estimates of sales to consumers by its retail dealers. There seemed to be about a two-month lag, on the average, between dealer sales and the time

TABLE 15.11. How 1969–1974 Top Mutual Funds Performed in 1974–1979

FUND	RANK	PERCENT CHANGE, 3/31/69–3/31/74*	RANK	PERCENT CHANGE, 3/31/74–3/31/79*
International Investors	1	+307.61	421	−29.31
Templeton Growth	2	+116.70	19	+154.44
Canadian Fund	3	+55.38	395	+10.30
Founders Special	4	+54.82	171	+51.41
Transatlantic Fund	5	+49.66	157	+55.47
American Insurance & Industries	6	+41.85	142	+59.58
Putnam Investors	7	+37.37	277	+35.53
Chemical Fund	8	+35.64	294	+10.85
Investors Selective	9	+33.84	202	+47.29
Wade Fund	10	+20.54	378	+16.87

*Cumulative rate of return
Source: Lipper Analytical Distributors, New York

these sales were reflected in Polaroid shipments to its dealers. Polaroid executives felt that by the time they learned about changes in sales by their dealers, it was often too late to avoid many production and marketing problems brought about by the changes.

To more closely monitor dollar sales, Polaroid implemented a dealer panel consisting of more than three hundred dealers who furnished accurate and rapid information on their sales. It was felt that by monitoring sales of this dealer panel, changing sales trends at the retail level would be quickly apparent.

The dealers in the panel were classified into one of four size categories based upon the volume of their Polaroid sales. In reviewing the panel after one year, it was noticed that more than a third of the panel dealers in the lowest sales category had shifted to the next higher category. This disturbed some executives, because the total number of dealers in the lowest category had remained quite stable. Did this mean the panel members were somehow unrepresentative of the total dealer group?

a. Explain how the regression phenomenon pertains to the upward shift in categories of so many panel members initially in the bottom category.

b. Explain why the regression phenomenon would not necessarily cause a downward shift in categories of very many panel members initially in the top category. (Hint: Consider the dispersion of panel member sales in the top category as compared to the bottom category.)

c. The mean percentage increase in sales over the year was substantially larger for

TABLE 15.12. Annual Performance of Mutual Funds, 1977–1978

1977 RETURNS	1978 RETURNS				FUNDS	MEAN 1977	MEAN 1978
	−10% to 0%	0% to 10%	10% to 20%	20% to 30%			
−20% to −10%	0	7	1	0	8	−11.22%	7.75%
−10% to 0%	3	83	35	5	126	−4.39%	8.27%
0% to 10%	1	28	28	9	66	3.66%	11.84%
10% to 20%	0	3	12	10	25	15.07%	18.02%
20% to 30%	0	0	2	6	8	24.83%	21.86%

Source: Weisenberger Investment Company Service

the panel members than for all the dealers. Could the regression phenomenon account for this difference? Explain.

33. *Gasoline Consumption and Engine Size* An automobile manufacturer wants to express the gas mileage ratings Y of automobiles as a function of their engine size X. A sample of fifty automobiles of varying engine sizes is selected and the miles per gallon rating of each is determined. A quadratic regression model is proposed and the fitted regression equation is:

$$\hat{Y} = 43.1 - 8.3X - 0.18X^2$$

where the size X of the engine is measured in hundreds of cubic inches. Other relevant statistics are:

$$S_{b_2} = .0032 \text{ and } R^2 = .91$$

a. Sketch the regression curve (between $X = 1$ and $X = 4$).
b. Is there evidence that the quadratic term in the model improves the prediction of the miles per gallon rating Y? Use the .05 level of significance.
c. Use the model to estimate the mean miles per gallon rating for all cars with 300 cubic inch engines ($X = 3.0$).
d. Suppose a 95% confidence interval for the quantity estimated in Part c is (19.2, 20.4). Interpret this interval.
e. Suppose you purchase an automobile with a 300 cubic inch engine and determine that the miles per gallon rating is 16.4. Is the fact that this value lies below the confidence interval given in Part d surprising? Explain.

34. *Estimating the Behavior of Shipping Cost* A. P. Hughes was physical distribution manager at CC Pharmaceutical Company, a newly formed but rapidly expanding supplier of products to medical laboratories. Hughes became concerned about the cost of shipping the company's main product line, diagnostic preparations. The firm assigns each product a shipping cost based on the ratio (over all its products) of shipping cost to manufacturing cost. Little effort has been made to learn how shipping cost depends on the number of units shipped, weight, packaging, and its classification as regular or emergency shipment.

Based upon experience at an established drug firm, Hughes believes that there are economies of scale in shipping. Consequently, the cost curve for shipping ought to appear non-linear, flattening out at a higher volume of output shipped. Hughes has the assistant manager conduct an investigation. It is found that over the last 24 monthly periods the cost function can be well estimated by a linear regression equation. But it has an intercept term which is unrealistically high as an estimate for the fixed cost of the shipping department. Statistical testing of the intercept term shows it to be significantly different from zero (the intercept term is several times larger than its standard error). The assistant manager, having had a course in statistics, assures Hughes that they can proceed to use the linear model and need not be concerned about an unrealistically high positive intercept term regardless of its significance. The assistant points out that the firm is not going to be shipping at low volumes anyway (around the intercept term), but rather it is expanding its volume.
a. Do you agree with the assistant manager's conclusion that the large positive intercept is not important in determining the validity of the model?
b. Should Hughes abandon the view that the cost function should have a non-linear shape? Should they use the linear curve estimated?

Multiple Regression

Preview. In Chapter Fourteen, for purposes of prediction and planning and control a dependent variable was linked to one independent variable by a regression equation. For example, returns of a security were linked to general market returns, delivery labor time usage was linked to delivery distance. Sometimes this approach is inadequate. Frequently more than one independent variable has to be linked to the dependent variable to improve the accuracy of prediction of Y. In the case of planning and control, the *multiple regression equation* allows each independent variable to demonstrate its separate contribution to the value of Y. Assuming the regression model assumptions are met, the use of independent variables, say X_1 and X_2, will permit us to answer such questions as "what will happen to Y if there is a 3 unit increase in X_1 and simultaneously a 2 unit decrease in X_2?"

In dealing with a multiple regression equation, an important issue is the correlation between the several independent variables. For the prediction of Y, the correlation between the independent variables is irrelevant since the concern is with the regression equation as a whole, not individual effects of selected independent variables. If the separate effect of individual variables is desired, high correlation seriously affects the reliability of the estimates.

For example, suppose that the sale of expensive jewelry is the dependent variable, and the price of gold and the price of silver are the two independent variables. In addition, suppose manufacturers want to predict the overall volume of jewelry sales and there is a high correlation between the price level of gold and the price level of silver. The high correlation would not affect the prediction of Y. The regression equation, as a unit, integrates the effect of prices in predicting Y. But if the manufacturer wishes to quantify the separate impact of gold prices versus silver prices on the value of Y, then the focus will be on the quality of the regression equation's estimates, b_1 and b_2. The values b_1 and b_2 will likely be unreliable figures in this case. This problem can be ameliorated by alternative specification of the independent variables or additional data.

16.1. The Multiple Regression Model

The advent of the computer opened the door to the exploration of business issues by means of multiple regression. Let us examine some business examples where the multiple regression estimate becomes important:

> GM wants to estimate the equation linking the sales of diesel cars and two key determinants of sales, the price of the car and the consumer's personal income.

> Strategic Planning Institute in Boston will distribute to its corporate members the equation estimating the relation between the level of executive compensation and the characteristics of firms, such as the size of the company's assets, the company's sales growth rate over the past five years, and the company's average return on equity over the past three years.

> Price Waterhouse's management consultant division is called on to evaluate the firm's cost accounting regression equation that links the company's operating costs, its level of output, and its mix of product lines.

In each of these situations, the multiple regression equation stems from a set of assumptions concerning the underlying regression model. The nature of these assumptions will now be set out.

The Basic Equation

A linear regression model extended to include more than one independent variable is called a multiple linear regression model. In the general case, for K independent variables, $X_1, \ldots, X_k$, the basic equation expressing the multiple regression model is:

$$Y = \alpha + \beta_1 X_1 + \beta_2 X_2 \ldots \beta_k X_k + \epsilon$$

The expression shows the dependent variable Y written as a function of the independent variables $X_1, X_2, \ldots, X_k$ and the random error term ϵ. The α and β terms are the linear regression parameters or coefficients.

For simplicity of exposition, our discussion in this chapter will deal with two independent variables only. That is:

$$Y = \alpha + \beta_1 X_1 + \beta_2 X_2 + \epsilon$$

Importantly, the conclusions reached for the two independent variable case can be generalized.

Assumptions About the Error Term, ϵ

The conditions assumed about the distribution of the term ϵ for the multiple regression model are identical to those assumed for the simple regression model.

1. The expected value of ϵ must be zero.

2. Successive values of ϵ must be independent.

3. The variance of ϵ values must be constant and not depend on the values of the independent variables; that is, $\sigma_\epsilon^2 = $ constant.

4. The distribution of ϵ is normal.

Population Scatter Diagram

In the two independent variable case, each observation will have a value for variables Y, X_1, and X_2. Graphing the entire population of observations produces a three dimensional scatter cloud as shown by the dotted outline in Figure 16.1.

The Population Regression Plane

For any particular pair of X_1X_2 values there are a host of different Y values. The large dashed arrow in Figure 16.1 shows the many Y values in the scatter cloud associated with $X_1 = 9$ and $X_2 = 7$. In the population, there is an *average relationship* between Y and the independent variables over the relevant range of X_1 and X_2. It defines a plane in which each point on the plane is a mean of Y at a particular X_1X_2 coordinate. The mean of Y is expressed by the relationship:[1]

$$\mu_{Y.12} = \alpha + \beta_1X_1 + \beta_2X_2$$

In other words, the *entire set of mean values* $\mu_{Y.12}$, *form a regression plane* which cuts the population cloud of observations as shown in Figure 16.1.

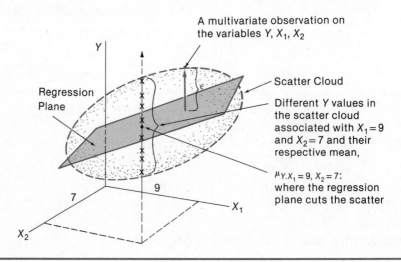

FIGURE 16.1 Three Dimension Population Scatter Diagram

The "ε" Term

The discrepancy between the population regression plane $\mu_{Y.12}$ and a particular value of Y measured in terms of vertical distance is labeled the error term, ϵ. That is,

$$\epsilon = Y - \mu_{Y.12}$$

What does ϵ represent? It represents the aggregate effect on Y of random factors not identified by the regression plane. Each individual value of Y then is a composite of *systematic forces* represented by the regression plane and of *random forces* represented by the term ϵ. To summarize,

$$Y = \text{systematic portion} + \text{random portion}.$$

If only the systematic forces are operating, all the Y values would lie on the population regression plane. In that case all the "ε" terms would be zero. Finding Y values off the plane is attributable to the random factor ϵ.

The Regression Plane Computed from Sample Data

The population of observations is rarely available. If it were available, the cost of handling the mass of data would probably prohibit its use. Availability and reliability of sample information encourage the use of a sample *estimate* of the population regression plane. The sample estimate is the regression plane cutting through the sample scatter cloud. It is expressed by the equation:

$$\hat{Y}_{12} = a + b_1X_1 + b_2X_2$$

where a, b_1, and b_2 are estimates of the population values α, β_1, and β_2.

The "e" Term

The discrepancy between the *actual* Y value and $\hat{Y}_{12}$, the corresponding value on the sample regression plane, is the residual term e. That is,

$$e = Y - \hat{Y}_{12}$$

Why use e rather than ϵ? The term e makes explicit the fact that the error term was computed using the sample regression plane and not the population regression plane. Generally the value of e differs from the value of ϵ. In other words, the observed discrepancy between Y and $\hat{Y}_{12}$ is not identical to the discrepancy between Y and $\mu_{Y.12}$. Why the difference? The *sample* regression plane with coefficient values a, b_1, and b_2 is not identical (miracles aside) to the *population* regression plane with the true values α, β_1, and β_2. The use of the sample regression plane therefore only permits us to obtain an estimate e of the true ϵ value.

The Least Squares Regression Plane

The most popular method employed to compute the sample regression plane is the least squares method. The technique determines the estimated regression plane, often termed the *computed regression plane,* or the *least squares regression plane.* It cuts the sample scatter cloud so as to minimize the sum of the squared discrepancies as shown in Figure 16.2. The plane sets

$$\sum e^2 = \sum (Y - \hat{Y}_{12})^2 \text{ at a minimum.}$$

In other words,

> the least squares regression plane minimizes the sum of the squared vertical distance of the Y observations from the surface of the $\hat{Y}_{12}$ plane.

Recall that e is measured in terms of vertical distances, indicated in Figure 16.2 by the vertical lines connecting the Y observations to the small crosses on the regression plane. The crosses on the plane represent the predicted Y values at the X_1, X_2 coordinates associated with the actual observations.

In summary:

1. the values of $\hat{Y}_{12}$ are the surface of the computed regression plane;

2. *they represent the least squares predictions of Y* computed from the regression equation for the various $X_1 X_2$ coordinates.

For example, suppose the computed least squares regression equation is

$$\hat{Y}_{12} = 40 + 3X_1 + 5X_2$$

and the values of the independent variables X_1 and X_2 are 30 and 20 respectively. The least squares prediction of Y for the values of the independent variables would be:

$$\hat{Y}_{12} = 40 + 3(30) + 5(20) = 230$$

which would be a point on the regression plane.

16.2. Determining the Multiple Regression Equation

The calculation of the coefficients a, b_1, b_2 of the least squares plane is an extension of the technique used in calculating the coefficients in simple regression. The solution requires that the number of unknown coefficients (a, b_1, b_2) equal the number of equations to be solved simultaneously. For three unknowns these equations are:

$$\sum \mathbf{Y} = na + b_1 \sum \mathbf{X_1} + b_2 \sum \mathbf{X_2}$$

$$\sum \mathbf{X_1 Y} = a \sum \mathbf{X_1} + b_1 \sum \mathbf{X_1^2} + b_2 \sum \mathbf{X_1 X_2}$$

$$\sum \mathbf{X_2 Y} = a \sum \mathbf{X_2} + b_1 \sum \mathbf{X_1 X_2} + b_2 \sum \mathbf{X_2^2}$$

The terms in bold print indicate operations performed on the data set. The results of these operations are inserted into the normal equations to yield solutions for a, b_1, and b_2.

If necessary, the required calculations can be made manually with the help

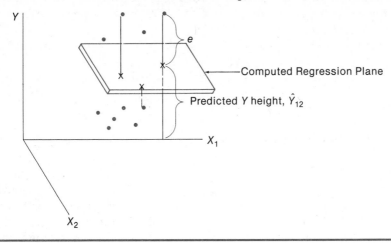

FIGURE 16.2 Computed Regression Plane

of a small calculator. Usually the computations are done by computer by assessing the multiple regression option of a software package. Some of the software packages which are very popular for business applications are: SPSS, BMDO2R, ESP, MINITAB, and IDA. IDA and MINITAB are interactive, meaning that once data have been entered, the investigator can obtain results almost instantaneously.

16.3. Interpretation of Regression Coefficients

What is the interpretation of the term α in the multiple regression? The symbol α or its sample counterpart "a" always designates the "Y intercept". The parameter α is the "Y intercept" of the population regression plane and the statistic "a" is the "Y intercept" of the *computed* regression plane, regardless of whether we are talking about simple or multiple regression. It represents the mean effect of the factors that affect Y, but are not included as independent variables.

Interpretation of the βs

The slope regression coefficients of the multiple regression model (βs) and of the computed multiple regression plane (bs) do *not* translate in the same way in multiple regression as in simple regression.

In the multiple linear regression model

the constant β_1 represents the amount of change, on average, in Y associated with one-unit changes in X_1 regardless of the level at which X_2 is held unchanged. Similarly, β_2 represents the amount of change in Y on average for unit changes in X_2 regardless of the level at which X_1 is held unchanged.

Since b_1 and b_2 are the *estimated* values of β_1 and β_2, the term

b_1 expresses the change on average in $\hat{Y}_{12}$ (the predicted Y values from the estimated regression plane) for one-unit changes in X_1, no matter at which level X_2 is held constant.

Likewise,

b_2 expresses the average change in $\hat{Y}_{12}$ for one-unit changes in X_2, no matter at which level X_1 is held constant.

Simultaneous Changes in the Independent Variables

Seemingly, the *interpretation* of b_1 and b_2 implies that only one of the independent variables is allowed to change at a time. In actuality the values of X_1 and X_2 are both likely to be changing. What, then, is the interpretation of b_1 and b_2 if neither X_1 nor X_2 is "held constant?" When the values of *both* independent variables change, the values of b_1 and b_2 *segregate statistically* the total movement of Y into two components, one attributable to X_1, the other to X_2. More precisely,

b_1 is the *part* of the movement in $\hat{Y}_{12}$ per unit change in X_1, *net* of the changes in $\hat{Y}_{12}$ attributable to a *concurrent* change in X_2.

In light of this operational interpretation, b_1 and b_2 are usually called the *estimated partial (or net) regression coefficients*.

16.4. An Illustration of Computer Output for Multiple Regression

Actually computing a multiple regression equation by employing a computer multiple regression package is not a very difficult procedure. But the intelligent application of the multiple regression *concept* to business problems *is* a challenging task. Through the MINITAB program, loaded on a Control Data Corporation computer serving eight Illinois universities, let's investigate a cost accounting problem adapted from Chapter 25 of *Managerial Cost Accounting* by Charles Horngren.[2]

━━━━━━ ───

Example 16.4. **Multiple Regression in Cost Accounting: Ralph's Precision Instrument Co.**

Ralph's Precision Instruments is a manufacturer of custom-built electronic instruments. Ralph's is a "job shop"; that is, all "jobs" are built to customer specifications. In preparing bids on jobs, it is important to identify as accurately as possible the expected marginal or incremental manufacturing cost of the job to be bid. The job's manufacturing cost consists of both *direct* and *indirect* costs due to the use of labor and material.

It is relatively easy to "cost out" the direct cost due to material and labor the job is expected to use since the accounting department keeps track of the material and labor *directly* charged to similar jobs. The problem lies with indirect cost. Most often *indirect* labor and material costs that are incurred for each job are *not* assigned to each job. How, then, are these relevant but indirect job costs handled by the cost accountants? As a matter of practice, cost accountants often *lump and report* the *indirect costs* of *all jobs* under one "catch-all" cost category, *manufacturing overhead.*

Typically, total manufacturing overhead consists of three components:

1. *Fixed components of overhead manufacturing costs* are usually *unrelated to any specific job;* rent and insurance typically fall into this category, as well as the costs of administrative personnel and handling, shipping, and receiving;

2. *Indirect material costs* which are related to specific jobs, but not in a way that can be directly measured; an example would be precision shearing punches subject to eventual wear out; these costs must be allocated over all jobs using the punches;

3. *Indirect labor costs* which also must be allocated to jobs; janitorial services and routine machine maintenance are examples.

The only part of manufacturing overhead cost relevant to a specific job's marginal cost are those which increase when a job is undertaken. Fixed manufacturing overhead is *not* included in marginal manufacturing cost of a specific job, since it is incurred regardless of whether a specific job is undertaken. Indirect material and indirect labor costs are relevant since there is an increase in these costs when a job is undertaken.

But how can one estimate the marginal manufacturing overhead cost due to a specific job's usage of indirect material and indirect labor? One approach is to utilize the link between indirect costs and direct costs. In that way, knowledge of the latter gets us the former. This relationship between indirect costs and direct costs is exploited by using multiple regression.

A multiple regression equation was computed for the data on Ralph's Precision Instrument Co. Total manufacturing overhead cost was the dependent variable in the regression. Direct Labor, X_1, and Direct Material, X_2, were the independent variables. The regression serves to *partition* total manufacturing overhead into its three components:

1. the fixed overhead cost component.

2. the (total) variable overhead cost due to indirect labor usage. This component of overhead cost is linked to usage of direct labor but not to usage of direct material.

3. the (total) variable overhead cost due to indirect materials. This component of overhead cost is linked to usage of direct material, but not to usage of direct labor.

In equation form we have

$$\hat{Y}_{12} = a + b_1X_1 + b_2X_2$$

Estimated Total Manufacturing Overhead Cost	=	Fixed Component of Overhead Cost	+	Variable Contribution to Overhead of Indirect Labor	+	Variable Contribution to Overhead of Indirect Materials

The slope coefficient b_1 represents the average change in the indirect labor *cost component of manufacturing overhead per unit (hour) change of direct labor.*

The variable X_1 indicates the total amount of direct labor used on all jobs.

Thus, the product $b_1 X_1$ represents indirect labor's *variable contribution to overhead* on all jobs for that time period.

Likewise, the product of the slope coefficient b_2 and the amount of direct material X_2 can be interpreted as the *variable contribution to overhead of indirect material, $(b_2 X_2)$,* on all jobs for the time periods to which the data refer.
The intercept term a

estimates the *average* fixed component of manufacturing overhead cost, or those costs which are *not related to either direct labor or direct material.* It is the average per period over the time periods considered.

Figure 16.3 shows graphically the meaning of the regression equation coefficients, b_1 and b_2, to be estimated.
Simulated data representing 16 observations on each variable is presented in Table 16.1. The data are monthly recordings.

TABLE 16.1. Simulated Cost Data

ROW	Y TOTAL MAN. OVERHEAD	X_1 DIRECT LABOR	X_2 DIRECT MATERIAL
1	24921.7	1297.38	612.69
2	28473.7	1064.55	1157.58
3	23529.8	905.30	724.85
4	30489.8	1280.13	1048.06
5	29585.2	1235.71	898.93
6	32937.2	1480.78	702.44
7	26415.1	1005.92	802.25
8	24286.4	837.36	823.39
9	27285.2	927.75	878.83
10	25519.4	829.29	975.63
11	25854.3	770.47	922.92
12	28028.4	1219.05	692.70
13	27231.9	765.26	1187.46
14	24790.0	852.28	1165.98
15	27604.8	1220.09	697.77
16	26891.6	866.34	1071.95

Computer output for this problem is shown in Figure 16.4.
The estimated regression equation is:

Estimated Total Manufacturing Overhead = 9737 + 10.72(D.L.) + 7.00(D.M.)
$$(1.95) \qquad (2.33)$$

The figures shown in brackets below the coefficient are the standard errors of the regression coefficient. Dividing the standard error of the coefficient into the value of the coefficient, we find that the coefficient of direct labor is 5.49 times its standard error and the coefficient of direct material is 3 times its standard error. Since both coefficients have a value several times their respective standard errors, the level of

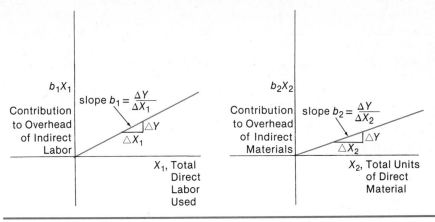

FIGURE 16.3 Graphical View of Contribution of X_1 and X_2 to Y, Total Manufacturing Overhead Cost

```
THE REGRESSION EQUATION IS
Y = 9737. + 10.72 X1 + 7.00 X2

                                          ST. DEV.    T-RATIO =
        COLUMN              COEFFICIENT    OF COEF.    COEF/S.D.
        --                   9737.          3601.        2.70
  X1    C2(DIRECT LABOR)     10.72          1.95         5.49
  X2    C3(DIRECT MATERIAL)   7.00          2.33         3.01

THE ST. DEV. OF Y ABOUT REGRESSION LINE IS
S =       1444.
WITH (  16- 3) =  13 DEGREES OF FREEDOM

R-SQUARED = 69.9 PERCENT
R-SQUARED = 65.3 PERCENT, ADJUSTED FOR D.F.
```

FIGURE 16.4 Multiple Regression for Ralph's Precision Instrument Problem

total manufacturing overhead in this company appears to be related to both the level of direct labor usage and the level of direct materials usage. In summary, we can say:

1. The b_1 value of 10.72 indicates that one additional hour of direct labor usage results in a corresponding estimated increase of $10.72, on the average, in manufacturing overhead cost, whatever the level of X_2 considered.

2. The b_2 value of 7.00 indicates that an increase of one unit in direct materials results, on the average, in an estimated increase of $7.00 in manufacturing overhead, no matter what level of X_1 is considered.

So, the coefficient values of b_1 and b_2 are *net* contributions to total manufacturing overhead cost with a one unit change in the direct labor variable X_1 and the direct materials variable X_2.

The intercept term of $9,737 indicates the average amount of manufacturing overhead cost *not* attributable to either additional direct labor usage or direct materials usage per monthly period.

It is the manufacturer's average level of *overhead cost* incurred, regardless of how much labor or material are used that month. The plausibility of the three estimates depends upon the assumption that there is reasonable linearity of overhead cost throughout the ranges of the data observed on direct labor and direct material usage.

16.5. Standard Deviation of Residuals and R^2 in Multiple Regression

As in the case of simple regression, the standard deviation of residuals and R^2 represent "goodness of fit" measures in multiple regression. The measures offer complementary views of how well the regression equation fits and explains the Y variation in the sample data. Let's examine the usefulness of these two measures in interpreting the worth of the regression equation.

In multiple regression with two independent variables, the standard deviation of residuals is defined as

$$S_{Y.12} = \sqrt{\frac{\Sigma(Y - \hat{Y}_{12})^2}{n - 3}}$$

The $n - 3$ represents the degrees of freedom. The 3 shows that 3 parameters (a, b_1, b_2) result when two independent variables are used. In the general case, the degrees of freedom equals $n - (k + 1)$ where k equals the number of independent variables and $k + 1$ equals the number of parameters to be estimated. As with simple regression,

> the standard deviation of residuals measures the standard deviation of Y about the regression plane and thus specifies the amount of prediction error $(Y - \hat{Y}_{12})$ incurred on average when the least squares regression equation values $\hat{Y}_{12}$ are used to predict Y.

A smaller value of the standard deviation of residuals shows

1. the closer the fit of the regression equation to the scatter of observations,

2. the more that has been done in explaining the variation of the actual Y values.

Therefore, smaller values of the standard deviation are more desirable and larger values are less desirable.

In the cost accounting problem, the standard deviation of residuals is shown in Figure 16.4 by the symbol S and has a value of 1444. This indicates $1444 of overhead cost, on average, has *not* been explained by the computed regression plane predictions. The figure $1444 appears to be a large amount left unexplained. However, relative to the magnitude of the typical Y values, which cover a range from 23529.8 to 30489.8, it is not large. Assuming the error term assumptions are satisfactory, the figure $1444 can be interpreted as the typical size error likely (approximately two thirds of the time) if the estimated regression equation is used to make predictions.

Multiple Correlation Coefficient and Multiple *R* Squared

The multiple correlation coefficient, called multiple R, is a summary measure of the estimated multiple regression that parallels the role and meaning of r in simple regression. Multiple R is the simple correlation between the actual Y values and their corresponding predicted Y values obtained from the multiple regression equation. The square of the multiple correlation coefficient yields R^2 which is called the *multiple coefficient of determination*. Similar to the construction and interpretation of r^2 in simple regression, the R^2 value is a ratio that indicates the proportional reduction in the variance of prediction errors that has been accomplished by the use of the regression equation. That is,

$$R^2 = \frac{\text{Variance of Prediction Error Without Regression} - \text{Variance of Prediction Error Using Regression}}{\text{Variance of Prediction Error Without Regression}}$$

$$= \text{Proportional Reduction of Prediction Error}$$

Properly treating the variances for their respective degrees of freedom gives the *adjusted* R^2, which is commonly a measure found on computer output. Importantly, changes in adjusted R^2 register the *net effect* of including an additional variable to the regression equation. It adjusts for the loss of degrees of freedom. The unadjusted R^2 rises automatically (or at worst remains unchanged) with the addition of another variable. For this reason the R^2 value more appropriate to be used to evaluate results is the adjusted R^2. It has not been common practice in published studies to specify whether the adjusted R^2 is used, but the difference between the adjusted R^2 and the unadjusted R^2 is generally not large enough to be of any great concern, especially when large samples are used. The main merit of using the adjusted R^2 is its role as a precise index of whether there has been a net gain with the addition (or elimination) of a variable to the equation.

The size of the R^2 indicates the degree to which the selected independent variables of the regression equation are useful in making a prediction of Y or in explaining the variation observed in Y. Reading the adjusted R^2 value in Figure 16.4, we see that the selected variables, direct labor and direct material, account for 65.3 percent of the observed variation in total manufacturing overhead, the Y variable.

The two measures of "goodness fit," the standard deviation of residuals and adjusted R^2, provide guidance in avoiding the simplistic notion that suggests eliminating a variable from the regression equation solely because the hypothesis test on its coefficient (H_0: $\beta = 0$) can't be clearly rejected. The regression equation including a variable may be more capable of predicting Y than the regression equation excluding the variable even though the hypothesis test cannot reject H_0. The rule of thumb suggests that if a variable's regression coefficient has a t value above one, the variable will be beneficial for Y prediction. When faced with the task of performing selected elimination of variables, one should start with the variable which has the lowest t value below one. Each beneficial elimination should show a decline in the standard deviation of residuals. If prediction of Y is the objective, an elimination which results in a rise of the standard deviation of residuals should not be undertaken.

The investigator may, however, set aside the rule of thumb if the regression equation is for planning and control and policy variables are involved. A variable may be retained in the regression equation if, in the investigator's judgment, sound economic or financial theory suggest it or some policy action on that variable is under consideration. Such judgment calls arise more often with small size samples in which the limited information of a small sample makes it difficult to obtain statistically strong results.

The rise or fall of adjusted R^2 is a complementary indicator of an additional variable's usefulness for prediction but not a direct substitute for the standard deviation of residuals. A rise in the adjusted R^2 value shows the additional variable inclusion (exclusion) was beneficial and is consistent with a fall in the standard deviation of residuals. A high adjusted R^2 clearly means that much has been accomplished in reducing prediction error on a percentage basis. It does not however state *explicitly* the size of the typical error that must be faced. For this reason, a high R^2, say at .8 or .9, ought not to be construed as saying "there is little *meaningful* reduction in prediction error that can be accomplished by an additional variable." The worth of a modest gain in reducing prediction error is a business question, not a statistical one, and the best indicator of what size error reduction has been accomplished is not the reduction of multiple R^2, but the reduction in the size of the standard deviation of residuals.

Additionally, one should remember that a high R^2 is not a guarantee of high accuracy in predicting Y. If the assumption that the Y values are independently distributed is violated, the value obtained for R^2 will be misleading. Interdependence of Y values is common for observations taken over several time intervals and is evident when successive Y observations show a strong tendency to trend or cycle. As first mentioned in Chapter Fourteen, this problem shows up in examining a residual plot and is known as the serial correlation problem. It will be dealt with in Chapter Nineteen on business forecasting.

16.6. Comparison of Multiple and Simple Regression Results

Does multiple regression simply offer an estimate of β_1 that would have been obtained from a simple regression of Y on X_1, or an estimate of β_2 that would have been obtained from a simple regression of Y on X_2?

The advantage of multiple regression over simple becomes evident by comparing the results of multiple and simple regression for the same sample data. Let's examine the display in Figure 16.5. The figure shows results of two simple regressions: Y on X_1 and Y on X_2. For evaluation purposes, the sample data were generated by computer simulation from a population in which the true regression relationship has an intercept term (α) of $10,000, a direct labor coefficient (β_1) of $10, and a direct materials coefficient (β_2) of $8.00. Comparing the results between Figure 16.4 and Figure 16.5 we find:

> The slope coefficient for direct labor obtained from multiple regression ($10.72) more closely estimated the true value ($10.00) than the one obtained from simple regression ($7.66)—an error of 72¢ versus an error of $2.34.

```
THE REGRESSION EQUATION IS
Y = 19188. + 7.66 X1 ◄────DIRECT LABOR
    ╲TOTAL MANUFACTURING OVERHEAD

                                      ST. DEV.      T-RATIO =
            COLUMN         COEFFICIENT OF COEF.      COEF/S.D.
            --              19188.      2209.        8.69
    X1      C2(DIRECT LABOR)  7.66      2.09         3.67

THE ST. DEV. OF Y ABOUT REGRESSION LINE IS
S =    1812.
WITH ( 16- 2) = 14 DEGREES OF FREEDOM




THE REGRESSION EQUATION IS
Y = 26818. + .331 X2 ◄────DIRECT MATERIAL
    ╲TOTAL MANUFACTURING OVERHEAD

                                      ST. DEV.      T-RATIO =
            COLUMN         COEFFICIENT OF COEF.      COEF/S.D.
            --              26818.      3193.        8.40
    X2      C3(DIRECT MATERIAL) .33     3.49         .09

THE ST. DEV. OF Y ABOUT REGRESSION LINE IS
S =    2536.
WITH ( 16- 2) = 14 DEGREES OF FREEDOM
```

FIGURE 16.5 Simple Regressions for Ralph's Precision Instrument Problem

The slope coefficient for direct material obtained from multiple regression ($7.00) more closely estimates the true value ($8.00) than the one obtained from simple regression (33¢)—an error of $1.00 vs. an error of $7.67.

The typical error in predicting the dependent variable (overhead) implied by the standard deviation of residuals is lower for the multiple regression equation ($1444) than the typical error implied for each of the simple regressions ($1812 and $2536).

The message is clear. Since the purpose of the regression analysis in this problem is planning and control, accurate estimates of β_1 and β_2 are needed and are better attained by multiple regression than by simple regression. Similarly, if prediction of Y is the purpose, multiple regression again has the advantage. It provides a more accurate forecast of Y than does simple regression, as is shown by the lower standard deviation of residuals for the multiple regression equation.

Advantages of Multiple Regression with Small Samples

Multiple regression can yield more reliable regression coefficients than simple regression. The gain in reliability, reflected by lower standard error of the coefficients, is typically substantial if two conditions are present:

1. the variable for which we want to estimate the coefficient accounts for only a small portion of the total variation in the dependent variable;

2. the number of sample observations is small, say less than a dozen.

When these two conditions are present, the simple regression coefficient will generally not be reliable, that is, it will show a high standard error and a low *t*-ratio. What's the reason for this? Plainly stated, *simple* regression is inadequate. It does not provide the appropriate framework to isolate a quantitatively small effect in the midst of a large amount of sampling variation that typically accompanies small samples. Under such conditions, using simple regression commonly, and too often erroneously, yields the conclusion that the underlying population regression coefficient of the small effect is zero.

This situation can be remedied often by using multiple regression and entering a second independent variable which accounts for a substantial portion of the variation in *Y*. This approach provides the needed reduction in the standard deviation of residuals and, importantly, lowers the standard error of the regression coefficient which is directly linked to the standard deviation of residuals. The reduction in the standard error will increase the regression coefficient's *t*-ratio and, possibly, enough to substantiate the *X* variable's contribution in explaining *Y*.

The inclusion of a second independent variable can be advantageous even though it may not be of any policy interest to the investigator. Its important role is in helping to separate out the net effect of the variable which *is* of interest.

Example 16.6.   The Effect of Inflation on Corporate Cash Balances

Business firms and individuals act alike when it comes to leaving money in their checking accounts. They only like to keep as much money in the accounts as they have to. Banks pay low interest on checking account balances, so excess cash balances could be earning higher interest. Why do firms keep checking account balances at all? The most important reason is that every day some bills have to be paid and enough money must be available to pay them.

What happens when inflation strikes? Excess cash balances in the checking accounts become even more expensive for corporations to hold. Inflation means that the purchasing power of money declines because a dollar in the future won't buy as much as that same dollar today. During inflation, money sitting idle in checking accounts loses purchasing power more rapidly and therefore becomes more costly to hold idle. Does rising inflationary pressure cause corporations to reduce their checking account balances?

Suppose an investigator on the research staff at the Federal Reserve Bank of San Francisco wants to isolate and measure the effect of inflation on corporate checking account balances. Trying to explain the variation in checking account balances (the dependent variable) by the rate of inflation (the independent variable) in a simple regression model is *not* likely to produce a regression coefficient representing the true effect of the rate of inflation. Why not? Checking account balances are mainly geared to business activity and the flow of daily business transactions that require payment; any variation in checking account balances due to changing inflationary pressures is likely to go unnoticed because there is a greater day to day variation in balances associated with routine business transactions.

What is the solution? The solution is a *multiple* regression, a multiple regression equation in which both the rate of inflation *and* transactions demands are represented as independent variables affecting the dependent variable, the level of checking account balances. The second independent variable, the demand for money due to routine business transactions, has a specific purpose. It is included to block out enough variation so that the net inflation effect on the level of cash account balances can be isolated.

The Intercept Term

The intercept term can be expected to have a value in multiple regression different than its value in simple regression. The intercept term is the average level of Y not explained by the level of the independent variables. Thus,

> with only a direct labor variable included as an independent variable in the manufacturing overhead regression equation, the impact of direct materials on overhead (left out of the equation) must show up in the intercept term.

Including the direct materials usage effect in overhead as a separate independent variable removes its effect from the intercept term. The computer output illustrates this. It shows that:

> the $19,188 intercept term in the equation having only direct labor as an independent variable falls dramatically to $9737 when direct material is included as a second independent variable.

The closeness of the estimated intercept to the true intercept value, $\alpha = \$10,000$, indicates the worth of the addition.

16.7. Specification Bias

How important is it to correctly specify the regression equation with respect to the independent variables? Is it necessary that *all* the variables having an important effect on the dependent variable be included as independent variables in the regression equation? What if one or more of these important variables are omitted? By how much will the accuracy of the regression equation in predicting the value of the dependent variable, or in estimating parameters, be impaired?

The answers to these questions were analyzed by comparing different regression equations for Ralph's Precision Instrument Company. It was found that the answers depend on the *degree of correlation between the important independent variables.* Let's see why this is so.

The multiple regression computer output for Ralph's Precision Instrument shows a modest *sample* correlation of $-.522$ between the two independent variables. Actually, the true population correlation between X_1 and X_2 is zero.[3] This lack of correlation in the population is an important fact. Even though an important variable may have been left out, the lack of population correlation insures that the regression coefficient in simple regression (for either X_1 and X_2) will be an *unbiased* estimate of the true net effect of the independent variable. But unbiased estimates merely lend confidence of accuracy on *average* rather than an assuredness of accuracy for each estimation. As the results in Figure 16.5 show, this estimation was quite inaccurate.

Can the inclusion of another variable with its additional relevant information bring accuracy to the estimation? A regression equation with both X_1 and X_2 as independent variables will provide not only *unbiased* estimates, but importantly more *efficient* estimates. This will give the multiple regression coefficients lower standard errors than their simple regression coefficients. This means that less uncertainty and more reliability is assigned to the coefficient estimates of the multiple regression.

The important points of the discussion are two:

1. zero population correlation between X_1 and X_2 guarantees unbiased estimation of the computed regression coefficient even though one of the important independent variables is left out of the regression equation;

2. including both variables when available gains greater reliability of the estimates.

But what if direct labor and direct material are *highly* correlated? Does omitting one of these independent variables bias the estimate of the coefficient of the remaining variable in the regression equation? Unfortunately, bias *will* occur because the remaining variable has to bear the burden of representing simultaneously not only its own true net effect, but also the effect of the variable highly correlated with it but omitted from the equation. This problem is known as *specification bias.*

High correlation between direct labor and direct material would distort the slope coefficient of a simple regression equation of manufacturing overhead on direct labor. The direct labor coefficient would no longer be the unbiased estimate of direct labor's true net impact on manufacturing overhead.

Instead, it becomes a *biased* estimate of the net effect. Actually, the estimate value reflects the gross effect of itself, the direct material variable, and all other correlated variables omitted from the equation. *The specification bias problem is relieved if all of the omitted independent variables are added to the regression equation; in this case each variable represents its own net effect.* However, this approach solves the problem only if the entering independent variable and the existing independent variables are not *too* highly correlated. Too high correlation creates a different problem called multicollinearity, which is discussed shortly in Section 16.8.

A modification of the Ralph's Precision Instrument example demonstrates the specification bias problem.

Example 16.7A.   A Computer Output Demonstration of Specification Bias

Ralph's Precision Instruments was described as a job shop operation producing electronic instruments custom-built to individual customer specifications. Direct materials usage and direct labor usage were specified to be uncorrelated in the population. Let's now change that. Let's assume Ralph's electronic instruments are manufactured by a standard production line with material and labor contributing in a fixed fashion in making a standardized product. When the demand for the product is high, both direct labor and direct material needs simultaneously go to high levels. When product demand is low, both direct labor and direct material usage fall below their respective averages. Under this production line arrangement, direct labor and direct material are highly correlated.

Computer simulated data for 25 periods of operations are shown in Table 16.2.

TABLE 16.2. Computer Simulated Data

ROW	Y	X_1	X_2
1	33272.8	1352.00	1139.85
2	23806.4	872.00	722.43
3	28209.4	1229.00	1066.43
4	26098.0	896.00	745.00
5	27498.3	1097.00	960.28
6	21865.4	711.00	616.43
7	29507.3	1125.00	929.28
8	19164.8	617.00	551.86
9	25715.0	861.00	771.00
10	21816.4	760.00	627.43
11	24500.0	917.00	815.00
12	30363.1	1189.00	1021.14
13	21172.3	642.00	553.28
14	34458.3	1377.00	1214.28
15	18379.3	551.00	487.28
16	21492.1	783.00	654.14
17	28312.5	1032.00	844.57
18	20436.4	648.00	544.43
19	28793.7	1129.00	977.71
20	32823.8	1338.00	1136.85
21	34273.8	1345.00	1146.85
22	28939.0	1162.00	958.00
23	27691.8	1100.00	912.85
24	26069.7	905.00	753.71
25	27896.8	1023.00	884.85

The data were generated from the same underlying parameter equation as before, but now the correlation between direct labor and direct materials is .99 in the population.

The computer output in Figure 16.6 shows what happens to the estimated regression coefficients when one of the independent variables is omitted.

The analysis shows:

A simple regression of overhead on direct labor (direct material omitted from the equation) results in the equation

$$\hat{Y} = 8610 + 18.1X_1$$
$$\quad (829) \quad (.815)$$
$$t = 10.39 \quad t = 22.26$$

Since the true value of $\beta_1 = 10$, the estimate is erroneous by $18.1 - 10 = 8.1$ dollars per direct labor hour.

```
THE REGRESSION EQUATION IS
Y =   8610. +  18.1 X1
```

COLUMN		COEFFICIENT	ST. DEV. OF COEF.	T-RATIO = COEF/S.D.
	--	8610.	829.	10.39
X1	C2	18.138	.815	22.26

```
THE ST. DEV. OF Y ABOUT REGRESSION LINE IS
S =    1003.
WITH (  25- 2) =  23 DEGREES OF FREEDOM

R-SQUARED = 95.6 PERCENT
R-SQUARED = 95.4 PERCENT, ADJUSTED FOR D.F.

THE REGRESSION EQUATION IS
Y =   8729. +  21.1 X2
```

COLUMN		COEFFICIENT	ST. DEV. OF COEF.	T-RATIO = COEF/S.D.
	--	8729.	937.	9.32
X2	C16	21.12	1.08	19.56

```
THE ST. DEV. OF Y ABOUT REGRESSION LINE IS
S =    1133.
WITH (  25- 2) =  23 DEGREES OF FREEDOM

R-SQUARED = 94.3 PERCENT
R-SQUARED = 94.1 PERCENT, ADJUSTED FOR D.F.

THE REGRESSION EQUATION IS
Y =   8617. +  19.5 X1 -  1.58 X2
```

COLUMN		COEFFICIENT	ST. DEV. OF COEF.	T-RATIO = COEF/S.D.
	--	8617.	848.	10.17
X1	C2	19.48	7.85	2.48
X2	C16	-1.58	9.21	-.17

```
THE ST. DEV. OF Y ABOUT REGRESSION LINE IS
S =    1024.
WITH (  25- 3) =  22 DEGREES OF FREEDOM

R-SQUARED = 95.6 PERCENT
R-SQUARED = 95.2 PERCENT, ADJUSTED FOR D.F.
```

FIGURE 16.6 Comparison of Simple and Multiple Regression

A simple regression of overhead on direct materials (omitting direct labor) results in the equation:

$$\hat{Y} = 8729 + 21.12X_2$$
$$(937) \quad (1.08)$$
$$t = 9.32 \quad t = 19.56$$

Since the true value of $\beta_2 = 8$, the estimate is in error by $(21.12) - 8 = 13.12$ dollars per hour of direct material.

Examining the difference between the computed regression coefficients and the true population values is revealing. In terms of the number of standard deviations, the direct labor coefficient errs by $8.1/.815 = 10$ standard deviations; the direct material coefficient errs by $13.12/1.08 = 12$ standard deviations. The large size of these errors highlight the extent of the bias incurred. In summary, the analysis shows that the *estimates are biased and grossly miss their target values.* Moreover, the standard errors of the regression coefficients *failed to signal* the large bias!

To see this distorting effect at first hand, let us use the extreme case of specification bias—*when X_1 and X_2 are perfectly correlated.* In particular, let us say that whenever direct material changes by a unit there is a corresponding change in direct labor by a unit. Thus, with a $10 price tag on direct labor cost per unit and an $8 price tag on direct material, the *total* cost change per additional unit increase in direct labor and material is $18.

This joint cost effect is reflected in the regression coefficient for the independent variable whether Y is regressed against X_1 alone or X_2 alone. For instance,

> the regression coefficient for direct labor will have a value near $18 rather than the appropriate $10 if Y is regressed against X_1 only.

Even with X_2 missing from the equation, the coefficient of X_1 registers the influence of X_2, its perfectly correlated cousin. This confounding effect virtually rules out the estimation of the true effect of X_1 on Y. *Without prior knowledge of the confounding effect, the $18 cost could erroneously be thought to be the cost change in Y induced directly* by a one-unit change in X_1. Under these conditions, regression analysis is helpless in detecting and correctly specifying how much of the change in Y is directly associated with a one unit change in X_1 from the amount *indirectly* induced through X_1 by X_2.

Inability to Establish Net Effect

Generally, the ability of a regression analysis to discern the net effect of a variable is lost any time the independent variable is highly correlated with an omitted variable. Since any change in the included independent variable will always be accompanied by a change in the omitted variable, the regression coefficient will not represent the true net effect of the included independent variable. Instead, it will represent the gross effect of both the included and omitted variables.

> Say the included variable is X_1. Then the coefficient of X_1 in the regression equation will reflect the combined effect of both X_1 and X_2 on Y even though X_2 is not included as an independent variable in the regression equation.

The potential distorting effects due to inadequate specification should caution the investigator to use regression analysis carefully because one can not always expect that each variable's coefficient will reflect only its own true effect on Y.

Specification Bias and the Purpose of the Regression Analysis

Threatening as specification bias may sound, the consequence depends on the managerial decisions at hand.

If the purpose of the regression analysis is *planning and control,* the use of biased coefficients will likely lead to *misguided decision making,* since the individual value of the regression coefficients is a key input to devising a decision strategy.

Alternatively, if the objective is *forecasting* the dependent variable Y, the possibly biased coefficients will *not* hamper the reliability of the prediction.

As mentioned earlier in the chapter, in forecasting with regression concern is not for the individual regression coefficient but for the accuracy of the entire equation as a unit in predicting the value of Y. For this purpose, it is actually possible in certain circumstances for specification bias to *benefit* the predictive accuracy of the regression equation.

Example 16.7B.   Once a Problem but Not Always a Problem

Suppose a variable influencing Y is not included in the regression equation but is highly correlated with one of the independent variables which are included. Then much of the omitted variable's effect on Y will be reflected by the included correlated independent variable's (biased) coefficient. Thus, in this case, the predictive accuracy of the regression may be little affected by whether a variable is included or omitted from the regression equation. For moderate to large sample sizes the predictive accuracy will likely be improved by including it, as reflected by a lower standard deviation of residuals. For very small sample sizes, the conclusion is surprisingly different! Including a highly correlated variable in the equation may, instead, *increase* the value of the standard deviation of residuals, thereby *decreasing* predictive accuracy.

But how can the uncertainty about predicting Y—reflected by the standard deviation of residuals—*increase* by adding another explanatory variable? Let's take a numerical example with two independent variables. Suppose the numerator of the standard deviation of residuals—called the "unexplained" variation—has a value of 1100. The sample size is 14 and there will be 3 constants to be estimated (a, b_1, b_2). Thus, the standard deviation of residuals would be

$$\sqrt{\frac{\sum(Y - \hat{Y})^2}{n - k}} = \sqrt{\frac{1100}{14 - 3}} = \sqrt{100} = 10$$

Now, suppose bringing in another explanatory variable reduces the unexplained variation in the numerator by five percent—an achievement, at first blush. But the calculation of the denominator, $n - k$, handicaps the use of additional independent variables k if the sample size remains unchanged. The net effect is a standard deviation of residuals of:

$$\sqrt{\frac{\sum(Y - \hat{Y})^2}{n - k}} = \sqrt{\frac{1045}{14 - 4}} = \sqrt{104.5} = 10.22$$

—an increase overall of .22. Although this reflects only slightly more uncertainty and a net loss in predictive ability, the important point is that there may be a negative aspect to adding marginally valuable variables to the regression equation.

16.8. Multicollinearity

Specification bias occurs if one of two highly correlated explanatory variables is *omitted* from the regression equation. But if both variables are included, a new parameter estimation problem, designated by the term *multicollinearity*, may occur.

High correlation between two independent variables X_1 and X_2 makes it extremely difficult to distinguish the separate effect of each variable; in the extreme case of perfect positive correlation, it is impossible to estimate each variable's separate influence. Graphically, as shown in Figure 16.7, the three-dimensional scatter cloud of observations collapses into a *line* of points to which no unique regression plane (equation) can be claimed to be best fitting, whereas any one of several planes will incorporate the line of values.

The acuteness of the multicollinearity problem depends on

the degree of correlation between the independent variables *and* the size of the sample.

The higher the correlation and the smaller the sample, the more serious is the problem of estimating reliable regression coefficients. In Example 16.7A, direct labor and direct material are very highly correlated ($r = .991$). With this extremely high intercorrelation, it is likely that the estimate of each variable's separate effect will be highly inaccurate. The multiple regression equation computed for a sample of 25 observations (Table 16.2) is:

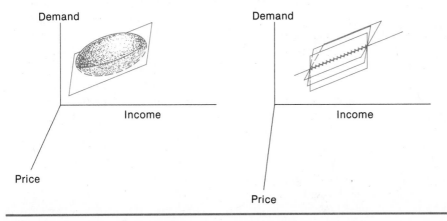

FIGURE 16.7 The Effect of Multicollinearity on Regression Plane Estimation

$$\hat{Y}_{12} = \begin{array}{ccc} 8617 & + 19.48X_1 & - 1.58X_2 \\ (848) & (7.85) & (9.21) \\ t = 10.17 & t = 2.48 & t = -.17 \end{array}$$

$R^2 = 95.2\%$

The coefficients of direct labor (19.48) and direct materials (-1.58) are *not* biased, although they are quite inaccurate compared to the true values of 10 and 8 respectively. In a large sample, greater accuracy could be expected. The critical point, however, is:

> multiple regression in which the independent variables are highly multi-collinear will generally produce highly inaccurate coefficients with *much higher* standard errors for the coefficients than multiple regression equations in which the independent variables are *not* highly correlated.

Comparing standard errors of the regression coefficients, one sees that with multicollinearity the standard error of the direct labor coefficient exploded from 0.82 to 7.85; the standard error of the direct material coefficient leaped from 1.08 to 9.21—both showing that the multicollinearity has been disruptive, to the point that the statistical evidence (low t value) suggests the variable to be unimportant as an explanatory variable determining Y. Therefore, highly disruptive multicollinearity undermines the ability of the regression coefficient to accurately estimate the underlying parameter and damages the ability to establish the importance of individual variables from t-tests.

How can the multicollinearity problem be alleviated? The simplest way is to increase sample size—bring more evidence to bear on distinguishing the net effect of each independent variable. However, this is generally not possible, nor does it guarantee a satisfactory reduction in the standard errors. Another approach is to obtain separate estimates of one or more of the coefficients from outside resources such as suggested by some studies in this area. Inserting them into the regression equation may make it possible to obtain reliable estimates of the remaining coefficients.

A complete presentation of the regression results including the regression coefficients, their standard errors, R^2, and the standard deviation of residuals for the regressions of manufacturing overhead on direct labor and direct materials is found in Table 16.3. The table gives an overview of the statistical impacts caused by independent variable correlation. The model has intercept term $\alpha = \$10,000$, direct labor coefficient $\beta_1 = \$10$, and direct materials coefficient $\beta_2 = \$8$.

Let us summarize briefly the points to be recognized in Table 16.3. There are two extreme situations between the independent variables (1) where X_1 and X_2 are uncorrelated in the population, $\rho_{X_1 X_2} = 0$; (2) where X_1 and X_2 show nearly perfect positive correlation, $\rho_{X_1 X_2} = .99$.

The first situation where $\rho_{X_1 X_2} = 0$ is presented by the top three equations. It shows that as long as X_1 and X_2 are independent, a simple regression leaving an important variable out will result in an inefficient estimation for the coefficient of the included variable. The regression coefficient estimate however will be unbiased but more inaccurate on average than it would be had a multiple regres-

TABLE 16.3. Comparison of Simple and Multiple Regression when Independent Variables are Uncorrelated and Highly Correlated

	R^2 (%)	Standard Deviation of Residuals	INTERCEPT TERM	
			Estimate	Standard Error
$\rho_{X_1 X_2} = 0$				
1. Multiple Regression	91.7	1049	8573	1310
2. Simple Regression on X_1	80.6	1608	14,129	1329
3. Simple Regression on X_2	36.0	2921	14,229	3422
$\rho_{X_1 X_2} = .99$				
1. Multiple Regression	95.2	1024	8617	848
2. Simple Regression on X_1	95.4	1003	8610	829
3. Simple Regression on X_2	94.1	1133	8729	937

	DIRECT LABOR COEFFICIENT, X_1			DIRECT MATERIALS COEFFICIENT, X_2		
	Estimate	Standard Error	t-ratio	Estimate	Standard Error	t-ratio
$\rho_{X_1 X_2} = 0$ (contd.)						
1. Multiple Regression	11.352	.908	12.50	8.00	1.41	5.66
2. Simple Regression on X_1	13.12	1.31	10.04	—	—	—
3. Simple Regression on X_2	—	—	—	14.08	3.70	3.81
$\rho_{X_1 X_2} = .99$ (contd.)						
1. Multiple Regression	19.48	7.85	2.48	−1.58	9.21	−.17
2. Simple Regression on X_1	18.138	0.82	22.26	—	—	—
3. Simple Regression on X_2	—	—	—	21.12	1.08	19.56

sion been used. The simple regressions suffer for prediction also, as indicated by substantially lower adjusted R^2 values and higher standard deviation of residuals.

The second situation, presented by the lower three equations in Table 16.3, assumes a very high degree of correlation between X_1 and X_2, $\rho_{X_1 X_2} = .99$. Looking at the goodness of fit measures, the standard deviation of residuals and adjusted R^2, one sees that for prediction purposes the simple regression with X_1 is preferred. The addition of X_2 in the multiple regression equation brings a t value of $-.17$ which depresses both goodness of fit measures since it is less than 1. If the purpose of the regression is reliable estimation of the regression coefficients for planning and control, the high correlation between X_1 and X_2 causes the multiple regression to yield coefficients that are highly inaccurate and even a nonsensical negative value. The simple regressions with one variable left out suffer from specification bias. This causes the computed regression coefficient of the included variable to be an inaccurate and biased estimate of the true coefficient value which we specified beforehand. Normally, of course, the true values will not be available to measure the extent of the bias, but more importantly the insidious specification bias will arise unsuspectingly because the investigator, unaware of the key missing variable, will not have tried the multiple regression which we, by hindsight, illustrated in our example. The specification bias problem, therefore, is difficult to handle because: (1) the investigator may not be aware of the key omitted variables correlated with the included variable, and (2) if aware, no data are available on the omitted key variables to alleviate the extent of the bias.

The presence of the multicollinearity problem is somewhat simpler to detect since high multicollinearity between a variable currently in the equation and an entering variable causes the standard error of the regression coefficient currently in the equation to rise dramatically and the t value to drop noticeably.

Moving from simple regression equation 2 to multiple regression equation 1, we find the extent of the statistical impact of entering X_2 on the standard error of the direct labor coefficient. A similar view of the standard error inflation is found by noticing the rise of the standard error of the direct material coefficient in moving from equation 3 to equation 1 when X_1 is entered. Such a statistical impact becomes completely disruptive if: (1) for prediction, any computed t value of a variable falls below 1, thus lowering the adjusted R^2 and the standard deviation of residuals; (2) for planning and control, any coefficient takes on a nonsensical sign contrary to economic or financial theory. Multiple regression equation 1 shows both of these symptoms.

One should recognize that multicollinearity and specification bias are interrelated issues. Relieving the multicollinearity problem by excluding a highly correlated independent variable creates a specification bias problem for the remaining independent variable. Faced with such a dilemma, one will tend to avoid specification bias and tolerate degrees of multicollinearity since: (1) the problem may not be acute enough to be completely disruptive; (2) one has the statistical signpost of the standard error to judge how disruptive the problem is; (3) regardless of the extent of the inaccuracy multicollinearity causes, the estimated coefficients will be unbiased.

A schematic flow chart describing the steps to consider in performing a regression analysis is found in Figure 16.8.

16.9. Measuring the Importance of a Variable in Determining Y

In multiple regressions, the size of the computed regression coefficients (the b values) does not directly indicate the importance of each independent variable in determining the variation and level of Y. For example, suppose a publishing company markets three magazines identified as 1, 2, and 3. A multiple regression of the company's monthly profits Y in thousands of dollars and unit sales of the three magazines in tens of thousands gives

$$\hat{Y} = -2 + 6X_1 + 3X_2 + 1X_3$$

We can distinguish the importance of the independent variables in the equation in two statistical senses.

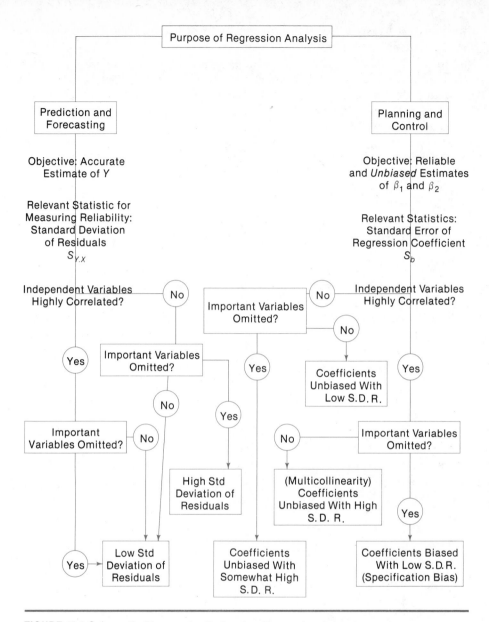

FIGURE 16.8 Schematic Diagram for Performing Regression Analysis

1. *Statistical Importance with Respect to the Variation in Y.* Importance in this sense refers to Y variation attributable to a particular variable's variation. The variable's variation is viewed as the means of predicting the variability in Y that actually takes place. Suppose that X_1 and X_3 exhibit little variation with standard deviation of $S_1 = .1$ and $S_3 = .1$, while X_2 shows considerably more variability ($S_2 = 1$). The actual variation in Y, say $S_Y = 2$, depends both upon how large an impact on Y the respective change in X will have when it happens, and on how

frequently it happens. The former is measured by the b values of X, the latter by the standard deviations of the X variables. We measure the combined effect by the *standardized regression coefficient*. The standardized regression coefficient adjusts the computed regression coefficient b for the variation (standard deviation) in both Y and the particular independent variable X. For each X variable, this is the product of b—the net regression coefficient—and the ratio of the independent variable's standard deviation, S_i, to the standard deviation of Y, S_Y. For the three independent variables, the values of the standardized regression coefficients are:

variable, i:	X_1	X_2	X_3
stand. b, $b\left(\dfrac{S_i}{S_Y}\right)$	$6(.1/2) = .3$	$3(1/2) = 1.5$	$1(.1/2) = .05$

Variable X_2 is the most important variable in this sense of importance. Its interpretation in this case means that for every increase of one standard deviation in X_2, profits are expected to increase by 1.5 standard deviations. Notice that an independent variable with small standard deviation S_i will tend to have a small standardized regression coefficient. This implies that a variable with a small standard deviation is of relatively little importance in predicting Y variation since its values exhibit little movement over the range of the observations.

2. *Statistical Importance with Respect to the Mean Level of Y.* It may appear that the third variable has no claim to importance whatsoever. It has the lowest net regression coefficient value and the lowest standardized regression coefficient value. However, suppose mean sales volume of the third magazine is $\overline{X}_3 = 20$, while $\overline{X}_2 = 2$ and $\overline{X}_1 = 1$. Calculating the mean level of monthly profitability we find

$$\overline{Y} = a + b_1\overline{X}_1 + b_2\overline{X}_2 + b_3\overline{X}_3$$
$$= -2 + 6(1) + 3(2) + 1(20)$$
$$= 30$$

The contribution of variable X_3 to mean level profits is

$$\frac{b_3\overline{X}_3}{\overline{Y}} = \frac{1(20)}{30} = \frac{2}{3}$$

This compares with

$$\frac{b_2\overline{X}_2}{\overline{Y}} = \frac{3(2)}{30} = \frac{1}{5} \text{ and } \frac{b_1\overline{X}_1}{\overline{Y}} = \frac{6(1)}{30} = \frac{1}{5}$$

Thus variable X_3 makes the most important contribution to the mean level of monthly profit.

16.10. Shifting Intercept: Using Zero-One (0, 1) Dummy Variables

The use of *dummy variables* makes it possible to include a qualitative variable in the regression equation and to estimate the change in Y attributable to changes in the value of the qualitative variable. For example, consider Figure 16.9.

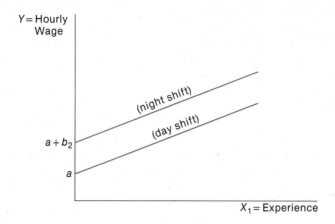

FIGURE 16.9 Shifting Effect of a Qualitative Variable

Plotted on the Y axis is hourly nurses' wages and plotted on the X axis is years of nursing experience. Suppose now we want to measure the differential hourly wage for the qualitative variable, night shift/day shift. The two parallel lines show the differential impact that day (bottom line) and night (top line) employment have on earnings Y. The lines verify that the night shift workers on average earn a differential of b_2 dollars per hour above the day shift. A qualitative variable that causes such a parallel shift differential is handled in a regression equation by a dummy independent variable, X_2, which takes on the value one ($X_2 = 1$) when the shift differential is present and the value zero ($X_2 = 0$) when it is absent. The regression equation is

$$\hat{Y}_{12} = a + b_1 X_1 + b_2 X_2$$

where X_1 is the quantitative variable, experience, and X_2 is the dummy variable for the qualitative variable, night/day shift. The value of b_2 estimates the amount the intercept shifts when the night shift is working. This intercept change can be recognized easily by rewriting the regression equation as follows:

$$\hat{Y}_{12} = \underbrace{(a + b_2 X_2)}_{\text{intercept}} + b_1 X_1$$

So the Y intercept is the value a if $X_2 = 0$ (day shift) and $a + b_2$ if $X_2 = 1$ (night shift). Hence, as Figure 16.9 suggests, b_2 is the distance between the two Y intercept terms of the two parallel lines.

Notice that this means that the average impact on Y of the day shift serves as the base of comparison since its effect resides in a when the dummy variable is zero. If the first three observations proved to be for two night shift nurses whereas the third was for a day shift nurse, the data matrix would appear as follows:

Y	X_1	X_2
6	3	1 (night shift)
5	2	1 (night shift)
4	3	0 (day shift)

A test on whether the difference b_2 is statistically significant will again be checked by the size of the t value for b_2. A reduction of the standard deviation of residuals with the addition of X_2 would indicate that X_2 provides a *net* beneficial gain for prediction.

The dummy variable approach can also accommodate a qualitative variable of several attribute categories. For example, suppose a manufacturing production line produces type A, type B, and type C silicon computer chips. To deal with this, one specifies two dummy variables (always one less than the number of categories) such that each dummy variable shows a zero or one value as follows for each observation:

Observation	Type	First Dummy Variable, X_2	Second Dummy Variable, X_3
1st	A present	0	0
2nd	B present	1	0
3rd	C present	0	1

Type A has been designated the base of comparison for the other types. The effect of type A resides in the intercept term a. The effect of type B is shown by $a + b_2$ and so differs from type A by the value b_2. The effect of type C is represented by $a + b_3$ and differs from type A by the value b_3.

16.11. Managerial Issues in Practice—Review Exercise I: The Sperry and Hutchinson Company Food Expenditure Study

The Sperry and Hutchinson Company, providers of "S & H Green Stamps" to retailers, conducted a nationwide survey to gain information on food shopping behavior and attitudes. A multiple regression equation was run of weekly household food expenditures on three independent variables:

X_1 = family size
X_2 = family income (in thousands of dollars)
X_3 = price consciousness (1 if price conscious, 0 if not)
$n = 312$

The computed regression equation was:

$$\hat{Y}_{123} = 10.86 + 2.64X_1 + .97X_2 - .47X_3$$

Standard Errors	(.31)	(.14)	(1.24)
t values	8.52	6.93	0.37

Standard Deviation of Residuals: 10.79

$R^2 = .31$

$\overline{Y} = 27.637, S_Y = 13.068$

$\overline{X}_1 = 3.843, S_{X_1} = 1.947$

$\overline{X}_2 = 7.091, S_{X_2} = 4.597$

$\overline{X}_3 = 0.449, S_{X_3} = 0.498$

a. Estimate weekly food expenditures for a family of four earning $20,000 per year for whom price is important.

$$\hat{Y}_{123} = \$10.86 + \$2.64(4) + \$.97(20) - \$.47(1)$$
$$= \$40.35.$$

b. Which independent variables are statistically significant?

The t values for the three independent variables are computed as follows:

$$t_1 = \frac{b_1}{S_{b_1}} \qquad t_2 = \frac{b_2}{S_{b_2}} \qquad t_3 = \frac{b_3}{S_{b_3}}$$

$$\frac{\$2.64}{.31} = 8.52 \qquad \frac{.97}{.14} = 6.93 \qquad \frac{-.47}{1.24} = -0.37$$

The number of degrees of freedom is $312 - 4 = 308$ so the critical value of t at the 5 percent level of significance is 1.96. Thus, X_1 (with t value of 8.52) and X_2 (with t value of 6.93) are statistically significant. However, X_3 (with t value of 0.37) is not statistically significant.

c. Which independent variable is most important in explaining variablity of family food expenditures?

Standardized Regression Coefficients are:

$$X_1 : b_1 \frac{S_{X_1}}{S_Y} = .393$$

$$X_2 : b_2 \frac{S_{X_2}}{S_Y} = .341$$

$$X_3 : b_3 \frac{S_{X_3}}{S_Y} = -.018$$

Therefore, X_1 is most important.

d. What is the interpretation of $2.64, $.97, and $-$.47, the coefficients of family size, income, and price consciousness, respectively?

Among families having the same income and classified in the same price conscious category, an average of $2.64 per week is spent on food per additional family member.

Among same-sized families classified in the same price-consciousness category, an extra $.97 per week on average is spent on food for each additional $1000 of family income.

Among same-sized families earning the same income, families that are conscious of prices spend an average of $.47 less per week than families that are not classified as price conscious.

A new multiple regression equation is run, this time on six independent variables. The additional variables take into account the number of toddlers under age 6 (X_4), youngsters age 6–18 (X_5), and the amount of education of the head of the household (X_6). The coefficient of the family size and family income variables in the new equation and their standard errors are:

Variable	Variable Name	Regression Coefficient	Standard Error of Reg. Coef.	t value
X_1	Family Size	1.33	.40	3.325
X_2	Family Income	.80	.15	5.33

Constant Term	10.37 ⎰ Note: These values are identical
Standard Deviation of Residuals	10.37 ⎱ only by coincidence
R^2	.36

e. Did adding the three additional variables substantially improve the predictability of family food expenditures? Explain. (Refer to Section 16.5.)

Not much. The standard deviation of residuals decreased only from 10.79 to 10.37.

f. Specific variables are included for toddlers and youngsters, but not for adults. In which variable is the effect on food expenditures of adults found? (Hint: what interpretation must be given to the family size coefficient in the second equation? Is it the same interpretation that applies to the first equation?)

There is an important difference in the interpretation of the family size coefficient between the two equations. In the first equation, the coefficient of family size ($2.64) refers to the average extra weekly spending on food per additional family member *measured over all family compositions*, including those with youngsters and toddlers. In the second equation, the coefficient of family size ($1.33) refers to a more narrowly defined group of families. An increase in family size, X_4 and X_5 *held unchanged*, implies that the additional family member is an *adult*. Intuitively, this makes sense. Since toddlers and youngsters have been given their own variables, the only persons who could be left in the family (for the coefficient of the family size variable to measure) are adults.

g. What is the increase in average weekly food expenditures associated with an increase of one adult in the family with toddlers, youngsters, and all other variables held constant?

$1.33 is the coefficient of X_1 in the second equation. Note that this is less than the $2.64 originally obtained for X_1.

h. The toddler variable has a coefficient of $1.37. Does this mean that toddlers on average consume $1.37 of food per week?

No. For a *given family size*, and given values of all the other independent variables, each additional toddler adds an average of $1.37 to the weekly food bill. However, note that when family size and number of youngsters are held constant, the number of toddlers can only increase if the number of adults *decreases* by one. For example, if the original values of X_1, X_4, and

X_5 were 5, 1, 2 respectively, this would imply families having two adults. If X_4 increases by one to 2, the average weekly food bill increases by \$1.33 if X_1 and X_5 stay at 5 and 2 respectively. But this implies that the number of adults is only 1 in this group of families. That is, these families have one more toddler than the original families, but they also have one fewer adult.

i. It seems surprising that for *same* size families (holding family size constant), the food bill, on average, is higher by \$1.33 per week for families in which one toddler replaces one adult. Does this mean that toddlers eat more than adults?

No. It only means that families of a given size, etc. tend to eat more if they include toddlers. It *doesn't* imply that toddlers are the ones doing the extra eating. Nor does it imply that replacing some adults in a given family by toddlers will increase the food bill. The comparison is across *different* families. Quite possibly, the families with toddlers have younger (and therefore, hungrier) than average adults.

j. How could you test that hypothesis?

By adding age of, say, the head of household as an independent variable. If the families with toddlers do have younger, hungrier than average adults, the coefficient of the toddler variable should fall towards zero, or perhaps become negative.

k. Would this be an illustration of specification bias (that is, if the toddler coefficient becomes negative or zero when age is included)?

Yes. The omission of age when age is correlated with numbers of toddlers means that the toddler variable picks up part or all of the age effect. Putting age in as an independent variable removes that source of bias in the toddler coefficient.

Several other aspects of the Sperry and Hutchinson study are raised in the problems at the end of the chapter.

16.12. Managerial Issues in Practice—Review Exercise II: Estimating Unit Variable Assembly Cost for a Multiple Product Department

A manufacturer of electric motors for vacuum cleaners produces two styles, standard and deluxe. The manufacturer wishes to estimate the unit variable cost of assembling each type of motor in the assembly department. Records indicating the *total* cost incurred by the assembly department, the number of standard motors assembled, and the number of deluxe motors assembled are given in Table 16.4 for fifteen accounting periods.

Issue: Reliable Values for Unit Variable Assembly Cost

Question: Can reliable estimates of the unit variable assembly cost for each motor type be obtained?

TABLE 16.4. Raw Data for Total Assembly Department Cost and Units Assembled

ACCOUNTING PERIODS	(1) TOTAL ASSEMBLY COST	(2) STANDARD UNITS PRODUCED	(3) DELUXE UNITS PRODUCED
1	$10,350	819	760
2	10,710	855	790
3	8,710	651	700
4	17,560	1323	1360
5	16,180	1279	1250
6	17,250	1303	1280
7	16,980	1249	1250
8	18,040	1438	1330
9	17,250	1351	1240
10	16,990	1266	1290
11	14,770	1201	1150
12	10,600	831	840
13	10,880	909	840
14	15,970	1224	1220
15	11,480	891	900
	Mean: 14,248	Mean: 1106	Mean: 1080

Source: Data adapted from the text *Cost Accounting* by Charles Horngren, Chapter 25.

Suggested Procedure: Apply simple and multiple regression analysis with assembly cost as dependent variable, number of standard motors assembled and number of deluxe motors assembled as independent variables.

Results and Comment:

Equation 1:

   Assembly Cost vs. Standard Units Assembled
   Dependent Variable = 1   (Total Assembly Cost)

Independent Variable	Coefficient	Std. Error	t-Value
Constant	−414.90	624.3	−.66
2 (Std. Units)	13.257	.5515	24.03

   $r^2 = .976$ and Standard Deviation of Residuals = 513.9

Equation 2:

   Assembly Cost vs. Deluxe Units Assembled
   Dependent Variable = 1   (Total Assembly Cost)

Independent Variable	Coefficient	Std. Error	t-Value
Constant	−609.3	533.7	−1.14
3 (Del. Units)	13.756	.4831	28.47

   $r^2 = .983$ and Standard Deviation of Residuals = 435.1

Equation 3:

   Assembly Cost vs. Standard Units Assembled and DeLuxe Units Assembled
   Dependent Variable = 1   (Total Assembly Cost)

Independent Variable	Coefficient	Std. Error	t-Value
Constant	−674.	411.9	−1.63
2 (Std. Units)	5.662	1.802	3.14
3 (Del. Units)	8.018	1.864	4.30

$R^2 = .990$ and Standard Deviation of Residuals $= 335.4$

The regression coefficients measure the average unit variable cost. They show how much assembly department cost changes with a one unit increase in the number of units assembled. The simple regressions for each type are:

$$\hat{Y} = -414.90 + 13.257 \text{ (STD. UNITS)}$$
$$\hat{Y} = -609.3 + 13.756 \text{ (DEL. UNITS)}$$

Equation 1 shows a negative intercept term (-414.9) and a computed average unit variable cost per standard unit of 13.26. The r^2 value of .976 reflects a close fit of the points around the estimated regression line. But is \$13.26 really a plausible estimate of the average unit variable assembly cost incurred with the assembly of one additional standard unit? It would not seem so because multiplying the \$13.26 unit variable cost by the *average number of assembled standard motors* (1106 units) gives an amount, adjusted for the constant term, of 14,665 − 415 = 14,250. This figure is approximately equal to *total* average assembly department cost! Shouldn't the deluxe motors account for some of that cost too?

Equation 2 also shows a negative intercept term (-609.3) with a 13.76 (rounded) computed variable cost for a one unit change in the number of deluxe motors assembled. The r^2 value of .983 indicates that the regression line represents well the scatter of recorded observations on assembly department cost and units assembled as the deluxe type over the periods.

The regression line slope for the deluxe motors equation is surprisingly similar to the value found in equation 1. Multiplying the \$13.76 unit variable cost by the *average number of deluxe units* assembled (1080) gives us a product, adjusted by the constant of 14,860 − 609 = 14,251. Again this figure just about equals the *total* assembly department cost. Surely standard and deluxe units, considered individually, cannot *both* account for the entire assembly department cost. What is the problem here?

Checking the correlation between the quantities of deluxe units assembled and the standard units assembled, one finds a very high value ($r_{23} = .98$). This suggests that a simple regression suffers from a *specification error*. The inclusion of only one of the two motor types as the independent variable will cause the included variable's coefficient value to reflect more than its own impact on Y; the coefficient value will also reflect the effect of the highly correlated excluded variable. To isolate the individual impact of each motor type both motor type variables must be included in the same multiple regression equation.

$$\hat{Y} = -674 + \$5.66 \text{ (STD UNITS)} + \$8.02 \text{ (DEL UNITS)}$$

The regression of assembly department cost on both the number of standard assembled motors and deluxe motors assembled gives a regression coefficient of \$5.66 for the standard motor and \$8.02 for the deluxe motor. These represent the estimated average unit variable cost of the two motor types. They are unbiased estimates, *despite the high multicollinearity*. The effect of the high multicollinearity is to make the coefficients less reliable estimates of the true unit variable costs. The decreased reliability is reflected in the values of the standard error of regression coefficients, 1.80 in the case of the standard motors, 1.86 in the case of deluxe motors. Both of these standard error values are higher than they would be if multicollinearity were not present. Nevertheless, the regression coefficients of standard motors and deluxe motors have, respectively, t ratios of 3.14 and 4.30. That means that the regression coefficients lie over 3 and over 4 standard deviations away from the value of zero. Thus, whatever the reduction in reliability attributable to multicollinearity, it certainly has not been sufficient to render the computed regression coefficients useless as estimates of the true unit variable assembly costs.

If the goal of the analysis is prediction of assembly department cost rather than the estimation of unit variable cost, would equation 3 still be the most preferable to use? Yes, it would in this case. The key statistic is the standard deviation of residuals. It is a component of the standard error of prediction. Its value is lower in equation 3 than in the other two equations. Predictions using the multiple regression will have tighter confidence bands for any particular confidence level than either of the simple regressions.

16.13. Managerial Issues in Practice— Review Exercise III: Job Evaluation at M & M Industries (continued)

In Chapters Fourteen and Fifteen, we dealt with a linear relationship between the management consultant's evaluation of a job's total content points (TOTAL) and the actual salary M & M pays (SALARY) for the job position. We found that converting the original variables TOTAL and SALARY to log form, LOGTOT and LOGSAL, provides a more appropriate approach to deal with the variations of the data. That is, the log version gives a statistical fit more in conformity with the linear regression model assumption of constant residuals. The log-linear relationship between total points and salary proved to be strong (high r^2) and positive. This means that a one percentage point increase in total content points was compensated, on average, by a *constant* percentage increase in salary. Important as this relationship is in making an external and internal evaluation of the M & M compensation structure, it doesn't address other important managerial issues.

> *Issue 1:* Does an additional point of a particular job component as "know-how" receive more compensation than a point of "accountability" (or vice versa)? If there is a difference in compensation, it means jobs with the same total content points but different job components will be paid differently. This can be an important finding if the firm is planning new hirings with new job descriptions and job components.

> *Issue 2:* Does an additional point in the engineering area receive more compensation than an additional point in the administrative area? If a pronounced difference in compensation exists, it means jobs equal in each job component will show differences in salary partly due to the functional area of the job. This may reflect an overall perception at M & M of which group represents the key personnel of the company.

We see in Table 16.5 the full data file available to the consultant. It shows not only a detailed breakdown of the points given to each job component (KNOWHOW, PROBSOLV, ACCTBIL) that make up the total, but also the qualitative variable, CLASS. The column of data under CLASS shows a code number assigned to each of the 64 job positions. Since CLASS is a qualitative variable the code numbers themselves merely *indicate* the particular functional area of M & M Industries. Therefore, jobs in the same functional area have the same code number in the CLASS column. The coding is as follows:

2	Major Division 1
3	Major Division 2
4	Major Division 3
5	Engineering
7	Administration
10	Sales

In this exercise we will pursue a statistical analysis of Managerial Issue One. The second managerial issue on functional status influence is left as a student assignment and is presented in the Student Solutions Manual.

1. *Managerial Issue:* Are point increases in the three different job components (KNOWHOW, PROBSOLV, ACCTBL) compensated at the same rate as presumed by the management consulting firm, since they summed the individual components to obtain the total points variable? Or are they in actuality compensated at different rates so that explaining existing salaries requires all three components?

Suggested Procedure: Run a multiple regression of SALARY, Y, as dependent variable on the three components of job content as independent variables to obtain the net effect of each component. See Figure 16.10.

Comment: The computed regression equation with job content component as independent variables was found to be:

$$\widehat{SAL} = \$10,122 + \$150.61 \text{ KNOWHO} - \$128.45 \text{ PROBSO} + \$61.27 \text{ ACCTBL}$$

This is the average relationship that gives the best fit by the least squares criterion between the salary variable and the three job content components. The net effect on salary of an additional one point increase of a particular job component, while the other components of job content are held unchanged, is measured by the designated component's regression coefficient. Except for the variable PROBSO, the regression coefficients are all several times their standard error, indicating that there is a high probability that the true values are different from zero. The reduced reliability and marginal significance of PROBSO is likely the symptom of multicollinearity between the job component variables. The simple correlation matrix given in Figure 16.10 shows that the simple correlations between the three independent variables are all above .9. This, of course, makes difficult the current attempt to distinguish explicitly the individual net effects of each variable.

Managerial Implication: The numerical values of $150.61 for KNOWHO, $-$128.45 for PROBSO and $61.27 for ACCTBL indicate large differences among the three components in the additional salary compensation for an additional

TABLE 16.5. Data File on M & M Industries

COLUMN COUNT ROW	C1 64 CLASS	C2 64 KNOWHOW	C3 64 PROBSOLV	C4 64 ACCTBIL	C5 64 TOTAL	C6 64 SALARY
1	2.	528.	304.	460.	1292.	77220.
2	3.	460.	264.	460.	1184.	77220.
3	5.	528.	304.	304.	1136.	87516.
4	4.	460.	264.	400.	1124.	60000.
5	7.	460.	230.	264.	954.	54000.
6	10.	400.	200.	350.	950.	69420.
7	7.	400.	175.	230.	805.	48048.
8	7.	400.	200.	200.	800.	48048.
9	5.	400.	175.	200.	775.	65520.
10	5.	304.	115.	175.	594.	64740.
11	2.	264.	100.	175.	539.	47580.
12	3.	264.	100.	175.	539.	49296.
13	10.	230.	100.	132.	462.	42120.
14	10.	230.	100.	132.	462.	37830.
15	7.	230.	87.	132.	449.	45006.
16	7.	230.	76.	115.	421.	42003.
17	5.	230.	76.	115.	421.	50700.
18	5.	230.	87.	100.	417.	39000.
19	5.	230.	87.	100.	417.	41340.
20	7.	200.	87.	100.	387.	36000.
21	7.	200.	76.	100.	376.	35880.
22	7.	200.	76.	100.	376.	36036.
23	7.	200.	76.	87.	363.	36900.
24	5.	200.	76.	87.	363.	35880.
25	7.	200.	66.	87.	353.	35100.
26	7.	175.	66.	100.	341.	34320.
27	2.	175.	57.	100.	332.	36660.
28	3.	175.	57.	100.	332.	39780.
29	7.	175.	57.	100.	332.	29640.
30	2.	175.	57.	100.	332.	37440.
31	3.	175.	57.	100.	332.	39000.
32	2.	175.	57.	100.	332.	39780.
33	3.	175.	57.	100.	332.	37440.
34	4.	175.	57.	87.	319.	37440.
35	7.	175.	57.	87.	319.	34320.
36	2.	175.	57.	87.	319.	36192.
37	3.	175.	57.	87.	319.	33540.
38	2.	175.	57.	87.	319.	27300.
39	3.	175.	57.	87.	319.	28860.
40	5.	175.	66.	76.	317.	29640.
41	5.	175.	66.	76.	317.	30600.
42	7.	175.	57.	76.	308.	30420.
43	7.	175.	57.	76.	308.	35100.
44	5.	175.	66.	66.	307.	30000.
45	7.	152.	50.	87.	289.	32760.
46	7.	152.	50.	76.	278.	27300.
47	3.	152.	50.	76.	278.	35100.
48	2.	152.	50.	76.	278.	29640.
49	3.	152.	50.	76.	278.	35100.

COLUMN	C1	C2	C3	C4	C5	C6
COUNT	64	64	64	64	64	64
ROW	CLASS	KNOWHOW	PROBSOLV	ACCTBIL	TOTAL	SALARY
50	5.	152.	50.	66.	268.	28080.
51	5.	152.	43.	66.	261.	31980.
52	2.	152.	43.	66.	261.	29952.
53	2.	152.	43.	66.	261.	31980.
54	3.	152.	43.	66.	261.	32760.
55	3.	152.	43.	66.	261.	32760.
56	2.	152.	43.	66.	261.	32760.
57	3.	152.	43.	66.	261.	31980.
58	3.	152.	43.	66.	261.	31980.
59	7.	152.	43.	66.	261.	24960.
60	5.	152.	43.	66.	261.	28080.
61	2.	152.	43.	66.	261.	32760.
62	3.	152.	43.	66.	261.	32760.
63	4.	152.	43.	66.	261.	31980.
64	7.	152.	43.	57.	252.	29640.

```
SAL VS KNOWHO, PROBS, ACCT


THE REGRESSION EQUATION IS
Y =   10122 + 150.61X1 -128.45 X2 + 61.27 X3


                                         ST. DEV.    T-RATIO =
          COLUMN      COEFFICIENT        OF COEF.    COEF/S.D.
          --           10122             3903.        2.59
  X1    C2 KNOW        150.61            42.13         3.57
  X2    C3 PROBSOL    -128.45            73.56        -1.75
  X3    C4 ACCT         61.27            22.42         2.73


THE ST. DEV. OF Y ABOUT REGRESSION LINE IS
S =     1682.
WITH ( 64- 4) = 60 DEGREES OF FREEDOM


R-SQUARED = 86.0 PERCENT
R-SQUARED = 85.3 PERCENT, ADJUSTED FOR D.F.


CORRELATION MATRIX

            C1      C2      C3      C4      C5
C2 KNOWHO  .168
C3 PROBSO  .156    .989
C4 ACCTBL  .076    .935    .951
C5 TOTAL   .134    .989    .993    .977
C6 SALARY  .059    .918    .904    .895    .919
```

FIGURE 16.10 Computer Output (Including Correlation Matrix) for Multiple Regression of SALARY on KNOWHO, ACCTBL, and PROBSO

job point. An additional point of KNOWHO is the most highly compensated. The negative 128.45 coefficient for PROBSO indicates that an additional point of problem solving ability, on average, has a depressant effect on salary when the other job components are left unchanged. This is quite an unusual result since *a priori*, additional points in any job component would be thought to have an enhancing effect on salary. This points out the type of implausible result multi-collinearity causes.

2. Statistical Issue: Reducing Multicollinearity for More Reliability One way to possibly reduce the multicollinearity problem and simultaneously to estimate more reliably the net effect of the job components is to create new variables which represent the present variables but are not so highly correlated. In this case, we try relative job component variables together with log total points as the independent variables.

Suggested Procedure: Run a multiple regression of LOGSAL, Y, on the independent variables: LOGTOT, *relative* Knowhow (RELKNO), and *relative* accountability (RELACC). Relative knowhow is the variable KNOWHO expressed as a percentage of the variable TOTAL; relative accountability is the variable ACCTBL expressed as a percentage of TOTAL. It is important to note that the effect of the variable PROBSO has not been lost. The variable LOGTOT is serving to capture its net effect. A more detailed discussion of this issue can be found in Problems 26 and 27 in the problem set of this chapter. See Figure 16.11 for the regression results.

Comment: All three independent variables have positive coefficients several times larger than their standard errors (high *t* values). This indicates that there is little chance that the true values of the coefficients are zero. The interpretation that follows is that, holding unchanged the relative weight of each job content component, RELKNO and RELACC, a one percentage point increase in total evaluation points leads to a 0.77 percentage increase in salary compensation. In addition, the significance of the coefficients of RELKNO and RELACC indicate there also exists an important effect of the job's component mix in salary determination.

For prediction purposes, the multiple regression exhibits greater reliability than the simple log salary-log total regression. This is indicated by the reduction of the standard deviation of residuals from .110 for the simple regression of LOGSAL vs. LOGTOT to .103 for the multiple. The adjusted R^2 value increased from 84.3 to 86.2 percent.

3. Statistical Issue: Residual Adequacy Is the problem of non-constant residuals still in evidence?

Suggested Procedure: Construct a scatterplot of the standardized residuals on the Y axis and the standardized predicted Y values on the X axis. See Figure 16.12.

Comment: The plot indicates the non-constant scatter problem of residuals (heteroskedasticity). A few outlying residuals can be found at the upper ranges of the data. Our visual assessment suggests that a strong cone-like pattern is not present and so the problem is not serious.

LOG SAL VS LOG TOT, RELKNOW, RELACC
                %TERMS %TOTAL

```
THE REGRESSION EQUATION IS
Y =  3.215 +  .768 X1 +  .0359 X2 +  .0306 X3


                                       ST. DEV.     T-RATIO =
             COLUMN      COEFFICIENT    OF COEF.     COEF/S.D.
             --     .       3.215         1.40         2.29
X1           C11 LOGTOT     .7683         .0891        8.62
X2           C8  RELKNO     .0359         .0128        2.80
X3           C9  RELACC     .03063        .00948       3.23


THE ST. DEV. OF Y ABOUT REGRESSION LINE IS
S =      .103
WITH ( 64- 4) = 60 DEGREES OF FREEDOM


R-SQUARED = 86.8 PERCENT
R-SQUARED = 86.2 PERCENT, ADJUSTED FOR D.F.
```

FIGURE 16.11 Computer Output for Multiple Regression of LOGSAL on LOGTOT, RELKNO, and RELACC

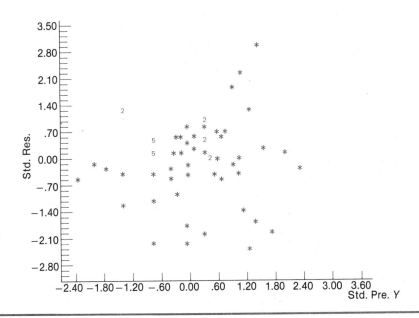

FIGURE 16.12 Scatterplot: Standardized Residuals of LOGSAL vs. Predicted LOGSAL

4. *Managerial Issue:* For a newly created management job evaluated at, say, 700 total points by the consulting firm, what salary level would be consistent with the current salaries assigned to other M & M management jobs, assuming 30 percent weight on Knowhow and 40 percent on Accountability?

Suggested Procedure: Using the computed equation for the regression of LOGSAL on the independent variables LOGTOT, RELKNO, and RELACC together with the specified values of the independent variables, the estimate of LOGSAL is:

$$\widehat{\text{LOGSAL}} = 3.22 + .7683(6.551) + .0359(30) + .0306(40) = 10.554$$

Then, taking the antilog of 10.554 gives \$38,330 as the salary estimate for the new position.

Further Exploration: Can you suggest additional analysis and effects not yet tested for? (Hint: Check the M & M data file for unused variables. This issue is explored further in the Student Solutions Manual.)

16.14. Concluding Comments

This chapter attempted to show that the multiple regression model is an important and valuable extension of the simple regression model. It allows one to take into account the effect of several independent variables in determining the value of Y.

For planning and control, the goal is the estimation of reliable regression coefficients that represent the *net effect* of each independent policy variable. The net effect provides us with the means of specifying the impact on Y of a policy variable change regardless of the movement that occurs in other variables. Reliability is established by the size of a variable's computed t statistic. The higher the t value, the greater the assurance that there exists a true association between the variables X and Y. Variables with low t values (below one as a rule of thumb) are generally discarded unless there is strong *a priori* evidence that suggests they should remain in the equation.

For purposes of prediction, the focus of concern is not on the net effect of individual variables but rather on the overall reliability of the entire equation in predicting Y. The criteria for judging the overall value of the equation to predict Y is the multiple adjusted R^2 and the standard deviation of residuals. If the addition of a variable lowers the multiple adjusted R^2 or raises the standard deviation of residuals, the variable should be left out of the equation. If, on the other hand, the R^2 rises and the standard deviation of residuals falls, the variable should be retained.

As well as the same statistical problems of residual behavior that accompany simple and multiple regression, the use of multiple regression poses the potential problems of multicollinearity and specification bias. Multicollinearity is essentially a sparse data problem in which the net effect (regression coefficient) of the variable becomes unreliable. The problem is characterized by a dramatic increase in the standard error of the coefficient often causing the computed t statistic to collapse, with the implication that the variable should be dropped for purposes of prediction but not necessarily for purposes of planning and control. Larger sample sizes are one way of possibly relieving the problem. Unfortunately, larger sample sizes for much of the observational data used are simply not available. An alternative is transformation of the original variables, which was done in the M & M review exercise.

Specification bias poses a different problem since we have no specific statistic to signal that it exists in a given situation. When present, it renders the regression coefficient inaccurate as well as biased. We will once again encounter the use of multiple regression in Chapter 19, on business forecasting. There we will explore more thoroughly the use and the pitfalls of multiple regression analysis with time series data.

Footnotes and References

[1] When the mean value of Y is a function of the independent variables X_1 and X_2, it is denoted by $\mu_{Y.X_1X_2}$, indicating it represents the mean value of Y given particular values of X_1 and X_2. However, this notation can become quite cumbersome when there are several independent variables. Hence, in this chapter we use simpler notation: $\mu_{Y.12}$.

[2] Charles Horngren, *Managerial Cost Accounting*, Chapter 25, Prentice-Hall, 1977 (Fourth Edition).

[3] Since a computer simulation was instructed to generate the sample data for illustrating important issues and problems, it is noteworthy to point out that X_1 and X_2 were devised with specification of a true zero correlation value between them.

Questions and Problems

1. Suppose the computed multiple regression equation is:

$$\hat{Y}_{123} = 52 + 1.7X_1 - 7X_2 + 4X_3$$

a. For values of $X_1 = 6, X_2 = 2,$ and $X_3 = 1,$ what is the predicted value of $\hat{Y}_{123}$?
b. What statistics would be used to assess the goodness of fit of the entire equation?
c. What statistic would be used to assess the reliability of the coefficient of X_1?

2. What are the advantages of using multiple linear regression on variables Y, X_1, and X_2, rather than using two simple linear regressions, one with Y and X_1, the other with Y and X_2? (Refer to the discussion in Section 16.6.)

3. How is the number of independent variables in a regression model related to the number of degrees of freedom available for estimating the standard deviation of residuals? If the addition of an independent variable does not reduce the unexplained variance, what must have happened to the standard deviation of residuals? What conclusion does this bring you to?

4. A multiple regression of household milk consumption in quarts per week (Y), on annual household income in thousands of dollars (X_1), and size of family (X_2) resulted in the following regression equation:

$$\hat{Y}_{12} = -.025 + .05X_1 + 1.14X_2$$

From this, would it be valid to conclude that

a. the coefficient of determination is $(-.025 + .05)/1.14$? Explain.
b. negative milk consumption occurs in very small, poor families? Explain.
c. changes in annual household income have about twice the effect on variability of milk consumption as does the intercept term? Explain.
d. a family of four people with $20,000 annual income will consume about 5.54 quarts of milk per week? Explain.

5. Explain why a regression equation is most appropriate over the range of values used for its development. (Refer to the discussion in Section 15.4 and 15.5.)

6. The (unadjusted) value of R^2 never decreases when a new independent variable is added to the regression equation. Therefore, it is tempting to add many variables to the model to force (unadjusted) R^2 to

be near one. Is this an appropriate procedure? Bearing in mind that the number of degrees of freedom is reduced by one when a new independent variable is added, what benefit does the adjusted R^2 provide? (Refer to Section 16.5.)

7. Comment on the statement: "The standard deviation of the dependent variable is always larger than the standard deviation of residuals in a useful regression."

8. The least squares multiple linear regression of Y on X_1 and X_2 has been estimated to be $\hat{Y}_{12} = a + b_1 X_1 + b_2 X_2$. Indicate in a few sentences why you agree or disagree with the following statements.

a. If b_2 is 7 times as large as b_1, then we may infer that X_2 is considerably more important than X_1 in accounting for the variation in Y.

b. The expected change in Y in response to a unit change in X_2 with X_1 held contant is b_2.

For all of the remaining statements, suppose that R^2 has a very high value, say $R^2 = 0.97$. Again, indicate in a few sentences why you agree or disagree that the statements below follow from this information.

c. The coefficients a, b_1, and b_2 must all have very high t values.

d. The computed regression plane is a very close approximation to the true regression plane.

e. The observed Ys cannot on average vary by much from the predicted Ys, $\hat{Y}$.

f. The variations in X_1 and X_2 account for a substantial proportion of the observed total variation in Y.

g. The observed residuals ($e = Y - \hat{Y}$) show no systematic pattern.

h. Dropping either X_1 or X_2 and estimating the simple regression of Y on the remaining variable would not reduce R^2 very much.

9. After a regression equation is fit to a set of data, a confidence interval for the *mean value of Y* at a given setting of the independent variables will ALWAYS be narrower than the corresponding prediction interval for a *particular value of Y* at the same setting of the independent variables. Why? (Refer to the discussion in

Sections 14.10 and 14.11. The answer to this question is the same whether multiple or simple regression is used.)

10. In estimating the regression slope coefficients, which of the following are we most desirous of obtaining? (Refer to the discussion in Sections 16.5, 16.7, and 16.8.)

a. a high R^2

b. independent variables which are uncorrelated with important omitted variables

c. a small standard error of slope coefficient

d. a small standard deviation of residuals

e. low multicollinearity

f. a high t ratio

11. In forecasting the dependent variable using multiple regression techniques, which of the following are we most desirous of obtaining? (Refer to the discussion in Sections 16.5, 16.7, and 16.8. Assume no serial correlation exists.)

a. a low standard deviation of residuals

b. low collinearity

c. a high R^2

d. independent variables which are uncorrelated with omitted variables

e. an unbiased regression coefficient with a high t ratio

12. Annual sales of the Jackson Beer Company in millions of dollars (Y) are thought to be correlated with U.S. disposable personal income in billions of dollars (X_1) and company marketing expenditures in millions of dollars (X_2). Data are collected over an 18 year period. Regressions of sales on the independent variables are as follows (assume all t ratios are above 2 and no serial correlation exists):

$$\hat{Y}_X = 216 + 19X_1 \text{ (simple regression)}$$
$$\hat{Y}_{12} = 182 + 7X_1 + 12X_2 \text{ (multiple regression)}$$

(Refer to the discussion in Section 16.7.)

a. What factors are likely to have caused the change in the coefficient of disposable income (X_1) from 19 in the simple regression equation to 7 in the multiple regression equation?

b. Suppose marketing expenditures were to be the same next year as this year (X_2 held constant). Would you estimate the sale response to a $1 billion increase in disposable income to be an increase of $19 million or an increase of $7 million? Explain.

13. *Demand for New Mainframe Computers* In a study of the demand for mainframe computers by *Fortune 500* during the period 1960–1981, the equation estimated was

$$\hat{Y}_{1234} = a + b_1X_1 + b_2X_2 + b_3X_3 + b_4X_4$$

where Y is expenditures (in hundred million dollars) in new computers for the year t; X_1 is the price index for all mainframes, new and used, for period t; X_2 is the estimated age of the total stock of mainframes in years; X_3 is the average firm earnings during year t (in billion dollars); and X_4 is the growth rate of firm sales over the last three years.

The following regression equation was fitted to the data:

$$\hat{Y}_{1234} = 75.436 - .118X_1 + 2.12X_2 + .173X_3 + .068X_4$$

$-.118X_1: (.029)$
$+2.12X_2: (.690)$
$+.173X_3: (.069)$
$+.068X_4: (.133)$

Variable	Mean	Std. Dev.
Y	101.44	6.52
X_1	115.08	35.22
X_2	10.20	1.26
X_3	99.36	12.58
X_4	10.50	7.73

$R^2 = 0.714$

The figures in parentheses are the standard errors of the respective regression coefficients.

Indicate briefly for each of the statements following why you agree or disagree with it. Assume no serial correlation of residuals is present.

a. Price had a more important effect in determining the variation in expenditures for mainframes than did average earnings.
b. If price increased one index point in a given year, other things being equal, expenditures for mainframes would decline by $11.8 million, on the average.
c. The relationship between price and expenditure for mainframes is not statistically significant.
d. About 29 percent of the variance in expenditures for new mainframes must be explained by variables other than stock of mainframes, price, and average firm earnings.
e. The fact that the coefficient of X_2 is approximately 18 times as large as the coefficient of X_1 means that X_2 explains considerably more of the variability in Y than does X_1.
f. The residuals ($e = Y - \hat{Y}_{1234}$) are necessarily independent of each other.

14. *Predicting Sales Potential* The human resources director of the Sure-Hands Insurance Company wishes to find out whether the sales talent of sales representatives can be predicted from their education and age. If found useful, these criteria would provide a valuable aid in screening the candidates for employment. As a start, ten sales reps are selected at random and are rated by their supervisor as to sales ability, education, and age. The rating on sales potential covers a seven point scale, from "Poor" (0) to "Excellent" (6). The education scale varies from "none" (0) to "Has master's degree" (4). The age scale extends from "Age 20–29 (0) to "Age 60–69" (4). The results are shown in Table 16.6.

a. Compute the multiple linear regression equation by the method of least squares to estimate sales potential from business education and age. Show all relevant statistics.
b. What is the meaning of the net regression coefficient b_1 in this particular case? How would this value differ in meaning from the regression coefficient of business education in the simple regression of sales potential on business education?
c. How long would the reliability of b_1 be affected if the younger reps generally had more business education than the older persons?
d. Would it be important to know whether age and business education had been used as criteria in hiring? Explain.
e. Is the "truncated distribution trap" discussed in Chapter 15 relevant to this problem?

TABLE 16.6. Sales Potential, Business Education, and Age

SALES REP	SALES POTENTIAL Y	BUSINESS EDUCATION X_1	AGE X_2
1	1	0	2
2	2	1	3
3	4	2	0
4	6	3	0
5	1	0	3
6	2	2	4
7	6	4	1
8	1	1	4
9	4	4	2
10	3	3	1
Sum	30	20	20

15. Compute the standard deviation of residuals in Problem 14 and interpret its meaning for purposes of predicting the sales potential of the sales representatives.
b. Compute the multiple coefficient of determination and interpret its meaning in describing the relationship between sales potential, business education, and age.

16. *Recruiting New Dealers*   A company sells women's hosiery in special display racks directly to supermarkets and drug stores. This company wants to determine the relationship, if any, between the percentage of stores who agree to carry its product and two independent variables: price, X_1, and years of experience of the salesperson, X_2. Thirty salespersons employed by the company are randomly assigned to sell the product to retail dealers, six salespersons for each of five different prices, ranging from 63¢ to $2.49 per pair. Each salesperson makes a sales presentation to forty prospective new dealers, and the percentage of new accounts is recorded. The thirty observations (six salespersons for each of five prices) are used to determine the least squares regression equation:

$$\hat{Y}_{12} = -28 - 1.2X_1 + 12X_2,$$
with $S_{b_1} = 0.4$, $S_{b_2} = 3.0$ and $R^2 = .88$

a. Interpret the values of b_1 and b_2. (Refer to the discussion in Section 16.3.)
b. Using a "*t*" test and the 5% level of significance, test the hypothesis that the inde-

pendent variables are useful in the equation for predicting Y.
c. Do the data support the conclusion that higher prices decrease dealer willingness to carry the product? Explain.
d. Does the evidence indicate that additional experience increases the ability of salespersons to secure additional dealers? Explain.

17. *Interpretation of Negative Intercept* In Problem 16, the intercept term has a value of -28. Suppose it is argued that this estimate cannot be correct, since a negative percentage of dealer acceptances is impossible. How would you refute this argument? (Hint: The discussion in Section 15.5 for simple regression also applies for multiple regression.)

18. *Identifying Determinants of Absenteeism*   A small manufacturer of men's ties experienced a very high rate of absenteeism among its workers and the absenteeism has tended to fluctuate considerably from week to week. The president of the company believes union organizers are the source of the absenteeism problem. Absenteeism and employee complaints have been encouraged by the organizers to apply pressure to management. A measure of the activity of the organizers is provided by the number of union-supported complaints appearing in the employee suggestion box each week. The plant manager believes the absenteeism results from the president's policy of not increasing the

workforce during peak demand periods. Any increase in demand must be met through overtime. He claims the workers "just don't want to work more than 45 hours a week." Excessive overtime assignments lead many workers to stay home rather than accumulate extra work hours. You decide to try to find out which factor is the more influential in causing the fluctuations in absenteeism. Accordingly, you compile the appropriate data over the past 4 weeks (all figures are in hundreds). Let Y be the number of worker-hours absent in a given week, X_1 the total number of overtime hours required in that week, and X_2 the number of union-supported complaints in the suggestion box that week.

The data are summarized in the following sums of squares and cross products.

$$\sum Y = 18 \qquad \sum X_2^2 = 23$$
$$\sum X_1 = 10 \qquad \sum YX_1 = 48$$
$$\sum X_2 = 9 \qquad \sum YX_2 = 43$$
$$\sum X_1^2 = 30 \qquad \sum X_1X_2 = 22$$

a. Write the normal equations to determine the net regression coefficients b_1 and b_2. (Refer to Section 16.2.)
b. Given the following solution for the multiple regression equation,

$$\hat{Y} = .407 + .704X_1 + 1.037X_2$$
$$[.046] \qquad [.053]$$

interpret the meaning of the coefficients.
c. Using the standard errors of the coefficients shown in brackets in Part b, determine which factor is more significant statistically. Does the larger t value mean that the factor is more important in explaining the variation in absenteeism? Explain.

19. *Appraising the Value of Single Family Homes* Table 16.7 lists the sales price Y and four assumed related predictor variables $X_1, X_2, X_3,$ and X_4 for each of 40 single-family residences sold by a realtor the previous month.
Which variables would you include in the regression equation if you want to estimate the market value of:
a. enlarging an existing house to add one bathroom?

b. adding one bathroom without enlarging the house?
c. Suppose older houses generally have fewer bathrooms for a given house size than do newer houses. What effect, if any, would this have on the reliability of the coefficients b_3 and b_4 in a regression with the four independent variables?
d. Suppose age of the house is thought to have an important influence on the house's market value. A regression of Y on $X_1, X_2, X_3,$ and X_4 gives coefficients for $X_1, X_2,$ and $X_3,$ that are highly statistically significant. The coefficient of X_4 is not significant, having a t value well below one. Would you include X_4 in a regression equation used to predict selling price of a house? Explain.
e. Should your answer to Part d depend on the sign of b_4? Explain.

20. Using the data set in Problem 19,
a. Fit a multiple linear regression equation $\hat{Y}_{1234} = a + b_1X_1 + b_2X_2 + b_3X_3 + b_4X_4$ using a standard computer regression analysis program.
b. Interpret the computer output for this analysis.
c. Use the computed multiple regression equation to estimate selling price for each of five residences currently on the market. The data are given in Table 16.8.

21. *Predicting the Selling Price of Undeveloped Lots* A real estate developer wanted to construct a multiple regression model to use for estimating the selling price of wooded lots for vacation homes near a Vermont ski resort. To do so she recorded data on the following variables for each of 28 lots recently sold:

Y = sale price of the wooded lot (in \$1000 units)
X_1 = area of the lot (in hundreds of square feet)
X_2 = elevation of the lot
X_3 = slope of the lot

Using a computer software regression analysis program, the real estate developer obtained the output in Table 16.9.

TABLE 16.7. Measurements Taken on 40 Single-family Residences

SALES PRICE $Y(\times \$1000)$	SQUARE FEET $X_1(\times 100)$	NO. OF STORIES X_2	NO. OF BATHROOMS X_3	AGE X_4
33.1	8.9	1	1	2
45.3	9.5	1	1	6
45.8	12.4	2	1.5	5
48.3	10.5	1	1	11
41.7	10.7	1	1.5	15
54.0	13.8	2	1.5	10
54.1	12.6	2	1.5	11
54.4	12.9	2	1.5	8
54.9	15.5	2	1	9
57.3	16.5	1	1.5	15
59.5	16.0	2	1	11
59.9	16.7	2	1	12
60.3	17.5	2	2	13
60.8	17.9	2	1.5	18
61.0	19.0	2	1	22
63.5	17.6	1	1	17
66.1	18.1	2	1.5	5
66.5	17.0	3	2	2
66.8	20.4	2	1.5	16
66.9	20.0	2	1.5	12
69.2	21.9	2	1.5	10
69.5	20.6	2	1.5	11
72.9	19.9	1	1.5	13
75.0	21.8	2	2	8
75.1	20.5	1	2	9
76.6	22.2	2	1.5	10
78.9	22.0	2	2.5	6
81.8	22.5	2	1.5	11
84.0	24.3	2	1.5	17
84.7	23.5	2	2.5	12
89.0	25.0	2	1.5	11
92.0	25.4	1	2	12
99.8	25.1	2	2	8
105.3	26.8	2	2.5	6
107.1	22.7	2	2	18
114.0	25.6	2	2	10
118.4	24.0	2	2	13
119.0	31.2	3	2.5	25
123.0	21.6	2	2.5	18
155.0	40.8	3	4	12

TABLE 16.8. Data for Five Residences

RESIDENCE i	SQUARE FEET $X_1(00)$	BATHROOMS X_2	TOTAL ROOMS X_3	AGE X_4
1	20.4	2	7	17
2	15.8	2	6	6
3	19.2	1	7	4
4	21.7	3	8	22
5	30.0	2	9	11

TABLE 16.9. Undeveloped Lots—Computer Output

R SQUARE	.90
STD. DEV. OF RESIDUALS	.53
PRICE MEAN	5.23
PRICE STD. DEV.	1.27

INDIVIDUAL ANALYSIS OF VARIABLES

VARIABLE	MEAN	STD. DEVIATION	COEFFICIENT, b	STD. ERROR OF b
CONSTANT	—	—	.604	
AREA	16.38	3.09	.124	.048
ELEVATION	5.49	3.22	.251	.070
SLOPE	175.24	23.57	.007	.008

a. Give the prediction equation that the real estate developer would use to relate selling price to the area, elevation, and slope of a wooded lot near the ski resort?

b. Which of the predictor variables is statistically the most important contributor to the variation in Y?

22. Suppose that before you collected the data for the analysis of Problem 21 you had a theory that sloping lots were preferred over those with lesser slope. Do the data provide sufficient evidence to indicate that sales price increases as the slope increases? (Hint: Test H_0: $\beta_3 = 0$ against the one-sided alternative H_a: $\beta_3 > 0$. Use $\alpha = .05$.)

23. *Measuring Advertising Productivity* An advertising agency sponsors a consumer panel study to determine the productivity of advertising for a client's brand of frozen mixed fruit. A multiple regression equation known as an *advertising response function* is computed regressing a family's dollar purchases of the brand (Y) on two independent variables: (1) the amount of exposure opportunities to the brand's advertising (X_1), and (2) the amount of exposure opportunities to a competing brand's advertising (X_2).

The computed regression equation is:

$$\hat{Y}_{12} = .22 + .235X_1 - .110X_2$$

a. What interpretation should be given to the two regression coefficients in the advertising response function?

b. For a family having 10 exposure opportunities to the brand's advertising and none to the competitor's advertising, what

is the estimated expenditure on the brand?

c. Suppose a family is given five exposure opportunities to the brand's advertising, and Brand 2 retaliates by advertising its own brand to the point that 2 of its ads are seen by the family in question. What is the expected expenditure of the family on Brand 1?

d. Does advertising of a brand of frozen mixed fruit appear to stimulate sales of that brand only, or does it stimulate sales of competing brands as well? (Hint: Interpret the coefficient of X_2.)

24. In Problem 23 assume that the manufacturer's variable costs of producing and distributing the product amount to 30 percent of a family's dollar purchases of the brand. Thus the manufacturer's marginal revenue of an advertising exposure net of these costs is 70 percent of the family's increased spending.

a. How much would it be worth paying for one additional family exposure opportunity (assuming no competitive retaliation)?

b. The cost of reaching a family with an additional exposure opportunity is generally thought to increase with additional exposure opportunities, because the least expensive media for reaching the family are ordinarily used first. Suppose the marginal cost of advertising is given by the equation:

$$C = .02 + .01X + .001X^2$$

The most profitable number of exposure opportunities occurs when the manufacturer's net marginal revenue from an additional exposure to the ad is equated to the marginal cost of the additional exposure. At what number of exposures would this equality occur?

c. Suppose that there are diminishing marginal revenues as advertising exposure opportunities increase. How would this change the form of the advertising response function?

25. In Problem 23 suppose that a major factor not considered which contributes to sales variation among the families in the consumer panel is the amount of purchases of mixed frozen fruit in the past. That is, families which have already developed a habit of purchasing this product will likely have comparatively large expenditures on frozen fruit with or without advertising in the product period. What effect does the omission of the past sales variable have on the regression coefficient if:

a. past sales among families are highly correlated with present sales? Explain. (Hint: would specification bias be present?)

b. past sales among families are *not* highly correlated with present sales? Explain.

26. *M and M Industries (Continued)* In the M and M Industries Review Exercise, numerous regressions were run to explain salary levels by various combinations of independent variables. It is important to note that the value and *interpretation* of a particular independent variable's coefficient critically depends on what other independent variables are in the equation. This can be illustrated by considering the four computed equations given below. The questions which follow refer to the changing interpretation of the variables.

General Regression Equation

$$\hat{Y}_{123456} = a + b_1 \text{ KNOWHO}$$
$$+ b_2 \text{ PROBSO}$$
$$+ b_3 \text{ ACCTBL}$$
$$+ b_4 \text{ TOTAL}$$
$$+ b_5 \text{ RELKNO}$$
$$+ b_6 \text{ RELACC}$$

Computed Equation

1. $\hat{Y}_{14} = 19,218 + 47.6 \text{ TOTAL}$
2. $\hat{Y}_{123} = 10,122 + 151 \text{ KNOWHO}$
$$- 128 \text{ PROBSO}$$
$$+ 61 \text{ ACCTBL}$$

3. $\hat{Y}_{134} = 10,122 + 279 \text{ KNOWHO}$
$$+ 189 \text{ ACCTBL}$$
$$- 128 \text{ TOTAL}$$
4. $\hat{Y}_{456} = -26,878 + 51 \text{ TOTAL}$
$$+ 523 \text{ RELKNO}$$
$$+ 608 \text{ RELACC}$$

a. What difference is there in the interpretation of b_4, the coefficient of the variable TOTAL, between equation number 1 (simple regression) and equation 4 (multiple regression)?

b. Equations 3 and 4 are both multiple regression equations which include the variable TOTAL as an independent variable. Does b_4, the coefficient of TOTAL, have the same interpretation in both equations? If so, why do the two values of b_4 differ so sharply? If not, what is the difference in interpretation? Hint: refer to the changing interpretation of the family size coefficient in Review Exercise I.

c. Is it coincidence that the value of b_4 in equation 3 is identical to the value of b_2 in equation 2? Explain.

d. Is it coincidence that the value of b_1 in equation 3 is the difference between b_1 and b_2 in equation 2? Explain. Hint: how is the interpretation of KNOWHO affected if PROBSO is replaced by TOTAL in the regression equation.

e. Is it coincidence that the value of b_3 in equation 3 is the difference between b_2 and b_3 in equation 2? Explain.

27. *M and M Industries (Continued)* In the M and M Industries Review Exercise one of the regressions included the three variables TOTAL, RELKNO, and RELACC:

$$\hat{Y}_{456} = -26878 + 51 \text{ TOTAL}$$
$$+ 523 \text{ RELKNO}$$
$$+ 608 \text{ RELACC}$$

On the surface, the coefficients of RELKNO and RELACC have a routine interpretation. For instance, estimated salary increases 523 dollars when RELKNO, which is KNOWHO expressed as a percentage of the total, is increased by one percentage point, given TOTAL and RELACC held constant. But for KNOWHO (as a percentage of the total) to increase as TOTAL is held constant, there must be a decrease in the contribution of some other component of

TOTAL by the same amount. It must be that the job component *problem solving ability*, PROBSO (not included explicitly in the equation), decreases. It *cannot* be accountability, because RELACC is included in the equation and is assumed to be held constant when RELKNO is increased. Thus, 523 dollars interprets as the estimated increase in salary for each one percentage point *shift of total job points out of PROBSO into KNOWHOW.*

a. What interpretation should be given to the coefficient of RELACC?

b. Why was RELPRO excluded from the regression equation which included RELKNO and RELACC?

28. *Multicollinearity Effect* James C. Boyd is the owner and general manager of a custom carpet shop servicing an urban trade area in Southern California. One of Boyd's problems is that he must give firm price quotations to his customers even though his cost is not determined until the job is completed. Labor cost is particularly difficult to estimate. Using the technique of multiple regression analysis which he learned in business school, Boyd has recently developed the following forecasting equation for estimating the labor cost of a job:

$$\widehat{LC} = 36.1 + 12.3MC + .7D - 11.3YD$$
$$t = 3.5 \quad t = 3.7 \quad t = -.4$$

$$R^2 = .98 \quad n = 57$$

where LC = total labor cost per job order; MC = material cost per yard for the job; D = total distance traveled from shop to job location; and YD = yardage used per job.

"Not relevant," said Boyd as he examined the computer output. "That minus 11.3 for the yardage coefficient doesn't make sense. Total labor cost can't decline the more carpet that is laid on the job." "Well," said his sales manager, who had also studied multiple regression analysis, "at least the negative coefficient value has a very low t value." "No matter," said Boyd. "I just can't feel confident about an equation which suggests such nonsense." Just as Boyd was about to pass final judgment on the result, the sales manager placed in front of him a comparison of the predicted labor cost using the equation versus the actual figure for labor cost for the last five jobs. See Table 16.10.

Boyd's jaw dropped. "My goodness, look at that," he said. "Our current estimation method based only upon the number of yards used doesn't come close in predictive accuracy to this approach." He thought a while, leaned over his desk toward the sales manager, and wondered out loud, "How can such a formulation work so well when we all know that the value for the yardage variable coefficient can't possibly be the true value?"

a. Can you suggest a plausible reason for a negative sign associated with the variable YD? (Hint: Refer to the discussion in Section 16.8.)

b. Should the variable YD be interpreted as the least important of the variables considered (because of its low t value)? (Hint: Refer to Section 16.9.)

c. Can Boyd, despite the negative YD coefficient, legitimately use the equation to predict labor cost for similar jobs now being planned?

d. Can the predictive accuracy of the equation likely be improved upon without using any more data?

29. *Forecasting Production Costs* Bob Johnson, production manager for the

TABLE 16.10. Comparison of Predicted and Actual Labor Costs

JOB	ACTUAL LABOR COST	PREDICTED LABOR COST	DIFFERENCE
1	147.2	145	2.2
2	176.1	175.4	.7
3	155.4	157.5	−2.1
4	201	204.2	−3.2
5	185	183.5	1.5

CONRAK division of Intek Corporation, had a conversation with his boss that ended with: "Bob, no more shot-in-the-dark guesses at your costs. Give me better divisional cost predictions or else I'll find somebody who will!" Johnson felt sure that the number of labor hours used (shown in Table 16.11a) and the hourly labor cost must figure somewhere into the divisional cost forecast. Hourly labor costs had risen from an average of $6.80 three years ago to $7.44 two years ago, and $8.09 one year ago, typically in lumps at the start of each year according to the union contract.

Machine breakdowns and other production line stoppages (shown in Table 16.11b) usually resulted in costs of some kind, although they did not always result in actual bills that had to be paid. Frequently, the cost was in the form of reduced production. In Bob Johnson's mind this made their effect difficult to discern.

The cost of materials other than aluminum wire was another factor to be considered. The production process required at least a half-dozen kinds of other materials, generally of the non-ferrous metal variety. Johnson obtained from purchasing an index of selected non-ferrous metal prices that might be useful in accounting for this factor (shown in Table 16.11c). Looking over the index, Johnson could see no specific way to involve this information in his forecast.

Although this mass of statistics was perplexing, Johnson realized that the time was right for him to show initiative and make a concerted effort to improve his forecasting record.

a. On the basis of data through June one year ago given in the case, formulate a regression equation which can be used to forecast monthly divisional operating costs. Assume that hourly labor usage is scheduled before the cost forecast is made.

b. Evaluate the adequacy of the forecasting equation, employing various statistical tests in your reasoning process.

c. Evaluate the reliability of the obtained results by checking that the statistical assumptions of the regression model are being met.

d. Prepare a cost forecast for the last six months using the data not included in constructing the model.

30. Refer to Review Exercise I, the Sperry and Hutchinson study.

a. Are there further analyses you might like to perform on this data to improve the prediction of food expenditures? Explain.

b. What additional data would you like to have?

c. Suppose that all the variables are subject to considerable measurement error which is not consistently in the same direction. If the effect of this measurement error is to increase the amount of unexplained variation which is in the residuals, what would be the effect on the computed value of R^2 and on the computed regression coefficients?

TABLE 16.11a. Hourly Labor Use (man-months)

	THREE YEARS AGO	TWO YEARS AGO	ONE YEAR AGO
January	243	235	250
February	250	254	255
March	255	258	264
April	260	266	275
May	281	210	282
June	262	213	278
July	241	207	260
August	220	210	248
September	214	210	241
October	212	280	239
November	218	260	261
December	224	241	280

TABLE 16.11b. Number of Production Line Stoppages

	THREE YEARS AGO	TWO YEARS AGO	ONE YEAR AGO
January	16	19	21
February	32	26	15
March	8	16	16
April	13	18	17
May	19	24	18
June	22	19	19
July	18	17	22
August	24	25	20
September	21	22	18
October	23	20	23
November	19	24	22
December	25	17	20

TABLE 16.11c. Selected Nonferrous Metal Prices (dollars) per pound

	THREE YEARS AGO	TWO YEARS AGO	ONE YEAR AGO
January	0.85	0.87	0.79
February	0.83	1.00	0.66
March	0.82	1.01	0.61
April	0.69	0.88	0.70
May	0.64	0.96	0.81
June	0.62	0.89	0.84
July	0.52	1.05	0.88
August	0.62	1.04	1.43
September	0.70	1.01	1.37
October	0.76	1.08	0.91
November	0.82	0.94	1.23
December	0.84	0.90	0.82

TABLE 16.11d. Operating Costs

	THREE YEARS AGO	TWO YEARS AGO	ONE YEAR AGO
January	280,310	279,210	296,005
February	284,950	290,110	295,420
March	287,010	293,100	299,250
April	291,610	300,040	303,925
May	300,990	321,700	307,900
June	291,870	325,500	295,005
July	281,680	322,660	298,200
August	271,110	326,342	294,210
September	270,700	324,900	292,900
October	268,420	311,010	293,510
November	269,720	298,050	307,410
December	272,310	287,120	317,618

TABLE 16.12a. Coding of Three Types of Bananas

BANANA TYPE AND SHIPPING METHOD	CODED QUALITY VALUE, Q
Regular—Stem	−1
Creamed—Stem	0
Superior—Boxed	1
PRICE	**CODED PRICE VALUE, P**
2¢ per pound below prevailing retail	−1
Prevailing retail price	0
2¢ per pound above prevailing retail	+1

31. Suppose the income (X_2) and education (X_6) variables in Review Exercise I are correlated. What effect would this have on the coefficient of the income variable in:
a. the first regression equation?
b. the second regression equation?

32. Refer again to Review Exercise I.
a. The data for the study were collected during the 1960s. Subsequent inflation during the 1970s and early 1980s pushed both incomes and food prices to much higher levels than prevailed at the time the study was taken. However, the computed regression equation includes an income variable to account for the effect of higher income on food spending. Would you, therefore, expect the estimates of weekly food spending provided by the computed regression in the 1980s to be nearly as reliable as when the survey was conducted? Explain.
b. Would the computed regression pro-

vide the basis for an unbiased estimate of the additional weekly food expenditures accompanying a $3,000 increase in a particular family's income? Explain. (Hint: Consider the regression phenomenon and regression fallacy discussed in Chapter 15.)

33. *The Demand for Chiquita Bananas: Price and Quality Determinants* Hoping to carve out a market niche and to avoid an intense price war with Ecuadorian bananas, the United Fruit Company devised a strategy to market a superior quality banana at a premium price under the brand name "Chiquita" banana. Superior quality bananas necessitate using a higher cost method of boxing bananas on the tropical plantations instead of the traditional method of shipping bananas on the stem. The boxing method would reduce breakage, bruising, and deterioration. In general it would facilitate a more stringent quality

TABLE 16.12b. Follow-up Study on Banana Sales

LOCATION	SALES IN POUNDS PER WEEK PER THOUSAND CUSTOMERS (Y)	(Q) QUALITY	(P) PRICE
1	390	+1	+1
2	388	+1	+1
3	278	0	+1
4	316	0	+1
5	578	+1	0
6	598	+1	0
7	490	0	0
8	512	0	0
9	228	−1	0
10	392	−1	0
11	452	0	−1
12	602	0	−1
13	390	−1	−1
14	420	−1	−1

control program than presently existed in the industry. But would consumers perceive this and pay extra for the "Chiquita" bananas? With the cooperation of a supermarket chain United Fruit conducted a marketing research study encompassing 14 locations. The numerical coding scheme in Table 16.12a was used to distinguish three quality levels and three price levels.

The following multiple regression equation summarized the results of the study:

$$\hat{Y} = 514 - 718P + 124Q$$

Standard Deviation of Residuals $= 58$

where Y is the pounds bought per week per thousand customers.

a. What is the estimated demand for superior quality boxed bananas at the prevailing retail price? At 2¢ per pound above the prevailing retail price?

b. Describe the extent of uncertainty about the demand for superior quality boxed bananas at 2¢ per pound above the prevailing retail price.

c. How does the estimated volume of superior boxed bananas at 2¢ per pound premium compare with estimated volume of better quality ("creamed") stem fruit at the prevailing retail price?

d. Explain how dummy variables using only 0 or 1 as values could have been used to measure the quality effect and indicate any advantages or disadvantages of this method. Hint: would the degrees of freedom change? How would the dummy variable estimation change the current estimation that assumes equal quality gaps from regular to creamed and creamed to

superior? (Refer to Section 16.10, p. 605.)

e. A later follow-up study at the same 14 locations was conducted to determine the permanence of the first study results. With the data from the follow-up study given in Table 16.12b, compute an estimated multiple regression equation and compare the results with the finding of the original study. Do the findings of the follow-up study confirm or contradict the conclusion reached in the original study?

34. *Employee Turnover* "High employee turnover is hurting us badly," said Iris Korne, the personnel manager at Continuous Lens, a growing contact lens producer on the West Coast. "I bet it's having a negative impact on our productivity; besides, it's disruptive to be continually recruiting and training new personnel. Maybe we're hiring too many of the wrong type of employee—the type that just has little company loyalty." After some further thought on the matter Korne decides that an in-house study of current and former employee traits may give some insight into the kind of individual that should be sought. The data in Table 16.13 were collected.

a. Calculate and interpret the regression coefficients a, b_1, and b_2.

b. Describe how Korne might use the multiple regression equation for prediction.

c. Compute and interpret the multiple coefficient of determination.

d. What is the value of the standard deviation of residuals and how might Korne use it?

e. Calculate the simple correlation coeffi-

TABLE 16.13. Employee Traits and Turnover

EMPLOYEE	X_1 GROUP ORIENTATION INDEX	X_2 COMMUNITY SERVICE INDEX	Y YEARS WITH CONTINUOUS LENS
A	85	70	1
B	120	125	4
C	125	135	6
D	100	80	2
E	110	90	3
F	90	75	2
G	130	150	8
H	115	110	5

cients and discuss what purpose an examination of their values may serve.

f. Would it be important to know whether the two indexes had been used to initially screen applicants for employment at Continuous Lens? Explain. (Hint: refer to the discussion in Section 15.8.)

35. *Predicting the Need for Temporary Help* Wyman's, a large Chicago-based department store serving the downtown Chicago area, uses many part-time clerical and sales employees to supplement the regular staff during busy selling periods. The supplementary work force is hired on a day to day basis as needed by the personnel manager. To better implement this plan a marketing research consultant was brought in to identify the factors that determine daily sales. "Accurate forecasts of daily sales will hold down the cost of hiring unneeded help, yet it will let us take advantage of sales opportunities," exclaimed the personnel manager. The consultant isolated and quantified two factors thought to be useful predictors of the fluctuating daily sales. They are listed with the daily sales records in Table 16.14.

a. As personnel manager, use regression analysis to evaluate how effectively the consultant's factors predict daily sales.

b. Should the personnel manager use the regression equation as a practical method of hiring the temporary work force?

c. Suggest alternative factors or relationships, which the consultant overlooked, that might be used to predict daily sales. (Hint: consider seasonality).

36. *The E. I. du Pont de Nemours Co., Inc.* The E. I. du Pont de Nemours Co. conducted a series of marketing experiments among 25 different geographic trading areas to determine the effect of normal advertising expenditures and other marketing variables on the sales of one of its consumer products. At the conclusion of the experiments, marketing executives were presented with a multiple regression equation relating the product's market share in its trading area to three marketing variables. The equation was of the form:

$$MS = a + b_1 AVL + b_2 DP \\ + b_3 \frac{(A - A^*)}{A^*}$$

where MS = market share in the trading area; AVL = *availability*, measured by the percentage of dealers, in the trading area stocking the product; DP = *dealer push*, measured by the percentage of salespersons in the trading area specifying the product; A = current year advertising expenditures in the trading area; and A^* = previous year advertising expenditures in the trading area.

The predicted market share was multiplied by estimated industry-wide sales (S) in a trading area to derive a prediction of DuPont sales. This, in turn, was multiplied by marginal profit per unit (P) to get predicted profit:

TABLE 16.14. Predictors of Daily Sales

DAYS	Y DAILY SALES (000 Dollars)	X_1 DAILY NEWSPAPER ADVERTISING (000 Dollars)	X_2 DAILY WEATHER SUITABILITY (Scaled 0 [Poor] to 9 [Excellent])
1	20	1	1
2	36	5	9
3	34	6	8
4	40	10	8
5	32	8	5
6	28	2	7
7	32	4	9
8	33	7	7
9	26	9	0
10	29	3	8

Trading Area Profit $= PS(MS) - A$.

a. Members of the review committee considering the report of the experiments expressed concern that market sales was *linearly* related to advertising expenditures, implying that *if* advertising expenditures in an area were profitable, further expenditures would be profitable without limit. Comment. (Refer to the discussion in Section 15.3.)

b. The profit equation was said to imply an in-out advertising strategy because the increase in *this* year's profit for a given level of current year advertising is inversely related to *last* year's advertising. Areas receiving heavy expenditures one year would receive little or none the next year. The advertising group was very skeptical of this and felt the regression equation must be useless if it gives this result. (1) Use a numerical illustration to verify the inverse relationship. (2) Does the inverse relationship imply an "in-out" advertising strategy? Explain. (3) The research director noted that the equation resulted from a study designed only to determine the effect of *increased* advertising expenditures. The equation would be useful for this purpose, but should not be used to estimate the effect of decreased advertising expenditures. Is the research director correct? Explain.

Analysis of Time Series Data

Preview.   The beginning of each new year affords us the chance to look back at the sequence of events of the past year. If we can discover a pattern that we expect will continue, we can either take full advantage of it if it provides positive benefits, or prepare to lessen its impact if it is going to produce unfavorable consequences. Economists and business people share our basic concern about past events, but they typically deal with a longer historical series and take a more formal approach. The economist tries to recognize the sequential pattern of such series as the level of GNP, the rate of inflation, the index of production, and the level of money supply. Someone in business starts with the economist's analysis of the pattern of these historical economic series and compares them to the patterns in the financial data for the particular company or industry. The hope is that the comparison will yield a usable historical relationship that can be exploited in planning for the future. This chapter presents the statistical means for decomposing a historical data series into its time series components. Their usefulness in business analysis is then discussed. The chapter deals with past data on a purely descriptive basis to gain historical perspective. In the following chapter procedures are presented for the construction of index number series to represent the aggregate movement in more than one time series. Then in Chapter 19, the analysis is extended to forecasting purposes.

17.1. Introduction

Since Chapter Two, the organization and analysis of data has been discussed without much regard to the sequence in which the observations occurred. It is perfectly logical to ignore sequence if no useful information is contained therein. Let us explore a situation where the chronological sequence is of no importance.

Example 17.1A. Sequence Doesn't Always Matter: Mail Surveys

Suppose 2000 responses to a marketing research survey on consumer attitudes towards a new laundry product arrive in the mail on the same day. Would it be important to record the *order* in which the responses are received? Almost certainly the sequence of the data values will follow a random ordering pattern. In this case, the order of response provides no useful information about the answer to questions which the survey was designed to answer. In this particular situation, it would likely be quite safe to *disregard the sequence of the observations.*

However, business and economic series frequently show consecutive data values that are *not* random order. In these cases, the sequence of data collection and recording should not be ignored, otherwise valuable information about the behavior of the data series will be lost. The main effort of this chapter is to supply a model for the underlying sequential pattern of data.

Are There Time Dependent Patterns?

Recordings made sequentially at periodic time intervals are called *time series* data. Time series *analysis* concentrates on identifying and characterizing the time dependent patterns in time series data. For example, monthly department store sales are very much dependent upon the time of year; it would not be unusual for forty percent of a store's sales for the year to be made during the (November-December) Christmas selling season. The basic assumption of this type of analysis is that observations at successive time intervals are statistically dependent; that is, the value of the variable at one particular point in time is statistically related to the value of that variable in another time period.

Once knowledge has been gained about the observed underlying time dependency of the series, one frequently can assume that the pattern will persist into the future. Planning and control can then be attempted. But why do observed time sequential observations show a time dependent pattern? Basically because there is an important element of consistency and continuity in the economic environment.

Whether we are in a period of recession, inflation, or both simultaneously, people still need food, shelter, and basic transportation capabilities. Thus, aggregate consumer buying patterns generally do not change overnight. Purchasing generally remains fairly stable (although even small changes overall can have a major impact on certain industries). The corporate sector's production plans also modify slowly. This relative stability of buying patterns, corporate operations, and other underlying forces which determine the behavior of firms and individuals is reflected in the data. Therefore, the observed values of each business or economic data series (GNP, corporate sales, the demand for fast food) are closely linked over time. What is an implication of this? The following example provides some indication.

Example 17.1B.   Feast or Famine at McDonalds?

Can you imagine what would happen to McDonalds if one week practically everyone came in to eat a hamburger, but unexpectedly no one came to eat a hamburger for the next month? Even worse, what if the duration of this feast-famine syndrome constantly changed unpredictably? Surely business operations and customer service would be devastated. How could fresh meat orders be matched to customer demand? How could employees be scheduled? McDonald's needn't worry, though, because the underlying forces which stimulate fast-food purchases don't change rapidly from week to week.

More disruptive and far-reaching would be a situation in which the industrial capital and labor force producing this year's GNP suddenly were destroyed or lost; next year's GNP would take a nosedive. Fortunately, however, short of a global war or some calamitous act of God, continuity of behavior and preservation of structure are part of man's economic attitude and make-up.

Since structure and behavior are seldom destroyed or radically altered over a short period of time, repetitive patterns in data series from period to period are to be expected. But does the lack of *radical* change mean no change at all? Certainly not. Change is inevitable as economic, social, and political forces exert their influence. Gradually but inexorably, the influence of old factors on data values wanes. It is this mixed setting of persistent, recurring, and newly evolving influences that business decision makers must face and understand to develop effective plans for their business operations. The objective of time series analysis in the planning process is to isolate, identify, and *describe* for analysis the various components which combine to give movement to the observed data series.

17.2. The Classical Time Series Model

Causal forces underlie discernible patterns in observed data. They are of two fundamentally different kinds:

> *Some persist for long periods of time,* their influence being quite stable (although perhaps becoming somewhat more pronounced or somewhat less evident the longer the time period);

Other causal forces come and go more rapidly; their frequency of occurrence can be either at regular intervals or at irregular intervals.

The empirical patterns observed in time series data are the *net result of all* the underlying causal forces.

The best known methods for describing empirical patterns in time series data are based upon the *classical time series model.* This model views time series variation as the result of four component sources:

1. *Secular movements* or trend
2. *Periodic variation* (such as seasonal variation)
3. *Compensatory* or cyclical variation (of varying duration)
4. *Random variation*

Secular Movements or Trend

Secular movement, or *trend,* refers to a pattern of steadily increasing or steadily decreasing data values over extended periods of time. These phenomena may be

demographic in origin (such as population growth)
economic (such as growth in GNP)
technological (such as the use of nuclear energy)

Secular or long-run movements are considered to be those of generally ten to fifteen years duration. The secular movement component can be pictured as a smooth curve rising or declining steadily with successive time periods. The smooth curve may be either linear or non-linear, as shown in Figure 17.1.

Periodic Seasonal Variation

Fluctuations in data which re-occur according to a stable, *periodic* pattern of a year's duration or less are often described as *seasonal* variation. The periodicity may be of various lengths; for example, the four quarters or the twelve months of a year, the seven days of a week, etc. However, for a particular series of data the periodicity must be stable in length and occur at the same calendar time period. To illustrate:

if we were charting textbook sales to students over the years according to quarters, we would expect the sales to peak consistently during the fall quarter and to be at their low point during the summer quarter.

The main causal forces underlying seasonal variation are

institutional arrangements such as the school year, the five-day work week, the Friday paycheck;

social customs such as exchange of gifts at a particular time of year—the Christmas season;

weather influences such as the cold season of the year which lead to the

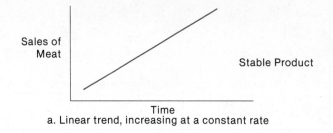

Sales of Meat

Stable Product

Time

a. Linear trend, increasing at a constant rate

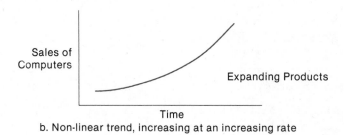

Sales of Computers

Expanding Products

Time

b. Non-linear trend, increasing at an increasing rate

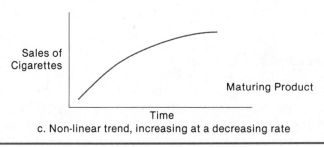

Sales of Cigarettes

Maturing Product

Time

c. Non-linear trend, increasing at a decreasing rate

FIGURE 17.1 Different Types of Increasing or Positive Trends

purchase of wool clothing, the pre-summer months which signal purchases of bathing suits, the temperate periods of the year which are favorable for housing starts.

In all of these examples, the so-called seasonal influence is really a reflection of the underlying institutional arrangement, social custom, or weather changes.

Today's seasonal patterns may be altered by tomorrow's change in institutional arrangements and behavior patterns. For example, a full-year academic program will significantly smooth out the textbook sales cycle; shifting to a four-day work week would alter many weekend shopping patterns; staggering work hours in metropolitan areas would modify the rush hour traffic density; an increase in the popularity of recreational skiing would likely alter the vacationing patterns of many people from the summer to the winter months; the increased popularity of air conditioning has already shifted the peak demand for electricity from the winter to the summer months.

Compensatory Variation

Compensatory variation is activity that departs from a stable level or trend; the activity, when broken down into components, cancels itself out. The following example shows how the intervention of a key event can set *compensatory variation* in motion.

Example 17.2.   New Orders for Steel Before and After Labor Negotiations

The pre- and post-strike deadline behavior of new orders in a basic industry like steel exhibits compensatory variation when a strike is anticipated, but in fact does not materialize. Prior to the anticipated strike, customers typically place unusually large orders for steel so as not to be caught short if the strike takes place. However, if the strike is avoided, customers cut back orders *below* the normal level to work off the excess inventories which were accumulated in anticipation of the strike. When the inventory level is reduced to a normal level, new orders for steel return to their normal level. In other words, post-deadline orders are kept unusually low to *compensate* for the unusually high pre-deadline order level.

Notice that compensatory variation produces a complete cycle from the normal level to a peak (or trough), then down to a trough (or up to a peak) and back to normal again. Compensatory variation is portrayed graphically in Figure 17.2. The area above the normal level to the left of the strike deadline date is fully offset by the area below the normal level to the right of the strike deadline date. Note that the pre-deadline peak is further above the normal level than the post-deadline trough is below the normal level. This reflects the fact that

1. *inventory buildup*, a variable under the control of the production manager, can be rapid;

2. the depletion of inventory is normally more gradual since it is constrained by the technical limitation of plant capacity and also by the consumption rate of the final user of the product.

Cyclical Variation

If the compensatory variation is caused by strike anticipations, there would be no reason to expect that the observed cycle would be *immediately followed* by a second cycle. But in other situations, it may happen that the end of one cycle marks the beginning of another. This situation could arise because anticipations always turn out to be somewhat in error, necessitating continual adjustments

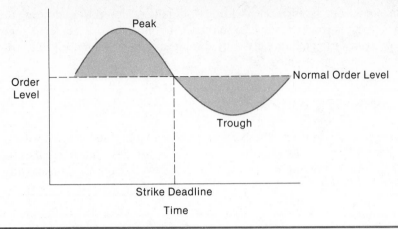

FIGURE 17.2 Compensatory Variation

to the order level, or it could be for entirely different reasons. Whatever the reason, a pattern of *recurring* cycles is often referred to as *cyclical variation*. Agricultural production data often exhibit cyclical tendencies, such as the seven year cattle cycle.

Random Fluctuations

Random fluctuations are non-periodic movements for which the causative factors are very transitory and very often non-recurring. These factors run the gamut from bizarre conditions of nature such as hurricanes, floods, and blights to unpredictable situations such as wars, strikes, and global political crises. For example,

the Southern corn blight in 1969–1970 caused corn prices to jump 50 per cent above the previous year's prices;

the inflationary spiral of 1974 depressed stock market prices 150 points on the Dow Jones Index;

the PATCO air controllers strike in 1981 caused air traffic to drop immediately by twenty-five percent.

At times, it is not just one random shock which causes a dramatic rise or fall in the time series, but rather a series of unpredictable happenings in conjunction with each other.

Cycles in Business

The name "business cycle" arises from the observation that business fluctuations are often characterized by recurring (although non-periodic) complete oscillations from peak to peak or trough to trough. A typical business cycle is described as going through four phases in one complete oscillation: recovery, boom, recession, and depression.

Recovery and boom are often referred to as the *expansionary* phases.

Recession and depression comprise the *contractionary* phases.

Cyclical fluctuations in the time series of sales of individual goods can be the result of general business cycle conditions in the economy and disequilibrium conditions between supply and demand for the product. For other non-economic time series, changes in institutional structure and in the political climate are the main determinants for wave-like oscillations. Cycles may be completed in a relatively short span of two years or persist for as long as fifteen years. For example, the Great Depression which began in the early thirties persisted through many of the years of that decade.

Cycles are not regarded as one of the stable components of the classical time series model. Strictly speaking, only secular movement and seasonality are characterized by stable patterns from one time period to another. Hence, if cycles exist, they are usually isolated as a residual of the data after secular movement and seasonality have been filtered out.

17.3. The Component Parts Approach: A Simple Example

The main purpose of time series analysis is to isolate the stable, measurable components of the time series data. Let us consider the hypothetical data in Table 17.1. It represents five years of quarterly sales of air conditioners for the Kool-Breeze Company.

TABLE 17.1. Quarterly Sales of Air Conditioners—Kool-Breeze Company (Millions of Dollars)

	QUARTER	1976 $j = 1$	1977 $j = 2$	1978 $j = 3$	1979 $j = 4$	1980 $j = 5$	ROW TOTAL	$\bar{Y}$	S
Winter	1	5	6	7	8	9	35	7	-5
Spring	2	12	13	14	15	16	70	14	$+2$
Summer	3	16	17	18	19	20	90	18	$+6$
Autumn	4	7	8	9	10	11	45	9	-3
Column Total		40	44	48	52	56	240		0
$\bar{Y}_j$		10	11	12	13	14			
T_j		-2	-1	0	$+1$	$+2$	0		
$M = 240/20 = 12$									

In this series, there is clearly an upward trend. Yearly totals are rising. Seasonal influence is also present. There are relatively higher sales in the second and third quarters of the year than for the rest of the year. For simplicity, we shall assume:

1. that the seasonal and trend influences operate independently, so that the combined effect is merely the sum of the two separate influences,

2. that the seasonal influences remain stable from year to year,

3. that other sources of variation—compensatory and random—are not present.

The trend and seasonal influences can be identified rather easily in this simple example. Let Y_{ij} equal sales in the ith quarter where $i = 1, 2\ 3, 4$ of the jth year where $j = 1, 2, 3, 4, 5$; M equals the grand or overall mean of the entire quarterly data series on Y; $\overline{Y}_i$ equals the mean of the ith season; $\overline{Y}_j$ equals the mean of the jth year; S_i equals the effect of the ith season, calculated as $\overline{Y}_i - M$; T_j equals the effect of the particular j^{th} year, calculated as $\overline{Y}_j - M$; and S_i and T_j are viewed as deviations from the overall mean M, and thus are measured in deviation units from M.

The value of a single observation is given by:

$$Y_{ij} = M + T_j + S_i.$$

For instance, the value of sales in the ith quarter of the jth year equals the overall mean M modified by the particular trend value for that year T_j and the particular effect of that quarter S_i. Thus, sales for the winter quarter of 1979 are found from $Y_{14} = M + T_4 + S_1 = 12 + 1 - 5 = 8$.

Recalling from Chapter 6 that the sum of the deviations around the mean is zero, we can state that:

$\sum_{\text{all } j} T_j = 0$; the net trend deviations from M is zero; differently stated, the sum of the trend deviations of the j years from the overall mean M must equal zero;

$\sum_{\text{all } i} S_i = 0$; the net seasonal effect is zero; differently stated, the sum of the seasonal deviations of the i seasons from the overall mean M must equal zero.

Measuring Seasonal Influence By "Blocking Out" Trend

To find a particular season effect, we simply take the difference between the mean of all the values in the row representing the same season and the overall mean M. Symbolically

$$S_i = \overline{Y}_i - M,$$

where $\overline{Y}_i$ represents the mean of the ith season. In our example, the seasonal effect of the winter (first) quarter is:

$$S_i = 7 - 12 = -5.$$

The interpretation of this result is that in the winter, sales of Kool-Breeze air conditioners are $5 million less than the average for all seasons. The other seasonal effects are computed the same way and show in the far right-hand column of Table 17.1.

Why does this method of isolating the seasonal effect work? Because averaging data for the same season over all five years effectively "blocks out" or eliminates the trend effect, leaving only the particular seasonal effect to explain the difference between the seasonal mean and the overall mean. Considered over all 5 years, $\sum T_j = 0$. Algebraically,

$$
\begin{aligned}
Y_{11} &= M + T_1 + S_1 \\
Y_{12} &= M + T_2 + S_1 \\
Y_{13} &= M + T_3 + S_1 \\
Y_{14} &= M + T_4 + S_1 \\
\underline{Y_{15}} &= \underline{M + T_5 + S_1} \\
\end{aligned}
$$

$$
\begin{aligned}
\sum Y_{1j} &= 5M + \sum T_j + 5S_1 \\
&= 5M + 0 + 5S_1 \\
\end{aligned}
$$

$$
\overline{Y}_1 = \frac{\sum_j (M + S_1)}{\text{no. of yrs.}} = \frac{5(M + S_1)}{5} = M + S_1
$$

$$
S_1 = \overline{Y}_1 - M
$$

Measuring Trend By "Blocking Out" Seasonal Influences

To measure the *trend effect for a particular year*, we compute the difference between the *mean of all the values in the column representing that year and the overall mean M*. Symbolically,

$$
T_j = \overline{Y}_j - M
$$

where T_j represents the trend effect of the jth year. In our example, the trend effect of the first year (1976) is:

$$
T_1 = 10 - 12 = -2
$$

The interpretation of this result is that quarterly sales of Kool-Breeze air conditioners in 1976 (year 1) fall $2 million below the average for all five years included in the series.

The other trend effects are computed the same way and are shown in the bottom row of Table 17.1. The procedure works because averaging data over all four seasons of a year essentially "blocks out" or eliminates any seasonal effect. This leaves trend to explain the difference between the mean for a particular year and the overall mean.

The simple methods presented in this section for isolating trend and seasonal components of time series are actually powerful tools for analyzing statistical variation of all kinds. For example, this method is extensively used for effective statistical planning and design. For the present, we shall turn to a consideration of some aspects of time series analysis which are not brought out by the present example.

Residual Component

The analysis of Table 17.1 was made simpler by the absence of compensatory and random variation. However, random variation will be present in real time series data, in which case the value of a single observation Y_{ij} is expressed by

$$Y_{ij} = M + T_j + S_i + R_{ij}$$

where R_{ij} is the individual random component.

The Multiplicative Model

An alternative to the additive component version of the classical time series model is the *multiplicative* component version. In the latter version the *product* rather than the sum of the components defines the value of the dependent variable Y. Symbolically,

$$Y_{ij} = MT_jS_i$$

Interestingly, the multiplicative version is often transformed to an additive version for ease of computation. This is accomplished by expressing the terms in log form; either natural or common logs can be used. Taking the natural logs of both sides of the multiplicative version, the following log-additive expression results:

$$\ln Y_{ij} = \ln M + \ln T_j + \ln S_i$$

where $\ln Y_{ij} = \log_e Y_{ij}$, $\ln M = \log_e M$ and so forth. In this expression, the trend component is identified with T_j, the seasonal component with S_i. The natural logarithms of the data in Table 17.1 are shown in Table 17.2.

TABLE 17.2. Natural Logarithms of Quarterly Sales of Air Conditioners, Kool-Breeze Company

	1976 $j = 1$	1977 $j = 2$	1978 $j = 3$	1979 $j = 4$	1980 $j = 5$	Row Total	$\overline{Y}_i$	$\ln S_i$
Winter $i = 1$	1.609	1.792	1.946	2.079	2.197	9.623	1.925	−.483
Spring $i = 2$	2.485	2.565	2.639	2.708	2.773	13.170	2.634	.226
Summer $i = 3$	2.773	2.833	2.890	2.944	2.996	14.436	2.887	.479
Autumn $i = 4$	1.946	2.079	2.197	2.303	2.398	10.923	2.185	−.223
Column Total	8.813	9.269	9.672	10.034	10.364	48.152	9.630	0*
$\overline{Y}_j$	2.203	2.317	2.418	2.509	2.591			
$\ln T_j$	−.205	−.091	.010	.101	.183	0*		
$\ln M = 48.152/20 =$	2.408							

*Note: Sum across row of $\ln T_j$ and sum down column of $\ln S_i$ deviates from zero due to rounding error.

To see how Y can be determined from the values in this table, consider the equation for summer of 1979;

$$\ln Y_{34} = \ln M + \ln T_4 + \ln S_3$$
$$\ln Y_{34} = 2.408 + .101 + .479$$
$$= 2.988 \text{ (Note: deviation from Table 17.2 due to rounding error.)}$$
$$Y_{34} = e^{2.988} = 19.85$$

Individually the value of the overall mean and the particular trend and seasonal components are:[1]

$$M = e^{2.408} = 11.112$$
$$T_4 = e^{.101} = 1.106$$
$$S_3 = e^{.479} = 1.614$$

Notice that M, T_4, and S_3 have values that are close to, but not the same as, the values obtained using the additive model. In fact, the value of M multiplied by constant factors S_i and T_j to give Y_{ij}, will generally not be the same value of M to which constant factors S_i and T_j are *added* to give Y_{ij}.

Interpreting the Trend and Seasonal Adjustments

The value of M represents the mean value of air conditioner sales per quarter for the *entire* series. The value of T_4 indicates that in 1979 the mean value should be adjusted upwards by $100(1.106 - 1) = 10.6$ percent to reflect a positive trend in air conditioner sales. The value of S_3 indicates that the mean value should be adjusted upwards by $100(1.614 - 1) = 61.4$ percent to reflect higher than average sales in the summer compared to other quarters of the year. The complete set of trend and seasonal adjustments for air conditioner sales is given in Table 17.3.

TABLE 17.3. Trend and Seasonal Adjustments for Air Conditioner Sales

TREND ADJUSTMENT (as percentage of series mean) Example: $T_4 \times 100$ = 1.106 × 100 = 110.6		SEASONAL ADJUSTMENT (as percentage of series mean) Example: $S_3 \times 100$ = 1.614 × 100 = 161.4	
1976	81.5	Winter	61.7
1977	91.3	Spring	125.4
1978	101.0	Summer	161.4
1979	110.6	Fall	80.0
1980	120.1		

Since the values of the seasonal and trend adjustments depend upon whether an additive or a multiplicative model is employed, a choice between the two models must be made. That choice should be dictated by the logic of the situation. If the magnitudes of seasonal changes are unrelated to the base value, then the additive model is appropriate. If the seasonal changes are related to the base value (larger with a larger base value, smaller with a smaller base value), the multiplicative model is more appropriate.

17.4. Using the Least Squares Method to Compute Trend and Seasonal Components

A common practice in time series analysis is to fit a *mathematical function* to capture the trend component. The most popular approach to mathematical trend fitting is based upon the method of least squares.

Using Time as an Independent Variable

The determination of trend and seasonal components by the method of least squares regression commonly assumes a linear trend. Using time as the independent variable, the linear trend equation for the actual Y series would be:

$$\hat{Y}_t = a + bt,$$

where t = the time period (the first time period is generally assigned the value of one, $t = 1$; the second time period has $t = 2$, etc.); $\hat{Y}_t$ = height of the trend line at time period t; b = the trend line slope (the rise in the trend line per period); and a = the intercept term.

Fitting a trend line with time as the independent variable means that time stands for all the (causal) variables which grow with the passage of time and which influence on a consistent basis the Y series. For example, if a trend line is fitted to air conditioner sales, time might stand for changes in variables such as population and disposable income.

The Use of Dummy Variables to Measure Seasonal Variation

Least squares regression can handle seasonal variation by including *dummy independent variables* to represent the different seasons. A dummy variable has just two possible values, zero or one. It is used to indicate the presence (value = 1) or absence (value = 0) of an attribute. The procedure is as follows:

1. One season, say winter, is arbitrarily selected as the reference season. Its effect on the Y series resides in the intercept term "*a*".

2. One dummy variable is included for each of the other seasons (spring, summer, fall); that is, for four seasons in all, there would be only three dummy variables.

3. A seasonal dummy variable is assigned the value one or zero. When the observation refers to that particular season, the dummy variable for that season is assigned the number one; otherwise assign zero.

Thus, if the observation in the actual Y series refers to the summer season, a value of one is assigned to the summer dummy and a value of zero to the seasonal dummies for spring and fall. *For any particular observation, no more than one dummy variable can be assigned a value of one;* if the observation refers to the reference season (winter), *all* the dummy variables will have a value of zero. If the data is quarterly, the regression equation for both trend and the four seasonal components is of the form:

$$\hat{Y}_t = a + b_1 t + b_2 X_2 + b_3 X_3 + b_4 X_4.$$

where a = the intercept term representing the effect on Y of the reference winter season; t = successive integer values representing the time variable; X_2 = the dummy variable representing the spring season; X_3 = the dummy variable representing the summer season; X_4 = the dummy variable representing the fall season; b_1 = the linear trend coefficient; and b_2, b_3, b_4 = the regression coefficients for the spring, summer, and fall seasons respectively.

Example 17.4. Trend and Seasonal Components of Soft Drink Sales

The A.C. Nielson Co. is the largest marketing research firm in the world. Its most widely used source is the reporting of retail store sales for numerous consumer products. The reports are issued bimonthly—every two months.

Bimonthly case-equivalent sales estimates of the soft drink industry prepared by the Nielson Co. for the period beginning in June, 1964 and ending in September, 1972 are shown in Table 17.4. Fifty bimonthly observations are reported.

TABLE 17.4. Bimonthly Soft Drink Case Sales—June-July, 1964 to August-September, 1972 (Millions of Case-Equivalents)

	1964–1965	1965–1966	1966–1967	1967–1968	1968–1969	1969–1970	1970–1971	1971–1972	1972
June-July	178	188	215	222	248	261	271	304	312
August-September	172	184	204	214	247	259	275	289	314
October-November	141	152	162	179	202	205	224	243	
December-January	144	158	169	187	207	211	234	249	
February-March	136	148	162	182	193	201	227	239	
April-May	161	174	183	211	223	235	256	270	

Glancing over the data, one observes that soft drink sales are *consistently higher in the summer months* than the winter. This periodic fluctuation during the year and the growth over the years present a good opportunity to examine seasonal and trend components.

The regression equation to estimate the coefficients or weights of the trend and seasonal components is:

$$\hat{Y}_t = a + b_1 t + b_2 X_2 + b_3 X_3 + b_4 X_4 + b_5 X_5 + b_6 X_6$$

where $\hat{Y}_t$ = estimated case sales of soft drink sold in period t; t = sequence number of bimonthly periods (integers 1 to 50); X_2 = a (0, 1) dummy variable representing

August–September (X_2 has value of one if the Y observation is an Aug.–Sept. observation, otherwise X_2 has value of zero); X_3 = a (0, 1) dummy variable representing Oct.–Nov.; X_4 = a (0, 1) dummy variable representing Dec.–Jan.; X_5 = a (0, 1) dummy variable representing Feb.–March; and X_6 = a (0, 1) dummy variable representing April–May.

Note: Since the June–July observation serves as the base of comparison for the seasonal dummies, zeros are assigned to variables X_2 through X_6 when a J/J observation on sales occurs. The June–July seasonal effect on sales is represented by the "*a*" intercept value.

The multiple regression equation and related statistics computed for this by the method described in Chapter 16 are:

$$\hat{Y}_t = 178 + 2.67t - 8.80X_3 - 53.5X_3 - 49.8X_4 - 61.3X_5 - 35.8X_6$$

$$\text{std. errors:} \quad (0.05) \quad (2.44) \quad (2.44) \quad (2.44) \quad (2.44) \quad (2.44)$$

$R^2 = 98.8\%$

Standard Deviation of Residuals: 5.14 million cases

Trend: Since trend is measured by the coefficient of t, the regression equation indicates an upward trend in the case volume of soft drink sales. For this data the estimated average increase is 2.67 million cases per bimonthly period.

Seasonality: Seasonal influences are measured by the coefficients of variables X_2 through X_6 relative to the base effect of the June–July season, which has an estimated average ("*a*" value) of 178. The negative values of the dummy coefficients indicate a lower level of sales for all of the other seasons. Thus, the hot months of June–July (the base) are the estimated peak season for soft drink sales.

The value of -8.8 for the August–September dummy indicates a moderate decline in sales for the August–September season relative to the sales effect of the June–July season. Much larger relative sales declines occur during the other seasons. The largest negative dummy variable coefficient is $b_5 = -61.3$ for the February–March season; it indicates that the average seasonal drop-off in soft drink sales between June–July and February–March is estimated to be 61.3 million cases.

Using the Regression Equation: By inserting the value of t and the values of X_2 through X_6 into the regression equation, a trend estimate of case sales adjusted for seasonal influences can be obtained. For example, this value estimated for Oct.–Nov. 1964 ($t = 3$) would be $Y_3 = 178 + 2.67(3) - 53.5(1) = 132.5$. The difference between this value and 141 (the actual value for that period) is the estimated effect of random factors specific to the Oct.–Nov. 1964 period.

It should be noted that the trend adjusted case sales value is nothing more than the application of the *average* growth rate for all 50 periods to each individual period. Thus, the trend adjusted value of 132.5 indicates what seasonally adjusted sales would have been in the Oct.–Nov. 1964 period had the growth trend occurred at a steady pace of 2.67 case equivalents *every* period.

It should also be noted that the trend effect of 2.67 per period described in these computations *specifically* refers to the average change per bimonthly period experienced for the 50 periods between June–July 1964 and Aug.–Sept. 1972. Had a different number of periods been used, or if the 50 periods were for some period other than June–July 1964 to Aug.–Sept. 1972, a value different from 2.67 could arise. In fact, one should not be surprised to find considerable change in the trend value depending on the particular years and number of periods considered in the computation.

Overly Optimistic Estimates of Reliability Due to Serial Correlation

It is appropriate to use the regression equation as a purely descriptive device for disaggregating the sales data into trend and seasonal components. But as we shall see from Chapter 19, its use as a forecasting tool is open to question. The problem is the behavior of the *residuals* when the regression equation is considered an estimation of an underlying probabilistic model.

The presumption of the probabilistic model is that the residuals about the trend line are uncorrelated (true correlation of zero). This is not likely to be correct because consecutive sales figures tend to have similar values, as the values shown in Table 17.4 suggest. The correlation between successive residuals for such data is usually found to be substantial: in this case, it is .455. Such a violation is called *serial correlation;* the value of the standard deviation of residuals is *underestimated,* as are standard errors of the regression coefficients. In other words, the calculated values of the standard deviation of residuals and the standard errors of the regression coefficients are unfortunately *not* reliable estimates of their true population values, and so the construction of a confidence interval for the trend line prediction would be unjustified in the sense that it would overstate the degree of confidence by an unknown amount. The problem of serially correlated residual values about the trend line is important. It was first raised in Chapter 16 and is more fully discussed in Chapter 19, where problems of business forecasting are considered.

Curvilinear Trend Fitting

Often fitted for its ease of interpretation, the linear trend line might more appropriately be replaced by a curvilinear trend line to achieve a better fit to the data at hand. Exponential and parabolic equations are two of the most popular curve forms used in least squares curvilinear trend fitting. For instance, one approach to fitting a parabolic curve to the Y series uses time, t, and time squared, t^2, as the independent variables and follows the same least squares procedure.

Trend and seasonal least-squares fitting are conceptually insightful and computationally practical. But time-dependent series generally follow more complicated patterns than that presumed by the simple trend and seasonality model. To accommodate this fact, additional devices for giving a more complete description of the time series have become popular. One such device is the moving average.

17.5. Smoothing by Moving Averages: Screening Out Seasonal and Random Influences

One of the most popular methods for capturing the main movements in the data series is to screen out the random and seasonal influences by constructing a *moving average* series for the Y values. A moving average series is a sequence of averages that overlap in their use of the original Y observations. Consider the quarterly sales data given in Table 17.1. A *four quarter moving average* series would consist of the averages of sales per quarter for successive four quarter periods. The first three averages in the series would be computed as in Table 17.5.

TABLE 17.5. A Four Quarter Moving Average

WINTER 1976	SPRING 1976	SUMMER 1976	FALL 1976	WINTER 1977	SPRING 1977	FOUR QUARTER AVERAGE
5	12	16	7			40/4 = 10.00
	12	16	7	6		41/4 = 10.25
		16	7	6	13	42/4 = 10.50

Each moving average term in the series averages an equal number of Y terms but not the same Y terms. Thus each moving average term covers the same fixed number of time periods as the other moving average terms in the series. The difference between each successive moving average term is only one different Y observation. By design, each new moving average term is constructed by dropping one Y observation from the previous moving average term and adding a new Y observation.

> If the Y series are monthly, the moving average series is constructed for a 12-month moving average. This is intended to deal with the seasonality over the year.

> If the Y series is reported quarterly, the series is a *four quarter* moving average. Again the seasonality of the year is captured.

The Y series on soft drink industry sales shown in Table 17.6 and graphed in Figure 17.3 was collected bimonthly, so a moving average of this series is called a *6-bimonth* moving average—once again to accommodate a year's seasonality.

First Step: Moving Totals

The procedure for calculating moving averages for soft drink case sales begins with 6-bimonth moving totals shown in Column 3 of Table 17.6. The steps are:

> 1. The values for the first six consecutive bimonthly periods (June–July of 1964 through and including April–May of 1965) are summed to obtain the initial 6-bimonth total (932). This is illustrated in Table 17.7.

> 2. The next total in the series is obtained by replacing the June–July, 1964, value by the June–July value for 1965. Thus, the second 6-bimonth total now contains the value 188 instead of 178.

TABLE 17.6. Soft Drink Sales—Cases Sold—Moving Totals, Moving Averages, and Ratios-To-Moving Average

(1) TIME PERIODS	(2) CASES SOLD (Millions)	(3) SIX PERIOD MOVING TOTAL	(4) TWO OF SIX MOVING TOTAL	(5) MOVING AVERAGE = MOVING TOTAL/12	(6) RATIO-TO-MOVING AVERAGE, DESEASONALIZED AS % OF M.A.
June–July '64	178	—	—	—	—
Aug.–Sept.	172	—	—	—	—
Oct.–Nov.	141	932	—	—	—
Dec.–Jan. '64–'65	144	942	1874	156.17	92.21
Feb.–March	136	954	1896	158	86.08
April–May	161	965	1919	159.92	100.68
June–July	188	979	1944	162	116.05
Aug.–Sept.	184	991	1970	164.17	112.08
Oct.–Nov.	152	1004	1995	166.25	91.43
Dec.–Jan. '65–'66	158	1031	2035	169.59	93.17
Feb.–March	148	1051	2082	173.5	85.30
April–May	174	1061	2112	176.75	98.44
June–July	215	1072	2133	177.75	120.96
Aug.–Sept.	204	1086	2158	179.83	113.44
Oct.–Nov.	162	1095	2181	181.75	89.13
Dec.–Jan. '66–'67	169	1102	2197	183.08	92.31
Feb.–March	162	1112	2214	184.5	87.80
April–May	183	1129	2241	186.75	97.99
June–July	222	1147	2276	189.67	117.05
Aug.–Sept.	214	1167	2314	192.83	110.98
Oct.–Nov.	179	1195	2362	196.83	90.94
Dec.–Jan. '67–'68	187	1221	2416	201.33	92.88
Feb.–March	182	1254	2475	206.25	88.24
April–May	211	1277	2531	210.92	100.04
June–July	248	1297	2574	214.5	115.62
Aug.–Sept.	247	1308	2605	217.08	113.79
Oct.–Nov.	202	1320	2628	219	92.24
Dec.–Jan. '68–'69	207	1333	2653	221.08	93.63
Feb.–March	193	1345	2678	223.17	86.48
April–May	223	1348	2693	224.42	99.37
June–July	261	1352	2700	225	116
Aug.–Sept.	259	1360	2712	226	114.60
Oct.–Nov.	205	1372	2732	227.67	90.04
Dec.–Jan. '69–'70	211	1382	2754	229.5	91.94
Feb.–March	201	1398	2780	231.67	86.76
April–May˙	235	1417	2815	234.58	100.18
June–July	271	1440	2857	238.08	113.83
Aug.–Sept.	275	1466	2906	242.17	113.56
Oct.–Nov.	224	1487	2953	246.08	91.03
Dec.–Jan. '70–'71	234	1520	3007	250.58	93.38
Feb.–March	227	1534	3054	254.5	89.19
April–May	256	1553	3087	257.25	99.51
June–July	304	1568	3121	260.08	116.89
Aug.–Sept.	289	1580	3148	262.33	110.17
Oct.–Nov.	243	1594	3174	264.5	91.87
Dec.–Jan. '71–'72	249	1602	3196	266.33	93.49
Feb.–March	239	1627	3229	269.08	88.82
April–May	270	—	—	—	—
June–July	312	—	—	—	—
Aug.–Sept.	314	—	—	—	—

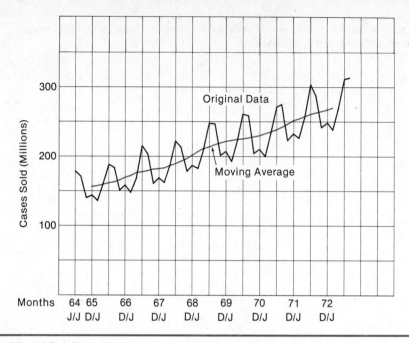

FIGURE 17.3 Soft Drink Sales and Its Moving Average Series

3. The procedure continues until the last bimonthly period, August–September 1972, has been included in a total.

Notice that each 6 bimonthly total has a one year duration with no bimonthly period represented twice. Each successive total moves the series along, replacing the earliest observation with the value one year later. Thus, in the third total, the August–September, 1964 value of 172 is replaced by the August–September, 1965 value of 184.

TABLE 17.7. Moving Total Calculations for Soft Drink Sales

1964	June–July	178	
	Aug.–Sept.	172	
	Oct.–Nov.	141	
	Dec.–Jan.	144	$178 + 172 + 141 + 144 + 136 + 161 = 932$
1965	Feb.–March	136	$172 + 141 + 144 + 136 + 161 + 188 = 942$
	April–May	161	$141 + 144 + 136 + 161 + 188 + 184 = 954$
	June–July	188	
	Aug.–Sept.	184	

Centering the Averages

Once the moving totals have been calculated, division of each total by six would give a moving average series. However, to correctly match the points in time to which the moving averages refer with the points in time of the original sales series, an adjustment known as *centering* the average must be made. Because this particular moving average is for an even number of periods, the moving totals fall at a point in time which does not coincide with an actual observation.

> For example, the first total (932) of the soft drink data is centered *between* the first three and last three bimonthly values in the first year. Thus, it is centered between the October-November, 1964 value and the December-January, 1964-1965 value, not coinciding with either one.

The mismatching continues for the second total (942), centered between December-January and February-March.

How is the moving total (and moving average) made to align properly with the time period reported with the sales series? By averaging two consecutive totals.

> For instance, adding the first two totals, 932 and 942 respectively (see Table 17.7), and then dividing the sum, 1874, by twelve (12 bimonthly periods in the sum) gives 156.17, a moving average centered exactly at the point of the December-January, 1965 sales figure of 144.

The other properly centered values are shown in column 5 of Table 17.6 and plotted in Figure 17.3 as a rising trend line. Notice the reduced variability of the moving average series in Figure 17.3 compared to the original data series shown in that same figure. Both series of values tend to move upward to the right, but the visual impression of a persistent upward trend and its magnitude is more easily discerned from the moving average series than from the original data series.

Why the Moving Average Method Is Useful

The key to the usefulness of the moving average method is that *all of the* seasons are included in each average. Therefore, *in comparing the value of two averages, the differences observed cannot be due to different seasonal influences*. An added feature of the averaging process is that short term random influences which occur during a year, raising or lowering the bimonthly sales level from what it would otherwise have been, should also be smoothed out. Thus, *the net effect of the moving average is to block out seasonal and irregular influence* and to isolate the main long term trend and cyclical fluctuation.

17.6. The Ratio-to-Moving Average Method of Measuring Seasonal Influence

Management responsibility for production, work scheduling, advertising, and cost control are but a few from a long list of business activities which require good advance planning. And good planning means that management knows what portion of the yearly total activity normally falls (on average) in particular months, particular days, or a particular quarter. Consider some specific issues:

> The Pontiac division of GM, in reviewing its plans for spring car production, has just received the January sales figures for current models. The January

sales amount to only 1/15th of the total sales planned for the year. Is this bad? Are consumers purchasing fewer cars than GM had planned? Should production be cut back? Not necessarily. You can't say until you know what fraction of yearly sales *normally* are made in January. That is, given the seasonal weight the January month normally commands, what projection do the *actual* January sales suggest should be made for the entire year? And, are the present production plans consistent with this forecast?

Sales for the Wendy's Hamburger chain grew rapidly in the late 1970s and early 1980s. The firm has plans for more expansion. As first quarter 1983 sales come in, the company must review its cash flow projections to detect unexpected changes. Are first quarter sales in line with projected cash revenues (inflows) for the year? If not, should the controller set up contingent lines of credit to meet possible cash shortages?

Seasonal Weights

One popular technique used both in government and business is the *ratio to moving average method*. This method produces *seasonal weights* for adjusting seasonal differences between weeks, months, or quarters of the year. The bimonthly soft drink industry sales data are used to illustrate the procedure.

1. Using the previously calculated moving average figures, the seasonal weights are computed by dividing the *actual* soft drink sales volume for each period by its *corresponding moving average*.

2. Multiplication by 100 expresses the actual bimonthly sales figures as a *percentage of the yearly moving average corresponding to it*.

These percentages, shown in column 6 of Table 17.6, are the *ratios to moving average* and the seasonal weights for the particular periods. The first seasonal weight is the one for December-January, 1964-1965; it equals 92.21, computed as follows:

$$\frac{\text{Actual Sales, Dec.-Jan., '64-'65}}{\text{Moving Average, Dec.-Jan., '64-'65}} \times 100 = \frac{144}{156.17} \times 100 = 92.21\%$$

Calculating the Seasonal Indexes

The calculation of the *seasonal indexes* requires the following.

1. The percentages of moving average should be arranged by season as shown in Table 17.8.

2. Either the median percentage for each column should be located or a modified percentage should be calculated. The modified mean is obtained by eliminating the highest-valued and lowest-valued observations for each season and then obtaining the mean for the remaining values. For example, the highest valued observation for the June–July season was 120.96; the

lowest valued observation was 113.83. With these two values eliminated, the modified mean is:

$$\frac{116.05 + 117.05 + 115.62 + 116 + 116.89}{5} = 116.32$$

3. The seasonal indexes are the products of the modified mean and an adjustment factor.

4. The adjustment factor, which is the same value for each seasonal index, is calculated by adding the modified means for all the seasons and dividing the sum into the product of 100 and the number of seasons.

TABLE 17.8. Calculation of the Seasonal Indexes

Percentage of Moving Average, by Season

	June–July	Aug.–Sept.	Oct.–Nov.	Dec.–Jan.	Feb.–March	April–May
	—	—	—	92.21	86.08	100.68
	116.05	112.08	91.43	93.17	85.30	98.44
	120.96	113.44	89.13	92.31	87.80	97.99
	117.05	110.98	90.94	92.88	88.24	100.04
	115.62	113.79	92.24	93.63	86.48	99.37
	116	114.60	90.04	91.94	86.76	100.18
	113.83	113.56	91.03	93.38	89.19	99.51
	116.89	110.17	91.87	93.49	88.82	—
Average	116.32	112.77	91.06	92.91	87.36	99.51

Total Modified Means = 599.93
Adjustment Factor   =   1.0001 = (600/599.93)

Seasonal Indexes

June–July	(116.32)(1.0001) = 116.33
August–September	(112.77)(1.0001) = 112.78
October–November	(91.06)(1.0001) = 91.07
December–January	(92.91)(1.0001) = 92.92
February–March	(87.36)(1.0001) = 87.37
April–May	(99.51)(1.0001) = 99.52
	600.04

For the soft drink data, the calculation for the adjustment factor is:

$$\text{adjustment factor} = \frac{100 \times \text{no. of seasons}}{\text{sum of modified means}}$$

$$= \frac{100 \times 6}{(116.32 + 112.77 + 91.06 + 92.91 + 87.36 + 99.51)}$$

$$\frac{600}{599.93} = 1.0001$$

The seasonal index for June–July is:

$$116.32 \times 1.0001 = 116.33$$

Table 17.8 shows the six seasonal indexes for the soft drink data. The sum of the indexes should be 600 except for rounding error. This forces the mean of the six seasonal indexes to be 100 (600/6 = 100), so the actual indexes can be compared to this base 100 figure. The adjustment factor was required in order to make the sum of the modified means equal to 600.

How should the seasonal indexes for particular periods be interpreted? Values above 100 indicate a positive seasonal effect for that period; values below 100 indicate a negative seasonal effect. The difference between a particular seasonal index and 100 indicates the percentage by which values for that season exceed or fall below the (moving) annual average. For example,

the value of 116.33 for June–July indicates that soft drink sales for the June–July season average 16 percent more than the annual average for all seasonal periods.

This is nearly 29 percentage points (116.33 − 87.37) above the low-seasonal point which occurs in February–March.

Dividing each seasonal index by the number of seasons in the moving average gives the percentage of the yearly total associated with a particular season. Since the soft drink data includes six seasons, the percentage associated with the June–July season is obtained by dividing 116.33 by 6:

$$\text{Season's percentage of yearly total} = \frac{\text{seasonal index}}{\text{No. of seasons}} = \frac{116.33}{6} = 19.39$$

Thus, on average, somewhat more than 19 percent of the yearly sales occur during the peak June–July season.

One can now realize how a corporate executive can advantageously use seasonal indexes. Knowing both the actual figure for the season and the season's normal percentage of the yearly total, the likely year's total activity can be projected. And on that basis, the executive can plan or revise production-work scheduling, advertising campaigns, and cash management policies. In the next section we explain how the seasonal indexes obtained with the ratio-to-moving average method are used to deseasonalize the original data and what managerial questions are best answered with deseasonalized data.

17.7. Deseasonalizing Data

How much of the variation in the actual series from one period to the next is attributable to the particular season of the year? How much is not? Can it be that there is a short-term change in the trend? The first question (addressed indirectly in the previous section) is answered by comparing the seasonal indexes for the different periods. The second and third questions are linked to *deseasonalizing* the data. By dividing each period's actual observation by its seasonal index and then multiplying by 100, the original data is adjusted to give the *deseasonalized* or *seasonally adjusted* data. The seasonally adjusted data for the soft drink sales data are shown in column 4 of Table 17.9.

The value for the first period, June–July '64, is obtained as follows:

$$\frac{\text{Actual value, June–July '64}}{\text{June–July Seasonal Index}} = \frac{178}{116.33} \times 100 = 153.01$$

TABLE 17.9. Deseasonalized Data Compared to Original Data and Moving Average

(1) TIME PERIODS	(2) CASES SOLD (MILLIONS)	(3) MOVING AVERAGE= MOVING TOTAL/12	(4) DESEASONALIZED DATA ORIGINAL/SEASONAL INDEX
June–July '64	178	—	153.01
Aug.–Sept.	172	—	152.51
Oct.–Nov.	141	—	154.83
Dec.–Jan. '64–'65	144	156.17	154.97
Feb.–March	136	158	155.66
April–May	161	159.92	161.78
June–July	188	162	161.61
Aug.–Sept.	184	164.17	163.15
Oct.–Nov.	152	166.25	166.90
Dec.–Jan. '65–'66	158	169.59	170.04
Feb.–March	148	173.5	169.39
April–May	174	176.75	174.84
June–July	215	177.75	184.82
Aug.–Sept.	204	179.83	180.88
Oct.–Nov.	162	181.75	177.89
Dec.–Jan. '66–'67	169	183.08	181.88
Feb.–March	162	184.5	185.42
April–May	183	186.75	183.88
June–July	222	189.67	190.84
Aug.–Sept.	214	192.83	189.75
Oct.–Nov.	179	196.83	196.55
Dec.–Jan. '67–'68	187	201.33	201.25
Feb.–March	182	206.25	208.31
April–May	211	210.92	212.02
June–July	248	214.5	213.19
Aug.–Sept.	247	217.08	219.01
Oct.–Nov.	202	219	221.81
Dec.–Jan. '68–'69	207	221.08	222.77
Feb.–March	193	223.17	220.90
April–May	223	224.42	224.08
June–July	261	225	224.36
Aug.–Sept.	259	226	229.65
Oct.–Nov.	205	227.67	225.10
Dec.–Jan. '69–'70	211	229.5	227.08
Feb.–March	201	231.67	230.06
April–May	235	234.58	236.13
June–July	271	238.08	232.96
Aug.–Sept.	275	242.17	243.84
Oct.–Nov.	224	246.08	245.96
Dec.–Jan. '70–'71	234	250.58	251.83
Feb.–March	227	254.5	259.81
April–May	256	257.25	257.23
June–July	304	260.08	261.33
Aug.–Sept.	289	262.33	256.25
Oct.–Nov.	243	264.5	266.83
Dec.–Jan. '71–'72	249	266.33	267.97
Feb.–March	239	269.08	273.55
April–May	270	—	271.30
June–July	312	—	268.20
Aug.–Sept.	314	—	278.42

The other values are obtained in similar fashion. Notice that the deseasonalized values given in column 4 differ from the moving average values given in column 3. Both columns of figures are purged of seasonal influences. However, the moving average figures given in column 3 are also purged of the irregular or random component, whereas the deseasonalized values given in column 4 are not. For this reason, the deseasonalized data in column 4 are more volatile than the values given in column 3.

Compare the moving average figure of 156.17 for Dec.–Jan. '64–'65 with the deseasonalized value for that period of 154.97. The lower deseasonalized value indicates that random or irregular factors adversely affected sales for this period. Since the positive and negative seasonal influences offset each other over the year, multiplying a deseasonalized figure for a period by the number of periods in a year (six in this instance) gives a projection (estimate) of twelve month sales (929.82 using Dec.–Jan. '64–'65). The projection indicates what twelve month sales would be if the factors affecting sales exert the same influence on sales over the entire year as this period. Thus, if sales are depressed this period because of retailer inventory reductions, the twelve month projection of this period's deseasonalized sales would indicate the hypothetical annual sales if retailers continue to reduce their inventories. Multiplying the bimonthly *moving average* figure by six, on the other hand, gives 937.02 as the twelve month projection of sales if the irregular forces affecting this period's sales were not present.

A final point to notice in comparing columns 3 and 4 of Table 17.9 is that values in the six period moving average series cannot be computed for the first three or for the last three periods. A moving average value in this series refers to the midpoint of a six period time interval. The earliest midpoint of a six period interval occurs after the first three periods; the latest possible midpoint occurs prior to the last three periods' observations.

Changes in the seasonally adjusted series may provide useful hints in analyzing changes in underlying trend movement of the series. Deseasonalizing a series eliminates the worry about whether the change in the data may be caused merely by seasonal influences. Thus in using seasonally adjusted sales data over successive periods, one can attribute any observed difference in values between the periods to the short term trend effects.

17.8. Concluding Comments

The decomposition of a historical data series according to the classical time series scheme identifies four components: trend, seasonality, cyclic movement, and random fluctuation. We have descriptive statistical tools that allow one to isolate and measure the first two components, trend and seasonality, since they exhibit recurring patterns. The other two components are not directly isolated but are derived residually once trend and seasonality have been removed. There are two types of classical time series schemes: one assumes that the components are additive factors in determining Y; the other assumes multiplicative components in determining Y. Using a descriptive regression equation, the trend component is represented by a time variable and seasonality by dummy variables. Estimation by the least squares criterion provides calculated coefficients for the equation.

The time coefficient describes the average change in Y over the time span of observations due to the trend line from period to period. The coefficients for each dummy variable show the particular seasonal adjustment once the reference season's effect has been captured in the intercept term. The moving average method is a descriptive technique that isolates trend by averaging out seasonality and the random component (assuming no pronounced cyclical movement). Seasonal indexes which isolate seasonal influences can also be obtained using the moving average series. Seasonal indexes divided into the original Y series convert the original series to a deseasonalized or seasonally adjusted basis. This means that an investigator, using deseasonalized data, will no longer assume seasonality as the cause of the fluctuations still observed.

Footnotes and References

[1]Applying the multiplicative form, (the product of the trend, seasonal, and mean factors) would also yield the value of Y_{34}. That is

$$Y_{34} = M \, T_4 \, S_3$$
$$Y_{34} = (11.112) \, (1.106) \, (1.614) = 19.85$$

Questions and Problems

1. Explain what is meant by the statement "the data are deseasonalized."

2. The least squares trend line equation found for the monthly sales of gasoline in one division of a large oil company is $\hat{Y} = 105 + 4.5t$ ($t = 1$ in January, 1978), where sales are expressed in millions of gallons. What would be the trend equation values by month for the year 1982?

3. Which of the four classical times series components of demand would account for the following pattern of sales?
a. growth in demand due to population increases
b. growth in demand due to increasing consumer awareness and market penetration
c. decreased sales due to a production stoppage arising from a strike or from curtailment of raw material supply
d. the effect of a heatwave or a cold spell
e. the effect of Christmas or Easter gift buying

4. The sales level for a given month has been decomposed into the following components (expressed in millions):

Overall Mean $M = 10.732$
Trend, $T = 1.541$
Seasonal, $S = 1.113$

Using the multiplicative form of the classical time series, how would these components be combined to calculate the sales value for this month?

5. Is the fitting procedure by least-squares in regression analysis the same as it is for least squares trend fitting in time series analysis? Is there a difference in interpretation?

6. Name four products which experience substantial seasonal variation in sales.

7. As a recently hired market analyst with the Polaroid Company, you are told that recently the company's monthly dollar value of film sales showed a downturn. How would you use the component approach to the time series of past monthly sales to analyze whether the downturn reflects an underlying trend or a temporary fluctuation?

8. Define "seasonal component" in a time series model. In the multiplicative time series model, the seasonal component rep-

resents a percentage of Y; what is the different perspective of the seasonal component in the additive time series model?

9. The adjustment of monthly data for variation in important calendar events is sometimes necessary before analyzing weekly seasonal indexes. Explain some of these circumstances.

10. Seasonal effects sometimes change gradually over time. What should the analyst observe in the seasonal indexes if this has been happening? What modification of the seasonal adjustment procedure might be desirable with a changing seasonal effect?

11. Before carrying out time series analysis, sales are sometimes computed on a daily average basis. Explain why this might be necessary or useful.

12. What is the main disadvantage of the moving average method of smoothing data?

13. For each of the following series, indicate which of the components (trend, seasonal, residual) are included in the series:
a. original data
b. moving average series
c. ratio-to-moving average
d. deseasonalized data series
e. series remaining after subtracting the moving average values from the deseasonalized values

14. Discuss the difference between compensatory variation and cyclical variation and give an example of each.

15. Which time series component should be linked with the following:
a. long term decline?
b. seasonality?
c. an unanticipated and nonrecurring event?

16. After isolating and removing the seasonal and trend components of a series, analysts may scrutinize the behavior of the residuals. What information might the residuals provide in studying a time series?

17. The "lite" beers introduced in the late 1970s became an important and growing product class. Which sales component (trend, seasonal, residual) would an ana-

lyst likely study in analyzing the growth of this type of beer?

18. Schlitz brand beer began to encounter stiff sales resistance during the mid 1970s. Reportedly there was a change in the taste of the beer. Which time series component (trend, seasonal, residual) would permit the analyst to assess this sudden unpopularity of the brand?

19. The brand manager of Sunburst brand bath towels has been asked to summarize the important characteristics of the brand's sales history. Questions 19 to 23 pertain to this request and refer to the sales data shown in Table 17.10 for the three years this brand has been on the market.

TABLE 17.10. Actual Sales of Sunburst Bath Towels (Not Seasonally Adjusted, 100s)

QUARTER	YEAR		
	1st Year	2nd Year	3rd Year
1	3253	4056	3882
2	2879	3619	2639
3	2279	3336	2278
4	4002	3412	2473

a. What is the mean sales per quarter?
b. Using the additive component parts approach described in Section 17.3, determine the seasonal effects, if any, by "blocking out" trend effects.
c. Determine the (three) year trend effects by "blocking out" seasonal effects.
d. Compute the residual component of sales for each quarter.
e. Do the computations suggest that the sales fluctuations that have occurred are largely due to effects other than seasonality and trend? Explain.
f. Is there a persistent pattern to the yearly trend effects? Explain.
g. Are the sales declines in the three most recent quarters plausibly explained by trend and seasonal factors? Explain.
h. Use your findings in parts a through g to write a brief review of the Sunburst brand's sales history.

20. Using the multiplicative model rather than the additive model, carry out the

same analysis of the Sunburst sales history as in Problem 19. Note any substantial differences in results.

21. Applying linear least squares trend procedure to this data presumes that actual sales are expanding in a steady incremental way. Would that notion make sense in analyzing this data? Explain.

22. Construct a 4-quarter moving average series to isolate the main movements in the Sunburst sales data.

23. Use the multiplicative model and the data series in Problem 19.
a. Construct a ratio-to-moving-average series for the Sunburst data.
b. Construct seasonal indexes for the data.
c. Construct a deseasonalized series.
d. Both the moving average series and the deseasonalized series remove the seasonal effect. Which one of the two series still includes the random effect?
e. Comment on the sales history of the Sunburst brand based on the deseasonalized data series.

24. At one time Camel brand cigarettes were the top-selling brand in the United States. In recent decades, however, sales have fallen drastically from their all-time highs. Annual sales for a 25 year period are given in Table 17.11.
a. Compute a least squares trend equation for the data.
b. Interpret the equation.

25. In 1964 the U.S. Surgeon General issued a report linking cigarette smoking to increased risk of cancer. This report is widely thought to have adversely affected sales of cigarettes, particularly nonfilter brands such as Camel.
a. Use a 0,1 dummy variable to account for any possible effect of the Surgeon General's report (that is, zero for the years before 1964 and one for the years after). Recompute the trend equation.
b. Interpret the dummy variable coefficient.
c. Does the adverse effect appear to be a short-lived phenomenon, or more persistent in nature? Explain the criterion you used in drawing your conclusion.

TABLE 17.11. Annual Sales of Camel Cigarettes, 1953–1977

YEAR	SALES (BILLIONS)
1953	99.0
1954	84.0
1955	77.0
1956	72.5
1957	66.0
1958	62.5
1959	63.5
1960	66.5
1961	67.0
1962	66.0
1963	63.0
1964	52.5
1965	49.1
1966	48.1
1967	44.9
1968	40.1
1969	35.3
1970	32.9
1971	31.6
1972	29.9
1973	29.9
1974	28.9
1975	27.4
1976	26.0
1977	24.3

26. Construct a five year moving average for the data on Camel brand sales given in Problem 24.

27. Best Foods, a manufacturer of salad dressing, contracts with your marketing research firm for an objective study to assess trends in container preferences among customers. You decide to examine reports on shipments of mayonnaise, salad dressing, and related products. Table 17.12 gives the information you found.
a. Compute trends for the sales of each container size by the least squares procedure.
b. Recommend which container sizes should be sold and in what proportions for 1972.

28. Use the data given in Problem 27:
a. Compute three-year moving averages for each container size.
b. Do you reach any different conclusions from those given in 27?

TABLE 17.12. Shipments of Mayonnaise, Salad Dressing, and Related Products by Size of Container (Percent of Shipment)

CONTAINER SIZE	1971	1970	1969	1968	1967	1966	1965	1964	1963	1962
8 ounces (half pint)	12.0	12.4	12.8	13.0	13.2	12.8	12.8	13.3	13.3	14.0
16 ounces (pint)	13.7	14.0	13.6	14.0	15.3	15.9	16.9	17.5	18.6	20.9
32 ounces (quart)	37.3	37.7	38.7	39.4	38.8	39.0	38.3	39.8	40.3	39.1
128 ounces	22.7	22.5	21.8	21.6	21.0	20.6	19.8	19.3	18.3	17.5

TABLE 17.13. 4day Tire Stores Dollar Sales

	1st Q	2nd Q	3rd Q	4th Q
1st year	1,666,896	1,942,136	1,856,700	1,722,577
2nd year	1,657,794	1,969,692	2,144,877	2,098,829
3rd year	2,035,646	2,242,968	2,447,295	2,190,975
4th year	2,467,032	2,739,593	2,989,866	2,590,964
5th year	2,442,404	2,966,955	3,136,669	3,016,982

29. Quarterly sales data for the 4day Tire Store chain located in Southern California are given in Table 17.13 for a five year period 1973–1977. Answer Questions a through e of Problem 19 using this data.

30. From the data given in Problem 29, construct a four-quarter moving average series; then using the centered ratio-to-moving-average method, determine seasonal indexes.

31. Deseasonalize the data given in Problem 29 with the indexes constructed in Problem 30.

32. Construct a chart showing the moving average series, the deseasonalized data series based on the ratio-to-moving-average method, and the actual data. Do all three series convey the same trend message? Are the components left in the moving average and the deseasonalized series the same? Explain.

33. If the least squares program is available on computer, consider the data in Problem 29. Let the quarterly dummy variables, X_2, X_3, X_4, take on the value one when that particular quarter is present and a zero otherwise.
a. Estimate the following regression equation for isolating trend and the quarterly influences with the first quarter as the base quarter.

$$\hat{Y} = a + b_1 t + b_2 X_2 + b_3 X_3 + b_4 X_4$$

b. Interpret the coefficients of the quarterly dummy variables.
c. Chart the original Y series.
d. Fit a linear trend by eye.
e. Since the first quarter was adopted (arbitrarily) as the base quarter, it makes sense to shift the trend line to pass as close as possible to first quarter points. This allows us to gain a rough estimate of how much higher the second quarters rise on average above this base level. Repeat this procedure for the third and fourth quarter.

34. *Kind of Trend—Arithmetic or Logarithmic?* As part of a financial analyst's study of the food industry, you are asked to estimate and analyze the growth trend in the retail food store industry's sales for the data in Table 17.14.
a. Plot this series on an arithmetic chart.
b. If the growth is roughly linear, fit a straight line trend by the method of least squares.
c. Would a logarithmic straight line of form $\overline{\text{Log } Y} = a + bt$ improve the fit by the r^2 criterion?
d. To be in conformity with least squares theory about residuals, what would you

TABLE 17.14. Growth Trend in the Food Industry

YEAR	RETAIL STORES—FOOD INDUSTRY (Sales per Store)
60	293.76
61	302.82
62	311.17
63	318.81
64	331.89
65	339.20
66	367.21
67	377.07
68	399.19
69	439.97
70	464.40
71	482.38
72	526.29
73	563.16
74	588.26
75	657.67
76	619.18
77	660.00

choose: the percentage (logarithmic) deviations or the absolute (natural values) deviations? Hint: Is the problem of serial correlation present?

e. How does serial correlation affect the validity of the standard deviation of residuals and related measures of reliability?

35. The manager of a recently opened supermarket specializing in natural foods is reviewing the store's four month sales history in preparation for merchandise and employment planning. The first month sales were affected by grand opening promotions to introduce the store to customers in the trade area. Sales in the three subsequent months exhibited considerable growth, although there was substantial variation from day to day. The manager felt the daily sales history reflected normal shopping patterns within the week combined with rapidly increasing market penetration as the store and its policies became better known in the community. To effectively plan merchandise and employment requirements the store manager needs to get some dimensions on the sales growth picture. The data on daily sales (expressed in thousands of dollars) for the last three months is given in Table 17.15.

a. Construct a seven-day moving average to reveal how rapidly and how steadily sales have been growing during the last three months. Then plot the computed moving-average values on a chart. Note: if a computer is not available, consider only the last 5 weeks.

b. Give a verbal description of the sales growth pattern exhibited by the moving average series.

36. The manager of the store described in Problem 35 is anxious to identify any regular pattern to daily sales within the week that will be useful in scheduling employees

TABLE 17.15. Daily Sales in a Natural Food Store for the Previous Three Months

WEEK	SUNDAY	MONDAY	TUESDAY	WEDNESDAY	THURSDAY	FRIDAY	SATURDAY
1	4.80	5.01	4.88	5.04	6.59	7.39	7.58
2	4.97	5.18	4.89	5.28	6.83	7.74	7.80
3	5.31	5.55	5.23	5.32	6.97	7.85	8.30
4	5.51	5.78	5.43	5.65	7.20	8.26	8.38
5	5.84	5.85	5.53	5.76	7.59	8.78	8.81
6	5.77	6.23	5.53	5.99	7.73	9.06	9.34
7	6.00	6.45	5.93	6.17	8.17	9.30	9.83
8	6.20	6.45	6.02	6.01	8.24	9.37	9.94
9	6.43	6.65	6.26	6.49	8.37	9.95	10.40
10	6.92	6.91	6.49	6.56	8.85	10.67	10.38
11	6.92	7.23	6.55	6.58	8.93	10.46	10.75
12	7.14	7.58	7.09	7.15	9.37	10.76	11.25
13	7.17	7.48	7.31	7.48	9.35	11.10	11.24

and merchandise deliveries.

a. Compute "daily indexes" for each day of the week using the ratio-to-moving-average method.

b. On which days of the week should the manager schedule the most employees and plan to have the greatest stock of merchandise available on the shelves for customer purchases?

37. The store manager in Problem 35 is aware that existing trade area competitors are trying retaliatory promotions to keep their own customers from "straying". "Have they had any measureable effect on the new store's sales?" is what the manager is trying to find out.

a. "Deseasonalize" the sales data by dividing the actual sales by the daily index for that day for the last three weeks. Plot this series on a chart.

b. Compute the least squares trend line from the deseasonalized data.

c. Explain how the store manager might use the residuals from the trend line of the deseasonalized data to examine the possible impact of a competitor's retaliatory promotions.

38. You are a well-known consultant on executive compensation and have been called in by a conglomerate's board of directors to mediate an executive compensation dispute. John Wilson, recently hired president of one of a corporate conglomerate's subsidiaries, is claiming that he is entitled to a substantial bonus for third quarter profits. The third quarter represents Mr. Wilson's first quarter at the helm. His compensation contract specifies that he is eligible for a substantial bonus as soon as the profit picture of the subsidiary improves. Mr. Wilson attributes the sharp profit rise of the third quarter over the profits earned in the second quarter by his predecessor to his "bold initiatives and necessary actions" upon taking over the reins of the company. The corporate board has another view of third quarter profits. Current third quarter profits are down from the third quarter of last year. The board feels this better measures Mr. Wilson's early performance as president and

under that measure profits have not improved.

a. Is Mr. Wilson's interpretation of profit improvement as the increase over the preceding quarter wrong?

b. Is the corporate board of directors' interpretation of profit improvement as the increase over the previous year's third quarter wrong?

c. The consultant recommends a different basis for measuring profit than either Mr. Wilson or the board used. Can you suggest an approach that overcomes the major deficiencies of the comparison with the preceding quarter or with the previous year's quarter? Explain.

39. A hospital administrator is looking for a better way to understand the demand for nursing services in three hospital cost centers: maternity, radiology, and emergency room. Monthly data on patient hours in these three departments are given in Table 17.16 for a five year period. Can you make some suggestions? Table 17.16 can be found on pages 666 and 667.

a. Compute 12-month moving averages for each series of data and plot the three moving average series on one chart.

b. Compare the trends in the three departments.

40. For the data given in Problem 39, compute monthly seasonal indexes for each series. Does a strong seasonal effect exist? If so, is it the same among the different departments?

41. a. Compute by the method of least squares the trend and seasonal effects for the data given in Problem 39. Use dummy variables to measure the monthly seasonal effects.

b. Compare the trend and seasonal effects, if any, among the different departments.

c. Is there a substantial difference among the departments in the amount of variation in patient demand which can not be assigned to trend or seasonal effects?

d. Compute the residuals for each series.

e. Do the residuals for any of the departments exhibit a pattern that deserves investigation? Explain.

42. *"Low Price Earnings Strategy"* Security analysts believe that it is worthwhile to use the price earnings ratio (the ratio of the market price of a stock to its annual earnings) as a way of screening stocks prior to considering them for intensive analysis. Firms with low price earnings ratios might be "undervalued" relative to their earnings potential. If so, the market would supposedly "discover" their mistake and raise the price, thereby creating capital gains for persons who bought before this discovery. Some evidence in fact suggests that firms with low price-earnings ratios form a preferred subset of stocks for the purpose of more rigorous financial analysis. But what type of earnings calculation should the analyst use? To reflect the impact that earnings reports during the year have on price movements, it is advantageous to use monthly or quarterly rather than annual earnings-per-share. However, few firms issue monthly earnings reports. Thus, perhaps the most practical choice is quarterly since firms issue quarterly financial reports. Multiplying each of the quarterly earnings-per-share as shown in column 3 in Table 17.17 by four allows earnings to be annualized so that the price-earnings ratio (P/E) calculation now becomes conventionally stated in annual terms.

But there is a problem in using price-earnings ratios based on unadjusted quarterly earnings-per-share (EPS) measurements. An obvious seasonal influence exists on earnings. If no adjustment is made, the EPS figures will not be comparable from quarter to quarter and therefore not useful in calculating meaningful P/E values that can be compared.

Can the procedures of statistical time series analysis identify normalized earnings—the stable component of earnings remaining after the disruptive seasonal and random components of earnings have been eliminated? Normalized earnings are what security analysts want to use to construct P/E ratios. They want the ratios to be appropriate for comparisons of the firm's P/E ratio with that of other firms and with that of the same firm at earlier points in time. Their strategy of seeking out and

TABLE 17.17. Quarterly Earnings

(1) YEAR	(2) QUARTER	(3) EARNINGS PER SHARE
1979	1	1.98
	2	.78
	3	.48
	4	1.76
1980	1	2.10
	2	.80
	3	.58
	4	2.02
1981	1	2.10
	2	.75
	3	.56
	4	1.84
1982	1	2.50
	2	.78
	3	.62
	4	2.10
1983	1	2.75
	2	1.05
	3	.70
	4	2.50

recommending as "bargains" stocks with low price-earnings ratios requires the earnings on which the ratios are based to be comparable.

a. One approach that adjusts the series to eliminate the seasonal and random elements is the four-quarter moving total. Calculate these values from the 1st quarter of 1979 until the 4th quarter of 1983.

b. Does this procedure completely resolve the issue of identifying normalized earnings? What information is lost?

43. Another approach to normalizing the quarterly earnings data given in Problem 42 is to deseasonalize the original series through the centered ratio-to-moving average method.

a. Calculate the seasonal indexes through the ratio-to-moving average method.

b. Deseasonalize the original EPS series.

c. What advantage is there in using the deseasonalized series rather than the moving total series as in 42?

d. What assumption about seasonality is being made in constructing the deseasonalized series? What can you point to in your

TABLE 17.16. Monthly Data on Patient Hours Spent in Three Departments

TIME PERIOD	MATERNITY	EMERGENCY ROOM	RADIOLOGY
1	3935	5666	855
2	3850	5405	870
3	3580	5001	866
4	4240	4688	859
5	4605	5492	862
6	4660	5231	855
7	4377	4813	857
8	3972	4780	839
9	3523	4611	847
10	3675	5201	836
11	3679	5136	876
12	3573	5124	873
13	3866	6149	865
14	3264	6202	860
15	3585	5808	846
16	4308	5572	839
17	4078	7069	852
18	4369	6839	864
19	4281	6104	884
20	3423	6812	878
21	4097	8367	874
22	3646	8130	865
23	3603	7525	868
24	3848	6918	855
25	4024	6737	857
26	3416	6800	865
27	3671	6112	861
28	3762	6717	853
29	4444	7937	860
30	5375	7647	863

calculations that show this is reasonable?

44. A normalized series of earnings with seasonal and random elements removed can also be achieved by least squares trend analysis. Normalized earnings are the trend line EPS values read from the computed least-squares line from the equation:

$$\widehat{EPS}_t = a + b\,t$$

The quarterly EPS values are annualized (multiplied by 4) to give values of the dependent variable. Time, t, is the independent variable with a starting value of 1 for the 1st quarter of 1979 and rising by one for each successive quarter.

a. Calculate the least-squares trend line for the original quarterly EPS (now annualized) series. (Do not use deseasonalized data.)

b. Determine the trend line values, $\widehat{EPS}$, from the computed equation.

c. Compare the original EPS (annualized) values with the trend line values. Should one expect only a little or considerable discrepancy between the two? Why?

d. If on average there is substantial deviation between the two, does this suggest that the trend line fitting was an ill-advised undertaking?

e. The least-squares trend line analysis suggested for the original quarterly EPS (annualized) series could be applied to the deseasonalized quarterly EPS data in annualized form to determine normalized earnings. Repeat the procedures. Do you expect to find a substantially different trend line from that found originally? Explain the reason for your answer. Which trend line,

TABLE 17.16. Monthly Data (continued)

TIME PERIOD	MATERNITY	EMERGENCY ROOM	RADIOLOGY
31	3752	6993	882
32	2884	8089	876
33	3324	9279	883
34	3133	9547	875
35	3048	8064	861
36	3163	8188	864
37	3217	8889	869
38	3106	8655	875
39	3196	7161	871
40	3118	6912	878
41	3305	8059	876
42	4667	8701	879
43	3555	7345	891
44	3101	8023	885
45	3507	8890	871
46	3131	10089	861
47	3639	8620	848
48	2762	9742	821
49	2929	12345	814
50	3137	12031	800
51	2975	10433	814
52	3274	12770	816
53	3422	13819	819
54	4507	15038	790
55	3254	15518	754
56	3426	12623	763
57	2983	10887	758
58	2724	9766	748
59	2974	8861	743
60	2561	11380	762

according to the r^2 criterion, gives a better fit?

45. Compare the deseasonalized series value for EPS (Problem 43) and the trend $\widehat{EPS}$ values calculated from the least-square method on the deseasonalized quarterly EPS in annualized form (Problem 44e).

a. Which would you suspect to have the most stable series? Why?

b. What conclusion would you draw about the relative merit of these two techniques in adjusting quarterly EPS? If both techniques produced very similar results would you want to re-check your calculations?

Index Numbers and the Measurement of Business Change

Preview. Times are always changing. To keep abreast of change, government officials, business managers, and investors have become avid index watchers. Numerous indexes—gold prices, housing starts, unemployment, industrial production, to name just a few—are followed closely for hints about the future. Because of increased concern about inflation and its consequences, no indexes attract more attention than the *Consumer Price Index* and the accompanying *Producer Price Index*. This chapter focuses on general principles of index series construction and then considers the construction, value, and use of the two key indexes just mentioned.

The 1976 presidential campaign saw Jimmy Carter, Democratic nominee for President of the United States, coin the term "misery index". The index was defined as the sum of the nation's unemployment rate and the inflation rate. Carter urged voters to vote for him, not the incumbent President Gerald Ford, because, among other things, Carter claimed that it was Ford who was responsible for the misery index reaching what he considered an unacceptable double digit value. Carter was elected, but four years later the misery index Carter had used in his first presidential campaign came back to haunt him. During the 1980 presidential election, President Carter was now on the defensive. The Republican challenger Ronald Reagan made reference to this Carter-inspired index to dramatize the failure of the Carter administration to cure, or even to ameliorate, the nation's economic ills. In the closing days of the campaign, with the "misery index" hovering around the twenty percent mark, Reagan stressed the issue of the economy and argued that by applying Carter's own misery criterion, President Carter didn't deserve to be re-elected President in 1980.

Is the index a valid measure of economic prosperity? What would it have been during the Great Depression? It will be the purpose of this chapter to determine just what can be safely and usefully said by using indexes.

18.1. Introduction

18

The key indexes used to measure business and economic change are neither as simply constructed nor as straightforwardly interpreted as the "misery index" of former President Carter. Nevertheless, business analysis is greatly aided by their availability. However, to assure proper usage of the popular indexes, it is important that their nature and composition be understood.

Inflation: The Indexes Tell the Story

Inflation. It's a four letter word today, an inescapable fact of life like death and taxes. Inflation became a serious national economic problem in the 70s despite the many governmental efforts to curtail it. Consumers found that their increased dollar incomes bought fewer goods and services. Investors saw wealth stored in savings accounts erode. Interest rates charged by lending institutions rose to record high levels, virtually choking off new home mortgage loans. Businesses found that high interest rates dampened plans for expansion. Uncertainty about inflation made long-term borrowing difficult. It also affected a business's ability to predict future sales levels, and therefore clouded strategic business planning.

Is the meaning of inflation intuitive and straightforward? It may seem so when one pays five times the pre-1973 price for a gallon of gasoline. But the meaning of inflation becomes less obvious when one pays $395 for a programmable, sleek, high speed electronic pocket-size calculator instead of $300 for the bulky, slow, mechanical one of a decade or two ago. The meaning of this important phenomenon can be ambiguous. The meaning of inflation is dependent on how it is measured by an index number; once measured, the question becomes how this index measurement is interpreted.

Index Numbers and Index Series

An index in its simplest form requires a comparison of two values of the same series at different time periods. The comparison is done by making a ratio of the two values. The denominator of the ratio is the period value designated as the standard against which the values at other periods are measured. It is called the base period value. The top of the ratio is the period value which is being compared to the base period value. For instance, if the 1975 value of the series is to serve as the base period, the ratio for 1977 would be formed as follows:

$$\frac{\text{The 1977 Value of the Series}}{\text{The 1975 (Base Period) Value of the Series}} = \text{Ratio for 1977}$$

This ratio is generally multiplied by 100 to show the top period value as a percent of the base period value. That is,

$$\frac{\text{The 1977 Value of the Series}}{\text{The 1975 (Base Period) Value of the Series}} \times 100 = I_{1977}$$

The calculated I_{1977} is the index number for 1977 that would be cited in newspapers and used by business economists. The conversion of the original values of a particular time sequences series into a series of index numbers with a common base period generates a new time series called an *index time series*.

Simple Indexes of Price and Quantity

Index series can be constructed for a single commodity or item like pork chops, or for a collection of items like the weekly grocery store shopping list. If the index is for only one item, it's called a *simple* index. If the measurement is on price, the index is a *simple price index*. Let's illustrate this type by considering the prices of the glittering metal, gold, over the years.

Example 18.1A.   The "Gold Bugs": What Does the Simple Price Index for Gold Say About Their Investment Advice?

Eliot Janeway, a noted investment adviser, waxes poetic when discussing gold. He, along with other "gold bugs," sees gold as a good (and perhaps the only) refuge for inflation weary investors. As Figure 18.1 visually shows, gold did distinguish itself as "the" investment medium of the inflationary Seventies.

But the surge in gold prices during the late Seventies and early Eighties can be better described by *indexing* the rate of change in gold prices. In 1971 the U.S. government decided to abandon the gold standard. The government made trading in gold legal and removed the legal price for it ($35 per ounce) letting market forces reign. Using 1971 as the base period, Table 18.1 shows how much a $100 investment in gold made in 1971 was worth in subsequent years.

TABLE 18.1. The Gold Price Index

START OF THE YEAR	GOLD PRICE PER OZ.	GOLD PRICE INDEX (BASE 1971)
1971	$ 40.80	100.0
1972	58.10	142.4
1973	97.20	238.2
1974	159.10	390.0
1975	161.10	395.0
1976	124.00	303.9
1977	147.70	362.0
1978	190.00	465.7
1979	300.00	735.3
1980	508.50	1246.3
1981	589.75	1445.5
1982	397.50	974.3

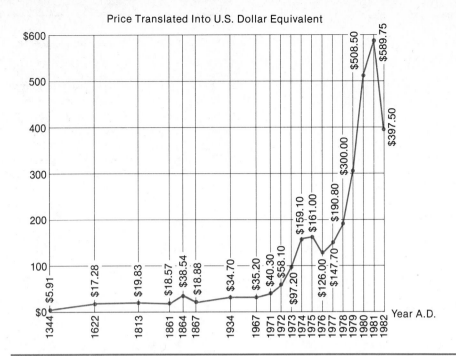

FIGURE 18.1 Gold Price, Per Ounce, Down Through the Centuries:
Price at the First of the Year

Source: *San Diego Union*, December 31, 1979; Data for years 1981 and 1982 from *Business Week*, January 11, 1982

The column on the right is the simple price index series for gold. The index shows that from 1971 to 1981 gold rose in price dramatically, unexpectedly surpassing the most optimistic predictions of the "gold bugs". This rise was continuous except during 1975 when it suffered approximately a 23% decline. By the end of the decade the overall percentage increase was 1446%! But the drop in the index in the subsequent year showed that gold gave up in only one year about one third of the gain it made in the entire decade.

The index series facilitates without graphics a quick mental image of the relative change in gold price. Knowing that the index is 1266, say, compared to the base period value of 100, we quickly recognize a twelve-fold increase in price. Moreover, the base year can be set to coincide with an important event (such as the 1971 government decision). This way, ratio comparisons of subsequent prices with the price in the year the important event took place can be made directly.

Price is not the only variable which can be or usually is indexed. Business decisions often require information on relative *quantity* changes over time. A simple *quantity index series* shows the quantity changes over time relative to the quantity in the base period. As the following example shows, quantity need not be a count of physical items; it can be a count by measurement units.

Example 18.1B. **A Quantity Index Series Shows the Boom and Bust Years for the Airlines**

The decade of the '60s marked the golden years of the airline industry. Passenger service business expanded at a phenomenal rate, as did profits. After installing its new jet capacity in the early part of the decade, the airline industry enjoyed the fruits of a growing economy and a U.S. populace that became more travel-minded in response to comparatively lower rates for distance traveled. The data from 1964 to 1969 in Table 18.2 highlight this boom of the late Sixties. Indexing the passenger revenue miles expansion for the latter half of the Sixties starting with 1964 and ending with 1969 shows that service more than doubled in 5 years, going from an index level of 100 to an index level of 232.7.

TABLE 18.2. Growth of Domestic Air Carriers Scheduled Service

YEAR	PASSENGER REVENUE MILES (in Billions)	INDEX
		1964 = 100
1964	44.14	100.0
1965	51.89	117.6
1966	60.59	127.2
1967	75.49	171.0
1968	87.51	198.2
1969	102.72	232.7
1970	104.15	236.0
1971	106.44	240.1
1972	118.14	267.6
1973	126.32	286.1
1974	129.73	292.2
1975	131.73	298.3
1976	145.27	329.1
1977	156.61	354.8
1978	182.67	413.8
1979	208.46	472.3
1980	200.09	453.3

Source: *Aerospace Facts and Figures,* 1981/82

The index series in the right column also reveals that the growth in scheduled domestic airline traffic did not continue at that pace in the Seventies. A recession began in 1969 and continued into the early Seventies. Along with sharply reduced growth of airline travel came declining airline earnings. A similar growth slowdown together with revenue and profits decline came in the 1973–1975 period. The 1980 index figure shows that growth actually became negative for the first time since the golden 60s.

Quantity index series such as this one are useful for comparing operating performance in the industry. For example, security analysts, drawing up their recommendations on particular airline stocks, construct quantity index series for TWA, United Airlines, American Airlines, and others, and compare these quantity index series to the above industry index series. The comparisons show the relative growth performance of a particular airline as the industry traffic expands and contracts. Indeed, without this index series, comparison of a specific airline's growth to the entire industry's growth would be difficult to make.

The Consumer Price Index—An Important Price Aggregate

The most widely used indexes are *aggregate* price indexes; that is, indexes which measure price changes for more than one commodity or item at a time. The most popular of these is the index millions of Americans use as the report card on inflation—the *Consumer Price Index*. Published by the U.S. Bureau of Labor Statistics and popularized by evening news reporters, the Consumer Price Index has given nearly every U.S. household a blow-by-blow account of the dizzying rise in prices. There are other important indexes published by government and private organizations that are inflation indicators. The Producer Price Index and the GNP Implicit Price Deflator are two (discussed later in this chapter). But the Consumer Price Index by far is more closely watched than any other economic index. When double-digit rises are registered, consumer confidence in the economy suffers and business reduces investment plans. Many cost-of-living clauses of labor contracts are tied to the Index as well as a great majority of other contracts that have indexation clauses. Because of its importance, much of the remainder of this chapter is devoted to an analysis of its construction and interpretation. The following example from *Fortune* magazine illustrates the magnitude of its impact.

Example 18.1C.   CPI Changes Directly Affect Millions of Americans

A change of 1 percent in the index can trigger a billion dollars' worth of income transfers, affecting about a half of the population. All 31 million Social Security recipients have their payments tied to the CPI by a cost-of-living escalator, as do 2 million retired members of the civil service and the military.

Changes in the index also directly affect the food-stamp allotments for 20 million recipients, the subsidies for the 25 million children who are served under the National School Lunch Act and the Child Nutrition Act, and benefits for millions more who partake of health and welfare programs with "poverty level" eligibility requirements tied to the CPI. Then, too, there is the growing number of private contracts governed by a CPI escalator. The contracts may cover such things as rent and child-support payments, but most notably the wages of nine million unionized workers whose cost-of-living escalators are tied to the CPI.[1]

18.2. Simple Aggregative Indexes: Implementing the Concept of an Average Price

Inflation is commonly understood to mean "rapidly rising prices." But does it have to mean "rapidly rising prices of everything?" After all, the prices of certain calculators and digital watches, to name just a few things, have declined over the last decade. The idea of inflation, like the idea of an aggregate price index, points to the concept of an *average* price. Like any other average, the value of an aggregate price index refers in *general* to the items considered in the average, but *not* necessarily to any specific item included in the average. So when we speak of an inflation index we do not necessarily mean that the prices of *all* goods actually went up. Nor is it meant that the percentage changes in prices of all the items comprising a price aggregate index have to conform to the percentage change in the value of the index. The intent of an aggregate index series is to use the movement in the value of the index as a *substitute* for the individual changes in the prices of items in the aggregate.

The concept of a general price level and the changes in it sounds workable— at least until one tries to measure it. Suppose an individual wishes simply to compare today's food prices with yesterday's food prices. Certainly this could be done on an item-to-item basis. For example, someone attempting to compare today's grocery prices with those paid 5 years ago might write down the prices given in Table 18.3.

TABLE 18.3. Consumer Shopping List

ITEM	TODAY'S PRICE ($)	PRICE 5 YEARS AGO ($)	PRICE CHANGE	INDIVIDUAL PRICE INDEX
Chicken (lb.)	.79	.59	.20	134
T-Bone Steak (lb.)	3.29	1.79	1.50	184
Ground Beef (lb.)	1.39	.99	.40	140
Bacon (lb.)	1.69	1.19	.50	142
Loaf of Bread (lb.)	.89	.62	.27	144
Coffee (lb.)	2.75	1.00	1.75	275
Sugar (lb.)	.24	.17	.07	141
Eggs (doz.)	.89	.73	.16	122
Milk (gal.)	1.69	1.29	.40	131
Potatoes (lb.)	.25	.20	.05	125
Margarine (lb.)	.59	.39	.20	151
Apples (lb.)	.49	.39	.10	126
	$14.95	$9.35		

There are twelve food items on this list. The items all have different prices and most of the price changes are different too. While a simple price index series *could* be constructed for each of the twelve items and inflation measured by reporting the changes in all twelve indexes, this would not ordinarily be done. It is too difficult to absorb the meaning of twelve individual comparisons as a measure of inflation. Instead, the information contained in all the individual price series is condensed and summarized into a single *aggregate price index*. This way inflation can be measured by a single comparison. Changes in the aggregate series are easier to comprehend, even though it is known full well that the changes in this series do not directly apply to a particular product included in the aggregate.

Average of Price Relatives

The price increases of the 12 items in the food shopping list varied considerably. The increases ranged from a low of 22% (eggs) to a high of 175% (coffee). One simple way to describe the inflation in the prices of the 12 food items is to *average* the price relatives.

$$\text{Index}_{TB} = \sum \left(\frac{P_T}{P_B}\right) \times \frac{100}{n} = (1816) \times \frac{100}{12} = 151.33 \text{ or } 151$$

where P_T is the price of the item in a *particular* year and P_B is the price of the same item in the *base* year. Finding a value of 151 in this example indicates that the average of the 12 different price inflation rates has been 51% (on average, the price levels are 151% of their level in the base period).

Although this index is useful in summarizing the inflation rate of different items, it is *not* a good index of the *impact* of inflation. The failure of the index stems from the fact that it ignores the different levels of price of the various products. Thus, the 25% increase in the price of 20¢ potatoes gets the same weight as the 84% increase in the price of $1.79 T-bone steak. If steak and potatoes are used together, the increase in steak price has a greater dollar impact than would the same percentage increase in potatoes because of the higher price of steak. This deficiency of the average price relatives index in measuring inflation can be overcome by using an index which averages *dollar* price changes rather than *percentage* price changes.

The Simple (Unweighted) Aggregate Index

The simple aggregate index of all commodities in the market basket is a ratio of the sum of the prices in a particular year, $\sum P_T$, to the sum of the prices in the base year, $\sum P_B$, times 100.

$$I_{TB} = \frac{\sum P_T}{\sum P_B} \times 100 = \frac{\text{Sum of Prices Today of Market Basket}}{\text{Sum of Prices Base Period of Market Basket}} \times 100$$

Making five years ago the base period, today's prices would have an index number of:

$$\frac{\$14.95}{\$9.35} \times 100 = 159.89$$

What is the interpretation of this simple aggregate index of 159.89? It indicates that the prices of the 12 items in this market basket increased 59.89% on average over the five year period. This procedure implicitly gives greater importance to the item that has the largest absolute price change. In this case that item was coffee, which increased $1.75.

An Unweighted Aggregate Index Ignores Purchase Frequency

A simple (unweighted) aggregate index is useful in measuring the inflation in the purchase expenditure to buy one of each of the items in the market basket. But as a measure of the *impact* of inflation on the consumer budget, it too has a serious deficiency which is shared with the average price relatives index. *Both of these indexes ignore the difference in frequency of purchase of the items in the market basket.*

The fact is a household *seldom purchases equal amounts of each item.* For instance, the average individual consumes nearly 200 lbs. of meat each year but uses only 14 pounds of coffee. Thus, the increase in a pound of meat, though smaller than the increase in a pound of coffee, is paid 200 times annually compared to only 14 times annually for the coffee. So simply aggregating unweighted prices item-by-item computes an index that assumes something that's just not so—equal importance in the consumer budget for each item. This leads to an erroneous impression about the increase in the cost of living.

What is needed is a consumer "market basket" which reflects, as nearly as possible, actual consumer purchases. The consumer "market basket" is a term specifying the sample of items upon which an index is based.

18.3. The Argument for a Weighted Index

In measuring inflation, a distinction must be made between what has happened to the prices of things people buy and the *impact* those price changes have on the standard of living.

> Of two items purchased equally frequently, a 10% decline on a $1 item does not offset a 10% increase in a big-ticket item costing $1,000.

The decrease on the $1 item amounts to only 10 cents, while the increase on the $1000 item amounts to $100. This is why the Average Price Relatives Index gives a misleading picture of inflation's impact.

> Of two items having identical prices in the base period, a 10% decline in the one purchased every two years does not offset a 10% increase in the one purchased every two weeks.

For example, suppose both items cost $1. The reduction in expenditures on the one purchased every two years amounts to $.10 over the two year period. This does not offset the increase of ($1 times 104/2)10% = $5.20 on the item purchased every two weeks. This is why the simple unweighted aggregate index gives a misleading impression of inflation's impact.

To measure the *impact* of price changes on a standard of living, it is necessary to measure the *change in spending* required to obtain the market basket of goods which defines the living standard. Consider two items having identical prices in the base period and also having identical price increases. *If one of the items is purchased six times as frequently as the other, it will have six times the inflationary impact* because of the greater proportion of the budget devoted to it. Thus, to get a true picture of the impact of inflation, the question which must be answered is, "How much additional expenditure is required to buy the market basket of goods which defines the given standard of living?" This question can only be answered by *weighting* the prices of the market basket items by their *purchase frequencies.*

Which Market Basket Defines the Living Standard? The Substitution Effect Problem of Shifting Relative Prices

The weight given to an individual item's price is determined by the purchase quantity in the market basket which defines the living standard. It might seem that the choice of market basket would be obvious; it is not. The problem is that, even in an inflationary period when all prices are rising, prices do not all rise at the same rate. When the prices of goods in the market basket change relative to each other, consumers tend to change their purchase quantities, substituting relatively cheaper goods for the more expensive ones whenever they can. So the market basket changes. Since the market basket is not constant, there is a problem in deciding which market basket should be used to define the standard of living. This problem will be considered in detail in a later section. For the present, we turn to a measure of inflationary impact utilizing the base period market basket. This is the most popular of the weighted indexes and, importantly, the one used in constructing the Consumer Price Index.

18.4. The Laspeyres Weighted Aggregate Price Index

The impact of inflation is most commonly measured by answering the following question:

> How much would it cost today relative to the base period to purchase the same market basket of goods that was purchased in the base period?

The price index which answers this question is called the *Laspeyres Index.* A Laspeyres price index is constructed by choosing *quantities purchased in the base period as weights* and holding these weights constant in computing the index for subsequent periods. The Laspeyres index for the current period is:

$$L_{0,1} = \left[\sum (p_1 q_0) / \sum (p_0 q_0) \right] \times 100$$

The index is a *weighted aggregative* type since it is the ratio of two expenditures— the numerator representing the items purchased in the base period q_0 at current prices p_1, and the denominator being the actual expenditures $q_0 p_0$ of the base period. Because the weights are constant and determined by the purchase quantities in the base period, it is also referred to as a *fixed-weight, fixed base* type of weighted aggregate index.

A Numerical Example

To illustrate the construction of a Laspeyres price index, suppose that our consumer's total budget consisted of five items and the expenditures on these five items were known for a period of four years. The five items in essence constitute our consumer's "market basket." Table 18.4 details this.

The *Laspeyres index* for 1982 with base year 1980 is computed as follows:

$$L_{1980,1982} = \frac{\sum p_{1982} q_{1980}}{\sum p_{1980} q_{1980}} \times 100 = \frac{12,897.5}{11,302.5} \times 100 = 114.11$$

Note that even though $4803 was spent in 1979 (a car was not purchased), the index is based on base year quantities, and therefore determined *as if* a car had been purchased.

A straightforward interpretation of the calculated value 114.11 is that if the consumer desires to purchase the identical "market basket" in 1982 as in year 1980, it would cost 14.11 percent more (on average, the price levels are 114.11% of their level in the 1980 base period). Similarly, the same bundle of items of the base year would cost 23.11 percent more in 1983 than in the 1980 base year: the price level in 1983 is 123.11% of the level in the base year.

The Laspeyres index series for the data in Table 18.4 is given below.

	1980	1981	1982	1983
Laspeyres (Base Year 1980)	100.0	106.68	114.11	123.11

The Consumer Price Index Is a Laspeyres Index

The Consumer Price Index is a Laspeyres index which is constructed according to the same principles as illustrated by the Laspeyres series just computed. Of course, far more than five items are included in the index. To assure the accuracy expected of the index, the Bureau of Labor Statistics expends a great deal of time and effort gathering the extraordinarily detailed data necessary for the index's construction, as the following example suggests.

Example 18.4A.   CPI Data Gathering

Verena Brunner, a field economist for the Labor Department, begins her day at a small, scruffy supermarket in New York City's Harlem. The "ambiente" is cordial there, and staccato Spanish punctuates the air as Miss Brunner quietly goes about her business, moving past bins of melons and mangos, searching for a predetermined list of groceries that make up part of the consumer price index. Miss Brunner isn't buying; rather, she's on a "quality assurance" mission for the Bureau of Labor Statistics. She has replaced the regular data collector for the day to make sure the "regular" hasn't been doing sloppy work or "curbstoning" (the BLS term for faking it, while sitting, presumably, upon a curbstone).

TABLE 18.4. Prices and Quantities Purchased—Consumer With a Hypothetical Five-Item "Market Basket"

| ITEM | YEARS | | | |
| | 1980 | | 1981 | |
	p_{1980}	q_{1980}	p_{1981}	q_{1981}
Automobiles, each	$ 7000.00	1	$ 7400.00	1
Rent, per month	280.00	12	305.00	12
Bread, per loaf	.70	250	.75	275
Movie tickets, each	2.75	10	3.00	6
Suits, each	185.00	4	195.00	4
Total Expenditures	$11,302.50		$12,064.25	

| ITEM | YEARS | | | |
| | 1982 | | 1983 | |
	p_{1982}	q_{1982}	p_{1983}	q_{1983}
Automobiles, each	$7900.00	0	$ 8400.00	1
Rent, per month	325.00	12	360.00	12
Bread, per loaf	.82	275	.88	300
Movie tickets, each	3.25	10	3.50	10
Suits, each	215.00	3	235.00	1
Total Expenditures	$4803.00		$13,254.00	

Note: Subscripts represent years, and p and q represent prices and quantities, respectively.

As Miss Brunner travels from the ghetto grocery store far uptown to a department store on the fashionable East Side and a half dozen more establishments throughout midtown Manhattan, store clerks recognize her by the dark blue notebook she carries under her arm. Emblazoned with the legend, "Consumer Price Index," it's the trademark of the 500 BLS data collectors across the country who visit stores selected by computers in Washington and note the prices of various items also picked by the computers in accord with sophisticated statistical techniques.[2]

The Consumer Price Index is published both on an all-items basis and for some major categories—food, housing, medical care, and the cost of energy. What does the index say about the course of inflation in recent years? Let's look at the index in the following example.

▰▰▰▰▰

Example 18.4B. Inflation Has Been Rampant and Widespread According to the CPI

The index numbers in Table 18.5 and their graph in Figure 18.2 clearly show the acceleration in price increases during the 1965–1981 time period. Prices overall rose steadily over the sixteen year period. Prices averaged a year to year 4.3 percent inflation rate during the five years 1966 through 1970, an even higher average 6.8 percent year to year rate for 1970 through 1975, and a spiraling average 9.1 percent rate for the years from 1976 through 1981.

As a result of these yearly increases, the all-item Consumer Price Index was 172 percent higher in 1981 than it was in 1967. The inflationary spiral peaked in 1980 at the 13.5 percent rate. It achieved double digit increases also in 1974, 1979, and 1981.

In comparing the different indexes shown in Figure 18.2, it becomes evident that the index of energy prices increased more overall since 1967 than did the other indexes selected. The dramatic 25% increases in 1974 and 1979 were due largely to the OPEC cartel world oil prices. A geographic breakdown of the Consumer Price Index for 28 Standard Metropolitan Statistical Areas for which indexes are published (as well as for 57 other areas) indicates that inflation has reached all areas of the country, exhibiting the kind of rapid price increase that has been typical of the U.S. at large for the past several years.

Why the Consumer Price Index Overstates the Impact of Inflation

Because the Consumer Price Index uses base period weights, it in essence defines the standard of living as that maintained in the base period. The Consumer Price Index reports how much extra income would be required in the current period as a result of inflation to buy the same market basket of goods as in the base period. However, if you give the consumer the extra money to maintain the base period market basket, you'll probably be in for a surprise. The consumer will no longer buy the same market basket. And if the same market basket is no longer

TABLE 18.5. Consumer Price Index (1967 = 100)

	ALL ITEMS	FOOD	HOUSING	MEDICAL	ENERGY	YEAR TO YEAR % CHANGE–ALL ITEMS (Inflation Rate)*	
1965	94.5	94.4	94.9	89.5	96.3		
66	97.2	99.1	97.2	93.4	97.8	2.9	
67	100.0	100.0	100.0	100.0	100.0	2.9	Average 4.3
68	104.2	103.6	104.0	106.1	101.3	4.2	
69	109.8	108.9	110.4	113.4	104.2	5.4	
70	116.3	114.9	118.2	120.6	107.0	5.9	
71	121.3	118.4	123.4	128.4	111.2	4.3	
72	125.3	123.5	128.1	132.5	114.3	3.3	
73	133.1	141.4	133.7	137.7	123.5	6.2	Average 6.8
74	147.7	161.7	148.8	150.5	159.7	11.0	
75	161.2	175.4	164.5	168.6	176.6	9.1	
76	176.5	180.8	174.6	184.7	189.3	5.8	
77	181.5	192.2	186.5	202.4	207.3	6.5	
78	195.4	211.4	202.8	219.4	220.4	7.7	Average 9.1
79	217.4	234.5	227.6	239.7	275.9	11.0	
80	247.0	254.6	263.6	265.9	361.1	13.5	
81	272.4	274.6	293.5	294.5	410.0	10.3	

*Example: 1969 inflation rate = [(109.8 − 104.2)/104.2] × 100 = 5.4
Source: U.S. Bureau of Labor Statistics

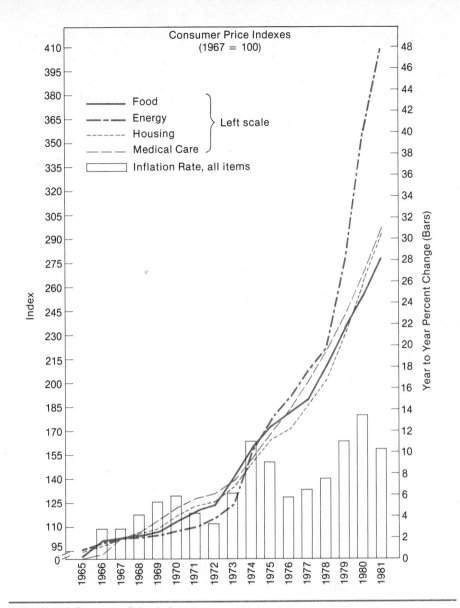

FIGURE 18.2 Consumer Price Indexes

Source: U.S. Bureau of Labor Statistics

purchased, we'll have to check to see whether the new market basket amounts to a higher or lower standard of living. As it turns out in this situation, we can be sure the new market basket gives an *improved* standard of living.

Why does the consumer not buy the base period market basket when given enough extra money to do so? And why can we be so sure the new market basket will give a higher standard of living than that maintained in the base period? In any inflationary period, some prices rise faster than others. At the new relative prices the consumer will want to cut back on goods that have advanced fastest in price, even if given money to compensate for the price increases. For example, suppose steak and chicken are both priced at $1 per pound in the base period and a consumer purchases equal amounts of each. If steak goes to $3.30 and chicken to $1.10 per pound, the consumer will cut back on steak consumption relative to chicken even if given enough extra money to maintain the original consumption pattern. When steak is three times the price of chicken the consumer does not find it desirable to consume as much steak relative to chicken as when the prices were equal. What the consumer does is substitute chicken for some of the steak formerly consumed and then use the leftover money to buy other wanted goods. However, since the CPI calculation is based on giving enough extra money to the consumer to buy the same market basket as before, and the consumer chose a *different* market basket (one with more chicken in it), it must be assumed that the consumer prefers the new market basket ($\sum q_1$) to the old ($\sum q_0$). Therefore, the *new* market basket represents a *higher* standard of living.

The Consumer Price Index calculation procedure hypothetically gives the consumer enough extra income to buy the base period market basket at the new prices. However, because of the substitution effect, the consumer chooses a *different* market basket. Since the original market basket *could* have been purchased with the same expenditure, but was not, the market basket actually chosen must be preferred to the original one. In this sense, we know the consumer is at a higher standard of living than in the base period. Since the outlay implied by the CPI is one that gives the consumer a higher standard of living than in the base period, it follows that too much extra outlay was given. That is, the *same* standard of living as in the base period could have been reached with a *smaller* outlay than implied by the CPI. That is why the CPI *overstates* the impact of inflation.

Example 18.4C.   Developing the "Market Basket" for the Consumer Price Index is a Monumental Job

The "market baskets" for the current Consumer Price Indexes are based upon a Consumer Expenditure Survey conducted during the 1972–1973 period. The Survey covered approximately 40,000 families divided into two samples, and it was the most comprehensive expenditure survey ever undertaken. One sample was designed to gather data on major expenditures. It was administered by the Bureau of the Census, who interviewed 20,000 families quarterly over a two-year period. The other sample was designed to develop a "market basket" of smaller, more personal, and less memorable purchases of goods and services. The data from this sample were taken from expenditure diaries that the families were asked to keep over a two-week period.

18.5. The Paasche Index

Since the Consumer Price Index implies a different standard of living in the base period than in the current period, and since the base period may be several years in the past, an index that recognizes the *present* standard of living may be desired. The *Paasche weighted aggregate index* accomplishes this by defining the market basket using *current* period quantities as weights rather than base period quantities. The Paasche index relates the actual current period expenditure, $\sum p_1 q_1$, in the numerator to a contrived base period expenditure for the current market basket in the denominator, $\sum p_0 q_1$.

$$P_{0,1} = \left(\sum p_1 q_1 / \sum p_0 q_1 \right) \times 100$$

By using current period weights, the Paasche index tells how much it currently costs the consumer to obtain the standard of living indicated by today's market basket relative to how much it would have cost to obtain today's market basket in the base period.

The Paasche index is frequently employed to show the decline in the purchasing power of the dollar, as in the statement "the same goods that it takes a dollar to buy in 1981 could have been purchased for 52¢ in 1967."

Using the data in Table 18.4 for illustration, the Paasche index for 1982 with base year 1980 is determined as follows:

$$P_{1980,1982} = \frac{\sum p_{1982} q_{1982}}{\sum p_{1980} q_{1982}} \times 100 = \frac{4803}{4135} \times 100 = 116.15$$

The appropriate interpretation of the Paasche index number is that "it would cost 16.15 percent more to purchase the market basket of the current period (in this case 1982) than that market basket would have hypothetically cost in the base year (in this case 1980)." The computed Paasche indexes for each of the four years is given below:

PAASCHE SERIES	1980	1981	1982	1983
	100.0	106.68	116.15	122.92

Example 18.5. Price Deflated GNP

The Gross National Product is perhaps the best known and most widely used measure of economic activity. It measures the value of all the goods and services produced by the economy for the year. When the economy is growing, this shows up in the form of a large increase in the GNP, as it is called. When the GNP starts to level off, that's a sure sign of slowdown in the economy. However, since the GNP measures the *value* of goods and services (the amount someone spent on them), GNP changes reflect price changes as well as quantity changes. Thus, changes in the GNP reflect two kinds of changes: (1) changes in the real level of output and (2) price inflation.

During inflationary times it's important to know how much of the change in GNP is due to real growth in the economy and how much is due to inflated prices. A measure known as the *constant dollar GNP* or the *price deflated GNP* removes the inflationary component. It measures expenditures in *this year's market basket* of goods and services at the prices prevailing in a base period. Because the quantity weights are for the current year rather than the base year, price deflated GNP is a Paasche type index rather than a Laspeyres type.

With a Paasche Index Series
the Base Is Fixed But Not the Weights

Like the Laspeyres, the Paasche index is a *ratio of weighted aggregate* expenditures on a specific market basket of goods and services. And in constructing a Paasche index series, like in constructing a Laspeyres series, the denominator always refers to expenditures on the market basket in a specific base year which remains constant. For this reason a Paasche index series, like a Laspeyres series, is said to have a *fixed base*.

In a Laspeyres index series, the denominator used to compute each index in the series is the same—it represents expenditures on the base period market basket at prices prevailing at that time. The reason the denominator never changes is that a Laspeyres series uses *fixed weights*, namely the quantities for the base period. Thus, finding succeeding values in the series simply requires computing a new numerator each year—updating expenditures on the same market basket to reflect the new price level.

In a Paasche index series, the denominator used to compute each index in the series is *not* the same. In a Paasche series, the *market basket changes each year* to reflect changes in the pattern of consumption which have taken place over the year. Thus the Paasche index series does *not* have fixed quantity weights. So the denominator in the indexes has to change each year to reflect expenditures on the *shifting market basket*. Consequently, computations involved in obtaining a Paasche series are not quite as simple as with a Laspeyres series. Both numerator *and* denominator must be recomputed each year.

The Paasche Index Understates Inflation

The Laspeyres type index was shown to *overstate* the impact of inflation. The Paasche type index has the opposite problem. It *understates* the impact of inflation.

By using current period quantities as weights, the Paasche index gives only enough expenditures in the base period to buy today's market basket at the (previously lower) prices prevailing then. But given that amount of money to spend at those prices, would the consumer have chosen the same market basket? No. Given that prices of some goods (steak) advanced faster than others (chicken) over the interim, the consumer could achieve greater satisfaction by spending a larger proportion of the money in goods that were *relatively* cheaper (steak) at the then prevailing prices. That is, the consumer could use the money that *would* buy the same market basket of goods to *actually* buy a market basket giving a *higher* level of satisfaction (more steak). Suppose steak advanced faster in price than chicken between 1980 and 1982, so that steak was cheaper relative to chicken in 1980 than in 1982. Given enough money in 1980 to buy the 1982 quantities of steak and chicken means the *same standard of living* could have been achieved with *less expenditure* than the amount necessary to buy the *same (current period) market basket*. In other words, the Paasche index suggests more expenditure is needed in the base period than is actually required to attain the standard of living maintained in the current period. But what does this overstatement of how much expenditure is needed in the base period mean? It means that the monetary difference between the current dollar expenditure and the Paasche base period dollar expenditure to maintain an equivalent living standard is going to be stated *smaller* than it actually should be. Suggesting what? That less inflation occurred than has actually been the case. Thus, the Paasche index *understates* the actual impact of inflation.

One disadvantage of a Paasche index series compared to a Laspeyres index series is that using the Paasche series, it is not possible to determine the percentage change in prices between two periods from the index numbers corresponding to the two years. Consider the years 1981 and 1982 for the data in Table 18.4. What was the percentage change in prices between these years? Neither the Laspeyres nor the Paasche index series gives this information *directly*. However, the figure is easily computed from the Laspeyres series index numbers.

> The calculations made from Table 18.4 show the Laspeyres index to be 106.7 in 1981 and 114.1 in 1982. This represents a 6.9 percent change in the cost of the "market basket" between 1981 and 1982 ([(114.1 − 106.7)/106.7] × 100 = 6.9). Thus, the "market basket" that the consumer purchased in the base period would cost 6.9 percent more in 1982 than it would have in 1981.

No similar interpretation of the change in the Paasche index between these two years can be made. Each successive Paasche index number applies the *current period "market basket"* directly to the *base year prices.* The items *actually purchased* in 1982 cost the consumer 16.2 percent more than it would have cost in the base year, 1980, and the items *actually purchased* in 1981 cost 6.6 percent more than it would have cost in the base year, 1980. Since the particular selection of items being priced changes between years 1981 and 1982, a direct comparison of the index numbers to measure price *changes* between the two years would be like comparing apples and oranges.

Widening Discrepancy between Laspeyres and Paasche Indexes over Time

If consumption patterns were frozen over time, both Laspeyres and Paasche indexes would give the same value. However, new products are continually being introduced, supplanting older ones in consumption expenditure importance. These changing consumption patterns lead to a discrepancy between the Laspeyres and Paasche indexes because the Laspeyres index is based on the old consumption pattern and the Paasche index is based on the new consumption pattern. Of course, the greater the change in the pattern of consumption, the greater the discrepancy between the values of the two indexes. Since change in consumption patterns tends to be greater over longer periods of elapsed time, the gap between the Laspeyres and Paasche indexes usually widens with time.

> Consider the Laspeyres and Paasche indexes for 1981 for the data in Table 18.4. Both indexes are constructed with a 1980 base. A comparison of the indexes for 1981 shows the index numbers to be quite close in value: 106.7 to 106.6. The lack of variation in the quantities purchased between 1980 and

1981 is why the Paasche and Laspeyres index numbers are almost identical in value. But if, for example, the consumer had not bought an automobile in 1981, the Paasche index would have increased in 108.24. The Laspeyres for 1981, on the other hand, would have been unaffected and remained at 106.7, since only base period (1980) quantities are relevant in its construction.

Because the Paasche index is based on current consumption patterns, it would seem to be a more important index statistic than the Laspeyres index, particularly if a long time period exists between the base period and the current period. However, because the Paasche index requires constant revision, a generalized version of the Laspeyres is more commonly used.

18.6. Revising Weights and Shifting the Base Period: Important Considerations in Selecting an Index Number

The Paasche method is handicapped by the need to revise and tabulate the quantity measured each period. With quantity information expensive to gather or unavailable, it is more convenient and cheaper to do this just once for the base year than to have to do it every year for the base year. Also, the base period's weighted aggregate expenditure for the current market basket must be recomputed on each year's current market basket if the Paasche method is used. If it later becomes desirable to change the base period, the new base period expenditure must be recomputed for each period covered by the index.

High Cost of Paasche Series Versus Frequent Base Period Updating of Laspeyres Series

The nuisance and high cost of constantly revising weights is avoided with the Laspeyres method because it uses fixed base period weights. The disadvantage, of course, is that it becomes out of date as consumer purchase patterns change. To overcome the difficulties of shifting consumption patterns, the base period may be revised from time to time to bring a Laspeyres index more in tune with the current market basket. Although the Laspeyres is cheaper relative to the Paasche series if the base period is not changed, the Laspeyres series cost is still substantial. The following example explains that an important government index such as the Consumers Price Index is revised infrequently, presumably because of the high cost involved.

Example 18.6. Revising the Consumers Price Index: How Frequently and at What Cost?

The Bureau of Labor Statistics expends a great deal of time and effort gathering the extraordinarily detailed data necessary for construction of a revised *index*. The 1978 revision was the first major revision of the index since 1964. A "major" revision, in the case of the Consumer Price Index, usually indicates changes in the "market basket" of goods and services to be priced. In the case of the 1978 revision, the "market basket" was indeed updated, but the revision included a number of other major changes as well. The most publicized change was the publication of an entirely new index.

Before 1978, the Consumer Price Index was designed to reflect expenditure patterns only for urban wage earners and clerical workers. Since the revision, the BLS has published another Consumer Price Index as a companion to the old one that is designed to reflect expenditure patterns for *all* urban consumers rather than just urban wage earners and clerical workers. The new index is thus broader than the old, covering the expenditures of approximately 80 percent of the urban population.

The new Consumer Price Index not only has revised weights assigned to the components of the market basket, but it also includes different items and items priced at different kinds of retail outlets.

The form of the index, which is a slightly modified Laspeyres-type weighted aggregate index, was not changed by the 1978 revision.

What's the price tag on a revision of this magnitude? The index revision in early 1978 was the result of eight years of research, costing approximately $50 million.

18.7. Fisher's Ideal Index

One might suspect that an index somewhere between the Laspeyres and Paasche indexes would be ideal. This is the reason for the use of *Fisher's Ideal Index*. The Fisher index is the geometric mean (discussed in the appendix to Chapter Four) of the Laspeyres and Paasche indexes and therefore lies between the two. Computationally,

$$\text{Fisher's Index} = \sqrt{(\text{Laspeyres index})(\text{Paasche index})} \times 100$$

The desirable properties of the Fisher's index have been overshadowed by the computational difficulties involved in its practical application. It requires that both the Laspeyres and the Paasche indexes be calculated. For this reason, and partly because an index which must be explained as the square root of the product of two other indexes does not have an intuitive appeal, it has never become very popular.

18.8. The Problem of Changing Product Quality

Dealing with quality changes in goods and services is one of the most difficult problems faced in compiling a price index. This problem has probably generated more discussion in the literature on consumer prices than any other single statistical issue. Both the Laspeyres and the Paasche indexes are computed on the assumption that the market basket is *held constant* throughout the series. This means that the products in the market basket are identical and have not been improved in any way between the base period and the current period. But actually, as time passes, new products do come into existence and old ones are phased out. So both indexes ignore technological progress that affects the quality of items included in the index between the base period and the current period. As a practical matter, the rapidity of technological progress has made quality change a major problem in the construction of indexes of consumer and industrial prices.

These problems are more serious in an index that measures prices of finished *goods* than in one that measures prices of basic commodities.

> It is obvious that a television set purchased in 1982 is quite different from one purchased in 1957. It is a higher quality, more sophisticated piece of equipment. The same is true of many (although clearly, not all) consumer goods and services as well as equipment used by industry. The prices of many of these items have risen in recent years. Part of the price increase, however, results from the quality improvement and should somehow be eliminated in measuring the price change associated with the original "market basket."

Is there a generally satisfactory solution to this problem? Not in a base-weighted index. On one hand, the "market basket" must be kept reasonably constant in order that price comparisons be meaningful. But, in fact, products and consumption patterns continually change. If the "market basket" isn't changed frequently, the price changes will refer to market baskets which are no longer relevant.

Magnitude of the Measurement Problem

The magnitude of the measurement problem is difficult to estimate, but, because of the rapidity of technological change, it must be taken seriously.

Example 18.8A. **How Serious is the Quality Problem in the Consumer Price Index?**

No one seriously denies that biases exist; the debate is over their magnitude. Yale economist Richard Ruggles offers one of the larger estimates. He suggests that if the CPI had taken improvements in the quality of products into account, prices would be seen to have fallen steadily from 1949 to 1966, whereas the CPI had them rising 36 percent in that period. (Ruggles concedes that prices *have* been going up since 1966, though less than the index indicates.) The CPI simply fails to adjust adequately when the higher price of, say, a color TV set reflects only the higher costs of building improved circuitry. The consumer may be paying more, but getting more, too. And while the BLS continues to price that particular model, the consumer is free to switch to a cheaper one.[3]

A Partial Solution

To reduce this kind of criticism, the BLS has attempted a partial solution. The BLS observes the cost of both the old and the new item when both are available in the market at the same time. The difference between such values is assumed to be a measure of the quality change, and that amount is adjusted out of the price of the new item.

What if Old Goods and Their Replacements Are Not Simultaneously Available?

With many goods and services, both the old and the new (or the old and the improved) are not available at the same time in the market. In such cases, an attempt is made to determine the difference in manufacturers' *costs*. This difference is then considered a measure of the quality change and is adjusted out of the new price. Quality changes, however, continue to require a great deal of judgment on the part of the statistician.

Automobile Price Increases: How Much Is for Higher Quality?

Automobile prices in the CPI must be adjusted yearly to ensure that new model quality improvements are not measured as price increases. The BLS estimates the additional cost associated with producing the change in quality by evaluating manufacturing costs and adding the established mark-up. In this way, new features that reflect quality changes are then priced and adjusted out of the index. The difficult question for the BLS, of course, is which new features are quality improvements and which are not. Generally, quality improvements in automobiles have been defined to include "structural and engineering changes that affect safety, environment, reliability, performance, durability, economy, carrying capacity, maneuverability, comfort, and convenience."

In practice, however, this definition is of *little* help in distinguishing quality improvements. In many cases, quality is subjective, and as the following situation illustrates, attempts to measure it can be contentious.

Example 18.8B.   Antipollution Equipment: BLS Loses a Big One

A famous case in BLS folklore arose in 1971 when automobiles acquired antipollution equipment. The BLS decided that the anti-smog gear represented a price increase without a quality increase, since performance wasn't improved and maintenance became more expensive. But an interagency committee set up by the Office of Management and Budget overruled the bureau, arguing that society as a whole would benefit from cleaner air. The cost of the equipment was kept out of the CPI, and the decision still rankles at the BLS. Says John Laying, the assistant commissioner in charge of price statistics: "That was one of the big ones we lost."[4]

18.9. Linking: Measuring Price Changes in a World of Changing Products

The problem of adjusting for quality changes is indeed difficult. But although the *form* of the product has changed, at least the product is *available* in both periods. What if the product isn't available in both periods? How do you measure the change in price between two periods of a product that only existed in one of the periods? Fifty years ago garters, bedwarmers, and washtubs were commonplace. Now these products have largely vanished from the product scene. Replacing them are entirely new products such as pantyhose, electric blankets, and automatic washers.

Over short periods of time, the problem of changing product availability may not be serious. The problem must be confronted over longer time periods.

Over a long period of time (several decades) there are few *directly* comparable items common to both the beginning period's market basket and the ending period's market basket (a car in 1983 is no longer simply a Model T Ford, as it probably would have been in 1920). Having the price changes of only a few *directly* comparable items would be inadequate in constructing what should be a representative broad base price index series. A way to lessen somewhat this transition problem is to *link* the different price series, each of which is representative over a shorter period of time (for example, a decade). Because each series takes price readings on a much shorter interval (for example, each year), the price change reflected in the price index essentially monitors a "similar" market basket from year to year. What changes in quality and product availability that do occur from year to year are gradual and not the dramatic and distorting ones found when observing individual time periods several decades apart. Smooth change makes the price readings on the items meaningful for comparison and linking. The point is that over a long time span, linking several index series, as in the following example, gives a more representative index than one using only a single fixed base period for the reference prices or quantities.

Example 18.9. A Twentieth Century Index

Suppose it is desired to construct a consumer price index series for the Twentieth Century. Surely, consumption patterns have changed. But greater similarity of consumption patterns is more likely to be found between nearby years (say between the year 1900 and 1910) than between years farther apart (say between the year 1900 and the year 1930). Therefore, it is appropriate to construct an index using 1900 as the base year and 1910 as the ending year. Similarly, another index series might be constructed using 1910 as the base year and 1920 as the ending year. The third series would have 1920 as the base year and 1930 as the ending year. Note that an overlapping year is needed. Table 18.6 shows details of the various index series and the linked index.

The linking of the separate index series to form the linked index was accomplished by:

1. dividing each number in the table by 100 to get "reduced" index numbers

2. multiplying the index number for the reference year by the bottom index number in each preceding column (for example, 1911: 1.024 × 1.206 = 1.235)

3. multiplying the product by 100 (1.235 × 100 = 123.5) as indicated by the arrows and multiplication signs.

TABLE 18.6. Three Price Index Series and the Linked Index

YEARS	INDEX I 1900 = 100	INDEX II 1910 = 100	INDEX III 1920 = 100	LINKED INDEX 1900 = 100
1900	100.0			100.0
1901	103.2			103.2
1910	120.6	100.0		120.6
1911		102.4	× 100 =	123.5
1920		115.1	100.0	138.8
1921			101.7	
1930			127.3	× 100 = 176.7

This calculation follows logically since:

   1. the index numbers of the 1910 base (Index II) series tell us that the index number for the 1911 value is 102.4% of the 1910 value and

   2. the 1920 value is 115.1% of the 1910 value.

Similarly then, the 1930 link index number using 1900 as the base would be found by:

   1. multiplying together each appropriate reduced index number, (1.206 × 1.151 × 1.273 = 1.767)

   2. multiplying the product by 100 (1.767 × 100 = 176.7) as indicated by the arrows and multiplication signs.

To find the 1980 index using 1900 as the base year, eight separate reduced indexes would be multiplied together and the product multiplied by 100 to again get a linked index number.

18.10. Additional Considerations in the Construction and Interpretation of the Consumer Price Index

The published indexes of producer and consumer prices are regarded as general-purpose price indexes. That is, the coverage of items is very broad, so that the indexes represent the behavior of prices in general. However, a number of statistical problems are encountered in the construction of all the commonly used aggregate indexes of producer and consumer prices. Consequently, there are important limitations to the interpretations that may be made from these general purpose indexes. Let's consider some additional features of the Consumer Price Index.

Sampling of Items

Is it feasible to derive a price index for consumers that includes *all* of the goods and services that they buy? No. Too much effort would be required to collect the information. Indexes intended for broad usage, like the Consumers Price Index, rely on *samples* of items that are thought to be representative. Thus, the design of the sample critically affects the representativeness of the index. However, representativeness is a bit like the "will o the wisp":

> Just as there are important differences in spending patterns among urban and rural families, central-city and suburban families, and northern and southern families, there are important differences among individual families within each of these groups.

For these reasons, no aggregate index can be applicable to individual consumers. However, the Consumer Price Index for all Urban Consumers covers the expenditures of approximately 80 percent of the population. Thus, although its market basket might not pertain to any specific consumer, it nevertheless represents well the "average" of urban consumers.

The Consumer Price Indexes are currently based upon a point-of-purchase survey conducted in 1974. This survey of approximately 23,000 families was designed to find out where various population groups purchased their goods and services. It provides the guidelines for the month-to-month sampling of items conducted by the Bureau of Labor Statistics. The following example points out the impact this change had on the field agent's data collection.

Example 18.10A. **Store-Specific-Pricing Reduces the Problem of Unstocked Items**

The 1978 revisions introduced an improved method of item selection. This method is called "store specific pricing."[5] In essence, the technique allows the pricing agent more leeway in selecting the items to be priced at a particular store. Prior to 1978, agents were limited to a list of 400 specific items. This limitation caused difficulties because a particular retail outlet might not stock the particular item that was to be priced. Store-specific pricing allows, within limits determined by probability calculations, agents to pick the items to be priced at a particular outlet from more general categories. They will then continue to price that specific item chosen periodically.

Sampling over Geographic Areas

Are the commonly used aggregate price indexes representative of the nation as a whole? Most are designed with that in mind. What must be remembered, however, is that an *average* price change for the nation as a whole may not apply to *any* particular geographic region. Moreover, its applicability is *not* necessarily the same in all parts of the nation. Just as general economic conditions vary widely among regions, price changes may vary widely by area, too. This variability is particularly applicable to indexes of consumer prices, which include numerous services and highly processed goods. Items that are essentially the same everywhere, for which highly organized national markets exist, and for which there is little variation in costs of production and delivery, are less subject to this problem (for example, some of the items included in the index of industrial materials prices).

What does it take for a price index of consumer items to be a representative "average" for a wide geographic area? Obviously, because of different prices in different places, it is essential to devise a means of sampling among different places. Also, a method of aggregating the data is required. The Consumer Price Index is calculated by averaging indexes from narrower regions. Although it is clearly not practical to construct price indexes for every city or area in the nation, it *is* possible to vary the sample cities on a probability sampling basis. This permits objective evaluation of the error involved in the estimate of the national figure.

Since early 1978, prices have been observed in 85 areas rather than only in 56, as was the case in the preparation of the old CPI. Separate indexes are now computed for 28 cities rather than 24, and, for the first time, indexes for four regions stratified by five different sizes of city population are published. But as the following example points out, caution needs to be exercised if one is comparing the indexes between cities.

Example 18.10B. Catch 22: Geographic Price Indexes Don't Tell You Where to Find Lower Cost of Living

The city and regional indexes provide measures of price *changes* for particular areas, but they cannot be used to compare living costs among the various places. The reason is simple. Although it is possible to measure the percentage *increase* in the index for one city or area relative to the *increase* in the index for another, the price levels in the two areas may have been quite different to begin with.

The Seasonal Adjustment Problem

The need to adjust the Consumer Price Index and its components for seasonal variation was recognized by BLS, and seasonally adjusted indexes were first published in 1966. The adjusted series are published only for the components that have been determined to have significant patterns of seasonal variation. Studies have shown that much of the seasonal variation takes place in prices of food, apparel, and private transportation and that the all-items index is affected only slightly by seasonal movement.

Seasonal factors, which may be used to adjust the series, were made available beginning in 1953, several years before seasonally adjusted indexes were published by the BLS. The methodology developed by the BLS for seasonal adjustments—the BLS Seasonal Factor Method—is now generally available so that comparable factors can be computed for those series for which no factors or adjusted series are published. The method employed is the traditional ratio-to-moving-average procedure with considerable refinement and with a means for frequently and periodically adjusting the seasonal factors for changes in the underlying pattern.

Sampling Over Time

Once the coverage of the index as to groups of consumers or industries is defined and the selection of items in the "market basket" is specified, an important question remains. How frequently should the prices of the items included be observed? Should the index be published monthly, quarterly, annually, or by some other period? Under theoretically ideal circumstances, a continuous observation of prices would be desired. But for obvious reasons, the cost of such a procedure would exceed the theoretical benefit. Fortunately, a satisfactory compromise on the problem can be reached if:

1. periodic samples of prices are used and

2. acceptable means of estimating interim prices can be derived for those periods between benchmark samples.

For instance, what if it is desired that a price index be published monthly and samples of prices are obtained every three months? In this case, previous experience with the "market basket" may provide sufficient information to allow estimation of prices, and therefore of the index, for the intervening months. Short-term movements in an index obtained on this basis are, of course, subject to error, particularly as underlying economic circumstances change.

Example 18.10C. **Monthly Reporting Doesn't Mean Monthly Sampling**

The Consumer Price Indexes, although published monthly, do not, strictly speaking, reflect month-to-month changes in prices. Some items are observed frequently (monthly) in every location; some are taken less frequently (bi-monthly) in every location; some are observed frequently in selected locations only; and some are observed less frequently in selected locations only. Food items are among the most frequently sampled, and monthly sampling is the general rule in the five largest metropolitan areas. Even after the 1978 revisions, only 53 percent of the items are priced every month compared to 48 percent earlier.

Sampling Error in Indexes

One kind of statistical problem, sampling error, occurs even under the best of circumstances. However, an important feature of sampling error is that its magnitude can be estimated, and it generally decreases as the sample size increases. This feature makes it possible to estimate with some degree of confidence (at some level of probability) how far the calculated value of the index can be expected to diverge from its true value. It can be a mistake, however, to interpret estimates of sampling error as estimates of *total* error. Sampling design considerations and data problems render all major indexes in current use less than perfect on grounds other than sampling error. As the following suggests, the degree of sampling error is a negligible factor overall.

Example 18.10D.   **Sampling Error in the Consumer Price Index**

In 1964, the BLS introduced the procedure of replicated (repeated) sampling in an effort to provide better estimates of sampling error. Estimates of the standard errors of changes in major components of the Consumer Price Index have been published monthly by the BLS since January 1967. Recent research concluded that the published estimates are reasonable approximations of the sampling error in the index.[6] It further showed that changes in the published index—either monthly, quarterly, or for longer periods—greater than 0.2 percent are significant changes at the .05 probability level (published figures with greater than .2 percent error are highly unlikely).

Actually, monthly or quarterly changes of 0.1 percent or more are statistically significant, but since the published index numbers are rounded, a 0.1 percent change in the published data could come about as a result of a much smaller change in the rounded data. A 0.2 percent change for a one-month period, however, is almost always statistically significant.

As the following example illustrates, too much can be made of small changes in the Consumers Price Index.

Example 18.10E.   **Exaggerating the Importance of Small CPI Changes**

If the value of the index were 100.0, a monthly change in the index to 100.1 or to 99.9 might not be of importance. Smaller changes have a high likelihood of resulting from random fluctuations in the sample of data rather than reflecting any actual change in the level of prices. Thus, the user of the index should be wary of attaching too much attention to small changes in the index. Since the changes in the index are often blown up to annual rates, their actual significance is sometimes quite misleading.

Expenditure Weighting: Changing Prices Affect Relative Weights

Although in principle prices are weighted by actual quantities, in practice the BLS uses "expenditures" as weights. Thus, even though quantity remains unchanged, relative expenditure weights of the items in the "market basket" change between surveys.

Example 18.10F.   Adjusting Expenditure Weights to Get Quantity Weights

As a hypothetical example, suppose that a consumer was spending a total of $100 per week in 1972 and allocating $25 (or 25 percent) to food and $10 (or 10 percent) to apparel. Suppose that the same consumer in 1977 was spending a total of $200 per week. If the 1972 expenditure weights were used, $50 would be allocated to food items and $20 to apparel items. But if food prices had increased 150 percent during the interim and apparel prices only 50 percent, the consumer spending $50 on food and $20 on apparel would be purchasing relatively fewer food items and more apparel items than that purchased in 1972. Thus, in order to keep the consumer's "market basket" in constant proportions, the changes in relative prices are adjusted out by changing the expenditure weights.

Table 18.7 compares the relative expenditure weights used for the "market basket" of the Consumer Price Index over the years to the weights derived from the 1972–1973 Consumer Expenditure Survey. It can be seen from the table that the expenditure weighting structure in December 1977 is different from that of 1972–1973 even though both are based on the 1972–1973 survey of consumer expenditures. These differences reflect changes in relative prices of the various items since the revision, not changes in the "market basket" as such. Table 18.7 shows that for all urban consumers, food price increases kept pace relative to other price increases between the 1972–1973 survey and December 1977, whereas apparel prices did not increase as rapidly as other prices.

18.11. The Producer Price Index

One of the oldest continually published index of prices is the Wholesale Producer Price Index. It is a Laspeyres weighted aggregative index just as the Consumer Price Index. The index is calculated on a 1967 base and it currently covers about 2800 commodities. Its purpose is to measure both price levels and changes in prices of items at the stage of their most important commercial transaction.

The Wholesale Producer Price Index uses base value weights that have been updated since the original base period. The weights used are expenditures for items measured by net value of products shipped (rather than produced) of producers in particular industries and sectors. With the revision made in 1976, the current weights represent the net selling value of commodities in 1972.

Table 18.8 shows the relative weights of items included in the Producer Price Index by industry and by stage of processing both before and after the recent revision. See page 698.

The following example suggests the linkage and a comparative view of the changes shown by the Consumer Price Index and the Producer Price Index over the recent years.

TABLE 18.7. Relative Weights of Major Consumer Price Index Components

| MAJOR GROUP | WAGE EARNERS AND CLERICAL WORKERS | | | | | All Urban Consumers 1972–73[4] | All Urban Consumers Dec. 1977[5] |
	1935–39[1]	1952[2]	1963[3]	1972–73[4]	Dec. 1977[5]		
Food and alcoholic beverages	35.4	32.2	25.2	20.4	20.5	18.8	18.8
Housing	33.7	33.5	34.9	39.8	40.7	42.9	43.9
Apparel	11.0	9.4	10.6	7.0	5.8	7.0	5.8
Transportation	8.1	11.3	14.0	19.8	20.2	17.7	18.0
Medical Care	4.1	4.8	5.7	4.2	4.5	4.6	5.0
Entertainment	2.8	4.0	3.9	4.3	3.9	4.5	4.1
Personal Care	2.5	2.1	2.8	1.8	1.8	1.7	1.8
Other goods and services	2.4	2.7	2.9	2.7	2.6	2.8	2.6

[1]Relative importance for the survey period 1934–1936 (updated for price change).
[2]Relative importance for the survey period 1947–1949 (updated for price change).
[3]Relative importance for the survey period 1960–1961 (updated for price change).
[4]Relative importance for the survey period 1972–1973.
[5]Relative importance for the survey period 1972–1973 (updated for price change).

Example 18.11A. Tracking Changes in Producer Prices

Figure 18.3 shows the Product Price Index for total finished goods, farm products, industrial commodities as well as annual change of total finished goods. The 2800 commodities covered by the indexes include not only finished goods, but also intermediate and crude materials. Movements in producer prices for finished goods ultimately translate into changes in consumer prices. For this reason they signal ahead of time important near-term movements in the Consumer Price Index.

Like consumer goods prices, producer prices were rising at a moderate pace during the latter half of the 1960s and early 1970s. But in the 1973–1981 period, however, the total finished goods index increased at a faster rate (9.8 percent) than the Consumer Price Index (9.0 percent) average rate of advance. As is clear from the graph, the most rapid increases in overall producer prices came in the 1974–1975 and 1979–1980 time periods. Farm products showed a very erratic pattern, with extremely sharp increases in the 1972–1973 period.

Such price variation has been particularly characteristic of farm products, where changes in the short-run supply and demand conditions affect prices significantly.

Transactions Prices Versus List Prices

Theoretically, all price indexes require prices used in calculating the index to be the *actual* prices at which transactions are made. Often, however, quoted prices (which are easier to obtain) do not change while substantial changes occur in prices actually paid. Experience has shown this to be a problem, particularly

TABLE 18.8. Relative Importance of Commodities Included in the Consumer Price Index in December 1975

	1963 WEIGHTS	1972 WEIGHTS
BY INDUSTRY		
Farm products	11.28	8.40
Processed foods and feeds	16.55	14.37
Textile products and apparel	5.76	5.78
Hides, skins, leather, and related products	1.08	.76
Fuels and related products, and power	10.39	10.34
Chemicals and allied products	6.55	7.17
Rubber and plastic products	2.02	2.80
Lumber and wood products	2.54	2.23
Pulp, paper, and allied products	4.75	5.28
Metals and metal products	13.45	13.00
Machinery and equipment	11.32	11.84
Furniture and household durables	2.86	3.44
Nonmetallic mineral products	3.05	2.82
Transportation equipment	6.26	8.61
Miscellaneous products	2.14	3.19
BY STAGE OF PROCESSING		
Crude materials for further processing	12.31	11.33
Foodstuffs and feedstuffs	7.84	6.97
Nonfood materials except fuel	3.18	3.15
Crude fuel	1.29	1.21
Intermediate materials, supplies, and components	47.28	47.11
Materials and components for manufacturing	25.62	25.59
Materials and components for construction	8.45	7.94
Processed fuels and lubricants	4.53	4.85
Containers	1.58	1.39
Supplies	7.09	7.35
Finished goods (including raw foods and fuel)	40.41	41.56
Consumer goods	31.47	29.71
Producer finished goods	8.94	11.85

Source: William H. Wallace and William E. Cullison, *Measuring Price Changes: A Study of the Price Indexes,* Federal Reserve Bank of Richmond, 4th Edition, April, 1979.

in the measurement of industrial prices. A number of the industrial prices used in the Producer Price Index, for example, are seller's list prices, which may bear little resemblance to the prices actually paid. In the steel industry, for example, list prices may be only the starting point in price negotiations, much as consumers "haggle" over the discount from list price on their automobiles. The Bureau of Labor Statistics is aware of this difficulty and uses list prices *only* when transactions prices are unavailable. Nevertheless,

> to the extent that *list* prices continue to be used, industrial prices may be *overstated* by failing to take account of discounts, special offers, and price shading.

Thus, the Producer Price Index may not always accurately represent the effect of changing economic conditions. It should be noted, however, that the index is considerably better in this respect than it once was.

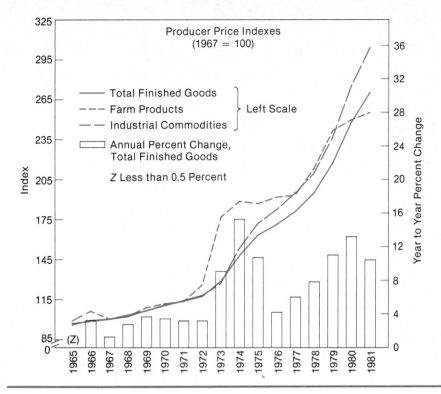

FIGURE 18.3 Producer Price Indexes
Source: U.S. Bureau of Labor Statistics

The Consumer Price Index has not been subject to the same criticism, since price observers function like buyers and obtain prices they know in most instances represent the prices at which the goods and services can be purchased.

Updating the Producer Price Series

Prices were updated from 1972 to December 1975, however, in order that the expenditure weights would reflect the most current prices at the time of the index revision. But the base of the index was not changed by the recent revision, so it continues to be 1967. The construction of the base weights for the Producer Price Index is clearly less complex than for the Consumer Price Index. The current policy of the Bureau of Labor Statistics is to revise the base weights every five years in coordination with Bureau of Census' updated information on manufacturing and mining. The BLS is currently engaged in an extensive revision of the Producer Price Index that is scheduled to be completed in 1984. The revision program is designed to eliminate several problems. One of the problems was the name of the index, which the BLS corrected since the writing of the following article.

Example 18.11B.   How Does the Producer (Wholesale) Price Index Err?

Let us count the ways. Even its name is misleading, for the WPI doesn't measure wholesalers' prices. Instead, it gauges prices from producers in mining, manufacturing, and agriculture. To measure price changes, the BLS sends out forms each month to about 3000 firms that have volunteered to report their prices on about 10,000 items. The quotations are used to construct separate price indexes for 2800 commodities. These are then combined into averages, weighted by the quantity of goods shipped back in 1972.

However, the BLS adequately prices only 27 percent of the products made by 550 major U.S. industries, and many of the price changes listed in the WPI are based on reports from only one or two firms. Worse than that, the selection of the items to be priced is arbitrary and frequently out of date, a major source of upward bias in the WPI. The index for office machinery, he [Commissioner John Laying] notes, has shown increasing prices just during those years when electronic computing equipment offered dramatic reductions in price per computation. Whereas in 1952 it cost $1.26 to do 100,000 multiplications, now they can be done for less than a penny. Yet the WPI has missed the price drop because most types of modern office equipment, including computers, aren't even priced by the BLS.

"The WPI is based on very thin data," admits Commissioner Laying. "We have pushed the data base too far, basing 2800 price series on 10,000 quotes." And if the prices quotes are too few in number, their quality is highly suspect, for many companies habitually report only their list prices. These may equal transactions prices when demand is strong. But in the doldrums of recession, producers shave prices through cash discounts, or by offering free shipment to buyer's warehouse, or by any number of other devices. Thus, industrial prices rise and fall more sharply with fluctuating demand than the WPI indicates.

"Businessmen are too secretive about their prices," complains Laying. "We think we're getting good price quotes, but it's hard to tell. Price is a sensitive topic to most businessmen." He concedes that the BLS doesn't always get to the bottom of the matter. "For instance, in the steel industry there are firms that have large sales forces with some pricing latitude. Now, we go into the accounting department for detailed prices, but it may not be aware of the discounts used by salesmen."

Laying has pointed out that the WPI is biased because it gets its reports mostly from the bigger firms, leaving out smaller and perhaps more competitive ones. Upward bias creeps in because the WPI, like the CPI, isn't properly adjusted for quality improvements. This bias is especially strong when it comes to durable goods such as electric appliances, which, he notes, have grown increasingly energy efficient and reliable.

The WPIs biggest distortion of all comes from double, triple, and even more redundant counting of price changes. If the price of cotton rises, and the price hike is passed on to yarn producers, and by them to cotton-fabric producers, and by them to finished-cotton-fabric makers, and finally to shirtmakers, the price increase will have been counted five times in the WPI.

The problem led Laying's predecessor, Joel Popkin, to upgrade three supplementary series—for raw goods, intermediate goods (those sold from one producer to another for further processing), and finished goods ready for sale to distributors. Late last year, the BLS officially recognized the deficiency of the original "all commodities" WPI by announcing that it was switching emphasis from this measure to one of Popkin's improved indexes, the finished-goods series.[7]

Other Producer Indexes

The BLS at present publishes, in addition to the stage-of-processing indexes and the All Commodities Index, component indexes by durability of product and by industry groups and subgroups. In the stage-of-processing category, separate indexes are constructed for crude materials, intermediate materials, consumer finished goods (at the wholesale level), and producer finished goods. These indexes enable analysts to isolate major price changes by stage of production. The "durability of product" classification facilitates price comparisons between durable and nondurable goods. Industry subgroup indexes carry this breakdown further and permit detailed comparisons of price movements. Since prices are obtained by industries or sectors, the Producer Price Index has no area breakdown, as does the Consumer Price Index.

Seasonal Adjustments

The BLS does not publish seasonally adjusted indexes for the detailed commodity groupings of the Producer Price Index. However, it does provide seasonally adjusted monthly percentage changes. Seasonally adjusted index numbers are published for stage-of-processing indexes.

Sampling Errors

Estimates of sampling error for the Producer Price Index are not produced by the BLS. The sample employed for the index does not lend itself to the measurement of sampling error, since it is selected purposively rather than on a random sampling basis.

Also, the number of reporters from whom price information is obtained is very small for many of the individual commodities, and the methods of aggregation used—by industry, durability of product, and stage of processing—result in heterogeneous groupings of individual items. Although the sample is already very large, an even larger sample would be needed, in view of the diversity of products covered, in order to develop reliable estimates of sampling error.

18.12. Can the Producer (Wholesale) Price Index Predict the CPI?

Journalists frequently use the producer price index (PPI) as a leading indicator of what will happen to consumer prices later on. It is informative to see a comparison of the two indexes for the Seventies. Figure 18.4a indicates the soothsaying ability of the PPI for all commodities by matching it with the CPI for all items for the following quarter. As can be observed, the all commodities index doesn't show a good track record of predicting the movement of the CPI. Figure 18.4b shows a contrast of the three major price indexes—the CPI (unlagged), the PPI, and the GNP deflator. The PPI seems to run the more erratic course.

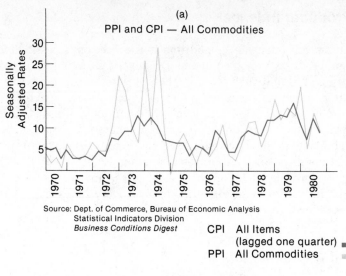

(a)

PPI and CPI — All Commodities

Source: Dept. of Commerce, Bureau of Economic Analysis
Statistical Indicators Division
Business Conditions Digest

CPI All Items
     (lagged one quarter)
PPI All Commodities

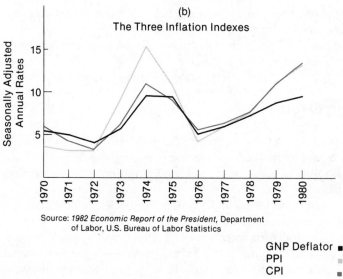

(b)

The Three Inflation Indexes

Source: *1982 Economic Report of the President*, Department
of Labor, U.S. Bureau of Labor Statistics

GNP Deflator
PPI
CPI

FIGURE 18.4 Predictors of the CPI

18.13. Concluding Comments

The persistent and high level of inflation in the past decade has caused corporate management, government bureaucrats, and financial advisers to require up-to-date information on price changes. This need has generally been satisfied by the Bureau of Labor Statistics which monthly constructs and distributes two key indexes on price movements—the *Consumer Price Index* and the *Producer Price Index*. Corporate managers who can use such information and successfully incorporate the rate of inflation in their investment strategy in the Eighties could very well be providing the difference between corporate failure and financial success. Government officials who fail to foresee inflationary changes will be at a loss to explain the differences between estimated and actual expenditures. Although index construction and its interpretation as a measure of inflation are beset by problems, in the case of the CPI, at least, much work has been done to refine techniques to make the CPI more than a rough indicator of changes in price.

Footnotes and References

[1] Excerpt from "Our Flawed Inflation Indexes," Edward Meadows, *Fortune*, April 24, 1978, pp. 66–67.

[2] *Ibid*, p. 66.

[3] *Ibid*, p. 67.

[4] *Ibid*, p. 67.

[5] For a detailed discussion, see Julius Shiskin, "The Consumer Price Index: How Will the 1977 Revision Affect It?" U.S. Department of Labor, Bureau of Labor Statistics, Washington D.C. 1975.

[6] Marvin Wilkerson "Sampling Error in the Consumer Price Index," *Journal of the American Statistical Association*, September 1967.

[7] Meadows, *op cit.*, p. 70–71.

Questions and Problems

1. Domestic automobile production in 1983 was given an index value of 132.4; what does this mean if the base year is 1981? If the base year is 1982?

2. What is meant by the phrase "constant dollar" GNP?

3. The phrase "real income" is sometimes used to describe the ratio of current income to the CPI. Is the result the number of base-period dollars it would take to buy the current market basket of goods and services?

4. What is meant by the phrase "purchasing power of the dollar"? How is it related to inflation?

5. A given year's CPI is 142.2. The base period is six years earlier. One dollar in the given year will buy a bundle of goods that could have been purchased with how many dollars in the base period?

6. Between 1982 and 1983 a cosmetics company increased its television advertising by 8%. A trade association index of national television advertising increased from 118 in 1982 to 126 in 1983. Did the cosmetics

company increase its usage of television advertising more than, less than, or the same as other companies, on the average?

7. Explain whether or not a price index measures changes in:
a. consumption patterns
b. product quality

8. Does the change in the cost of a market basket measured by a price index reflect the price change actually experienced by all individual consumers? Explain.

9. During the 1980 election campaigns, Democrats, who then controlled the White House and both houses of Congress, defended their record on inflation by saying that measuring inflation by the increase in the CPI overstated the true cost of living increase. Do you agree? Explain.

10. Your apartment rents for $300 per month in a city with rent control. The rent control ordinance indexes rent increases. Rent increases cannot exceed the increase in the CPI. At the time you rented the apartment, the CPI stood at 121. Three

years later your rent is raised to $340 per month. The CPI had increased to 143 by that time. You complained that the rent increase was larger than the ordinance allowed. Was your complaint justified?

11. With respect to Problem 10, do you think the CPI is constructed to serve as an appropriate measure for judging the fairness of a rent increase? Explain.

12. Current consumers' credit buying seems to reflect the attitude of "buy now with borrowed money, pay back later with cheaper dollars." What is implicitly assumed by this statement about changes in the CPI?

13. In the spring of 1980, President Carter, running for renomination as his party's choice for president, had to defend his administration's record on the economy. Facing double-digit CPI increases, backers of the President blamed much of the CPI increase on only one CPI component, the huge increases in the cost of mortgage money (the interest rate). Since high mortgage rates affected only the small percentage of the population purchasing homes at that time, the cost of living increases for the rest of the population was vastly overstated. Comment.

14. List and describe four uses of index numbers.

15. What kinds of averages may be used to combine price relatives into a price index?

16. What weights are normally used to compute a Laspeyres type index?

17. Why is the Laspeyres type of index more frequently used than a Paasche type of index?

18. Upon what weighting system is the CPI based?

19. What type of index is the Producer Price Index?

20. The Standard and Poor's 500 Stock Price Index is based on many prices and the stocks are weighted by the value of the outstanding shares. Does this make the Standard and Poor's a better market indicator than the more widely quoted Dow Jones Averages which contains about 30 unweighted prices? Explain.

21. Discuss alternative methods of handling a substantial quality change for an item included in a price index.

22. The CPI for San Francisco is typically higher than the CPI for Chicago. Does this assure you that the relative cost of living is higher in San Francisco than the relative cost of living in Chicago?

23. What major problem would be faced in constructing an index of record player prices over the last three decades?

24. What is the principal disadvantage in using value indexes?

25. What is the major difference between a weighted aggregate index and a weighted average of relatives index?

26. The local Board of Realtors of a major city publishes an index of housing prices for the city. It is constructed by dividing the median purchase price for a random sample of homes purchased in the given period by the median price of a sample of homes purchased in the base period. Discuss some of the problems in interpreting this housing price index (for example, financing terms of sale, quality changes, neighborhood effects).

27. In a different city than the one discussed in Problem 26, real estate appraisers were using an index of housing prices constructed by comparing the median selling prices in the given year and the base year of homes which were actually sold in both years. Is this a better index than the one computed in the previous problem? Explain.

28. Discuss the criteria for choosing the base of an index.

29. Under what conditions is the simple aggregative method satisfactory for the construction of a composite price index?

30. Why might we use the weighted average of relatives method to compute an index rather than the weighted aggregative method?

31. Why might it be necessary to shift the base of an index?

32. Labor unions are anxious to have an automatic wage adjustment clause in the work contract based on the CPI or other price index series. These clauses have been criticized as overstating the wage increase required to maintain the same standard of living. Do you agree? Why?

33. When averaging price relatives, value weights are used, whereas quantity weights are used when averaging unit prices. Explain why different weights are required.

34. If the CPI increases from 210 to 230 during the year, what is the annual rate of inflation?

35. Inflation is inversely related to purchasing power. Explain why the purchasing power of the dollar can never decline by more than 100% whereas the rate of inflation can be astronomical.

36. The CPI increased from 97.2 to 170 during the ten years ending in 1976. The Dow Jones Industrial Average showed almost no change over the exact same period. It closed at 990 in 1966 and at 970 in 1976. What should the DJIA have closed at in 1976 in order for stocks to stay just even with inflation?

37. A San Diego distributor holds exclusive bottling and distribution rights for beer and soft drinks of the P and M parent company. The distributor examined the changes in average prices paid and quantities of materials purchased for 1980 and 1983. Table 18.9 shows the price and quantity figures for the two years.

Determine each of the following:

a. the simple price index for each material in 1983 using 1980 as a base year.

b. the unweighted average of price relatives index.

c. the simple aggregate index, using 1980 as the base year.

d. the weighted aggregate price index for 1983 using base period quantities (the Laspeyres index).

e. the weighted aggregate price index using nonbase period (1983) quantities (Paasche index).

38. The production and costs of pocket electronic calculators has changed dramatically in a short period of years. Table 18.10 includes the prices of four different kinds of pocket electronic calculators at two time periods eight years apart and the quantities at the initial year.

a. Compute a quantity-weighted index of the price change in calculators over the eight years.

TABLE 18.9. Changes in Price and Quantity of Materials, 1980 and 1983

| MATERIAL | 1980 | | 1983 | |
	PRICE ($)	QUANTITY (Millions)	PRICE ($)	QUANTITY (Millions)
Bottles	$.25	1.7	$.29	2.0
Caps	.02	2.0	.03	2.2
Labels	.01	1.7	.02	2.0
Cartons	.03	.5	.05	.7

TABLE 18.10. Change in Price of Electronic Calculators

MODEL	INITIAL YEAR PRICE	PRICE EIGHT YEARS LATER	INITIAL YEAR QUANTITY
Basic Four Function	$55	$9	13 million
Single Memory	$79	$12	10 million
Scientific	$180	$19	3 million
Programmable	$390	$58	0.5 million

b. Which type of index did you calculate, Laspeyres or Paasche?

The ending year quantities for the calculators are given in Table 18.11.

TABLE 18.11. Calculators—Ending Year Quantities

MODEL	ENDING YEAR QUANTITY
Basic Four Function	30 million
Single Memory	48 million
Scientific	27 million
Programmable	19 million

c. Using the ending year quantities, compute a quantity weighted index of the price change in calculators over the eight year period.

d. Which type of index did you calculate, Laspeyres or Paasche?

e. Compare your answer with the one given before. Which index indicates the greater price change? Does this depend on whether prices increase or decrease over the period? Is the magnitude of the difference between the two calculator indexes your computed substantial or negligible, or is the magnitude not comparable?

39. Use the data given in Problem 38.

a. Compute the price relatives for the four calculator models using the initial year as the base period. Do the values of the price relatives differ substantially or negligibly?

b. Compute the average of price relatives index for the four calculator models using the initial year as the base period. Describe a situation for which this index would be particularly useful.

c. Compute the simple aggregate index of calculator prices based on the four models. Which type of index is this, weighted or unweighted? Describe a situation in which this index might be particularly useful. Compare the interpretations of this index and the one computed in Part b.

d. Describe a situation in which the simple aggregate index of calculator prices would serve better than a Laspeyres or a Paasche index.

e. Compute the Fisher index for the calculator data. What are the advantages and disadvantages of this index compared to a Laspeyres or Paasche index?

40. Changes in the technology of computers have seen tubes replaced by tiny, more powerful silicon chips. The production of electronic computers has already gone through several generations. The IBM Model 1401, regarded as one of the "workhorses" of the computer industry, has long since been discontinued by its manufacturer, along with its immediate replacement. But since the Model 1401 performs some of the tasks current models do, some 1401s may still be in regular use.

a. Describe some of the problems one confronts in constructing a price index for computers for the quarter of a century since 1957.

b. What steps would you propose to deal with the problems of constructing a computer industry price index?

c. Are there any problems in constructing a computer industry price index that you feel cannot be adequately resolved? Explain.

41. Customarily, General Motors Corporation and other United States automobile manufacturers, when revising posted prices on their various car models, publish a figure representing the "average" percentage increase. Suppose you were trying to develop an index of new car prices based on these announced average percentage increases. Discuss the possible effect of the following:

a. the manufacturer's announced number is an unweighted average of the percentage increases on all their various models.

b. the announced average increase is a calculated ratio of the sum of the posted prices on all the models after the increase, to the sum of the posted prices before the increase announcement.

c. the announced average increase is computed by weighting each model's price increase by the number of vehicles sold of that model.

d. the posted price after the increase refers to the same model but the model now includes improvements that were not previously available.

e. the posted price after the increase includes equipment now standard which was optional before.

f. when the equipment referred to in Part e was optional, the manufacturer deliberately priced it high to discourage sales.

The manufacturer had been lobbying against government action to make this item mandatory. The manufacturer knew the government case would be weaker if it became public knowledge that consumers wouldn't buy the equipment when its purchase was optional.

Business Forecasting

Preview. The patterns of the past are often important in planning for the future. The descriptive techniques of time series analysis examined in Chapter 17 enabled us to describe the major historical trend and seasonal movement of the observed data. This chapter uses these techniques and extends the analysis to time series forecasting beyond the range of the observed data. The chapter also discusses the methodology of more elaborate time dependent methods of forecasting. An application to sales data is fully illustrated. One should keep in mind that all forecasting techniques rest critically on the assumption that the patterns of the past will persist into the future and therefore can be used as a basis for projecting future values. If such an assumption does not hold, systematic bias and large forecasting errors are likely consequences.

19.1. Business Forecasting—An Overview

Few business activities are more carefully followed or more hotly debated in the executive suite than business forecasting. It has always been an integral part of management planning and control. The roller coaster business cycle of ups and downs of the seventies and early eighties has seemingly intensified interest in forecasting. Future value forecasts of sales, cash flow, and material costs are focal points in making profit performance projections and in guarding against cash insolvency.

Will there be a continuance of the recent trend in a critical economic factor that affects sales, cash flow, material costs? Or is a near term change in the offing? If so, what will be the magnitude of the change? Published forecasts of key economic factors, such as the growth of the money supply, the inflation in wholesale prices, and the rate and level of inventory accumulation, are closely watched by alert executives who don't want to be caught napping in a changing economic climate. If published forecasts don't suffice, private forecasting services can be retained to develop forecasts of the specific series needed.

The demand for independent forecasters has spawned a cadre of business consulting firms—Predicasts, Chase Econometrics, Data Resources, Michael Evans Associates, Wharton Econometrics Forecasting Associates. Their steady growth and success is proof that there is a ready market for their delphic forecasts. The forecasting models employed by firms and consulting agencies generally can be classified as one of two types: (1) time dependent models which use only the pattern in the historical series of the variable itself to forecast future values of the variable; (2) structural models in which the interrelationship between economic variables over time are simultaneously considered to obtain a future value of the variable of interest. The structural type of model ranges from the single equation variety with several economic variables involved (similar to the multiple regression equation studied in Chapter 16) to a complex interlocking multi-equation variety, which requires estimation by sophisticated econometric techniques. This chapter will restrict its presentation and discussion to the time dependent type of forecasting using the historical series of a variable alone. This choice provides: (1) a view of an adequate short term approach that is widely used and that can be easily used by available computer business programs, such as Apple's Business Graphics program; (2) an approach that gives bench mark forecasts which can be compared to the econometric model approach. Let us begin the explanation of time dependent extrapolation by considering forecasting by a trend-line regression and by a moving average regression.

19.2. Extrapolation of a Time Series: Least Squares Trend Projections

Projecting future values by the least squares trend line procedure is a straightforward application of a regression equation. Let us suppose the regression equation of the least squares line has been computed for 20 quarterly periods (1 thru 20) and includes dummy variables for seasonal variation with the winter effect (the base season) captured by the intercept term; that is,

$$\hat{Y} = 400 + 30t + 100X_2 + 400X_3 - 50X_4$$

where t = time period value assigned; $X_2 = 1$ if spring season, 0 otherwise; $X_3 = 1$ if summer season, 0 otherwise; and $X_4 = 1$ if fall season, 0 otherwise. Note that it is not necessary to include a variable for the winter season because winter will correspond to the values 0, 0, 0 for X_1, X_2, and X_3 respectively.

In projecting a value for the coming fall period (t = period 21), the following equation is solved for $\hat{Y}$.

$$\hat{Y}_{21} = 400 + 30(21) + 100(0) + 400(0) - 50(1) = 980$$

Thus, 980 is the projected value of the series in period 21. Assuming the regression equation estimation is in conformity with the error assumption of an underlying regression model, one can form prediction intervals around the point prediction 980. That is, the .95 prediction interval for an individual Y value will be:

$$980 \pm t_{.025, \text{d.f.}} \text{ (standard error of prediction for an individual Y value)}$$

Where $t_{.025, \text{d.f.}}$ is the t table value that leaves two and a half percent in each tail of a t distribution with d.f. degrees of freedom.

Let's say that the standard error of prediction for the next individual Y value, $\hat{Y}_{21}$, is calculated to be 7.25. Since the degrees of freedom $= n - 5 = 15$ for the twenty observations used, the .95 prediction interval is:

$$980 \pm 2.131(7.25)$$
$$980 \pm 15.45$$

This interval therefore covers the range from 964.55 to 995.45. For a larger number of observations, say 30, there would be more degrees of freedom ($30 - 5 = 25$ d.f.) so that $t_{.025}$ would be smaller and the prediction interval would be narrower.

Forecasting by regression equations is an improvement over convenient at-hand approaches which add or subtract five or ten percent to last year's figures to obtain next year's value. But forecasting by a least squares trend line regression equation also has its shortcomings and its use must be tempered by the recognition that potential pitfalls do exist.

For instance, one needs to exercise caution when extrapolating a least squares trend line beyond the range of the data, as first mentioned in Chapter 15. The standard error of forecast will be larger in the extrapolation range than in the interpolated range (because $X - \overline{X}$ increases). A potentially more serious problem is the reliance one places on the estimated relationship. Its form, adequate for the observed data, may not be an appropriate model for extrapolation, as the following example suggests.

Example 19.2.   **Uncertainties in Extrapolation**

Suppose the true path of the time series over time is curvilinear. For the observed time range a straight line may give a good fit to the observed data and provide a good approximation to the true relationship. But there is a risk if one intends to

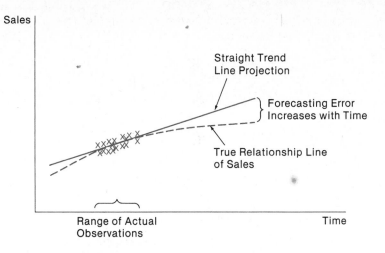

FIGURE 19.1 Extrapolation Revisited

extrapolate and project future values of the series with the belief that the linear relationship will continue. The situation illustrated in Figure 19.1 shows sales, on average, increasing at a decreasing rate, yet the fitted straight trend line to past sales assumes sales increase at a *constant* rate. To forecast future sales by the trend line would give overly optimistic sales forecasts. It can be seen that the forecast error will increase the farther into the future the forecasts are made.

Forecasting mechanically always leaves the possibility of dramatic failure. As the causal elements determining the series change, the trend will intensify or moderate. Significant change can even cause a change in direction. For example, projecting a steady growth in passenger automobile miles driven in the United States into the distant future could be quite risky, particularly if U.S. gasoline prices rise to the level found in most other parts of the world.

Do the hazards of mechanically using time series methods outweigh the benefits? Without a crystal ball to gaze into the future, one's dependency on a mechanical use of models for forecasting should be limited to the short range at best. Forecasting beyond a short time horizon borders on pure speculation.

The problem of forecasting by trend line should be adjusted for when possible. For instance, knowledge of diminishing sales returns to high dosages of advertising or of accelerating cost at full capacity production represent opportunities where one might directly incorporate the non-linearity into the estimating equation of sales and cost, respectively. The following discussion shows how to deal with a moving average series and its non-linear trend component.

Forecasting with Moving Averages

With a moving average series, a non-linear long-run trend component can be computed by regressing the moving average terms against time and time squared. Once the next period's forecast of the trend component is made from the moving average trend equation, seasonal adjustments can be made using the seasonal indices. For example, suppose the moving average trend equation for periods 1 through 12 is estimated by least squares regression to be:

$$\hat{Y}_{M.A.} = 300 + 50t + .5t^2 : \text{Moving Average (M.A.) Trend Component}$$
$$\text{recognizing the non-linearity}$$

This equation implies a rapid growth in $\hat{Y}$ which increases at an increasing rate. The seasonal indices are:

Winter = 84   Summer = 120
Spring = 92   Fall = 105

The projection for period 13, the summer season, will be:

$$\hat{Y}_{M.A.} = 300 + 50(13) + .5(13)^2$$
$$= 300 + 650 + 84.5 = 1034.5$$

$\hat{Y}_{M.A.} = 1034.5(1.20)$: M.A. Trend Component adjusted seasonally to arrive at the projected value for the original series for period 13

$$= 1241.4$$

19.3. Serial Correlation

Beginning users of time series analysis can readily see that projecting a linear trend beyond the range of the observed data *can* result in large non-random errors. But there are also some devastating statistical problems encountered in trend line fitting projections that are subtle and not at all easy to see. The *serial correlation* problem in time series analysis is one of them.

The problem surfaces when two conditions are present.

1. The value of the time series is influenced by a strong random influence which lingers longer above or below the long term trend line than is expected (given a random model), and

2. this persistence lasts much longer than the time interval at which individual measurements on the time series are taken.

Let's illustrate this problem in an example.

———————

Example 19.3.   Estimating in the Face of Carryover Effects

A corporate economist for the Northern Illinois Gas Company is doing a time series analysis for home (non-industrial) consumption of natural gas. *Weekly* data are used. But this past winter unseasonally cold Canadian winds have caused the thermometer to record consistently below-zero temperatures. The spring has been unseasonally warm with Southwest and Texas hot winds sweeping into the Midwest from the South. As one might expect, consumption of natural gas was above the long-term trend during the winter and below the long-term trend during the spring.

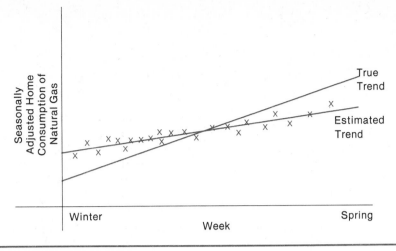

FIGURE 19.2 Serial Correlation

A projection of the trend based on the data for the winter and spring weeks would be seriously misleading, *even if the trend line fitting is seasonally adjusted.* This effect can be seen in Figure 19.2. The computed trend line of seasonally adjusted consumption has a lower slope than the true trend.

Notice that it took several weekly periods for the effect of the random influence (unexpected severe winter weather) to die out and reach the true trend line. This lingering effect of the weather causes adjacent residuals about the *true* trend line to be correlated. In other words, if the residual at a particular time t is above the true trend line (positive), the residual for the next period $t + 1$ is also likely to be above the true trend line (positive) and also nearby. This tendency for the residuals to be sequentially correlated is called serial correlation.

No Bias, But Decreased Accuracy

What estimating distortions result?

> Serial correlation causes the slope of the computed trend line to be either *smaller* or *larger* than the true trend value.

The estimating error will depend on the direction of the random influence and whether it occurs at the beginning or end of the entire period considered. The slope coefficient will be *smaller* than that of the true trend line slope if

1. the random event causes the beginning of the series to increase and slowly settle down towards the true trend line or if

2. the random event has a depressant effect at the end of the series with slow recovery.

Both these situations are depicted in Figure 19.2 where the computed trend has a lower slope than the true trend line. The opposite situation, a computed slope *larger* than that of the true trend line, occurs if the event

1. initially has a depressant effect slowly recovering or

2. an ending effect which inflates the series with a declining effect as time moves on.

Whichever direction, serial correlation causes the computed slope trend line to be consistently *off-target.*

Interestingly, the estimates of the true values are neither systematically biased high nor systematically biased low. Although the slope estimates are off-target, the direction of the bias is *not* predictable. The estimates have as much a chance of being too high as being too low as compared to their true values. In sum, the real net effect of serial correlation is simply a loss of accuracy in estimating the true slope term. With the direction and size of the error unknown, knowing that the trend slope estimate is off-target isn't very comforting, but it does point to the need for correcting the problem.

Deceptive Confidence Intervals

There are other negative consequences resulting from the presence of serial correlation. It destroys the usefulness of conventional computed statistics, say the value of the standard deviation of residuals, used to validate regression output.

From Figure 19.2, one can sense that serial correlation tends to produce deviations of the actual observations from the *computed* trend line that are smaller than the deviations calculated from the *true* line. This surprisingly *good* fit of the *computed* trend line for the observations produces a low sample standard deviation of residuals. So, if we were to construct, say, a .95 confidence interval for the true trend line slope using the computed standard deviation of residuals, we would find ourselves in trouble. With repeated samplings, far less than 95 percent of the intervals computed would include the true slope. Thus, the presence of serial correlation causes *overly optimistic statements about the reliability of the confidence interval for the true slope coefficient.*

19.4. Exponential Smoothing

A method of smoothing the variation in the time-series data for the purpose of forecasting the next future observation in the series is called *exponential smoothing.* Its growing popularity owes much to the method's ability to provide inexpensive forecasts which quickly reflect changes in underlying conditions generating the value of the series. This feature is particularly important when forecasts must be made for a large number of different data series.

Supermarkets, drugstores, and some other retail businesses generally carry 10,000
or more different items of merchandise in their inventory. Typically, the items have
a price tag of only a few dollars or less, so the per-unit profit is quite small. Many of
the items have high turnover and require frequent reordering.

Retailers aim to keep enough inventory on hand to meet customer demand until
the next reordering cycle. But limited storeroom space and high holding costs discourage retailers from carrying too large a stock of any one individual item. Establishing a satisfactory inventory level requires knowing how much demand to expect
in a given period. For many of these products, the demand fluctuations are substantial from period to period, making it difficult to know how much demand to
expect from one period to the next.

What are the sources of the fluctuation in period-to-period demand at a retail
store for such consumer products as Crest toothpaste? Generally, several different
factors can be cited. A family moving into a neighborhood would be a source of a
relatively permanent upward shift in toothpaste demand. Shifts in demand with considerably less staying power are associated with special deals on toothpaste at a
competitive store, or cents-off coupons mailed to consumers by the toothpaste
manufacturer. External forces, such as a gasoline shortage, can also lead to temporary demand shifts. Customers would be inclined to make less frequent shopping
trips for the duration of the shortage. The transitory nature of these latter forces
may be viewed largely as random from the retailer's perspective—unpredictable
in frequency and duration. Over time, changes in demand linked to transitory random
factors tend to offset each other. That is, the random factors increasing sales
balance off the factors decreasing sales.

But what if the time period is short? Then it is more likely for a particular random
factor to be the dominant influence—even swamp temporarily a permanent gradual
upward or downward shift in demand.

What should the retailer's inventory policy be in this environment? Should time
and money be spent predicting sales of individual brands?

Prediction of random factors and their impact is impossible; moreover, even
if it could be accomplished it would be unprofitable in terms of the benefits gained
and the cost incurred. The retailer's real advantage lies in an inexpensive means
of detecting the more *permanent* shifts in demand: a procedure programmed into
a computer, easily used, routinely producing reasonably accurate forecasts with
little or no human intervention for the thousands of individual products. Exponential
smoothing fits these requirements and for that reason has become a popular
planning tool.

Exponential Smoothing Gives Greatest Weight to Recent Observations

How does exponential smoothing work? What advantage does it have over
the moving average method? Recall that the moving average method produces
smoothed values of the time series by averaging equally-weighted data in blocks,

each of one year duration. The exponential approach likewise smooths. It averages the original data to produce a smoothed series of values, but differs from the moving average method of smoothing in two important respects:

1. all the previous values of the series are incorporated into each new smoothed value.

2. the greatest weight is given to the most recent actual measurement.

Let the *actual* value of the data series at time sequence t be A_t, and the corresponding *smoothed* value be S_t. The *first smoothed value* in exponential smoothing, S_1, is defined to be the first actual value of the series, A_1. Thus $S_1 = A_1$. Subsequent smoothed values, S_t, are computed from the most recent actual data value A_t and the previous smoothed value S_{t-1}. The latter term stands for all the previous A values. We have then,

$$S_t = wA_t + (1 - w)S_{t-1}$$

where w is a smoothing constant or weight assigned to the actual data value A_t. The value of w ranges from zero to one and determines the weight $1 - w$ attached to S_{t-1}.

TABLE 19.1. Illustration of Exponential Smoothing ($w = .3$)

PERIOD t	ACTUAL DEMAND A_t	EXPONENTIALLY SMOOTHED Demand S_t
1	1000	1000
2	1020	1006
3	950	989.20
4	1410	1115.44
5	1380	1194.81
6	1400	1256.37
7	1430	1308.46
8	1390	1332.92

Table 19.1 illustrates the exponential smoothing method for computer simulated data exhibiting a large positive shift in period 4. To start the process, the actual figure for period 1 is used as the smoothed value for period 1. That is, $S_1 = A_1 = 1000$. Using a smoothing constant of $w = .3$, the calculation of the next two smoothed values is given below:

$$S_2 = .3(1020) + (1 - .3)(1000)$$
$$= 306 + 700$$
$$= 1006$$

$$S_3 = .3(950) + (1 - .3)(1006)$$
$$= 285 + 704.2$$
$$= 989.2$$

Forecasting with Exponential Smoothing

Since the smoothed value S_t takes into consideration the most recent value of A as well as the weighted average of previous values of A, it can serve as our best guess for the unknown *next* future observation. Thus, for forecasting future observations (the period $t + 1$ and beyond), the smoothed value at the current period t, S_t, is used as the *forecast* for period $t + 1$, F_{t+1}. Likewise one can view S_{t-1} as the forecast for period t, F_t. That is:

$$F_{t+1} = S_t \text{ and } F_t = S_{t-1}$$

and by substitutions for S_t and S_{t-1}, we have

$$F_{t+1} = wA_t + (1 - w)F_t$$

Now one can see that the forecast for $t + 1$ is expressed as a function of the *current actual value* A_t and the forecast for t. Rearranging terms, one obtains,

$$F_{t+1} = F_t + w(A_t - F_t)$$

This means that the forecast for $t + 1$ is the forecast at t with an adjustment for the error between the current actual value A_t and the forecast at t, F_t.

Adaptive Forecasts

The last expression indicates that exponential smoothing is an *adaptive forecasting* process. Each forecast is a revision of the previous forecast, recognizing and adapting to the error just made $(A_t - F_t)$. The smoothing constant w indicates the degree of adaptation.

The When and Why of Exponential Smoothing

The basic exponential smoothing forecasting model is intended to accommodate situations where demand, always subject to random variation, suddenly shifts to a new *permanent* level about which the random variation now takes place (see Figure 19.3).

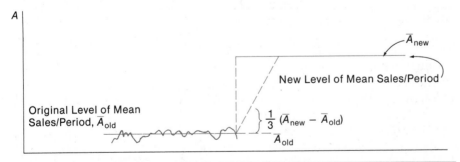

FIGURE 19.3 Response of Exponentially Smoothed Forecast to Shift in Mean Sales Level

The goal of the basic exponential smoothing model is to distinguish between:

1. a permanent shift in demand to the new (higher, in this case) level, and

2. a transitory movement due to a dominant random event.

How is a permanent shift distinguished from transitory movement? In the case of a permanent shift, the model's intent is to revise subsequent forecasts in the direction of the shift. The guiding principle at work is that the persistence of the actual values near the new permanently higher level (as shown in Figure 19.3) will cause positive forecast errors. These lead to a sequence of upward revisions on subsequent forecasts. Eventually this adjustment process brings the forecasts in line with the new permanent level, $\bar{A}$.

Choosing the Smoothing Constant

Regulation of the adjustment process is accomplished by the smoothing constant w which determines how quickly the revised forecast adapts to the shift. Figure 19.4b shows that for a $w = .33$, each new forecast will move up one-third of the distance between the current forecast and the new permanent level $\bar{A}_{new}$. The size of w will depend upon the degree of random fluctuation in the series.

The panels (a, b, c) of Figure 19.4 show three types of fluctuation. With *no* random fluctuation, the proper adjustment will be an immediate jump to the new permanent level and will equal the entire error currently observed, $A_t - F_t$. A weight of one, $w = 1$, properly reflects this situation.

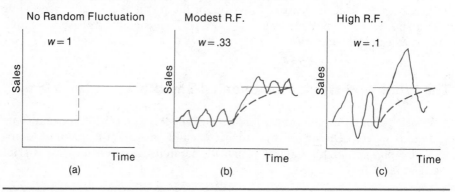

FIGURE 19.4 Effect of Smoothing Constant on Forecast Response to Permanent Shifts

An extremely volatile series in which all changes are purely random is the opposite extreme. In this case the observed error ought not to be considered as information for the purpose of revising the previous forecast. Highly volatile series will have low w values closer to 0. These low weights for w reflect the fact that most of the fluctuation that caused the observed error can be discounted as random and should not be given significant weight as evidence of a shift in the series to a new permanent level.

Table 19.2 illustrates the adaptive forecasting feature of the exponential smoothing method. The data is the same as that shown in Table 19.1. The forecast for period 2 is the actual figure for period 1. That is, $F_2 = A_1 = 1,000$. The next two forecasts are computed as follows:

$$F_3 = F_2 + w(A_2 - F_2)$$
$$= 1000 + .3(1020 - 1000)$$
$$= 1000 + 6$$
$$= 1006$$

$$F_4 = F_3 + w(A_3 - F_3)$$
$$= 1006 + .3(950 - 1006)$$
$$= 1006 - 16.8$$
$$= 989.2$$

The adaptive feature is illustrated by the error shown in the last column. Note that after the large error in period 4, subsequent errors diminish as the forecasts adapt to the errors made. Also note that the smoothed values in column 3 (taken from Table 19.1) correspond to the forecasted values for the next period.

TABLE 19.2. Forecasting by Exponential Smoothing, $w = .3$

PERIOD t	ACTUAL DEMAND A_t	FORECAST FOR PERIOD t, MADE IN PERIOD $t - 1$ F_t	ERROR $(A_t - F_t)$
1	1000	—	—
2	1020	1000	20
3	950	1006	−56
4	1410	989.20	420.8
5	1380	1115.44	264.56
6	1400	1194.81	205.19
7	1430	1256.37	173.63
8	1390	1308.46	81.54

Because exponential smoothing requires storage for only two numbers, computers can easily handle forecast updating for several thousand products. And since the forecasting process is self-correcting, it does not depend on human intervention.

Exponential smoothing averages for three different values of w (.1, .5, .9) are shown in Figure 19.5 for the soft drink industry data. As can be seen, the constant .1 smooths the data much more than .9. Setting w at .9 assigns more importance to current values and brings a more rapid response to demand changes. The objective of applying several values of w to past representative data is to gain perspective on the size and fluctuation of the forecast error associated with each w value. The optimal value of w to choose for forecasting is the one that minimizes the overall magnitude and variability of the forecast error.

Other Exponential Smoothing Models

Variations of the basic exponential smoothing model also exist. These variants are more appropriate for particular series in which the shifts that take place tend not just to be to a new permanent plateau but follow a more complicated pattern.

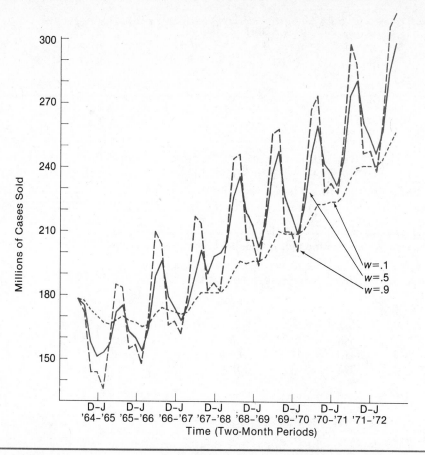

FIGURE 19.5 Exponential Smoothing of Soft Drink Data at Various Values of *w*

Variants of the basic exponential smoothing model described here are available. They are appropriate when there is a linear trend to the shift, if there is a non-linear trend, or if there is a pronounced pattern of seasonal variation.

19.5. Evaluating Forecasts

In this section, we will discuss three commonly employed summary measures used in assessing forecasting: the mean absolute deviation (MAD), the mean squared error (MSE), and the mean absolute percentage error (MAPE).

Table 19.3 adds to the figures first introduced in Table 19.2 illustrating exponential smoothing and the absolute and squared deviations needed in the calculation of MAD and MSE.

The mean absolute deviation is defined as

TABLE 19.3. Summary Error Measurement for Exponential Smoothing Forecasting Model—Calculating MAD and MSE

(1) TIME PERIOD t	(2) ACTUAL DEMAND A_t	(3) FORECAST FOR PERIOD t MADE IN PERIOD $t-1$ F_t	(4) ACTUAL ERROR $A_t - F_t$	(5) ABSOLUTE ERROR $|A_t - F_t|$	(6) SQUARED ERROR $(A_t - F_t)^2$
1	1000	—			
2	1020	1000	20	20	400
3	950	1006	−56	56	3136
4	1410	989.2	420.8	420.8	177,072.64
5	1380	1115.44	264.56	264.56	69,991.99
6	1400	1194.81	205.19	205.19	42,102.94
7	1430	1256.37	173.63	173.63	30,147.38
8	1390	1308.46	81.54	81.54	6648.77
Sum			**1109.72**	**1221.72**	**329,499.72**

$$\text{MAD} = \frac{\Sigma(|A_t - F_t|)}{n}$$

where A = Actual value for the given period; F = Forecasted value for the given period; and n = number of forecasts considered.

From the data presented in column 5, Table 19.3, we have

$$\text{MAD} = \frac{1221.72}{7} = 174.53$$

The value obtained interprets as the average size of the forecasting error for the forecasts considered regardless of the direction of the error. In this case, the demand forecasts are on average 174.53 units off per forecasting period. But notice that the sum of the actual deviations was 1109.72 and not a value of zero or near zero. This implies that the exponential trend-line is not balancing out the directional error above and below the line. In fact, the larger and more positive the value of the sum, the greater the difference between the actual values and the forecasted values. In this case, the forecasting model is too conservative, producing smaller forecasted values than actually appear.

The use of this summary statistic as a measure of forecasting ability suggests that management is not overly concerned about the direction of the forecasting error since the calculation of MAD routinely treats negative and positive errors equally. That is, forecasting that falls short and produces positive error must *not be viewed less favorably* than forecasting that is over optimistic and yields negative errors.

Another condition that one should note about MAD is that large size forecasting errors are not given special importance. Small forecasting errors arithmetically equivalent to a single large forecasting error are treated exactly alike in the MAD calculation. This ignores a pervasive managerial attitude that the consequences of a single large error are much more devastating than the cumulative effect of many small forecasting errors. For instance, the large 1981 forecasting shortfall in demand for cars, with the subsequent massive inventory buildups and billion dollar losses, has brought some major producers to the brink of bankruptcy, whereas minor shortfalls through the years have been adjusted for smoothly. The desire to penalize relatively more for large size errors of forecasting than for small size errors of forecasting is recognized in a summary measure for assessing forecasts called the *mean squared error.*

The mean squared error is defined as:

$$MSE = \frac{\Sigma(A_t - F_t)^2}{n}$$

where A_t = actual value for a given period t; F_t = forecasted value for the given period t; and n = number of forecasts considered. From the data in column 6 in Table 19.3, we have

$$MSE = \frac{329,499.72}{7} = 47,071.39$$

The MSE figure shows that, on average, the forecasts face a mean squared error of 47,071.39 per period forecast. If two forecasting methods yield identical or comparable MAD measures, the technique with the larger MSE would be less preferred by management whenever there is a strong concern for minimizing large errors in forecasting.

The last summary measure of forecasting error that we will discuss and illustrate is the *mean absolute percentage error* (MAPE). This measure serves as an indication of the extent to which the forecast error is keeping pace with the actual level of the quantity being forecasted. The MAPE is a summary statistic computed as:

$$MAPE = \frac{\Sigma\left(\left|\frac{A_t - F_t}{A_t}\right|\right)}{n} \cdot 100$$

where again the symbols A, F, and n have the same meaning as before—actual, forecasted, and number of forecasted values.

Table 19.4 illustrates the calculation of MAPE from the data introduced in Table 19.3.

The calculation of MAPE from column 5 of Table 19.4 is:

$$MAPE = 89.53/7 = 12.79\%$$

The MAPE figure shows that *on average* the absolute value of the forecast error represents about 12.79% of the level of actual demand. Whether this percentage error is adequate for the needs of management and acceptable partly depends on the availability and cost of alternative forecasting and the value of the MAPE measure along with the other forecasting error measures. Let us now examine one approach to that issue.

TABLE 19.4. Summary Error Measurement for Exponential Smoothing Forecasting Model—Calculating MAPE

(1) TIME PERIOD t	(2) ACTUAL DEMAND A_t	(3) FORECAST FOR PERIOD t MADE IN PERIOD $t-1$ F_t	(4) ABSOLUTE ERROR $|A_t - F_t|$	(5) ABSOLUTE PERCENTAGE ERROR $\left(\left|\dfrac{A_t - F_t}{A_t}\right|\right) \cdot 100$
1	1000	—	—	
2	1020	1000	20	$(20/1020) \cdot 100 = 1.96$
3	950	1006	56	$(56/950) \cdot 100 = 5.89$
4	1410	989.2	420.8	$(420.8/1410) \cdot 100 = 29.84$
5	1380	1115.44	264.56	$(264.56/1380) \cdot 100 = 19.17$
6	1400	1194.81	205.19	$(205.19/1400) \cdot 100 = 14.66$
7	1430	1256.37	173.63	$(173.63/1430) \cdot 100 = 12.14$
8	1390	1308.46	81.54	$(81.54/1390) \cdot 100 = 5.87$
				sum = **89.53**

19.6. Judging Forecasting Methods

In order to gain some perspective on error measurement of alternative forecasting methods, a generally acceptable standard is needed. One approach is to employ a so-called "naive model" as a standard of comparison. A naive model is a simplistic forecasting procedure which requires no statistical analysis for interpretation, can be easily used, is inexpensive to run, and requires no judgment decision on the part of the user. One naive model which is frequently used assumes the forecasted value for the period to be identical to the previous period's actual value: $F_t = A_{t-1}$. From Table 19.5, we see the calculated error summary measures MAD, MSE, and MAPE associated with this naive model approach.

TABLE 19.5. Summary Error Measurement for Naive Forecasting Model—Calculating MAD, MSE, and MAPE

1 TIME PERIOD t	2 ACTUAL DEMAND A_t	3 FORECAST FOR PERIOD t MADE IN PERIOD $t-1$ F_t	4 ABSOLUTE ERROR $|A_t - F_t|$	5 SQUARED ERROR $(A_t - F_t)^2$	6 ABSOLUTE PERCENTAGE ERROR $[|(A_t - F_t)/A_t|]100$
1	1000				
2	1020	1000	20	400	1.96%
3	950	1020	70	4900	7.37
4	1410	950	460	211,600	32.62
5	1380	1410	30	900	2.17
6	1400	1380	20	400	1.43
7	1430	1400	30	900	2.10
8	1390	1430	40	1600	2.88
Sums			**670**	**220,700**	**50.53**

MAD = 670/7 = 95.71	MSE = 220,700/7 = 31,528.57	MAPE = 50.53/7 = 7.22%

In Table 19.6, let's compare the calculated values of MAD, MSE, and MAPE for the two forecasting methods considered—the exponential smoothing forecasting model and the naive forecasting model, the assumed standard.

TABLE 19.6. An Error Measurement Comparison Between Forecasting by the Exponential Smoothing Model and the Naive Model

METHOD	MAD	MSE	MAPE
Exponential Smoothing	174.53	47,071.39	12.79%
Naive	95.71	31,528.57	7.22%

Over the period of comparison, it does appear that the naive model does a better job of forecasting, on average, from period to period no matter whether the summary error measures (MAD, MSE, or MAPE) are considered separately or as a group. Since the naive model is less complicated to operate and is less costly to maintain, it would seem to be the preferable one to employ on this data for demand projections. Of course, if management is dissatisfied with the error record of both models, the search for another forecasting device would proceed.

In the following section, we will follow a detective-like approach to uncover patterns in the data, to model those patterns, and to forecast from the model.

19.7. Exploratory Data Analysis—A Sequence Plot

Considerable insight about the sequential pattern that observations follow is obtained visually by constructing a *sequence plot*. A sequence plot is simply a two dimensional graph plotting the value of each observation in the exact sequence in which it appears and is reported. The values are calibrated horizontally, with the sequence order shown vertically. For example, let's examine the data block of monthly returns on IBM common stock from January, 1969 (the first observation), through December, 1975 (the 84th observation), shown in Table 19.7.

A sequence plot of the IBM data running from the first observation (top) to the eighty-fourth observation (bottom) is shown in Figure 19.6. What conclusions can we draw from the plot? Is the path of the observations around the median return line sequentially patternless?

A Simple Test

Consider a pair of observations in sequence, say the first two observations, −.05952 and −.00700. Now, suppose you are attempting to predict or guess-estimate the next observation (the third one).

Would you change your "guesstimate" if the order of appearance (sequence) of the observations had been reversed—that is, −.00700 came first, followed by −.05952?

TABLE 19.7. Data File on Monthly IBM Returns

COLUMN COUNT ROW	C5 B4	ROW		ROW	
1	−.05952	29	.08232	57	−.14236
2	−.00700	30	−.03058	58	.08624
3	.07030	31	−.08123	59	−.05042
4	.04459	32	.04824	60	−.06887
5	−.02500	33	−.00082	61	−.00608
6	.05878	34	−.01070	62	−.02485
7	−.03923	35	.02097	63	−.00893
8	.06626	36	.10147	64	−.03606
9	.00072	37	.09361	65	−.05927
10	.04417	38	.00503	66	.00118
11	.00693	39	.03731	67	−.05229
12	.02101	40	.00981	68	−.04030
13	−.08025	41	.03394	69	−.17187
14	.01849	42	−.01446	70	.18947
15	−.00514	43	.02232	71	.05486
16	−.11965	44	.02271	72	−.05219
17	−.06309	45	−.00490	73	.12054
18	−.10072	46	−.05166	74	.15272
19	.01380	47	.01777	75	−.04118
20	.05550	48	.02813	76	.01573
21	.09577	49	.08333	77	.03157
22	.01183	50	−.00597	78	−.02791
23	.04507	51	.00000	79	−.08971
24	.03417	52	−.05446	80	−.01183
25	.02439	53	−.03226	81	.01074
26	.03779	54	.00715	82	.12749
27	.06241	55	−.00789	83	.07479
28	.00070	56	−.03936	84	−.00939

Do you attach any importance to the consecutive negative sign, or to the fact that the magnitude of the value is increasing (−.00700 to −.05952) or decreasing (−.05952 to −.00700)?

If changing the order of the first two observations alters your opinion about the "guesstimate" of the third one, then you do not really believe the series is "patternless". You are suggesting that the order of appearance of an observation with its magnitude and sign carries information which is relevant in making predictions. The presence of relevant informational content in the sequence of observations implies that analysis of the sequence can lead to improved forecasts of future values of the series.

On the other hand, if you hold to your prediction of the third observation when the sequence of the first two observations is switched, you must be concluding that no useful information for prediction can be obtained from knowing the sequence of the observations. In short, your conclusion is that predictive ability cannot be enhanced by knowing the sequence of observations. Herein lies a crucial checkpoint.

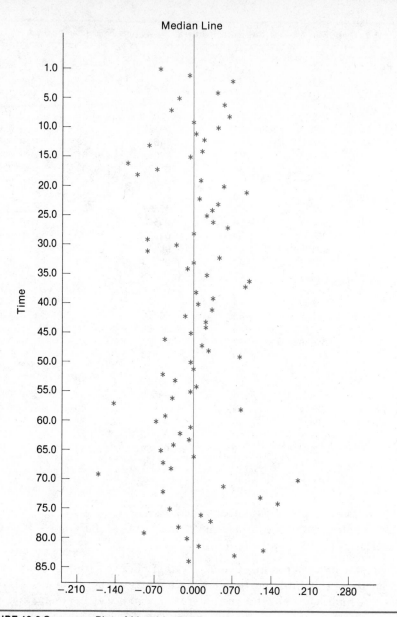

FIGURE 19.6 Sequence Plot of Monthly IBM Returns

If sequence of observations *matters*, then one can predict the value of a coming observation from knowledge of the direction and value of a previous observation or perhaps the time path of the previous observations. Statistical tools are available to identify and represent (model) the informational patterns exploitable for prediction. If sequence *doesn't* matter, one can disregard the *sequence* of observations for predictive purposes.

Tracking the Observations

What should one keep in mind to detect *patterns* from a sequence plot? What type of clues should the sequence of observations have in order to be useful in predicting the next observation?

One diagnostic which can be used for detecting patterns is *anticipatory tracking*. Here is how it works.

1. Place a piece of paper over the entire sequence plot and slide it back slowly from the first observation, gradually uncovering the series one by one.

2. While performing these mechanics, make a mental note of a possible emerging pattern.

3. See whether you can anticipate the position of the next observation after you already have seen the path of the previous one.

You should grant yourself complete liberty to concoct whatever underlying scheme you think will be useful for the prediction job.

Points to Ponder

Here are some sequence patterns to look for:

1. Do you detect a strong tendency for the value of an observation to be more *similar to that of the previous observation* than to the value of observations further removed in the sequence?

2. Do you detect a persistent tendency for the value of successive observations to drift (trend) mainly upward or mainly downward?

3. Do you detect a successive series of observations exhibiting a wave-like (cyclical) movement with some semblance of regularity?

4. Do you detect any abrupt shifts of level?

Such visual data analysis has been called the Interocular Traumatic Test (IOTT)—in other words, patterns of sequence ought to hit you between the eyes.[1]

What Does It Mean if None of These Things Are Observable?

To conclude that your data exhibits no systematic movement that can be exploited for prediction means that *sequence does not matter*. We call this state of patternless sequence *"randomness"* and we say that the data exhibits *random behavior*, or is in general conformity to the *model* of random behavior.

Do IBM Monthly Returns Follow a Pattern?

Let us consider the sequence plot in stages to detect possible evolving patterns. Place Figure 19.6 sideways and read from left to right the *first ten* observations.

The values seem to show no persistent drift and are pretty well scattered around the median value line, located at .00035.

Furthermore, a line drawn across from the median position seems to separate equally the number of observations above and below the line.

Now, make an "intelligent guess" as to the position (and therefore the value) of the next observation. Wouldn't you guess from what you just saw a return near zero for the eleventh observation?

Moving on to consider the *first twenty observations* changes things a bit. There seems to be a perceptible downdrift of the observations. A best guess of the twenty-first observation would suggest a value in the negative return range. Does this pattern continue when twenty more observations are studied? No. By the fortieth observation, a counterbalancing effect is detectable, with the apparent creation of cycles centered near the middle value of zero. Thus, the best guess of the forty-first observation seems to revert back to a zero rate of return. After the fiftieth observation, a gentle down drift (observations 50 to 70) seems to emerge again, but subsequent observations (70 to 84) show no apparent continuation of the drift.

What's the Conclusion at this Point?

Our visual examination of the sequence plot revealed no obvious significant sequential pattern in the data.

Overall, however, the scatter about the median value line, located at .00035, showed some tendency for successive observations to cluster near each other, creating the appearance of some cycles and a tendency for modest drifts.[2] This apparent non-random type behavior suggests that we ought to have reservations about the conformity of the data to a random behavior model. Certainly the possibility of non-random type clustering of observations above and below the median should be checked more thoroughly. For this, we turn to a formal statistical procedure known as the *runs test*.

Runs Test

A run is defined as a cluster or streak of observations all on the same side of the median value.

The runs test postulates randomness as a working hypothesis and provides a statistic for testing the hypothesis. More specifically, it provides the means of answering the question: What is the chance of getting observations with as much or more clustering on either side of the median line as shown by this data if truly the changes in the returns are randomly behaved. The answer is determined by comparing the number of runs *observed* versus the number of runs *expected* if the data is behaving randomly.

Strong non-random patterns like those generated by trends and seasonal variation result in either a deficient number or excessive number of runs compared to the expected number for random behavior.

Strong trends have *fewer* runs than randomly generated data.

If the trend is upward, early values fall *below* the median, whereas the later values show up *above* the median. The reverse pattern is obtained with a downward trend. In either case, strong trends diminish the observed runs count. Strong short term seasonal variation shows mechanical toothsaw movement in the data and produces excessive crisscrossing of the median.

The net result of seasonal variation is many more runs than expected for a random series.

The runs test is discussed more thoroughly in Chapter 22. Here we concentrate on learning how to interpret the summary statistics found on the computer printout of the runs test. For example, the MINITAB printout for the IBM data lists

ACTUAL NUMBER OF RUNS = 35
EXPECTED NUMBER OF RUNS = 42.78
SIGNIFICANT AT .0793 LEVEL

There are 35 runs for the IBM returns data. If the particular sequence of the IBM returns conformed to the random model specification, the number of runs expected is 42.78—the mean of the probability distribution for the number of runs. The last value is the key summary statistic of the runs test. It indicates how probable it is to find as extreme a value as 35 runs, if the expected value is 42.78. In this case the chance is only .0793, not very likely for a random series, prompting us to have some reservations about the random specification for the IBM returns. On the other hand, the value of .0793 is *not overwhelming* evidence against the random specification. A hypothesis test of randomness at the .05 level of significance could not be rejected.

19.8. Probabilistic Time Dependent Modeling

Probabilistic time dependent modeling is a forecasting scheme which exploits the non-random, time dependent patterns found in most time series data. Its working procedure is:

1. *Identification:* use various data transformations, if necessary, on the original series to decompose the series into two components—the time dependent component and the *random* (non-time dependent) component:

Y series ⤙ time dependent
          random portion

Properly done, the series has now achieved stationarity. That is, the process we are attempting to use to forecast is quite stable.

2. *Estimation:* develop a *predictive equation* (autoregressive model) *for the time dependent portion.*

3. *Diagnostic Checking:* test to make sure that the residuals conform to a random model specification.

4. *Forecasting A:* forecast from the predictive equation the next (future) value of the *transformed* series.

5. *Forecasting B:* trace back through the transformation to obtain a forecast of the *original* series.

Ideally this procedure accomplishes two things:

1. reveals the time dependent movements in the data series;

2. extracts and models these time dependent movements for forecasting purposes, leaving only random (non-predictable) movement remaining.

Extrapolating into the future the time dependent patterns which were discovered permits us to make forecasts of the value of the original variable.

Strive for Random Residuals

The key to the strategy of probabilistic time-dependent modeling is to formulate a model of the time dependent factors so that the "residual" component is indeed behaving randomly. None of the time dependent factors are left to exploit in the residual component.

The statistical investigation at this point has reached a stage in which further analysis of the sequence of the residuals component would not be a worthwhile endeavor. No usable information for building the forecasting model is any longer available.

The key difference between the classical time series model and the probabilistic model we now describe is that the latter does not impose the existence of trends, seasonality, and cycles in any predetermined way. Instead, whatever time-dependent patterns are in the data are extracted in the estimation process, leaving only random residuals. The revealed time-dependent patterns then become building blocks of the forecasting model.

Let us now begin such an analysis on the time series of bimonthly case sales for soft drinks. This data was first described in Table 17.9 in deseasonalized form. Table 19.8 shows the formatted original data in column 3 and subsequent transformations in columns 4, 5, 6, and 7 from the MINITAB computer program printout. We shall describe these transformations and their purposes after examining a scatterplot of the original data.

An Example

Turned on its side, the sequence plot of the original data on case sales is given in Figure 19.7; sequentially, the observations are numbered one to fifty. The plot shows:

1. *an upward trend* with noticeable periodic waves around the upward trend. This is evidence of a nonstationary process since a stationary process is trendless.

2. *wavelike fluctuations* with somewhat wider swings towards the end of the data—approximately the last 10 observations

TABLE 19.8. Data File of Original Data and Transformed Data on Bimonthly Case Sales of Soft Drinks on MINITAB

COLUMN ROW	C3 ORIGINAL CASE SALES, Y	C4 FIRST DIFFERENCES, D	C5 DOUBLE DIFFERENCES, DD	C6 LAG ONE OF DD	C7 LAG SIX OF DD
1	178.				
2	172.	−6.			
3	141.	−31.			
4	144.	3.			
5	136.	−8.			
6	161.	25.			
7	188.	27.			
8	184.	−4.	2.		
9	152.	−32.	−1.	2.	
10	158.	6.	3.	−1.	
11	148.	−10.	−2.	3.	
12	174.	26.	1.	−2.	
13	215.	41.	14.	1.	
14	204.	−11.	−7.	14.	2.
15	162.	−42.	−10.	−7.	−1.
16	169.	7.	1.	−10.	3.
17	162.	−7.	3.	1.	−2.
18	183.	21.	−5.	3.	1.
19	222.	39.	−2.	−5.	14.
20	214.	−8.	3.	−2.	−7.
21	179.	−35.	7.	3.	−10.
22	187.	8.	1.	7.	1.
23	182.	−5.	2.	1.	3.
24	211.	29.	8.	2.	−5.
25	248.	37.	−2.	8.	−2.
26	247.	−1.	7.	−2.	3.
27	202.	−45.	−10.	7.	7.
28	207.	5.	−3.	−10.	1.
29	193.	−14.	−9.	−3.	2.
30	223.	30.	1.	−9.	8.
31	261.	38.	1.	1.	−2.
32	259.	−2.	−1.	1.	7.
33	205.	−54.	−9.	−1.	−10.
34	211.	6.	1.	−9.	−3.
35	201.	−10.	4.	1.	−9.
36	235.	34.	4.	4.	1.
37	271.	36.	−2.	4.	1.
38	275.	4.	6.	−2.	−1.
39	224.	−51.	3.	6.	−9.
40	234.	10.	4.	3.	1.
41	227.	−7.	3.	4.	4.
42	256.	29.	−5.	3.	4.
43	304.	48.	12.	−5.	−2.
44	289.	−15.	−19.	12.	6.
45	243.	−46.	5.	−19.	3.
46	249.	6.	−4.	5.	4.
47	239.	−10.	−3.	−4.	3.
48	270.	31.	2.	−3.	−5.
49	312.	42.	−6.	2.	12.
50	314.	2.	17.	−6.	−19.

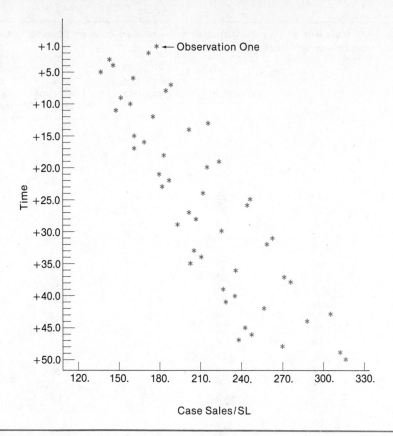

FIGURE 19.7 Sequence Plot of Original Data of Bimonthly Soft Drink Sales

3. *persistence of nearby observations* confirmed by runs count (twelve observed runs compared to twenty-six expected for a random series). The size of the difference between the actual number of runs and the expected number does *not* support the random model specification.

These conclusions point to a time dependent (non-random) pattern. How should we separate out the time dependent regularity? Recognizing the existence of an upward trend pattern, can we go on to identify and characterize the time dependent consistency in the cyclical fluctuation about the rising trend levels?

First Differences Reveal Time-dependent Consistency

Since our ultimate interest is forecasting the next sales level from the present sales level, perhaps a good starting point is to consider the pattern of changes in the level of sales at successive time periods. Interesting time-dependent consistency from year to year may be revealed. To test this conjecture, the interactive command 'Diff' is executed, using either the IDA or MINITAB computer program. The mathematical operation of 'Diff' takes the difference between successive

sales levels, $Y_t - Y_{t-1}$, one time period apart. These are called *first differences*:
$D_t = Y_t - Y_{t-1}$.

The first difference of the soft drink sales data are shown in column C4 of Table 19.8. Thus, $-6 = 172 - 178$ and $-31 = 141 - 172$, etc. The sequence plot shown in Figure 19.8, when turned on its side, reveals a pleasant surprise. A dramatic pattern appears. *First differences, six periods (one year) apart, seem to be positioned similarly on the graph.* This indicates that bimonthly sales have similar changes at the same seasonal point during the year. The similar "first difference" terms are encircled by the same geometric shape.

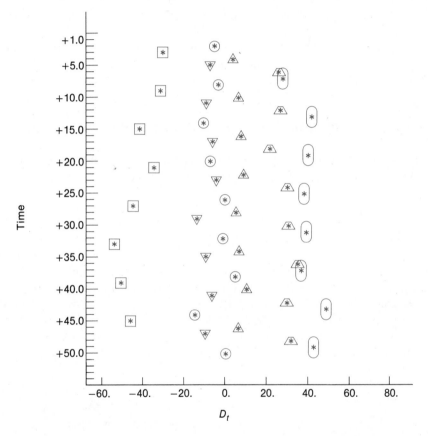

1 Missing Observation

FIGURE 19.8 Sequence Plot of First Differences of Bimonthly Soft Drink Sales

First Difference Autocorrelation Function

The strong tie between *every sixth pair* of "first differences" shows up numerically in the six order autocorrelation statistic from the *autocorrelation function*.

The autocorrelation function monitors the strength of the correlation between a variable's terms separated by a specific number, g, of time periods (Y_t, Y_{t-g}). If $g = 1$, the paired terms are one time period apart and the autocorrelation is a first-order autocorrelation. Correlating pairs two periods apart, $g = 2$, yields a *second order* autocorrelation, etc. Therefore the first-order autocorrelation coefficient relates all the pairs represented by Y_t, Y_{t-1}; the second order autocorrelation coefficient relates all the pairs represented by Y_t, Y_{t-2}, and so forth.

The sixth order autocorrelation coefficient is of particular interest. It is the correlation between bimonthly changes spaced one year apart. That is, it relates all the changes represented by the pairs D_t, D_{t-6}. Column C4 of Table 19.8 lists the first differences. The first pair (D_t, D_{t-6}) is found in rows 8 and 2 ($D_8 = -4$, $D_2 = -6$); the second pair is found in rows 9 and 3 ($D_9 = -32, D_3 = -31$); the third pair is (6, 3), etc. The correlation between the first number of the pair and the second number of the pair is .866. This is the sixth order autocorrelation coefficient. Its value in this case indicates that bimonthly changes are highly correlated with the bimonthly change one year (six periods) earlier.

Autocorrelation Function Reveals Seasonality

Figure 19.9 is a correlogram, a graphical display of the autocorrelations existing between the observations spaced by a constant interval of time. The numbers in the first column indicate which autocorrelation is referred to in that row. For example, the number 6 in column one indicates that this row refers to the sixth order autocorrelation. The value of the sixth order correlation, .866, is given in the second column of the row. This value is represented graphically by the length and position of the string of Xs in the row, measured along the horizontal scale given at the top of the table. A string of Xs to the right of zero indicates positive autocorrelation; to the left, negative autocorrelation. Scanning the rows, one notices considerable differences among the autocorrelations of different order. Some are strong (many Xs), some are weak (few Xs). Some are positive; some are negative. The strongest autocorrelation is the sixth order and it is positive.

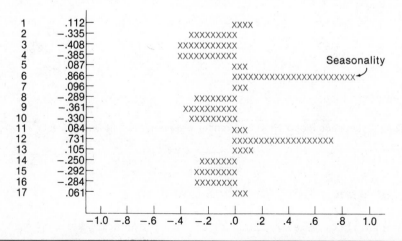

FIGURE 19.9 Autocorrelation Function of First Differences of Bimonthly Soft Drink Sales

As noted above, the large positive autocorrelation value of .866 found at the sixth order (between all pairs represented by D_t, D_{t-6}) indicates a strong kinship between pairs one year (6 bimonthly periods) apart. Since these pairings of first difference terms link the same period of each year they therefore represent a strong case of seasonality. The interpretation of seasonality in this case is that *changes in sales* reach a similar level *at the same time each year.*

Once this time dependent seasonality has been identified, the next step is to *filter out* the seasonality to permit the identification of other time dependent consistencies that may exist. Differencing once again, with a gap of 6 (6 bimonths), factors out the year to year seasonal effect. Differencing now by a gap of 6 *periods* gives new difference terms represented by $DD_t = (D_t - D_{t-6})$.

These differences are given in column C5 of Table 19.8. For example, the value of 2 in row 8 of that table represents the difference between the first difference of -4 given in row 8 of column C4 and the first difference of -6 (six periods earlier) given in row 2 of that same column.

The original Y series has now been *double differenced*, initially at a gap of one to give first-differenced terms D_t and then again with a gap of six between D_t terms to give DD_t terms. What now remains is the double differenced *series* which is shown in column C5 of Table 19.8. Let us show how the calculation of first double-differenced value in column C5 corresponds to the notation we are using.

DD_t denotes the double differenced series.

$$DD_t = D_t - D_{t-6}$$
$$= (Y_t - Y_{t-1}) - (Y_{t-6} - Y_{t-7})$$
$$= Y_t - Y_{t-1} - Y_{t-6} + Y_{t-7}$$

where Ys denote the original observations. Thus,

$$DD_1 = Y_8 - Y_7 - Y_2 + Y_1$$
$$= 184 - 188 - 172 + 178$$
$$= 2$$

which is the first value in column C5.

Is There a Pattern in the Double Difference Series?

The sequence plot of data after the two differencing operations (column C5 of Table 19.8) is shown in Figure 19.10. It is hard to tell visually whether it is a "patternless" sequence. To formally check the double-differenced series for lack of conformity with a random model specification, a *Runs Test* (for random sequences) is applied. (This test is described more fully in Chapter 22.) This diagnostic in MINITAB shows:

OBSERVED NUMBER OF RUNS = 25
EXPECTED NUMBER OF RUNS = 22.4884
TEST SIGNIFICANT AT .2826
CANNOT REJECT AT ALPHA = .05

These statements mean: Under the assumption that a random model is operative, 22.5 runs is the expectation and the probability of finding a result as extreme as twenty-five (our observed number) or more runs is .2836. The observed evidence is not improbable enough for the specification of randomness of the series to be rejected at the five percent significance level. The runs test probability value of .2826 does indicate, however, that there is a modestly low chance of finding such extreme results if the random model specification is operative. Therefore we ought to hold some reservations about assuming the random model specification. Can we check more thoroughly for time dependencies in the double differences that may be useful for prediction?

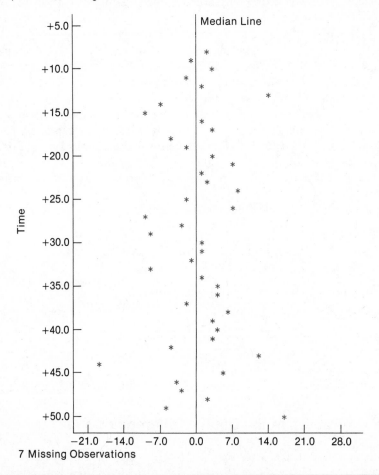

FIGURE 19.10 Sequence Plot of the Double Differences of Bimonthly Soft Drink Sales

Cyclical Residuals

Figure 19.11 shows the autocorrelations for the double differences as a function of the order. It is interpreted the same way as Figure 19.9 except that the auto-correlations row refers to the double differenced values.

A check of the plot of the different order autocorrelation values in Figure 19.11 for the double-differenced series shows "large" autocorrelation of the first order and sixth order. In both cases, the correlation is *negative*.

The negative sign of the sixth order autocorrelation coefficient ($-.409$) of the double-differenced terms in this case means that if the value of the current double-differenced term is low, its value 6 bimonthly periods (one year) back is likely high and vice versa.

The next step is to exploit this statistical time dependency at the first and sixth order for forecasting in an autoregressive moving average model.[3]

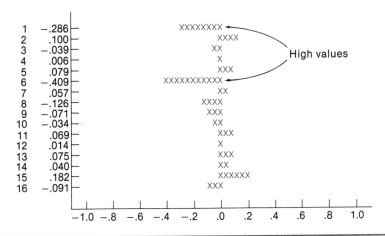

FIGURE 19.11 Autocorrelation Function of Double Differences of Bimonthly Soft Drink Sales

Multiple Regression with Autoregressive Terms

Our objective at this point is to formulate and estimate a predictive equation that can forecast future values of the double-differences series. Lagged variables (variables of one or more periods back, such as $t - 1$, $t - 2$) of the double-differences terms are used as independent variables in a multiple regression equation. For instance, forecasting the double difference term DD_t requires an equation which is some variant of the following form:

$$\widehat{DD}_t = a + b_1 DD_{t-1} + b_2 DD_{t-2} \cdots + b_g DD_{t-g}$$

In this equation, the independent variables on the right hand side are lagged double differences.

How many double-differenced lagged terms should be used as independent variables is suggested by the following useful guidelines:

1. Limit the number of lagged (independent) variables to a few.

2. Give priority to recent lagged variables, particularly the first two.

3. Employ independent variables that show a substantial autocorrelation at the seasonal lag.

4. Drop any lagged variable which, when included in the equation, fails to lower the standard deviation of residuals. Typically a variable with *t* ratio below one in absolute value will be dropped.

The soft drink double-differenced data shown in column C5 of Table 19.8 represent the dependent variable. The multiple regression uses as independent variables the two lag terms at the first and sixth periods back (columns C6 and C7) and starts with row 14. The computer output for the autoregression is shown in Figure 19.12. The *t* ratio of each lagged variable's coefficients far exceeds the absolute value of one. This means that each of the two lagged terms contributes to the predictive gain of the equation by lowering the standard deviation of residuals. Forecasting the next value of the dependent variable DD_t will then be more reliable if these variables are included in the forecasting equation for DD_t.

```
THE REGRESSION EQUATION IS
Y = - .0435 -  .322 X1 -  .500 X2


     37 CASES USED
     13 CASES CONTAINED MISSING VALUES


                                       ST. DEV.     T-RATIO =
          COLUMN      COEFFICIENT     OF COEF.     COEF/S.D.
          --            -.044           .936          -.05
     X1   C6 LAG1       -.322           .144          -2.23
     X2   C7 LAG6       -.500           .147          -3.39


THE ST. DEV. OF Y ABOUT REGRESSION LINE IS
S =       5.69
WITH (  37- 3) =   34 DEGREES OF FREEDOM


R-SQUARED = 33.6 PERCENT
R-SQUARED = 29.7 PERCENT, ADJUSTED FOR D.F.
```

FIGURE 19.12 Computer Output of Multiple Regression on Double Differences and its Lagged Terms, Lag 1 and Lag 6

To be confident in using the regression equation as a forecasting device, one must find conformity between the actual behavior of the calculated residuals and the regression model assumptions made about the behavior of the disturbance term. A runs test checks on the randomness of the observed residuals. The observed residuals gave the following diagnostics:

OBSERVED NUMBER OF RUNS = 22
EXPECTED NUMBER OF RUNS = 19.4865
TEST SIGNIFICANT AT .4018
CANNOT REJECT AT ALPHA = .05

From the evidence one cannot reach the conclusion that the random model specification should be rejected. The evidence shows:

Assuming an underlying random model with an expectation of 19.5 runs, the probability of obtaining as extreme as 22 or more runs is somewhat likely (.4018).

Clearly this evidence is not accusatory enough to reject the random model specification at alpha = .05 level.

The plot of the *autocorrelation values* of the double-differenced series is given in Figure 19.13.

This figure shows the autocorrelations for the *residuals* from the multiple regression forecasts of DD_t as a function of the order. It is interpreted the same way as Figure 19.9, except that the autocorrelation row refers to the residuals. These are obtained by subtracting from DD_t values the estimates of these values computed from the multiple regression analysis.

Figure 19.13 shows *virtually no trace of a strong time dependent pattern remaining*. Nor does it show a correlation (positive or negative) between the different order of residuals high enough to invalidate the specification of a random pattern for the residuals.

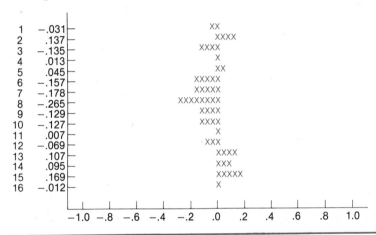

FIGURE 19.13 Autocorrelation Correlogram of Residuals from Double Difference Multiple Regression

A final visual check on the scatter of the residuals given in Figure 19.14 shows a scatter around the computed regression line value (horizontally tilted for ease of inspection) in conformity with the constant scatter assumption.

Finding no curvature pattern of residuals (suggestive of non-linearity) lets us give a satisfactory verdict on the linearity assumption also.

Having now filtered out time dependency patterns to the point where the residuals conform reasonably to a random (non-time dependent) specification, we turn to using the identified time dependent patterns to predict future observations. From Figure 19.12, we can see that the model for forecasting the double differences is:

$$\widehat{DD}_t = -.044 - .322DD_{t-1} - .500DD_{t-6}$$

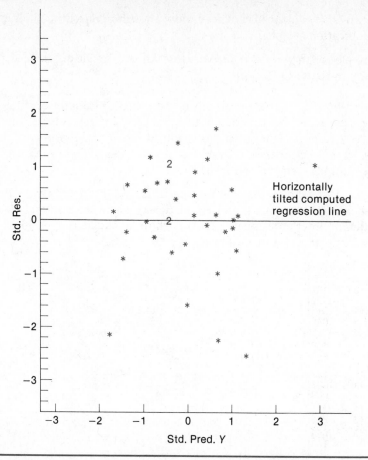

FIGURE 19.14 Plot of Residuals vs. Predicted Y for Double-Difference Multiple Regression

19.9. Prediction by the Autoregressive Model

Our diagnostic checks on the residuals of the double-differenced autoregressive equation revealed no alarming evidence supporting model inadequacy. The double differenced equation $\widehat{DD}_t = -.044 - .322DD_{t-1} - .500DD_{t-6}$ can now be used to predict the next double difference value. With the time dependent pattern identified for the entire already observed fifty bimonthly periods, the ultimate objective is to make a prediction for the level of the case sales for the fifty-first period, November/December. Predicting the fifty-first observation is accomplished in two steps:

1. The prediction for the double differenced term, DD_{51}, is made *from the estimated autoregressive equation.* The procedure is to substitute values in the computed regression equation for the double-differenced variables one and six periods back. The predictive equation is:

$$\widehat{DD}_t = -.044 - .322DD_{t-1} - .500DD_{t-6}$$
$$\widehat{DD}_{51} = -.044 - .322(DD_{50}) - .500(DD_{45})$$

2. The forecast of case sales Y_{51} will be obtained by using the forecast DD_{51} and earlier Y values.

Step One: Predicting DD_{51}

To follow the procedure of Step One more easily, Figure 19.15 is presented showing the last six bimonthly double differenced terms, DD from DD_{50} to DD_{45} with their associated DD value obtained from Table 19.8, column C5.

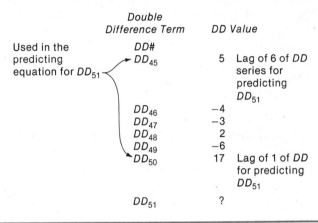

FIGURE 19.15 Selected Set of Double Difference Terms

The values of DD_{50} and DD_{45} are historical and so available from the original Y data series as known values. Substituting the values of DD_{50} and DD_{45} into the predictive equation we get a prediction for DD_{51}.

$$
\begin{aligned}
\widehat{DD}_{51} &= -.044 - .322(DD_{50}) - .500(DD_{45}) \\
&= -.044 - .322(17) - .500(5) \\
&= -.044 - 5.474 - 2.5 \\
&= -8.018
\end{aligned}
$$

Step Two: Retrieving Y, Case Sales

Because we have differenced twice the original Y series—once to isolate *consecutive* changes in Y levels from the trend ($Y_t - Y_{t-1} = D_t$), and the other to deseasonalize ($DD_t = D_t - D_{t-6}$)—the procedure for retrieving the original case sales requires a little careful arithmetic. With Y representing the original case sales series where $Y_1 \cdots Y_{50}$, we can write the value $\widetilde{DD}_{51}$ in terms

$$
\widetilde{DD}_{51} = \tilde{D}_{51} - D_{45}
$$
$$
\widetilde{DD}_{51} = (\tilde{Y}_{51} - Y_{50}) - (Y_{45} - Y_{44})
$$

Comment: Since the fiftieth observation is the last available, both $\tilde{Y}_{51}$ and $\widetilde{DD}_{51}$ are *future* observations. At the present time, their values are unknown and can only be estimated. This is shown by the tilde (~ or $\sim$) symbol over the variable. The values of Y_{50}, Y_{45}, and Y_{44} are already known from the original Y series.

Since our objective is to forecast $\tilde{Y}_{51}$, we rearrange the elements of $\widetilde{DD}_{51}$ to isolate $\tilde{Y}_{51}$, to get:

$$\tilde{Y}_{51} = \widetilde{DD}_{51} + Y_{50} + Y_{45} - Y_{44}$$

The point forecast of $\widetilde{DD}_{51}$ was just computed to be -8.018 by the autoregressive predictive model. The next step is to plug in the missing value of case sales at Y_{50}, Y_{45}, and Y_{44}. Looking at the Y case sales series in Table 19.9 we can pick out these values.

TABLE 19.9. Y Case Sales, Observations 43–50

OBSERVATION NUMBER Y #	Y
43	304
44	289
45	243
46	249
47	239
48	270
49	312
50	314

Plugging the known values into the expression, the forecast of Y at $t = 51$ comes out to be:

$$\begin{aligned} \tilde{Y}_{51} &= \widehat{DD}_{51} + Y_{50} + Y_{45} - Y_{44} \\ &= -8.018 + 314 + 243 - 289 \\ &= 260 \text{ million cases (rounded)} \end{aligned}$$

The figure 260 million cases is our point estimate of the number of millions of cases that will be sold for the October/November 1972 bimonthly period. It is the best guess of next period case sales given the time dependent patterns that the double-differenced procedure has identified and modeled.

Can forecasts be made beyond the next period, that is beyond October/November, 1972? For instance, can we project case sales for period $\tilde{Y}_{52}$? If so, how?

Forecasting More Than One Period into the Future

The procedure again uses the double-difference autoregressive forecasting model to obtain a point estimate of $\widehat{DD}_{52}$. More precisely,

$$\widehat{DD}_t = -.044 - .322(\widehat{DD}_{t-1}) - .500(DD_{t-6})$$
$$\widehat{DD}_{52} = -.044 - .322(\widehat{DD}_{51}) - .500(DD_{46})$$

The equation shows that the $\widehat{DD}_{52}$ calculation requires the value for the term $\widetilde{DD}_{51}$ (for which we don't have an observed past value) and the value of DD_{46} (which we do know). But the term $\widetilde{DD}_{51}$ is still an unrealized value from the vantage point of our last Y observation at $t = 50$. The solution of $\widehat{DD}_{52}$ becomes possible *by using an estimate of* $\widetilde{DD}_{51}$—*the point forecast* value of $\widetilde{DD}_{51}$ just calculated. With the estimated value of $\widetilde{DD}_{51}$ and the known value of DD_{46} of -4 from column C5 of Table 19.8 substituted in the expression, we find:

$$\widehat{DD}_{52} = -.044 - .322(-8.018) - .500(-4)$$
$$= -0.044 + 2.582 + 2$$
$$= 4.538$$

And since

$$\widetilde{DD}_{52} = (\tilde{Y}_{52} - \tilde{Y}_{51}) - (Y_{46} - Y_{45})$$

rearranging the terms isolates $\tilde{Y}_{52}$:

$$\tilde{Y}_{52} = \widetilde{DD}_{52} + \tilde{Y}_{51} + Y_{46} - Y_{45}.$$

Given the observed data on Y_{46} and Y_{45} (column C3 in Table 19.8) and using point estimates for $\tilde{Y}_{51}$ and $\widetilde{DD}_{52}$, we arrive at:

$$\tilde{Y}_{52} = 4.538 + 260 + 249 - 243$$
$$= 270 \text{ million cases (rounded)}$$

So our point estimate of $\tilde{Y}_{52}$ is the value 270. It represents (in millions of case equivalents) the forecasted sales for the bimonthly period, December 1972/January 1973.

Forecasting case sales for periods 53 and beyond unavoidably relies on estimates of the unrealized series beyond the latest available value of the series, in this case Y_{50}. For instance, the forecast value of $\widehat{DD}_{52}$ needed estimates of $\widehat{DD}_{51}$ and the known double-difference DD_{47}. All uses of regression for predicting values rest on the assumption that the structural process generating the series remains stable. If it doesn't, prediction becomes highly speculative—more so, the further we go beyond the range of the observed data. Predictive confidence suffers critically if the consistent structure assumption does not remain tenable.

The main feature of autoregressive forecasting is its efficiency. It incorporates into a predictive scheme the time dependent consistencies observed in the past. This integration is accomplished by transforming the data to reveal their systematic time dependent patterns and then using the regression framework to exploit the patterns into making predictions.

19.10. Concluding Comments

The term forecasting means the problem of understanding the past in order to predict the level of activity in the future. The past can be analyzed on two bases— a time-dependent model and a causal model. The building of a time-dependent model expresses the belief that merely the passage of time is needed to forecast values for the variable of interest. The hope in this case is to identify the time dependent pattern in observed data, capture its systematic movement in equation form, and estimate it quantitatively. A causal model, on the other hand, requires knowledge of the interrelationship between key variables (for example, interest rates, disposable income, etc.) and the variable that is being predicted (for example, mobile home sales).

The chapter concentrated on the formulation, assumptions, and implementation of time dependent models, such as time series regression, exponential smoothing, and autoregression. Because forecast accuracy varies across forecasting devices, summary measures of error (MAD, MSE, MAPE) help to pinpoint the advantage of choosing one forecasting method over another. One can safely conclude that there is no single best forecasting technique for all occasions. Simplistic (naive) time-dependent models that require little or no resources provide a benchmark standard to consider before making a commitment to a very complex modeling approach that requires care and feeding: for example, autoregressive modeling and its estimation. Note that the utility of a model which on the surface appears to be working well will be destroyed if the underlying assumptions of a regression are not met. Adequacy tests that check residual conformity to the assumptions of regression are a prerequisite for forecasting.

Footnotes and References

[1] The name of the IOTT test was used by Professor Harry Roberts, University of Chicago
[2] Perhaps the fact that the median monthly stock return of only .00035 (approximately 0.4 percent per year) for a respected company like IBM suggests why investors were so leary of the stock market during the early 1970s.
[3] A full treatment of the theoretical usefulness of auto regression time series prediction is given in the book *Time Series Analysis* by Box and Jenkins (Holden-Day, 1970). A more applied version is found in *Applied T Series Analysis* by Charles R. Nelson (Holden-Day), 1973.

Questions and Problems

1. What assumption are we making in forecasting beyond the range of the observed data using a model based on past data? When may this be appropriate? When will it not be appropriate?

2. Why should a forecasting tool's performance not be measured by simply summing its forecasting error over the period of interest?

3. If the least square trend line always balances out the errors, ($\sum$ residuals $= 0$), why is there a concern that the residuals are serially correlated? Be specific.

4. Exponential smoothing gives heaviest weight to recent observations. Why is this an important advantage over the moving average method?

5. Explain fully the rationale behind the structure of the forecasting equation, $F_{t+1} = F_t + w(A_t - F_t)$.

6. What is the reason for examining the actual forecast errors for patterns?

7. Comment: Highly volatile series should place the greatest weight on the most recent observation to respond quickly to sudden changes in the series.

8. If a set of data is declared to be random, does that mean that the series is haphazard and out of control and generally of no informational interest? Explain.

9. Comment: Is there a strategic difference between performing classical time series analysis on a set of data and probabilistic modeling? After all, don't they both try to have only a random component left over?

10. How's business? "We don't mind letting our sales figures speak for themselves," said Phil Washington, a principal in charge of marketing for the 30 unit chain of 4 Day Tire Stores. "The tire business is supposed to be in a decline but we haven't noticed it." The possibility of an eventual downturn was somewhat disconcerting to Doris Carr, another principal of business, whose responsibilities are in the area of financial control and forecasting. "Perhaps we are getting more than our fair share," Carr beamed aloud, "but we ought to model our past growth so that we can better forecast our future growth. Let's see what we can find in our quarterly figures." (See Table 19.10.)

a. Compute the coefficients of the trend equation with dummy variables for the respective quarters through 1978 setting the first quarter as the base quarter, that is estimate

$$\hat{Y}(\text{sales}) = a + b_1 t + b_2 Q_2 + b_3 Q_3 + b_4 Q_4$$

entering the first observation as 230,313; 1; 0; 0; 0; for the variables Y; t; Q_2; Q_3; Q_4 respectively.

b. Interpret the meaning of the calculated coefficients.

c. Judge the worth of the dummy variables as a group. Do they improve the equation's forecasting ability by lowering the standard deviation of residuals? If not, eliminate them from the forecasting equation.

d. From Part c, select the forecasting regression equation which comparatively offers better forecast through a lower standard deviation of residuals. Forecast quarterly sales for the years 1979 and 1980 using the comparatively better forecasting equation (obtain the predicted $\hat{Y}$ values for the last 8 quarters). Calculate the forecasting errors given the actual values of 1979 and 1980. Use MAD and MAPE as summary measures.

e. Had the annual data only been used in a simple trend equation $\hat{Y}(\text{annual sales}) = a + bt$, what would be the forecasting equation? Interpret the coefficients and describe how a quarterly forecast would be made. Discuss the advantage or disadvantage of this approach.

11. (Note: This problem draws on procedure discussion in Chapter 17.) Refer to the quarterly sale data of 4 Day Tire Stores in Problem 10. To get some comparative performance of different forecasting tech-

TABLE 19.10. Quarterly Sales for 4 Day Tire Stores

	1st QUARTER	2nd QUARTER	3rd QUARTER	4th QUARTER	TOTAL
1970	230,313	333,537	409,018	415,177	1,388,045
1971	466,557	620,211	699,411	727,220	2,513,399
1972	860,505	1,244,259	1,574,046	1,281,289	4,960,099
1973	1,666,896	1,942,136	1,856,700	1,722,577	7,188,309
1974	1,657,794	1,960,692	2,144,877	2,098,829	7,862,192
1975	2,035,646	2,242,968	2,447,295	2,190,975	8,916,684
1976	2,467,032	2,739,593	2,989,866	2,590,964	10,787,445
1977	2,442,404	2,966,955	3,136,669	3,016,982	11,563,010
1978	2,857,033	3,683,926	4,342,306	3,808,919	14,692,184
1979	3,907,138	4,167,928	4,273,815	3,938,207	16,287,088
1980	3,966,566	4,553,981	5,125,848	4,404,604	18,050,999

Source: Company records

niques, Doris Carr wants to try the merit of forecasting this data with the moving averages trend component approach.

a. Compute the centered four quarter moving average series.

b. Using the ratio-to-moving average method, calculate the seasonal indexes.

c. Compute the moving average trend line

$$\hat{Y}(\text{sales}) = a + b_1 t + b_2 t^2$$

eliminating t^2 if its inclusion does not improve (lower) the standard deviation of the residuals.

d. With the moving average trend equation settled on in Part c, forecast the quarterly sales trend component for the 8 quarter periods in 1979 and 1980. Now apply the seasonal indices to arrive at the seasonally adjusted forecast.

e. Compare the forecast values with the actual quarterly data and obtain the forecasting error. Summarize the error performance by calculating MAD and MAPE.

12. Refer to the quarterly sales data of 4 Day Tire Stores in Problem 10. Another forecasting technique that Doris Carr wished to evaluate is the technique of exponential smoothing.

a. Calculate the exponential smoothing forecasts F_t using the exponential weight $w = .1$.

b. Compute the forecast error for the quarters of 1979 and 1980, and summarize by calculating MAD and MAPE.

c. Calculate the exponential smoothing forecasts F_t using the exponential weight $w = .4$.

d. Compute the forecast errors for the quarters in 1979 and 1980 and summarize by MAD and MAPE.

e. Repeat steps a and b using $w = .8$.

f. Compare the MAD and MAPE across the different weights used. Which seems to do the best smoothing adjustment on the basis of MAD and MAPE?

g. Plot the original series and the forecasts based on the smoothing factor .1, .4, .8. Discuss. Does one value of w consistently produce forecasts that tend to be low? Tend to overshoot at the turning points?

13. Refer to each forecasting equation used so far: in Problem 10, the trend equation with dummy variables; in Problem 11, the seasonally adjusted moving average trend equation; and lastly, Problem 12, the exponential smoothing forecast equation.

a. Forecast sales for quarter 1 in year 1980 by each equation.

b. Actual 4 Day Tire Store sales for the 1st Quarter in 1980 was 3,966,566. Compute the forecast error for each technique. Which was the lowest? Did this agree with the technique you expected to be best on the basis of the previously computed MAD and MAPE statistics?

14. In the early Seventies the stock market went through the doldrums. The broad based index of all New York Stock Exchange companies, the NYSE index, registered a negative .1% return monthly on average (annualized at -1.2%).

Market analysts claim that one can make high returns whether the market is going up (buy long) or the market is going down (sell short). Either way streaks exist and knowing when they occur can turn a small amount of cash into a large amount.

a. Look at the actual sequence plot of NYSE returns shown below for a seven year period. Can one use *anticipatory tracking* to predict successive observations by "reading the past sequence?" What emerging pattern do you see that can provide a useful prediction tool? Mention cycles, downdrift, trend, and runs.

b. Map out the runs for the NYSE sequence plot placing a $+$ or a $-$ when an observation falls above or below the median line respectively. Count the number of runs.

c. The runs test format shows

Actual Number of runs	
Expected Number of runs	42.62
Test significant at	0.0793

Report the actual number of runs value. What conclusion can one draw about randomness and predictability?

15. Longhorn Sand and Cement is a Texas based regional producer of cement. Top management is currently involved in its five-year planning process. At the last plan-

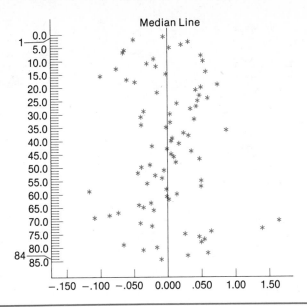

Median Line

| | −.150 | −.100 | −.050 | 0.000 | .050 | 1.00 | 1.50 |

PROBLEM 19.14

ning session it requested a breakdown of cement consumption by major markets and a forecast of cement demand on an annual basis for the next five years. Your boss wants you to report your results before the next meeting, which is in 10 days.

Your preliminary reports summarized by Table 19.11 show that the bulk of Longhorn's cement production is shipped to concrete ready-mix plants which supply non-residential building. A substantial portion also goes to public highway construction. The remainder over the years has been divided between the residential construction market and dam building. The latter factor has been generally on a hit-or-miss basis.

TABLE 19.11. Cement Shipments to Purchaser (Percent of Total)

MARKET	THIS YEAR	LAST YEAR
Non-Residential	55%	48%
Highways	33%	42%
Residential	7%	8%
Dams	5%	2%

With this information in hand you get to work on the problem immediately and collect 17 years of data on Longhorn's shipments of cement and two associated indicators of what determines demand, as shown in Table 19.12.

a. Compute the least squares trend line forecasting equation

$$\hat{Y} \text{ (Shipments)} = a + bt \text{ (annual periods).}$$

b. Plot the observations with shipments on the vertical axis and the annual time periods on the horizontal axis. Draw in the least squares line. Is there any evidence of curvilinearity?

c. Forecast shipment values from the computed equation for the next five year annual time periods. Is there any evidence of serial correlation? If there is, how would you adjust your forecast?

16. Refer to the data in Problem 15 on the 17 annual time periods collected for Longhorn Sand and Cement on the variables *cement shipments, highway construction,* and *building contracts.*

a. Compute the equation relating the dependent variable *cement shipments* and the independent variable *highway construction.* From a scatter plot check the adequacy of the linearity assumption. Interpret the coefficients of the equation.

TABLE 19.12. Seventeen Years of Longhorn Cement Data

ANNUAL TIME PERIOD	SHIPMENTS (MILLIONS OF BARRELS)	HIGHWAY CONSTRUCTION (MILLIONS OF DOLLARS)	BUILDING CONTRACTS (TEXAS) (MILLIONS OF DOLLARS)
1	.570	7.90	18.96
2	.572	10.32	20.82
3	.684	13.42	29.10
4	.818	10.76	31.60
5	.814	8.74	33.66
6	.914	12.32	34.98
7	.872	11.20	39.64
8	1.174	15.94	47.62
9	1.202	11.72	63.32
10	1.250	12.32	68.44
11	1.036	8.60	70.28
12	1.222	11.28	72.94
13	1.266	13.44	73.26
14	1.214	11.18	74.38
15	1.322	13.96	82.70
16	1.566	15.36	91.34
17	1.664	15.60	94.86

Source: Company Records, Construction Industry Publications

b. Would the coefficients change if the variables were measured in different units? Would the forecasting ability of the equation change? Explain.

c. Calculate the standard deviation of the residuals and r^2 and interpret.

d. Repeat steps a and c for the relationship between the variables *cement shipments* and *building contracts*.

e. Alamo Resources, a Texas based business forecasting group to which Longhorn Cement subscribes, has provided at your request forecasts of the levels of highway construction and building contracts for the next five years. They are shown in Table 19.13.

TABLE 19.13. Forecast of Highway Construction and Building Contracts

PERIOD	HIGHWAY CONSTRUCTION (Millions of dollars)	BUILDING CONTRACTS (Millions of dollars)
18	19.26	103.60
19	19.06	107.60
20	16.32	109.18
21	20.02	121.34
22	20.78	130.22

Using the equation computed in Part a, forecast Longhorn's cement shipments for each of the next five years.

f. Repeat this forecasting analysis using the equation computed in Part d.

g. From the statistical measures, which equation do you feel should provide a better forecast? Explain.

h. Actual Longhorn cement shipments in periods 18 through 22 were 1.806, 1.894, 1.896, 2.098, 2.304. Compare the forecasting performance of the two equations calculating the MAD, MSE, and the MAPE figures. Did the comparative performance agree with your impressions about which would be the better forecasting equation?

i. Compare the forecasting performance found in Part h with the calculated MAD, MSE and MAPE figures for the trend forecasting equation computed in Problem 15. Evaluate. Do the statistical measures (standard deviation of residuals, r^2) suggest the observed difference in performance?

17. Refer again to the data on the 17 annual time periods collected for Longhorn Sand and Cement on the variables *cement shipments, highway construction,* and *building contracts.*

a. Calculate the multiple regression equation that relates the dependent variable *cement shipment* to the two independent variables *highway construction* and *building contracts*.

b. Interpret the meaning of the regression coefficients.

c. How well do these explain the variation in Longhorn's cement shipments?

d. Calculate the standard deviation of the residuals. Explain why the comparison of the same statistic for each simple regression performed would indicate the forecasting gain that has been made.

e. On the basis of the projected data given in 16e for highway construction and building contracts for periods 18 through 22, forecast cement shipments over periods 18 to 22.

f. Is there any evidence of multicollinearity? If there was, would it render unreliable your forecast of cement shipment? Explain.

g. Calculate the MAD, MSE, and MAPE values for the five forecasts versus the actual values given in 16h. How does the forecasting performance compare with the single equation discussed in Problem 16?

h. Plot the residuals from the multiple regression against the predicted Y values (fitted Y values). Is there any evidence of curvilinearity?

i. Now plot the residuals against the variable *time*. Is there any evidence of serial correlation? If there were serial correlation, how would you adjust your forecast?

18. Refer to the data presented in Problem 16 on Longhorn Sand and Cement. The three variables *cement shipments, highway construction,* and *building contracts* exhibit a growth rate over the seventeen periods. One approach recommended to lessen the curvilinearity and serial correlation that accompanies a strong growth component in the data is to transform the variables to annual percentage changes and then to perform the regression analysis on the transformed variables. Table 19.14 shows the 16 observations of yearly percentage changes for the three variables of interest.

a. Estimate the multiple regression equation relating annual percentage changes in shipments to annual percentage changes in highway construction and building contracts.

b. Interpret the meaning of each of the regression coefficients.

c. How well do the independent variables explain the percentage changes in shipments now that the growth component previously linking the variables has been eliminated? Does this suggest that the fore-

TABLE 19.14. Yearly Percentage Changes, Longhorn Cement

| OBSERVATION | PERCENTAGE CHANGES FOR THE THREE VARIABLES | | |
	Shipments	Highway Construction	Building Contracts
1	0.351	30.633	9.810
2	19.580	30.039	39.769
3	19.591	−19.821	8.591
4	−0.489	−18.773	6.519
5	12.285	40.961	3.922
6	−4.595	−9.091	13.322
7	34.633	42.321	20.131
8	2.385	−26.474	32.969
9	3.993	5.119	8.086
10	−17.120	−30.195	2.688
11	17.954	31.163	3.785
12	3.601	19.149	0.439
13	−4.107	−16.815	1.529
14	8.896	24.866	11.186
15	18.457	10.029	10.447
16	6.258	1.563	3.854

casting ability of the multiple regression equation using percentage change is inferior to the original multiple regression equation estimated in Problem 17 on the previous page?

d. Evaluate the statistical significance of the regression coefficient and discuss whether this is an issue to consider in using the equation for forecasting.

e. The merit of retaining a variable in the forecasting equation can be judged by its effect on the standard deviation of residuals, a component of the standard error of forecast. A variable ought to be dropped if its exclusion from the equation lowers the standard deviation of residuals. According to this criterion, test each independent variable that seems to make only a marginal contribution. What do you conclude? Is there multicollinearity in the problem that renders the regression coefficient unreliable?

f. Plot the residuals against the predicted Y values (fitted Y values). Is there any evidence of curvilinearity?

g. Plot the residuals against time. Has the serial correlation evidenced in Problem 17 been reduced?

h. For the forecasted data for highway construction and building contracts given in Problem 16e, compute percentage changes for the forecasts for annual time periods 18–22. Forecast shipments for period 18 through period 22 using the multiple regression equation found in Part e.

i. How does the performance of the multiple regression model in Part h compare to the performance of the multiple regression model in 17g? Use MAD, MSE, and MAPE as measures of relative performance. Evaluate.

j. Can you suggest another way to improve the model? Explain.

19. Aware that sales represent the lifeblood of the large retail food store, Safeway management is engaged in strategic planning and wishes to have a quantitative model for projecting the company's future sales. The company's program advocates building larger stores and expanding its product line to include specialty departments (pharmacies, cheese shops, bakeries, etc.)

This will improve its profit margin because of the higher markups such products afford and offer consumers the type of attractive multi-purpose store they have come to expect. Since the company markets over a wide geographical area in the United States, its sales will be directly linked to the consumer's disposable income as well as Safeway's ability to meet the competition. Correlating past sales with the growth of U.S. personal disposable income and its own store area expansion ought to provide the basis for sales projections. Let us use regression analysis to verify whether such a useful relationship can be found and relied upon to do sales forecasting. Table 19.15 gives the respective figures over the last 18 years.

a. Plot Safeway sales and disposable income for 1963–1980. Does the relationship appear linear?

b. Fit a least squares line with Safeway sales as the dependent variable and disposable income as the independent. Interpret the coefficient.

c. How well does disposable income explain sales? Compute R^2.

d. Compute the standard deviation of the residual. To assess its validity, plot the residuals against the predicted Y values (fitted Y, Y). Does it reveal serial correlation?

e. Realizing that both sales and disposable income exhibit growth rates, perhaps log transformation would be a more appropriate model. Repeat steps a through d again assessing whether the serial correlation persists.

f. Discuss the inherent danger in using such an equation for forecasting. Do you have any recommendations at this point?

20. Refer to Safeway data presented in Problem 19. Now consider the variable *time* as an additional independent variable along with disposable income to explain the growth trend of Safeway sales.

a. Plot Safeway sales against the variable *time*. Does it reveal a strong trend in sales over the 18 years?

b. Estimate a multiple regression equation between Safeway sales as the dependent variable and disposable income and time as the independent variables.

TABLE 19.15. Safeway Sales, U.S. Disposable Income, and Store Area Employed, 1963–1980

YEAR	SAFEWAY SALES (Billions of Dollars)	DISPOSABLE INCOME (Billions of Dollars)	TOTAL SQ. FEET OF STORE (End of Year, Thousands)
1963	2.649	403	28,765
1964	2.817	437	30,795
1965	2.939	472	32,951
1966	3.345	510	35,402
1967	3.360	544	37,850
1968	3.685	588	39,033
1969	4.099	630	40,169
1970	4.860	686	41,769
1971	5.358	743	42,752
1972	6.057	801	44,844
1973	6.773	902	46,480
1974	8.185	985	50,159
1975	9.716	1087	51,854
1976	10.422	1184	52,223
1977	11.249	1305	55,184
1978	12.559	1462	57,461
1979	13.717	1641	59,470
1980	15.102	1821	62,069

Source: *Survey of Current Business,* Safeway *Annual Reports*

c. How does the equation compare with the simple regression equation excluding time performed in Problem 19 in accounting for the variability in Safeway sales? Specifically, compare the standard deviation of residuals and reliability of the coefficient for time.

d. Plot the residuals versus predicted Y values (fitted Y). Assess whether the serial correlation found in Problem 19 has been reduced. What do you conclude?

e. Repeat steps a through d but for the multiple regression of log Safeway sales versus log disp. inc. and the natural values of time. Do you see an improvement in the equation's diagnostics that would merit its consideration as a forecasting tool?

21. Refer to the data on Safeway stores presented in Problem 19. Now consider the use of the variable *store area* as an additional variable in the regression equation. It may be that the variability of Safeway sales can be attributable to the fact that store space is changing.

a. Plot Safeway sales against the variable *store area*. Does it reveal that both variables experienced strong growth?

b. Compute a multiple regression equation with Safeway sales as dependent variable and disposable income and store area as explanatory variables. Interpret the coefficients. Do you think the store area variable was "too large" a number to be used in the regression?

c. Compare the standard deviation of residuals and R^2 of this equation with the simple regression equation excluding store area computed in Problem 19. How well does this compare?

d. Plot residuals versus predicted value of Y (Fitted Y). Has the serial correlation problem been lessened by the inclusion of the variable *store area*? What is the implication for the equation as a forecasting tool now?

22. Refer to the quarterly data on 4 Day Tire Stores presented in Problem 10. Doris Carr, in her search for a sales forecasting tool that relies only on time pattern in the data itself, has in a recent business seminar come across the Box Jenkins approach. Although she has only 44 observations and a minimum of 50 is recommended, she thought she should give it a try. The following steps were taken:

Step 1   Upon inspection of the sequence plot of the original 44 quarters of sales and its autocorrelation function ACF, first differences were thought appropriate.

Step 2   First differences were taken. Upon viewing their sequence plot and auto correlation function, fourth differencing of the first differences was performed. The original series now has been double-differenced.

Step 3   The autocorrelation of the double-differences suggested an autoregression with the double difference term DD_t as the dependent variable and with two lag terms DD_{t-1} (lag one of DD) and DD_{t-4} (lag four of DD) as dependent terms; $\widehat{DD}_t = f(DD_{t-1}, DD_{t-4})$.

Table 19.16 presents the data of the original series and the series after differencing the original data. The computer output that follows shows the analysis and appropriate diagnostics used. The output is from the Minitab program.

a. Elaborate more fully on each of the steps taken in the analysis commenting on its rationale, on what has been accomplished, and on what needs to be accomplished subsequently.

b. Perform the multiple regression using the last three columns of data in the table as suggested in Step 3. Discuss the merits of retaining each of the lags.

c. Predict from your analysis the first two quarters of 1981 sales for 4 Day Tire Stores.

d. Actual sales of 4 Day Tire Stores came in at 4,466,812 and 5,322,532. What is your forecast error? What percentage does it represent of the actual sales figure?

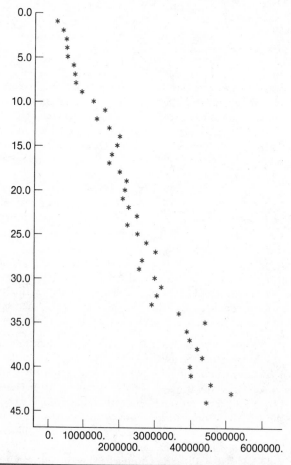

Step 1a Sequence Plot of Original 4 Day Time Sales

TABLE 19.16. Data for 4 Day Tire Stores

		COLUMN			
	1	2	3	4	5
ROW	ORIGINAL SALES	FIRST DIFFERENCES	DOUBLE DIFFERENCES	LAG ONE OF DD	LAG FOUR OF DD
1	230313.				
2	333537.	103224.			
3	409018.	75481.			
4	415177.	6159.			
5	466557.	51380.			
6	620211.	153654.	50430.		
7	699411.	79200.	3719.	50430.	
8	727220.	27809.	21650.	3719.	
9	860505.	133285.	81905.	21650.	
10	1244259.	383754.	230100.	81905.	50430.
11	1574046.	329787.	250587.	230100.	3719.
12	1281289.	−292757.	−320566.	250587.	21650.
13	1666896.	385607.	252322.	−320566.	81905.
14	1942136.	275240.	−108514.	252322.	230100.
15	1856700.	−85436.	−415223.	−108514.	−250587.
16	1722577.	−134123.	158634.	−415223.	−320566.
17	1657794.	−64783.	−450390.	158634.	252322.
18	1960692.	302898.	27658.	−450390.	−108514.
19	2144877.	184185.	269621.	27658.	415223.
20	2098829.	−46048.	88075.	269621.	158634.
21	2035646.	−63183.	1600.	88075.	−450390.
22	2242968.	207322.	−95576.	1600.	27658.
23	2447295.	204327.	20142.	−95576.	269621.
24	2190975.	−256320.	−210272.	20142.	88075.
25	2467032.	276057.	339240.	−210272.	1600.
26	2739593.	272561.	65239.	339240.	−95576.
27	2989866.	250273.	45946.	65239.	20142.
28	2590964.	−398902.	−142582.	45946.	−210272.
29	2442404.	−148560.	−424617.	−142582.	339240.
30	2966955.	524551.	251990.	−424617.	65239.
31	3136669.	169714.	−80559.	251990.	45946.
32	3016982.	−119687.	279215.	−80559.	−142582.
33	2857033.	−159949.	−11389.	279215.	−424617.
34	3683926.	826893.	302342.	−11389.	251990.
35	4342308.	658382.	488668.	302342.	−80559.
36	3808919.	−533389.	−413702.	488668.	279215.
37	3907138.	98219.	258168.	−413702.	−11389.
38	4167928.	260790.	−566103.	258168.	302342.
39	4273815.	105887.	−552495.	−566103.	488668.
40	3938207.	−335608.	197781.	−552495.	−413702.
41	3966566.	28359.	−69860.	197781.	258168.
42	4553981.	587415.	326625.	−69860.	−566103.
43	5125848.	571867.	465980.	326625.	−552495.
44	4404604.	−721244.	−385636.	465980.	197781.

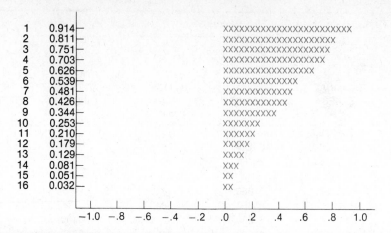

1	0.914
2	0.811
3	0.751
4	0.703
5	0.626
6	0.539
7	0.481
8	0.426
9	0.344
10	0.253
11	0.210
12	0.179
13	0.129
14	0.081
15	0.051
16	0.032

Step 1b Autocorrelation Function of Original Sales

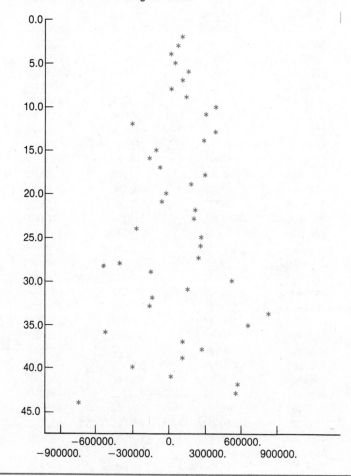

Step 2a Sequence Plot of First Differences

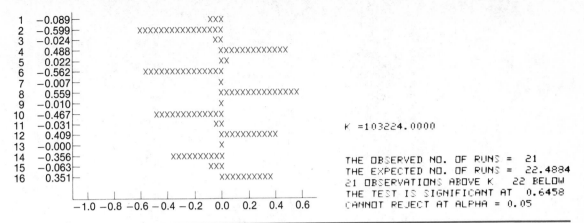

1	−0.089	XXX
2	−0.599	XXXXXXXXXXXXXXX
3	−0.024	XX
4	0.488	XXXXXXXXXXXXX
5	0.022	XX
6	−0.562	XXXXXXXXXXXXXX
7	−0.007	X
8	0.559	XXXXXXXXXXXXXXX
9	−0.010	X
10	−0.467	XXXXXXXXXXXX
11	−0.031	XX
12	0.409	XXXXXXXXXX
13	−0.000	X
14	−0.356	XXXXXXXXXX
15	−0.063	XXX
16	0.351	XXXXXXXXX

K = 103224.0000

THE OBSERVED NO. OF RUNS = 21
THE EXPECTED NO. OF RUNS = 22.4884
21 OBSERVATIONS ABOVE K   22 BELOW
THE TEST IS SIGNIFICANT AT   0.6458
CANNOT REJECT AT ALPHA = 0.05

Step 2b Autocorrelation Function of First Differences

Step 2c Runs Test on First Differences

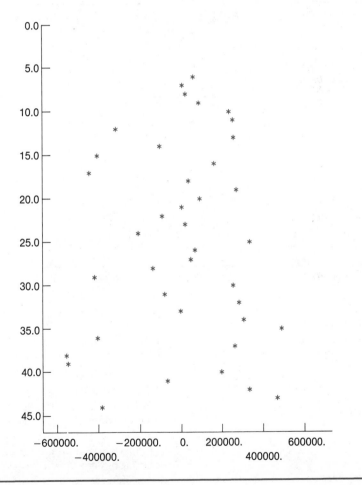

Step 2d Sequence Plot of Double Differences

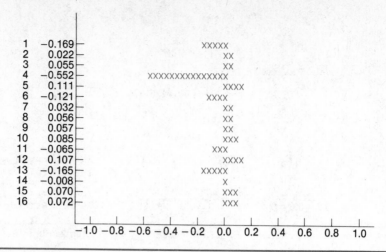

Step 2e Autocorrelation Function of Double Differences

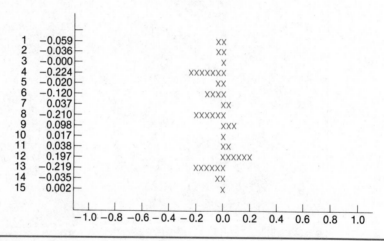

Step 3a Autocorrelation Function of Residuals of Autoregression of DD

23. Is multicollinearity a problem that one should be concerned about given that the correlation matrix of the variables used in Problem 21 shows the following:

	Sales	Disposable Income
Disposable Income	.995	
Store Area	.971	.971

Explain.

b. If the equation computed in Prob 21 shows notable improvement for forecasting (lower serial correlation, lower standard deviation of residuals) over the simple regression excluding area, forecast 1981 Safeway sales using 1945 billion dollars as income projection and the company report of an additional store area of 3 million square feet.

24. Refer to the data on Safeway stores presented in Problem 19. Convert the original 18 observations on the three variables to annual percent changes (17 observations).

a. Estimate the multiple regression equation relating percentage changes in Safeway sales to percentage changes in the independent variables *disposable income* and *store area*.

b. Explain the meaning of the multiple

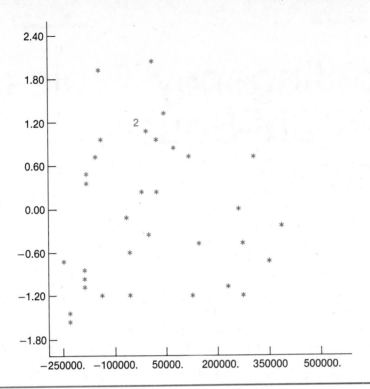

Step 3b Scatter Plot of Residuals Versus Fitted Y of Autoregression of DD

regression equation coefficients.

c. How well does the percentage change in the independent variables explain the percentage changes in Safeway sales? Compute R^2. Have we lost considerable explanatory power with this equation compared to multiple regression estimated in Problem 21? Explain.

d. Plot residuals versus predicted values of Y (Fitted Y). Has the use of the three variables in percentage change terms improved the serial correlation problem plaguing Problem 21? What did this accomplish for forecasting purposes?

e. Forecast 1981 Safeway sales on the basis of 1945 billion dollars as income projection and company projection of an additional store area of 3 million square feet.

Contingency Tables and Chi-Square Analysis

Preview. Analysis of bivariate relationships was first studied in Chapter 14. There, regression and correlation analysis were applied to quantitative bivariate data. In this chapter we turn to the case of categorical variables such as brand of laundry detergent or marital status. Bivariate analysis of categorical data focuses on the relationship, if any, between the two variables. The principle tool of analysis is a table of bivariate frequencies known as a *contingency table*.

The bivariate relationship found in a particular set of sample data does not necessarily generalize to the population from which the data were drawn. It could merely be a sampling fluke. To find out whether the relationship between the variables is present in the population, the null hypothesis can be tested using a sample statistic known as the chi-square statistic.

20.1. Introduction

A telling characteristic of an effectively functioning business organization is its comprehension and exploitation of the relationship between key business variables. The statistical procedures for the analysis of bivariate relationships between two quantitative variables were discussed in Chapter 14. Those procedures required numerical measurements on both variables. Since categorical variables do not involve numerical measurements, the procedures studied in Chapter 14 are not applicable. In this chapter, our study is extended to include some statistical tests designed to detect bivariate relationships between two categorical variables. In the next chapter our study will be extended to one quantitative and one categorical variable—a hybrid situation.

Once a relationship is confirmed, the follow-up step is to examine the extent (nature) of the relationship.

20.2. Cross Classification

What is your age? Where do you live? Are you male or female? These are standard questions on survey research questionnaires. Such personal background information "demographics" are routinely sought along with information on the individual's behavior, activities, interests, and attitudes towards particular topics. The individual responses to each question are typically summarized for the group surveyed and the summaries organized to fashion a "group profile". If the group consists of chief executive officers (CEOs), a "CEO profile" is developed; if the group members are newly graduated MBAs, a "newly graduated MBA profile" is produced.

A partial view of a questionnaire surveying the career advancement of middle managers is shown in Figure 20.1.

FIGURE 20.1. Survey of Middle Managers

Please check the appropriate box:

SEX:	MARITAL STATUS:	PROMOTIONAL STATUS:
MALE ☐	SINGLE ☐	PROMOTED IN LAST 3 YEARS ☐
FEMALE ☐	MARRIED ☐	NOT PROMOTED IN LAST THREE YEARS ☐
	DIVORCED ☐	

This particular questionnaire asks from the respondent demographic information on three categorical variables: sex, marital status, and the respondent's promotional history.

The Quest for Generalizations

Why ask for such demographic information in a study of career advancement? Is it important to know more than that one individual, J. T. Jones, was promoted and that another individual, M. R. Smith, wasn't? What is gained by knowing, for example, that J. T. Jones is a man and that M. R. Smith is a woman?

J. T. Jones or M. R. Smith are seldom of interest to researchers *per se;* that is, as unique individuals. But *generalizations* about their distinguishing features often are of interest. In other words, do the individuals who are classified into a particular category have one or more identifiable features in common? If so, what are these common features and do they distinguish individuals in the category from individuals not in the category? For instance,

> what common features distinguish the group of promoted persons from the group who haven't been promoted? Could one of the features be that the members of the promoted group are predominantly male?

A generalization like this would be of much greater interest than a mere list of the names of promoted individuals, especially if it is the issue of equal opportunity for women that is being investigated. The investigator would surely want the questionnaire to include a male/female checkoff together with the promotion variable to find out whether gender (along with job performance) plays a role in career advancement.

Note that the information is collected on individuals. The study, however, focuses on generalizations pertaining to groups, not individuals. How can information collected on individuals be organized to infer generalizations about members of a group, say of the promotion history of male versus female executives? Let us illustrate.

Cross-classification

The process of making generalizations about groups begins by classifying individuals into groups according to characteristics that are common to members of the group. Suppose each executive queried in the survey possesses a title indicating his or her position within the organization. By defining the categorical variable "executive position", the many titles can be organized into sub-groups or categories. Any particular executive can be classified according to his or her specific title as an observation on some particular category: production manager, director of industrial relations, etc. After all the individuals are classified into categories, analysis can be done by category rather than by individuals.

Typically, the classification of individuals into categories is done according to more than one grouping or categorical variable. For instance, executives can be characterized by their seniority as well as by their title. So any particular executive possessing a specific title *and* a specific seniority can be *cross-classified* as a bivariate observation on a particular combination of the title and seniority categories. Combinations of specific categories on two different categorical variables are called *cross-classification cells*. The entire set of cross-classification cells can be organized into a cross-classification table. Figure 20.2 is an example of such a table.

FIGURE 20.2. Cross-classification of Promotional Status and Gender

		PROMOTIONAL STATUS	
		P	Not P
GENDER	F	F & P	F & not P
	M	M & P	M & not P

Counting the Cross-classification Possibilities

How many cross-classification cells are possible? The total number depends, of course, on how many categories there are for each categorical variable.

There are two categories for gender and two for promotional status. There are then $2 \times 2 = 4$ cross-classification cells.

For any two categorical variables, the number of cross-classification cells will be $M \times N$, where M is the number of categories for one variable and N the number of categories for the second variable.

The different cross-classification cells can have differences in meaning which are very important to a manager. For example, an advertising manager surely will not be indifferent to the cross-classifications of persons according to product usage potential and readership status of the company's advertising.

It is the job of the advertising manager to match the audience of the company sponsored advertising messages and the people who use, or at least might potentially use, the product the company sells. Allocating the advertising budget to an audience composed of persons who aren't good prospects for the company's products is an unproductive use of cash which severely limits the firm's ability to reach prospective buyers of the products.

How can a cross-classification table help the advertising manager to zero in on a media use problem?

Example 20.2.   An Advertising Placement Problem

Suppose a large bicycle manufacturer like Schwinn faces a decision of whether or not to go promotionally heavy in a specialty magazine, *Cycling*. Figure 20.3 shows four cross-classification cells, one for each possible match up between the membership status in the target market of prospective bicycle purchasers and the readership status of *Cycling*.

FIGURE 20.3. Cross-classification of Purchasing Status and *Cycling* Reader

		READERSHIP STATUS	
		Reader	Not Reader
PURCHASING STATUS	Prospect	Prospect Reader Match	Unreached Prospect
	Non-Prospect	Wasted Advertising	No Gain No Loss

The four cross-classification cells in Figure 20.3 have totally different implications for the advertiser.

The top left quadrant matches readers and prospects. That is, prospective purchasers are reached by the advertising. The more people found in this cell, the more productive are advertising expenditures.

The bottom left cell represents people reached by the advertising but who are not prospective purchasers. Unfortunately, the advertiser is charged for the magazine's total circulation and that includes the people in this cell. This cell represents wasted advertising dollars, so the fewer the people in this cell, the better the situation for the advertiser.

The top right cell represents an unreached segment of the target market of prospective purchasers. Because they don't read *Cycling* Magazine, they cannot be reached by advertising in it. It would also be advantageous for the advertiser if the number of people in this cell was minimal.

The bottom right cell represents a cell of no particular interest to the advertiser. These are people who don't read *Cycling* and therefore won't be exposed to advertising in it, and who are not in the market for a bicycle anyway. No advertising dollars will be spent reaching these non-prospects. The number of people in this cell is of no concern to the advertiser.

What does this cross-classification accomplish? The joint frequencies of the cells can now be analyzed to uncover the underlying relationship or *association* between the two categorical variables. Job performance evaluations, credit operations, bank loan operations, and marketing operations are just a few of the many situations in which contingency tables are used to define important relationships between two variables.

20.3. Contingency Tables

The number of bivariate observations in each cell of a cross-classification table is known as the *joint frequency of the cell.* The entire set of cells with their joint frequencies is commonly called a *contingency table.* A contingency table segments the entire surveyed group into subgroups defined by the cross-classification cells.

Using a Contingency Table to Assess Effectiveness of Advertising Media

The four cross-classifications given in Figure 20.3 are the cells of the contingency table shown in Table 20.1. A hypothetical population of 200 million adults has been classified according to two variables—purchasing status (with respect to purchasing a new bicycle) and readership status (with respect to *Cycling* Magazine). The former variable has two categories (prospect and non-prospect) given in the *rows* of the table. The latter variable indicates subscription status with respect to *Cycling* Magazine. The two categories of this variable (reader and non-reader) are given in the *columns* of the table.

TABLE 20.1. Contingency Table for Purchasing and Readership Status of *Cycling* Magazine in a Hypothetical Community of 200 Million Persons

VARIABLE: PURCHASING STATUS	VARIABLE: READERSHIP STATUS Reader (R) (Millions of Persons)	Non-Reader (R')	Row Totals	Marginal Frequencies
Prospects (P)	1.9	18.1	20.0	(of P)
Nonprospects (P')	0.1	179.9	180.0	(of P')
Column Totals	2.0	198.0	200.0	
Marginal Frequencies	(of R)	(of R')		

The column on the extreme right shows the row totals. These row totals are the *marginal frequencies* of the two categories of the purchase status variable.

The marginal frequencies indicate that of the 200 million persons in the population, 20 million are prospective bicycle purchasers and 180 million are not.

The frequencies in the bottom row represent the *column totals.* These column totals are the marginal frequencies for the two categories of the readership variable.

Of the 200 million persons in the population, the marginal frequencies are 2 million for the readers of *Cycling* Magazine, and 198 million for those persons who are not readers of *Cycling.*

The four joint frequencies in the cells of the table are collectively called *cross-tabulations* or "cross-tabs" by survey researchers. Segmenting the 200 million population into these four cells reveals the following information of potential value to a bicycle manufacturer considering *Cycling* as an advertising medium:

The figure in the top left cell reveals that 1.9 million prospective purchasers read *Cycling* and can therefore be reached by advertising in the magazine.

The frequency in the bottom left cell shows that there are only 0.1 million magazine readers who aren't prospective bicycle purchasers. Compared with the above information that 1.9 million prospective purchasers are reached, it appears that very little advertising money would be wasted on non-prospects.

Of more concern is the 18.1 million prospective purchasers in the upper right cell who can't be reached by advertising in *Cycling*. Some other means would have to be found for reaching them, and they constitute the larger segment of the total market.

Finally, it is noted that 179.9 million persons, the overwhelming majority of the population, are neither prospects for a new bicycle nor readers of *Cycling*.

How large is the market of potential purchasers of new bicycles?

Twenty million persons, the marginal frequency of *prospective purchasers*.

How popular is *Cycling* Magazine?

Two million is the marginal *readership frequency*.

And how is readership *related* to purchasing status? That is revealed through an analysis of the *joint* frequencies.

Table 20.1 reports absolute frequencies. However, contingency tables can also be constructed to report the cell's joint *relative* frequencies. The joint relative frequency of a cell is the ratio of a cell's joint absolute frequency to the sum of the joint absolute frequencies of *all* the cells in the table. Why use relative frequencies? They are usually easier to interpret than absolute frequencies and are more useful in analyzing a relationship. Table 20.2 shows the results of the conversion to relative frequencies from the absolute frequencies presented in Table 20.1.

TABLE 20.2. Contingency Table for Purchasing Status and Readership of *Cycling* Magazine in a Hypothetical Population of 200 Million Persons (Relative Frequencies)

PURCHASING STATUS	READERSHIP STATUS		Row Totals
	R	R'	
P	.0095	.0905	.1000
P'	.0005	.8995	.9000
Column Totals	.0100	.9900	1.0000

Useful Properties of Contingency Tables

Analyzing the rows of the table, notice that:

1. the joint relative frequencies across any row sum to the marginal relative frequency for that row. For the two purchase categories, P and P', we have

.0095 + .0905 = .1000 = Marginal Relative Frequency of P

.0005 + .8995 = .9000 = Marginal Relative Frequency of P'

2. the summation of the row marginal relative frequencies (in the Totals column) for the two purchase status categories must equal one.

.1000 + .9000 = 1.000

Likewise, in analyzing the columns, note that:

3. the joint relative frequencies down each column sum to the marginal relative frequency for that column. For the two readership categories, R and R', we have

.0095 + .0005 = .0100 = Marginal Relative Frequency of R

.0905 + .8995 = .9900 = Marginal Relative Frequency of R'

4. the summation of the column marginal relative frequencies of the readership categories (in the Totals row) must equal one.

.0100 + .9900 = 1.000

What properties are common to all bivariate relative frequency tables? There are two:

1. the *sum* of *joint* relative frequencies across a particular row or down a particular column equals the marginal relative frequency of that row or column, and

2. the sum of the *row* marginal relative frequencies must sum to one, as must the sum of the *column* marginal relative frequencies.

20.4. Conditional Relative Frequencies: Interpretations and Misinterpretations

The boldface numbers in Table 20.3 are the result of forming a ratio from corresponding relative frequencies in Table 20.2. The ratios are calculated by dividing each joint relative frequency by the appropriate column marginal relative frequency. For example:

.950 = .0095/.01   .091 = .0905/.99
.050 = .0005/.01   .909 = .8995/.99

These calculated numbers (boldface in Table 20.3) are called (column) *conditional* frequencies. Conditional frequencies can also be calculated using row marginal frequencies as divisors. The row conditional frequencies differ in value from the column conditional frequencies.

Relationships in the reported data are indicated by a comparison of the appropriate conditional relative frequencies. Table 20.3, for example, reports the

TABLE 20.3. Purchase Status, Given Readership Status

PURCHASE STATUS	READERSHIP STATUS	
	(R)	(R')
(P)	.950	.091
(P')	.050	.909
Totals	1.000	1.000

relationship between purchase status and the classification with respect to reader-ship status. Note the difference in the incidence of purchasers between *readers* and *nonreaders*. The .950 value for readers means that 95 percent of *Cycling's* 2 million readers are prospective purchasers. This percentage is more than ten times the incidence of prospective purchasers among nonreaders of *Cycling*. Only 9.1 percent of nonreaders are prospective purchasers. The greater prevalence of prospective purchasers among readers than among nonreaders of *Cycling* magazine describes a strong *relationship* or association between purchase status and readership status among the group of persons surveyed. That is, knowing that the person is a reader, the chances of that person being a prospective pur-chaser would be (subjectively assessed as) ten times more likely than if that person were known to be a nonreader of *Cycling*.

Exploiting Differences in Conditional Relative Frequencies

Management can often exploit the relationship found between conditional relative frequencies. In this case, *Cycling's* management would use the rela-tionship between purchase status and readership status to attract "paid ads". The profits of *Cycling*, as with many specialty magazines, ride the paid-ads roller coaster—plunging when ads drop off dramatically, climbing rapidly as total revenue increases. Recognizing this sensitivity of profits to advertising, *Cycling's* management tries to promote more advertising by disseminating the type of infor-mation in which media buyers are keenly interested. *Cycling* surveys its sub-scription readers, obtaining demographic characteristics and purchase habits. *Cycling's* pitch to the Schwinn media buyers would be expected to emphasize advertising *purity*—that *Cycling* readers are prime prospects for new bicycle equipment and that very little money spent on advertising in *Cycling* is wasted on non-prospective purchasers. In short, an ad in *Cycling* would be the best buy for the money.

A Pitfall in Interpreting Conditional Frequencies

With the profile of *Cycling* readers matching closely Schwinn's target customers, *Cycling* ads do offer a low cost per prospective customer. This is an intuitively appealing procedure for allocating advertising expenditures, but there is a basic flaw. What percentage of Schwinn's target market does *Cycling* reach? Regardless of the fact that *Cycling* may offer the lowest cost per prospect, it *may not reach enough prospects*. It may be as Figure 20.4 shows—solid on purity but short on reach.

For a given size advertising budget, the purpose of Schwinn advertising is not to maintain purity but to maximize target market reach—a goal better satisfied perhaps by a general purpose magazine like *Time* or *Sports Illustrated*. Advertis-ing in *Cycling* may simply be duplicating a portion of the target audience already reached by the general purpose magazines.

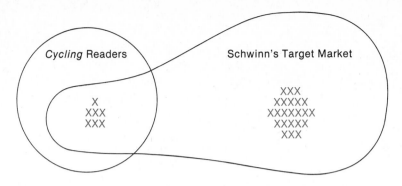

Cycling Readers

Schwinn's Target Market

X
XXX
XXX

XXX
XXXXX
XXXXXXX
XXXXX
XXX

FIGURE 20.4 Every *Cycling* Reader Is in Schwinn's Target Market but not Vice Versa

The "Convenient Data" Trap

The degree of advertising purity is given by column R in Table 20.3. Advertising reach is not given. Unless the Schwinn media buyers are keyed in to the fact that high advertising purity is not synonymous with high advertising reach, they might *not* insist on having the necessary information prior to choosing the media. After all, it would not be in the best interest of *Cycling* to point out the purity vs. reach problem, nor would one expect *Cycling* to hand over the relevant reach statistics on a silver platter, even if they were available. So unless Schwinn has a complete list of its target market purchase prospects and knows what percentage of them are readers of *Cycling*, it is understandable why Schwinn's media buyers could be pressured to work with the purity information *Cycling* is gladly willing to supply. But by using *Cycling's* advertising purity as a guideline to place the company's ads, Schwinn's media buyers would fall victim to the prevalent "convenient data" trap: using the most conveniently available information rather than the relevant information.

The Schwinn advertising manager needs evidence on advertising reach. This is not available directly and is not equivalent to the advertising purity evidence which is available. The manager appears to be stymied. However, is there a way of *indirectly* converting evidence on advertising purity to evidence on advertising reach?

Before attempting to answer this question, let us examine in closer detail the distinction between advertising purity and advertising reach and the relationship that links the two.

Different Types of Relationships Between Conditional Relative Frequencies:
Advertising Purity Versus Advertising Reach

Cycling's advertising purity is defined by a particular conditional relative frequency. It is the incidence of purchase prospects among readers of *Cycling* magazine. Algebraically it can be expressed as

$$RF(P|R) = \frac{RF(R \text{ and } P)}{RF(R)}$$

The three parts of this equation are as follows:

$RF(P \text{ and } R) = .0095 =$ the *joint* relative frequency of purchase prospects and *Cycling* readers

$RF(R) = .01 =$ the *marginal* relative frequency of *Cycling* readership

$RF(P|R) = \dfrac{.0095}{.01} = .95 =$ the conditional relative frequency of purchase prospects among the readers of *Cycling*

The conditional relative frequency defining *Cycling's* advertising reach is the incidence of readership among prospective purchasers. Algebraically, it then follows

$$RF(R|P) = \frac{RF(R \text{ and } P)}{RF(P)} = \frac{.0095}{.10} = .095$$

The two new parts of this equation are:

$RF(P) = .10 =$ the marginal frequency of prospective purchasers

$RF(R|P) =$ the conditional frequency of *Cycling* readers among purchase prospects $= .095$

Why is advertising purity *not the same* as advertising reach? The numerator $RF(R \text{ and } P)$ for both expressions is identical. But the denominators differ—$RF(R)$ in the case of advertising purity versus $RF(P)$ in the case of advertising reach. A little reordering of terms establishes the link between them:

$$RF(R \text{ and } P) = RF(R) \times RF(P|R) = RF(P) \times RF(R|P)$$

$$RF(R|P) = RF(P|R)\frac{RF(R)}{RF(P)}$$

$$.095 = .95\left[\frac{.01}{.10}\right]$$

Therefore, advertising reach = advertising purity $\times$ the ratio of readers to prospects. In this instance, advertising reach is only one-tenth the value of advertising purity, because the ratio of readers to prospects is only one to ten.

Taking Advantage of Indirect Evidence

As one can see, advertising reach can be obtained *indirectly* from two pieces of information:

1. advertising purity, the incidence of prospective buyers among subscribers to *Cycling* Magazine, and

2. the ratio of readers to prospective buyers.

Since the first piece of information (.95 value) will likely be supplied by *Cycling's* "promotional" effort, we need only obtain the ratio figure. The numerator of the ratio, *Cycling's* total readership, should be readily available from the publisher. Schwinn's market analysts should have estimates of the total market potential for bicycles. So Schwinn executives should be able to piece together an estimate of this ratio. If these two figures are not available or are of a highly doubtful quality, Schwinn could commission a bicycle user survey with media readership questions. Whichever information route is used, one can estimate

the number of prospective bicycle buyers to the number of readers of a special interest magazine on bicycling.

From this knowledge alone it follows that the incidence of readers among prospective buyers ($RF(R|P)$, *Cycling's* reach) must be only some fraction of the .95 value (for $RF(P|R)$, *Cycling's* purity). Hence, it would be rather foolhardy for a media buyer to assume that the conveniently available figure on *Cycling's* advertising purity could be perfectly substituted for the needed figure on *Cycling's* advertising reach.

Let us reinforce this important point. Assume that information on the incidence of *Cycling* readership, $RF(R)$, to the incidence of prospective buyers, $RF(P)$, have been gathered. Reordering of the expression linking purity to reach shows that an equivalence can be established between two ratios:

$$\frac{RF(R|P)}{RF(P|R)} = \frac{RF(R)}{RF(P)}$$

The left hand term is the ratio of the conditional relative frequency expressing *Cycling's* advertising reach to the conditional relative frequency expressing *Cycling's* advertising purity; whereas the right hand term is the ratio of *Cycling's* readership prevalence in the population to prospective bicycle purchaser prevalence in the population.

Assuming that the market research indicates ten times as many bicycle purchasing prospects as readers of *Cycling* Magazine, that is, the ratio $RF(R)/RF(P) = .01/.10$, what important point can be inferred? Using the equivalence ratios, it is logical to infer that *Cycling advertising purity must be ten times greater than Cycling advertising reach.* No matter how high the advertising purity, *Cycling* will not have high reach. But knowing the purity and the ratio in the population of *Cycling's* readership prevalence to prospective bicycle purchaser prevalence, the correct reach figure can be established. Once it has been learned, a decision can be made as to whether advertising in *Cycling* is worth its cost.

The lesson in this example can be summarized in three key points with respect to purity and reach in particular, and between different types of conditional relative frequencies in general.

1. You should know the difference between advertising purity and advertising reach; that is, the difference between $RF(P|R)$ and $RF(R|P)$.

2. You should know that figures on reach and purity are not direct substitutes for each other. You cannot use $RF(P|R)$ when you need $RF(R|P)$.

3. You should know how to indirectly compute reach from purity or vice versa. To illustrate: if there are five times as many prospective purchasers

of a product as readers of a magazine in which the product is advertised, the magazine's reach is only one-fifth its purity.

20.5. The Relationship Between Two Categorical Variables: Samples Versus Populations

Suppose an investigator finds a relationship in cross-classified sample data. Can it be legitimately assumed that there exists a corresponding bivariate relationship in the population? Not necessarily. Just as in the univariate case, the cause of the sample relationship could merely be sampling variability. In other words, the sample relationship could be spurious—a random sampling fluke which would disappear if the entire population was considered. Recognizing this, how can an investigator proceed to make an inferential statement about the population relationship?

Is the Observed Relationship a Sampling Fluke?

One common approach to bivariate inference is devising a rigorous test procedure. The test procedure first sets up a null hypothesis that claims that there is no population bivariate relationship. Then it requires calculating the probability of finding a sample value as extreme as the one observed would if we consider the null hypothesis as true. If the chances (prob-value) are very low, then the null hypothesis of no population relationship between the two cross-classified categorical variables can be rejected. The investigator can now be very confident that the observed sample relationship is not a fluke but rather a true reflection of the relationship that exists in the bivariate population. An inferential statement confirming this belief can then be made.

Equivalent to the null hypothesis claim of no bivariate population relationship is the statement that the two categorical variables are *statistically independent*. The following example employs such an "independence" test in a business situation.

Example 20.5. Television Advertising and Brand Usage

"Buying air time" stands high on the list of responsibilities that go with an (advertising) media manager's job. The assumption is that a good ad placed on a T.V. program with the right audience will get the exposure that leads to increased usage of the advertised brand.

Which programs have the right audience? The media manager's job depends on providing good answers to this question. A hunch is not likely to satisfy the ad agency's client. The client usually wants the initial and continued commitment of funds to be based on measured ad effectiveness. How is the effectiveness of an ad campaign verified? One way is to establish the existence of a bivariate relationship between viewer and brand usage. If the ad campaign is to be effective, the expectation is that a higher incidence of brand usage will be found among viewers than among nonviewers of a program on which the ad is shown.

Consider measuring the effectiveness of ads for a liquid starch brand aired on the "Hollywood Squares" program. Are they helping the sales of the brand? (This problem was first discussed in Chapter 2.)

A survey program using a random sample of consumers asks questions on both viewership of "Hollywood Squares" and usage of liquid starch. The original data tabulations are shown in Table 20.4[1] Table 20.5 shows the same data converted to relative frequencies.

TABLE 20.4. Advertised Brand Usage of Liquid Starch Versus Viewership of *Hollywood Squares*

| | VIEWERSHIP | | |
BRAND USAGE	Viewer	Nonviewer	Total
Use Adv. Brand	76	204	280
Use Another Brand	80	402	482
Do Not Use Product	133	725	858
	289	1331	1620

TABLE 20.5. Advertised Brand Usage Versus Viewership (in Relative Frequencies)

| | VIEWERSHIP | | |
BRAND USAGE	Viewer	Nonviewer	Total
Use Adv. Brand	.047	.126	.173
Use Another Brand	.049	.248	.297
Do Not Use Product	.082	.448	.530
	.178	.822	1.000

Have the television ads on Hollywood Squares been effective in increasing sales? To find out, look at the data comparing brand usage with viewership shown in Table 20.4. Among the 289 viewers of the program, 76 or 26.3% use the advertised brand. This is 11 percentage points more than the advertised brand's usage among non-viewers. What is the source of this increased brand usage? Are its new converts coming from former nonusers who have seen the ads and been converted to users? Or are the ads effective at luring away customers from other competing brands? A *yes* answer to either question indicates that advertising on the Hollywood Squares program has been an effective way to generate new business for the advertised brand of spray starch. However, there is a third, less favorable possibility. Perhaps both interpretations are incorrect.

Could the source of the observed 11 percentage point difference in usage simply be the expected random sampling variation that comes with surveying only 1620 persons from a population of millions of people?

A *yes* answer to this question has important implications. It would imply, for example, that substantially increasing the sample size would cause the observed relationship to disappear, indicating no meaningful relationship between viewership and usage. The main issue, then, is to assess the magnitude and plausibility of encountering such a sampling quirk, if in fact viewership and usage are unrelated (independent) categorical variables as the null hypothesis claims.

To assess the plausibility of the null hypothesis, its implications for sampling must be understood. This requires understanding a bivariate sampling statistic known as *chi-square*.

20.6. Understanding the Chi-Square Statistic

If viewership and usage are independent variables, what are the chances that a randomly selected person in a sample survey would be both a viewer and a user of the advertised brand? In the case of independent events, the probability of one event occurring does not affect the chance of the other event occurring (this topic was first discussed in Chapter 6). So the chance or joint probability of finding both events occurring together is simply the product of their separate or individual *marginal* probabilities. In other words:

> to calculate the joint probability of finding an individual with both features of two independent categorical variables, one would simply multiply the marginal probability of finding each feature separately.

For example, in the Schwinn-*Cycling* example, suppose the probability of a prospective Schwinn purchaser was .10 and the probability of a *Cycling* reader was .01. If the two events were independent, the probability of a Schwinn prospect who reads *Cycling* would be $(.10)(.01) = .001$. Thus, the joint probability of surveying at random and finding a viewer of "Hollywood Squares" who is also a user of the advertised liquid starch brand is:

$$P\left(\begin{matrix}\text{viewer of program and}\\ \text{user of the brand}\end{matrix}\right) = P\,(\text{program viewer}) \times P\,(\text{brand user})$$

The joint probabilities of the various combinations of viewership and brand usage are shown in Table 20.6 as the product of the respective marginal probabilities.

TABLE 20.6. Joint Probability Table for Viewership and Brand Usage Assuming Independence

BRAND USAGE	VIEWERSHIP	
	Viewer, V	Nonviewer, V'
User of Adv. Brand, B	$P(V)\,P(B)$	$P(V')\,P(B)$
User of Alternative Brand, A	$P(V)\,P(A)$	$P(V')\,P(A)$
Nonuser of Product, N	$P(V)\,P(N)$	$P(V')\,P(N)$
Marginal Probability	$P(V)$	$P(V')$

How do we find the specific marginal probability values in this table to use in computing the joint probabilities? We don't. At least not their exact values, since that would imply having full knowledge of the respective populations. However, the marginal probabilities should be close in value to the marginal relative frequencies given in the table. Regardless of whether viewership and usage are dependent or independent variables:

Step 1: The (five) marginal probabilities can be *estimated* by using as estimates the marginal *relative frequencies* of the sample.

Table 20.7 shows the relative frequencies as estimates of the marginal probabilities.

TABLE 20.7. Estimated Marginal Probabilities of Viewership and Brand Usage

BRAND USAGE	VIEWERSHIP Viewer V	Nonviewer V'	(Estimated) Marginal Probability
B			.173
A			.297
N			.530
(Estimated) Marginal Probability	.178	.822	1.000

Step 2: If viewership and brand usage are independent categorical variables, the estimated joint probabilities for the various cross-classifications are the product of the estimated *row* marginal probability and estimated *column* marginal probability for the respective categories.

For example, the estimated joint probability of finding in the brand survey a person who is both a viewer and user of the advertised brand is:

$$P(V\&B) = P(V)P(B) = (.178)(.173) = .030794$$

The joint probability table assuming independence is shown in Table 20.8.

TABLE 20.8. Joint Probability Table Assuming Independence

BRAND USAGE	VIEWERSHIP V	V'
B	.030794	.142206
A	.052866	.244134
N	.094340	.435660

The probabilities in this table refer to the chance that when (any) one person is surveyed, he or she will be found to have the particular joint characteristics. But what does this tell us about the implications for the sample of *all* persons canvassed in the survey? Using the estimated joint probabilities, we:

Step 3: Calculate for each cross-classification cell the *expected* (or mean) number of persons in the sample having the specific joint characteristics. Designate this value by E_{ij}, where i represents the row number and j the column number.

Since the persons in the survey are assumed to be randomly drawn (hence independent of one another), the probability distribution for the number of persons falling into a given cross-classification category will follow a *binomial* sampling distribution with parameters n and p. In this case,

n represents the sample size of 1620 and
p represents the estimated joint probability of the cross-classification in question.

The mean or expected number of persons falling into this category in a sample size of n is np. Thus, the *expected frequency* for the specific cross-classification ($V\&B$) "viewers who use the advertised brand" in a sample of 1620 persons would be:

$$E_{ij} = np_{ij} = (1620)(.030794) = 49.8863 \text{ persons}$$

Designate the actually observed frequency in row i and column j by O_{ij}. The actual or *observed* frequency found in this particular survey is 76 persons. Table 20.9 shows the expected frequencies as well as the observed frequencies for each possible cross-classification:

TABLE 20.9. Expected Frequencies Versus Observed Frequencies (Bracketed)

BRAND USAGE	VIEWERSHIP	
	V	V'
B	49.8863 [76]	230.3737 [204]
A	85.6429 [80]	395.4971 [402]
N	152.8308 [133]	705.7692 [725]

Step 4: For each cross-classification cell, the degree of "unusualness" of the observed frequency from the expected frequency is measured by the *deviation* of the actually observed frequency O_{ij} from the expected frequency E_{ij}.

If only one cross-classification were involved, the normal probability distribution could be used to determine how unusual a particular deviation is. However, each cross-classification cell cannot be considered in isolation, but in fact is linked with the others. The expected frequency values in the table, when totaled across rows and down columns of the cells, must give the row and marginal totals shown in Table 20.4.

The statistic used to test the independence assumption is known as the *chi-square* statistic, and its specialized distribution is the *chi-square distribution*.

The chi-square statistic is defined as:

$$\chi^2 = \sum_{ij}[(O_{ij} - E_{ij})^2/E_{ij}]$$

The χ^2 statistic is the sum over all cells of the ratio of the squared difference between observed and expected cell frequencies, to the expected cell frequency.

Step 5: Designate the calculated value of chi-square by χ_c^2 to distinguish it from the value we shall subsequently obtain from the chi-square table in testing the null hypothesis at a given level of significance.

The computation is:

$$\chi_c^2 = \frac{(O_{11} - E_{11})^2}{E_{11}} + \frac{(O_{12} - E_{12})^2}{E_{12}} + \frac{(O_{21} - E_{21})^2}{E_{21}} + \frac{(O_{22} - E_{22})^2}{E_{22}}$$
$$+ \frac{(O_{31} - E_{31})^2}{E_{31}} + \frac{(O_{32} - E_{32})^2}{E_{32}}$$
$$= \frac{(76 - 49.8863)^2}{49.8863} + \frac{(204 - 230.3737)^2}{230.3737} + \frac{(80 - 85.6429)^2}{85.6429}$$
$$+ \frac{(402 - 395.4971)^2}{395.4971} + \frac{(133 - 152.8308)^2}{152.8308} + \frac{(725 - 705.7692)^2}{705.7692}$$
$$= 13.6696 + 3.0193 + 0.3718 + 0.1069 + 2.5732 + 0.5240$$
$$= 20.265$$

In the next section, this computed value of chi-square is used to test the null hypothesis of independence between viewership status and usage status.

20.7. The Chi-Square Distribution and the Chi-Square Test for Independence

What conclusions can be reached based upon the calculated value of 20.265 obtained in the previous section? Before addressing this question, let us formulate a hypothesis to be tested.

Our claim in calculating the expected value E is that the two categorical variables are independent. Therefore, it follows that the null hypothesis H_0 and its alternative H_A are:

H_0: no relationship exists between the advertised brand's usage and *Hollywood Squares* viewing ($p_{ij} = p_i p_j$ for all i and all j)
H_A: viewership of *Hollywood Squares* is associated with the advertised brand's usage ($p_{ij} \neq p_i p_j$ for all i and all j)

If the null hypothesis is true, what values of χ_c^2 would be anticipated? The more accurate the hypothesis claim, the smaller the anticipated deviations of the observed frequency O_{ij} from the expected frequency E_{ij}. In fact, if the observed frequency in each cross-classification were perfectly matched to the expected frequencies, the calculated χ_c^2 will be *zero*. Why? Because each numerator calculation $(O_{ij} - E_{ij})^2$ would equal zero as would each term. Therefore, so would the sum of the terms χ_c^2. This means that when H_0 is true, the value of χ_c^2 will tend to be close to zero. Why wouldn't O_{ij} always equal E_{ij} when H_0 is true? Sampling variation typically causes an individual sample frequency to deviate from its expected frequency. Since the difference between the frequencies $O_{ij} - E_{ij}$ is squared, the squared difference will always be a non-negative term with minimum value of zero. When H_0 is true, sample frequencies will tend to be close to the expected frequencies, so it would be much more likely to find the χ_c^2 value close to zero. This tendency for sample values of χ^2 to concentrate near zero when H_0 is true is expressed by the *sampling distribution of* χ^2. Figure 20.5 shows the range of values that the χ^2 statistic assumes and the associated probabilities (area under the curve associated with the χ^2 values) when H_0 is true. Note that although values near zero are common, the value of exactly zero has very low probability.

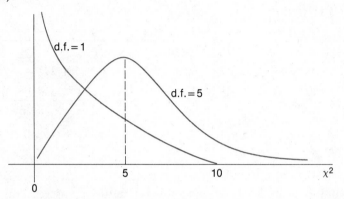

FIGURE 20.5 Chi-Square Distribution When H_0 Is True

The shape of the χ^2 distribution and therefore the probability associated with different χ^2 values changes with the number of degrees of freedom associated with the entire cross-classification table. The degrees of freedom for a particular table is given by the product

(number of table rows $-$ 1)(number of table columns $-$ 1)

It follows then that there exists a *family* of chi-square distributions, of which one is associated with each degree of freedom value.

Specifically, how is the chi-square distribution used to test the hypothesis of independence of the two categorical variables?

Step 6: The calculated value of the chi-square statistic from the sample data, χ_c^2, is compared to the published value of the chi-square distribution for a predetermined α, the maximum acceptable probability of Type I error.

The hypothesis is rejected if the larger of the two chi-square values is the one computed from the sample.

A table of the chi-square values at two commonly used values of $\alpha - .05$ and .01—is given in the Appendix. In the viewer-usage example, the appropriate chi-square distribution has

(rows $-$ 1)(columns $-$ 1) = (3 $-$ 1)(2 $-$ 1) = 2

degrees of freedom. With two degrees of freedom and the assumption that the null is true, Table 20.10 shows the published χ^2 values for selected values of α.

TABLE 20.10. Chi-Square Values for Selected Values of α, df = 2

χ^2 STATISTIC	AT α VALUE
2.77	0.25
4.61	0.10
5.99	0.05
9.21	0.01
13.80	0.001

The computed value of chi-square, χ_c^2, in the viewership-brand usage survey for the *Hollywood Squares* program has a value of 20.265. This exceeds the 13.80 chi-square value associated with α value of .001. This means that the prob-value associated with 20.265 would be considerably less than .001. What does this imply about the probability of getting a chi-square statistic as large as or larger than the 20.265 actually observed, assuming brand usage is independent of viewership of the *Hollywood Squares?* It must be less than one in one thousand. Thus, the sample evidence is *not* supportive of the independence premise. It instead strongly suggests that the two variables are *not* independent, a necessary condition for the ads on the *Hollywood Squares* to be considered effective in stimulating sales.

20.8. Analysis After Rejecting the Independence Hypothesis

Although the chi-square test has led to the important conclusion that brand usage is linked with the ads on the *Hollywood Squares*, it provides no insight into the *extent* of association or the exact nature of the relationship that links the two. No single measure of association is universally used to measure the association. A discussion of formal measures is given in Hays and Winkler.[2] For the decision maker who must take action based on the relationship, an *ad hoc* procedure that may be considered is to:

> assume that the table of joint relative frequencies computed from the sample data describes the relationship between the two categorical variables in the population. Thus, the joint frequencies given in Table 20.5 would be used in the *Hollywood Squares* example.

Now turn to an analysis of the difference in usage of the advertised brand between viewers and nonviewers. Suppose this difference is attributed to the advertising; what is the source of the new customers buying the advertised brand? Are they primarily converted nonusers? Or are they former users of a rival liquid starch brand switching to our advertised brand?

The answer appears to be a little of both according to the conditional relative frequencies given in Table 20.11. To see this, we shall compare usage percentages between viewers and nonviewers and assume that the differences are attributable to advertising (and not the motivation for doing the advertising).

> Usage of competing brands was 30.2 percent among nonviewers and 27.5 percent among viewers, a 2.7 percentage point difference. This suggests a

"capture rate" of $2.7/30.2 = 8.9$ percent of the competitor's customers. To evaluate the conversion rate of nonusers to users, we again compare *viewers* with *nonviewers*. Nonusers of the product amounted to 54.5 percent of the *Hollywood Squares* nonviewers and 46.1 percent of the viewers. We assume this difference would not have existed in the absence of *Hollywood Squares* advertising. The drop of 8.4 percentage points suggests a 15.4 percent conversion rate of the former nonusers.

Thus, although new customers come from both the nonusers and other brand user groups, nonuser conversions appear to be progressing more rapidly.

TABLE 20.11. Conditional Relative Frequencies of Usage of the Advertised Brand, Given Viewership Status

	VIEWERSHIP STATUS	
USAGE STATUS	Viewer	Nonviewer
User of the Advertised Brand	.264	.153
User of Competing Brand	.275	.302
Nonuser	.461	.545
	1.000	1.000

20.9. Concluding Comments

The contingency table is a valuable tool for analyzing relationships between two categorical variables. Different combinations of bivariate categories typically have different meanings to the decision maker. The prevalence of any particular combination of categories is given by the *joint frequency* of the combination, or in relative terms by the *joint relative frequency*. The latter is the number of observations in the cell representing that combination to the total number of observations. A comparison of the joint relative frequencies may reveal much of what needs to be known about the relationship. However, conditional and marginal relative frequencies also provide useful information. Conditional relative frequencies are obtained by dividing all frequencies by their corresponding row or column totals. Marginal relative frequencies are the row and column frequencies divided by the total number of observations. If the two cross-classified categorical variables are independent, the conditional relative frequencies corresponding to the cells of any given row or given column of the contingency table will also equal the marginal relative frequency for that row or column, except for sampling error differences. This is not true when the two variables are related; that is, when the category of one variable is dependent upon the category of the other variable.

For every cell in the contingency table, a row conditional relative frequency and a column conditional relative frequency can be computed. In general, these two values are not equal. The former is equal to the latter multiplied by the ratio of the corresponding row and column marginal relative frequencies.

If a bivariate relationship has been observed in sample data, it does not necessarily follow that the two variables are also related in the population from which the sample was drawn. To test the hypothesis of independence (or no relationship) between the two variables in the population, the chi-square test can be used. The upper-tail prob-value should be used with a chi-square distribution having (rows-1)(columns-1) degrees of freedom.

Failure to reject the null hypothesis indicates that the observed relationship in the sample is plausibly due merely to sampling variability and not to a relationship in the population considered as a whole.

Footnotes and References

[1] The data are reported in the "Staten Manufacturing Company" case, H. Boyd, R. Westfall, and S. Stasch, *Marketing Research: Text and Cases*, 4th edition, Richard D. Irwin Co., 1977.

[2] Hays and Winkler, *Statistics: Probability, Inference, Decisions*, Holt, Rinehart and Winston, 1970.

Questions and Problems

1. Explain how a contingency table might be useful in investigating the issue of sexual discrimination in job promotions.

2. Suppose a contingency table is constructed by cross-classifying a population of people according to two different categorical variables, gender and soft drink brand preference. In terms of the numbers in the table what would it mean to say that:
a. the two categorical variables are not related in this population.
b. the two categorical variables are related (or associated) in this population.

3. Suppose the population referred to in Problem 2 is also cross-classified according to occupational status and soft drink brand

preference. Assume that these two categorical variables are found to be related, and also that gender and soft drink preferences are found to be related. Is there an obvious way to determine which of the two relationships is stronger? Explain.

4. Suppose a contingency table is constructed which cross-classifies a population of cigarette smokers according to gender and whether or not the person smokes the Marlboro brand. A second contingency table is constructed for this same population using occupational status rather than gender as the variable cross-classified against Marlboro status.
a. What numerical comparisons would you make to determine whether smoking the

TABLE 20.12. Population of Cigarette Smokers

MARLBORO STATUS	(a) GENDER			(b) OCCUPATIONAL STATUS		
	Male	Female	Total	Blue Collar	White Collar	Total
Smoke Marlboro	400	50	450	250	200	450
Do Not Smoke Marlboro	800	750	1550	750	800	1550
Total	1200	800	2000	1000	1000	2000

Marlboro brand is related to gender? Occupational status?

b. Assume that smoking status of the Marlboro brand is found to be related both to gender and to occupational status. What numerical comparisons would you make to determine whether smoking of the Marlboro brand is more strongly related to gender than to occupational status?

c. Based upon contingency tables (Tables 20.12a and b) for a population of cigarette smokers, describe and compare the relationships between Marlboro smoking and (1) gender and (2) occupational status.

5. Suppose a contingency table for a population of employees reveals that promotional status is related to gender. Does it follow that sexual discrimination in promotion is the cause of the relationship? If not, give an alternative explanation.

6. Suppose a contingency table for a population of employees reveals that promotional status is related to gender. Assume that sexual discrimination in promotion is the (only) cause of the relationship.

a. Does it follow that sexual discrimination is an important factor in job promotions? Explain.

b. How would you measure and report the importance of sexual discrimination as a factor in job promotion?

7. A contingency table is constructed which cross classifies two categorical variables: marital status and type of residence. The marital status categories are: single (never married), presently married, presently divorced, widow or widower. The type of residence categories are: single family home, high rise apartment or condominium, low-rise apartment or condominium, mobile home, other.

a. How many cells are in the contingency table?

b. How many cells would there be if each of the marital status categories were split into two new categories, indicating the presence or absence of children?

8. Is there a difference between the meanings of the terms "joint frequency" and "cross-tabulations"? Explain.

9. Does it matter whether a contingency table reports absolute or relative frequencies? Explain.

10. Is it true that the sum of the row marginal frequencies must equal the sum of the column marginal frequencies? Explain.

11. Suppose a conditional relative frequency is obtained by dividing a particular joint relative frequency by the marginal relative frequency for that row. A second conditional relative frequency is obtained by dividing the same joint relative frequency by the marginal relative frequency for that column. Is it true that the two conditional relative frequencies must have the same value? Explain.

12. A brand manager targets her brand at 18–35 year old single females with above average income and education. She learns that *Cosmopolitan* magazine's reader profile closely matches the description of her target market. If 75% of *Cosmopolitan* readers are in her target market:

a. does it follow that *Cosmopolitan* reaches a high percentage of her target market?

b. is 75 the percentage of her target market reached by *Cosmopolitan*?

c. why might it be more convenient for the brand manager to work with the *Cosmopolitan* readership profile rather than to develop the target market reach figures directly from the target market?

d. would it help the brand manager to know that *Cosmopolitan* readership is 6 million and her target market is 18 million persons? Explain.

13. Is it true that the claim of no bivariate relationship between two categorical variables is equivalent to claiming the two variables are statistically independent? What numeral implication follows for the cross-classified population data if the two variables are statistically independent?

14. Suppose an advertisement is highly effective at stimulating usage of the advertised brand.

a. Would you expect the two categorical variables "brand usage" and "exposure to advertising" to be statistically dependent or statistically independent? Explain.

b. What would you look for in the cross-tabs for a set of sample data as evidence of a relationship between the two variables?

c. Suppose a relationship is found in the sample data between exposure to advertising and brand usage. How would you establish the likelihood of the observed relationship merely being a sampling fluke from a population in which there is no relationship?

15. Reconsider the advertising brand usage problem described in Problem 14.

a. If it is concluded that a bivariate population relationship exists between exposure to advertising and brand usage, does it follow that the advertising is an effective way to stimulate brand usage? Why or why not?

b. Suppose the observed sample data result from a carefully designed statistical experiment. What figures would you compose to estimate the increased brand usage attributable to exposure to the advertising?

c. Suppose the observed sample data are obtained by a survey rather than a statistical experiment. Give an alternative explanation for the value you estimated in Part b as the increased brand usage attributable to exposure to advertising.

16. Would your answers to any of the questions in Problem 15 change if you learned that the advertiser was a beer company which placed advertisements only on television programs and in magazines known to be popular among beer drinkers? Explain.

17. An employment discrimination suit brought against a company charges it with discriminating against women in promotions to executive positions. As evidence, a contingency table is presented which ex-hibits a relationship between gender and promotional status. The data are for the entire population of employees rather than a sample of them. Yet the expert witness called by the defense claims that the observed relationship is merely a sampling fluke. Can you suggest a plausible basis for this explanation?

18. How many degrees of freedom does a χ^2 distribution have if it is based on a cross-classification of two categorical variables, one of 6 categories, the other of 4 categories?

19. Consider the possible values of χ^2 obtained from a contingency table.

a. What is the lowest value possible?

b. Why are values near zero unlikely even if the null hypothesis of statistical independence is true?

20. A study was undertaken to measure the attitudes of new imported car purchasers towards a particular brand R. A questionnaire was designed and administered to a sample of new car purchasers classified by brand purchased and by sex. The results of each questionnaire were classified as favorable, neutral, or unfavorable towards brand R. The data are given in Table 20.13.

a. Test the hypothesis that attitudes towards Brand R are independent of gender (over both purchaser categories).

b. Test the hypothesis that attitude is independent of brand purchased (over both sexes).

c. Using the designations male Brand R purchaser, female Brand R purchaser, male purchaser of brand other than R, and female purchaser of brand other than R as

TABLE 20.13. Attitudes of New Imported Car Purchasers Concerning Brand R

| ATTITUDE TOWARDS BRAND R | PURCHASERS OF | | | |
| | BRAND R | | BRAND OTHER THAN R | |
	Male	Female	Male	Female
Favorable	8	10	36	40
Neutral	6	10	46	34
Unfavorable	14	12	30	24
Total	28	32	112	98

a category set, test the hypothesis that attitude is independent of this categorization.

21. A survey of 200 users of hair shampoo led to the contingency table given (Table 20.14).

TABLE 20.14. Users of Hair Shampoo

USAGE RATE	GENDER Male	GENDER Female	Total
Light	48	32	80
Medium	38	42	80
Heavy	14	26	40
Total	100	100	200

A manufacturer of personal care products noted in the survey that more women than men are heavy users and more men than women are light users.

a. Is the percentage of heavy users who are women the same as the percentage of women who are heavy users? If not, compare the two percentages.

b. If the manufacturer wanted to target a new shampoo at the heavy user segment, which of the two percentages in Part a would be more pertinent? Would your answer change if the manufacturer wanted to target the shampoo especially for women?

c. Considering the possibility that the observed relationship in the sample between gender and usage rate might just be a sampling fluke, use the chi-square distribution to test the hypothesis of no relationship between usage rate and gender.

22. Department stores are usually concerned about the image of their store as perceived by customers and by prospective customers who do not shop at their store. In response to a market survey, the results in Table 20.15 were obtained for a particular department store.

a. Calculate the chi-square statistic for this data.

b. Test the independence hypothesis at $\alpha = .10$.

23. In the market survey conducted by the department store in Problem 22, the additional data in Table 20.16 were obtained:

a. If the observed relationships in these two data sets and in the data set given in Problem 22 accurately reflect the population relationship, what can you conclude about the image of this department store?

b. Calculate the chi-square values for the two data sets given in this problem.

c. It is argued that the observed relationships in data sets could well be attributable solely to sampling variation and that a rela-

TABLE 20.15. Department Store's Image (1)

Where would a construction or mill worker buy casual shoes?	Customers of this store	Noncustomers of this store
At this store	13	15
Elsewhere or no response	175	290

TABLE 20.16. Department Store's Image (2)

Where would a bank teller or draftsman buy casual shoes?	Customers of this store	Noncustomers of this store
At this store	111	119
Elsewhere or no response	77	186

Where would a doctor or lawyer buy casual shoes?	Customers of this store	Noncustomers of this store
At this store	124	147
Elsewhere or no response	64	158

TABLE 20.17. Amount of Information Sought By Automobile Buyers (1)

Number of Automobiles Previously Purchased	AMOUNT OF INFORMATION-SEARCH EFFORT			
	Very Little	Some	Moderate	Very Intensive
0–2	4	10	8	9
3–5	16	14	14	10
6 or more	16	13	16	16

TABLE 20.18. Amount of Information Sought By Automobile Buyers (2)

Number of Previous Purchases of this Brand	AMOUNT OF INFORMATION-SEARCH EFFORT			
	Very Little	Some	Moderate	Very Intensive
0	5	10	17	18
1–2	15	17	11	13
3 or more	16	10	10	4

tionship would not be observed in a larger sample. Use the computed chi-square values to test the plausibility of this argument.

24. Frustrated marketers have long noticed that some eventual purchasers of their products are very hard to reach with information the marketer feels prospective buyers should have before a decision is made. Yet other buyers are easy to reach; many go out of their way to seek out pertinent information for evaluating products and brands. Why are some buyers so hard and others so easy to reach? According to one theory, it is the inexperienced buyers of the product who are easiest to reach because they know they need the information. The "old hands" have often settled into a routine pattern of acquiring the product and are not on the lookout for information to the same extent. The following contingency table (Table 20.17) presents data from a study on the amount of information sought by automobile buyers having different degrees of previous automobile buying experience. In the table, previous buying experience includes any brand.
a. Calculate the value of the chi-square statistic.

b. Test the independence hypothesis at $\alpha = .10$ risk of Type I error.
c. Do the data provide evidence supporting the theory that persons with more car buying experience tend to put forth less effort searching for information when they shop for a new car? Explain.
(Note: Data in this and the following problem are reported in Peter Bennett and Robert Mandell, "Prepurchase Information Seeking Behavior of New Car Purchasers— The Learning Hypothesis," *Journal of Marketing Research*, Vol 6 (Nov. 1969), pp 430–433.)

25. A second set of data is given in Table 20.18 from the same study described in Problem 24. Here, however, the definition of previous buying experience is restricted to the same brand as presently purchased.
a. Calculate the value of the chi-square statistic.
b. Test the independence hypothesis at the 1% level of significance.
c. Do the data provide evidence that the more times a buyer of a particular brand of new car has purchased this same brand in the past, the less is the effort that tends to be put into shopping for the new car? Explain.

Analysis of Variance

Preview. Bivariate relationships involving two quantitative variables were introduced in Chapter 14 (regression and correlation analysis). In the previous chapter, contingency tables and chi-square analysis were introduced to study relationships between two categorical variables. In this chapter the study of bivariate relationships is extended to the hybrid situation in which one variable is categorical and the other is quantitative. For instance, the buying agent for an auto parts retail chain needs to find out whether the several makes of 12 volt batteries under consideration (categorical variable) have on average the same operative life (quantitative variable); the plant manager of a utility company may have to show the State Public Utility authorities that there is a relationship between fuel types used in generating power (categorical variable) and the pollution costs that result (quantitative variable); the personnel manager screening candidates for employment wants to know whether applicant personality type (categorical variable) is related to productivity on the job (quantitative variable). The common feature in each of these situations is that one variable is quantitative and the other is categorical. Moreover, the categorical variable can be viewed as the set of options available to the decision maker. The quantitative variable can be viewed as a measurement which reflects the response to a particular option. The common concern involves knowing whether there is a link between the quantitative response variable and the categorical options available to the decision maker.

A special case of the hybrid situation was encountered in Chapter 13. There the t test was used in experimental designs to test for the difference between means of two populations (categories). However, the t test is not applicable when the number of means to be compared is more than two. When there are three or more categories or populations, we can often turn to a distribution known as the F distribution. This distribution and associated techniques known collectively as the *analysis of variance* are the subject of this chapter.

21.1. Hybrid Bivariate Data: One Variable Quantitative, One Variable Categorical

21

Consider the hybrid bivariate relationships just mentioned in which a quantitative (response) variable is related to a categorical (options) variable.

Quantitative (*response*) Variable	is related to	Categorical (options) Variable
Length of operative life	⟺	Different makes of 12 volt battery
Pollution costs	⟺	Different fuel types
Job productivity	⟺	Different personality types

Upon examination it seems that for the three examples given, the type of potential relationship to be investigated is the same. It is that,

the categorical variable represents management's set of decision options (alternatives);[1]

the quantitative variable describes the numerical response associated with each of the decision option categories.

The level of response—be it revenue, cost, productivity, or profits—typically reflects the degree of business impact that comes from choosing one decision alternative rather than another. The objective of the statistical analysis is to determine whether the average value of the response materially depends upon the different decision option taken.

If average profits, revenue, costs, or productivity *do* respond differently to the decision options considered, the next step would be to specify the exact nature of the relationship.

What importance does finding *no* relationship have?

If average profits, revenue, costs, or productivity *do not* respond differently to the decision options considered, other reasons will have to serve as the basis for the decision option chosen.

A Business Situation

To closely examine a decision relying on the analysis of hybrid data, let us consider the situation facing the fast-food segment of the restaurant industry. In this highly competitive business, success or failure can come quickly. Establishing and maintaining a favorable reputation for quality, price, and service determines whether the profit and loss (P & L) statement ends up in the black or the red. Many believe that the market dominance of McDonald's in the fast food business is built on a strategy of consistently providing high quality food with fast and courteous service at reasonable prices. But today, prices face inflationary pressure. Franchises must cope with a new and persistent element in the business environment. To hold prices at affordable levels, franchises give vigilant attention to cost cutting schemes wherever and whenever quality is not adversely affected. The battle to hold down costs (or "control expenses") was the key topic of a recent business conference and was reported in this way:

> If there was one theme to this year's National Restaurant Association meeting it was "Control, Control, Control".[2]

The following example shows how the desire to control costs does lead to the analysis of hybrid data.

Example 21.1. Cooking Oil Procurement at Chick'N Chips

A West Coast chain, Chick'N Chips, in an effort to check inflationary pressure on prices, is considering new cost control measures. One suggestion is to switch to a less expensive cooking oil for its "specialty" fries. Along with the currently used cooking oil, two less expensive alternative oils are being tried on an experimental basis by the franchise chain. The suppliers of the alternatives, hoping to replace the currently used cooking oil, contend that the cooking performance of their oils is equivalent to the currently used oil.

A variable believed important in discriminating performance between different cooking oil brands is the length of time an oil maintains its cooking integrity before breaking down. Worn out oil is rancid. If not replaced, poor tasting food comes from the deep fat fryer. Changing worn out oil, however, requires shutting down the deep fryer and, importantly, interrupting customer service on heavily ordered items. Additionally, the more frequently oil needs changing, the greater is the burden on an already quick moving and often harried staff. The common result is that other jobs will be rushed or skipped in order for the oil to be changed on time.

Such foreboding consequences prompt the chain to investigate carefully and thoroughly the cooking oil life of brands proposed by prospective suppliers.

The chain's management randomly assigns to three groups the chain's fifty-one restaurants. Then the three brands of oil are assigned to the three groups of restaurants in a way that gives each brand an equal chance of being assigned to each group. The approach makes certain that the cooking oil experiment does not systematically favor one particular brand over the others, effectively eliminating possible assignment bias.

With this accomplished, each franchise manager is instructed to record how long (days and fraction of a day) the oil remains usable. Oil should be discarded when its color and its reaction to heat matches the description of "worn out oil" given in the manager's handbook.

The managers' recordings from the 51 restaurants were received and assembled as shown in Table 21.1.

The *overall* sample mean is denoted by $\overline{\overline{Y}}$ (read Y-double bar). It equals 3.2737 for the 51 observations. The highest individual brand mean $\overline{Y}_1$ is for the cooking oil supplied by Superior, the current supplier. But what is the meaning of the shorter average life of the two cooking oils offered by the other suppliers? Do these less expensive oils not measure up to the quality of the oil supplied by Superior? Or is the difference small enough that it could well be due merely to the normal variation in kitchen conditions that affect oil life at different franchises?

TABLE 21.1. Sample of Cooking Oil Life by Supplier Type (Days and Fraction of a Day)

SUPPLIER TYPE:	SUPERIOR SUBSAMPLE (current; $j = 1$)	AGRA SUBSAMPLE (alternative; $j = 2$)	RCW SUBSAMPLE (alternative; $j = 3$)
	3.93	4.70	2.43
	3.45	4.15	2.98
	2.00	4.55	3.04
	2.28	3.31	4.94
	3.49	2.13	3.15
	4.25	4.69	2.46
	2.33	2.68	3.34
	3.02	2.36	2.38
	3.26	3.93	2.27
	4.03	1.56	2.52
	3.67	4.29	3.10
	2.94	1.74	3.53
	5.90	2.17	3.06
	2.18	1.97	2.51
	5.39	4.69	3.48
	2.74	2.87	5.94
	3.49	3.17	2.52
Brand Mean:	$\overline{Y}_1 = 3.4324$	$\overline{Y}_2 = 3.2329$	$\overline{Y}_3 = 3.1559$
Brand Std. Dev.:	$S_1 = 1.0707$	$S_2 = 1.1390$	$S_3 = 0.96481$
Brand Size:	$n_1 = 17$	$n_2 = 17$	$n_3 = 17$

Overall Mean, $\overline{\overline{Y}} = 3.2737$ for overall sample size, $N = 51$
$$= (3.4324 + 3.2329 + 3.1559)/3 = 3.2737$$

Source: Adapted Data: Harry V. Roberts, University of Chicago

---

These questions are a natural extension of the questions asked in Chapter 13 pertaining to the comparison of the mean performance measurement of two (independent normal) populations. The t test used there cannot be employed because the investigator is interested in comparing *several* means, not just two. The hypothesis that the investigator is interested in testing is that all brands have identical (mean) life μ, which in essence means that useful cooking life is *not related to brand* of cooking oil. The null hypothesis that follows is:

$$H_0: \mu_1 = \mu_2 = \ldots = \mu_K = \mu$$

where $K = 3$ for the cooking oil experiment. The alternative hypothesis is:

H_A: non-identical long run (mean) useful life among the brands, *or,*

in other words, useful life *is* related to the brand of cooking oil supplied. In this latter case the investigator may wish to analyze the *nature* of the relationship. For example, the cooking oil with the largest sample mean value could be identified as the one expected to have the longest life. Also, numerical estimates of the pairwise differences between means, called *contrasts*, may be obtained (for example, $\overline{Y}_2 - \overline{Y}_1, \overline{Y}_2 - \overline{Y}_3, \overline{Y}_1 - \overline{Y}_3$). The contrasts would indicate the estimated differences in mean lives among the brands.

Is there a replacement for the *t* test procedure used with two independent samples that is applicable to situations in which the hybrid variable has more than two categories? A formal statistical analysis using the procedure called ANOVA, the *analysis of variance*, can often be used.

21.2. Analysis of Variance— ANOVA and the Logic Behind It

Before analyzing this specific set of observed sample data, let us discuss three very different possibilities for the brand populations, any one of which could represent the underlying distributions from which the sample data are drawn.

Possibility I: Extraneous Variation and No Brand Effect

If there is no distinct brand effect, all of the brand populations show the same variance with identical means for the measured responses on cooking oil life, as Figure 21.1 shows.

The fact that there is variation in the response observations is not unexpected. Regardless of whether there is a meaningful brand effect or not, there will be an inherent variability in the observations. It is virtually impossible to totally control for the numerous factors that give rise to this variability. Since these factors typically are extraneous to the issue being investigated, the response variability they cause is commonly called "extraneous variation". It can be attributed to several sources:

1. Variation among experimental units (restaurants) in the sampling frame that are assigned to use the same brand of cooking oil. These include operating factors not specifically standardized, such as age of the deep fry cooker, experience of the operators, ventilation system in each unit, etc.

2. Variation if repetitions of the experiment for the same restaurant were

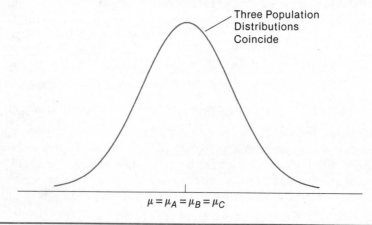

FIGURE 21.1 Identical Cooking Oil Life Populations for the Three Brands (Extraneous Variation and No Brand Effect)

recorded. This is due to the instability of operating conditions over time: flow of customers at peak hours, intensity of orders on the deep fry cooker, shifts of personnel in the kitchen.

Possibility II: Brand Effect Large Compared to Extraneous Variation

What would happen to the variation among observations for a given brand if there is a distinct brand effect operating on cooking life? Would there be a tendency to have a greater amount of extraneous variability than before? *No*, because the sources of extraneous variation which were previously present have not disappeared or changed in any way. However, the presence of a strong differential brand effect on cooking oil life *will cause each brand population to project a more distinctive and separable display* of observations, as shown in Figure 21.2.

On the surface it would seem simple to distinguish sample data for this latter situation (Possibility II) from sample data in which identical brand populations generated the data (Possibility I). If the brand populations are identical, the sample of different brands would

1. contain observations which greatly overlap and

2. have brand sample means which are very similar in value.

In the case of a brand effect as portrayed in Figure 21.2, the observations don't overlap. The brand populations produce brand samples having means which are not all similar in value. In short, the populations are so distinct, it would seem that the brand samples would always reflect their underlying populations. Unfortunately, such clear distinctions as portrayed in Figure 21.2 are not always present, even when the brand effect is strong. The reason is that extraneous sources of variation are also present. Only if extraneous variation is swamped by the brand effect will the brand samples reflect underlying populations.

Possibility III: Brand Effect Small Compared to Extraneous Variation

If the brand effect is small compared to the extraneous sources of variation, the observations will overlap. It will be difficult to tell whether the differences among sample means reflect a brand effect. Consider the hypothetical brand situation in Figure 21.3.

Which panel better describes the population situation that generated the brand sample observations? If Panel I is generating the brand observations, then the observed variation among the observations only reflects extraneous variation (since no brand effect exists). On the other hand, if Panel II is the underlying population situation, it means that the observed variation reflects both the extraneous variation and the variation due to the differences between the underlying means of the brand populations. Thus, if we could correctly identify which panel (I or II) describes our situation, we would know whether or not the brand means are different.

Individual values in one sample (□, X, or ○) do not correspond to any other values in the other samples

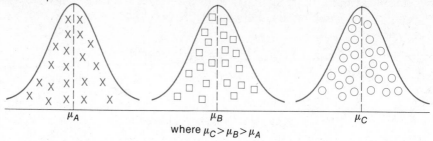

where $\mu_C > \mu_B > \mu_A$

FIGURE 21.2 Display of Hypothetical Brand Populations for Strong Brand Effect Compared to Extraneous Variation

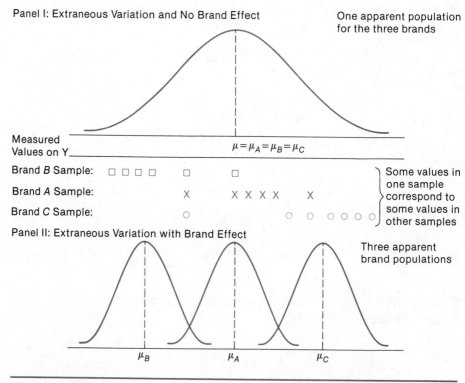

Panel I: Extraneous Variation and No Brand Effect

One apparent population for the three brands

Measured Values on Y

$\mu = \mu_A = \mu_B = \mu_C$

Brand *B* Sample: □ □ □ □   □   □

Brand *A* Sample: X   X X X X   X

Brand *C* Sample: ○   ○ ○ ○ ○ ○

} Some values in one sample correspond to some values in other samples

Panel II: Extraneous Variation with Brand Effect

Three apparent brand populations

μ_B μ_A μ_C

FIGURE 21.3 Displaying the Underlying Populations Considered by ANOVA

21.3. MS Within: A Standard of Comparison

How can this choice between Panel I (no brand effect) and Panel II (brand effect) be resolved? The resolution would be easy if there were a *universal* standard of comparison indicating how much extraneous variation to expect. Unfortunately, this is not the case. The true underlying (population) amount of extraneous variation indicated by σ^2 is specific to the situation and generally unknown.

Nevertheless, sample observations can provide an estimate of the extraneous variance, thereby providing a standard of comparison that is relevant to the specific data being analyzed. In the cooking oil example, three estimates of extraneous variance can be obtained by computing the sample variance S^2 for *each* brand's sample observations. However, the three calculated estimates can also be pooled, giving the estimate, S_p^2. The pooling (averaging) results in a better estimate than any of the three individually because the pooled estimate is based on a larger number of degrees of freedom. This pooled estimate is commonly referred to as the *within sample mean-square* estimate or simply MS WITHIN.

The value of MS WITHIN is given by the expression

$$\text{MS WITHIN} = S_p^2 = \frac{\sum S_j^2}{K} = \frac{S_1^2 + S_2^2 + \ldots + S_K^2}{K}$$

where $S_1^2, S_2^2, \ldots S_K^2$ are the respective sample variances for the K different brands of cooking oil. For the cooking oil example,

$$S_p^2 = \frac{\sum S_j^2}{K} = \frac{(1.0707)^2 + (1.1390)^2 + (0.96481)^2}{3}$$

$$= 1.12486$$

21.4. MS Between:
The Estimate to Be Compared with the Standard

How is this "pooled sample" estimate S_p^2 of the extraneous variance used as a "standard of comparison" in assessing whether there is a brand effect reflected in the mean life of the different cooking oil brands? The essence of the ANOVA test procedure is to make another estimate of the extraneous variance called MS BETWEEN by an entirely different method and then devise a test for comparing the two.

MS BETWEEN is calculated by a two step process:

1. First estimate $\sigma_{\bar{Y}}^2$ (the variance of *means* of samples of size n) by computing $S_{\bar{Y}}^2$ from the sample.

The value of $\sigma_{\bar{Y}}^2$ is related to the amount of the extraneous variance σ^2 there is among the individual observations. The expression linking the two terms is,

$$\sigma_{\bar{Y}}^2 = \frac{\sigma^2}{n}$$

which can be written as

$$n\sigma_{\bar{Y}}^2 = \sigma^2$$

From this latter expression it can be seen that

2. $n(\text{estimate of } \sigma_{\bar{Y}}^2) \xrightarrow{\text{gives}} \textit{estimate of } \sigma^2$

Thus, substituting $S_{\bar{Y}}^2$ for $\sigma_{\bar{Y}}^2$ lets us estimate σ^2 by the product of n and $S_{\bar{Y}}^2$.

$$\text{MS BETWEEN} = nS_{\bar{Y}}^2$$

For the cooking oil data,

$$
\begin{aligned}
S_{\bar{Y}}^2 &= \frac{(\bar{Y}_1 - \bar{\bar{Y}})^2 + (\bar{Y}_2 - \bar{\bar{Y}})^2 + (\bar{Y}_3 - \bar{\bar{Y}})^2}{K - 1} \\
&= \frac{(3.4324 - 3.2737)^2 + (3.2329 - 3.2737)^2 + (3.1559 - 3.2737)^2}{3 - 1} \\
&= \frac{.0251857 + .0016646 + .0138768}{2} = \frac{.0407271}{2} \\
&= .0203636
\end{aligned}
$$

$$\text{MS BETWEEN} = nS_{\bar{Y}}^2 = 17(.0203636) = .346181$$

The central premise of ANOVA is that the relationship between MS BETWEEN and MS WITHIN *changes* depending on whether H_0 is true or not.

21.5. Comparing the Two Estimates: The Role of the *F* Distribution in ANOVA

Under the assumption that

1. H_0 is true;

2. the aggregative effects of extraneous variation on the observations are:
a. independent of each other,
b. follow a normal distribution,
c. have zero mean, and
d. have common variance;

3. the dependent variable is an interval or ratio scaled quantitative variable;

the expressions MS BETWEEN and MS WITHIN will be independent estimates of the extraneous variance σ^2. Their ratio, called the *F Statistic*, equals

$$F = \frac{\text{Between brand mean square}}{\text{Within brand mean square}} = \frac{\text{MS BETWEEN}}{\text{MS WITHIN}} = \frac{nS_{\bar{Y}}^2}{S_p^2}$$

For the cooking oil samples,

$$F_c = \frac{.346181}{1.12486} = .308 = .31 \text{ (rounded)}$$

The value of these statistics will help us determine which panel (I or II) in Figure 21.3 correctly describes our situation. Thus it helps us determine whether or not the three brands all have the same mean life. The statistic follows an *F distribution with $K - 1$ and $N - K$ degrees of freedom where N is total sample size*. The $K - 1$ refers to the number of degrees of freedom in MS BETWEEN; $N - K$ refers to the number of degrees of freedom in MS WITHIN.

F Distribution

The *F* sampling distribution shown in Figure 21.4 pictures all the possible values of the *F* statistic along the horizontal axis with the area above representing their chances of appearing in a sample. The *F* statistic should have a value near one when H_0 is true, but *F* will sometimes be lower and sometimes substantially higher than its expected value. The exact value for a particular sample depends on the amount of sampling variability present in the population.

The shape of the *F* sampling distribution changes as shown in Figure 21.4b. There is a *family* of F distributions; each member of the family has a different shape and probability of obtaining the various F values. What determines the shape of the appropriate F distribution? As with the *t* distribution, the size of sample or, more precisely, the degree of freedom value is the determining factor. But the *F* statistic is a ratio. Whereas each member of the *t* distribution is associated with a unique degree of freedom value *d.f.*, each member of the F distribution requires *two* degrees of freedom values: one for the numerator of the ratio and one for the ratio's denominator.

> *Numerator:* DF_B, which depends on the number of different alternatives compared
>
> *Denominator:* DF_W, which considers the overall sample size involved

ANOVA When H_0 Is Not True

What if the null hypothesis is not true? Then MS BETWEEN "blows up". Why? Because in addition to extraneous variation, the term includes the variation due to the differences among the brand means. The larger these differences, the greater their contribution to the overall variation as compared to the contribution of extraneous variation. Hence the greater will be the value of MS BETWEEN (which includes *both* sources of variation) compared to MS WITHIN (which includes only extraneous variation). The relative expansion of the numerator

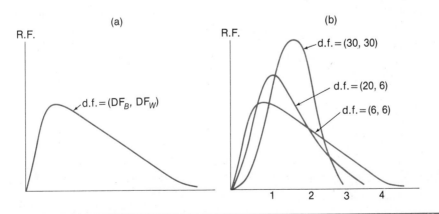

FIGURE 21.4 *F* Sampling Distribution at Various Degrees of Freedom

generates a larger computed F statistic, F_c, indicating that there exists a meaningful brand effect. This is why the F ratio serves as the key statistic in ANOVA. By analyzing variance, we can draw an inference about the population means.

Testing Procedure

Procedurally, the testing requires that the prob-value associated with the calculated F statistic F_c (shaded area under the F distribution in Figure 21.5) be compared with alpha, the maximum acceptable probability of Type I error. When the computations are made on a computer using one of the standard software packages, the prob-value is usually printed out.

F values corresponding to numerous prob-values can be found in the F distribution table in the Appendix. This table can also be used to test the null hypothesis at any chosen level of significance, alpha. The computed F statistic F_c is compared against the published value of F for the chosen values of alpha— usually .10, .05, or .01. The larger the F_c value, the smaller is its prob-value and the less plausible is the null hypothesis of no cooking oil brand effect on useful life. If F_c exceeds the published value of F corresponding to the alpha level chosen, the conclusion is that the brand of cooking oil *does* make a difference on average in obtaining useful cooking life: the longevity of the different brands of oil is not the same. Let us test the null hypothesis in the cooking oil example at the 5 percent level of significance. The published value of F for $K - 1 = 2$ and $N - K$ $= 48$ degrees of freedom is 3.19. Since $F_c = .31$ is far less than 3.19, the null hypothesis claiming that the cooking oils have the same mean useful life cannot be rejected.

The interpretation of the test results is considered further in Section 21.8. First, however, we review some useful aspects for the computational procedure and then in Section 21.7 we present a popular shortcut computational procedure.

21.6. The ANOVA Format and Computational Steps: The Sums-of-Squares Approach

An illustrative and useful way of formating the calculations leading to the F_c statistic is displayed in Table 21.2. The format displayed is called the sums-of-squares approach. This approach leads to the same value of F_c as previously calculated. However, the computational procedure differs slightly from that described in

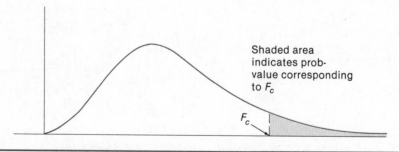

Shaded area indicates prob-value corresponding to F_c

F_c

FIGURE 21.5 Testing the Hypothesis Using the F Distribution

the previous section. An intermediate calculation of the sums of squared deviations of individual sample item values from their sample means is required. The sums-of-squares approach offers three computational advantages over the basic conceptual approach described in Section 21.5. First, it facilitates numerical accuracy by providing a handy accounting scheme of cross-checking calculations made at intermediate steps. Second, when used in conjunction with the shortcut method discussed in the following section, computations are simpler and faster. Third, it facilitates computation of the F ratio when sample sizes are unequal.

TABLE 21.2. Conceptual ANOVA Table Format

COL. 1	COL. 2	COL. 3	COL. 4
		Degrees of	
Source of Variation	Sum of Squares	Freedom	Variance Estimate
Row			
1. Between Brands ("Explained" Variation)	SS BETWEEN = 0.69	$DF_B = 2$	MS BETWEEN (.69/2)
2. Within Brands ("Extraneous" Variation)	SS WITHIN = 53.99	$DF_w = 48$	MS WITHIN (53.99/48)
3. Total (check figures)	SS TOTAL = 54.68	$DF_T = 50$	

The first row shows calculations for the numerator of the F_c statistic, MS BETWEEN. The value of MS BETWEEN is computed as the ratio of two intermediate calculations, the between-sum-of-squares (SS BETWEEN) and the degrees of freedom (DF_B):

$$\text{MS BETWEEN} = nS_{\overline{Y}}^2 = \frac{n\Sigma(\overline{Y}_j - \overline{\overline{Y}})^2}{K - 1} = \frac{17(.0407271)}{2}$$

$$= \frac{.692361}{2} = \frac{\text{SS BETWEEN}}{DF_B}$$

Thus, SS BETWEEN $= .692361$ and $DF_B = 2$. Their ratio, .346181, is MS BETWEEN. This is the same value obtained in the previous section.

The second row shows calculations for the denominator of the F_c statistic, MS WITHIN. The value of MS WITHIN is computed as the ratio of two intermediate calculations, the within-sum-of-squares (SS WITHIN) and the degrees of freedom (DF_W):

MS WITHIN

$$= \frac{\Sigma S_j^2}{K} = \frac{S_1^2 + S_2^2 + \ldots + S_k^2}{K}$$

$$= \frac{\frac{\Sigma(Y_{i1} - \overline{Y}_1)^2}{n - 1} + \frac{\Sigma(Y_{i2} - \overline{Y}_2)^2}{n - 1} + \ldots + \frac{\Sigma(Y_{iK} - \overline{Y}_K)^2}{n - 1}}{k}$$

$$= \frac{\Sigma\Sigma(Y_{ij} - \overline{Y}_j)^2}{K(n - 1)}$$

$$= \frac{\sum(Y_{i1} - \overline{Y}_1)^2 + \sum(Y_{i2} - \overline{Y}_2)^2 + \ldots + \sum(Y_{iK} - \overline{Y}_K)^2}{K(n-1)}$$

$$= \frac{\text{SS WITHIN}}{\text{DF}_W}$$

The notation $\sum\sum$ means "double summation". Thus, to compute SS WITHIN, the squared deviations are first summed for each column. Then the three column sums are summed.

SS WITHIN
$$= (3.93 - 3.43235)^2 + \ldots + (2.52 - 3.15588)^2$$
$$= 53.993$$

The third row provides a system of checks on the intermediate calculations. The sum of SS BETWEEN and SS WITHIN in column (2) must equal the *total* sum-of-squares (SS TOTAL) which is independently computed from the expression

SS TOTAL
$$= \sum\sum(Y_{ij} - \overline{\overline{Y}})^2$$
$$= \sum(Y_{i1} - \overline{\overline{Y}})^2 + \sum(Y_{i2} - \overline{\overline{Y}})^2 + \ldots + \sum(Y_{ik} - \overline{\overline{Y}})^2$$
$$= (3.93 - 3.27372)^2 + \ldots + (2.52 - 3.27372)^2$$
$$= 54.685$$

The sum of DF_B and DF_W must equal the total degrees-of-freedom (DF_T) independently computed from the expression

$$\text{DF}_T = \text{DF}_B + \text{DF}_W = (K-1) + K(n-1) = nK - 1$$
$$= 17(3) - 1 = 50.$$

21.7. A Shortcut Computational Procedure

The procedure for calculating sums of squares described in the previous section demonstrates what is meant by sums of squares, but is rarely used in actually computing the sums of squares. It requires computing squared deviations from a mean—a tedious and time consuming calculation. Instead an alternative *shortcut* method is recommended. It leads to the same end results while offering several advantages. The alternative shortcut method will

reduce potential rounding error

be less cumbersome and more efficient

offer a general format for handling the case where the number of observations for the different brands are unequal.

Data Format and Computational Steps

The computational tasks in an ANOVA table can be simplified by expressing the sums of squares in an algebraically equivalent form in terms of *totals*. This conversion is shown in Table 21.3. In this table T_j is the sum or total of all the values in the j_{th} column. $T_j = \sum Y_{ij}$. Thus, the totals of the values in the columns for Superior, Agra, and RCW cooking oils are 58.35, 54.96, and 53.65 respectively.

TABLE 21.3. Computational ANOVA Table Format

(1) Source of Variation	(2) Sum of Squares	(3) Degrees of Freedom	(4) Variance Estimate
Between Brands	SS BETWEEN	DF_B	MS BETWEEN
("Explained" Variation)	$= \sum \left[\dfrac{T_j^2}{n}\right] - \dfrac{(\sum T_j)^2}{N}$	$= K - 1$	$= 0.69/2$
	$= 547.27 - 546.58$	$= 3 - 1$	$= 0.345$
	$= .69$	$= 2$	
Within Brands	SS WITHIN	DF_W	MS WITHIN
("Extraneous" Variation)	$= \sum\sum (Y_{ij})^2 - \sum \left[\dfrac{T_j^2}{n}\right]$	$= N - K$	$= 54.00/48$
	$= 601.27 - 547.27$	$= 51 - 3$	$= 1.125$
	$= 54.00$	$= 48$	
Total	SS TOTAL	DF_T	
	$= \sum\sum (Y_{ij})^2 - \dfrac{(\sum T_j)^2}{N}$	$= 51 - 1$	
	$= 601.27 - 546.58$	$= 50$	
	$= 54.69$		

$$F_c = \frac{.345}{1.125}$$

Let us now follow a step by step procedure supplying intermediate computations to show how the mean squares are calculated:

Step 1. Organize the observations by column according to the categorical variable (brands of cooking oil) as in Table 21.4.

Step 2. Square the value for each observation Y_{ij}^2. Obtain the sum of the squares.

$$\sum\sum (Y_{ij})^2 = (3.93)^2 + (3.45)^2 + (2.00)^2 + \ldots + (2.52)^2 = 601.27$$

Step 3. Square each of the column brand totals to get T_j^2. Then divide each T_j^2 by the number of brand observations, n for that brand. Sum together the T_j^2/n to get the sum.

$$\sum (T_j^2)/n = \frac{(58.35)^2}{17} + \frac{(54.96)^2}{17} + \frac{(53.65)^2}{17}$$

TABLE 21.4. Data on Cooking Oil Life—Brands

	Superior, $j = 1$	Agra, $j = 2$	RCW, $j = 3$
	3.93	4.70	2.43
	3.45	4.15	2.98
	2.00	4.55	3.04
	2.28	3.31	4.94
	3.49	2.13	3.15
	4.25	4.69	2.46
	2.33	2.68	3.34
	3.02	2.36	2.38
	3.26	3.93	2.27
	4.03	1.56	2.52
	3.67	4.29	3.10
	2.94	1.74	3.53
	5.90	2.17	3.06
	2.18	1.97	2.51
	5.39	4.69	3.48
	2.74	2.87	5.94
	3.49	3.17	2.52
Column Totals, T_j:	58.35	54.96	53.65
Brand Observations, n:	17	17	17

Grand Total $= \Sigma T_j = 166.96$
Total Observations $= N = 51$

$$= 200.28 + 177.68 + 169.31$$
$$= 547.27$$

Step 4. Square the grand total ΣT_j and divide by the total number of sample observations.

$$\frac{(\Sigma T_j)^2}{N} = \frac{(166.96)^2}{51}$$
$$= 546.58$$

Step 5. Subtract the computation made in Step 4 from the one in Step 2 to obtain the sum of squares total, SS TOTAL.

$$\text{SS TOTAL} = \sum\sum (Y_{ij})^2 - \frac{(\Sigma T_j)^2}{N}$$
$$= 601.27 - 546.58$$
$$= 54.69$$

Step. 6. Subtract the computation made in Step 4 from the one in Step 3 to obtain the sum of squares between brands, SS BETWEEN.

$$\text{SS BETWEEN} = \sum \left[\frac{T_j^2}{n} \right] - \frac{(\Sigma T_j)^2}{N}$$
$$= 547.27 - 546.58$$
$$= 0.69$$

Dividing by $K - 1$ gives the mean square between brand treatments, MS BETWEEN.

$$MS\ BETWEEN = SS\ BETWEEN/(K - 1)$$
$$= \frac{.69}{2}$$
$$= 0.345$$

Step 7. Subtract the computation made in Step 3 from the one made in Step 2 to obtain the sum of squares within brands, SS WITHIN.

$$SS\ WITHIN = \sum\sum (Y_{ij})^2 - \sum \left[\frac{T_j^2}{n}\right]$$
$$= 601.27 - 547.27$$
$$= 54.00$$

Dividing by $N - K$ obtains the mean square within brands, MS WITHIN.

$$MS\ WITHIN = SS\ WITHIN/(N - K)$$
$$= 54.00/48$$
$$= 1.125$$

Step 8. Obtain the calculated F ratio by dividing the mean square between brands by the mean square within brands.

$$F_c = \frac{MS\ BETWEEN}{MS\ WITHIN} = \frac{.345}{1.125} = .307 = .31\ (rounded)$$

Step 9. Compare the calculated F value F_c to the published F value found in the Appendix table for the chosen level of alpha and having $K - 1$ and $N - K$ degrees of freedom. Draw a conclusion on the null hypothesis of no brand effect. The null hypothesis is *rejected* if the larger of the two F values is F_c. For degrees of freedom of 2 and 48 at the typically used alpha levels of .01 and .05, the F ratios are

$$F_{2, 48, .01} = 5.08\ and\ F_{2, 48, .05} = 3.19.$$

F_c of 0.31 is substantially below both of these published F values, so one is not able to reject H_0 using either alpha of .01 or .05 as a criterion. Thus, the hypothesis that the mean length of life of the three cooking oil brands are equal is not rejected on the basis of the sample evidence.

Step 10. Construct a table such as Table 21.5. Summarize the following: the partitioning of the variation, the appropriate degrees of freedom, sum of squares, and means square.

TABLE 21.5. Summary of Cooking Oil Variation

Variation due to	DF	Sum of Squares	Mean Square	F_c ratio
Between Brands: $K - 1 = 2$		SS BETWEEN = 0.69	MS BETWEEN = 0.345	.31
Within Brands: $N - K = 48$		SS WITHIN = 54.00	MS WITHIN = 1.125	
Total: $N - 1 = 50$		SS TOTAL = 54.69		

21.8. Interpreting the Test Results

The brand-effect component of the total variation is small compared with the extraneous variation component. This is inferred from the calculated F statistic, which has a value less than one. Since the approximate expected numerical value of the F statistic when H_0 is true is one, and since the prob-value of F values below the expected F values exceed .5, it can be surmised that the prob-value for the calculated F statistic exceeds .5. Consequently the null hypothesis is not rejected. Had the reverse been true, that is, had there been a large brand effect compared with the extraneous variation, would the conclusion about the null hypothesis be reversed? Perhaps. Certainly the larger SS BETWEEN (the component measuring the variation among restaurants using different cooking oil brands) compared to SS WITHIN (the component measuring variation within the same restaurant),[3] the more inclined the investigator would be (given no other *a priori* evidence) to abandon the null hypothesis.

$$H_0: \mu = \mu_1 = \mu_2 = \mu_3 \text{ (no brand effect)}.$$

In this particular example, the calculated F statistic F_c indicates that the evidence brought to bear on H_0 was not substantial enough to reject H_0 at the maximum tolerable level of Type I error (alpha).

What is the decision-making implication of failing to reject the null hypothesis?

> The implication is that useful life of the cooking oil can safely be disregarded in deciding whether to switch to a supplier selling a different brand of cooking oil.

Thus, the decision maker can concentrate attention on other factors such as price, delivery frequency, credit terms, and possible change-over costs in reaching a decision.

Assumptions

Certain preconditions (given in Section 21.5) must be met to make the ANOVA technique reliable.

> Presumably the preconditions of *independent cooking life observations* has been assured by assigning the different brands *randomly* to the restaurants.

> The assumption of *equality of population variance* of cooking life response for each brand also seems not to have been violated. A comparison of these estimated brand standard deviations (Table 21.6) shows no gross disparity.

TABLE 21.6. Brand Standard Deviations of Cooking Oil Life

BRAND TREATMENT	SAMPLE SIZE	SAMPLE ST. DEVIATION
Superior	17	1.07
Agra	17	1.14
RCW	17	.96

The *normality* condition requires that measured response on useful life be approximately normally distributed for each brand subsample. Conformity with this assumption is likely, if the *numerous* untested factors (age of cooking fryer, experience of operating help, cleaning maintenance of the cooker) can be considered relatively independent of each other. Together the separate factors give an aggregate effect which follows a normal distribution.

> Although normality is difficult to verify in this case given the small number of each brand's observations, independence is assured by the experiment's design. Also, there is no strong *a priori* reason for believing otherwise.

Our example presented a simplified situation for the purpose of presenting the underlying logic of ANOVA and showing a basic application of the ANOVA technique. In practice, the situation is typically more complicated—sample sizes may be unequal for each brand, other factors are involved, interval estimates of the pairwise difference must be handled. Fuller discussion of these topics can be found in texts that deal almost exclusively with ANOVA, as the one by Scheffe.[4]

In the case where it is not plausible to assume normality of the underlying population, nonparametric tests, discussed in the next chapter, become more appropriate to use instead of ANOVA.

21.9. Concluding Comments

Analysis of variance is a powerful approach to the study of the relationship between the means of several different populations. Required assumptions are that (1) the dependent variable be quantitative, measured on an interval or ratio scale, (2) the K different populations of measurements must all be normally distributed with (3) common variance, σ^2. If one or more of these assumptions are highly implausible, an alternative is nonparametric methods discussed in the next chapter.

The null hypothesis tested is that all K populations of measurements have the same mean value. The test is based on the F statistic, which is the ratio of the "between means" estimate of the common population variance and the "within means" estimate of this value. The prob-value for a computed F statistic depends on the number of degrees of freedom in the numerator of the ratio, $K - 1$, and in the denominator, $K(n - 1)$.

The example of cooking oil life brings out a number of issues pertaining to the interpretation of the F statistic.

Failing to reject the null hypothesis led to a straightforward decision implication—cooking oil life can be eliminated as a factor in the supplier selection decision. But what if the null hypothesis is rejected? Mere knowledge that a difference exists among the population means for at least one pair of brands usually does not solve the decision maker's problem. Let's distinguish two situations:

> 1. *The decision rests only on the difference in life of the cooking oil, if any differences exist.* Rejection of the null hypothesis implies a statistical difference between the brands' cooking oil life. In the absence of any prior information about the difference among cooking oil life, one infers that the

brand which truly has the longest population mean useful life is the one that generated the longest sample mean useful life of the three observed.

2. *Differences in cooking oil life between brands is only one factor to be weighed against differences in factors* such as price and supplier reliability. In this case the pairwise differences in sample mean life can be computed to provide *contrasts.* Contrasts are point estimates of the corresponding population mean differences. The brand differences provide an input in making the final selection of the cooking oil brand.

Footnotes and References

[1]Other ways are often used to describe the categorical variable and its subgroups: for example, treatment and treatment levels, factor and factor levels.

[2]Business section of the *Chicago Tribune,* Monday, May 26, 1980.

[3]Note: there is another valid interpretation of SSs. The ratio of SS BETWEEN to SS TOTAL is equal to the unadjusted R^2. The unadjusted R^2 represents the ratio of explained variation to the total variation and is interpreted as the contribution that the systematic components (brand effects) have made in explaining, in an accounting sense, the total variation.

[4]Scheffe, Henry. *The Analysis of Variance,* John Wiley and Sons, Inc. 1959.

Questions and Problems

1. In Chapter 13 the t statistic was employed to test the null hypothesis of no difference between the means of the populations compared. Why can't the t statistic be employed to test the null hypothesis in the cooking oil example?

2. What are contrasts? If the categorical variable represents four decision options available to management, how many contrasts can be computed?

3. If the null hypothesis of no difference among brand effects is true, will the observed sample brand means be identical? If not, what would account for the differences?

4. Is there a rule of thumb for estimating how much variation to expect among sample means drawn from 4 separate, but identical, populations? If so, what is it?

5. Each of the sample variances computed from each brand's sample observations is an unbiased estimate of the extraneous variance. Does it matter which one is used

to estimate the extraneous variance? What procedure is usually followed in estimating the extraneous variance? Why?

6. If H_0 is true, MS BETWEEN is an unbiased estimate of the extraneous variance, σ^2. However, the sample variance on which MS BETWEEN is based is not computed directly for a sample of extraneous variation. It is derived from the estimated variance of a different sampling distribution, from which a sample of size K is drawn. What is this other sampling distribution? What is the relationship between its variance and the variance of the distribution of extraneous variation?

7. The value of MS WITHIN is an unbiased estimator of σ^2 *whether or not H_0 is true.* MS BETWEEN is an unbiased estimator of σ^2 only if H_0 is true. Explain how a comparison of the two values can be useful in drawing a conclusion as to whether H_0 is true.

8. If samples of size 9 are to be drawn from

each of 4 distinct populations having identical distributions:

a. what is the probability that the computed F ratio will exceed 4²?

b. what is the minimum value of F_c to reject H_0 at the .10 level of significance?

9. In order that ANOVA procedures be applicable, it is necessary that each of the K populations have the same variance and be normally distributed. Although these requirements seem quite restrictive, there are many actual situations in which both conditions are satisfied at least approximately. Explain.

10. For the Cooking Oil data given in Table 21.1, use the conceptionally based procedure described in section 21.6 to compute:

a. SS BETWEEN
b. SS WITHIN
c. SS TOTAL

Verify your answers by checking for agreement with the figures given in Table 21.3 obtained by the shortcut method.

11. Reconsider the Cooking Oil data given in Table 21.1 using only the first thirteen observations from each brand.

a. Use the shortcut computational procedure described in Section 21.7 to find the new values corresponding to the ones given in Table 21.3.

b. Test H_0 at the 5% level of significance.

12. If H_0 is rejected on the basis of F_c, does it follow that the means of the K populations are all different? Explain.

13. What is the decision making implication of:

a. failing to reject H_0?
b. rejecting H_0?

14. Given 5 degrees of freedom in the numerator and 7 in the denominator for the F distribution, determine F values where

a. 0.01 of the distribution lies to the right
b. 0.05 of the distribution lies to the right
c. 0.25 of the distribution lies to the right

15. Find the critical values of F assuming that the critical region is in the right tail and the degrees of freedom and level of significance are as given in Table 21.7.

16. Test H_0: $\mu_1 = \mu_2 = \mu_3 = \mu_4$ at the .05 level of significance, given the following results:

$n_1 = 3$ $n_2 = 3$
$n_3 = 3$ $n_4 = 3$
$\overline{X}_1 = 50.6$ $\overline{X}_2 = 45.63$
$\overline{X}_3 = 49.42$ $\overline{X}_4 = 44.8$

SS BETWEEN = 170.6
SS WITHIN = 41.4

17. The data in Table 21.8 are from three populations known to be normally distributed with equal variances.

TABLE 21.8. Three Normal Populations with Equal Variances

A	B	C
62	51	51
55	57	43
69	66	69
79	68	54

a. Develop the ANOVA table.

b. Test the hypothesis H_0: $\mu_A = \mu_B = \mu_C$ at the .05 level of significance.

18. *Scheduling Sales Calls* A study is being made of the amount of time sales representatives with a certain chinaware company spend on a sales call. The purpose is to determine whether schedules for sales calls should take into consideration the types of account being called upon. Twelve customer prospects are selected at random from each of three types

TABLE 21.7. Critical Values of F

	DEGREES OF FREEDOM IN NUMERATOR	DEGREES OF FREEDOM IN DENOMINATOR	LEVEL OF SIGNIFICANCE	CRITICAL VALUE OF F
a.	3	5	.05	____
b.	8	12	.10	____
c.	10	6	.01	____

TABLE 21.9. Time Spent on Sales Call, By Account Type

ACTIVE	INACTIVE	NEW PROSPECT
36	35	38
34	36	34
27	34	45
31	42	39
29	36	44
32	31	48
32	30	40
29	39	42
26	37	46
38	39	42
36	39	40
25	30	43

TABLE 21.10. "Whiteness" Ratings of Laundry Detergents, By Brand

A	B	C	D
32.0	31.4	30.9	33.1
34.5	32.6	29.4	36.8
29.5	35.1	33.1	36.2
32.2	36.8	32.7	34.5
28.7	29.5	31.5	35.9
28.9	33.4	29.6	35.4
30.9	35.2	35.3	33.6
31.4	30.7	31.2	31.4
27.1	34.9	32.0	29.8

of accounts in a large city. The number of minutes spent on each call is recorded. The data are given in Table 21.9.

a. Construct the ANOVA table.

b. Assuming that the three populations are normally distributed with equal variances, test the hypothesis that the mean length of call is identical for all three types of account.

c. Can you provide a plausible explanation why the populations might be approximately distributed as normal distributions with equal variances? What would you do if this assumption is not plausible?

19. *Validating Advertising Claims—A* A manufacturer of laundry detergent wants to advertise that one of its brands makes clothes look "whiter" on average than other brands. However, this claim must first be substantiated before it is aired. A random sample of 36 consumers, 9 for each of 4 detergent brands, participate in the experiment. Each participant does a regular load of laundry using the assigned detergent (with brand unidentified). At the completion of the wash load, the consumer rates the laundry for "whiteness" on a scale of 1 to 10.0. This is repeated three times and the ratings are summed. The results recorded are shown in Table 21.10.

a. Compute the ANOVA table for these data.

b. Test the hypothesis H_0: $\mu_A = \mu_B = \mu_C = \mu_D$ at the .05 level of significance.

c. What assumptions are required in order to justify the test in Part b?

d. Do the results substantiate the claim of a difference in "whiteness" as perceived by consumers? (Brand D is the brand in question.)

20. *Validating Advertising Claims—B* Refer to the experiment in Problem 19.

a. It is argued that the experiment conducted cannot be a fair test of the advertising claim because the same person did not try all four brands. Comment.

b. It is pointed out that different washing machines, different water temperatures, different water hardness levels, and different "degrees of dirtiness" of the wash to begin with could all have contributed to differences in the results. It is argued that the experiment cannot be a fair test of the advertising claim, since these conditions are not held constant. Comment.

c. It is argued that the design of the experiment does not facilitate identification of conditions in which the detergent is effective from conditions in which it is not effective. Without this distinction, consumers might mistakenly suppose it to be effective in all conditions. Comment.

d. It is argued that the failure to replicate the experiment under conditions which might exist in a household (same washing machine, same water hardness, etc.) means it is impossible to estimate the variability in "whiteness" a consumer could expect to experience. Comment.

21. *Management Style and Sales Representative Productivity* A large department

TABLE 21.11. Sales by Management Style

A	B	C	D
388	375	436	475
496	450	421	490
452	333	508	515
470	468	497	509

store chain conducted an experiment to learn whether management style changes the productivity of its retail sales force. Sixteen sales reps were randomly assigned to four different groups. The groups were given different managerial styles and the output was subsequently measured. The data in Table 21.11 are the sales for a one month period.

a. Construct the ANOVA table.

b. Test the null hypothesis at the 5 percent level of significance.

c. What assumptions are necessary to justify the test you conducted in Part b?

22. Suppose the four styles in Problem 21 are as follows:

A. No change from existing style.

B. Same as A except that periodic official notes remind employees that punctuality, courteousness, attentiveness, etc., are expected of employees.

C. Management participates with employees in monthly "brainstorming" sessions.

D. Management asks employees to participate in storesponsored "personal improvement" workshops on sales techniques.

a. How would you develop a point estimate of the sales change attributable to implementing style D?

b. How would you develop a point estimate of the differential effect of style C as compared to style D?

23. *Sales Impact of Container Size* A firm is market testing three alternative container sizes for its instant breakfast. The alternatives refer to different ways of boxing 144 packages in a case. Alternative 1 is a case of 24 6-package boxes; Alternative 2 is 16 9-package boxes, and Alternative 3 is 12 12-package boxes. Each alternative is placed in 9 stores and the sales measured over a period of one month. The sales in cases per month are shown in Table 21.12.

TABLE 21.12. Sales Per Month, By Alternative Container Size

1			2			3		
33	12	87	40	43	22	45	17	21
76	39	45	46	58	62	60	9	12
48	45	107	78	25	37	58	43	36

a. Compute the mean sales per month for each brand.

b. Use the analysis of variance procedure to test at the 5 percent level the null hypothesis of no difference in mean sales among the three alternatives.

c. A critic of the test notes that a choice must be made among the three alternatives whether or not the null hypothesis is rejected. The critic says the test serves no useful purpose, because there is no decision implication unless the null hypothesis is rejected. Can you suggest a way in which the null hypothesis test might fit into a decision framework for choosing among the brands?

Nonparametric Statistics

Preview.   With a single exception, the inferential procedures we have considered are characterized by two themes. First, they are concerned with *population parameters* (the population mean; the population proportion). Second, their applicability depends upon the validity of a set of assumptions about the data and distribution of the population (for example, that the data are interval-scaled and normally distributed). These inferential procedures are called *parametric* procedures. Parametric procedures are extremely useful, yet have limitations which greatly restrict their versatility. For example, in the case of small samples, the Student t test statistic if strictly applied can only be used for hypothesis testing if the population is normally distributed (Chapter 12). What if this condition cannot be met? Does it rule out hypothesis testing? Are there alternative tests which do not require a normally distributed population?

Fortunately, there is an important class of statistical methods available to appropriately test hypotheses in a wide assortment of small sample and other situations where the requirements of parametric testing are not met. These methods are called *distribution-free* or *nonparametric* tests. They are distinguished from parametric tests in that they are not concerned with population parameters, or do not depend for their validity upon the data being interval-scaled or upon specific assumptions (for example, normality) about the distribution of population values. The one nonparametric inferential procedure we studied is the chi-square test of independence. In this chapter we shall study eight other nonparametric tests and the situations which make it advantageous to employ them. Some of the nonparametric tests have parametric counterparts; others do not.

22.1. Introduction

In previous chapters we have considered test procedures dependent on normally distributed data. These are *parametric* tests. In this chapter we consider alternative methods which have in common three highly desirable features:

> freedom from *a priori* conditions as to the specific type of underlying populations generating the sample data; the population can be normal or non-normally distributed.

> freedom from prerequisite *parameter* conditions about the population; for example, if we wish to decide whether a sample is random or non-random, we use a nonparametric test. No reference to parameters is involved.

> freedom from severe restrictions about the *kinds of data* that can be analyzed. Consumers, for example, may be asked to rank their preferences for several brands of soft drinks; ranks are measured on an ordinal scale (more preferred to less preferred, without specifying how much). This is a weaker scale than the interval scale required by most parametric tests.

These freedoms overcome the inadequacies of the t tests and F tests. The t test used with sampling from two populations (Chapter 13) and the F test used with sampling from more than two populations (Chapter 21) require interval scaled normal populations with equal population variance parameters. The alternative tests considered in this chapter do not. They are free of these restrictions and for this reason are called *distribution free* or *nonparametric* tests.

Nonparametric Tests Offer Greater Flexibility

To see the great flexibility of nonparametric tests with regard to kinds of data, consider the classification scheme for variables in Figure 22.1. (Note: measurement scales were first discussed in Section 2.7.)

Parametric tests are confined to data measured on nominal, interval, or ratio scales; they cannot handle data *ordinally* scaled (ranked). Many of the nonparametric tests are not handicapped by this restriction.

FIGURE 22.1. Classification Scheme for Variables

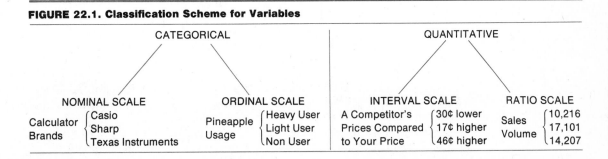

Parametric Tests Are More Sensitive—
But Are Their Conclusions More Reliable?

Not all parametric tests have nonparametric counterparts and vice versa. However, in many situations a parametric and a nonparametric test can both be used. What guideline should direct the choice of test?

> Provided the assumptions for using the parametric test are valid, the *parametric* test is preferable.

Why? Because the parametric test provides a greater sensitivity than its nonparametric counterpart in detecting differences and relationships between populations. On the other hand, using a parametric test in the face of strong reservations about the validity of the assumptions can lead to an unreliable conclusion. Thus, the efficiency of the parametric test is preferable, but not at the price of an unreliable conclusion.

Let's be more specific. In testing the difference between the means of two populations both parametric and nonparametric methods could be used. If both populations are normally distributed with equal variance, the *parametric t* test studied in Chapter 12 has an advantage. Under these conditions and for any level of type I error assumed tolerable, the parametric *t* test offers, with a 5 percent smaller sample size, the same assurance of detecting a real difference in populations means (if there is one) than would the comparable nonparametric test. However, a serious departure from the parametric requirements of normality and equal variance undermines the trustworthiness of the *t* test. Importantly, its use under these circumstances would create a false sense of confidence in whatever conclusions are reached. Thus if the assumptions of the parametric test are met, the parametric test should be used. It requires a smaller sample size to achieve the same degree of reliability. When doubt exists about the validity of these assumptions, the nonparametric counterpart offers greater reliability for the same sample size.

The first nonparametric test we consider is one which has no parametric counterpart. It is the runs test for sequential randomness.

22.2. Runs Test for Sequential Randomness

In the Wall Street situation described in the next example, it is important to know whether there is a sequential pattern to the data. The parametric methods we have studied are not applicable. A nonparametric approach is required.

────────

Example 22.2A.   Stock Splits: A Special Profit Opportunity or Not?

In the financial world, a corporation's action to issue without charge additional shares of stock to its stockholders is known as a *stock split*. For example, a stockholder owning 100 shares might receive an additional 100 shares gratis. This would be a "two-for-one" split, in that the stockholder ends up with two shares for every one held initially. After the split, the price of the shares will drop to reflect the larger number of shares outstanding. For example, if one share was selling for $100 before the two-for-one split, a price drop to $50 per share after the split would make the two shares equal in value to the one held initially. If the stock traditionally has been priced in the $50 range but has recently risen to $100, the corporation might split the stock to bring it back to the price range where it traditionally sells.

A stock split is viewed by some financial analysts as more than merely an exercise in arithmetic. They interpret the split as a signal from corporate management that the recent stock price increase is based on solid earnings potential and is not just a temporary speculative bubble soon to be burst by disappointing earnings news. Consequently, they view the split as a good omen for earnings to come, and hence for future stock price gains that would outperform the market.

Is a stock split a piece of information a financial analyst can parlay into profit by buying on news of the split? That is, does the market soon give a higher value to the two new shares than the one original share? Among some people who regard themselves as financially astute, the idea of a stock split creating value is pure hogwash—one of the many myths of the stock market. Some think differently. For example, a recent article notes:

> "Stock splits are generally bullish," says *Outlook,* the advisory published by Standard & Poor's. "An issue usually will rise in price at the time a company's directors propose a split. Searching for split candidates can be a rewarding undertaking."[1]

Take the pro-side of the stock-split question. Suppose investors believe that stocks which split will subsequently outperform the market. Suppose the investors gradually back their beliefs with a willingness to pay a higher price for the stocks. After the split, what should be the pattern of successive stock price levels?—A *discernible upward pattern.* That is, an investor buying the stock at the time of the split announcement and holding it should presumably soon be rewarded by positive above-average gains.

On the other hand, take the con-side of the stock-split question. What if the market reacts very quickly so that the market price reflects the news of the stock-split immediately? Or what if investors do not regard a stock-split as a fundamental piece of information affecting the stock's true worth? In these cases, what will an examination of the sequential pattern of price changes after the split show? Not a systematic upward trend but, instead, a *patternless series* of stock price changes conforming to a random process, offering no positive above-average returns opportunity.

What are the measurable symptoms of a random sequential process? That is, how does one distinguish between *random* sequential price change patterns and the *systematic* price change patterns such as trends and periodic movements we discussed in Chapter 17? In general, how does one establish from a sequence of observations on price changes that there are *no* systematic patterns?

A hypothesis test seems appropriate to resolve this issue. But note that this situation is quite different from all previous situations in which hypotheses were tested. First, we have no information on the *type of distribution* for price changes. We don't know whether it is a normal distribution. Second, we are not testing a hypothesis about a *parameter value* of the price change distribution (for example, its mean or standard deviation), as would have to be the case with a parametric test. Instead our hypothesis is about the pattern or *sequence* of changes. So this will have to be a nonparametric test. The nonparametric *runs test* provides a formal statistical procedure for making such an investigation.

Runs Above and Below the Median

Sequential randomness: how is it tested? With sample (quantitative) data, a very useful starting point is to dichotomize the data into opposite categories. For example, for a consecutive series of stock price changes, each period's stock price change could be classified as above ($+$) or below ($-$) the median stock price change (or some other dividing line) of the series. Described in this way, the data become a string of categorical designations. For example,

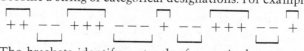

The brackets identify a *streak* of a particular category. The streak, called a *run*, is an important notion in testing for randomness. More specifically, the *number* of runs in the sequence is a statistic used to judge whether there is randomness (or lack of it) in a sequence of observations. The number of runs in a *nonrandom* sequence tends to be very different from the number in a random sequence of the same length.

At one extreme, there are nonrandom patterns which show strong *persistent* movements in the same direction—trends which continue for many periods. This kind of a systematic pattern produces very *few* runs. For example, in the following sequence of 13 observations there are only two runs.

```
         1
   ┌──────────┐
   + + + + + + +   - - - - - -
               └──────────────┘
                      2
```

At the other end of the spectrum, there are nonrandom patterns which exhibit an excessive frequency of *abrupt reversals* in direction. This kind of a systematic pattern results in an *overabundance* of runs. For example, in the following sequence of 13 observations there are 13 runs.

```
  1     3     5     7     9    11    13
  ┌┐    ┌┐    ┌┐    ┌┐    ┌┐    ┌┐    ┌┐
  +  -  +  -  +  -  +  -  +  -  +  -  +
     └┘    └┘    └┘    └┘    └┘    └┘
     2     4     6     8    10    12
```

So for any sample sequence,

the least runs count is two, and

the most runs one can have is one more than twice the number of observations in the smaller of the two categories.

For example, in the last sequence of 13 observations there are alternating pluses and minuses. This leads to the highest possible runs count for any sequence of 13 observations. The smaller category was minuses. There were six. Twice this number plus one gives 13, the maximum number of runs for the sequence of 7 pluses and six minuses.

For a *nonrandom* sequence, the count tends to be near one of these two extremes. For a *random* sequence, the runs count tends to lie somewhere between the two extremes—larger than the extremely small number of runs associated with persistent movement in the same direction; smaller than the extremely large number of runs associated with frequent abrupt reversals of direction.

The Sampling Distribution for the Number of Runs (Assuming Randomness)

For a random process, the length of runs varies considerably and in no fixed pattern. It is found that the distribution of the number of runs R, for repeated samples of n observations drawn from such a process, will be a hypergeometric distribution encountered in sampling without replacement from a finite population (see Chapter 9). Fortunately the tedious task of computing the hypergeometric probability of obtaining a specific number of runs for a particular sample sequence can be avoided. A standard normal table can be used instead to calculate the probability of R. The normal distribution is a very good approximation of the probability distribution of R if the number of sample observations exceeds twenty and the number of $+$ and $-$ are each greater than ten, a condition often found.

The normal distribution approximating the Hypergeometric distribution of R has a mean or expected value of

$$\mu_R = \frac{2n_1 n_2}{n_1 + n_2} + 1$$

where n_1 and n_2 are the number of positive and negative marks. Its standard deviation is:

$$\sigma_R = \sqrt{\frac{2n_1 n_2 (2n_1 n_2 - n_1 - n_2)}{(n_1 + n_2)^2 (n_1 + n_2 - 1)}}$$

Alternative Hypotheses

Alternative hypotheses express competing beliefs about the nature of the process generating the observed runs. They are:

Null, H_0: the sequential pattern is in conformity with a random process.

Alternative, H_A: the sequential pattern is in conformity with a nonrandom process.

The test statistic used in testing the alternative belief is the standard normal value, Z, for the difference between the actual number R and expected number μ_R of runs:

$$Z = \frac{R - \mu_R}{\sigma_R}$$

For example, if the distribution of R has a mean of 10 and a standard deviation of 2, the value of Z corresponding to $R = 15$ runs would be

$$Z = \frac{15 - 10}{2} = 2.5$$

The prob-value for the calculated Z value is obtained from the probability table for the standardized normal distribution. A two-sided test is usually employed since a departure from randomness can result from either too few or too many runs. In the example that follows, the stock split hypothesis described in Example 22.2A is tested using the nonparametric runs test.

Example 22.2B. Using the Runs Test to Investigate the Reaction of the Market to Stock Splits

The data graphed on the right side of the vertical line in Figure 22.2 represent the *path of monthly abnormal returns* for a hypothetical stock subsequent to splitting.

The positive marks (+) indicate those post-splitting months that the splitting stock has percentage price changes *above* what is expected, given the risk of the stock and the movement of the market. The negative mark (−) indicates a return (percentage price change) below what is expected, given the risk of the stock and the movement of the market.

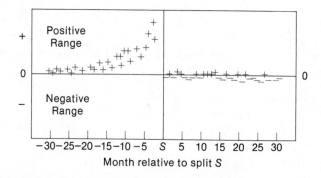

FIGURE 22.2 The Behavior of Price Changes of a Split Stock

Is there a sequential nonrandom pattern of the returns for the post-splitting period? Concluding that there is would suggest exploiting such post-splitting patterns for better than normal profits. Stated as competing hypotheses:

Null, H_0: the sequence of the stock's abnormal returns after the split follows a *random* process.

Alternative, H_A: the sequence of the stock's abnormal returns after the split follows a *nonrandom* pattern.

The pattern of + and − marks and number of runs in the post-splitting period is:

$$-\underset{1}{+}-\underset{2}{+}\underset{3}{+}\underset{4}{---}\underset{5}{+}-\underset{6}{-}\underset{7}{+}\underset{8}{+++}\underset{9}{--}\underset{10}{+}\underset{11}{-}\underset{12}{+}\underset{13}{-}\underset{14}{+}\underset{15}{----}\underset{16}{+}\underset{17}{---}$$

Runs Number

Solution: There are 12 +, 18 − and seventeen runs. The sample size is 30 so the sampling distribution of R will approximate the standard normal distribution with mean and standard deviation values of:

$$\mu_R = \frac{2n_1 n_2}{n_1 + n_2} + 1 = \frac{2(12)(18)}{30} + 1 = \underline{\underline{15.4}}$$

$$\sigma_R = \sqrt{\frac{2n_1 n_2(2n_1 n_2 - n_1 - n_2)}{(n_1 + n_2)^2(n_1 + n_2 - 1)}}$$

$$= \sqrt{\frac{173{,}664}{(900)(29)}} = \sqrt{6.653793104} = \underline{\underline{2.5795}}$$

The calculated Z test statistic is therefore:

$$Z_c = \frac{R - \mu_R}{\sigma_R}$$

$$Z_c = \frac{17 - 15.4}{2.5795} = \underline{\underline{0.6203}}$$

Again, it is important to note that μ_R and σ_R are *not* parameters of the stock price change distribution, which would be required in order for the test to be parametric.

The two-tail-test prob-value associated with Z represents the area under both the lower and upper tails beyond $Z = 0.6203$. From the standardized normal probability table the prob-value is found to be $1 - .4648 = .5352$.

Using the traditional significance levels of .05 and .01 the null hypothesis cannot be rejected. Only for significance levels above .5352 would the null hypothesis H_0 be rejected. The testing suggests that the observed difference between the sample value of 17 and the expected value of 15.4 under the null was likely the work of chance variation.

What does the conclusion of the hypothesis test imply about the value of stock splits? Since the null hypothesis was not rejected, the evidence is in strong conformity with the belief that the abnormal returns follow a *random* and not a systematic sequential pattern. Without a systematic pattern, the idea that a stock split is a bullish influence on future price changes is not credible. Moreover, even if the randomness hypothesis had been rejected, the fact that eighteen out of the 30 monthly abnormal returns are negative would suggest a *bearish, not bullish* investor attitude prevailing subsequent to the split.

Two additional items must be mentioned before concluding this example. First, although the company is fictitious, the data are not. They are taken from a famous study by Fama, Fisher, Jensen, and Roll, and represent the *average* abnormal returns to some 940 split stocks examined in the study.[2] Second, note the upward pattern of abnormal returns shown on the *left* side of the figure. This pattern is *not* random and indicates a substantial price rise *before* the announcement is made to the public.

This suggests that there *is* an association between stock price increases and stock splits, but not one that you can take advantage of by buying in after the stocks have split. By that time the split-adjusted price has already peaked, perhaps in *anticipation* of the split (inside information?).

22.3. Two Independent Samples: The Wilcoxon Ranked Sum Test and the Mann-Whitney Test

Suppose independent samples of quantitative data have been drawn from two populations to test whether these populations have identical distributions. Under some circumstances the large-sample and small-sample parametric tests discussed in Chapter 12 are applicable. How limited are these circumstances? What nonparametric procedures are available if the parametric tests cannot be used?

1. *Large Samples: the Z test* If (a) the sample is large enough and (b) the data are on an interval scale, then the parametric Z test (based on the standardized normal distribution) for the difference between two population means would be appropriate.

2. *Small Samples: the t-test* For small samples (a) based on interval data from (b) two normally distributed populations with (c) equal variances, the t test is appropriate.

Both large and small sample parametric tests require interval data. What if the available data are only on an *ordinal* scale? It may be that the original interval data have been transformed into rank data and are now inaccessible, or that the original data were never on an interval scale to begin with. Or what if the populations are not expected to have a common variance or to be normally distributed? In these cases both the large and small sample parametric procedures would be inappropriate and a nonparametric test would be needed.

Two nonparametric tests would be suitable and lead to the same result—the Wilcoxon test and the Mann-Whitney U test.

The *Wilcoxon test* for ranked-sums is desirable because it is simpler. The *Mann-Whitney U test* is desirable to know because it is encountered in the research literature.

Both tests will be illustrated in the following example.

Example 22.3. **Automobile Life**

Does the make of automobile you drive have a longer road life than the make of automobile your neighbor drives? For consumers this is an important question, so manufacturers have to take it seriously too. In fact, several automobile makers (Volvo, Mercedes-Benz) have gone so far as to publish the claims of satisfied owners on how many miles they have put on the cars that are still running satisfactorily.

Are these the exceptions? How can a manufacturer determine the road life (in miles driven) of the cars it produces? Why not survey the automobile scrap yards, the burial ground for worn out automobiles?

Suppose AMC wants to find out if its brand S compact lasts as long as the GMC brand M compact. A visit to local scrap yards by the AMC product researcher gives the small sample data shown in Table 22.1. Procedurally, the sample is collected to include all automobiles other than those scrapped because of collision accident damage. For the vehicles sampled on which the odometer had obviously passed 100,000 miles, 100,000 is added to the odometer reading.

TABLE 22.1. Odometer Reading at Scrappage (thousands of miles)

SAMPLE BRAND S:	Size 18	SAMPLE BRAND M:	Size 17
99.2	113.9	107.0	79.7
100.8	102.5	75.6	106.9
96.7	83.8	102.9	86.8
94.5	87.4	101.5	106.8
80.0	94.9	105.5	83.6
89.4	90.2	77.4	88.7
119.0	92.6	81.7	91.7
82.8	87.0	93.1	99.3
94.9	81.8	81.3	

Similar auto longevity studies suggest that the underlying distribution is highly skewed to the right with some autos reaching unusually high mileage before scrappage. Therefore, the parametric t test requirement of a normal population is not likely to be met. The nonparametric Wilcoxon test does not require a normal population and can be used with the skewed distribution provided the variances and the shapes are the same.

The null hypothesis to be tested is:

H_0: there is no difference in the population between brands S and M in mean mileage upon scrappage; $\mu_S = \mu_M$

H_A: $\mu_S \neq \mu_M$

The Wilcoxon Two-sample Ranked Sum Test

To test the null hypothesis using the Wilcoxon Two-sample Ranked Sum Test, the test statistic W must be computed. A four step procedure is followed:

1. *pool* the samples, arraying the absolute values of the pooled observations from low to high (column 3 and 6 of Table 22.2).

2. *rank* the low to high arrayed values, with the lowest value a rank of 1.

3. working with the ranks, *assign the rank to its appropriate brand.* For example, since the observation with value 75.6 was a Brand M car, its rank of 1 is listed in the Brand M column.

If the mean mileage life of Brand S and Brand M do not differ, the rankings ought to be more or less evenly dispersed between the two brands. But if there is a brand effect on mileage life, the automobiles of the longer-mileage brand ought to have higher rankings. An examination of the rankings does not clearly show whether the observed differences are due to the brands or simply to chance variation.

4. To examine this, the test statistic W is computed by *summing the ranks* for the particular brand with the *smaller sample size.* In this case brand M has the smaller sample size. It's rank sum is:

$W = 1 + 2 + 3 + \ldots + 33 = 294$

TABLE 22.2. Ranked Observations from Table 22.1.

COL. 1 RANK BRAND S	COL. 2 RANK BRAND M	COL. 3 OBSERVATION	COL. 4 RANK BRAND S	COL. 5 RANK BRAND M	COL. 6 OBSERVATION
	1	75.6		19	93.1
	2	77.4	20		94.5
	3	79.7	21.5		94.9
4		80.0	21.5		94.9
	5	81.3	23		96.7
	6	81.7	24		99.2
7		81.8		25	99.3
8		82.8	26		100.8
	9	83.6		27	101.5
10		83.8	28		102.5
	11	86.8		29	102.9
12		87.0		30	105.5
13		87.4		31	106.8
	14	88.7		32	106.9
15		89.4		33	107.0
16		90.2	34		113.9
	17	91.7	35		119.0
18		92.6			

If the two samples are of the *same size,* it does not matter which one is used to compute W.

What distribution does the statistic W follow for most sample sizes encountered? For samples larger than 10 and under the assumption that the null hypothesis is true, the distribution of W can be approximated accurately by the normal curve with mean

$$\mu_W = \frac{n_1(n_1 + n_2 + 1)}{2} = \frac{17(17 + 18 + 1)}{2} = 306$$

The standard deviation is

$$\sigma_W = \sqrt{\frac{n_1 n_2 (n_1 + n_2 + 1)}{12}} = \sqrt{\frac{(17)(18)(17 + 18 + 1)}{12}} = 30.299$$

where n_1 and n_2 are the respective sizes of the smaller and larger samples.

To calculate the standardized normal test statistic Z, the following expression is used:

$$Z = \frac{W - \mu_W}{\sigma_W}$$

Thus the calculated Z test statistic is

$$Z_c = \frac{W - \mu_W}{\sigma_W} = \frac{294 - 306}{30.299} = -.396$$

From the standardized normal probability table, the two-tail probability of finding a Z statistic as extreme, or more so, as the $-.396$ found is $1 - .31 = .69$. For the commonly used levels of .05 and .01, the null can't be rejected. Thus, this sample evidence is consistent with the null hypothesis of equal mean mileage for the two brands.

What does the finding of no significant difference between the two brands of cars imply about their relative longevity? It implies that the mileage differences among cars of the *same brand* can reasonably be thought to account for what appears to be a *difference between* the brands. That is, the observed greater average mileage of Brand S cars over Brand M cars in the two samples is not sufficiently large to rule out the plausibility of the hypothesis that the two brands have equal mileage longevity on average. Thus the conclusion is that the longer mean life of Brand S cars in the scrap yard sample is attributable to nothing more than the chance variation that came with sampling.

How are ties handled in computing the rankings? Ties are given a rank equal to the *average rank of the tied observations*. That is, if three observations tied for ranks 4, 5, and 6, each observation would be given *rank 5*. In Table 22.2 two observations are tied for ranks 21 and 22, so each is given rank 21.5.

The Mann-Whitney *U* Test

The Mann-Whitney U Test, another nonparametric test, is equivalent to, but procedurely different from, the Wilcoxon Two-Sample Ranked Sum test. The Mann-Whitney U test also requires the calculations of ranked sums. The following test statistic is used:

$$U = n_1 n_2 + \frac{n_1(n_1 + 1)}{2} - W$$

In the automobile mileage example, the value of U is:

$$U = (17)(18) + \frac{(17)(18)}{2} - 294$$

$$= 306 + 153 - 294 = 165$$

The sampling distribution for U can also be approximated by the normal distribution. This approximation will be adequate when both n_1 and n_2 are larger than 10. In this case the calculated Z test statistic using the mean and standard deviation for the U statistic is:

$$\mu_U = \frac{n_1 n_2}{2}$$

$$= \frac{(17)(18)}{2} = 153$$

$$\sigma_U = \sqrt{\frac{n_1 n_2 (n_1 + n_2 + 1)}{12}}$$

$$= \sqrt{\frac{(17 \times 18)(17 + 18 + 1)}{12}} = 30.299$$

$$Z = \frac{U - \frac{n_1 n_2}{2}}{\sigma_U} = \frac{165 - 153}{30.299} = \frac{12}{30.299} = .396$$

Thus, the value of Z in the Mann-Whitney U test is the same in absolute terms as in the Wilcoxon test; so the prob-value and conclusions are also the same. Although the U test involves some additional computations, it is good to know because many research studies (particularly earlier ones) have used it.

22.4. Matched Pairs Differences: The Wilcoxon Signed-Rank Sum Test and the Sign Test

The Wilcoxon Ranked-Sum and the Mann-Whitney tests were used to test the difference between two *independent* samples. They are not applicable to testing the difference between a *matched pair* of samples. Other nonparametric techniques must be used in analyzing the difference between matched pairs of observations. The choice among the two most widely used techniques depends upon the measurement scale of the data.

> The *Wilcoxon Signed-Rank Sum Test* is preferred when the matched pairs of differences are *interval* (or ratio) measurements.

> The *Sign Test* is used when the matched pairs of differences are only *ordinal* (ranked) measurements.

The Wilcoxon Signed-Rank Sum Test

The Wilcoxon Rank Sum Test for *independent* samples from two populations ranked the *absolute values* of two *pooled* sets of observations. In dealing with two sets of observations which are *paired* and *differenced*, it is the absolute values of the *paired differences* which are ranked.

A five step procedure is used to compute the Wilcoxon Signed-Rank Sum Statistic, denoted by V.

1. Compute the difference for each matched pair formed from the two samples.

$$d_i = X_{1_i} - X_{2_i}$$

For example, if the first pair of observations are $X_{1_i} = 12$ for the first sample and $X_{2_i} = 16$ for the second sample, then the first period difference is $d_1 = 12 - 16 = -4$.

2. Take the *absolute value* of the differences (ignore signs), $|d_i|$. Thus, $|d_i| = |-4| = 4$.

3. Rank the absolute value of the d_i. (If a difference is zero, do not use it; don't assign it a rank.) Establish two groups, one for positive d_i, the other for negative d_i.

4. Allocate each rank to one of two groups according to the sign of the original matched pair difference. Suppose $d_i = -4$ had a rank of 7 in step 3. Then 7 would be assigned to the negative difference group.

5. Calculate the sum of the *ranks* of the differences for each group (positive and negative sign groups). The smaller sum is V.

When n is large (25 or larger) the sampling distribution for V can be approximated by a normal distribution with mean:

$$\mu_V = \frac{n(n + 1)}{4}$$

and standard deviation:

$$\sigma_V = \sqrt{\frac{n(n + 1)(2n + 1)}{24}}$$

Thus, the Z statistic is calculated from:

$$Z_c = \frac{V - \dfrac{n(n + 1)}{4}}{\sqrt{\dfrac{n(n + 1)(2n + 1)}{24}}}$$

The prob-value associated with the Z_c statistic will depend on whether the null hypothesis implies a one or two tailed test.

In the following example, a marketing experiment is described. The data for the experiment are appropriately analyzed using the Wilcoxon Signed-Rank Sum test.

Example 22.4A.   The Effect of Supermarket Shelf Position on Product Sales

Wheaties, Ultra-Brite, and Alberto VO-5. Do these and other brands achieve greater consumer sales if the products are displayed at eye level on supermarket shelves? If they do, supermarket retailers want to know so they can put their most profitable products on the "best" shelves. Manufacturers want to know, too. They must decide whether or not to commit armies of sales representatives to the battle for the best supermarket shelf space.

The answer for both the retailer and the manufacturer rests on the shopping habits of consumers. If consumers are "product visibility" buyers or "impulse" buyers, brand exposure through eye level shelf display will be a strong stimulant to sales. On the other hand, if "brand loyalty" dominates consumer thinking on what to buy, consumers will search for and select a brand regardless of its shelf space position. With consumer behavior of the latter type, any attempt to improve profit by gaining eye level shelf space for a particular brand will be a misdirected use of time, effort, and possibly sales force resources.

An effective way to determine whether the position of the shelf space affects product sales is a statistical experiment using a randomized block design. Such a study was conducted for several products at 24 different stores. The stores were first grouped into 12 pairs according to similarity of weekly sales. Then one of the stores in each pair was picked randomly to display at eye level shelf space the brand product. The other store displayed the brand product with shelf space "above or

TABLE 22.3. Packages of the Breakfast Product Sold in Test Store

COL. 1 Store Pair	COL. 2 Sample 1 Non-Eyelevel Shelf Pos.	COL. 3 Sample 2 Eyelevel Shelf Pos.	COL. 4 Original Diff.	COL. 5 Absolute Value of Diff.	COL. 6 Ranks of Absolute Val. of Diff.	COL. 7 Positive Diff. Ranks	COL. 8 Negative Difference Ranks
1	71	111	−40	40	10		10
2	121	150	−29	29	9		9
3	133	130	3	3	2	2	
4	126	154	−28	28	8		8
5	93	67	26	26	6	6	
6	49	112	−63	63	12		12
7	109	84	25	25	5	5	
8	96	123	−27	27	7		7
9	27	71	−44	44	11		11
10	58	62	−4	4	3		3
11	36	38	−2	2	1		1
12	37	51	−14	14	4		4
						$V = 13$	65

below eye level." The results for breakfast products are shown in Table 22.3. The hypothesis tested is:

H_0: Sales of the product exposed on shelf space above or below eye level are at least as great as the sales of the brand when exposed at the eye level shelf.

The alternative hypothesis is:

H_A: Sales of the product when displayed on shelf space above or below eye level are less than the sales associated with the product exposed at the eye level position.

The investigator must decide whether to assume that the observed differences, d_i are drawn from a normal sampling distribution. If this assumption is made, the parametric t test could be used appropriately to test whether there is a real difference in sales due to shelf exposure level. But is the assumption of normality justified in this problem? It would be a shaky assumption if its basis is the observed sample distribution of only twelve differences. Given this reservation, a safer approach is to use the nonparametric Wilcoxon test which doesn't require normality.

The V statistic for Table 22.3 is calculated as follows.

1. For each store pair, the difference between the sample observations gives the original differences in Col. 4.

2. Ignoring signs leads to the absolute value of differences shown in Column 5.

3. Column 6 shows ranks, assigned to the 12 absolute differences, starting with 1 for the lowest.

4. Then the ranks are assigned to a positive or negative group based on the sign of the original difference (Columns 7 and 8).

5. Just as in the Wilcoxon Rank Sum Test for independent samples, the sum of the ranks is taken for either the positive or negative grouping, whichever is smaller. In this case the sum of the three positive rank differences is picked:

$V = 2 + 6 + 5 = 13$

The null hypothesis implies a one-tail test. The Z statistic that follows is

$$Z = \frac{V - \dfrac{n(n+1)}{4}}{\sqrt{\dfrac{n(n+1)(2n+1)}{24}}} = \frac{13 - \dfrac{12(13)}{4}}{\sqrt{\dfrac{(12)(13)(25)}{24}}} = \frac{-26}{\sqrt{162.5}} = -2.040$$

This Z statistic has a prob-value of .0207, indicating that the null hypothesis would be rejected at the 5% level of significance. Thus, assuming that the experiment was properly designed, it appears that eye level shelf positions do stimulate sales for the breakfast product. Whether the amount of sales stimulation is worth fighting over is another question and has not been answered by the test.[3]

Ties in determining the ranks are resolved by assigning to each tied difference the *average of the tied ranks.* For example, if two differences were tied for the 4th and 5th ranked positions, they would both be assigned a rank of 4.5. If more than one-fourth of the differences are involved in ties, the Wilcoxon method should not be used.

Differences of zero are simply eliminated and the number of pairs reduced accordingly.

The Sign Test

The Wilcoxon Signed-Rank Sum test calculations implicitly assume that the d_i are interval measurements. Thus, for paired differences measured on an *ordinal* scale, the Wilcoxon Signed-Rank Sum test is not applicable. One would not be able to calculate the value of the d_i, only their signs. The appropriate nonparametric test is the *sign test*, which in principle can be used to test *any* type of matched pair differences. However, its use in practice should be limited to data that are on an ordinal scale because the Wilcoxon test is more likely to reject a false null if the differences are interval data.

A situation in which the sign test proves to be very useful is given in the following example.

Example 22.4B. Bond Rating Services: Are Moody's and Standard and Poor's Equally Conservative?

Tens of thousands of corporate and municipal bonds are periodically rated for "investment quality" by two rating services: Moody's and Standard and Poor's. A simplified description of the ratings categories is given in Table 22.4.

Are the two rating services equally conservative in rating investment quality? To find out, a hypothesis test can be conducted on the difference in ratings published by the two organizations. Because each bond issue is rated by both services, matched pairs rather than an independent sample test is appropriate. However, the Wilcoxon Signed-Rank Sum Test used in the previous example is *not* applicable. The problem is that the difference between a Moody's rating and the corresponding Standard and Poor's rating is not an interval measurement. A Moody's rating of Aaa

TABLE 22.4. Comparison of Bond Rating Categories

QUALITY CHARACTERIZATION	SYMBOLS	
	Moody's	Standard and Poor's
Prime	Aaa	AAA
Excellent	Aa	AA
Upper Medium	A, A-1	A
Lower Medium	Baa, Baa-1	BBB
Marginally Speculative	Ba	BB
Very Speculative	B, Caa	B
Default	Ca, C	D

is higher than a Standard and Poor's AA rating. (This can be denoted by assigning a + sign to the difference.) But there is no way to measure how much Moody's rating exceeds that of Standard and Poor's.

Can the null hypothesis of no difference in rating investment quality still be tested? Fortunately, yes. Even when the differences can only be denoted as + or − as in this case, a nonparametric test is applicable. The *sign test* is used. It tests for the significance of the difference between the number of + actually observed and the number which could be expected from chance sampling variation.

The basic idea of the sign test is quite simple. If there is no real difference between two populations, then in comparing the results of a random draw from each, there is *just as good a chance that the larger of the two values will be from one population as the other.* Thus, if we denote by a + sign a larger value for a particular one of the two populations, the probability of a + in any one sample pair will be .5, providing we agree not to use ties (which do not matter). In a sample of *n* pairs (excluding ties) the sampling distribution for the number of + will be binomial with $p = .5$ and $n =$ the number of pairs sampled. For large samples, the normal approximation to the binomial can be utilized. Thus, for a sample of size n, the mean and standard deviation of the number of + is:

$$\mu = np = n(.5)$$

$$\sigma = \sqrt{np(1 - p)} = \sqrt{n(.5)(.5)} = .5\sqrt{n}$$

From these, the computed value of the standardized normal variable Z for X number of + can be obtained by:

$$Z = \frac{X - \mu}{\sigma} = \frac{X - .5n}{.5\sqrt{n}} = \frac{2X - n}{\sqrt{n}}$$

A problem at the end of the chapter asks you to draw your own sample of bond ratings so you can find out for yourself whether Moody's and Standard and Poor's are equally conservative.

Numerical calculations are illustrated in the following real estate example which requires a sign test.

Example 22.4C. Which Realtor Sells Homes the Fastest?

Jane Wells is a real estate broker who has reciprocal listing agreements with two other brokers in her community. When Wells secures a listing on a home, the other two brokers are quickly informed. She would like to know whether there is any real difference in the mean number of days it takes the other brokers to sell the houses listed with them. The faster a buyer can be found, the greater the probability that she can sell the house and earn the commission before her listing expires. If there is a difference, she might be inclined to stress closer cooperation with and courtesies for the faster selling broker, even if this means somewhat impaired relations with the other broker. The last thirty sales made through one of them are regarded as a random sample of reciprocal listings.

This problem differs from previous matched pairs examples in an important way. A measurement is available on *only one member* of the pair, namely the broker that actually sold the house. It is *not known* how long it would have taken the other broker to sell the house—but it would *have* to be *longer*. Thus, the *sign* of the difference *can* be determined, even though the *amount* of the difference cannot. For instance, suppose A sold it in 14 days. Therefore B would take more than 14 days, indicated by $14+$. Table 22.5 shows the comparative success of the two brokers

TABLE 22.5. Length of Time to Sell a House (Days)

LISTING	BROKER A	BROKER B	A − B
1	14	14+	−
2	22+	22	+
3	9+	9	+
4	27	27+	−
5	16+	16	+
6	13+	13	+
7	36+	36	+
8	25	25+	−
9	17	17+	−
10	3	3+	−
11	22+	22	+
12	19	19+	−
13	34+	34	+
14	29	29+	−
15	15+	15	+
16	11	11+	−
17	42	42+	−
18	5+	5	+
19	19	19+	−
20	23+	23	+
21	12+	12	+
22	11+	11	+
23	18	18+	−
24	26+	26	+
25	20	20+	−
26	39	39+	−
27	7+	7	+
28	13	13+	−
29	25	25+	−
30	16	16+	−

for the thirty listings. A plus sign in the last column means that Broker *B* sold the house; a minus sign indicates that Broker *A* sold the house.

H_0: On the average, no difference exists in the length of time it takes the two brokers to sell a house.

H_A: The length of time it takes the two brokers to sell a house is not the same on the average.

In this sample there are fourteen pluses. For a value of $X = 14$, the computed Z value is:

$$Z = \frac{2X - n}{\sqrt{n}} = \frac{2(14) - 30}{\sqrt{30}} = \frac{-2}{5.477} = -.3651$$

The prob-value of the calculated $Z = -.3651$ for a two-sided null hypothesis is .7114. It represents the area under both the lower and upper tails beyond $Z = \pm.3651$. Only for significance levels above .7114 would the null hypothesis be rejected. For the .05 or .01 significance levels commonly used, the null hypothesis would not be rejected. Thus the sample evidence strongly suggests that chance is causing the observed differences between the two brokers.

22.5. Comparing More Than Two Populations: The Kruskal-Wallis Test for Independent Samples

The Wilcoxon Rank Sum Test described in Section 22.3 is an appropriate test for comparing the means of *two* populations, particularly if the normality assumption necessary for a t test cannot be justified. However, when there are three or more populations, the Wilcoxon test cannot be employed. Fortunately, an extension of it, the *Kruskal-Wallis* test, is applicable. It is the non-parametric replacement for the parametric *F* test described in the previous chapter.

The null hypothesis is that all the populations possess the same mean. Under this hypothesis, the Kruskal-Wallis test statistic K is:

$$K = \frac{12}{n(n + 1)} \left(\sum_{}^{m} \frac{T_j^2}{n_j} \right) - 3(n + 1)$$

where m = the number of categories; n_j = the number of observations in the jth category; $n = \Sigma n_j$, the total number of observations in all the categories; and T_j = the sum of ranks for each category (the ranks are for the pooled sample and therefore range from 1 to n). The sampling distribution of K is approximately chi-square with $m - 1$ degrees of freedom. The approximation is accurate if the sample size for each group is greater than three.

Calculations for the Kruskal-Wallis test are illustrated in the next example.

Example 22.5. **Do Better Built Homes Appreciate in Value Faster?**

It is often said in home-building circles that homes constructed with higher quality materials are a worthwhile investment. It is believed that such houses hold their value longer or appreciate in value faster. Is there any truth to this belief? The Kruskal-Wallis test can be helpful in providing an answer.

Table 22.6 presents data on the average annual percentage change in value of 20 randomly selected California single family homes in a particular geographical area classified according to materials and construction quality of the home.

TABLE 22.6. Average Annual Percentage Change in Housing Value of Twenty Homes According to Four Types of Housing Quality (Ranks Shown in Parentheses)

QUALITY			
A	B	C	D
16 (1)	21 (11)	31 (19.5)	19 (6)
22 (13.5)	27 (17)	20 (8.5)	19 (6)
21 (11)	17 (2.5)	23 (15)	30 (18)
26 (16)	18 (4)	17 (2.5)	19 (6)
22 (13.5)	31 (19.5)	20 (8.5)	21 (11)
$T_A = 55$	$T_B = 54$	$T_C = 54$	$T_D = 47$
$T_A^2 = 3025$	$T_B^2 = 2916$	$T_C^2 = 2916$	$T_D^2 = 2209$
$\dfrac{T_A^2}{n_A} = 605$	$\dfrac{T_B^2}{n_B} = 583.2$	$\dfrac{T_C^2}{n_C} = 583.2$	$\dfrac{T_D^2}{n_D} = 441.8$

$n_A = n_B = n_C = n_D = 5$

The null and alternative hypotheses are:

H_0: No difference exists among the mean rates of appreciation and value of homes of different construction quality.

H_A: The mean rates of appreciation in value of homes of different construction quality is not the same.

Solution:

$$K = \frac{12}{n(n+1)} \left(\sum_{}^{m} \frac{T_j^2}{n_j} \right) - 3(n+1)$$

$$= \frac{12}{20(21)} (605 + 583.2 + 583.2 + 441.6) - 3(21)$$

$$= 0.23$$

Since there are four quality types, $m = 4$. The χ^2 value with $m - 1 = 3$ degrees of freedom at the 5% level of significance is 7.81. This far exceeds 0.23, the calculated value of K. It therefore seems that the null hypothesis of no difference among the rates of appreciation of homes of differing construction quality can't be rejected on the basis of the sample evidence. In fact, the computed K value has a prob-value in excess of .95, indicating it is extremely likely to get a calculated K value of this size or greater merely by chance when the null is true.

Perhaps those who think that higher quality construction in this geographical area enhances the prospects for appreciation in value should do some further checking.

22.6. Comparing Several Population Means: The Friedman Test for Matched Samples

Suppose we wish to compare the means of several populations, but *cannot* assume that the populations are normally distributed and have a common variance. Then the parametric analysis of variance techniques described in the previous chapter are not applicable. The Kruskal-Wallis test can be used instead, but *only* if the samples are independently drawn from the different populations. What if matched samples are used? The Wilcoxon Signed-Rank Test would apply if there were only two populations, but cannot be used for more than two. In this situation the Friedman test is used. The following example illustrates the Friedman test.

Example 22.6. Executive Transfers: Silk Purse or Sow's Ear?

I.B.M.—that means "I've Been Moved!" For many years transfers at IBM Corporation were so common that the company's initials became synonymous with executive relocation. Many other large corporations also transfer executives frequently among districts, often sweetening the moves with a promotion. Sales executives are particularly susceptible to transfers. Why play geographic musical chairs with executive talent? From the company's point of view the relocations appear to offer several advantages. Not the least of these is the assurance that their sales executives won't have time to develop strong personal ties with customers and then leave the company, taking the customers with them.

From the executives' point of view the transfers are a two-edged sword. On the one hand it provides an excellent opportunity to demonstrate that the good performance in the present position is real and not a fluke. On the other hand, it can be a performance trap because of the sales quota assigned the territory.

A key marketing decision by top management in designing sales territories of different sizes, say small, medium, large, is the sales quota of the territory. Within each size category, the intent is to make the sales potential as equal as possible. What if the territories' sales potential has been overestimated? Overestimating a district's sales potential sets up a performance evaluation trap for the transferred sales executive. Transfer to a district destined (because of overestimated potential) to produce "below quota sales," no matter who heads it, is a sure way to deflate the corporate image of the executive. The consequence can be detrimental to both the individual and the structure of corporate management. Superior sales performance may go unrecognized, the executive reward systems becomes disrupted, and the confidence of the best performers becomes undermined. But how can a corporation find out whether a group of territories really do have the same sales potential?

One way to learn about the effect, if any, of territory design on sales is to apply the Friedman test to sales data of sales executives in different districts. The data in Table 22.7 illustrate the approach. Shown in the table are the sales performance records of eight sales executives, each of whom has been transferred among the same four sales districts. The null and alternative hypotheses are:

H_0: Sales potential of the four districts is identical.

H_A: Sales potential of the four districts is not identical.

TABLE 22.7. Sales Performance of Eight Sales Executives (in millions of dollars)

SALES EXECUTIVE	PITTSBURGH SALES DISTRICT		DALLAS SALES DISTRICT		LOS ANGELES SALES DISTRICT		KANSAS CITY SALES DISTRICT	
	$	District Rank	$	District Rank	$	District Rank	$	District Rank
1	2	(2)	3	(3)	13	(4)	1	(1)
2	12	(3)	11	(2)	13	(4)	10	(1)
3	10	(3)	3	(1)	11	(4)	9	(2)
4	4	(1)	12	(4)	10	(2)	11	(3)
5	10	(4)	4	(2)	5	(3)	3	(1)
6	10	(4)	4	(2)	7	(3)	3	(1)
7	14	(4)	4	(2)	7	(3)	2	(1)
8	3	(2)	2	(1)	4	(3)	13	(4)
K	$T_1 = (23)$		$T_2 = (17)$		$T_3 = (26)$		$T_4 = (14)$	

The numbers in parentheses across a row in the table rank (from a low of 1 to a high of 4) each sales executive's personal performance among the four districts. *If the district really has no effect on sales performance, and if the assignment pattern of executives to the districts can be considered random, then the expected average rank of each district would be identical (2.5).* Likewise, the *sum* of ranks in each column should differ only due to chance variation. What if there tend to be pile-ups of high or low ranks in particular districts? This is evidence *against* the null hypothesis of no effect of sales district on performance. The Friedman test measures the strength of this evidence.

The Friedman statistic, F_r, is calculated from:

$$F_r = \frac{12}{KJ(J + 1)} \left(\sum T_j^2 \right) - 3K(J + 1)$$

where K = the number of pairings, J = the number of categories, and T_j = the sum of the ranks for each category. In the executive transfer example given above, $K = 8$ and $J = 4$. Values of the T_j are given in Table 22.7. Thus, the Friedman statistic is calculated as follows:

$$F_r = \frac{12}{8(4)(5)} (23^2 + 17^2 + 26^2 + 14^2) - 3(8)(5)$$

$$= 6.75$$

What is the prob-value of this statistic? Is it statistically significant? The Friedman statistic is distributed as χ^2 with $J - 1 = 3$ degrees of freedom. We find from the tables of χ^2 that the computed statistic has a prob-value just under .10.

With this prob-value the null hypothesis would be rejected at the 10% level, but not at the 1% or 5% levels. Thus, although the evidence against the null hypothesis is not strong enough to convincingly discredit the claim, it is not very reassuring either. Apprised of these results, executives slated for transfer to the Kansas City district would probably have second thoughts about the desirability of accepting it.

22.7. Rank Correlation

In Chapter Fourteen, the linear correlation coefficient r was introduced as a measure of the degree of linear association between two quantitative variables. There are many situations where a measure of association between two variables is desired but the linear correlation coefficient is not applicable.

> What if the data are curvilinear rather than linear? Strictly speaking, the linear correlation coefficient would not be applicable.

> What if the data available on a variable indicate only the *order* of magnitude of the values and not the *amount* by which they differ?

Again the linear correlation coefficient is not applicable. This situation might arise in the business world in the following way:

Example 22.7A.   Soft Drink Preferences Correlation

Suppose a person's favorite soft drink brands are Coke, Pepsi, Seven-Up, and RC, in that order. Unless it is also known by *how much* the liking for Coke exceeds that of Pepsi, Seven-Up, etc., it is not possible to compute a value of r measuring the association between soft drink preference and some other variable of interest.

Spearman's Rank Correlation Coefficient

There is a way of measuring correlation when the restrictive assumptions about the form of the relationship and the nature of the data for computing r cannot be met. If the two variables of interest are the *ranks* within their respective series, a procedure identical to that used to calculate the value of the simple correlation coefficient r can be used. The statistic known as *Spearman's rank correlation coefficient*, r_s, is a measure of the degree of association that exists between the *ranks* of the bivariate values.

Coefficient r_s is an indicator of the degree of consistency in the comovement of the two variables (*monotonicity*), not of whether the *form* of the relationship is linear or nonlinear.

How versatile is the rank correlation coefficient? Can it provide a valid measure of the association between two variables regardless of the nature of the relationship? No, not always. It does provide a valid measure for any relationship which is either *consistently* (*monotonic*) *increasing* (as one variable increases the other does too) or *consistently* (*monotonic*) *decreasing* (one variable increases and the other decreases)—but not for relationships which change direction.

Three examples are presented below: the first one is monotonic decreasing, the second is monotonic increasing, and the third is not monotonic. In the first two examples, the rank correlation coefficient provides a useful measure of association for situations where the simple (linear) correlation coefficient is not applicable. The third example illustrates a situation in which the rank correlation coefficient is not applicable.

Curvilinear Demand Curve In the demand curve described in Section 15.2, a decrease in price led to an increase in quantity demanded at every price level; thus, it was a monotonic increasing relationship. But the relationship was *curvilinear* rather than linear. That is, although a given price change always led to a quantity change in the opposite direction, the *amount* of the change depended upon the quantity level before the change in price. The simple linear correlation coefficient r could *not* be relied upon, but the rank correlation coefficient r_s would provide a valid ordinal measure of the association between price and quantity changes.

Ordinal Evaluations of Medical School Applicants Twenty-two applicants to medical school are ranked independently by a faculty admissions committee and by an advisory committee of practicing physicians. From the rankings alone, it would not be possible to compare the *amount* of preference either committee had for the top ranked candidates over the other candidates. Nevertheless, using the rank correlation coefficient one can establish a measure of the ordinal association between the preferences of the two committees.

Humidity and Employee Grievances A U-shape parabola describes the relationship between humidity and employee complaints in Example 15.1. In one portion of the parabola, an increase in humidity leads to a *decrease* in complaints, whereas in another portion of the parabola, an increase in humidity leads to an *increase* in complaints. Therefore, the relationship is not monotonic. The rank correlation coefficient cannot be relied on to give a valid measure of association.

Calculating the Rank Correlation Coefficient

Many of the inexpensive electronic pocket calculators have a correlation coefficient key. If the data entered are ranks, this key computes the value of r_s. Otherwise, the Spearman rank correlation coefficient can be computed by a quick and easy shortcut formula so long as neither variable has any repeated values (in other words, no tie rankings are assigned within each variable).

$$r_s = 1 - \frac{6 \Sigma d_i^2}{n(n^2 - 1)}$$

Here d_i is the *difference* between ranks of the two variables for each individual or elementary unit.

The sampling distribution of r_s is symmetrical about zero. It approaches normality as the sample size becomes large. For samples of size 20 or more, the standardized normal distribution can be used to test the significance of r_s. The null hypothesis for the population rank correlation coefficient can be tested by computing the Z statistic which has an approximately standard normal distribution.

$$Z = \frac{r_s - 0}{\text{std. error of } r_s}$$

where the standard error of $r_s = \sqrt{\dfrac{1}{n-1}}$.

For samples of ten or more a two-tailed significance test can be made using the Student t distribution with $n - 2$ degrees of freedom. In that case the test statistic is the t statistic

$$t = r_s \sqrt{\frac{n-2}{1-r_s^2}}$$

We shall illustrate the calculation of r_s and its use in testing the null hypothesis in the following example on executive succession.

Example 22.7B.   Climbing the Executive Ladder: Which Way is Up?

Do corporate executives who attain positions of high responsibility for their age travel a particular route to the top? Does persistence in the same organization provide internal promotions to the top? Or is the best strategy to the executive suite the outside promotional route with timely switches from one organization to another? Or is executive ladder climbing generally unrelated to the particular route travelled?

Suppose a panel of judges (beginning with one for the highest value) ranked ten executives on two variables: (1) achievement level with respect to age and (2) advancement by internal promotion within the organization versus advancement by switching in from the outside. Do the data given in Table 22.8 confirm an association between how fast the executive ladder is climbed and the means of climbing it?

TABLE 22.8. Rank, By Category

EXECUTIVE	EXECUTIVE LADDER CLIMBING SPEED	RELIANCE UPON INTERNAL PROMOTIONS	d	d^2
A	7	6	1	1
B	8	8	0	0
C	9	10	−1	1
D	3	4	−1	1
E	2	2	0	0
F	6	3	3	9
G	10	9	1	1
H	4	7	−3	9
I	5	5	0	0
J	1	1	0	0
				$\Sigma d^2 = 22$

$$r_s = 1 - \frac{6\Sigma d_i^2}{n(n^2 - 1)}$$

$$= 1 - \frac{(6)(22)}{10(100 - 1)}$$

$$= 1 - .13$$

$$= .87$$

The null and alternative hypotheses are:

H_0: No association between the rank on the speed with which the executive has climbed the executive ladder and the rank in using internal promotions to climb the ladder; in other words,

H_0: population rank correlation $= 0$
H_A: population rank correlation $\neq 0$

The test statistic is

$$t = r_s \sqrt{\frac{n-2}{1-r_s^2}} = .87 \sqrt{\frac{10-2}{1-(.87)^2}} = 4.99$$

At $n - 2 = 8$ degrees of freedom, the two-tailed value of t at the 1% level of significance is 3.36. The result is significant at the 1% level, so the null hypothesis is rejected.

Conclusion: The high positive value of r_s equaling .87 shows a strong positive association between the ranked variables, suggesting that internal promotions, contrary to popular opinion, may be the faster route. Although the data above are hypothetical and intended only to demonstrate the use of rank correlation and its computational procedure, in an actual study conducted by Donald Helmich similar conclusions were reached.[4]

22.8. Concluding Comments

Nonparametric tests differ from parametric tests in that they are not concerned with population parameters, or do not depend for their validity upon the data being interval-scaled or upon specific assumptions (for example, normality) about the distribution of population values. Nevertheless, nonparametric methods should be restricted to those situations in which assumptions required for the parametric counterpart are not met. Parametric tests, when feasible, offer greater efficiency.

The type of nonparametric test to be used depends on the hypothesis to be tested. To test for sequential randomness in time series data, the *runs* test is appropriate. To test for ordinal association between two variables, Spearman's rank correlation coefficient is computed and tested for significance. To test the null hypothesis of no difference between or among means of different populations, the choice depends (1) on how many populations are compared, and (2) whether the data were collected from independent samples or a matched pair (randomized block) design. The six nonparametric procedures given in this chapter for comparing population means are presented in Table 22.9 together with their parametric counterparts (t and F tests).

For independently drawn samples from two populations, either the Mann-Whitney U test or the Wilcoxon Two-Sample Ranked Sum test should be used. These tests are equivalent and it does not matter which one is chosen. Their parametric counterpart is the t test. If the samples are independently drawn from three or more populations, the Kruskal-Wallis test should be used. Its parametric counterpart is the F test.

For matched samples from two populations, the Wilcoxon Signed-Rank

TABLE 22.9. Classification of Some Nonparametric Tests

SAMPLES	TWO (replaces parametric *t* test)	MORE THAN TWO (replaces parametric *F* test)
Independent (Completely Randomized)	Mann-Whitney U or Wilcoxon Two-Sample Ranked Sum	Kruskal-Wallis
Matched (Randomized Block)	Sign Wilcoxon Signed Rank Sum (Interval Data)	Friedman

test should be used if the data are measured on an interval or ratio scale. If the data are measured only on an ordinal scale, the sign test is used. The sign test is particularly valuable in what might be termed "ruined samples" of the type illustrated by Example 22.4C. Once the number of days required to sell the house is known for the realtor who makes the sale, it "ruins" the opportunity of the other realtor to sell it, and therefore ruins the opportunity for the investigator to learn how many days the second broker would have required. The sign test only requires knowing *which* realtor made the sale and is therefore advantageously used to test the null hypothesis of no difference between the two realtors in mean selling time. The parametric counterpart to both the Wilcoxon Signed-Rank test and the sign test is the *t* test.

For matched samples from three or more populations, the Friedman test is used. Its parametric counterpart is the *F* test.

Finally, we note that the chi-square test discussed in Chapter 20 is also considered a nonparametric test. It was included in a separate chapter because of its prevalent use in statistical practice.

Footnotes and References

[1] *The Outlook*, published by Standard & Poor's Corporation, February 25, 1980, pp. 908–909.

[2] Eugene Fama, Lawrence Fisher, Michael Jensen, and Richard Roll, "The Adjustment of Stock Price to New Information," *International Economic Review*, X, No. 1, (February, 1969), pp. 1–21.

[3] A study of this problem is reported in Ronald Frank and William Massy, "Shelf Position and Space Effects on Sales," *Journal of Marketing Research*, February 1970, pp. 59–66.

[4] Donald Helmich, "Managerial Achievement Aspirations and Successor Characteristics," *Business and Economic Perspective*, Spring 1977, pp. 27–36.

Questions and Problems

1. What distinguishes a nonparametric from a parametric hypothesis test?

2. In general, what are the advantages of a nonparametric test over its parametric counterpart?

3. Is there a parametric counterpart to every nonparametric test? Explain.

4. Do parametric and nonparametric tests give identical test results (expressed in prob-values or significance levels)? Explain.

5. Is it fair to say that a nonparametric test should replace its parametric counterpart only if the assumptions of the parametric test are not met? Explain.

6. Nonparametric tests are credited with more versatility than parametric tests. What is meant by versatility in this case?

7. The sign test is applicable in every situation that the Wilcoxon Signed-Rank Sum test is used and also in certain situations in which the Wilcoxon Signed-Rank Sum test is *not* applicable. Why then should the Wilcoxon Signed-Rank Sum test not be discarded in favor of the sign test?

8. The sign test is widely used in certain types of situations involving matched-pair samples. Is the sign test also applicable when the samples are independently drawn? Explain.

9. Does a runs test for randomness of regression residuals duplicate as a diagnostic check what a scatter diagram of residuals accomplishes? Explain.

10. Can a Friedman test and a Kruskal-Wallis test be interchanged? Explain.

11. The more versatile Kruskal-Wallis test could be used in the two sample cases in which the Wilcoxon Two-Sample Rank Sum test would be applicable. Why then bother with the Wilcoxon Two-Sample Rank Sum test at all?

12. In situations where the Wilcoxon Signed-Rank Sum test would be applicable the Friedman test could be substituted. Why then bother with the Wilcoxon Signed-Rank Sum test at all?

13. Are there any situations in which the correlation between two interval-valued variables should be measured by the rank correlation coefficient rather than the correlation coefficient used in Chapter 14? Explain.

14. How do ties affect the nonparametric tests involving ranks? What procedure should be followed to handle ties?

15. *Supplier Delivery Capabilities* Steel mill R and steel mill L are alternate suppliers of specially ordered alloy steel. Two independent random samples of ten orders each are taken from each supplier. The number of days that lapse between the placing of the order and the receipt of shipment is recorded. The results and their rankings are given in Table 22.10.
a. Calculate the value of the rank sum.
b. What is the value of the standard normal deviate?
c. Test the null hypothesis of no difference between the suppliers in the distribution of time until an order is received, using the 5% level of significance.

16. Steel mill U is a third source of supply of alloy steel along with the two others described in Problem 15. A random sample of ten orders is taken from this supplier and the number of days until receipt of

---

TABLE 22.10. Ranking of Order Fulfillment Time at Two Steel Mills

									STEEL MILL											
	R	R	R	R	L	R	R	R	L	L	R	L	R	L	R	L	L	L	L	L
No. of days	28	29	31	32	33	34	35	36	38	41	42	44	45	47	49	51	53	54	57	60
Ranking	1	2	3	4	5	6	7	8	9	10	11	12	13	14	15	16	17	18	19	20

the shipment is recorded. Test the hypothesis of no difference among the suppliers in the distribution of time until an order is received. The number of days elapsed until the order was received is given as follows: 17, 29, 42, 24, 37, 38, 39, 26, 49, and 50.

17. Use the Mann-Whitney distribution to test the null hypothesis for the steel supplier data given in Problem 15.

18. The following case history of an industrial design experiment is reported by Dr. Donald R. Herzog.[1]

This problem occurred in the development of a new component of a piston ring which was required for modern high speed, high compression engines. It is one part of a multiple piece steel oil control ring called a "segment". This "segment" is essentially a ribbon of steel coiled on edge to form a ring. However, this coiling must result in a shape so uniform that when placed in a cylindrical gage, each point on the circumference of the ring makes contact with the surface of the gage. This characteristic of contact in older ring specifications was described in loose general terms, such as "full contact with only fringe light permitted," or "intermittent light extending not over X^0 at any one point."

A system of point measurement was first developed since it became obvious that no comparative tests could be made unless a scale of measurement was provided. Once we had the scale of measurement, we began to consider the nature of the information available. First, we had several suppliers of steel, Mill A, B, and C. These were all quite reputable sources. The chemical and physical properties of their steel met our specifications. There were, however, feelings expressed in the shop about the rolling ability of one steel or another, and the tendency of one steel or another to form "dog legs." These were straight sections in the circumference of the ring, causing objectionable "open light."

One basic question was, "Is the steel a factor in our ability to produce the desired shape in our segments?" The steel was supplied in rolls which are quite long. When once placed on the machine, it was necessary to run the entire reel. However, steel had been supplied to the various machines and operators randomly in the past. While the steel identity was maintained, that of the operator and machine were not. There were sampling results of the rings produced by each roll of steel, in terms of the numerical scale of light. This is the basic information for a one-way classification by steel sources. Data which represented all the machines, all the operators, and the three steels were arranged by steel supplier, as in Table 22.11.

TABLE 22.11. Steel Suppliers and "Open Light"

	A	B	C
	14	9	12
	13	11	10
	10	0	6
	6	13	20
	23	−6	15
	1	−5	23
	−1	5	13
	16	5	19
	16	−4	4
	6	13	13
Total	104	41	135

Assuming that machine and operator effects are randomly distributed in columns A, B, and C, is there any evidence of a steel supplier effect? (Test the null hypothesis at the 5% level of significance.)

19. This problem is a continuation of the case study by Dr. Donald R. Herzog described initially in Problem 18.

In addition to the three sources of steel, there were also four rolling machines of essentially the same design, but made over a period of years, as requirements increased. Each machine was attended by an operator. There were feelings in the shop that particular combinations of machines and operators were superior to others.

A series of tests were made in which each of the three steels were randomly assigned in normal production to each

TABLE 22.12. Steel Suppliers, Machines, and "Open Light"

	STEEL	MACHINE-OPERATOR COMBINATION				STEEL TOTALS
		1	2	3	4	
	A	11.5	8.2	7.1	9.9	36.7
	B	6.1	7.0	6.8	4.9	24.8
	C	12.0	12.5	8.7	11.2	44.4
Machine Total		29.6	27.7	22.6	26.0	105.9

TABLE 22.13. Length of Tenancy, By Realtor

	Tenancy (No. of Months)									
Realtor A	8	19	15	11	23	10	16	20	18	18
Realtor B	15	19	16	13	17	20	18	22	19	18

machine-operator combination.

When a total of approximately five samples (rolls) had been run for each steel with each machine-operator combination, Table 22.12 was prepared. The data are mean values for the 5 samples.

a. Is there any evidence of a machine-operator effect?

b. Is there evidence of a steel supplier effect? If so, is it stronger or weaker evidence than obtained in Problem 18?

20. *Evaluating Realtors' Ability to Select Tenants* Dale Max, owner of an apartment building, wants to know whether there is any difference in the length of time tenants obtained by two different realtors stay before moving out. Records on ten tenants who rent on a month-to-month basis obtained by each realtor are given in Table 22.13. Assume that these data can be regarded as independent random samples. Test the null hypothesis of no difference at the 10% level of significance.

21. In Example 22.4A, the effect of supermarket shelf position on product sales was investigated. Suppose the experiment was altered to include a third location, namely, a special display at the end of an aisle, producing the data given in Table 22.14.

a. What would be an appropriate nonparametric statistic to use in testing the null hypothesis?

b. What is the prob-value of this test?

TABLE 22.14. Aisle Display Effect on Sales

STORE GROUP	SALES AT END AISLE LOCATION
1	121
2	159
3	132
4	160
5	73
6	120
7	89
8	136
9	82
10	66
11	71
12	54

22. In Example 22.6, the effect of four sales territories on executive performance was investigated. Suppose that data were available only for Pittsburgh and Dallas.

a. What would be an appropriate nonparametric statistic to use in testing the null hypothesis?

b. What would be the prob-value of this test?

23. In Example 22.3, the longevity of automobile life was compared for two brands of automobiles using the Wilcoxon Rank Sum test. This test is not applicable if more than two brands are to be compared. Sup-

pose 18 observations on a third brand F are collected with the following results:

82.4	88.1	82.8	91.3	106.6	88.5
104.0	103.6	111.4	115.0	76.7	84.9
102.6	96.0	78.5	93.7	94.2	82.9

a. What nonparametric test would be appropriate to test the null hypothesis of no difference in mean mileage longevity among the three brands?

b. Conduct the test identified in Part a.

24. *Spotting Fashion Merchandise Winners* Marilyn Jansen, a buyer for a chain of women's wear stores sought a method for quickly spotting winners in the fashion merchandise derby each buying season. Much of her merchandise was of a staple nature, not subject to fashion fads. For this type of merchandise there was no particular pattern to the variation in demand among the stores in the chain. However, certain stores in the chain were located in areas where "fashion leaders," typically younger single women, shopped. Their wearing of an item seemed to set off, or at least signal, a buying wave for that particular item. If this is true and the stores could be identified, the buyer could capitalize on the information by making an early reorder. If she were confident of sufficient "bandwagon" demand at the other stores later in the season, she could place a reorder before her competitors realized how popular the item would become. In doing so, she would avoid getting caught in the order backlog that would soon develop at the manufacturers and cause delivery delays beyond the selling season.

Studying the history of previous fashion "winners" Jansen hypothesized that stores 1, 5, 7, 8, 9, 12, 16, 17, 18, and 20 were the "early-reorder" stores in fashion winners. She decided to test her theory out on the next "winner." The sequence of store stockouts was as follows:

7, 12, 6, 9, 8, 17, 15, 20, 1, 11, 18, 2, 4,
5, 14, 19, 16, 13, 3, 10

a. Compute the prob-value for the null hypothesis.

b. What conclusion do you draw about her method of spotting fashion merchandise winners?

25. *Price Fixing* A trade association for the electric utility industry is investigating the firms Grace Nuclear and Wilcox Interstate, the two major suppliers of turbine generators. The charge is price fixing. The association suspects that the firms have agreed not to undercut each other on price and to divide the market by some predetermined formula. To accomplish their objectives, the firms would have arranged a bid submission game plan. One firm would put in an unacceptably high bid opening the way for the other firm to get the contract at a comfortably high price level. Is there any information the trade association could examine and test to uncover any pattern that exists for past winners of large contracts for turbines? The sequence of winning bids follows (read across first).

G W G W W G G W W G W
G W G G W G G W G W G

If a disconcerting pattern is found, a complaint may be filed with the Justice Department.

a. Is the exact sequence of bids a critical information element for answering the issue of price fixing?

b. Use a runs test to find the prob-value of the hypothesis that the winning bidder sequence follows a random pattern.

c. If the randomness hypothesis is rejected and a type I error has not been made, can you suggest an alternative explanation to conspiracy?

d. If the turbine suppliers are conspiring to fix prices, will the randomness hypothesis necessarily be rejected? Explain.

26. *Systematic Versus Random Factors in Overbidding* Grace Nuclear, one of the two major firms producing turbine generators for electric power plants, has been examining the success of its bids on recent contracts. The firm wants to determine whether a change in its bidding procedure might be desirable. The company's success for the last 22 bids in sequence of occurrence are given below, where G = Grace Nuclear and W = Wilcox Interstate. (Read across first.)

G W G W W G G W W G W
G W G G W G G W G W G

The variability in the bidding outcomes is partly attributable to the difficulty of accurately estimating the cost elements which represent the basis for a bid. It is recognized also that different people normally arrive at different estimates for the same set of specifications. Both factors operating together unavoidably produce random variability in the bidding outcomes. The major concern centers on the possibility that random variability may mask any difference in the mean bidding level of the two competitors.

a. Using the sign test, find the prob-value of the test statistic under the null hypothesis that the company's bids are at least as low as the competitor's.

b. At the 5% level of significance, test the null hypothesis stated in A.

c. Calculate the prob-value for the hypothesis that the competitor's bids are at least as low as the company's bids.

d. Is it important to know the sequence of success occurrence in order for the question of interest to be resolved? Compare and contrast with the concern of Problem 25.

27. A target market's preference for a type of wine and the price of the wine were the factors measured in a consumer wine tasting experiment conducted to determine the extent of association. The wines were tasted and ranked in order of descending preference without knowledge of price. A dummy label was affixed over the bottle label to avoid any contaminating brand effect. The results are given in Table 22.15.

a. Compute the rank correlation coefficient for the above data.

b. Test the null hypothesis of no association at the 1% level of significance.

28. *Impact of Price on Perceived Wine Quality* A rerun of the wine tasting experiment described in Problem 27 was performed except that the subjects were permitted to see a "suggested list price" on the dummy label. The results are given in Table 22.16.

a. Compute the rank correlation coefficient for the above data.

TABLE 22.15. Wine Ranked by Taste, Price Unknown

WINE	RANK BY TASTING PANEL	PRICE
A	9	$2.45
B	8	$4.50
C	3	$2.75
D	6	$3.80
E	4	$6.00
F	1	$9.25
G	7	$5.50
H	2	$8.00
I	5	$7.00
J	10	$2.95

TABLE 22.16. Wine Ranked By Taste, Price Known

WINE	RANK BY TASTING PANEL	PRICE
A	9	$2.45
B	5	$4.50
C	10	$2.75
D	8	$3.80
E	4	$6.00
F	1	$9.25
G	6	$5.50
H	2	$8.00
I	3	$7.00
J	7	$2.95

b. Test the null hypothesis of no association at the 1% level of significance.

c. What is the rank correlation coefficient between the rankings by the panel with price known (this problem) and without price known (Problem 27)?

Footnotes

[1] Further details and elaboration on designed experiments in industry are found in Dr. Herzog's book, *Industrial Engineering: Methods and Practice*, Reston Publishing, 1983.

Decision Theory

Preview.   Managers make many decisions of uncertain outcome. The trick is to reduce uncertainty as much as possible. Procedures should be developed to reduce uncertainty. For many of the small decisions made daily, *ad hoc* methods may suffice. However, where fortunes and careers are at stake, formal decision making procedures are advantageous. In this chapter we consider an approach called *decision theory analysis* or DTA by some of its practitioners.

The analysis begins with the simplest case, in which a decision must be made using only information presently available. This analysis is extended to (1) the decision of whether to wait for decisive information, (2) the upper limit of value for information that would eliminate the uncertainty, (3) the decision to buy information that is less than perfect, (4) the use of indirectly relevant information to reduce uncertainty, (5) the case of a quantitative decision variable, and (6) attitudes of the decision maker toward risk.

"Lookit all this stuff." Feinstein said.

Inside all the boxes were 20,000 pairs of men's, ladies, and children's winter footwear, all rubberized and waterproof. Enough galoshes, rubbers, and boots to keep every person in a good-sized town as dry as toast while winter storms rage around them.

Twenty thousand pair of winter footwear that Jack Feinstein is about to get stuck with because the deity that makes it snow has been taking the season off this year.

"I need a big snow," Feinstein said mournfully. Seven, 8, 9 inches, maybe. I'm not hoping for 90 inches, like last year. Just one good blizzard."

In July, when he ordered $250,000 worth of rubber footwear from his suppliers, most of whom are foreign importers, things looked bullish. Another snowy winter seemed in the offing, and the retail shoestores Feinstein sells to were almost sure to have customers beating their doors down for galoshes and boots.

In addition, Feinstein reasoned happily, the stores were starting from scratch. They had no leftover stock from last year because the horrible winter had left their shelves cleaned out.

What Feinstein expected were big initial orders and then a season of steady profitable repeat orders. What he got was $140,000 worth of initial orders and then nothing.

"I haven't had an order in ages," he said. He dug into an open carton and pulled out a blue pair of "Moon Boots," huge things manufactured in Korea. He ran his fingers slowly over the ridged black soles, with a "Why me, Lord?" expression on his face.

"In the shoe business," he said, "the stores buy their opening needs and they expect the wholesaler to hold their stock for them the rest of the season.

"If there's a lot of play, with customers demanding a certain item, they call the wholesaler up and reorder. If there's no play," he sighed, gesturing sweepingly at his floorful of inventory, "then the wholesaler's left holding the bag. That's me."[1]

Jack Feinstein knows the dire consequences that can follow from decisions made in the face of uncertainty. He couldn't control the weather, and the galoshes manufacturer wouldn't wait till winter for his orders. So he had to decide how many pairs to order for inventory, take his chances on the weather, and live with his decision even if it meant he'd be the one left "holding the bag." Could Jack Feinstein have been helped by modern business decision theory? Perhaps the unwelcome left-over inventory could have been considerably less than it was.

23.1. Introduction

During recent decades, important analytical techniques have been developed to handle many types of management decisions. One pivotal tool, of particular importance because of its flexibility and essential simplicity, is *decision theory analysis*, or DTA, as it has come to be known in management circles.

The essential elements of a decision theory problem are not difficult to grasp. The manager must be prepared to give explicit answers to the following five questions.

1. What are the options to the decision maker?   (Acts)

2. What are the possible occurrences which can directly affect the decision at hand?   (Events)

3. What probabilities can be assigned subjectively or empirically to the possible occurrences?   (Probabilities of Events)

4. What are the monetary consequences corresponding to each act-event combination?   (Payoffs)

5. What decision criterion can appropriately be used?

23.2. How Decision Theory Analysis Works

An approach to DTA made popular by business decision theorists at the Harvard Business School utilizes the "decision tree" technique. A decision tree is simply a graphic device logically presenting the series of events and decisions which an executive considers important in decision making. Once constructed, the decision tree becomes the framework for expressing the process of logical decision making. Let us take an example involving a hypothetical, but realistic, business decision.

Example 23.2.   **Decision on a California Real Estate Option**

A steep rise in interest rates accompanied by a slowdown of construction has produced for a California real estate broker an interesting land acquisition opportunity. The broker has been offered an option to buy 10 acres of prime commercial land from a cash-poor land developer at an advantageous price—$50,000 an acre. But the local government does not always grant permits for commercial development. The broker knows this and assesses the chances as 50-50 that the local government will deny the commercial construction request. In case of a denial, the option to buy would not be exercised, and the option price of $10,000 per acre (which would have been applied to the sale price) would be forfeited. Since other brokers in the area have been contacted also, our broker feels an immediate decision must be made. Previous sales figures on comparable parcels of land suggest that an acre will sell for $80,000 if the local government will issue a commercial building permit.

A decision tree for the real estate problem is shown in Figure 23.1. Three points should be noted:

1. The branches on the decision tree indicate the "acts" and "events" being considered.

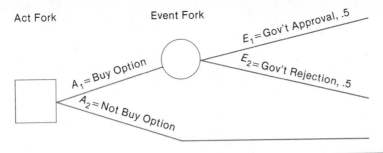

FIGURE 23.1 Decision Tree Illustrating the Act-Event Forks

2. A fork is the set of branches displaying the act or event alternatives at that point.

3. Each fork must always represent a set of mutually exclusive and collectively exhaustive acts or events. This means that the event probabilities on each event fork must sum to one.

The symbol used to indicate the fork tells one whether a fork represents acts or events. Whenever a *box* is used it indicates that the choice between alternative *acts* (in this case, the decision whether or not to buy the option) is in the hands of the decision maker (real estate broker). To emphasize that at that point the decision maker faces an *event fork* (the approval or refusal of the building license), a *circle* is used. The events at the fork are out of the hands of the decision maker.

We call the real estate broker's choice a decision "problem" because the uncertainty surrounding the license makes it impossible to be certain in advance which is the "best" act to choose. Every path through the tree corresponds to a unique sequence of acts and events with its own economic consequence. For example, if our broker decides to buy the option and the license application is rejected, the option cost (assuming a penalty of $10,000 an acre) of $100,000 would be non-reclaimable. So the problem is that the best act depends on the event which occurs, yet the event occurrence is beyond the control of the decision maker.

Assessing the Event Probabilities

Good decisions require good assessment of the probabilities assigned to the events. What event probabilities must the real estate broker take into account? Clearly, the probabilities required are for the two events, approval or refusal of the building license. With an estimated profit potential of $300,000, it is easy to see that, if the broker assesses a high probability of approval, it would be wise to go ahead and buy the land option. But assigning only a 50-50 chance to approval means that there is a 50% chance of obtaining $300,000 against an equal chance of losing $100,000. These estimates of the gains and losses are shown on the extreme right end of each branch of the decision tree in Figure 23.2.

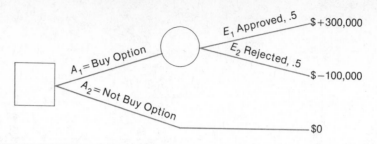

FIGURE 23.2 Decision Tree Illustrating the Act-Event Forks and Monetary Consequences

Table 23.1 summarizes the elements involved.

TABLE 23.1. Summary Table for Decision Tree of Figure 23.2

PROBABILITY	EVENTS	ACTS: A_1	A_2
		Buy Option	Not Buy Option
.5	E_1: permit issued	Profit: $300,000.00	Profit: 0
.5	E_2: permit not issued	Profit: $-$100,000.00	Profit: 0

Establishing the Decision Criterion

Which act should be preferred? The answer will depend on the criterion used to compare results. The choice among decision critera should reflect the broker's attitude toward the possible financial consequences. Suppose as a general policy the broker believes in "playing the averages" and is not at all averse to taking risks. What decision criterion would be consistent with this posture? An often used decision criterion suggested for these conditions is the *expectation rule of monetary consequences.*

Expectation Rule

According to this widely accepted criterion for solving DTA problems, the act which produces the highest expected value for profit is the optimal act. This profit is called the *Expected Monetary Value.*

Computationally, the expected value of an act is analogous to the calculation for the expected value of a discrete random variable X, previously shown as

$$E(X) = \sum X \cdot P(X)$$

where the product of the variable's value and its probability are summed over the possible values of X. For example, the expected profit of an act is found by calculating,

$$E(\text{Profit}) = \sum (\text{Profit})(\text{Probability of Event})$$

where the summation involves each event branch of the event fork following the act.

The formal analysis of the decision tree can now begin:

1. Starting at the extreme right end of the decision tree, compute the expected consequence that corresponds to each event fork.

2. Treat the expected value calculated as *if it were a certain* monetary consequence. In this case, there is only one event fork (governmental approval or rejection of the permit) on the tree; its expectation calculation is ($300,000)(.5) + (−$100,000)(.5) = $100,000. The substitution is accomplished in Figure 23.3 by placing the calculated expected profit of $100,000 in the circle representing the origin of the event fork and then eliminating the event fork. Had there been several event forks on the right, this same procedure would have been repeated on each fork. That is, each calculated expected consequence would replace the event fork and be placed in the event fork's circle origin. Of course the monetary consequence of the act "Not Buy Option" with no event fork is a certain value of zero. Therefore, zero is circled.

Decision Rule

Since the one event fork in this case is now eliminated, only the act fork remains. The act fork consists of a "Buy Option" branch with a consequence of $100,000 and a "Not Buy Option" branch with a consequence of zero. A decision rule can now be applied:

Decision rule: The act on the act fork with the highest expected profit (least opportunity cost) consequence is the optimal act.

The "Buy Option" act maximizes profit and so can be singled out as the optimal course of action. The analysis of the problem is now complete.

Reflections

Is it worth going to the trouble of a formal analysis for such a simple problem? Perhaps not, but it does get us started on this method of thinking. When does

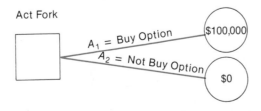

FIGURE 23.3 Reduced Decision Tree by Applying the Expectation Rule

the real pay-off likely come? The decision maker is in need of such a system for problems in which the separable elements that have an impact on the decision cannot reasonably be handled by an individual's memory. Typically these cases involve more than two tiers of act-event forks in a decision tree, and several event forks at each tier. A repetitive application of the method just described systematically eliminates event forks and act forks until the origin of the tree is reached on the left-hand side. The act placed at the origin of the tree represents the best decision act. The DTA procedure has demonstrated a way to find an optimal strategy and its expected consequence.

23.3. Seeking Definite Information

Much has been gained by presenting in tree form (Figure 23.1) the broker's initial considerations about his decision problem. But more insight can perhaps be achieved if some additional forethought would be included. For instance, are the acts "Buy Option" and "Don't Buy Option" the only ones immediately available? As in most business problems, a decision may be forestalled until information is gathered. This expanded view can be incorporated into the decision tree. The additional options and the consequences of every set of act-event sequences must appear as branches on the decision tree. Then the optimal act can be determined by the same procedure as was followed before.

Example 23.3. **Question First, Act Later?**

Let us suppose the broker is searching for a fresh approach on the matter. It occurs to the broker that it might be sensible to apply for government permission *before* finalizing the purchase of the option. The disadvantage is that the deal may no longer be open by the time the answer comes. Upon reflection the broker thinks this is quite likely; in fact, there is believed to be only a 30 percent chance that the government's answer will come while the option is still available.[2]

The broker's new decision situation can be pictured by the decision tree shown in Figure 23.4.

The new perspective on the problem shows:

1. a segment that confronts the "Buy-Not Buy" business decision straightforwardly, and

2. an information gathering route which, if undertaken, precedes the "Buy-Not Buy" with the intent of improving this business decision.

What if the broker has no intention of applying for government permission first? The information gathering upper segment of Figure 23.4 will be eliminated and the lower segment will represent the only relevant network. Thus, Figure 23.4 becomes identical with Figure 23.2, both having the same expected consequences of +$100,000.

The prospect of being closed out of the deal looms large if the broker does

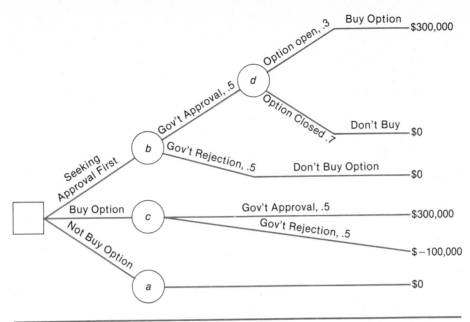

FIGURE 23.4 Decision Tree Seeking Government Approval Before Exercising Option

apply for the permit before deciding on the land option. But this action does simplify the "Buy-Not Buy" business decision. Before the broker acts on the option, the uncertainty surrounding two events will be resolved. That is

1. the government will have approved or refused the application, and

2. the offer to buy the option will either be still open or it will not.

If the offer is no longer open, there is no decision to make. If the government refuses the building permit, the offer to buy the option is rejected. The combination of government approval and of a still-open option to buy shown by the uppermost branch is the best of all worlds. The broker can assume a $300,000 payoff, exercising the available option to buy. For this combination the "Don't Buy" alternative on an act fork no longer appears, illustrating a general DTA rule.

> There is no need to evaluate a possible act if we are satisfied in advance that it is not going to be selected.

Backward Induction Is the Key to Decision Tree Analysis

Having entered the probabilities in Figure 23.4, the series of events and decisions can be evaluated by a process known as *backward induction*. The process of backward induction applies the expectation rule to successive stages of the decision tree. Working from right to left, the intent is to determine the optimal act. The actual solution process begins by taking the right-most event fork. An event fork by its nature has probabilities on its branches, the expected value of the monetary consequences at the end of its branches can be computed by using the respective probabilities on the branches.

1. The first event fork encountered is the event fork d. For this event fork the expected value is

Expected Monetary Gain of $d = .3(\$300,000) + .7(0)$

$$= \$90,000$$

The expected monetary gain of $90,000 can now be inserted inside the circle of event fork d. Since $90,000 is the expected value of the event fork, it can be said that this particular event situation with its two branches can be summarized and replaced by the single value of $90,000. See Figure 23.5.

2. Now moving further left, the next event fork encountered with all its branches leading directly to an end position is event fork b. The expected value operation is again repeated at this stage and computed to be

Expected Monetary Gain of $b = .5(\$90,000) + .5(0)$

$$= \$45,000$$

The expected monetary gain of $45,000 now summarizes event fork b and can be placed in the circle of event b with two branches eliminated. Replacing the original Figure 23.4 with these new results combined with the expected monetary consequence found in Figure 23.3, the reduced decision tree is shown in Figure 23.6.

Now that all event forks have been reduced to their respective expected consequences, the broker faces a choice among:

1. the act "Seeking Permission" with an expected consequence of $+\$45,000$,

2. the act "Buy Option" with an expected consequence of $+\$100,000$,

3. the act "Don't Buy Option" with a zero consequence.

Clearly the second alternative is preferable on the basis of its most favorable expected outcome.

The decision tree has shown us that the broker ought not to petition at the outset for a government license. Instead the broker (assuming a risk accepter) should plan to buy the option without collecting this information in the way proposed.

Reflections

The modification of our original problem has resulted in this more complex and interesting variant. The changed decision elements are:

1. a wide range of opening options by adding the act "seek approval first,"

2. a recognition of additional uncertainty by quantifying the chances that the land option may or may not still be open.

The elements unchanged are:

3. the financial consequences, and

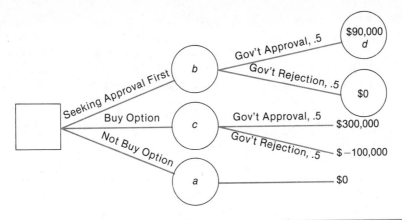

FIGURE 23.5 Reduced Decision Tree Applying the Expectation Rule: Intermediate Stage

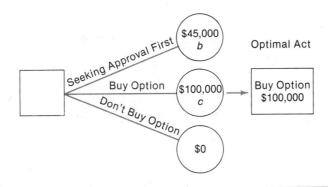

FIGURE 23.6 Reduced Decision Tree Applying the Expectation Rule: Final Stage

4. the decision criteria.

Additional insights will soon be considered that will broaden further the four decision elements.

23.4. Expected Value of Perfect Information

Informative as the "question first-act later" guideline seems, it is a somewhat shortsighted approach. Why? It views the gathering of information passively. It dismisses the age-old adage, *carpe diem* — seize the day. It assumes that the broker must sit back and let events happen. It presumes no direct initiative in resolving the uncertainty on the part of the decision maker. Isn't there a way to forestall losing the opportunity by neglect?

Since the basis of the broker's decision problem lies with uncertainty, any means that would alleviate the uncertainty without jeopardizing the opportunity to buy would be welcomed. One way that has been used to accomplish this is to buy relevant information. A consultant, expert at sizing up such situations, could be hired. Otherwise, a research group can be commissioned to study the problem. Whatever means are employed, the end result must be relevant information lessening the uncertainty and permitting a better prediction of that event. For example, a marketing decision on the introduction of a new product usually hinges on the extent and speed of acceptance of the new product. Various types of marketing research including test marketing can be purchased to improve assessment of the product's acceptance.

Is the information worth its price tag? This is the bottom-line question. When confronted with proposals purporting to reduce uncertainty through the acquisition of relevant information, is there a way to screen the proposals? One feasible approach is to compare purchase prices to a standard known as the *Expected Value of Perfect Information*, or EVPI. The EVPI is the maximum amount that should be paid for information that completely eliminates the uncertainty. Presumably any actual research study or advice from a consultant will fall short of eliminating all uncertainty. Hence, its worth cannot exceed the EVPI value. Thus the EVPI serves as an upper spending limit for new information. Any research project or consultant's advice with a price tag higher than the EVPI value is overpriced for the decision at hand.

The EVPI is calculated by finding the *difference* between two expected values. The first is the expected value of the optimal action knowing that perfect foresight will be acquired prior to the time the course of action must be chosen. This is designated by EVPF, or Expected Value with Perfect Foresight. For the real estate broker this situation corresponds to hiring a lawyer-consultant who is certain to find out whether or not the government will approve the project. The second component of EVPI is the expected value of the optimal action when the course of action is chosen *without* acquiring additional information. This is the component previously calculated in Section 23.2 as $100,000. Thus the gain in expected value from acquiring perfect information is:

$$EVPI = EVPF - (\text{Expected Value of Optimal Act})$$

The steps are as follows:

1. Calculate EVPF. This calculation refers to the broker's expectation prior to acquiring the lawyer-consultant's report on what the government will do. However, since the lawyer-consultant has perfect foresight into the government's reaction to the request, the consultant can (for a fee) tell the broker with certainty what event will occur. Now one may ask what is the probability that the consultant will conclude (with certainty) that E_1 will occur? Since the consultant doesn't control the government's decision on licensing, the probability of license approval E_1 and license disapproval E_2 will still be .5. If the consultant concludes E_1 will occur, the broker will choose A_1 which gives $300,000 profit. The consultant's conclusion that E_2 will occur will cause the broker to choose A_2 which gives a zero profit. Linking the probabilities of E_1 and E_2 with the profit consequences implies that $300,000 and zero will each have .5 probability of occurring. These conditions are expressed in Table 23.2.

TABLE 23.2. Determining the EVPF

If This Event Occurs	Then the Best Act Is	And the Profit Will Be	And the Probability of This Profit Is
E_1	A_1	$300,000	.5
E_2	A_2	0	.5

The EVPF computation is simply the expected value of the economic consequences that follows from (1) choosing the best act knowing the event, (2) weighted by the event's probability of occurrence. That is,

$$300,000(.5) = \$150,000 \text{ (if license is approved)}$$
$$+ \$0(.5) \quad = \quad \underline{\qquad 0} \text{ (if license is rejected)}$$
$$\$150,000$$

2. Calculate the expected value of the optimal action assuming that the event which will occur is not known in advance. In the real estate problem, this calculation was made in Section 23.2, leading to an expected value of $100,000.

3. Find the difference between the expected values in steps 1 and 2. This is the EVPI. In the real estate problem, the EVPI is $150,000 − $100,000 = $50,000.

Thus, no matter how prophetic a consultant or research service claims to be, $50,000 is the most that should be paid for the information provided.

23.5. Seeking Imperfect Information

The EVPI calculation of the last section suggests that if imperfect information is obtainable, the broker should pay at most some dollar amount under $50,000. But how can the broker determine whether or not a proposal with a specific price tag on it is worth accepting? The price paid ought to depend on how good the information is. More precisely, how well does the imperfect information reduce (not eliminate) the uncertainty?

Example 23.5.   Is Imperfect Information Worth Its Price?

Suppose a local lawyer wants to "sound out" the government position on this particular option for a $1000 fee. Realizing that the lawyer has a fairly good, but not perfect, record on such matters, the question is, "Should the broker pay a thousand dollars to hire the lawyer as a consultant?"

Simplifying the Decision Tree

The decision tree shown in Figure 23.7 is an augmented version of Figure 23.4. The segment identical to Figure 23.4 shows some act branches with double

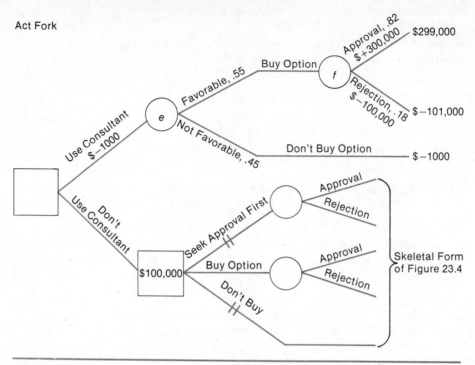

FIGURE 23.7 Augmented Decision Tree: Using a Consultant for $1000 Fee

slashes. This indicates that these branches have been eliminated from further considerations. Using the decision criterion of choosing the act branch with the highest expected value, all act branches at a given fork except one will be ruled out.

What about the intent of the broker in hiring the consultant? It is assumed that the recommendations are a basis for action. It would make little sense to incur the cost of a consultant if you disregard the appraisal and follow an already decided course of action. This means that a favorable appraisal from the consultant should cause the broker to exercise the option to buy the land parcel. Since it is clear that the act to choose based on a *favorable* consultant's report is the *Buy Option*, it is unnecessary at that point to show on the tree a Don't Buy branch as a possibility. Likewise, a *Buy* branch as a possibility is ruled out and not shown if the consultant's report is unfavorable. This elimination avoids clutter in constructing the decision tree. More importantly, possible confusion in reading the tree is reduced. Thus, only those act branches thought to be in actual contention for the best act are shown on the act fork.

Does the broker need to come up with any new probabilities now that a consultant is going to be considered? Yes. With the extension of two additional event forks there is an assessment required of:

1. the chances that the consultant's report will be favorable or unfavorable; that is, the probabilities on event fork e;

2. if the report is known to be favorable, the chances that the government will or will not approve the deal; that is, the probabilities on event fork f.

Is there a redundancy here? After all, the broker already assessed the possible government approval as .5 probability. Why ask for that probability again? The .5 probability value assessed in the absence of the consultant's report is the uncertainty surrounding government approval without the benefit of knowing that the consultant's report was favorable. Aided by the information of a favorable report, the probability of approval is a conditional probability which will be higher than 0.5. There is no redundancy because the two probabilities of approval refer to different situations.

It is clear that a favorable consultant's report provides information that improves the chance that the forthcoming government decision will be an approval. Thus, it must be recognized that the probability assigned to the event "government approval" is always conditional (dependent) on the information available before the event. On a decision tree, this means all the events and acts to the left of the event and on the same branch of the tree provide relevant information. Consequently, the event "approval" may and probably will have a different chance of occurring depending on where on the decision tree it resides.

The consultant's report to the broker, if favorable, causes the broker to believe that government approval is more probable (.82) than the .5 value used prior to receiving the report. Subtracting the $1000 consulting fee from all the monetary consequences intended to be at end positions introduces the consultant's cost explicitly into the problem. Intermediate monetary consequences are placed beneath each act and event branch, as shown in Figure 23.7, to help derive the net end monetary consequences, which become difficult to track as the tree becomes larger and more complex.

Reducing the Tree

The process of reducing the tree is the result of choosing the highest consequences on a fork. The part of the tree that carries over from Figure 23.4 and shown in skeletal form in Figure 23.7 is now summarized in Figure 23.8 by the expected monetary consequence of $100,000 found by choosing *Buy* as the optimal act.

Calculating the expected value that will replace the *f* event fork, we find

$$\$299,000(.82) - \$101,000(.18) = \$227,000$$

which we find encircled in *f* in Figure 23.8.

For event *e*, the expected value computed is

$$\$227,000(.55) - \$1000(.45) = \$124,400$$

The end result is the decision tree in Figure 23.9.

Comparing the act "Use Consultant" with its expected value of $124,400, to the expected value of $100,000 resulting from the series of acts "Don't Use Consultant" followed by the act "Buy Option," shows that using the consultant and paying the $1000 fee provides a greater expected gain than if the service and imperfect information were foregone.

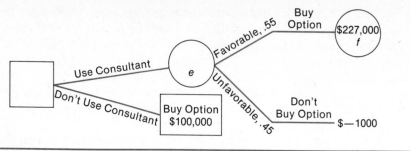

FIGURE 23.8 Reduced Decision Tree: Using a Consultant

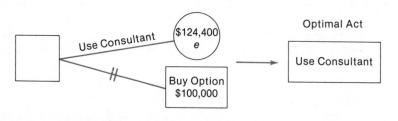

FIGURE 23.9 Final Reduced Decision Tree Using a Consultant

Information is gathered to minimize the uncertainty surrounding a decision. Both the "use consultant" and the "seeking government clearance" are information gathering decisions. One difference between the two resides in the quality of information gathered. The former supplies only imperfect information which may substantially reduce but never totally eliminate the risk that the act chosen is the wrong decision. It was learned that in spite of the imperfection of the consultant's information and its associated cost, its immediate availability made it quite attractive. Perfect but delayed information obtained through formal application for clearance suffered because it took so long to obtain it.

In this example the information provided by the consultant reduced the uncertainty enough to be worth the $1000 asking price. But the key point to bear in mind at this stage is that the information which avoids costly errors will be valuable to the decision maker. Moreover, better decisions will accrue to those decision makers who take advantage of the way relevant information generally reduces uncertainty surrounding the outcome of a business decision.

23.6. Indirectly Relevant Information

What makes relevant information valuable to managers? In the context of DTA, relevant information raises the expected monetary consequence of the optimal act chosen. For example, in the real estate broker's problem, acquisition of the consultant's opinion raised the expected monetary consequence by $24,400. How does this boost come about? The initial event probabilities are revised to reflect the importance of the acquired information. As before, the selection of the optimal act would require applying the expectation rule to the monetary consequence of the acts. But now the revised probabilities will replace the initial event probabilities. Relevant information incorporated in the revised probabilities will give a higher expected monetary consequence for the optimal act than the optimal act chosen using the initial event probabilities. Note that this rise in expected value required no change in the actual value of the possible monetary consequences. The increased expected value is attributable to a higher probability of choosing the act that gives the higher monetary value.

Specifically, how can the manager take advantage of relevant information? It requires knowing a procedure for reassessing the initial event probabilities. The next four steps describe such a procedure.

Recall in the real estate broker's problem that initially the assessed probability of government license approval was 0.5. Letting event $A = E_1$ means $P(A) = .5$. Likewise, letting event $R = E_2$ means $P(R) = .5$. Now, along comes information of a favorable consultant's report. What is the significance of this report?

Step One: Identifying the Set of Discriminating Circumstances

The decision process can be reviewed in four steps. First, there must exist an identifiable condition or set of conditions which are directly linked to and tend to discriminate between the occurrence and non-occurrence of the event in question.

> The lawyer engaged as a consultant by the real estate broker devotes time and effort to study key conditions determining government decisions. The record shows that conformity to zoning and performance standard conditions such as curb cut locations and building height and setback are important factors in gaining approval of the license. That is, they can be identified as being linked to the government's decision to approve or reject a license. Specifically, publicly available government data over the past few years show that conformance to these conditions are found in 90 percent of license approvals but only 20 percent of license rejections.

Step Two: Defining the Elementary Events

The initial event possibilities coupled with the status position of the discriminating condition become joint events. These joint events can be viewed as elementary events and the building blocks to use to define the events of interest. Each elementary event will be associated with a joint probability. Essentially the real estate broker's problem boils down to four elementary events:

1. license approval, A, and favorable conditions present, $F \Rightarrow (A\&F)$
2. license approval, A, and favorable conditions absent, $F^1 \Rightarrow (A\&F^1)$
3. license rejection, R, and favorable conditions present, $F \Rightarrow (R\&F)$
4. license rejection, R, and favorable conditions absent, $F^1 \Rightarrow (R\&F^1)$

Step Three: Establish Whether the Discriminating Conditions Are Present

Are the conditions identified as discriminating in step one absent or present? This revelation, in light of the incidence rates of the four elementary events presented in step 2, constitutes relevant information on which event (accepted or rejected) will likely occur.

> Does the broker's proposed license application have the proper curb cut, building setback, etc. conditions? If so, the application conforms to all the forementioned conditions most closely associated with approved applications. The consultant will verify this and issue a favorable opinion.

Step Four: Revising Event Probabilities By Reversing the Probability Tree

The initial probabilities of the events need to be updated in view of the relevant information from the consultant's report on the discriminating conditions.

> The broker's initial assessment of the event "license approval" or the event "license rejection" is combined with the conditional probabilities given by the consultant for the particular "license" event. A revised assessment of approval and rejection results.

How does the mechanism of revising probabilities work once the initial probabilities and conditional probabilities for the discriminating conditions are known? First, it is important to recognize that the probabilities of the newly coined elementary events are the end products of two different but equally legitimate probability trees. By knowing the probabilities on the branches of one of these trees, as in the broker example, the probabilities of the elementary events and the required probabilities on the other tree can be determined. The procedure is called "reversing the probability tree."

Finding the Joint (Elementary Event) Probabilities

Figure 23.10 portrays two probability trees in tandem for the real estate example. Each tree is a combination of two event forks, the "accept-reject" event fork and the consultant's "favorable-unfavorable" event fork. The left tree starts with the accept-reject event fork and proceeds to combine that fork with the "favorable-unfavorable" event fork. Therefore the probabilities of "favorable-unfavorable" events occurring will be conditional probabilities.

> The upper network shows the "favorable-unfavorable" event fork, given the accept branch as its starting branch. The probabilities shown on the two branches of the "favorable-unfavorable" event fork then are the conditional probabilities of F given A and of not F given A.

> The lower network shows the "favorable-unfavorable" fork given the rejec-

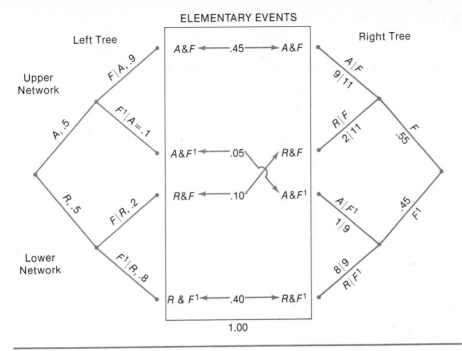

ELEMENTARY EVENTS

Left Tree

Right Tree

Upper
Network

$F|A, .9$

$A\&F \longleftarrow .45 \longrightarrow A\&F$

$A|F$

$9/11$

$F'|A = .1$

$A, .5$

$R|F$

$2/11$

$A\&F^1 \longleftarrow .05$

$R\&F$

F

.55

$R, .5$

$F|R, .2$

$R\&F \longleftarrow .10$

$A\&F^1$

$A|F^1$

$1/9$

.45

F^1

Lower
Network

$F'|R, .8$

$R\&F^1 \longleftarrow .40 \longrightarrow R\&F^1$

$8/9$

$R|F^1$

1.00

FIGURE 23.10 Reversing the Probability Trees

tion branch as the starting branch. The probabilities on the two branches of the "favorable-unfavorable" event fork are conditional probabilities of F given R and not F given R.

There are three known probabilities $P(A)$, $P(F|A)$, $P(F|R)$. The latter two, from the consultant's findings, were .9 and .2 respectively. All the other probabilities on this probability tree can be determined from the fact that the sum of all the (joint) probabilities at the end positions must equal one. The probability of each end position is the probability of one of the four resulting elementary events $(A\&F^1)$, $(A\&F^1)$, $(R\&F)$, $(R\&F^1)$. The values are obtained from the probabilities derived for each branch route. Thus,

$$P(A\&F) = P(A)P(F|A) = (.5)(.9) = .45 \text{ etc.}$$

Finding Revised Probabilities on the Right-Hand Tree

Once the (joint) probabilities of the four elementary events are determined, the probabilities on the right (inverted) probability tree can be computed. For example, the probability of a favorable opinion is the sum of the (joint) probabilities at the end positions of the F branch. These two probabilities $P(A\&F)$ and $P(R\&F)$ have previously been computed. Thus,

$$P(F) = P(A\&F) + P(R\&F) = .45 + .10 = .55$$
$$P(F^1) = 1 - .55 = .45 \text{ is the complementary probability.}$$

But what about the four required conditional probabilities on the right tree? These probabilities can now easily be found from the fact that the product of the probabilities along any branch of the tree must give the (known) joint probability for the elementary event at the end position of that branch. Thus,

$$P(F) \qquad\qquad P(A|F) \quad = \quad P(A\&F)$$

$$\uparrow \qquad\qquad\quad \uparrow \qquad\qquad\qquad \uparrow$$

Known	Unknown	Known
.55	$P(A\|F)$	= .45

$$P(A|F) = \frac{.45}{.55} = \frac{9}{11}$$

Following the same procedure the other conditional probabilities can be ascertained:

$$P(F)P(R|F) = P(R\&F)$$
$$.55P(R|F) = .10$$
$$P(R|F) = .10/.55 = 2/11$$
$$P(F^1)P(A|F^1) = P(A\&F^1)$$
$$.45P(A|F^1) = .05$$
$$P(A|F^1) = .05/.45 = 1/9$$
$$P(F^1)P(R|F^1) = P(R\&F^1)$$
$$.45P(R|F^1) = .40$$
$$P(R|F^1) = .40/.45 = 8/9$$

A Caveat

Notice that the consultant's research is based only on the applications which had already been processed: *approved* applications and *rejected* applications. That is, a randomly chosen approved application could be said to have a .9 probability of possessing the consultant's discriminating conditions, and therefore be classified as favorable, $P(F|A) = .9$. This is *not* the same as saying a randomly chosen favorable opinion has a .9 probability of approval. That is,

$$P(F|A) \neq P(A|F)$$
$$.9 \neq 9/11$$

Likewise, a randomly chosen rejected application could be said to have a .2 probability of possessing the consultant's discriminating conditions, $P(F|R) = .2$, which is *not* the same as saying a randomly chosen favorable opinion has a .2 probability of rejection. That is,

$$P(F|R) \neq P(R|F)$$
$$.2 \neq 2/11$$

To obtain one probability from the other is the reason the decision tree had to be reversed. So reversing the probability trees to obtain $P(A|F)$ from $P(F|A)$ and $P(R|F)$ from $P(F|R)$ clearly demonstrates that the pair $P(F|A)$ and $P(A|F)$ and the pair $P(F|R)$ and $P(R|F)$ are indirectly related probabilities. Importantly, the procedure gained for us the revised probabilities of approval and rejection,

$P(A|F)$ and $P(R|F)$, given the relevant information of a favorable opinion. These key probabilities can now replace the initial event probabilities in DTA analysis.

How does the acquisition of the information contained in the consultant's report alter the decision process so as to bring about a higher expected monetary consequence? The reader should refer back to Figure 23.6 and 23.9. The latter figure shows the decision tree based upon the use of the consultant. The expected monetary consequence in that situation is $124,400. The other figure shows the decision tree when the consultant is not used. The expected monetary consequence is $100,000. The difference between the two expected monetary consequences is the expected profitability improvement, $24,400. That improvement is only attainable when the probabilities on the reversed probability tree have been determined.

23.7. Bayes' Theorem and Bayesian Inference

The use of indirectly relevant information (such as reversed probability trees) to revise probabilities was first articulated by a seventeenth century English minister, the Reverend Thomas Bayes. He proposed that an event A initially assessed $P(A)$ prior to learning the occurrence of another event B can have a new probability assessment *conditional* on B, $P(A|B)$. The occurrence of B will change the initial probability assessment for A provided A and B are not independent events. The value of $P(A|B)$ is given by the following expression, known as *Bayes' Theorem*:

$$P(A|B) = \frac{P(A)P(B|A)}{P(A)P(B|A) + P(A^1)P(B|A^1)}$$

The probability for A prior to knowing that the indirectly related event B has occurred is called the *prior* probability of A, $P(A)$. The probability for A assessed in light of the knowledge that event B has occurred is called the *posterior* probability of A, $P(A|B)$. Thus, the prior probability of A is unconditional; the posterior assessment is a conditional probability. The conditional probabilities $P(B|A)$ and $P(B|A^1)$ are called *likelihoods*. Thus, $P(B|A)$ is the likelihood of B having occurred if A is true, while $P(B|A^1)$ is the likelihood of B having occurred if A^1 is true. Note that these likelihoods need not sum to one; indeed, their sum is not meaningful, since the symbols $|A$ and $|A^1$ refer to different reduced sample spaces.

Bayes' Theorem is extremely useful. It allows us to obtain the posterior (revised) probability of an event without having to use the cumbersome forward and inverted probability trees. For instance, the posterior probability of government approval subsequent to a favorable consultant's opinion is calculated as follows, letting A = approval and A^1 = rejection.

$$P(A|F) = \frac{P(A)P(F|A)}{P(A)P(F|A) + P(A^1)P(F|A^1)}$$

$$= \frac{(.5)(.9)}{(.5)(.9) + (.5)(.2)}$$

$$= \frac{.45}{.55} = .82$$

This and other posterior probabilities are obtained from the left tree of Figure 23.10. This figure gives a graphical "proof" of Bayes Theorem. As can be seen, .82 is exactly the same value obtained from the reverse tree analysis. Once determined, the revised probabilities will replace initial probabilities and represent the relevant weights in the calculation of the expected monetary consequences of the acts under consideration in DTA analysis.

In the general case where we consider not just an event A and its complement A^1, but rather a set of K mutually exclusive events, designated by E_j, Bayes' Theorem is given by

$$P(E_j \mid B) = \frac{P(E_j)P(B \mid E_j)}{\sum\limits_{j=1}^{K} P(E_j)P(B \mid E_j)}$$

As before, B is an event not independent of the E_j. Thus the occurrence of B changes the probability of the E_j according to the above expression.[3]

23.8. Decision Tree Analysis for Quantitative Variables—The Bracket-Median Method

Up to this point the two-branch event forks investigated have had branches showing attribute alternatives. One branch points to the event occurring; the other branch shows the event not occurring. Business problems need not be of this kind. That is, they need not deal with attributes. Thus, the event fork could be a collection of the possible business quantities that could occur. For example, both sales and costs are typically quantitative variables with a large number of possible values.

Can the expected monetary value be computed, as before, by multiplying each possible event's monetary consequence by its probability and summing the products? Yes, if the quantitative variable is discrete. Analysis would be burdensome, though, if each possible value of the variable has to be considered. To keep things manageable, it is often feasible to reduce the entire range of values down to a few representative numbers. Each event branch then represents a limited *range* of values rather than a single value. By the "bracket median method," an equivalent distribution with a few values substitutes for the entire distribution of values. The bracket medians are structured to have equal probability.

Recalling the set of decisions faced by the real estate broker, assume that some misgivings have arisen about the selling price of the land parcels.

Fluctuation in interest rates have made uncertain the $80,000 per acre figure. A price between $50,000 and $100,000 per acre is now the range considered likely. How likely? The probabilities for specific values within this range are expressed by the cumulative distribution shown in Figure 23.11.

Can the bracket median technique offer the real estate broker any help? If so, in what form? First, thought must be given to the number of event branches

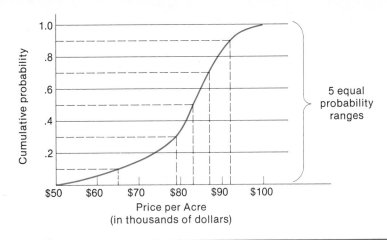

FIGURE 23.11 Cumulative Probability Distribution and Bracket Medians for Real Estate Problem

chosen for the accuracy desired. Let's say five branches are decided on. (Computer speed makes computationally feasible the use of a hundred or more branches.) The next step is to partition the total probability into five equal portions of .2 each. With each branch summarizing a range of price per acre figures, the bracket median for the branch corresponds with the midpoint of the probability assigned each range of values. These midpoints are the .10, .30, .50, .70 and .90 fractiles of the probability distribution. The price-per-acre "bracket medians" in this case are $65,000, $79,000, $83,000, $87,000 and $92,000 per acre.

The "equivalent-event fan" shown in Figure 23.12 is the direct result of grouping the original probability distribution in this way. The bracket median represents the range of values and each branch has an event probability of 0.2. According to the expectation rule, the "fan" can be eliminated and replaced by its expected consequence (net of cost) of $312,000. The decision analysis proceeds exactly as before. The approved-rejected fork is eliminated and replaced by its expected consequence of $106,000. The best action on the basis of highest expected consequence is still to buy the option.

23.9. Incremental Analysis

At times it is wise to simplify the decision tree analysis. Consider the circumstance confronting Jack Feinstein, the galoshes wholesaler described in the introduction to this chapter. Orders for galoshes from his suppliers must be placed in the summer before he knows what demand the winter weather will bring. A "bracket median" approach on the number of galoshes ordered could be tried but there is a simpler approach. The simplification would follow once

1. the problem of how many pairs to order can be viewed in terms of successive decision trees—one for each pair of galoshes ordered

2. with each decision tree having one two-branch act fork and one two-branch event fork

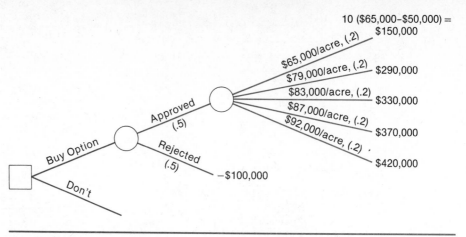

10 ($65,000–$50,000) = $150,000

$65,000/acre, (.2)

$79,000/acre, (.2) $290,000

$83,000/acre, (.2) $330,000

$87,000/acre, (.2) $370,000

$92,000/acre, (.2) $420,000

Approved (.5)

Buy Option

Rejected (.5) −$100,000

Don't

FIGURE 23.12 Equivalent-Event Fan for Real Estate Broker's Problem

3. and each successive decision tree having monetary consequences at the end of its branch paths identical to every other tree.

The monetary consequences reflect the loss on every available but unneeded pair and the unrealized *profit potential* on every needed but unavailable pair. This unrealized profit potential is called an *opportunity loss.* In order for the simplified approach to be applicable, this opportunity loss must also be identical on each pair. Under these conditions, the proper question to ask is "should this q^{th} pair be ordered?" Then proceed to subsequently ask and answer the same question for the $(q + 1)^{th}$ pair.

Supporting Jack Feinstein's profit picture is a $6 per pair profit margin for each sold pair prior to the February 1st closing out date. Losses amount to $2 per pair on every unsold pair in stock at that date because to sell enough galoshes to reduce his inventory sufficiently, substantial price markdowns are necessary. For each pair of galoshes the decision tree will resemble Figure 23.13.

From the expectation rule the event fork is replaced by the expected consequence

$$P_q(\$6) + (1 - P_q)(-\$2)$$
$$= 8P_q - 2$$

where P_q is the probability of selling the qth pair before the February closing date.

Should the qth pair of galoshes be ordered? That depends on whether the expected monetary consequence of the act *Buy* is greater than that of the act *Don't Buy.* When will that happen? Whenever

$$8P_q - 2 > 0$$
$$8P_q > 2$$
$$P_q > \tfrac{2}{8}$$

This equation puts a specific requirement on the value of P_q. It must exceed $\tfrac{2}{8}$ or .25 for the expected monetary consequence of the buy act to be preferred. This

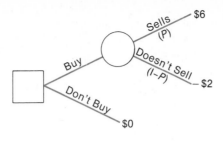

FIGURE 23.13 Decision Tree for q^{th} Pair of Galoshes

means that the qth pair of galoshes under consideration should not be ordered unless there is at least a .25 chance of selling them before the markdown date.

What about the $(q + 1)^{th}$ pair of galoshes? With the act-event consequence series the same as for the qth unit, the signal should again be "order" whenever P_{q+1} exceeds .25. Could P_{q+1} exceed P_q? That would be a bit farfetched. If the probability of demand of at least q galoshes does not exceed .25, then certainly the probability that demand equals an even higher value $(q + 1)$ cannot exceed .25 either. So,

> if the best decision on the qth unit is not to buy, the best decision on subsequent units must also be not to buy.

Stepping back a bit one can wonder whether the decision to buy the $(q + 1)^{th}$ pair of galoshes means that the decision on the qth pair must also be to buy that pair too. This must be true since it is recognized that the probability that galoshes demand exceeds q pairs can't be less than the probability that demand exceeds an even larger $(q + 1)$ number of pairs. Suppose q is 7. The probability that demand exceeds 7 can't be less than the probability of demand exceeding 8. So it is a principle of *incremental analysis* that a favorable decision on buying the qth item assures a favorable decision on any lower number of items. Thus a favorable decision on the 7th item means a favorable decision on buying items 1 to 6 also. Similarly the decision not to buy the qth item confirms that the decision on any higher number of items must also be not to buy. If the decision on the 7th item is not to buy it, the decision on the 8th, 9th, etc. items must also be not to buy them. With this principle in mind, an incredibly simple decision criterion can be given Jack Feinstein to use in buying his galoshes.

What stop-go rule results? Assigning K_o as the loss on any unsold pair and K_u as the profit foregone by not having on hand a pair that could have been sold, the rule suggests to

> continue to buy up to and including the last (highest) value of q at which P_q equals or exceeds the ratio $K_o/(K_u + K_o)$.

In the galoshes problem, $K_o = 2$ and $K_u = 6$. Therefore, the ratio $K_o/(K_u + K_o) = .25$. The value of q at this point would be the $(1 - P_q)$ fractile of the probability distribution for demand. At this point, $P_q = K_o/(K_u + K_o)$. Expressing the stop-go rule in terms of a fractile of the distribution for demand, it indicates that one should order the quantity indicated by the

$$\frac{K_u}{K_u + K_o}$$ fractile of the probability distribution.

For Jack Feinstein's case, this would have pointed to the

$$\frac{K_u}{K_u + K_o} = \frac{6}{6 + 2} = .75 \text{ fractile.}$$

How many pairs should he have ordered if he assigned the demand for his galoshes as a normal distribution with a mean of 40,000 pairs and a standard deviation of 15,000 pairs? The .75 fractile of a normal distribution (from the table of areas under the standardized normal distribution) occurs at a value 0.67 standard deviations above the mean. Knowledgeable about the rule, a prudent move on Jack Feinstein's part would have been an order of:

mean + .67(value of the standard deviation)
40,000 + (.67)(15,000) = 50,050 pairs.

That is, the optimal stock of galoshes for Jack Feinstein to have ordered for the coming winter season is 50,050 pairs.

23.10. Decision Making by Utility Theory

So far in this chapter the only decision guideline applied in choosing the optimal action among alternatives has been the expectation decision rule. By this rule the action that maximizes the expected gain or minimizes the expected loss is to be chosen among the alternatives available. As plausible and useful as this criterion has been, there are situations in which the application of the expected value decision rule would lead the business manager astray.

The major reservation with the use of the expectation rule as a universal managerial guideline is that it assumes the business organization will survive for the long run. To reap the benefits of this long-run view which is implied by the expected value calculation, the firm must be able to avoid bankruptcy in the short run. The famous British economist John Maynard Keynes dramatized this issue with his comment, "In the long run we are all dead." The implication of this statement is that long run objectives are irrelevant considerations if we neglect the short run. Thus, making decisions solely on the basis of a long run criterion can ignore some of the realities that the firm lives with and can produce poor managerial decisions.

Suppose the chief financial officer of a major airline has forecasted this coming year's income statement and recognized that, because of the recent unanticipated hikes in aviation fuel from 87¢ a gallon to $1.07 a gallon, operating expenses will be considerably overbudget and will devastate the hoped-for rate of return that he knows stockholders are expecting. Recognizing that seriously disappointing current stockholders will likely cut off future monies from prospective stockholders and will seriously impair the firm's ability to remain competitive by updating its fleet, the officer is contemplating different ways to resolve the situation. One option for paring expenses without causing a reduction in operating service is to cut the insurance expense line on the income statement.

The air traffic records indicate that the chance of an airplane crash where the plane would be lost is only two in 1000. The expected loss on a 50 million dollar plane would be

$$.002 \times \$50,000,000 = \$100,000 \text{ expected loss per plane.}$$

The insurance premium on the plane itself (passenger liability aside) has been costing the company $250,000. On the basis of the expectation rule (calculations shown in Table 23.3), the expected loss of $250,000 insurance premium exceeds the expected loss of $100,000 for an airline crash. This suggests that the insurance should be dropped if expected value is the decision criterion.

TABLE 23.3. Decision Matrix for Purchasing Airplane Insurance

PROBABILITY	EVENT	A_1 = BUY INSURANCE	A_2 = NOT BUY INSURANCE
.002	E_1 = Crash	−250,000	−50,000,000
.998	E_2 = No Crash	−250,000	0

$$E(A_1) = .002(-250,000) + .998(-250,000)$$
$$= -250,000$$

$$E(A_2) = .002(-50,000,000) + .998(0)$$
$$= -100,000$$

If this suggestion is followed for its fleet of 100 planes, the company would show an immediate 25 million dollar reduction in the insurance expense line on the income statement and an improved profit picture. What if the unexpected happens and one or possibly two planes crash during the year? The impact of a 50 or 100 million dollar capital loss would assuredly devastate whatever meager profits were forecast, would disillusion current and prospective stockholders, would put the firm's financial picture in comparatively poor light versus its competitors, and would probably cripple the firm's immediate chance of raising new capital for replacement and modernization. A predictable consequence would be the resignation of the financial manager. Despite the favorable impact on the reported income statement if no crash occurs, not buying insurance places in jeopardy the short run viability of the firm. Because of the dire consequences possible if the expectation rule is used as the decision criterion, the act that minimizes the expected loss ought to be discarded in this situation.

Expected-Utility Concept

An observation of the current management environment suggests that not every financial manager is an expected-value maximizer; otherwise, one would see many more managerial shake-ups and a higher frequency of corporate bankruptcies. The vast majority of financial managers seem to follow a risk aversion policy. This leads them to buy insurance to avoid catastrophic losses from unpredictable and uncontrollable events. There are, however, financial managers who commit capital to ventures which offer high speculative gain. What explains their behavior? The expected utility is introduced into decision making to add some additional insight. Suppose a financial manager accurately assesses the probability of various profit outcomes. Subsequently, the financial manager assigns values, or *utilities*, to the different possible amounts of profit. The utilities assigned and the different profit possibilities can be sketched by a *utility function*. A utility function maps out the levels of utility associated with different amounts of profit attained.

Three Types

Basically three types of managers can be identified: one who takes a risk-aversion posture, another who views risk neutrally, and another who can be labeled a risk lover. The three types have distinct attitudes toward profitability and utility, as shown in Figure 23.14.

A deliberating, conservative manager is shown by curve *A* and is categorized as risk averse. The zero profit point is located at the middle of the graph. A move to the right from the zero profit mark gains positive utility, but the utility gains are less than the utility loss suffered if an equal amount of loss is incurred. Risk averse managers regret their losses much more than they enjoy their gains. Their utility functions increase at a slower and slower pace with each increment in profit. Type *A* will reject investment opportunities in which substantial losses can occur.

Manager *B* is indifferent to risk. The utility function of this type of manager increases by a constant amount with each increment in profit. A move to the right from the zero point brings a positive utility amount equal to the utility loss associated with a move an identical distance to the left from zero.

Finally, Type *C* manager is a risk lover because the satisfaction that comes with high profits is more rewarding than the displeasure that comes from similar size losses.

One can observe from Figure 23.14 that a gain in profits from the zero profit point brings Type *C* managers a higher utility than a loss of the same amount would have decreased it. Type *C* managers are more likely to take on boom or

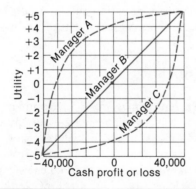

FIGURE 23.14 Three Types of Utility Curves

bust ventures which have very high profit potential, for example genetic engineering projects, deep sea ore mining, and oil exploration.

23.11. Concluding Comments

Decision theory analysis requires a decision maker to clearly delineate the decision options available, and for each of those to assess the probability of the possible consequences. The decision maker states a criterion for what is to be maximized. Then a *decision tree* is used to successively eliminate inferior decisions. *Backward induction* is a procedure used to deal with situations in which definite information can be sought to resolve the uncertainty, but only at the expense of less attractive consequences brought about by the delayed decision. The *expected value of perfect information* places an upper limit on the value of acquiring additional information to reduce uncertainty. In many decision situations, indirectly relevant information is available and can be advantageously used by proper application of *Bayes' theorem*.

For quantitative variables, the *bracket median method* facilitates the decision analysis by reducing to a manageable number the alternatives to be considered. In certain situations involving quantitative variables, the *incremental analysis approach* greatly simplifies the decision analysis. This approach requires that the opportunity loss from every available but unneeded unit be identical; the opportunity loss from every needed but unavailable unit must also be identical.

Footnotes and References

[1] Jeff Lyon, *Chicago Tribune*, Thursday, January 24, 1980.
[2] This situation is analogous to test marketing a product before launching it, with the risk that the delay may allow a competitor to get in first.
[3] A simple matrix method for solving this type of problem has been proposed by Donald Mann. It is very helpful in reducing the computational burden when there are numerous acts and events. See Donald Mann, "A Matrix Technique for Finite Bayesian Decision Problems," *Decision Sciences*, volume 3 (1972), pp. 129–136.

Questions and Problems

1. What is the purpose of a decision tree?

2. What is the purpose of a fork?

3. What is the difference between an act fork and an event fork?

4. Can both events and acts be shown on the branches of the same fork?

5. Can a decision tree be constructed with a succession of event forks but no act forks? With a succession of act forks but no event forks?

6. Why must the acts or events each fork represents be mutually exclusive? Collectively exhaustive?

7. If the sum of the event probabilities at an event fork does not equal one, does it mean the events are not mutually exclusive? Does it mean the events are not col-

lectively exhaustive? Does it mean the event fork has been invalidly constructed?

8. Every event on an event fork must be assigned a probability. Could the acts on an act fork of the decision tree also be shown with probabilities assigned?

9. What is the purpose of the expectation rule? Its limitation? Does it always indicate which actual payoff you will likely receive?

10. Summary Table 23.4 condenses a business decision tree which includes an initial act fork followed by event alternatives. Values in the table represent profits corresponding to particular Act-Event combinations.

a. Construct the decision tree from the information summarized in the table.

b. Applying the expectation rule, which act is optimal?

c. Since A_3 ("Don't Buy") never gives a profit, should it always be eliminated as an act to choose?

11. The values in Table 23.5 are the relevant conditional profits for a decision tree in which the starting act fork has 3 acts. Each act is subsequently followed by the three events of the event fork and its probabilities.

a. Draw the decision tree for the information presented in the table.

b. Applying the expectation principle, what is the optimal act (highest expected profit)?

12. The commercial lending department of a large western-based bank, B of W, is considering lending construction money to a builder. Provisions of the loan include a mortgage on the property and a $200,000 ownership position on the 12 unit each (1000 sq. feet) condominium complex to

be built at Laguna Niguel, California. The solid reputation of the builder and the fact that the complex will have an ocean view are considered attractive features of the venture. The bank thinks the chance of building permit approval is .9, whereas the chance of rejection of the permit, subsequent devaluation of the land parcel, and loss of equity is .1. But there is considerable uncertainty in the financial markets as to what will be the prevailing mortgage rates at the time the units are ready for sale.

If interest rates are high, price concessions will have to be granted to buyers. Low mortgage rates will create a strong demand and will permit the units to sell at full value prices. The bank's real estate appraisers, on the basis of historical data combined with their own judgment, have come up with prices ranging from $95,000 to $135,000 per unit on average. The probability distribution (p. 867) has been partitioned into five equal portions of .2 each. The cost per square foot for land and building is $85, therefore $85,000 per unit.

a. Using the cumulative probability graph, estimate to the nearest higher integer the price per unit associated with the midpoint of each .2 size partition.

b. Using the estimates found in Part a, show the profits (net of costs) with each branch of the equivalent-event fan.

c. Determine the optimal act by using backward induction for the decision tree diagram on the next page.

TABLE 23.5. Conditional Profits

PROBABILITY	EVENTS	A_1	A_2	A_3
.2	E_1	160	180	0
.2	E_2	120	20	180
.6	E_3	40	0	140

TABLE 23.4. Expected Profits

PROBABILITY	EVENTS		ACT:		
			A_1 = Buy	A_2 = Lease	A_3 = DON'T BUY OR LEASE
.3	low demand	= E_1	100	120	0
.3	moderate demand	= E_2	105	100	0
.4	high demand	= E_3	80	60	0

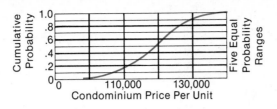

PROBLEM 23.12

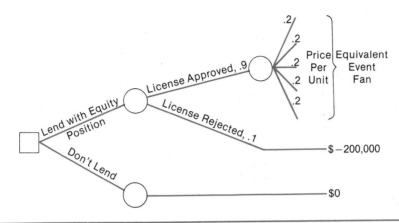

PROBLEM 23.12C

13. Suppose in Problem 23.12 B of W learned that since this condominium complex was situated along the California coast, permission to build had to be granted by the California Coastal Commission. Assume that the decision on the local building permit would be the same as that reached by the Coastal Commission. The bank real estate appraiser believes that there is better than a fifty-fifty chance that approval would be granted. But news of approval would drive the cost of the land up considerably and result in an overall cost of $100 sq. ft., thus lowering the profits. A reconstructed decision tree diagram for this is shown on page 868.

a. Recompute the values for the adjusted equivalent event fan.

b. Determine the optimal act by backward induction.

14. *Computech A* Computech is a pio-

neering high technology firm located in Silicon Valley, California. It has been very successful introducing a personal home microcomputer, Systems 5. It is now considering moving into the profitable commercial word processing business, which is in its infancy stage of growth. Since the technology for a word processor is essentially the same as for the microcomputer it now produces, Computech feels that its only current resource commitment would be taking out a lease option on additional plant capacity. If the economy becomes depressed, demand for commercial word processors will also be sluggish. In that case, Computech will not exercise the lease option, forfeiting the money it paid to obtain the option. A healthy economy with expanding business needs will show a strong demand for word processors. The lease option is expected to cost $25,000 and the chances of a low demand from a weak

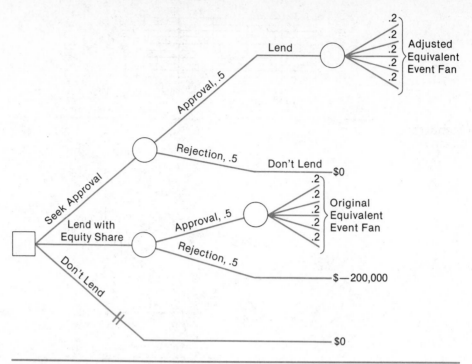

PROBLEM 23.13

economy are assessed at .4, whereas a .6 chance is given for high demand from a strong economy with a prospect of $75,000 profit.

a. Set up a decision tree with act-event forks and monetary consequences.

b. Formulate a summary table for the decision tree.

c. Using the expectation rule, select the optimal act.

15. *Computech B* The corporate vice president of finance at Computech has another plan for the expansion into word processing. The VP feels that Computech should redirect its efforts towards government purchasing by the GAO (Government Accounting Office) which would yield the same $75,000 profit prospect if successful. The new administration's push toward efficiency in government and its promise to trim down the use of government personnel should present Computech with a selling opportunity. Since Computech has done research for the gov-

ernment before, it knows how to deal with government machinery and the bidding process. They estimate the chances of winning the GAO bid as .7. This approach offers Computech three possibilities: (1) buy option; (2) not-buy option; (3) seek bid approval before finalizing the option purchase. Although the latter act seems to wisely suggest "looking before leaping," the approach is flawed. Currently, little excess plant capacity is to be found in Silicon Valley because of the high level of growth going on. This competition for facilities combined with the time lapse before the government acts on the bid significantly reduces Computech's chances to purchase the lease option to .5.

a. Draw a decision diagram for the decision situation above.

b. Use backward induction to choose the best act.

c. Calculate the EVPF and explain what it means.

d. Calculate the EVPI and explain what it means.

16. *Lie Detector Screening for Bank Theft*
A large bank has been defrauded of funds in excess of one million dollars. It is believed that an inside accomplice was involved, but it would be possible for any one of five thousand employees to have obtained the information crucial to the scheme's success. All five thousand employees are given a lie detector test. The test itself is regarded as perfectly reliable if properly administered, but there is a .1 probability of erroneous results each time the test is administered. The errors occur randomly and are not related to the subject or the subject's status with respect to the crime. To minimize the chances of erroneous conclusions the test is administered four times on four separate occasions to each of the 5000 employees. Only one employee, Richard Gerain, failed any of the tests. Moreover, of the four tests administered to Gerain, he failed on three occasions, passing only once. Assuming that the accomplice is one who took the test,

a. what is the probability that the accomplice is Gerain?

b. If the company's decision criterion is not to take action against the suspected culprit unless the odds are at least three to one that he is the accomplice, should action be taken? Explain.

17. *Determining Customer Service Levels*
Management of the Top-Value Liquor Company wants to determine the *optimal* stocking level for Beefeater's Gin, a popular brand with strong brand loyalty. Management believes stock-out cost is equal to the gross profit of *$10 per case*, on the assumption that customers will simply buy Beefeater's elsewhere, if Top-Value is temporarily out of stock. The cost of Beefeater's is *$56 per case*. Holding charges over the order cycle are comprised of interest cost ($2.25 per case) for financing $56 per case and shelf space rent ($.46 per case). There are no obsolescence or deterioration charges.

The probability distribution for Beefeater demand is estimated to have a mean of 134 cases. Errors are normally distributed, with mean zero and standard deviation equal to 46 cases.

a. What is the value of K_u, the foregone profit (opportunity loss) per case understocked?

b. What is the value of K_o?

c. What is the optimal stocking level, expressed as a fractile of the probability distribution for demand?

d. How many cases should be on hand at the beginning of the order cycle?

e. What would be the loss per case from overstocking, if the cost per case were $39? (Hint: Interest costs vary with case cost, but shelf space rent is fixed cost per case.)

18. A merchant carries a perishable good in inventory. Each item costs $9 and sells for $15. At the end of the day any unsold items must be thrown away (become valueless). Demand for this item is given by the distribution in Table 23.6. Assume that future customer demand is not altered by a stock-out this period.

TABLE 23.6. Demand for a Perishable Good

DEMAND	PROBABILITY
0	0
1	.3
2	.4
3	.2
4	.1
5 or more	0
	1.0

a. How many items should the merchant stock in order to maximize Expected Monetary Value? (Hint: Use Incremental Analysis.)

b. What is the Expected Monetary Value?

19. In Problem 18 suppose the demand is given by a binomial distribution with $n = 10$ and $p = .3$.

a. How many items should the merchant stock? (Hint: Use Incremental Analysis.)

b. What is the Expected Monetary Value?

20. In Problem 18 suppose the demand is given by a Poisson distribution with mean of 4 units.

a. How many items should the merchant stock?

b. What is the Expected Monetary Value?

Appendix

TABLE 1. Binomial Probabilities

Example: $P(X = 3 | n = 5, p = 0.30) = 0.1323$

n	x	.01	.05	.10	.15	.20	.25	p .30	.35	.40	.45	.50
1	0	.9900	.9500	.9000	.8500	.8000	.7500	.7000	.6500	.6000	.5500	.5000
	1	.0100	.0500	.1000	.1500	.2000	.2500	.3000	.3500	.4000	.4500	.5000
2	0	.9801	.9025	.8100	.7225	.6400	.5625	.4900	.4225	.3600	.3025	.2500
	1	.0198	.0950	.1800	.2550	.3200	.3750	.4200	.4550	.4800	.4950	.5000
	2	.0001	.0025	.0100	.0225	.0400	.0625	.0900	.1225	.1600	.2025	.2500
3	0	.9703	.8574	.7290	.6141	.5120	.4219	.3430	.2746	.2160	.1664	.1250
	1	.0294	.1354	.2430	.3251	.3840	.4219	.4410	.4436	.4320	.4084	.3750
	2	.0003	.0071	.0270	.0574	.0960	.1406	.1890	.2389	.2880	.3341	.3750
	3	.0000	.0001	.0010	.0034	.0080	.0156	.0270	.0429	.0640	.0911	.1250
4	0	.9606	.8145	.6561	.5220	.4096	.3164	.2401	.1785	.1296	.0915	.0625
	1	.0388	.1715	.2916	.3685	.4096	.4219	.4116	.3845	.3456	.2995	.2500
	2	.0006	.0135	.0486	.0975	.1536	.2109	.2646	.3105	.3456	.3675	.3750
	3	.0000	.0005	.0036	.0115	.0256	.0469	.0756	.1115	.1536	.2005	.2500
	4	.0000	.0000	.0001	.0005	.0016	.0039	.0081	.0150	.0256	.0410	.0625
5	0	.9510	.7738	.5905	.4437	.3277	.2373	.1681	.1160	.0778	.0503	.0312
	1	.0480	.2036	.3280	.3915	.4096	.3955	.3602	.3124	.2592	.2059	.1562
	2	.0010	.0214	.0729	.1382	.2048	.2637	.3087	.3364	.3456	.3369	.3125
	3	.0000	.0011	.0081	.0244	.0512	.0879	.1323	.1811	.2304	.2757	.3125
	4	.0000	.0000	.0004	.0022	.0064	.0146	.0284	.0488	.0768	.1128	.1562
	5	.0000	.0000	.0000	.0001	.0003	.0010	.0024	.0053	.0102	.0185	.0312
6	0	.9415	.7351	.5314	.3771	.2621	.1780	.1176	.0754	.0467	.0277	.0156
	1	.0571	.2321	.3543	.3993	.3932	.3560	.3025	.2437	.1866	.1359	.0938
	2	.0014	.0305	.0984	.1762	.2458	.2966	.3241	.3280	.3110	.2780	.2344
	3	.0000	.0021	.0146	.0415	.0819	.1318	.1852	.2355	.2765	.3032	.3125
	4	.0000	.0001	.0012	.0055	.0154	.0330	.0595	.0951	.1382	.1861	.2344
	5	.0000	.0000	.0001	.0004	.0015	.0044	.0102	.0205	.0369	.0609	.0938
	6	.0000	.0000	.0000	.0000	.0001	.0002	.0007	.0018	.0041	.0083	.0156
7	0	.9321	.6983	.4783	.3206	.2097	.1335	.0824	.0490	.0280	.0152	.0078
	1	.0659	.2573	.3720	.3960	.3670	.3115	.2471	.1848	.1306	.0872	.0547
	2	.0020	.0406	.1240	.2097	.2753	.3115	.3177	.2985	.2613	.2140	.1641
	3	.0000	.0036	.0230	.0617	.1147	.1730	.2269	.2679	.2903	.2918	.2734
	4	.0000	.0002	.0026	.0109	.0287	.0577	.0972	.1442	.1935	.2388	.2734
	5	.0000	.0000	.0002	.0012	.0043	.0115	.0250	.0466	.0774	.1172	.1641
	6	.0000	.0000	.0000	.0001	.0004	.0013	.0036	.0084	.0172	.0320	.0547
	7	.0000	.0000	.0000	.0000	.0000	.0001	.0002	.0006	.0016	.0037	.0078

TABLE 1. Binomial Probabilities (continued)

n	x	.01	.05	.10	.15	.20	p .25	.30	.35	.40	.45	.50
8	0	.9227	.6634	.4305	.2725	.1678	.1002	.0576	.0319	.0168	.0084	.0039
	1	.0746	.2793	.3826	.3847	.3355	.2670	.1977	.1373	.0896	.0548	.0312
	2	.0026	.0515	.1488	.2376	.2936	.3115	.2965	.2587	.2090	.1569	.1094
	3	.0001	.0054	.0331	.0839	.1468	.2076	.2541	.2786	.2787	.2568	.2188
	4	.0000	.0004	.0046	.0185	.0459	.0865	.1361	.1875	.2322	.2627	.2734
	5	.0000	.0000	.0004	.0026	.0092	.0231	.0467	.0808	.1239	.1719	.2188
	6	.0000	.0000	.0000	.0002	.0011	.0038	.0100	.0217	.0413	.0403	.1094
	7	.0000	.0000	.0000	.0000	.0001	.0004	.0012	.0033	.0079	.0164	.0312
	8	.0000	.0000	.0000	.0000	.0000	.0000	.0001	.0002	.0007	.0017	.0039
9	0	.9135	.6302	.3874	.2316	.1342	.0751	.0404	.0207	.0101	.0046	.0020
	1	.0830	.2985	.3874	.3679	.3020	.2253	.1556	.1004	.0605	.0339	.0176
	2	.0034	.0629	.1722	.2597	.3020	.3003	.2668	.2162	.1612	.1110	.0703
	3	.0001	.0077	.0446	.1069	.1762	.2336	.2668	.2716	.2508	.2119	.1641
	4	.0000	.0006	.0074	.0283	.0661	.1168	.1715	.2194	.2508	.2600	.2461
	5	.0000	.0000	.0008	.0050	.0165	.0389	.0735	.1181	.1672	.2128	.2461
	6	.0000	.0000	.0001	.0006	.0028	.0087	.0210	.0424	.0743	.1160	.1641
	7	.0000	.0000	.0000	.0000	.0003	.0012	.0039	.0098	.0212	.0407	.0703
	8	.0000	.0000	.0000	.0000	.0000	.0001	.0004	.0013	.0035	.0083	.0176
	9	.0000	.0000	.0000	.0000	.0000	.0000	.0000	.0001	.0003	.0008	.0020
10	0	.9044	.5987	.3487	.1969	.1074	.0563	.0282	.0135	.0060	.0025	.0010
	1	.0914	.3151	.3874	.3474	.2684	.1877	.1211	.0725	.0403	.0207	.0098
	2	.0042	.0746	.1937	.2759	.3020	.2816	.2335	.1757	.1209	.0763	.0439
	3	.0001	.0105	.0574	.1298	.2013	.2503	.2668	.2522	.2150	.1665	.1172
	4	.0000	.0010	.0112	.0401	.0881	.1460	.2001	.2377	.2508	.2384	.2051
	5	.0000	.0001	.0015	.0085	.0264	.0584	.1029	.1536	.2007	.2340	.2461
	6	.0000	.0000	.0001	.0012	.0055	.0162	.0368	.0689	.1115	.1596	.2051
	7	.0000	.0000	.0000	.0001	.0008	.0031	.0090	.0212	.0425	.0746	.1172
	8	.0000	.0000	.0000	.0000	.0001	.0004	.0014	.0043	.0106	.0229	.0439
	9	.0000	.0000	.0000	.0000	.0000	.0000	.0001	.0005	.0016	.0042	.0098
	10	.0000	.0000	.0000	.0000	.0000	.0000	.0000	.0000	.0001	.0003	.0010
11	0	.8953	.5688	.3138	.1673	.0859	.0422	.0198	.0088	.0036	.0014	.0005
	1	.0995	.3293	.3835	.3248	.2362	.1549	.0932	.0518	.0266	.0125	.0054
	2	.0050	.0867	.2131	.2866	.2953	.2581	.1998	.1395	.0887	.0513	.0269
	3	.0002	.0137	.0710	.1517	.2215	.2581	.2568	.2254	.1774	.1259	.0806
	4	.0000	.0014	.0158	.0536	.1107	.1721	.2201	.2428	.2365	.2060	.1611
	5	.0000	.0001	.0025	.0132	.0388	.0803	.1321	.1830	.2207	.2360	.2256
	6	.0000	.0000	.0003	.0023	.0097	.0268	.0566	.0985	.1471	.1931	.2256
	7	.0000	.0000	.0000	.0003	.0017	.0064	.0173	.0379	.0701	.1128	.1611
	8	.0000	.0000	.0000	.0000	.0002	.0011	.0037	.0102	.0234	.0462	.0806
	9	.0000	.0000	.0000	.0000	.0000	.0001	.0005	.0018	.0052	.0126	.0269
	10	.0000	.0000	.0000	.0000	.0000	.0000	.0000	.0002	.0007	.0021	.0054
	11	.0000	.0000	.0000	.0000	.0000	.0000	.0000	.0000	.0000	.0002	.0005
12	0	.8864	.5404	.2824	.1422	.0687	.0317	.0138	.0057	.0022	.0008	.0002
	1	.1074	.3413	.3766	.3012	.2062	.1267	.0712	.0368	.0174	.0075	.0029
	2	.0060	.0988	.2301	.2924	.2835	.2323	.1678	.1088	.0639	.0339	.0161
	3	.0002	.0173	.0852	.1720	.2362	.2581	.2397	.1954	.1419	.0923	.0537
	4	.0000	.0021	.0213	.0683	.1329	.1936	.2311	.2367	.2128	.1700	.1208

TABLE 1 BINOMIAL PROBABILITIES 871

TABLE 1. Binomial Probabilities (continued)

n	x	.01	.05	.10	.15	.20	.25	.30	.35	.40	.45	.50
								p				
	5	.0000	.0002	.0038	.0193	.0532	.1032	.1585	.2039	.2270	.2225	.1934
	6	.0000	.0000	.0005	.0040	.0155	.0401	.0792	.1281	.1766	.2124	.2256
	7	.0000	.0000	.0000	.0006	.0033	.0115	.0291	.0591	.1009	.1489	.1934
	8	.0000	.0000	.0000	.0001	.0005	.0024	.0078	.0199	.0420	.0762	.1208
	9	.0000	.0000	.0000	.0000	.0001	.0004	.0015	.0048	.0125	.0277	.0537
	10	.0000	.0000	.0000	.0000	.0000	.0000	.0002	.0008	.0025	.0068	.0161
	11	.0000	.0000	.0000	.0000	.0000	.0000	.0000	.0001	.0003	.0010	.0029
	12	.0000	.0000	.0000	.0000	.0000	.0000	.0000	.0000	.0000	.0001	.0002
13	0	.8775	.5133	.2542	.1209	.0550	.0238	.0097	.0037	.0013	.0004	.0001
	1	.1152	.3512	.3672	.2774	.1787	.1029	.0540	.0259	.0113	.0045	.0016
	2	.0070	.1109	.2448	.2937	.2680	.2059	.1388	.0836	.0453	.0220	.0095
	3	.0003	.0214	.0997	.1900	.2457	.2517	.2181	.1651	.1107	.0660	.0349
	4	.0000	.0028	.0277	.0838	.1535	.2097	.2337	.2222	.1845	.1350	.0873
	5	.0000	.0003	.0055	.0266	.0691	.1258	.1803	.2154	.2214	.1989	.1571
	6	.0000	.0000	.0008	.0063	.0230	.0559	.1030	.1546	.1968	.2169	.2095
	7	.0000	.0000	.0001	.0011	.0058	.0186	.0442	.0833	.1312	.1775	.2095
	8	.0000	.0000	.0001	.0001	.0011	.0047	.0142	.0336	.0656	.1089	.1571
	9	.0000	.0000	.0000	.0000	.0001	.0009	.0034	.0101	.0243	.0495	.0873
	10	.0000	.0000	.0000	.0000	.0000	.0001	.0006	.0022	.0065	.0162	.0349
	11	.0000	.0000	.0000	.0000	.0000	.0000	.0001	.0003	.0012	.0036	.0095
	12	.0000	.0000	.0000	.0000	.0000	.0000	.0000	.0000	.0001	.0005	.0016
	13	.0000	.0000	.0000	.0000	.0000	.0000	.0000	.0000	.0000	.0000	.0001
14	0	.8687	.4877	.2288	.1028	.0440	.0178	.0068	.0024	.0008	.0002	.0001
	1	.1229	.3593	.3559	.2539	.1539	.0832	.0407	.0181	.0073	.0027	.0009
	2	.0081	.1229	.2570	.2912	.2501	.1802	.1134	.0634	.0317	.0141	.0056
	3	.0003	.0259	.1142	.2056	.2501	.2402	.1943	.1366	.0845	.0462	.0222
	4	.0000	.0037	.0349	.0998	.1720	.2202	.2290	.2022	.1549	.1040	.0611
	5	.0000	.0004	.0078	.0352	.0860	.1468	.1963	.2178	.2066	.1701	.1222
	6	.0000	.0000	.0013	.0093	.0322	.0734	.1262	.1759	.2066	.2088	.1833
	7	.0000	.0000	.0002	.0019	.0092	.0280	.0618	.1082	.1574	.1952	.2095
	8	.0000	.0000	.0000	.0003	.0020	.0082	.0232	.0510	.0918	.1398	.1833
	9	.0000	.0000	.0000	.0000	.0003	.0018	.0066	.0183	.0408	.0762	.1222
	10	.0000	.0000	.0000	.0000	.0000	.0003	.0014	.0049	.0136	.0312	.0611
	11	.0000	.0000	.0000	.0000	.0000	.0000	.0002	.0010	.0033	.0093	.0222
	12	.0000	.0000	.0000	.0000	.0000	.0000	.0000	.0001	.0005	.0019	.0056
	13	.0000	.0000	.0000	.0000	.0000	.0000	.0000	.0000	.0001	.0002	.0009
	14	.0000	.0000	.0000	.0000	.0000	.0000	.0000	.0000	.0000	.0000	.0001
15	0	.8601	.4633	.2059	.0874	.0352	.0134	.0047	.0016	.0005	.0001	.0000
	1	.1303	.3658	.3432	.2312	.1319	.0668	.0305	.0126	.0047	.0016	.0005
	2	.0092	.1348	.2669	.2856	.2309	.1559	.0916	.0476	.0219	.0090	.0032
	3	.0004	.0307	.1285	.2184	.2501	.2252	.1700	.1110	.0634	.0318	.0139
	4	.0000	.0049	.0428	.1156	.1876	.2252	.2186	.1792	.1268	.0780	.0417
	5	.0000	.0006	.0105	.0449	.1032	.1651	.2061	.2123	.1859	.1404	.0916
	6	.0000	.0000	.0019	.0132	.0430	.0917	.1472	.1906	.2066	.1914	.1527
	7	.0000	.0000	.0003	.0030	.0138	.0393	.0811	.1319	.1771	.2013	.1964
	8	.0000	.0000	.0000	.0005	.0035	.0131	.0348	.0710	.1181	.1647	.1964
	9	.0000	.0000	.0000	.0001	.0007	.0034	.0116	.0298	.0612	.1048	.1527

TABLE 1. Binomial Probabilities (continued)

							p					
n	x	.01	.05	.10	.15	.20	.25	.30	.35	.40	.45	.50
	10	.0000	.0000	.0000	.0000	.0001	.0007	.0030	.0096	.0245	.0515	.0916
	11	.0000	.0000	.0000	.0000	.0000	.0001	.0006	.0024	.0074	.0191	.0417
	12	.0000	.0000	.0000	.0000	.0000	.0000	.0001	.0004	.0016	.0052	.0139
	13	.0000	.0000	.0000	.0000	.0000	.0000	.0000	.0001	.0003	.0010	.0032
	14	.0000	.0000	.0000	.0000	.0000	.0000	.0000	.0000	.0000	.0001	.0005
	15	.0000	.0000	.0000	.0000	.0000	.0000	.0000	.0000	.0000	.0000	.0000
16	0	.8515	.4401	.1853	.0743	.0281	.0100	.0033	.0010	.0003	.0001	.0000
	1	.1376	.3706	.3294	.2097	.1126	.0535	.0228	.0087	.0030	.0009	.0002
	2	.0104	.1463	.2745	.2775	.2111	.1336	.0732	.0353	.0150	.0056	.0018
	3	.0005	.0359	.1423	.2285	.2463	.2079	.1465	.0888	.0468	.0215	.0085
	4	.0000	.0061	.0514	.1311	.2001	.2252	.2040	.1553	.1014	.0572	.0278
	5	.0000	.0008	.0137	.0555	.1201	.1802	.2099	.2008	.1623	.1123	.0667
	6	.0000	.0001	.0028	.0180	.0550	.1101	.1649	.1982	.1983	.1684	.1222
	7	.0000	.0000	.0004	.0045	.0197	.0524	.1010	.1524	.1889	.1969	.1746
	8	.0000	.0000	.0001	.0009	.0055	.0197	.0487	.0923	.1417	.1812	.1964
	9	.0000	.0000	.0000	.0001	.0012	.0058	.0185	.0442	.0840	.1318	.1746
	10	.0000	.0000	.0000	.0000	.0002	.0014	.0056	.0167	.0392	.0755	.1222
	11	.0000	.0000	.0000	.0000	.0000	.0002	.0013	.0049	.0142	.0337	.0667
	12	.0000	.0000	.0000	.0000	.0000	.0000	.0002	.0011	.0040	.0115	.0278
	13	.0000	.0000	.0000	.0000	.0000	.0000	.0000	.0002	.0008	.0029	.0085
	14	.0000	.0000	.0000	.0000	.0000	.0000	.0000	.0000	.0001	.0005	.0018
	15	.0000	.0000	.0000	.0000	.0000	.0000	.0000	.0000	.0000	.0001	.0002
	16	.0000	.0000	.0000	.0000	.0000	.0000	.0000	.0000	.0000	.0000	.0000
17	0	.8429	.4181	.1668	.0631	.0225	.0075	.0023	.0007	.0002	.0000	.0000
	1	.1447	.3741	.3150	.1893	.0957	.0426	.0169	.0060	.0019	.0005	.0001
	2	.0117	.1575	.2800	.2673	.1914	.1136	.0581	.0260	.0102	.0035	.0010
	3	.0006	.0415	.1556	.2359	.2393	.1893	.1245	.0701	.0341	.0144	.0052
	4	.0000	.0076	.0605	.1457	.2093	.2209	.1868	.1320	.0796	.0411	.0182
	5	.0000	.0010	.0175	.0668	.1361	.1914	.2081	.1849	.1379	.0875	.0472
	6	.0000	.0001	.0039	.0236	.0680	.1276	.1784	.1991	.1839	.1432	.0944
	7	.0000	.0000	.0007	.0065	.0267	.0668	.1201	.1685	.1927	.1841	.1484
	8	.0000	.0000	.0001	.0014	.0084	.0279	.0644	.1134	.1606	.1883	.1855
	9	.0000	.0000	.0000	.0003	.0021	.0093	.0276	.0611	.1070	.1540	.1855
	10	.0000	.0000	.0000	.0000	.0004	.0025	.0095	.0263	.0571	.1008	.1484
	11	.0000	.0000	.0000	.0000	.0001	.0005	.0026	.0090	.0242	.0525	.0944
	12	.0000	.0000	.0000	.0000	.0000	.0001	.0006	.0024	.0081	.0215	.0472
	13	.0000	.0000	.0000	.0000	.0000	.0000	.0001	.0005	.0021	.0068	.0182
	14	.0000	.0000	.0000	.0000	.0000	.0000	.0000	.0001	0004	.0016	.0052
	15	.0000	.0000	.0000	.0000	.0000	.0000	.0000	.0000	.0001	.0003	.0010
	16	.0000	.0000	.0000	.0000	.0000	.0000	.0000	.0000	.0000	.0000	.0001
	17	.0000	.0000	.0000	.0000	.0000	.0000	.0000	.0000	.0000	.0000	.0000
18	0	.8345	.3972	.1501	.0536	.0180	.0056	.0016	.0004	.0001	.0000	.0000
	1	.1517	.3763	.3002	.1704	.0811	.0338	.0126	.0042	.0012	.0003	.0001
	2	.0130	.1683	.2835	.2556	.1723	.0958	.0458	.0190	.0069	.0022	.0006
	3	.0007	.0473	.1680	.2406	.2297	.1704	.1046	.0547	.0246	.0095	.0031
	4	.0000	.0093	.0700	.1592	.2153	.2130	.1681	.1104	.0614	.0291	.0117

TABLE 1 BINOMIAL PROBABILITIES 873

TABLE 1. Binomial Probabilities (continued)

n	x	.01	.05	.10	.15	.20	.25	p .30	.35	.40	.45	.50
	5	.0000	.0014	.0218	.0787	.1507	.1988	.2017	.1664	.1146	.0666	.0327
	6	.0000	.0002	.0052	.0301	.0816	.1436	.1873	.1941	.1655	.1181	.0708
	7	.0000	.0000	.0010	.0091	.0350	.0820	.1376	.1792	.1892	.1657	.1214
	8	.0000	.0000	.0002	.0022	.0120	.0376	.0811	.1327	.1734	.1864	.1669
	9	.0000	.0000	.0000	.0004	.0033	.0139	.0386	.0794	.1284	.1694	.1855
	10	.0000	.0000	.0000	.0001	.0008	.0042	.0149	.0385	.0771	.1248	.1669
	11	.0000	.0000	.0000	.0000	.0001	.0010	.0046	.0151	.0374	.0742	.1214
	12	.0000	.0000	.0000	.0000	.0000	.0002	.0012	.0047	.0145	.0354	.0708
	13	.0000	.0000	.0000	.0000	.0000	.0000	.0002	.0012	.0045	.0134	.0327
	14	.0000	.0000	.0000	.0000	.0000	.0000	.0000	.0002	.0011	.0039	.0117
	15	.0000	.0000	.0000	.0000	.0000	.0000	.0000	.0000	.0002	.0009	.0031
	16	.0000	.0000	.0000	.0000	.0000	.0000	.0000	.0000	.0000	.0001	.0006
	17	.0000	.0000	.0000	.0000	.0000	.0000	.0000	.0000	.0000	.0000	.0001
	18	.0000	.0000	.0000	.0000	.0000	.0000	.0000	.0000	.0000	.0000	.0000
19	0	.8262	.3774	.1351	.0456	.0144	.0042	.0011	.0003	.0001	.0000	.0000
	1	.1586	.3774	.2852	.1529	.0685	.0268	.0093	.0029	.0008	.0002	.0000
	2	.0144	.1787	.2852	.2428	.1540	.0803	.0358	.0138	.0046	.0013	.0003
	3	.0008	.0533	.1796	.2428	.2182	.1517	.0869	.0422	.0175	.0062	.0018
	4	.0000	.0112	.0798	.1714	.2182	.2023	.1491	.0909	.0467	.0203	.0074
	5	.0000	.0018	.0266	.0907	.1636	.2023	.1916	.1468	.0933	.0497	.0222
	6	.0000	.0002	.0069	.0374	.0955	.1574	.1916	.1844	.1451	.0949	.0518
	7	.0000	.0000	.0014	.0122	.0443	.0974	.1525	.1844	.1797	.1443	.0961
	8	.0000	.0000	.0002	.0032	.0166	.0487	.0981	.1489	.1797	.1771	.1442
	9	.0000	.0000	.0000	.0007	.0051	.0198	.0514	.0980	.1464	.1771	.1762
	10	.0000	.0000	.0000	.0001	.0013	.0066	.0220	.0528	.0976	.1449	.1762
	11	.0000	.0000	.0000	.0000	.0003	.0018	.0077	.0233	.0532	.0970	.1442
	12	.0000	.0000	.0000	.0000	.0000	.0004	.0022	.0083	.0237	.0529	.0961
	13	.0000	.0000	.0000	.0000	.0000	.0001	.0005	.0024	.0085	.0233	.0518
	14	.0000	.0000	.0000	.0000	.0000	.0000	.0001	.0006	.0024	.0082	.0222
	15	.0000	.0000	.0000	.0000	.0000	.0000	.0000	.0001	.0005	.0022	.0074
	16	.0000	.0000	.0000	.0000	.0000	.0000	.0000	.0000	.0001	.0005	.0018
	17	.0000	.0000	.0000	.0000	.0000	.0000	.0000	.0000	.0000	.0001	.0003
	18	.0000	.0000	.0000	.0000	.0000	.0000	.0000	.0000	.0000	.0000	.0000
	19	.0000	.0000	.0000	.0000	.0000	.0000	.0000	.0000	.0000	.0000	.0000
20	0	.8179	.3585	.1216	.0388	.0115	.0032	.0008	.0002	.0000	.0000	.0000
	1	.1652	.3774	.2702	.1368	.0576	.0211	.0068	.0020	.0005	.0001	.0000
	2	.0159	.1887	.2852	.2293	.1369	.0669	.0278	.0100	.0031	.0008	.0002
	3	.0010	.0596	.1901	.2428	.2054	.1339	.0716	.0323	.0123	.0040	.0011
	4	.0000	.0133	.0898	.1821	.2182	.1897	.1304	.0738	.0350	.0139	.0046
	5	.0000	.0022	.0319	.1028	.1746	.2023	.1789	.1272	.0746	.0365	.0148
	6	.0000	.0003	.0089	.0454	.1091	.1686	.1916	.1712	.1244	.0746	.0370
	7	.0000	.0000	.0020	.0160	.0545	.1124	.1643	.1844	.1659	.1221	.0739
	8	.0000	.0000	.0004	.0046	.0222	.0609	.1144	.1614	.1797	.1623	.1201
	9	.0000	.0000	.0001	.0011	.0074	.0271	.0654	.1158	.1597	.1771	.1602
	10	.0000	.0000	.0000	.0002	.0020	.0099	.0308	.0686	.1171	.1593	.1762
	11	.0000	.0000	.0000	.0000	.0005	.0030	.0120	.0336	.0710	.1185	.1602
	12	.0000	.0000	.0000	.0000	.0001	.0008	.0039	.0136	.0355	.0727	.1201
	13	.0000	.0000	.0000	.0000	.0000	.0002	.0010	.0045	.0146	.0366	.0739
	14	.0000	.0000	.0000	.0000	.0000	.0000	.0002	.0012	.0049	.0150	.0370

TABLE 1. Binomial Probabilities (continued)

n	x						p					
		.01	.05	.10	.15	.20	.25	.30	.35	.40	.45	.50
	15	.0000	.0000	.0000	.0000	.0000	.0000	.0000	.0003	.0013	.0049	.0148
	16	.0000	.0000	.0000	.0000	.0000	.0000	.0000	.0000	.0003	.0013	.0046
	17	.0000	.0000	.0000	.0000	.0000	.0000	.0000	.0000	.0000	.0002	.0011
	18	.0000	.0000	.0000	.0000	.0000	.0000	.0000	.0000	.0000	.0000	.0002
	19	.0000	.0000	.0000	.0000	.0000	.0000	.0000	.0000	.0000	.0000	.0000
	20	.0000	.0000	.0000	.0000	.0000	.0000	.0000	.0000	.0000	.0000	.0000
25	0	.7778	.2774	.0718	.0172	.0038	.0008	.0001	.0000	.0000	.0000	.0000
	1	.1964	.3650	.1994	.0759	.0236	.0063	.0014	.0003	.0000	.0000	.0000
	2	.0238	.2305	.2659	.1607	.0708	.0251	.0074	.0018	.0004	.0001	.0000
	3	.0018	.0930	.2265	.2174	.1358	.0641	.0243	.0076	.0019	.0004	.0001
	4	.0001	.0269	.1384	.2110	.1867	.1175	.0572	.0224	.0071	.0018	.0004
	5	.0000	.0060	.0646	.1564	.1960	.1645	.1030	.0506	.0199	.0063	.0016
	6	.0000	.0010	.0239	.0920	.1633	.1828	.1472	.0908	.0442	.0172	.0053
	7	.0000	.0001	.0072	.0441	.1108	.1654	.1712	.1327	.0800	.0381	.0143
	8	.0000	.0000	.0018	.0175	.0623	.1241	.1651	.1607	.1200	.0701	.0322
	9	.0000	.0000	.0004	.0058	.0294	.0781	.1336	.1635	.1511	.1084	.0609
	10	.0000	.0000	.0000	.0016	.0118	.0417	.0916	.1409	.1612	.1419	.0974
	11	.0000	.0000	.0000	.0004	.0040	.0189	.0536	.1034	.1465	.1583	.1328
	12	.0000	.0000	.0000	.0000	.0012	.0074	.0268	.0650	.1140	.1511	.1550
	13	.0000	.0000	.0000	.0000	.0003	.0025	.0115	.0350	.0760	.1236	.1550
	14	.0000	.0000	.0000	.0000	.0000	.0007	.0042	.0161	.0434	.0867	.1328
	15	.0000	.0000	.0000	.0000	.0000	.0002	.0013	.0064	.0212	.0520	.0974
	16	.0000	.0000	.0000	.0000	.0000	.0000	.0004	.0021	.0088	.0266	.0609
	17	.0000	.0000	.0000	.0000	.0000	.0000	.0001	.0006	.0031	.0115	.0322
	18	.0000	.0000	.0000	.0000	.0000	.0000	.0000	.0001	.0009	.0042	.0143
	19	.0000	.0000	.0000	.0000	.0000	.0000	.0000	.0000	.0002	.0013	.0053
	20	.0000	.0000	.0000	.0000	.0000	.0000	.0000	.0000	.0000	.0001	.0016
	21	.0000	.0000	.0000	.0000	.0000	.0000	.0000	.0000	.0000	.0000	.0004
	22	.0000	.0000	.0000	.0000	.0000	.0000	.0000	.0000	.0000	.0000	.0001
30	0	.7397	.2146	.0424	.0076	.0012	.0002	.0000	.0000	.0000	.0000	.0000
	1	.2242	.3389	.1413	.0404	.0093	.0018	.0003	.0000	.0000	.0000	.0000
	2	.0328	.2586	.2277	.1034	.0337	.0086	.0018	.0003	.0000	.0000	.0000
	3	.0031	.1270	.2361	.1703	.0785	.0269	.0072	.0015	.0003	.0000	.0000
	4	.0002	.0451	.1771	.2028	.1325	.0604	.0208	.0056	.0012	.0002	.0000
	5	.0000	.0124	.1023	.1861	.1723	.1047	.0464	.0157	.0041	.0008	.0001
	6	.0000	.0027	.0474	.1368	.1795	.1455	.0829	.0353	.0115	.0029	.0006
	7	.0000	.0005	.0180	.0828	.1538	.1662	.1219	.0652	.0263	.0081	.0019
	8	.0000	.0001	.0058	.0420	.1106	.1593	.1501	.1009	.0505	.0191	.0055
	9	.0000	.0000	.0016	.0181	.0676	.1298	.1573	.1328	.0823	.0382	.0133
	10	.0000	.0000	.0004	.0067	.0355	.0909	.1416	.1502	.1152	.0656	.0280
	11	.0000	.0000	.0001	.0022	.0161	.0551	.1103	.1471	.1396	.0976	.0509
	12	.0000	.0000	.0000	.0006	.0064	.0291	.0749	.1254	.1474	.1265	.0806
	13	.0000	.0000	.0000	.0001	.0022	.0134	.0444	.0935	.1360	.1433	.1115
	14	.0000	.0000	.0000	.0000	.0007	.0054	.0231	.0611	.1101	.1424	.1354
	15	.0000	.0000	.0000	.0000	.0002	.0019	.0106	.0351	.0783	.1242	.1445
	16	.0000	.0000	.0000	.0000	.0000	.0006	.0042	.0177	.0489	.0953	.1354
	17	.0000	.0000	.0000	.0000	.0000	.0002	.0015	.0079	.0269	.0642	.1115
	18	.0000	.0000	.0000	.0000	.0000	.0000	.0005	.0031	.0129	.0379	.0806
	19	.0000	.0000	.0000	.0000	.0000	.0000	.0001	.0010	.0054	.0196	.0509

TABLE 1 BINOMIAL PROBABILITIES 875

TABLE 1. Binomial Probabilities (continued)

n	x	.01	.05	.10	.15	.20	.25	p .30	.35	.40	.45	.50
		.0000	.0000	.0000	.0000	.0000	.0000	.0000	.0003	.0020	.0088	.0280
	21	.0000	.0000	.0000	.0000	.0000	.0000	.0000	.0001	.0006	.0034	.0133
	22	.0000	.0000	.0000	.0000	.0000	.0000	.0000	.0000	.0002	.0012	.0055
	23	.0000	.0000	.0000	.0000	.0000	.0000	.0000	.0000	.0000	.0003	.0019
	24	.0000	.0000	.0000	.0000	.0000	.0000	.0000	.0000	.0000	.0001	.0006
	25	.0000	.0000	.0000	.0000	.0000	.0000	.0000	.0000	.0000	.0000	.0001
40	0	.6690	.1285	.0148	.0015	.0001	.0000	.0000	.0000	.0000	.0000	.0000
	1	.2703	.2706	.0657	.0106	.0013	.0001	.0000	.0000	.0000	.0000	.0000
	2	.0532	.2777	.1423	.0365	.0065	.0009	.0001	.0000	.0000	.0000	.0000
	3	.0068	.1851	.2003	.0816	.0205	.0037	.0005	.0001	.0000	.0000	.0000
	4	.0006	.0901	.2059	.1332	.0475	.0113	.0020	.0003	.0000	.0000	.0000
	5	.0000	.0342	.1647	.1692	.0854	.0272	.0061	.0010	.0001	.0000	.0000
	6	.0000	.0105	.1068	.1742	.1246	.0530	.0151	.0031	.0005	.0000	.0000
	7	.0000	.0027	.0576	.1493	.1513	.0857	.0315	.0080	.0015	.0002	.0000
	8	.0000	.0006	.0264	.1087	.1560	.1179	.0557	.0179	.0040	.0006	.0001
	9	.0000	.0001	.0104	.0682	.1386	.1397	.0849	.0342	.0095	.0018	.0002
	10	.0000	.0000	.0036	.0373	.1075	.1444	.1128	.0571	.0196	.0047	.0008
	11	.0000	.0000	.0011	.0180	.0733	.1312	.1319	.0838	.0357	.0105	.0021
	12	.0000	.0000	.0003	.0077	.0443	.1057	.1366	.1090	.0576	.0207	.0051
	13	.0000	.0000	.0001	.0029	.0238	.0759	.1261	.1265	.0827	.0365	.0109
	14	.0000	.0000	.0000	.0010	.0115	.0488	.1042	.1313	.1063	.0575	.0211
	15	.0000	.0000	.0000	.0003	.0050	.0282	.0774	.1226	.1228	.0816	.0366
	16	.0000	.0000	.0000	.0001	.0019	.0147	.0518	.1031	.1279	.1043	.0572
	17	.0000	.0000	.0000	.0000	.0007	.0069	.0314	.0784	.1204	.1205	.0807
	18	.0000	.0000	.0000	.0000	.0002	.0029	.0172	.0539	.1026	.1260	.1031
	19	.0000	.0000	.0000	.0000	.0001	.0011	.0085	.0336	.0792	.1194	.1194
	20	.0000	.0000	.0000	.0000	.0000	.0004	.0038	.0190	.0554	.1025	.1254
	21	.0000	.0000	.0000	.0000	.0000	.0001	.0016	.0097	.0352	.0799	.1194
	22	.0000	.0000	.0000	.0000	.0000	.0000	.0006	.0045	.0203	.0565	.1031
	23	.0000	.0000	.0000	.0000	.0000	.0000	.0002	.0019	.0106	.0362	.0807
	24	.0000	.0000	.0000	.0000	.0000	.0000	.0001	.0007	.0050	.0210	.0572
	25	.0000	.0000	.0000	.0000	.0000	.0000	.0000	.0003	.0021	.0110	.0366
	26	.0000	.0000	.0000	.0000	.0000	.0000	.0000	.0001	.0008	.0052	.0211
	27	.0000	.0000	.0000	.0000	.0000	.0000	.0000	.0000	.0003	.0022	.0109
	28	.0000	.0000	.0000	.0000	.0000	.0000	.0000	.0000	.0001	.0008	.0051
	29	.0000	.0000	.0000	.0000	.0000	.0000	.0000	.0000	.0000	.0003	.0021
	30	.0000	.0000	.0000	.0000	.0000	.0000	.0000	.0000	.0000	.0001	.0008
	31	.0000	.0000	.0000	.0000	.0000	.0000	.0000	.0000	.0000	.0000	.0002
	32	.0000	.0000	.0000	.0000	.0000	.0000	.0000	.0000	.0000	.0000	.0001
50	0	.6050	.0769	.0052	.0003	.0000	.0000	.0000	.0000	.0000	.0000	.0000
	1	.3056	.2025	.0286	.0026	.0002	.0000	.0000	.0000	.0000	.0000	.0000
	2	.0756	.2611	.0779	.0113	.0011	.0001	.0000	.0000	.0000	.0000	.0000
	3	.0122	.2199	.1386	.0319	.0044	.0004	.0000	.0000	.0000	.0000	.0000
	4	.0015	.1360	.1809	.0661	.0128	.0016	.0001	.0000	.0000	.0000	.0000

TABLE 1. Binomial Probabilities (continued)

n	x	.01	.05	.10	.15	.20	.25	p .30	.35	.40	.45	.50
5		.0001	.0658	.1849	.1072	.0295	.0049	.0006	.0000	.0000	.0000	.0000
6		.0000	.0260	.1541	.1419	.0554	.0123	.0018	.0002	.0000	.0000	.0000
7		.0000	.0086	.1076	.1575	.0870	.0259	.0048	.0006	.0000	.0000	.0000
8		.0000	.0024	.0643	.1493	.1169	.0463	.0110	.0017	.0002	.0000	.0000
9		.0000	.0006	.0333	.1230	.1364	.0721	.0220	.0042	.0005	.0000	.0000
10		.0000	.0001	.0152	.0890	.1398	.0985	.0386	.0093	.0014	.0001	.0000
11		.0000	.0000	.0061	.0571	.1271	.1194	.0602	.0182	.0035	.0004	.0000
12		.0000	.0000	.0022	.0328	.1033	.1294	.0838	.0319	.0076	.0011	.0001
13		.0000	.0000	.0007	.0169	.0755	.1261	.1050	.0502	.0147	.0027	.0003
14		.0000	.0000	.0002	.0079	.0499	.1110	.1189	.0714	.0260	.0059	.0008
15		.0000	.0000	.0001	.0033	.0299	.0888	.1223	.0923	.0415	.0116	.0020
16		.0000	.0000	.0000	.0013	.0164	.0648	.1147	.1088	.0606	.0207	.0044
17		.0000	.0000	.0000	.0005	.0082	.0432	.0983	.1171	.0808	.0339	.0087
18		.0000	.0000	.0000	.0001	.0037	.0264	.0772	.1156	.0987	.0508	.0160
19		.0000	.0000	.0000	.0000	.0016	.0148	.0558	.1048	.1109	.0700	.0270
20		.0000	.0000	.0000	.0000	.0006	.0077	.0370	.0875	.1146	.0888	.0419
21		.0000	.0000	.0000	.0000	.0002	.0036	.0227	.0673	.1091	.1038	.0598
22		.0000	.0000	.0000	.0000	.0001	.0016	.0128	.0478	.0959	.1119	.0788
23		.0000	.0000	.0000	.0000	.0000	.0006	.0067	.0313	.0778	.1115	.0960
24		.0000	.0000	.0000	.0000	.0000	.0002	.0032	.0190	.0584	.1026	.1080
25		.0000	.0000	.0000	.0000	.0000	.0001	.0014	.0106	.0405	.0873	.1123
26		.0000	.0000	.0000	.0000	.0000	.0000	.0006	.0055	.0259	.0687	.1080
27		.0000	.0000	.0000	.0000	.0000	.0000	.0002	.0026	.0154	.0500	.0960
28		.0000	.0000	.0000	.0000	.0000	.0000	.0001	.0012	.0084	.0336	.0788
29		.0000	.0000	.0000	.0000	.0000	.0000	.0000	.0005	.0043	.0208	.0598
30		.0000	.0000	.0000	.0000	.0000	.0000	.0000	.0002	.0020	.0119	.0419
31		.0000	.0000	.0000	.0000	.0000	.0000	.0000	.0001	.0009	.0063	.0270
32		.0000	.0000	.0000	.0000	.0000	.0000	.0000	.0000	.0003	.0031	.0160
33		.0000	.0000	.0000	.0000	.0000	.0000	.0000	.0000	.0001	.0014	.0087
34		.0000	.0000	.0000	.0000	.0000	.0000	.0000	.0000	.0000	.0006	.0044
35		.0000	.0000	.0000	.0000	.0000	.0000	.0000	.0000	.0000	.0002	.0020
36		.0000	.0000	.0000	.0000	.0000	.0000	.0000	.0000	.0000	.0001	.0008
37		.0000	.0000	.0000	.0000	.0000	.0000	.0000	.0000	.0000	.0000	.0003
38		.0000	.0000	.0000	.0000	.0000	.0000	.0000	.0000	.0000	.0000	.0001

TABLE 1 BINOMIAL PROBABILITIES 877

TABLE 2. Cumulative Binomial Probability Tables

Table values give the probability that the random variable X assumes a value less than or equal to x:

$$P(X \leq x|n, p) = \sum_{0}^{x} P(x) = P(0) + P(1) + \ldots + P(x); \text{Example: } P(X \leq 5|n = 7, p = .7) = .671$$

$n = 1$

x	.01	.05	.10	.20	.30	.40	p .50	.60	.70	.80	.90	.95	.99
0	.990	.950	.900	.800	.700	.600	.500	.400	.300	.200	.100	.050	.010

$n = 2$

x	.01	.05	.10	.20	.30	.40	p .50	.60	.70	.80	.90	.95	.99
0	.980	.903	.810	.640	.490	.360	.250	.160	.090	.040	.010	.003	.000
1	1.000	.998	.990	.960	.910	.840	.750	.640	.510	.360	.190	.097	.020

$n = 3$

x	.01	.05	.10	.20	.30	.40	p .50	.60	.70	.80	.90	.95	.99
0	.970	.857	.729	.512	.343	.216	.125	.064	.027	.008	.001	.000	.000
1	1.000	.993	.972	.896	.784	.648	.500	.352	.216	.104	.028	.007	.000
2	1.000	1.000	.999	.992	.973	.936	.875	.784	.657	.488	.271	.143	.030

$n = 4$

x	.01	.05	.10	.20	.30	.40	p .50	.60	.70	.80	.90	.95	.99
0	.961	.815	.656	.410	.240	.130	.063	.026	.008	.002	.000	.000	.000
1	.999	.986	.948	.819	.652	.475	.313	.179	.084	.027	.004	.000	.000
2	1.000	1.000	.996	.973	.916	.821	.688	.525	.348	.181	.052	.014	.001
3	1.000	1.000	1.000	.998	.992	.974	.938	.870	..760	.590	.344	.185	.039

$n = 5$

x	.01	.05	.10	.20	.30	.40	p .50	.60	.70	.80	.90	.95	.99
0	.951	.774	.590	.328	.168	.078	.031	.010	.002	.000	.000	.000	.000
1	.999	.977	.919	.737	.528	.337	.188	.087	.031	.007	.000	.000	.000
2	1.000	.999	.991	.942	.837	.683	.500	.317	.163	.058	.009	.001	.000
3	1.000	1.000	1.000	.993	.969	.913	.812	.663	.472	.263	.081	.023	.001
4	1.000	1.000	1.000	1.000	.998	.990	.969	.922	.832	.672	.410	.226	.049

$n = 6$

x	.01	.05	.10	.20	.30	.40	p .50	.60	.70	.80	.90	.95	.99
0	.941	.735	.531	.262	.118	.047	.016	.004	.001	.000	.000	.000	.000
1	.999	.967	.886	.655	.420	.233	.109	.041	.011	.002	.000	.000	.000
2	1.000	.998	.984	.901	.744	.544	.344	.179	.070	.017	.001	.000	.000
3	1.000	1.000	.999	.983	.930	.821	.656	.456	.256	.099	.016	.002	.000
4	1.000	1.000	1.000	.998	.989	.959	.891	.767	.580	.345	.114	.033	.001
5	1.000	1.000	1.000	1.000	.999	.996	.984	.953	.882	.738	.469	.265	.059

TABLE 2. Cumulative Binomial Probability Tables (continued)

n = 7

x	.01	.05	.10	.20	.30	.40	p .50	.60	.70	.80	.90	.95	.99
0	.932	.698	.478	.210	.082	.028	.008	.002	.000	.000	.000	.000	.000
1	.998	.956	.850	.577	.329	.159	.063	.019	.004	.000	.000	.000	.000
2	1.000	.996	.974	.852	.647	.420	.227	.096	.029	.005	.000	.000	.000
3	1.000	1.000	.997	.967	.874	.710	.500	.290	.126	.033	.003	.000	.000
4	1.000	1.000	1.000	.995	.971	.904	.773	.580	.353	.148	.026	.004	.000
5	1.000	1.000	1.000	1.000	.996	.981	.938	.841	.671	.423	.150	.044	.002
6	1.000	1.000	1.000	1.000	1.000	.998	.992	.972	.918	.790	.522	.302	.068

n = 8

x	.01	.05	.10	.20	.30	.40	p .50	.60	.70	.80	.90	.95	.99
0	.923	.663	.430	.168	.058	.017	.004	.001	.000	.000	.000	.000	.000
1	.997	.943	.813	.503	.255	.106	.035	.009	.001	.000	.000	.000	.000
2	1.000	.994	.962	.797	.552	.315	.145	.050	.011	.001	.000	.000	.000
3	1.000	1.000	.995	.944	.806	.594	.363	.174	.058	.010	.000	.000	.000
4	1.000	1.000	1.000	.990	.942	.826	.637	.406	.194	.056	.005	.000	.000
5	1.000	1.000	1.000	.999	.989	.950	.855	.685	.448	.203	.038	.006	.000
6	1.000	1.000	1.000	1.000	.999	.991	.965	.894	.745	.497	.187	.057	.003
7	1.000	1.000	1.000	1.000	1.000	.999	.996	.983	.942	.832	.570	.337	.077

n = 9

x	.01	.05	.10	.20	.30	.40	p .50	.60	.70	.80	.90	.95	.99
0	.914	.630	.387	.134	.040	.010	.002	.000	.000	.000	.000	.000	.000
1	.997	.929	.775	.436	.196	.071	.020	.004	.000	.000	.000	.000	.000
2	1.000	.992	.947	.738	.463	.232	.090	.025	.004	.000	.000	.000	.000
3	1.000	.999	.992	.914	.730	.483	.254	.099	.025	.003	.000	.000	.000
4	1.000	1.000	.999	.980	.901	.733	.500	.267	.099	.020	.001	.000	.000
5	1.000	1.000	1.000	.997	.975	.901	.746	.517	.270	.086	.008	.001	.000
6	1.000	1.000	1.000	1.000	.996	.975	.910	.768	.537	.262	.053	.008	.000
7	1.000	1.000	1.000	1.000	1.000	.996	.980	.929	.804	.564	.225	.071	.003
8	1.000	1.000	1.000	1.000	1.000	1.000	.998	.990	.960	.866	.613	.370	.086

n = 10

x	.01	.05	.10	.20	.30	.40	p .50	.60	.70	.80	.90	.95	.99
0	.904	.599	.349	.107	.028	.006	.001	.000	.000	.000	.000	.000	.000
1	.996	.914	.736	.376	.149	.046	.011	.002	.000	.000	.000	.000	.000
2	1.000	.988	.930	.678	.383	.167	.055	.012	.002	.000	.000	.000	.000
3	1.000	.999	.987	.879	.650	.382	.172	.055	.011	.001	.000	.000	.000
4	1.000	1.000	.998	.967	.850	.633	.377	.166	.047	.006	.000	.000	.000
5	1.000	1.000	1.000	.994	.953	.834	.623	.367	.150	.033	.002	.000	.000
6	1.000	1.000	1.000	.999	.989	.945	.828	.618	.350	.121	.013	.001	.000
7	1.000	1.000	1.000	1.000	.998	.988	.945	.833	.617	.322	.070	.012	.000
8	1.000	1.000	1.000	1.000	1.000	.998	.989	.954	.851	.624	.264	.086	.004
9	1.000	1.000	1.000	1.000	1.000	1.000	.999	.994	.972	.893	.651	.401	.096

TABLE 2 CUMULATIVE BINOMIAL 879

TABLE 2. Cumulative Binomial Probability Tables (continued)

$n = 11$

x	.01	.05	.10	.20	.30	.40	p .50	.60	.70	.80	.90	.95	.99
0	.895	.569	.314	.086	.020	.004	.000	.000	.000	.000	.000	.000	.000
1	.995	.898	.697	.322	.113	.030	.006	.001	.000	.000	.000	.000	.000
2	1.000	.985	.910	.617	.313	.119	.033	.006	.001	.000	.000	.000	.000
3	1.000	.998	.981	.839	.570	.296	.113	.029	.004	.000	.000	.000	.000
4	1.000	1.000	.997	.950	.790	.533	.274	.099	.022	.002	.000	.000	.000
5	1.000	1.000	1.000	.988	.922	.753	.500	.247	.078	.012	.000	.000	.000
6	1.000	1.000	1.000	.998	.978	.901	.726	.467	.210	.050	.003	.000	.000
7	1.000	1.000	1.000	1.000	.996	.971	.887	.704	.430	.161	.019	.002	.000
8	1.000	1.000	1.000	1.000	.999	.994	.967	.881	.687	.383	.090	.015	.000
9	1.000	1.000	1.000	1.000	1.000	.999	.994	.970	.887	.678	.303	.102	.005
10	1.000	1.000	1.000	1.000	1.000	1.000	1.000	.996	.980	.914	.686	.431	.105

$n = 12$

x	.01	.05	.10	.20	.30	.40	p .50	.60	.70	.80	.90	.95	.99
0	.886	.540	.282	.069	.014	.002	.000	.000	.000	.000	.000	.000	.000
1	.994	.882	.659	.275	.085	.020	.003	.000	.000	.000	.000	.000	.000
2	1.000	.980	.889	.558	.253	.083	.019	.003	.000	.000	.000	.000	.000
3	1.000	.998	.974	.795	.493	.225	.073	.015	.002	.000	.000	.000	.000
4	1.000	1.000	.996	.927	.724	.438	.194	.057	.009	.001	.000	.000	.000
5	1.000	1.000	.999	.981	.882	.665	.387	.158	.039	.004	.000	.000	.000
6	1.000	1.000	1.000	.996	.961	.842	.613	.335	.118	.019	.001	.000	.000
7	1.000	1.000	1.000	.999	.991	.943	.806	.562	.276	.073	.004	.000	.000
8	1.000	1.000	1.000	1.000	.998	.985	.927	.775	.507	.205	.026	.002	.000
9	1.000	1.000	1.000	1.000	1.000	.997	.981	.917	.747	.442	.111	.020	.000
10	1.000	1.000	1.000	1.000	1.000	1.000	.997	.980	.915	.725	.341	.118	.006
11	1.000	1.000	1.000	1.000	1.000	1.000	1.000	.998	.986	.931	.718	.460	.114

$n = 13$

x	.01	.05	.10	.20	.30	.40	p .50	.60	.70	.80	.90	.95	.99
0	.878	.513	.254	.055	.010	.001	.000	.000	.000	.000	.000	.000	.000
1	.993	.865	.621	.234	.064	.013	.002	.000	.000	.000	.000	.000	.000
2	1.000	.975	.866	.502	.202	.058	.011	.001	.000	.000	.000	.000	.000
3	1.000	.997	.966	.747	.421	.169	.046	.008	.001	.000	.000	.000	.000
4	1.000	1.000	.994	.901	.654	.353	.133	.032	.004	.000	.000	.000	.000
5	1.000	1.000	.999	.970	.835	.574	.291	.098	.018	.001	.000	.000	.000
6	1.000	1.000	1.000	.993	.938	.771	.500	.229	.062	.007	.000	.000	.000
7	1.000	1.000	1.000	.999	.982	.902	.709	.426	.165	.030	.001	.000	.000
8	1.000	1.000	1.000	1.000	.996	.968	.867	.647	.346	.099	.006	.000	.000
9	1.000	1.000	1.000	1.000	.999	.992	.954	.831	.579	.253	.034	.003	.000

TABLE 2. Cumulative Binomial Probability Tables (continued)

10	1.000	1.000	1.000	1.000	1.000	.999	.989	.942	.798	.498	.134	.025	.000
11	1.000	1.000	1.000	1.000	1.000	1.000	.998	.987	.936	.766	.379	.135	.007
12	1.000	1.000	1.000	1.000	1.000	1.000	1.000	.999	.990	.945	.746	.487	.122

n = 14

							p						
x	.01	.05	.10	.20	.30	.40	.50	.60	.70	.80	.90	.95	.99
0	.869	.488	.229	.044	.007	.001	.000	.000	.000	.000	.000	.000	.000
1	.992	.847	.585	.198	.047	.008	.001	.000	.000	.000	.000	.000	.000
2	1.000	.970	.842	.448	.161	.040	.006	.001	.000	.000	.000	.000	.000
3	1.000	.996	.956	.698	.355	.124	.029	.004	.000	.000	.000	.000	.000
4	1.000	1.000	.991	.870	.584	.279	.090	.018	.002	.000	.000	.000	.000
5	1.000	1.000	.999	.956	.781	.486	.212	.058	.008	.000	.000	.000	.000
6	1.000	1.000	1.000	.988	.907	.692	.395	.150	.031	.002	.000	.000	.000
7	1.000	1.000	1.000	.998	.969	.850	.605	.308	.093	.012	.000	.000	.000
8	1.000	1.000	1.000	1.000	.992	.942	.788	.514	.219	.044	.001	.000	.000
9	1.000	1.000	1.000	1.000	.998	.982	.910	.721	.416	.130	.009	.000	.000
10	1.000	1.000	1.000	1.000	1.000	.996	.971	.876	.645	.302	.044	.004	.000
11	1.000	1.000	1.000	1.000	1.000	.999	.994	.960	.839	.552	.158	.030	.000
12	1.000	1.000	1.000	1.000	1.000	1.000	.999	.992	.953	.802	.415	.153	.008
13	1.000	1.000	1.000	1.000	1.000	1.000	1.000	.999	.993	.956	.771	.512	.131

n = 15

							p						
x	.01	.05	.10	.20	.30	.40	.50	.60	.70	.80	.90	.95	.99
0	.860	.463	.206	.035	.005	.000	.000	.000	.000	.000	.000	.000	.000
1	.990	.829	.549	.167	.035	.005	.000	.000	.000	.000	.000	.000	.000
2	1.000	.964	.816	.398	.127	.027	.004	.000	.000	.000	.000	.000	.000
3	1.000	.995	.944	.648	.297	.091	.018	.002	.000	.000	.000	.000	.000
4	1.000	.999	.987	.836	.515	.217	.059	.009	.001	.000	.000	.000	.000
5	1.000	1.000	.998	.939	.722	.403	.151	.034	.004	.000	.000	.000	.000
6	1.000	1.000	1.000	.982	.869	.610	.304	.095	.015	.001	.000	.000	.000
7	1.000	1.000	1.000	.996	.950	.787	.500	.213	.050	.004	.000	.000	.000
8	1.000	1.000	1.000	.999	.985	.905	.696	.390	.131	.018	.000	.000	.000
9	1.000	1.000	1.000	1.000	.996	.966	.849	.597	.278	.061	.002	.000	.000
10	1.000	1.000	1.000	1.000	.999	.991	.941	.783	.485	.164	.013	.001	.000
11	1.000	1.000	1.000	1.000	1.000	.998	.982	.909	.703	.352	.056	.005	.000
12	1.000	1.000	1.000	1.000	1.000	1.000	.996	.973	.873	.602	.184	.036	.000
13	1.000	1.000	1.000	1.000	1.000	1.000	1.000	.995	.965	.833	.451	.171	.010
14	1.000	1.000	1.000	1.000	1.000	1.000	1.000	1.000	.995	.965	.794	.537	.140

TABLE 2 CUMULATIVE BINOMIAL 881

TABLE 2. Cumulative Binomial Probability Tables (continued)

n = 16

x	.01	.05	.10	.20	.30	.40	p .50	.60	.70	.80	.90	.95	.99
0	.851	.440	.185	.028	.003	.000	.000	.000	.000	.000	.000	.000	.000
1	.989	.811	.515	.141	.026	.003	.000	.000	.000	.000	.000	.000	.000
2	.999	.957	.789	.352	.099	.018	.002	.000	.000	.000	.000	.000	.000
3	1.000	.993	.932	.598	.246	.065	.011	.001	.000	.000	.000	.000	.000
4	1.000	.999	.983	.798	.450	.167	.038	.005	.000	.000	.000	.000	.000
5	1.000	1.000	.997	.918	.660	.329	.105	.019	.002	.000	.000	.000	.000
6	1.000	1.000	.999	.973	.825	.527	.227	.058	.007	.000	.000	.000	.000
7	1.000	1.000	1.000	.993	.926	.716	.402	.142	.026	.001	.000	.000	.000
8	1.000	1.000	1.000	.999	.974	.858	.598	.284	.074	.007	.000	.000	.000
9	1.000	1.000	1.000	1.000	.993	.942	.773	.473	.175	.027	.001	.000	.000
10	1.000	1.000	1.000	1.000	.998	.981	.895	.671	.340	.082	.003	.000	.000
11	1.000	1.000	1.000	1.000	1.000	.995	.962	.833	.550	.202	.017	.001	.000
12	1.000	1.000	1.000	1.000	1.000	.999	.989	.935	.754	.402	.068	.007	.000
13	1.000	1.000	1.000	1.000	1.000	1.000	.998	.982	.901	.648	.211	.043	.001
14	1.000	1.000	1.000	1.000	1.000	1.000	1.000	.997	.974	.859	.485	.189	.011
15	1.000	1.000	1.000	1.000	1.000	1.000	1.000	1.000	.997	.972	.815	.560	.149

n = 17

x	.01	.05	.10	.20	.30	.40	p .50	.60	.70	.80	.90	.95	.99
0	.843	.418	.167	.023	.002	.000	.000	.000	.000	.000	.000	.000	.000
1	.988	.792	.482	.118	.019	.002	.000	.000	.000	.000	.000	.000	.000
2	.999	.950	.762	.310	.077	.012	.001	.000	.000	.000	.000	.000	.000
3	1.000	.991	.917	.549	.202	.046	.006	.000	.000	.000	.000	.000	.000
4	1.000	.999	.978	.758	.389	.126	.025	.003	.000	.000	.000	.000	.000
5	1.000	1.000	.995	.894	.597	.264	.072	.011	.001	.000	.000	.000	.000
6	1.000	1.000	.999	.962	.775	.448	.166	.035	.003	.000	.000	.000	.000
7	1.000	1.000	1.000	.989	.895	.641	.315	.092	.013	.000	.000	.000	.000
8	1.000	1.000	1.000	.997	.960	.801	.500	.199	.040	.003	.000	.000	.000
9	1.000	1.000	1.000	1.000	.987	.908	.685	.359	.105	.011	.000	.000	.000
10	1.000	1.000	1.000	1.000	.997	.965	.834	.552	.225	.038	.001	.000	.000
11	1.000	1.000	1.000	1.000	.999	.989	.928	.736	.403	.106	.005	.000	.000
12	1.000	1.000	1.000	1.000	1.000	.997	.975	.874	.611	.242	.022	.001	.000
13	1.000	1.000	1.000	1.000	1.000	1.000	.994	.954	.798	.451	.083	.009	.000
14	1.000	1.000	1.000	1.000	1.000	1.000	.999	.988	.923	.690	.238	.050	.001
15	1.000	1.000	1.000	1.000	1.000	1.000	1.000	.998	.981	.882	.518	.208	.012
16	1.000	1.000	1.000	1.000	1.000	1.000	1.000	1.000	.998	.977	.833	.582	.157

TABLE 2. Cumulative Binomial Probability Tables (continued)

$n = 18$

x	.01	.05	.10	.20	.30	.40	p .50	.60	.70	.80	.90	.95	.99
0	.835	.397	.150	.018	.002	.000	.000	.000	.000	.000	.000	.000	.000
1	.986	.774	.450	.099	.014	.001	.000	.000	.000	.000	.000	.000	.000
2	.999	.942	.734	.271	.060	.008	.001	.000	.000	.000	.000	.000	.000
3	1.000	.989	.902	.501	.165	.033	.004	.000	.000	.000	.000	.000	.000
4	1.000	.998	.972	.716	.333	.094	.015	.001	.000	.000	.000	.000	.000
5	1.000	1.000	.994	.867	.534	.209	.048	.006	.000	.000	.000	.000	.000
6	1.000	1.000	.999	.949	.722	.374	.119	.020	.001	.000	.000	.000	.000
7	1.000	1.000	1.000	.984	.859	.563	.240	.058	.006	.000	.000	.000	.000
8	1.000	1.000	1.000	.996	.940	.737	.407	.135	.021	.001	.000	.000	.000
9	1.000	1.000	1.000	.999	.979	.865	.593	.263	.060	.004	.000	.000	.000
10	1.000	1.000	1.000	1.000	.994	.942	.760	.437	.141	.016	.000	.000	.000
11	1.000	1.000	1.000	1.000	.999	.980	.881	.626	.278	.051	.001	.000	.000
12	1.000	1.000	1.000	1.000	1.000	.994	.952	.791	.466	.133	.006	.000	.000
13	1.000	1.000	1.000	1.000	1.000	.999	.985	.906	.667	.284	.028	.002	.000
14	1.000	1.000	1.000	1.000	1.000	1.000	.996	.967	.835	.499	.098	.011	.000
15	1.000	1.000	1.000	1.000	1.000	1.000	.999	.992	.940	.729	.266	.058	.001
16	1.000	1.000	1.000	1.000	1.000	1.000	1.000	.999	.986	.901	.550	.226	.014
17	1.000	1.000	1.000	1.000	1.000	1.000	1.000	1.000	.998	.982	.850	.603	.165

$n = 19$

x	.01	.05	.10	.20	.30	.40	p .50	.60	.70	.80	.90	.95	.99
0	.826	.377	.135	.014	.001	.000	.000	.000	.000	.000	.000	.000	.000
1	.985	.755	.420	.083	.010	.001	.000	.000	.000	.000	.000	.000	.000
2	.999	.933	.705	.237	.046	.005	.000	.000	.000	.000	.000	.000	.000
3	1.000	.987	.885	.455	.133	.023	.002	.000	.000	.000	.000	.000	.000
4	1.000	.998	.965	.673	.282	.070	.010	.001	.000	.000	.000	.000	.000
5	1.000	1.000	.991	.837	.474	.163	.032	.003	.000	.000	.000	.000	.000
6	1.000	1.000	.998	.932	.666	.308	.084	.012	.001	.000	.000	.000	.000
7	1.000	1.000	1.000	.977	.818	.488	.180	.035	.003	.000	.000	.000	.000
8	1.000	1.000	1.000	.993	.916	.667	.324	.088	.011	.000	.000	.000	.000
9	1.000	1.000	1.000	.998	.967	.814	.500	.186	.033	.002	.000	.000	.000
10	1.000	1.000	1.000	1.000	.989	.912	.676	.333	.084	.007	.000	.000	.000
11	1.000	1.000	1.000	1.000	.997	.965	.820	.512	.182	.023	.000	.000	.000
12	1.000	1.000	1.000	1.000	.999	.988	.916	.692	.334	.068	.002	.000	.000
13	1.000	1.000	1.000	1.000	1.000	.997	.968	.837	.526	.163	.009	.000	.000
14	1.000	1.000	1.000	1.000	1.000	.999	.990	.930	.718	.327	.035	.002	.000
15	1.000	1.000	1.000	1.000	1.000	1.000	.998	.977	.867	.545	.115	.013	.000
16	1.000	1.000	1.000	1.000	1.000	1.000	1.000	.995	.954	.763	.295	.067	.001
17	1.000	1.000	1.000	1.000	1.000	1.000	1.000	.999	.990	.917	.580	.245	.015
18	1.000	1.000	1.000	1.000	1.000	1.000	1.000	1.000	.999	.986	.865	.623	.174

TABLE 2 CUMULATIVE BINOMIAL   883

TABLE 2. Cumulative Binomial Probability Tables (continued)

n = 20

x	.01	.05	.10	.20	.30	.40	p .50	.60	.70	.80	.90	.95	.99
0	.818	.358	.122	.002	.001	.000	.000	.000	.000	.000	.000	.000	.000
1	.983	.736	.392	.069	.008	.001	.000	.000	.000	.000	.000	.000	.000
2	.999	.925	.677	.206	.035	.004	.000	.000	.000	.000	.000	.000	.000
3	1.000	.984	.867	.411	.107	.016	.001	.000	.000	.000	.000	.000	.000
4	1.000	.997	.957	.630	.238	.051	.006	.000	.000	.000	.000	.000	.000
5	1.000	1.000	.989	.804	.416	.126	.021	.002	.000	.000	.000	.000	.000
6	1.000	1.000	.998	.913	.608	.250	.058	.006	.000	.000	.000	.000	.000
7	1.000	1.000	1.000	.968	.772	.416	.132	.021	.001	.000	.000	.000	.000
8	1.000	1.000	1.000	.990	.887	.596	.252	.057	.005	.000	.000	.000	.000
9	1.000	1.000	1.000	.997	.952	.755	.412	.128	.017	.001	.000	.000	.000
10	1.000	1.000	1.000	.999	.983	.872	.588	.245	.048	.003	.000	.000	.000
11	1.000	1.000	1.000	1.000	.995	.943	.748	.404	.113	.010	.000	.000	.000
12	1.000	1.000	1.000	1.000	.999	.979	.868	.584	.228	.032	.000	.000	.000
13	1.000	1.000	1.000	1.000	1.000	.994	.942	.750	.392	.087	.002	.000	.000
14	1.000	1.000	1.000	1.000	1.000	.998	.979	.874	.584	.196	.011	.000	.000
15	1.000	1.000	1.000	1.000	1.000	1.000	.994	.949	.762	.370	.043	.003	.000
16	1.000	1.000	1.000	1.000	1.000	1.000	.999	.984	.893	.589	.133	.016	.000
17	1.000	1.000	1.000	1.000	1.000	1.000	1.000	.996	.965	.794	.323	.075	.001
18	1.000	1.000	1.000	1.000	1.000	1.000	1.000	.999	.992	.931	.608	.264	.017
19	1.000	1.000	1.000	1.000	1.000	1.000	1.000	1.000	.999	.988	.878	.642	.182

n = 21

x	.01	.05	.10	.20	.30	.40	p .50	.60	.70	.80	.90	.95	.99
0	.810	.341	.109	.009	.001	.000	.000	.000	.000	.000	.000	.000	.000
1	.981	.717	.365	.058	.006	.000	.000	.000	.000	.000	.000	.000	.000
2	.999	.915	.648	.179	.027	.002	.000	.000	.000	.000	.000	.000	.000
3	1.000	.981	.848	.370	.086	.011	.001	.000	.000	.000	.000	.000	.000
4	1.000	.997	.948	.586	.198	.037	.004	.000	.000	.000	.000	.000	.000
5	1.000	1.000	.986	.769	.363	.096	.013	.001	.000	.000	.000	.000	.000
6	1.000	1.000	.997	.891	.551	.200	.039	.004	.000	.000	.000	.000	.000
7	1.000	1.000	.999	.957	.723	.350	.095	.012	.001	.000	.000	.000	.000
8	1.000	1.000	1.000	.986	.852	.524	.192	.035	.002	.000	.000	.000	.000
9	1.000	1.000	1.000	.996	.932	.691	.332	.085	.009	.000	.000	.000	.000
10	1.000	1.000	1.000	.999	.974	.826	.500	.174	.026	.001	.000	.000	.000
11	1.000	1.000	1.000	1.000	.991	.915	.668	.309	.068	.004	.000	.000	.000
12	1.000	1.000	1.000	1.000	.998	.965	.808	.476	.148	.014	.000	.000	.000
13	1.000	1.000	1.000	1.000	.999	.988	.905	.650	.277	.043	.001	.000	.000
14	1.000	1.000	1.000	1.000	1.000	.996	.961	.800	.449	.109	.003	.000	.000
15	1.000	1.000	1.000	1.000	1.000	.999	.987	.904	.637	.231	.014	.000	.000
16	1.000	1.000	1.000	1.000	1.000	1.000	.996	.963	.802	.414	.052	.003	.000
17	1.000	1.000	1.000	1.000	1.000	1.000	.999	.989	.914	.630	.152	.019	.000
18	1.000	1.000	1.000	1.000	1.000	1.000	1.000	.998	.973	.821	.352	.085	.001
19	1.000	1.000	1.000	1.000	1.000	1.000	1.000	1.000	.994	.942	.635	.283	.019
20	1.000	1.000	1.000	1.000	1.000	1.000	1.000	1.000	.999	.991	.891	.659	.190

TABLE 2. Cumulative Binomial Probability Tables (continued)

n = 22

x	.01	.05	.10	.20	.30	.40	p .50	.60	.70	.80	.90	.95	.99
0	.802	.324	.098	.007	.000	.000	.000	.000	.000	.000	.000	.000	.000
1	.980	.698	.339	.048	.004	.000	.000	.000	.000	.000	.000	.000	.000
2	.999	.905	.620	.154	.021	.002	.000	.000	.000	.000	.000	.000	.000
3	1.000	.978	.828	.332	.068	.008	.000	.000	.000	.000	.000	.000	.000
4	1.000	.996	.938	.543	.165	.027	.002	.000	.000	.000	.000	.000	.000
5	1.000	.999	.982	.733	.313	.072	.008	.000	.000	.000	.000	.000	.000
6	1.000	1.000	.996	.867	.494	.158	.026	.002	.000	.000	.000	.000	.000
7	1.000	1.000	.999	.944	.671	.290	.067	.007	.000	.000	.000	.000	.000
8	1.000	1.000	1.000	.980	.814	.454	.143	.021	.001	.000	.000	.000	.000
9	1.000	1.000	1.000	.994	.908	.624	.262	.055	.004	.000	.000	.000	.000
10	1.000	1.000	1.000	.998	.961	.772	.416	.121	.014	.000	.000	.000	.000
11	1.000	1.000	1.000	1.000	.986	.879	.584	.228	.039	.002	.000	.000	.000
12	1.000	1.000	1.000	1.000	.996	.945	.738	.376	.092	.006	.000	.000	.000
13	1.000	1.000	1.000	1.000	.999	.979	.857	.546	.186	.020	.000	.000	.000
14	1.000	1.000	1.000	1.000	1.000	.993	.933	.710	.329	.056	.001	.000	.000
15	1.000	1.000	1.000	1.000	1.000	.998	.974	.842	.506	.133	.004	.000	.000
16	1.000	1.000	1.000	1.000	1.000	1.000	.992	.928	.687	.267	.018	.001	.000
17	1.000	1.000	1.000	1.000	1.000	1.000	.998	.973	.835	.457	.062	.004	.000
18	1.000	1.000	1.000	1.000	1.000	1.000	1.000	.992	.932	.668	.172	.022	.000
19	1.000	1.000	1.000	1.000	1.000	1.000	1.000	.998	.979	.846	.380	.095	.001
20	1.000	1.000	1.000	1.000	1.000	1.000	1.000	1.000	.996	.952	.661	.302	.020
21	1.000	1.000	1.000	1.000	1.000	1.000	1.000	1.000	1.000	.993	.902	.676	.198

n = 23

x	.01	.05	.10	.20	.30	.40	p .50	.60	.70	.80	.90	.95	.99
0	.794	.307	.089	.006	.000	.000	.000	.000	.000	.000	.000	.000	.000
1	.978	.679	.315	.040	.003	.000	.000	.000	.000	.000	.000	.000	.000
2	.998	.895	.592	.133	.016	.001	.000	.000	.000	.000	.000	.000	.000
3	1.000	.974	.807	.297	.054	.005	.000	.000	.000	.000	.000	.000	.000
4	1.000	.995	.927	.501	.136	.019	.001	.000	.000	.000	.000	.000	.000
5	1.000	.999	.977	.695	.269	.054	.005	.000	.000	.000	.000	.000	.000
6	1.000	1.000	.994	.840	.440	.124	.017	.001	.000	.000	.000	.000	.000
7	1.000	1.000	.999	.928	.618	.237	.047	.004	.000	.000	.000	.000	.000
8	1.000	1.000	1.000	.973	.771	.388	.105	.013	.001	.000	.000	.000	.000
9	1.000	1.000	1.000	.991	.880	.556	.202	.035	.002	.000	.000	.000	.000
10	1.000	1.000	1.000	.997	.945	.713	.339	.081	.007	.000	.000	.000	.000
11	1.000	1.000	1.000	.999	.979	.836	.500	.164	.021	.001	.000	.000	.000
12	1.000	1.000	1.000	1.000	.993	.919	.661	.287	.055	.003	.000	.000	.000
13	1.000	1.000	1.000	1.000	.998	.965	.798	.444	.120	.009	.000	.000	.000
14	1.000	1.000	1.000	1.000	.999	.987	.895	.612	.229	.027	.000	.000	.000

TABLE 2 CUMULATIVE BINOMIAL 885

TABLE 2. Cumulative Binomial Probability Tables (continued)

$n = 23$ (continued)

x	.01	.05	.10	.20	.30	.40	p .50	.60	.70	.80	.90	.95	.99
15	1.000	1.000	1.000	1.000	1.000	.996	.953	.763	.382	.072	.001	.000	.000
16	1.000	1.000	1.000	1.000	1.000	.999	.983	.876	.560	.160	.006	.000	.000
17	1.000	1.000	1.000	1.000	1.000	1.000	.995	.946	.731	.305	.023	.001	.000
18	1.000	1.000	1.000	1.000	1.000	1.000	.999	.981	.864	.499	.073	.005	.000
19	1.000	1.000	1.000	1.000	1.000	1.000	1.000	.995	.946	.703	.193	.026	.000
20	1.000	1.000	1.000	1.000	1.000	1.000	1.000	.999	.984	.867	.408	.105	.002
21	1.000	1.000	1.000	1.000	1.000	1.000	1.000	1.000	.997	.960	.685	.321	.022
22	1.000	1.000	1.000	1.000	1.000	1.000	1.000	1.000	1.000	.994	.911	.693	.206

$n = 24$

x	.01	.05	.10	.20	.30	.40	p .50	.60	.70	.80	.90	.95	.99
0	.786	.292	.080	.005	.000	.000	.000	.000	.000	.000	.000	.000	.000
1	.976	.661	.292	.033	.002	.000	.000	.000	.000	.000	.000	.000	.000
2	.998	.884	.564	.115	.012	.001	.000	.000	.000	.000	.000	.000	.000
3	1.000	.970	.786	.264	.042	.004	.000	.000	.000	.000	.000	.000	.000
4	1.000	.994	.915	.460	.111	.013	.001	.000	.000	.000	.000	.000	.000
5	1.000	.999	.972	.656	.229	.040	.003	.000	.000	.000	.000	.000	.000
6	1.000	1.000	.993	.811	.389	.096	.011	.001	.000	.000	.000	.000	.000
7	1.000	1.000	.998	.911	.565	.192	.032	.002	.000	.000	.000	.000	.000
8	1.000	1.000	1.000	.964	.725	.328	.076	.008	.000	.000	.000	.000	.000
9	1.000	1.000	1.000	.987	.847	.489	.154	.022	.001	.000	.000	.000	.000
10	1.000	1.000	1.000	.996	.926	.650	.271	.053	.004	.000	.000	.000	.000
11	1.000	1.000	1.000	.999	.969	.787	.419	.114	.012	.000	.000	.000	.000
12	1.000	1.000	1.000	1.000	.988	.886	.581	.213	.031	.001	.000	.000	.000
13	1.000	1.000	1.000	1.000	.996	.947	.729	.350	.074	.004	.000	.000	.000
14	1.000	1.000	1.000	1.000	.999	.978	.846	.511	.153	.013	.000	.000	.000
15	1.000	1.000	1.000	1.000	1.000	.992	.924	.672	.275	.036	.000	.000	.000
16	1.000	1.000	1.000	1.000	1.000	.998	.968	.808	.435	.089	.002	.000	.000
17	1.000	1.000	1.000	1.000	1.000	.999	.989	.904	.611	.189	.007	.000	.000
18	1.000	1.000	1.000	1.000	1.000	1.000	.997	.960	.771	.344	.028	.001	.000
19	1.000	1.000	1.000	1.000	1.000	1.000	.999	.987	.889	.540	.085	.006	.000
20	1.000	1.000	1.000	1.000	1.000	1.000	1.000	.996	.958	.736	.214	.030	.000
21	1.000	1.000	1.000	1.000	1.000	1.000	1.000	.999	.988	.885	.436	.116	.002
22	1.000	1.000	1.000	1.000	1.000	1.000	1.000	1.000	.998	.967	.708	.339	.024
23	1.000	1.000	1.000	1.000	1.000	1.000	1.000	1.000	1.000	.995	.920	.708	.214

$n = 25$

x	.01	.05	.10	.20	.30	.40	p .50	.60	.70	.80	.90	.95	.99
0	.778	.277	.072	.004	.000	.000	.000	.000	.000	.000	.000	.000	.000
1	.974	.642	.271	.027	.002	.000	.000	.000	.000	.000	.000	.000	.000
2	.998	.873	.537	.098	.009	.000	.000	.000	.000	.000	.000	.000	.000
3	1.000	.966	.764	.234	.033	.002	.000	.000	.000	.000	.000	.000	.000
4	1.000	.993	.902	.421	.090	.009	.000	.000	.000	.000	.000	.000	.000

TABLE 2. Cumulative Binomial Probability Tables (continued)

x	.01	.05	.10	.20	.30	.40	.50	.60	.70	.80	.90	.95	.99
5	1.000	.999	.967	.617	.193	.029	.002	.000	.000	.000	.000	.000	.000
6	1.000	1.000	.991	.780	.341	.074	.007	.000	.000	.000	.000	.000	.000
7	1.000	1.000	.998	.891	.512	.154	.022	.001	.000	.000	.000	.000	.000
8	1.000	1.000	1.000	.953	.677	.274	.054	.004	.000	.000	.000	.000	.000
9	1.000	1.000	1.000	.983	.811	.425	.115	.013	.000	.000	.000	.000	.000
10	1.000	1.000	1.000	.994	.902	.586	.212	.034	.002	.000	.000	.000	.000
11	1.000	1.000	1.000	.998	.956	.732	.345	.078	.006	.000	.000	.000	.000
12	1.000	1.000	1.000	1.000	.983	.846	.500	.154	.017	.000	.000	.000	.000
13	1.000	1.000	1.000	1.000	.994	.922	.655	.268	.044	.002	.000	.000	.000
14	1.000	1.000	1.000	1.000	.998	.966	.788	.414	.098	.006	.000	.000	.000
15	1.000	1.000	1.000	1.000	1.000	.987	.885	.575	.189	.017	.000	.000	.000
16	1.000	1.000	1.000	1.000	1.000	.996	.946	.726	.323	.047	.000	.000	.000
17	1.000	1.000	1.000	1.000	1.000	.999	.978	.846	.488	.109	.002	.000	.000
18	1.000	1.000	1.000	1.000	1.000	1.000	.993	.926	.659	.220	.009	.000	.000
19	1.000	1.000	1.000	1.000	1.000	1.000	.998	.971	.807	.383	.033	.001	.000
20	1.000	1.000	1.000	1.000	1.000	1.000	1.000	.991	.910	.579	.098	.007	.000
21	1.000	1.000	1.000	1.000	1.000	1.000	1.000	.998	.967	.766	.236	.034	.000
22	1.000	1.000	1.000	1.000	1.000	1.000	1.000	1.000	.991	.902	.463	.127	.002
23	1.000	1.000	1.000	1.000	1.000	1.000	1.000	1.000	.998	.973	.729	.358	.026
24	1.000	1.000	1.000	1.000	1.000	1.000	1.000	1.000	1.000	.996	.928	.723	.222

n = 50

x	.01	.05	.10	.20	.30	.40	p .50	.60	.70	.80	.90	.95	.99
0	.605	.077	.005	.000	.000	.000	.000	.000	.000	.000	.000	.000	.000
1	.911	.279	.034	.000	.000	.000	.000	.000	.000	.000	.000	.000	.000
2	.986	.541	.112	.001	.000	.000	.000	.000	.000	.000	.000	.000	.000
3	.998	.760	.250	.006	.000	.000	.000	.000	.000	.000	.000	.000	.000
4	1.000	.896	.431	.018	.000	.000	.000	.000	.000	.000	.000	.000	.000
5	1.000	.962	.616	.048	.001	.000	.000	.000	.000	.000	.000	.000	.000
6	1.000	.988	.770	.103	.002	.000	.000	.000	.000	.000	.000	.000	.000
7	1.000	.997	.878	.190	.007	.000	.000	.000	.000	.000	.000	.000	.000
8	1.000	.999	.942	.307	.018	.000	.000	.000	.000	.000	.000	.000	.000
9	1.000	1.000	.975	.444	.040	.001	.000	.000	.000	.000	.000	.000	.000
10	1.000	1.000	.991	.584	.079	.002	.000	.000	.000	.000	.000	.000	.000
11	1.000	1.000	.997	.711	.139	.006	.000	.000	.000	.000	.000	.000	.000
12	1.000	1.000	.999	.814	.223	.013	.000	.000	.000	.000	.000	.000	.000
13	1.000	1.000	1.000	.889	.328	.028	.000	.000	.000	.000	.000	.000	.000
14	1.000	1.000	1.000	.939	.447	.054	.001	.000	.000	.000	.000	.000	.000
15	1.000	1.000	1.000	.969	.569	.096	.003	.000	.000	.000	.000	.000	.000
16	1.000	1.000	1.000	.986	.684	.156	.008	.000	.000	.000	.000	.000	.000
17	1.000	1.000	1.000	.994	.782	.237	.016	.000	.000	.000	.000	.000	.000
18	1.000	1.000	1.000	.997	.859	.336	.032	.001	.000	.000	.000	.000	.000
19	1.000	1.000	1.000	.999	.915	.446	.059	.001	.000	.000	.000	.000	.000

TABLE 2 CUMULATIVE BINOMIAL 887

TABLE 2. Cumulative Binomial Probability Tables (continued)

$n = 50$ (continued)

x	.01	.05	.10	.20	.30	.40	p .50	.60	.70	.80	.90	.95	.99
20	1.000	1.000	1.000	1.000	.952	.561	.101	.003	.000	.000	.000	.000	.000
21	1.000	1.000	1.000	1.000	.975	.670	.161	.008	.000	.000	.000	.000	.000
22	1.000	1.000	1.000	1.000	.988	.766	.240	.016	.000	.000	.000	.000	.000
23	1.000	1.000	1.000	1.000	.994	.844	.336	.031	.000	.000	.000	.000	.000
24	1.000	1.000	1.000	1.000	.998	.902	.444	.057	.001	.000	.000	.000	.000
25	1.000	1.000	1.000	1.000	.999	.943	.556	.098	.002	.000	.000	.000	.000
26	1.000	1.000	1.000	1.000	1.000	.969	.664	.156	.006	.000	.000	.000	.000
27	1.000	1.000	1.000	1.000	1.000	.984	.760	.234	.012	.000	.000	.000	.000
28	1.000	1.000	1.000	1.000	1.000	.992	.839	.330	.025	.000	.000	.000	.000
29	1.000	1.000	1.000	1.000	1.000	.997	.899	.439	.048	.000	.000	.000	.000
30	1.000	1.000	1.000	1.000	1.000	.999	.941	.554	.085	.001	.000	.000	.000
31	1.000	1.000	1.000	1.000	1.000	.999	.968	.664	.141	.003	.000	.000	.000
32	1.000	1.000	1.000	1.000	1.000	1.000	.984	.763	.218	.006	.000	.000	.000
33	1.000	1.000	1.000	1.000	1.000	1.000	.992	.844	.316	.014	.000	.000	.000
34	1.000	1.000	1.000	1.000	1.000	1.000	.997	.904	.431	.031	.000	.000	.000
35	1.000	1.000	1.000	1.000	1.000	1.000	.999	.946	.553	.061	.000	.000	.000
36	1.000	1.000	1.000	1.000	1.000	1.000	1.000	.972	.672	.111	.000	.000	.000
37	1.000	1.000	1.000	1.000	1.000	1.000	1.000	.987	.777	.186	.001	.000	.000
38	1.000	1.000	1.000	1.000	1.000	1.000	1.000	.994	.861	.289	.003	.000	.000
39	1.000	1.000	1.000	1.000	1.000	1.000	1.000	.998	.921	.416	.009	.000	.000
40	1.000	1.000	1.000	1.000	1.000	1.000	1.000	.999	.960	.556	.025	.000	.000
41	1.000	1.000	1.000	1.000	1.000	1.000	1.000	1.000	.982	.693	.058	.001	.000
42	1.000	1.000	1.000	1.000	1.000	1.000	1.000	1.000	.993	.810	.122	.003	.000
43	1.000	1.000	1.000	1.000	1.000	1.000	1.000	1.000	.998	.897	.230	.012	.000
44	1.000	1.000	1.000	1.000	1.000	1.000	1.000	1.000	.999	.952	.384	.038	.000
45	1.000	1.000	1.000	1.000	1.000	1.000	1.000	1.000	1.000	.982	.569	.104	.000
46	1.000	1.000	1.000	1.000	1.000	1.000	1.000	1.000	1.000	.994	.750	.240	.002
47	1.000	1.000	1.000	1.000	1.000	1.000	1.000	1.000	1.000	.999	.888	.459	.014
48	1.000	1.000	1.000	1.000	1.000	1.000	1.000	1.000	1.000	1.000	.966	.721	.089
49	1.000	1.000	1.000	1.000	1.000	1.000	1.000	1.000	1.000	1.000	.995	.923	.395

TABLE 3. Cumulative Probability Values for the Poisson Distribution

$P(X \le x|\mu)$; Example: $P(X \le 4|\mu = 1.8) = .9636$

μ x	0.1	0.2	0.3	0.4	0.5	0.6	0.7	0.8	0.9	1.0
0	0.9048	0.8187	0.7408	0.6703	0.6065	0.5488	0.4966	0.4493	0.4066	0.3679
1	0.9953	0.9825	0.9631	0.9384	0.9098	0.8781	0.8442	0.8088	0.7725	0.7358
2	0.9998	0.9989	0.9964	0.9921	0.9856	0.9769	0.9659	0.9526	0.9371	0.9197
3	1.0000	0.9999	0.9997	0.9992	0.9982	0.9966	0.9942	0.9909	0.9865	0.9810
4	1.0000	1.0000	1.0000	0.9999	0.9998	0.9996	0.9992	0.9986	0.9977	0.9963
5	1.0000	1.0000	1.0000	1.0000	1.0000	1.0000	0.9999	0.9998	0.9997	0.9994
6	1.0000	1.0000	1.0000	1.0000	1.0000	1.0000	1.0000	1.0000	1.0000	0.9999
7	1.0000	1.0000	1.0000	1.0000	1.0000	1.0000	1.0000	1.0000	1.0000	1.0000

μ x	1.1	1.2	1.3	1.4	1.5	1.6	1.7	1.8	1.9	2.0
0	0.3329	0.3012	0.2725	0.2466	0.2231	0.2019	0.1827	0.1653	0.1496	0.1353
1	0.6990	0.6626	0.6268	0.5918	0.5578	0.5249	0.4932	0.4628	0.4338	0.4060
2	0.9004	0.8795	0.8571	0.8335	0.8088	0.7834	0.7572	0.7306	0.7037	0.6767
3	0.9743	0.9662	0.9569	0.9463	0.9344	0.9212	0.9068	0.8913	0.8747	0.8571
4	0.9946	0.9923	0.9893	0.9857	0.9814	0.9763	0.9704	0.9636	0.9559	0.9473
5	0.9990	0.9985	0.9978	0.9968	0.9955	0.9940	0.9920	0.9896	0.9868	0.9834
6	0.9999	0.9997	0.9996	0.9994	0.9991	0.9987	0.9981	0.9974	0.9966	0.9955
7	1.0000	1.0000	0.9999	0.9999	0.9998	0.9997	0.9996	0.9994	0.9992	0.9989
8	1.0000	1.0000	1.0000	1.0000	1.0000	1.0000	0.9999	0.9999	0.9998	0.9998
9	1.0000	1.0000	1.0000	1.0000	1.0000	1.0000	1.0000	1.0000	1.0000	1.0000

μ x	2.1	2.2	2.3	2.4	2.5	2.6	2.7	2.8	2.9	3.0
0	0.1225	0.1108	0.1003	0.0907	0.0821	0.0743	0.0672	0.0608	0.0550	0.0498
1	0.3796	0.3546	0.3309	0.3084	0.2873	0.2674	0.2487	0.2311	0.2146	0.1991
2	0.6496	0.6227	0.5960	0.5697	0.5438	0.5184	0.4936	0.4695	0.4460	0.4232
3	0.8386	0.8194	0.7993	0.7787	0.7576	0.7360	0.7141	0.6919	0.6696	0.6472
4	0.9379	0.9275	0.9162	0.9041	0.8912	0.8774	0.8629	0.8477	0.8318	0.8153
5	0.9796	0.9751	0.9700	0.9643	0.9580	0.9510	0.9433	0.9349	0.9258	0.9161
6	0.9941	0.9925	0.9906	0.9884	0.9858	0.9828	0.9794	0.9756	0.9713	0.9665
7	0.9985	0.9980	0.9974	0.9967	0.9958	0.9947	0.9934	0.9919	0.9901	0.9881
8	0.9997	0.9995	0.9994	0.9991	0.9989	0.9985	0.9981	0.9976	0.9969	0.9962
9	0.9999	0.9999	0.9999	0.9998	0.9997	0.9996	0.9995	0.9993	0.9991	0.9989
10	1.0000	1.0000	1.0000	1.0000	0.9999	0.9999	0.9999	0.9998	0.9998	0.9997
11	1.0000	1.0000	1.0000	1.0000	1.0000	1.0000	1.0000	1.0000	0.9999	0.9999
12	1.0000	1.0000	1.0000	1.0000	1.0000	1.0000	1.0000	1.0000	1.0000	1.0000

μ x	3.1	3.2	3.3	3.4	3.5	3.6	3.7	3.8	3.9	4.0
0	0.0450	0.0408	0.0369	0.0334	0.0302	0.0273	0.0247	0.0224	0.0202	0.0183
1	0.1847	0.1712	0.1586	0.1468	0.1359	0.1257	0.1162	0.1074	0.0992	0.0916
2	0.4012	0.3799	0.3594	0.3397	0.3208	0.3027	0.2854	0.2689	0.2531	0.2381
3	0.6248	0.6025	0.5803	0.5584	0.5366	0.5152	0.4942	0.4735	0.4533	0.4335
4	0.7982	0.7806	0.7626	0.7442	0.7254	0.7064	0.6872	0.6578	0.6484	0.6288
5	0.9057	0.8946	0.8829	0.8705	0.8576	0.8441	0.8301	0.8156	0.8006	0.7851
6	0.9612	0.9554	0.9490	0.9421	0.9347	0.9267	0.9182	0.9091	0.8995	0.8893
7	0.9858	0.9832	0.9802	0.9769	0.9733	0.9692	0.9648	0.9599	0.9546	0.9489
8	0.9953	0.9943	0.9931	0.9917	0.9901	0.9883	0.9863	0.9840	0.9815	0.9786
9	0.9986	0.9982	0.9978	0.9973	0.9967	0.9960	0.9952	0.9942	0.9931	0.9919

TABLE 3 CUMULATIVE POISSON 889

TABLE 3. Cumulative Poisson (continued)

μ / x	3.1	3.2	3.3	3.4	3.5	3.6	3.7	3.8	3.9	4.0
10	0.9996	0.9995	0.9994	0.9992	0.9990	0.9987	0.9984	0.9981	0.9977	0.9972
11	0.9999	0.9999	0.9998	0.9998	0.9997	0.9996	0.9995	0.9994	0.9993	0.9991
12	1.0000	1.0000	1.0000	0.9999	0.9999	0.9999	0.9999	0.9998	0.9998	0.9997
13	1.0000	1.0000	1.0000	1.0000	1.0000	1.0000	1.0000	1.0000	0.9999	0.9999
14	1.0000	1.0000	1.0000	1.0000	1.0000	1.0000	1.0000	1.0000	1.0000	1.0000

μ / x	4.1	4.2	4.3	4.4	4.5	4.6	4.7	4.8	4.9	5.0
0	0.0166	0.0150	0.0136	0.0123	0.0111	0.0101	0.0091	0.0082	0.0074	0.0067
1	0.0845	0.0780	0.0719	0.0663	0.0611	0.0563	0.0518	0.0477	0.0439	0.0404
2	0.2238	0.2102	0.1974	0.1851	0.1736	0.1626	0.1523	0.1425	0.1333	0.1247
3	0.4142	0.3954	0.3772	0.3595	0.3423	0.3257	0.3097	0.2942	0.2793	0.2650
4	0.6093	0.5898	0.5704	0.5512	0.5321	0.5132	0.4946	0.4763	0.4582	0.4405
5	0.7693	0.7531	0.7367	0.7199	0.7029	0.6858	0.6684	0.6510	0.6335	0.6160
6	0.8736	0.8675	0.8558	0.8436	0.8311	0.8180	0.8046	0.7908	0.7767	0.7622
7	0.9427	0.9361	0.9290	0.9214	0.9134	0.9049	0.8960	0.8867	0.8769	0.8666
8	0.9755	0.9721	0.9683	0.9642	0.9597	0.9549	0.9497	0.9442	0.9382	0.9319
9	0.9905	0.9889	0.9871	0.9851	0.9829	0.9805	0.9778	0.9749	0.9717	0.9682
10	0.9966	0.9959	0.9952	0.9943	0.9933	0.9922	0.9910	0.9896	0.9880	0.9863
11	0.9989	0.9986	0.9983	0.9980	0.9976	0.9971	0.9966	0.9960	0.9953	0.9945
12	0.9997	0.9996	0.9995	0.9993	0.9992	0.9990	0.9988	0.9986	0.9983	0.9980
13	0.9999	0.9999	0.9998	0.9998	0.9997	0.9997	0.9996	0.9995	0.9994	0.9993
14	1.0000	1.0000	1.0000	0.9999	0.9999	0.9999	0.9999	0.9999	0.9998	0.9998
15	1.0000	1.0000	1.0000	1.0000	1.0000	1.0000	1.0000	1.0000	0.9999	0.9999
16	1.0000	1.0000	1.0000	1.0000	1.0000	1.0000	1.0000	1.0000	1.0000	1.0000

μ / x	5.1	5.2	5.3	5.4	5.5	5.6	5.7	5.8	5.9	6.0
0	0.0061	0.0055	0.0050	0.0045	0.0041	0.0037	0.0033	0.0030	0.0027	0.0025
1	0.0372	0.0342	0.0314	0.0289	0.0266	0.0244	0.0224	0.0206	0.0189	0.0174
2	0.1165	0.1088	0.1016	0.0948	0.0884	0.0824	0.0768	0.0715	0.0666	0.0620
3	0.2513	0.2381	0.2254	0.2133	0.2017	0.1906	0.1801	0.1700	0.1604	0.1512
4	0.4231	0.4061	0.3895	0.3733	0.3575	0.3422	0.3272	0.3127	0.2987	0.2851
5	0.5984	0.5809	0.5635	0.5461	0.5289	0.5119	0.4950	0.4783	0.4619	0.4457
6	0.7474	0.7324	0.7171	0.7017	0.6860	0.6703	0.6544	0.6384	0.6224	0.6063
7	0.8560	0.8449	0.8335	0.8217	0.8095	0.7970	0.7842	0.7710	0.7576	0.7440
8	0.9252	0.9181	0.9106	0.9026	0.8944	0.8857	0.8766	0.8672	0.8574	0.8472
9	0.9644	0.9603	0.9559	0.9512	0.9462	0.9409	0.9352	0.9292	0.9228	0.9161
10	0.9844	0.9823	0.9800	0.9775	0.9747	0.9718	0.9686	0.9651	0.9614	0.9574
11	0.9937	0.9927	0.9916	0.9904	0.9890	0.9875	0.9859	0.9840	0.9821	0.9799
12	0.9976	0.9972	0.9967	0.9962	0.9955	0.9949	0.9941	0.9932	0.9922	0.9912
13	0.9992	0.9990	0.9988	0.9986	0.9983	0.9980	0.9977	0.9973	0.9969	0.9964
14	0.9997	0.9997	0.9996	0.9995	0.9994	0.9993	0.9991	0.9990	0.9988	0.9986
15	0.9999	0.9999	0.9999	0.9998	0.9998	0.9998	0.9997	0.9996	0.9996	0.9995
16	1.0000	1.0000	1.0000	0.9999	0.9999	0.9999	0.9999	0.9999	0.9999	0.9998
17	1.0000	1.0000	1.0000	1.0000	1.0000	1.0000	1.0000	1.0000	1.0000	0.9999
18	1.0000	1.0000	1.0000	1.0000	1.0000	1.0000	1.0000	1.0000	1.0000	1.0000

TABLE 3. Cumulative Poisson (continued)

μ x	6.1	6.2	6.3	6.4	6.5	6.6	6.7	6.8	6.9	7.0
0	0.0022	0.0020	0.0018	0.0017	0.0015	0.0014	0.0012	0.0011	0.0010	0.0009
1	0.0159	0.0146	0.0134	0.0123	0.0113	0.0103	0.0095	0.0087	0.0080	0.0073
2	0.0577	0.0536	0.0498	0.0463	0.0430	0.0400	0.0371	0.0344	0.0320	0.0296
3	0.1425	0.1342	0.1264	0.1189	0.1119	0.1052	0.0988	0.0928	0.0871	0.0818
4	0.2719	0.2592	0.2469	0.2351	0.2237	0.2127	0.2022	0.1920	0.1823	0.1730
5	0.4298	0.4141	0.3988	0.3837	0.3690	0.3547	0.3407	0.3270	0.3137	0.3007
6	0.5902	0.5742	0.5582	0.5423	0.5265	0.5108	0.4953	0.4799	0.4647	0.4497
7	0.7301	0.7160	0.7018	0.6873	0.6728	0.6581	0.6433	0.6285	0.6136	0.5987
8	0.8367	0.8259	0.8148	0.8033	0.7916	0.7796	0.7673	0.7548	0.7420	0.7291
9	0.9090	0.9016	0.8939	0.8858	0.8774	0.8686	0.8596	0.8502	0.8405	0.8305
10	0.9531	0.9486	0.9437	0.9386	0.9332	0.9274	0.9214	0.9151	0.9084	0.9015
11	0.9776	0.9750	0.9723	0.9693	0.9661	0.9627	0.9591	0.9552	0.9510	0.9466
12	0.9900	0.9887	0.9873	0.9857	0.9840	0.9821	0.9801	0.9779	0.9755	0.9730
13	0.9958	0.9952	0.9945	0.9937	0.9929	0.9920	0.9909	0.9898	0.9885	0.9872
14	0.9984	0.9981	0.9978	0.9974	0.9970	0.9966	0.9961	0.9956	0.9950	0.9943
15	0.9994	0.9993	0.9992	0.9990	0.9988	0.9986	0.9984	0.9982	0.9979	0.9976
16	0.9998	0.9997	0.9997	0.9996	0.9996	0.9995	0.9994	0.9993	0.9992	0.9990
17	0.9999	0.9999	0.9999	0.9999	0.9998	0.9998	0.9998	0.9997	0.9997	0.9996
18	1.0000	1.0000	1.0000	1.0000	0.9999	0.9999	0.9999	0.9999	0.9999	0.9999
19	1.0000	1.0000	1.0000	1.0000	1.0000	1.0000	1.0000	1.0000	1.0000	0.9999
20	1.0000	1.0000	1.0000	1.0000	1.0000	1.0000	1.0000	1.0000	1.0000	1.0000

μ x	7.1	7.2	7.3	7.4	7.5	7.6	7.7	7.8	7.9	8.0
0	0.0008	0.0007	0.0007	0.0006	0.0006	0.0005	0.0005	0.0004	0.0004	0.0003
1	0.0067	0.0061	0.0056	0.0051	0.0047	0.0043	0.0039	0.0036	0.0033	0.0030
2	0.0275	0.0255	0.0236	0.0219	0.0203	0.0188	0.0174	0.0161	0.0149	0.0138
3	0.0767	0.0719	0.0674	0.0632	0.0591	0.0554	0.0518	0.0485	0.0453	0.0424
4	0.1641	0.1555	0.1473	0.1395	0.1321	0.1249	0.1181	0.1117	0.1055	0.0996
5	0.2881	0.2759	0.2640	0.2526	0.2414	0.2307	0.2203	0.2103	0.2006	0.1912
6	0.4349	0.4204	0.4060	0.3920	0.3782	0.3646	0.3514	0.3384	0.3257	0.3134
7	0.5838	0.5689	0.5541	0.5393	0.5246	0.5100	0.4956	0.4812	0.4670	0.4530
8	0.7160	0.7027	0.6892	0.6757	0.6620	0.6482	0.6343	0.6204	0.6065	0.5926
9	0.8202	0.8096	0.7988	0.7877	0.7764	0.7649	0.7531	0.7411	0.7290	0.7166
10	0.8942	0.8867	0.8788	0.8707	0.8622	0.8535	0.8445	0.8352	0.8257	0.8159
11	0.9420	0.9371	0.9319	0.9265	0.9208	0.9148	0.9085	0.9020	0.8952	0.8881
12	0.9703	0.9673	0.9642	0.9609	0.9573	0.9536	0.9496	0.9453	0.9409	0.9362
13	0.9857	0.9841	0.9824	0.9805	0.9784	0.9762	0.9739	0.9714	0.9687	0.9658
14	0.9935	0.9927	0.9918	0.9908	0.9897	0.9886	0.9873	0.9859	0.9844	0.9827
15	0.9972	0.9968	0.9964	0.9959	0.9954	0.9948	0.9941	0.9934	0.9926	0.9918
16	0.9989	0.9987	0.9985	0.9983	0.9980	0.9978	0.9974	0.9971	0.9967	0.9963
17	0.9996	0.9995	0.9994	0.9993	0.9992	0.9991	0.9989	0.9988	0.9986	0.9984
18	0.9998	0.9998	0.9998	0.9997	0.9997	0.9996	0.9996	0.9995	0.9994	0.9993
19	0.9999	0.9999	0.9999	0.9999	0.9999	0.9999	0.9998	0.9998	0.9998	0.9997
20	1.0000	1.0000	1.0000	1.0000	1.0000	0.9999	0.9999	0.9999	0.9999	0.9999
21	1.0000	1.0000	1.0000	1.0000	1.0000	1.0000	1.0000	1.0000	1.0000	1.0000

TABLE 3 CUMULATIVE POISSON   891

TABLE 3. Cumulative Poisson (continued)

μ \ x	8.1	8.2	8.3	8.4	8.5	8.6	8.7	8.8	8.9	9.0
0	0.0003	0.0003	0.0002	0.0002	0.0002	0.0002	0.0002	0.0002	0.0001	0.0001
1	0.0028	0.0025	0.0023	0.0021	0.0019	0.0018	0.0016	0.0015	0.0014	0.0012
2	0.0127	0.0118	0.0109	0.0100	0.0093	0.0086	0.0079	0.0073	0.0068	0.0062
3	0.0396	0.0370	0.0346	0.0323	0.0301	0.0281	0.0262	0.0244	0.0228	0.0212
4	0.0941	0.0887	0.0837	0.0789	0.0744	0.0701	0.0660	0.0621	0.0584	0.0550
5	0.1822	0.1736	0.1653	0.1573	0.1496	0.1422	0.1352	0.1284	0.1219	0.1157
6	0.3013	0.2896	0.2781	0.2670	0.2562	0.2457	0.2355	0.2256	0.2160	0.2068
7	0.4391	0.4254	0.4119	0.3987	0.3856	0.3728	0.3602	0.3478	0.3357	0.3239
8	0.5786	0.5647	0.5508	0.5369	0.5231	0.5094	0.4958	0.4823	0.4689	0.4557
9	0.7041	0.6915	0.6788	0.6659	0.6530	0.6400	0.6269	0.6137	0.6006	0.5874
10	0.8058	0.7955	0.7850	0.7743	0.7634	0.7522	0.7409	0.7294	0.7178	0.7060
11	0.8807	0.8731	0.8652	0.8571	0.8487	0.8400	0.8311	0.8220	0.8126	0.8030
12	0.9313	0.9261	0.9207	0.9150	0.9091	0.9029	0.8965	0.8898	0.8829	0.8758
13	0.9628	0.9595	0.9561	0.9524	0.9486	0.9445	0.9403	0.9358	0.9311	0.9262
14	0.9810	0.9791	0.9771	0.9749	0.9726	0.9701	0.9675	0.9647	0.9617	0.9585
15	0.9908	0.9898	0.9887	0.9875	0.9862	0.9847	0.9832	0.9816	0.9798	0.9780
16	0.9958	0.9953	0.9947	0.9941	0.9934	0.9926	0.9918	0.9909	0.9899	0.9889
17	0.9982	0.9979	0.9976	0.9973	0.9970	0.9966	0.9962	0.9957	0.9952	0.9947
18	0.9992	0.9991	0.9990	0.9989	0.9987	0.9985	0.9983	0.9981	0.9978	0.9976
19	0.9997	0.9996	0.9996	0.9995	0.9995	0.9994	0.9993	0.9992	0.9991	0.9989
20	0.9999	0.9999	0.9998	0.9998	0.9998	0.9997	0.9997	0.9997	0.9996	0.9996
21	1.0000	0.9999	0.9999	0.9999	0.9999	0.9999	0.9999	0.9999	0.9998	0.9998
22	1.0000	1.0000	1.0000	1.0000	1.0000	1.0000	1.0000	0.9999	0.9999	0.9999
23	1.0000	1.0000	1.0000	1.0000	1.0000	1.0000	1.0000	1.0000	1.0000	1.0000

μ \ x	9.1	9.2	9.3	9.4	9.5	9.6	9.7	9.8	9.9	10.0
0	0.0001	0.0001	0.0001	0.0001	0.0001	0.0001	0.0001	0.0001	0.0001	0.0000
1	0.0011	0.0010	0.0009	0.0009	0.0008	0.0007	0.0007	0.0006	0.0005	0.0005
2	0.0058	0.0053	0.0049	0.0045	0.0042	0.0038	0.0035	0.0033	0.0030	0.0028
3	0.0198	0.0184	0.0172	0.0160	0.0149	0.0138	0.0129	0.0120	0.0111	0.0103
4	0.0517	0.0486	0.0456	0.0429	0.0403	0.0378	0.0355	0.0333	0.0312	0.0293
5	0.1098	0.1041	0.0987	0.0935	0.0885	0.0838	0.0793	0.0750	0.0710	0.0671
6	0.1978	0.1892	0.1808	0.1727	0.1650	0.1575	0.1502	0.1433	0.1366	0.1301
7	0.3123	0.3010	0.2900	0.2792	0.2687	0.2584	0.2485	0.2388	0.2294	0.2202
8	0.4426	0.4296	0.4168	0.4042	0.3918	0.3796	0.3676	0.3558	0.3442	0.3328
9	0.5742	0.5511	0.5479	0.5349	0.5218	0.5089	0.4960	0.4832	0.4705	0.4579
10	0.6941	0.6820	0.6699	0.6576	0.6453	0.6330	0.6205	0.6080	0.5955	0.5830
11	0.7932	0.7832	0.7730	0.7626	0.7520	0.7412	0.7303	0.7193	0.7081	0.6968
12	0.8684	0.8607	0.8529	0.8448	0.8364	0.8279	0.8191	0.8101	0.8009	0.7916
13	0.9210	0.9156	0.9100	0.9042	0.8981	0.8919	0.8853	0.8786	0.8716	0.8645
14	0.9552	0.9517	0.9480	0.9441	0.9400	0.9357	0.9312	0.9265	0.9216	0.9165
15	0.9760	0.9738	0.9715	0.9691	0.9665	0.9638	0.9609	0.9579	0.9546	0.9513
16	0.9878	0.9865	0.9852	0.9836	0.9823	0.9806	0.9789	0.9770	0.9751	0.9730
17	0.9941	0.9934	0.9927	0.9919	0.9911	0.9902	0.9892	0.9881	0.9869	0.9857
18	0.9973	0.9969	0.9966	0.9962	0.9957	0.9952	0.9947	0.9941	0.9935	0.9928
19	0.9988	0.9986	0.9985	0.9983	0.9980	0.9978	0.9975	0.9972	0.9969	0.9965

TABLE 3. Cumulative Poisson (continued)

20	0.9995	0.9994	0.9993	0.9992	0.9991	0.9990	0.9989	0.9987	0.9986	0.9984
21	0.9998	0.9998	0.9997	0.9997	0.9996	0.9996	0.9995	0.9995	0.9994	0.9993
22	0.9999	0.9999	0.9999	0.9999	0.9998	0.9998	0.9998	0.9998	0.9997	0.9997
23	1.0000	1.0000	1.0000	0.9999	0.9999	0.9999	0.9999	0.9999	0.9999	0.9999
24	1.0000	1.0000	1.0000	1.0000	1.0000	1.0000	1.0000	1.0000	0.9999	0.9999
25	1.0000	1.0000	1.0000	1.0000	1.0000	1.0000	1.0000	1.0000	1.0000	1.0000

μ	11.0	12.0	13.0	14.0	15.0	16.0	17.0	18.0	19.0	20.0
x										
0	0.0000	0.0000	0.0000	0.0000	0.0000	0.0000	0.0	0.0	0.0	0.0
1	0.0002	0.0001	0.0000	0.0000	0.0000	0.0000	0.0000	0.0000	0.0000	0.0
2	0.0012	0.0005	0.0002	0.0001	0.0000	0.0000	0.0000	0.0000	0.0000	0.0000
3	0.0049	0.0023	0.0011	0.0005	0.0002	0.0001	0.0000	0.0000	0.0000	0.0000
4	0.0151	0.0076	0.0037	0.0018	0.0009	0.0004	0.0002	0.0001	0.0000	0.0000
5	0.0375	0.0203	0.0107	0.0055	0.0028	0.0014	0.0007	0.0003	0.0002	0.0001
6	0.0786	0.0458	0.0259	0.0142	0.0076	0.0040	0.0021	0.0010	0.0005	0.0003
7	0.1432	0.0895	0.0540	0.0316	0.0180	0.0100	0.0054	0.0029	0.0015	0.0008
8	0.2320	0.1550	0.0998	0.0621	0.0374	0.0220	0.0126	0.0071	0.0039	0.0021
9	0.3405	0.2424	0.1658	0.1094	0.0699	0.0433	0.0261	0.0154	0.0089	0.0050
10	0.4599	0.3472	0.2517	0.1757	0.1185	0.0774	0.0491	0.0304	0.0183	0.0108
11	0.5793	0.4616	0.3532	0.2600	0.1847	0.1270	0.0847	0.0549	0.0347	0.0214
12	0.6887	0.5760	0.4631	0.3585	0.2676	0.1931	0.1350	0.0917	0.0606	0.0390
13	0.7813	0.6815	0.5730	0.4644	0.3632	0.2745	0.2009	0.1426	0.0984	0.0661
14	0.8540	0.7720	0.6751	0.5704	0.4656	0.3675	0.2808	0.2081	0.1497	0.1049
15	0.9074	0.8444	0.7636	0.6694	0.5681	0.4667	0.3714	0.2866	0.2148	0.1565
16	0.9441	0.8987	0.8355	0.7559	0.6641	0.5660	0.4677	0.3750	0.2920	0.2211
17	0.9678	0.9370	0.8905	0.8272	0.7489	0.6593	0.5640	0.4686	0.3784	0.2970
18	0.9823	0.9626	0.9302	0.8826	0.8195	0.7423	0.6549	0.5622	0.4695	0.3814
19	0.9907	0.9787	0.9573	0.9235	0.8752	0.8122	0.7363	0.6509	0.5606	0.4703
20	0.9953	0.9884	0.9750	0.9521	0.9170	0.8682	0.8055	0.7307	0.6472	0.5591
21	0.9977	0.9939	0.9859	0.9711	0.9469	0.9108	0.8615	0.7991	0.7255	0.6437
22	0.9989	0.9969	0.9924	0.9833	0.9672	0.9418	0.9047	0.8551	0.7931	0.7206
23	0.9995	0.9985	0.9960	0.9907	0.9805	0.9633	0.9367	0.8989	0.8490	0.7875
24	0.9998	0.9993	0.9980	0.9950	0.9888	0.9777	0.9593	0.9317	0.8933	0.8432
25	0.9999	0.9997	0.9990	0.9974	0.9938	0.9869	0.9747	0.9554	0.9269	0.8878
26	1.0000	0.9999	0.9995	0.9987	0.9967	0.9925	0.9848	0.9718	0.9514	0.9221
27	1.0000	0.9999	0.9998	0.9994	0.9983	0.9959	0.9912	0.9827	0.9687	0.9475
28	1.0000	1.0000	0.9999	0.9997	0.9991	0.9978	0.9950	0.9897	0.9805	0.9657
29	1.0000	1.0000	1.0000	0.9999	0.9996	0.9989	0.9973	0.9940	0.9881	0.9782
30	1.0000	1.0000	1.0000	0.9999	0.9998	0.9994	0.9985	0.9967	0.9930	0.9865
31	1.0000	1.0000	1.0000	1.0000	0.9999	0.9997	0.9992	0.9982	0.9960	0.9919
32	1.0000	1.0000	1.0000	1.0000	0.9999	0.9999	0.9996	0.9990	0.9978	0.9953
33	1.0000	1.0000	1.0000	1.0000	1.0000	0.9999	0.9998	0.9995	0.9988	0.9973
34	1.0000	1.0000	1.0000	1.0000	1.0000	1.0000	0.9999	0.9997	0.9994	0.9985
35	1.0000	1.0000	1.0000	1.0000	1.0000	1.0000	0.9999	0.9999	0.9997	0.9992
36	1.0000	1.0000	1.0000	1.0000	1.0000	1.0000	1.0000	0.9999	0.9998	0.9996
37	1.0000	1.0000	1.0000	1.0000	1.0000	1.0000	1.0000	1.0000	0.9999	0.9998
38	1.0000	1.0000	1.0000	1.0000	1.0000	1.0000	1.0000	1.0000	1.0000	0.9999
39	1.0000	1.0000	1.0000	1.0000	1.0000	1.0000	1.0000	1.0000	1.0000	0.9999
40	1.0000	1.0000	1.0000	1.0000	1.0000	1.0000	1.0000	1.0000	1.0000	1.0000

TABLE 3 CUMULATIVE POISSON 893

For ease of reference, Table 4, Areas under the Normal Curve, has been placed on the inside of the back cover.

TABLE 5. Normal Deviates for Statistical Estimation

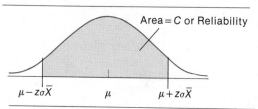

Reliability or Confidence Level $(1 - \alpha)$	Normal Deviate z
.80	1.28
.90	1.64
.95	1.96
.98	2.33
.99	2.57
.998	3.08
.999	3.27

TABLE 6. Critical Normal Deviates for Hypothesis Testing

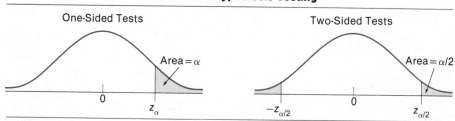

Significance Level α	Normal Deviate z_α	Significance Level α	Normal Deviate $z_{\alpha/2}$
.10	1.28	.10	1.64
.05	1.64	.05	1.96
.025	1.96	.025	2.24
.01	2.33	.01	2.57
.005	2.57	.005	2.81
.001	3.08	.001	3.27

Tables 5 and 6 from *Statistics for Modern Business Decisions*, second edition, by Lawrence Lapin. (c) 1978 by Harcourt Brace Jovanovich, Inc. Reprinted by permission of the publisher.

For ease of reference, Table 7, Student's *t* Distribution, has been placed on the inside of the back cover.

TABLE 8. Chi-Square Distribution

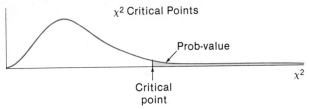

χ^2 Critical Points

Prob-value

Critical point

χ^2

d.f.	Prob-value						
	.250	.100	.050	.025	.010	.005	.001
1	1.32	2.71	3.84	5.02	6.63	7.88	10.8
2	2.77	4.61	5.99	7.38	9.21	10.6	13.8
3	4.11	6.25	7.81	9.35	11.3	12.8	16.3
4	5.39	7.78	9.49	11.1	13.3	14.9	18.5
5	6.63	9.24	11.1	12.8	15.1	16.7	20.5
6	7.84	10.6	12.6	14.4	16.8	18.5	22.5
7	9.04	12.0	14.1	16.0	18.5	20.3	24.3
8	10.2	13.4	15.5	17.5	20.1	22.0	26.1
9	11.4	14.7	16.9	19.0	21.7	23.6	27.9
10	12.5	16.0	18.3	20.5	23.2	25.2	29.6
11	13.7	17.3	19.7	21.9	24.7	26.8	31.3
12	14.8	18.5	21.0	23.3	26.2	28.3	32.9
13	16.0	19.8	22.4	24.7	27.7	29.8	34.5
14	17.1	21.1	23.7	26.1	29.1	31.3	36.1
15	18.2	22.3	25.0	27.5	30.6	32.8	37.7
16	19.4	23.5	26.3	28.8	32.0	34.3	39.3
17	20.5	24.8	27.6	30.2	33.4	35.7	40.8
18	21.6	26.0	28.9	31.5	34.8	37.2	42.3
19	22.7	27.2	30.1	32.9	36.2	38.6	32.8
20	23.8	28.4	31.4	34.2	37.6	40.0	45.3
21	24.9	29.6	32.7	35.5	38.9	41.4	46.8
22	26.0	30.8	33.9	36.8	40.3	42.8	48.3
23	27.1	32.0	35.2	38.1	41.6	44.2	49.7
24	28.2	33.2	36.4	39.4	32.0	45.6	51.2
25	29.3	34.4	37.7	40.6	44.3	46.9	52.6
26	30.4	35.6	38.9	41.9	45.6	48.3	54.1
27	31.5	36.7	40.1	43.2	47.0	49.6	55.5
28	32.6	37.9	41.3	44.5	48.3	51.0	56.9
29	33.7	39.1	42.6	45.7	49.6	52.3	58.3
30	34.8	40.3	43.8	47.0	50.9	53.7	59.7
40	45.6	51.8	55.8	59.3	63.7	66.8	73.4
50	56.3	63.2	67.5	71.4	76.2	79.5	86.7
60	67.0	74.4	79.1	83.3	88.4	92.0	99.6
70	77.6	85.5	90.5	95.0	100	104	112
80	88.1	96.6	102	107	112	116	125
90	98.6	108	113	118	124	128	137
100	109	118	124	130	136	140	149

From E. S. Pearson and H. O. Hartley, *Biometrika Tables for Statisticians*, Vol. 1, 3rd edition, Cambridge, 1966, Table 8. Reprinted by permission of the Biometrika Trustees.

TABLE 8 CHI-SQUARE DISTRIBUTION 895

TABLE 9. F Distribution

F Critical Points
Prob-value
Critical point
F

Degrees of Freedom for Denominator

	Prob-Value	\multicolumn{10}{c}{Degrees of Freedom for Numerator}
		1	2	3	4	5	6	8	10	20	40
1	.25	5.83	7.50	8.20	8.58	8.82	8.98	9.19	9.32	9.58	9.71
	.10	39.9	49.5	53.6	55.8	57.2	58.2	59.4	60.2	61.7	62.5
	.05	161	200	216	225	230	234	239	242	248	251
2	.25	2.57	3.00	3.15	3.23	3.28	3.31	3.35	3.38	3.43	3.45
	.10	8.53	9.00	9.16	9.24	9.29	9.33	9.37	9.39	9.44	9.47
	.05	18.5	19.0	19.2	19.2	19.3	19.3	19.4	19.4	19.4	19.5
	.01	98.5	99.0	99.2	99.2	99.3	99.3	99.4	99.4	99.4	99.5
	.001	998	999	999	999	999	999	999	999	999	999
3	.25	2.02	2.28	2.36	2.39	2.41	2.42	2.44	2.44	2.46	2.47
	.10	5.54	5.46	5.39	5.34	5.31	5.28	5.25	5.23	5.18	5.16
	.05	10.1	9.55	9.28	9.12	9.10	8.94	8.85	8.79	8.66	8.59
	.01	34.1	30.8	29.5	28.7	28.2	27.9	27.5	27.2	26.7	26.4
	.001	167	149	141	137	135	133	131	129	126	125
4	.25	1.81	2.00	2.05	2.06	2.07	2.08	2.08	2.08	2.08	2.08
	.10	4.54	4.32	4.19	4.11	4.05	4.01	3.95	3.92	3.84	3.80
	.05	7.71	6.94	6.59	6.39	6.26	6.16	6.04	5.96	5.80	5.72
	.01	21.2	18.0	16.7	16.0	15.5	15.2	14.8	14.5	14.0	13.7
	.001	74.1	61.3	56.2	53.4	51.7	50.5	49.0	48.1	46.1	45.1
5	.25	1.69	1.85	1.88	1.89	1.89	1.89	1.89	1.89	1.88	1.88
	.10	4.06	3.78	3.62	3.52	3.45	3.40	3.34	3.30	3.21	3.16
	.05	6.61	5.79	5.41	5.19	5.05	4.95	4.82	4.74	4.56	4.46
	.01	16.3	13.3	12.1	11.4	11.0	10.7	10.3	10.1	9.55	9.29
	.001	47.2	37.1	33.2	31.1	29.8	28.8	27.6	26.9	25.4	24.6
6	.25	1.62	1.76	1.78	1.79	1.79	1.78	1.77	1.77	1.76	1.75
	.10	3.78	3.46	3.29	3.18	3.11	3.05	2.98	2.94	2.84	2.78
	.05	5.99	5.14	4.76	4.53	4.39	4.28	4.15	4.06	3.87	3.77
	.01	13.7	10.9	9.78	9.15	8.75	8.47	8.10	7.87	7.40	7.14
	.001	35.5	27.0	23.7	21.9	20.8	20.0	19.0	18.4	17.1	16.4
7	.25	1.57	1.70	1.72	1.72	1.71	1.71	1.70	1.69	1.67	1.66
	.10	3.59	3.26	3.07	2.96	2.88	2.83	2.75	2.70	2.59	2.54
	.05	5.59	4.74	4.35	4.12	3.97	3.87	3.73	3.64	3.44	3.34
	.01	12.2	9.55	8.45	7.85	7.46	7.19	6.84	6.62	6.16	5.91
	.001	29.3	21.7	18.8	17.2	16.2	15.5	14.6	14.1	12.9	12.3
8	.25	1.54	1.66	1.67	1.66	1.66	1.65	1.64	1.63	1.61	1.59
	.10	3.46	3.11	2.92	2.81	2.73	2.67	2.59	2.54	2.42	2.36
	.05	5.32	4.46	4.07	3.84	3.69	3.58	3.44	3.35	3.15	3.04
	.01	11.3	8.65	7.59	7.01	6.63	6.37	6.03	5.81	5.36	5.12
	.001	25.4	18.5	15.8	14.4	13.5	12.9	12.0	11.5	10.5	9.92

TABLE 9. *F* Distribution (continued)

	Prob-Value	Degrees of Freedom for Numerator									
		1	2	3	4	5	6	8	10	20	40
9	.25	1.51	1.62	1.63	1.63	1.62	1.61	1.60	1.59	1.56	1.55
	.10	3.36	3.01	2.81	2.69	2.61	2.55	2.47	2.42	2.30	2.23
	.05	5.12	4.26	3.86	3.63	3.48	3.37	3.23	3.14	2.94	2.83
	.01	10.6	8.02	6.99	6.42	6.06	5.80	5.47	5.26	4.81	4.57
	.001	22.9	16.4	13.9	12.6	11.7	11.1	10.4	9.89	8.90	8.37
10	.25	1.49	1.60	1.60	1.59	1.59	1.58	1.56	1.55	1.52	1.51
	.10	3.28	2.92	2.73	2.61	2.52	2.46	2.38	2.32	2.20	2.13
	.05	4.96	4.10	3.71	3.48	3.33	3.22	3.07	2.98	2.77	2.66
	.01	10.0	7.56	6.55	5.99	5.64	5.39	5.06	4.85	4.41	4.17
	.001	21.0	14.9	12.6	11.3	10.5	9.92	9.20	8.75	7.80	7.30
12	.25	1.56	1.56	1.56	1.55	1.54	1.53	1.51	1.50	1.47	1.45
	.10	3.18	2.81	2.61	2.48	2.39	2.33	2.24	2.19	2.06	1.99
	.05	4.75	3.89	3.49	3.26	3.11	3.00	2.85	2.75	2.54	2.43
	.01	9.33	6.93	5.95	5.41	5.06	4.82	4.50	4.30	3.86	3.62
	.001	18.6	13.0	10.8	9.63	8.89	8.38	7.71	7.29	6.40	5.93
14	.25	1.44	1.53	1.53	1.52	1.51	1.50	1.48	1.46	1.43	1.41
	.10	3.10	2.73	2.52	2.39	2.31	2.24	2.15	2.10	1.96	1.89
	.05	4.60	3.74	3.34	3.11	2.96	2.85	2.70	2.60	2.39	2.27
	.01	8.86	5.51	5.56	5.04	4.69	4.46	4.14	3.94	3.51	3.27
	.001	17.1	11.8	9.73	8.62	7.92	7.43	6.80	6.40	5.56	5.10
16	.25	1.42	1.51	1.51	1.50	1.48	1.48	1.46	1.45	1.40	1.37
	.10	3.05	2.67	2.46	2.33	2.24	2.18	2.09	2.03	1.89	1.81
	.05	4.49	3.63	3.24	3.01	2.85	2.74	2.59	2.49	2.28	2.15
	.01	8.53	6.23	5.29	4.77	4.44	4.20	3.89	3.69	3.26	3.02
	.001	16.1	11.0	9.00	7.94	7.27	6.81	6.19	5.81	4.99	4.54
18	.25	1.41	1.50	1.49	1.48	1.46	1.45	1.43	1.42	1.38	1.35
	.10	3.01	2.62	2.42	2.29	2.20	2.13	2.04	1.98	1.84	1.75
	.05	4.41	3.55	3.16	2.93	2.77	2.66	2.51	2.41	2.19	2.06
	.01	8.29	6.01	5.09	4.58	4.25	4.01	3.71	3.51	3.08	2.84
	.001	15.4	10.4	8.49	7.46	6.81	6.35	5.76	5.39	4.59	4.15
20	.25	1.40	1.49	1.48	1.46	1.45	1.44	1.42	1.40	1.36	1.33
	.10	2.97	2.59	2.38	2.25	2.16	2.09	2.00	1.94	1.79	1.71
	.05	4.35	3.49	3.10	2.87	2.71	2.60	2.45	2.35	2.12	1.99
	.01	8.10	5.85	4.94	4.43	4.10	3.87	3.56	3.37	2.94	2.69
	.001	14.8	9.95	8.10	7.10	6.46	6.02	5.44	5.08	4.29	3.86
30	.25	1.38	1.45	1.44	1.42	1.41	1.39	1.37	1.35	1.30	1.27
	.10	2.88	2.49	2.28	2.14	2.05	1.98	1.88	1.82	1.67	1.57
	.05	4.17	3.32	2.92	2.69	2.53	2.42	2.27	2.16	1.93	1.79
	.01	7.56	5.39	4.51	4.02	3.70	3.47	3.17	2.98	2.55	2.30
	.001	13.3	8.77	7.05	6.12	5.53	5.12	4.58	4.24	3.49	3.07
40	.25	1.36	1.44	1.42	1.40	1.39	1.37	1.35	1.33	1.28	1.24
	.10	2.84	2.44	2.23	2.09	2.00	1.93	1.83	1.76	1.61	1.51
	.05	4.08	3.23	2.84	2.61	2.45	2.34	2.18	2.08	1.84	1.69
	.01	7.31	5.18	4.31	3.83	3.51	3.29	2.99	2.80	2.37	2.11
	.001	12.6	8.25	6.60	5.70	5.13	4.73	4.21	3.87	3.15	2.73

Degrees of Freedom for Denominator

TABLE 9 *F* DISTRIBUTION 897

TABLE 9. F Distribution (continued)

		Prob-Value	Degrees of Freedom for Numerator									
			1	2	3	4	5	6	8	10	20	40
	50	.05	4.03	3.18	2.79	2.56	2.40	2.29	2.13	2.02	1.78	1.63
		.01	7.17	5.06	4.20	3.72	3.41	3.18	2.88	2.70	2.26	2.00
	60	.25	1.35	1.42	1.41	1.38	1.37	1.35	1.32	1.30	1.25	1.21
		.10	2.79	2.39	2.18	2.04	1.95	1.87	1.77	1.71	1.54	1.44
		.05	4.00	3.15	2.76	2.53	2.37	2.25	2.10	1.99	1.75	1.59
		.01	7.08	4.98	4.13	3.65	3.34	3.12	2.82	2.63	2.20	1.94
		.001	12.0	7.76	6.17	5.31	4.76	4.37	3.87	3.54	2.83	2.41
	120	.25	1.34	1.40	1.39	1.37	1.35	1.33	1.30	1.28	1.22	1.18
		.10	2.75	2.35	2.13	1.99	1.90	1.82	1.72	1.65	1.48	1.37
		.05	3.92	3.07	2.68	2.45	2.29	2.17	2.02	1.91	1.66	1.50
		.01	6.85	4.79	3.95	3.48	3.17	2.96	2.66	2.47	2.03	1.76
		.001	11.4	7.32	5.79	4.95	4.42	4.04	3.55	3.24	2.53	2.11

Degrees of freedom for denominator

For values not listed in the table, an approximation can be obtained by linear interpolation. The example in Chapter 21 is based on 2 d.f. in the numerator and 48 d.f. in the denominator. Noting that 48 d.f. is $8/10$ of the way between 40 and 50, the critical value of F at the 5% level of significance can be approximated as follows:

$$F_{2,48} \approx 3.23 - .8(3.23 - 3.18)$$
$$\approx 3.23 - .8(.05)$$
$$\approx 3.19$$

Answers to Selected Problems

Chapter 2
39.c. 228 light 229 heavy
  d. 53 heavy half
40.a. 212
  b. overlap at 3
  c. 1596
  d. 1425
  e. 1846
  f. 77%
41. usage almost evenly split

Chapter 3
22. 7,9
37.a. Cum. r.f.: .13, .31, .4, .56, .69,
   .82, .93, 1.00
  d. upper 18% consume 36%
  of the cereal eaten

Chapter 4
7.a. mean
  b. mode
  c. median
10. geometric mean

17.b. 3.18
  c. 3
18. 2.167
19.a. 143
  c. 21
  d. 14.7%
21.a. 1
  b. mode
  c. 20%
25.a. 44.4%
  b. 73.4%
29.b. no more than 21%
31. 22 to 50 thousand
35.a. 96%
  c. 26.6%
  d. 66.7%
  e. about $\frac{1}{4}$ of employees
   account for about $\frac{2}{3}$ of the
   absences
41.a. arithmetic = 10.65%, geometric = 10.52%
  b. −20.21%, −20.63%

Chapter 5
8. 36
11. .075
20. .7
24.a. 0
  b. 36
  c. 2^{36}
29.a. $\frac{1}{3}$
  b. $\frac{2}{9}$
  c. $\frac{4}{9}$
  d. $\frac{5}{9}$
  e. 0
  f. $\frac{2}{3}$
  g. 0
  h. $\frac{4}{9}$
  i. 1
  j. $\frac{2}{3}$
32. .27
38. $\frac{4}{7}$
39.a. $\frac{30}{64}$
  b. $\frac{30}{56}$
40.a. $\frac{5}{8}$
  b. $\frac{5}{16}$

PROBLEM 37c. Household and Usage Concentration   (Chapter 3)

HOUSEHOLD CONCENTRATION: CUMULATIVE % HOUSEHOLDS (X AXIS)	USAGE X	FREQUENCY F	= USAGE DAYS	USAGE DAYS SUBTOTALS AS % OF TOTAL USAGE	USAGE CONCENTRATION: CUMULATIVE % USAGE DAYS (Y AXIS)
.13 × 100 = 13%	0	6	0	$\frac{0}{142}$ × 100 = 0	0
.31 × 100 = 31%	1	8	8	$\frac{8}{142}$ × 100 = 5.63%	5.63%
.40 × 100 = 40%	2	4	8	$\frac{8}{142}$ × 100 = 5.63%	11.26%
.56 × 100 = 56%	3	7	21	$\frac{21}{142}$ × 100 = 14.79%	26.05%
.69 × 100 = 69%	4	6	24	$\frac{24}{142}$ × 100 = 16.90%	42.95%
.82 × 100 = 82%	5	6	30	$\frac{30}{142}$ × 100 = 21.13%	64.08%
.93 × 100 = 93%	6	5	30	$\frac{30}{142}$ × 100 = 21.13%	85.21%
1.00 × 100 = 100%	7	3	21	$\frac{21}{142}$ × 100 = 14.79%	100.0%
			142		

Chapter 6

8.a. .85
  b. .15
10. .15
13. .42
15.a. .57
  b. .5
  c. .4
  d. .33
  e. .2
18.a. .3
  b. .65
  c. .545
23.d. .65
  f. $\frac{7}{13}$
  h. $\frac{1}{3}$
  j. $\frac{6}{13}$
  l. $\frac{2}{3}$
  m. .15
  p. .30
26.a. .36
  b. .48
  c. .16
30. .060
32.a. .5
  b. .25
33.a. .64
  b. .09
  c. .04
  d. no

Chapter 7

10.a. yes
  b. no
  d. 50
12.b. 0–3
  c. $P(3) = \frac{8}{27}$; $P(2)$ $\frac{12}{27}$; $P(1) = \frac{6}{27}$; $P(0) = \frac{1}{27}$
14.a. 8
  b. 8
  c. 8.05
15.b. RV from 2 to 12
  c. $P(2) = \frac{1}{36}$, $P(3) = \frac{2}{36}$, $P(4) = \frac{3}{36}$, $P(5) = \frac{4}{36}$, $P(6) = \frac{5}{36}$, $P(7) = \frac{6}{36}$, $P(8) = \frac{5}{36}$, $P(9) = \frac{4}{36}$, $P(10) = \frac{3}{36}$, $P(11) = \frac{2}{36}$, $P(12) = \frac{1}{36}$
  d. 7
16. 2.41
17. 2.17 to 11.83

20.d. 80% of time within 10% of cost
  e. $E(R) = 1.02$
  g. $\sigma_R = .116$
  h. no, no
21.a. $\mu_X = 12$, $\mu_Y = 10$
  b. cov $(XY) = -60$
  c. $\sigma_X = 7.48$, $\sigma_Y = 8.94$
  d. $\rho = -.896$
27.a. 16.5, $\sigma = 8.92$, $\sigma^2 = 79.5$
  b. 17, 9.31, 86.67
28.a. $\sigma^2 = 12$, $\sigma = 3.46$, $\sigma_W^2 = 26.67$, $\sigma_W = 5.16$
  b. $\sigma^2 = 72$, $\sigma = 8.49$, $\sigma_W^2 = 80$, $\sigma_W = 8.9$

Chapter 8

11.a. 1600
  b. 10
  c. 16,000
  d. 48,000
12. .384
21. .5443, .021
25.a. 8
  b. 8
  c. 9
  d. 12
  e. 12
  f. 12
  g. 11
27.a. .7393
  b. 7393
  c. .3590
29. .8891
35. .1643 and zero
38.a. almost zero
  b. almost zero
  c. .375
  d. .75
39.a. ± .447
  b. ± .354
  c. ± .071
  d. ± .045
46. $600
47.a. $P(0) = .1678$, $P(1) = .3355$, $P(2) = .2936$, $P(3) = .1468$, $P(4) = .0459$, $P(5) = .0092$, $P(6) = .0011$, $P(7) = .0001$
  b. 25.78 yes
  c. .2031

Chapter 9

5.a. 5040
  b. 4
  c. 10
7.a. $C_3^5 = 10$
  b. with: 70^3; without: 328,440
  c. with: 900; without: 870
  d. with: 3,087,000,000; without: 2,857,420,000
  e. with: 10,000,000,000; without: 9,034,500,000
  f. with: .3087; without: .316
22.a. .0377
  b. .0377
  c. .1563
  d. .1755
26.a. $C_6^{4000}(.002)^6(.998)^{3994}$
  b. too burdensome
  c. 8
  d. 7.98
  e. 8
  f. .122
32.a. .018
  b. .179
  c. .821
33.a. .38
  b. .0045
34.a. 7
  b. 120
35.a. .1736
36.a. .0183
  b. .0733
  c. .1954
  d. .5665
  e. .7619
  f. .4335
37.a. .6065
  b. .3033
  c. .0902
  d. .9856
  e. .0902
  f. .0256
38.a. .3679
  b. .6321
  c. .3679
  d. .0613
45.a. binomial
  b. .0302, virtually zero

Chapter 10

3.a. .1554

b. .1554
c. .2538
d. .2538
e. .0968
f. .7698
g. .9037
h. .8858
5.a. 2.33
  b. −1.645
  c. ±1
  d. 1.285
  e. −1.12
  f. ±1.645
  g. ±2.575
6.a. .49865
  b. .1587
  c. .3849
  d. .6826
  e. .5
  f. .9993
10. 27%
13. $E(Y) = 210$
14. 234 lamps
15. every 49 days
16. .02
20.a. .56
  b. .46
  c. .63
  d. .82
21. 1550 days
22.a. .9772
  b. .0668
  c. .0228
  d. almost zero
23.a. 4347.82
  b. .0537
  c. .999
26. $996

Chapter 11
9.a. .1974
  b. .5160
  c. .975
  e. $n = 106$
14.a. .2033
  b. $1.05 million per month or
    $12.77 million per year
16. 6.9 to 11.7 percent
22. UCL = 5.801; LCL = 3.199;
  .1357
25. UCL = .418, LCL = .142

28. UCL = 2.35 million, LCL =
  1.65 million
33.a. $n = 4268$
  b. $8936
38.a. 45 stores, $S_{\bar{X}} = 2.24$
  b. UCL = 164,970, LCL =
    123,030
  c. by 10,000 = .267, by 20,000
    = .0264

Chapter 12
33.a. normal
  b. normal
  c. normal
  d. normal
  e. normal
  f. t distribution
  g. normal
  h. none
35.a. .0027
  b. yes, prob-value < .01
  d. the first set
  e. $\beta_\mu \quad = .3372,$
    $\beta_\mu \quad = .9427$
36.a. .6892
  b. not rejected at 1% and 5%
  c. $\beta = .9439$
  e. $n = 1651$
37.a. $n = 182$
  b. .1357
  c. cannot reject H_0
39.a. accept if $9.87 \leq \bar{X} \leq 10.13$
  b. reject since $10.15 > 10.13$
41. reject since $80 < 89.5$
43.a. cannot reject since
    $117 < 116.5$
  b. .7422
  c. .0885
47.a. .2810
  b. 35
  c. reject since $7.25 < 7.32$

Chapter 13
18.a. $m_1 = 300, m_2 = 600$
  b. $\sigma_{\bar{X}_1} = 344.7$
  c. $\sigma_{\bar{X}_2} = 723.7$
  d. 345.6
  e. 53,600 miles; 2,680,000 miles
19.a. local: 31,324.4 to 32,675.6
    miles; intercity: 84,602.9 to
    87,397.1 miles

b. all: 52,923 to 54,277
26.a. $\mu = .013, \sigma_D = .01$
  b. .00001
  c. UCL = .016, LCL = .010
28.a. reject H_0, prob-value = .003
34.b. prob-value $\leq .01$, reject
35.a. $d = 2.2$
  b. $D = 6.2$
  c. S_D (pooled) = 4.427

Chapter 14
4. 1, C; 2, B; 3, A; 4, C; 5, B; 6, B; 7, B
5. no
6.a. $r = .185$
  b. $r^2 = .034$
7.a. $S_r = .288$
  b. no
11. 1.8
12.a. $b = 1.4236$
  b. $a = 6.61$
  c. $r = .847$
  d. $r^2 = .718$
  e. $\hat{Y} = 6.61 + 1.4236X$
  f. $\hat{Y} = 15.1516$
13.a. $S_{Y.X} = 3.924$
  b. $S_b = .3158$
17. no
21.a. $S_b = .3158$
  b. $S_{\hat{Y}.X} = 2.986$
  c. $S_{F.X} = 4.931$
  d. $S_a = 3.570$
  e. UCL = 2.152, LCL = .695
  f. UCL = 15.0
  g. UL = 26.0
23. $(\bar{X}, \bar{Y})$
26. (a)
32.a. disagree
  b. disagree
  c. disagree
  d. disagree
  e. disagree
  f. disagree
  g. agree
  h. disagree
42.a. $\hat{Y} = 57.09 + 12.2X$

43.b. UL = 169.5

c. UL = 183.5

d. UL = 95.9

e. 8 is least, 3 is most

f. yes

45.a. $\hat{Y} = 108.5 + 52.3X, R^2 = .76$

Chapter 15

15.a. $\widehat{\log Y} = 1.01 - .272 \log X;$
$R^2 = .97$

b. 27.2 % decrease

17.a. decrease by 2.30%

b. +16.9%

c. −1.15

23.c. (1) linear: $\hat{Y} = 7.99 + 1.39X;$
$r^2 = .912$ (2) log-log: $\log Y =$
$1.65 + .64 \log X; r^2 = .958$

33.b. yes

c. 16.58 m.p.g.

e. no

Chapter 16

1.a. 52.2

b. R^2, S_{YX}

c. S_{b_1}

13.a. agree

b. agree

c. disagree

d. agree

e. disagree

f. disagree

14.a. $\hat{Y} = 2.60 + .80X_1 - .60X_2$

15.a. $S_{Y.12} = \sqrt{\dfrac{4.4}{7}} = .7928$

b. adjusted $R^2 = .83$

23.b. $2.57

c. $1.175

d. no

24.a. $.1645

b. $8.02

25.a. no

b. no

29.a. $\widehat{OC} = 158, 327 - 59.28X_1$
$- 228.09X_2 + 46,211.4X_3$
$+ 16,060.6X_4;$ adjusted

$R^2 = .33$

33.a. 638 lb, 460 lb

b. standard deviation of
residuals = 58

c. 514 lb > 460 lb

34.a. $\hat{Y} = -8.896 + .449X_1 +$
$.690X_2$

Chapter 17

4. 18.407

13.a. trend, seasonal, random

b. trend and long term cyclical

c. seasonal and random

d. trend and random

e. residual

15.a. trend

b. periodicity

c. random

19.a. 3175.67

b. $S_1 = 554.66, S_2 = -130,$
$S_3 = -544.67, S_4 = 120$

c. $T_1 = -72.42, T_2 = 430.08,$
$T_3 = -357.67$

22. (first 3 values) 3203.625,
3396.5, 3621.125

24.a. $\hat{Y} = 16.073 + .273T$

25.a. $\hat{Y} = 23.23 + .239T - 5.5D$

34.b. $\hat{Y} = -1.159 + 23.44T$

c. yes

35.b. rises, levels off, rises again

37.b. $\hat{Y} = 8.07 + .041T$

Chapter 18

5. $.70

10. no: CPI + 18%, rent + 13%

36. DJIA = 1731.5

37.a. bottles = 116, caps = 150,
label = 200, cartons = 167

b. 158.25

c. 125.8

d. 123.1

e. 123.2

38.a. 14.4

b. Laspeyres

c. 13.9

d. Paasche

39.a. 4-function = 16.4; single
memory = 15.2; scientific
= 10.6; programmable
= 14.9

b. 14.3

c. 13.9

e. 14.1

Chapter 19

10.a. $\hat{Y} = -88,420 + 101,860T$
$+ 252,530Q_2 + 381,910Q_3$
$+ 25,123Q_4$

d. MAD = 139,102;
MAPE = 3.12%

e. $\hat{Y} = -305,346.29$
$+ 1,629,822.2T; R^2 = .99$

11.c. $\hat{Y} = 180,580 + 87,976T$
$+ 312.14T^2$

e. MAD = 249,472;
MAPE = 5.5%

12.b. MAD = 1,097,670;
MAPE = 25.32%

d. MAD = 339,093;
MAPE = 7.50%

14. 31 runs

16.a. $\hat{S} = -.026 + .091$ highway;
$r^2 = .47$

b. yes, no

d. $\hat{S} = .387 + .012B; r^2 = .91$

17.a. $\hat{S} = .081 + .033H + .011B$

c. adjusted $R^2 = .951$

d. $S_{Y.12} = .0733$ compared to
.241 and .098

22.b. $\widehat{DD}_t = 2351 - .147DD_{t-1}$
$- .648DD_{t-4}$

c. $\tilde{Y}_{81I} = 4,537,271; \tilde{Y}_{81II}$
$= 4,900,051$

d. $QI - 70,459: 1.6\%; QII$
422,481: 7.9%

Chapter 20

20.a. $\chi^2 = 1.484;$ at $\alpha = .10,$
cannot reject H_0

b. $\chi^2 = 7.01;$ at $\alpha = .05,$ reject
H_0

22.a. $\chi^2 = .77$

b. cannot reject H_0

23.b. $\chi^2 = 14.51$ (doctor-lawyers);
$\chi^2 = 18.69$ (bankers-
draftsman)

28.a. $\chi^2 = 4.43$

b. at $\alpha = .01,$ reject H_0

Chapter 21

8.b. $F_{3,32} > 2.28$

11.a. MS between = .555, MS
within = .959, F = .579

b. $F_{2, 36, \alpha=.05} = 3.26$; since $.579 < 3.26$ accept H_0

17.a. $F_c = 1.51$

b. cannot reject at $\alpha = .05$

21.b. $F_c = 2.720$, cannot reject at $\alpha = .05$

23.b. $F_c = 1.95$, accept H_0

Chapter 22

15.a. $W = 70$

b. $Z = -2.65$

c. prob-value $= .008$, reject H_0

16. $K = .882$, reject H_0

17. prob-value $= .008$

21.a. Friedman Test

b. prob-value $< .01$

22.a. Sign Test; binomial

b. prob-value $= .289$

23.a. Kruskal-Wallis Test

b. $\chi^2_{2, \alpha=.05} = 5.991 > .173$, accept H_0

25.a. yes

b. prob-value $= .025$

26.a. prob-value $= .67$

b. accept H_0

27.a. $r_s = .673$

b. $t_{d.f.=8, \alpha=.01} = 3.355 > 2.57$, cannot reject H_0

Chapter 23

10.b. buy option

14.c. lease

15.b. buy option

c. $35,000

d. $7500

17.a. $K_u = $10/case$

b. $K_o = $2.71/case$

c. .786 fractile

Index

defined, 37–38
scales, 37–41
Measurement, of location. *See*
Central tendency; Summary
measures
Median
in decision making, 125–26
defined, 105–6
and effect of skewness, 123–25
estimating, 110–11, 359–60
and probability distribution, 221
runs above and below, 810–11
See also Central tendency; Mean;
Mode; Summary measures
Mesokurtic degree of peakedness, 128
Miller, Merton, 101
Minor premise, 12
Mode
defined, 105
effect of skewness, 123–25
estimating, 110
and probability distribution, 219
See also Central tendency; Mean;
Median; Summary measures
Monotonicity, 828
Moody's Investment Service, 41
Moving average series
and business forecasting, 711–12
and ratio, 653–56
smoothing, in time series, 650–53
See also Business forecasting; Time
series analysis
MS between, 791–94
MS within, 790–91
MSE. *See* Mean squared error
Multicollinearity, 599–602
Multiple coefficient of determination,
589
Multiple regression
with autoregressive terms, 737–40
compared to simple regression
results, 590–93
computer output for, 584–88,
594–97
estimating assembling cost, 609–12
food expenditure study, 606–9
job evaluation, 612–18
and specification bias, 593–99
standard deviation of residuals and
R^2, 588–90
using 0, 1 dummy variables, 605–6
See also Regression
Multiple regression coefficients
interpretation of, 583–84
measuring importance of variable
in determining Y, 602–4
and multicollinearity, 599–602

and multiple correlation coefficient, 589–90
Multiple regression equation
defined, 579
determining, 582–83
and Y intercept:
determining, 602–4
shifting, 605–9
Multiple regression model
assumptions about error term ϵ,
579–80, 581
and "e" term, 581
equation, 579, 582–83
least square regression plane,
581–82
population regression plane, 580–81
population scatter diagram, 580
Multiplication rule
and advertising effectiveness,
196–97
and quality control, 195–96
sampling account receivable, 205–6
for statistically independent events,
198–99
Multiplicative model, time series,
644–45
Multivariate data, 30
Mutually exclusive events, 184–85
Mutually exclusive outcomes, 143–44

Nader, Ralph, 25, 26
Nelson, Gaylord, 3
Net regression coefficient, 604
Nominal scale, 38, 39
Nonlinearity and residuals, 503
Nonparametric tests
chi-square test of independence,
775–78
classification of, 832
defined, 807–8
for independent samples:
Kruskal-Wallis test, 824–25, 826
Mann-Whitney U test, 814–15,
817–18
Wilcoxon ranked sum test,
814–15, 824
Wilcoxon two-sample ranked
sum test, 815–17
for matched pair samples:
Friedman test, 826–27
Sign test, 818, 821–24
Wilcoxon signed-rank sum test,
818, 826
vs. parametric tests, 807–8
and rank correlation:
calculating, 829–31

Spearman's rank correlation
coefficient, 828–29
runs test, sequential randomness,
808–13
See also Chi-square statistic; Parametric tests
Nonrandom samples, 428
Nonrandom sampling, and sample
design, 423. *See also* Random
sampling
Nonrandom sequence, 810
Nonresponse bias, 427
Normal curves, bell-shaped, 319–21
Normal density functions, 86–87. *See
also* Standard normal density
function
Normal distributions
approximating binomial distributions, 329–33
an empirical demonstration of,
337–41
and normal curve:
bell-shaped, 319–21
central limit theorem, 341–43
using probability table for,
327–29
and normal model, 344–47
probability calculation for, 334–37
and sampling distribution of
sample mean, 343–44
in small size, two-sample design,
444
and standard normal density function, 321–27
wholesaling strategy, 347–49
See also Binomial distribution;
Standard normal density functions
Nuisance variables, 548–50
Null event
assigning probabilities for, 184
defined, 150
Null hypothesis
and categorical variables, 770–72
defined, 396
in hypothesis testing, 398–406
See also Alternative hypothesis;
Hypothesis testing
Numerical information. *See* Data

Observations
and forecasting new, 493–95, 598
and right class size, 75–81
tracking, 727
Ogives, 87–90
One-sample tests, 414–16

polynomial regression, 533–36
Regression equation, 462
Regression line
  and analyzing residuals, 501–5
  approximating curvilinear relation-
    ship, 540–41
  finding least squares line, 481,
    490–91:
    comparing prediction confidence
      intervals, 507–10
    improving prediction accuracy,
      510–13
  forecasting a new observation,
    493–95
  and least squares method of fitting,
    479–81
  sampling variation of computed,
    490–93
  simple linear, 478–79
  and standard deviation of, 491–93
  and standard deviation of residuals,
    484–87
Relative dispersion, 120–23. See also
  Dispersion
Relative frequencies, 59
  density, 70–71
  procedures, 152
  vs. probability distribution, 216–17
  See also Frequency distribution;
    Probability distribution
Relative frequency density, 70. See
  also Density histograms; Frequency histograms
Relative frequency distribution, 59.
  See also Frequency distribution
Reliability level
  defined, 275–76
  and larger samples, 277–78, 279
  and precision, 278
  and serial correlation, 649
Residual component, 644
Residual dependency, 502
Residuals
  analyzing, 501–2
  cyclical, 736–37
  and heteroskedasticity, 503
  and market model, 503–5
  and nonlinearity, 503
  standard deviation of, 484–86, 509:
    and R^2, 588–90
  and time series analysis, 659
  See also Time series analysis
Round method of grouping data,
  65–66
Runs
  in sequential randomness, 810–13
  test, 728–29, 735

Sample
  cluster, 434–36
  defined, 426
  discrete, 224
  and expert judgment, 16
  in inductive logic, 13
  quota, 428–29
  random, 15–17
  stratified, 432–34
  systematic, 431–32
  See also Random sample
Sample design
  and random sampling plans, 423,
    429–36
  and two-sample designs, 438–41:
    matched pairs, 443–44
    small samples, 444–47
  and types of bias, 426–29
  See also Experimental design;
    Sampling; Two-sample designs
Sample mean
  empirical distribution of, 337–41
  sampling distribution of, 272–76,
    343–44
  See also Mean
Sample median, 359–60. See also
  Median
Sample population, 247–48, 424–25,
  770–72
  and alternative population param-
    eters, 258–60
Sample proportion, sampling distribution of, 272–76, 299–300
Sample regression line. See Least
  squares line
Sample regression plane, 581
Sample size
  and binomial distributions, 319–21
  determining:
    in hypothesis testing, 412–13
    sampling with replacement,
      372–75
    sampling without replacement,
      376–78
  and diminishing returns, 282–87
  and effect on sampling distribution,
    276–79
  improving prediction accuracy,
    510–12
  and law of averages, 279–81
  and role in forecasting, 508–9
  vs. sample precision, 375–76
  See also Large samples; Small
    samples
Sample spaces, 145, 146–47, 149
  discrete, 224
  and random variables, 213–15

Sample statistic, 19, 249, 251
  and alternative population param-
    eters, 258–60
  and empirical experiments, 250–51
  and estimation. See Estimation
  and variation, 251–54, 256
Sampling
  and expert judgment, 16
  process, 361
  random, 16–17
  and sample design, 423
  unit, 425
Sampling bias
  and "larger is better" trap, 429
  measurement, 426–27
  nonrandom samples, 428
  nonresponse, 427
  quota samples, 428–29
  selection, 426
  volunteer, 427–28
Sampling distribution
  defined, 249–50
  effect of sample size on, 276–79
  and empirical experiment, 250–51,
    337–40
  mean of, 343–44
  and number of runs, 811
  probability calculations for, 334–37
  for sample proportions:
    sampling without replacement,
      299–300
    standard deviation of, 277
  See also Binomial distribution;
    Probability distribution
Sampling error, 19, 358–59
  of estimation, 248–49, 256–58
  in indexes, 694–95, 701
Sampling, over time and space. See
  Poisson distribution
Sampling plans. See Random sampling plans
Sampling with replacement, 198
  and binomial formula, 267–70
  defined, 158
  determining required sample size,
    372–75
  and number of elementary events,
    163
Sampling without replacement
  binomial approximation of hyper-
    geometric probabilities, 302–5
  defined, 158
  determining sample size, 376–78
  hypergeometric distribution,
    297–99, 301–2
  interval estimation for, 370–71
  permutations, 293–97

sampling distribution for sample
proportion, 299–300
Sampling terminology, 423–26
Sampling variation
and estimation error, 248–49,
256–58
and law of averages, 279–81
Sampling, and application of statistical methods to
coin tossing, 143–50, 151–52,
219–20
dice, 143, 149, 150, 185, 338–39
poker chips, 247–48, 251–53,
254–56, 274, 276, 279–85,
293–94
Scales
interval, 38–39
of measurement, 37–39
nominal, 38, 39
ordinal, 38, 39
ratio, 39
Scatter diagram
for population, 580
in regression analysis, 460–61
Seasonal adjustment
and autocorrelation function,
734–35
calculating seasonal indexes,
654–56
and Consumer Price Index, 693–94
and deseasonalizing data, 656–58
and indexes, 701
and least squares method, 646–49
ratio-to-moving averages method,
653–56
and seasonal variation, 637–39
and seasonal weights, 654
smoothing by moving averages,
650–53
and trend, 642–43, 645–46, 646–49
See also Business forecasting;
Indexes; Time series analysis;
Trend
Secular movements, 637
Selection bias, 426
Self-selection bias, 10
Semi-interquartile range, 114
Sequence,
and data analysis, 30–31
and random sampling, 247–48
See also Business forecasting; Time
series analysis; Trend
Sequence plot, business forecasting,
724–29
Sequential randomness, 808–13
Serial correlation,
and business forecasting, 712–14

defined, 502
and reliability level, 649
in time series, 649
Sets
equality of, 146
and random sampling ingredients,
146
and subsets, 147–49
Shifting intercept, multiple regression, 605–6
Sign test, 821–24
Significance level,
comparing with prob-value, 404–6
of test, 397, 398, 403
Simple aggregative indexes, 673–76
unweighted, 675–76
weighted, 676–77
Simple index, 670. *See also* Indexes
Simple linear model, 474–78. *See also*
Correlation; Regression
Simple random samples, 16–17,
156–58, 429–31. *See also* Random
samples; Random sampling;
Sampling
Simple regression. *See* Multiple regres-
sion
Six-fifteen rule, 82
Skewness
and binomial distributions, 319–21
defined, 102, 123–25
measures of, 127–28
See also Central tendency; Sum-
mary measures
Slope coefficient, 487–89
in regression analysis, 463
Small samples
advantages of, 591–92
and t test, 814
tests, 416–17
and two-sample design, 444–47
See also Large samples; Sample size
Smooth curves, 85–86
Smoothing, exponential, 715–17
Spearman's rank correlation coefficient, 828–31
Specification bias, 594–99
Split-sample comparison, 83
Sports, and statistical methods, 5, 279,
295, 557
Spurious correlation, 507. *See also*
Correlation
Standard deviation
of binomial distributions, 271–72
and Chebyshev's Inequality,
119–20, 301, 302
defined, 116–17
and distribution of sample proportions, 277

of forecast error, 493
of hypergeometric distribution, 301
of probability distribution, 222
of regression line, 491–93
of residuals, 484–86, 588–90
of sample proportions, 237
of stratified items, 434
See also Central tendency; Dispersion; Mean absolute deviation;
Summary measures
Standard error
of difference, 438
of estimate, 485, 533
of the mean, 343–44
of stratified sample, 433
Standard normal curve
decline in probability, 325–27
measurement of, 322–25
probability table for, 327–29
Standard normal density function
approximating binomial distributions, 329–33
and central limit theorem, 341–43
decline of probability, 325–27
defined, 319, 321–22
measuring probability for normal
curve, 322–25, 328
and table of areas, 326, 327–29
See also Normal density function
Standardized regression coefficient,
604
Statistical
array, 56–57
decision theory, 8, 19–20
description, 8, 18
design, 8, 18
estimates. *See* Estimation
independence, 197–99
reasoning, 12–15
sample, 19
sampling, 15–17
theory, 8
Statistical analysis
of bivariate quantitative data,
459–60
cross-section, 31
frequency, 31
sequence, 30–31
time series, 31
See also individual entries
Statistical independence. *See* Independence
Statistical inference
among alternative population
parameters, 258–60
about correlation coefficient,
472–74

TABLE 4. Areas Under the Normal Curve

Each entry is the proportion of the total area under a normal curve which lies under the segment between the mean and Z standard deviations from the mean. Example: $X - \mu = 31$ and $\sigma = 20$, so $Z = X - \mu/\sigma = 1.55$. The required area is .4394. The area in the tail beyond the point $X - \mu = 31$ is then $.5000 - .4394 = .0606$.

Z	.00	.01	.02	.03	.04	.05	.06	.07	.08	.09
0.0	.0000	.0040	.0080	.0120	.0160	.0199	.0239	.0279	.0319	.0359
0.1	.0398	.0438	.0478	.0517	.0557	.0596	.0636	.0675	.0714	.0753
0.2	.0793	.0832	.0871	.0910	.0948	.0987	.1026	.1064	.1103	.1141
0.3	.1179	.1217	.1255	.1293	.1331	.1368	.1406	.1443	.1480	.1517
0.4	.1554	.1591	.1628	.1664	.1700	.1736	.1772	.1808	.1844	.1879
0.5	.1915	.1950	.1985	.2019	.2054	.2088	.2123	.2157	.2190	.2224
0.6	.2257	.2291	.2324	.2357	.2389	.2422	.2454	.2486	.2518	.2549
0.7	.2580	.2612	.2642	.2673	.2704	.2734	.2764	.2794	.2823	.2852
0.8	.2881	.2910	.2939	.2967	.2995	.3023	.3051	.3078	.3106	.3133
0.9	.3159	.3186	.3212	.3238	.3264	.3289	.3315	.3340	.3365	.3389
1.0	.3413	.3438	.3461	.3485	.3508	.3531	.3554	.3577	.3599	.3621
1.1	.3643	.3665	.3686	.3708	.3729	.3749	.3770	.3790	.3810	.3830
1.2	.3849	.3869	.3888	.3907	.3925	.3944	.3962	.3980	.3997	.4015
1.3	.4032	.4049	.4066	.4082	.4099	.4115	.4131	.4147	.4162	.4177
1.4	.4192	.4207	.4222	.4236	.4251	.4265	.4279	.4292	.4306	.4319
1.5	.4332	.4345	.4357	.4370	.4382	.4394	.4406	.4418	.4429	.4441
1.6	.4452	.4463	.4474	.4484	.4495	.4505	.4515	.4525	.4535	.4545
1.7	.4554	.4564	.4573	.4582	.4591	.4599	.4608	.4616	.4625	.4633
1.8	.4641	.4649	.4656	.4664	.4671	.4678	.4686	.4693	.4699	.4706
1.9	.4713	.4719	.4726	.4732	.4738	.4744	.4750	.4756	.4761	.4767
2.0	.4772	.4778	.4783	.4788	.4793	.4798	.4803	.4808	.4812	.4817
2.1	.4821	.4826	.4830	.4834	.4838	.4842	.4846	.4850	.4854	.4857
2.2	.4861	.4864	.4868	.4871	.4875	.4878	.4881	.4884	.4887	.4890
2.3	.4893	.4896	.4898	.4901	.4904	.4906	.4909	.4911	.4913	.4916
2.4	.4918	.4920	.4922	.4925	.4927	.4929	.4931	.4932	.4934	.4936
2.5	.4938	.4940	.4941	.4943	.4945	.4946	.4948	.4949	.4951	.4952
2.6	.4953	.4955	.4956	.4957	.4959	.4960	.4961	.4962	.4963	.4964
2.7	.4965	.4966	.4967	.4968	.4969	.4970	.4971	.4972	.4973	.4974
2.8	.4974	.4975	.4976	.4977	.4977	.4978	.4979	.4979	.4980	.4981
2.9	.4981	.4982	.4982	.4983	.4984	.4984	.4985	.4985	.4986	.4986
3.0	.49865	.4987	.4987	.4988	.4988	.4989	.4989	.4989	.4990	.4990
3.1	.49903	.4991	.4991	.4991	.4992	.4992	.4992	.4992	.4993	.4993
3.2	.4993129	.4993	.4994	.4994	.4994	.4994	.4994	.4995	.4995	.4995
3.3	.4995166	.4995	.4995	.4996	.4996	.4996	.4996	.4996	.4996	.4997
3.4	.4996631	.4997	.4997	.4997	.4997	.4997	.4997	.4997	.4998	.4998
3.5	.4997674	.4998	.4998	.4998	.4998	.4998	.4998	.4998	.4998	.4998
3.6	.4998409	.4998	.4999	.4999	.4999	.4999	.4999	.4999	.4999	.4999
3.7	.4998922	.4999	.4999	.4999	.4999	.4999	.4999	.4999	.4999	.4999
3.8	.4999277	.4999	.4999	.4999	.4999	.4999	.4999	.5000	.5000	.5000
3.9	.4999519	.5000	.5000	.5000	.5000	.5000	.5000	.5000	.5000	.5000
4.0	.4999683									
4.5	.4999966									
5.0	.4999997133									

From Frederick E. Croxton and Dudley J. Cowden, *Practical Business Statistics* 2d ed., p. 511. Copyright 1948 Prentice-Hall, Inc. Through $Z = 2.99$, from Rugg's *Statistical Methods Applied to Education*, Houghton Mifflin Company. A much more detailed table of normal curve areas is given in Federal Works Agency, Work Products Administration for the City of New York, *Tables of Probability Functions* (New York: National Bureau of Standards, 1942), Vol. II, pp. 2–238. In this appendix values for $Z = 3.00$ through 5.00 were computed from the latter source.

$I E \quad Z = 1.22 = .3888$